Theologians and Contract Law

Legal History Library

VOLUME 9

Studies in the History of Private Law

VOLUME 4

The titles published in this series are listed at brill.com/lhl

Theologians and Contract Law

The Moral Transformation of
the *Ius Commune* (ca. 1500–1650)

With a new Preface

By

Wim Decock

BRILL | NIJHOFF

LEIDEN | BOSTON

Originally published in hardback in 2013.

Cover illustration: Marinus van Reymerswaele, *The Lawyer's Office*, Museum purchase through the Ella West Freeman Foundation Matching Fund, 70.7.

The Library of Congress has cataloged the hardcover edition as follows:

Library of Congress Cataloging-in-Publication Data

Decock, Wim, 1983–
    Theologians and contract law : the moral transformation of the ius commune (ca. 1500-1650) / By Wim Decock.
        p. cm. — (Legal history library volume ; 9) (Studies in the history of private law ; 4)
    Includes bibliographical references and index.
    ISBN 978-90-04-23284-6 (hardback : alk. paper) — ISBN 978-90-04-23285-3 (e-book)
    1. Liberty of contract—Europe—History. 2. Liberty of contract—Moral and ethical aspects.
    3. Contracts (Canon law) 4. Contracts (Roman law) 5. Contracts—Europe—History.
    6. Customary law—History. I. Title.

    KJC1726.D43 2012
    262.9'2—dc23
                                                                              2012021902

Typeface for the Latin, Greek, and Cyrillic scripts: "Brill". See and download: brill.com/brill-typeface.

ISSN 1874-1793
ISBN 978-90-04-53677-7 (paperback, 2023)
ISBN 978-90-04-23284-6 (hardback)
ISBN 978-90-04-23285-3 (e-book)

That general aim of all law is simply referable to the moral destination of human nature, as it exhibits itself in the Christian view of life; then Christianity is not to be regarded merely as a rule of life for us but it has also in fact changed the world so that all our thoughts, however strange and even hostile they may appear to it, are nevertheless governed and penetrated by it.

Friedrich Carl von Savigny[1]

[1] *System of the modern Roman law*, Translated by W. Holloway, Madras 1867, vol. 1, p. 43.

CONTENTS

ACKNOWLEDGMENTS

This book has grown out of a dissertation submitted with a view to obtaining the joint degree of Doctor in Laws (KU Leuven) and Dottore di ricerca in diritto europeo su base storico-comparatistica (Università Roma Tre). The research was initiated in the autumn of 2006 and the thesis was successfully defended in Leuven, Belgium, on 8 December 2011.

The debt one incurs over the course of a five-year research period, spent in five different countries, is tremendous. Thanks to the 6th Framework Program of the European Commission ('Structuring the European Research Area') I benefitted from a Marie Curie Early Stage Training grant from 1 October 2006 through 30 September 2009. It enabled me to participate in the research project on the 'History, Philosophy, Anthropology and Sociology of European Legal Cultures,' organized by the École des Hautes Études en Sciences Sociales (EHESS) in Paris, the Max-Planck-Institut für europäische Rechtsgeschichte (MPIER) in Frankfurt am Main, the Istituto Italiano di Scienze Umane (SUM) in Florence, and the London School of Economics (LSE). From 1 October 2009, I was able to continue my research at the Division for Roman Law and Legal History at the KU Leuven as a PhD Fellow of the Research Foundation Flanders (FWO). The FWO also granted financial support for a stay at Harvard Law School as a Visiting Researcher during the Spring Term of 2011.

I am indebted to many scholars across the boundaries of academic disciplines. Special thanks are owed to my supervisors, Professors Laurent Waelkens (KU Leuven) and Emanuele Conte (Università degli Studi Roma Tre). During the annual summer schools in Rome I received instructive feedback on my work-in-progress by Professors Italo Birocchi (Università 'La Sapienza'), David Deroussin (Université Lyon III) and Charles Donahue Jr. (Harvard Law School). I am grateful to my colleagues of the project on European Legal Cultures for enduring my overbearing enthusiasm for Lessius. The same goes true for my colleagues and friends at the Max-Planck Research School for Comparative Legal History in Frankfurt am Main, at the Harvard Law School Graduate Program, at the Dipartimento di Storia e Teoria Generale del Diritto of Roma Tre University, at the Institute of Legal History of Gent University, and at the Division for Roman Law and Legal History at KU Leuven and KU Leuven Campus Kortrijk.

I have had the chance to visit some of the most splendid libraries across the world from the Bibliotheca Palafoxiana in Puebla to the Library of Congress in Washington D.C. and the Biblioteca Nazionale in Rome. Special thanks are owed to Mr Bernard Deprez and Mr Hans Storme at the Maurits Sabbe Library of Theology (KU Leuven). I also benefitted from generous support by the library staff at the Max-Planck-Institut für europäische Rechtsgeschichte in Frankfurt, at the Archivum Historicum Societatis Iesu, the Pontificia Università Gregoriana and the Academia Belgica in Rome, at the Bibliothèque Nationale and the Bibliothèque du Saulchoir in Paris, and at Harvard's Langdell and Widener libraries. Their continuous help left me more time for the really important things in life: my wife and family. As a matter of course, my final word of thanks goes out to them.

PROLOGUE

Extremely vast. Extremely difficult. Extremely useful. These unambiguous adjectives prominently appear in the introduction to the Spanish Jesuit Pedro de Oñate's (1568–1646) four-volume treatise *On contracts*. They are meant to capture the essential features of contract law. The myriads of contracts concluded every day, Oñate warned his readership, make up an ocean that is deep, mysterious and capricious. Contracts are the inevitable means enabling man to navigate his way either to the salvation or to the destruction of his material goods—and of his soul. Therefore, he considered expert knowledge of the complex field of contract law to be indispensable for confessors who needed a nuanced solution to practical cases of conscience. Each contract was thought to express a moral choice for either virtue or vice, for avarice or liberality, for justice or fraud. To live is to enter into contracts, according to Oñate, and to live a God-pleasing life is to conclude contracts in a manner that is consistent with the imperatives of Christian morality. To help confessors decide how Christians of all trades, including princes and businessmen, have to live their lives, this Spanish Jesuit expounded what such a Christian view of contracts should look like.

Oñate's work stands at the end of a vibrant tradition of scholastic contract law, which will be subject to meticulous analysis in the chapters that follow. Scholastic contract law evolved all across Europe over a period of more than half a millenium. By the 1650s, it had come to fruition in the works of major theologians of the Spanish Golden Age, such as Domingo de Soto (ca. 1494–1560), Tomás Sánchez (1550–1610), and Leonardus Lessius (1554–1623). It had left its mark not only on the Catholic moral theological tradition, but also on canonists such as Diego de Covarruvias y Leyva (1512–1577), civilians such as Matthias van Wezenbeke (1531–1586) and natural lawyers such as Hugo Grotius (1583–1645). Slowly but effectively, the Roman law of the late medieval period used all across Europe, the *ius commune*, was transformed into the image of Christian morality. The consequence of this transformation, in Oñate's own words, was the restoration of 'freedom of contract' (*libertas contrahentibus restituta*). This 'freedom of contract' granted contracting parties the possibility to enter into whatever agreement they wanted on the basis of their mutual consent. They could then have their contract enforced before the tribunal of their choice. The following pages intend to analyze theologians' conception of this principle of 'freedom of contract' and its limits.

NOTES ON THE TEXT AND ITS MODES OF REFERENCE

We have followed the conventions for bibliographical reference as recommended by the *Tijdschrift voor Rechtsgeschiedenis* (*The Legal History Review*). References to modern journals or dictionaries have not been abbreviated so as to make sure that the text remains as accessible as possible to scholars coming from different academic backgrounds. The Latin and Greek are cited as they occur in the quotations, except for the punctuation, which has been slightly modernized. The most emblematic quotations have been translated into English, usually in a freer style than that used in the rendering of Latin texts in school exercises. For the form of names, the vernacular has been preferred to the Latinized forms unless the Latin name was more common. For example, Lenaert Leys is cited as Leonardus Lessius, while Charles Du Moulin is employed rather than Carolus Molinaeus. Sometimes both versions are used for stylistic purposes, particularly when the name is equally well-known in its vernacular as in its Latinized form, e.g. Martín de Azpilcueta besides Dr. Navarrus. The following abbreviations have been used for the citation of ancient and medieval legal texts:

D. 1,1,1	Digestum Justiniani, book 1, title 1, lex 1
C. 1,1,1	Codex Justiniani, book 1, title 1, lex 1
Inst. 1,1,1	Institutiones Justiniani, book 1, title 1, lex 1
Nov.	Novellae
Dist.1, c.1	Decretum Gratiani, Distinctio 1, canon 1
C.1, q.1, c.1	Decretum Gratiani, Causa 1, quaestio 1, canon 1
De pen.	Decretum Gratiani, De penitentia
X 1,1,1	Decretales Gregorii IX, book 1, title 1, canon 1
VI 1,1,1	Liber sextus Bonifatii VIII, book 1, title 1, canon 1
Clem.	Constitutiones Clementis V, book 1, title 1, canon 1

PREFACE TO THE PAPERBACK EDITION

Ten years have elapsed since the publication of the first edition of *Theologians and Contract Law*. In that brief space, dozens of scholars in the humanities and social sciences have found their way to the lifes and writings of the "theologian-jurists" (*teólogos-juristas*) of the early modern period. The literature has exploded in fields as diverse as legal history, political science, moral theology, early modern philosophy, Jesuit studies and the history of economic thought. Fortunately, since those days, companions and bibliographical tools have appeared which facilitate access to high-quality scholarship across those disciplines, for instance *A Companion to the Spanish Scholastics*, Leiden 2021, edited by Harald Braun, Erik De Bom and Paolo Astorri. Other examples include Celia Alejandra Ramírez Santos's and José Luis Egío García's "The Research on the School of Salamanca (2008–2019). A Conceptual and Multidisciplinary Bibliography", *Max Planck Institute for Legal History and Legal Theory Research Paper Series* (No. 2020–09), or the collected volume *Qué es la Escuela de Salamanca?*, Madrid 2021, edited by Simona Langella and Rafael Ramis Barceló. Earlier, I had the chance to publish, along with Christiane Birr, a succinct overview of both the primary source material and the secondary literature related to law and theology in early modern scholasticism (see *Recht und Moral in der Scholastik der Frühen Neuzeit, 1500–1750*, Berlin 2016).

This paperback edition of *Theologians and Contract Law* provides an unaltered version of the original text. Its aim is to make a monograph that met with unexpectedly high and diverse scholarly interest even more readily available to researchers and students in law, theology, philosophy, history, political science and economic thought across the globe. Readers may nevertheless want to take note of new perspectives that have since been developed in literature on early modern scholasticism in general, and the "theologian-jurists" steeped in the intellectual tradition of Salamanca, in particular. The global character of the normativity regimes developed by theologians in the framework of the early modern Spanish and Portuguese empires has now been thoroughly investigated by an international team of researchers led by Thomas Duve at the *Max Planck Institute for Legal History and Legal Theory* in Frankfurt; among their latest work, see T. Duve, J.L. Egío, C. Birr (eds.), *The School of Salamanca: A Case of Global Knowledge*

Production, Leiden 2021. Fresh perspectives on the history of international law such as Martti Koskenniemi's *To the Uttermost Parts of the Earth: Legal Imagination and International Power, 1300–1870*, Cambridge 2021, also provide new clues to analyze the complex normative fabric created by the early modern scholastics.

As far as the development of private law doctrines in early modern theological literature is concerned, important insights can be gained from new scientific work. Since the first edition of *Theologians and Contract Law*, there has been research on contract law in the work of specific early modern scholastic authors (e.g. Piotr Alexandrowicz's "Paolo Comitoli SJ (1545–1626) on Contracts", *Zeitschrift der Savigny-Stiftung für Rechtsgeschichte, Kanonistische Abteilung*, 107 (2021), 255–299). Theologians' engagement with the partnership contract (*societas*) has been analyzed in Luisa Brunori's *Societas quid sit. La société commerciale dans l'élaboration de la Seconde Scolastique*, Paris 2015. Scholastics' analysis of problems related to restitution and torts law have been thoroughly examined in several contributions by Nils Jansen (e.g. *The Structure of Tort Law: History, Theory and Doctrine of Non-Contractual Claims for Compensation*, Oxford 2021), Tilman Repgen (e.g. De restitutione – Fortsetzung der kommentierenden Einführung, in: De iustitia. Über die Gerechtigkeit. Francisco de Vitoria, Teil 3, herausgegeben, eingeleitet und ins Deutsche übersetzt von Joachim Stüben. Mit einer Einleitung von Tilman Repgen, Stuttgart – Bad Cannstatt 2020, VII–LVI) and in Joe Sampson's *The Historical Foundations of Grotius' Analysis of Delict*, Leiden 2018. Incidentally, the debate about the scholastic influences on Hugo Grotius has continued to draw attention, with critical approaches emerging in this line of historiography, as can be seen in Mark Somos' and Joshua Smeltzer's "Vitoria, Suárez and Grotius: James Brown Scott's Enduring Revival", *Grotiana*, 41 (2020), 137–162.

New research allows us to appreciate even more than before the similarities and the differences between Catholic and Protestant approaches to law and normativity in the early modern period. As regards contract law, in particular, Paolo Astorri's *Lutheran Theology and Contract Law in Early Modern Germany (ca. 1520–1720)*, Leiden 2019, offers a very precise insight into the continuities and discontinuities between the authors of the School of Salamanca and Biblical re-interpretations of contract law in early modern Protestant theological sources. At the same time, Mathias Schmoeckel has highlighted the transformative force, for the development of contract doctrine, of the parallel reception of Aristotle in the Protestant

world (see "Melanchthons Konzeption der Verträge. Archäologie der Privatautonomie", *Zeitschrift der Savigny-Stiftung für Rechtsgeschichte, Kanonistische Abteilung*, 104 (2018), 304–346). In addition, Schmoeckel's work on the epistemological impact of the Protestant revolution (*Das Recht der Reformation. Die epistemologische Revolution der Wissenschaft und die Spaltung der Rechtsordnung in der Frühen Neuzeit*, Tübingen 2014) offers an interesting point of contrast and comparison with the normative structures developed in the Catholic world of the sixteenth and seventeenth centuries.

Moreover, recent scholarship provides a fuller picture of the historical and political background of early modern theologians' engagements with law. A series of new monographs by Nicole Reinhardt (*Voices of Conscience. Royal Confessors and Political Counsel in Seventeenth Century Spain and France*, Oxford 2016), Stefania Tutino (e.g. *Uncertainty in Post-Reformation Catholicism. A History of Probabilism*, Oxford 2017), Rudolf Schüssler (*The Debate on Probable Opinions in the Scholastic Tradition*, Leiden 2019), Daniel Schwartz (*The Political Morality of the Late Scholastics: Civic Life, War and Conscience*, Cambridge 2019) and many other eminent scholars sharpen our insight into the intellectual historical and political background of the legal doctrines of the early modern scholastics. At the same time, more detailed historical accounts of the lives and writings of protagonists in *Theologians and Contract Law* such as Thomas Cajetan, Francisco de Vitoria, Domingo de Soto, Martín de Azpilcueta, Diego de Covarrubias y Leyva, Luis de Molina, Francisco Suárez and Tomás Sánchez are now more easily available in English thanks to the volumes on *Great Christian Jurists in Spanish History*, Cambridge 2018, edited by Rafael Domingo and Javier Martínez-Torrón, and *Law and the Christian Tradition in Italy*, London 2021, edited by Orazio Condorelli and Rafael Domingo.

Many challenges lie ahead. Despite the fact that studies on the "theologian-jurists" are flourishing, too many students and scholars in law, history, philosophy, theology, economics and political science are excluded from having access to the immense wealth of this tradition because of a linguistic barrier of a double kind. First of all, the Latin language barrier. Overcoming this obstacle requires an intense pursuit of the translation of pre-modern legal and theological texts into modern languages. Secondly, the writings of the early modern theologians are couched in the technical language of Roman law and canon law (the *ius commune*). Especially in Europe, the heartland of the *ius commune* tradition, upscaling the efforts to break down these barriers would be most welcome. In this connection,

I would like to reiterate my thanks to the many academic institutions, colleagues and friends who, over the past decade and much longer, have been so generous as to support my work in all kinds of ways. It has been an incredible intellectual and professional journey, and I hope that this paperback edition of *Theologians and Contract Law* may help ensure that others will embark on this inspiring path.

Louvain-la-Neuve, 19 July 2023

CHAPTER ONE

METHOD AND DIRECTION

1.1 RESEARCH HYPOTHESIS

The basic assumption that underlies this book is that the moral transformation of the *ius commune* in the writings on contracts of moral theologians led to the birth of a principle called 'freedom of contract'. 'Contractual freedom' is understood as the power of individuals to impose contractual obligation upon themselves by virtue of their wills and mutual consent alone. They can then enforce this agreement in court. This assumption is not thought of in a nineteenth-century, dogmatic manner. As is sufficiently well-known, the will theories of contract that were developed in modern times were held to be characterized by the absence of moral considerations. For example, the modern will theorists considered the idea of fairness in exchange to be at odds with 'freedom of contract'.[2] Needless to say, considerations of justice in exchange still played a major role for the theologians. However, it appears that in the work of the theologians there was no conflict between emphasizing the autonomy of the will and understanding contractual exchange in moral terms.

The move towards a consensualist doctrine of contract in the writings of theologians is brilliantly illustrated in Pedro de Oñate's treatise *On contracts*. Expounding on the bindingness of all agreements, Oñate happily concludes:[3]

---

[2] E.g. M.J. Horwitz, *The transformation of American law, 1780–1860*, Cambridge Mass. – London 1977, p. 160. For a good and critical synthesis of some of the major theses of this work, see C. Desan, *Beyond commodification, Contract and the credit-based world of modern capitalism*, in: D.W. Hamilton – A.L. Brophy (eds.), Transformations in American legal history, Essays in honor of professor Morton J. Horwitz, Cambridge Mass. 2010, vol. 2, p. 111–113.

[3] Pedro de Oñate, *De contractibus*, Romae 1646, tom. 1, tract. 1, disp. 2, sect. 5, num. 166, p. 40: 'Unde lex naturalis, lex canonica et lex Hispaniae omnino consentiunt et innumerae difficultates, fraudes, lites, iurgia hac tanta legum consensione et claritate sublata sunt, et contrahentibus consultissime libertas restituta ut quandocumque de rebus suis voluerint contrahere et se obligare, id ratum sit in utroque foro in quo convenerint et sancte et inviolabiliter observetur. Quare ius canonicum et ius Hispaniae corrigunt ius commune, concedentes pactis nudis omnibus actionem et obligationem civilem, quam illud negabat.'

© WIM DECOCK, 2013 | DOI:10.1163/9789004232853_002

Consequently, natural law, canon law and Hispanic law entirely agree, and innumerable difficulties, frauds, litigations and disputes have been removed thanks to such great consensus and clarity in the laws. To the contracting parties, liberty has very wisely been restored (*contrahentibus libertas restituta*), so that whenever they want to bind themselves through concluding a contract about their goods, this contract will be recognized by whichever of both courts [i.e. the civil or the ecclesiastical court] before which they will have brought their case and it will be upheld as being sacrosanct and inviolable. Therefore, canon law and Hispanic law correct the *ius commune*, since the former grant an action and civil obligation to all bare agreements, while the latter denied them just that.

We wish to flag three elements in this quotation. First, Oñate praises the evolution toward the general enforceability of all willful agreements. Second, he considers the universal adoption of this principle as a victory for the freedom or liberty of the contracting parties. Third, he explains the emergence of this principle through the transformation of the *ius commune* after the model of canon law.

The assumption that theologians played an important role in the development of an idea of 'contractual freedom' builds on previous scholarship by eminent legal historians such as Paolo Cappellini, Klaus-Peter Nanz, Robert Feenstra, James Gordley, Italo Birocchi and Thomas Duve. They have shown that the moral theologians played a vital role in the development of a so-called 'general category of contract'.[4] Such a 'general category of contract' is at odds with Roman contract law, which dominated legal thinking all through the Middle Ages. Roman contract law did not universally recognize the principle that agreements are enforceable by virtue of

---

[4] See P. Cappellini, *Sulla formazione del moderno concetto di 'dottrina generale del diritto'* (a proposito di Martin Lipp, *De Bedeutung des Naturrechts für die Ausbildung der allgemeinen Lehren des deutschen Privatrechts*, [Schriften zur Rechtstheorie, 88], Berlin 1980), Quaderni fiorentini per la storia del pensiero giuridico moderno, 10 (1981), p. 323–354; K.-P. Nanz, *Die Entstehung des allgemeinen Vertragsbegriffs im 16. bis 18. Jahrhundert*, [Beiträge zur neueren Privatrechtsgeschichte, 9], München 1985, p. 135–148; R. Feenstra – M. Ahsmann, *Contract, aspecten van de begrippen contract en contractsvrijheid in historisch perspectief*, [Rechtshistorische Cahiers, 2], Deventer 1988², p. 19–23; J. Gordley, *The philosophical origins of modern contract doctrine*, Oxford 1991, p. 69–111; I. Birocchi, *Causa e categoria generale del contratto, Un problema dogmatico nella cultura privatistica dell'età moderna, I. Il cinquecento*, [Il Diritto nella Storia, 5], Torino 1997, p. 203–269; Th. Duve, *Kanonisches Recht und die Ausbildung allgemeiner Vertragslehren in der Spanischen Spätscholastik*, in: O. Condorelli – F. Roumy – M. Schmoeckel (eds.), Der Einfluss der Kanonistik auf die Europäische Rechtskultur, Band 1: Zivil- und Zivilprozessrecht, [Norm und Struktur, 37], Köln – Weimar – Wien 2009, p. 389–408.

mutual agreement alone.[5] Roman contract law accepted the actionability on consensualist grounds alone only in regard to a limited set of contracts such as sale, lease, mandate and partnership. According to James Gordley, in particular, the foundations for a modern, consensualist doctrine of contract in both civil and common law jurisdiction were laid in the treatises of scholastics such as Domingo de Soto, Luís de Molina and Leonardus Lessius.[6] They achieved a great synthesis of Aristotelian-Thomistic moral principles and the medieval *ius commune* which led to the formulation of this 'general category of contract'.

In modern times, economic development is seen as the fundamental rationale behind 'freedom of contract'.[7] Therefore, if one asks for the reasons why a principle of 'freedom of contract' was gradually introduced in the sixteenth century, the obvious answer seems to be 'for the sake of economic progress'. As a matter of fact, historians have already argued that there is a connection between the rise of liberal economic views in the early modern scholastic writers and their profound engagement with contract law. For example, Paolo Prodi adheres to the thesis that the moral theological literature is a witness both to the rise of market capitalism and to the birth of a general law of contract.[8] He argues that new commercial transactions which could not be captured under the headings of the Roman body of legal texts, the *Corpus iuris civilis*, were regulated systematically for the first time in the moral theological literature. It remains to be seen in this monograph whether 'economic development' effectively was the main driving force behind theologians' advocating a principle of 'contractual freedom.'

---

[5] H. Dilcher, *Der Typenzwang im mittelalterlichen Vertragsrecht*, Zeitschrift für Rechtsgeschichte der Savigny-Stiftung, Rom. Abt., 77 (1960), p. 270–303. A standard account of Roman contract law can be obtained from reading any textbook on Roman law.

[6] Gordley, *The philosophical origins of modern contract doctrine*, p. 3–4 and 69–71. For a critical assessment of Gordley's thesis, see I. Birocchi's review in Tijdschrift voor Rechtsgeschiedenis, 61 (1993), p. 132–137. The argument has been extended to other fields of private law in J. Gordley, *Foundations of private law, property, tort, contract, unjust enrichment*, Oxford 2006, critically reviewed by M. Graziadei in The American Journal of Comparative Law, 58 (2010), p. 477–486.

[7] P.S. Atiyah, *The rise and fall of 'freedom of contract'*, Oxford 1979; P.A. Foriers, *Espaces de liberté en droit des contrats*, in: Les espaces de liberté en droit des affaires, Séminaire organisé à l'occasion du 50e anniversaire de la Commission Droit et Vie des Affaires, Bruxelles 2007, p. 25–28.

[8] P. Prodi, *Settimo non rubare, Furto e mercato nella storia dell'Occidente*, Bologna 2009, e.g. p. 237 and p. 246. See also Prodi's concluding remarks in: D. Quaglioni – G. Todeschini – M. Varanini (eds.), Credito e usura fra teologia, diritto e amministrazione (sec. XII–XVI), [Collection de l'École française de Rome, 346], Roma 2005, p. 291–295.

Research into the economic thought of the scholastics has blossomed over the past decades.[9] Importantly, the idea of the market was increasingly 'objectivized' and 'depersonalized' in the moral theological literature of the second half of the sixteenth century.[10] Studies show that the theologians valued economic prudence, the protection of private property, and the pursuit of self-interest.[11] This claim is confirmed by careful reading of the primary sources. A Jesuit such as Lugo stimulates commercial behavior that is driven by economic prudence (*prudentia oeconomica*) and private gains (*privata commoda*).[12] In other words, it is not improbable that the principle of 'freedom of contract' is tied to a liberal economic paradigm that also emerges in the work of sixteenth and seventeenth century theologians. By and large, there was a decidedly liberal element inherent in both the economic and legal theory espoused by the theologians. This

---

9   It would be impossible to give an exhaustive list of the research done in recent years on the economic thought of scholastics from the 12th until and including the 16th century. Major works include O.I. Langholm, *Economic freedom in scholastic thought*, History of Political Economy, 14 (1982), p. 260–283; O.I. Langholm, *Economics in the medieval schools, Wealth, exchange, value, money and usury according to the Paris theological tradition, 1200–1350*, [Studien und Texte zur Geistesgeschichte des Mittelalters, 29], Leiden 1992; F. Gómez Camacho, *Economía y filosofía moral, La formación del pensamiento económico europeo en la Escolástica española*, [Historia del pensamiento económico, 1], Madrid 1998; S. Piron, *Parcours d'un intellectuel franciscain, d'une théologie vers une pensée sociale, l'oeuvre de Pierre Jean d'Olivi (ca. 1248–1298) et son traité De contractibus*, Paris 1999 [unpublished doct. diss. EHESS]; G. Ceccarelli, *Il gioco e il peccato, economia e rischio nel tardo Medioevo*, Bologna 2003.

10   O.I. Langholm, *The legacy of scholasticism in economic thought, Antecedents of choice and power*, Cambridge 1998, p. 99. This thesis has been confirmed through a study of the case of the Merchant of Rhodes in W. Decock, *Lessius and the breakdown of the scholastic paradigm*, Journal of the History of Economic Thought, 31 (2009), p. 57–78.

11   Cf. H.M. Robertson, *Aspects of the rise of economic individualism, A criticism of Max Weber and his school*, [Cambridge Studies in Economic History, 1], Cambridge, 1933; W. Weber, *Wirtschaftsethik am Vorabend des Liberalismus, Höhepunkt und Abschluss der scholastischen Wirtschaftsbetrachtung durch Ludwig Molina SJ (1535–1600)*, [Schriften des Instituts für christliche Sozialwissenschaften der westfälischen Wilhelms-Universität Münster, 7], Münster 1959; A.A. Chafuen, *Faith and liberty, the economic thought of the late scholastics*, Lanham 2003 [= slightly re-worked version of A.A. Chafuen, *Christians for freedom, late-scholastic economics*, San Francisco 1986]; M.N. Rothbard, *An Austrian perspective on the history of economic thought*, vol. 1: *Economic thought before Adam Smith*, Aldershot – Brookfield 1995.

12   For a good illustration from the primary sources themselves, see Juan de Lugo, *De iustitia et iure*, Lugduni 1642, tom. 2, disp. 26, sect. 8, par. 2, num. 143, p. 337: 'Usus autem scientiae non est usus vel exercitium potestatis, sed est actus prudentiae oeconomicae, quae ordinatur ad privata commoda. Quare nullus est abusus, quod in ea commoda ordinetur.' See also W. Decock – J. Hallebeek, *Pre-contractual duties to inform in early modern scholasticism*, Tijdschrift voor Rechtsgeschiedenis, 78 (2010), p. 89–133.

was reflective of a more general liberal atmosphere.[13] Certainly in the first half of the seventeenth century, this liberalism is apparent also in the doctrine of moral probabilism, which was primarily, albeit not exclusively, the province of the Jesuits.[14]

However intriguing, the explication of the rise of 'freedom of contract' in terms of the concomitant rise of a liberal economic paradigm is not the immediate goal of this book. There are certainly parallels between both phenomena. Yet, we concentrate on the argumentations developed by theologians themselves to advocate 'freedom of contract'.[15] It turns out that their explicit reasoning relies upon religious and juristic arguments much more than upon economic policy considerations. The ambition of this book is to reveal the explications given by theologians themselves for their advocating 'contractual freedom'. These religious and juristic arguments merit attention, because they are likely to be highlighted less than the economic factors that were undoubtedly also at play. The internal, theological logic on which their argumentation relies, grants us a better insight into the idiosyncratic nature of the theologians' enterprise. It turns out that theologians were primarily concerned with the salvation of souls.

Oñate's statement on the restoration of 'freedom of contract' clearly indicates that moral theologians' defense of 'freedom of contract' is not wholly identical with modern versions of it. Oñate starts from a different logic. Modern conceptions of 'freedom of contract' are structured around the philosophy that private markets are the economic institutions which are best fit for the purpose of the efficient allocation of scarce goods

[13] F. Carpintero Benítez, Los escolásticos españoles en los inicios del liberalismo político y jurídico, Revista de estudios histórico-jurídicos, 25 (2003), p. 341–373.
[14] See Ph. Schmitz, Probabilismus—das jesuitischste der Moralsysteme, in: M. Sievernich – G. Switek (eds.), Ignatianisch, Eigenart und Methode der Gesellschaft Jesu, Freiburg – Basel – Wien 1990), p. 354–368; and Ph. Schmitz, Kasuistik, Ein wiederentdecktes Kapitel der Jesuitenmoral, Theologie und Philosophie, 67 (1992), p. 29–59. Probabilism will be discussed in the second chapter.
[15] H. Fleischer, Informationsasymmetrie im Vertragsrecht, eine rechtsvergleichende und interdisziplinäre Abhandlung zu Reichweite und Grenzen vertragsschlussbezogener Aufklärungspflichten, München 2001, p. 46. An example of the interdisciplinary approach which is recommended by Fleischer is offered by L. Baeck, The legal and scholastic roots of Leonardus Lessius's economic thought, [Leuven Centre for Economic Studies Discussion Papers], Leuven 1999, a slightly extended version of which has been published as L. Baeck, Die rechtlichen und scholastischen Wurzeln des ökonomischen Denkens van Leonardus Lessius, in: B. Schefold (ed.), Leonardus Lessius' De iustitia et iure, Vademecum zu einem Klassiker der Spätscholastischen Wirtschaftsanalyse, [Klassiker der Nationalökonomie], Düsseldorf 1999, p. 39–61.

and services.[16] 'Freedom of contract' is then seen as the appropriate juridical framework for supporting this economic paradigm. However, what
Oñate primarily cares about is finding the juridical principle that best
fosters peace and moral comfort. This logic approximates the canonical
understanding of freedom.[17] It is the freedom to develop virtuousness,
to express moral responsibility, and to strengthen mutual trust amongst
human beings. Moreover, the moral theologians shared with the canonists
a concern for the salvation of the soul (*cura animarum*), which has nearly
disappeared in modern times.

From a historiographical point of view, theologians' contract doctrines
have not only been studied for their own sake.[18] Much more frequently,
they have received attention in the context of scholarship on 'modern' natural lawyers such as Hugo Grotius (1583–1645).[19] This is hardly

---

[16] For a critical analysis of this paradigm, see M.J. Trebilcock, *The limits of freedom of contract*, Cambridge Mass. 1993, p. 1–22, a book which is itself subject to critical assessment in F. Parisi, *Autonomy and private ordering in contract law*, European Journal of Law and Economics, 1 (1994), p. 213–227.

[17] As described by R.H. Helmholz, *The spirit of classical canon law*, Athens (Ga.) – London 1996, p. 49.

[18] I. Birocchi, *Saggi sulla formazione storica della categoria generale del contratto*, Cagliari 1988, p. 36–41; J. Gordley, *The philosophical origins of modern contract doctrine*, p. 69–111; Birocchi, *Causa e categoria generale del contratto*, p. 203–269; A. Guzmán Brito, *La doctrina de Luis de Molina sobra la causa contractual*, in: A. Guzmán Brito, *Negocio, contrato y causa en la tradición del derecho europeo e iberoamericano*, Navarra 2005, p. 407–439; H. Rodríguez Penelas, *Ética y sistemática del contrato en el siglo de oro, La obra de Francisco García en su contexto jurídico-moral*, [Colleción de pensamiento medieval y renacentista, 82], Pamplona 2007, p. 69–121; Th. Duve, *Kanonisches Recht und die Ausbildung allgemeiner Vertragslehren in der Spanischen Spätscholastik*, p. 389–408.

[19] E.g. H. Thieme, *Natürliches Privatrecht und Spätscholastik*, in: H. Thieme (ed.), Ideengeschichte und Rechtsgeschichte, Gesammelte Schriften, Band II, [Forschungen zur neueren Privatrechtsgeschichte, 25], Köln – Wien 1986 [1953], p. 871–908; M. Diesselhorst, *Die Lehre des Hugo Grotius vom Versprechen*, [Forschungen zur neueren Privatrechtsgeschichte, 6], Köln – Graz, 1959, *passim*; F. Wieacker, *Privatrechtsgeschichte der Neuzeit unter besonderer Berücksichtigung der deutschen Entwicklung*, Göttingen 1967, p. 293–297; R. Feenstra, *De oorsprong van Hugo de Groot's leer over de dwaling*, in: L. Jacob (ed.), Met eerbiedigende werking, opstellen aangeboden aan Prof. Mr. L.J. Hijmans van den Bergh, Deventer 1971, p. 87–101; H. Thieme, *Qu'est ce que nous, les juristes, devons à la Seconde Scolastique espagnole?*, in: P. Grossi (ed.), La seconda scolastica nella formazione del diritto privato moderno, [Per la storia del pensiero giuridico moderno, 1], Milano 1973, p. 7–22; R. Feenstra, *L'influence de la Scolastique espagnole sur Grotius en droit privé, Quelques expériences dans des questions de fond et de forme, concernant notamment les doctrines de l'erreur et de l'enrichissement sans cause*, in: P. Grossi (ed.), La seconda scolastica nella formazione del diritto privato moderno, [Per la storia del pensiero giuridico moderno, 1], Milano 1973, p. 377–402, reprinted in his *Fata iuris romani*, Leiden 1974, p. 338–363; R. Feenstra, *Impossibilitas and clausula rebus sic stantibus, Some aspects of frustration of contract in continental legal history up to Grotius*, in: A. Watson (ed.), Daube noster, Essays in legal history for David Daube, Edinburgh – London 1974, p. 77–104, reprinted in his *Fata iuris*

surprising. The legal norms and concepts developed in the theological tradition were then adopted by the natural lawyers of the seventeenth and eighteenth centuries. Therefore, it will be a constant concern in this monograph to investigate how theologians' theories of contract left their mark on Hugo Grotius. In the eyes of allegedly 'modern' natural lawyers such as Grotius, contract remained to play the central role it had gotten in the moral theological tradition as the principal tool for the regulation of all human affairs, including international relations and the relations between citizens and the public authorities.[20]

The assumption of this book implies that modern contract law is indebted to theologians. The history of substantive doctrines of private law—which are currently undergoing a process of 'Ent-staatlichung'—can be understood also as a history which started with the 'Ver-staatlichung' in modern times of doctrines originally developed by actors other than the State.[21] It appears that those actors were not only learned jurists of the medieval *ius commune*. They were also moral theologians of subsequent centuries who transformed the civilian tradition. They belonged to an institution, the Roman Catholic Church, which, for centuries, vied for normative power with the secular authorities.[22] The Church was the author of a global normative structure that operated in the shadow of the 'State'.[23] In Prodi's historical analysis, the State emerged as the

---

romani, Leiden 1974, p. 364–391; Cappellini, *Sulla formazione del moderno concetto di 'dottrina generale del diritto'*, p. 323–354; Nanz, *Die Entstehung des allgemeinen Vertragsbegriffs im 16. bis 18. Jahrhundert*, p. 135–148; Feenstra – Ahsmann, *Contract*, p. 19–23; J. Gordley, *Natural law origins of the common law of contract*, in: J. Barton (ed.), Towards a general law of contract, [Comparative studies in continental and Anglo-American legal history, 8], Berlin 1990, p. 367–465; A. Somma, *Autonomia privata e struttura del consenso contrattuale, aspetti storico-comparativi di una vicenda concettuale*, [Problemi di diritto comparato, 4], Milano 2000, p. 71–73; M.J. Schermaier, *Die Bestimmung des wesentlichen Irrtums von den Glossatoren bis zum BGB*, [Forschungen zur neueren Privatrechtsgeschichte, 29], Wien-Köln-Weimar 2000, p. 124–143; R. Feenstra, *Grotius' doctrine of liability for negligence, Its origins and its influence in civil law countries until modern codifications*, in: E.J.H. Schrage (ed.), Negligence, The comparative legal history of the law of torts, [Comparative Studies in Continental and Anglo-American Legal History, 22], Berlin 2001, p. 129–172.

[20] R. Zimmermann, *The law of obligations, Roman foundations of the civilian tradition*, Cape Town – Wetton – Johannesburg 1990, p. 544.

[21] R. Zimmermann (ed.), *Globalisierung und Entstaatlichung des Rechts, Teilband II: Nichtstaatliches Privatrecht, Geltung und Genese*, Tübingen 2008, p. vi.

[22] F. Fukuyama, *The origins of political order*, London 2011, chapters 18 (*The Church becomes a State*) and 19 (*The State becomes a Church*).

[23] Th. Duve, *Katholisches Kirchenrecht und Moraltheologie im 16. Jahrhundert, Eine globale normative Ordnung im Schatten schwacher Staatlichkeit*, in: S. Kadelbach – K. Günther (eds.), Recht ohne Staat? Zur Normativität nichtstaatlicher Rechtsetzung, [Normative Orders, 4], Frankfurt am Main 2011, p. 147–174; W. Decock, *La transformation*

winner from this intense power struggle with the Church, but, in the process, absorbed a lot of the normative structures which had been developed by the moral theologians.[24] If it is permitted to employ the language of company law, the temporal authority launched a 'reverse take-over' effort over its spiritual assailant, defending its body through the acquisition, at least in part, of the soul of its rival.[25]

1.2   RESEARCH DESIGN

The rise of a principle of 'freedom of contract' in theological literature of the early modern period will be analyzed in three steps. First, the encounter between the legal tradition and the moral theological tradition will be contextualized. Second, the rise of 'freedom of contract' as a principle will be explained. Third, the natural, political, and moral limits to the principle of 'contractual freedom' will be explored. Sometimes these limitations are expressly mentioned by the theologians, sometimes they are implicit in their discussions of specific cases.

We will first highlight the background of the theologians' involvement with contract law in chapter 2. This effort to contextualize theologians' reflections on contracts will lead to a deeper historical understanding of the rise of 'freedom of contract.' The profound differences between the legal cultures of the past and those of the present will appear almost immediately. Moral theologians' grappling with contracts was possible because they lived in a society that was far less secularized than is the case in modern Western States. The political context was one of religious

---

de la culture juridique occidentale dans le premier 'tribunal mondial', in: B. Coppein –
F. Stevens – L. Waelkens (eds.), Modernisme, tradition et acculturation juridique, Actes des Journées internationales de la Société d'histoire du droit tenues à Louvain, 28 mai–
1 juin 2008, [Iuris scripta historica, 27], Brussel 2011, p. 125–135.

24 P. Prodi, *Eine Geschichte der Gerechtigkeit, Vom Recht Gottes zum modernen Rechtsstaat*, München 2003, p. 270: 'Der Kampf, der in der ersten Hälfte des 17. Jahrhunderts ausgefochten wird, findet sowohl in den katholischen wie in den reformierten Ländern als Kampf um die Errichtung eines juristischen Systems statt, das in gewisser Weise alternative oder in Dialektik zum politischen System steht. Dass der Staat ab der zweiten Hälfte des Jahrhunderts als Sieger aus diesem Konflikt hervorgeht und versucht, das neue Recht des Gewissens in seine Machtapparate aufzunehmen, ist erwiesen, und ich werde nicht darauf zurückkommen.'

25 The metaphor is borrowed from K. Geens, *Hoe het vennootschapsrecht zich met een reverse take over verweert tegen een overnamepoging door het 'beginsel van de juiste prijs'*, in: Synthèses de droit bancaire et financier, Liber amicorum André Bruyneel, Bruxelles 2008, p. 452.

and secular authorities rivaling for normative power. The juridical context was one of legal pluralism and the parallel existence of a variety of tribunals and enforcement mechanisms. The anthropological foundations upon which the theologians' jurisprudence rested was characterized by a dualistic view of man. Individual citizens believed they were composed not only of a body but also of a soul. Presumably, the seminal encounter between moral theology and contract law has almost completely disappeared from historical accounts of private law, precisely because these contextual elements have completely changed.

It is important to point out the differences between the past and the present. Yet at the end of the day, the legal historian is called upon to present the results of his research in a language that can be understood by scholars from other specializations within the field of law and beyond.[26] In this sense, 'freedom of contract' is a starting point which not only offers a legitimate perspective on early modern scholastic contract doctrine. It also resonates with jurists of the twenty-first century. Moreover, the concept 'freedom of contract' allows one to organize a vast and complex literature around one central idea without doing injustice to the sources. Concretely, we will first show in chapter 3 how theologians developed a general law of contract centered around the notions of freedom, the will and mutual consent. Subsequently, this book will examine the limits to this principle in chapters 4 through 7. More specifically, we will assess to what extent 'freedom of contract' was thought to be constrained through the vices of the will, formality requirements by the State, moral turpitude, and justice in exchange.[27]

To begin with, the 'natural' limitations to 'contractual liberty' will be assessed in chapter 4. The moral theologians reorganized the *ius commune*

---

[26] On the need to foster the dialogue between specialist historians and the wider public community, particularly professional jurists, see R.C. van Caenegem, *Clio and the humanities, Alma Mater and prodigal sons?*, in: L. Milis et al. (eds.), Law, history, the Low Countries and Europe: R.C. van Caenegem, London-Rio Grande 1994, p. 27–35. That this is not an easy, albeit quite laudable task can be derived from observations on the increasingly practical nature of legal education and legal research in universities and law schools across the world; cf. D. Heirbaut, *Law*, in: N. Hammerstein, Social sciences, history and law, in: W. Rüegg (ed.), A history of the universities in Europe, Universities since 1945, [A History of the University in Europe, 4], Cambridge 2011, p. 414–422. In regard to the Belgian context, in particular, see D. Heirbaut – M.E. Storme, *The Belgian legal tradition, From a long quest for legal independence to a longing for dependence?*, European Review of Private Law, 14 (2006), p. 654.

[27] This operational scheme is indebted to the framework for identifying and evaluating contract theories as proposed in S.A. Smith, *Contract theory*, Oxford 2004.

tradition on contracts around the meeting of individual wills as the natural, necessary and sufficient cause to create contractual obligation. Therefore, it is only natural to find that the so-called 'vices of the will' are treated
as the first possible impediment to 'freedom of contract'. Next, chapter 5
discusses the 'formal' limitations to 'freedom of contract'. Although individual citizens have the power to create any natural obligation they want
through contract, the public authorities can decide to put a brake on this
natural liberty for the sake of the common good. This political limitation
of 'contractual freedom' occurs through the imposition of form or solemnity requirements. Chapter 6 treats the frustration of 'freedom of contract'
on moral grounds.[28] One might expect that the moral restraints on the
contracting parties' autonomy were of particular relevance to moral theologians. Lastly, chapter 7 explicates the impact of fairness in exchange or
commutative justice on 'freedom of contract'.

A couple of preliminary warnings are needed before we can go on. They
have to do with the basic methodological assumption that legal cultures
and legal institutions change all the time. In particular, legal historians
share a commitment to the proposition that legal concepts and institutions change over time.[29] They have an innate tendency, therefore, to
resist easy generalizations and naïve conceptual genealogies. While the
development of legal thought cannot be fully grasped without a profound
sensitivity for the autonomy and the technicalities of the legal system,
it does not entirely reveal its secrets unless it is seen also as the product of particular and changing historical contexts.[30] Sound legal historical scholarship, then, needs both more history and more law.[31] In light
of these caveats, this book refuses to offer a teleological account of the
history of the development of 'freedom of contract' from the Romans to

---

[28] These limitations are called 'substantial' after Smith, *Contract theory*, p. 245–268.
[29] Ch. Donahue, Jr., *A crisis of law? Reflections on the Church and the law over the centuries*, The Jurist, 65 (2005), p. 3.
[30] N. Jansen, 'Tief ist der Brunnen der Vergangenheit', Funktion, Methode und Ausgangspunkt historischer Fragestellungen in der Privatrechtsdogmatik*, Zeitschrift für neuere
Rechtsgeschichte, 27 (2005), p. 227.
[31] See the plea for a renewed paradigm in the historiography of law which values both
an increased openness to the intrinsic technicality of law and the contextual sensitivity
going with a profound historical consciousness in E. Conte, *Diritto comune, Storia e storiografia di un sistema dinamico*, Bologna 2009, p. 40–42. A similar call for the increased
complementary of both disciplines can be derived from S. Lepsius, *Rechtsgeschichte und
allgemeine Geschichtswissenschaft, Zur Wahrnehmung einer Differenz bei den Historikern
Burgdorf und Zwierlein*, Zeitschrift für neuere Rechtsgeschichte, 27 (2005), p. 304–310.

the present, as if history reached its natural endpoint in today's codified legal systems.

A further preliminary remark derives from Michel Foucault's (1926–1984) warning that all continuity in concepts is but apparent.[32] It pertains to the elusive genius of the law of obligations to be in constant movement and still keep up the appearance of stability. This especially true for the 'law of contract'.[33] Today, the history of contract law is usually thought of as the history of Roman contract law. Yet this view is in no small measure the fruit of the genius of the nineteenth and twentieth century Pandectist movements, which included eminent legal historians such as Savigny, Vinogradoff and Koschaker.[34] Their erudite attempts at recovering the law of Rome in its ancient or medieval form and giving it an appropriate, systematic structure have turned out to be both impressive and extremely useful. However, it should be remembered that they served the practical purposes of their time in the first place.[35] To be sure, the texts of Roman law have provided the basis for Western thinking about obligations and contracts, but they were re-worked for many ages by many clever men coming from many different contexts.[36]

The law of contract has not come down to us in the form of a refurbished piece of static legal architecture from Rome. Throughout the ages,

---

[32] M. Foucault, *Les mots et les choses, Une archéologie des sciences humaines*, Paris 1966, preface.

[33] J.-L. Gazzaniga, *Domat et Pothier, Le contrat à la fin de l'Ancien Régime*, Droits, 12 (1990), p. 37–38.

[34] There is no need to try to emulate Francesco Calasso's respectful yet oft-repeated critique of the legal historical method and the ideological motives underlying the work of these eminent jurists; cf. the first chapter (*Tradizione e critica metodologica*) of his *Introduzione al diritto comune*, Milano 1951, p. 3–30, and *Il problema storico del diritto comune e i suoi riflessi metodologici nella storiografia giuridica europea*, in: Storicità del diritto, [Civiltà del diritto, 15], Milano 1966, p. 205–226 [originally published in Archives d'histoire du droit oriental, Revue internationale des droits de l'Antiquité, 2 (1953), p. 441–463].

[35] For a compelling reflection on the contextual elements that help to explain the use of Roman law as European *ius commune* after the second world war, particularly in the work of Paul Koschaker, see M. Stolleis, *The influence of 'ius commune' in Germany in the early modern period on the rise of the modern state*, Rivista internazionale di diritto comune, 11 (2000), p. 275–285, especially the introduction. For a detailed analysis of the fascinating attempt by the nineteenth century Pandectists to develop a systematic science of law on the basis of Roman categories for the purpose of unifying private law in the German areas, see the two-volume standard work by P. Cappellini, *Systema iuris*, [Per la storia del pensiero giuridico moderno, 17–19], Milano 1984–5.

[36] J.-F. Gerkens, *Comment enseigner le droit privé (romain) en Europe? L'enseignement du droit romain en Europe aujourd'hui (Trento, 12–13 novembre 2010)*, European Review of Private Law, 19 (2011), p. 339: 'Le droit romain de Domat, n'est pas celui de Savigny ou de Cujas, mais tous ont été très utiles pour leur époque et pour le futur.'

the written sources of the terrific outburst of juristic activity in ancient Rome have been re-created in the image of the needs of the time.[37] For example, in the West, the law of Rome was reshaped by its medieval heirs, the civilians, from the 12th century onwards. In this regard, one should insist that the transformations which the Roman law of Antiquity underwent during medieval and early modern times need not be regarded as repugnant forms of degeneration. Francesco Calasso (1904–1965), the father of post-second World War Italian legal historical scholarship, has warned against overly negative assessments of Roman law in its medieval form. The conception of the pure and original Roman law is fallacious. Calasso invites us to see medieval Roman law as a vivid witness to the dynamic and variegated life which Roman law has lived until today.[38]

Roman law lived one of its most intense, prolonged and productive stages by participating in the rich life of the Church. Not surprisingly, the Church is famously said to live by virtue of Roman law (*Ecclesia vivit lege romana*).[39] There is a general consensus that the seeds for a profound transformation of contract law were sown by the canon lawyers. One should not underestimate, though, the impact of the ideology of *laïcité* that spread along with the *Code Napoléon* and the repression of the *ancien régime*, not only on the actual, battered relationship between State and

---

[37] See H.J. Berman – Ch. J Reid, Jr., *Roman law in Europe and the ius commune, A historical overview with emphasis on the new legal science of the sixteenth century*, Syracuse Journal of International Law and Commerce, 20 (1994), p. 1–2, and L. Waelkens, *Civium causa, handboek Romeins recht*, Leuven 2008, p. 379–382.

[38] F. Calasso, *Diritto volgare, diritti romanzi, diritto comune*, in: Atti del congresso internazionale di diritto Romano e storia del diritto, 2, Milano 1951, p. 372. The argument has been taken up afresh by Emanuele Conte with critical observations on the ideological presuppositions that have often underlied legal historical scholarship over the last two centuries; cf. *Storia interna e storia esterna, Il diritto medievale da Francesco Calasso alla fine del XX secolo*, Rivista internazionale di diritto comune, 17 (2006), p. 299–322.

[39] A. Thier, *Ecclesia vivit lege Romana*, in: A. Cordes – H. Lück – D. Werkmüller (eds.), Handwörterbuch zur deutschen Rechtsgeschichte, Lieferung 5, Berlin 2007, cols. 1176–1177; J. Gaudemet, *Le droit au service de la pastorale (Décret de Gratien, C. XVI, q. 3)*, in: Formation du droit canonique et gouvernement de l'Église de l'Antiquité à l'Âge classique, Recueil d'articles, Strasbourg 2008, p. 339–340 [= reprint from *Società, istituzioni, spiritualità, Studi in onore di Cinzio Violante*, Spoleto 1994, p. 409–422]. For an invaluable article on the impact of Roman law on the early Church fathers; cf. J. Gaudemet, *L'apport du droit romain à la patristique latine du IVe siècle*, in: Formation du droit canonique et gouvernement de l'Église de l'Antiquité à l'Âge classique, Recueil d'articles, Strasbourg 2008, p. 41–54 [= reprint from *Les transformations de la société chrétienne au IVe siècle, Miscellanea historiae ecclesiasticae*, [Bibliothèque de la Revue d'Histoire Ecclésiastique, 67], Louvain-la-Neuve 1983, p. 165–181].

Church, but inevitably also on legal historical scholarship.[40] The Roman law of Antiquity has often been artificially stripped of its religious, as well as its philosophical, context.[41] Textbooks often do not fail to mention the contribution of canon law to the development of contract law. But in such instances, canon law is limited to a relatively tiny segment in its complex history, namely the so-called 'classical' period of canon law roughly between 1140 and 1298.[42] Moreover, the contribution by the theologians to the same field has been eclipsed almost completely, perhaps due to the quite pardonable tendency of the mind to project the secular tendencies of the present onto the past.

From these preliminary remarks it will be clear that we do not purport to enter into debates provoked by sweeping statements such as Henry Sumner Maine's dictum that the movement of progressive societies is from status to contract.[43] We are reluctant to subscribe to the Enlightenment proposition that history can be understood in terms of linear progress. Much less do we wish to apply conclusions taken from observed changes in legal doctrine in the early modern period to the history of the construction of social relations in modern times.[44] The 'labor question' formed the

---

[40] The dazzling impact of the strict division of State and Church today on legal historical scholarship is highlighted in G. Dolezalek, *The moral theologians' doctrine of restitution and its juridification in the sixteenth and seventeenth centuries*, in: T.W. Bennett e.a. (ed.), Acta Juridica, Essays in honour of Wouter de Vos, Cape Town – Wetton – Johannesburg 1992, p. 104–105. The rupture in legal culture brought about by the French Revolution is aptly described in J.-M. Carbasse, *Manuel d'introduction historique au droit*, Paris 2007[5], p. 241–300.

[41] Reacting against what it calls 'the biased view' that Roman law was the first 'autonomous legal science', O. Tellegen-Couperus (ed.), *Law and religion in the Roman Republic*, [Mnemosyne, Supplements, 336], Boston-Leiden 2011 highlights the profoundly religious dimension to Roman legal thought and practice. L.C. Winkel, for his part, has recently emphasized the Aristotelian influence on Gaius' outline of the Roman system of obligations; cf. *Alcune osservazioni sulla classificazione delle obbligazioni e sui contratti nominati nel diritto romano*, in: M. Talamanca (ed.), Bullettino dell'Instituto di Diritto Romano 'Vittoria Scialoja', IIIa serie, CIII–CIV (2000–2001), Milano 2009, p. 51–66. I am grateful to professor Winkel for drawing my attention to this article.

[42] Specialists are increasingly calling for more in-depth studies of the canon law in later periods, e.g. O. Condorelli, *Il diritto canonico nel tardo Medioevo, Secoli XIV–XV, Appunti per una discussione*, Rivista internazionale di diritto comune, 19 (2008), p. 263–267.

[43] H. Sumner Maine, *Ancient law, its connections with the early history of society and its relation to modern ideas*, London 1883[9], p. 168–170, also cited in R. Feenstra – M. Ahsmann, *Contract*, p. 61–63, num. 43.

[44] The modern debates in France about 'liberal' versus more 'socially responsible' accounts of contract law are aptly summarized in D. Deroussin, *Histoire du droit des obligations*, Paris 2007, p. 485–506. An elaborate study on the subject is offered by V. Ranouil, *L'autonomie de la volonté, naissance et évolution d'un concept*, [Travaux et recherches de l'Université de droit, d'économie et de sciences sociales de Paris, Série sciences

context for the famous American jurist Roscoe Pound's (1870–1964) scathing critique of 'freedom of contract'.[45] Yet the labor question is clearly
not the background against which the moral theologians promoted 'freedom of contract'. As a phrase, 'freedom of contract' came into circulation
only around the middle of the nineteenth century, during the debates on
whether joint stock corporations could be granted limited liability or not.[46]
Yet limited liability is of much greater concern to modern lawyers than it
was to theologians or, for that matter, jurists in the sixteenth century. The
victory of *laissez-faire* capitalism also postdates the writings of the moral
theologians, even though capitalism's march of conquest may have begun
precisely during their lifetime.[47]

1.3   SELECTION OF SOURCES

The focus of this monograph lies on texts—printed Latin sources composed by Catholic moral theologians and canon lawyers roughly between
1500 and 1650. One should keep in mind that there is an abundant Catholic theological literature on contracts written in the vernacular, but those
sources have not been employed for the present study, except for occasional references to Tomás de Mercado (c. 1530–1575).[48] By the same token,

---

historiques, 12], Paris 1980. For the Anglo-Saxon world, see P.S. Atiyah, *The rise and fall of
'freedom of contract'*, Oxford 1979. On the difference in scope between contemporary debates
and the moral theologians' conceptualization of 'freedom of contract', see W. Decock,
Jesuit freedom of contract, Tijdschrift voor Rechtsgeschiedenis, 77 (2009), p. 457–458,
and W. Decock, *Freedom, The legacy of early modern scholasticism to contract law*, in:
D. Heirbaut – X. Rousseaux – A.A. Wijffels (eds.), Histoire du droit et de la justice, Une
nouvelle génération de recherches / Justitie-en rechtsgeschiedenis, Een nieuwe onderzoeksgeneratie, Louvain-la-Neuve 2009, p. 233–245.
  45 R. Pound, *Liberty of contract*, Yale Law Journal, 18 (1909), p. 454–487.
  46 M. Lobban, *Contract*, in: The Oxford history of the laws of England, Vol. 12: 1820–1914:
Private law, Oxford 2010, p. 298.
  47 W. Decock, *In defense of commercial capitalism (Antwerp, Early 17th century), Lessius,
partnerships and the 'contractus trinus'*, in: W. Decock – F. Stevens – B. Van Hofstraeten
(eds.), Medieval and modern company law in Europe, [Iuris Scripta Historica], Brussels
2012 [forthcoming].
  48 On Mercado, see A. Botero Bernal, *Análisis de la obra 'Suma de tratos y contratos'
del Dominico Tomás de Mercado*, in: A. Botero Bernal (ed.), Diagnóstico de la eficacia
del derecho en Colombia y otros ensayos, Medellín 2003, p. 128–192. References to the
sixteenth-century literature on contracts in Spanish are contained, amongst others, in
Birocchi, *Causa e categoria generale del contratto*, p. 228–238, and Duve, *Kanonisches Recht
und die Ausbildung allgemeiner Vertragslehren in der Spanischen Spätscholastik*, p. 389–408.
See also I. Zorroza – H. Rodríguez-Penelas (eds.), *Francisco García, Tratado utilísimo y muy
general de todos los contratos (1583)*, [Colleción de pensamiento medieval y renacentista,
46], Pamplona 2003.

the elaborations on contract law in protestant moral theological literature fall outside the scope of this book. References to the work of civilians such as Matthias van Wezenbeke (1531–1586) and Antonio Gómez emerge occasionaly.

The appropriateness of the terms 'late scholasticism' (*Spätscholastik*),[49] 'late medieval scholasticism',[50] or 'second scholasticism' (*seconda scolastica*),[51] which are often employed to designate the moral theologians of the early modern period, is subject to endless debate.[52] Therefore, we have tried to avoid their use. In this monograph the terms '(moral) theologians' and 'early modern scholastics' will be preferred to English variants on *Spätscholastik* and *seconda scolastica*. There are both substantive and pragmatic reasons for this preference. Scholasticism can be succinctly defined as a method of academic research chiefly inspired by Aristotelian logic. It begins with the rise of the universities in the twelfth century and it continues on in sundry forms until the twentieth century.[53] Jurists as well as theologians applied scholasticism as a method of systematically treating a particular subject.[54] Therefore, by circumscribing the *doctores* as 'moral theologians' rather than as 'scholastics', the argument gains in

---

[49] E.g. F. Grunert – K. Seelmann (eds.), *Die Ordnung der Praxis, Neue Studien zur Spanischen Spätscholastik*, [Frühe Neuzeit, 68], Tübingen 2001

[50] E.g. J.H. Burns, *Scholasticism, Survival and revival*, in: J.H. Burns – M. Goldie (eds.), The Cambridge history of political thought, 1450–1700, Cambridge e.a. 1991, p. 132–133.

[51] E.g. A. Ghisalberti (ed.), *Dalla prima alla seconda scolastica, Paradigmi e percorsi storiografici*, Bologna 2000.

[52] For a critical discussion of the variegated categories that are being used, amongst which figure also 'Renaissance Aristotelianism', 'Baroque scholasticism', and 'post-Tridentine scholasticism', see M. Forlivesi, *A man, an age, a book*, in: M. Forlivesi (ed.), Rem in seipsa cernere, Saggi sul pensiero filosofico di Bartolomeo Mastri (1602–1673), Atti del Convegno di studi sul pensiero filosofico di Bartolomeo Mastri da Meldola (1602–1673), Meldola-Bertinoro, 20–22 settembre 2002, Padova 2006, p. 98–114. As the title of his contribution indicates, Jacob Schmutz proposes to use the term 'modern scholasticism' to indicate the theological and philosophical writings, associated with the 'schools', of the sixteenth and the subsequent centuries; cf. *Bulletin de scolastique moderne* (1), Revue thomiste, 100 (2000), p. 276–277.

[53] For an elaborated historical semantic analysis of the term 'scholasticism', see R. Quinto, *Scholastica, Storia di un concetto*, [Subsidia Mediaevalia Patavina, 2], Padova 2001.

[54] The tremendous influence of scholastic logic on the medieval *ius commune* is the subject of a compelling study by A. Errera, *The role of logic in the legal science of the glossators and commentators, Distinction, dialectical syllogism, and apodictic syllogism, An investigation into the epistemological roots of legal science in the late Middle Ages*, in: A. Padovani – P. Stein (eds.), The jurists' philosophy of law from Rome to the seventeenth century, [A treatise of legal philosopy and general jurisprudence, 7], Dordrecht 2007, p. 79–155. For a less recent contribution, see A. Van Hove, *De oorsprong van de kerkelijke rechtswetenschap en de scholastiek*, [Mededeelingen van de Koninklijke Vlaamsche

precision. If the term 'scholasticism' is nevertheless preferred, then it is appropriate to limit it on a chronological basis by adding the adjective 'early modern', to designate the phase of scholasticism between approximately 1500 and 1650.

Even allowing for the aforementioned limitations that are inherent in the selection of the sources, the mass of available material remains enormous in volume and formidable in nature. Almost desperate, Karl Friedrich Stäudlin (1761–1826) confessed that a historian loses heart when confronted with the complex and nuanced literature of the myriad Catholic moral theologians of the early modern period.[55] Indeed, the fact that the sources are so voluminous might explain why the history of the legal teachings of the Catholic moral theologians has not yet been written.[56] Another possible factor in this neglect is that, traditionally, the Catholic moral theological contribution to the history of law has been repressed both from within and from outside of the Catholic Church. Needless to say, the Jesuits, who are among the strongest advocates of the symbiosis of law and morality, have been under attack both from without and from within the Catholic Church.[57] Also, it has been submitted that the struggle between Protestantism and Catholicism, certainly during the German *Kulturkampf* (1871–1878) might have favored a bias against recognizing the Catholic legacy to juristic thought.[58]

Academie voor Wetenschappen, Letteren en Schoone Kunsten van België, Klasse der Letteren, Jaargang 6, Nr. 3], Antwerpen – Utrecht 1946.

[55] Karl Friedrich Stäudlin, *Geschichte der christlichen Moral seit dem Wiederaufleben der Wissenschaften*, [Geschichte der Künste und Wissenschaften, 2], Göttingen 1808, p. 441.

[56] But this can quickly change, if historical scholarship in canon law is anything to go by. Compare Ch. Donahue, Jr., *Why the history of canon law is not written*, London 1986 (arguing that the vast amount of source material was an important factor explaining the absence of general outlines of the history of canon law), and the response to it hardly a decade later: J. Brundage, *Medieval canon law*, London – New York 1995. See also R.H. Helmholz, *The Oxford history of the laws of England, Vol. 1: The canon law and ecclesiastical jurisdiction from 597 to the 1640s*, Oxford 2004.

[57] S. Knebel, *Wille, Würfel und Wahrscheinlichkeit, Das System der moralischen Notwendigkeit in der Jesuitenscholastik*, [Paradeigmata, 21], Hamburg 2000, p. 20–24; H. Callewier, *Anti-jezuïtisme in de Zuidelijke Nederlanden (1542–1773)*, Trajecta, 16 (2007), p. 30–50; P.-A. Fabre – C. Maire (eds.), *Les Antijésuites, Discours, figures et lieux de l'antijésuitisme à l'époque moderne*, Rennes 2010.

[58] We are grateful to Prof. Dr. Joachim Rückert for this suggestion, which merits further investigation that goes beyond the scope of this doctorate. On the *Kulturkampf* and the role it played in the historiography of canon law, see S. Ruppert, *Kirchenrecht und Kulturkampf, Historische Legitimation, politische Mitwirkung und wissenschaftliche Begleitung durch die Schule Emil Ludwig Richters*, [Ius Ecclesiasticum, 70], Tübingen 2002. From the polemical tone against the *papistae* among natural lawyers such as Christian Thomasius, as will be seen infra (e.g. pp. 47–48), one may infer that this historiographical struggle has been raging on for at least three centuries.

The focus on the Catholic tradition is certainly not meant to deny the profound influence of Protestant movements on the development of legal thought. Sixteenth-century jurists with a Calvinist or Lutheran background have made fundamental contributions to several fields of law.[59] Philip Melanchton (1497–1560) and John Calvin (1509–1564) are but two of the most famous examples.[60] Generally speaking, though, there is clear evidence that the reformed theologians understood the distinction between law and morality in much stronger terms than the 'followers of the Pope' (papistae). Hence, reformed moral theology appears to be much less juridical in nature than the confessional literature written by Catholics. In particular, Puritan ethics was inspired by high-minded devotional literature rather than technical legal argumentation.[61] Indeed, the alienation between law and morality, the strict separation between the realms of the jurists and the theologians, and the rise of the modern State would perhaps not have occurred if Luther had not condemned the legalistic outlook of medieval Christian morality in the first place.

From a methodological point of view, priority has been given to the study of the Antwerp-born Jesuit Leonard Lessius (1554–1623). The third section of the second book of his On justice and right (De iustitia et iure) is entirely dedicated to contract law.[62] Lessius is one of the foremost

---

[59] E.g. M. Schmoeckel, Das Gesetz Gottes als Ausgangspunkt christlicher Ethik? Zu calvinistischen Traditionen des 16. Jh.s im Hinblick auf ihre rechtshistorische Relevanz, in: Ius commune, 25 (1998), p. 347–366; J. Witte, Jr., Law and Protestantism, The legal teachings of the Lutheran Reformation, Cambridge 2002; H.J. Berman, Law and revolution II, The impact of the Protestant Reformations on the Western legal tradition, Cambridge Mass. 2003 (with an emphasis on Lutheran legal philosophy); Ch. Strohm, Calvinismus und Recht, Weltanschaulich-konfessionelle Aspekte im Werk reformierter Juristen in der Frühen Neuzeit, [Spätmittelalter, Humanismus, Reformation, 42], Tübingen 2008.

[60] Among the vast, recent secondary literature on Calvin, see H.J. Selderhuis (ed.), Calvin Handbuch, Tübingen 2008 and B. Pitkin, Calvin's mosaic harmony, Biblical exegesis and early modern legal history, The Sixteenth Century Journal, 41 (2010), p. 441–466; on Melanchton, see I. Deflers, Lex und Ordo, Eine rechtshistorische Untersuchung der Rechtsauffassung Melanchtons, [Schriften zur Rechtsgeschichte, 121], Berlin 2005.

[61] J.F. Keenan, Was William Perkins' 'Whole treatise of cases of conscience' casuistry? Hermeneutics and British practical divinity, in: H.E. Braun – E. Vallance (eds.), Contexts of conscience in early modern Europe, 1500–1700, Basingstoke 2004, p. 17. On Reformed moral theology, see also C. Selzner, Les forges des philistins, La problématique d'une casuistique réformée en Angleterre de William Perkins à Jeremy Taylor, in: S. Boarini (ed.), La casuistique classique, genèse, formes, devenir, Saint-étienne 2009, p. 73–86; M. Wisse – M. Sarot – W. Otten (eds.), Scholasticism reformed, essays in honour of Willem J. van Asselt, [Studies in theology and religion, 14], Leiden – Boston 2010.

[62] For further discussion, see chapter 2. What follows is a preliminary overview of the titles of the chapters in Lessius, De iustitia et iure ceterisque virtutibus cardinalibus, Antverpiae 1621, lib. 2, sect. 3 (De contractibus): 17. De contractibus in genere; 18. De promissione

representatives of scholastic moral theology in the early modern period outside of the Iberian peninsula.[63] His profound influence on the history of contract law has been confirmed by all of the abovementioned experts in the field.[64] The first edition of Lessius' treatise was published in 1605 with John Masius in Leuven.[65] In terms of chronology, this means that Lessius is an interesting starting point for yet another reason. First, the evolution of early modern scholastic contract doctrine during the sixteenth century, mainly in Spain, is already integrated in his work. Second, Lessius' treatise in turn inspired Hugo Grotius' *The right of war and peace* (*De iure belli ac pacis*), which was published only twenty years after the first edition of Lessius' *On justice and right*. Also, other Jesuit writers of the first half of the seventeenth century, such as the aforementioned Juan de Lugo and Pedro de Oñate, drew heavily on Lessius.

The initial, methodological concentration on Lessius as the main gateway to the much larger volume of moral theological literature on contracts has had a couple of consequences. First, Lessius runs as a 'red thread' through all of the chapters. The selection of other jurists and theologians has been largely, if not exclusively, based on their relevance for gaining a better understanding of the argumentation in Lessius.[66] This

et donatione; 19. De testamentis et legatis; 20. De mutuo et usura; 21. De emptione et venditione; 22. De censibus; 23. De cambiis; 24. De locatione, emphyteusi, et feudo; 25. De societate; 26. De ludo et sponsionibus; 27. De deposito et commodato; 28. De fideiussione, pignore et hypotheca.

[63] See Schmutz, *Bulletin de scolastique moderne*, p. 326–329; J.P. Doyle, *Hispanic scholastic philosophy*, in: J. Hankins (ed.), The Cambridge companion to Renaissance philosophy, Cambridge 2007, p. 263.

[64] Quoted supra, p. 2, n. 4.

[65] In this monograph, the fifth, augmented and corrected edition published in 1621 by the famous Antwerp printers Plantin-Moretus is used as a reference, since it is the last edition which appeared during Lessius' lifetime. An account of the successive editions of Lessius' *De iustitia et iure* is included in T. Van Houdt, *Leonardus Lessius over lening, intrest en woeker, De iustitia et iure, lib. 2, cap. 20, Editie, vertaling en commentaar*, [Verhandelingen van de Koninklijke Academie voor Wetenschappen, Letteren en Schone Kunsten van België, Klasse der Letteren, 162], Brussel 1998, p. xviii–xxv. Van Houdt's masterpiece has been reviewed by G.P. van Nifterik in Tijdschrift voor Rechtsgeschiedenis, 69 (2001), p. 164–166.

[66] The canonists who proved to be particularly influential on Lessius' thought appear to be Sinibaldus Flischus (Innocent IV) (c. 1195–1254), Nicolaus de Tudeschis (Abbas Panormitanus) (1386–1455), Felinus Sandaeus (1444–1503), Martinus de Azpilcueta (Dr. Navarrus) (1492–1586), Didacus Covarruvias y Leyva (1512–1577), and Tomás Sánchez (1550–1610). Among the civilians, we count Bartolus de Saxoferrato (1313–1357), Baldus degli Ubaldis (1327–1400), and Antonius Gomezius (1501–1561). There are, of course, references to the great manuals of confessors by Angelus Carlettus de Clavasio (c. 1414–1495) and Silvester Prierias (1456–1523). A great many theologians are cited by Lessius. Among the more important figure Thomas Aquinas (1225–1274), Bernardinus Senensis (1380–1444),

has not prevented us from occasionaly studying the work of authors who made a significant contribution to a particular topic, even though they are not cited by Lessius.[67] The focus lies on the great sixteenth century Spanish thinkers and on the contemporaneous civilians and canonists who have handed down the *ius commune* tradition to these moral theologians. Second, the choice of perspective has often been determined by questions and cases that gained particular relevance in Lessius. Conversely, themes that no longer play a direct role in Lessius' contract doctrine are omitted, even though, originally, they were important for the development of contract law, such as vow-making.[68]

Debate, disagreement, and pluralism of opinions are some of the most characteristic features of the writings of the doctors of both the *ius commune* and moral theology. From the twelfth century onward, jurists and theologians shared a method of doing research known as 'scholastic', because it was used in the schools and universities.[69] It is an essential tool for nuanced debate that both fully recognizes the existence of opposing opinions and tries to reconcile them through making distinctions, using interpretative reason and balancing the relative weight of authoritative opinions. In a dialectical manner, it seeks to discern how general moral or juridical principles apply to particular cases. Gratian's *Decretum* (c. 1140) stands out as one of the earliest illustrations of the splendid application of this method to legal argument. This method takes seriously Aristotle's warning that there is no such thing as absolute certainty to be attained in human affairs. There are several opinions with a certain degree of probability, but none of them can claim to tell the absolute truth. Generations of learned argumentations bring about a common

---

Antoninus Florentinus (1389–1459), Conradus Summenhart (1455–1502), Adrianus VI (1459–1523), Johannes Maior (c. 1467–1550), Cajetanus (1469–1534), Franciscus de Vitoria (1483/1492–1546), Dominicus Soto (1494–1560), Joannes Medina (1490–1546), and Ludovicus Molina (1535–1600). Biographical information on these authors will be provided in the course of the exposition.

[67] E.g. the Spanish *doctor utriusque iuris* Fortunius Garcia (1494–1543) in regard to the development of general actionability of naked agreements, and the Portuguese jurist Arias Piñel (1515–1563) concerning just pricing and *laesio enormis,* the French theologian Petrus Johannes Olivi (1248–1298) in regard to prostitution agreements, the Portuguese Jesuit Fernão Rebelo (1547–1608) concerning the vices of the will, and the Spanish Jesuit Gregorius de Valentia (1549–1603) in the section on just pricing.

[68] E.g. S. Piron, *Vœu et contrat chez Pierre de Jean Olivi,* Les cahiers du centre de recherches historiques, 16 (1996), p. 43–56.

[69] On the scholastic method, see P. Koslowski – R. Schönberger, *Was ist Scholastik?,* [Philosophie und Religion, Schriftenreihe des Forschungsinstituts für Philosophie Hannover, 2], Hildesheim 1991.

opinion (*communis opinio*).[70] This common opinion is highly authoritative, but it is not necessarily tantamount to eternal truth. There remains a place for debate and controversy.

The pluralistic character of legal and moral thought in the Middle Ages and the early modern period poses a challenge to the legal historian who wishes to make generalizations about the emergence of a principle of 'freedom of contract' in the writings of moral theologians over a period of about a century and a half. Sir Edward Coke (1552–1634) complained that the *ius commune* was a 'sea full of waves', and Blaise Pascal (1623–1662) famously noted that there were few cases in which one could not find one moral theologian saying yes and the other saying no.[71] However, we regard the respect for pluralism of opinions in scholarly debates as an attractive asset of the scholastic tradition in law and theology rather than as a hindrance. Much attention will be paid to conflict on a multitude of levels: conflict between arguments, conflict between principles and reality, conflict between the values underlying the choice for different legal rules.

---

[70] S. Lepsius, *Communis opinio doctorum*, in: A. Cordes – H. Lück – D. Werkmüller (eds.), Handwörterbuch zur deutschen Rechtsgeschichte, Band 1, Lieferung 4, Berlin 2006, cols. 875–877; I. Maclean, *Interpretation and meaning in the Renaissance, The case of law*, [Ideas in Context, 21], Cambridge 1992, p. 93; E. Andujar – C. Bazán, *Aequitas, aequalitas et auctoritas chez les maîtres de l'école espagnole du XVIe siècle*, in: D. Letocha (ed.), Aequitas, aequalitas, auctoritas, Raison théorique et légitimation de l'autorité dans le XVIe siècle européen, Actes du IIe colloque international (1990) du Centre de recherche en philosophie politique et sociale de l'Université d'Ottawa, [De Pétrarque à Descartes, 54], Paris 1992, p. 172–185.
[71] E. Coke, *Second part of the Institutes of the laws of England*, London 1642, Proeme, *in fine* (available online at *Early English Books Online*; last visited on May 20, 2011); B. Pascal, *Les Provinciales ou les lettres écrites par Louis De Montalte*, Amsterdam 1657, Lettre 5 (March 20, 1656), p. 69 (available online at *The Digital Libary of the Catholic Reformation*; last visited on May 20, 2011).

CHAPTER TWO

THEOLOGIANS AND CONTRACT LAW: CONTEXTUAL ELEMENTS

Before delving into the technicalities of the early modern theologians'
treatment of contract law, a couple of introductory notes may provide
familiarity with the historical and ideological background against which
these highly sophisticated legal doctrines were shaped. Sound legal history, just as sound comparative law, cannot just limit itself to the study of
the history of legal concepts. That would result in the narcisstic pursuit of
uncovering the image of the present in the past. Just like Don Quixote, a
dogmatic legal historian is bound to wake up in a strange world, incapable
of explaining why the legal universe that he is familiar with is not out
there.[72] In chapters three through seven, the legal vocabulary developed
by the theologians when discussing contract law will often convey a feeling of familiarity. This will lead one to feel that 'the past is never dead,
it is not even past'.[73] However, the impression that is likely to dominate
the reader's experience in the following paragraphs can be summarized
through that fine saying that 'the past is a foreign country, they do things
differently there'.[74]

One of the main differences between the past and the present is the
engagement with law by moral theologians. Medieval Roman and canon
law were unquestioned sources of wisdom to the Spanish theologians. For
one thing, the *ius commune* was one of the pillars of the secular jurisdictions they were dwelling in. For another thing, the theologians themselves
expressly recognized the authority of the civilian tradition. Without meaning to be exhaustive, the first part of this chapter seeks to highlight some
of the conditions that made the theologians' involvement with law possible. It will then be reminded in the second part that the symbiosis of law

---

[72] The metaphor is borrowed from M. Adams, *Wat de rechtsvergelijking vermag, Over
onderzoeksdesign*, Ars Aequi, 60, (2011), p. 195.
[73] Thus one of the famous lines from the American writer William Faulkner's (1897–
1962) *Requiem for a nun*.
[74] See the almost proverbial opening sentence of the British writer Leslie Poles Hart-
ley's (1895–1972) *The Go-between*, discussed in A. Rose, *Studying the past, The nature
and development of legal history as an academic discipline*, The Journal of Legal History,
31 (2010), p. 101–102.

and morality was already intrinsic to the Catholic tradition of manuals for confessors. In the course of the sixteenth and seventeenth centuries, this synthesis grew more intense, eventually resulting in the creation of systematic legal treatises, certainly in the wake of that buoyant yet diffuse Spanish tradition of moral theological, economic and juridical thought often associated with the 'School of Salamanca'. The third and the fourth part of this chapter explain why this particular form of moral theology can be conceived of in truly juridical terms.

2.1   THEOLOGIANS AND THE *IUS COMMUNE*

2.1.1   *Law and theology?*

At first sight, the idea of searching for sophisticated elaborations on contract law in Lessius and in the works of other learned men who were not necessarily professional jurists might seem counter-intuitive. Legal positivism forbids the introduction of theological narratives into the black-letter text of the law. It teaches that law should be strictly distinguished from morality and religion. And yet, evidence is mounting that many legal concepts are derived from theological traditions—not to mention the absolutely vital role which the canon law played in the shaping of Western law.[75] This is an established fact in the realm of public law and international law, not in the least thanks to the late Carl Schmitt, Ernst

---

[75] Naturally, the literature on the contribution of canon law to the civil and common law tradition is immense. In this context, of particular relevance are A. Lefebvre-Teillard, *Le droit canonique et la formation des grands principes du droit privé français*, in: H. Scholler (ed.), Die Bedeutung des kanonischen Rechts für die Entwicklung einheitlicher Rechtsprinzipien, [Arbeiten zur Rechtsvergleichung, Schriftenreihe der Gesellschaft für Rechtsvergleichung, 177], Baden-Baden 1996, p. 9–22; P. Landau, *Pacta sunt servanda, Zu den kanonistischen Grundlagen der Privatautonomie*, in: M. Ascheri et al. (eds.), Ins wasser geworfen und Ozeane durchquert, Festschrift für Knut Wolfgang Nörr, Köln-Weimar-Wien 2003, p. 457–474. Also it is worthwhile mentioning the ongoing project to give a systematic overview of the legacy of canon law to different fields of the law: O. Condorelli – F. Roumy – M. Schmoeckel (eds.), *Der Einfluss der Kanonistik auf die Europäische Rechtskultur*, Band 1: *Zivil- und Zivilprozessrecht*, [Norm und Struktur, 37], Köln-Weimar-Wien 2009. The influence of the canon law tradition on the common law is the subject of nuanced debate in R. Helmholz, *Roman canon law in Reformation England*, Cambridge 1990 and Ch. Donahue, Jr., *Ius commune, canon law and common law in England*, Tulane Law Review, 66 (1992), p. 1745–1780.

H. Kantorowicz and James Brown Scott,[76] but the legacy of theological learning in private law and commercial law has been equally recognized.[77]

---

[76] Recent literature in what seems to be an exploding field of study includes J.P. Doyle, *Francisco Suárez on the law of nations*, in: M.W. Janis – C. Evans (eds.), *Religion and international law*, London 1999, p. 103–120; N. Brieskorn, *Luis de Molinas Weiterentwicklung der Kriegsethik und des Kriegsrechts der Scholastik*, in: N. Brieskorn – M. Riedenauer (eds.), Suche nach Frieden, Politische Ethik in der Frühen Neuzeit, I, [Theologie und Frieden, 19], Barsbüttel 2000, p. 167–191; R. Lesaffer, *The medieval canon law of contract and early modern treaty law*, in: Journal of the history of international law, 2 (2000), p. 178–198; F. Hafner – A. Loretan – C. Spenlé, *Naturrecht und Menschenrecht, Der Beitrag der Spanischen Spätscholastik zur Entwicklung der Menschenrechte*, in: F. Grunert – K. Seelmann (eds.), Die Ordnung der Praxis, Neue Studien zur Spanischen Spätscholastik, [Frühe Neuzeit, 68], Tübingen 2001, p. 123–153; M.F. Renoux-Zagamé, *Du droit de Dieu au droit de l'homme*, Paris 2003; M. Stolleis, *Das Auge des Gesetzes, Geschichte einer Metapher*, München 2004; D. Bauer, *The importance of canon law and the scholastic tradition for the emergence of an international legal order*, in: R. Lesaffer (ed.), Peace treaties and international law in history, Cambridge 2004, p. 198–221; A. Boureau, *La religion de l'état, La construction de la République étatique dans le discours théologique de l'Occident médiéval (1250–1350)*, Paris 2006; G. Agamben, *Il regno e la gloria, Per una genealogia teologica dell'economia e del governo*, [Homo Sacer, II. 2], Vicenza 2007; M. Scattola, *Sklaverei, Krieg und Recht, Die Vorlesung über die Regula 'Peccatum' von Diego de Covarrubias y Leyva*, in: M. Kaufmann – R. Schnepf (eds.), Politische Metaphysik, Die Entstehung moderner Rechtskonzeptionen in der Spanischen Scholastik, [Treffpunkt Philosophie, 8], Frankfurt am Main 2007, p. 303–356; D. Recknagel, *Einheit des Denkens trotz konfessioneller Spaltung, Parallelen zwischen den Rechtslehren von Francisco Suárez und Hugo Grotius*, [Treffpunkt Philosophie, 10], Frankfurt am Main 2010; A. Pagden, *Gentili, Vitoria, and the fabrication of a natural law of nations*, in: B. Kingsbury – B. Straumann (eds.), The Roman foundations of the law of nations, Alberico Gentili and the justice of empire, Oxford-New York 2010, p. 340–362; J. Cruz Cruz, *Ius gentium bei Vitoria, Ein eindeutig internationalistischer Ansatz*, in: A. Fidora – M. Lutz-Bachmann – A. Wagner (eds.), Lex and Ius, Essays on the foundation of law in medieval and early modern philosophy, [Politische Philosophie und Rechtstheorie des Mittelalters und der Neuzeit, Series 2, Studies, 1], Stuttgart 2010, p. 301–332; J. Waldron, *A religious view of the foundations of international law*, [NYU School of Law, Public law and legal theory research paper series, 11–29], New York 2011; M. Koskenniemi, *Empire and international law, the real Spanish contribution*, University of Toronto Law Journal, 61 (2011), p. 1–36; K. Bunge, *Das Verhältnis von universaler Rechtsgemeinschaft und partikularen politischen Gemeinwesen, Zum verständnis des 'totus orbis' bei Francisco de Vitoria*, in: K. Bunge – A. Spindler – A. Wagner (eds.), Die Normativität des Rechts bei Francisco de Vitoria, [Politische Philosophie und Rechtstheorie des Mittelalters und der Neuzeit, Abt. 2: Untersuchungen, 2], Stuttgart 2011, p. 201–227; A. Wagner, *Francisco de Vitoria and Alberico Gentili on the legal character of the global commonwealth*, Oxford Journal of Legal Studies, 31 (2011), p. 565–582. A good overview of less recent literature on the Spanish contribution to international law is contained in David Kennedy, *Primitive legal scholarship*, Harvard International Law Journal, 27 (1986), p. 1–99, esp. n. 1–7.

[77] M.F. Renoux-Zagamé, *Origines théologiques du concept moderne de propriété*, [Travaux de droit, d'économie, de sciences politiques, de sociologie et d'anthropologie, 153], Genève 1987; J. Hallebeek, *The concept of unjust enrichment in late scholasticism*, [Rechtshistorische reeks van het Gerard Noodt Instituut, 35], Nijmegen, 1996; A.S. Brett, *Liberty, right and nature, Individual rights in later scholastic thought*, [Ideas in Context, 44], Cambridge 1997; R. Savelli, *Derecho romano y teología reformada, Du Moulin frente al problema del interés del dinero*, in: C. Petit (ed.), Del 'Ius mercatorum' al derecho mercantil, Madrid 1997,

It is no coincidence that the great Belgian private lawyer René Dekkers (1909–1976) did not hesitate to include in his *Bibliotheca Belgica Juridica* the mystic Geert Grote from Deventer (1340–1384) as well as theologians such as Leonardus Lessius from Brecht and Joannes Malderus from Sint-Pieters-Leeuw (1563–1633), who became the bishop of Antwerp.[78] In recent years, theological perspectives on the origins of the criminal law have been particularly thought-provoking.[79] The emphasis on the Reformation as a motor for the renewal of legal thought has been constant.[80] Theologians within the Catholic Church seem to be regaining awareness of its incredibly rich legal tradition.[81] Even during the twentieth century,

p. 257–290; A. Lefebvre-Teillard – F. Demoulin – F. Roumy, *De la théologie au droit*, in: R. Helmholz et al., Grundlagen des Rechts, FS Peter Landau, Paderborn 2000, p. 421–438; H. Dondorp, *Crime and punishment, Negligentia for the canonists and moral theologians*, in: E.J.H. Schrage (ed.), Negligence, The comparative legal history of the law of torts, [Comparative Studies in Continental and Anglo-American Legal History, 22], Berlin 2001, p. 101–128; F. Grunert – K. Seelmann (eds.), *Die Ordnung der Praxis. Neue Studien zur Spanischen Spätscholastik*, [Frühe Neuzeit, 68], Tübingen 2001; F. Carpintero Benítez, *El derecho subjetivo en su historia*, Cádiz 2003; M.I. Zorroza – H. Rodríguez-Penelas (eds.), *Francisco García, Tratado utilísimo y muy general de todos los contratos (1583)*, [Colección de pensamiento medieval y renacentista, 46], Pamplona 2003; D. Reid, *Thomas Aquinas and Viscount Stair, The influence of scholastic moral theology on Stair's account of restitution and recompense*, Journal of Legal History, 29 (2008), p. 189–214.

[78] R. Dekkers, *Bibliotheca Belgica Juridica, Een bio-bibliografisch overzicht der rechtsgeleerdheid in de Nederlanden van de vroegste tijden af tot 1800*, [Verhandelingen van de Koninklijke Vlaamse Academie voor Wetenschappen, Letteren en Schone Kunsten van België, Klasse der Letteren, Jaargang 13, Nr. 14], Brussel 1951, p. 72, p. 100, and p. 106, respectively. Geert Grote is said to have left behind a manuscript on contracts and usury (*De contractibus et usuris*).

[79] F. Grunert, *Punienda ergo sunt maleficia, Zur Kompetenz des öffentlichen Strafens in der Spanischen Spätscholastik*, in: F. Grunert – K. Seelmann (eds.), Die Ordnung der Praxis, Neue Studien zur Spanischen Spätscholastik, [Frühe Neuzeit, 68], Tübingen 2001, p. 313–332; D. Müller, *Schuld—Geständnis—Buße, Zur theologischen Wurzel von Grundbegriffen des mittelalterlichen Strafprozeßrechts*, in: H. Schlosser – R. Sprandel – D. Willoweit (eds.), Herrschaftliches Strafen seit dem Hochmittelalter, Formen und Entwicklungsstufen, Köln e.a. 2002, p. 403–420; H. Maihold, *Strafe für fremde Schuld? Die Systematisierung des Strafbegriffs in der Spanischen Spätscholastik und Naturrechtslehre*, [Konflikt, Verbrechen und Sanktion in der Gesellschaft Alteuropas. Symposien und Synthesen, 9], Köln 2005; A. Masferrer, *Contribución de la teología y ciencia canónica al derecho penal europeo moderno, Materiales y breves notas para su estudio*, in: Europa, sé tú misma, Actas del VI Congreso Católicos y vida pública (Madrid, 19–21 noviembre de 2004), Madrid 2005, vol. 1, p. 185–200; H. Pihlajamäki, *Executor divinarum et suarum legum, Criminal law and the Lutheran Reformation*, in: V. Mäkinen (ed.), Lutheran Reformation and the Law, [Studies in Medieval and Reformation Traditions, 112], Leiden-Boston 2006, p. 171–204; J.Q. Whitman, *The origins of reasonable doubt, Theological roots of the criminal trial*, New Haven – London 2008.

[80] E.g. Berman, *Law and revolution II, The impact of the Protestant Reformations on the Western legal tradition*.

[81] E.g. J. Porter, *Natural and divine law, Reclaiming the tradition for Christian ethics*, Ottawa-Grand Rapids 1999, p. 39–75; W. Waldstein, *Ins Herz geschrieben, Das Naturrecht*

which saw a period of relative 'antijuridicism' in the Church, the Supreme Pontiffs continued to emphasize that it would be mistaken to oppose a 'Church of charity' against a 'juridical Church'.[82]

It is not inconceivable that the legal historian misses at least some of the steps in the development of fundamental concepts in his field by ignoring the contribution of the theologians to the Western legal tradition.[83] The fact that theologians were preoccupied with legal matters, particularly concerning contracts and business, might still be surprising. As Max Weber (1864–1920) noted, modern man seems to be unable to escape the tendency to underrate the impact of religion in the history of Western societies.[84] Ironically, in his famous book on the history of commercial partnerships (*Zur Geschichte der Handelsgesellschaften im Mittelalter*, 1889), Max Weber himself underestimated the historical significance of canon law and theology for the development of commercial law. This was probably due to the influence exerted on him by the Lutheran jurist Rudolf Sohm (1841–1917).[85] Sohm notoriously advocated the thesis that there is a fundamental incompatibility between law and the Christian faith.[86] As is obvious from Weber's legal historical scholarship, this 'antinomianist' conception of the 'true' and 'original' Church has had profound consequences for the historiography of law. Traditional legal historical scholarship has often overlooked the contribution of Christian theology to the development of law.

---

als Fundament einer menschlichen Gesellschaft, Augsburg 2010; Pope Benedict XVI, *The listening heart, Reflections on the foundations of law*, Address of his Holiness Benedict XIV on the occasion of his visit to the Bundestag (Berlin, 22.09.2011) URL: http://www.vatican.va/ holy_father/benedict_xvi/speeches/2011/september/documents/hf_ben-xvi_spe_20110922_ reichstag-berlin_en.html (last visited 23.09.2011).

[82] W.L. Daniel, *The origin, nature, and purpose of canon law in the recent pontifical magisterium*, Studia Canonica, 45 (2011), p. 331–336.

[83] See the critical observations by A. Hespanha, *Panorama histórico da cultura jurídica europeia*, [Forum da história, 24], Mem Martins 1997, p. 16–22, esp. p. 21, as well as B. Clavero, *Religión y derecho. Mentalidades y paradigmas*, Historia, Instituciones y Documentos, 11 (1984), p. 67–92. See also A. Padovani, *Perché chiedi il mio nome? Dio, natura e diritto nel secolo XII*, [Il diritto nella storia, 6], Torino 1997, p. 11. The latter book is a compelling attempt to enliven the theological context behind the renaissance of European legal thinking in the 12th century.

[84] Quoted in Clavero, *Religión y derecho*, p. 92.

[85] G. Dilcher, *Einleitung*, in: G. Dilcher – S. Lepsius (eds.), Max Weber, Zur Geschichte der Handelsgesellschaften im Mittelalter, [Max Weber Gesammtausgabe, Abt. 1, Band 1], Tübingen 2008, p. 9.

[86] G. Agamben, *Opus Dei, Archeologia dell'ufficio*, [Homo Sacer, II. 5], Torino 2012, p. 21–22.

The inner renewal of legal history as a discipline will lie in a rediscovery of the theological and canonical roots of modern legal traditions.[87] In a book that exemplifies this inner renewal of legal history, James Whitman provides us with an important clue to understand why the history of law cannot be studied separately from the history of theology.[88] First of all, one needs to realize that the salvation of the soul was a major source of preoccupation for people living in deeply Christian societies in the West until not long ago. This preoccupation relied upon a fundamentally dualistic anthropology, namely the idea that man consists of body and soul (*homo ex corpore et anima constat*).[89] Not only the body, but also the soul were subject to jurisdictional power. This view of man was deeply ingrained in the minds of the pre-Enlightenment citizen.[90] In his manual of civil procedure, Joos de Damhouder (1507–1581) from Bruges was careful to remind judges of the importance of keeping the images of paradise and hell clearly before their eyes.[91] If he had to decide on earth, the judge was himself subject to God's judgment in the afterlife. Therefore, Cardinal Hostiensis, undoubtedly the most brilliant canonist of the thirteenth century, adviced judges to keep the Gospel carefully with them at any moment during the lawsuit.[92]

The second point which explicates the theologians' involvement with law is the fact that the soul was thought to be subject to rules and discipline.[93] Consequently, besides the jurisdiction over the external

---

[87] See M. Schmoeckel, *Rechtsgeschichte im 21. Jahrhundert, Ein Diskussionsbeitrag zur Standortbestimmung*, Forum Historiae Iuris (2000); cf. http://www.forhistiur.de/zitat/0005schmoeckel.htm, last visited on 25 July 2011.

[88] Whitman, *The origins of reasonable doubt*, p. 1–8.

[89] Francisco Suárez, *Tractatus de anima*, prooemium, in: Opera omnia, editio nova a D.M. André, canonico Rupellensi, Parisiis 1856, tom. 3, p. 463.

[90] The many paintings and sculptures of the Last Judgment in churches, court rooms and town halls across European cities are there to remind us that, ultimately, the soul was thought to be accountable for its acts to God on the Day of Doom; e.g. G. Martyn, *Painted Exempla Iustitiae in the Southern Netherlands*, in: R. Schulze (ed.), Symbolische Kommunikation vor Gericht in der Frühen Neuzeit, [Schriften zur Europäischen Rechts- und Verfassungsgeschichte, 51], Berlin 2006, p. 335–356; A.A. Wijffels, *Justitie en behoorlijk bestuur, Hans Vredeman de Vries' schilderijen in het stadhuis van Danzig (Gdánsk)*, Pro Memorie, 13 (2011), p. 103–118.

[91] See the *Beschrijvinghe vande Wereltsche Iustitie*, s.v. *Hel, Paradijs*, in: Joos de Damhouder, *Practycke in Civile Saecken*, 's Graven-hage 1626, ed. J. Monballyu – J. Dauwe, Gent 1999, [s.p.].

[92] Hostiensis (Henricus de Segusio), *Summa aurea*, Venetiis 1570, lib. 2, tit. 1, f. 117v, num. 10: 'Debet autem iudex evangelia a principio usque ad finem coram se tenere, sciturus quod sicut iudicat homines, et ipse iudicabitur a Deo.'

[93] E.g. P. Prodi – C. Penuti (eds.), *Disciplina dell'anima, disciplina del corpo e disciplina della società tra medioevo ed età moderna*, [Annali dell'Istituto storico italo-germanico, 40],

actions of man as we still know it today, there was a jurisdiction over man as a spiritual being that has now disappeared. The guardians of this realm of norms were the theologians. Bringing together natural law, divine law and positive law, they determined what the rights and obligations of persons in specific situations were, according to these different sets of norms, so as to be able to guide the flock on their earthly pilgrimage to God.[94] The tribunal where this parallel jurisdiction was 'enforced' was the 'court of conscience' (*forum conscientiae sive animae sive internum*)—confession. As will be developed later in this chapter, it is not entirely adequate to think of this parallel legal universe as being deprived of sanctions.[95] After all, the exclusive use of violence and sanctions became the monopoly of the secular State only from the moment the State had defeated—and partly absorbed—the rival sources of norms. Also, one should not forget that there were many linkages between *forum internum* and *forum externum*.[96]

The juristic notion of conscience up until the early modern period, also present in the English Court of Chancery—which was alternatively called the Court of Conscience—is fundamentally at odds with the contemporary notion of conscience.[97] Ever since the Reformation, conscience

---

Bologna 1994; R.J. Ross, *Puritan godly discipline in comparative perspective*, Legal pluralism and the sources of 'intensity'*, American Historical Review, 113 (2008), p. 975–1002.

[94] W. Decock, *From law to paradise, Confessional Catholicism and legal scholarship*, Rechtsgeschichte, Zeitschrift des Max-Planck-Instituts für europäische Rechtsgeschichte, 18 (2011), p. 14–20.

[95] Apart from the ultimate sanctions in the after-life, the law of conscience also legitimizes the use of self-help (*occulta compensatio*) in matters related to private law if that is the only way of obtaining the rights which are accorded to you as a matter of conscience; cf. W. Decock, *Secret compensation, A friendly and lawful alternative to Lipsius's political thought*, in: E. De Bom – M. Janssens – T. Van Houdt – J. Papy (eds.), (Un)masking the realities of power, Justus Lipsius and the dynamics of political writing in early modern Europe, Leiden – Boston 2011, p. 263–280. The 'juridical' nature of religious and moral norms in the Middle Ages is also subject to investigation in: E. Coccia, *Regula et vita, Il diritto monastico e la regola francescana*, Medioevo e Rinascimento, 20 (2006), p. 97–147.

[96] The interconnectedness between the *forum internum* and the *forum externum ecclesiasticum* can still be noticed in the ecclesiastical court of Bruges at the turn of the seventeenth century, see J. Monballyu, *Een kerkelijke rechtbank aan het werk in de contrareformatie, De rechtspraak van de officialiteit van Brugge in 1585–1610*, in: Liber amicorum Monique Van Melkebeke, Brussel 2011, p. 125–161. This is all the more true in both the secular and the ecclesiastical courts in the colonies of the Spanish empire, as the case study by Alejandro Agüero shows in *Las penas impuestas por el Divino y Supremo Juez, Religión y justicia secular en Córdoba del Tucumán, siglos XVII y XVIII*, in: Anuario de historia de América Latina, 46 (2009), p. 203–230.

[97] D.R. Klinck, *Conscience, equity and the Court of Chancery in Early Modern England*, Farnham 2010, p. 1–40.

has been gradually personalized, privatized and subjectivized. Allegedly, elements of the turn towards a more subjective understanding of conscience can already be perceived in the work of the Renaissance man Thomas More (1478–1535), who served as Lord Chancellor in the Court of Chancery.[98] Yet, generally speaking, the rules of conscience were originally thought to be almost as objective as legal rules. They could form the object of expert knowledge of specialists. These specialists were the moral theologians. Their literary production is the written imprint of a parallel jurisdiction which existed for centuries. These writings, therefore, are not merely 'law in the books', to use Roscoe Pound's famous expression from 1910 in a slightly different context. They are the only access we have to a 'law in action', which no longer exists and of which there is no better evidence than the manuals for confessors. It would be misleading to think of this literature as merely pertaining to doctrine or academic reflection. The moral theologians were usually actively involved in practice as advisers to princes, merchants and Christians of all walks of life.[99] They even debated whether they could bill the confessant for giving him advice in contractual affairs.

2.1.2   *The* ius commune *in Spain and its theological status*

Many of the preconceptions that prevent one from taking the 'texts' of the moral theologians seriously also apply to the study of the *ius commune*, which was one of the main juristic sources of inspiration for the

---

[98] J. Baker, *The Oxford history of the laws of England, Vol. 6: 1483–1558*, Oxford 2003, p. 177–179; R.B. Hein, *'Gewissen' bei Adrian von Utrecht (Hadrian VI.), Erasmus von Rotterdam und Thomas More, Ein Beitrag zur systematischen Analyse des Gewissensbegriffs in der katholischen nordeuropäischen Renaissance*, [Studien der Moraltheologie, 10], Münster 1999, p. 366–472; and B. Cummings, *Conscience and the law in Thomas More*, in: H.E. Braun – E. Vallance (eds.), The Renaissance conscience, [Renaissance Studies Special Issues, 3], Oxford 2011, p. 29–51.

[99] A typical example is Lessius, who was consulted on a frequent basis by businessmen and a personal adviser to the Hapsburg Archdukes Albert and Isabella (1598–1621). In the *Notitia iuris belgici*, Antverpiae 1675, lib. 4, p. 61, the jurist Zypaeus (1580–1650) from the Southern Netherlands recommends lawyers to read Lessius in order to get the best analysis of financial techniques used at the Antwerp Bourse. Lessius' private 'counsels' on specific cases have been collected posthumously by his nephew J. Wijns; cf. *Leonardi Lessii (…) in D. Thomam de beatitudine, de actibus humanis, de incarnatione Verbi, de sacramentis et censuris praelectiones theologicae posthumae. Accesserunt eiusdem variorum casuum conscientiae resolutiones*, Lovanii 1645, ed. I. Wijns.

theologians.[100] The *ius commune*, too, remains incomprehensible if the pluralistic nature of law in the pre-modern European context is not accepted.[101] Both phenomena provide evidence that it is possible to have legal order and legal reasoning in a political context different from the modern national State.[102] Incidentally, this is one of the reasons why there is currently a renewed interest in the *ius commune* and religious systems of private law.[103] After all, certainly in memberstates of the European Union, jurists are faced with the reality that the national legal order is no longer autonomous, but part of a larger normative universe.[104] Legal pluralism is again the defining characteristic of our legal universe.

It is true that the medieval canonists and civilians, as well as the moral theologians of the early modern period, did create marvellous intellectual constructs.[105] But that does not mean that they were merely intellectuals who did not exercize any form of power. The great medieval doctors of civil law and canon law were certainly not detached from legal practice. Certainly in respect to sixteenth century Spain, jurists working in the tradition of the so-called *mos italicus* were very actively engaged in practical dispute settlement.[106] The theologians, for their part, were frequent

---

[100] K. Pennington, *Learned law, droit savant, Gelehrtes Recht*, The tyranny of a concept, Rivista internazionale di diritto comune, 5 (1994), p. 197–209. This article highlights some of the absurdities historical scholarship has run into by taking this doctrinal view of the Roman canon tradition too seriously. Conte, *Diritto comune*, p. 83 points out the nineteenth century origins of this kind of misconception. It is important, indeed, to keep in mind that nineteenth century legal historical scholarship has often distorted on our view of the legal past. A famous example is the idea, promoted by influential jurists such as Otto von Gierke, Frederic William Maitland and Oliver Wendell Holmes, Jr., that the trust is a typically Anglo-American legal device; cf. R.H. Helmholz – R. Zimmermann, *Views of trust and Treuhand, An introduction*, in: R.H. Helmholz – R. Zimmermann (eds.), Itinera fiduciae, Trust and Treuhand in historical perspective, [Comparative Studies in Continental and Anglo-American Legal History, 19], Berlin 1998, p. 27–28 and p. 31–34.

[101] P. Grossi, *L'ordine giuridico medievale*, Roma-Bari, 1996², p. 52–56; P. Cappellini, *Storie di concetti giuridici*, Torino 2010, p. 123.

[102] P. Grossi, *Un diritto senza Stato*, Quaderni fiorentini, 25 (1996), p. 267–284.

[103] E.g. Ch. Donahue, Jr., *Private law without the State and during its formation*, in: N. Jansen – R. Michaels (eds.), Beyond the State, Rethinking private law, Tübingen 2008, p. 121–144; N. Jansen, *The making of legal authority, Non-legislative codifications in historical and comparative perspective*, Oxford-New York 2010, p. 20–44.

[104] This situation is clearly sketched in M. Adams – W. Witteveen, *Gedaantewisselingen van het recht*, Nederlands Juristenblad, 9 (2011), p. 540–546.

[105] The academic institutional background of the *ius commune* is highlighted in M. Bellomo, *L'Europa del diritto comune*, Roma 1989⁴, p. 119–146.

[106] F. Tomas y Valiente, *Manual de historia del derecho Español*, Madrid 1980², p. 298–299. The practical edge to the jurists' writings is instantiated by the flourishing of the *Consilia*-literature; cf. M. Ascheri – I. Baumgärtner – J. Kirshner (eds.), *Legal consulting*

advisers to the political authorities.[107] It would fall outside the scope of this introductory chapter to go deeper into this debate. Yet the vivid, concrete arguments that were exchanged among the theologians sufficiently witness that these men, however cultivated, were not just bookish types. Not surprisingly, jurists were amazed at Luis de Molina's (1535–1600) solid grasp of legal matters.[108] Franciscus Zypaeus (1580–1650), author of a book on Belgian law, recommended jurists to consult Lessius to gain a better understanding of the practice of money-exchange at the Bourse of Antwerp.[109] The local magistrates drew on Lessius and the Spanish canonists and theologians when compiling the last version of Antwerp customary law, the *Consuetudines compilatae* (1608), particularly in the field of contract law.[110]

A couple of notes might be welcome here on the use of the *ius commune* by the theologians. One of our main conclusions will be that the Roman law of contract, as found in a great variety of fragments and texts scattered all over the *Corpus iuris civilis*, was profoundly transformed over the course of centuries. This transformation was driven, not only by the canonists, but also by the theologians. The interpretation of the disparate Roman legal material on contracts in the Western legal tradition was profoundly shaped by the moral imperatives of Christianity. By *ius commune*, we understand, then, the juridical culture deriving from the interpretation of the Roman legal texts collected by Justinian in 529–534, which spread all across Europe from the so-called Renaissance of Roman law at the end of the eleventh century until approximately the sixteenth century

---

in the civil law tradition, Berkeley 1999; U. Falk, *Consilia, Studien zur Praxis der Rechtsgutachten in der frühen Neuzeit*, [Rechtsprechung, 22], Frankfurt am Main 2006.

[107] E.g. H.E. Braun, *Conscience, counsel and theocracy at the Spanish Habsburg court*, in: H.E. Braun – E. Vallance (eds.), Contexts of conscience in Early Modern Europe, 1500–1700, Basingstoke 2004, p. 56–66.

[108] See F.B. Costello, *The political philosophy of Luis de Molina S.J. (1535–1600)*, [Bibliotheca Instituti Historici S.I., 38], Rome 1974, p. 21, n. 72. For biographical details on Molina, see J.P. Donnelly, *Luis de Molina*, in: C. O'Neill – J. Domínguez (eds.), Diccionario histórico de la Compañía de Jesús, Biográfico-temático, Roma-Madrid 2001, vol. 3, p. 2716–2717.

[109] Zypaeus, *Notitia iuris belgici*, lib. 4, p. 61.

[110] The allegations to the late scholastic authors have been analyzed in B. Van Hofstraeten, *Juridisch humanisme en costumiere acculturatie, Inhouds- en vormbepalende factoren van de Antwerpse Consuetudines compilatae (1608) en het Gelderse Land- en Stadsrecht (1620)*, Maastricht 2008, p. 406–410. The *Consuetudines compilatae* have been carefully examined from the point of view of their significance for the development of commercial law in D. De ruysscher, *Naer het Romeinsch recht alsmede den stiel mercantiel, Handel en recht in de Antwerpse rechtbank (16de–17de eeuw)*, Kortrijk-Heule 2009.

and beyond.[111] A fundamental role in the creation and the spread of the *ius commune* was played by the universities. The concept 'ius commune' itself developed out of teaching practices in the university law schools.[112] The late medieval *ius commune* is not to be confounded with the present day development of a *ius commune Europaeum*, even though there are striking parallels.[113]

Until the fourteenth century, the *ius commune* referred mostly to Justinian's compilation of legal texts.[114] Bartolus de Saxoferrato and Baldus de Ubaldis identified *ius commune* primarily with the Roman legal texts and not with canon law.[115] This use of the term by the doctors was confirmed

---

[111] There is no way in which this rudimentary and pragmatic definition could substitute for the detailed accounts of the characteristics of the *ius commune* in standard contributions such as M. Caravale, *Alle origini del diritto europeo, Ius commune, droit commun, common law nella dottrina giuridica della prima età moderna*, [Archivio per la storia del diritto medioevale e moderno, 9], Bologna 2005, and Manlio Bellomo's textbook *L'Europa del diritto comune*. In an article expressly devoted to defining the *ius commune*, Bellomo adopts a distinction between two periods in the 'life' of the *ius commune*, namely the 12th–16th centuries, on the one hand, and the 16th–18th centuries, on the other hand, since the context of the *ius commune* in the latter period is fundamentally different from that of the former, given the rise of the national states. However, Bellomo warns against the interpretation that the *ius commune* of the first period derived its normative force from being considered the product of the legislative activity of the German emperor (*Kaiserrecht*). He argues instead that their character as authoritative and useful legal texts (*libri legales*) was decisive in their success. Importantly, Bellomo also refuses to recognize that the *ius commune* entered into a 'crisis' from the sixteenth century onwards, referring to the ongoing relevance of the *ius commune* in Latin America, on the one hand, and the *usus modernus pandectarum*, on the other hand; cf. M. Bellomo, *Condividendo, rispondendo, aggiungendo, Riflessioni intorno al 'ius commune'*, Rivista internazionale di diritto comune, 11 (2000), p. 287–296.

[112] J.A. Brundage, *Universities and the 'ius commune' in medieval Europe*, Rivista internazionale di diritto comune, 11 (2000), p. 237–253.

[113] For further discussion, see A.A. Wijffels, *Qu'est-ce que le ius commune?*, in: A.A. Wijffels (ed.), *Le Code civil entre ius commune et droit privé européen*, Bruxelles 2005, p. 643–661; J. Smits, *The making of European private law, Toward a ius commune Europaeum as a mixed legal system*, Antwerp – Oxford – New York 2002, p. 43–45.

[114] L. Mayali, *Ius civile et ius commune dans la tradition juridique médiévale*, in: J. Krynen (ed.), Droit romain, jus civile et droit français, [Études d'histoire du droit et des idées politiques, 3], Toulouse 1999, p. 201–217; N. Warembourg, *Le 'droit commun coutumier', Un exemple paradoxal d'acculturation juridique*, in: B. Coppein – F. Stevens – L. Waelkens (eds.), Modernisme, tradition et acculturation juridique, Actes des Journées internationales de la Société d'Histoire du Droit, Louvain 29 mai–1 juin 2008, [Iuris Scripta Historica, 27], Brussel 2011, p. 162–163.

[115] N. Horn, *Aequitas in den Lehren des Baldus*, [Forschungen zur neueren Privatrechtsgeschichte, 11], Köln-Graz 1968, p. 54–55. It might be noted, however, that the canon law also aspired to be a kind of *ius commune*, namely a law common to all Christian nations; cf. Bellomo, *L'Europa del diritto comune*, p. 72–74 and p. 80–83.

in the sixteenth century by Fernanda Vázquez de Menchaca (1512–1569).[116] A theologian such as Francisco Suárez also employed *ius commune* to designate the Roman civil law.[117] These Roman texts served as the default rules for legal practice and thinking across Europe. As such, *ius commune* contrasted with the *ius proprium, ius municipale,* or *ius patrium*—some of the concepts that were used to denote the legal system proper to a particular territory.[118]

Even though the interpretation of those Roman rules was often mingled with canonical legal thinking, inevitably leading to the simultaneous spreading of both Roman and canon law in the culture of the *ius commune,* the term *ius commune* is mostly distinguished from the term which denotes the interconnectedness of Roman and canon law, i.e. *utrumque ius.*[119] One should be careful, however, about being too rigid in employing these terms. Thirteenth century jurists sometimes employed the term *ius commune* in a broader sense to denote the two learned laws (*utrumque ius*).[120] Yet, in principle, the term *ius commune* was employed in the past and will be used throughout this book as signifying the Roman civil law (*ius civile Romanorum*) in its received form as a common legacy to many local jurisdictions in medieval and early modern Europe.

The theologians drew on almost the entire legal heritage to come to grips with complex cases involving contractual transactions. They combined this legal knowledge with Aristotelian-Thomistic philosophy to formulate principles for contract law in general.[121] A factor which undoubtedly contributed to the theologians' familiarity with the civilian tradition was that legal cultures on the Iberian peninsula had undergone the influence of

---

116 Fernando Vázquez de Menchaca, *Controversiae illustres aliaeque usu frequentes,* Francofurti 1668, lib. 1, cap. 45, num. 17, p. 180: '[jus commune] a doctoribus sumitur pro jure civili Romanorum'.

117 Cf. infra, p. 35.

118 I. Birocchi, *Alla ricerca dell'ordine, Fonti e cultura giuridica nell'età moderna,* [Il Diritto nella Storia, 9], Torino 2002, p. 51–54; A. Cavanna, *Storia del diritto moderno in Europa, Le fonti e il pensiero giuridico,* 1, Milano 1979, p. 59–62.

119 E.J.H. Schrage, *Utrumque Ius, Eine Einführung in das Studium der Quellen des mittelalterlichen gelehrten Rechts,* [Schriften zur europäischen Rechts- und Verfassungsgeschichte, 8], Berlin 1992.

120 Brundage, *Universities and the 'ius commune' in medieval Europe,* p. 239; E.J.H. Schrage, *Utrumque Ius, Über das römisch-kanonische ius commune als Grundlage europäischer Rechtseinheit,* Revue Internationale des Droits de l'Antiquité, 39 (1992), p. 383–412 [Reprinted in: E.J.H. Schrage, *Non quia Romanum sed quia ius, Das Entstehen eines europäischen Rechtsbewußtseins im Mittelalter,* [Bibliotheca Eruditorum, Internationale Bibliothek der Wissenschaften, 17], Goldbach 1996, p. 273–302].

121 Gordley, *The philosophical origins of modern contract doctrine,* p. 69.

the renaissance of Roman law in a specifically intense way from relatively early on.[122] In fact, the Roman tradition had never really ceased to inspire local rulers. This is true of many regions across Europe, but of Spain in particular.[123] From the *Lex Romana Visigothorum* (506) to the eight-century *Liber Iudiciorum* and the *Fuero Juzgo*, its thirteenth century Spanish translation, the Roman tradition continued its presence on 'Spanish territories'[124] from late Antiquity through the Middle Ages to the early modern period alongside local customs (*fueros*). Most conspicuously, Alfonso X El Sabio (1221–1284) unified the laws in the kingdom of Castile and Leon through the implementation of Roman law.

It is worthwhile briefly dwelling on the Spanish legal historical tradition, since the theologians often cited these sources. Alfonso X's legislative work in seven parts, the *Siete Partidas* (1265) is a jewel of juristic art which, despite its initial lack of impact on legal practice, remained influential in proto-codifications of Spanish law (*recopilaciones*) until the beginning of the nineteenth century. It also served as a source of inspiration for the *Ordenaçoes Alfonsinas* (1446) of the Portuguese king Alfonso V, intensifying the reception of the *ius commune* on Portuguese territory.[125] The *Ordenaçoes Alfonsinas* (1446), in turn, formed the basis of the *Ordenações*

---

[122] A. García y García, *Derecho romano-canónico medieval en la Península Ibérica*, in: J. Alvarado (ed.), Historia de la literatura jurídica en la España del antiguo régimen, vol. 1, Madrid-Barcelona 2000, p. 79–132.

[123] For an overview of the persistent influence of the Roman tradition in territories other than Spain ranging from the German kingdoms to Constantinople, see, for instance, chapter 8 (*In orbem terrarum*) in Calasso, *Introduzione al diritto comune*, p. 305–340, and Waelkens, *Civium causa*, p. 81–90 and p. 381–382.

[124] We use the rather indefinite term 'Spanish territories', since the political reality of the late medieval Iberian peninsula was diffuse and pluralistic in nature; see the caveat by A. Masferrer, *Spanish legal history, A need for its comparative approach*, in: K.A. Modéer – P. Nilsén (eds.), How to teach European comparative legal history, Lund 2011, p. 136–137. When the *ius commune* started to exercise its influence in the twelfth century, the response of the various local regimes was variegated. For a detailed account of the reception of the *ius commune* in each region, see Tomas y Valiente, *Manual de Historia del derecho Español*, chapters 12–14, p. 205–262. The opposition to Roman law was particularly vehement in Navarra and Aragón, where the local *fueros* were strong. For instance, only in 1576, when they were faced with the threat of Castile imposing its legal system, did the *cortes* of Pamplona accept the *ius commune* as subsidiary law in Navarra. Catalonia was more receptive to the *ius commune*. From the beginning, the texts of the *Corpus iuris civilis* were imported in practice to substitute for the *Liber Iudiciorum* and local *costumbres*. The *ius commune* was recognized as a subsidiary source of law in 1409 by the *cortes* of Barcelona. Compare Cavanna, *Storia del diritto moderno in Europa*, 1, p. 418–420.

[125] Cavanna, *Storia del diritto moderno in Europa*, 1, p. 426–427. The reception of the *ius commune* in Portugal is debated in M. Augusto Rodrigues, *Note sul 'ius commune' in Portogallo*, Rivista internazionale di diritto comune, 12 (2001), p. 265–287.

Filipinas (1603), ordered by King Philip II of Spain, which remained in force in Portugal until 1867.[126] Interestingly, the *Siete Partidas* already combined juridical, philosophical and theological sources in a manner that was to become even more typical of the moral theological literature. In addition to references to Roman and canon law jurisprudence, the *Siete Partidas* bear the marks of thinkers such as Aristotle, Seneca, and Thomas Aquinas. One of the express aims of the *Siete Partidas* as mentioned at the outset of the first law of this proto-codification, was to ensure that people knew how to keep their faith in Christ.[127] The *Siete Partidas* offer a good example, then, of the strong connections between legal and religious cultures on the Iberian peninsula—a relationship that would only be intensified in the sixteenth century.

While the *Siete Partidas* illustrate the early diffusion of the *ius commune* in the kingdom of Castile and Leon, they also show that this reception was instrumental for the unification of contemporary Spanish legal culture. The revival of Roman law was not an end in itself. Politically speaking, the reception of the *ius commune* was even a sensitive issue, since the spread of Roman law was profoundly associated with the imperialistic tendencies of the Holy Roman Empire.[128] Alfonso X used the revived law of Rome for the purpose of unifying his kingdom, not to cede his power to the Holy Roman Emperor. He declared that he recognized no superior in temporal affairs (*non habemos major sobre nos en lo temporal*).[129] The *ius commune* derived its authority as a subsidiary legal source from the promulgation by Alfonso X, not from the Holy Roman Emperor. Moreover, this 'nationalized' version of the *ius commune* achieved success in practice from the midst of the fourteenth century onwards. Until then, its implementation was impeded by local forces who abided by the local customary laws (*fueros*) and resisted the king's attempts to centralize power through the use of Roman law.

Eventually, the *ius commune* as absorbed into the *Siete Partidas* gained relevance as a source of law in Castilla and Leon through Alfonso XI's promulgation of the *Ordenamiento de Alcalá* (1348). The *Siete Partidas* was

---

126 Cavanna, *Storia del diritto moderno in Europa*, 1, p. 269.

127 Alfonso X El Sabio, *Las Siete Partidas, cotejadas con varios codices antiguos por la Real Academia de la Historia, y glosadas por Gregorio López*, Paris 1851, tom. 1, part. 1, tit. 1, l. 1, p. 1–2: 'Estas leyes de todo este libro son establecimientos como los homes sepan creer et guardar la fe de nuestro señor Jesu Christo complidamente asi come ella es (…).'

128 Cf. Cavanna, *Storia del diritto moderno in Europa*, 1, p. 56–59.

129 For discussion, see C. Petit, *Derecho común y derecho castellano*, Tijdschrift voor Rechtsgeschiedenis, 50 (1982), p. 157–158.

deemed to be subsidiary in force to the *fueros*, which occupied the second place in the hierarchy of norms, and to royal legislation, the primordial legal standard.[130] This hierarchy prevailed until the beginning of the nineteenth century, since many of the rules of the *Ordenamiento de Alcalá* were confirmed by the *recopilaciones*, the compilations of royal legislation. Two of the most famous such compilations were the *Ordenamiento de Montalvo* (1484) and the *Nueva Recopilación* (1567). The *Ordenamiento de Montalvo* was named after its drafter Alonso Díaz de Montalvo. It was also known as the *Ordenanças Reales de Castilla*. The *Nueva Recopilación* was promulgated by King Philip II.[131] In the meantime the *Leyes de Toro* (1505) were published. They contained seminal provisions of Castilian private law, and became a favorite subject of learned commentaries, for instance by Palacios Rubios (c. 1450–1524) and Antonio Gómez.[132] From the sixteenth century onward, the *ius commune* also filtered through into the laws of the Indies (*derecho indiano*).[133] In 1805, a year after Napoleon's *Code civil* had appeared in France, the early modern Spanish compilations were absorbed into the *Novísima Recopilación*, of which the first book was still dedicated to the 'Holy Church'.[134] In brief, the Iberian legal tradition, on which the moral theologians heavily drew, was one of the strongholds of the *ius commune* tradition.

Interestingly, the ambiguous approach to the *ius commune* in the Spanish realm is still apparent in Suárez's early seventeenth century *Treatise on the laws and God the legislator* (*Tractatus de legibus et legislatore Deo*). He recalls that the *ius commune* is a direct source of norms only in the territories that are directly subject to the power of the Holy Roman Emperor and in the lands that fall immediately under the power of the Roman Church.[135] In the kingdoms of Portugal and Spain, which are sovereign countries, the

---

[130] Tomas y Valiente, *Manual de Historia del derecho Español*, p. 243–244.

[131] Tomas y Valiente, *Manual de Historia del derecho Español*, p. 263–281.

[132] Petit, *Derecho común y derecho castellano*, p. 169–175, and Tomas y Valiente, *Manual de Historia del derecho Español*, p. 268–269 and p. 312–313.

[133] On the Spanish colonial law (*derecho indiano*) and its relationship to the *ius commune*, see Tomas y Valiente, *Manual de Historia del derecho Español*, p. 325–345; A. Pérez Martín, *Derecho Común, Derecho Castellano, Derecho Indiano*, in: Rivista internazionale di diritto comune, 5 (1994), p. 43–90; J. Barrientos Grandon, *El sistema del 'ius commune' en las Indias occidentales*, Rivista internazionale di diritto comune, 10 (1999), p. 53–137; M. Mirow, *Private law, lawyers and legal institutions in Spanish America, 1500–2000*, Leiden 2003 [= doct. diss.], p. 60–70, and M. Mirow, *Latin American law, A history of private law and institutions in Spanish America*, Austin, TX, 2004, esp. p. 45–53.

[134] Tomas y Valiente, *Manual de Historia del derecho Español*, p. 397–398.

[135] Suárez, *Tractatus de legibus et legislatore Deo*, lib. 3, cap. 8, num. 1, in: Opera omnia, editio nova a Carolo Berton, Parisiis 1856, tom. 5, p. 199.

ius commune, that is 'civil law' (*leges civiles*) or 'imperial law' (*leges imperatorum*), is not binding per se, not even as a subsidiary source of norms. In this regard, Suárez is critical of Antonio Gómez, who apparently claimed that, as a matter of custom, Roman law enjoyed subsidiary force in Spain.¹³⁶ In Suárez's view, only if there is no royal legislation on a particular matter can Roman law be used as a subsidiary source of law, provided that the King grants explicit authority to those specific, subsidiary provisions of Roman law.¹³⁷ In other words, Suárez confirms that ultimately, the King decides whether Roman law can be considered binding in a certain field. He recalls an old Spanish adage that states that 'citing from Roman law, that is the law of the Emperor, is punished with execution'. This principle was laid down by Kings Alfonso X and Alfonso XI. The *Leyes de Toro* and the *Nueva Recopilación* re-affirmed that the only laws that could be cited in court were the laws of the kingdom.¹³⁸ Consequently, 'imperial laws' or 'civil laws' are not in force in Spain. Still, it is permitted for academics to study the civilian tradition for the sake of the erudition and wisdom it contains. Moreover, to the extent that the 'civil laws' express natural law, they are binding by virtue of natural law, according to Suárez.¹³⁹ Even if

---

136 Suárez, *Tractatus de legibus et legislatore Deo*, lib. 3, cap. 8, num. 5, p. 201: 'Addunt vero aliqui consuetudine receptum esse in Hispania, ut jus civile servetur, ubi leges regni desunt. Ita tenet Burgos de Paz in l. 1 Tauri, num. 520, ubi etiam Antonius Gomezius num. 10 sentit leges civiles habere vim legis in Hispania, deficiente lege regni; non tamen affert jus in quo id fundetur, nec consuetudinis mentionem facit, sed tantum ait esse communem opinionem. Re tamen vera non habet sufficiens fundamentum; nam constat ex dictis illae leges ex vi suae originis non habere vim in Hispania.'

137 Suárez, *Tractatus de legibus et legislatore Deo*, lib. 3, cap. 8, num. 3, p. 200: 'Sic etiam in hoc regno Lusitaniae, quod eisdem titulis supremum est, quibus regnum Hispaniae, jus civile per se non obligat, eique per leges regni derogari potest, ac saepe derogatur: ubi autem deest lex regni, servatur civile, non vi sua, sed ex ordinatione propria ejusdem regni.'

138 Suárez, *Tractatus de legibus et legislatore Deo*, lib. 3, cap. 8, num. 4, p. 200–201: 'Idemque in Hispania expresse cautum est legibus regni (...) et refert Palacium Rub. dicentem Hispanos olim constituisse, ut qui leges imperatorum allegaret capite plecteretur. (...) Item in l. 1 Tauri refertur antiqua lex regis Alphonsi, quae ibi confirmatur et renovatur, in qua declaratur quo ordine et modo judicandum sit per proprias leges Hispaniae, nullaque ratio habetur juris civilis in ratione legis ac juris. Additur vero ibidem permitti nihilominus in Hispania leges civiles doceri in publicis Academiis, et interpretari propter earum eruditionem et sapientiam, non quia per illas judicandum sit. | Et in l. 2 Tauri adduntur illa verba, per leges regni, et non per alias judicandum esse, et omnia haec novissime confirmantur in nova recopilatione l. 1, ante librum 1, et lib. 2, l. 1 et 2. Ex quibus legibus manifestum est leges civiles in Hispania non habere vim legum quatenus leges positivae sunt.'

139 Suárez, *Tractatus de legibus et legislatore Deo*, lib. 3, cap. 8, num. 4, p. 201: 'Quatenus vero illae leges in multis continent et declarant ipsam naturalem legem, servandae erunt in vi legis naturalis, non in vi legis humanae. (...) Item quamvis non contineant naturalem

they are not expressive of a natural obligation, they can serve as a model of prudence and equity (*per modum exemplarium ad imitandam prudentiam et aequitatem*).

The *ius commune*, then, clearly was not merely present as an attenuated force. Instead, theologians consciously used it as a precious source of wisdom and argument. In a style reminiscent of the so-called *mos italicus*, the theologians fiercely debated the right interpretation of provisions contained in the texts of the civilian tradition. Using the dialectical and scholastic method also typical of the late medieval jurists, they entered into vigorous debates with authorities past and present to weigh the opinions on the correct meaning of legal texts from the Code, the Digest, the Institutes and the Novels. References to jurists of Orléans, such as Pierre de Belleperche (ca. 1247–1308) are not insignificant.[140] The theologians were much more heavily indebted, though, to the work of post-glossators such as Bartolus de Saxoferrato (1313–1357).[141] The theologians' predilection for Bartolus might have had to do with the fact that Bartolus had not been afraid of assimilating the principles of Aristotelian-Thomistic philosophy in the first place. It has been shown, indeed, that Bartolus deliberately integrated argumentations from theology and canon law into the field of civil law.[142]

By the same token, their involvement with the canon law tradition was profound. Their discussions on contract law are replete with references

---

obligationem, nec etiam per se obligent, deservire possunt per modum exemplarium ad imitandam prudentiam et aequitatem, quam frequentius continent, sive in taxandis poenis, sive in interpretandis testamentis, in conjecturanda mente defuncti, et similibus.'

[140] On Pierre de Belleperche (Petrus de Bellapertica), whose works are remembered mainly for their influence on Bartolus and Baldus thanks to the intermediation of Cino da Pistoia (c. 1270–1336/7), see F. Soetermeer, s.v. *Belleperche*, in: P. Arabeyre – J.-L. Halpérin – J. Krynen (eds.), Dictionnaire historique des juristes français, XIIe–XXe siècle, Paris 2007, p. 61–62; and K. Bezemer, *Pierre de Belleperche, Portrait of a legal puritan*, [Studien zur europäischen Rechtsgeschichte, 194], Frankfurt am Main 2005.

[141] On Bartolus, see the recent studies by S. Lepsius, *Der Richter und die Zeugen, Eine Untersuchung anhand des Tractatus testimoniorum des Bartolus von Sassoferrato, Mit Edition*, [Studien zur europäischen Rechtsgeschichte, 158], Frankfurt am Main 2003; and *Von Zweifeln zur Überzeugung, Der Zeugenbeweis im gelehrten Recht ausgehend von der Abhandlung des Bartolus von Sassoferrato*, [Studien zur europäischen Rechtsgeschichte, 160], Frankfurt am Main 2003.

[142] S. Lepsius, *Juristische Theoriebildung und Philosophische Kategorien, Bemerkungen zur Arbeitsweise des Bartolus von Sassoferrato*, in: M. Kaufhold (ed.), Politische Reflexion in der Welt des späten Mittelalters / Political thought in the ages of scholasticism, Essays in honour of Jürgen Miethke, [Studies in Medieval and Reformation traditions, 103], Leiden-Boston 2004, p. 287–304; S. Lepsius, *Taking the institutional context seriously, A comment on James Gordley*, The American Journal of Comparative Law, 56 (2008), p. 661–662.

to Gratian's *Decretum* and Pope Gregory IX's *Liber Extra*. The opinions of great canonists such as Nicolaus de Tudeschis (1386–1455), better known as Abbas Panormitanus or Abbas Siculus, are a constant point of reference.[143]

In the sixteenth century Spanish experience, the boundaries between legal and theological scholarship turn out to be rather porous. This is even more true of the Spanish legal tradition as it evolved in the Indies. The tremendous variety of sources quoted by a famous Spanish jurist from the first half of the seventeenth century such as Juan de Solórzano Pereira (1575–1655) evidences the syncretic nature of the Spanish legal culture in the early modern period. In his standard work on the law of the Indies (*De indiarum iure*), Solórzano Pereira quoted extensively from patristic sources, the *ius commune*, the humanist jurists and the moral theologians.[144]

Eminent scholars used to teach that the culture of the *ius commune* lost the battle against the rising power of *iura propria* in the course of the sixteenth century, since the *ius commune* came under the twin attack from legal humanism and the 'second scholastic'.[145] It is beyond doubt that the *ius commune* lost much of its significance in Europe at least from the middle of the sixteenth century onwards, as the nation state became the 'basic legal unit'.[146] There is also a certain amount of truth in the proposition that the 'second scholastic' and, even more so, legal humanism contributed to the demise of the the the *ius commune*. Both the humanist

---

[143] Nicolaus de Tudeschis was known under these synonyms, since he obtained the abbacy of Santa Maria di Maniace near Mount Etna in Sicily, even though he does not seem to have been present there very often; see K. Pennington, *Nicolaus de Tudeschis (Panormitanus)*, in: O. Condorelli (ed.), Niccolò Tedeschi (Abbas Panormitanus) e i suoi Commentaria in Decretales, [I libri di Erice, 25], Roma 2000, p. 9–36. M. Ascheri, *Nicola 'el monaco', consulente, con edizione di due suoi pareri olografi per la Toscana*, in: O. Condorelli (ed.), Niccolò Tedeschi (Abbas Panormitanus) e i suoi Commentaria in Decretales, [I libri di Erice, 25], Roma 2000, p. 9–36. Panormitanus was busy attending councils and giving legal advice, as is illustrated in the same volume by M. Ascheri, *Nicola 'el monaco', consulente, con edizione di due suoi pareri olografi per la Toscana*, p. 37–68.

[144] See the impressive number of authorities cited in his work, listed in Juan de Solórzano y Pereira, *De indiarum iure sive de iusta Indiarum Occidentalium inquisitione, acquisitione et retentione*, lib. 1: *De inquisitione Indiarum*, ed. C. Baciero e.a., [Corpus Hispanorum de Pace, Serie 2, 8], Madrid 2001, p. 615–640.

[145] Bellomo, *L'Europa del diritto comune*, p. 107. The author has acknowledged that this view on the alleged crisis of the *ius commune* in the sixteenth century is subject to revision; see M. Bellomo, *Condividendo, rispondendo, aggiungendo, Riflessioni intorno al 'ius commune'*, Rivista internazionale di diritto comune, 11 (2000), p. 295, n. 19. Since we cannot go into the subject of legal humanism in France and its attitude toward Roman law, we refer to Birocchi, *Alla ricerca dell'ordine*, p. 1–49 for a critical analysis of the authoritative status of Roman law among the legal humanists.

[146] This point is made with particular vehemence in D. Osler, *The myth of European legal history*, Rechtshistorisches Journal, 16 (1997), p. 393–410.

jurists and the moral theologians regarded the *ius commune* as a historical source of useful juridical tools rather than a set of immutable truths. Yet it is difficult to make sweeping generalizations on this topic, certainly when it comes to the transformation of the *ius commune* in the works of the 'late scholastics'. At any rate, the *ius commune* was continuously praised by theologians as a unique source of knowledge for confessional practice. A brief look at Melchor Cano will illustrate this.

In his posthumously published masterpiece on the hierarchy of theological sources, *De locis theologicis*, the Dominican friar Melchor Cano (c. 1509–1560) concluded that both canon law and civil law were an extremely useful and authoritative source of norms for the theologian.[147] The civilian tradition was praised as a unique source of elegant, technical legal vocabulary.[148] The fifty books of Justinian's Digest were called 'sacred' and 'a temple of wisdom'.[149] Also, Cano expressly criticized Juan Luis Vives' (1492/3–1540) typically humanist undermining of the authority of Roman law. Still, he did share Vives' lament about the corruption of the civilian tradition. Concretely, he dissuaded theologians from relying on the modern commentators of Roman law, since, in contrast to the Roman jurists, contemporary jurists frequently had no training in philosophy.[150]

Cano's praise of civil law and canon law as invaluable tools for the sound practice of moral theology was certainly not an exception. An anonymous dissertation preceding Alfonso de' Liguori's *Theologia moralis* expressly confirmed Cano's statement that the knowledge of civil and canon law

---

[147] Melchor Cano, *De locis theologicis*, edición preparada por Juan Belda Plans, [Biblioteca de Autores Cristianos Maior, 85] Madrid 2006, lib. 10, cap. 8 [Utilidad del Derecho Civil para el teólogo], p. 545–546: 'La verdad es que, contra lo dicho en capítulo anterior, los recursos del Derecho humano pueden ser aprovechados por el teólogo en muchas ocasiones. En efecto, si la ciencia canónica es necesaria al teólogo, y está tan próxima y ligada al conocimiento de las leyes que apenas pueden separarse una y otra cosa, entonces el teólogo debe considerar cosa suya tanto el Derecho Canónico como el Civil, relacionado con el anterior.'

[148] Cano, *De locis theologicis*, lib. 10, cap. 8, p. 547: 'En los anteriores ejemplos nos parece bien el vocabulario técnico de los jurisperitos, pues tampoco es oportuno que hablemos siempre con un lenguaje elegante; (...).'

[149] Cano, *De locis theologicis*, lib. 10, cap. 8, p. 548: 'Afirmo que aquella compilación [Digesto] es cosa santa; con razón lo llamó Justiniano *Templo de la sabiduría* [C. 1,17,1].'

[150] Cano, *De locis theologicis*, lib. 10, cap. 9 [Fuerza y valor del argumento tomado del derecho civil], p. 549: 'Y no podemos aprobar que Luis Vives se empeñe en minar toda la fuerza de las leyes romanas y desvirtuar su autoridad. Con frecuencia es demasiado indulgente consigo mismo cuando fustiga la corrupción de la disciplinas. (...) Por otra parte, una cosa es criticar las leyes civiles, sobre todo las sancionadas por la costumbre en una República bien constituida, y otra denunciar los errores de los comentaristas; aunque Luis, en lo que atañe a los jurisperitos, piensa lo mismo que nosotros.'

was not only useful for a moral theologian, but necessary. A theologian
claiming to be able to solve a case of conscience without the support of
the civilian and canon law tradition was considered to be arrogant.[151]

2.1.3   *A syncretic legal culture*

The works of the canonists Martín de Azpilcueta (1492–1586), alias
Dr. Navarrus, and of Diego de Covarruvias y Leyva (1512–1577), his student,
have been of particular relevance for stimulating the cross-fertilization
between the *ius commune*, the canon law tradition and the moral theological literature. Both stood at the crossroads of canon and civil legal
thought, humanism, and scholasticism. Their works are exemplary of the
syncretic nature of Spanish legal culture of the early modern period, both
on the peninsula and in the Spanish Netherlands.

Dr. Navarrus was born in Barásoain in Navarra to the noble family
Azpilcueta.[152] He studied the arts at Alcalá de Henares with doctor
Miranda, himself a pupil of the Scottish, nominalist philosopher John
Mair (1467–1550). Undoubtedly for political reasons, he left Spain in
1516 to study law in Toulouse, where he also taught for a couple years.
In France he was exposed to both the revival of Thomism and the rise
of legal humanism. To obtain his doctoral degree, Martin de Azpilcueta
went to Salamanca in 1524, where he became a professor of canon law
until Emperor Charles V called upon him in 1537 to teach at Coimbra. For

---

151   Alfonso de' Liguori, Bassani 1773, *Theologia moralis*, tom. 1, prol. (*Dissertatio prolegomena de casuisticae theologiae originibus, locis atque praestantia*), part. 2 (*Pars didactica*),
app. 1 (*De jure utroque canonico et civili deque ejus usu in morali theologia*), par. 1 (*Juris
utriusque canonici et civilis notitiam theologo morali necessarium esse*), p. lxiii: 'At pene
innumera sunt in morali theologia, quae sine canonum scientia definiri non possint. (…)
In his aliisque sexcentis hujus generis, theologus insolentissimus erit, si absque canonibus
atque jurisperitis inconsultis sententiam ferre ausus fuerit. Plura vide apud Canum de locis
theologicis (…). Atque hinc constare puto, juris quoque civilis notitiam non utilem modo
theologo morali esse, sed et necessariam. Nam multa sunt in theologia morali quae ex juris
civilis institutis pendent, neque aliter definiri possunt quam legibus.'

152   The following biographical details on Dr. Navarrus are borrowed from the detailed
account in V. Lavenia, *Martín de Azpilcueta (1492–1586), Un profilo*, Archivio Italiano per
la storia della pietà, 16 (2003), p. 15–148. See also E. Tejero, *El Doctor Navarro en la historia de la doctrina canónica y moral*, in: Estudios sobre el Doctor Navarro en el IV centenario de la muerte de Martín de Azpilcueta, Pamplona 1988, p. 125–180. Dr. Navarrus is
not only famous for his legacy as a moralist and a canonist, he also formulated ground-
breaking economic ideas, cf. B. Schefold (ed.), *Vademecum zu zwei Klassikern des spanishen
Wirtschaftsdenkens, Martín de Azpilcuetas 'Comentario resolutorio de Cambios' und Luis
Ortiz' 'Memorial del Contador Luis Ortiz a Felipe II'*, Düsseldorf 1998.

approximately the last two decades of his life, he worked as a counselor to the *Penitenzieria Apostolica*, the tribunal of conscience of the Holy See.[153] Covarruvias, one of Dr. Navarrus' students at Salamanca, was as difficult to put into a category as his master.[154] While drawing much inspiration from the scholastic tradition, they shared a love for the typically humanist ideal of writing perfect, limpid Latin.[155] Not without reason, Dr. Navarrus has been called a 'humanist jurist'.[156]

The 'Spanish Bartolus', as Covarruvias was nicknamed, quoted as easily from the classical authors, the theologians, and the humanists, as he did from the civilians. Perhaps the only category which would do justice to the hybrid thought of both Dr. Navarrus and Covarruvias is 'humanist scholastic canon law'—a neologism which shows the inadequacy of the traditional categories when applied to sixteenth century Spanish juridical thought. Then again, Covarruvias was not only a great academic, but also

---

[153] For an introduction to the jurisdiction of the *Penitenzieria Apostolica*, which cries out for further study, see P. Chouët, *La sacrée Pénitencerie Apostolique, Étude de droit et d'histoire*, Lyon 1908; L. Schmugge, *Verwaltung des Gewissens, Beobachtungen zu den Registern der päpstlichen Pönitentiarie*, Rivista internazionale di diritto comune, 7 (1996), p. 47–76; M. Maillard-Luypaert, *Les suppliques de la pénitencerie apostolique pour les diocèses de Cambrai, Liège, Thérouanne et Tournai (1410–1411)*, [Analecta Vaticano-Belgica, Série 1, 34], Bruxelles 2003, p. 27–53; and J. Ickx, *Ipsa vero officii maioris Penitentiarii institutio non reperitur? La nascità di un Tribunale della coscienza*, in: M. Sodi – J. Ickx (eds.), La penitenzieria apostolica e il sacramento della penitenza, Percorsi storici, giuridici, teologici e prospettive pastorali, Città del Vaticano 2009, p. 19–50.

[154] Tomas y Valiente, *Manual de Historia del derecho Español*, p. 309–310. Valiente acknowledges that Covarruvias escapes any attempt to classify him, but he treats Covarruvias in the same chapter that discusses the humanist jurists Antonio de Nebrija (1441–1522) and Antonio Agustín (1516–1568). Further biographical details on Covarruvias can be found in F. Merzbacher, *Azpilcueta und Covarruvias, Zur Gewaltendoktrin der spanischen Kanonistik im Goldenen Zeitalter*, in: G. Köbler – H. Drüppel – D. Willoweit (ed.), Friedrich Merzbacher, Recht-Staat-Kirche, Ausgewählte Aufsätze, [Forschungen zur kirchlichen Rechtsgeschichte und zum Kirchenrecht, 18], Wien-Köln-Graz 1989, p. 275–280; J. Finestres, *El humanismo jurídico en las universidades españolas, Siglos XVI–XVIII*, in: Rodríguez, L. – Bezares S. (eds.), Las Universidades Hispánicas de la Monarquía de los Austrias al Centralismo liberal, Salamanca 2000, vol. 1, p. 317–320; and N. Brieskorn, *Diego de Covarrubias y Leyva, Zum Friedens- und Kriegsdenken eines Kanonisten des 16. Jahrhunderts*, in: N. Brieskorn – M. Riedenauer (ed.), Suche nach Frieden, Politische Ethik in der Frühen Neuzeit II, Stuttgart 2002, p. 323–352.

[155] E.g. Martín de Azpilcueta, *In tres de poenitentia distinctiones posteriores commentarii*, Conimbricae 1542, [Ad auditores]: 'Cum enim illum erigere paulum potuerimus, ut multis potius quam paucis placeremus ac prodessemus usque ad plenam perspicuitatem illum deiecisse nos credimus a barbara voce ac phrasi quatenus per stilum scholasticum licuit abstinentes.'

[156] C. Zendri, *L'usura nella dottrina dei giuristi umanisti, Martin de Azpilcueta (1492–1586)*, in: D. Quaglioni – G. Todeschini – M. Varanini (eds.), Credito e usura fra teologia, diritto e amministrazione (sec. XII–XVI), [Collection de l'École française de Rome, 346], Rome 2005, p. 265–290.

actively engaged in forensic practice. Besides teaching canon law at Salamanca from 1543 onwards, he started his legal career as a judge in the
Chancillería of Granada, participated in the Council of Trent, served as the
bishop of Ciudad Rodrigo in 1560 and of Segovia in 1565, and eventually
became the president of the *Consejo Real de Castilla* in 1573.

Dr. Navarrus and Covarruvias are among the most important and direct
sources of juridical thought for theologians. However, the fusion of the traditions of civil law, canon law, and moral philosophy was not the exclusive
domain of Dr. Navarrus and Covarruvias. They were tapping into a wider
trend, which mixed legal and moral traditions. It found fertile ground in
many different regions in the early modern Spanish empire, such as the
Spanish Netherlands. The work of the sixteenth century jurists at the University of Leuven, too, drew on a mix of several traditions, such as Bartolism, legal humanism, and scholastic thought.[157] The general acceptance
in the sixteenth-century Netherlands that naked pacts are binding (*pacta
nuda sunt servanda*) might be due in no small measure to this singular
fusion of civil and canon law traditions at the University of Leuven.[158]

A seminal synthesis between civil law, canon law, and moral thought
was already being forged at the beginning of the sixteenth century in the
works of an exceptional jurist such as Nicolaas Everaerts (1463/4–1516), a
professor at the University of Leuven who went on to become the president of the Council of Malines.[159] Everaerts heralded in a tradition of
practice-oriented legal thought which combined a profound expertise in
Romano-canon law and a great sensitivity for moral thought.[160] He was

---

[157] L. Waelkens, *Was er in de zestiende eeuw een Leuvense invloed op het Europese contractenrecht?*, in: B. Tilleman – A. Verbeke (eds.), Actualia vermogensrecht, Brugge 2005,
p. 3–16. It is worthwhile noting with the author on p. 8–9 that despite King Philip II's
attempt to separate the study of civil law and canon law by founding three royal chairs in
law (1557), the influence of canon law persisted at the Faculty of Law of the University of
Leuven. For example, the calvinist jurist Elbertus Leoninus (1519/20–1598) taught canon
law for a certain period. Also, professor of Roman law Johannes Wamesius (1524–1590)
went on to occupy the chair of canon law.

[158] Waelkens, *Was er in de zestiende eeuw een Leuvense invloed op het Europese contractenrecht?*, p. 15–16.

[159] On the life and times of Everaerts, see the biograpy by D. van den Auweele in G. Van
Dievoet e.a. (eds.), *Lovanium docet, Geschiedenis van de Leuvense Rechtsfaculteit (1425–1914)*,
Cataloog bij de tentoonstelling in de Centrale Bibliotheek (25.5–2.7.1988), Leuven 1988,
p. 60–63, and O.M.D.F. Vervaart, *Studies over Nicolaas Everaerts (1462–1532) en zijn Topica*,
Arnhem 1994 [= doct. diss.], p. 3–25.

[160] On Everaerts' familiarity with the theologian Conrad Summenhart, in particular,
see Vervaart, *Studies over Nicolaas Everaerts*, p. 110–111. Compare L. Waelkens, *Nicolaas
Everaerts, Un célèbre méconnu du droit commun (1463/4–1532)*, Rivista internazionale di
diritto comune, 15 (2004), p. 182: 'Everaerts raisonne toujours *utroque iure*. En outre il ne

a friend of Erasmus and is considered to be a protagonist of the legal humanist movement at the University of Leuven.[161] The synthesis created by Everaerts not only inspired generations of jurists in the Low Countries, but also the Spanish theologian Francisco de Vitoria.[162] Whether a direct connection between Everaerts and Vitoria existed is unknown. But it is beyond doubt that they participated in the same tendency of fusing canon law, civil law, moral thought, and humanist mentality. This trend can be witnessed from the early sixteenth century onward, in the Southern Netherlands as well as on the Spanish mainland.

The theologians did not content themselves with absorbing the legal traditions. They also claimed to be superior to the civilians and canonists. They vindicated the power to evaluate positive law—contemporary statutory law, the law of the Church, and the *ius commune*—from the perspective of natural law. For example, Domingo de Soto argued that it was the task of theologians to evaluate the moral foundations of civil law.[163] Boasting of the superiority of their discipline, the theologians claimed to be able to speak with authority in all matters related to man's existence. As the opening sentence of Francisco de Vitoria's *Relectio de potestate civili* reads,[164] 'the office and calling of a theologian are so wide, that no argument or controversy on any subject can be considered foreign to his profession.'

---

cite pas seulement les légistes et les canonistes, mais également des moralistes et des pénitenciers comme Angelus de Clavasio, Astesanus de Asti ou Conrad Summenhart.'

[161] E.g. V. Brants, *La faculté de droit de l'Université de Louvain à travers cinq siècles, Étude historique*, Paris-Bruxelles 1917, p. 8–9; and R. Dekkers, *Het humanisme en de rechtswetenschap in de Nederlanden*, Antwerpen 1938, p. 1–36.

[162] Waelkens, *Civium causa*, p. 114. It is beyond doubt that jurists from Leuven did influence the Spanish moral theologians. This is very clear in Tomás Sánchez's work. References to Nicolaas Everaerts, in particular, are scarce but not absent, e.g. Sánchez, *Disputationes de sancto matrimonii sacramento*, Antverpiae 1620, tom. 1, lib. 1, disp. 65, num. 1, p. 111.

[163] Soto, *De iustitia et iure libri decem / De la justicia y del derecho en diez libros*, edición facsimilar de la hecha por D. de Soto en 1556 [Salamanca], con su versión castellana corrrespondiente, Introducción historica y teologico-juridica por Venancio Diego Carro, Versión española de Marcelino González Ordóñez, [Instituto de estudios políticos, Sección de teólogos juristas, 1], Madrid 1967 (hereafter: Soto, *De iustitia et iure*, ed. fac. V. Diego Carro – M. González Ordóñez), vol. 1, Prooemium, p. 5.

[164] Francisco de Vitoria, *On Civil Power*, prologue, cited from the translation in A. Pagden – J. Lawrance (eds.), *Francisco de Vitoria, Political writings*, Cambridge 2001 [= 1991], p. 3. We are grateful to Professor Charles Donahue Jr. for bringing this text to our attention.

2.2 FROM MANUALS FOR CONFESSORS TO SYSTEMATIC LEGAL TREATISES

2.2.1 *Symbiosis* versus *separation of law and morality*

The intense relationship between law and theology naturally reaches much farther back than the moral theologians of the sixteenth and seventeenth centuries.[165] During the Middle Ages, all monastic orders, even the most ascetic ones, became deeply involved with law.[166] It is unwise for an historian to divide the flux of historical events into neatly distinguished epochs, or worse still, to revise the existing *caesurae*. Were it not unwise, then it would be tempting to reconsider the Middle Ages as a thousand-year period beginning with Benedict of Nursia's famous maxim 'Ora et labora' as expressed during his Rule around 550, and ending with Luther's symbolic burning of Angelo Carletti de Chivasso's (ca. 1414–1495) famous manual for confessors, the *Summa Angelica* (1486) on December 10th, 1520 at Wittenberg. Let us explain this a little further.

Benedict's Rule had been an authentic exhortation to reconcile the active and the contemplative life. The medieval tradition of manuals for confessors—which enjoyed a boom from at least the fourth Lateran Council (1215) onwards[167]—had eventually tried to determine the practical

---

[165] The following paragraphs borrow in part from material previously published in Decock, *From law to paradise*, p. 14–33.

[166] Hence, the fundamental contribution of Franciscans such as Pier Giovanni Olivi (1248–1298) to contract law and economic thought; cf. S. Piron, *Marchands et confesseurs, Le Traité des contrats d'Olivi dans son contexte (Narbonne, fin XIIIe–début XIVe siècle)*, in: *L'Argent au Moyen Age, XXVIIIe Congrès de la SHMESP (Clermont-Ferrand, 1997)*, Paris 1998, p. 289–308. Olivi is also the subject of detailed study in several, fundamental contributions by G. Todeschini, e.g. *Il prezzo della salvezza, Lessici medievali del pensiero económico*, Roma 1994, and *I mercanti e il tempio, La società cristiana e il circolo virtuoso della ricchezza fra Medioevo ed Età Moderna*, Bologna 2002.

[167] The secondary literature on the manuals for confessors is abundant. See, for example, F.W.H. Wasserschleben, *Die Bussordnungen der abendländischen Kirche*, Halle 1851; H.J. Schmitz, *Die Bussbücher und Bussdisziplin der Kirche*, Mainz 1883; P. Michaud-Quantin, *Sommes de casuistique et manuels de confession au moyen âge (XIIe–XVIe siècles)*, Leuven-Lille-Montréal 1962; Ch. Bergfeld, *Katholische Moraltheologie und Naturrechtslehre*, in: H. Coing (ed.), Handbuch der Quellen und Literatur der neueren europäischen Privatrechtsgeschichte, Band II. Neuere Zeit (1500–1800), Das Zeitalter des gemeinen Rechts, Teilband I.1. Wissenschaft, München 1977, p. 999–1033; and O.I. Langholm, *The merchants in the confessional, Trade and price in the pre-Reformation penitential handbooks*, [Studies in Medieval and Reformation Thought, 93], Leiden 2003, p. 233–271; J. Goering, *The scholastic turn (1100–1500), Penitential theology and law in the schools*, in: A. Firey (ed.), A new history of penance, [Brill's Companions to the Christian Tradition, 14], Leiden – Boston 2008, p. 219–238; J. Goering, *The internal forum and the literature of penance and confession*, in: W. Hartmann – K. Pennington (eds.), The history of medieval canon law in

consequences of that ideal. The technical devices they used for bridg-ing the gap between the lofty principles of Christian spirituality and the realities of the active life were Roman and canon law. These legal sources were brought to bear on the qualms of conscience arising in all areas of life.[168] However, Luther no longer wanted legal argument to dominate the internal forum, as it did in the *Summa Angelica* and other manuals for confessors.[169] It is certainly no coincidence that Silvester Mazzolini da Prierio (1456–1523), the Dominican theologian who was the author of the other famous manual for confessors, the *Summa Silvestrina*, was one of the first who became involved in a direct polemic with Luther, notably on the subject of papal power.[170]

Significantly, two thirds of the references contained in Angelo Car-letti's *Summa Angelica* were taken from Roman law, canon law and medieval jurists. This deeply juridical character of the *Summa Angelica* is not surprising. For one thing, Angelo Carletti de Chivasso himself was a former professor of theology and law at the university of Bologna and a magistrate who eventually became a Franciscan friar.[171] For another thing, the juridical and the theological spheres already overlapped in earlier manuals as well, for instance in the *Speculum curatorum* drafted by Ran-ulph Higden (c. 1285–1364) from the Benedictine monastery in Chester, and in the *Gnotosolitos parvus* written by Arnold Gheyloven of Rotter-dam (c. 1375–1442), a regular canon at the Windesheim monastery at

---

the classical period, 1140–1234, From Gratian to the decretals of Pope Gregory IX, Washing-ton D.C. 2008, p. 379–428. Importantly, under the supervision of Prof. Dr. Thomas Duve, PD Dr. Christiane Birr is currently conducting research on the manuals for confessors in the late medieval and early modern period at the Max-Planck-Insitute for European Legal History (Frankfurt/Main).

[168] The result is that those manuals offer us a unique insight into late medieval Chris-tian societies, as has recently been noted in regard to the early fourteenth-century *Libro de las confesiones* in A. García y García – B. Alonso Rodríguez – F. Cantelar Rodríguez (eds.), *Martín Pérez, Libro de las confesiones, Una radiografía de la sociedad medieval española*, [Biblioteca de autores cristianos maior, 69], Madrid 2002. It is worthwhile noting that the *Libro de las confesiones* (c. 1312–1317) counts no less than 757 pages in its modern edition.

[169] Pihlajamäki, *Executor divinarum et suarum legum, Criminal law and the Lutheran Reformation*, p. 183.

[170] M. Scattola, *Eine interkonfessionelle Debatte, Wie die Spanische Spätscholastik die politische Theologie des Mittelalters mit der Hilfe des Aristoteles revidierte*, in: A. Fidora – J. Fried – M. Lutz-Bachmann – L. Schorn-Schütte (eds.), Politischer Aristotelismus und Religion in Mittelalter und Früher Neuzeit, [Wissenskultur und gesellschaftlicher Wandel, 23], Berlin 2007, p. 141, n. 9.

[171] For more biographical details, see S. Pezzella, in: *Dizionario Biografico degli Italiani*, 20 (1977), p. 136–138.

Groenendaal near Brussels.[172] The eminent legal historian Winfried Trusen has cogently argued that the manuals for confessors provided one of the highways through which the *ius commune* took root at the grassroots level of society.[173] This is even more true of the subsequent moral theological tradition. The literature of theologians such as Soto, Molina and Lessius contributed to no small extent to the ongoing diffusion of the texts of the *ius commune* and to their preservation as a repository of legal vocabulary and legal argument until the modern era.

Martin Luther almost succeeded in his *damnatio memoriae* of 1520. Until recently, little attention has been paid to the fact that the Catholic Church's antagonistic reaction to the Protestant movement actually strengthened the combination of law and theology that formed the nub of Luther's criticism.[174] The sixteenth-century Dominicans and Jesuits challenged Luther's heterodox view of morality by reinforcing precisely what he had condemned.[175] They gave spiritual advice to the flock by relying on pagan philosophy and the *ius commune*. Luther thought that personal faith, divine grace and the Bible were the principal agents in the process of justification. Moreover, he rejected the intermediary role of the Church as the guide of the individual's conscience. The Dominicans and the Jesuits,

---

[172] E. Crook – M. Jennings (ed. and transl.), *Ranulph Higden, Speculum Curatorum, A mirror for curates, Book 1, The commandments*, [Dallas Medieval Texts and Translations, 13], Leuven 2011; A.G. Weiler, *Het morele veld van de Moderne Devotie, weerspiegeld in de Gnotosolitos parvus van Arnold Gheyloven van Rotterdam, 1423, Een Summa van moraaltheologie, kerkelijk recht en spiritualiteit voor studenten in Leuven en Deventer*, [Middeleeuwse studies en bronnen, 96], Hilversum 2006, p. 41–72.

[173] W. Trusen, *Forum internum und gelehrtes Recht im Spätmittelalter, Summae confessorum und Traktate als Wegbereiter der Rezeption*, Zeitschrift der Savigny-Stiftung für Rechtsgeschichte, Kan. Abt., 57 (1971), p. 83–126; W. Trusen, *Zur Bedeutung des geistlichen Forum internum und externum für die spätmittelalterliche Gesellschaft'*, Zeitschrift der Savigny-Stiftung für Rechtsgeschichte, Kan. Abt., 76 (1990), p. 254–285.

[174] There are excellent studies, however, by M. Turrini, *La coscienza e le leggi, Morale e diritto nei testi per la confessione delle prima età moderna*, Bologna 1991; A. Prosperi, *Tribunali della coscienza, Inquisitori, confessori, missionari*, [Bibliotheca di cultura storica, 214], Torino 1996; E. Brambilla, *Giuristi, teologi e giustizia ecclesiastica dal '500 alla fine del '700*, in: M.L. Betri – A. Pastore (eds.), *Avvocati, medici, ingegneri, Alle origini delle professioni moderne (secoli XVI–XIX)*, Bologna 1997, p. 169–206; W. de Boer, *The conquest of the soul, Confession, discipline and public order in counter reformation Milan*, Leiden 2001; R. Rusconi, *L'ordine dei peccati, La confessione tra Medioevo ed età moderna*, Bologna 2002; V. Lavenia, *L'infamia e il perdono, Tributi, pene e confessione nella teologia morale della prima età moderna*, Bologna 2004.

[175] For a description of early modern Catholic legal culture as opposed to the Lutheran Reformation, see M. Schmoeckel, *Fragen zur Konfession des Rechts im 16. Jahrhundert am Beispiel des Strafrechts*, in: I. Dingel – W.-F. Schäufele (eds.), Kommunikation und Transfer im Christentum der Frühen Neuzeit, [Veröffentlichungen des Instituts für Europäische Geschichte Mainz, Beihefte, 74], Mainz 2008, p. 185–187.

on the other hand, remained faithful to the adage of Thomas Aquinas, that grace perfects nature, provided that the potential of nature has been developed in the first place (*gratia naturam praesupponit et perficit*). They also believed that the dictates of conscience could only be spelled out correctly by clerical experts. For Protestants, the individual's conscience was judge; for Catholics, the confessor was considered judge.[176]

It should not come as a surprise, then, that in comparison with their Catholic counterpart, the Protestant traditions in moral theology were characterized by relatively scarce references to sources other than the Gospel and the Old Testament. They emerged from the very condemnation by Luther of that symbiosis of law and morality as it had grown in the Catholic Church. This can clearly be seen in the work *On Conscience* by the Puritan theologian William Ames (1576–1633).[177] His work is devoid of almost any reference to Roman or canon law, in great contrast to that of the Catholic moral theologians. This is reflective of the wider protestant tradition. To quote Friedrich Balduin's (1575–1627) critique of Catholic 'casuists' such as Cajetan, Dr. Navarrus, and Azor: 'they derive the solutions to far too difficult cases not from the most limpid fountains of Israel (*ex limpidissimis Israelis fontibus*), but from their own scholastic pool and that of others, such as Thomas Aquinas, Tomás Sánchez, and Suárez, and they yield them up to the ignorant mob.'[178]

Scathing critiques of canon law and 'papalizing jurisprudence' were typical of the Protestant reformation. This phenomenon persisted, for instance in Heinrich Ernst Kestner's (1671–1723)' *Discourse on papalizing jurisprudence* (*Discursus de jurisprudentia papizante*).[179] However, the anti-papal

---

[176] See J.F. Keenan, *William Perkins (1558–1602) and the birth of British casuistry*, in: J.F. Keenan – Th.A. Shannon (eds.), The context of casuistry, Washington DC 1995, p. 112. The author goes on to remark, not without a certain sense of irony, that the near-conflicting roles of judge and consoler that perplexed Catholic confessors were absolutely irreconcilable in the personal conscience of the Reformed believer.

[177] This is illustrated in regard to the solution of a concrete case of conscience, namely the Merchant of Rhodes, in Decock, *Lessius and the breakdown of the scholastic paradigm*, p. 68.

[178] Friedrich Balduin, *Tractatus de casibus conscientiae*, Wittebergae 1628, Epistola dedicatoria, [s.p.]: '(...) qui non ex limpidissimis Israelis fontibus, sed propriis traditionum scholasticorum et aliorum, ut Thomae Aquinatis, Thomae Sanchez, Suarezii lacunis, decisiones difficiliorum casuum hauserunt et rudi populo propinarunt. 'On Balduin, see Wilhelm Gaß, *Balduin, Friedrich*, in: Allgemeine Deutsche Biographie, 2 (1875), p. 16–17 (URL: http://www.deutsche-biographie.de/pnd116883391.html?anchor=adb; last visited on 20.09.2011).

[179] Heinrich Ernst Kestner, *Discursus de jurisprudentia papizante*, Rintelii 1711, p. 14: 'Est autem nobis jurisprudentia papizans doctrina corrupta, sive ex papismo, sive ex

rhetoric employed by Protestant theologians and jurists should not make
us blind to their ongoing familiarity with the Catholic moral theological
and canon law tradition. This is obvious from Balduin's quoting names
of Spanish theologians in his *Treatise on cases of conscience*. The same is
true of the Lutheran jurist Dietrich Reinking (1590–1664). In his *Biblische
Policey* (1653), a famous example of the literature on *Gute Policey*,[180] he
shows himself quite familiar with the Spanish authors, for instance with
Covarruvias.[181] The ongoing presence of Catholic moral theology in seventeenth century reformed circles is also obvious from juridical dissertations supervised by an eminent theologian and jurist such as Samuel
Stryk (1640–1710). Stryk would become very close to typically anti-Catholic
protestant natural lawyers, such as Christian Thomasius (1655–1728). Stryk
was even a mentor to Justus Henning Boehmer (1674–1749), the famous
author of the *Ius ecclesiasticum protestantium*. A couple of dissertations
that were submitted to the faculty of law at the University of Frankfurt/
Oder under Stryk's supervision abound with references to Catholic moral
theologians such as Leonardus Lessius.[182]

Yet, generally speaking, to the protestant reformers, *ius commune* and
canon law are no longer valid sources for the solution of moral problems.
To return to the citation from Friedrich Balduin, only sacred texts of the
New and Old Testament (*limpidissimi Israelis fontes*) are justified in arbi-
trating the solution of moral cases. A starker contrast with Melchor Cano's

---

superstitione fluens, quando circa genuina jurisprudentiae principia aliud statuimus,
aliudque inferimus, quam quod recta ratio et vera legum natura exigunt.' For biographical
information on Kestner, who became a professor of law at Rintel after his studies at the
universities of Frankfurt/Oder and Halle (1671–1723), see F. von Schulte, *Kestner, Heinrich
Ernst*, in: Allgemeine Deutsche Biographie, 15 (1882), p. 664 (URL: http://www.deutsche-
biographie.de/pnd122950054.html?anchor=adb'; last visited on 20.09.2011).

[180] M. Stolleis, *Geschichte des öffentlichen Rechts in Deutschland, Band I: Reichspublizistik und Policeywissenschaft 1600–1800*, München 1988, p. 337–365.

[181] M.M. Totzeck, *A Lutheran jurist and the emergence of modern European states—
Dietrich Reinking and his late work 'Biblische Policey' (1653)*, Zeitschrift der Savigny-Stiftung
für Rechtsgeschichte, Kan. Abt., 97 (2011), p. 325, n. 70.

[182] References to Lessius, to name but one Catholic moral theologian, are contained in:
Disputatio juridica de conscientia partium in judicio, quam (…) praeside Samuele Strykio
(…) placido eruditorum examini submittit Johannes Christianus John (Francofurti ad Viadrum, 1677) [= Diss. jur., Frankfurt/Oder, 1677], e.g. p. 10, 12, 17, 26, 39, 47, 48, 51, 52, 53, 60,
63, 64, 67, 71, 72, 78. Similar observations apply to *Dissertatio de conscientia advocati*, quam
(…) praeside Samuele Strykio (…) placido eruditorum examini sistit Ephraim Nazius
(Francofurti ad Oderam, 1677) [= Diss. jur., Frankfurt/Oder, 1677], e.g. p. 31, 41, 42, 43, 50,
51, 66, 68, 69, 70. See also *Dissertatio juridica de credentiae revelatione*, quam (…) praeside
Samuele Strykio (…) publicae eruditorum disquisitioni exponit Henricus Andreas Breiger
(Francofurti ad Viadrum, 1675) [= Diss. jur., Frankfurt/Oder, 1675], e.g. p. 10, 72.

abovementioned insistence on the necessity of the study of Romano-canon law for confessors and moral theologians could hardly be imagined. In this manner, Balduin's statement heralds in the neat separation, not only of law and morality, but also of the disciplines of jurisprudence and moral theology. A brilliant account of this separation of distinct duties and disciplines was eventually formulated by the Lutheran professor of natural law Samuel von Pufendorf (1632–1694). In the wonderful introduction to his work *On Duties*, which is a true rhetorical masterpiece, Pufendorf distinguished three sources of duties, namely: reason, civil laws, and divine revelation. Contrary to the Catholic moral theologians, he held that it pertained to separate disciplines to analyze the obligations that followed from each of those sources, namely: natural law, civil law, and moral theology, respectively:[183]

> It is therefore manifest that mankind draws the knowledge of his duty, and of what he has to do because it is honest, and of what he has to omit because it it is turpid, from three fountains, so to speak, namely from the light of reason, from the civil laws, and from a peculiar revelation by God. (...). From this, three separate disciplines come forth, of which the first is natural law, which is common to all nations, the other is the civil law of each individual political community, of which there are as many as, or could be as many, as there are political communities in which mankind split up. The third discipline is considered to be moral theology, which is distinct from that part of theology in which the principles of faith are explained.

2.2.2   *The Dominicans at Salamanca and the renewal of the Catholic tradition*

While the protestant reformation was asserting itself with increasing force, the Catholics revived Thomistic moral philosophy. This is sufficiently

---

[183] Samuel von Pufendorf, *De officio, Ad lectorem*, in: G. Hartung (ed.), *Samuel Pufendorf, De officio*, in: W. Schmidt-Biggeman (ed.), *Samuel Pufendorf, Gesammelte Werke*, Band 2, Berlin 1997, p. 5: 'Manifestum igitur est, ex tribus velut fontibus homines cognitionem officii sui, et quid in hac vita sibi tanquam honestum sit agendum, tanquam turpe omittendum, haurire; ex lumine rationis, ex legibus civilibus, et ex peculiari revelatione divini numinis. [...] Inde et tres separatae disciplinae proveniunt, quarum prima est juris naturalis, omnibus gentibus communis: altera juris civilis singularum civitatum, quae tam multiplex est, aut esse potest, quot numero sunt civitates, in quas genus humanum discessit. Tertia theologia moralis habetur, illi parti theologiae contradistincta, quibus credenda exponuntur.'

well-known.[184] This revival coincided with the reinforcement of the Aristotelian moral tradition, which can generally be observed during the sixteenth and seventeenth centuries.[185] The victory of Thomas' *Summa* at
the expense of Lombard's *Sentences* has been ascribed, amongst other
reasons, to the more expressly juridical and technical character of the
Summa Theologiae. This characteristic made it more fit for the solution of
new and complex problems related to the discovery of the Americas and
the expansion of commercial capitalism.[186] It may be recalled that the
theologians were frequently consulted by merchants and bankers.[187]

A good example of the revival of Thomas at the threshold of the six-
teenth century can be seen in the work of the Dominican theologian
Pieter Crockaert (c. 1450–1514) from Brussels. In 1509, he replaced Peter
Lombard's (1095–1160) *Sententiae* with Thomas Aquinas' *Summa Theolo-
giae* as the main textbook in theology at the University of Paris. Crock-
aert also wrote a commentary on the *Summa*. However, it was the Italian
Dominican Tommaso de Vio (1469–1534), also named Cardinal Cajetanus
(Gaetano) after his birthplace Gaeta, who started publishing in 1508 what

---

[184] See M. Grabmann, *Geschichte der katholischen Theologie seit dem Ausgang der Väterzeit*, Freiburg im Breisgau 1933, p. 151–154, for an overview of the most important commentators of Thomas at the outset of the sixteenth century.

[185] On the renewed interest for Aristotle which is apparent in the jurists of the early
modern period, both in Catholic and Protestant circles, see Birocchi, *Alla ricerca dell'ordine*,
p. 159–164, and Stolleis, *Geschichte des öffentlichen Rechts in Deutschland, Band I: Reichspublizistik und Policeywissenschaft 1600–1800*, p. 80–90. The lines of development of Aristotelianism from the fifteenth to the seventeenth century are expounded in great detail
by Forlivesi, *A man, an age, a book*, p. 48–114, and by L. Bianchi, *Continuity and change in
the Aristotelian tradition*, in: J. Hankins (ed.). The Cambridge companion to Renaissance
philosophy, Cambridge 2007, p. 49–71. For a profound case-study of the reception of Aristotle's *Nicomachean Ethics* in Italy, see D.A. Lines, *Aristotle's Ethics in the Italian Renaissance (ca. 1300–1650), The universities and the problem of moral education*, [Education and
society in the Middle Ages and Renaissance, 13], Leiden-Boston 2002.

[186] B. Löber, *Das spanische Gesellschaftsrecht im 16. Jahrhundert*, Freiburg im Breisgau
1965, p. 8–9. The juridical nature of Thomas's thought is analyzed in J.-M. Aubert, *Le droit
romain dans l'œuvre de Saint Thomas*, [Bibliothèque Thomiste, 30], Paris 1955; T. Mayer-
Maly, *Die Rechtslehre des heiligen Thomas von Aquin und die römische Jurisprudenz*, in:
J.A. Ankum e.a. (ed.), Mélanges Felix Wubbe offerts par ses collègues et ses amis à l'occasion
de son soixante-dixième anniversaire, Fribourg 1993, p. 345–353; K. Seelmann, *Thomas von
Aquin am Schnittpunkt von Recht und Theologie, Die Bedeutung der Thomas-Renaissance für
die Moderne*, [Luzerner Hochschulreden, 11], Luzern 2000.

[187] For example, in 1530 the Antwerp bankers consulted the doctors of Paris on the
licitness of new types of bills of exchange; cf. M. Grice-Hutchinson, *The School of Salamanca, Readings in Spanish monetary theory, 1544–1605*, Oxford 1952, p. 120–126. See also
L. Vereecke, *Théologie morale et magistère, avant et après le Concile de Trente*, Le Supplément, Revue d'éthique et théologie morale, 177 (1991), p. 13.

was to become the standard commentary on Thomas' *Summa Theologiae*.[188] This commentary, particularly its expositions on the binding force of promises, became a point of reference in the Spanish theologians' treatises *On justice and right* and *On contracts*.

As the traditional story goes, it is to the credit of Francisco de Vitoria (1483/1492–1546), a pupil of Crockaert, to have imported Thomism from Paris into Salamanca, laying the foundations of the so-called 'School of Salamanca', famous for its fundamental contributions to theological, juridical and economic thought.[189] This traditional picture is now subject to qualification, in part because the very concept of the 'School of Salamanca' is under dispute.[190] Also, there is growing evidence that Thomism spread at Spanish universities long before Vitoria's appointment at a college in Valladolid in 1523 and, successively, at the University of Salamanca in 1526. Recent literature points out that Salamanca came under the spell of Thomism from the second half of the fifteenth century onwards through the pioneering work of Pedro Martínez de Osma (c. 1420–1480) and his student Diego de Deza (1443–1523).[191] Probably, the decisive moments in the move toward Thomism were the reformation of the Dominican monastery in Vallodolid in 1502 and the foundation of an establishment for higher learning called *Santo Tomás* in Seville in 1517.

Vitoria's commentary on Thomas Aquinas' *Summa Theologiae* turned out to be idiosyncratic enough to become very influential. He earned

---

[188] For biographical references, see E. Stöve, s.v. *De Vio, Tommaso*, in: Dizionario biografico degli Italiani; cf. http://www.treccani.it/enciclopedia/tommaso-de-vio_(Dizionario-Biografico)/ (website last visited on 12/09/2011).

[189] Among recent biographical introductions to Vitoria, see D. Deckers, s.v. *Vitoria, Francisco de*, in: Theologische Realenzyklopädie, vol. 35, Berlin – New York 2003, p. 169–173.

[190] For an analysis of the problematical history of the conception of 'School of Salamanca' in the twentieth century, see M. Anxo Pena González, *La Escuela de Salamanca, de la Monarquía hispánica al Orbe católico*, [Biblioteca de Autores Cristianos Maior, 90], Madrid 2009, p. 415–484. The term was promoted by Marjorie Grice-Hutchinson to designate a group of scholars who were either directly or indirectly influenced by Francisco de Vitoria in the context of her ground-breaking investigation of early Spanish economic thought; cf. *The School of Salamanca, Readings in Spanish monetary theory, 1544–1605*, Oxford 1952, and *The concept of the School of Salamanca, Its origins and development*, in: L.S. Moss – C.K. Ryan (eds.), Economic thought in Spain, Selected essays of Marjorie Grice-Hutchinson, Cambridge 1993, p. 23–29. Of late, Juan Belda Plans has written a monumental history of the school arguing that it was chiefly a movement for the renewal of scholastic theology; cf. J. Belda Plans, *La escuela de Salamanca y la renovación de la teología en el siglo XVI*, [Biblioteca de Autores Cristianos Maior, 63], Madrid 2000.

[191] Belda Plans, *La escuela de Salamanca*, p. 64–73.

himself a reputation as the 'Spanish Socrates'.[192] His commentaries on Thomas were considered to be more adapted to the concrete demands of the time than Cajetan's rather abstract and convoluted commentary of Thomas.[193] Since the revival of Thomas Aquinas' *Summa theologiae* was inspired by pragmatic motives as much as by dogmatic choices, it is not surprising that the moral theologians were not reluctant to deviate from the conclusions reached by the Doctor Angelicus. They frequently exposed themselves to other currents of thought, for instance to Scotist nominalism.[194] Vitoria's Thomism was intrinsically hybrid in nature. As was true of other theologians of the sixteenth century, Vitoria did not feel constrained by Thomas' viewpoints.[195] In time, the commentaries on Thomas grew into a new literary genre of treatises 'On justice and right' (*De iustitia et iure*). They dealt more specifically with ethical issues and attest to the birth of an autonomous discipline of moral theology.[196]

---

[192] He was named as such by Domingo de Bañez (1528–1604); cf. J. Barrientos García, *Un siglo de moral económica (1526–1629), Tom. 1: Francisco de Vitoria y Domingo de Soto*, [Acta Salmanticensia iussu Senatus Universitatis edita, Filosofía y letras, 164], Salamanca 1985, p. 27.

[193] Belda Plans, *La escuela de Salamanca*, p. 237–241, and A. Brett, *Liberty, right and nature, Individual rights in later scholastic thought*, [Ideas in Context, 44], Cambridge 1997, p. 123.

[194] It has been argued that the opposition between the *via antiqua* and the *via moderna* grew obsolete in the course of the sixteenth century; cf. M.J.F.M. Hoenen, *Via antiqua and via moderna in the fifteenth century, Doctrinal, institutional, and Church political factors in the Wegestreit*, in: R.L. Friedman – L.O. Nielsen (eds.), The medieval heritage in early modern metaphysics and modal theory, 1400–1700, [The new synthese historical library, Texts and studies in the history of philosophy, 53], p. 31. The influence of nominalistic philosophers such as John Mair and Jacques Almain is apparent in the works of the sixteenth century moral theologians and easily explicable in view of the training they received. For further discussion, see L. Vereecke, *Préface à l'histoire de la théologie morale moderne*, in: L. Vereecke, De Guillaume D'Ockham à Saint Alphonse de Liguori, Études d'histoire de la théologie morale moderne 1300–1787, [Bibliotheca Historica Congregationis Sanctissimi Redemptoris, 12], Rome 1986, p. 27–55; F. Gómez Camacho, *Later scholastics, Spanish economic thought in the 16th and 17th centuries*, in: S. Todd Lowry – B. Gordon (eds.), Ancient and medieval economic ideas and concepts of social justice, Leiden-New York-Köln 1998, p. 503–562.

[195] Similar observations on the 'liberal' use of Thomas by the scholastics of the early modern period can be found in M. Villey, *Bible et philosophie gréco-romaine, De saint Thomas au droit moderne*, in: Dimensions religieuses du droit et notamment sur l'apport de Saint Thomas D'Aquin, [Archives de Philosophie du Droit, 18], Paris 1973, p. 45–48; and F. Motta, *Bellarmino, Una teologia politica della Controriforma*, [Storia, 12], Brescia 2005, p. 553–554.

[196] See Van Houdt, *Leonardus Lessius over lening, intrest en woeker*, p. xxviii.

A student of Vitoria, the Dominican Domingo de Soto (c. 1494–1560), was the first to publish such a treatise *De iustitia et iure* in 1553.[197] Soto studied arts at Alcalá de Henares and went on to study theology in Paris, for instance at the Collège Sainte-Barbe where for a short time he studied under the nominalist logician Juan de Celaya (c. 1490–1558).[198] From 1532 onward, he taught at the University of Salamanca, after a short period of teaching metaphysics at the *Complutense*. Soto is noted for his advocating the rights of the poor during the grain crises and the famine in 1540 and 1545. He was appointed as the representative of Emperor Charles V at the Council of Trent, even becoming the emperor's confessor for a couple of years. In 1553 his *De iustitia et iure* was published for the first time, soon followed by an extended edition in 1556. It presented itself as a mirror-for-princes, dedicated to prince Carlos (1545–1568), the first and only child born out of Philip II's marriage to Maria Emanuala of Portugal. Hence, Soto called his work the *Carolopaedia*, by analogy with Xenophon's *Cyropaedia*, the Greek mirror-for-princes written in the early fourth century BC. He compared his mission to that of Aristotle teaching Alexander the Great, Seneca the future emperor Nero, and Plutarch the emperor Trajan.[199]

Many view Soto's work as even more juridical than that of his predecessors.[200] Some suggest that Soto played a major role in the development of a systematic law of contract.[201] There is certainly a good amount of truth in those propositions, although they should not be exaggerated. As a matter of fact, Soto remained quite dependent on the structure of Thomas Aquinas' argument. It is important not to overlook that other theologians, mainly coming from the German areas, contributed to

---

[197] Belda Plans, *La escuela de Salamanca*, p. 487–498. For a chronological overview of the treatises *De iustitia et iure* in the early modern period, see A. Folgado, *Los tratados De legibus y De iustitia et iure en los autores españoles del siglo XVI y primera mitad del XVII*, La Ciudad de Dios, 172.3 (1959), p. 284–291.

[198] For a detailed biographical account, see V. Beltrán de Heredia, *Domingo de Soto, O.P., Estudio biográfico documentado*, [Biblioteca de teologos españoles, 20], Salamanca 1960, p. 9–588.

[199] Soto, *De iustitia et iure* (ed. fac. V. Diego Carro – M. González Ordóñez, vol. 1), epistola dedicatoria, [p. 3]: 'Scripsit Xenophon Cyropediam, instituit Aristoteles Alexandrum, Neronem Seneca, et Traianum Plutarchus, atque alios alii. Ego vero, quamvis ea utaris sapientia paedagogia, ut a mea pusillitate nullius egeas obsequii, hanc interim tamen Carolopaediam claritudini tuae non sum offere veritus: ubi, uti dicere coeperam, decorem iustitiae, ac perinde foelicissimi principis vultum contempleris.'

[200] E.g. R. Feenstra, *Der Eigentumsbegriff bei Hugo Grotius im Licht einiger mittelalterlicher und spätscholastischer Quellen*, in: O. Behrends (ed.), Festschrift für Franz Wieacker zum 70. Geburtstag, Göttingen 1978, p. 219–226.

[201] Gordley, *The philosophical origins of modern contract doctrine*, p. 69–111.

the systematic treatment of contract law already back in the fourteenth and fifteenth centuries, that is much earlier than Soto.[202] From the point of view of the growth of autonomous works on contract law, they probably played an even bigger role than the Spanish Dominicans Vitoria and Soto. A good example is Matthäus von Krakau's (1330/1335–1410) *De contractibus*.[203] Another instance is the *Opus septipertitum de contractibus* by the magnificent Tübingen professor Conrad Summenhart von Calw (c. 1455–1502).[204] Summenhart's *De contractibus* was frequently cited by the Spanish scholastics, in particular by Juan de Medina (1490–1546), a star professor of nominalist theology at the University of Alcalá de Henares—from which he derived his nickname 'el Complutense'.[205] Medina authored a very successful treatise on penance, restitution and

---

202 These treatises fall outside the scope of this book. For an overview, see M. Nuding, *Geschäft und Moral, Schriften 'De contractibus' an mitteleuropäischen Universitäten im späten 14. und frühen 15. Jahrhundert*, in: F.P. Knapp – J. Miethke – M. Niesner (eds.), Schriften im Umkreis mitteleuropäischer Universitäten um 1400, Lateinische und volkssprachige Texte aus Prag, Wien und Heidelberg, Unterschiede, Gemeinsamkeiten, Wechselbeziehungen, [Education and Society in the Middle Ages and Renaissance, 20], Leiden – Boston 2004, p. 40–62; M. Bukała, *Oeconomica mediaevalia of Wroclaw Dominicans, Library and studies of friars and ethical-economic ideas, The example of Silesia*, [Studi del Centro Italiano di Studi sull'Alto Medioevo, 16], Spoleto 2010.

203 See M. Nuding (ed.), *Matthäus von Krakau, De contractibus*, [Editiones Heidelbergenses, 28], Heidelberg 2000; M. Nuding, *Matthäus von Krakau, Theologe, Politiker, Kirchenreformer in Krakau, Prag und Heidelberg zur Zeit des Großen Abendländischen Schismas*, [Spätmittelalter und Reformation, Neue Reihe, 38], Tübingen 2007.

204 On Summenhart, see the recent contributions by K.W. Nörr, *'Ein Muster damaliger Gelehrsamkeit', Kanonistische Bemerkungen zu zwei Abhandlungen Konrad Summenharts zum Thema der Simonie*, in: S. Lorenz – D. Bauer – O. Auge (eds.), Tübingen in Lehre und Forschung um 1500, Zur Geschichte der Eberhard Karls Universität Tübingen, Festgabe für Ulrich Köpf, [Tübinger Bausteine zur Landesgeschichte, 9], Ostfildern 2008, p. 207–221, and J. Varkemaa, *Conrad Summenhart's theory of individual rights*, [Studies in Medieval and Reformation Traditions, 159], Leiden-Boston 2012, p. 4–6 [= J. Varkemaa, *Conrad Summenhart's theory of individual rights and its medieval background*, Helsinki 2009, doct. diss., p. 3–4]. Summenhart joined Gabriel Biel (1420/1425–1495) to teach at the faculty of theology of the freshly founded University of Tübingen in 1491. He occupied a chair of the *via antiqua*, which in Tübingen was dedicated to Scotist philosophy. Before that time, he had been teaching at the faculty of arts – which explains his thorough familiarity with natural philosophy and physics. See also the discussion of Conrad Summenhart and of that other important German theologian, Johann Eck (1486–1543), in: I. Birocchi, *Tra elaborazioni nuove e dottrine tradizionali, Il contratto trino e la natura contractus*, Quaderni fiorentini per la storia del pensiero giuridico moderno, 19 (1990), p. 243–322. This article also offers a good illustration of the nominalistic influences in late medieval scholasticism in general, and in Summenhart, in particular.

205 Scant biographical notes on Medina, who has been the subject of very little scholarly interest, are contained in V. Heynck, *Johannes de Medina über vollkommene und unvollkommene Reue*, Franziskanische Studien, 29 (1942), p. 120–150.

contracts (*De poenitentia, restitutione, et contractibus*). He expressly addressed it to both theologians and jurists.[206]

2.2.3   *The Jesuits and the reinforcement of the symbiosis*

As time went by, the connection between law and theology grew ever stronger, at least in the Catholic tradition. The Council of Trent (1545–1563), which was attended by great Salamancan theologians such as Domingo de Soto, affirmed and reinforced the tendency within the late medieval manuals for confessors to use legal argument as an essential tool in solving cases of conscience. What is more, the role of the confessor was increasingly conceived of in juristic terms.[207] The confessors were expressly considered to be judges in an autonomous tribunal, namely the court of conscience (*forum internum*). Accordingly, they were required to have the knowledge of a judge (*scientia judicis*).[208] Their acts were considered to be tantamount to judicial acts.[209] There was a tendency to consider the decisions rendered by the supreme court of conscience in Rome (*praxis Sacrae Poenitentiariae*) as judicial precedent.[210] This intensification of a

---

[206] As is obvious from the complete title of his work; cf. Juan de Medina, *De poenitentia, restitutione et contractibus praeclarum et absolutum opus, in duos divisum tomos, non modo theologiae, sed et iurisprudentiae professoribus ac studiosis omnibus quam utilissimum*, Farnborough 1967 [= Ingolstadii 1581].

[207] Cf. D. Borobio, *The Tridentine model of confession in its historical context*, Concilium, 23 (1967), p. 21–37 and A. Prosperi, *La confessione e il foro della coscienza*, in: P. Prodi – W. Reinhard (eds.), Il concilio di Trento e il moderno, Atti della XXXVIII settimana di studio, 11–15 settembre 1995, [Annali dell'Istituto storico italo-germanico, 45], Bologna 1996, p. 225–254; M. Turrini, *Il giudice della coscienza e la coscienza del giudice*, Prodi, P. – Penuti, C. (eds.), Disciplina dell'anima, disciplina del corpo e disciplina della società tra medioevo ed età moderna, [Annali dell'Istituto storico italo-germanico, 40], Bologna 1994, p. 279–294. For the preceding model of the confessor, see A.T. Thayer, *Judge and doctor, Images of the confessor in printed model sermon collections, 1450–1520*, in K.J. Lualdi – A.T. Thayer (eds.), Penitance in the age of reformations, Aldershot 2000, p. 10–29.

[208] E.g. Vincenzo Figliucci, *Brevis instructio pro confessionibus excipiendis*, Ravenspurgi 1626, cap. 2 (*De scientia necessaria ad confessiones*), par. 1 (*De scientia quatenus est iudex*), p. 28–109.

[209] See the conclusions reached during session 14 on the doctrine of penance which was held at the Council of Trent on 25 November 1551, cited in M. Schmoeckel, *Der Entwurf eines Strafrechts der Gegenreformation*, in: M. Cavina, Tiberio Deciani (1509–1582), Alle origini del pensiero giuridico moderno, Udine 2004, p. 226, n. 138–142.

[210] E.g. Vincenzo Figliucci, *Morales quaestiones de Christianis officiis et casibus conscientiae ad formam cursus qui praelegi solet in Collegio Romano Societatis Iesu*, Lugduni 1622, tom. 1, Ad lectorem, [s.p.]: 'Ubi vero probabilium opinionum varietas est, adieci praxim Sacrae Poenitentiariae, sicuti etiam suis locis formam absolutionum et dispensationum, quae impendendae poenitentibus sunt iuxta praxim eiusdem Sacrae Poenitentiariae.'

form of 'moral jurisprudence', so to speak, is all the more salient as it happened both in concomitance with and in reaction to the separation of the moral and the legal spheres in the Reformed traditions of the sixteenth century. It has been sharply noted that post-Tridentine confession became judicialized at a moment when the analogy between the resolution of cases of conscience and adjudication in the external court lost its power in the Reformed traditions.[211]

After Trent, the Catholic conviction that spirituality and morality cannot be made operational unless they are articulated along legal lines was strengthened. This gave rise to a reinforcement of the synthesis of patristic-scholastic philosophy and Romano-canon law, which had characterised the medieval manuals for confessors. This is particularly evident in the works of the Jesuits.[212] From relatively thin manuals of confessors which mixed theological and juridical argument, the Jesuit confessional literature increasingly became all-comprehensive, systematic and doctrinal in nature. The Jesuits were adamant that sound moral theology could not function without putting the juridical tradition to use. Vincenzo Figliucci (1566–1622), member of the Penitentiary at Saint Peter's Basilica and the chair of moral theology at the Collegio Romano (1600–1604/1607–1613), pointed out that he did not content himself just to give the solution for moral cases.[213] As a methodological principle he would always make sure to elucidate the foundation of his solution. These grounds were to be found either in civil law, canon law, theological principles or natural reason.[214]

The following paragraphs will briefly go into relevant writings of some of the most important Jesuits, whose work will be touched upon in the next pages. Not surprisingly, the canonist Martin de Azpilcueta (1492–

---

[211] Schmoeckel, *Fragen zur Konfession des Rechts im 16. Jahrhundert am Beispiel des Strafrechts*, p. 187.

[212] E.g. N. Brieskorn, *Skizze des römisch-katholischen Rechtsdenkens im 16. Jahrhundert und seine Spuren im Denken der Societas Jesu und des Petrus Canisius*, in: R. Berndt (ed.), Petrus Canisius SJ (1521–1597), Humanist und Europäer, [Erudiri Sapientia, Studien zum Mittelalter und zu seiner Rezeptionsgeschichte, 1], Berlin 2000, p. 39–75.

[213] On Figliucci, see M. Zanfredini, *Vincenzo Figliucci*, in: C. O'Neill – J. Domínguez (eds.), Diccionario Histórico de la Compañía de Jesús, Biográfico-Temático, Roma-Madrid 2001, vol. 2, p. 1416.

[214] Figliucci, *Morales quaestiones*, tom. 1, Ad lectorem, [s.p.]: 'Quoad modum, non solae conclusiones et resolutiones quaestionum afferentur, sed etiam earum fundamenta, vel ex civili aut canonico iure, iuxta materiae exigentiam, vel ex theologicis principiis, vel naturalibus rationibus desumpta.'

1586), better known under the name Dr. Navarrus, left an indelible mark on Jesuit casuistry and moral theology.[215] The Jesuit Francisco de Toledo (1532–1596), a former student of Domingo de Soto at the University of Salamanca, who was to become a professor at the *Collegio Romano*, drew inspiration from Dr. Navarrus' famous manual (*Enchiridion sive manuale confessariorum et poenitentium*) as he prepared his own *Instruction for Priests and Penitants* (*Instructio sacerdotum ac poenitentium*). From its publication in 1596 it was to become an alternative within the Jesuit order to Juan Alfonso de Polanco's (1517–1576) high-minded *Short Directory for Confessors and Confessants* (*Breve directorium ad confessarii ac confitentis munus recte obeundum*), along with Valère Regnault's (1549–1623) *Praxis fori poenitentialis*. Incidentally, Regnault modelled his manual for confessors on the structure of Emperor Justinian's *Institutions*, as will be shown later in this chapter.

Rather than adding names to the impressive list of Jesuit manuals for confessors and casuistic treatises of moral theology, what matters here is to point out the increasing systematization of the Jesuits' involvement with law.[216] Of course, Francisco Suárez (1548–1617) from Granada is a famous case in point.[217] Although he had almost been refused as a novice when he entered the Jesuit order in Salamanca, Suárez was to become its most renowned metaphysician. He served as a professor of theology at the *Collegio Romano* (1580–1585), at Alcalá de Henares (1585–1592), at Salamanca (1592–1597), and at Coimbra (1597–1616). In Rome he taught Leonardus Lessius among many other young and bright Jesuits. The most juridical of his works is the treatise on *The Laws and God the Legislator* (1612). It contains some of the most thorough and systematic discussions

---

[215] On the good relations between Dr. Navarrus and the Society of Jesus, see Lavenia, *Martín de Azpilcueta (1492–1586), Un profilo*, p. 103–112.

[216] For a comprehensive account of early Jesuit manuals for confessors, see the priceless list in R.A. Maryks, *Saint Cicero and the Jesuits, The influence of the liberal arts on the adoption of moral probabilism*, Aldershot – Rome 2008, p. 32–47, which is but a selection of the more extensive overview in R.A. Maryks, *Census of the books written by Jesuits on sacramental confession (1554–1650)*, Annali di Storia moderna e contemporanea, 10 (2004), p. 415–519. The role of the Jesuits as confessors to princes is discussed in H. Höpfl, *Jesuit political thought, The Society of Jesus and the State c. 1540–1630*, [Ideas in context, 70], Cambridge 2004, p. 15–19.

[217] An introduction to the study of the transformation of the Roman legal tradition in Suárez's work can be found in C. Bruschi, *Le 'Corpus iuris civilis' dans le premier livre du 'De legibus' de François Suárez*, in: Les représentations du droit romain en Europe aux temps modernes, Collection d'histoire des idées politiques, Aix-Marseille 2007, p. 9–41.

of the concept of 'law' that have ever been written.[218] Suárez elaborates on pairs of concepts that in a similar, albeit not entirely identical form, continue to play a role in legal thinking today. One is the distinction between the promulgation (*promulgatio*) of a law and its divulgation (*divulgatio*) among the people. In Suárez's view, the promulgation is the moment when a law theoretically starts to have binding force. The divulgation is the moment when the citizens can really be considered to be bound by it because they have effectively been able to take notice of the newly promulgated law.[219] A short overview of the titles of the ten books of *The Laws and God the Legislator* will make the rich variety of legal theoretical subjects treated by Suárez abundantly clear:[220]

> Book 1: On the nature of laws in general, their causes, and their effects
> Book 2: On eternal law, natural law, and the law of nations
> Book 3: On human positive law in itself (as it can be seen in the pure nature of man), also called civil law
> Book 4: On canon positive law
> Book 5: On the variety of human laws, particularly on criminal laws and laws that are being detested
> Book 6: On the interpretation of human laws, their changeability and ending
> Book 7: On the non-written laws, called custom
> Book 8: On favorable human law, viz. on privileges
> Book 9: On the old divine positive law
> Book 10: On the new divine law

Although Suárez is undoubtedly the Jesuit most widely known for the fundamental contribution he made to legal thinking, he is by no means the only Jesuit who excelled in legal studies.[221] Perhaps he even borrowed

---

218 For an introduction, see N. Brieskorn, *Lex Aeterna, Zu Francisco Suárez' Tractatus de legibus ac Deo legislatore'*, in: F. Grunert – K. Seelmann (eds.), Die Ordnung der Praxis, Neue Studien zur Spanischen Spätscholastik, [Frühe Neuzeit, 68], Tübingen 2001, p. 49–74.

219 Suárez, *Tractatus de legibus et legislatore Deo*, lib. 3, cap. 16, num. 3 , p. 238: '*Distinctio inter promulgationem et divulgationem legis.*—Ut autem explicem clarius qualis promulgatio sufficiat ac necessaria sit, distinguo inter promulgationem et divulgationem legis. Promulgationem appello illam publicam propositionem seu denuntiationem legis, quae fit aut voce praeconis, aut affigendo legem scriptam in publico loco, aut alio simili modo. Divulgationem autem appello applicationem illius primae promulgationis ad notitiam vel aures subditorum absentium, qui aut legere aut audire primam illam promulgationem non potuerunt: utrumque ergo explicandum est: nam re vera utrumque potest esse aliquo modo necessarium, et in utroque oportet aliquos dicendi modos extreme contrarios cavere.'

220 Suárez, *Tractatus de legibus et legislatore Deo*, Index librorum et capitum.

221 Recent introductions to Suárez include J.-F. Schaub, *Suárez, Les lois*, in: O. Cayla – J.-L. Halpérin (eds.), Dictionnaire des grandes oeuvres juridiques, Paris 2008, p. 565–570,

many ideas from his colleagues, which is hardly surprising. Back from a mission to China, François Noël (1651–1729) composed a companion to Suárez's theology in which he pointed out that Suárez's mind may have been far too speculative to be able to dwell on rather vulgar and practical day-to-day affairs.[222] Consequently, he decided to add a summary of Tomás Sánchez's *On Marriage* and of Leonardus Lessius' *On Justice and Right* to the companion.[223] These additions were praised as being the most frequently studied works in Jesuit colleges on these practical matters worldwide.

The Jesuit Tomás Sánchez (1550–1610), from Cordoba, wrote an influential treatise *On the holy sacrament of Marriage* (*Disputationes de sancto matrimonii sacramento*) amongst several other important moral-juridical treatises.[224] Its first volume appeared in 1602, the remaining two volumes were published in 1605.[225] Because of its vastness and detail, Sánchez's *On marriage* surpasses the earlier and rather modest attempt by Jesuit Enrique Henríquez (1536–1608) to treat the canon law of marriage. Henríquez studied in Alcalá de Henares and became a professor of theology in

---

and V.M. Salas (ed.), *J.P. Doyle, Collected studies on Francisco Suárez (1548–1617)*, [Ancient and Medieval philosophy, De Wulf-Mansion Centre, Series 1, 37], Leuven 2010, p. 1–20.

[222] Noël is known for his *Sinensis imperii libri classici sex*, Pragae 1711, a Latin translation of classical Chinese philosophy which formed the basis for Christian Wolff's observations on Chinese culture. For biographical details on Noël, see P. Rule, *François Noël, SJ and the Chinese rites controversy*, in: W.F. Vande Walle – N. Golvers (eds.), The history of the relations between the Low Countries and China in the Qing Era (1644–1911), [Leuven Chinese Studies, 14], Leuven 2003, p. 137–165. I am grateful to Dr. Noël Golvers for bringing this contribution to my attention.

[223] F. Noël, *Theologiae Francisci Suarez e Societate Jesu summa seu compendium in duas partes divisum, duobusque tractatibus adauctum; primo de justitia et jure, secundo de matrimonio*, Coloniae, 1732, *Appendix ad Suarez*, p. 1–2. Curiously, the economic historian Raymond De Roover attributes the short discussion on bills of exchange, which is included in this anthology, to Suárez, while it is actually part of the supplement *On Justice and Right*, which is a summary of Lessius' legal and economic thought; cf. R. De Roover, *L'Évolution de la lettre de change (14e–18e siècles)*, [Affaires et gens d'affaires, 4], Paris 1953, p. 202.

[224] On Sánchez, see E. Olivares, *Más datos para una biografía de Tomás Sánchez*, Archivo Teológico Granadino, 60 (1997), p. 25–50; J.M. Viejo-Himénez, s.v. *Sánchez*, in: M.J. Peláez (ed.), Diccionario crítico de juristas españoles, portugueses y latinoamericanos (hispánicos, brasileños, quebequenses y restantes francófonos), 2.1, Zaragoza-Barcelona 2006, p. 480–481; and F. Alfieri, *Nella camera degli sposi, Tomás Sánchez, il matrimonio, la sessualità (secoli XVI–XVII)*, [Annali dell'Istituto storico italo-germanico in Trento, 55], Bologna 2010, p. 21–48.

[225] E. Olivares, *En el cuarto centenario de la publicación del tratado de Tomás Sánchez, De sancto matrimonii sacramento (1602)*, Archivo Teológico Granadino, 65 (2002), p. 5–38. Parts of the ninth book (*De debito conjugali*) were censured; cf. E. Olivares, *Ediciones de las obras de Tomás Sánchez*, Archivo Teológico Granadino, 45 (1982), p. 160–178.

Salamanca, Cordoba, Granada and Sevilla.[226] He dedicated an entire book of his *Summa Theologiae Moralis* to marriage law, which was simply cited as his *On Marriage* by subsequent authors such as Sánchez.[227] Sánchez's *On Marriage* would remain one of the works referenced in post-Tridentine matrimonial law. The eminent French natural lawyer Robert-Joseph Pothier (1699–1772) appears to have been familiar with Sánchez's *On Marriage*, in spite of his Jansenist sympathies. At the beginning of the twentieth century, Pietro Gasparri (1852–1934), the Secretary for the Commission for the Codification of Canon Law, drew heavily on Sánchez for the canons on marriage law as he prepared the new Code of Canon Law of 1917.[228]

Studying Sánchez requires a certain amount of courage and perseverance, not in the least because his argument is often floating and self-contradictory, even if the general structure of his treatise is systematic and clear. Yet no one runs the risk of being disappointed by Sánchez's stimulating reasoning and prudent counsels in very concrete matters. The expressive terms in which he describes the casuistry surrounding certain impediments to a valid marriage have struck eminent historians of canon law as being almost tantamount to mild forms of pornographic literature.[229] The editor of an early seventeenth century compendium of Sánchez's *On marriage* honestly expressed his wonder at how well Sánchez had scrutinized the most intimate secrets of wedlock—an amazing performance, for somebody to teach all the details of the bride-bed without sleeping in it (*Quam bene scrutatur thalami penetralia Sánchez! Mirum! Qui docuit, nesciit ipse torum*)![230] Charles Louis de Secondat, alias Montesquieu (1689–1755), took Sánchez as a prime example of those casuists who revealed all the secrets of the night, and were capable of rounding up all the monsters which the demon of love produced.[231]

---

[226] E. Moore, *Enrique Henríquez*, in: C. O'Neill – J. Domínguez (eds.), Diccionario Histórico de la Compañía de Jesús, Biográfico-Temático, Roma-Madrid 2001, vol. 2, p. 1900–1901.
[227] In the Venice edition of 1600, the canon law of marriage is dealt with autonomously by Enrique Henríquez in book 11 of his *Summa theologiae moralis tomus primus*.
[228] Cf. C. Fantappiè, *Chiesa Romana e modernità giuridica*, Tom. 1: *L'edificazione del sistema canonistico (1563–1903)*, [Per la storia del pensiero giuridico moderno, 76], Milano 2008, p. 447–458.
[229] See J. Brundage, *Law, sex and Christian society in medieval Europe*, Chicago – London 1990, p. 564–567; M. Madero, *Peritaje e impotencia sexual en el De Sancto Matrimonio de Tomás Sánchez*, Eadem utraque Europa (2008), p. 105–136.
[230] Cited in Alfieri, *Nella camera degli sposi, Tomás Sánchez, il matrimonio, la sessualità*, p. 11.
[231] Alfieri, *Nella camera degli sposi, Tomás Sánchez, il matrimonio, la sessualità*, p. 13.

When it comes to the development of contract law, we will see that Sánchez's elaborations on duress have been seminal. This is due to the fact that much of Sánchez's detailed analyses in regard to the validity of marital consent were then applied by other Jesuits, such as Lessius, to other contracts. The table of contents from Sánchez's work *On Marriage* gives a rough idea of his systematic approach to marriage law and its relevance to other domains of contract law:[232]

Book 1: On engagement
Book 2: On the essence of marriage and marital consent
Book 3: On clandestine consent
Book 4: On coerced consent
Book 5: On conditional consent
Book 6: On donations between spouses, premarital gifts, and jointures
Book 7: On marital impediments
Book 8: On dispensations
Book 9: On marital obligations
Book 10: On divorce

For historians of moral theology, as well as historians of law, it is useful also to consider Sánchez's commentary on the precepts contained in the Decalogue (*Opus morale in praecepta Decalogi*) and his collection of counsels (*Opuscula sive consilia moralia*). The latter contains a vast number of cases dealing with what is now known as the law of persons and family law, inheritance, sale contracts, and the morality of judging. However, at this point these works will not be further investigated due to limited space and the need to consider the other Jesuit whose work was thought to be of such importance that it must be added to the anthology of Suárezian thought: Leonardus Lessius.[233] Ever since the Renaissance of Thomism, driven by Pope Leo XIII in the late nineteenth century, this renowned Jesuit from Antwerp has drawn much attention for his masterpiece *On Justice and Right and the other Cardinal Virtues* (*De iustitia et iure ceterisque virtutibus cardinalibus*), by historians of moral, economic, and legal thought.[234]

---

[232] Sánchez, *Disputationes de sancto matrimonii sacramento*, index.

[233] For details on Lessius' life and times as well as references to secondary literature, see Decock, *Breaking the limits*, p. 35–53; T. Van Houdt – W. Decock, *Leonardus Lessius, Traditie en vernieuwing*, Antwerpen 2005, p. 11–54. Especially worthy of mentioning in this context is T. Van Houdt, *De economische ethiek van de Zuid-Nederlandse jezuïet Leonardus Lessius (1554–1623), Een geval van jezuïtisme?*, De zeventiende eeuw, 14 (1998), p. 27–37.

[234] Throughout the ages, interest in Lessius never entirely faded. He was singled out as an original thinker, for instance, by Carl von Kaltenborn-Stachau (1817–1866), the famous jurist from Halle, in *Die Vorläufer des Hugo Grotius auf dem Gebiete des Ius Naturae et Gentium sowie der Politik im Reformationszeitalter*, vol. 1: *Literarhistorische Forschungen*,

Impressed with Roberto Bellarmino's (1542–1621) fiery sermons during his studies at the Arts faculty in Leuven, Lessius entered the Society of Jesus in 1572 and soon became a teacher of Aristotelian philosophy at the Collège d'Anchin in Douai—a job which left him enough spare time to teach himself Roman and canon law.

Upon finishing his theological studies at the *Collegio Romano*, Lessius became a professor of moral theology at the Jesuit College of Leuven in 1585. For the exercises in practical ethics and casuistry, which he considered to be the hallmark of the Jesuit order, he made use of Dr. Navarrus' *Manual for Confessors*. Even if Lessius is best known among theologians for his tenacious defence of molinism in the debate on grace and free will, his moral theological and juridical masterpiece is the treatise *On Justice and Right*, which enjoyed numerous re-editions across Europe until the nineteenth century.[235]

Lessius' *On Justice and Right* played a vital role in the history of the law of obligations. In his *On the Right of War and Peace (De iure belli ac pacis)* the alleged father of modern natural law, Hugo Grotius (1583–1645), frequently gives an elegant summary of the extensive arguments that were first developed by Lessius and other moral theologians. Embarrassingly, this often leads Grotius to copy the same incorrect references as Lessius did.[236] Also in regard to the history of commercial law, Lessius' work is not insignificant. For instance, in order to get the best analysis of financial techniques used by merchants and bankers at the Antwerp Bourse, the jurist Zypaeus (1580–1650), from the Southern Netherlands, recommends that lawyers read Lessius' *De iustitia et iure*.[237] Given his reputation for sharp economic analyses, it should not come as a surprise that Lessius became a source of inspiration for Kaspar Klock from Soest (1583–1655)

Leipzig 1848, p. 151–157. Emblematic for the renewed interest in Lessius at the beginning of the twentieth century are the studies by the Leuven historian, philosopher and economist Victor Brants; e.g. V. Brants, *Les théories politiques dans les écrits de L. Lessius (1554–1623)*, Revue Néo-Scolastique de Philosophie, 19 (1912), p. 42–85; V. Brants, *L'économie politique et sociale dans les écrits de L. Lessius (1554–1623)*, Revue d'Histoire ecclésiastique, 13 (1912), p. 73–89. The last years have seen a revival of the interest in Lessius' economic thought; cf. B. Schefold (ed.), *Leonardus Lessius' De iustitia et iure, Vademecum zu einem Klassiker der Spätscholastischen Wirtschaftsanalyse*, Düsseldorf 1999, which contains contributions by Louis Baeck, Barry Gordon, Toon Van Houdt, and Bertram Schefold.

[235] T. Van Houdt, *Leonardus Lessius over lening, intrest en woeker*, p. xviii–xxv.

[236] Feenstra, *L'influence de la Scolastique espagnole sur Grotius en droit privé, Quelques expériences dans des questions de fond et de forme, concernant notamment les doctrines de l'erreur et de l'enrichissement sans cause*, p. 377–402.

[237] F. Zypaeus, *Notitia iuris belgici*, Antverpiae 1675, lib. 4, p. 61.

in the more technical parts of his *De aerario*, a comparative study of state financing.[238]

In any event, in Lessius' *On Justice and Right*, the casuistry of the legal and moral tradition is ordered within a systematic whole.[239] Since Lessius' elaborate concept of law has already been mentioned, it should suffice here to point out an element in the construction of Lessius' book which is symptomatic of the shift towards systematic legal thinking. Before discussing the particulars of property law, Lessius gives an account of justice in general (*de iustitia in genere*) and right in general (*de iure in genere*). By the same token, his comprehensive analysis of illicit acts or torts is preceded by a chapter on injustice and restitution in general (*de iniuria et restitutione in genere*). Last but not least, his treatment of particular contracts follows his treatment of general contract law (*de contractibus in genere*). A quick look at the contents of the second book of Lessius' treatise shows us how thoroughly and systematically the law of property, torts and contracts were discussed by Lessius, next to selected topics in procedural law, tax law and canon law.[240]

Section I. On justice, right, and the specific types of right
1. On justice in general
2. On right in general
3. On dominion, usufruct, use and possession, which are specific types of rights
4. On who is capable of having dominion and over what
5. On the mode of acquiring dominion over goods that belong to nobody or over goods which are common to all, particularly on servitudes, hunting, fishing, fowling and treasures
6. On the mode of acquiring dominion over someone else's good, particularly on prescription

Section II. On injustice and damage in all kinds of human goods and their necessary restitution
7. On injustice and restitution (which is an act of justice) in general
8. On injustice against spiritual goods
9. On injustice against the body through homicide or mutilation
10. On injustice against the body through adultery and fornication

---

[238] Cf. K. Klock, *Tractatus juridico-politico-polemico-historicus de aerario, sive censu per honesta media absque divexatione populi licite conficiendo, libri duo*, mit einer Einleitung herausgegeben von Bertram Schefold, Hildesheim – Zürich – New York 2009, *passim*; reviewed in: Tijdschrift voor Rechtsgeschiedenis, 78 (2010), p. 463–466.

[239] Decock, *La transformation de la culture juridique occidentale dans le premier 'tribunal mondial'*, p. 125–135.

[240] Lessius, *De iustitia et iure*, lib. 2, p. 13–14.

Lessius' work is a relatively concise treatise on legal and moral problems written in a crystal-clear style. The six-volume treatise, *On Justice and Right*, by his friend and colleague Luís de Molina, which was published over the period 1593–1609, was more detailed and voluminous.[241] It is obvious from a quick glance at the sheer titles of the six volumes constituting Molina's impressive *On Justice and Right* that this is an extremely rich treatise, which deals not only with vast areas of private law, but also with those of public law:[242]

Volume 1: On justice, rights, property law, family law, successions
Volume 2: On contracts
Volume 3/1: On primogeniture and taxes
Volume 3/2: On delicts and quasi-delicts
Volume 4: On commutative justice in corporeal goods and goods belonging to people connected to us
Volume 5: On commutative justice in the goods of honour and reputation, and also in spiritual goods
Volume 6: On judgment and the execution of justice by the public authorities

Molina had been the first Jesuit to adopt the type of moral theological literature known as *On Justice and Right*. As mentioned before, the first work of its kind was written by the Salamancan Dominican Domingo de Soto in 1553. These treatises actually grew out of commentaries on Thomas Aquinas' *Secunda Secundae* as can still be seen in the *Commentarii theologici* of Gregorio de Valentia (1550–1603), a Spanish Jesuit who taught at the University of Ingolstadt. Yet these commentaries soon became increasingly independent from their source. This eventually led to the creation of an autonomous genre of moral theological literature at the university of Salamanca, where an important renewal of theological thought took place in the course of the sixteenth century. Due to this increased autonomy, at the very outset of his treatise, *On Justice and Right*, Molina both acknowledges and minimizes Thomas Aquinas' contribution to his discussion on justice:[243]

---

[241] On Molina, see F.B. Costello, *The Political Philosophy of Luis de Molina,* Rome 1974; F. Gómez Camacho, *Luís de Molina, La teoría del justo precio,* Madrid 1981; and D. Alonso-Lasheras, *Luis de Molina's De iustitia et iure, Justice as virtue in an economic context,* [Studies in the history of Christian traditions, 152], Leiden – Boston 2011.

[242] Luís de Molina, *De iustitia et iure tomi sex,* Moguntiae 1659.

[243] Molina, *De iustitia et iure,* tom. 1, col. 1: 'Licet autem, quae per has 23. quaestiones Divus Thomas de iustitia tradit, sapientissime ut et caetera alia, dicta sint, Ecclesiae tamen utile theologisque pergratum, immo et necessarium fore iudicamus, si rem hanc multo copiosius tractaremus, multa, quae D. Thomas de contractibus et plerisque aliis rebus praetermisit, disputantes. Ita enim fiet, ut theologi in enodandis hominum conscientiis,

Granted, the things that the divine Thomas hands down to us through those twenty-three questions on justice have been expressed as wisely as the rest, but we are of the opinion that it will be useful for the Church and pleasant for the theologians, if not necessary, to treat this subject much more extensively, and to elaborate on many of the things concerning contracts and other things which the divine Thomas omitted. In this manner, the theologians will no longer find themselves stuck when untangling the consciences of men. Consequently, they will feel more confident and will be more adapted for the task of helping their neighbors and keeping them away from sin. They will grow more useful for exercizing the ecclesiastical offices and the government of the Church.

In contrast to Soto's work, the Jesuits' treatises, *On Justice and Right*, were far more systematic, voluminous and technical. The Jesuits were much more acquainted with the *ius commune* and the juridical thinking of their time. Molina's references to contemporary Portuguese and Spanish law or commercial practices are even more copious than Lessius' useful observations on contemporary law and commercial customs in the Low Countries.[244] Molina's citations of scholastic authorities also outnumber those in Lessius. In this respect, Lessius appears to have integrated the humanist critique on scholastic methodology to a greater extent. He also cared more about the reader-friendliness of his book. Yet, the general scope of both treatises is the same, namely to give a systematic outline of law for the purpose of spiritual guidance. As a result, the Romano-canon legal tradition and Aristotelian-Thomistic moral philosophy were united in Lessius' and Molina's, *On justice and right*.

The third Jesuit who wrote a successful treatise, *On Justice and Right*, was Juan de Lugo (1583–1660), a canon lawyer by training, who went on to become a professor of theology at the Collegio Romano before being named a Cardinal by Pope Urban VIII in 1643, the year after the publication of his *Disputations on Justice and Right* (*Disputationes de iustitia et iure*).[245] He shared a thorough understanding with Molina and Lessius

---

passim non haereant, audacioresque proinde, aptioresque multo sint ad proximos suos iuvandos, et a peccatis eruendos, atque ut praelaturis, regiminique toti Ecclesiae longe evadant utiliores.'

244 I am grateful to Prof. Dr. Wolfgang Forster (Universität Gießen) for sending me along his unpublished paper *Das kastilische Privatrecht in der Spanischen Spätscholastik, Luis de Molina S.J. (1535–1600)*, delivered at the symposium *Spanische Spätscholastik- noch Mittelalter oder schon Moderne?* (Hamburg 14–17.09.2008).

245 For further details, see E. Olivares, *Juan de Lugo (1583–1660), Datos biográficos, sus escritos, estudios sobre su doctrina y bibliografía*, Archivo Teológico Granadino, 47 (1984), p. 5–129.

of different kinds of law and their application to qualms of conscience, but he also had a tremendous insight into the actual functioning of life, particularly in regard to business and economic affairs.[246] In regard both to form and content, Lugo seems to be heavily indebted to Lessius, although he is certainly not a servile imitator. Lugo further developed the Jesuits' systematic approach to law and morality, but sometimes could not avoid the pitfalls of casuistry. It is worthwhile noting to the modern reader that Lugo also treated a number of subjects that are considered to be 'juridical', such as marriage law, in his collection of practical moral responses (*Responsa moralia*).[247]

By the mid-seventeenth century we witness the birth of vast, systematic and influential books on various branches of law. An exciting example of this turn towards a Jesuit legal science, notably in regard to contract law, is the Spanish Jesuit Pedro de Oñate's (1568–1646) four-volume treatise, *On Contracts*, published posthumously in 1646 (*De contractibus*).[248] Pedro de Oñate, who had been a student of Suárez at Alcalá de Henares, became provincial of the Jesuit order in Paraguay in 1615. By the end of his term, he had co-founded the University of Córdoba (Argentina) and eleven colleges. In 1624 he was designated professor of moral theology at the Colegio San Pablo in Lima (Peru). His treatise, *On Contracts*, is one of the most extensive treatises on both general and particular contract law that has ever been written. In it, Oñate discusses all contracts from the point of view of Aristotelian-Thomistic philosophy. He borrows extensively from the Romano-canon legal tradition, as well as from Molina, Sánchez and Lessius, but has the merit of giving an ultimate synthesis of all the problems pertaining to contract law. It is a three-volume testament to a five hundred year-old tradition in scholastic contract doctrine, which is unparalleled in its comprehensiveness.

The first volume of Pedro de Oñate's *On Contracts* is a systematic account of general contract doctrine (*de contractibus in genere*). The

---

[246] F. Monsalve Serrano – O. De Juán Asenjo, *Juan de Lugo y la libertad en economía, El análisis económico escolástico en transición*, Procesos de mercado, Revista europea de economía política, 2 (2006), p. 217–243.

[247] E.g. Juan de Lugo, *Responsa moralia*, Lugduni 1651, lib. 1, dub. 35–46, p. 55–80.

[248] See E. Holthöfer, *Die Literatur zum gemeinen und partikularen Recht in Italien, Frankreich, Spanien und Portugal*, in: H. Coing (ed.), Handbuch der Quellen und Literatur der neueren europäischen Privatrechtsgeschichte, 2.1, München 1977, p. 368 and p. 491; Birocchi, *Causa e categoria generale del contratto*, p. 271–289; E. Fernández, s.v. *Oñate*, in: C. O'Neill – J. Domínguez (eds.), Diccionario histórico de la Compañía de Jesús biográfico-temático, vol. 3, Roma-Madrid 2001, p. 2870–2871.

second volume deals with gratuitous contracts (*de contractibus lucrativis*), e.g. donations, agency, dowry, etc., and the third offers a meticulous analysis of all onerous contracts (*de contractibus onerosis*), e.g. sale-purchase, rents, bills of exchange, etc. At the outset of his treatise, Oñate warns his reader that contract law is both an extremely vast (*vastissimum*) and difficult (*difficillimum*) field of study. Distinguishing between more than thirty particular contracts, he admits that contract law is an immense ocean or, rather, an infinite chaos. Contract law is founded upon unstable ground, which prevented any scholar before him to treat it as thoroughly. Moreover, contract law is very difficult. According to Oñate, this has to do with the avarice of man, which mainly expresses itself through the use of contracts, since contracts are the juridical means by which money and property are exchanged. On top of this, various legislators have tried to rule on the same matter in different ways and have issued a plethora of different laws.

Pedro de Oñate points out that understanding contract law is extremely useful (*utilissimum*). Contract law is essential not only to businessmen, lawyers, judges and public officials, but to theologians as well. A sound knowledge of contract law is absolutely necessary for theologians, certainly for those who are involved in the sacrament of confession (*est materia haec theologis, iis maxime qui sacris aures confessionibus praebent, pernecessaria*).[249] The reason is simple: on the earthly pilgrimage towards God, it is impossible not to enter into contracts. In the course of the twentieth century, certainly after the Second Vatican Council, mainstream theology seems to have lost touch with this tradition of moral jurisprudence.[250] Influential theologians, such as the Henri de Lubac (1896–1991), have called for a return to the allegedly more authentic Christian spirit found in the writings of the Fathers of the Church. The Church's age-long involvement with Roman law and Aristotelian moral philosophy—the pillars of the scholastic—bore the brunt of Lubac's criticism. It is actually easy to forget that Lubac belonged to the same Jesuit order that had previously went to such great lengths to promote the synthesis of law and theology.

---

[249] Oñate, *De contractibus*, tom. 1, tract. 1, pr., num. 3, p. 1.

[250] See J.F. Keenan, *A history of Catholic moral theology in the twentieth century, From confessing sins to liberating consciences*, London – New York 2010, and the remarks in chapter 8.

2.3 MORAL JURISPRUDENCE AND THE COURT OF CONSCIENCE

2.3.1 *A court for the soul and the truth*

A lawyer by training, Alfonso de' Liguori (1696–1787), founder of the Redemptorist order, patron saint of moral theologians, and doctor of the Church, agreed to define moral theology properly as 'a kind of moral jurisprudence and civil science' (*quasi moralis iurisprudentia ac scientia civilis*), not so much consisting in the memorization of written laws, at least not exclusively, but a jurisprudential science capable of finding out what is right if the existing laws remain silent'.[251] Clearly, in the eighteenth century, the Catholic fusion of law and theology was still very much alive. The prerequisite for being called a good theologian was showing a certain prowess to study law. As Lessius noted, the knowledge (*scientia*) a good confessor must possess pertains not only to theology but also to canon law.[252] As a matter of fact, Liguori's treatise on moral theology (*Theologia moralis*) abounded with references to the Jesuit confessional literature of the preceding centuries, especially to Hermann Busembaum's (1600–1668) *Medulla theologiae moralis*.[253] Although definitely not as elaborated as the expositions on contract law contained in the treatises, *De iustitia et iure*, by Jesuits such as Molina and Lessius, Liguori's masterpiece still contained chapters on contract law in general and on the particular contracts. Even

---

[251] This definition figures in the apologetic part of an anonymous dissertation preceding Liguori's books on moral theology. Since Liguori supervised the publication of the 1773 edition, which is used here, he at least approved of this dissertation, if he was not its author. The passage is directly attributed to Liguori by Alfieri, *Nella camera degli sposi, Tomás Sánchez, il matrimonio, la sessualità*, p. 75. For the Latin text, see Liguori, *Theologia moralis*, tom. 1, prol. (*Dissertatio prolegomena de casuisticae theologiae originibus, locis atque praestantia*), part. 3 (*pars apologetica*), cap. 1, p. lxv: 'Est enim theologia illa moralis quasi jurisprudentia, ac scientia civilis, quae si bene definiatur, non in eo sita est, quod quispiam memoria leges omnes scriptas teneat, quamvis et id non sit extra ipsam, sed quod ubi leges nihil dicunt, norit id, quod rectum est invenire.'

[252] Lessius, *In III Partem D. Thomae de Sacramentis et Censuris*, quaest. 8, art. 5, dubium 8 (*quanta requiratur scientia in confessario?*), num. 50, in: *De beatitudine, de actibus humanis, de incarnatione Verbi, de sacramentis et censuris praelectiones theologicae posthumae. Acceserunt variorum casuum conscientiae resolutiones*, ed. I. Wijns, Lovanii 1645, p. 240.

[253] Busembaum, a famous Jesuit moral theologian, taught humanities, philosophy and theology at Münster and Köln. He became rector of the Jesuit colleges of Hildesheim and Münster, and was a confessor to the prince-bishop of Münster; cf. P. Schmitz, *Hermann Busembaum*, in: C. O'Neill – J. Domínguez (eds.), Diccionario Histórico de la Compañía de Jesús, Biográfico-Temático, Roma-Madrid 2001, vol. 1, p. 578.

in the details, for instance, in the solution of practical cases of conscience, Liguori showed himself a fine expert of Jesuit casuistry.[254]

Those jurisprudential qualities required of confessors and moral theologians served the settlement of cases of conscience in the so-called court of conscience (*forum conscientiae*) or internal forum (*forum internum*).[255] The reality of this tribunal of conscience may well come across as counterfeit to a modern ear. Yet it was part and parcel of legal cultures in the early modern period, certainly on the Iberian and Italian peninsulas.[256] This is an essential insight not only if one wants to come to grips with the moral theological literature of the time, but also with the first systematic treatises on commercial law, such as the *Tractatus de commerciis et cambio* by Sigismondo Scaccia (c. 1564–1634).[257] Its existence was still obvious to eighteenth century luminaries such as the Italian historian Ludovico Antonio Muratori (1672–1750) and the French jurist Robert-Joseph Pothier. Muratori spoke of the jurisdiction over the soul of man which the moral theologians had (*i teologi morali che hanno giurisdizione sull'anima dell'uomo*).[258] Pothier, for his part, proposed to investigate the law of obligations from the perspective of both the *forum externum* and the *forum*

---

254 For an illustration in regard to speculation in the market and insider trading, see Decock, *Lessius and the breakdown of the scholastic paradigm*, p. 67.

255 G. Minnucci, *Foro della coscienza e foro esterno nel pensiero giuridico della prima età moderna*, in: G. Dilcher – D. Quaglioni (eds.), Gli inizi del diritto pubblico, 3: Verso la costruzione del diritto pubblico tra medioevo e modernità, [Annali dell'Istituto Storico Italo-Germanico in Trento, Contributi, 25], Bologna-Berlin 2011, p. 55–81.

256 This is further attested by the abundant presence of cases of conscience literature in legal libraries in the early modern period; see D.J. Osler, *Jurisprudence of the Baroque, A Census of Seventeenth Century Italian Legal Imprints*, [Studien zur Europäischen Rechtsgeschichte, 235–237, Bibliographica Juridica, 4–6], Frankfurt am Main 2009, A–G (vol. 235), H–S (vol. 236), T-Z (vol. 237).

257 See the caveat in W. Endemann, *Studien in der romanisch-kanonistischen Wirthschafts- und Rechtslehre bis gegen Ende des siebenzehnten Jahrhunderts*, Berlin 1874, tom. 1, p. 59: 'Dabei muss bemerkt werden, dass er [sc. Scaccia] und viele andere Juristen stets zweierlei Gerichte (*fora*) im Auge haben. Nicht blos das weltliche Gericht, sondern auch der Beichtstuhl wird als Gericht, Beichte und Absolution als eine Art von gerichtlicher Prozedur betrachtet. Es gibt also ein Gewissens- oder inneres Forum (*forum conscientiae, interius, animae, poli*), in dem Gott richtet durch den Mund des Priesters, und ein irdisches Gericht (*forum terrestre, fori, exterius*), in dem Menschen urtheilen. In jenem wird nach dem göttlichem und natürlichem Recht, nach der Wahrheit, namentlich nach der wahren Absicht geurtheilt, um Gott genug zu thun; in diesem nach dem weltlichen Gesetz, nach Präsumtionen, die der Wahrheit, welche hier oft verborgen bleibt, vorgehen, um dem Gemeinwesen und den Betheiligten genug zu thun.'

258 Cited in Prodi, *Una storia della giustizia*, p. 430, n. 89.

internum in his famous *Treatise on obligations according to the rules of the court of conscience as well as the external court.*[259]

The court of conscience was not just a metaphor. The procedural character of the notion of conscience in the medieval tradition was real. The introduction to the manual for confessors by the Jesuit Valère Regnault, who expressly modelled his book after the structure of Justinian's *Institutions*, is quite telling:[260]

> This manual subdivides into three parts according to the three basic elements of adjudication in the external courts: persons (*personae*), actions (*actiones*), and things (*res*). The first part concerns the persons in the court of conscience, namely those who participate in the sacrament of penance: the confessor, who is the legitimate judge in this court, and the penitent sinner, who is at the same time the guilty party and the witness, his own defendant and plaintiff, as if he were pleading the cause of God, who is offended by his acts against himself. The second part concerns the actions that are used in the process of confession. For the penitent, those actions involve inner contrition, oral confession, and satisfaction through works; for the confessor, performing the sacrament of absolution. The former constitute the material of the sacrament of penitence, the latter its form. Lastly, the third part concerns the things which the practice of confession is about, namely the sins committed by the penitent after his baptism.

One of the clearest descriptions of the court of conscience was offered by the Carthusian Juan de Valero (1550–1625), author of a splendid work on *The Differences between both courts, that is between the judicial court and*

---

[259] R.-J. Pothier, *Traité des obligations, selon les regles, tant du for de la conscience, que du for extérieur*, nouvelle édition, Paris – Orléans 1777. The fact that the original, also moral context of Pothier's law of obligations has been obscured may be part of what has been called the 'Enlightenment myth' surrounding the study of the French natural lawyers Domat and Pothier—a myth which emphasizes the legacy of both luminaries for the *Code civil*, without sufficiently taking into account the profound roots their thought had in the pluralist legal culture of the *ancien régime*; cf. Birocchi, *Alla ricerca dell'ordine*, p. 153–157.

[260] Valère Regnault, *Praxis fori poenitentialis ad directionem confessarii in usu sacri sui muneris. Opus tam poenitentibus quam confessariis utile*, Lugduni 1616, pr.: '[…] Institutiones […] digessi tripartitas, pro triplice genere attinentium ad iudiciale forum: personarum, inquam, actionum, et rerum, ita ut prima pars complectatur spectantia ad personas fori poenitentialis, tanquam eas ex quibus dependet sacramenti poenitentiae usus. Sunt autem confessarius, tanquam iudex legitimus in illo foro; et peccator poenitens, tanquam reus simul et testis, adeoque advocatus accusator sui, tanquam is qui a se offensi Dei causam agat contra semetipsum. Secunda vero pars contineat spectantia ad actiones, in quibus idem usus consistit; quae sunt, quoad poenitentem quidem, contritio cordis, confessio oris et satisfactio operis. Quoad confessarium vero, absolutio sacramentalis. Illaeque sacramenti poenitentiae materiam constituunt et haec formam. Tertia demum pars […] sit de rebus, circa quas idem usus versatur. Eae autem sunt peccata poenitentis post Baptismum commissa […].'

the court of conscience.[261] He opposed the exterior court (*forus exterior*) as a human court presided by judges to the interior court (*forus interior*) as the court of God pertaining to confessors and to every Christian.[262] The rigor of justice and the laws attended in the exterior court yielded to equity in the court of conscience—conscience being the dictate of right reason in a good and virtuous man. Valero distinguished between the interior tribunal as it related to the sacrament of penance (*alter ad sacramentum poenitentiae*), and the interior tribunal as an instrument to appease the soul's scruples about obligations regardless of the sacrament of confession (*alter ad sedandam animam ab scrupulis et eius obligationibus extra sacramentum*).[263] By the same token, Valero differentiated in regard to the external court between the judicial forum (*alter judicialis*) and the customary practice of men (*alter usus et practica inter homines*).[264]

The interior court had two objectives, according to Valero, the first being the preservation of the soul (*conservatio animae*), and the second being the restitution of what belonged to the estate of another (*restitutio alieni patrimonii*). Indeed, restitution of goods taken from another person without justification was considered an essential prerequisite for the salvation of the soul. Every form of unjust enrichment was considered to be an offence against the seventh commandment not to steal.[265] Hence, commutative justice was as important a rule in contracts as mutual consent. In light of the overriding importance of saving souls, it should not come as a surprise that canon law, which the Church laid down precisely for the sake of spiritual salvation, was thought to be immediately binding

---

[261] A graduate from the universities of Valencia and Salamanca, Juan de Valero was the head of the Carthusian monastery of Palma de Mallorca from 1613 till 1621. He was closely connected to the Jesuits as can be seen from a letter written by Michael Julian (1557–1621), the rector of the Jesuit college at Mallorca, to Valero. This letter was included as a dedication to the *Differentiae*. Valero heavily draws on Leonardus Lessius throughout his treatise. More biographical details can be found in A. Gruys, *Cartusiana, vol. 1: Biblioghraphie générale et auteurs cartusiens*, Paris 1976, p. 169.

For other works dealing with the differences between the court of conscience and the external courts, see J.F. von Schulte, *Die Geschichte der Quellen und Literatur des canonischen Rechts von Gratian bis auf die Gegenwart*, Graz 1956 [= Stuttgart 1877], vol. 2 (*Gregor IX. Bis auf das Concil von Trient*), p. 508.

[262] Juan de Valero, *Differentiae inter utrumque forum, iudiciale videlicet et conscientiae*, Cartusiae Maioricarum 1616, praeludia, num. 1.

[263] Valero, *Differentiae*, praeludia, num. 2. On the post-Tridentine origins of the distinction between a sacramental and an extra-sacramental side to the court of conscience, see A. Mostaza, *Forum internum—forum externum, En torno a la naturaleza jurídica del fuero interno*, Revista Española de derecho canonico, 23 (1967), p. 274–284.

[264] Valero, *Differentiae*, praeludia, num. 28.

[265] See chapter 8.

in the court of conscience. Yet there was an important qualification to this principle. If a rule of canon law was based on a presumption (*praesumptio*) which was manifestly in contradiction with the truth, then the truth had to prevail in the internal court.[266] Presumptions applied in the external courts did not bind the confessor.[267] In other words, the court of conscience was considered to be simultaneously the court of the soul (*forus animae*), the court of equity (*forus aequitatis*) and the court of truth (*forus veritatis*).

2.3.2   A minimalistic concept of morality

Even though the ultimate standard of judgment in the *forum internum* was truth and not presumption, its objective was expressly not to enforce the highest ideals of Christian virtue. Up until the beginning of the twentieth century, moral theologians would assert, just as Valero did, that one of its two main objectives was to offer relief to overburdened consciences.[268] Since the very idea of overburdened consciences may sound improbable to a modern ear, it is worthwhile remembering that the famous theologian Jean Gerson (1363–1429), at one point the Chancellor of the University of Paris, already raised alarm about the pestiferous effects of scrupulosity in his *Doctrine against too strict and scrupulous conscience*. Gerson expressed the need to dam up the spread of scruples of conscience, since those unduly burdensome feelings of guilt risked to turn into a counterproductive sense of moral defeatism.[269] Throughout the centuries, theologians would not cease to repeat this fundamental truth. They were well aware of the danger of perplexity that abstract ideals and vague aspirational norms carry with them. If at any time and in all spheres life man is called upon to live in accordance with the highest norms, then life becomes

---

[266] Valero, *Differentiae*, praeludia, num. 7; and s.v. *lex*, diff. 11, num. 1, p. 181.
[267] Compare Lessius, *De iustitia et iure*, lib. 2, cap. 7, dub. 6, num. 30, p. 79: '(…) nos loquimur in foro interiori, ubi praesumptio non habet locum (…).'
On the development of the doctrine of presumptions in the *ius commune*, see M. Schmoeckel, *Humanität und Staatsraison, Die Abschaffung der Folter in Europa und die Entwicklung des gemeinen Strafprozeß- und Beweisrechts seit dem hohen Mittelalter*, Köln e.a. 2000, p. 228–232.
[268] Keenan, *A history of Catholic moral theology in the twentieth century*, p. 9–34.
[269] For Gerson's notion of conscience, see R. Schüßler, *Jean Gerson, moral certainty and the renaissance of ancient skepticism*, in: H.E. Braun – E. Vallance (eds.), The Renaissance conscience, [Renaissance Studies Special Issues, 3], Oxford 2011, p. 11–28.

unbearable. All-pervasive obligations deprive man of his freedom.[270] In the introduction to his treatise on the sacrament of penance, Juan de Lugo asked confessors to proceed tactfully in applying the abstract rules of consciences in confessional practice. He admonished them not to turn this soft and sweet remedy against evil into an impossible, dysfunctional, scary machine that would unsettle man, certainly the scrupulous one, in his fragility.[271] Transposed in the economic language of today—which, in many respects, has replaced the religious grammar and vocabulary of times past—unduly burdensome tax rates risk to unsettle the State rather than fill its treasury.

The minimalistic approach to morality is closely related to the notoriously complex debates on decision-making in a context of uncertainty, which flourished in early modern scholasticism. The historiography on this subject, which touches on thorny issues such as tutiorism and probabilism, has often been distorted by internecine strife between rival theological schools. Many of these distortions have now been rectified through Rudolf Schüßler's *magnum opus* on the subject.[272] It would be inappropriate to open the Pandora box on probabilism in this context. A couple of notes may contribute, though, to understanding the juridical bent of

---

[270] It would seem that modern legislators, who have a tendency to formulate norms in rather vague and aspirational terms (e.g. 'the emission of toxic substances should be as low as reasonably achievable'), have a lot to learn from the early modern theologians in this regard; cf. P.C. Westerman, *Some objections to an aspirational system of law*, in: N.E.H.M. Zeegers et al. (eds.), Social and symbolic effects of legislation on the rule of law, Lewiston 2004, p. 299–315, and P.C. Westerman, *The emergence of new types of norms*, in: L.J. Wintgens (ed.), Legislation in context, Essays in legisprudence, Aldershot 2007, p. 117–133.

[271] Juan de Lugo, *Disputationes scholasticae et morales de virtute et sacramento poenitentiae*, Lugduni 1638, *Ad lectorem*, [s.p.]: 'Ut suo loco iterum monebimus, ad praxim huius sacramenti considerandum non solum est, quid utcumque verum quasi in abstracto sit, sed quid etiam moraliter et humano modo fieri possit ac deceat, ita ut remedium hoc suavitate ac dulcedine plenum non fiat sua difficultate impossibile vel horrorem nimium ingerat humanae fragilitati. Quod multo magis circa conscientias scrupulosas prae oculis habendum est (…).'

[272] On the vicissitudes of probabilism as a moral problem solving method from Antiquity till modern times, see G. Otte, *Der Probabilismus: eine Theorie auf der Grenze zwischen Theologie und Jurisprudenz*, in: P. Grossi, (ed.), La seconda scolastica nella formazione del diritto privato moderno, [Per la storia del pensiero giuridico moderno, 1] Milano 1973, p. 283–302; L. Vereecke, *Le probabilisme*, Le Supplément. Revue d'Ethique et Théologie Morale, 177 (1991), p. 23–31, and Rudolf Schüßler's magnum opus *Moral im Zweifel*, [Perspektiven der analytischen Philosophie, Neue Folge], Paderborn, Band I: *Die scholastische Theorie des Entscheidens unter moralischer Unsicherheit*, 2003, and Band II: *Die Herausforderung des Probabilismus*, 2006. See also R. Schüßler, *Moral self-ownership and ius possessionis in late scholastics*, in: V. Mäkinen – P. Korkman (eds.), Transformations in medieval and early modern rights discourse, [The new synthese historical library, Texts and studies in the history of philosophy, 59], Dordrecht 2006, p. 149–172.

early modern theology and the minimalistic character of Catholic moral theology until before the Second Vatican Council. Probabilism holds that in a situation of uncertainty one may follow an expert opinion, at least if that opinion is simply 'probable' (*opinio probabilis*), despite the fact that a 'more probable' opinion (*opinio probabilior*) exists. Generally speaking, a probable opinion is a standpoint endorsed by an authoritative expert or by sound argument.

Although the Jesuits would become the fiercest advocates of moral probabilism, it was defended for the first time in 1577 by the Dominican Bartolomé de Medina (1527–1581), a student of Francisco de Vitoria.[273] Medina held that even if the arguments for the other position were very good, an opinion could be followed as long as it was probable, even if the opposite opinion was more probable.[274] Medina defended his position on four grounds. Firstly, he reasoned that if an opinion was deemed probable from a theoretical point of view, i.e. it could be followed without running the risk of being intellectually mistaken, then it was also to be deemed probable from a practical point of view, i.e. it could be followed without the risk of sin.[275] Secondly, an opinion is called probable precisely because it can be followed without reprehension or vituperation. Consequently, it is a contradiction in terms to maintain that an opinion is probable, but that it is nevertheless illicit to follow it.[276] Thirdly, a probable opinion is in conformity with right reason and the assessment of prudent and wise men. Hence, to follow it does not amount to sin.[277] Lastly, the advocates

---

[273] I. Kantola, *Probability and moral uncertainty in late medieval and early modern times*, [Schriften der Luther-Agricola-Gesellschaft, 32], Helsinki 1994, p. 124–130. Whether Medina really espoused probabilism is cast in doubt, though, by F. O'Reilly, *Duda y opinion, La conciencia moral en Soto y Medina*, [Cuadernos de pensamiento español, 32], Pamplona 2006, p. 81–90.

[274] Bartolomé de Medina, *In primam secundae divi Thomae*, Bergomi 1586, ad quaest. 19, art. 7, p. 179: 'Certe argumenta videntur optima, sed mihi videtur, quod si est opinio probabilis, licitum est eam sequi, licet opposita probabilior sit.'

[275] Medina, *In primam secundae divi Thomae*, ad quaest. 19, art. 7, p. 179: 'Nam opinio probabilis in speculativis ea est, quam possumus sequi sine periculo erroris et deceptionis. Ergo opinio probabilis in practicis ea est, quam possumus sequi sine periculo peccandi.'

[276] Medina, *In primam secundae divi Thomae*, ad quaest. 19, art. 7, p. 179: 'Secundo, opinio probabilis ex eo dicitur probabilis, quod possumus eam sequi sine reprehensione et vituperatione. Ergo implicat contradictionem, quod sit probabilis et quod non possumus eam licite sequi.'

[277] Medina, *In primam secundae divi Thomae*, ad quaest. 19, art. 7, p. 179: 'Tertio, opinio probabilis est confirmis rectae rationi et existimationi virorum prudentum et sapentium. Ergo eam sequi non est peccatum.'

of the contrary opinion admit that it is licit to teach and propose a probable opinion in academia. It is also licit, then, to advise it.[278]

Probabilism is related to a theory of moral action centered around the quite liberal assumption that the human will is the owner of its actions (*voluntas domina suorum actuum*).[279] Put differently, human will is basically free to choose any course of action it wants, as long as that course of action has not been forbidden by a superior law. For example, Lessius argued that making extra profits on the basis of insider trading was not forbidden for individual businessmen, since there was no law forbidding them to avail themselves of the knowledge of a future statute (*nulla lex vetat ne utar notitia illius decreti in meum commodum*).[280] Freedom is the principle, restriction the exception. As a matter of fact, the human will is its own legislator in the context of a hierarchy of laws. Superior laws can break the obligation which the individual will imposes upon itself. Therefore, the political authorities can impose formality requirements by virtue of which the citizens' freedom to contract is limited.[281] Superior laws can also create an obligation for the individual will. Yet, if superior laws want to impose an obligation on an individual, then they must be clearly promulgated and convincing.

One of the basic requirements which a law must meet to be able to bind the individual is sufficient promulgation. According to a fundamental rule of scholastic legal philosophy, a doubtful law is not binding (*lex dubia non obligat*).[282] A doubtful law is not binding for the following reasons. First, the individual possesses its freedom before a law comes

---

[278] Medina, *In primam secundae divi Thomae*, ad quaest. 19, art. 7, p. 179: 'Quarto, licitum est opinionem probabilem in scholis docere et proponere, ut etiam adversarii nobis concedunt. Ergo licitum est eam consulere.'

[279] Lessius, *De gratia efficaci, decretis divinis, libertate arbitrii et praescientia Dei conditionata disputatio apologetica*, Antverpiae 1610, cap. 5, num. 11, p. 53. There is some controversy on whether possession of the self as defended in the scholastic tradition prefigures modern conceptions of liberalism or not. See the critical remarks by Janet Coleman on the contributions by Rudolf Schüßler and Brian Tierney in the same volume; cf. J. Coleman, *Are there any individual rights or only duties?, On the limits of obedience in the avoidance of sin according to late medieval and early modern scholars*, in: V. Mäkinen – P. Korkman (eds.), Transformations in medieval and early modern rights discourse, [The new synthese historical library, Texts and studies in the history of philosophy, 59], Dordrecht 2006, p. 27–32.

[280] Lessius, *De iustitia et iure*, lib. 2, cap. 21, dub. 5, num. 47, p. 279.

[281] See Chapter 5 (Formal limitations on 'freedom of contract').

[282] See L. Vereecke, *Le Concile de Trente et l'enseignement de la théologie morale*, in: id., De Guillaume D'Ockham à Saint Alphonse de Liguori, Études d'histoire de la théologie morale moderne, 1300–1787, [Bibliotheca Historica Congregationis Redemptoris, 12], Romae 1986, p. 495–508; L. Vereecke, *Théologie morale et magistère, avant et après le*

to claim that it has the right to restrict that fundamental freedom. Second, the position of the possessor is the stronger.[283] In other words, the moral theologians applied a fundamental rule of property law to the field of human action. They used it as an argument both in disputes regarding property and in questions concerning the obligation or not which rested on an individual's conscience. As an example of the former, Lessius argued in the footsteps of Covarruvias that he who starts to doubt the good faith with which he acquired a good continues to be the rightful possessor of that good. Hence, he continues to benefit from acquisitive prescription. To buttress his view, Lessius expressly cited the maxim that, in equal doubt, the position of he who possesses is stronger than that of he who does not possess (*in pari dubio melior est conditio possidentis quam non possidentis*).[284]

The Spanish Jesuit Antonio Perez (1599–1649) claimed with reason that this maxim was the cornerstone of moral theology.[285] Juan de Salas (1553–1612) likened man's possession of liberty and his right to do what is most useful to him to the position of the possessor of an external good.[286] Put differently, the building blocks of a strikingly liberal strand of moral theology were provided by the *ius commune*. The theologians reasoned from Romano-canon property law to ethics. The rule that the position of

---

Concile de Trente, Le Supplément, Revue d'Ethique et Théologie Morale, 177 (1991), p. 7–22; J. Mahoney, *The making of moral theology*, Oxford 1987, p. 227.

[283] Compare S. Pinckaers, *Les sources de la morale chrétienne, Sa méthode, son contenu, son histoire*, [Études d'éthique chrétienne, 14], Fribourg 1985, p. 279: 'La liberté 'possède' la place, tant qu'une loi certaine ne vient pas l'en déloger.' Similarly, L. Vereecke, *Le probabilisme*, Le Supplément, Revue d'Ethique et Théologie Morale, 177 (1991), p. 29.

[284] Lessius, *De iustitia et iure*, lib. 2, cap. 6, dub. 3, num. 11, p. 56.

[285] Antonio Perez, *De iustitia et iure et de poenitentia opus posthumum*, Romae 1668, tract. 2, disp. 2, cap. 4, num. 78, p. 174. Perez, who studied arts and theology in Medina del Campo and Salamanca, succeeded Juan De Lugo in 1642 as a theology professor at the Collegio Romano. He made an important contribution to the conceptualization of intellectual property and copyright; cf. J. Escalera, s.v. *Perez*, in C. O'Neill – J. Domínguez (eds.), Diccionario histórico de la Compañía de Jesús biográfico-temático, vol. 3, Roma-Madrid 2001, p. 3089–3090.

[286] Juan de Salas, *Disputationes in primam secundae*, Barcinonae 1607, tom. 1, tract. 8, disp. 1, sect. 6, num. 67, p. 1205: 'ut in dubiis melior est conditio possidentis rem aliquam externam aut ius percipiendi aliquem fructum (...), ita etiam melior est conditio possidentis libertatem suam et ius efficiendi quod sibi utile fuerit'. A graduate from Salamanca and a theology professor at the Collegio Romano, he and his colleague Suárez were accused by Miguel Marcos of deviating too much from Thomas Aquinas's standard teaching; cf. V. Ordóñez, s.v. *Salas*, in C. O'Neill – J. Domínguez (eds.), Diccionario histórico de la Compañía de Jesús biográfico-temático, vol. 4, Roma-Madrid 2001, p. 3467.

the possessor is the stronger can be traced back through to the Digest.[287]
It also figured in the titles on the general principles of law of both Justinian and Pope Boniface VIII (*in pari delicto vel causa potior est conditio
possidentis*).[288] This is another example of the profound interconnectedness of law and theology in premodern times. Although the exact scope of
application of the rule remained a matter of debate, the moral theologians
would continue to endorse this view of freedom of action as an undis-
puted right possessed by the will and protected by the '*melior est conditio possidentis*-rule'. The Jesuit Ignaz Schwarz (1690–1763), for instance,
maintained that this maxim held true as a matter of justice not only in
the external courts, but also in conscience, since man's right to possess his
freedom was certain, while the right of the law which intended to limit
that freedom was doubtful.[289]

The relationship between man's basic freedom, on the one hand, and
laws trying to impose obligations on the individual, on the other, was
essentially conceived of in antagonistic terms. It was analyzed as a conflict which opposed a plaintiff against a defendant in the tribunal known
as the court of conscience. As Antonio Perez explained, the side favoring

---

[287] E.g. D. 43,33,1,1 in *Corporis Iustinianaei Digestum novum, Commentariis Accursii,
scholiis Contii, paratitlis Cujacii, et quorundam aliorum doctorum virorum observationibus novae accesserunt ad ipsum Accursium Dionysii Gothofredi notae*, Lugduni 1604
[= 1588] (hereafter: ed. Gothofredi), tom. 3, col. 782: 'Si colonus res in fundum duorum
pignoris nomine intulerit, ita ut utrique in solidum obligatae essent; singuli adversus
extraneum Salviano interdicto recte experientur, inter ipsos vero si reddatur hoc inter-
dictum, possidentis conditio melior erit.' See also D. 43,33,2 cum glossa *Ad Servianum*, l.c.:
'In Salviano interdicto, si in fundum communem duorum pignera sint ab aliquot invecta,
possessor vincet, et erit eis descendendum ad Servianum iudicium [Gl.: in quo id veniet,
ut sit possidentis conditio melior].'

[288] VI, Reg. iur., 65, *Corpus juris canonici* (ed. Gregoriana), part. 3, col. 844, l. 9–10.
The gloss *In pari* rightly draws the attention to the procedural consequence of this rule:
that the defendant has the benefit of the doubt (*et nota quia hic exhibetur favor reo, quia
absolvitur in pari causa vel delicto*). Boniface VIII's formulation of the rule combines
D. 50,17,128pr. (*in pari causa possessor potior haberi debet*) and D. 50,17,154 (*cum par delictum est duorum, semper oneratur petitor et melior habetur possessoris causa*); cf. *Corporis
Iustinianaei Digestum novum* (ed. Gothofredi), tom. 3, col. 1915 and col. 1921.

[289] Ignaz Schwarz, *Institutiones iuris universalis naturae et gentium*, Venetiis 1760, part.
1, tit. 1, instruct. 5, par. 4, resp. 2, p. 126: 'Ista regula, *quod melior sit conditio possidentis* non
tantum valet in materia iustitiae, sed etiam conscientiae. Ratio est, quia in hac homo habet
ius certum possessionis *quoad suam libertatem*; lex vero *jus dubium* obligationis. Ergo homo
non debet deturbari a sua possessione, nisi oppositum efficaciter probetur. Porro tunc
libertas hominis censetur *esse in possessione*, quando dubium est *de obligatione contracta*,
secus, quando dubium est *de obligationis contractae satisfactione* seu *exemptione*.'
Ignaz Schwarz was a professor of history at the University of Ingolstadt; cf. H. Dickerhof,
*Land, Reich, Kirche im historischen Lehrbetrieb an der Universität Ingolstadt, Ignaz Schwarz
(1690–1763)*, Berlin 1967.

the imposition of an obligation was like a plaintiff (*actor*), since it claimed a debt, while the other side acted as a defendant (*reus*) who fought for his freedom. Moreover, the burden of proof lay with the law trying to impose an obligation on the individual, since it is up to the plaintiff to prove his claim (*actoris est probatio*) that the individual owes it something. It lay in the nature of things that the defendant was unable to prove that he was not under an obligation.[290] More interesting still, is that Perez defended the view that he who doubts the existence of a certain precept remains free (*dubitans est possessor suae libertatis*). He reasoned that this kind of principles promoted freedom of action and relieved men of innumerable obligations (*favent libertati operandi, et ab innumeris obligationibus homines liberant*).[291]

Perez's argumentation brings us back to the interior forum's role as the place where Christians are healed from unduly burdensome obligations, as the Carthusian monk Valero pointed out. Consequently—and this point needs emphasis—the court of conscience was not the place for the enforcement of lofty moral principles or 'thick morality'. It was the place for determining the rights and obligations a person had in the light of truth and justice. For example, following Lessius, Perez maintained that one is not bound as a matter of justice to rescue people from drowning. It is important to understand what he means by that. Perez explained that you could not be bound as a matter of justice, that is, legally speaking, to prevent someone from incurring damage by omitting certain actions. This means that you are only bound to prevent damage if you are under a duty to do so by your office or by contract (*ex officio aut contractu*).[292] If you do

---

[290] Perez, *De iustitia et iure*, tract. 2, disp. 2, cap. 4, num. 100, p. 182: 'Ultimo idem probari potest, quia pars obligationi favens est, quasi actor, petit enim debitum; altera est quasi reus, defendit enim suam libertatem. At semper actoris est probatio, non vero rei: actor enim dicit sibi deberi; reus solum negat: negatio autem per rerum naturam probari non potest, ut passim iuris periti dicunt.'

[291] Perez, *De iustitia et iure*, tract. 2, disp. 2, cap. 4, num. 78, p. 174.

[292] Perez, *De iustitia et iure*, tract. 2, disp. 3, cap. 7, num. 122, p. 236: 'Quaeritur primo, utrum qui non impedit damnum alterius, cum posset facile impedire, teneatur semper ad restitutionem? Caietanus verbo restitutio, et alii affirmant. Contraria sententia est communis, et vera, teste Lessio lib. 2, cap. 13, dub. 10. Et ratio est, quia quando meam operam in alterius commodum non impendo, si ad id ex officio, aut contractu non tenear, nihil proprium illius, nihil ipsi ex iustitia debitum aufero: alioquin, si quando alius mea opera indiget, tenerer ex iustitia eam non omittere, non possem pro opera petita pretium exigere, quod est absurdum. Secundo, quia durissimum esset, omnes homines esse obligatos ex iustitia, et cum obligatione restitutionis ad praestandam mutuam operam, quando damnum timetur, cum ad finem societatis humanae sufficiat obligatio misericordiae et charitatis.'

not care for the good of your neighbor and you are not under a (quasi-) contractual or official obligation to do so, then you cannot be bound to make restitution if your neighbor suffers damages that you could have prevented. You are certainly under obligation as a matter of charity, but you are not under an obligation as a matter of justice. You are not infringing upon your neighbor's natural rights by failing to take action. Consequently, your confessor cannot oblige you to make restitution.

The focus on restitution and the rights and obligations existing between people as a matter of justice explains the minimalistic character of the penitential literature, or, according to the modern understanding of the role of 'law', its 'legalistic' nature.[293] Their conception of 'justice' was minimalistic in the first place, in the sense that it did not dictate the rules that allowed one to become the most virtuous person ever. As Niklas Luhmann noted, the scholastics reduced the moral notion of 'justice' to its legal aspects.[294] The theologians were concerned, primarily, with what jurists such as Pothier would call 'perfect obligations' (obligations parfaites). Unlike imperfect obligations (obligations imparfaites), perfect obligations created legal debt, whether those obligations were enforceable in the exterior fore or in the interior fore. Like Pothier, the theologians recognized that moral debt (debitum morale seu debitum ex honestate) brought about a natural obligation, but not the kind of natural obligation which was enforceable in the court of conscience. The only enforceable natural obligation was the natural obligation rooted in the body of law called natural law (debitum ex iure naturali).[295] Imperfect natural obligations,

---

293 See the positivistic definition of law as the ethical minimum in Georg Jellinek's (1851–1911) Die sozialethische Bedeutung von Recht, Unrecht und Strafe, Berlin 1908, p. 45: 'Das Recht ist nichts anderes, als das ethische Minimum. Objektiv sind es die Erhaltungsbedingungen der Gesellschaft, soweit sei vom menschlichen Willen abhängig sind, also das Existenzminimum ethischer Normen, subjektiv ist es das Minimum sittlicher Lebenstätigung und Gesinnung, welches von den Gesellschaftsgliedern gefordert wird.' Also cited in O. Behrends, Die rechtsethischen Grundlagen des Privatrechts, in: F. Bydlinski – T. Mayer-Maly (eds.), Die ethischen Grundlagen des Privatrechts, Wien-New York 1994, p. 28.

294 N. Luhmann, Das Recht der Gesellschaft, [Suhrkamp Taschenbuch Wissenschaft, 1183], Frankfurt am Main 1995, p. 232, n. 50: 'Die alteuropäische Tradition hatte, zumindest in einem ihrer Stränge, eher dazu tendiert, den ethischen Begriff der Gerechtigkeit inhaltlich auf Recht zuzuschneiden—etwa in dem Sinne, daβ Gerechtigkeit sich auf äuβeres Handeln (operationes, actus) im Hinblick auf andere (ad alterum) beziehe und auf das nach dem Recht Geschuldete (sub ratione debiti legalis), wie es in Formeln der Scholastik heiβt.'

295 Valero, Differentiae, praeludia, num. 24–25, p. 3: 'Naturalis tantum obligatio est duplex, ut constat ex D. Thoma 2.2., quaest. 106, art. 4, 5, 6. Una, quae est vera et propria, ex iure et lege naturae producta, quae in re gravi obligat in conscientia sub poena peccati mortalis. [...] Altera est naturalis obligatio, quae ab honestate morali deducitur, insurgitque

for instance natural obligations stemming from moral debt but not based on natural law (e.g. the duty to be grateful to somebody who makes you a gift) did not grant a right to another person, not even in the court of conscience.[296] Natural obligations based on natural law, on the contrary, were considered to be enforceable in the court of conscience both by the moral theologians and by Pothier.[297]

The moral theologians made a sharp distinction between precepts (*praeceptum*) and counsels (*consilium*). It drew on medieval antecedents and persisted unaltered in the work of Hugo Grotius.[298] Precepts were binding for all Christians, while counsels became enforceable only on condition that one assented to making them binding for oneself through a vow (*votum*).[299] Counsels show the way to the plenitude of Christian life, but they are not binding.[300] They are the object of works of supererogation (*supererogatio*), not of justice. They go beyond what is demanded

---

ex honestate et debito morali. Ut est illa recipientis beneficium qua quis tenetur ad anti-dora et ad gratam remunerationem loco et tempore convenienti.'

[296] Pothier, *Traité des obligations, selon les regles, tant du for de la conscience, que du for extérieur*, tom. 1, article préliminaire, p. 1.

[297] Pothier, *Traité des obligations, selon les regles, tant du for de la conscience, que du for extérieur*, tom. 1, part. 2, chap. 2, p. 174–175: 'Au contraire, les obligations naturelles, dont nous avons traité dans ce chapitre, donnent à la personne, envers qui nous les avons contractées, un droit contre nous, non pas, à la vérité, dans le for extérieur, mais dans le for de la conscience. C'est pourquoi si j'ai fait une dépense de cent livres dans un cabaret du lieu de mon domicile, ce cabaretier est vraiment mon créancier de cette somme, non dans le for extérieur, mais dans le for de la conscience; et si j'avois de mon côté une créance de pareille somme contre lui qui fût prescrite | il pourroit dans le for de la conscience se dispenser de me la payer, en la compensant avec celle qu'il a contre moi.' As will be explained below, one of the favorite enforcement mechanisms in the court of conscience was compensation.

[298] E.g. Hugo Grotius, *De jure belli ac pacis libri tres in quibus ius naturae et gentium item iuris publici praecipua explicantur*, Curavit B.J.A. De Kanter – Van Hettinga Tromp, Editionis anni 1939 exemplar photomechanice iteratum, Annotationes novas addiderunt R. Feenstra et C.E. Persenaire, adiuvante E. Arps-De Wilde, Aalen 1993 [hereafter cited as Ed. De Kanter-Van Hettinga Tromp – Feenstra – Persenaire], lib. 1, cap. 2, par. 9, num. 4, p. 81. On the thirteenth century roots of this distinction, see Pinckaers, *Les sources de la morale chrétienne*, p. 292–293, and D. Witschen, *Zur Bestimmung supererogatorischer Handlungen, Der Beitrag des Thomas von Aquin*, Freiburger Zeitschrift für Philosophie und Theologie, 51 (2004), p. 30–38. The *praeceptum—consilium* pair already played a vital role in the Franciscan Pierre Jean d'Olivi's (1248–1298) treatise on contracts, see S. Piron, *Le devoir de gratitude, Émergence et vogue de la notion d'antidora au XIIIe siècle*, in: D. Quaglioni – G. Todeschini – M. Varanini (eds.), Credito e usura fra teologia, diritto e amministrazione (sec. XII–XVI), [Collection de l'École française de Rome, 346], Rome 2005, p. 73–101.

[299] This is the theme of Coccia, *Regula et vita*, p. 97–147.

[300] T. Van Houdt – N. Golvers – P. Soetaert, *Tussen woeker en weldadigheid, Leonardus Lessius over de Bergen van Barmhartigheid (1621), Vertaling, inleiding en aantekeningen*, Leuven-Amersfoort 1992, p. 129.

from ordinary Christians. For example, Lessius conceded that following the counsels of Christ was the safest way to paradise, but he refused to acknowledge that they were binding as a matter of necessity. Otherwise, he quipped, all people would be bound to abstain from doing business.[301] The *forum internum*, then, merely pretended to be a place where rights and obligations deriving from precepts could be reinforced. The confessors did not mean to transform character.[302] It was their task to make sure that ordinary Christians passed the exam, so to speak, at the Day of Last Judgment. If people strived for honors, as they were encouraged to do through homilies and preaching, they would turn their attention to devotional and spiritual literature, not to manuals for confessors.

2.3.3   *A plurality of legal sources*

The sources of obligations that threatened to limit the will's possession of its freedom of action were manifold. Contrary to the Protestants, the Catholics did not think that the 'New Law', that is the Gospel,[303] was sufficient to decide what obligations a man needed to fulfill in a particular circumstance in order to please God. Moral theologians such as Lessius had a comprehensive and systematic view of the various bodies of law that

---

[301] Lessius, *De beatitudine (…) praelectiones theologicae posthumae. Accesserunt eiusdem variorum casuum conscientiae resolutiones*, Lovanii 1645), quaest. 19, art. 6, dub. 7, num. 44: 'Fateor tamen tutius esse facere quam non facere in tali casu. Non tamen ideo necessarium est facere, alioqui omnes deberent sequi consilia Christi: hoc enim est tutius; omnes tenerentur exequi omnes bonas inspirationes, omnes tenerentur abstinere a negotiatione.'

[302] E. Leites, *Casuistry and character*, in: E. Leites (ed.), Conscience and casuistry in Early Modern Europe, Cambridge 2002 [= 1988]), p. 120; M. Sampson, *Laxity and liberty in seventeenth-century English political thought*, in: E. Leites (ed.), Conscience and casuistry in early modern Europe, Cambridge 2002 [= 1988], p. 82; J.F. Keenan, *The casuistry of John Mair, Nominalist professor of Paris*, in: J.F. Keenan – Th.A. Shannon (eds.), The context of casuistry, Washington DC 1995, p. 96.

[303] Since, to a modern ear, which is influenced by the Protestant tradition, the Gospel is considered to be a source of morality instead of law, it might be worthwhile recalling that the Gospel used to be considered a source of law by the Catholics. Indeed, the post-Tridentine moral theologians emphasized that seeing it otherwise was a form of heresy. Cf. Francisco Suárez, *Tractatus de legibus et legislatore Deo*, lib. 10, cap. 1 (*De lege nova et legislatore Christo*), num. 3, in: Opera omnia, editio nova a Carolo Berton, Parisiis 1856, tom. 6, p. 550: 'Catholica veritas Christum Dominum non solum fuisse Redemptorem, sed verum et proprium legislatorem.—Dicendum vero primo est Christum Dominum non solum fuisse redemptorem, sed etiam fuisse verum et proprium legislatorem. Haec assertio est de fide, definita in Concilio Tridentino, sessione 6, can. 21.'

rule human behavior.[304] The main distinction Lessius made was between natural law and positive law. Natural law (*ius naturale*) was considered to derive from rational nature and the natural condition of things.[305] Contrary to positive law, the rectitude of natural law was determined not by a human or divine voluntary disposition, but rather by the inherent nature of things themselves (*ex ipsa rerum natura*).[306] Hence, natural law was also said to be immutable. Positive law (*ius positivum*), on the other hand, derived from a voluntary disposition.[307] As Lessius explained, positive law depended on the free will of God or mankind. Hence, it was subject to change.

Positive law was subdivided into two main categories depending on whether a positive legal disposition stemmed from God (*ius divinum*) or from mankind (*ius humanum*). Divine law itself was divisible into old divine law and new divine law. Old divine law (*ius divinum vetus*) coincided with God's legislation in the Old Testament, for example concerning rituals and governance. New divine law (*ius divinum novum*) encompassed the Gospel and, as Lessius added in a truly anti-protestant vein, the sacraments. Human law subdivided into three categories. Apart from the laws that were common to all nations (*ius gentium*), there existed civil law (*ius civile*) as constituted by secular rulers, and canon law (*ius canonicum*) as issued by virtue of the authority of the Pope or the Council. It should suffice here to note that positive law was thought to be divine at least in an indirect sense, since God was the ultimate legislator. Therefore, it was commonly accepted by Catholic moral theologians that human laws were

---

[304] See Lessius, *De iustitia et iure*, lib. 2, cap. 2, dub. 2, num. 9, p. 20: 'Si [ius] accipiatur secundo modo, pro lege, dividitur sicuti lex. Itaque *ius* aliud est naturale, aliud positivum; *ius positivum* alius est divinum, aliud humanum. *Ius divinum* aliud est vetus, aliud novum. *Ius humanum* aliud est ius gentium, aliud ius canonicum, aliud civile.'

[305] Lessius, *De iustitia et iure*, lib. 2, cap. 2, dub. 2, num. 9, p. 20: 'Ius naturale dicitur quod ex ipsis rerum naturis oritur, scilicet ex natura rationali et naturali conditione operum de quibus hoc ius disponit. Unde eius rectitudo, supposita existentia naturae humanae, non pendet ex aliqua libera ordinatione Dei vel hominis, sed ex ipsa rerum natura.'

[306] The 'nature of things' remains an elusive and ubiquitous argument in the history of jurisprudence; cf. H. Holzhauer, *Natur als Argument in der Rechtswissenschaft*, in: G. Köbler – H. Nehlsen (ed.), Wirkungen europäischer Rechtskultur, Festschrift für Karl Kroeschell zum 70. Geburtstag, München 1997, p. 395–417.

[307] On the origins of the concept of 'positive law' in the canon law tradition, see S. Kuttner, *Sur les origines du terme 'droit positif'*, Revue Historique de Droit Français et Étranger, 15 (1936), p. 728–740 [reprinted in S. Kuttner, *The history of ideas and doctrines of canon law in the Middle Ages*, [Variorum Collected Studies Series, 113], London 1980, n. III], and J.M. Finnis, *The truth in legal positivism*, in: R.P. George (ed.), The autonomy of law, Essays on legal positivism, Oxford 1996, p. 195–214 [reprinted in J.M. Finnis, *Philosophy of law, Collected essays*, Oxford 2011, vol. 4, p. 174–188].

binding in conscience, as long as they were just.[308] As Suárez explained,
all secular laws derive from God as their first cause (*causa prima*), even
if their direct cause (*causa proxima*) is the work of the secular legislator.[309]
The indirectly divine nature of statutory law legitimized the theologians'
involvement with positive secular law in the first place.[310]

Not only did moral theologians such as Lessius draw up a cartography
of laws, they also found an important connection between objective laws
and subjective rights—rights being defined in terms of power based on
law (*potestas legitima*).[311] Therefore, depending on whether they correspond to natural law or positive law, men dispose of natural rights (*ius
naturale*) or positive rights (*ius positivum*). Conversely, Lessius and his
colleagues also developed the important conceptual notion that a debt or
an obligation (*debitum*) is the other side of a right.[312] The Jesuits arrived
at a detailed and scientific analysis of the 'system' of law to which Hugo
Grotius was highly indebted.[313] Developing these highly influential theoretical observations on laws and rights at the outset of their manuals for
confessors, the moral theologians could then proceed to answer the question about which concrete rights and which laws were at play in a particular case of conscience. A moral theologian needed to have a sound

---

308 E.g. Francisco de Vitoria, *Commentarii in IamIIae De lege*, quaest. 96, art. 4 (*Utrum
lex humana imponat homini obligationem in foro conscientiae*), num. 5, in: Francisco de
Vitoria, *Comentarios a la Secunda secundae de Santo Tomás*, edición preparada por
V. Beltrán de Heredia, tom. 6, appendice 1 (*De lege*), [Biblioteca de Teólogos Españoles, 17],
Salamanca 1952, p. 433: 'Communis tamen opinio theologorum est quod leges humanae
possunt obligare virtute sua ad mortale [peccatum].'
309 For discussion, see W. Decock, *Counter-reformation diplomacy behind Francisco
Suárez's constitutionalist theory*, Ambiente Juridico, 11 (2009), p. 68–92.
310 Suárez, *Tractatus de legibus et legislatore Deo*, tom. 5, Prooemium, p. ix–x; and
Suárez, *Defensio fidei catholicae adversus Anglicanae sectae errores*, lib. 3, cap. 2, num. 1,
in: Opera Omnia, editio nova a Carolo Berton, Parisiis 1859, tom. 24, p. 206. Compare C.
Larrainzar, *Una introducción a Francisco Suárez*, Pamplona 1976, p. 135.
311 Lessius, *De iustitia et iure*, lib. 2, cap. 2, dub. 2, num. 10, p. 20: 'Si ius accipiatur tertio modo, scilicet pro *potestate legitima*, dividi potest, primo ex parte principii, nempe
secundum divisionem legum quibus oritur. Unde aliud est *naturale*, quod lege vel con-
cessu naturae competit; aliud *positivum*, quod lege positiva vel concessione libera Dei vel
hominum competit, et sic deinceps in aliis membris.'
312 Lessius, *De iustitia et iure*, lib. 2, cap. 2, dub. 1, num. 7, p. 20: 'Ex iure enim ipsius in
me vel mea, nascitur in me debitum praestandi id, quod illud ius impleat et exhauriat.'
313 The same idea has been stressed in the context of demonstrating the profound
indebtedness of Hugo Grotius (1583–1645) to Jesuit moral theological thought by P. Haggenmacher, *Droits subjectifs et système juridique chez Grotius*, in: L. Foisneau (ed.), Politique,
droit et théologie chez Bodin, Grotius et Hobbes, Paris 1997, p. 73–130; and in B. Tierney,
The idea of natural rights, Studies on natural rights, natural law, and Church law, 1150–1650,
[Emory studies in law and religion, 5], Grand Rapids – Cambridge 2001, p. 316–342.

knowledge of all sources of law to be able to determine the rights and obligations of the penitents with precision. In Suárez's words:[314]

> The road to salvation passes through free actions and moral rectitude. Since moral rectitude strongly depends on law's being, as it were, the rule of human actions, the study of law is a major part of theology. In treating of laws, the sacred doctrine of theology investigates nothing less than God himself in his function as a legislator. (...) It is the task of a theologian to care for the consciences of the pilgrims on earth. Yet the rectitude of consciences is dependent on observing the law just like moral depravity is dependent on breaking the law, since a law is every rule which leads to the acquisition of eternal salvation if observed—as it must be—and which leads to the loss of eternal salvation when it is broken. The study of law, then, pertains to theologians, to the extent that law binds conscience.

Jurisdiction over the souls required a profound knowledge of a plurality of legal sources. Learned experts in moral jurisprudence needed to assist confessors with the task of judging in the internal forum, just as knowledgeable doctors of laws had to assist judges in the external forum. Adjudication in the internal forum was perhaps even more demanding than it was in the external forum, at least from an intellectual point of view. The Jesuit Juan Azor (1536–1603) added to the title of his famous *Moral Institutes* (*Institutiones morales*) that the material of his treatise was based not only on the doctrine of theology, but also on canon law, civil law, and history, as well as on commentaries by the experts in each of those fields.[315] Also, the field of application of moral jurisprudence was less limited than in the external forum, even in a territorial sense. Its territory and field of application was the soul. As a result, whereas a judge in either a secular

---

[314] Suárez, *Tractatus de legibus et legislatore Deo*, Prooemium, p. ix–x: 'Quoniam igitur hujus salutis via in actionibus liberis morumque rectitudine posita est, quae morum rectitudo a lege tanquam ab humanarum actionum regula plurimum pendet; idcirco legum consideratio in magnam theologiae partem cedit; et dum sacra doctrina de legibus tractat, nihil profecto aliud quam Deum ipsum ut legislatorem intuetur. (...) Deinde theologicum est negotium conscientiis prospicere viatorum; conscientiarum vero rectitudo stat legibus servandis, sicut et pravitas violandis, cum lex quaelibet sit regula, si ut oportet servatur, aeternae salutis assequendae; si violetur, amittendae; ergo et legis inspectio, quatenus est conscientiae vinculum, ad theologum pertinebit.'

[315] Juan Azor, *Institutiones morales, in quibus universae quaestiones ad conscientiam recte aut prave factorum pertinentes breviter tractantur. Omnia sunt vel ex theologica doctrina, vel ex iure canonico vel civili, vel ex probata rerum gestarum narratione desumpta, et confirmata testimoniis vel theologorum, vel iuris canonici aut civilis interpretum, vel summistarum, vel denique historicorum*, Lugduni 1612. For a biographical introduction to Juan Azor, see A.F. Dziuba, *Juan Azor S.J., Teólogo moralista del s. XVI–XVII*, Archivo Teológico Granadino, 59 (1996), p. 145–156.

or an ecclesiastical external court had no legitimate jurisdiction beyond
his own territory, a parish priest could confess his flocks and absolve
them wherever on earth he was.[316] The jurisdiction of the soul as well
as its accompanying science, moral jurisprudence, were all-encompassing
in scope.

2.4   ENFORCEMENT MECHANISMS

2.4.1   *Norms and force*

It is natural to take the law of one's own time and country as a norm,
and, hence, to consider it as 'normal'. If carried to excess, however, this
tendency easily leads to an impoverishment of our understanding of the
historical development of legal doctrine and of human conflict management in the past. Awareness of the deeply religious consciousness that
shaped the lives of more than a minority of the people until well into
modern times is a fundamental prerequisite for gaining a better insight
into the functioning of 'law' in the *ancien régime*.[317] This study will reveal
some of the roots of modern contract doctrine in an area where they
ought not have grown according to the tenets of legal positivism. The
theological roots of Western legal cultures are hidden behind the view—
which relies on the philosophies of legal thinkers such as John Austin and
Max Weber—that rules of conduct can properly be called laws only when
force stands behind them, and that the secular State is endowed with
the monopoly over the legitimate use of such force. In Michael Barkun's
description of this positivistic creed:[318] 'The coercive power of the state,
exercised or brandished, makes the difference between the pious hopes
of morality and the grim certitudes of law.'

One may wonder whether it is useful at all to approach the theologians' treatment of contract from the perspective of the current distinction between 'morality' and 'law'. We have just seen that the theologians

---

316 Valero, *Differentiae*, s.v. *sententia*, num. 1, p. 323: 'Iudex ferens sententiam extra locum
consuetum et territorium proprium nulliter agit. [...] At parochus ubicumque locorum et
terrarum potest audire confessiones suorum parochianorum et eos absolvere. [...]'.

317 S. Kuttner, *Kanonistische Schuldlehre von Gratian bis auf die Dekretalen Gregors IX,
systematisch auf grund der handschriftlichen Quellen dargestellt*, [Studi e testi, 64], Città
del Vaticano 1935, p. 1–3.

318 Michael Barkun, *Law without sanctions, Order in primitive societies and the world
community*, New Haven – London 1968, p. 8.

themselves conceived of their job in terms of moral jurisprudence. They also made a distinction between 'moral' norms that were unenforceable and 'moral' norms that were enforceable in the court of conscience. To put it in their own vocabulary, they distinguished between 'moral debt' and 'legal debt'. In addition, the normative universe developed by the theologians was not entirely perceived, at least in their times, to be unenforceable. If we follow Hart's concept of law as rules of recognition, then, the theologians' norms should be considered, even according to certain strands in contemporary legal philosophy, not as 'morality' but as 'law'. Furthermore, it is a matter of debate whether norms need to be enforceable to qualify as 'legal' in the first place. As Donahue has argued with reference to Jewish and Islamic legal systems as well as the Roman legal system in many of its periods, the absence of the possible use of public force might not be a necessary element in a system of private law at all.[319]

To return from contemporary legal philosophy to the facts of history, it is clear that the theologians were the self-promoted guardians of a realm of norms which ran parallel to State legislation and were coupled with jurisdiction. In the following paragraphs, a tentative hint is given of how the normative universe of the theologians rose to the surface in the material life of pre-modern societies. We will first draw attention to a well-known mechanism for the enforcement of moral norms through the ecclesiastical courts which is known as evangelical denunciation (*denunciatio evangelica*). Originally, evangelical denunciation was meant as a charitable act of fraternal correction (*correctio fraterna*) for the good of the soul of one's brother. Eventually, however, it evolved into a mechanism for enforcing one's patrimonial claims against a sinful defendant. Therefore, evangelical denunciation came close to the appeal to the judge's office (*officium judicis*), which allowed the vindication of one's material interests through urging the judge to have the defendant comply with his moral duties. The second enforcement mechanism that will offer us a glimpse into the material implications of the moral theologians' normative universe is secret compensation (*occulta compensatio*). This is a form of legal

---

[319] Donahue, *Private law without the State and during its formation* p. 123. The author goes on to argue, however, that the possibility of using force makes the practical application of any system of private law more effective. Also, even if religious authorities (e.g. the rabbis of the Talmud), developed a private law system with little regard for whether the system ever got applied to actual disputes, they, or their students, were often involved in the resolution of real-world cases (p. 124–125).

self-help promoted by the theologians (and Grotius), in the event that the
external courts are defective in giving litigants their due.

2.4.2 *Evangelical denunciation and the power of the keys*

An in-depth study of the use of evangelical denunciation in classical
canon law has been provided by Piero Bellini.[320] It may be recalled that
the precept of fraternal correction (*correctio fraterna*) takes its roots from
the Gospel of Matthew (Mt. 18:15–17). In short, it holds that every Christian is under a duty to talk to his brother about his misbehavior. If the
brother in question refuses to listen to him, then he should try to persuade him by appealing to one or two witnesses. In the event that even
this second warning fails, the wrongs should be reported to the Church.
Canonists such as Dr. Navarrus insisted on the necessity of following each
step in this procedural order (*ordo*). The secret, fraternal correction had
to occur first (*primo fraterna et secreta correctio*), then the appeal to witnesses (*deinde testium adhibitio*), and, finally, the denunciation in court
(*postremo denunciatio*).[321] At any rate, a Christian who sees his brother
committing a sin must try to dissuade him. The combat against sin and
the promise of salvation are at the heart of Christianity, and of the Church
as an institution, in particular. It is no coincidence, then, that the precept
of fraternal correction precedes the verse that lays the foundation of the
Church's power of the keys (Mt. 18:18).

The Church's power of the keys (*potestas clavium*), that is the power
to bind and loose sins, was central to the Church's claim to spiritual

---

320 P. Bellini, *'Denunciatio evangelica' e 'denunciatio iudicialis privata'*, Un capitolo di
storia disciplinare della Chiesa, Milano 1986. Earlier studies of importance include Ch.
Lefebvre, *Contribution à l'étude des origines et du développement de la 'denunciatio evangelica' en droit canonique*, in: Ephemerides iuris canonici, 6 (1950), p. 60–93; H. Coing,
English equity and the 'denunciatio evangelica' of the canon law, Law Quarterly Review,
71 (1955), p. 223–241; Ch. Lefebvre, *Gratien et les origines de la dénonciation évangélique,
De l'accusatio à la denunciatio*, Studia Gratiana, 4 (1956), p. 231–250; J. Barton, *Equity in
the medieval common law*, in: R.A. Newman (ed.), Equity in the world's legal systems,
A comparative study, Brussels 1973, p. 154–155. Recent literature includes G. Jerouschek –
D. Müller, *Die Ursprünge der Denunziation im Kanonischen Recht*, in: H. Lück-B. Schildt
(eds.), Recht – Idee – Geschichte. Beiträge zur Rechts- und Ideengeschichte für Rolf Lieberwirth anlässlich seines 80. Geburtstages, Köln e.a. 2000, p. 3–24.
321 Azpilcueta, *Relectio in cap. Novit de iudiciis*, not. 5, num. 1, in: Opera Omnia, Venetiis
1601, tom. 3: Commentarii et tractatus relectionesve, f. 76r.

jurisdiction.[322] The power of the keys is a judicial power, exercised through a tribunal of its own. According to Suárez, the orthodox Catholic faith subscribes on pain of heresy to the tenet that Christ established a kind of tribunal in the Church, crowding it with judges to whom cases of conscience and sinners are to be brought.[323] As Diego de Covarruvias y Leyva explains, the power of the keys falls directly to all priests by virtue of the sacrament of holy orders or ordination.[324] The power of the keys grants priests the power to absolve penitants from sin in the court of conscience (*potestas absolvendi a peccatis in foro animae*). However, Covarruvias is careful to point out that the actual exercise of the power of the keys presupposes that a priest has first been granted the power of jurisdiction (*potestas iurisdictionis*) from the Pope or from a bishop, as when the care over a particular group of souls is committed to him. In other words, the power of jurisdiction is as it were the force which sets in motion the power of the keys (*potestas iurisdictionis tamquam vis motiva clavium*). Generally speaking, from the moment a priest is punished with excommunication, he loses his jurisdictional power both in the ecclesiastical court and in the court of conscience.[325]

---

[322] In a remarkable book, *The reformation of the keys, Confession, conscience, and authority in sixteenth-century Germany*, Cambridge Mass. 2004, Ronald K. Rittgers rightly finds it surprising that so little scholarly attention has been paid to the change in the conception of the power of the keys during the Reformation (p. 3).

[323] Francisco Suárez, *Commentaria in tertiam partem Divi Thomae, a quaestione 84 usque ad finem*, disp. 16 (*De potestate clavium*), sect. 1, coroll. (*potestatem hanc esse per modum judicii*), num. 10, in: Opera omnia, editio nova a Carolo Berton, Parisiis 1861, tom. 22, p. 340: 'Ex quibus facile etiam colligitur, potestatem hanc esse judiciariam, seu per modum judicii exercendam; quod etiam est de fide, ut constat ex Conc. Trid., sess. 14, cap. 1, ubi propterea can. 9 definit absolutionem esse actum judicii et sententiae prolationem. Quod etiam maxime confirmatur ex traditione Ecclesiae, quae in illis verbis semper intellexit, constituisse Christum Dominum in Ecclesia sua quoddam tribunal, et reliquisse judices, apud quos peccatorum et conscientiarum causae tractarentur; quod verba illa Christi, *remittendi et retinendi peccata, ligandique et solvendi*, satis indicant, ut disp. seq. sect. 2 latius expendam.'

[324] Merzbacher, *Azpilcueta und Covarruvias*, p. 294–295.

[325] Francisco Suárez, *Disputationes de censuris in communi et in particulari de excommunicatione, suspensione et interdicto, ac praeterea de irregularitate*, disp. 14 (*De sexto effectu excommunicationis majoris, qui est privatio jurisdictionis ecclesiasticae*), in: Opera omnia, editio nova a Carolo Berton, Parisiis 1861, tom. 23, p. 366: 'Hic est ultimus effectus excommunicationis pertinens ad privationem spiritualem bonorum, in quo nihil addere oportebat de jurisdictione spirituali pertinente ad forum poenitentiae; nam in superioribus dum ostendimus excommunicatum privatum esse potestate administrandi sacramenta, satis est consequenter ostensum, esse privatum jurisdictione judicandi in illo foro. Solum ergo hic agimus de jurisdictione in foro exteriori.' For the details, see pp. 367–385.

Fraternal correction was thought to be a binding precept for every Christian. It was considered to pertain to justice as well as charity. Huguccio of Pisa and, later, Hostiensis forcefully asserted that every Christian was bound as a matter of charity to correct the sins of his brother.[326] As Thomas Aquinas explained in his elaborate question *De correctione fraterna*, fraternal correction is an act of charity in that it liberates the sinner from an evil, and an act of justice since it sets a good example for Christians other than the sinner in question.[327] If the sinner would not listen to the corrections of his brother, he could be taken to court by virtue of evangelical denunciation. There were three ways of bringing a criminal to trial.[328] The first was the *accusatio*, in which the prosecution was initiated by an individual, mostly the person who had suffered from the crime; the second was the *inquisitio*, in which the prosecution was initiated by the judge; the third was the *denuntiatio*, which started through an individual's denunciation under oath and was then carried forward by the judge. Contrary to the *accusatio*, the proceedings initiated by evangelical denunciation were not primarily geared towards the punishment of the criminal act, but towards the emendation of the sinner (*ad emendationem delinquentis*), as Thomas Aquinas explained.[329]

Of great importance, at least to the decretists of the twelfth century, was the intention with which sinful behavior was denounced. The admissibility of evangelical denunciations depended on the good zeal (*bonus zelus*) of the denouncer to correct and emend the behavior of his brother. If driven by bitterness, pride or dishonesty, Rufinus warned, the denouncer himself was guilty of sin and malice.[330] Thomas Aquinas admonished that the manner in which fraternal correction was practiced mattered as much as the observation of the precept itself. Most importantly, the goal

---

326 Bellini, *'Denunciatio evangelica' e 'denunciatio iudicialis privata'*, pp. 52–53.
327 Thomas Aquinas, *Summa Theologiae*, IIaIIae, quaest. 33, art. 1 (*Utrum fraterna correctio sit actus caritatis*), in: *Opera omnia iussu impensaque Leonis XIII edita*, tom. 8: *Secunda secundae a quaestione I ad quaestionem LVI cum commentariis Cardinalis Cajetani*, Romae 1895 [hereafter: Ed. Leonina, tom. 8]), p. 262–263. This interpretation was followed by Guido de Baysio (Archidiaconus), cf. Bellini, *'Denunciatio evangelica' e 'denunciatio iudicialis privata'*, p. 46, n. 76.
328 For a brief introduction to these separate procedures, see Helmholz, *The spirit of classical canon law*, p. 293–296.
329 Aquinas, *Summa Theologiae* (Ed. Leonina, tom. 8), IIaIIa, quaest. 33, art. 1, concl., p. 262. Cited in Bellini, *'Denunciatio evangelica' e 'denunciatio iudicialis privata'*, p. 47, n. 79.
330 Bellini, *'Denunciatio evangelica' e 'denunciatio iudicialis privata'*, p. 62, n. 100.

of fraternal correction, namely virtue, had to be kept in mind.[331] Consequently, the benefits bestowed upon the denouncer through the emendation of the sinner were thought to be merely accidental, and they could
certainly not be strived for as an end in themselves. For example, if a
vendor had violated the just price, then he could not be absolved from
his sin unless he made restitution to the buyer of the surplus—which
is a clear external, material act benefitting the buyer. However, if the
buyer principally intended this restitution, without cheerfully intending
the moral emendation of the vendor in the first place, then he sinned by
denouncing the vendor.[332] In the absence of good zeal, the denouncer
could be excluded through the exception of malice (*malitia*).[333] As Guillaume Durand cynically remarked, the lawyers of the defence found an
easy ground for the reproval of denouncers in the criterion of the good
zeal.[334]

Although, initially, evangelical denunciation could grant the victim of a
sinful act committed by his 'brother' only an indirect means of relief, such
as the sinner not being absolved from sin except by making restitution,
this was bound to change gradually. A major role in this evolution was
played by Pope Innocent III. In one of his most important decretals, *Novit
ille* (X 2,1,13), which actually deals with the larger problem of the relationship between the Pope, the ecclesiastical courts and secular authority,[335]

---

[331] Aquinas, *Summa Theologiae* (Ed. Leonina, tom. 8), IIaIIa, quaest. 33, art. 2, concl.,
p. 263: 'Sed actus virtutum non quolibet modo fieri debent, sed observatis debitis circumstantiis quae requiruntur ad hoc quod sit actus virtuosus: ut scilicet fiat ubi debet,
et quando debet, et secundum quod debet. Et quia dispositio eorum quae sunt ad finem
attenditur secundum rationem finis, in istis circumstantiis virtuosi actus praecipue atten-
denda est ratio finis, quia est bonum virtutis (...). Correctio autem fraterna ordinatur ad
fratris emendationem. Et ideo hoc modo cadit sub praecepto, secundum quod est necessaria ad istum finem: non autem ita quod quolibet loco vel tempore frater delinquens
corrigatur.'

[332] Bellini, 'Denunciatio evangelica' e 'denunciatio iudicialis privata', p. 72–73.

[333] Bellini, 'Denunciatio evangelica' e 'denunciatio iudicialis privata', p. 60 and 73.

[334] Guillaume Durand, *Speculum iudiciale illustratum et repurgatum a Giovanni Andrea
et Baldo degli Ubaldi*, Aalen 1975 [= anastatic reprint of the Basel 1574 edition], tom. 2, lib.
3, partic. 1, num. 1, p. 24: 'Quis denunciare possit? Et certe qui bonae famae, vitae et conver-
sationis est, et non criminosus nec excommunicatus nec odii fomite denuncians (...)
Et has exceptiones non ignorant procuratores praelatorum in Curia Romana degentes,
quia, cum aliqua summo Pontifici de eorum dominis nunciantur, statim dicunt: Pater
sancte, ille non est audiendus, quia ex odio movetur; odit enim dominum meum ex tali
causa. Item est criminosus, et sic frequenter litteras impediunt, ut videmus. (...) Item
opponitur contra denunciantem quod non charitative proponit, quod facere debuit (...)'.
Also cited in Bellini, 'Denunciatio evangelica' e 'denunciatio iudicialis privata', p. 92, n. 25.

[335] Responding to an appeal of King John of England that King Philip August of France
was wrongly waging war against him, Pope Innocent III explained that he could not

he favored the use of evangelical denunciation as a way of obtaining relief for the infringement of one's patrimonial rights.[336] Canon *Novit ille* paved the way for a utilitaristic rather than a charitable recourse to fraternal correction. Furthermore, in a gloss on X 5,19,13, which was undoubtedly inspired by Tancred, it was expressly stated that the victim of a usurious loan could denounce the usurer for the sake of his private good (*ob privatum commodum*).[337] The turn towards the 'interested' as opposed to the 'disinterested' use of evangelical denunciation was completed in the work of Sinibaldo de' Fieschi, the later Pope Innocent IV. In his commentary on canon *Novit ille* (X 2,1,13), this famous canonist held that if it was in this patrimonial interest, one could denounce a debtor and claim that he could not repent his sin unless he performed his obligation.[338] Thus, the use of evangelical denunciation for 'temporal', 'patrimonial' or 'secular' ends became common currency.

As will be demonstrated in the next chapter, Innocent IV proposed that naked pacts be enforceable through evangelical denunciation.[339] Having parted with the original, purely charitable function of fraternal correction, denunciation could now evolve into a remedy to enforce one of the most important principles in the history of contract law. Previously, canonists such as Huguccio had had to propose an alternative remedy for the enforcement of naked pacts, namely the recourse to the office of the judge.[340] This is conclusive, since at the end of the eleventh and during the twelfth centuries, evangelical denunciation was still conceived of very strictly in terms of the emendation of one's neighbor. It was intimately connected to the requirement of *bonus zelus* and charity. Although the enforcement of temporal interests on moral grounds was thought to be a proper task of the ecclesiastical courts, it nonetheless had to occur through remedies other than evangelical denunciation. In fact, canon law developed a general rule according to which the office of the judge could be implored if an ordinary remedy did not exist for the enforcement of

---

interfere in a case of feudal law, cleverly submitting at the same time that the Pope could only judge *ratione peccati*, thus leaving open the possibility of interference in matters of sin; cf. K. Pennington, *Panormitanus' Additiones to 'Novit ille' (X.2.1.13)*, Rivista internazionale di diritto comune, 13 (2002), p. 43.

[336] Bellini, *'Denunciatio evangelica' e 'denunciatio iudicialis privata'*, p. 98–99.

[337] Bellini, *'Denunciatio evangelica' e 'denunciatio iudicialis privata'*, p. 104, n. 39. See also p. 105, n. 41 for another testimony by Tancred that the denouncer cannot be reproved if he is primarily motivated by his private interests.

[338] Bellini, *'Denunciatio evangelica' e 'denunciatio iudicialis privata'*, p. 106, n. 43.

[339] Cf. infra, p. 128–129.

[340] Cf. infra, p. 124–125.

moral principles (*deficiente actione datur officium judicis*).[341] Thus, in the ecclesiastical courts, the office of the judge became an instrument which granted the judge a certain flexibility to account for moral considerations in resolving a lawsuit.[342] For example, by adding the so-called *clausula salutaris* to his statement of claim, the plaintiff could grant the judge extended powers to construct the legal argument of the case and decide which remedy (*actio*) was most appropriate.[343]

Pope Innocent IV was able to advocate evangelical denunciation instead of the recourse to the office of the judge as the proper way of enforcing promises, since, by his time, fraternal correction was no longer dependent on exclusively charitable intentions. In his view, all material interests deriving from natural obligations could be vindicated through the remedy of evangelical denunciation.[344] Of paramount importance in this context is that the two chief principles of contract law, namely the prohibition of unjustified enrichment and the bindingness of naked pacts, were considered to be naturally binding. This was stated, for instance, by Bartolus de Saxoferrato.[345] Consequently, the re-balancing of one-sided contracts and the enforcement of a naked pact could be obtained through private evangelical denunciation. As has been pointed out by Kenneth Pennington in his study of a manuscript of Abbas Panormitanus' *Additiones* to *Novit ille*,

---

[341] Ch. Lefebvre, *L'officium iudicis d'après les canonistes du Moyen Âge*, L'Année canonique, 2 (1953), p. 120, n. 29.

[342] Lefebvre, *L'officium iudicis*, p. 116–117. The appeal to the office of the judge was dependent on the pre-existence of some kind of moral obligation. For example, illegitimate children could claim alimentation from their parents by virtue of the office of the judge since those parents were bound to supply alimentation as a matter of natural equity. Similarly, the duty to observe promises was grounded on the moral principle that a Christian's word should be as trustworthy as an oath. The appeal did not need to be based on a legitimate text from the civil law or the canon law. Indeed, the office of the judge was invoked as a subsidiary remedy, but it had to be motivated at least by natural equity (p. 123). For an example of the use of evangelical denunciation and the office of the judge for enforcing trusts, see M. Graziadei, *The development of 'fiducia' in Italian and French law from the 14th century to the end of the Ancien Régime*, in: R.H. Helmholz – R. Zimmermann (eds.), Itinera fiduciae, Trust and Treuhand in historical perspective, [Comparative Studies in Continental and Anglo-American Legal History, 19], Berlin 1998, p. 340–341. For more details on the role of the office of the judge in Roman and canon law, see Horn, *Aequitas in den Lehren des Baldus*, p. 134–149.

[343] K. Mizuno, *Das 'officium iudicis' und die Parteien im römisch-kanonischen Prozess des Mittelalters, Eine Betrachtung über die 'clausula salutaris'*, Zeitschrift der Savigny-Stiftung für Rechtsgeschichte, Kan. Abt., 97 (2011), p. 76–111, esp. p. 95–111 (approaches to the *clausula salutaris* by late medieval canonists in their commentaries on X 2,1,6 and X 2,10,2).

[344] Bellini, *'Denunciatio evangelica' e 'denunciatio iudicialis privata'*, p. 118.

[345] Bellini, *'Denunciatio evangelica' e 'denunciatio iudicialis privata'*, p. 122, n. 64.

the Sicilian jurist adopted and expanded upon Bartolus' observations in
the recension of his commentary on X 2,1,13. It reads as follows:[346]

> And conclude that when the enforcement of the civil law would nurture a
> sin, as in a natural obligation that arises from consent or when someone is
> enriched at the expense of another, recourse can be made to the Church.

In this manner, Panormitanus pushed Pope Innocent IV's treatment of
evangelical denunciation to its logical conclusion. Evangelical denunciation became a universal remedy to guarantee the protection of material
interests. Also, this quotation is indicative of the expansion of ecclesiastical jurisdiction by virtue of sin (*ratione peccati*). Indirectly, that is for
reason of sin, all human affairs were claimed to be subject to the jurisdictional authority of the Church.[347] While the doctrine of the two swords,
as developed by Pope Gelasius (d. 496), held that temporal and spiritual
authorities were autonomous and equal powers, each with its own sphere
of competence, Innocent IV's views exemplify the increased assertiveness
of the Church during the first three centuries of the second millenium.
In that period, of which the symbolic starting point is the pontificate of
Gregory VII (d. 1085), the hierocratic claim gained ground that the spiritual was superior to the temporal.[348] It was canon *Novit ille*, precisely,
through which one of Innocent IV's predecessors, Pope Innocent III, had
laid down that the Pope could always judge in a matter of sin.

The improper use of evangelical denunciation to defend the temporal
interests of the denouncer rather than to promote the spiritual salvation of
the sinner led to a reconceptualization of denunciation in the second half
of the thirteenth century. To distinguish the original, charitable form of
denunciation from its improper use, in his commentary on canon *Romana*
(VI 3,20,1) Cardinal Hostiensis made an influential distinction between
'evangelical denunciation' (*denunciatio evangelica*), 'judicial denunciation' (*denunciatio judicialis*), and 'canonical denunciation' (*denunciatio
canonica*).[349] True to its authentic meaning, evangelical denunciation

---

346 Own translation from the Latin text in Appendix num. 18 (Vat. Lat. 2551) as transcri-
bed in Pennington, *Panormitanus' Additiones to 'Novit ille' (X.2.1.13)*, p. 51: 'Et conclude quod
ubi iuris civilis observatione nutriretur peccatum, ut in obligatione naturali, que oritur ex
consensu vel cum quis locupletatur cum alterius iactura, potest ad ecclesiam recurri, ut in
c.i. de pact. [X.1.35.1] et c. Cum haberet, de eo qui duxit in matrimon. [X.4.7.5].'
347 Bellini, *'Denunciatio evangelica' e 'denunciatio iudicialis privata'*, p. 108–117.
348 Helmholz, *The spirit of classical canon law*, p. 339–343.
349 Hostiensis' commentary on this canon was originally published as a commentary on
Pope Innocent IV's Novels (*Lectura in Novellas Innocentii IV*). We have used the following

intended to bring a sinner to confession and penitence.[350] Judicial denunciation was either public or private. Private judicial denunciation was the instrument for the creditor to defend his interests (*ratione interesse*).[351] Those interests had been wronged by the inappropriate behavior of the sinner, and the aim of private judicial denunciation was to have the sinner make restitution or compensate the wronged party. Public judicial denunciation also serves the enforcement of interests, but it is initiated by virtue of public office, for instance by a bishop.[352] Canonical denunciation was used, among other things, to remove clerics from their benefices or to correct ecclesiastical judges.[353]

Hostiensis was anxious to neatly distinguish between judicial denunciation and evangelicial denunciation, noting that despite the apparent similarities, they were entirely different in substance, scope, and procedure.[354] The distinction between 'interested' and 'disinterested' forms of denunciation, initiated by Innocent III and further developed by Innocent IV and Hostiensis, had a tremendous impact.[355] Giovanni d'Andrea (c. 1275–1348), one of the luminaries of later medieval canon law, remained

---

edition: Hostiensis, *In sextum Decretalium librum commentaria*, Torino 1965 [= anastatic reprint of the Venice 1581 edition], ad VI 3,20,1, f. 26v–27r, num. 29–38.

[350] Hostiensis, *In sextum Decretalium librum commentaria*, ad VI 3,20,1, f. 26v, num. 29: 'Evangelica est illa quae fit ad hoc tantum, ut peccator confiteatur peccatum et poenitentiam agat, et habet locum in peccato non omnino occulta.'

[351] Hostiensis, *In sextum Decretalium librum commentaria*, ad VI 3,20,1, f. 26v, num. 32: 'Privata vero iudicialis potest dici illa quae ratione interesse competit, ut si aliquis mihi iniurietur vel rem meam auferat.'

[352] Hostiensis, *In sextum Decretalium librum commentaria*, ad VI 3,20,1, f. 26v, num. 32: 'Publica iudicialis potest dici illa quae competit ex officio suo in qua nec monitio requiritur (....), et ad hanc denuntiationem episcopus inquirere tenetur (...), et si episcopus nollet inquirere, archiepiscopus de hoc inquiret.'

[353] Hostiensis, *In sextum Decretalium librum commentaria*, ad VI 3,20,1, f. 27r, num. 35–36: 'Canonicarum vero denuntiationem alia potest dici specialis, alia generalis. Specialis canonica denuntatio competit illi soli cuius interset habere bonum praelatum vel bonum subditum ecclesiasticum, et fit ad hoc ut quid de beneficio suo removeatur. (...) Canonica generalis et publica potest dici quando agitur de numero dissolvendo vel impediendo, vel quando agitur de peccato in iudicio ecclesiastico corrigendo, in quo principaliter aliquod non includitur interesse (...)'.

[354] Hostiensis, *In secundum Decretalium librum commentaria*, Torino 1965 [= anastatic reprint of the Venice 1581 edition], ad X 2,1,13, f. 6r, num. 13: 'Nihil enim est idipsum cui simile est (...). Licet autem sit ei similis quantum ad formam, est tamen dissimilis quod ad substantiam, in evangelica enim agitur ad hoc, ut peccator poenitentiam agat, nec scriptura proponitur, neque litigator. In ista vero ad hoc agitur, ut res restituatur, sive ut laesus indemnis servetur et denunciatio in scripturis porrigitur et examinatur et tandem in ea pronunciatur.'

[355] Its relevance is emphasized by Bellini, '*Denunciatio evangelica*' e '*denunciatio iudicialis privata*', p. 166, n. 5.

faithful to Hostiensis' opinions on private judicial denunciation.[356] Less than three centuries after Hostiensis had developed the distinction between the three forms of denunciation, it shows up in an only slightly refined version in the work of the Spanish canonist Dr. Navarrus. Alongside mixed forms of denunciation, he distinguished between 'pure evangelical denunciation' (*denunciatio evangelica pura*), 'pure judicial denunciation' (*denunciatio judicialis pura*), and 'pure canonical denunciation' (*denunciatio canonica pura*).[357] While pure evangelical denunciation was seen in direct relationship with penance (*ad poenitentiam*), the aim of pure judicial denunciation was said to be restitution (*ad restitutionem*), and the aim of pure canonical denunciation was geared toward the removal from office (*ad remotionem officii*).

As Hostiensis sharply noted, the existence of the remedy of evangelical denunciation implied that legal disputes could almost universally be brought before the ecclesiastical courts *ratione peccati*. Moreover, the prospect of evangelical denunciation being used on a general scale for the sake of enforcing private interests threatened to make secular jurisdiction almost redundant (*laicis iurisdictionem subtrahere*).[358] To avoid just that, Hostiensis was careful to stress that the use of private judicial denunciation must be restricted to a limited set of cases, for instance, if secular jurisdiction was deficient or if *miserabiles personae* were involved.[359]

---

[356] Giovanni d'Andrea, *In secundum Decretalium librum novella commentaria*, Torino 1963 [= anastatic reproduction of the Venice 1581 edition], f. 9v, num. 6.

[357] Azpilcueta, *Relectio in cap. Novit de iudiciis*, not. 5, num. 3, f. 76r.

[358] Hostiensis, *In sextum Decretalium librum commentaria*, ad VI 3,20,1, f. 26v–27r, num. 33: 'Sic ratione peccati quasi omnis causa coram judice ecclesiastico agi potest (…) sed hoc intelligendum puto quando iuramentum intervenit, vel agitur de pacis foedere, vel in defectum iustitiae, vel ubi denunciantes pauperes sunt et oppressi, vel quando notorium est delictum (…) Alioquin si hoc generaliter intelligeres nihil aliud esset quam laicis totam iurisdictionem suam subtrahere, quod non est faciendum.'

Hostiensis, *In secundum Decretalium librum commentaria*, ad X 2,1,13, f. 5v, num. 6: 'Tamen iudex ecclesiasticus hanc denunciationem non debet admittere indistincte, nisi in defectum iustitiae, vel ratione pacis, vel iuramenti, vel secundum dictum numerum quando alias non audiretur in foro civili, puta quoniam obligatio naturalis tantum est, super quod vide quod numero supra de pactis, c. 1, vel quando notorium est peccatum, ut probatur in inferioribus, vel quando hanc proponit persona miserabilis et depressa, secundum ea quae numero supra de officium et potestatem iudicis delegati significantibus. (…) Alioquin si hoc generaliter intelligeres haec absurditas exinde sequeretur, quia periret iurisdictio temporalis gladii, et omnis causa per hanc viam ad ecclesiam deferretur.'

[359] See the quotes from Hostiensis in the previous footnote. The legitimate intervention of ecclesiastical judges in temporal affairs in the event of the breakdown of secular jurisdiction or for the sake of disadvantaged persons is subject to elaborate discussion in Helmholz, *The spirit of classical canon law*, p. 116–144. On the subject of the Church's authority to interfere with temporal affairs to protect *miserabiles personae*, in particular,

Hostiensis deemed it absurd that the jurisdiction of the temporal sword, to use Gelasius' metaphor, would vanquish due to the greediness of the ecclesiastical courts (*periret iurisdictio temporalis gladii*).[360] The innate tendency of ecclesiastical jurisdiction to expand its scope *ratione peccati* and to intrude into the sphere of competence of the secular courts continued to stir controversy until well into the modern age. While Giovanni d'Andrea contented himself to repeat Hostiensis' conclusion almost word for word,[361] Dr. Navarrus re-invigorated the Church's claims to indirect power in temporal affairs by reason of sin. His relectio on canon *Novit ille* contained a dauntless defence of the enforcement of the moral principle of justice in exchange—the second pillar of contract law besides the principle that all agreements are binding—by means of ecclesiastical remedies.

Interestingly, Dr. Navarrus advocated evangelical denunciation as the proper means to restore the equilibrium of unduly one-sided contracts in the framework of an exposition on the nature of power and the scope of the Church's jurisdictional competence.[362] In this theoretical preface, he espoused the doctrine of the indirectly divine nature of political power a generation before it was to gain such prominence among the Jesuits.[363]

---

see Th. Duve, *Sonderrecht in der Frühen Neuzeit, Studien zum ius singulare und den privilegia miserabilium personarum, senum und indorum in Alter und Neuer Welt*, [Studien zur europäischen Rechtsgeschichte, 231], Frankfurt am Main 2008.

[360] Hostiensis, *In secundum Decretalium librum commentaria*, ad X 2,1,13, f. 5v, num. 6 (cited above), discussed in Bellini, '*Denunciatio evangelica' e 'denunciatio iudicialis privata*', p. 200.

[361] D'Andrea, *In secundum Decretalium librum novella commentaria*, f. 9v, num. 6: 'Tamen licet iudex ecclesiasticus praecedentem denunciationem [sc. evangelicam] admittat indistincte, istam [sc. iudicialem privatam] indistincte non debet admittere, quia non nisi in defectum iustitiae vel si crimen de sui natura est ecclesiasticum, vel ratione pacis, vel iuramenti, vel quando crimen est notorium, vel quando non auditur in foro seculari, ut quia obligatio est naturalis tantum, vel si hanc proponit miserabilis et depressa persona (…). Alias, si indistincte admitteretur, periret temporalis gladii iurisdictio, et omnis causa per hanc viam deferretur ad ecclesiam.'

[362] For Dr. Navarrus' treatment of the interconnected themes of commutative justice, unjustified enrichment and *laesio enormis*, see corollary 13 of notabile 6 of his *Relectio in cap. Novit de iudiciis*. For his political views, see *Relectio in cap. Novit de iudiciis*, notabile 3; for his treatment of evangelical denunciation, see *Relectio in cap. Novit de iudiciis*, notabile 4–6.

It has been noted with reason that the Relectio in canon *Novit* contains the kernel of Dr. Navarrus' political philosophy; cf. R. Martínez Tapia, *Filosofía política y derecho en el pensamiento español del s. XVI, El canonista Martín de Azpilcueta*, Granada 1997, p. 122.

[363] See Dr. Navarrus' definition of lay power (*potestas laica*) in *Relectio in cap. Novit de iudiciis*, not. 3, num. 85, f. 69r: '(…) esse potestas naturaliter a Deo immediate data mortalium communitati ad sese gubernandum in rebus naturalibus, ut bene beateque vivant secundum rationem naturalem.'

By the same token, he asserted the Holy See's indirect power in temporal affairs (*potestas indirecta*), besides affirming the Church's direct power in regard to the supernatural spheres of life.[364] As a matter of fact, these ideas were part and parcel of sixteenth-century Spanish political thought.[365] It should not come as a surprise, then, that Dr. Navarrus cited Cajetan and Vitoria to buttress his claim that the Pope could interfere with temporal affairs, if, and only if, spiritual interests were at stake.[366] A little later on in the sixteenth century, the Jesuit Roberto Bellarmino would become one of the most famous advocates of the theory of the indirect secular power of the Pope.[367] What is striking about Dr. Navarrus' exposition is the straightforward manner in which he applied relatively widespread political ideas to concrete contractual disputes. As will be explained, Dr. Navarrus feared no pain in challenging both lay and ecclesiastical judges through his insistence on the enforcement of justice in exchange.[368]

Despite his deploring the lack of concern for the salvation of the soul in secular jurisdictions, Dr. Navarrus went far in recognizing the autonomy of the temporal sphere. Significantly, he emphasized more than other canonists of his time, such as Fortunius Garcia, that the principal aim of civil law was fundamentally different from the scope of canon law.[369] Against Fortunius, Dr. Navarrus held that civil law could not be concerned

---

364 See Dr. Navarrus' definition of ecclesiastical power (*potestas ecclesiastica*) in *Relectio in cap. Novit de iudiciis*, not. 3, num. 85, f. 69v: '(...) est potestas a Christo instituta immediate et supernaturaliter, ad gubernandos fideles secundum legem Evangelicam in supernaturalibus, et quatenus ad illa est opus etiam in naturalibus.'

365 E.g. B. Hamilton, *Political thought in sixteenth-century Spain, A study of the political ideas of Vitoria, De Soto, Suárez, and Molina*, Oxford 1963. For further discussion, see infra, chapter 8.

366 Azpilcueta, *Relectio in cap. Novit de iudiciis*, not. 3, num. 41, f. 66v: 'Ita quod, ut dixit Franciscus a Victoria, de potestate Ecclesiastica, q. 5, versic. octava propositio, Papa in ordine ad supernaturalia habet amplissimam potestatem supra omnem temporalem qua uti potest, quando et quantum necesse est ad finem supernaturalem; et potest non solum omnia quae possunt principes saeculares, sed et facere novos principes et tollere alios et imperia dividere et pleraque alia, adeo quod verum dici possit illud illustrissimi Caietani, tom. 1, tract. 2 de auctoritate Papae et Concilii, cap. 13, ad 8, in haec verba: *Papa habet supremam potestatem in temporalibus et non habet supremam potestatem in temporalibus: affirmativa namque est vera in ordine ad spiritualia, negatio vero est vera directe, seu secundum seipsa temporalia.* Haec ille.'

367 S. Tutino, *Empire of souls, Robert Bellarmine and the Christian Commonwealth*, Oxford 2010, p. 24–47 and p. 159–210.

368 Cf. infra, chapter 7.

369 For his critical assessment of Fortunius Garcia, see Martín de Azpilcueta, *Commentarius de finibus humanarum actuum, in cap. Cum minister (C. 23 q.5)*, num. 29, f. 210v–211r, in: *Opera omnia*, Venetiis 1601, tom. 1. On Fortunius Garcia's conception of the end of the civil laws, see infra, chapter 8.

with the supernatural aim of saving souls, at least not directly. The end of
the civil laws must be in accordance with the nature of man as a human
and as a citizen. Crucially, the natural end must correspond to the natural
means, and no human being has the natural capacity to conceive of the
end of human life in supernatural terms by natural reason alone (*ratio
et cognitio naturalis non attingit supernaturalia*).[370] The true, eternal, and
Christian form of happiness is perceived through the supernatural light of
faith, not through the light of natural reason (*beatitudo vera, quae Christiana est, supernaturali tantum lumine cognoscitur*).[371] It is attained by following the laws issued through that supernatural power with which the
Church alone has been endowed.[372]

Dr. Navarrus made a separation, then, between the natural and the
supernatural spheres of life, between secular power and ecclesiastical
power, between the citizen and the Christian. Dr. Navarrus carefully articulated the distinction between mortals (*mortales*) in so far as they were
Christians (*quatenus sunt Christiani*) and in so far as they were merely
human beings or citizens (*quatenus homines tantum vel cives*).[373] In this
way, Dr. Navarrus tapped into a tradition, initiated by Cajetan, which
rebuked the classical scholastic idea that man has a natural appetite for
the supernatural. Cajetan paved the way for the conception of man as man,
and of a purely human form of morality without reference to the realm of
grace and eternal happiness. Cajetan would not deny, of course, that there
is a supernatural dimension to life. Yet instead of seeing the relationship
of man to God in terms of a natural rational desire, he described the connection between the supernatural and the natural in terms of voluntary
obedience.[374] This would eventually lead to the doctrine of man 'in the

---

[370] Azpilcueta, *Commentarius de finibus humanarum actuum*, num. 29, par. *Omissa
tamen*, f. 211r.

[371] Azpilcueta, *Commentarius de finibus humanarum actuum*, num. 29, par. *Tertius*,
f. 211r.

[372] Naturally, this general statement must be qualified. For example, Dr. Navarrus conceded that the civil laws laid down by Roman emperors such as Justinian also attained
the supernatural end of human life, since these were Christian Emperors. Even though in
theory their power was merely natural, therefore striving only at natural ends, they were
'infused by the knowledge of the Christian faith' (*habent cognitionem fidei infusam*). From
this he infers, importantly, that Justinian's laws must be interpreted in conformity with
the canon law; *Commentarius de finibus humanarum actuum*, num. 29, par. *Quartum* et
par. *Ex quibus*, f. 211r.

[373] Azpilcueta, *Relectio in cap. Novit de iudiciis*, not. 3, num. 169, f. 75v.

[374] See F. Todescan, *Lex, natura, beatitudo, Il problema della legge nella scolastica Spagnola del sec. XVI*, [Pubblicazioni della Facoltà di Giurisprudenza dell'Università di Padova,
65], Padova 1973, p. 39–46; F. Todescan, *Etiamsi daremus, Studi sinfonici sul diritto naturale*,

state of pure nature'. Cajetan's and Dr. Navarrus' ideas herald in a more anthropocentric worldview, later reinforced by the Jesuits, which is at odds with the more theocentric conception of man's existence promoted by medieval theologians such as Thomas Aquinas.[375]

A further testimony to the increasing respect for the autonomy of the secular sphere in Dr. Navarrus' thought is his subtle modification of some of the standpoints concerning the scope of ecclesiastical jurisdiction formulated by famous thirteenth century jurists such as Guillaume Durand and Hostiensis. Prefiguring, at least to a certain extent, the modern advocates of 'forum-shopping', Durand had allegedly stated that Christian citizens were granted an option to submit any cause either to the ecclesiastical or the lay courts.[376] Dr. Navarrus subscribed to Durand's proposition that a Christian citizen, inasmuch as he is a Christian, is subject to ecclesiastical jurisdiction. Yet he called the right of 'forum-shopping' into question, as well as the proposition that ecclesiastical courts could be approached in all affairs.[377] His argumentation is sophisticated, but it is clear that it stemmed from the fear that the secular courts would be weakened. At the same time, Dr. Navarrus tried to temper those fears. Paradoxically, he did so by expressly rejecting Hostiensis' statement that the ecclesiastical courts can merely step in when the secular courts are deficient.

Against Hostiensis, Dr. Navarrus affirmed that, in principle, the ecclesiastical courts had the right to investigate any affair by reason of sin, even in the absence of negligent or impotent lay tribunals. However, he shared Hostiensis' commitment not to make the secular courts superfluous. Therefore, he suggested a new argument to limit the scope of ecclesiastical jurisdiction and to guarantee the survival of lay adjudication.[378] Even if, in principle, no objection could be made to the competence of the ecclesiastical judge to investigate a case by virtue of sin, Dr. Navarrus argued that the defendant could use another remedy to take the case away from the Church's jurisdiction. This remedy was not dependent

---

Studio 3: *Amore, socialità et legge nella filosofia e teologia del diritto del sec. XVII*, [Biblioteca di Lex naturalis, 1], Padova 2003, esp. p. 54–58.

[375] Todescan, *Lex, natura, beatitudo*, p. 55–81.

[376] Azpilcueta, *Relectio in cap. Novit de iudiciis*, not. 6, num. 8 et num. 16–18, f. 76v–77v.

[377] Azpilcueta, *Relectio in cap. Novit de iudiciis*, not. 6, num. 18, f. 76v–77v: 'Respondeo igitur (…), et quod fallitur Durandus quatenus ait, omnem Christianum esse utriusque fori quoad omnia et actoris esse optionem eum conveniendi coram quo iudice maluerit, ecclesiastico scilicet vel saeculari.'

[378] Azpilcueta, *Relectio in cap. Novit de iudiciis*, not. 6, num. 22, f. 78r: 'Qua nova ratione illa Hostiensis et Joannis Andreae a quibus nemo recedit antiqua doctrina defenditur, quam etiam satis sensisse videtur Innocentius, num. 4.'

on the competence of the judge but on the behavior of the plaintiff. The defendant could object that the plaintiff took him to the ecclesiastical court through malice, deceit and fraud, leaving aside the secular court, even though he, the defendant, would have been prepared to stand by the decision of the secular court.[379] Dr. Navarrus also indicates why the ecclesiastical courts must abide by this exception. If they did not, the Church would appear arrogant, envious and greedy for power rather than justice.[380] In other words, Dr. Navarrus gives lay tribunals space to breathe by telling the Church that she should practice greater modesty.

2.4.3 Secret compensation

The debate on evangelical denunciation has revealed some of the structural elements of a fundamental tension between Church and State, which determined legal and theological thinking from the late Middle Ages through to the early modern period. This tension strikes the contemporary Western ear as almost entirely alien. In the eyes of a modern legal positivist, the assumption that evangelical denunciation must allow judges in the ecclesiastical courts to enforce Christian moral principles comes across as preposterous. Accordingly, other conceptions, too, which were at the heart of this past tension between rival normative powers, such as 'secret compensation' (*occulta compensatio*), cannot but sound strange. This should not hide the fact that they lived on in the work of so-called modern natural lawyers such as Hugo Grotius.

Secret compensation was a way of satisfying and enforcing rights in secret, without recourse to a public institution. It was still recognized by the famous Dutchman from Delft.[381] It existed alongside the public alternative to enforce rights in court, notably when the courts failed to render your due as a matter of natural law. It offered a way for the plaintiff to take the law in his own hands in the event that the public court system was

---

[379] Azpilcueta, *Relectio in cap. Novit de iudiciis*, not. 6, num. 22, f. 78r: 'Reum autem excipere posse, non quidem quod iudex ecclesiasticus non est competens ad cognoscendum de tali causa tali modo proposita, sed quod actor malitiose, dolo ac fraude videtur eum trahere ad forum ecclesiasticum, omisso saeculari, cuius iudicio se ait paratum stare.'

[380] Azpilcueta, *Relectio in cap. Novit de iudiciis*, not. 6, num. 22, f. 78r: 'Et si Ecclesia non admitteret eiusmodi exceptionem, arrogans videretur, et alieni cupida, et potius velle quaerere potentiam quam facere iustitiam.'

[381] A succinct comparison of 'Selbshilfe' in Francisco de Vitoria and Hugo Grotius is offered by G. Otte, *Das Privatrecht bei Francisco de Vitoria*, [Forschungen zur neueren Privatrechtsgeschichte, 7], Köln-Graz 1964, p. 142–145.

deficient. For example, if an employee did not receive just salary for the service he rendered, and if he could not obtain his compensation through the courts, then the theologians would allow him to take the law in his own hands and procure secret compensation, for instance by stealing. As was sharply remarked by Domingo de Soto, we are talking here about taking the law into our own hands, or private justice (*Selbsthilfe*), in the field of what is now known as 'patrimonial law' (*ius externorum bonorum*), not in criminal affairs.[382] Curiously, private justice in matters of private law has received little attention in the past, while the historical use of *Selbsthilfe* in criminal affairs has been a rather popular topic of interest.

As a private enforcement mechanism, secret compensation was naturally controversial and politically sensitive.[383] It posed a threat to the political authorities' claim to exclusivity in regulating human affairs. Not surprisingly, it became suspect and even forbidden by the theologians themselves in the mid-seventeenth century as the State celebrated its victory over concurring normative universes, and as the secular authorities claimed the monopoly in settling disputes at the expense of rival tribunals, such as the ecclesiastical court and the *forum internum*. The following paragraphs will briefly concentrate on Hugo Grotius' adoption of the moral theologians' teachings on secret compensation. The aim of this quick glance at secret compensation is to show that enforcement mechanisms then were not entirely conceived of in the same way as they are today. As a preliminary remark, it should be noted that Grotius did not use the term secret compensation (*occulta compensatio*) expressly, preferring the term *acceptatio* instead, as other scholastics, such as Cajetan, had done before him.

Grotius set out to explain that as a matter of natural law the alienation of property occurs either through the satisfying of right (*expletio iuris*) or through succession. The satisfying of right denotes that every time something is not yet mine but is due to me, I take something of equal value from the person who is my debtor.[384] For example, the Israelites stole

---

[382] Soto, *De iustitia et iure* (ed. fac. V. Diego Carro – M. González Ordóñez, vol. 3), lib. 5, quaest. 3, art. 3, dub. 3, p. 423.
[383] The political significance of secret compensation is highlighted in Decock, *Secret compensation*, p. 263–280.
[384] Grotius, *De jure belli ac pacis* (Ed. De Kanter-Van Hettinga Tromp – Feenstra – Persenaire), lib. 2, cap. 7, par. 2, num. 1, p. 268: 'Lege naturae, quae ex ipsa dominii natura ac vi sequitur, dupliciter fit alienatio, expletione iuris et successione. Expletione iuris fit alienatio, quoties id quod meum nondum est, sed mihi dari debet, aut loco rei meae, aut mihi debitae, cum eam ipsam consequi non possum, aliud tantundem valens [Sic ipso

goods from the Egyptians to compensate for the unpaid services which they rendered to Pharaoh. Through this example, Grotius immediately betrayed his indebtedness to the scholastic tradition. He even literally cited the passage in Thomas Aquinas' *Secunda Secundae* which contained this illustration. Furthermore, he adduced the passage in Sylvester Prieras' manual for confessors, in which Sylvester acknowledged that if the judicial system was deficient, the creditor was allowed to take the law in his own hands.[385] Grotius indicated that, in principle, taking the law in your own hands went against Roman laws prohibiting self-justice (*legibus civilibus vetitum sibi ius dicere*). His observation that it also ran counter to the existence of the judicial system as a public institution was reminiscent of Thomas. From this he inferred that secretly enforcing private rights was only allowed if the judicial system entirely collapsed.[386]

Following the sixteenth-century Dominican theologians Cajetan and Soto, Grotius went on to claim, however, that under certain conditions self-help in private affairs could be allowed. The statutory prohibition on self-justice yielded to the principles of natural law if there could be no doubt about the creditor's right (*ius certum*), and if, simultaneously, there was moral certainty that the courts were not capable of rendering the creditor his due for lack of formal proof.[387] Grotius' thought clearly bears

---

naturae iure defendit Hebraeos Irenaeus quod in compensationem operae res Aegyptiorum ceperint] accipio ab eo qui rem meam detinet, vel mihi debet [Thom. 2.2., 66, art. 5]. Nam iustitia expletrix quoties ad idem non potest pertingere, fertur ad tantundem, quod est morali aestimatione idem. [Sylv. v. bellum, p. 2, q. 13].'

[385] Sylvester Prierias, *Summa sylvestrina*, part. 1, s.v. *bellum* 2 (*bellum privatum*), num. 13, Lugduni 1553, p. 9: 'Alioquin, si non potest [recuperare rem suam per iudicem], potest dominus in defectu iudicis rem suam violenter recuperare, si aliter non potest.'

[386] Grotius, *De jure belli ac pacis* (Ed. De Kanter-Van Hettinga Tromp – Feenstra – Persenaire), lib. 2, cap. 7, par. 2, num. 2, p. 268–269: 'Legibus quidem civilibus [D. 41,2,5; D. 47,8,2, 18; D. 4,2,13; D. 48,7,7–8] scimus vetitum esse sibi ius dicere; adeo quidem ut vis dicatur, siquis quod sibi debitum est, manu reposcat, et multis in locis ius crediti amittat qui id fecerit. Imo etiamsi lex civilis hoc non directe prohiberet, ex ipsa tamen iudiciorum institutione sequeretur hoc esse illicitum. Locum ergo habebit quod diximus ubi iudicia continue cessant; quod quomodo contingat explicavimus supra: ubi vero momentanea est cessatio, licita quidem erit acceptatio rei, puta si alioqui nonquam tuum recuperare possis, aufugiente forte debitore. Sed dominium a iudicis addictione erit exspectandum, quod fieri solet in repressaliis, de quibus infra erit agendi locus.'

[387] Grotius, *De jure belli ac pacis* (Ed. De Kanter-Van Hettinga Tromp – Feenstra – Persenaire), lib. 2, cap. 7, par. 2, num. 2, p. 268–269: 'Quod si ius quidem certum sit, sed simul moraliter certum per iudicem iuris explementum obtineri non posse, puta quia deficiat probatio; in hac etiam circumstantia, cessare legem de iudiciis, et ad ius rediri pristinum verior sententia est. [Soto, de Iust, q. 3, a. 2; Caiet., a. 66].'

It might be noted that the marginal references to Soto and Cajetan have been linked to the subsequent paragraph (3) in Grotius' text, which deals with succession. Yet, those

the marks, then, of the existence of parallel jurisdictions, and, accordingly, of a plurality of enforcement mechanisms, which was so typical of the medieval and early modern theologians. Grotius also repeated his standpoint further on in his discussion of compensation in general. If there is no other way of enforcing your rights and obtaining your due, he recalled, you can compensate by several means. You can take something of equal value from your creditor (*accipere*), you can retain something of equal value (*retinere*), or you can refrain from performing a promise (*non praestari*).[388]

---

references seem more likely to pertain to Grotius' discussion of secret compensation in paragraph 2. On Cajetan's and Soto's teachings on secret compensation, which marked a clear departure from Thomas Aquinas, see Decock, *Secret compensation*, p. 271–274.

[388] Grotius, *De jure belli ac pacis* (Ed. De Kanter-Van Hettinga Tromp – Feenstra – Persenaire), lib. 3, cap. 19, par. 15, p. 822: 'Compensationis originem alibi indicavimus, cum diximus nos, si quod nostrum est aut quod nobis debetur consequi aliter non possumus, ab eo qui nostrum habet aut nobis debet tantundem in re quavis accipere posse: unde sequitur ut multo magis possimus id quod penes nos est sive corporale est sive incorporale retinere. Ergo quod promisimus poterit non praestari si non amplius valet quam res nostra quae sine iure est penes alterum.'

CHAPTER THREE

TOWARD A GENERAL LAW OF CONTRACT

3.1 INTRODUCTION

'All accepted offers are binding.' 'Liberty has wisely been restored to the contracting parties.' 'The will, possessing its freedom, imposes contractual obligation upon itself as a private legislator.' There are many ways to describe the legacy of the early modern scholastics to the development of a general law of contract, but these three quotes should definitely form part of any standard account. They may create surprise, or they may sound familiar. Either way, the scope of this chapter is to give an introduction to the moral theologians' understanding of contractual obligation against the background of a particularly rich, varied and age-old tradition of thinking about the words that bind men together as yokes join the oxen. The first part of this chapter proposes to explore the long and manifold roads that led to the consensualist approach to contractual obligation, which was more or less unanimously adopted from the sixteenth century onward. The second part is devoted to the elaboration of a voluntaristic and general law of contract in the moral theological literature of the early modern period.

Without taking into account the fundamentally pluralistic character of law before the age of the codifications, it seems hard to come to grips with the historical development of contract law.[389] How can one understand the enforceability of all contracts in most secular courts from the sixteenth century onwards without taking into account the alluring influence of ecclesiastical jurisdiction? How is it possible to explain the emergence of the canonical principle that all bare agreements are binding in the first place, if not by reference to the parallel normative order governed by the

---

[389] J.-L. Halpérin, *Le fondement de l'obligation contractuelle chez les civilistes français du XIX siècle*, in: J.-F. Kervégan – H. Mohnhaupt (eds.), Gesellschaftliche Freiheit und vertragliche Bindung in Rechtsgeschichte und Philosophie / Liberté sociale et lien contractuel dans l'histoire du droit et la philosophie, [Ius commune, Sonderhefte, 120], Frankfurt am Main 1999, p. 325: 'Il convient de se demander à chaque fois de quelle loi (loi divine, loi naturelle fondée sur l'équité ou la raison, loi du for intérieur et de la conscience, loi romaine, loi du royaume...) il est question.'

law of conscience? How should one make sense of the French humanists' reluctance to grant actionability to all agreements without awareness of the denaturation of the original Roman law of contract in the civilian tradition? To summarize, by concentrating on the multi-dimensional nature of the normative universe up until and including the early modern period, the first part of this chapter intends to shed light on the gradual victory of the consensualist principle from natural law over canon law to civil law.

Arguably, it is no coincidence that the scholastic movement of the early modern period came up with a singularly systematic and in-depth treatment of contract as promise and acceptance. After all, its roots lay on the Iberian peninsula, and Spain has undoubtedly been one of the most exciting laboratories for the development of a consensualist and open category of contract. Already back in the early sixteenth century, Fortunius Garcia (1494–1543) argued from natural law and canon law that all agreements, however naked, ought to be enforceable in the civil courts.[390] He could do so because there was evidence that Spanish statutory law had always been favorable to the general actionability of agreements. A couple of decades later, the consensualist principle of contract was made sacrosanct by Antonio Gómez, one of the favorite jurists of the theologians. Hence, by the time scholastics such as Molina applied their sophisticated method of analyzing human business to contract law, the idea that *pacta quantumcumque nuda sunt servanda* had gained firm ground.

What will be of concern in the second part of this chapter is the broader, anthropological foundations on which the moral theologians rested the consensualist account of contractual obligation. The elaboration of a general category of contract based on free consent could gain such weight in their writings, because, unlike the jurists, theologians could formulate it on the basis of a broader theory of the will and its freedom of action.[391] Another concern in the second part will be to analyze the basic require-

---

[390] For short biographical notices, see J.F. von Schulte, *Die Geschichte der Quellen und Literatur des canonischen Rechts*, Band 3.1: *Von der Mitte des 16. Jahrhunderts bis zur Gegenwart*, Graz 1956, p. 715. M.J. Peláez, s.v. *García de Arteaga de Ercilla, Fortún (1494–1543)*, in: M.J. Peláez (ed.), Diccionario crítico de juristas Españoles, Portugueses y Latinoamericanos (Hispánicos, Brasileños, Quebequenses y restantes francófonos), vol. 1 (A–L), Barcelona – Zaragoza 2005, p. 344. Fortunius Garcia is briefly mentioned without further details in A. Van Hove, *Prolegomena ad Codicem iuris canonici*, [Commentarium Lovaniense in Codicem iuris canonici, 1.1], Mechliniae – Romae 1945, p. 510, num. 477.

[391] Incidentally, Luis de Molina boasted that the theologians were superior to the jurists in that they had a firmer grasp and a methodic understanding of underlying principles; cf. *De iustitia et iure*, tom. 1, col. 1: 'Cum enim via et ratione ex suisque principiis res intelligent, in quo longo intervallo iurisperitos superant (…).'

ments that the theologians singled out for contracual obligation to arise. The basic principle that all offers are binding was developed through the meticulous linguistic and psychological analysis that the theologians were able to bring to bear on contract law. The three basic ingredients of contractual obligation were considered to be the will of the promisor, the outward communication of his *animus obligandi,* and the acceptance of the offer by the promisee. In addition, the impact of the voluntaristic account of contract will be measured in what the theologians had to say about the right way of interpreting contractual obligation.

3.2   THE LONG ROADS TO CONSENSUALISM

3.2.1   *Haunted by the Romans*

'If our jurisprudence, now burgeoning, bore the fruits of industry, I would impose, through solid arguments, the view which denies naked pacts any action.' These are the words of Callidemus, a Greek polymath staged by Étienne Forcadel (c. 1519–1578) in a fictitious dialogue with the Roman jurists Triphoninus and Julianus.[392] Through Callidemus' mouth, Forcadel, a top-notch professor of law at the university of Toulouse, aired a view fashionable amongst many humanist jurists of his glorious age. As part of a more general effort to revive the pristine law of ancient Rome, the great majority of jurists belonging to the so-called *mos gallicus* held that the actionability of naked agreements was to be considered a contradiction in terms. In so asserting, the humanists sacrificed four centuries of ecclesiastical jurisprudence on the altar of strict obedience to the ancient sources. Concurrently, they dismissed the civilian tradition as a denaturation of original Roman contract law.

---

[392] Étienne Forcadel, *Necyomantiae sive occultae jurisprudentiae tractatus,* in *Opera S. Forcatuli,* Parisiis 1595, part. 1, dialogo 69, num. 1, p. 160: 'Si nostra iurisprudentia, quae nunc in herbis est, fructum ferret industriae, urgerem validis argumentis pro illa sententia, quae pactis nudis actionem adimit.' For details on Forcadel's life and writings, see F. Joukovsky (ed.), *Étienne Forcadel, Œuvres poétiques, opuscules, chants divers, encomies et élégies,* Genève 1977 and G. Cazal's biographic note s.v. *Forcadel,* in P. Arabeyre – J.-L. Halpérin – J. Krynen (eds.), Dictionnaire historique des juristes français, XIIᵉ–XXᵉ siècle, Paris 2007, p. 337–338. For an illustration of Forcadel's typically Renaissance blending of legal argument and classical literature, see W. Decock, *Law on love's stage, Étienne Forcadel's (c. 1519–1578) Cupido Jurisperitus,* in: V. Draganova – S. Kroll – H. Landerer – U. Meyer (eds.), Inszenierung des Rechts, Law on Stage, München 2011, p. 17–36.

The jurists of the late medieval *ius commune* had been engaged in a strenous effort to overcome the *Typenzwang*[393] characteristic of original Roman contract law. The closed Roman system of contracts implied that, except in the case of a limited set of expressly designated contracts, namely *emptio-venditio, locatio-conductio, mandatum* and *societas*, mutual consent alone could not produce obligation. What was needed was either the conveyance of the thing in question (real contracts) or the construction of the agreement in the solemn form of a *stipulatio*.[394] Agreements falling outside these categories were called contracts 'without name' or innominate contracts.[395] They could be enforced through an *actio praescriptis verbis* in the presence of *causa*, if the plaintiff had already performed.[396] Consequently, neither an open system of contracts, nor a general law of contract, let alone a universal principle of 'freedom of contract' could be constructed on the basis of the *Corpus Justinianeum*. Through increasingly far-stretching interpretations, the civilians nonetheless tried to bring the sacred text of Justinian in line with the changing needs of their own societies. The canonists, for their part, advocated the bindingness of sufficiently motivated naked pacts as a matter of Church law on the basis of moral principles.

The following paragraphs are devoted to the medieval jurists' attempt at liberating themselves from the Roman tradition and the sixteenth century reaction to it. Competing with the canonists, the medieval civilians were eager to open up the closed system of contracts by making ever more exceptions to law *Iusgentium* while trying to remain faithful to the Roman principle that naked pacts are not binding. The reaction this provoked with the humanistically minded jurists and canonists of the sixteenth century will be the next subject of examination.

---

[393] Dilcher, Der *Typenzwang im mittelalterlichen Vertragsrecht*, p. 270–303.

[394] Apart from its formal nature, the flexibility of the *stipulatio* probably granted the Romans more 'freedom of contract' than is usually accepted; see Birocchi, *Causa e categoria generale del contratto, Un problema dogmatico nella cultura privatistica dell'età moderna, 1. Il cinquecento*, Torino 1997, p. 47–48.

[395] S. Lepsius, *Innominatkontrakt*, in: A. Cordes – H. Lück – D. Werkmüller (eds.), Handwörterbuch zur Deutschen Rechtsgeschichte, Band 2, Lieferung 13 (2011), cols. 1225–1226.

[396] As we will see below, there is a seemingly unending debate about the meaning of *causa*. Yet in D. 2,14,7,4, to which we come back in the following pages, the meaning of *causa* seems to be 'a preceding juridical act'. On account of his performance, the plaintiff has sufficient interest to be worthy of 'consideration' by the courts; cf. L. Waelkens, *De oorsprong van de causaliteit bij contractuele verbintenissen*, in: B. Dauwe e.a. (eds.), Liber Amicorum Ludovic De Gryse, Brussel 2010, p. 675.

3.2.1.1 *The civilian tradition*

The multi-layered nature of 'law' in medieval societies calls for a nuanced approach to the question whether bare agreements were deemed binding by the jurists of that period. The glossators and the postglossators, also known as the 'civilians', acknowledged that naked pacts are binding as a matter of natural law. They also recognized that the bindingness of bare agreements, as a matter of natural law, had some major consequences in the realm of civil law.[397] Yet, at the same time, they advocated the principle of non-actionability of naked agreements in the secular courts, as a matter of civil law. This can be seen, for instance, in the commentary on D. 2,14,7,4 by the most famous among the commentators, Bartolus de Saxoferrato.[398] Consequently, Bartolus argued, even if I promised you today by virtue of a bare agreement that I would go to Rome for you, but no *causa* intervened, no obligation or civil remedy would be created for you to enforce my promise.[399] The meaning of *causa* in this context is simply *datio* or *factum*, as will be explained below.

It appears that evolutions in statutory law, legal practice and canon law—all of which will be briefly touched upon below—urged the postglossators to gradually adapt their reading of Roman contract law to the rising tenet that all agreements should be binding in principle. It will be seen that this process of adaptation proceeded along the lines of the theory of the 'clothes of agreements' (*vestimenta pactorum*). For example, immediately after he had set out the rule that bare agreements are not binding, Bartolus set out to explain this theory of the clothes that could make naked agreements binding.[400] This process came to fruition in the work of late medieval civilians such as Giasone del Maino, who carefully argued that, for the sake of the salvation of souls, naked agreements should be actionable even in the civil courts. As Ennio Cortese remarked in more general terms, the pressure of morality and religion urged the

---

[397] Aptly summarized in Lessius, *De iustitia et iure*, lib. 2, cap. 17, dub. 4, num. 23, p. 198. For further discussion, see below.

[398] Bartolus de Saxoferrato, *In primam Digesti veteris partem*, Venetiis 1570, ad D. 2,14,7,4, par. *Igitur*, f. 81r: 'Nuda pactio non parit actionem, igitur nuda pactio non parit obligationem, neque actionem civilem, sed quaeritur an exceptionem pariat? Et respondetur quod sic, licet hoc non inferatur ex praemissis, sed suo motu ponitur hic a iurisconsulto.'

[399] Bartolus, *In primam Digesti veteris partem*, ad D. 2,14,7,4, par. *Sed cum nulla*, f. 81r: 'Unde si etiam hodie promitterem tibi nudo pacto ire pro te Romam, nulla adiecta causa, nulla oriretur obligatio, neque actio.'

[400] Bartolus, *In primam Digesti veteris partem*, ad D. 2,14,7,5, par. *Quinimo*, f. 81v.

civilians not only to contemplate the ultimate ideal of natural law, but also to apply it in the civil court.[401]

From a doctrinal perspective, it is not unlikely that it was canon law doctrine that eventually provided the decisive incentive for the civilians to search for a middle ground somewhere in between the natural law and the civil law point of view, regarding the actionability of bare agreements. The canonists' idea that pacts, however naked, bring about an obligation that can be enforced before an ecclesiastical court, undoubtedly acted as a magnet attracting the civilians to stretch the interpretation of the Roman texts far enough to get closer to the dictates of natural reason and Church authority. There was definitely more involved in this act of *rapprochement* than mere passion for consistency in between the logic of the various legal orders. If the civilians wished to keep up with the highly successful ecclesiastical courts, they had to develop their doctrines more into the direction of the Church's law.

The story of how the medieval jurists bent and stretched the Roman texts on contract law has formed the subject of many excellent studies.[402] Hence, it seems both refreshing and more fruitful for present purposes to concentrate on the reflection of the civilian tradition in the writings of the early modern jurists and theologians. Arguably, the upshot of previous studies is that the civilians left the closed Roman system of enforceable contracts intact, while widening the scope for actionability through the doctrine of the so-called 'clothes' (*vestimenta*), which can enforce naked agreements (*pacta nuda*).[403] At the centre of all debates stood paragraph *Sed cum nulla* of law *Iurisgentium* taken from Justinian's Digest (D. 2,14,7,4). It held that, in the absence of *causa*, a naked pact could bring forth an exception but not an action.[404]

---

[401] E. Cortese, *La norma giuridica, Spunti storici nel diritto comune classico*, [Ius nostrum, 6], Milano 1962, vol. 1, p. 91. It should be noted that the gradual, moral transformation of the civilian tradition occurred already in the work of the 12th century glossators. For example, Martinus Gosia's defence of specific performance was indebted to 'moral' ideas about the bindingness of promises, particularly on the typical idea that breaking a promise amounts to perjury, cf. T. Repgen, *Vertragstreue und Erfüllungszwang in der mittelalterlichen Rechtswissenschaft*, [Rechts- und Staatswissenschaftliche Veröffentlichungen der Görres-Gesellschaft, Neue Folge, 73], Paderborn e.a. 1994, p. 325–326.

[402] Among recent contributions, see R. Volante, *Il sistema contrattuale del diritto comune classico, struttura dei patti e individuazione del tipo, glossatori e ultramontani*, [Per la storia del pensiero giuridico moderno, 60], Milano 2001.

[403] Nanz, *Die Entstehung des allgemeinen Vertragsbegriffs im 16. bis 18. Jahrhundert*, p. 31–45.

[404] D. 2,14,7,4 (Ulpian): 'Sed cum nulla subest causa, propter conventionem hic constat non posse constitui obligationem: igitur nuda pactio obligationem non parit, sed parit exceptionem.'

'A naked pact is a pact to which, besides consent and agreement, nothing is added from the outside,' Covarruvias explains,[405] 'as if this kind of agreement were naked since it had not been turned into a contract of its own with a specific and proper name and had not received any support from outside.' Crucially, from D. 2,14,7,4 it is inferred that naked pacts are not binding as a matter of civil law and, hence, not actionable.[406] Metaphorically speaking, the only way naked pacts can become enforceable as a matter of civil law is through their getting clothes, being dressed up and becoming 'hot'. As Baldus explained two centuries earlier, naked pacts are as dysfunctional as naked men. While the naked body grows numb and stiff with the cold, the body's vigor and force (*virtus*) is aroused by the external heat brought to it by clothes. By the same token, naked agreements, such as innominate contracts, require an external cloth (*vestimentum*) if they wish to gain enforceability.[407]

The aforementioned Triphoninus apparently elaborated on Baldus' metaphor:[408] 'a clothed agreement produces an action, inasmuch as it is

---

[405] Diego de Covarruvias y Leyva, *Relectio in cap. quamvis pactum de pactis, libro 6*, part. 2, par. 5, num. 12, in: Opera omnia, Augustae Taurinorum 1594, tom. 2, p. 273: 'Primum, pactum nudum id dici, cui praeter consensum et conventionem nihil extrinsecus accedit, quasi ea pactio, quae in propriam et speciale nomen contractus minime transierit, nec aliquod extrinsecus fomentum acceperit, nuda sit.'

[406] Covarruvias, *Relectio in cap. quamvis pactum*, part. 2, par. 5, num. 13, p. 273: 'Secundo principaliter constituendum est, iure civili ex pacto nudo nec nasci civilem obligationem nec itidem actionem civilem dari.'

[407] See Baldus de Ubaldis, *Super Decretalibus*, Lugduni 1564, ad X 1,6,16, num. 1, f. 57r: '(…) et vestiuntur isti contractus [innominati] vestimento extra rem sicut homo qui calefit ab igne calefit calore extraneo et non calore innato. Et ita est natura contractuum frigidorum sive innominatorum, quia secundum glossam iuris civilis frigide naturae sunt et non vestiuntur nisi per vestimentum appositum eis ad similitudinem hominis nudi, ut not. ff. de pactis, l. iurisgentium, par. quinimmo, et ad similitudinem hominis qui nascitur nudus. Item hominis qui frigore contrahit nervos, et propter frigiditatem non est aptus ad aliquid agendum, riget enim corpus propter frigiditatem et extenditur virtus eius propter caliditatem, et philosophi legum imitati sunt philosophos naturae.' Also cited in M. Kriechbaum, *Philosophie und Jurisprudenz bei Baldus de Ubaldis*, 'Philosophi legum imitati sunt philosophos naturae', Ius commune, 27 (2000), p. 302–303.

[408] Forcadel, *Necyomantiae*, dialogo 69, num. 2, p. 161: 'Ergo vestitum pactum actionem tribuit, utpote calentius, nuditateque seposita multo excellentius ac pulchrius, quemadmodum Nausicaa Alcionos, Odysseae lib. 6 cum nudum Ulyssem invenisset, ac deinde vestes pretiosas eum induisset, ait Ulyssem, qui antea visus foedissima specie: νῦν δὲ θεοῖσιν ἔοικε, τοὶ οὐρανὸν εὐρὺν ἔχουσιν [= Odysseia 6, 243], id est, *Nunc instar divûm, caelum, quos detinet amplum*.' A minor note regarding the Latin translation of the Greek might be that, although there is no doubting the poetic quality of the Latin verse, it would have been more consonant with the grammar of the original Greek verse if the Gods, instead of Ulysses, had been taken as the subject of the verb 'detinet' (which in the Greek original is actually an active present participle masculine dative plural added as an adjective to the Gods). This is confirmed by Murray's translation in Homer, *The Odyssey*, Books 1–12, with an English translation by A.T. Murray revised by George E. Dimock, [Loeb Classical

hotter, more excellent and more beautiful once it has covered its nudity.'
In a burst of poetic inspiration, Triphoninus even goes as far as comparing
the transformation of a naked pact into a vested agreement with Ulysses'
rebirth from a naked vagabond into the godlike hero praised by the lovely
Nausicaa after she had dressed him up. Would any serious person have
doubted the connection between Eros, attire and legal enforceability?
In any case, Triphoninus rather sanctimoniously ends by deploring the
vocabulary of clothing used by the medieval doctors, which, he says, was
uncommon to the Roman jurists.[409]

So if these 'clothes' were so powerful, what did they look like in the
eyes of the medieval jurists? In a brief synthesis of the civilian tradition,
for which he is clearly inspired by Accursius' gloss, Leonardus Lessius concludes that a bare agreement can get dressed up through one of the following six *vestimenta pactorum*:[410] 1) performance on the part of one of
the parties (*reipsa*); 2) the use of formal wording (*verbis*), for instance a
stipulatio; 3) the use of writing (*litteris*), as in the case of an *acceptilatio*;
4) being a nominate contract (*specifico nomine contractus*), although it
should be kept in mind that not all nominate contracts are consensual
contracts;[411] 5) coherence with a vested agreement (*cohaerentia cum contractu vestito*), according to the maxim that an accessory thing goes with
the principal (*accessorium sequitur principale*); 6) confirmation through
an oath (*iuramento*).

The history of the doctrine of vested agreements reaches back to the
glossators. Traditionally, the twelfth-century jurist Placentinus, a disci-
ple of Martinus Gosia and founder of the law school at Montpellier, is

---

Library, 104], Cambridge Mass. – London 1995, p. 239: 'Before, he seemed to me uncouth,
but now he is like the gods, who hold broad heaven.'

[409] Forcadel, *Necyomantiae*, dialogo 69, num. 3, p. 161: 'Utinam tamen abstinuissent
doctores hoc nomine, vestiti, in pactis, iurisconsultis inusitato.'

[410] Lessius, *De iustitia et iure*, lib. 2, cap. 17, dub. 3, num. 18, p. 197. Compare with glossa
Quinimo ad D. 2,14,7,5 in *Corporis Iustinianaei Digestum vetus*, tom. 1, col. 263.

[411] Consequently, as a matter of civil law, the establishment of other nominate contracts depends either on the conveyance of a thing (*re*), the use of writing (*scriptura*) or the
expression of solemn formulas (*verbis*). As long as they consist of mere mutual consent,
these contracts, however nominate, are not enforceable in civil courts: 'ante traditionem,
dum in solis verbis consistunt, dicuntur pacta nuda, quae non pariunt obligationem
civilem, nisi ex aliquo iuris privilegio'; see Lessius, *De iustitia et iure*, lib. 2, cap. 17, dub. 2,
num. 7, p. 196. Interestingly, Lessius notes, firstly, that the *stipulatio* is only of relevance to
the secular courts, and, secondly, that even in the daily business of those courts, stipulations have become extremely rare (*parvum usum nunc habent*); cf. *De iustitia et iure*, lib. 2,
cap. 17, dub. 2, num. 11, p. 196.

cited as the father of the theory.[412] In a modest attempt to systematize Roman contract law, he first made a distinction between *pactum* as the generic term and *contractus* as a specific class of agreements. Contracts were those agreements that were enforceable and, therefore, coincided with the vested pacts. In a certain sense, Placentinus thereby substituted the distinction between vested pacts and naked pacts for the Roman distinction between nominate and innominate contracts. The *vestimenta* he recognized coincided with the four substantial elements of the nominate contracts (*consensus, res, scripta, verba*).[413]

By the time Accursius wrote his gloss to law *Iurisgentium*, other 'clothes' had been added to this list. As is rightly noted by Lessius, the so-called *pacta praetoria*, e.g. the *constitutum debiti*, and the *pacta legitima*, e.g. the *pactum donationis*, became considered as actionable.[414] More importantly, with the advent of the postglossators from the fourteenth century onwards, a shift occurred in the approach to the question of naked pacts. While the glossators gave a more systematic expression to the Roman texts, successive generations of jurists increasingly searched for exceptions to the rule that naked pacts are not producing civil obligations.[415] This often led to lengthy catalogues of cases in which law *Iurisgentium* did not apply. A notorious example is André d'Exea's (†1575) list of sixty-four exceptions to the Roman rule that naked pacts are not binding.[416]

The cracks in the civilian tradition become apparent in the list of sixteen exceptions to law *Iusgentium* singled out by Giasone del Maino (1435–1519), the famous professor of law who taught at Pisa, Padova, and Pavia, where he counted Andrea Alciati (1492–1550) among his students.[417]

---

[412] However, Birocchi, *Causa et categoria generale del contratto*, p. 48–49 raises the possibility that the doctrine of *vestimenta pactorum* found its expression even earlier on in (Anglo-)Norman sources, particularly in the *Ulpianus de edendo*, a treatise on procedure that now is said to have been influenced by Placentinus in the first place; see A. Gouron, *Un traité écossais du douzième siècle*, Tijdschrift voor Rechtsgeschiedenis, 78 (2010), p. 1–13.

[413] For a more detailed account of Placentinus' reflections on contract law in his *Summa Codicis*, lib. 2, tit. 3, see Birocchi, *Causa et categoria generale del contratto*, p. 50–52.

[414] Lessius, *De iustitia et iure*, lib. 2, cap. 17, dub. 4, num. 24, p. 198. Compare Birocchi, *Causa et categoria generale del contratto*, p. 52–54.

[415] Birocchi, *Causa et categoria generale del contratto*, p. 63–67.

[416] Birocchi, *Tra tradizione e nuova prassi giurisprudenziale, La questione dell'efficacia dei patti nella dottrina italiana dell'età moderna*, in: J. Barton (ed.), Towards a general law of contract, [Comparative Studies in Continental and Anglo-American Legal History, 8], Berlin 1990, p. 275–277, n. 135.

[417] For biographical information, see the notice by F. Santi in the online Dizionario biografico degli Italiani (URL: http://www.treccani.it/enciclopedia/giasone-del-maino_ (Dizionario_Biografico)/, last visited 20.09.2011).

One of the exceptions flagged by Giasone reads as follows:[418] 'Even though it is not possible to sue on the basis of a naked pact as a matter of civil law, performance can still be demanded by virtue of evangelical denunciation, *even in the civil court.*' Certainly, the commentators of Roman law knew that different rules than the one expressed in D. 2,14,7,4 prevailed in the canon law. Yet, through statements of this kind, Giasone del Maino was attacking the civilian system from within. It is therefore baffling to find him claiming that by means of a remedy based on canon law, naked pacts can in fact become actionable as a matter of civil law. Giasone del Maino's argument would be cited later in the sixteenth century by Matthias van Wezenbeke, who also claimed that bare agreements were actionable as a matter of civil law.

By the beginning of the sixteenth century, the Roman way of thinking about contractual obligation met with growing skepticism. Some scholars expressly stated that the civil law tradition should conform to the canon law of contract. As Covarruvias is perplexed to find,[419] 'some believe, against the common opinion, that even as a matter of civil law a civil obligation and action arise out of a naked pact.' Covarruvias is taking issue here with Fortunius Garcia. This eminent jurist, born in the same year as Domingo de Soto, argued that in contractual affairs, civil courts should abide by canon law (*in foro civili standum est iuri pontificio*), since violating contractual obligations is a matter of sin.[420] Remarkably, Covarruvias, one of the foremost canonists of the Spanish Golden Age, does not follow Fortunius' opinion.

---

[418] Giasone del Maino, *In primam Digesti Veteris partem commentaria*, Venetiis 1579, ad D. 2,14,7,4, num. 14, limitatione 4, f. 138r: 'Quamvis ex pacto nudo agi non possit de iure civili, tamen potest peti executio per viam denunciationis evangelicae *etiam in foro civili* (...).' [the italics are ours]

[419] Covarruvias, *Relectio in cap. quamvis pactum*, part. 2, par. 5, num. 13, p. 274: 'Quidam autem adversus communem opinantur, etiam iure civili ex pacto nudo obligationem civilem nasci et actionem competere, idque probare conantur, primo, quia in materia peccati adhuc in foro civili standum est iure pontificio, quo datur ex pacto nudo actio, non civili.'

[420] See Fortunius Garcia, *Repetitio super cap. 1 de Pactis*, in: *Commentaria in titulum Digesti de Pactis, difficilem, uberrimum, omniumque contractuum parentem cum repetitione cap. 1 Extra in eodem titulo*, Francoforti 1592, num. 118, p. 119: 'Hinc singulariter constat quod in utroque foro hodie ex pacto nudo habebimus ius agendi. (...) Cum ergo in iustitia pactorum nudorum ius civile negligenter se habuerit, quia ea praetermisit, succedit regula iuris canonici etiam foro seculari (ut credo) observanda, qua regula pactis ius ministratur.' For further discussion of Fortunius Garcia's seminal contribution to the development of a general law of contract, see below.

3.2.1.2 *Classical convulsions*

Covarruvias' resistance against Fortunius Garcia's far-stretching, if not slightly dishonest interpretation of law *Iurisgentium*, is part of a general trend in the early modern period to protest against the denaturation of the classical Roman law of contract. The aforementioned opinion by Callimachus expressed in Forcadel's dialogues is but one of many examples of this. One should not infer from their resistance against the denaturation of Roman contract law that critics such as Covarruvias did not recognize the need for an open system of contracts or the general actionability of bare agreements. On the contrary, they would insist that, as a matter of canon law, or, for that matter, natural law, all pacts should be binding. Again, it seems crucial to bear in mind the multi-layered nature of law until the rise of the State's monopoly on the creation of norms and the settlement of conflict.

Barring exceptions, these classical convulsions, as we might call them, are symptomatic of what was a general concern to carefully distinguish between different levels of normativity, rather than a reluctance to stimulate the development of a general law of contract in practise and canon law. Moreover, the crusade for a philologically correct understanding of Justinian's *Corpus* had the ironical effect of making original Roman law increasingly irrelevant. Whether that was an intended or an unintended consequence of the humanist jurists is beyond the scope of this argument.

Equally uncertain is whether a sharp distinction between so-called humanist jurisprudence and traditional legal scholarship, or, alternatively, between humanism (*mos gallicus*) and Bartolism (*mos italicus*), is adequate in the first place, if we want to come to grips with contract doctrine in the early modern age.[421] It is not unthinkable that in distinguishing too sharply between *mos gallicus*, the 'French' way of teaching law, and *mos italicus*, the 'Italian' way of teaching law, traditional historiography has been deceived by the polemic tone of the sources. In addition, preconceptions about the positive or negative meaning of terms

---

[421] The inadequacy of this pair of terms in dealing with sixteenth century jurists has already been illustrated in regard to André d'Exea; see Birocchi, *Causa e categorie generale del contratto*, p. 66, n. 106. Some authors suggested that d'Exea belongs to a movement in between *mos italicus* and *mos gallicus*; cf. F. Carpintero Benitez, '*Mos italicus*', '*mos gallicus*' *y el humanismo racionalista, Una contribución a la historia de la metodología jurídica*, Ius commune, 6 (1977), p. 143; Carpintero has been followed by R.C. van Caenegem, *An historical introduction to private law*, Cambridge 1992, p. 58, n. 52.

such as 'scholasticism' and 'humanism' have played a sad role in historical scholarship.[422] Modern scholarship rightly places the emphasis on the
interaction between humanism and Bartolism in the sixteenth century.[423]
It has been suggested that overly excessive emphasis on the distinctive
ways of teaching law in the late fifteenth and the sixteenth centuries
might be the misleading result of unduly nationalistic tendencies. One
should not forget that in the late nineteenth and early twentieth century,
when a lot of legal histiographical scholarship emerged, France and Italy
were at political loggerheads with each other.[424]

Consider Covarruvias' fierce rebuttal of Andrea Alciati's suggestion that
naked pacts might be actionable even as a matter of civil law if sin cannot
be prevented otherwise.[425] The writings of both authors unite characteristics usually thought to be in the almost exclusive province of either a
'humanistic' or a 'scholastic' jurist. With a commitment to authenticity
typical of the humanists, the rather 'scholastic' Covarruvias wants the
original meaning of paragraph *Sed cum nulla* to be respected at all costs,
whereas the allegedly 'humanistic' Alciati overstretches the interpretation of the same law with a sense of pragmatism typically associated with
the scholastics. Particularly in this context, it should not be omitted that
Alciati studied under Giasone del Maino.

There were also more subtle ways that genuine Roman contract law
could be undermined and, consequently, needed to be refuted. One of
them concerned the standard explanation for the non-actionability of
naked pacts in Roman law. According to that account, the Romans had
been careful not to make bare agreements enforceable, since that would
have led to the actionability of ill-considered and rash promises. In other
words, if a promise had been made through a naked pact, the Romans

---

[422] Invaluable warnings against the tenacity of the misconceptions on this distinction
can be found in D. Maffei, *Gli inizi dell'umanesimo giuridico*, Milano 1972³, p. 15–23. Birocchi,
Alla ricerca dell'ordine, p. 236, n. 17 notes that, if anything, the typically sixteenth century
polemic was closed by the Protestant and humanist jurist Alberico Gentili (1552–1608),
whose *De iuris interpretibus* (1582) was designed as a defence of the *mos italicus*.

[423] R. Lesaffer, *European legal history, A cultural and political perspective*, Cambridge
2009, p. 353.

[424] See the critical analysis in M. Bellomo, *Perché lo storico del diritto europeo deve occuparsi dei giuristi indiani?*, Rivista internazionale di diritto comune, 11 (2000), p. 30–32.

[425] See the argumentation by Andrea Alciati in *Paradoxa iuris civilis ad Pratum*, Lugduni 1532, lib. 5, cap. 3, p. 79, and the reaction it provoked in Covarruvias, *Relectio in cap.
quamvis pactum*, part. 2, par. 5, num. 13, p. 274: 'Unde manifeste errare videtur Andreas
Alciatus in rubr. ff. de verborum obligatione, num. 13 et lib. 5 Parad., cap. 5 (sic), dum
scribit ex pacto nudo iure etiam civili actionem oriri in his casibus quibus eiusdem pacti
violatio mortalem culpam habet.'

rightfully presumed that it ensued from levity (*praesumptio levitatis*). This opinion can be traced back at least to Andrea Alciati, who attributes it in a not wholly convincing way to Alexander Tartagni of Imola (1424–1477).[426] It became widespread among the jurists in the sixteenth century and endures in textbooks to this day.

Covarruvias is anxious to express his misgivings about the *praesumptio levitatis*-theory for explaining the Roman law of contract.[427] If paragraph *Sed cum nulla* rests on a presumption, then it must be a conclusive presumption (*iuris et de iure*), according to Covarruvias. Yet even a conclusive presumption can be rebutted if he in whose favor it has been established provides evidence through confession that the presumption is not true.[428] However, D. 2,14,7,4 would not admit of such a confession, since it establishes a general rule. In other words, even if it could be proven that consent had been made deliberately, then paragraph *Sed cum nulla* would still not make a bare agreement actionable. Consequently, the assumption that the non-enforceability of naked pacts in Roman law rests on a presumption of levity is false.

There is a second argument why the non-actionability of naked pacts cannot rest on a presumption of lack of deliberation.[429] Does not

---

[426] E.g. Alciati, *Paradoxa*, lib. 5, cap. 3, p. 79: '...ratio cur ex pacto iure civili actio non nascebatur, ea tradita est, quod improvide huiusmodi promissio facta praesumitur (Alex. in rub. de verb. oblig.).'

The reference to Tartagni is suspiciously imprecise and probably not justified. Perhaps the following passage could be cited, though, to argue that Tartagni was indeed of the opinion that the non-actionability of naked pacts must be ascribed to a lack of proof that consent had been given deliberately; cf. Alexander Tartagnus Imolensis, *Lectura novissima de verborum obligatione*, rubr., num. 9 (*factum ad interrogationem dicitur magis deliberate fieri*), in *Ad frequentiores Pandectarum titulos, leges et paragraphos*, Venetiis 1595, f. 158r.

On Tartagni and his counsels, see A.A. Wijffels, *La bonne foi en droit savant médiéval, Bona fides—mala fides dans les consilia d'Alexander Tartagnus (Imolensis)*, in: La bonne foi, [Cahiers du centre de recherches en histoire du droit et des institutions, 10], Bruxelles 1998, p. 23–52.

[427] Interestingly, Covarruvias levels his criticism against Tartagni instead of Alciati, although it seems unlikely that Covarruvias read Tartagni directly, given that he copies Alciati's reference with the same lack of precision. In any case, Tartagni did not state the *praesumptio levitatis*-idea with the same clarity as Alciati.

[428] Covarruvias, *Relectio in cap. quamvis pactum*, part. 2, par. 5, num. 13, p. 274: 'Adhuc tamen haec ratio Alexandri et aliorum minime satisfacit, quippe quae convinceret, si vera foret actionem iure civili dari ex pacto nudo ubi per confessionem constaret animus deliberatus, cum praesumptio iuris et de iure in contrarium admittat confessionem illius pro quo praesumitur secundum communem (...) et vere, si communi omnium sententiae standum est et ipsis quidem iuris civilis responsis, plane dicendum erit etiam in hoc casu actionem ex pacto nudo minime dari, nec obligationem oriri.'

[429] Covarruvias, *Relectio in cap. quamvis pactum*, part. 2, par. 5, num. 13, p. 274: 'Praesertim ratio Alexandri ex eo deficit, quod ius ipsum civile fatetur ex pacto nudo oriri

D. 2,14,7,4 itself recognize that even a naked pact produces legal effects of some kind? After all, a bare agreement produces an exception. The Romans would certainly not have granted this remedy to an agreement they considered to be unthoughtful. Moreover, the *praetores* would not have granted actionability to a limited set of pacts if they had considered them as being indeliberate. Last, if the non-enforceability of naked pacts truly rested on a presumption of lack of deliberate consent, then there would be no distinction between the civil law, the canon law and the law of conscience. Under the assumption of rash consent, naked pacts cannot be enforced in the ecclesiastical courts and the court of conscience either (*praesumpta levitate nec iure pontificio nec in animae iudicio pacta nuda servanda sunt*).

Clearly, the spectre of confusion between the different levels of normativity was abhorred by Covarruvias. Yet if the distinct character of Roman law could not be explained by reference to a presumption of levity, then what was the true foundation of its rule that naked pacts are not actionable (*quid ergo ius civile hac in re statuit*)? In the footsteps of earlier canonists, Covarruvias gives an explanation that fully integrates the basic, pre-modern insight that 'law' is a multi-layered phenomenon. Within this multi-dimensional reality, a different objective is pursued at each level, all of the objectives and the levels being complementary. The civil law, in particular, aims at the preservation of society without necessarily striving for the highest degree of morality. As Antonio de Butrio (ca. 1338–1408) pointed out when explaining why civil law does not enforce naked pacts: 'it is not the chief aim of civil law to attain the end of divine law, but primarily to pursue the end of public utility (*finis publicae utilitatis*)'.[430] Covarruvias assented to this argument. It became standard among the early modern theologians.

Because the overextension of the courts were a major evil, according to Covarruvias, D. 2,14,7,4 laid down that naked pacts are not enforceable,

---

naturalem obligationem debiti quidem legalis ad retinendum, ad excipiendum et compensandum. Quae profecto minime oriretur praesumptione constituta non deliberatae promissionis. Nam praetor ipse adversus iuris civilis praesumptionem non defenderet pacta nuda ratione consensus minus perfecti non praemissa animi integra deliberatione, imo praesumpta levitate quadam. Quo casu si de hoc constet nec iure pontificio nec in animae iudicio pacta nuda servanda sunt, cum deficiat consensus ad conventionem necessarius, l. 1 de pactis.'

[430] Antonio de Butrio, *Super Decretalibus commentarii*, Torino 1967 [= anastatic reproduction of the Venice 1578 edition], tom. 2, ad X 1,35,1, f. 94v, num. 7: 'Et si dicatur secundum leges datur concursus iuris divini, et tamen non oritur, dico quod ideo, quia ius civile principaliter non insequitur finem iuris divini sed finem publicae utilitatis.'

in order to prevent the courts from being flooded by an endless stream of useless disputes (*actionem civilem pactis nudis negavit ad utilitatem rei-publicae ut tot lites foris cederent*).[431] For the same reason, the civil law tolerated prostitution, did not grant an action but for lesion beyond moiety, and did not impose an obligation of remuneration on the donee. Covarruvias' explanation of the non-actionability of bare agreements as a matter of civil law became standard doctrine among the moral theologians. The view that Roman law neither actively promoted, nor actively resisted bare agreements (*pacto nudo lex civilis nec adsistit nec resistit*) became equally standard.[432] It left room for the theologians to argue that bare pacts are still enforceable as a matter of natural law without having to go against Roman law.

Covarruvias' critical attitude towards the degeneration of Roman law was not an isolated case, of course. Classical convulsions could be seen, too, in the works of illustrious French jurists such as François Le Douaren (1509–1559), Jacques Cujas (1520–1590) and Hugues Doneau (1527–1591). Their standpoint resembles that of their less well-known but equally impressive compatriot Étienne Forcadel. Their aversion to medieval jurisprudence is notorious; their penchant for philological acriby widely praised. In view of the relative insignificance of the *mos gallicus* to the development of early modern scholastic contract law, they cannot receive extended study here. It is sufficient to say that Cujas plainly confirms the Roman rule that bare agreements produce an exception but not a civil action.[433] The same goes for Doneau (Donellus), who expressly rejects the medieval doctrine of the *vestimenta pactorum*.[434] Perhaps Le Douaren

---

[431] Covarruvias, *Relectio in cap. quamvis pactum*, part. 2, par. 5, num. 13, p. 274.

[432] Covarruvias, *Relectio in cap. quamvis pactum*, part. 2, par. 5, num. 10, p. 273.

[433] Jacques Cujas, *Paratitla in libros quinquaginta Digestorum seu Pandectarum Imperatoris Iustiniani*, Coloniae 1570, ad D. 2,14, p. 25: 'Ex pacto autem datur exceptio vel replicatio, formatur actio contractus, sed non datur vel tollitur actio, nisi lege confirmatum sit.'

[434] Hugues Doneau, *Commentaria iuris civilis*, Hanoviae 1612, lib. 12, cap. 9, p. 575: 'Quod si neutrum horum erit, id est, neque conventio transibit in proprium nomen, neque praeter conventionem quidquam datum aut factum erit, ut vicissim dares aut faceres, tum sit illa pactio, quae Ulpiano et veteribus dicitur nuda pactio et nudum pactum, ex quo obligatio et actio non nascitur (…).' For Doneau's rejection of the medieval doctrine of the *vestimenta pactorum*, see lib. 12, cap. 11, p. 578–580 (*quae solo consensu non pariunt obligationem conventiones, quibus rebus accedentibus confirmentur et pariant. Eas res esse, quae vulgo vocant vestimenta pactorum. In horum tum appellatione, tum divisione quam vulgo erretur, et refutatus in eo error vulgaris*). Doneau would argue that Roman law merely recognized two 'clothes', namely the *rei vel facti traditio* and the *stipulatio* (p. 578). For a more profound discussion of Doneau's views on contract law, see Birocchi, *Causa e categoria generale del contratto*, p. 178–188.

merits somewhat more attention, because his commentary is typical of
the humanist attitude toward contract law as well as canon law.

While emphasizing that the Roman pretor acknowledged that all agreements were binding as a matter of equity and fidelity, Le Douaren concedes that the civil law as such did accord actionability only to a limited
set of contracts out of policy considerations. The performance of agreements that fell outside of this peculiar category was purely a matter of
honesty, religion and fidelity.[435] In his commentary on D. 2,14,7*pr*, Le
Douaren recalls that the Romans did not want to grant an action for all
agreements, because that would have proved detrimental to society: if all
contracts were enforceable, then the courts would be overextended.[436] At
the same time, he recognizes that this is merely a regulation as a matter
of civil law. The absence of a general category of enforceable contract is
neither necessary nor natural. Le Douaren begrudgingly admits that this
explains why not all people have followed the same path as the Romans,
but sometimes developed a rule which grants binding force to all agreements, even if they are naked.[437] Not without a certain sense of irony, he
goes on to indict the canon law for having abolished the Roman laws of
contract. He suggested that, in his view, the world would have been a better place if this irreverend act had not occurred.[438]

Le Douaren expressly attacked the late medieval juridical tradition,
certainly its papalist character, and launched the Ciceronian program of
ius in artem redigere, which he exposed in his famous letter of 1544 on
the way to teach and to study law (*Epistola ad Andream Guillartum de*

---

[435] François Le Douaren, *Commentarius in tit. De pactis*, in: Opera omnia, Lugduni 1554,
f. 26r: 'Supra ostendimus, veteribus Romanis utile visum non fuisse, passim ex quibusli-
bet conventionibus actiones dari, ideoque paucas quasdam ex multis delegisse eos, quas
ad agendum utiles esse ducerent. Caeteras honestae cuiusque voluntati, religioni, et fidei
reliquisse.'

[436] Le Douaren, *Commentarius in tit. De pactis*, f. 26r: 'Nulla est igitur alia istius iuris
ratio, quam quae supra a nobis commemorata est, ne videlicet litibus immodicis, conten-
tionibusque abundet civitas, quibus minuendis potissimum studere legislatorem oportet.'

[437] Le Douaren, *Commentarius in tit. De pactis*, f. 26r: 'Cum autem ea ratio tantum civilis, ac probabilis sit, non necessaria et naturalis (ut diximus), mirum profecto videri non
debet, si non aeque omnes ei assentiantur, adeo ut quorundam populorum legibus cautum
esse acceperimus, ne ex pactione ulla, quamlibet nuda, ac simplici, denegetur actio.'

[438] Le Douaren, *Commentarius in tit. De pactis*, f. 26r: 'Ac merito sophistas nescio quos
perstringit [Aristoteles] nihil facilius esse confirmantes quam multis legibus in unum
locum collatis, optimas eligere, quibus, utinam neque nostra haec aetas, neque superiora
secula similes aliquando tulissent. Non enim tam multa praeclare et utiliter legibus ac
iure civili comparata, pontificum quorundam sanctionibus abrogata iacerent, et felicius
aliquanto, mea sententia, cum rebus humanis ageretur.'

ratione docendi discendique iuris). It consecrated the legal humanist movement (*mos gallicus*) already set in motion in France by his master Guillaume Budé (1468–1540). It would stimulate generations of jurists to get a
deeper historical understanding of pristine Roman contract law without
preventing them from being creative in systematizing the Roman legacy
in new ways. Particularly important, in this respect, is François Connan's
(1508–1551) entirely idiosyncratic doctrine of contract based around the
notion of *synallagma*. Connan only recognized the enforceability of synallagmatic contracts as a matter of civil law. He went as far as denying that
naked pacts produce natural obligation.[439] Connan would draw heavy
criticism of Hugo Grotius for his 'unscholastic' standpoints.

3.2.2   *The refreshing spirit of canon law*

If the weight of the Roman legal tradition turned out to be so oppressive
as to stifle almost any attempt to overturn D. 2,14,7,4, then how could the
consensualist principle eventually emerge? From where did the attempts
made by some of the medieval jurists to open up the civilian tradition
draw their inspiration? From where did the pressure to change the civil
law, or even to depart from the Roman legacy altogether, come?

   In the past, eminent legal historians have pointed out the crucial role
played by at least two factors in the rise of the consensualist principle:
the law of the Church and the courts of merchants.[440] At least from the
fourteenth century onward, the doctors agreed that naked agreements
were binding in a mercantile court.[441] An analysis of the development
of contract law among merchants would, however, take us far afield. Suffice it to cite here the opinion of Benvenuto Stracca (1509–1578) in his
De mercatura that 'in a court of merchants, where questions are decided

---

[439] For an in-depth discussion, see Birocchi, *Causa e categoria generale del contratto*,
p. 95–136. Also noteworthy is Nanz's observation that Connan's extreme positions not only
drew heavy criticism by Hugo Grotius but also by Matthias van Wezenbeke; *Die Entstehung des allgemeinen Vertragsbegriffs im 16. bis 18. Jahrhundert*, p. 65–69 and p. 88–89.
Other notes on Connan's understanding of contract law and the way in which it formed
a counter-example for Grotius, can be found in Diesselhorst, *Die Lehre des Hugo Grotius
vom Versprechen*, p. 31–34.

[440] See, for instance, the syntheses of the historical development of the principle of
'freedom of contract' in W. Scherrer, *Die geschichtliche Entwicklung des Prinzips der Vertragsfreiheit*, [Basler Studien zur Rechtswissenschaft, 20], Basel 1948, p. 16–30; Nanz, *Die
Entstehung des allgemeinen Vertragsbegriffs im 16. bis 18. Jahrhundert*, p. 46–64.

[441] Ch. Donahue, Jr., *Equity in the courts of merchants*, Tijdschrift voor Rechtsgeschiedenis, 72 (2004), p. 23–31.

according to the good and the equitable, the *exceptio nudi pacti* is not accepted; rather, the received opinion is that naked pacts are actionable'.[442] Stracca expressly relied on post-glossators such as Baldus to support his standpoint.[443]

The following paragraphs will mainly focus on the canonists' development of the principle that all agreements are binding, since the canon law tradition had a relatively major impact upon early modern scholastic contract doctrine. We thereby heavily draw upon previous scholarship.[444]

3.2.2.1 Pacta quantumcumque nuda servanda

The legacy of canon law to contract doctrine can be aptly summarized through the title put above the famous canon *Antigonus* (X 1,35,1) in the *Liber Extra* (1234): all pacts, however naked, are binding (*pacta quantumcumque nuda servanda sunt*).[445] This canon can be traced back to the Council of Carthago (348 AD), when bishop Antigonus accused bishop Optantius of not observing an agreement in which they had fixed the boundaries of their power (*cum inter se pactum fecissent quod alter non*

---

[442] Benvenuto Stracca, *De mercatura*, Venetiis 1553, f. 77r, num. 1: '(...) in curia mercatorum, in qua quaestiones sunt de bono et aequo, huiusmodi exceptio quod ex pacto nudo actio non oriatur reiicitur, quinimo ex eo agi posse receptum est.' Also quoted in Donahue, *Equity in the courts of merchants*, p. 31.

[443] Stracca cites Baldus' commentary to C. 4,35,10, but he could as well have cited Baldus' testimony in his commentary to X 1,35,1; cf. Baldus, *Super Decretalibus*, ad X 1,35,1, num. 8, f. 112r.

[444] L. Seuffert, *Zur Geschichte der obligatorischen Verträge*, Nördlingen 1881; F. Spies, *De l'observation des simples conventions en droit canonique*, Paris 1928; J. Roussier, *Le fondement de l'obligation contractuelle dans le droit de l'Église*, Paris 1933; P. Fedele, *Considerazioni sull'efficacia dei patti nudi nel diritto canonico*, Tolentino 1937, p. 5–90 [= Estratto degli Annali della R. Università di Macerata, 11]; P. Bellini, *L'obbligazione da promessa con oggetto temporale nel sistema canonistico classico con particolare riferimento ai secoli XII e XIII*, [Università degli Studi di Roma, monografie dell'istituto di diritto pubblico della facoltà di giurisprudenza, nuova serie, 19], Milano 1964; O. Behrends, *Treu und Glauben, Zu den christlichen Grundlagen der Willenstheorie im heutigen Vertragsrecht*, in: L. Lombardi Vallauri – G. Dilcher (eds.), Christentum, Säkularisation und modernes Recht, [Per la storia del pensiero giuridico moderno, 11–12], Baden-Baden/Milano 1981, p. 957–1006; Feenstra – Ahsmann, *Contract*; R.H. Helmholz, *Contracts and the canon law*, in: J. Barton (ed.), Towards a general law of contract, [Comparative Studies in Continental and Anglo-American Legal History, 8], Berlin 1990, p. 49–66; P. Landau, *Pacta sunt servanda, Zu den kanonistischen Grundlagen der Privatautonomie*, in: M. Ascheri et al. (eds.), Ins wasser geworfen und Ozeane durchquert, Festschrift für Knut Wolfgang Nörr, Köln – Weimar – Wien 2003, p. 457–474.

[445] *Corpus juris canonici emendatum et notis illustratum, Gregorii XIII iussu editum*, Romae 1582 (= ed. Gregoriana), part. 2, col. 440, l. 10–24: 'Antigonus episcopus dixit: et infra. Aut inita pacta suam obtineant firmitatem, aut conventus (si se non cohibuerit) ecclesiasticam sentiat disciplinam. Universi dixerunt, pax servetur, pacta custodiantur.'

subtraheret alterius populos).[446] The council ruled that the agreement was binding because peace must be maintained and agreements observed (*pax servetur, pacta custodiantur*). The Council of Carthago's settling of this particular dispute is emblematic of the Church's deep-seated conviction that promises are binding. This is witnessed by several decisions taken by its authorities in subsequent centuries, which eventually found their way into Gratian's *Decretum*, such as canon *Quicumque suffragio* (C.12, q.2, c.66), canon *Quia Johannes* (C.12, q.5, c.3) and canon *Iuramenti* (C.22, q.5, c.12).[447]

The ruling by the council of Carthago on the bindingness of agreements was handed down to the medieval canonists through the 7th century *Collectio Hispana* only to re-appear in Bernardo di Pavia's *Breviarium Extravagantium* (1188). He could not have borrowed it from either Burchard von Worms or Yves de Chartres, yet probably took it from the Pseudo-Isidorian decretals.[448] Bernardo di Pavia also excerpted a passage from a letter by Pope Gregory I (600 AD) where he urges the bishop of Cagliari to be sure that promises are kept (*studiose agendum est ut ea, quae promittuntur, opere compleantur*).[449] Remarkably, he did not feel the need to put forward strong arguments as to why naked pacts should be deemed binding. It makes the argumentation of his contemporary and probable master, Huguccio, all the more important.

Indeed, in the same crucial year 1188—which Landau not improperly calls the year of birth of *pacta sunt servanda*—Huguccio published his famous *Summa* of Gratian's *Decretum*.[450] In it, we find a gloss on canon *Quicumque suffragio* (C.12, q.2, c.66) which explains why and how bare agreements should be enforced.[451] Importantly, the argumentation of this early canonist is fundamentally 'moral' in nature, at least from the

---

[446] See gloss *Antigonus episcopus* ad X 1,35,1 in *Corpus juris canonici* (ed. Gregoriana), part. 2, col. 439, l. 65–72.

[447] F. Calasso, *Il negozio giuridico, Lezioni di storia del diritto italiano*, Milano 1967², p. 264–266.

[448] Landau, *Pacta sunt servanda*, p. 458, n. 7 and p. 464–467.

[449] 1 Comp. 1,26,3 (= X 1,35,3); cf. E. Friedberg (ed.), *Quinque compilationes antiquae nec non collectio canonum Lipsiensis*, Lipsiae 1882, p. 10.

[450] On the date of composition of Huguccio's *Summa decretorum*, see W.P. Müller, *Huguccio*, [Studies in Medieval and Early Modern Canon Law, 3], Washington D.C. 1994, p. 68–73.

[451] See C.12, q.2, c.66 in *Corpus juris canonici* (ed. Gregoriana), part. 1, cols. 1345–1346: 'Quicumque episcopi suffragio cuiuslibet aliquid ecclesiasticae utilitatis providerint, et pro eo quodcumque commodum in remunerationem promiserint, promissi solutionem eos exolvere oportebit, ita ut id ad concilium provinciale deferatur, ut eorum conniventia confirmetur, quia (sicut Paulus ait), dignus est operarius mercede sua.'

perspective of the modern reader.[452] According to Huguccio, agreements should be enforced because he who breaks a promise commits a sin. Moreover, he cites the argument, amply discussed in Gratian's *Decretum* (C.22, q.5, c.12) that God does not want there to be a difference between what a Christian says and what he swears. In other words, simple promises are as binding as oaths. Moreover, Huguccio considers circumstances which render the performance of a promise more difficult to be tests of virtuousness.[453]

From the moral foundation of the bindingness of bare agreements, Huguccio infers that the procedural means to demand enforceability is not a normal juridical remedy, i.e. an *actio*. In Huguccio's view, the proper remedy to enforce a naked pact is a typically canonical technique, namely the *officium iudicis*.[454] In this manner he avoids a straightforward confrontation with D. 2,14,7,4, which says that no *actio* lies for naked pacts. However, whether the *officium iudicis* is the appropriate procedural means to enforce a naked pact remains a bone of contention among the canonists.[455] Even if the bindingness of naked promises was never questioned, finding the proper remedy to enforce this principle gave rise to controversy.[456] As we will see below, Pope Innocent IV opted for the *denunciatio evangelica*,

---

The standard gloss *Promiserint* ad C.12, q.2, c.66 (which naturally postdates Huguccio's gloss) states the principle that naked pacts are binding in more express terms, adducing canon *Iuramenti*; cf. *Corpus juris canonici* (ed. Gregoriana), part. 1, col. 1345: 'Videtur quod aliquis obligetur nudis verbis, licet non intercessit stipulatio, ut extra de testa. indicante 22 q.5, et i.e. q.5 quia Ioannes; quod verum est; et potest dici quod competit actio ex nuda promissione, sc. condictio ex canone illo i. 22 q. 2 iuramenti.'

[452] Landau, *Pacta sunt servanda*, p. 463: 'Er begründet den Erfüllungszwang beim einfachen Versprechen mit dem Rückgriff auf den christlichen Sündenbegriff, also mit einer moralischen Kategorie. Darin liegt zweifellos eine Tendenz zur Moralisierung des Rechts, der sog. *Rigor iuris* Huguccios.'

Paradoxically, the end of the sixteenth century witnesses the opposite process of the moralization of canon law, namely the juridification of the moral theology of promise-keeping. For instance, according to Lessius, promises are binding, not merely because the promiser who does not perform commits a sin, but, fundamentally, because promising entails the transfer of a right upon the promisee. Cf. infra.

[453] Müller, *Huguccio*, p. 70–71.

[454] Huguccio, *Summa*, ad C.12, q.2, c.66, cited in Landau, *Pacta sunt servanda*, p. 463, n. 31: 'Sed quam actionem proponet cum ex nudo pacto non oriatur actio? Sed non exigitur ut semper proponatur actio sed simpliciter proponatur factum et postuletur officium iudicis ut ille cogatur ad solvendum promissum.'

On the *officium iudicis* as an *auxilium extraordinarium*, particularly as a way of sanctioning promises in Huguccio, see Roussier, *Le fondement de l'obligation contractuelle*, p. 106–136.

[455] For a brief synthesis of this discussion, see Spies, *De l'observation des simples conventions en droit canonique*, p. x–xi.

[456] Calasso, *Il negozio giuridico*, p. 277–279.

rather than the office of the judge, although Johannes Teutonicus' view would prevail. Teutonicus held that pacts should be enforced through a *condictio ex canone juramenti*, at least in cases involving clergymen.

There are few examples in the history of law that offer as clear evidence to the decisive impact of Christian morality on the formation of the Western legal tradition as the emergence of the consensualist principle in contract law.[457] The call for peace, authenticity and truthfullness that pervades Christianity ended up laying the foundation for a basic legal concept in Western legal culture. Numerous passages from Scripture and the Church Fathers attest to the paramount importance of these moral values.[458] In a text that eventually found its way into the *Liber Extra* (X 5,40,11), Isidore of Seville (ca. 560–636) explained that peace is a condition for agreement. Hence, he claimed that agreement (*pactum*) was etymologically derived from, as well as logically posterior to, peace (*pax*).[459]

Of course, some of the humanist jurists, such as Forcadel,[460] would poke fun at Isidore's naive philosophical account (claiming from a more down-to-earth perspective that peace is the outcome rather than the precondition of agreement), but his etymological effort brilliantly illustrates the intimate connection that was supposed to exist between sound contract law and the establishment of peace. At the apex of scholastic contract doctrine, the Jesuit Pedro de Oñate boasts that 'a vast number of

---

[457] Behrends, *Treu und Glauben*, p. 974–994; H.J. Berman, *The religious sources of general contract law, An historical perspective*, in: Faith and order, The reconciliation of law and religion, [Emory studies in law and religion, 3], Grand Rapids – Cambridge 1993, p. 187–208 [= reprint from Journal of law and religion, 4 (1986), p. 103–124.

[458] For a more detailed overview of the Greek and Latin Church Fathers' insistence on the moral duty to keep promises, see Spies, *De l'observation des simples conventions en droit canonique*, p. 1–22.

[459] Isidore of Seville, *Etymologies*, 5,24,18, in: *Isidori Hispalensis Etymologiarum sive originum libri XX*, recognovit brevique adnotatione critica instruxit W.M. Lindsay, [Scriptorum classicorum bibliotheca Oxoniensis], Oxonii 1911, tom. 1, [s.p.]: 'Pactum dicitur inter partes ex pace conveniens scriptura, legibus ac moribus comprobata.'

[460] In his *Cupido Jurisperitus*, Lugduni 1553, cap. 2, num. 7, p. 16, Forcadel cynically remarks that along Isidore's lines one can at least understand why love affairs fall apart so easily: 'Pactum a pace deduxit Isidorus (...) ne mirum sit pacta amantium non servari, cum pax eorum parvo duret tempore, vigent bella, et quaedam induciae, mox utcunque redeunt in gratiam (...).'
With other humanist jurists, Forcadel shares a low opinion of Isidore, preferring the classical Roman jurists and their rejection of a general law of contract to Isidore's absurd etymological deductions and the Catholic views they hide; see Forcadel, *Necyomantiae sive occultae jurisprudentiae tractatus*, in *Opera S. Forcatuli*, Parisiis 1595, part. 1, dialogo 69, num. 6, p. 159: 'Menander: Non expedit in iis rescriptis quae canonica vocant diem deterere, neque in nugis non prorsus mali grammatici nec boni iurisconsulti Isidori (cuius dicta pro oraculo pontificibus passim referuntur) in cap. pactum de verb. signific.'

irritating and useless disputes and lawsuits have been removed thanks to the conformity of natural law, canon law and Spanish law in regard to the enforceability of naked pacts.'[461] In the eyes of these Christian writers, enforcing agreements, however naked, fosters peace. *Pax* and *pactum* are intrinsically intertwined with one another.

Typically, Biblical and patristic sources found their way into late medieval canon law through Gratian's epochal attempt to harmonize the Christian normative traditions and adopt them to the solution of practical cases. Salient for its impact is canon *Iuramenti* (C.22, q.5, c.12),[462] the preceding rubric of which is telling enough: for Christians, there should be no difference between an oath and a simple statement (*inter iuramentem et locutionem fidelium nulla debet esse differentia*). Hence, breaking a promise is tantamount to perjury and lying.[463] It poses a serious threat to the salvation of the soul. Put differently, in the *Decretum*, the enforceability of contracts is not a theme as such, but forms part of a moral exhortation against lying and falsehood.[464] It is basically a corollary of the moral duty of the promisor to keep his promise. The promisee is able to hold the promisor to the agreement merely in an indirect way, by accusing the promisor with the sin of breaking a promise.

Gratian's *Decretum* in itself, without the gloss, does not contain the principle that naked pacts are binding, let alone a general law of contract. As mentioned before, several canons express the idea that promises are binding. Yet the adage *pacta nuda sunt servanda* emerged only in the glosses of Bernardo di Pavia and Huguccio at the end of the twelfth century.[465]

---

[461] Oñate, *De contractibus*, tom. 1, disp. 2, sect. 5, num. 166, p. 40. For a more ample discussion of Oñate, see below.

[462] See C.22, q.5, c.12 in *Corpus juris canonici* (ed. Gregoriana), part. 1, cols. 1703–1704: 'Iuramenti haec causa est: quia omnis, qui iurat, ad hoc iurat, ut quod uerum est, eloquatur. Et ideo Dominus inter iuramentum, et loquelam nostram, nullam vult esse distantiam: quia, sicut in iuramento nullam convenit esse perfidiam; ita quoque in verbis nostris nullum debet esse mendacium: quia utrumque et periurium et mendacium diuini iudicii poena damnatur, dicente scriptura: Os, quod mentitur, occidit animam. Quisquis ergo verum loquitur, iurat, quia scriptum est: Testis fidelis non mentitur.'

[463] Compare Gratian's d.p. C.22, q.2, c.2 in *Corpus juris canonici* (ed. Gregoriana), part. 1, cols. 1658–1659: 'Item qui falsum iurat, mentitur. Mentiendo autem iurare, nihil aliud est quam peierare. Cum ergo omnes, qui loquuntur mendacium perdendi sint, iuxta illud Psalmistae: Perdes omnes qui loquuntur mendacium, multo magis damnabiles sunt, qui mentiendo peierare convincuntur: quia nomen Dei sui in vanum assumunt.'

[464] The moral foundations of *pacta sunt servanda* are emphasized in Roussier, *Le fondement de l'obligation contractuelle*, p. 1–20.

[465] It remains true, nonetheless, that the enunciation of the *pacta sunt servanda*-rule formed an indispensable stage in the subsequent development of a general law of contracts; see H. Coing, *Common law and civil law in the development of European civilization—*

Moreover, given the fundamentally moral character of the early decretists' emphasis on the bindingness of naked agreements, the decretist had to cope with the question of how this principle could be enforced as a matter of canon law altogether. Huguccio resolved the conundrum by proposing a remedy through the judge's office (*officium judicis*). However, the canonists felt increasingly uncomfortable with this more or less external solution to the problem, trying to found the enforceability on the canons themselves instead. This ambition was accomplished by Johannes Teutonicus in his *Glossa ordinaria* (ca. 1215) on the *Decretum*.

Johannes Teutonicus worked out a solution that would become the majority opinion at least until the fourteenth century.[466] For this, he drew inspiration from a Roman technique to introduce new remedies: the so-called *condictio ex lege*. This is an action that is not mentioned, as such, in the *Corpus Iustinianeum*, and therefore no *actio* in the true sense of the word, but which nevertheless relies on a legal basis.[467] By the same token, Teutonicus argued, there is sufficient textual evidence in the canon law that there should be a remedy to enforce promises. A *condictio ex canone* for the actionability of promises could be construed around C.22, q.5, c.12, regardless of the absence of any express remedy to enforce promises. Accordingly, Johannes Teutonicus calls this action the *condictio ex canone Iuramenti*.[468] For the first time, then, an ordinary juridical means was developed to sanction the breaking of an agreement.[469] Still, the practical significance of this juridical enforcement mechanism remained limited, since it only applied to the clergy. Only if the promise had been joined with an oath could contracts between laymen become subject to the Church's spiritual jurisdiction.[470]

---

possibilities of comparisons, in: H. Coing – K.W. Nörr (eds.), Englische und kontinentale Rechtsgeschichte, Ein Forschungsprojekt, [Comparative studies in continental and Anglo-American legal history, 1], Berlin 1985, p. 36.

[466] For its adoption by Hostiensis, Guillaume Durand and Baldus, amongst many other canonists, see Spies, *De l'observation des simples conventions en droit canonique*, p. 40–65 and p. 72–94.

[467] D. 13,2,1: 'Si obligatio lege nova introducta sit nec cautum eadem lege, quo genere actionis experiamur, ex lege agendum est.'

[468] Glossa *Promiserint* ad C.12, q.2, c.66 in *Corpus juris canonici* (ed. Gregoriana), part. 1, col. 1345: 'Videtur quod aliquis obligetur nudis verbis, licet non intercessit stipulatio (...), quod verum est et potest dici quod competit actio ex nuda promissione, scilicet condictio ex canone illo infra 22, q. 2 (sic) Iuramenti.'

[469] Roussier, *Le fondement de l'obligation contractuelle*, p. 137–148.

[470] See the *caveats* by Helmholz, *Contracts and the canon law*, p. 51.

In 1234, the principle that naked pacts are binding becomes a definitive and substantial part of the canon law through its consecration in X 1,35,1. However, Johannes Teutonicus' proposal that this principle should be enforced through a *condictio ex canone* soon met with fierce and relatively short-lived criticism, coming from a quite unexpected quarter. Trying to reconcile *pacta sunt servanda* with the Roman idea that there lies no action for a naked agreement, Pope Innocent IV recommended an alternative way of enforcing bare agreements: evangelical denunciation (*denuntiatio evangelica*), which, if the convicted person persisted in his sin, could result in excommunication. Innocent thought of naked pacts as producing a natural obligation. In addition, he considered the *denuntiatio evangelica* as the appropriate, universal remedy to enforce natural obligations in the ecclesiastical court.[471] He would have any party bring a claim in the ecclesiastical court by virtue of evangelical denunciation out of charity or even to pursue his own interest.

Pope Innocent IV's argumentation was not taken very seriously by his contemporaries. For example, Hostiensis rejected Innocent's extensive view of the *denunciatio evangelica* as a universal remedy to enforce natural obligations, calling instead for a more restrained use of the remedy.[472] Only later, with canonists such as Francisco Zabarella (1335–1417) and Giovanni d'Imola (ca. 1372–1436), is the enforcement of bare agreements through a *condictio ex canone* being contested again.[473] Yet, at the same time, Innocent IV's establishing evangelical denunciation as the interface in between natural law and canon law might explain why he was widely appreciated by moral theologians. Pope Innocent IV's alternative solution is not insignificant for the simple reason that even the advocates of Teutonicus' opinion considered the field of application of the *condictio ex canone iurmanenti* to be restricted to the clergy. As Baldus de Ubaldis (1327–1400) and Felinus Sandaeus (1444–1503) famously put it, excluding the lands of the Church, the common opinion does not concern lay

---

471 Innocentius IV, *Apparatus in quinque libros Decretalium*, Francoforti ad Moenum 1570, ad X 2,1,13, f. 193r, num. 4: 'Item dicimus quod iste modus agendi habet locum ubi aliquod temporale, in quo est reus naturaliter obligatus, debet dari vel fieri, etiam si ad illud petendum nulla competit actio civilis vel canonica ut quando quis iuravit dare vel facere sine stipulatione locum habet denunciatio ut hîc. Et est idem in omnibus aliis quae debent dari vel fieri et peccat qui promisit nisi promissum impleat, ut hîc, ubi dicit quod ad papam pertinet de omni peccato mortali quemlibet corripere.'
472 Landau, *Pacta sunt servanda*, p. 471, n. 66.
473 Spies, *De l'observation des simples conventions en droit canonique*, p. 98–113, and Bellini, *Denunciatio evangelica*, p. 120 and p. 128.

people.[474] Consequently, lay people have to appeal to the *denunciatio evangelica* if they wish to enforce a promise. Baldus' and Sandaeus' opinion would become mainstream in the moral theological tradition.[475] Still, dissenting opinions circulated. It should not be forgotten, for instance, that Abbas Panormitanus advocated the universal applicability of a canonical remedy for enforcing promises, for laymen as well. Panormitanus cared less about the appropriateness of a specific remedy than about its general availability.[476]

Apart from the initial discussions on the appropriate remedy for enforcing naked pacts, canonists throughout the late Middle ages unanimously agreed on the religious foundations of *pacta sunt servanda*. Famous *doctores utriusque iuris* such as the aforementioned Antonio de Butrio remained very explicit about the moral grounds for enforcing naked pacts as indicated in Gratian (C.22, q.5, c.12). 'Canon law strives for the good and the equitable in God's eyes (*bonum et aequum secundum Deum*) and God does not distinguish between oaths and simple statements,' he remarks.[477] Butrio infers from this that 'consequently, as a matter of canon law, a pact, however naked, has force, since it has force in the eyes of God.' Another reason he gives for the canon law to enforce naked pacts is that canon

---

[474] Baldus de Ubaldis, *Commentaria in quartum et quintum Codicis libros*, Lugduni 1585, ad C. 4,32,16, num. 16–18, f. 107v: 'Illud c. [novit] intelligitur in clericis vel laicis subiectis ecclesiae quo ad temporalem iurisdictionem. In aliis autem nullum est remedium nisi per viam evangelicae denunciationis, in qua requiritur peccatum et qui denunciatur sciat vel scire debeat se teneri (...). Cum non scit, facit contra conscientiam; est autem conscientia sensus animi cognoscentis bonum et malum; cum vero debet scire, habet conscientiam erroneam et ideo cogitur ad correctionem erroris. Nam errare in eo in quo non est errandum, est peccatum (...).'; Felinus Sandaeus, *Commentaria in quinque libros Decretalium*, Basileae 1567, ad X 1,35,1, part. 1, col. 1402, num. 10: 'Inter laicos subiectos imperio non habet locum ista communis opinio (...) Sed inter eos habet locum denunciatio evangelica, quam possunt practicare in curia episcopi, secundum omnes hîc (...) Sed in terris subiectis ecclesiae, bene habet locum communis opinio etiam in foro seculari, quia in terris ecclesiae praevalet canon legi, et in foro seculari.'

[475] See Molina, below.

[476] Abbas Panormitanus, *Commentaria super Decretalibus*, Augustae Taurinorum 1577, tom. 2 (*Super secunda parte libri primi Decretalium*), ad X 1,35,1, f. 132v, num. 5: '(...) in effectu non refert, an detur actio seu condictio ex lege, vel officii imploratio, dummodo concludamus in iudicem ecclesiasticum posse etiam laicum praecise compellere ad observantiam pacti.'

[477] Antonio de Butrio, *Super Decretalibus commentarii*, ad X 1,35,1, f. 94v, num 7: 'Item ius canonicum assequitur bonum et aequum secundum Deum, sed Deus inter simplicem loquelam et iuramentum non facit differentiam, 22, q.5 iuramenti: ergo secundum ius canonicum pactum habet firmitatem, quantumcumque nudum, quia habet quantum ad Deum.'

law conforms to the ends of natural law, bare agreements being binding as a matter of natural law, which for him is synonymous with divine law.

Similar reference to divine order (*divina ordinatio*) as the basis for *pacta quantumcumque nuda sunt servanda* is contained in Baldus de Ubaldis' commentary on X 1,35,1.[478] However, Baldus also qualifies the rule that all agreements are binding in a way that has troubled scholars from the Middle Ages till the present day:[479] 'In that text, nl. *pacta custodiantur etc.*, no distinction is made between naked and vested agreements, since God and good conscience do not make that distinction either, provided that there is a *causa* which could be brought into a stipulation.' Having been trained both as a canonists and a civilian, Baldus infuses the canon law of naked pacts with a notion, *causa*, derived from the Roman law on innominate contracts and stipulations, which had already formed the subject of brief annotations by the glossators. Yet, at least from the renaissance of Aristotelian metaphysics in the 13th century and its Christian reformulation in Thomas Aquinas, this concept simultaneously evoked associations with the Greek philosophy of being. Some of that philosophical tradition resonates in Baldus, for instance when he states that 'there is no caused thing where there is no cause', inferring from this that the action to a pact, being a caused thing, cannot exist without there being a cause for its being.[480] The elusiveness of *causa* might derive, at least in part, from this coming together of different legal and intellectual traditions.

3.2.2.2   Causa

Given the multiple contexts in which the notion of *causa* comes to the fore, it is not surprising to find that the meaning of *causa* remains obscure, despite generations of scholars having given full rein to their exegetical creativity when trying to find its historically correct interpretation. Already in the late sixteenth century, Molina complained that the jurists had made a mess out of the doctrine of *causa*. Given our methodological focus on the early modern scholastics, it falls outside the scope of this monograph to settle the dispute regarding the multiple significations of

---

478 Baldus, *Super Decretalibus*, ad X 1,35,1, num. 5, f. 112r.

479 Baldus, *Super Decretalibus*, ad X 1,35,1, num. 5, f. 112r: 'In tex. ibi pacta custodiantur non distinguunt inter nuda et vestita: quia nec Deus nec bona conscientia distinguit dummodo talis causa subsit quae esset deducibilis in stipulationem.'

480 Baldus, *Super Decretalibus*, ad X 1,35,1, num. 8, f. 111v: 'Ubi non est causa ibi non est causatum, et immo ex pacto nudo non insurgit actio, quia actio est quoddam causatum, ergo non potest sine causa oriri (...)'.

causa throughout the centuries. We cannot afford to investigate the possible connections and disconnections between the continental tradition on *causa* and the common law notion of *consideration* either.[481] Modesty demands that we rely on recent scholarship to lift just a tiny corner of the veil that covers the meaning of *causa* in general contract law. In any case, we think that future scholarship on this topic will continue to fail to come to grips with *causa* unless the following caveats expressed by two outstanding scholars in Roman law are taken seriously.

In his study advocating a procedural understanding of *causa* in the Roman texts on *stipulatio*, Laurent Waelkens points out that *causa* received a plethora of different meanings over the centuries. As regards the *stipulatio sine causa*, for instance, he advocates a methodology in three steps to come closer to the truly historical meaning of D. 44,4,2,3.[482] Firstly, the medieval, early modern and contemporary layers of interpretation that condition our understanding of the *stipulatio sine causa* should be bracketed out. Secondly, awareness is needed of the fundamentally procedural character of Roman law as opposed to the substantial approach to law during the medieval *ius commune* and in contemporary civil legal systems. Thirdly, a linguistic sensitivity is required to the different meanings

---

[481] It should be sufficient to note here that at least in regard to certain notions of *causa* and certain notions of *consideration*, prominent scholars have found evidence of interaction between the continental and common law traditions; see A. Guzmán Brito, *La doctrina de la consideration en Blackstone y sus relationes con la causa en el ius commune*, in: id., Actio, negocio, contrato y causa en la tradición del derecho Europeo e Iberoamericano, Navarra 2005, p. 441–477 [= reprint from Revista de estudios histórico-jurídicos, 25 (2003), p. 375–406].
Gordley suggests that, despite similarities that persist until Blackstone and occasionally even beyond, the common law eventually departed from the doctrine of *causa* because the purpose of the common law judges was to limit the promises that could be enforced in *assumpsit*, therefore refusing to enforce gratuitous promises, even though, in terms of the *ius commune*, liberality could constitute a legitimate *causa*; cf. Gordley, *The philosophical origins of modern contract doctrine*, p. 137–139. However, clear indications of the exclusion of gratuitous agreements from the domain of enforceable contracts can already be found in the fourteenth and fifteenth century common law; cf. D. Ibbetson, *A Historical introduction to the law of obligations*, Oxford 1999, p. 80–83.
For a study of the sixteenth century notion of *consideration* in the common law, see J. Baker, *Origins of the 'doctrine' of consideration, 1535–1585*, in: M.S. Arnold (ed.), On the laws and customs of England, Essays in honor of Samuel E. Thorne, Chapel Hill 1981, p. 336–358; D. Ibbetson, *Consideration and the theory of contract in sixteenth century common law*, in: J. Barton (ed.), Towards a general law of contract, [Comparative studies in continental and Anglo-American legal history, 8], Berlin 1990, p. 67–123; Baker, *The Oxford history of the laws of England, Vol. 6: 1483–1558*, p. 862–868.
[482] L. Waelkens, *La cause de D. 44,4,2,3*, Tijdschrift voor Rechtsgeschiedenis, 75 (2007), p. 204.

of *causa* in other contexts within the *Corpus Iustinianeum* itself.[483] All in all, this is a much wider applicable methodology, which makes operational the lucid plea for a functional approach to the history of private law as promoted by the late Yan Thomas. Undoubtedly inspired by Derrida's deconstructivist analysis of language, Thomas warned historians of law not to turn a largely contingent concept such as *causa* into an absolute entity leading a sort of metaphysical life.[484]

In recent years, a similar concern to find a historically correct understanding of *causa* seems to have been at the basis of at least three contributions to the debate by Antonio Guzmán Brito, Raffaele Volante, and Italo Birocchi. In an impressive article, Guzmán Brito writes the history of *causa* from ancient times until the present, carefully paying attention to discontinuities and ruptures as well as to apparent similarities.[485] In his frequently cited monograph, Birocchi analyzes the emergence of *causa* in conjunction with the rise of a general law of contract in the sixteenth century. In a more specialized volume, Volante dwells on the distinction

---

[483] The upshot of the application of this methodology to D. 44,4,2,3 is that *causa* must be taken in that context to mean something like a juridical act; cf. Waelkens, *La cause*, p. 209: 'A chaque fois que la signification la plus conforme au sens général de *causa* semble être celle d'acte juridique. L'expression *sine causa* apparaît plusieurs fois en dehors de D. 44,4,2,3 et sa meilleure traduction semble également être "sans acte juridique" et quelquefois "sans procès". (...) Vu tout ce qui précède, nous sommes tentés de la traduire par une stipulation faite sans problèmes, sans conflit, sans controverse. (...) En tout cas il n'est pas nécessaire d'y voir ni la causalité des Temps Modernes ni l'absence de contreprestation des romanistes qui ont combiné la causalité moderne avec la *causa finalis* médiévale.'

[484] Y. Thomas, review of Carlos Cossio, *La causa y la comprension en el derecho*, Buenos Aires 1969, in: *Dimensions religieuses du droit et notamment sur l'apport de Saint Thomas D'Aquin*, [Archives de philosophie du droit, 18], Paris 1973, p. 464–467: 'Le problème soulevé par la présence éventuelle du concept de causa dans un système juridique donné doit être traité à partir des seuls éléments de ce système. C'est dire que toute recherche sur ce sujet devrait se ramener à la question de savoir si tel droit (par exemple, le droit romain; la common law; le droit français à partir du code civil) fait appel à la notion de cause (...) et, dans l'affirmative, quelle fonction remplit, au sein du système, un tel instrument. Or, d'une part, il n'est pas évident que tous les systèmes utilisent ou aient utilisé une notion qui n'a rien d'universel: à cet égard, une approche philosophique du sujet risque de poser en absolu ce qui n'est qu'un moyen relatif, dans le temps et dans l'espace, que le droit peut se donner.' Compare the methodological remarks in Y. Thomas, *Le langage du droit romain, Problèmes et methodes*, in: Le langage du droit, [Archives de philosophie du droit, 19], Paris 1974, p. 339–346 and in E. Falzone, *Poena et emenda, Les sanctions pénale et non pénale dans le droit canonique médiéval et la pratique des officialités*, in: M.-A. Bourguignon – B. Dauven – X. Rousseaux (eds.), La sanction juridique du XIIIe au XXe siècle, Actes des journées d'étude (19–20 octobre, Louvain-la-Neuve), Louvain 2012 [forthcoming].

[485] See A. Guzmán Brito, *Causa del contrato y causa de la obligación en la dogmática de los juristas romanos, medievales y modernos y en la codificación europea y americana*, in: id., Actio, negocio, contrato y causa en la tradición del derecho Europeo e Iberoamericano, Navarra 2005, p. 197–406 [= reprint of Revista de estudios histórico-jurídicos, 23 (2001), p. 209–367].

between *causa finalis* and *causa impulsiva*, famously made by Azo in his commentary on title *De condictionibus ob causam datorum*.[486] He concludes that the distinction between these two *causae* should not be understood in modern terms as a differentiation between the intrinsic, State-guaranteed, socio-economic function of a contract (*causa finalis*) and the highly personal motivation (*causa impulsiva*) that lies behind the contract.[487] According to Volante, even the final cause merely points to 'a relation between facts that have acquired normative value through the preceding agreement between the parties'.[488]

Interestingly, Birocchi associates the penetration of the State into contract law through the concept of *causa* with Hermann Vultejus (1555–1634) amongst others.[489] In Vultejus' view, only those agreements that are backed up by the civil law, or, as he puts it, those agreements that have *causa*, are enforceable.[490] In this context, *causa* is closely intertwined

---

[486] Azo, *Summa codicis et institutionum*, Venetiae 1499, lib. 4, ad C. 4,6, f. 67r: 'Inducit autem istam actionem [sc. condictionem ob causam datorum] causae defectus ut ff. de condictione ob turpem causam, lex prima, § ob rem igitur [= D. 12,5,1,1]; hoc ita si causa fuerit finalis, id est qua finita vel non completa voluit uterque restitui quod datum est. Secus si fuerit impulsiva causa id est in corde tradentis retenta ob quam impellebatur animo suo ad dandum illa, nam non secuta non parit repetitionem, ut puta dedi tibi ut te mihi redderem amiciorem vel ut te provocarem ad proficiscendum mecum nec profectus es nec amicior factus es, non ideo datur repetitio.' This text has been considered as seminal in the development of a theory of 'causa negoziale' by E. Cortese, *Il diritto nella storia medievale, II. Il basso medioevo*, Roma 1995, p. 189.

[487] Volante, *Il sistema contrattuale del diritto comune classico*, p. 294–300 and p. 307.

[488] Volante, *Il sistema contrattuale del diritto comune classico*, p. 297.

[489] Hermann Vultejus, *Jurisprudentia Romana a Justiniano composita*, Marpurgi Cattorum 1628, lib. 1, cap. 26, p. 157: 'Causa summa, quae omnibus aliis juris effectibus est communis, est jus: inferior hominis factum, quod obligationi occasionem magis praebet, quam ut obligationem inducat. Etsi enim ut obligatio constituatur mens atque voluntas ut plurimum sit necessaria, ex ea tamen obligatio oritur, non quod homo ita velit, sed quod jus ex facto ejusmodi obligationem oriri concedat; et e diverso saepe fit, ut homo obligari nolit, obligetur tamen nihilominus, si ejusmodi aliquid fecerit, ex quo jus ipsum obligari voluit. Jus igitur causa obligationis est proxima, factum hominis remota: et haec sine qua non, illa principalis.' This passage is partially cited in Birocchi, *Causa e categoria generale del contratto*, p. 143, n. 17.

See also Birocchi, *Causa e categoria generale del contratto*, p. 176–177: 'Si può parlare di una dialettica tra *causa proxima* (individuata nel *ius*) e *causa remota* (individuata nella volontà delle parti), in cui però tutta l'enfasi è posta sulla prima: il contratto—inteso obiettivamente come effetti che si producono—è tale non tanto perché le parti l'hanno voluto (questo è solo il presupposto), quanto perché l'ordinamento così ha disposto.' Birocchi also discusses similar tendencies to introduce the approbation of State power into contract law in Hugues Doneau and Giulio Pace; see *Causa e categoria generale del contratto*, p. 137–202.

[490] Vultejus, *Jurisprudentia Romana*, lib. 1, cap. 30, p. 168: 'Conventio quae causam habet, contractus dicitur, unde contractum definio quod sit conventio cum causa. Causa autem negocium est, quod cum a jure probatum sit, facit ut obligatio ex contractu sit, et ex contractu actio.'

with a new theory of law trying to explain the transition from facts to norms by the intervention of an institution, namely the State, which has the monopoly over civil law to decide what facts are of normative value by granting *causa* to it. At the same time, this new doctrine of *causa* instantiates the separation of the individual and the community, or, alternatively, of the private and the public.[491] This sounds very modern. Not surprisingly, Vultejus was familiar with the thought of French jurists such as Jean Bodin and Hugues Doneau. Incidentally, he had been a student of Doneau at Heidelberg somewhere between 1571 and 1574,[492] eventually publishing his *Jurisprudentia Romana* in 1590, at about the same moment Doneau's *Commentaria iuris civilis* appeared.[493] In Doneau, the same dichotomy is present between the factual consent of the parties and its endorsement by the civil law as a necessary condition for its enforceability.[494]

It is precisely in the work of Hugues Doneau, or, better still, in the Aristotelian interpretation of Doneau by Oskar Hilliger, that Laurent Waelkens perceives the problems of the modern notion of *causa*.[495] As we have mentioned in the section on the classicial convulsions in 16th century law, the humanist jurists, mostly protestants, could not identify with the canon law tradition. They scornfully rejected the canonists as servants of 'papal law'. What they wanted was to restore the pristine Roman law of contract. What is distinctly modern about this return to Roman law is the reduction

---

491 See I. Birocchi, *Causa e definizione del contratto nella dottrina del Cinquecento*, in: L. Vacca (ed.), Causa e contratto nella prospettiva storico-comparatistica, II Congresso Internazionale ARISTEC, Palermo, 7–8 giugno 1995, Torino 1997, p. 212: 'Quell'istanza è dunque, nel contempo, un'istanza di liberazione dell'individuo, che rientra in primo luogo nel processo di separazione dell'individuo dalla comunità o, il che è lo stesso, del privato dal pubblico; e, come è noto, è allora che comincia ad acquistare autonomia lo studio e l'insegnamento del diritto pubblico.'

492 See A. Mazzacane, *Umanesimo e sistematiche giuridiche in Germania alla fine del Cinquecento, equità e giurisprudenza nelle opere di Herman Vultejus*, Annali di Storia del Diritto, 12–13 (1968–1969), p. 257–319.

493 The *Commentaria iuris civilis* successively appeared in 1589 (books 1–5), 1590 (books 6–11) and 1595–1596 (books 12–28); cf. Birocchi, *Causa e categoria generale del contratto*, p. 179, n. 132.

494 Cf. Doneau, *Commentaria iuris civilis*, lib. 12, cap. 6: 'Duorum pluriumve consensus in hoc, ut unus alteri quid det aut faciat, jure ad eam rem et praestationem comprobatus.' Compare Birocchi, *Causa e categoria generale del contratto*, p. 186–187: 'Come a più riprese ribadiva il giurista ugonotto, l'*approbatio* significava che l'accordo teso a stabilire una obbligazione di dare o fare raggiungeva il suo fine solo a certe condizioni previste dall'ordinamento. Salvo ritornare su questo punto centrale della dottrina di Doneau, si può dire comunque che concretamente esso svolgesse le funzioni che nella concezione di Vultejus erano assegnate alla *causa*.'

495 L. Waelkens, *De oorsprong van de causaliteit bij contractuele verbintenissen*, in: B. Dauwe e.a. (eds.), Liber Amicorum Ludovic De Gryse, Brussel 2010, p. 676–679.

of the plurality of normative sources—typical of the medieval period—to the State-backed civil law as the only source of legal validity. In a fairly conservative manner, Doneau repeats D. 2,14,7,4, stating that no action lies for a pact unless there is *causa*. However, he unwittingly implements the ideas of the canonists by interpreting pact as any agreement.[496] Now let us combine this with the insight, revealed by Birocchi, that *causa* in Doneau is to be understood as the approval by the State. Then perhaps one could argue that in Doneau, *causa* comes close to the function it seems to have in, for instance, art. 1131 of the French Civil Code.

The early modern theologians did not think along the lines of Vultejus or Doneau. They still lived in the late medieval universe where several competing legal orders co-existed. This is one of the reasons why their thought is often considered as 'early modern' and not as 'modern'.[497] Moreover, when taking a closer look at the early modern scholastic writings, one has to admit that, in fact, *causa* is not the subject of autonomous discussions in their treatises in the first place. We may not have to infer from this that the concept of *causa* did not play any role for them. At first sight, their notion of *causa* was chiefly related to their consensualist doctrine of contract, a lack of *causa* indicating mistake and, hence, the absence of a ground for the contract to exist because of lack of consent. Distinctions such as between *causa finalis* and *causa impulsiva*, or between *causa proxima* and *causa remota*, do not appear to be fundamental concepts in their thinking on contracts. This should not come as a surprise. As we have seen, the context in which these pairs of concepts were created by Azo and Vultejus, respectively, radically differ from the context in which the scholastics dealt with contract law.

Interestingly, while scholars such as Vultejus were reshaping the debate on *causa* and contract, adapting it to a new type of society, Luís de Molina was writing his voluminous treatise *De iustitia et iure*, published, partially posthumously, between 1593 and 1609. Its second volume was entirely dedicated to contract law. Even more curiously, at the outset of his discussion on the bindingness of agreements, we find him making a unique effort to explain the meaning of the doctrines of *causa* in the civilian tradition and the canon law tradition, respectively. The scope of his exposition is to clarify the meaning of *causa*. He does not mean to be original. Yet his

---

[496] Waelkens, *De oorsprong van de causaliteit*, p. 678.

[497] Compare M. Meccarelli, *Ein Rechtsformat für die Moderne, Lex und Iurisdictio in der spanischen Spätscholastik*, in: C. Strohm – H. de Wall (eds.), Konfessionalität und Jurisprudenz in der frühen Neuzeit, [Historische Forschungen, 89], Berlin 2009, p. 285–311.

synthesis of both normative traditions brilliantly highlights that he as well as other moral theologians of the early modern period fully realized that the meaning of *causa* within the system of canon law was fundamentally different from the role *causa* plays in the civilian tradition. It also gives us an exceptional insight into the moral theologians' perception of the meaning of *causa* in normative traditions other than natural law.

Addressing the question of the enforceability of innominate contracts in the civilian tradition, Molina cites paragraph *Sed cum nulla* (D. 2,14,7,4). In other words, if there is *causa* to the bare agreement or innominate contract, then the general rule that bare agreements are not actionable as a matter of civil law does not apply. Molina's phrasing is more precise and is worthwhile mentioning:[498]

> An exception lies [against an action to enforce an innominate contract] unless an act (*factum*) intervenes or a cause (*causa*) that lies in the nature of things and on account of which something is owed beyond the agreement, or unless those bare agreements are added and sticked directly, not after a certain time, to a nominate contract or to a contract in which an act or cause intervenes.

Molina illustrates what he means by this through the following example.[499] Let us assume that we agree that I exchange twenty sheep for your one ox. This is a bare agreement or an innominate contract, since this type of exchange has not received a particular name in Roman law. Therefore, a *vestimentum* is needed to make this agreement enforceable. One possibility is to use solemn verbs so as to turn this agreement into a *stipulatio*. Another possibility, though, is that I give you the twenty sheep. Through this act of conveyance (*traditio*), or, put differently, through this objective

---

[498] Molina, *De iustitia et iure*, tom. 2 (*De contractibus*), tract. 2, disp. 255, col. 13, num. 1: 'Excipitur nisi vel interveniat factum seu causa posita in rerum natura, ob quam, ultra conventionem, sit iam aliquid debitum, vel nisi eiusmodi pacta in continenti et non ex intervallo cohaereant et coniungantur cum contractu aliquo nominato, aut cum contractu in quo intervenit factum seu causa.'

[499] Molina, *De iustitia et iure*, tom. 2 (*De contractibus*), tract. 2, disp. 255, col. 14, num. 4: 'Simili modo, si eodem nudo pacto de commutandis viginti ovibus pro uno bove superveniret, non quidem stipulatio, sed traditio ex altera parte, quia vel tu traderes alteri viginti oves, vel alter traderet tibi bovem, eo ipso pactum illud maneret vestitum ea traditione et causa, propter quam, ultra pactum, is qui nondum ex sua parte contractum implevit, obligatus civiliter maneret ei, qui implevit, ac proinde huic, qui implevit, conceditur actio, quam iura praescriptis verbis aut in factum vocant, qua, si alter tempore debito ex sua parte non impleat, cogere illum potest, vel ad interesse, nempe ut, quod promisit, solvat, aut quantum id solvisse sua intererat, vel ut condictio seu actio ut sibi restituat, quod accepit, tanquam datum ob causam, causa non sequuta, optioque est penes eum qui implevit, ut agat, quo ex his duobus maluerit modis.'

act (*causa posita in rerum natura*), I have an action in court to claim the ox or to claim compensation. The foundation of this action lies beyond the agreement itself. The action is called an *actio praescriptis verbis* or an *actio in factum*. Because of my preceding act, it becomes now possible for me to demand in court either that your promise be enforced or that I get a full compensation. Alternatively, I can urge you to give back what I gave you through a *condictio causa data causa non secuta*. It is up to me to decide whether I want to use rather the *actio* or the *condictio*.

The disjunction of *factum* and *causa* might require some historical explanation.[500] Originally, the Romans would only consider an innominate contract in which the first performance was a *datio* as a bare agreement that could be enforced by virtue of the preceding *causa*.[501] This is notably the case in the innominate contracts *do ut des* and *do ut facias*. However, the glossators held that the same regime must apply to the two other types of innominate contracts, involving a *factum* as the first act, namely *facio ut des* and *facio ut facias*.[502] Consequently, *causa* in the Roman sense of a preceding act that makes an innominate contract enforceable beyond the agreement itself consisted of either a *datio* or a *factum*. The Accursian gloss clearly indicates this.[503] Probably Molina wanted to separate the original Roman meaning of *causa* from the medieval extension of its meaning by using the expression *factum seu causa*, thus implying that *causa* originally coincided with *datio*.[504]

Having explained the civilian notion of *causa*, Molina then goes on to elucidate the meaning of *causa* in the canon law tradition. His direct sources of inspiration appear to be Felinus Sandaeus and Diego de Covarruvias y Leyva. He sets out by recalling the motivation behind the canon

---

[500] For which we rely on the considerations in A. Guzmán Brito, *La doctrina de Luis de Molina sobra la causa contractual*, in: id., Actio, negocio, contrato y causa en la tradición del derecho Europeo e Iberoamericano, Navarra 2005, p. 413–415 and p. 420–423.

[501] D. 2,14,7,2.

[502] D. 19,5,5,1.

[503] Glossa *Causa* ad D. 2,14,7,2 in *Corporis Iustinianaei Digestum vetus* (ed. Gothofredi), tom. 1, col. 261: 'id est datio vel factum quod vestiet pactum'; Compare glossa *Causa* and glossa *Igitur* ad D. 2,14,7,4 in *Corporis Iustinianaei Digestum vetus* (ed. Gothofredi), tom. 1, col. 262.

[504] On other occasions, though, he seems to use *causa* as a generic term, mentioning *factum* and *traditio* as its species. Then, *traditio* seems to be tantamount to *datio*. Cf. Molina, *De iustitia et iure*, tom. 2 (*De contractibus*), tract. 2, disp. 255, col. 13, num. 3: 'Ratio est, quoniam contractus ille est innominatus, do ut des, ex nulloque capite transit in contractum nominatum et ex neutra parte intervenit traditio, factum, seu causa, unde, ultra pactum, unus alteri teneretur, neque cohaeret in continenti cum aliquo alio contractu.'

law enforcing naked pacts:[505] for the sake of reason (*ratio*) and the salvation of the soul (*salus animarum*), canon law must conform to the dictates of the court of conscience, where there is no doubt whatsoever regarding the natural obligation ensuing from a bare agreement. Still, this principle is to be qualified in two ways. First of all, the enforceability of naked pacts is limited to the clergy and to lay people living in territories ruled by the Church. In other cases, laymen have to enforce their claims indirectly through evangelical denunciation. Secondly, the *causa* underlying the naked agreement should be expressed. Both qualifications can be ultimately traced back to Baldus.[506]

The expression of cause (*causae expressio*) is a notorious requirement for the actionability of bare agreements in the ecclesiastical courts. It shifts the burden of proof to the plaintiff if he wants to enforce the obligation of the defendant despite there being no cause expressed. Conversely, if the cause is expressed, then the defendant can now only discharge himself of his obligation by proving that he was actually mistaken about the cause or that there actually was no cause at all. The fundamental reason why the expression of *causa* was deemed essential for an agreement to becoming binding as a matter of canon law, is because the canonists modelled the canon law of contract on the Roman *stipulatio*.[507] As Covarruvias explains:[508]

---

505 Molina, *De iustitia et iure*, tom. 2 (*De contractibus*), tract. 2, disp. 257, col. 19, num. 2: 'Cum enim ex pacto nudo naturalis obligatio oriatur, hominesque in conscientiae foro nudis pactis, ut ostensum est, stare teneantur, utique ratio, animarumque salus ac bonum postulabant, ut canonico iure ex pacto nudo actio concederetur, quod et factum est.'

506 Cf. supra, p. 130.

507 Molina, *De iustitia et iure*, tom. 2 (*De contractibus*), tract. 2, disp. 257, col. 20, num. 9: 'Confirmant doctores citati, quando causa non est expressa, aut aliunde non sufficienter probatur, iure canonico non concedi actionem ex pacto nudo, qua reus pactum implere cogatur, quoniam non plus iure canonico conceditur actio ex pacto nudo, quam iure civili ex stipulatione concedatur. Sed iure civili ex stipulatione non conceditur actio, qua promittens stare cogatur promissis, nisi expressa fuerit promissionis causa, sive ea fuerit donationis titulus sive aliqua alia, ut patet l. 2, par. circa, ff. de doli exceptione. Quamvis enim de stipulatione et promissione subsequuta constet, si tamen causa talis promissionis non fuit expressa, potest, qui promisit, opponere ei, qui iudicio secum contendit ut stet promissis, dolo malo agere, eo quod adimpleta non sit causa, ob quam promisit. Dicet namque, se promisisse dare illi centum tali die propter totidem, quae mutuo ab eo erat accepturus, neque accepit vel propter aliam similem causam, quae non extitit, et tunc ad actorem pertinebit probare, causam fuisse impletum aut donationis titulo ea promisisse. Eadem ergo ratione ex pacto nudo non concedetur actio iure canonico, nisi de causa constet ob quam aliquid fuit promissum.'

508 Covarruvias, *Relectio in cap. quamvis pactum*, part. 2, par. 5, num. 14, p. 274: 'Nam pactum iure canonico non habet maiorem vim, quam habeat stipulatio iure civili, sed stipulatio sine causa non habet actionem quo ad effectum, l. 2, par. circa, ff. de doli exceptio [= D. 44,4,2,3], igitur nec pactum nudum'. Whether the canonists were reading the

As a matter of canon law, a pact does not have more force than a stipulation as a matter of civil law. Now a stipulation without cause does not have an action in regard to its effect, as can be derived from D. 44,4,2,3. Hence, neither does a naked pact.

The shadow of the Roman *stipulatio* sometimes complicated matters, notably in regard to the question whether a pact without expressed cause should be presumed to be a donation. Felinus argued on the basis of law *Campanus* (D. 38,1,47) that since there was a presumption of gift in stipulations without cause, the same presumption should lie in naked pacts as a matter of canon law.[509] Following Covarruvias, Molina rejected this argument. A presumption of donation in a pact without expressed cause could only lie if, first, the promisee proved that the promisor knew that there was no other cause for promising at the moment of concluding the agreement. Also, a presumption of donation could lie if it was an established fact that the promisee disposed of this knowledge, excluding doubt or mistake. Yet in principle, a pact without cause must not be presumed to have a gift as its cause.[510]

The fact that donation is not presumed as a cause does not mean that the *animus donandi* or liberality cannot constitute a valid *causa* producing a remedy to enforce an agreement.[511] This may be especially worthwhile

---

Roman text in its authentic sense here, could be disputed on the grounds of Waelkens, *La cause*, supra n. 483.

[509] Felinus, *Commentaria in quinque libros Decretalium*, col. 1404, num. 15. It is not entirely clear, though, how Felinus could have inferred this conclusion from law *Campanus*; cf. *Infortiatum*, in: *Corpus Iustinianeum* (ed. Godofredi), tom. 2, col. 1929: 'Campanus scribit, non debere praetorem pati donum, munus, operas imponi ei qui ex fideicommissi causa manumittatur. Sed si cum sciret posse se id recusare, obligari se passus sit, non inhibendam operarum petitionem, quia donasse videtur.'

[510] Molina, *De iustitia et iure*, tom. 2 (*De contractibus*), tract. 2, disp. 257, col. 20, num. 5: 'Quod si quis ita obijciat, qui absque causae expressione promittit, donare voluisse praesumitur, iuxta l. Campanus, ff. de operis libertorum, quando ergo in scriptura continetur debitum, neque expressa est causa, praesumendum est fuisse donationem, isque qui promisit, cogendus est solvere, nisi ipse contrarium probet. Dicendum est, id intelligendum esse, quando constat, aut sufficienter probatur, eum, qui promisit, habuisse scientiam dum promittebat, nullam aliam subesse causam, ex qua promitteret, ut ex verbis eiusdem legis constat; tunc enim donasse praesumitur. Si tamen constet, promittentem credidisse aliquam subesse causam, quae non erat, aut simus in dubio an forte ductus causa aliqua, quae non suberat, vel quae non est sortita effectum, promisit, tunc non tam vehementer praesumitur donare voluisse, ut cogatur stare pacto nudo.'

[511] This point has been stressed by James Gordley, who emphasizes that the late scholastics thought of contract as 'either acts of commutative justice or acts of liberality'; cf. Gordley, *The philosophical origins of modern contract doctrine*, p. 73. When speaking of the Jesuit moral theologians such as Molina, Lessius and Oñate, it could perhaps be slightly more precise to say that they conceived of the *causa* of a contract to be either onerous

noticing, given that contemporary courts in the common law are reluctant to enforce gratuitous promises for want of consideration. As Molina observes, donation is a title that grants sufficient *causa* for the donee to claim the gift in court. If the deed of gift expressly mentions this title, then the contract is enforceable. By the same token, if the donee convincingly proves that liberality or compassion was the cause behind the contract, then he can claim the gift in court. Moreover, this holds not only true in the ecclesiastical courts, but also in the secular courts. For, allegedly, by virtue of law *Si quis argentum* (C. 8,53,35), the naked pact to make a gift was turned into a *pactum legitimum* which is enforceable in court.[512]

Last, Molina addresses the question to what extent the concept of *causa* in the civil law tradition and the requirement of *causa* in the canon law are the same or differ. He expressly makes an attempt at elucidating a point, which, to say the least, has been treated by others in inferior manners (*non ut oportet loquantur*).[513] He concludes that the difference of the understanding of *causa* by the canonists and the civilians is huge.[514] Molina also explains why:[515]

---

or gratuitous, while considering the rights and obligations ensuing from contract to be governed by the virtue of commutative justice.

[512] Along with the so-called *pacta praetoria*, the *pacta legitima* were recognized as exceptions to D. 2,14,7,4. On these agreements, which were privileged by the praetor or the law, see Deroussin, *Histoire du droit des obligations*, p. 128–130.

[513] Molina, *De iustitia et iure*, tom. 2 (*De contractibus*), tract. 2, disp. 257, col. 22, num. 11: 'In hac doctrina doctores omnes Hispani videntur convenire, (…) tametsi quidam ex eis [sc. Antonius Gomezius et Antonius Padilla] et nonnulli alii non ut oportet loquantur, non attendentes ad varias illas acceptiones causae paulo ante explicatas.' Compare *De iustitia et iure*, tom. 2 (*De contractibus*), disp. 257, col. 22, num. 10, *in fine*.

[514] Molina, *De iustitia et iure*, tom. 2 (*De contractibus*), tract. 2, disp. 257, col. 21, num. 10: 'Illud postremo circa hanc secundam partem huius disputationis est observandum, latissimum esse discrimen inter ius civile et ius canonicum, dum dicimus iure civili non concedi actionem ex pacto nudo, si tamen vestiatur superventu causae dari eodem civili iure actionem, ut disp. 255 ostensum est; et dum hac disputatione dicimus, ut ex pacto nudo actio iure canonico concedatur, qua adversarius stare pacto nudo compellatur, necessariam esse causae expressionem aut probationem.'

[515] Molina, *De iustitia et iure*, tom. 2 (*De contractibus*), tract. 2, disp. 257, col. 21, num. 10: 'Illic namque sermo est de causa exequutioni mandata, quae proinde pactum vestit, neque illud relinquit intra limites pacti nudi. Hîc vero sermo est de causa expressa in ipso pacto aut aliunde probata, vel quam reus confiteatur, sive illa exequutioni sit mandata, sive non. Verbi gratia, si Petrus paciscatur cum Ioanne, se illi daturum mutuo centum, neque illa tradiderit, cum mutuum includat causam onerosam, nempe ut Ioannes totidem postea restituat, de iure canonico concedetur Ioanni actio adversus Petrum, ut illa mutuo det. De iure vero civili actio ei denegabitur, eo quod illud sit pactum nudum, ex neutraque parte facta sit ulla traditio seu adimpletio; quae adimpletio causae, pactum nudum vestiens appellatur.'

The latter [civil law] speaks of a *causa* which has been performed, therefore vesting the pact and not leaving it within the limits of a naked pact; the former [canon law] speaks of a *causa* which is expressed in the pact itself, or proven from elsewhere, or confessed by the defendant, regardless of whether or not it has been performed.

This fundamental insight is illustrated by our Jesuit theologian in the following way. Let us assume that Peter concludes an agreement with John to lend John a hundred guilders. From the perspective of canon law, John will be able to enforce this agreement even though nothing else has happened subsequent to the agreement. The reason John gets his *actio* is that a money-loan (*mutuum*) includes an onerouse cause, since John will have to render the money when due. As a matter of civil law, however, the agreement is not actionable, since as long as neither of the parties has performed, there is no *causa* to the agreement in the sense of D. 2,14,7,4. It is only subsequent to *causa* in the sense of the performance of one of the obligations, that the agreement becomes enforceable in favor of the party who has already performed. From the civilian perspective, the *causa* is not intrinsic to the pact but an external cloth which vests the bare agreement.

In a similar vein, Covarruvias had insisted almost a generation before that the civil law and the canon law understanding of *causa* should not be confounded:

It is beyond doubt that there is a big difference between the law of the Pope and the civil law. For, as a matter of civil law, a pact which is normally naked gets support from *causa* only when the effect of that *causa* has already taken place and not simply by that *causa* being attached to it. Hence, the naked pact is supported by the effect of the *causa* as is indicated in law *Iurisgentium.*

To summarize, the sixteenth century witnessed a growing awareness that *causa* is an essential element for the actionability of contracts in both the civil and the canon law tradition, albeit in radically different ways. Moreover, at the very moment that jurists and theologians claimed to have found the true meaning of *causa* in the *ius commune* tradition, the concept itself may have started to play a different role. In the work of Herman Vultejus, *causa* seems to be used as a device to introduce the State's approval into the law of contract. Also, the discrepancy between civil and canon law had apparently been superseded in practice in a number of countries, particularly in Spain. Last but not least, even though he came up with a brilliant synthesis of the canonical and civilian sources, Molina himself was actually proposing an even more interesting, natural

law account of the whole story. It is precisely to these emerging perspectives on the bindingness of bare agreements that we will now turn our
attention.

3.2.3   A new world: the victory of consensualism

After this brief tour d'horizon of the attempts by the medieval civilians
to adapt Roman law to their own societies and of the canonists' effort
to promote the bindingness of agreements on the basis of simple moral
principles, it is probably difficult to prevent readers from sympathizing
with Molina's call for harmonization and simplification:[516]

> All those subtle rather than useful concoctions, invented and introduced as
> a matter of civil law by pagans about naked agreements and vested agree-
> ments, innominate contracts and nominate contracts, should be abolished
> (aboleri deberent)...

More precisely, what Molina urges lawmakers to do is to follow the example of the Kings of Castile and accommodate statute law to the canon law,
or, better still, to accommodate civil and ecclesiastical jurisdiction to the
court of conscience. As he goes on to say, the contrived arguments of the
civilians should be abolished,[517]

> ...as has occurred, in conformity with the canon law, almost completely
> in the Kingdom of Castile; and the external court should be brought into
> line with the court of conscience (exterius forum conscientiae foro aequari
> deberet).

In Molina's view, harmonizing positive law with the law of nature would
help political society to achieve its ambition of maintaining peace. As
has been pointed out before, the traditional argument to explain Roman

---

516 Molina, *De iustitia et iure*, tom. 2 (*De contractibus*), tract. 2, disp. 258, col. 25, num. 9:
'Quin omnia etiam, quae de pacto nudo et vestito, et contractibus innominatis et nomi-
natis, subtiliter potius quam utiliter de iure civili ab ethnicis hominibus inventa atque
introducta sunt, aboleri deberent...'
   Given this call by Molina to radically depart from the civilian tradition, Guzmán Brito
criticizes Birocchi for his interpretation that Molina did not feel dissatisfied by the doctrine of *vestimenta pactorum*; cf. Guzmán Brito, *La doctrina de Luis de Molina sobre la causa
contractual*, p. 434, n. 86.
517 Molina, *De iustitia et iure*, tom. 2 (*De contractibus*), tract. 2, disp. 258, col. 25, num. 9
(continuation of sentence in previous footnote): '...ut in Regno Castellae, l. illa 3 citata,
aut omnino aut magna ex parte, consentanee ad ius canonicum factum est, exteriusque
forum conscientiae forum aequari deberet.'

law's refusal to enforce naked agreements in D. 2,14,7,4 was that the courts would otherwise be overextended. Molina reverses this argument: the principle that all agreements are binding will promote rather than disturb civil peace.[518] He even urges the Pope to intervene and abrogate the civil laws that are contrary to canon law, because these civil laws promote sin and strife, not in the least because they are so complex.

So, if the court of conscience was considered to be the ultimate standard for advocating the bindingness of all bare agreements in the temporal courts, what did the natural law tradition really say about the consensualist foundations of contractual obligation? Moreover, to what extent were the natural law principle of the universal bindingness of agreements, the canon law of contract and statute law imbricated in the Castilian law of contract in the early modern period? To what extent did the civil jurisdictions in practice already adhere to the consensualist principle of natural and canon law? The following section proposes to successively answer these questions.

3.2.3.1   Natural law

In order to come to grips with the expositions on contract law of Molina and his fellow moral theologians, awareness of the thoroughly pluralistic character of European legal cultures until at least the seventeenth century is material. Although frequently bracketed out from legal historical scholarship, the court of conscience as a truly juridical notion has played a vital role in the shaping of legal doctrine throughout the Middle Ages and the early modern period, only to gradually stop making sense with the natural lawyers of the seventeenth and eighteenth centuries. References to natural law and conscience are still rife in jurists such as Pothier, but it is not clear whether they could still function as more than a theoretical and moral frame of reference to 'law' properly called so.

Natural law was principally understood as the law that applies to man as man. This law has not as its chief aim to regulate man's behavior as a member of a particular civil or religious community, but as a man in his naked condition before the ultimate judge of his existence, God. Naturally, this approach to natural law gained increasing currency with the

---

[518] Molina, *De iustitia et iure*, tom. 2 (*De contractibus*), tract. 2, disp. 258, col. 25, num. 9: 'Nec dubito ea ratione minuerentur potius, quam augerentur lites, hominesque liberarentur a difficili admodum harum rerum praescrutatione, prout hactenus sparsim atque involute iure civili traditae sunt.'

discovery of the Americas. It was considered the task of the moral theologian to anticipate the Last Judgment in the afterlife for all men, pagans included, by reasoning with *recta ratio* what the law applying to man as man was and what it meant in concrete circumstances of life. This was far from being a mere intellectual enterprise. In trying to figure out the dictates of natural law, and by designing the sacrament of penitence as a court of conscience, the Church essentially helped people to prepare for the day of Last Judgment.[519] Through its power of the keys, the Catholic Church claimed the power to make decisions in conscience that would affect Last Judgment.

The imminent reality of the Last Judgment is obvious from even the most superficial of historical tourist trips through any European city. It requires a belief in the soul and the afterlife, though, which, for better or for worse, falls on deaf ears in the majority of European countries today. Still, Lessius' juridical treatise *De iustitia et iure*, to cite but a famous example, does not make any sense without reference to his equally successful treatise *On divine providence and the immortality of the soul* (*De providentia numinis et animi immortalitate*).[520] This needs to be stressed, here, since natural law appears to have been the fundamental motor behind the drive towards contractual consensualism and a general law of contract. This is not exactly the same 'natural law', though, that was adhered to by some of the intellectual coryphaei mentioned at the outset of this section. Yet without taking the literature for confessors, i.e. the judges in the court of conscience whose task it is to enforce natural law, seriously, it is impossible to get a sense of why the development of contractual consensualism could have arisen in the first place. Given the predominance of the soul over the body and the spiritual over the temporal, even the civilians could not escape regarding natural law and the court of conscience as benchmarks for their own juridical thought.

As a tribunal where natural law is enforced, the court of conscience is a jurisdiction parallel to the ecclesiastical and the civil courts. For centuries, it allowed its secular counterparts to look at themselves in a mirror *sub specie aeternitatis*. It permitted jurists and theologians to go straight to the essence of things and leave historical contingencies as well as practical considerations aside. Hence, the court of conscience is the court of equity

---

[519] For more details on the 'court of conscience', see higher, chapter 2.

[520] A work considered of such importance that it was even translated into Chinese by Martino Martini s.j. (1614–1661).

and truth. As Juan de Valero remarks,[521] 'the sophistication and subtleties of law are not allowed in the court of conscience, nor are they a matter of concern, nor a source of excuse.' Ideally, equity (*aequitas*) as the basic principle of judgment in the court of conscience is enforced in space and time through evangelical denunciation before the ecclesiastical courts— the bishop being for Catholics what the praetor was for the Romans, to wit, the guarantor of equity.

Interestingly, for his definition of the court of conscience, Valero expressly relies on jurists usually not remembered for their familiarity with the moral theological tradition, such as Pieter Peck (1529–1589) and Francisco Vivio (1532–1616). Peck argued in true Aristotelian-Thomistic fashion that just laws were binding in the court of conscience, admitting, at the same time, that the subtleties and the rigidness of laws could not apply in that court.[522] In his overview of the practical decisions issued by the Royal Court of Naples, Vivio showed himself thoroughly familiar with the scholastic teachings on mistake and deceit, citing all of the famous scholastic theologians and canonists by name, ranging from Adrian of Utrecht over Domingo de Soto to Diego de Covarruvias y Leyva. He defined the court of conscience as the court of the good and the equitable.[523] It was oriented towards the salvation of the soul and regarded truth and justice in an absolute sense. The rigor and the subtlety of the laws could play no role

---

[521] Valero, *Differentiae*, s.v. *Iudicium*, diff. 3, p. 209, num. 1 and 3: 'Apices et subtilitates iuris in foro conscientiae non admittuntur nec curantur neque excusant. (...) Et hinc institutum fuit et adinventum tribunal praetorium pro aequitate servanda instar cuius inter Catholicos habetur ille recursus ad episcopos per denunciationem evangelicam.'

[522] Pieter Peck, *Tractatus de amortizatione bonorum a principe impetranda*, cap. 7 (*an clerus tuta conscientia legem amortizationis fraudare possit*), in: *Opera omnia*, Antverpiae 1679, p. 445–446: 'Propositae quaestionis decisio ex iustitia vel iniustitia constitutionis, quia necessitas petendae amortizationis indicitur, tota dependet. Nam si iniusta sit constitutio, conscientias humanas non obstringit, ut nec aliae quaecumque leges, quae vel pietatem laedunt, vel a non habente potestatem legis ferendae, latae sunt. (...) Sin autem iusta sit et legitima, nihil dubium, quin etiam conscientias nostras alliget (...). Licet in foro conscientiae summi ac rigidi iuris apices remitti solent. (...) Si conscientia ligat, quem natura ligat (...) natura porro eos ligat quos proprius consensus ligat (...), quae temeritas est, libertatem fraudandae legis illis permittere qui a tot annis in legem consenserunt.'

[523] Francisco Vivio, *Decisiones regni Neapolitani*, Venetiis 1592, lib. 1, decis. 160, num. 10–11, p. 229: 'Et tanto libentius concurro cum opinione ista communi, quanto quod ubi agitur de salute animae, non attenduntur ápices iuris (...), et ulterius concludit Baldus multum eleganter (...) quod apices iuris in foro conscientiae non excusant. Et sic subtilitas seu subtilizatio in materia rescriptorum et similium, penitus et omnino vitanda est, cum in illis non veniat aliter de apicibus iuris disputandum (...). Forum enim conscientiae, secundum Baldum (...) est forum boni et aequi coniuncti, quae perfecta iustitia requirit. Ideo vocari debet tribunal veritatis non fictionis (...).'

in conscience. Both Peck and Vivio expressly borrowed from the following passage in Baldus for their description of the court of conscience:[524]

> The court of conscience is the court of the good and the equitable taken together. It is the court of truth and not of fiction, for when the equitable is found in opposition and contradictory to the good, then divine justice embraces the equitable rather than that which is called good by the civil law. This is obvious from the beginning of the first title of the Digest *On justice and right*, where it is stated that perfect justice requires both the good and the equitable simultaneously.

A major consequence of the irrelevance of the subtleties of Roman law in conscience is that the provisions regarding the *stipulatio* in the Digest, Code and Institutes are of no importance to the moral theologians. 'What the jurists laid down regarding stipulations is of no concern in the court of conscience,' Valero explains,[525] 'because all that matters as a matter of conscience is consent between the parties (*consensus paciscentium*) and natural obligation (*naturalis obligatio*).' In other words, the view *sub specie conscientiae* allowed the Western legal tradition to depart from the classical legacy and radically re-think the foundations of contract law. From the point of view of conscience, the ultimate point of reference for measuring contractual obligation is mutual consent between the parties, not the solemn wording of promises.

The fact that they were not constrained by the Roman legal tradition did not entirely prevent the keepers of the court of conscience from caring about what the *Corpus Iustinianeum* said. After all, there was a certain mutual understanding among civilians, canonists and theologians that each had its own distinct yet legitimate role to play in society. As mentioned before, Covarruvias' view that civil law neither actively promotes nor actively resists bare agreements (*pacto nudo lex civilis nec adsistit nec resistit*) would be repeated time and again by the moral theologians.[526] By the same token, much emphasis was laid on the fact that D. 2,14,7,4 still

---

524 Baldus de Ubaldis, *Commentaria in septimum, octavum, nonum, decimum et undecimum Codicis libros*, Lugduni 1585, ad C. 7, 59, 1, num. 3, f. 99v: 'Forus enim conscientiae est forus boni et aequi coniunctim, et est tribunal veritatis et non fictionis, nam quando aequum bono opponitur contradictione, divina iustitia potius amplectitur aequum quam id quod ius civile vocat bonum, ut ff. de iustitia et iure, l. 1 in princip. Perfecta enim iustitia requirit haec duo simul, ut ibi patet.'
525 Valero, *Differentiae*, s.v. *contractus*, diff. 5, p. 70: 'Decreta a iurisconsultis circa stipulationes in foro conscientiae non curantur. Quia in eo solum attenditur consensus paciscentium et naturalis obligatio; licet nulla intervenerit solemnitas et interrogatio ultra pactum nudum.'
526 Covarruvias, *Relectio in cap. quamvis pactum*, part. 2, par. 5, num. 10, p. 273.

recognized that, on account of the *ius gentium*, an *exceptio* followed from a naked agreement. The *ius excipiendi* was generally taken to mean that the Romans recognized that a natural obligation (*obligatio naturalis*) ensued from a bare agreement. This could easily be inferred from the Accursian gloss, which held that obligations ensuing from *ius gentium* were tantamount to natural obligations.[527] The Accursian gloss went even as far as expressly stating that a natural obligation ensues from a naked pact.[528] The medieval jurists would not cease to repeat this.[529]

Proof for the claim that bare agreements produce natural obligation was found in the consequences that Roman law attached to naked pacts even as a matter of civil law.[530] The most obvious juridical effect in the civil court is the *exceptio* mentioned in paragraph *Sed cum nulla*, of course, but other consequences were recognized. For example, the right for the

---

[527] See glossa *Obligationes* ad D. 1,1,5 in *Corporis Iustinianaei Digestum vetus* (ed. Gothofredi), tom. 1, col. 58: 'Item quaero de qua obligatione dicit hîc, quod est de iure gentium, cum duae tantum sunt obligationes, sc. civilis et naturalis. De civili non. Item de naturali non videtur. Sed dic de naturali, quia obligatio iuris gentium dicitur naturalis et e converso.'

[528] See glossa *Is natura* ad D. 50,17,84 in *Corporis Iustinianaei Digestum novum* (ed. Gothofredi), tom. 3, col. 1894: 'Naturaliter autem quis tenetur de iure gentium nudo pacto.'

[529] E.g. Baldus, *Commentaria in quartum et quintum Codicis libros*, ad C. 4,32,16, num. 18, f. 107v: '(...) quia licet de iure civili non oriatur civilis obligatio propter defectum solemnitatis et contractus, tamen de iure gentium oritur naturalis, ut ff. de pactis, l. iurisgentium, par. igitur nuda.'

See also Volante, *Il sistema contrattuale del diritto comune classico*, p. 150–156 on the glossators' discussion of the result of a *pactum de non petendo*, which naturally binds the creditor not to claim anymore the debt owed to him on the basis of a preceding contract, and a successive *pactum de petendo*, through which this natural obligation following from the *pactum de non petendo* is removed again.

[530] For a quick overview of the effects of naked pacts in the secular court which were thought to be following from the natural obligation inherent in bare agreements, see Molina, *De iustitia et iure*, tom. 2 (*De contractibus*), tract. 2, disp. 257, cols. 18–19, num. 1: 'Quamvis ex nudis pactis concedere noluerit civilem obligationem et actionem (paucis quibusdam pactis exceptis, ut disput. 255 ostensum est) nihilominus vim suam, quam, stando in solo naturali ac gentium iure ad naturaliter obligandum habebant, ab eis non abstulit, quin potius, propter illam, varios ex illis effectus introduxit. Nempe, ut is cui ex pacto nudo aliquid debebatur, quamvis exigere illud in foro exteriori non posset, posset tamen id sibi semel solutum in eodem exteriori foro retinere, neque posset cogi illud reddere. Item ut, si ipse eidem aliquid deberet, posset facere compensationem in eo, quod sibi ex pacto nudo creditor debebat, neque in exteriori foro compelli posset plus solvere, quam incrementum. Praeterea (et fere in idem recedit) posset excipere adversus exigentem esse sibi ex pacto nudo tantum vel tantum, debitum aut remissum, neque teneri id solvere. (...) Item propter obligationem ex pacto nudo remanentem, quamvis non detur civilis actio adversus ita paciscentem, datur tamen adversus fideiussorem, si fideiussor pro talis pacti impletione est datus, retinerique eadem ratione potest pignus, si pro nudo pacto implendo sit datum (...).' Compare Lessius, *De iustitia et iure*, lib. 2, cap. 17, dub. 4, p. 198, num. 23.

creditor of a naked pact to hold back what he had already received from the debtor or to retain what had been given to him by the debtor as a pledge (*ius retinendi*). In any case, the debtor could no longer claim back what he had already paid. Also, the right for a creditor to compensate (*ius compensandi*) his own debt with the outstanding debt owed to him by virtue of the naked pact.[531] Last but not least, even though the debtor himself was only bound as a matter of natural law, his guarantor (*fideius-sor*) was bound on account of civil law (D. 46,1,16,3).

The insight that bare agreements produce natural obligation was cru-cial for the argument that naked pacts are enforceable in the court of conscience, and, hence, in the ecclesiastical court. As Valero put it:[532]

> The reason why in the ecclesiastical court a naked pact produces an obliga-tion efficacious enough for bringing an action is related by Fortunius Garcia (...), namely that a natural obligation arises out of a naked pact. Whenever you are bound as a matter of natural law (*obligatus naturaliter*), you are bound in the court of conscience and, hence, in the ecclesiastical court, at least by way of denunciation.

That Valero expressly relied on Fortunius Garcia for this syllogism is no coincidence. Fortunius was a constant and major source of inspiration for theologians and jurists on the Iberian peninsula in the early modern period. What is more, he did pioneering work in transforming the civilian tradition of thinking about contracts from within by arguing that pacts could be enforced even as a matter of civil law. Granted, Fortunius was very circumspect in making his argument. He did not put forward his con-clusion straight away. Yet, led by a deep desire to find out the truth and to know what true justice is like (*investigandi ac iustitiae cognoscendae dulcedine captus*), he dared question and doubt conventional wisdom.[533] As occasionally happens when people are driven by such lofty feelings,

---

[531] Lessius only recognized this effect in the court of conscience.

[532] Valero, *Differentiae*, s.v. *obligatio*, diff. 10, p. 300, num. 2: 'Rationem autem quare in foro canonico ex nudo pacto oriatur obligatio efficax ad agendum, tradit Fortunius Gar-cia d.c. 1, col. 5 et in l. 1 col. 2 et in l. legitima, num. 14, ff. de pact., scilicet quia ex dicto pacto oritur obligatio naturalis. At ubi quis est obligatus naturaliter, est obligatus in foro conscientiae et consequenter in foro canonico, saltem per viam denunciationis, ut docent dd. In c. novit.'

[533] See Fortunius Garcia, *Repetitio super cap. 1 de Pactis*, num. 52, p. 1002–1003: 'Septimo ex superioribus inferri potest talis dubitatio, an de iure civili ex nudo pacto oriatur actio? At dices stultum et iuris ignarum tale dubium, cum tam iureconsulti quam imperatores saepissime dicant, ex tali pacto actionem non nasci (...) Sed etsi nunquam aliquis de hoc dubitaverit, quod ego dubitaverim, libidini non referas, non enim lascivia, non sequor | vulgum, sed investigandi ac iustitiae cognoscendae dulcedine captus.'

the outcome of his systematic doubt was shocking. His conclusion that naked pacts are actionable as a matter of civil law would have stunned generations of civilians and canonists.[534]

In fact, Fortunius Garcia's is a wonderful illustration of the natural law and the canon law calling forth traditional jurisprudence to alter its course. Eventually, the civilian tradition collapsed before the vigorous consensualist drive inherent in the theologians' and the canonists' account of contractual obligation. Dozens of manuals for confessors used all over Europe, and, eventually, all across the world, kept hammering on the bindingness of bare agreements in the court of conscience. For example, Sylvester Prierias—Dominican friar famous not only for his dispute with Martin Luther, but also for his extraordinarily successful manual for confessors—considered not performing a bare agreement to constitute a mortal sin, at least in serious affairs, since pacts, however naked, produce an obligation in conscience.[535] Angelo Carletti de Chivasso, whose equally influential manual for confessors was ostentatiously burned by Martin Luther, propagated exactly the same view.[536]

The central role of consent in the natural law tradition, particularly as mirrored in the manuals for confessors, is closely intertwined with both the theologians' and the canonists' notion of *causa*. In the court of conscience, as in the ecclesiastical courts, *causa* expresses the concern that, given the definition of contract as mutual consent, there is true, motivated, and reasonable consent on the part of the assenting parties. Needless to say, this is a notion of *causa* that is far away from the Roman discussions on the enforceability of innominate contracts on account of a previous juridical act. For the theologians and the canonists, *causa* intervenes at the level of the will of the parties. This seems to have been so evident that there was hardly any need of convoluted theories about the meaning of *causa* among the theologians. In the writings of the early

---

[534] Fortunius employed all rhetorical strategies to convince his audience; cf. *Repetitio super cap. 1 de Pactis*, num. 60, p. 1007: 'Responde, quod confirmari pacta a lege civili non est contra leges civiles, quia pacta erant praeter eas, ut in d. l. stipulatio, § alteri. Unde si confirmas id, quod numquam infirmasti, non tibi contradicis.'

[535] See Sylvester Prierias, *Summa Sylvestrina*, Lugduni 1520, part. 2, s.v. *pactum*, num. 4, f. 192r: 'Quarto quaeritur, utrum ex sola promissione sive ex pacto quis obligetur in conscientia? Et dico, quod sic sub peccato mortali, in rebus scilicet alicuius importantiae.'

[536] Angelo Carletti de Chivasso, *Summa Angelica de casibus conscientiae*, Lugduni 1512, s.v. *pactum*, num. 4, f. 267v: 'Utrum ex nudo pacto sive ex sola promissione homo obligetur? Respondeo quod de iure canonico et in conscientia sic sub poena mortalis peccati.'

modern scholastics, there is no single *dubitatio*—the standard format to raise a controversial or a major issue—which deals with *causa*.

Among the few instances in which the notion of *causa* is paused upon for reflection, we find an interesting passage from the *Summa Sylvestrina*. Still, it basically deals with the enforceability of agreements in the ecclesiastical courts, for which, as is generally known, the expression of *causa* is needed. In line with expectations, Sylvester explains that the expression of *causa* is needed, because otherwise the agreement is presumed to rest on mistake (*error*).[537] In that case, no natural obligation can be presumed to ensue from the agreement, without which even in conscience the contracting parties are not bound. In the event of mistake, there is no way to invoke a natural obligation, since nothing is as contrary to consent as mistake (*sic allegari non potest obligatio naturalis, cum nihil sit tam contrarium consensui quam error*). Incidentally, the will to make someone a gift out of pure liberality is a sufficient *causa* for creating an obligatory agreement.

Perhaps more unique, and certainly a bit more elaborated, are a couple of paragraphs devoted to *causa* by the canonist Dr. Navarrus in the context of his definition of a promise that binds on pain of mortal sin. He defines such a promise as 'every true, deliberate, and voluntary promise, however naked, with a licit, possible and notable object, which cannot be enervated by changed circumstances.[538] Dr. Navarrus expounds on *causa* in clarifying the first element of the definition, namely that a promise should be true (*vera*). In other words, a promise should not be fake (*ficta*), as when parties enter into an agreement without intending to bind themselves (*animo non obligandi*). Granted, such a false promise cannot constitute mortal sin, but it does not create contractual obligation. 'A promise of which the principal cause is not true,' Dr. Navarrus concludes, 'is not binding'.[539] He also indicates, that the *causa* need not

---

537 Sylvester Prierias, *Summa Sylvestrina*, part. 2, s.v. *pactum*, num. 3, f. 192r: 'Tertio quaeritur, utrum ex nudo pacto seu sola promissione obligetur homo iure canonico? Et dico, quod sic (…) quando exprimitur causa, ut promitto tibi decem, quia vendidisti mihi tale rem, vel mutuo concessisti et huiusmodi, quia si sit nudum, sic quod nulla causa sit adiecta, non obligat etiam in conscientia, quia praesumitur quis per errorem promisisse, et sic allegari non potest obligatio naturalis, cum nihil sit tam contrarium consensui quam error.'

538 Azpilcueta, *Enchiridion sive manuale confessariorum et poenitentium*, Antverpiae 1575, cap. 18, num. 6, p. 407: 'Promissio autem quae obligat ad mortale est omnis vera, deliberata et voluntaria, etiam nuda, rei licitae, possibilis et notabilis, quam mutatio rerum status non enervavit.'

539 Azpilcueta, *Enchiridion sive manuale confessariorum et poenitentium*, cap. 18, num. 6, p. 407: 'Ex quo infertur, non obligare promissionem cuius causa principalis non est vera,

be expressed for there to be a contractual obligation in the court of conscience (*nec refert quoad forum conscientiae utrum causa exprimatur aut taceatur*), since conscience does rely on the truth rather than on presumptions. This was part of the common opinion, repeated time and again by theologians and jurists including Hugo Grotius.

Consequently, there is nothing mysterious about the doctrine of *causa* among the theologians and canonists. The simplicity of the doctrine explains why it need not be the subject of lengthy expositions in the first place. As a caused thing (*causatum*) consisting of mutual consent, an agreement simply cannot exist if it is founded on vicious consent.[540] The absence of *causa* is tantamount to the absence of reasonable consent and, by defintion, impedes the birth of an agreement. Where there is no cause, there is no caused thing (*ubi non est causa, ibi non est causatum*). If any, the remarks of early modern theologians such as Lessius on *causa* are even more cursory. They rehearse the common opinion that an agreement lacks *causa* if it is founded on mistake. In the following, Lessius' explanation is quoted for why the canon law does not enforce agreements unless *causa* is expressed:[541]

> Since it has been founded for the sake of the salvation of souls, the canon law observes the obligation in conscience and orders that it be fulfilled, unless it presumes mistake or fraud. Therefore, the canon law does not grant an action to enforce the promise if the reason why the promise was made (*causa sur sit promissum*) is not expressed, as Sylvester explains. Otherwise, the canon law does not presume that the promise has been made seriously and freely (*alioquin non praesumit serio et libere promissum*).

Lessius' quote also offers another illustration of the determining role of the law of conscience for the canon law of contracts. The relevance of the concurrent jurisdiction of conscience to the spelling out of a consensualist doctrine of contract becomes even more obvious if we turn to one of the

---

si ei qui promisit non erat animus se obligandi absque ea, nec refert quoad forum conscientiae utrum causa exprimatur aut taceatur. (...) Qui expressionem causae requirunt, intelligitur in foro exteriori, in quo absque ea, animus obligandi non praesumitur (...), non autem in foro conscientiae in quo soli veritati standum est.'

[540] To a certain extent, one could say, then, that the meaning of the doctrine of *causa* in early modern scholasticism can be investigated in an indirect manner through studying their elaborate discussions on the vices of the will.

[541] Lessius, *De iustitia et iure*, lib. 2, cap. 17, dub. 4, num. 23, p. 198: 'Ratio est, quia ius canonicum, cum sit conditum ad salutem animarum, respicit obligationem conscientiae, eamque iubet impleri, nisi forte praesumat errorem vel fraudem, quam ob causam non concedit actionem ad exigendum promissum, nisi exprimatur causa cur sit promissum. Sylvester supra. Alioquin non praesumit serio et libere promissum.'

fundamental statements made by Lessius on the bindingness of all contracts in the court of conscience:[542]

> Every contract, even if it is naked, which has been freely and spontaneously
> made (*sponte libereque factus*), if the parties have the capacity to contract,
> produces a natural obligation in the court of conscience, so that you cannot
> rescind the contract against the other party's will, unless it is void through
> positive law or if positive law gives you the power to void it.

This statement, which comes down to a general principle of 'freedom of
contract', is motivated by Lessius in two ways.[543] First, the distinction
between naked and vested agreements is superseded by the law of nature
(*iure naturae nulla est inter haec distinctio*). So both gratuitous and onerous promises are binding as long as the promisee accepts the promise.
Second, all that is required to bind yourself is a will expressed in words
and accepted by the other party to the contract (*ad obligandum sese sufficit animus verbis expressus and acceptatus*). One could rightly wonder if
there is any more clear expression of consensualism as the basis of contract than Lessius asserting that the will of the parties constitutes the basis
of contractual obligation.

    In principle, then, parties are free as a matter of natural law to agree
on any agreement they want. The primary concern now in dealing with
contracts becomes the will and its vices (as will be discussed in the next
chapter 4). Also, Lessius would concede that the will can be restrained by
the public authorities, who can limit 'freedom of contract' by imposing
formality requirements for the sake of public utility (as will be discussed

---

542 Lessius, *De iustitia et iure*, lib. 2, cap. 17, dub. 4, num. 19, p. 197: 'Omnis contractus,
etiam nudus, sponte libereque factus, si contrahentes sint habiles, parit obligationem naturalem seu in foro conscientiae, ita ut parte invita non possis rescindere, nisi iure positivo
sit irritus vel detur irritandi potestas.'

543 Lessius, *De iustitia et iure*, lib. 2, cap. 17, dub. 4, num. 19, p. 197: 'Probatur primo,
quia iure tenetur quisque praestare quod promisit, altero acceptante, sive promiserit titulo
gratuito sive oneroso. Nec refert an pacto nudo an vestito promiserit, quia iure naturae
et gentium nulla est inter haec distinctio, sed solo iure civili, quae etiam solum forum
externum respicit. Secundo, quia ad obligandum sese, sufficit animus verbis expressus et
acceptatus, ut communiter docent Theologi.'
    Compare Molina, *De iustitia et iure*, tom. 2 (*De contractibus*), tract. 2, disp. 257, col. 18,
num. 1: 'Doctores communiter consentiunt (...) ex pacto nudo naturalem oriri obligationem, quae paciscentes in conscientiae foro tenentur illis stare (...). Ratio est, quoniam,
stando in solo iure naturali ac gentium, antequam civile ius introduceretur, nulla erat differentia inter contractus nominatos et innominatos (...) neque item inter pacta nuda et
vestita. Quare in conscientiae foro, spectata ipsa rei natura, ex omnibus oriebatur obligatio
quam ea de causa naturalem appellamus, ut a civili, ex qua actio civili iure conceditur,
eam distinguamus.'

in chapter 5), and by basic principles of morality, such as sexual discipline and the virtue of commutative justice (as will be discussed in chapters 6 and 7, respectively).

3.2.3.2   In utroque foro hodie ex pacto nudo habebimus ius agendi

Previous scholarship shows that over the course of the sixteenth century, several public authorities across Europe and their jurists adopted the canon law principle that all agreements, however naked, are binding. Clearly, the pressure on the civilian tradition to conform to the moral theological and to the canon law tradition became irresistible, certainly because they were complied with in practice (*usu*). In a period that witnessed an increased desire among would-be absolutist princes to centralize and monopolize juridical power, parallel sources of norms and jurisdiction were neutralized by 'swallowing' them. The days of medieval legal pluralism were over. Better still, attempts were rife at integrating non-State jurisdictions into a renewed, single power structure controlled by the State.

Many examples of the civil law 'swallowing' the canon law tradition could be set forth.[544] In English legal history, there is evidence that suggests a link between the rise of *assumpsit* as a general contractual remedy over the course of the sixteenth century and the demise of ecclesiastical jurisdiction *pro laesione fidei*, which was moribund by the 1520s.[545] In France, the *ordonnance de Villers-Cotterêts* (1539) denied ecclesiastical courts all competence in contractual affairs. Only a couple of decades later, Charles Du Moulin (1500–1566) noted that in practice, all agreements were binding, in the secular courts as well.[546] The *aequitas naturalis* of the canon

---

[544] This is a constant theme in Waelkens, *Civium causa*, illustrated in regard to the law of obligations on p. 300–302.

[545] For the nuances, see Helmholz, *Contracts and the canon law*, p. 59–65, and Helmholz, *The canon law and ecclesiastical jurisdiction from 597 to the 1640s*, p. 366–368.

[546] Charles Du Moulin, *Nova et analytica explicatio Rubricae et legum 1. et 2. de verborum obligationibus ex lectionibus tam Tubingensibus quam Dolanis*, Parisiis 1562, num. 42 (*hodie nuda conventio serio conclusa stipulationi aequipollet*), p. 19: 'Sed hodie in praxi hae et omnes leges et theoriae de formulis stipulationum supervacuae sunt, quia etiam extra scripturam publicam vel privatam, sive confessione partis sive testibus aut alias legitime appareat de conventione serio pacta et conclusa in re licita nec prohibita, nec inter prohibitos aut inhabiles, pro stipulatione habetur et oritur efficax actio, juxta no. in c. 1, Extra de pactis, quod ita debet intelligi et restringi, et ita in utroque foro seculari et ecclesiastico observatur, nec de verborum forma aut solemnitate curatur, ita ut multorum prolixae et operosae commentationes supervacuae sint.'
For further discussion, see Spies, *De l'observation des simples conventions en droit canonique*, p. 217–225 and J. Bart, *Pacte et contrat dans la pratique française (XVIᵉ–XVIIIᵉ siècles)*, in: J. Barton (ed.), Towards a general law of contract, [Comparative Studies in

law had been adopted by the civil courts. As the French jurist Antoine
Loysel (1536–1617) famously put it, making a slight variation on the common medieval expression *verba ligant homines, taurorum cornua funes*:[547]
'on lie les bœufs par les cornes, et les hommes par les paroles, et autant
vaut une simple promesse que les stipulations du droit romain'.[548]

In Italy, the civilian tradition persisted until the eighteenth century.
However, as early as the sixteenth century the superior courts enforced
bare agreements on account of the judge's office (*officium iudicis*).[549] The
remark by Giulio Cesare Ruginelli (†1628) is significant in this respect:[550]
'it cannot be denied that before whichever judge, equity (*aequitas*) and
faith (*fides*) have force in pacts even though they are naked'. As elsewhere
in Europe, the commercial courts in Italy enforced bare agreements, as
is witnessed by Sigismondo Scaccia (1564–1634).[551] The evolution of the
doctrine on naked pacts reached its height in Giovanni Battista de Luca
(1614–1683), a major Italian jurist and cardinal whose *Theatrum veritatis et iustitiae* is reminiscent of the work of the Spanish theologians and
canonists.[552] In a rather familiar passage, De Luca concludes that the

---

Continental and Anglo-American Legal History, 8], Berlin 1990, p. 125–127. Spies, *De
l'observation des simples conventions en droit canonique*, p. 253 wonders why Du Moulin
was still aware of the canon law origins of the development of the principle that all agreements are binding, while this historical consciousness seems to have been completely lost
by natural lawyers of the eighteenth century (with the exception of De Boutaric; cf. p. 253,
note 2).

[547] See Glossa *Iuris vinculum* ad Inst. 3,14 in *Corporis Iustinianaei Institutiones* (ed.
Gothofredi), tom. 4 (*Volumen parvum*), col. 333: 'Ut enim boves funibus visualiter ligantur,
sic homines verbis ligantur intellectualiter. Additio: iuxta illud, verba ligant homines, taurorum cornua funes; cornu bos capitur, voce ligatur homo.'
    For further discussion, see G. Sautel – M. Boulet-Sautel, *Verba ligant homines, tauro-
rum cornia funes,* in: Études d'histoire du droit privé offertes à Pierre Petot, Paris 1959,
p. 507–517.

[548] Antoine Loysel, *Institutes coustumieres ou manuel de plusieurs et diverses reigles, sentences, et proverbes tant anciens que modernes du droict coustumier et plus ordinaire de la
France*, Paris 1637, lib. 3, tit. 1 (*De conventions*), num. 2, p. 642.

[549] Birocchi, *Tra tradizione e nuova prassi giurisprudenziale*, p. 306–330.

[550] G. Ruginelli, *Practicarum quaestionum rerumque iudicatarum liber singularis*, Venetiis 1610, cap. 1, num. 117: 'Negari non potest, quin coram quocunque iudice vigeat aequitas
et fides in ipsis pactis quamvis nudis.' Also quoted in Birocchi, *Tra tradizione e nuova
prassi giurisprudenziale*, p. 309.
    On Ruginelli, a lawyer from Milan, see M.G. di Renzo Villata, *Diritto comune e diritto
locale nella cultura giuridica Lombarda dell'età moderna*, in: Diritto comune e diritti locali
nella storia dell'Europa, Milano 1980, p. 361–362.

[551] Birocchi, *Tra tradizione e nuova prassi giurisprudenziale*, p. 303–306.

[552] It is therefore not surprising that, as is pointed out by Birocchi, *Tra tradizione e
nuova prassi giurisprudenziale*, p. 335, n. 399, De Luca's argumentation on the bindingness
of naked pacts seems to borrow directly from Covarruvias.

distinction between naked pacts and *stipulationes* is no longer of relevance in the courts, since all that matters is the truth as a matter of natural law, namely consent.[553]

As far as the Southern Netherlands are concerned, the Great Council of Malines claimed jurisdiction over canonical affairs from the early sixteenth century onwards. Its one time president Nicolaas Everaerts brought the fusion of canon law and civil law to unknown heights.[554] As the ultimate court of appeals, the Council was also used as an instrument in centralizing power, first by the Burgundians, from the late fifteenth century onwards, and then by the Habsburgs.[555] Both tendencies have been associated with intensified Byzantine influences on Western European jurisdictions.[556] Regarding contracts, the consequences of the absorption of canon law jurisdiction into the civil law were forthcoming. In 1568, Matthias van Wezenbeke noted in his commentary on the Digest that all agreements were considered binding now also in the civil courts.[557]

Wezenbeke's argument is emblematic of a more general influence of the law of conscience, canon law and practice on the reshaping of civil contract law in the sixteenth century. He sets out his argument in the spirit of the theologians with the observation that the subtleties of the civilian

---

[553] Giovanni Battista de Luca, *Theatrum vertiatis et iustitiae*, lib. 8 (*de credito et debito, creditore et debitore, cum recentissimis Sacrae Rotae Romanae decisionibus*), Venetiis 1716, disc. 74, num. 9, p. 137: 'Hodie siquidem a foro, ob dictas limitationes in suis casibus veras exulasse videntur subtilitates iuris civilis circa distinctionem inter pacta nuda et stipulationes, sed principaliter attenditur substantia veritatis, an scilicet debitum alienum, pro quo quis se constituat, vere subsistat necne, quoniam eo non subsistente, corruit obligatio ex capite erroris, seu falsi praesuppositi. Unde propterea cum iste sit defectus naturalis, utpote proveniens a defectu consensus, istum non supplent neque iuramentum neque canonica aequitas vel mercatorum stylus, cum haec omnia percutiant solum remotionem subtilitatum iuris civilis, non autem ea quae sunt iuris naturae ipsamque veritatem percutiunt (...).'

[554] See Waelkens, *Nicolaas Everaerts*, p. 181–182.

[555] See L. Waelkens, *Le rôle de l'appel judiciaire romain dans la formation des Pays Bas au seizième siècle*, in: Podział władzy i parlamentaryzm w preszłosci i współczesnie, Prawo, doktryna, praktyka, Warschau 2007, p. 75–85.

[556] L. Waelkens, *Réception ou refoulement? Pour une lecture grecque de l'histoire du droit de la Renaissance*, in: B. Coppein – F. Stevens – L. Waelkens (ed.), Modernisme, tradition et acculturation juridique, Actes des Journées internationales de la Société d'Histoire du Droit, Louvain 29 mai–1 juin 2008, [Iuris Scripta Historica, 27], Brussel 2011, p. 145.

[557] For a discussion of Wezenbeke's insight that bare agreements are also binding as a matter of civil law, see Nanz, *Die Entstehung des allgemeinen Vertragsbegriffs im 16. bis 18. Jahrhundert*, p. 85–94 and R. Feenstra, *Pact and contract in the Low Countries from the 16th to the 18th century*, in: J. Barton (ed.), Towards a general law of contract, [Comparative Studies in Continental and Anglo-American Legal History, 8], Berlin 1990, p. 198–201.

tradition (*iuris veteris subtilitates*) are no longer in use today.[558] Subsequently, he cites two reasons for why that is the case. First, all agreements are now binding as a matter of canon law. Second, all supreme courts, in which judgments are rendered *ex aequo et bono*, such as the highest courts of the princes and the merchants, considered all agreements to be actionable. Wezenbeke concludes that it is the common opinion of his day as well as daily practice that all agreements, regardless of whether they are naked or vested, are enforced in the civil courts (*indistincte ex pactis nudis etiam in foro civili hodie detur actio*). He notes that there is discussion about the application of this principle in the lower civil courts.

Wezenbeke then goes on to give personal endorsement to this allegedly common opinion. Interestingly, the reason he adduces for doing so has received little attention in the secondary literature.[559] Only recently has it been noticed that Wezenbeke's statements are a typical expression of the deep moral theological impact on the evolution of contract law.[560] It is essentially religious in nature and a confirmation of the persistent influence of the law of nature and the court of conscience:[561]

> Still, it is common opinion, and so it is observed in practice, that today all agreements are indiscriminately actionable, even in the civil courts. I think this opinion is true and must be followed. For since agreements are binding naturally and as a matter of equity (*obligant naturaliter et ex bono et aequo*), it follows that he who does not keep an agreement acts and sins

558 Matthias van Wezenbeke, *Paratitla in Pandectas iuris civilis ab authore recognita et aucta*, Basileae 1568, ad D. 2,14, p. 110: 'Etsi autem hac de re plura subtiliter disputari possunt, tamen modus aliquis adhibendus est, maxime cum hae iuris veteris subtilitates hodie non sint in usu. Nam primum iure pontificio ex quolibet pacto oritur actio. Deinde hodie idem obtinet in omni foro ubi ex aequo et bono et ex suprema potestate iudicatur, ut sunt curiae summorum principum, arbitratorum, mercatorum et similium. Etsi autem longa disputatio est, an in reliquis curiis, in quibus secundum ius civile pronunciatur, ius pontificium obtinere debeat, tamen communis opinio est, et ita usus observat, ut indistincte ex pactis nudis, etiam in foro civili hodie detur actio. Quod verum puto et sequendum. Nam pacta cum obligent naturaliter et ex bono et aequo, sequitur eum qui pacta non servat contra naturam, conscientiam, atque adeo contra officium boni viri facere ac peccare, ut volunt canonistae, mortaliter; ac certe divus Paulus ad Rom. 1 asunthetas, hoc est, eos qui pacta non servant, in illus numerat qui capitaliter delinquunt. Est autem definitum inter doctores ut quotiescunque agitur de cavendo peccato, deque causa conscientiae, toties etiam in foro civili ius pontificium debeat observari.'
559 For example, the citation in Feenstra, *Pact and contract in the Low Countries*, p. 201, note 11 breaks off at '(...) etiam in foro civili hodie detur actio.'
560 G. Hartung, *Zur Genealogie des Versprechens, Ein Versuch über die begriffsgeschichtlichen und anthropologischen Voraussetzungen der modernen Vertragstheorie*, in: M. Schneider (ed.), Die Ordnung des Versprechens, Naturrecht—Institution—Sprechakt, [Literatur und Recht, 1], München 2005, p. 285.
561 The Latin text is quoted supra, note 558.

against nature, conscience and, therefore, against the duty of a good man. As the canonists wish, this is a mortal sin (*peccare mortaliter*). And, surely, in his first letter to the Romans, Paul includes those who do not keep their agreements among those who commit a capital crime. Now it is established among the doctors that each time we are dealing with the protection from sin and a matter of conscience (*causa conscientiae*), even in the civil court the canon law has to be observed.

Not surprisingly, Wezenbeke cites Giasone del Maino, whose argument we have discussed before, to support his view. After all, Wezenbeke's standpoint was not that unique in the early modern period. In France, too, similar viewpoints were aired, for instance by Charles Du Moulin—much to the displeasure of humanists such as the aforementioned Forcadel. Still, Wezenbeke deserves credit as a constant point of reference among later writers of the *usus modernus pandectarum* in the Dutch- and German-speaking territories.[562] His authority seems to have been as important in the development of the general enforceability of agreements as the self-promoted belief that German culture rested on *Treu und Glauben* from its early beginning—for which support was found in sources as early as Tacitus' *Germania*.[563] Wezenbeke's influence in German territories is not surprising, given his careers at Jena and Wittenberg after his escape from the Southern Netherlands, where the Spanish were prosecuting the Protestants. It has been suggested by Feenstra that Wezenbeke drew inspiration from Fortunius Garcia, who was a quite popular author in the Southern Netherlands throughout the sixteenth century.[564]

---

[562] See Nanz, *Die Entstehung des allgemeinen Vertragsbegriffs im 16. bis 18. Jahrhundert*, p. 85. I. Birocchi, *La questione dei patti nella dottrina tedesca dell'Usus modernus*, in: J. Barton (ed.), Towards a General Law of Contract, [Comparative Studies in Continental and Anglo-American Legal History, 8], Berlin 1990, p. 144–145 critically observes that the authors of the *usus modernus pandectarum* quoted a plethora of Spanish jurists and theologians (Fortunius Garcia, Gómez, Covarruvias, Molina, Fernando Vázquez de Menchaca) as much as Wezenbeke to defend the actionability of naked pacts.

[563] Behrends, *Treu und Glauben*, p. 994–1006 and Birocchi, *La questione dei patti nella dottrina tedesca dell'Usus modernus*, p. 165–183. For critical observations on the distinct nature of 'German' legal culture, see F. Schäfer, *Juristische Germanistik, Eine Geschichte der Wissenschaft vom einheimischen Privatrecht*, [Juristische Abhandlungen, 51], Frankfurt am Main 2008, and L. Waelkens, *Droit germanique, La fin d'un mythe? À propos d'un ouvrage récent*, Revue historique de droit français et étranger, 87 (2009), p. 415–426.

[564] Feenstra, *Pact and contract in the Low Countries*, p. 201, note 17. Feenstra's assumption relies partly on the fact that Wezenbeke cites Fortunius Garcia in one of his *Consilia*, precisely for the purpose of defending the rule that all agreements are binding.
The fact that Fortunius Garcia was widely read in the Southern Netherlands is shown by the presence of his writings in the libraries of important jurists such as Pierre Lapostole (d. 1532), *doctor iuris utriusque*, member of the Great Council of Malines and professor at Leuven university; cf. R. van Caenegem, *Ouvrages de droit romain dans les catalogues des*

If questions of originality matter at all, then the Iberian peninsula seems to have been the first place where the civilian tradition definitively managed to recreate itself in the image of the twin traditions of moral theology and canon law. Fortunius Garcia's sublime commentaries on Roman and canon contract law are a significant case in point. Unfortunately, we are not well informed about the life and works of this compelling jurist.[565] After obtaining a doctorate in canon law at Bologna and receiving a doctorate in civil law from Rome, Fortunius was apparently called back to Spain by Emperor Charles V as supreme royal judge of Navarra, where he later became president of the council. He refused a teaching position at the university of Pisa. Besides his commentaries on contracts (*Commentaria de pactis in titulum Digestorum de pactis*) and justice (*Commentaria in titulum Digestorum de iustitia et iure*), Fortunius wrote a book on property law and unjustified enrichment (*De expensis et meliorationibus sumptis bonae et malae fidei possessorum*), and a more philosophical treatise on the aim of civil and canon law (*De ultimo fine iuris canonici et civilis*). Peláez mentions that an unpublished manuscript of his on the political tensions between France and Spain (*Discurso histórico y jurídico del desafío del emperador Carlos V y Francisco I rey de Francia*) is preserved in the Biblioteca Nacional de Madrid.

In the person of Fortunius Garcia we meet a legal jack-of-all-trades whose work lies at the crossroads of civil law, canon law, and moral theology—a fusion typical of many authors across the Spanish empire at the threshold of the sixteenth century.[566] Fortunius considers juridical problems consistently from the threefold perspective of civil law, canon law, and the law of conscience. This is very obvious in his large commentary on title *De iustitia et iure* in which he discusses a plethora of subjects including natural obligation, slavery and self-defence. For example, Fortunius argues against the gloss that killing an offender is not a sin. The gloss had interpreted the licence to kill by virtue of self-defence as only holding true in the civil and ecclesiastical courts. Yet, following the theologians,

anciens Pays-Bas méridionaux (XIIIᵉ–XVIᵉ siècle), Tijdschrift voor Rechtsgeschiedenis, 28 (1960), p. 405 and p. 432.
[565] Scant biographical details can be found in Peláez, *García de Arteaga de Ercilla, Fortún*, p. 344. Von Schulte, *Prolegomena ad Codicem iuris canonici*, p. 715 admits that he cannot see on which grounds Fortunius Garcia could have been praised so highly by his contemporaries. This honest confession probably helps to explain why Fortunius Garcia has been overlooked in modern historical scholarship.
[566] In the Low Countries, similar observations could be made on Nicolaas Everaerts and Adrian of Utrecht, who were active about roughly the same period.

Fortunius claims that killing out of self-defence is permitted in the court of conscience, too, since this licence is founded both on natural reason and on the right to self-preservation instilled in all men by divine providence.[567]

This compelling synthesis of law and morality is even more clear in Fortunius' commentary on the ultimate goal of canon law and civil law. The title of this work bears of its own witness to the Aristotelian-Thomistic, teleological world view underlying his entire juridical enterprise.[568] Canon law and civil law are like sailors leaving the harbour, Fortunius says: they first determine what their destination will be, only afterward do they start preparing their ships, otherwise they would be pointlessly bobbing up and down on the sea. Hence, defining the scope of canon law and civil law is crucial before laying down its provisions (*finem praeponere oportet*).[569] Moreover, the ultimate standard by which to judge any secular law is natural reason and the court of conscience (*et quid sit tenendum ipsa iustitia*). Secular laws are subordinated to the law of nature just as the second mover is dependent on the first mover.[570] This is why Fortunius argues, for instance, that the civil laws allowing moneylenders to charge interest need to be altered and brought in line with conscience, since interest-taking is forbidden as a matter of natural law.[571]

With a strange reference to the Greek orator Demosthenes, Fortunius claims that the ultimate aim of all laws must be to correct sin (*finis universalis legum peccata corrigere*) and to lead man to the felicity of eternal

---

[567] Fortunius Garcia, *Commentarius in l. ut vim, ff. de iustitia et iure*, num. 16–18, in: *Tractatus in materia defensionis*, Coloniae 1580, p. 528–529. The commentary on law *Ut vim* was published separately in this collection of treatises on self-defence, but originally formed part of Fortunius' greater commentary on title *De iustitia et iure*.

[568] Fortunius Garcia, *De ultimo fine iuris civilis et canonici, de primo principio et subsequentibus praeceptis, de derivatione et differentiis utriusque iuris et quid sit tenendum ipsa iustitia*, Coloniae Agrippinae 1585.

[569] Fortunius Garcia, *De ultimo fine iuris civilis et canonici*, num. 2, p. 31: 'Itaque ut rectum cursum dirigamus finem praeponere oportet. Veluti nautae, qui antequam navem solvant atque expeditam velis et vento committant, constituunt portum ad quem sit navigandum, deinde ad cursum necessaria et convenientia parant. Cognito enim fine determinantur principia, quae tendant ad ipsum. Et hoc est quod philosophi dicunt, in omnibus agendis finem esse principium.'

[570] Fortunius Garcia, *De ultimo fine iuris civilis et canonici*, num. 14, p. 36: 'De legibus vero civilibus idem dicendum est: nam omnes pendent a lege naturae et in tantum habent de ratione legis in quantum participant de lege aeterna. (...) In omnibus enim quae ordinate moventur, necesse est, ut virtus moventis secundi derivetur et pendeat a virtute primi motoris. Nam motor secundus non movet, nisi ut movetur a primo, quod in his inferioribus facile colligimus.'

[571] Fortunius Garcia, *De ultimo fine iuris civilis et canonici*, num. 93, p. 74.

life (*foelicitas ad vitam aeternam*).[572] Also, in the context of maintenance duties of a child born out of incestuous wedlock toward his father, he insists that the canon law must prevail over civil law whenever it is based on natural reason.[573] In regard to contract law this means that naked pacts must be enforceable also in civil courts, since they are actionable as a matter of canon law for the sake of felicity and the avoidance of sin.[574] It is worth recalling Fortunius Garcia's famous statement in his treatise on contracts, which was published for the first time in Bologna in 1514:[575]

> It is therefore firmly and singularly established that today we shall have in both courts a right of action by virtue of a bare agreement (*in utroque foro hodie ex pacto nudo habebimus ius agendi*). For since the civil law showed itself negligent in regard to the justice of bare agreements, because it omitted them, the principle of canon law steps in, which (as I believe) has to be observed also in the secular court. Through this rule, justice will be effected in agreements.

Apart from the obvious canonical foundations of Fortunius' bold statement, what might have made it easier for Fortunius to claim that bare agreements are enforceable in civil courts is a long tradition in Spanish statutory law, which acknowledges at least some sort of force to naked pacts.[576] It may be recalled that, at the end of the sixteenth century, Luís de Molina called upon other regions and public authorities to abolish the subtleties of the civilian tradition precisely by citing the praiseworthy example of Casitilian law. 'In the Kingdom of Castile, just as in canon law and in the court of conscience,' Molina notes,[577] 'there is no place for changing your mind and withdrawing from an innominate contract.'

---

[572] Fortunius Garcia, *De ultimo fine iuris civilis et canonici*, num. 32, p. 44–45 and num. 45, p. 51.

[573] Fortunius Garcia, *De ultimo fine iuris civilis et canonici*, num. 109–122, p. 83–93.

[574] Fortunius Garcia, *De ultimo fine iuris civilis et canonici*, num. 164, p. 121: 'sed cum iustitia pacti observandum sit utilis et tendat ad foelicitatem humanam (...) et ius canonicum ad evitandum peccatum praecipiat pacta observari, ut omnes fatentur in c. 1 [X 1,35,1], sequitur ab omnibus et in quocunque foro servanda (...).'

[575] Fortunius Garcia, *Repetitio super cap. 1 de Pactis*, num. 118, p. 119: 'Hinc singulariter constat quod in utroque foro hodie ex pacto nudo habebimus ius agendi. (...) Cum ergo in iustitia pactorum nudorum ius civile negligenter se habuerit, quia ea praetermisit, succedit regula iuris canonici etiam foro seculari (ut credo) observanda, qua regula pactis ius ministratur.' Unfortunately, we have not been able to check whether there are any differences between the first edition (1514) and subsequent editions.

[576] Feenstra-Ahsmann, *Contract*, p. 15.

[577] Molina, *De iustitia et iure*, tom. 2 (*De contractibus*), tract. 2, disp. 258, col. 25, num. 8: 'Quinta conclusio. In Regno Castellae non est locus poenitentiae in contractibus innominatis, sicut nec de iure canonico, nec in foro conscientiae.'

The relevant passage from Castilian law is the famous *Ley Paresciendo*, which Molina cites from the *Ordenamiento de Montalvo* or the *Ordenanças Reales de Castilla* (1484). It can be traced back, though, to the *Ordenamiento de Alcalá* (1348) and reappears in the *Nueva Recopilación* (1567). Opening with an invocation of the Holy Trinity, the *Ordenamiento de Alcalá* is famous for its moral and religious undertone. In the 1774 edition of the *Ordenamiento*, the passage on the alleged enforceability of bare agreements reads that whether a man binds himself to another by promise, contract or otherwise, he is bound to fulfill his obligation.[578] He cannot object that he was bound through no stipulation (*non pueda ser puesta excebcion que non fue fecha estipulacion*). Hence, Molina concludes, bare agreements are as binding in the Castilian civil courts as they are before ecclesiastical courts.[579] Molina does not pronounce explicitly whether *causa* is required for the actionability of naked pacts as a matter of Castilian law, since *Ley Paresciendo* does not mention *causa* in the first place.[580]

From *Ley Paresciendo* it was not immediately inferred that all agreements were binding as a matter of civil law. The *Ordenamiento de Alcalá* was mostly interpreted in a restrictive way. It was held, for instance, that it applied to unilateral contracts but not to the synallagmatic, innominate contracts. Yet this restrictive interpretation was definitively refuted by Antonio Gómez, the influential professor of Roman law at Salamanca. In his *Variae resolutiones*, published for the first time in 1552, he reaches the conclusion that 'today, in our Kingdom, there shall be no place in innominate contracts for claiming back what has been performed because you

---

[578] *El ordenamiento de leyes que Alfonso XI hizo en las cortes de Alcalá de Henares (1348)*, ed. I.J. de Asso y del Rio – D.M. de Manuel y Rodriguez, Madrid 1774, tit. 16 (*de las obligaciones*), l. 1 (come vale la obligacion entre absentes, aunque non aya y estipulacion): 'Paresciendo que se quiso un Ome obligar a otro por promision, o por algund contracto, o en alguna otra manera, sea tenudo de aquellos a quienes se obligò, e non pueda ser puesta excebcion que non fue fecha estipulacion, que quiere decir: prometimiento con ciertas solepnidades nel derecho; o que fue fecha a Escribano publico, o a otra persona privada en nombre de otro entre absentes; o que se obligò uno de dar, o de façer alguna cosa a otro: mas que sea valedera la obligacion o el contracto que fueren fechos en qualquier manera que paresca que alguno se quiso obligar a otro e façer contracto con el.' [= Ordenamiento de Montalvo, lib. 3, tit. 8, l. 3 = Nueva Recopilación, lib. 5, tit. 16, l. 2]
[579] Molina, *De iustitia et iure*, tom. 2 (*De contractibus*), tract. 2, disp. 257, col 22, num. 11: 'Eo modo quo de iure canonico explicatum est dari ex pacto nudo actionem, affirmandum esse dari ex eodem pacto nudo in regno Castellae in foro seculari.'
[580] Guzmán Brito, *La doctrina de Luis de Molina sobre la causa contractual*, p. 438 and Birocchi, *Causa e categoria generale del contratto*, p. 261 are divided on this matter.

changed your mind or because the other party's juristic act did not follow.'[581] So at least by the time Molina wrote, there was sufficient authoritative support for the view that Castilian law enforced bare agreements *tout court*. However, at the time Fortunius Garcia pleaded for the actionability of all bare agreements in the civil courts, there was no adequate support.

The arguments produced by Gómez to defend his extensive interpretation of the *Ordenamiento de Alcalá* are telling of the consensualist turn in early modern contract law, certainly on the Iberian peninsula.[582] The *Ordenamiento* enforces every agreement that is based on consent, according to Gómez, so innominate contracts should also be considered actionable, since they are based on consent and, therefore, they have cause (*datur consensus, ergo et causa*).[583] He also insists on the natural obligation that ensues from an innominate contracts as a matter of the *ius commune*, again because innominate contracts are based on consent (*oritur obligatio naturalis virtute consensus partium*). Finally, the *Ordenamiento* is said to go even a step further than the canon law, since it does not even require mutual consent for one of the parties to be bound. In Gómez's interpretation, the sole will and intent to be bound are sufficient for the promisor to be bound on account of the *Ordenamiento* (*sufficit sola voluntas et animus obligandi*).

3.3   THE MAKING OF CONTRACTUAL OBLIGATION

By the time the moral theologians started writing about contract law, there was a general feeling that consensualism was the basis of contractual obligation. Generally speaking, the formerly divergent legal traditions had been attuned to the natural law principle that all agreements are binding. The contribution of the early modern scholastics consists in their consecrating and systematizing this new paradigm. First, they highlighted the anthropological and religious foundations of the principle of 'freedom of contract'. Second, they thoroughly analyzed the making of contractual

---

[581] Antonio Gómez, *Commentarii variaeque resolutiones iuris civilis, communis et regii, Accesserunt adnotationes Emanuelis Soarez a Ribeira*, Francoforti ad Rhenum 1572, tom. 2, cap. 8, num. 5, p. 288: 'Ex quibus notabiliter infero, quod hodie in nostro Regno in contractu innominato non habebit locum repetitio ex capite poenitentiae vel causae non secutae.'

[582] This is further evidenced with reference to more vulgarizing Spanish legal literature by Duve, *Kanonisches Recht und die Ausbildung allgemeiner Vertragslehren in der Spanischen Spätscholastik*, p. 389–408.

[583] Gómez, *Commentarii variaeque resolutiones*, tom. 2, cap. 8, num. 4, p. 287.

obligation. More specifically, three elements were thought to be essential to create contractual obligation: the will of the promisor to be bound, the external communication of his promise, and the acceptance of the offer by the promisee. Hence, all accepted offers are binding. Third, the early modern scholastics elaborated on what the voluntarist account of contractual obligation implied for its interpretation. To summarize, they provide us with a unique, systematic insight into the fabric of contract law.

3.3.1 *Liberty and the will*

3.3.1.1 Contrahentibus libertas restituta

The gradual turn towards an open and consensualist doctrine of contract reached one of its apogees in the writings of the Jesuit moral theologians of the late sixteenth and early seventeenth century. They cherished the fact that by their time, the legal traditions that had something to say about contractual obligation had been brought into harmony with each other. Moreover, their explicit reason for being so happy about the outcome of the above-sketched evolution resided in the fact that it stimulated 'freedom of contract'. The universal enforceability of agreements guaranteed one of the values they esteemed to be priceless: freedom (*libertas*). The Spanish Pedro de Oñate (1567–1646), a tremendously busy Jesuit who founded dozens of colleges all across South America besides being the author of a voluminous treatise *On Contracts* (*De contractibus*), conveys his feeling of awe at the bindingness of all agreements stipulated by *Ley Paresciendo* this way:[584]

> Consequently, natural law, canon law and Hispanic law entirely agree and innumerable difficulties, frauds, litigations and disputes have been removed thanks to such great consensus and clarity in the laws. To the contracting parties, liberty has very wisely been restored (*contrahentibus libertas restituta*), so that whenever they want to bind themselves through concluding a contract about their goods, this contract will be recognized by whichever of both courts before which they will have brought their case and it will be

---

[584] Oñate, *De contractibus*, tom. 1, tract. 1, disp. 2, sect. 5, num. 166, p. 40: 'Unde lex naturalis, lex canonica et lex Hispaniae omnino consentiunt et innumerae difficultates, fraudes, lites, iurgia hac tanta legum consensione et claritate sublata sunt, et contrahentibus consultissime libertas restituta ut quandocumque de rebus suis voluerint contrahere et se obligare, id ratum sit in utroque foro in quo convenerint et sancte et inviolabiliter observetur. Quare ius canonicum et ius Hispaniae corrigunt ius commune, concedentes pactis nudis omnibus actionem et obligationem civilem, quam illud negabat.'

upheld as being sacrosanct and inviolable. Therefore, canon law and Hispanic law correct the *ius commune*, since the former grant an action and civil
obligation to all bare agreements, while the latter denied them just that.

Few would disagree that Oñate delivers a brilliant synthesis here of the
turn towards 'freedom of contract' in the early modern period. At the
expense of the civilian tradition (*ius commune*), natural law, canon law
and Hispanic law have prevailed. The result is that 'freedom of contract'
has been restored to the contracting parties. Moreover, Oñate believes
that the universal bindingness of agreements promotes peace rather than
disturbing it. This is a point that was also made by Molina.[585] However,
traditionally, the argument put forward to defend the Roman law principle that naked pacts are not binding was precisely the opposite: enforcing
all agreements will overextend the courts and disrupt justice and peace.
There is an obvious discrepancy in views, then, between moral theologians such as Oñate and the traditional jurists regarding the impact of the
legal rule which stipulates that all agreements are binding.[586]

Oñate's statement also highlights the theologians' custom of conceiving of contract as essentially being a legal instrument to convey property
rights, or, as they would call it, types of lordship or *dominium* in a wider
sense. At the outset of his discussion on contracts, Molina indicates that
the scope of his argumentation will be to make intelligible to what extent
dominium is transferred or not by virtue of the will of the contracting
parties (*quousque contrahentium voluntate transferatur aut non transferatur domimium*).[587] Francisco de Vitoria remarks that *dominium* includes
a variety of property rights ranging from use over usufruct to ownership
and possession.[588] More importantly, in raising the question how property rights are acquired after the original division of things, Vitoria points

---

585 Molina, *De iustitia et iure*, tom. 2 (*De contractibus*), tract. 2, disp. 258, col. 25, num. 9,
cited supra, n. 516.
586 Compare the observations made by Birocchi, *Saggi sulla formazione storica della
categoria generale del contratto*, p. 54.
587 Molina, *De iustitia et iure*, tom. 2 (*De contractibus*), tract. 2, disp. 252, col. 1, num. 1:
'A disputatione 124 huius secundi tractatus de iustitia dicere coepimus de translatione
dominii, propria domini prioris voluntate, indeque hucusque egimus de ultimus voluntatibus. Nunc vero de contractibus est disserendum, ut intelligatur, quousque contrahentium
voluntate transferatur aut non transferatur dominium, et quantum iuris ex unoquoque
contractu aut quasi contractu comparetur. Prius autem dicemus de contractibus in genere,
sumpto latissime vocabulo contractus, deinde vero ad singulos descendemus.'
588 Vitoria, *Commentarii in IIamIIae*, quaest. 62, art. 1, num. 8, in: Francisco de Vitoria,
Comentarios a la Secunda secundae de Santo Tomás, edición preparada por V. Beltrán de
Heredia, tom. 3: *De justitia* (qq. 57–66), [Biblioteca de Teólogos Españoles, 4], Salamanca
1934, p. 67 (hereafter: ed. Beltrán de Heredia, tom. 3): 'Et in materia de restitutione indif-

out three mechanisms: through the will of the lord (*ex voluntate domini*), by virtue of the authority of the prince and by prescription.[589]

The scholastics consider contract to be the vehicle of a *dominus'* will to dispose of his property rights. It is not surprising to find, then, that two paragraphs after he has praised the now universal principle of the bindingness of all agreements, Oñate classifies all specific contracts into a three-column scheme depending on what type of property right they transfer: ownership (*dominium*), usufruct (*ususfructus*) or use (*usus*).[590] In this context, he evidently employs *dominium* in its strict, Roman sense as meaning ownership. It is also worthwhile noting that the focus on property and goods did not prevent the scholastics from taking into consideration what are now called service contracts. Following the medieval jurists, though, they conceived of service contracts in terms of lease and hire of a right of labor use (*locatio conductio*).

One of the major consequences of the fact that contractual obligation gravitates around man as the lord of his property is that the limits of 'contractual liberty' depend on the limits of the capability of a *dominus* to freely dispose of his goods. This is clear from the work of Domingo de Soto, who suggests that every systematic treatment of contract law must begin with an elucidation of *dominium*, because this concept is the basis and foundation of all things done through exchange (*dominium basis fundamentumque omnium contractuum*).[591] With Soto, the question of the limits to 'freedom of contract' is expressed in terms of the limitations imposed on the free exchange of *dominium*. Incidentally, Soto takes *dominium* in a narrower sense than Vitoria. Likewise, the Dominican theologian Domingo de Bañez (1528–1604) treats contract law in his discussion of the transfer

---

ferenter utemur dominio, scilicet sive sit dominus, sive usuarius, sive usufructuarius, sive possessionarius, quia in eo etiam cadit injuria quae est obnoxia restitutioni.'

[589] Vitoria, *Commentarii in IIamIIae* (ed. V. Beltrán de Heredia, tom. 3), quaest. 62, art. 1, num. 27, p. 81: 'Quomodo ergo isti qui modo sunt, facti sunt domini? (...) Facta prima divisione et appropriatione, duobus praecise modis et duobus tantum titulis potuit quis adquirere dominium rerum. Nam etiam duobus potest transferri dominium ad nos ab uno in alium. Et hoc est quod exspectat ad restitutionem. Primo ergo modo potuit transferri dominium ad nos voluntate prioris domini. Alio modo auctoritate principis.' Prescription as a third mode of acquiring dominium is dealt with in Vitoria, *Commentarii in IIamIIae* (ed. V. Beltrán de Heredia, tom. 3), quaest. 62, art. 1, num. 46–48, p. 102–105 (ed. B. de Heredía).

[590] See the scheme in Oñate, *De contractibus*, tom. 1, tract. 1, disp. 2, sect. 5, num. 166, p. 40.

[591] Soto, *De iustitia et iure* (ed. fac. V. Diego Carro – M. González Ordóñez, vol. 2), lib. 4, prooem., p. 278.

of *dominium* by virtue of the will of the *dominus*.[592] Other authors, such as Molina, treat contract law separately from their lengthy discussions on *ius* and *dominium*, but on a conceptual level they continue to stress the connections between property and contract.

Although it is worthwhile being aware of the expressly instrumental character of contract in scholastic thought, modesty demands that scholastic property law falls outside the scope of this dissertation. Already back in the sixteenth century, there were several diverging opinions on what ownership, possession, and property actually signify. The debate was complicated by at least three theologically sensitive issues: the creation of man as *dominus* in the image of God as *Dominus*, the *dominium* of Christ over the Church, and, eventually over the whole world, and, last but not least, the Franciscan poverty controversy. There was so much confusion about the meaning of *dominium* among theologians and jurists alike that Bañez's commentary on *quaestio* 62 of Thomas Aquinas' *Summa Theologiae* was preceded by a lengthy *Praeambulum de dominio Christi* in which he made a praiseworthy attempt to reconcile all opposite positions. Many thought-provoking studies could be written on this *praeambulum* alone.

3.3.1.2   Voluntas libertatem possidens

What should be retained from previous research is that the early modern scholastics had a remarkably liberal concept of property. As Paolo Grossi has convincingly demonstrated, this tendency towards liberalism is particularly present in the Jesuit moral theologians.[593] It is sufficient to recall that Lessius thinks it is the very sign of ownership that he who owns goods has the arbitrary power also to destroy them even out of pure lust (*perimere voluptatis causa*).[594] Gregorio de Valentia (1549–1603) talks about the right to love one's own things (*ius amandi proprias res*).[595] Juan de Lugo confirms that a private person only needs to look after his own interest

---

[592] Domingo de Bañez, *De iure et iustitia decisiones*, Salmanticae 1594, ad quaest. 62, p. 154.
[593] See the ground-breaking article *La proprietà nel sistema privatistico della Seconda Scolastica*, in: P. Grossi (ed.), La seconda scolastica nella formazione del diritto privato moderno, [Per la storia del pensiero giuridico moderno, 1], Milano 1973, p. 117–222.
[594] Lessius, *De iustitia et iure*, lib. 2, cap. 3, dub. 2, num. 8, p. 22: 'Proprium est perfecti dominii ut possis re tua uti pro tuo arbitratu eam vel tibi servando vel vendendo vel donando vel vastando.' And Lessius, *De iustitia et iure*, lib. 2, cap. 4, dub. 10, num. 58, p. 40: 'Proprium veri dominii est rem pro arbitratu suo posse perimere etiam voluptatis causa.'
[595] Gregorio de Valentia, *Commentaria theologica in Secundam Secundae D. Thomae*, Ingolstadii 1603, tom. 3, disp. 5, quaest. 10, punct. 5, litt. a–c, p. 1315.

(*privata commoda*), considering that to be an essential part of economic prudence (*prudentia oeconomica*).[596] Further evidence of the liberal tendencies in Jesuit thought can be found throughout this study.

Also, previous scholarship by Rudolf Schüssler has highlighted the development of the liberal notion of self-ownership in early modern scholasticism, which is again particularly evident in Jesuit writers.[597] How the notions of possession of the self and freedom of action tie in with the development of the doctrine of 'freedom of contract' has been the subject of previous study.[598] Lessius' statement in the controversy on grace and free will may be recalled here to the effect that human will is the owner of its very actions (*voluntas domina suorum actuum*) and therefore not just a passive agent in the process of salvation.[599] Tomás Sánchez literally mentions the individual will's indisputable right of possessing its own liberty (*ius certum possessionis libertatis*).[600] The result of which was, of course, that the medieval law of property, particularly the maxim that the position of the possessor is the stronger (*melior est conditio possidentis*) could be applied to human freedom and moral agency.

Practically speaking, this means that man is free in principle to do what he wants to do, unless there is a superior law that can sufficiently demonstrate that in a particular case it limits the will's freedom.[601] This law will then be in the position of the plaintiff in a court who has to prove that the defendant is no rightful possessor of his liberty. In the meantime, the defendant is free to do as pleases him. As long as there is doubt if there is a legal constraint of liberty, the will preserves its freedom of action, according to the principle that in a doubtful case the condition of the possessor is the stronger (*in pari delicto vel causa potior est conditio possidentis*). This is an excellent illustration of how medieval procedural law

---

[596] Lugo, *De iustitia et iure*, tom. 2, disp. 26, sect. 8, par. 2, num. 143, p. 337. Cited supra, n. 12.

[597] R. Schüßler, *Moral self-ownership and ius possessionis in late scholastics*, in: V. Mäkinen – P. Korkman (eds.), Transformations in medieval and early modern rights discourse, [The new synthese historical library, Texts and studies in the history of philosophy, 59], Dordrecht 2006, p. 149–172. For an older but still valuable contribution, see E. Ruffini Avondo, *Il possesso nella teologia morale post-tridentina*, Rivista di storia del diritto italiano, 2 (1929), p. 63–98.

[598] See our *Jesuit freedom of contract*, Tijdschrift voor Rechtsgeschiedenis, 77 (2009), p. 423–458.

[599] See Lessius, *De gratia efficaci, decretis divinis, libertate arbitrii et praescientia Dei conditionata*, cap. 5, num. 11, p. 53.

[600] T. Sánchez, *Opus morale in praecepta Decalogi*, Antverpiae 1614, tom. 1, lib. 1, cap. 10, num. 11, p. 41.

[601] For a more detailed account, see *Jesuit freedom of contract*.

and property law helped the moral theologians, especially the Jesuits, to formulate freedom of action in the first place. As the Jesuit Antonio Perez (1599–1649) witnesses, they did so with the specific purpose of promoting liberty (*quia favent libertati operandi, et ab innumeris obligationibus homines liberant*).[602]

What these brief encounters with the moral theological conceptions of ownership of the self and liberty show is how the juridical treatment of contracts is now being set against the background of a much larger philosophy. It explains why contract law is suddenly being debated in much more general terms and from a broader anthropological perspective than in the *ius commune*. The theologians' way of grappling with contract law is distant from Romano-canon casuistry or dry juristic craftsmanship. Contract law becomes part of a broader theological story about man, his goods and the divine *telos* of life on earth. As we have seen Suárez explaining in the second chapter, human life is basically understood in terms of a pilgrimage in which the individual human being stays on the right track toward his eternal destination by following the right directions— directions essentially given to man by a multiplicity of laws ranging from natural law over canon law to statute law and laws which man has imposed upon himself through promise and contract (*promissio lex privata*).[603]

The theological elevation of man's will into a private legislator who can or cannot decide to impose an obligation upon itself through contract rests on a long-standing tradition. On the basis of D. 50,17,23 (*legem contractus dedit*) it was not unusual for the jurists of the *ius commune* to think of contract as an act of private legislation.[604] It would find one of its most famous expressions in article 1134 of the French Civil Code. Yet, again, in the grand universe of lofty theological argument it would resonate stronger than before. If Jesuits such as Molina, Lessius and Sánchez had prepared this rise of the will as a private legislator, Oñate definitively consecrated the principle that the individual will is the measure of all things in matters contractual. Without the reserve that could still be found in earlier moral theologians, Oñate straightforwardly holds that contractual obligation merely depends on the will of the person willing to incur it,

---

602 Perez, *De iustitia et iure*, tract. 2, disp. 2, cap. 4, num. 78, p. 174.

603 Juan de Lugo, *De iustitia et iure*, Lugduni 1642, tom. 2, disp. 23, sect. 1, num. 4, p. 103.

604 Compare D.16,3,1,6 and VI 5,13,85. On the Roman and medieval origins of the notion that a contract takes the place of law for the parties who make it, as well as Domat's programmatic restatement of it, see I. Birocchi, *Notazioni sul contratto*, Quaderni fiorentini per la storia del pensiero giuridico moderno, 19 (1990), p. 637–659, and P.J. du Plessis, *The Roman concept of 'lex contractus'*, Roman Legal Tradition, 3 (2006), p. 69–94.

from the moment he is willing to incur it and to the extent that he is willing to incur it (*nemo ex contractu se obligat nisi qui vult, et quando vult, et
quantum vult*).[605]

Oñate extolls the principle that the sole measure of contractual obligation is the will as the lynchpin and the basis of the entire doctrine of
contract (*cardo et basis totius materiae contractuum*). Not surprisingly,
property law is invoked to motivate this highly liberal principle. An especially powerful argument is derived from the famous Roman maxim contained in C. 4,35,21 that everybody is moderator and arbiter of his own
things (*suae quidem quisque rei moderator et arbiter*). Moreover, Oñate
explains, not only is everybody the moderator and arbiter of his own
things, but also of the rights and obligations that are derived from those
things.[606] Hence, it is possible not only to transfer the goods to another
person, but also the right to claim those goods and your obligation to
transfer them. This obligation is almost tantamount to the thing itself: it
is its substitute and vicar. So if property law allows you to dispose of your
goods as freely as you wish, and obligations are rights acting as substitutes
of these real things, it is equally allowed to freely impose obligations upon
yourself regarding these goods.

Hence, the freedom to incur all kinds of obligations through promise and contract rests on a liberal conception of private property. The
extent of this personally imposed obligation is also determined by the
will. Consequently, not every promise results in an enforceable obligation
as a matter of justice, according to Oñate. Some promises can be merely
binding as a matter of honesty or friendship. The measure of the seriousness of the obligation entirely depends on the will of the private legislator.
Using highly theological vocabulary, Oñate derives this from man's being
created in God's image. Created in God's image, man is capable of having *dominium* over the goods of the world and over his will and actions.
Hence, the measure of obligation must be the extent to which he wishes
to bind himself:[607]

---

[605] Oñate, *De contractibus*, tom. 2, tract. 9, disp. 29, sect. 6, num. 93, p. 114.

[606] Oñate, *De contractibus*, tom. 2, tract. 9, disp. 29, sect. 7, num. 86, p. 112: 'Quia in
hoc casu promissio est quasi quaedam donatio, non quidem ipsius rei promissae quae
tunc non traditur neque est praesens, sed obligationis loco illius quae tantumdem valet
ac ipsa res promissa ; quae obligatio ex tunc donata et tradita per acceptationem alterius
est substituta rei promissae et quasi vicaria illius. (....) Quia ergo unusquisque suae rei est
moderator et arbiter, sicut rem suam donare posset si ad manum haberet, ita loco rei istam
obligationem de qua loquimur, donat.'

[607] Oñate, *De contractibus*, tom. 2, tract. 9, disp. 29, sect. 6, num. 74, p. 108: 'Reliquit
Deus hominem in manu consilii sui Eccles. 15, 14 sine dubio inter alia, quia reliquit Deus
in voluntate eius ut se obligaret, quando vellet, et sicut actiones agentium non operantur

God left man the freedom to take care of himself, as is expressed in Ecclesi-
astes 15, 14, one of the reasons being, no doubt, that He left it to man's will to
bind himself when he wanted (*reliquit Deus in voluntate eius ut se obligaret
quando vellet*). Now actions do not operate beyond the will and the intention of the agents, but in accordance with their will and intention.

As if to underline his fundamental belief in genuine, or, at least, typically
Jesuit 'freedom of contract', he continues:[608]

Otherwise man would not be the true and perfect owner of his goods (*alias
non esset homo vere et perfecte dominus rerum suarum*), that is, unless he
could give them when he wants, to whom he wants, in whatever way he
wants, and unless he has the additional capacity to enter into contractual
obligation when he wants and in whatever way he wants.

It would be hard to find a more limpid formulation of 'contractual liberty'.
Oñate's particularly clear-cut phrases are the climax of a trend, witnessed
among the scholastic theologians over a period of at least one century and
a half, to re-found the law of contract on the autonomous will of the free
individual. Not all moral theologians were as bold, though, as to spell out
their belief in 'freedom of contract' so straightforwardly. There has always
been an astounding plurality amongst the early modern scholastics all the
more so as we move away from the limited set of core shared principles.

3.3.1.3   De contractibus in genere

The rise of a general law of contract has often been connected with the
birth of the notion of individual autonomy. In conformity with widespread beliefs, Lipp and Diesselhorst therefore concluded that, although
the influence of scholasticism on Grotius' doctrine of promising is substantial, the cradle of general contract law still lies in Grotius' *De iure
belli ac pacis*. It is to the credit of Paolo Cappellini to have qualified these
views by pointing out that the early modern scholastics, particulary Jesuit
authors such as Molina, Lessius, Lugo and Oñate, formulated both the idea
that contactual obligation rests on the autonomous will of the promisor
and the first doctrines of contract as a general category.[609] We think it is

---

ultra voluntatem et intentionem eorum, ita operantur iuxta voluntatem et intentionem
eorum.'

   [608] Oñate, *De contractibus*, tom. 2, tract. 9, disp. 29, sect. 6, num. 76, p. 108: 'Quia alias
non esset homo vere et perfecte dominus rerum suarum si non posset eas dare quando, et
cui vult, et quomodo vult, et obligationem etiam contrahere, quando et quomodo vult.'

   [609] See Paolo Cappellini's fundamental *Sulla formazione del moderno concetto di 'dottrina generale del diritto'*. Lipp's treatment of the Spanish scholastics can be found in *Die
Bedeutung des Naturrechts*, p. 126–129.

obvious from the above paragraphs that there is no reason whatsoever to doubt Cappellini's observations on the rise of general contract law in the Jesuit scholastics. The concept of the will's self-ownership has hardly been described in more explicit terms than in the early modern Jesuit writers.

Having singled out the will's liberty to bind itself as the centerpiece of all contractual obligation, the early modern scholastics could now go on to develop a general law of contract even before discussing the particulars of the specific contracts. At least originally, this turn towards a systematic introduction to the general law of contract seems to have been the province of the Jesuit moral theologians. The efforts toward systematization are still very modest in scholastics such as Domingo de Soto, who, following Thomas Aquinas, did elaborate on contractual promise, but rather rapidly and merely in the margin of a discussion on the binding force of vows.[610] The same could be said of Domingo Bañez. The Jesuits, on the contrary, explicitly devoted one chapter to general contract law (*de contractibus in genere*) before systematically treating the specific contracts. 'We will first talk about contracts in general, using the word 'contract' in its most wide sense,' Molina admonishes his readers,[611] 'next we will descend to the specific contracts.'

A glimpse at the table of contents of the first three sections of Lessius' *De iustitia et iure* is revealing of a trend toward systematization of legal doctrine, not only in regard to contract law, but also property law and torts:[612]

Section I. On justice, right, and the specific types of right
1. On justice in general (*De iustitia in genere*)
2. On right in general (*De iure in genere*)
3. On dominion, usufruct, use and possession, which are specific types of rights
4. On who is capable of having dominion; on the objects of dominion
5. On the mode of acquiring dominion over goods that belong to nobody or over goods which are common to all, particularly on servitudes, hunting, fishing, fowling and treasures
6. On the mode of acquiring dominion over someone else's good, particularly on prescription

---

[610] Soto, *De iustitia et iure* (ed. fac. V. Diego Carro – M. González Ordóñez, vol. 4), lib. 7, quaest. 2 (*De voti vigore ac virtute*), art. 1 (*Utrum omne votum obliget ad sui observationem*), p. 628–639.

[611] Molina, *De iustitia et iure*, tom. 2 (*De contractibus*), tract. 2, disp. 252 (*pactum et contractus quid sint et de obligatione civili et naturali*), col. 1, num. 1: 'Prius autem dicemus de contractibus in genere, sumpto latissime vocabulo contractus, deinde vero ad singulos descendemus.'

[612] Lessius, *De iustitia et iure*, p. 13–14.

Section II. On injustice and damage and their necessary restitution

    7. On injustice and restitution in general (*De iniuria et restitutione in genere*)

    8. On injustice against spiritual goods

    9. On injustice against the body through homicide or mutilation

    10. On injustice against the body through adultery and fornication

    11. On injustice against reputation and honour through detraction and defamation

    12. On injustice against property through theft, robbery or damage.

    13. On cooperating to theft or injury

    14. On restitution by virtue of the good received and the receiver of restitution

    15. On the respective order and the way in which restitution has to be made, where restitution must be made and what to do with the expenses

    16. On the factors which excuse from restitution

Section III. On contracts

    17. On contracts in general (*De contractibus in genere*)

    18. On promise and donation

    19. On testaments and legacies

    20. On loan for consumption and usury

    21. On sale-purchase

    22. On rents

    23. On money-exchange

    24. On lease-hire, emphyteusis and feudal contracts

    25. On partnerships

    26. On games and gambling

    27. On deposit and loan

    28. On suretyship, pawn, mortgage

Arguably, the sheer organization of Lessius' exposition on contracts points toward the birth of a general law of contract. Similar examples could be given for the other Jesuit authors mentioned.[613] By the time Oñate published his treatise on contracts, the entire first volume of his voluminous work, which is more than seven hundred in folio pages, were dedicated to contract law in general:

Vol. 1. On contracts in general (*De contractibus in genere*)

    1. On the nature and the divisions of contract

    2. On the causes of contract

    3. On the effects of contract

    4. On the qualities of contract

---

[613] Cappellini, *Sulla formazione del moderno concetto di 'dottrina generale del diritto'*, p. 354–355, n. 53.

5. On adjacent pacts and other accidentals
6. On the termination and dissolution of contract
7. On quasi-contracts and distracts

VOL. 2. ON THE SPECIFIC, LUCRATIVE CONTRACTS (*De singulis contractibus lucrativis*)

8. On the four sacred contracts
9. On promise and stipulation
10. On donation in general and its species
11. On dowry
12. On loan for use
13. On mandate
14. On mandataries
15. On the duties of the mandator
16. On agency
17. On tutelage and curatorship
18. On sureties
19. On contracts of deposit
20. On pawn and mortgage

VOL. 3. ON THE SPECIFIC, ONEROUS CONTRACTS (*De singulis contractibus onerosis*)

21. On sale-purchase
22. On rents, certainly Spanish rents
23. On the invalid contract of simony
24. On money-exchanges
25. On the contract of exchange
26. On settlement agreements
27. On arbitration agreements
28. On the partnership contract
29. On loan for consumption
30. On usury
31. On the contract of emphyteusis
32. On feudal contracts
33. On usufruct, use and habitation
34. On rustic and urban servitudes
35. On lease-hire
36. On the four aleatory contracts: insurance, gambling, lottery, gaming

Many pages could be spent describing the great variety of attempts for formulating an adequate definition of contract. It may suffice here to quote Oñate's simple and elegant definition of contract as an agreement which is binding as a matter of commutative justice (*contractus est pactum obligans ex iustitia commutativa*).[614] What is worthwhile noting is that,

---

[614] Oñate, *De contractibus*, tom. 1, tract. 1, disp. 1, sect. 3, num. 26, p. 7. In the preceding numbers (12–25), Oñate rebukes the definitions offered by Labeo, Jean Gerson, Conrad

following Lessius, Oñate puts an end to the controversy surrounding the status of lucrative contracts. In his view, the definition of contract as an agreement binding by virtue of justice in exchange allows one to think of lucrative contracts as contracts in the proper sense of the word, because even lucrative contracts are binding as a matter of justice for one of the parties involved (*etiam omnis contractus lucrativus obligat ex iustitia ex uno latere*).[615]

The problematic status of gifts as contracts derived not in the least from the Roman jurist Labeo's famous definition of contract as *synallagma*.[616] Since *synallagma*, or reciprocity in exchange, was deemed an essential feature of contracts, it was usually held that lucrative contracts such as gifts could not constitute true contracts.[617] Such was the authoritative opinion, for instance, of Domingo de Soto. He claimed that gifts were in the moral realm of liberality, which had nothing to do with justice. Therefore, Soto heavily criticized Summenhart's subtle attempt to consider gifts as contracts by stretching the Roman definition of contract.[618] As frequently occurred, Summenhart prepared the way for change and modernity by introducing clever distinctions that in the long run allowed

---

Summenhart and Paolo Comitoli. For a thorough discussion of Gerson's and Summenhart's definitions of contract, see Birocchi, *Causa e categoria generale del contratto*, p. 208–218.

[615] Oñate, *De contractibus*, tom. 1, tract. 1, disp. 1, sect. 3, num. 27, p. 7.

[616] D. 50,16,19: 'Labeo libro primo praetoris urbani definit, quod quaedam agantur, quaedam gerantur, quaedam contrahantur: et actum quidem generale verbum esse, sive verbis sive re quid agatur, ut in stipulatione vel numeratione: contractum autem ultro citroque obligationem, quod Graeci *synallagma* vocant, veluti emptionem venditionem, locationem, conductionem, societatem: gestum rem significare sine verbis factam.'

[617] On this debate regarding the status of gratuitous contracts, see the short notices in Cappellini, *Sulla formazione del moderno concetto di 'dottrina generale del diritto'*, p. 342–343 and in W. Decock, *Donations, bonnes mœurs et droit naturel, Un débat théologico-politique dans la scolastique des temps modernes*, in: M. Chamocho Cantudo (ed.), Droit et mœurs, Implication et influence des mœurs dans la configuration du droit, Jaén 2011, p. 185–188. Given the divergence of the historical traditions, it is not surprising to find that the status of gifts is still a point of dispute in today's scholarly literature; cf. R. Barbaix, *Het contractuele statuut van de schenking*, Antwerpen-Oxford 2008, p. 1013–1044.

[618] Soto, *De iustitia et iure* (ed. fac. V. Diego Carro – M. González Ordóñez, vol. 3), lib. 6, quaest. 2, art. 1, p. 541: 'Contractus namque omnis, si de suo nomine perpendas, actus iustitiae est, utramque colligantis partem. Laxant tamen alii latius nomen usque ad illas actiones ex quibus ex altera tantum parte oritur vinculum: veluti est donatio et simplex promissio. Et ideo Baldus, quem Sylvester citat in verbo, contractus, et Conradus sequitur, q. 16, distinguit de nomine contractus, quod accipiatur proprie, quando obligatio oritur ex utraque parte, et impropriissime quando ex neutra nascitur. Sed revera abusivae istae acceptiones abusu essent abigendae. Hoc enim est nomina a sua nativa significatione abalienare, siquidem neque donatio neque simplex promissio ad iustitiam attinent, sed sunt actus liberalitatis.'

other theologians to advocate new opinions.[619] Concretely, Summenhart introduces a distinction between three different conceptions of contract. The second, improper definition of contract includes donations.[620]

Summenhart's subtle efforts to open up the definition of contract were brought to fruition in the writings of the late sixteenth century theologians. The Dominican Francisco García (1525–1585), who co-founded and taught at the University of Tarragona, argued that donations were contracts in the proper sense of the word. He defined contract in terms of mutual consent regardless of its synallagmatic nature, rejecting Soto's viewpoint and Summenhart's traditional conclusion as being too scrupulous.[621] Famous Jesuits such as Molina and Lessius continued García's line of reasoning, even though it is not clear whether they were familiar with his thought. Molina and Lessius argued that gifts could be properly called contracts. For example, Molina fiercely rebuked Soto's standpoint, stressing that even though donations are motivated by liberality and not by an act of justice, once they have been concluded, they are binding as a matter of justice (*quamvis ex liberalitate profecta, ex ea resultavit obligatio iustitiae*).[622] Summenhart had not yet gone so far in his reasoning. Citing C. 4,21,17, in which donations are called contracts, Lessius suggests that Roman law itself considered gifts to be contracts. Lessius defines contract as an

---

[619] Cappellini, *Sulla formazione del moderno concetto di 'dottrina generale del diritto'*, p. 341, n. 42 interestingly notes in making the threefold distinction in the conception of contract, Summenhart might have combined ideas that can be traced back to the late medieval jurists.

[620] Conradus Summenhart, *Opus septipertitum de contractibus*, [Augustae Vindelicae 1515], quaest. 16, par. *Distinctio*, [s.p.]: 'Secundo modo capitur improprie, et sic est factum vel actus ex quo oritur tantum ex una parte obligatio seu in quo tantum una pars obligatur. Hoc modo donatio, mutuatio et stipulatio sunt contractus et non primo modo.'

[621] Francisco García, *Tratado utilísimo y muy general de todos los contratos*, Valencia 1583, cap. 1 in: I. Zorroza – H. Rodríguez-Penelas (eds.), [Colleción de pensamiento medieval y renacentista, 46], Pamplona 2003, p. 61: 'Contrato es un legítimo consentimiento de muchos, que sobre alguna cosa convienen; del cual consentimiento nace en ambas partes, o en una tan solamente, alguna obligación. (...) Dijimos "o en una tan solamente", por causa de la promisión, de la donación, del depósito, de la prenda y semejantes contratos, en los cuales de la una parte tan solamente nace la obligación, como en la explicación de la naturaleza de estos claramente se verá. No ignoramos haber algunos doctores que dijeron tales conciertos no ser contratos; de cuyo número fueron: Soto (...) y Conrado (...), tratando esta materia algo escrupulosamente con los juristas y canonistas, los cuales no quieren que sea contrato, sino el que por ambas partes produce obligación.'

[622] Molina, *De iustitia et iure*, tom. 2 (*De contractibus*), tract. 2, disp. 252, col. 3, num. 6: 'Etenim quamvis promissio illa ex liberalitate donantis sit profecta, fueritque proinde actus liberalitatis promittentis et non iustitiae, ex ea tamen resultavit obligatio iustitiae, qua promittens eo ipso ex iustitia astrictus mansit ad id implendum, quod sola liberalitate ductus, promisit, ut inferius suo loco fusius explicabitur.'

agreement between two parties creating an obligation for at least one of them (*contractus est conventio duorum obligationem saltem in alter-utro pariens*), so that lucrative contracts are truly contracts.[623] Lessius expressly indicates that he uses the term 'contract' in a wide sense so as to be identical to 'agreement' and to include gratuitous contracts.[624] Oñate claimed that Lessius' was the right definition and that it was mirrored in his own definition.

Oñate not only followed Lessius in considering unilateral, lucrative agreements as true contracts. He also endorsed Lessius' interpretation of Labeo (*contractus est ultro citroque obligatio*), to the effect that the synallagmatic aspect of a contract regards its effect rather than its formal structure.[625] This might need some explanation. Formally speaking, Lessius explains, a contract is something that is made up of a verbal expression, a written document or another external sign. Through these external signs, people express their mind, bind themselves toward each other, and exchange rights. A contract is not identical with contractual obligation. It is merely the cause of the obligation.[626] The obligation is the effect of the contract. Moreover, contract is an external sign producing obligation by virtue of the underlying consent of the contracting parties (*contractus est signum externum practicum ultro citroque obligationem ex consensu contrahentium pariens*).

If we wish to understand the general law of contract as developed by the Jesuit moral theologians, it is indispensable to turn to their discussion of promise (*promissio*). This may sound bizarre, but it need not be. As a matter of fact, 'promise' was used as a general term to denote the very abstract concept of contract. Its function was to serve as a kind of

---

[623] Lessius, *De iustitia et iure*, lib. 2, cap. 17, dub. 1, num. 4–5, p. 196.

[624] Lessius, *De iustitia et iure*, lib. 2, cap. 17, dub. 1, num. 5, p. 196: 'Nos nomine *contractus* utimur hîc ample, ut idem sit quod *pactum* et comprehendat contractus gratuitos, qui sunt veluti semicontractus.'

[625] Oñate, *De contractibus*, tom. 1, tract. 1, disp. 1, sect. 3, num. 17, p. 6: 'Referens praedictam definitionem [Labeonis], sic explicans, est pactum ex quo ultrocitroque oritur obligatio, quo fit ut illa Labeonis enunciatio formalis non sit, sed sit effective interpretanda, Lessius (…) cum hac definitione consentit.'

[626] Lessius, *De iustitia et iure*, lib. 2, cap. 17, dub. 1, num. 1, p. 195: '*Contractus est ultro citroque obligatio, quod Graeci synallagma vocant*. Ita habetur l. 19, Labeo, ff. de verborum significatione, quae definitio non sic est intelligenda quasi contractus sit formaliter obligatio (obligatio enim est effectus per contractum productus in contrahentibus) sed quod sit causa obligationis. Est enim formaliter locutio vel scriptura vel aliud externum signum, quo hominess exprimunt mentem suam et sese vicissim alter alteri obligant et iura commutant. Itaque *contractus* est signum externum practicum ultro citroque obligationem ex consensu contrahentium pariens, quod nomine Graeco clarius indicatur.'

generic concept around which the general principles of contract could be built. It could refer both to onerous and gratuitous contracts. As Lessius put it:[627] 'It needs to be remarked that the term 'promise' is general in character (*nomen promissionis esse generale*), and that it can be extended to all contracts (*posseque extendi ad omnes contractus*), just as the term 'stipulation' can, since I can promise something in exchange for something (*sub onere*), e.g. a price or a good, or for free (*gratis*). On the other hand, the term promise can be used to denote a specific contract, namely a gratuitous promise, which is motivated by liberality or gratitude.

A most delightful analysis of the term 'promise' is offered by Oñate. Although it certainly builds on the work of the previous scholastics, it seems to be quite unique. It is not sure, therefore, whether all moral theologians would have seen things as clearly as Oñate did. In any case, Oñate's analysis is quite remarkable because he seems to have found a vocabulary with which to express ideas that are in conformity with the scholastic tradition but prefigure much later developments in the history of private law, particularly in nineteenth century Germany. He distinguishes between three different meanings of *promissio*: 1) *promissio* as a part of every contract, namely the offer, which, along with the acceptance, constitutes the basic skeleton of every contract; 2) *promissio* as the combination of offer and acceptance which precedes every contract; 3) *promissio* as a specific contract—which falls outside the scope of the following discussion.

In its first sense, 'offer', *promissio* comes down to the proposal (*propositum*) to do something that is of use to another person with the intention of obligation even before the other party has accepted the offer. Hence, *promissio* in the sense of 'offer' is part and parcel of every contract, since every single contract consists of the promise, that is the offer, to transfer a property right, on the one hand, and the acceptance of that offer, on the other hand (*omnes contractus ex promissione et acceptatione constant*).[628] In this first sense, promise is different from contract in the way that a

---

[627] Lessius, *De iustitia et iure*, lib. 2, cap. 18, dub. 1, num. 1, p. 216: 'Notandum est, nomen *promissionis* esse generale, posseque extendi ad omnes contractus, sicut et nomen stipulationis. Possum enim promittere rem aliquam sub aliquo onere (v.g. ut detur pretium aut res alia) vel gratis.'

[628] Oñate, *De contractibus*, tom. 2, tract. 9, disp. 29, sect. 1, num. 6, p. 87: 'Primo pro proposito aliquid faciendi in utilitatem alterius cum intentione se obligandi ante acceptationem, et sic est pars cuiusque contractus, quia omnes quotquot sunt contractus ex promissione transferendi dominium vel partem et acceptatione constant et conflantur.'

substantial part differs from the whole (*tamquam pars a toto differt*). For, as Oñate vividly explains:[629]

> Every contract is composed of a conflation of promise and acceptance, just as a physical thing is composed of matter and form, or a human being of soul and body. Now if promise is understood in the second manner, then it does not differ from contract, just as a man does not differ from the combination of his soul and body, or just as the whole universally does not differ from the united combination of its two parts.

In its second sense, *promissio* denotes precisely that fundamental fusion of offer and acceptance that forms the backbone of contract understood both in generic and specific terms (*promissio simul cum acceptatione et sic est contractus*).[630] Here, promise coincides with contract in the way that man coincides with the combination of his body and soul. Is there a more plastic way conceivable to elucidate the doctrine of offer and acceptance?

3.3.2   *All accepted promises are binding*

3.3.2.1   *First requirement*: animus obligandi

Voluntary intention as the foundation of contractual obligation was beyond doubt for the early modern scholastics. The most direct expressions of this principle can be found in the Jesuit writers. Lessius holds that the entire power of promise to bind stems from intention (*omnis vis obligandi promissionis est ab intentione*).[631] Lugo couples this basic insight to the metaphor of contract as an act of private legislation. Promise is seen as a private law, which the promisor imposes upon himself and by virtue of which he binds himself.[632] In the absence of will there can be

---

629 Oñate, *De contractibus*, tom. 2, tract. 9, disp. 29, sect. 1, num. 7, p. 87: 'Componitur enim et conflatur omnis contractus ex promissione et acceptatione tanquam ex materia et forma compositum physicum, vel tanquam homo ex anima et corpore. Si vero secundo modo sumatur, non differt promissio a contractu, sicut nec homo non differt ab anima et corpore simul sumptis, nec totum aliquod in universum differt a duabus partibus suis simul sumptis et unitis.'

630 Oñate, *De contractibus*, tom. 2, tract. 9, disp. 29, sect. 1, num. 6, p. 87: 'Secundo pro quacumque promissione simul cum acceptatione, et sic est contractus, et omnia genera et species contractus (quia omnes sunt promissiones quaedam) pervagatur.'

631 Lessius, *De iustitia et iure*, lib. 2, cap. 18, dub. 1, num. 6, p. 216.

632 Lugo, *De iustitia et iure*, tom. 2, disp. 23, sect. 1, num. 4, p. 103: 'Promissio enim est lex privata quam promittens sibi imponit et qua se ligat, ubi ergo ex defectu animi non se ligat, non est lex nec promissio.'

no talk of a binding promise, since a law cannot be properly called a law
if its outward expression does not rest on the inner will to bind.[633] If a
legislator lacks the will to bind, his subjects are not bound. By the same
token, if the promisor does not have the will to bind himself, then there
will not be a private law or a promise (*deficiente animo se obligandi non
erit lex privata nec promissio*).[634]

Not only is the will to be bound essential to contractual promise, Jesuits
such as Lessius, Lugo and Oñate insist that contractual obligation also
requires that the promisor intends to bind himself as a matter of commutative justice. The object of the intent of obligation must be the exchange
of legally enforceable rights and obligations. We will come back to this
point further in this text. It is sufficient to note here that the moral theologians were careful to distinguish between mere promises out of friendship
or liberality and truly juridical promises. To put it in modern terminology,
the theologians were aware that not all agreements are exactly the same
as contracts. There is promising out of social convenience, gentleman's
agreements, and serious contracts.

What also preoccupied theologians was the need to distinguish promises from other assertions about future action. As Soto put it in the margin
of his treatment of the force of a vow (*votum*)—which is basically a promise between man and God instead of a promise in between men—a simple assertion about the future, e.g. 'I will do', is not necessarily a promise
(*simplex assertio futuri non est semper promissio*).[635] The difference is that
plans can be changed whereas promises cannot. The distinction between
a plan or resolution (*propositum*) and a promise (*promissio*) went back

---

[633] Lugo, *De iustitia et iure*, tom. 2, disp. 23, sect. 1, num. 4, p. 103: 'Et quidem in hac
quaestione de nomine placet magis quod deficiente voluntate interna non dicatur promissio, quia promissio simpliciter dicitur actus humanus inducens obligationem, sicut etiam
lex exterius proposita sine voluntate obligandi non est lex proprie et in rigore, et sicut
matrimonium externum sine consensu interno non est matrimonium et votum externum
sine voluntate se obligandi non est verum votum, et sic de aliis.'

[634] Lugo, *De iustitia et iure*, tom. 2, disp. 23, sect. 1, num. 4, p. 103–104: 'Sicut si in legislatore desit animus ligandi et obligandi subditos, quantumvis proponat exterius et fingat
se velle obligare, non obligat, nisi per accidens propter ignorantiam, qua subditi putant
voluisse legislatorem obligare, ergo | deficiente animo illa non est lex vera, sed apparens.
Sic ergo lex privata, deficiente animo se obligandi, non erit lex privata nec promissio.'

[635] Soto, *De iustitia et iure* (ed. fac. V. Diego Carro – M. González Ordóñez, vol. 4),
lib. 7, quaest. 2, p. 631: 'Praeter haec ex superioribus recolendum est simplicem assertionem futuri non esse semper promissionem. Si enim dicas, faciam, id tantum exprimens
quod in proposito habes, non subinde obligaris nisi illo id sensu proferas quod est, promitto facere, ut puta dum quis ex te quidpiam petit, et respondes, faciam. Alias iam supra
diximus posse te mutare propositum.'

to Thomas Aquinas' succinct analysis of the making of a vow. In Thomas' view, a vow comes about in three successive stages:[636] 1) deliberation (*deliberatio*); 2) the resolution of the will (*propositum voluntatis*); 3) promise (*promissio*). In the early modern period, this became a popular way to analyze not only promises to God, but also promises between men.

The debate on the distinction between *deliberatio*, *propositum* and *promissio* truly began with Tommaso da Vio Cajetan. Unfortunately, Cajetan's commentaries often made Thomas' thoughts more complex than they were. A point in case is his explanation of the meaning of *deliberatio*. What one might wish to retain from his lengthy exposition is that deliberation does not simply signify voluntariness in this context.[637] Deliberation presupposes an intellectual act, namely the assessment and comparison (*collatio*) of a large set of different courses of action, and an act of will, namely the determination (*determinatio*) to pursue one chosen course of action.[638] In Cajetan's view, this element of determination constitutes true *deliberatio*. It is different from *propositum*, because a plan always regards the future whereas the determination of the will to follow one particular course of action after careful rational analysis is irrespective of time.[639] Also of interest is the conclusion that the words 'I will do' should not necessarily be interpreted as constituting a binding promise. Unless the promisor is motivated by a true *animus promittendi*, 'I will do' can also express the intent to do something in the future (*enuntiatio propositi*) or the impending, factual realisation of an act (*enuntiatio eventus*).[640]

For many generations, moral theologians struggled with the distinction between *propositum* and *promissio*. Molina insisted that a *propositum* is

---

636 Aquinas, *Summa Theologiae* (Ed. Leonina, tom. 9), IIaIIae, quaest. 88 (*De voto*), art. 1, concl., in: *Opera omnia iussu impensaque Leonis XIII edita*, tom. 9: *Secunda secundae a quaestione LVII ad quaestionem CXXII cum commentariis Cardinalis Cajetani*, Romae 1897 [hereafter: Ed. Leonina, tom. 9], p. 234: 'Promissio autem procedit ex proposito faciendi. Propositum autem aliquam deliberationem praeexigit, cum sit actus voluntatis deliberatae. Sic igitur ad votum tria ex necessitate requiruntur, primo quidem, deliberatio; secundo, propositum voluntatis; tertio, promissio, in qua perficitur ratio voti.'
637 Tommaso de Vio Cajetanus, *Commentaria ad Secundam Secundae divi Thomae*, in: *Sancti Thomae Aquinatis opera omnia iussu impensaque Leonis XIII edita*, tom. 9: *Secunda secundae Summae Theologiae a quaestione LVII ad quaestionem CXXII*, Romae 1897 [hereafter: Cajetanus, *Commentaria ad Secundam Secundae divi Thomae* (Ed. Leonina, tom. 9)], ad quaest. 88, art. 1, p. 235, num. 3.
638 Cajetanus, *Commentaria ad Secundam Secundae divi Thomae* (Ed. Leonina, tom. 9), ad quaest. 88, art. 1, p. 236, num. 4.
639 Cajetanus, *Commentaria ad Secundam Secundae divi Thomae* (Ed. Leonina, tom. 9), ad quaest. 88, art. 1, p. 236, num. 4 (in fine).
640 Cajetanus, *Commentaria ad Secundam Secundae divi Thomae* (Ed. Leonina, tom. 9), ad quaest. 88, art. 1, p. 235, num. 1.

entirely different from a *promissio*. More precisely, it is different to have the firm and deliberate will and purpose (*propositum*) to do somebody a favor, expressing this will and purpose linguistically through the use of a future verb, and to constrain oneself (*astringere seipsum*) out of liberality and through one's own will to do something in favor of somebody, also expressing this through the use of a future verb.[641] In other words, what preoccupied the theologians was whether a statement such as 'tomorrow I will give you a horse' automatically produced obligation or not. As is frequently the case, not until Pedro de Oñate was a more or less clear, systematic, and persuasive linguistic analysis of statements such as these finally brought forward. Oñate holds that the proposition 'I will give you a horse tomorrow' can have no less than five meanings (*quincuplex sensus*). Only two of them involve obligation of some kind.

The first meaning of statements such as 'I will give you a horse tomorrow' or 'I will give you a hundred' is a mere affirmation of what is going to happen in the future. It is neither a plan nor a promise, but an objective statement of a future event.[642] The speaker merely intends to make a proposition (*propositio*). In its second meaning, 'I will give you a horse tomorrow' involves a certain *propositum*, but it is not a *propositum* in the proper sense of the word and it is not binding. It is a mere affirmation of a present intention which can still be altered. The speaker does not intend to bind himself irrevocably. At the very moment he makes this statement, he can already be aware of the fact that he probably is not going to give the horse because of the 'fragility of human nature'…[643]

---

[641] Molina, *De iustitia et iure*, tom. 2 (*De contractibus*), tract. 2, disp. 262, cols. 36–37, num. 1: 'Illud ante omnia est observandum, longe diversa esse, aliquem habere propositum voluntatemve deliberatam ac firmam quippiam in gratiam alicuius faciendi, idque verbo futuri temporis exprimere, dicendo faciam hoc, vel dabo tibi hoc, aut illud; et aliquem ex sua liberalitate seipsum propria voluntate astringere ad quippiam faciendum, idque verbo futuri temporis exprimere, dicendo, promitto me facturum vel daturum tibi hoc, aut tali die dabo tibi hoc, aut in gratiam tui faciam hoc, aut illud.'

[642] Oñate, *De contractibus*, tom. 2, tract. 9, disp. 29, sect. 1, num. 4, p. 85: 'Primo ut solum affirmet quod futurum est vel ipse credit futurum, sicut posset affirmare quamcumque aliam veritatem, quia hae propositiones etiam si sint de futuro contingenti determinatam habent veritatem in se ipsis, licet non habeant determinatam in causis.'

[643] Oñate, *De contractibus*, tom. 2, tract. 9, disp. 29, sect. 1, num. 4, p. 85–6: 'Secundo modo potest esse intentio illam propositionem proferentis non affirmare eam veritatem futuram, scilicet se daturum centum Petro, sed praesentem suam intentionem dandi, sive postea sit impleturus sive non. (…) Sicut qui confitetur vel sacerdos qui audit confessionem, potest valide et licite asserere se habere de praesenti intentionem et simul credere se propositum illud ex fragilitate humana, irruentibus occasionibus et tentationibus non esse impleturum. Et ipse hoc credens licite confitetur et sacerdos confessionem excipiens et idem credens licite eum absolvit.'

The element of mutability distinguishes the second from the third meaning of, 'I will give you a horse tomorrow'. If there is an intention of permanence, then there is a *propositum* in the proper sense, and a promise in an improper sense.[644]

What distinguishes the three aforementioned *propositiones* from true promises is the element of obligation. Yet, obligatory statements, in turn, subdivide into two categories.[645] On the one hand, there are propositions such as 'I will give you a horse tomorrow', which involve the intent of producing obligation as a matter of justice in exchange (*cum animo se obligandi ex iustitia commutativa*). These propositions are contracts in the proper sense of the word. On the other hand, there are agreements between two persons in which the promisor merely binds himself as a matter of—what we would now consider to be—morality (*cum animo se obligandi ex aliis virtutibus, ut ex gratitudine, pietate, misericordia, liberalitate vel ex honestate*). These agreements are truly agreements if they are accepted by the promisee, but they are not contracts properly speaking, according to Oñate's definition of contract as an agreement which is binding as a matter of commutative justice (*pactum obligans ex iustitia commutativa*).

To conclude, no matter how sophisticated or unsophisticated their respective linguistic and psychological accounts of promisory statements were, the moral theologians insisted that the primary condition for any binding promise in the technical sense of an offer to contract required *animus obligandi*.

3.3.2.2 *Second requirement*: promissio externa

If the will is the measure of all things contractual, then it would seem that the production of obligation is not dependent on any externalization through signs of communication. As Francisco de Vitoria notes in

---

644 Oñate, *De contractibus*, tom. 2, tract. 9, disp. 29, sect. 1, num. 4, p. 86: 'Tertio potest proferre illa verba dabo tibi centum ita ut non solum asserat se habere de praesenti intentionem dandi sed etiam asseveret se in ea intentione permansuram, quam conceperit in utilitatem et gaudium eius cum quo agit et ut sciat eam et certam habens disponat quod sibi magis expedit, quia ipse acturus est et curaturus ut in effectum deducatur, ita tamen ut neque velit se obligare ex iustitia nec saltem ex honestate, neque securum reddere illum de illius intentionis effectu, quia non tenetur ex veracitate illam propositionem veram facere sed veram dicere et hoc est propositum, scilicet actus voluntatis efficax faciendi aliquid quod includit etiam intentionem perdurandi et permanendi in eadem voluntate (...).'
645 Oñate, *De contractibus*, tom. 2, tract. 9, disp. 29, sect. 1, num. 4, p. 86, col. 2.

regard to gratuitous promises, the declaration of promise does not add any obligation to the obligation which already exists by virtue of the will. The outward statement of promise is merely declarative. The roots of a promise lie in the will (*radix promissionis in voluntate*).[646] Consequently, Vitoria takes the view that the mere interior intent to bind yourself is sufficient, at least in simple promises.[647] He acknowledges that in 'contracts', namely onerous contracts, external communication is required for the promisor to be bound. Perhaps confused by Vitoria's argumentation, Domingo de Soto concludes that one could argue either way, namely that external signs are required or that they are not. Moreover, he points out that this is primarily a problem from the point of view of conscience (*hoc forte problema est stando in iure mero naturae et in conscientia*).[648] In practise, external signs are always required.

Through making the distinction between simple promises and contracts, which roughly corresponds to the distinction between gratuitous contracts and onerous contracts, Vitoria was able to go around a particularly authoritative argument for the contrary opinion. This contrary opinion, which was to become the clear majority opinion by the end of the sixteenth century, held that exteriorization was absolutely required for contractual obligation to arise. It can be traced back to Thomas Aquinas' discussion on vows. In articulating the difference between vows and human promises, Thomas stressed that obligations between men require that the will of the promisor to bind himself be expressed through words or other signs (*per verba vel quaecumque exteriora signa*).[649] There is an

---

[646] See Francisco de Vitoria, *Commentarii in IIamIIae*, quaest. 88, art. 1, num. 5, in: *Comentarios a la Secunda secundae de Santo Tomás*, edición preparada por V. Beltrán de Heredia, tom. 4: *De justitia* (qq. 67–88), [Biblioteca de Teólogos Españoles, 5], Salamanca 1934, p. 329 (hereafter: ed. Beltrán de Heredia, tom. 4).

[647] Vitoria, *Commentarii in IIamIIae* (ed. Beltrán de Heredía, tom. 4), quaest. 88, art. 1, num. 5, p. 329: 'Sed ego puto quod bene posset quis per solum actum interiorem obligari alteri, quia videtur mihi quod argumentum illud convincat, scilicet quia verba exteriora non obligant nec inducunt aliquam obligationem. (...) Et ad verba sancti Thomae, dico quod vult dicere quod homo non potest pacisci, id est facere pactum cum homine altero nec potest facere contractum obligatorium nisi per verba exteriora. Et haec sunt de obligatione simplicis promissionis et assertionis.'

[648] Soto, *De iustitia et iure* (ed. fac. V. Diego Carro – M. González Ordóñez, vol. 4), lib. 7, quaest. 2, p. 613: 'Aliquantulo autem difficilius dubium est an promissio quam apud te sola mente homini facias, sit obligatoria. Visus est sanctus Thomas, artic. 1, id negare. (...) Hoc forte problema est, stando in iure mero naturae et in conscientia. Nam in foro exteriori manifestum est mentalem obligationem, imo neque omnem quae fit absenti, ligare. Sed in conscientia de utraque forte parte opinari quisque potest.'

[649] Aquinas, *Summa Theologiae* (Ed. Leonina, tom. 9), IIaIIae, quaest. 88, art. 1, concl., p. 234: 'Sed promissio quae ab homine fit homini, non potest fieri nisi per verba vel

outward declaration needed for the promise to become binding toward another human being. Conversely, God or the angels can see inside man, so that vows, which are basically promises to God, need not be communicated in order to become binding.

As has been explained before, the Jesuit moral theologians did not adhere to the distinction between gratuitous promises and contracts anymore, so that they would have to find other arguments than Vitoria if they wished to counter Aquinas' standpoint. As will be illustrated in the next paragraphs, the only Jesuit who seemed willing to go against the common opinion was Luís de Molina. In practice, he argued, external signs are always needed, since they are required by positive law, and a promise can be revoked as long as it has not been accepted by the promisee.[650] Yet the crux of the matter is, and in sorting out this crux Molina deviated from the common opinion, whether outward expression of a promise is also needed as a matter of natural law—the will being the foundation of contractual obligation according to natural law. It may well be that civil law added a further condition to make promises binding besides the *animus obligandi*, namely exteriorization, but should we infer from this that external communication of the promise is also needed for the promisor to be bound in conscience? In other words, does the requirement to express a promise through external signs merely pertain to civil law or also to natural law?[651]

In Molina's view, the requirement to signify the promise to the promisee is merely civil in nature. Adducing paragraph *Per traditionem* (Inst. 2,1), he argues that nothing is as naturally equitable as to observe the will of the owner. The will is both a necessary and a sufficient source of contractual obligation. Words or other external signs cannot add anything to this obligation, which is founded on the will. They do not contribute to the formation of contractual obligation.[652] Signs are merely vehicles to express

---

quaecumque exteriora signa. Deo autem potest fieri promissio per solam interiorem cogitationem, quia ut dicitur I Reg. XVI, *homines vident ea quae parent, sed Deus intuetur cor*.'

[650] Molina, *De iustitia et iure*, tom. 2, tract. 2, disp. 266, col. 63, num. 7: 'Sane ea quaestio parum utilitatis habet ad praxim, cum enim iure civili, in commune reipublicae bonum, facta sit potestas revocandi promissiones et donationes antequam acceptentur, etiam si verbo aut scripto factae sint, atque adeo, etiam si exterius sint manifestatae (...).'

[651] Molina, *De iustitia et iure*, tom. 2 (*De contractibus*), tract. 2, disp. 266, col. 63, num. 8: 'Quod ergo hoc loco potissimum disputare intendimus est, utrum seclusa dispositione iuris civilis, standoque solum intra limites iuris naturalis, donatio mere interna, qua quis diceret secum, dono talem rem meam Petro, aut promitto Petro me daturum illi hanc rem, obliget in foro conscientiae sic donantem aut promittentem (...).'

[652] Molina, *De iustitia et iure*, tom. 2 (*De contractibus*), tract. 2, disp. 266, col. 64, num. 9: 'Primo, quoniam voces et scripta sunt signa conceptuum, neque vim habent obligandi nisi ex interiori actu quem exprimunt, atque ex voluntatis intentione se obligandi et promit-

the will (*significatio solum instrumentum*).[653] In Molina's view, exteriorization of the promise has been laid down by statute law for the sake of the
common good, because promises need to be accepted in order to become
binding as a matter of civil law. However, Molina denies that acceptance
is necessary as a matter of natural law in the first place.[654] This is precisely the other point on which his view radically differs from the common opinion of the moral theologians. We will come back to it below.

Another argument which Molina brings forward to argue against the
necessity of exteriorizing the promise is taken from the Roman law of
property (e.g. D. 41,2,3,8). Possession of a thing can be lost if only one does
not will to possess it anymore (*possessio sola voluntate non possidendi
amittitur*).[655] Even ownership of a thing can be lost, if one does not will to
own that thing anymore and possession of it is lost. It is then considered
to be abandoned and becomes the property of the first person who occupies it. Molina illustrates this through the example of boatsmen who do
not take the pain to lift the anchors of their ships out of the water when
they set out to leave the harbour. They wittingly part with their property
and leave it behind. These anchors then become the property of the first
person who takes them.[656] By the same token, the right to claim the gift is
transferred to the promisee by the mere inner will of the promisor.

Molina acknowledged that his view ran counter to the majority opinion. Moreover, he provided his adversaries with the arguments to rebutt
his view. In regard to the argument from property law, for instance, he
suggested that the analogy did not hold water, since transferring a right is
more difficult than parting with it.[657] Lessius gratefully accepts Molina's

---

tendi (…); ac plane, si ab externa promissione aut donatione auferas voluntatem et intentionem internam se obligandi, tollis in foro conscientiae illius obligationem. Ergo donatio
aut promissio mere interna, quantum est ex se, vim habet obligandi in foro conscientiae,
non solum si Deo fiat, sed etiam si fiat homini.'

[653] Molina, *De iustitia et iure*, tom. 2 (*De contractibus*), tract. 2, disp. 266, col. 64, num. 11.

[654] Molina, *De iustitia et iure*, tom. 2 (*De contractibus*), tract. 2, disp. 266, col. 64,
num. 10: 'Secundo, acceptatio, stando in solo iure naturali, necessaria non est ut promissio
aut donatio sit valida et irrevocabilis, sed iure positivo in commune bonum introductum
est, ut regulariter sit conditio ad id requisita.'

[655] Molina, *De iustitia et iure*, tom. 2 (*De contractibus*), tract. 2, disp. 266, col. 64, num. 12.

[656] Molina, *De iustitia et iure*, tom. 2 (*De contractibus*), tract. 2, disp. 266, col. 65,
num. 12: '(…) anchoras a propriis dominis relictas in portubus, quia recedunt nolentes
sumptus facere aut industriam apponere in eis extrahendis aut quaerendis dicimus haberi
pro derelictis et fieri primo occupantis easque extrahentis, ergo pari ratione donatio aut
promissio mere interna erit satis stando in solo iure naturali ut donatarius comparet ius a
nobis supra explicatum ad rem sibi ita donatam aut promissam.'

[657] Molina, *De iustitia et iure*, tom. 2 (*De contractibus*), tract. 2, disp. 266, col. 66, num. 19:
'Ad quartum dicat, licet actus internus sufficiat ut, qui illum exercet, aliquid in seipso

suggestion:[658] 'even though possession and ownership can be lost through an internal act, as when a thing is considered to be abandoned, they cannot be transferred to another person, since that requires many things.' One of the decisive elements in Lessius' rebuttal of Molina is the idea that inner acts of the will are not capable of conveying rights by themselves. External signs are not merely instruments of the will. In a remarkabe piece of pragmatic linguistics, Lessius argues that external signs have the effect of making the inner volition effective and real. Language does not passively convey the act of will, it actively creates the very reality it signifies (*sunt signa quaedam practica efficientia id ipsum quod significant*).[659]

In all, Lessius epitomizes the majority opinion according to which obligation depends on the will as a necessary, but not as a sufficient condition. Or as Lugo puts it,[660] 'albeit that words without inner will do not bind, neither does an inner will without external sign'. To return to Lessius, the will cannot be the cause of obligation 'immediately', that is without the medium of external signs.[661] Similarly, a judge's sentence (*iurisdictio*) is not rendered effective until it is pronounced. Rights cannot be transferred or accorded to other persons through mere inner volition of the promisor alone. Contractual exchange of rights and obligations is a social

---

amittat, non tamen ut transferat ius in alterum, nisi accedat conditio sine qua non, hoc est, manifestatio externa eiusdem actus.'

[658] Lessius, *De iustitia et iure*, lib. 2, cap. 18, dub. 5, num. 32, p. 219: 'Ad secundum, etsi possessio et dominium possunt amitti actu interno, ut cum res habetur pro derelicto, non tamen transferri in alterum. Ad hoc enim plura requiruntur. Facilius enim est aliquid desinere quam incipere esse aut in altero produci. Unde nec ius alteri dari per internam promissionem potest.'

[659] Lessius, *De iustitia et iure*, lib. 2, cap. 18, dub. 5, num. 30–31, p. 219: 'Probabilius tamen videtur, promissionem donationemque internam iure naturae esse insufficientem et invalidam ad obligandum. (...) Ratio est, quia promissio et donatio sunt signa quaedam practica, efficientia id ipsum quod significant. Qui enim dicit, promitto tibi, do tibi, non solum significat internam cogitationem et affectum dandi, sed etiam ipsum actum donationis et promissionis, qui in hisce verbis sub tali intentione prolatis formaliter consistit, et effectum eius, scilicet obligationem, quae nascitur in promittente, et ius, quod nascitur in promissario. Quare cum actus interni non sint idonea signa ad alteri significandum, non sunt etiam instrumenta ad se alteri obligandum, nam haec aptitudo fundatur in significatione ad alterum.'

[660] Lugo, *De iustitia et iure*, tom. 2, disp. 23, sect. 2, num. 34, p. 112: 'Respondeo ex dictis [ad Molinam], verba sine voluntate interna non posse quidem obligare, sed nec voluntatem internam sine signo externo, quia non sufficit ad connexionem sensibilem ponendam, quae fundet ius praelationis ad alios, ut diximus.'

[661] Lessius, *De iustitia et iure*, lib. 2, cap. 18, dub. 5, num. 33, p. 219: 'Etsi tota vis obligandi sit a voluntate, tamen voluntas non potest eam immediate in homine causare absque actu externo tamquam instrumento, alioquin hoc ipso quo interius vellem, alter haberet ius in omnia bona mea, nec possem ea alteri dare vel retinere. Hinc fit, ut etiam iurisdictio sine actu externo dari nequeat, ut communiter theologi docent.'

phenomenon that requires the promisee to participate in the transaction by knowing, by virtue of external communication, what is going on. This leads us to the third indispensable stage in the making of contractual obligation: acceptance by the promisee.

3.3.2.3 *Third requirement*: promissio acceptata

Although it would become standard contract doctrine in the natural law tradition that acceptance is required for an offer to be binding, the question of the status of *pollicitationes*,[662] or mere unilateral, unaccepted offers, was an endless source of controversy throughout the centuries.[663] It is probably to the credit of Jesuit moral theologians such as Lessius to have insisted on acceptance as an essential stage in the formation of contractual obligation. This is not to say that all the Jesuits, or, all moral theologians subscribed to that view. On the contrary, Lessius was urged to expound and defend his views precisely in rebuking the argument to the contrary as advocated by Molina. While Lessius underlined the element of mutual consent in the definition of contract, thus requiring the acceptance of the offer by the promisee, Molina focused on the will's capacity of binding itself, regardless of what the promisee did.

The debate on the obligatory nature of a unilateral, unaccepted promise (*pollicitatio*) was particularly vivid among the decretalists. For present purposes, a brief look at Panormitanus should suffice. The inconsistency of his thought on *pollicitationes* mirrors the confusion that reigned among the canonists more generally. In his commentary on canon *Qualiter* (X 1,35,3), Panormitanus argues that *pollicitationes*—understood as promises to an absent party—are enforceable in the ecclesiastical courts.[664] Yet in commenting upon canon *Cum inter universas* (X 1,6,18) he doubts the actionability of *pollicitationes* as a matter of canon law.[665] In the

---

[662] D. 50,12,3*pr.*: 'Pactum est duorum consensus atque conventio, pollicitatio vero offerentis solius promissum.' Compare Gómez, *Commentarii variaeque resolutiones*, tom. 2, cap. 9, num. 1 p. 289: 'Pollicitatio est nuda et simplex offerentis promissio, non secuta acceptatione creditoris tacite nec expresse (....)'. Gómez took the view that *pollicitatio* is not binding as a matter of civil or canon law.

[663] It still is today, see C. Cauffman, *De verbindende eenzijdige belofte*, Antwerpen 2005.

[664] Panormitanus, *Commentaria super Decretalibus*, tom. 2 (*Super secunda parte primi Decretalium libri*), ad X 1,35,3, f. 132v: 'Et sic videtur quod cum verbum promissio sit multum generale, nedum in pacto quod est duorum, sed in pollicitatione, quae est unius tantum, debet habere locum iste textus, nam ex significato huius verbi promittuntur non requiritur quod intervenerit pactum, sed sufficit nuda promissio unius tantum (....).'

[665] Panormitanus, *Commentaria super Decretalibus*, tom. 1 (*Super prima parte primi Decretalium libri*), ad X 1,6,18, f. 135v, num. 13: '(...) ex simplici pollicitatione non agitur

mid-sixteenth century, Covarruvias attests to the ongoing nature of the
controversy and adds grist to the mill of confusion. He sets out pretty
straightforwardly, saying that offers are binding as a matter of canon law.[666]
In the context of promises strengthened by oath, he claims that equity
demands that offers should be binding without there being a mutual
agreement, since the promisor's will is the measure of all things as a matter of natural law (*naturalis obligatio quantum ad meipsum attinet a meo
consensu deducitur*).[667] Yet the discussion meant to buttress the opposite
view takes the lion's share of his exposition.

Covarruvias points out that, 'regularly', the canon law considers
unaccepted promises as not binding (*regulariter etiam iure canonico ex
pollicitatione actio non oritur*).[668] His reasoning is fundamental: a *pollicitatio* does not produce natural obligation, because natural obligation in
contracts arises out of the consent of two parties. This remained a major
argument to affirm that acceptance is a necessary stage in the making
of contractual obligation, for instance in Lessius (*obligatio non nascitur
nisi mutuo duorum consensu*).[669] Moreover, the requirement of acceptance was not even doubted by Molina. He endorses what he considers
to be the common opinion, namely that, as a general rule, *pollicitationes*
are not binding either as a matter of civil or canon law.[670] At the same
time, he points out why this rule only applies in principle. There is a list

de iure civili (…) nec etiam ex pacto nudo (…). Sed de iure canonico posset dubitari et
ubi intervenisset pactum recurrendum esset ad c. 1 de pactis. Sed in simplici pollicitatione
esset magis dubitandum. Et pollicitatio differt a pacto quia pollicitatio est unius, cum sine
pacto promitto tibi aliquid. Pactum vero est duorum (…). Verum simplici pollicitatione
non credo quod possit alius agere pro interesse suo, quia c. 1 loquitur de pacto, sed peccat
retrocedens, iuxta illud psalmistae, Quae procedunt de labiis meis, non faciam irrita.'
    666 Covarruvias, *Relectio in cap. quamvis pactum*, part. 2, par. 5, num. 15, p. 275: 'Quarto
principaliter est hic adnotandum iure pontificio actionem oriri et dari ex pollicitatione,
quae est unius promissio absenti non praesenti facta.'
    667 Covarruvias, *Relectio in cap. quamvis pactum*, part. 2, par. 5, num. 16, p. 276: 'Etenim
utcumque sit de illa controversia si pollicitationi iuramentum accesserit, aequissimum erit
quod ex ea obligatio oritur et actio detur, idemque iure verius videtur, si vim iuramenti
diligenter consideremus. Nec enim video quid impediat me naturaliter absenti obligari
adhuc nullo cum eo pacto inito, siquidem naturalis obligatio quantum ad meipsum attinet a meo consensu deducitur. Qui consensus perfectissimus est, nisi lex impediat, donec
absens ille cui promisi expresse vel tacite obligationem istam remittat.'
    668 Covarruvias, *Relectio in cap. quamvis pactum*, part. 2, par. 5, num. 15, p. 275: 'Igitur
regulariter etiam iure canonico ex pollicitatione actio non oritur. Et praeterea constat haec
opinio ex eo, quod pollicitatio non producit naturalem obligationem, quae ex consensu
duorum oritur.'
    669 Lessius, *De iustitia et iure*, lib. 2, cap. 18, dub. 6, num. 34, p. 220.
    670 Molina, *De iustitia et iure*, tom. 2 (*De contractibus*), tract. 2, disp. 263, col. 40,
num. 1: 'Convenerunt doctores, promissionem antequam acceptetur, atque adeo antequam

of exceptions going back to Roman law (D. 50,12) which concern simple offers to support public projects (*pollicitatio civitati*).[671] These offers are binding, indeed, from the moment of their expression.

The *pollicitationes civitati* lead us to the heart of one of the biggest points of conflict between Molina and Lessius. The dispute concerned the issue of whether the foundation of the requirement that said that offer needs to be accepted lies in civil law or in natural law. The terms of the debate are similar, then, to the one on the second requirement for promises to be binding, namely exteriorization. Although there was agreement on the practical solution, there was disagreement on the theoretical foundations of the requirement. Another parallel concerns the outcome of the controversy. Molina eventually lost against Lessius. The reason why the *pollicitationes civitati* became the bone of contention around which the debate crystallized is because their bindingness seemed to imply that there was a natural obligation ensuing from an unaccepted promise. The reason why the moral theologians thought this way requires some explanation. It was thought that positive obligation could not exist unless there was an underlying natural obligation. In addition, positive law was thought to be able to qualify or to remove natural obligation.

Molina derives from the existence of positive legal obligation in certain *pollicitationes civitati* the existence of an underlying natural obligation.[672] But given that, as a rule, offers are not binding from the point of view of

---

in pactum transeat, regulariter neque obligationem civilem, neque actionem in seculari foro parere (....).'

[671] See laws *Pactum* (D. 50,12,3*pr.*), which holds that if an offer is made for the sake of honor (*ob honorem*), debt is created, just as in the case where the works promised have effectively been started (*coeptum opus*); *Propter incendium* (D. 50,12,4), which declares an offer binding if it is made for the benefit of the republic in situations of natural disaster (*propter incendium vel terrae motum vel aliquam ruinam*); *Ob casum* (D. 50,12,7), which stipulates that the promisor is bound to perform whatever he promised with an eye on a certain act of God (*ob casum*), even if eventually nothing evil happens. Compare Molina, *De iustitia et iure*, tom. 2, tract. 2, disp. 263, col. 61, lit. b–d.

[672] Molina, *De iustitia et iure*, tom. 2 (*De contractibus*), tract. 2, disp. 263, cols. 46–47, num. 12: 'Hanc sententiam primo persuadet id, quod supra ostendimus, nempe de iure civili ex promissione facta civitati aut reipublicae concedi actionem, esto acceptata non fuerit. Si namque ea promissio, spectata sola ipsius natura, vim obligandi non haberet, sane civile ius numquam supra suam naturam et vim id illi tribueret. Licet enim ius aliquando in commune bonum consueverit vim obligandi, quam ex sua natura habent, ab aliquibus contractibus aut actibus auferre, ut ab alienationibus factis a minoribus, aut ab Ecclesiis sine solemnitatibus ad id constitutis, ab alienatione fundi dotalis, a donationibus sine insinuatione factis ultra certam summam et a multis aliis, non tamen consuevit vim actibus ad alienandum supra ipsorum naturam tribuere, praesertim quando alienatio est mere gratuita, qualis ea est, de qua nunc disputamus.'

positive law, he also holds that this natural obligation has in most cases been qualified by positive law. In Molina's view, simple, unilateral and unaccepted promises are binding in principle as a matter of natural law. Only afterward did positive law make this natural obligation dependent on acceptance in all offers, excluding the *pollicitationes civitati*. As a matter of principle and for the sake of the common good, positive law introduced acceptance as a *conditio sine qua non* for offers to become binding. However, citing Covarruvias, Molina claims that the true source of promissory obligation is founded on the promise itself and not on the acceptance, so that offers out of themselves produce natural obligation. This is certainly true in gratuitous promises, where the liberality of the promisor must not be thwarted by the State.[673] In all, then, the foundation of the acceptance requirement is positive law (*ius positivum*), according to Molina.[674]

Although Lessius did not entirely reject Molina's opinion—which he deemed probable—he still thought the contrary opinion to be nearer to the truth: acceptance is required not merely as a matter of positive law, but primarily as a matter of natural law (*ius naturale seu ius gentium*).[675] Also, it is worthwhile noticing that Lessius made a genuine effort at expounding the principles of a general law of contract. In Molina and Covarruvias the argument wavers somewhat confusingly in between the law of gratuitous promises and the law of promises in general. Lessius tries to harmonize the rules that govern all kinds of promises.

In Lessius' view, the common opinion holding that gratuitous promises regularly do not produce civil or natural obligation until they are accepted is equally applicable to gratuitous promises as it is to all other contracts (*idem in omnibus aliis contractibus*).[676] Because of the right to revoke a promise before acceptance in onerous contracts, Lessius argues that the

---

673 Molina, *De iustitia et iure*, tom. 2 (*De contractibus*), tract. 2, disp. 263, col. 47, num. 12: 'Quarto idem persuadet ratio cui Covarruvias loco citato nititur, nempe in gratuitis promissionibus acceptatis obligationem promittentis ex natura rei non oriri ex acceptatione sed ex promissione ipsa, quae ex liberalitate promittere vult ac se obligare donatario sine ulla recompensatione aut mutua obligatione ex parte donatarii.'
On this tension between the imperatives of the State and the Christian practicing of the virtue of liberality, see Decock, *Donations, bonnes mœurs et droit naturel*, p. 195–197.
674 Molina, *De iustitia et iure*, tom. 2 (*De contractibus*), tract. 2, disp. 263, col. 47, num. 12: 'Sicut autem ius positivum acceptationem donatarii introduxit tamquam conditionem sine qua promissio non obligaret, ita in aliquibus potuit illam omnino remittere, ut in promissionibus civitati factis (…).'
675 Lessius, *De iustitia et iure*, lib. 2, cap. 18, dub. 6, num. 39, p. 220: 'Dico secundo, verius videri quod promissio et donatio non habeant vim obligandi ante acceptationem, id provenire non tantum ex iure civili sed etiam ex iure naturali vel iure gentium.'
676 Lessius, *De iustitia et iure*, lib. 2, cap. 18, dub. 6, num. 34, p. 219–220.

same must hold true in gratuitous contracts, as long as positive law does not decide otherwise.[677] Moreover, Lessius argues that both onerous and gratuitous contracts contain a tacit condition (*tacita conditio*), which in the case of onerous contracts can be circumscribed as, 'if the other party wants to be bound in his turn', and 'if they will be accepted' in gratuitous promises and contracts.[678] The ultimate reason, however, why he disagrees with Molina, is that he interprets D. 50,12 and its stipulations concerning *pollicitationes civitati* in a different manner. According to Lessius, law *Pactum* (D. 50,12,3*pr.*) does not attribute irrevocable obligation to a *pollicitatio civitati*.[679] What law *Pactum* does, in Lessius' view, is to prohibit the promisor from arbitrarily revoking his promise.

Even though Lessius' exegesis might come down to the same result as Molina's in practice, it constitutes a different explanatory story with significant consequences on a doctrinal level. While Molina was pressured to assume that offer without acceptance creates a natural obligation in order to explain D. 50,12, Lessius denies that there is any kind of obligation in the special case of *pollicitationes civitati*. What makes these offers particular, in Lessius' opinion, is that they seem to be binding without acceptance, while, in fact, positive law merely denies their promisor the right to revoke his promise (*impedit ne possit revocari*).[680] Generally speaking, an offer only creates an obligation that is dependent on the suspending or resolutory condition that the offer will be accepted or revoked (*obligatio veluti conditionata et suspensa*).[681] Positive law does limit natural law in

---

[677] Lessius, *De iustitia et iure*, lib. 2, cap. 18, dub. 6, num. 39, p. 220: 'Probatur primo, quia in contractibus onerosis ante acceptationem licitum est ubique gentium poenitere et revocare suam oblationem (…), ergo idem licitum erit in promissionibus et donationibus gratuitis, nisi lex positiva adimat hanc potestatem.'

[678] Lessius, *De iustitia et iure*, lib. 2, cap. 18, dub. 6, num. 39, p. 220: 'Secundo, sicut promissio vel oblatio onerosa, qua quis se obligat, habet tacitam conditionem, nempe, *Si alter vicissim se velit obligare*, ita etiam promissio et donatio habent tacitam conditionem, *Si acceptentur.*'

[679] Lessius, *De iustitia et iure*, lib. 2, cap. 18, dub. 6, num. 40, p. 220: 'Ad primam rationem respondeo, ius civile non efficere ut pollicitatio facta civitati vim habeat absolutam ante acceptationem (nihil enim tale colligi potest ex ulla lege toto titulo de pollicitationibus) sed ne possit revocari pro libito, sicut ex natura rei posset, ut patet ex l. 3 eodem titulo. Unde fit ut talis promissio semper possit acceptari et promissum peti; quae petitio videtur necessaria ut teneris solvere ut iisdem legibus indicatur.'

[680] Lessius, *De iustitia et iure*, lib. 2, cap. 18, dub. 6, num. 40, p. 220: 'Unde tunc ius civile non tribuit proprie pollicitationi vim quam iure naturali vel gentium non habet, sed impedit ne possit revocari.'

[681] Lessius, *De iustitia et iure*, lib. 2, cap. 18, dub. 6, num. 40, p. 220: 'Itaque ex pollicitatione omni nascitur quaedam obligatio veluti conditionata et suspensa donec acceptetur vel revocetur, quam revocationem ius positivum potest impedire.'

regard to offers, but not through making the alleged natural obligation that arises out of mere promises dependent on acceptance. Acceptance is required by nature itself. If positive law limits nature in the special case of *pollicitationes civitati*, it is through limiting the natural right to revoke an offer, so long as that offer has not been accepted.

Lessius' view that offers require acceptance as a *conditio sine qua non* for producing natural as well as civil obligation was adopted by later Jesuits such as Laymann, Lugo and Oñate. Paul Laymann (1574–1635), a professor of canon law at the University of Dillingen and a confessor to the Emperor Ferdinand II, took sides with Lessius against Molina to conclude that promises are always to be understood in relational terms (*omnis promissio suapte natura respectiva*).[682] The consent by the promisee is of the essence for the creation of obligation. Lugo reminds us that it is impossible to convey ownership or possession of a thing without the consent of the promisee.[683] Oñate considers acceptance an essential part of all contracts (*acceptatio de essentia omnium contractuum*). Along with the offer, acceptance is the second essential juristic act which constitutes the essence of contract (*altera pars essentialis contractuum*).[684] The view that acceptance is necessary also became an integral part of Grotius', Domat's and Pothier's natural law doctrine on the making of contractual obligation.

3.3.3   *The interpretation of contractual obligation*

3.3.3.1   *Fictitious and doubtful promises*

If contractual obligation primarily relies on the will and the intent of the promisor (*animus obligandi*), then how can the promisee's reliance on the

---

[682] Paul Laymann, *Theologia moralis*, Monachii 1630, lib. 3, tract. 4 (*De pactis et contractibus*), cap. 1, num. 3, p. 371: 'Sed Sotus, Gomez, Lessius loc. cit., Sanchez lib. 1 de matrim. disp. 7 num. 24 et alii plerique contrarium sentiunt, omnem promissionem suapte natura respectivam esse, cuius proinde vis et obligatio ex alterius partis consensu, tamquam a forma sua, dependeat.'
On Laymann, see R.L. Bireley, *Paul Laymann*, in: C. O'Neill – J. Domínguez (eds.), Diccionario Histórico de la Compañía de Jesús, Biográfico-Temático, Roma-Madrid 2001, vol. 3, p. 2297–2298.
[683] Lugo, *De iustitia et iure*, tom. 2, disp. 23, sect. 3, num. 39, p. 114: 'Ratio itaque petenda est ex supra dictis, quia licet aliquis possit sua sola voluntate amittere dominium vel possessionem rei suae, non tamen potest sola sua voluntate facere quod res sua ad alium pertineat. Ad hoc enim requiritur etiam consensus illius ad quem pertinere debet.'
[684] Oñate, *De contractibus*, tom. 2, tract. 9, disp. 29, sect. 4, num. 45, p. 100: 'Moveor quia acceptatio est de essentia omnium contractuum et altera pars omnium essentialis eorum, ut saepissime in hoc opere probavi.'

external declaration of promise be protected if the promise turns out to lack *animus obligandi*? If the obligation of the promisor is only apparent, then what remedies are granted to the promisee? Put more technically, what is the status of a fictitious promise (*promissio ficta*)? Not surprisingly, this is a question that was treated extensively by Tomás Sánchez in his treatise on marriage law. Fictitious marriages or marriages of convenience, in which at least one of the parties declares marriage without having the intent of truly binding him- or herself, have preoccupied theologians and jurists until the present day. Sánchez's emphasis on the presence of *animus obligandi* for the marriage contract to be binding was in line with the scholastic tradition and eventually prevailed, although, at first, it met with fierce criticism from Gabriel Vázquez.

Sánchez elaborates on the value of fictitious promises in the context of his doctrine of engagement contracts (*sponsalia*). As a preliminary remark, he excludes the possibility of doubt about the status of engagements entered into with the intent of obligation (*animus obligandi*) but without intent of fulfilling the obligation (*animus non implendi*). Indisputably, that kind of promise is binding, if only because such a morally objectionable intention (*pessima intentio non implendi*) cannot exempt one from the natural obligation that is produced by the *animus obligandi*.[685] Hence, the real crux of the matter concerns promises that have been entered into with the intention of making a promise, but without the intention of binding oneself. The question is whether those fictitious promises are binding either as a matter of contract law, or as a matter of torts law.[686]

Sánchez concludes that it is nearest to the truth to hold that fictitious promises are not binding by virtue of the promise itself, since the *animus obligandi* is of the essence of promise.[687] 'Every obligation which does not

---

[685] Sánchez, *Disputationes de sancto matrimonii sacramento*, tom. 1, lib. 1, disp. 9, num. 2, p. 29–30: 'Certum igitur est si promittentes animum se obligandi habeant | non tamen implendi, esse vera sponsalia, obligareque, quia pessima non implendi intentio rem promissam non eximit ab obligatione quae ex ipsa promissione animo se obligandi emissa naturaliter consurgit.'

[686] Sánchez, *Disputationes de sancto matrimonii sacramento*, tom. 1, lib. 1, disp. 9, num. 2, p. 30: 'Tota igitur difficultas est, quando promittens habuit promittendi animum et positive habuit animum se non obligandi. Et de huiusmodi promissionis fictae obligatione bifariam disputari potest: 1. an obliget ex vi promissionis et sponsalium; 2. an saltem obliget ratione fraudis ad resarciendam iniuriam illatam.'

[687] Sánchez, *Disputationes de sancto matrimonii sacramento*, tom. 1, lib. 1, disp. 9, num. 5, p. 30: 'Secunda sententia verior affirmat nec esse sponsalia nec ex vi promissionis obligare. Probatur ex c. fin. de condit. appos. ubi conditio contraria substantiae matrimonii ipsum annullat, licet verba et intentio essent contrahendi. Ergo cum de natura promissionis et sponsalium sit animus se obligandi, ubi contrarius animus adfuerit, nulla erunt.'

ensue from a law comes into existence through the private will of man', Sánchez argues,[688] 'so where the will to bind is absent, the obligation is absent.' He further adduces the metaphor of contract as a private law:[689] 'promissary obligation arises out of a private law which the promisor imposes upon himself, but no law is binding unless the legislator intends it to be binding (*nulla lex obligat nisi legislator obligare intendat*).' Consequently, the will is the measure of contractual obligation. The promisor cannot be bound by virtue of his fictitious promise. However, Sánchez proceeds to explain that he can be bound to perform his promise on account of the harm he inflicted upon the promisee through his fraudulent behavior (*ratione fraudis et iniuriae illatae*). In other words, fictitious promises can give rise to delictual liability.

There is a lot of casuistry involved in Sánchez's determining what the consequences of fictitious promises of engagement are in terms of the obligations that follow from the harm done to the promisee. By way of an illustration, imagine the typical situation of a man who promises to marry a virgin in order to have intercourse with her, only to leave her after the first night they spent together.[690] He pretends that he had not made the promise to marry her with the intention of being bound. The question raised by Sánchez is whether restitution of the harm done through this fictitious promise, namely defloration, consists in monetary compensation or in specific performance. He concludes that the man must marry her on pain of mortal sin, since justice in exchange is not observed by merely paying damages.[691] Again, this solution is subject to qualifications. For example, since the girl should have known that this man was only trying to have sex with her, because he belonged to a more noble class than

---

688 Sánchez, *Disputationes de sancto matrimonii sacramento*, tom. 1, lib. 1, disp. 9, num. 5, p. 30: 'Probatur quia omnis obligatio quae non est ex lege oritur ex privata hominis voluntate, ergo ubi deest se obligandi voluntas deficit obligatio.'

689 Sánchez, *Disputationes de sancto matrimonii sacramento*, tom. 1, lib. 1, disp. 9, num. 5, p. 30: 'Tandem, quia obligatio promissionis consurgit ex lege privata, quam promittens sibi imponit, nulla autem lex obligat, nisi legislator obligare intendat.'
On the Roman origins of the concept of contract as a law, see the literature cited supra, n. 604.

690 Sánchez, *Disputationes de sancto matrimonii sacramento*, tom. 1, lib. 1, disp. 10, num. 2, p. 33: 'Quaestio prima. An ficte promittens matrimonium et sub ea spe deflorans virginem teneatur eam ducere.'

691 Sánchez, *Disputationes de sancto matrimonii sacramento*, tom. 1, lib. 1, disp. 10, num. 3, p. 33: 'Omnino tamen dicendum est teneri sub culpa lethali eam ducere. Probatur quia iustitia commutativa non tantum petit reddi aequale, sed ut idemmet reddatur ex iustitia debitum, ut si equum furatus sum, nulla restituta pecunia satisfaciam, unum enim pro alio invito creditore solvi non potest, l. 2, par. Matri, ff. Si cert. petat.'

she did, or because it was clear from his words, perhaps she should blame herself for her naivety.[692]

The most fierce attack against Sánchez's opinion that fictitious promises cannot be binding by virtue of the promise itself was launched by one of his fellow Jesuits, Gabriel Vázquez. In his relatively thin, posthumously published treatise on the sacrament of marriage, Vázquez argued that the declaration of the promise to marry was sufficient to bring about contractual obligation, regardless of the *animus obligandi*.[693] His was definitely not to become the majority opinion.[694] This should not come as a surprise. There was little in the late medieval and early modern legal tradition that supported a declaration theory of contract interpretation.[695]

Lessius transposed the discussions on fictitious *sponsalia* on a more general level and applied Sánchez's conclusion to all contracts. He argued that a declaration of promise without the underlying, serious intention to be bound could not be enforced by virtue of the promise itself. On the other hand, he acknowledged that the promisee's reliance on the promisor's declaration should be protected through the law of torts, so that the fictitious promisor could still be bound by virtue of the harm he inflicted upon the promisee.[696] 'Faith in contractual affairs (*fides contractuum*) would crumble,' Lessius warned,[697] 'if promisors could free themselves of their obligation simply by saying that they had made a fictitious promise.'

---

[692] Sánchez, *Disputationes de sancto matrimonii sacramento*, tom. 1, lib. 1, disp. 10, num. 5–7, p. 33–34.

[693] Gabriel Vázquez, *De matrimonii sacramento*, in: Commentaria ac disputationes in tertiam partem Summae Theologiae divi Thomae, Lugduni 1631, tom. 4, disp. 6, p. 348–354.

[694] See the lengthy refutation of Vázquez's argumentation in Lugo, *De iustitia et iure*, tom. 2, disp. 23, sect. 1, num. 6–10, p. 104–106.

[695] For a more ample discussion on the tension between *verba* and *voluntas*, and the late medieval jurists' general preference for *voluntas* in the interpretation of contracts, see A. Massironi, *Nell'officina dell'interprete, La qualificazione del contratto nel diritto comune (secoli XIV–XVI)*, Milano 2012, p. 46–54.

[696] Lessius, *De iustitia et iure*, lib 2, cap. 18, dub, 8 num. 59, p. 225: 'Si tamen promissarius putaret alterum serio promisisse et inde postea contingeret illum damno affici (ut quia non potest solvere ad diem condictum) promissor tenetur implere sub peccato mortali, quia illo modo promittendi illum decepit, eaque deceptio est causa sine qua non damni secuti, quod ut evitetur, debet promissum praestare.'

[697] Lessius, *De iustitia et iure*, lib 2, cap. 18, dub, 8 num. 60, p. 225: 'Adde, nullam fore fidem contractuum inter homines, si hac ratione se possent expedire, dicendo se ficte promisisse.'

The fact that Lessius' theory of promising is essentially reliance-based has already been noted by L. Böttcher, *Von der Lüge zur Mentalreservation, Über den Einfluss von Moralphilosophie und -theologie auf das Bürgerliche Recht*, Göttingen 2007, p. 164.

An issue that was often raised in conjunction with fictitious promises concerned the interpretation of a doubtful promise (*promissio dubia*). While fictitious promises create confusion because of the disparity between the promisor's intention and the promisee's perception of the promise, the status of doubtful promises is not even clear to the promisor himself. Basically, the promisor is in doubt whether he has promised with the intention of truly binding himself or not. This is probably a typically moral theological rather than a juridical question, but the solutions that were forged to deal with are another testimony to the juridical manner in which theologians resolved what we now consider to be moral problems. As can easily be expected from what has been discussed before, the solution to the issue of doubtful promises turned on probabilism. More specifically, a crucial role was to be played by the probabilistic maxim—borrowed from the law of property and procedure—that if in doubt, the condition of the possessor is stronger (*in dubiis melior est conditio possidentis*).

From the propositions that a promisor is in doubt about his *animus obligandi*, and, that if in doubt, the condition of the possessor is the stronger, one might be tempted to infer that doubtful promises are not binding. However, the debate about the bindingness of doubtful vows and doubtful contractual promises runs into casuistical analysis, which would need much more attention than can be afforded in this chapter.[698] Interesting discussions that witness the central role played in this debate of the conceptions of liberty, possession and probabilism can be found in Sánchez and Lugo.[699] Let it suffice here to quote Lessius' intermediary standpoint. On the one hand, he sets out by confirming the principle that in both courts no obligation should be imposed if there is doubt about the promisor's intention. Yet he goes on to state that a doubtful promise should be interpreted so as to be binding (*in dubio in utroque foro interpretandum valere*).[700]

---

[698] Soto's allegedly trail-blazing application of the *possidentis*-principle to doubtful vows is discussed by R. Schüßler, *Moral self-ownership and ius possessionis in scholastics*, in: V. Mäkinen – P. Korkman, Transformations in medieval and early modern rights discourse, [The New Synthese Historical Library, 59], Dordrecht 2006, p. 156–159.

[699] Sánchez, *Disputationes de sancto matrimonii sacramento*, tom. 1, lib. 1, disp. 9, num. 11–14, p. 31–33; and Lugo, *De iustitia et iure*, tom. 2, disp. 22, sect. 5, num. 65–66, p. 17–18.

[700] Lessius, *De iustitia et iure*, lib 2, cap. 18, dub. 1, num. 7, p. 216–217: 'Dices, quid si promissor sit dubius quo animo verbis promissoriis usus sit? Respondeo, in utroque foro inclinandum esse in eius favorem, quia in dubio non est imponendum onus, quod, nisi sponte, non suscipitur. Ita multi doctores. Verius tamen puto, si verba expressam promis-

Lessius' position on doubtful promises is motivated by the concern to find a balance between the will of the promisor and the protection of the promisee's reliance on the verbal expression of the promise. In fact, Lessius argues that there is no *paritas conditionis*, since there is certainty about the promissory declaration, which is in favor of the promisee, while there is uncertainty about the intention of the promisor.[701] Only if it can be established in an equally certain way that the promisor had no *animus obligandi*—which is hardly the case in practice—does the probabilistic maxim apply.

3.3.3.2 *Legally* vs *morally binding promises*

One of the reasons why the early modern, Catholic moral theologians' engagement with contract law has proven to be elusive is the difference between the modern and the early modern understanding of the relationship between law and morality. As highlighted above, the modern, Protestant way of distinguishing law from morality, which becomes evident in thinkers such as Pufendorf, limits the task of the moral theologians to the study of duties as they derive from divine Revelation, reserving the study of *ius naturale* to natural lawyers and the knowledge of *ius positivum* to civil jurists. Yet the Catholic moral theologians in the early modern period failed to make these distinctions. As highlighted above, all bodies of law (*iura*) were considered to be relevant sources of norms guiding man on his earthly pilgrimage to God. Therefore, the theologians had to know all of those sources of norms. Morality was thought of in legal terms, and law could not escape from its embeddedness in a moral universe. This is where a short digression into question 80 of Thomas Aquinas' *Secunda Secundae* may prove helpful.

In fact, theologians did make the distinction between morality and law. Yet they did so on another level, namely inside the system of virtues—a concept that nowadays is commonly associated with the realm of morality. As Thomas explains, there is a difference between moral debt (*debitum morale*) and legal debt (*debitum legale*). Legal debt is ruled by the virtue of justice itself, while moral debt is governed by virtues connected

---

sionem prae se ferunt, in dubio in utroque foro interpretandum valere et obligationem induci, maxime in voto.'

[701] Lessius, *De iustitia et iure*, lib 2, cap. 18, dub. 1, num. 7, p. 217: 'Confirmatur quia hic non est par conditio promissoris et promissarii. Nam constat de verbis promissionis, quae favent promissario, ergo haec servanda, nisi aliunde constet defuisse animum.'

to justice.[702] Thomas explains that some types of human exchange cannot fall within the scope of the virtue of justice, strictly understood, because they fall short of perfect equality.[703] In principle, the virtue of justice is geared towards giving another person his due so that equality in between these persons is maintained. Borrowing from Aristotle, Thomas argues that it will not always be possible to render the exact counter-value in human relationships. For example, a child can never make up for the gift of life and the education it received from its parents. Therefore, this type of relation will be governed by virtues connected to justice, e.g. piety (*pietas*).

The first conclusion to be drawn from Thomas is that legal debt is owed by virtue of justice (*iustitia*), while moral debt is owed by the related virtue of honesty (*honestas*). Thomas goes on to explain that not all moral debt must necessarily be rendered for the virtue of honesty to be observed. He distinguishes between moral debt that must be rendered lest honesty be violated, and moral due that does not break honesty, even if it is not rendered. Examples of the former include moral debt owed as a matter of truthfulness in speaking to others (*veritas*), gratefulness in compensating another person for a benefit (*gratia*), and vindication in 'compensating' another person for an evil act (*vindicatio*). Performing this type of moral debt is absolutely required if moral honesty is to be preserved (*sine eo honestas morum conservari non potest*).[704] Examples of the latter type of

---

702 Aquinas, *Summa Theologiae* (Ed. Leonina, tom. 9), IIaIIae, quaest. 80, art. 1, concl., p. 174: 'A ratione vero debiti iustitiae defectus potest attendi secundum quod est duplex debitum, scilicet morale et legale, unde et philosophus, in VIII Ethic., secundum hoc duplex iustum assignat. Debitum quidem legale est ad quod reddendum aliquis lege adstringitur, et tale debitum proprie attendit iustitia quae est principalis virtus. Debitum autem morale est quod aliquis debet ex honestate virtutis.'

703 Aquinas, *Summa Theologiae* (Ed. Leonina, tom. 9), IIaIIae, quaest. 80, art. 1, concl., p. 174: 'Ratio vero iustitiae consistit in hoc quod alteri reddatur quod ei debetur secundum aequalitatem, ut ex supradictis patet. Dupliciter igitur aliqua virtus ad alterum existens a ratione iustitiae deficit, uno quidem modo, inquantum deficit a ratione aequalis; alio modo, inquantum deficit a ratione debiti. Sunt enim quaedam virtutes quae debitum quidem alteri reddunt, sed non possunt reddere aequale.'

704 Aquinas, *Summa Theologiae* (Ed. Leonina, tom. 9), IIaIIae, quaest. 80, art. 1, concl., p. 174–175: 'Debitum autem morale est quod aliquis debet ex honestate virtutis. Et quia debitum necessitatem importat, ideo tale debitum habet duplicem gradum. Quoddam enim est sic necessarium ut sine eo honestas morum conservari non possit, et hoc habet plus de ratione debiti. Et potest hoc debitum attendi ex parte ipsius debentis. Et sic ad hoc debitum pertinet quod homo talem se exhibeat alteri in verbis et factis qualis est. Et ita adiungitur iustitiae veritas, per quam, ut Tullius dicit, *immutata ea quae sunt aut fuerunt aut futura sunt, dicuntur*. Potest etiam attendi ex parte eius cui debetur, prout scilicet aliquis recompensat alicui secundum ea quae fecit. Quandoque quidem in bonis. Et sic adiungitur iustitiae gratia, in qua, ut Tullius dicit, *amicitiarum et officiorum alterius memoria, remunerandi voluntas continetur alterius*. Quandoque vero in malis. Et sic adiungitur

moral debt, which is conducive to virtue but not absolutely necessary, include what is due by virtue of liberality (*liberalitas*), affability (*affabilitas*), or friendship (*amicitia*). These types of debt are much less coercive. Moral rectitude can be attained without practicing liberality or friendship (*sine quo honestas conservari potest*).[705] It will merely make life less complete from a moral point of view.

The early modern scholastics developed Thomas' taxonomy of debt and virtue further while respecting the main lines of his argument. Of principal concern in this context is how the distinction between moral and legal debt was brought to bear on contractual obligation. In a controversial piece of commentary on question 113 of Thomas' *Secunda Secundae*, Cardinal Cajetan claimed that promises were enforceable merely as a matter of moral debt. Moreover, he opined that promises were only binding on pain of venial sin.[706] Cajetan's standpoint produced a storm of critique for more than a century. Although theologians remained divided on the question of how to determine the extent of promissory obligation exactly, the early modern scholastics universally agreed that what distinguishes contracts properly speaking from social agreements is the creation of juridically enforceable rights and obligations.

Cajetanus argues that the promisor is merely bound to perform by virtue of honesty (*honestas*) and not by justice, since fulfilling promises is a

---

iustitiae vindicatio, per quam, ut Tullius dicit, *vis aut iniuria, et omnino quidquid obscurum est, defendendo aut ulciscendo propulsatur.*'

[705] Aquinas, *Summa Theologiae* (Ed. Leonina, tom. 9), quaest. 80, art. 1, concl., p. 175: 'Aliud vero debitum est necessarium sicut conferens ad maiorem honestatem, sine quo tamen honestas conservari potest. Quod quidem debitum attendit liberalitas, affabilitas sive amicitia, et alia huiusmodi. Quae Tullius praetermittit in praedicta enumeratione, quia parum habent de ratione debiti.'

[706] If the secondary literature is reliable, then it does not seem easy to give a short answer to the question of what differentiates venial sin (*peccatum veniale*) from mortal sin (*peccatum mortale*). From the almost five hundred columns devoted to the distinction in the *Dictionnaire de Théologie Catholique*, the following sentence may be retained: 'Le péché est mortel qui fait contracter au coupable la dette d'une peine éternelle, véniel qui n'emporte l'obligation que d'une peine temporelle.' Cf. M. Jugie, s.v. *Péché*, in: Dictionnaire de Théologie Catholique, Paris 1933, tom. 12, 1, col. 227. Alternatively, the following elucidation may be cited for what it is worth: 'By mortal sin, a created good is preferred to God Himself, in fact, the sinner places his last end in the creature and turns away from God as his natural and supernatural destiny'; cf. W.A. Huesman, *The doctrine of Leonard Lessius on mortal sin*, Excerpta ex dissertatione ad lauream in Facultate Theologiae Pontificae Universitatis Gregorianae, Romae 1947, p. 34. Turning to the primary sources does not bring much relief. See, for instance, the seemingly unending and overly subtle discussion in Francisco Suárez, *Tractatus de vitiis et peccatis*, disp. 2, in: Opera omnia, editio nova a D.M. André, canonico Rupellensi, Parisiis 1856, tom. 4, p. 519–542.

matter of fidelity (*fidelitas*) and truth (*veritas*).[707] He infers from this that promises are to be fulfilled on pain of venial sin, since the virtues of fidelity and truth are merely binding on pain of venial sin.[708] The only situation in which he can imagine the promisor to be bound on pain of mortal sin is in the case that the non-fulfillment seriously harms the promisee, thus going against charity. Cajetan's analysis drew a scathing critique from Soto:[709] 'promising is not simply a matter of truth, but of commutative justice'. Soto's critique was amplified by Lessius. The Antwerp Jesuit insists that promising does not merely come down to a factual affirmation of what the promisor is going to do or give in the future. Promising is about the creation of obligation (*obligatio*) and, hence, the conveyance of a right (*ius*), so that the promisee can enforce the promise. Promise is debt, namely legal debt. To say that promises are merely binding by virtue of *veritas* is to confound promises and declarations about the future.[710]

Importantly, Lessius maintains that all contractual obligations are binding as a matter of justice (*omnis obligatio contractuum est obligatio iustitiae*), regardless of whether they are produced by onerous or gratuitous contracts.[711] This point is stressed by all his successors. As mentioned before, Oñate eventually defined contract as an agreement that is binding as a matter of commutative justice (*contractus est pactum obligans ex iustitia commutativa*).[712] We have also seen him expressly distinguishing promises binding by virtue of moral debt (*ex aliis virtutibus, ut ex gratitudine, pietate, misericordia, liberalitate vel ex honestate*) and truly contractual

---

[707] Birocchi, *Causa e categoria generale del contratto*, p. 120, n. 69.

[708] Cajetanus, *Commentaria ad Secundam Secundae divi Thomae* (Ed. Leonina, tom. 9), ad quaest. 113, art. 2, p. 440, num. 8: 'Nam ex sola ratione promissionis violatae, licet ratio peccati habetur, quia est contra rationis naturalis rectitudinem, non tamen habetur ratio peccati mortalis, nisi ad aliquid contra caritatem Dei aut proximi descendatur.'

[709] Soto, *De iustitia et iure* (ed. fac. V. Diego Carro – M. González Ordóñez, vol. 4), lib. 7, quaest. 2, art. 1, p. 630: 'Enimvero promittere non pertinet simpliciter ad virtutem veritatis, sed reducitur ad commutativam iustitiam. Non enim est utcumque verum asserere, sed obstringendo alteri fidem.'

[710] Lessius, *De iustitia et iure*, lib 2, cap. 18, dub. 8, num. 52, p. 223–224: '(…) hoc fundamentum Cajetani non est verum. Primo, quia promittere non tantum est affirmare se daturum vel facturum, sed ulterius est se obligare | alteri et consequenter ius illi tribuere ad exigendum. Unde dici solet, *promissionem parere debitum*. Secundo, quia inde sequeretur, eum qui promittit non magis obligari quam eum qui absque promissione affirmat se facturum, quod constat esse falsum communi hominum usu et sensu.'

[711] Lessius, *De iustitia et iure*, lib 2, cap. 18, dub. 8, num. 55, p. 224: 'Omnis obligatio contractuum est obligatio iustitiae, et non oritur nisi promissione. Ergo promissio inducit obligationem iustitiae.'

[712] Oñate, *De contractibus*, tom. 1, tract. 1, disp. 1, sect. 3, num. 26, p. 7.

promises binding by virtue of justice (*ex iustitia commutativa*).[713] The criterion he used for distinguishing these legally binding promises from morally binding promises was the foundation of obligation, namely the will. However, this was something the moral theologians were not entirely unanimous about. Whether the ultimate criterion to decide whether a promise is legally or morally binding must be entirely subjective or rather take into account objective circumstances led to lengthy argumentation on both sides.

Apart from the almost general rejection of Cajetanus' quite monolithic statement that promises are binding as a matter of truth or fidelity, two opinions circulated on the extent to which promises are binding. Lessius defended the view that not only subjective, but also objective factors should play a role in determining whether a promise produces moral or legal debt. The motivation behind this balanced view recalls Lessius' concern for the rights of the promise, which we have seen in his interpretation of dubious promises. In notable matters (*materia notabilis*), he holds that serious gratuitous promises (*promissio serio facta*) are binding on pain of mortal sin, amongst other reasons, because it is common opinion that onerous promises, once accepted, must be performed on pain of mortal sin.[714] A matter is 'notable' if the thing exchanged is notable, that is, if it is considered notable in theft.[715]

Lessius also holds that the fiction of promise created by the apparent meaning of a declaration can create true contractual obligation.[716] Assume that a person suffers damage from relying on a statement that he mistakenly considers to be a promise. The perceived promisor is then bound to perform the apparent promise on pain of mortal sin, even though he

---

[713] Oñate, *De contractibus*, tom. 2, tract. 9, disp. 29, sect. 1, num. 4, p. 86, col. 2.

[714] Lessius, *De iustitia et iure*, lib 2, cap. 18, dub. 8, num. 55, p. 224: 'Tertia sententia est communior doctorum, promissio si materia notabilis est, obligare sub peccato mortali. Pro qua dico primo, omnis promissio serio facta animo promittendi in re magni momenti, ubi acceptata fuerit, obligat sub peccato mortali ad sui impletionem. (...) Probant secundo, promissio onerosa acceptata obligat lege iustitiae, ut omnes fatentur, ergo etiam gratuita.'

[715] Lessius, *De iustitia et iure*, lib 2, cap. 18, dub. 8, num. 56, p. 225.

[716] Lessius, *De iustitia et iure*, lib 2, cap. 18, dub. 8, num. 58, p. 225: 'Dico secundo, si quis utatur verbis promissoriis non quidem animo serio promittendi sed tantum ad significandum firmum propositum vel ad firmius asseverandum, ut ei credatur, non obligabitur sub peccato mortali ad implendum quod ita promisit, nisi ratione damni inde secuti. (...) Si tamen promissarius putaret alterum serio promisisse et inde postea contingeret illum damno affici (ut quia non potest solvere ad diem condictum) promissor tenetur implere sub peccato mortali, quia illo modo promittendi illum decepit, eaque deceptio est causa sine qua non damni secuti.'

was not serious about making a promise (*non animo serio*). This standpoint would have been much more difficult to defend by Molina, Lugo,
and Oñate, who insisted that the sole criterion to determine the extent
of promissory obligation was the subjective intention of the promisor
(*ex intentione*)—an opinion that Lessius also found probable but less convincing than his own point of view.[717] In the case of dubious promises,
Molina argues that the will of the perceived promisor is decisive for interpreting whether there is an obligation as a matter of justice or merely as a
matter of honesty (*ad proferentis animum recurrendum*).[718] Lugo endorses
Molina's opinion: if you promise with the intent of binding yourself legally,
then you are bound on pain of mortal sin, while promises made with the
intent of producing moral debt bind on pain of venial sin. The will is the
measure of everything (*pendet ex animo promittentis*).[719]

3.3.3.3   *Implied conditions and changed circumstances*

If the will is the measure of all things contractual from the perspective of
natural law, then what impact do changed circumstances have on contractual obligation? The short and straightforward answer to this question
is implicit in the Portuguese Jesuit Manuel de Sá's (1528–1596) successful
booklet of aphorisms: 'In a general obligation, even if strengthened by an
oath, those things which you did not intend are not included. Those things
seem to be all the things to which you would not have bound yourself if
you had then thought about them'.[720] The implication is clear: changed

---

[717] Lessius, *De iustitia et iure*, lib 2, cap. 18, dub. 8, num. 54, p. 224: 'Secunda sententia est, obligationem promissionis pendere ex intentione promittentis. Si enim promissor intendat se solum obligare ex honestate morali, solum tenebitur sub peccato veniali.
Si vero intendat se obligare stricte et ex iustitia, tunc tenebitur sub peccato mortali. Ita
Molina supra, estque probabilis, sed non satis explicat vim promissionis, quantum ipsa per
se, praecisa intentione extrinseca, obliget.'

[718] Molina, *De iustitia et iure*, tom. 2 (*De contractibus*), tract. 2, disp. 262, col. 37,
num. 2. Incidentally, Molina expressly associated debt pertaining to the virtue of honesty,
as opposed to debt deriving from justice, with morality and politics. Telling, in this respect,
is his employing the fixed expression 'moral or political honesty' (*honestas politica ac moralis*); e.g. *De iustitia et iure*, tom. 2 (*De contractibus*), tract. 2, disp. 262, col. 39, num. 10:
'Illud postremo observa circa promissionem, qua quis solum *ex honestate politica ac morali*
intendit se obligare, quod cum obligatio, quae ex ea resultat, et sit ad alterum, et non sit
ex iustitia, sed ex morali solum honestate, consequens est, ut fidei virtus, qua quis ex ea
promissione tenetur, et sit virtus iustitiae annexa, quatenus est ad alterum, et nihilominus
deficiat a perfecta ratione iustitiae, quatenus, quod ex ea est debitum, est solum debitum
ex honestate morali.' [italics are ours]

[719] Lugo, *De iustitia et iure*, tom. 2, disp. 23, sect. 6, num. 90, p. 127–128.

[720] Manuel de Sá, *Aphorismi confessariorum ex doctorum sententiis collecti*, Antverpiae
1599, s.v. *obligatio*, num. 2, p. 239–240: 'In obligatione generali, etiam cum iuramento, non

circumstances that negatively affect the position of the promisor do not fall within the scope of contractual obligation. An even more concise formulation of this idea is contained in the common expression that nothing is willed if it has not been foreseen (*nil volitum quin praecognitum*).[721] Following an alternative formulation of this common dictum (*voluntas non fertur in incognitum*), Lessius maintains that the will does not cover what is unknown.[722] Hence,[723]

> Every dissoluble contract contains the following tacit condition (*tacita conditio*) as a matter of the law of nations, namely that the contracting party will remain loyal to the contract unless he finds out that he has been gravely mistaken, namely through such mistake (*error*) which is the cause of the contract (*causa contractus*).

In other words, the quite classical idea that contracts do no longer bind if circumstances change considerably now becomes part of the doctrine of the vices of the will. Changed circumstances and mistake are two sides of the same coin. In both cases, the decisive reason for entering into a contract is lack of sufficient knowledge. Whether the legitimate ground to annul the contract exists before you enter into the contract (*causa praecedens*), as in the case of what we now call error, or only supervenes once you have concluded the contract (*causa superveniens*), as in the case of changed circumstances, the promisor's will turns out to have chosen a course of action which it would not have taken under full knowledge. In both cases, the will turns out to be deceived. Therefore, all contractual obligation is entered into under the tacit or implied condition (*tacita conditio*) that the will is not mistaken in regard to past, present or future circumstances. As Reinhard Zimmermann has sharply noted, once the foundation of contractual obligation came to rest on the will, the frustration of contractual obligations also had to be formulated in terms of the

---

veniunt ea quae non intendebas. Talia autem videntur esse quae si tunc cogitasses ad ea te non obligasses.' For biographical details on Sá, who taught theology at Alcalá and at the Collegio Romano, see A. Leite, *Sá, Manuel de*, in: C. O'Neill – J. Domínguez (eds.), Diccionario histórico de la Compañía de Jesús biográfico-temático, Roma-Madrid 2001, vol. 4, p. 34–54.

[721] *Pro ceteris*, Sánchez, *Disputationes de sancto matrimonii sacramento*, tom. 2, lib. 7, disp. 18, num. 1, p. 69.

[722] Lessius, *De iustitia et iure*, lib. 2, cap. 17, dub. 11, num. 74, p. 214.

[723] Lessius, *De iustitia et iure*, lib. 2, cap. 17, dub. 5, num. 29, p. 199: 'Unde omnis contractus solubilis iure gentium videtur habere hanc tacitam conditionem, quod contrahens stabit contractu nisi deprehenderit se graviter deceptum, id est, tali errore qui sit causa contractus.'

will.[724] This is exactly what we see happening in the moral theologians' doctrine of contract.

As Tomás Sánchez remarks, prenuptial agreements include the following implied condition: 'if things will have remained in the same state' (*si res in eodem statu permanserint*), or, put differently, 'if no cause supervenes, or a preceding cause comes fresh to light which is legitimate to dissolve the contract of engagement (*causa legitima ad ea dissolvenda*)'.[725] Lessius defends the voidability ensuing from mistake in the modern sense of the word by making reference to changed circumstances:[726] 'If such happened after the conclusion of contract, he would not be bound to perform any more, since the state of the things have notably changed (*status rerum notabiliter mutatus*). Consequently, he will also not be bound to perform anymore if that which was hidden at the outset comes to light during the contract.' The reason for the analogy is obvious: 'To supervene afresh (*supervenire de novo*), to be brought to light (*proferri in lucem*), or to begin to be known (*incipere cognosci*) are the same.'[727]

The incorporation of the teachings on changed circumstances into the doctrine of mistake did not happen immediately. For example, Soto contents himself to repeat the traditional view without more, namely that promises are no longer binding if performance has become unuseful, noxious, impossible or pernicious.[728] This idea reaches back at least to Cicero and Seneca.[729] Cicero reasoned that the reason why promises were

724 R. Zimmermann, 'Heard melodies are sweet, but those unheard are sweeter' – Conditio tacita, implied condition und die Fortbildung des Europäischen Vertragsrechts, Archiv für die civilistische Praxis, 193 (1993), p. 167.

725 Sánchez, Disputationes de sancto matrimonii sacramento, tom. 1, lib. 1, disp. 67, num. 2, p. 112: 'Sponsalia autem habent tacitam conditionem, si res in eodem statu permanserint, id est, si causa non superveniat aut praecedens nove cognoscatur legitima ad ea dissolvenda'.

726 Lessius, De iustitia et iure, lib. 2, cap. 17, dub. 5, num. 33, p. 200: 'Quia si tale quid post contractum eveniret, non teneretur illum implere, eo quod status rerum sit notabiliter mutatus, ergo etiam non tenebitur, si id quod ab initio latebat, postea se aperiat. Nam paria sunt, supervenire de novo, et proferri in lucem seu incipere cognosci.'

727 Curiously, Lessius rejects precisely this analogy (used as an argument by Juan de Medina) in solving the case of the Merchant of Rhodes; cf. Lessius, De iustitia et iure, lib. 2, cap. 21, dubit. 5, num. 41–42.

728 Soto, De iustitia et iure (ed. fac. V. Diego Carro – M. González Ordóñez, vol. 4), lib. 7, quaest. 2, art. 1, p. 631: 'Ut si quid tibi promisi tibi postea sit inutile aut nocuum, ut si gladium tibi promisi quo postea video te velle abuti, aut si promittenti factum est impossibile aut perniciosum, ut si promisi pecuniam quam postea ob infortunium reddere non possum, aut si mihi ingratitudinis signa exhibuisti.'

729 For a brief historical introduction to the doctrine of changed circumstances, see the contribution by Andreas Thier in: E. Hondius – H.C. Grigoleit (eds.), Unexpected cir-

to be kept was that, under normal circumstances, this principle contributed to the achievement of two principles that were even more important,
namely the do-no-harm principle and the principle that the common good
must be served.[730] However, if the achievement of these principles gets
frustrated through keeping a promise, then it is better not to observe the
promise in the first place. The rule that one ought to keep one's promises
is subordinate to other rules of justice. Hence, it is appropriate in certain
cases to deviate from the principle that promises are binding, otherwise
justice would turn into injustice (*summum ius, summa iniuria*).[731] Cicero
narrates the story of a lawyer who promised to litigate but whose son
suddenly fell ill, needing the care of his father.[732] In a utilitarian manner,
it is concluded that since the utility in staying at home with his son is
greater than the utility in going to court, the lawyer can break his promise. By the same token, he thinks it is a duty to refuse to return a sword
to a depositor who has gone mad by the end of the deposit contract.[733]
Cicero thus laid the foundations of a general principle of frustration of
contract by virtue of changed circumstances.[734] Seneca confirmed this.
He claimed that promises always come on condition that circumstances
remain unchanged (*si nihil inciderit quod inpediat*).[735]

Another important step toward a general application of the doctrine of
frustration, particularly under the guise of the *tacita conditio*, came with
Thomas Aquinas. He firmly adhered to Seneca's principle that promises
are binding on condition that circumstances remain the same. In this

---

cumstances in European contract law, [The common core of European private law], Cambridge 2011, p. 15–32.

[730] Cicero, *De officiis*, 1, 10, 31, in: *Cicéron, Les devoirs, Livres 1*, Texte établi et traduit par
Maurice Testard, [Collection des Universités de France], Paris 1965, vol. 1 (hereafter: Ed.
Testard, vol. 1), p. 119: 'Referri enim decet ad ea, quae posui principio, fundamenta iustitiae, primum ut ne cui noceatur, deinde ut communi utilitati serviatur. Ea cum tempore
commutantur, commutatur officium et non semper est idem.'

[731] Cicero, *De officiis* (Ed. Testard, vol. 1), 1, 10, 33, p. 120.

[732] Cicero, *De officiis* (Ed. Testard, vol. 1), 1, 10, 32, p. 119–120.

[733] Cicero, *De officiis*, 3, 25, 95, in: *Cicéron, Les devoirs, Livres 2–3*, Texte établi et traduit
par Maurice Testard, [Collection des Universités de France], Paris 1970, vol. 2 (hereafter:
Ed. Testard, vol. 2), p. 122.

[734] Cicero, *De officiis* (Ed. Testard, vol. 1), 1, 10, 32, p. 119: 'Nec promissa igitur servanda
sunt ea quae sint iis quibus promiseris, inutilia, nec, si plus tibi ea noceant quam illi pro-
sint cui promiseris, contra officium est maius anteponi minori.'

[735] Seneca, *De beneficiis*, 4, 34, 4, in: *Sénèque, Des bienfaits*, [Collection des Universités
de France], Paris 1961, vol. 1, p. 134: 'Non mutat sapiens consilium omnibus his manentibus,
quae erant, cum sumeret; ideo numquam illum paenitentia subit, quia nihil melius illo
tempore fieri potuit, quam quod factum est, nihil melius constitui quam constitutum est;
ceterum ad omnia cum exceptione venit: 'si nihil inciderit, quod inpediat'.

manner, Thomas is able to excuse Saint Paul's not fulfilling his promise to travel to Corinth. If the conditions of persons and the business in general change (*mutatae conditiones personarum et negotiorum*), then a promisor can be excused from not fulfilling his promise.[736] A promisor binds himself under the implicit assumption of the due conditions (*subintellectis debitis conditionibus*). If these conditions are frustrated, he is no longer bound. Cleverly generalizing the teachings of his master, Cajetan summarizes them as follows: 'all things must remain unchanged if agreements are to be binding' (*omnia debent esse immutata si pacta servanda sunt*).[737] He concludes that it is necessary for right reason (*recta ratio*) to take into consideration the circumstances of place, time, persons and business in general and weigh them against the initial promise.[738]

The role of right reason in deciding whether a contract could be avoided on account of changed circumstances returns in Lessius' exposition under the guise of the prudent man. This recalls the canon law tradition, expressed for instance in Dr. Navarrus, according to which it pertained to the office of the judge to decide if a contract could be avoided by virtue of changed circumstances.[739] Moreover, Lessius connects the debate on changed circumstances to the metaphor of contracts as private legislation.

---

[736] Aquinas, *Summa Theologiae* (Ed. Leonina, tom. 9), IIaIIae, quaest. 110, art. 3, ad 5, p. 425–426: 'Ad quintum dicendum quod ille qui aliquid promittit, si habeat animum faciendi quod promittit, non mentitur, quia non loquitur contra id quod gerit in mente. Si vero non faciat quod promisit, tunc videtur infideliter agere per hoc quod animum mutat. Potest tamen excusari ex duobus. Uno modo, si promisit id quod est manifeste illicitum, quia promittendo peccavit, mutando autem propositum bene facit. Alio modo, si sint mutatae conditiones personarum et negotiorum. Ut enim Seneca dicit, in libro de Benefic., ad hoc quod homo teneatur facere quod promisit, requiritur quod omnia immutata permaneant, alioquin nec fuit mendax in promittendo, quia promisit quod habebat in mente, subintellectis debitis conditionibus; nec etiam est infidelis non implendo quod promisit, quia eaedem conditiones non extant. Unde et apostolus non est mentitus, qui non ivit Corinthum, quo se iturum esse promiserat, ut dicitur II Cor. I, et hoc propter impedimenta quae supervenerant.'

[737] Cajetanus, *Commentaria ad Secundam Secundae divi Thomae* (Ed. Leonina, tom. 9), ad quaest. 113, art. 2, p. 440, num. 8: 'Auctor autem, sequens Senecam, unum universalem casum posuit in qu. 110, scilicet mutationem, dum dixit quod omnia debent esse immutata si pacta servanda sunt.'

[738] Cajetanus, *Commentaria ad Secundam Secundae divi Thomae* (Ed. Leonina, tom. 9), ad quaest. 113, art. 2, p. 440, num. 8: 'Oportet ergo considerare impedimenta supervenientia et conferre cum re promissa, et, collatione facta, quod recta tunc ratio suadet, pensatis conditionibus locorum, personarum, temporum et negotiorum, honestum exequi.

[739] For Dr. Navarrus, see *Enchiridion sive manuale confessariorum et poenitentium*, cap. 18, num. 7, p. 408: '(...) Quae non sunt intelligenda de qualibet mutatione, sed de illa qua si promittens praecogitasset, non promisisset, cui fides habenda est in foro conscientiae (...) et etiam exteriori si iudicio prudentis viri consideratis negotii circumstantiis, nequaquam promisisset si illud praecogitasset (...).'

Since an accepted promise is like a binding law, the principle applies that says that the law is not binding in those cases that have expressly or tacitly been excluded from the scope of the law by the legislator:[740] 'a promise is a particular kind of law (*lex quaedam particularis*) that someone spontaneously imposes on himself, so it will not bind in those cases that the promisor is considered, according to the interpretation of prudent men (*ex prudentum interpretatione*), to have excluded explicitly or implicitly.'

The analogy from the legislator can be traced back to Molina and attained its climax in Oñate. In addition, Oñate declared the principle of changed circumstances a universal principle of contract law (*regula semper universalis*).[741] He based it on equity and the idea of contractual obligation as a private law:[742] 'Just as under those changing circumstances *epikeia* is to be applied to the laws and constitutions of the princes, so will it be equitable to apply *epikeia* to the promises made by private persons. For promises are like laws which private persons impose upon themselves.' Luis de Molina had expressed roughly the same view before, also arguing that nobody could be considered a better interpreter of the obligation than the promisor himself.[743] Oñate insists that it could never be considered the intent of the promisor to bind himself in the event of changed circumstances. Hence, every promise must be interpreted as being quasi-conditional, namely 'unless a notable change affects the promise' (*nisi notabilis mutatio accidit circa promissionem*).[744]

---

[740] Lessius, *De iustitia et iure*, lib. 2, cap. 18, dub. 10, num. 71, p. 227: 'Confirmatur quia lex quae absolute lata est, non obligat in illis casibus, quos legislator expresse vel interpretative voluit exceptos. Atqui promissio est lex quaedam particularis, quam sibi quis sponte imponit, ergo non obligabit in illis casibus, quos expresse vel tacite ex prudentum interpretatione censetur excepisse.'

[741] Oñate, *De contractibus*, tom. 2, tract. 9, disp. 29, sect. 11, num. 153, p. 128.

[742] Oñate, *De contractibus*, tom. 2, tract. 9, disp. 29, sect. 11, num. 152, p. 128: '(...) sicut in simili in legibus et constitutionibus principum *epikeia* locum habet, ita eam in promissionibus privatorum locum habere aequum est, cum promissiones sint quaedam leges, quas sibi ipsis privati imponunt'.

[743] Molina, *De iustitia et iure*, tom. 2 (*De contractibus*), tract. 2, disp. 272, col. 84, num. 2: 'Etenim quemadmodum in legibus locum habet epicheia ad excipiendos eventus de quibus dubitandum non est, si legislatori occurrerent, illos excepisset, qui proinde eiusmodi legibus non censentur comprehensi, esto legislator nihil de eis, quando legem tulit, cogitaverit, sic etiam in promissione, quae est velut lex quaedam quam sibi promittens imponit, non censentur comprehensi eventus quos tunc promittens excepisset, si ipsi occurrerent aut proponerentur. Neque alius potest esse melior interpres suae propriae promissionis quam promittens ipse, esto absolute promiserit, neque quicquam de eventibus tunc inopinatis cogitaverit.'

[744] Oñate, *De contractibus*, tom. 2, tract. 9, disp. 29, sect. 11, num. 151, p. 128.

However, not all moral theologians were willing to give the principle of changed circumstances such a universal application. Many authors were quite inconsistent in their views of frustration of contract, as for instance Tomás Sánchez.[745] Even though the doctrine of changed circumstanced reached unknown heights in the writings of the scholastics, some argued that changed circumstances should not be allowed as a universal principle. Their principal argument was legal certainty and security of business. Juan de Lugo considered a general application of the tacit condition highly problematic (*regula illa generalis difficillima*).[746] He feared that all contractual exchange would become unstable (*sequeretur nullum in rebus humanis contractum firmum manere*). Generally speaking, Lugo pleaded for a very restricted use of changed circumstances as a remedy. The detailed casuistry he developed on the basis of this restrictive principle falls outside the scope of the present study.[747]

3.4   GROTIUS

'If the positive laws and natural law are not to be confounded,' Grotius briefly notes at the end of his chapter on promises,[748] 'it should also not be omitted that, no more than gifts, promises which lack an expressed cause (*causa expressa*) are not void as a matter of natural law.' As opposed to canon law, natural law does not require that the parties expressly mention the cause behind the promise in order for that promise to become enforceable. This is standard scholastic doctrine. In just one single, dense and almost cryptic phrase, Grotius divulges the same idea. In doing so, the jurist and theologian from Delft does not make any explicit reference to the moral theologians or to the literature on the *forum internum*. Yet it seems unlikely that the meaning of his remark can be fully grasped if not read against the background of the observations on *causa* by the medieval canonists and the early modern jurists and theologians.

---

[745] For a critical assessment of Sánchez's confusing teachings on the subject, see Lugo, *Disputationes de iustitia et iure*, tom. 2, disp. 22, sect. 6, num. 87, p. 23.

[746] Lugo, *De iustitia et iure*, tom. 2, disp. 22, sect. 6, num. 87, p. 23.

[747] For a detailed account, see Lugo, *De iustitia et iure*, tom. 2, disp. 22, sect. 6, num. 88–95, p. 23–25.

[748] Grotius, *De jure belli ac pacis* (Ed. De Kanter-Van Hettinga Tromp – Feenstra – Persenaire), lib. 2, cap. 11, par. 21 (*promissiones sine causa, naturaliter non esse irritas*), p. 339: 'Hoc quoque omittendum non est, ne iura civilia cum naturali iure confundantur, neque promissiones quae causam expressam non habent naturaliter esse irritas, non magis quam rerum donationes.'

What this citation means to suggest is not that Grotius' legal doctrine could be reduced to the teachings of the scholastics. While reductionist visions appear to be naive in the first place, they more sadly threaten to kill the very poetry behind the changing faces of legal history. A restless traveller and an intellectual polymath, Grotius was exposed to many different strands of thought. If scholasticism and legal humanism undoubtedly count among the more powerful catalysts of his legal thinking, Grotius transformed those traditions into a unique product of his own. His larger ambition of fostering peace among the divided nations of Europe may also not have been wholly identical with the moral theologians' chief concern, namely to prepare the soul for the day of Last Judgment. Still, the fact that Grotius was not afraid of being inspired by his scholastic sources seems almost undeniable.

Regarding the essence and the formation of contract, there is clear evidence that reading the *De iure belli ac pacis* against a scholastic background can shed fresh light on Grotius' argumentation. On a macro-level, it is probably no coincidence that Grotius first opens with a chapter on promises before dedicating a chapter to contracts. After all, the scholastics structured their new views on the creation of contractual obligation around the notion of promise, thereby superseding the old *ius commune* discussions on naked and clothed pacts, nominate and innominate contracts, etc. Moreover, Grotius' attempt to distinguish between three different scales of obligation (*veritas* / *debitum constantiae sive fidelitatis* / *iustitia*) depending on the kind of enunciation (*assertio* / *pollicitatio* / *perfecta promissio*) bears striking similarities to the strenuous efforts made by the scholastics to differentiate between, roughly speaking, mere indicative statements about future action, morally binding statements of intention, and juridically binding promises.[749]

Importantly, Grotius follows the majority opinion of the scholastics that acceptance of a promise is required for the promisor's legal obligation and the promisee's enforceable right to come into existence.[750] The promisor

---

[749] Grotius, *De jure belli ac pacis* (Ed. De Kanter-Van Hettinga Tromp – Feenstra – Persenaire), lib. 2, cap. 11, par. 2–4, p. 328–329. Grotius does not use the expression 'debitum iustitiae' explicitly, as some of the scholastics did, but it is implicit in his description of perfect promises; see below. Grotius' indebtedness to the scholastics for his three-stage theory of promise has already been pointed out, *inter alia*, in F. Wieacker, *Die vertragliche Obligation bei den Klassikern des Vernunftrechts*, in: G. Stratenwerth et al. (eds.), Festschrift für Hans Welzel zum 70. Geburtstag, Berlin – New York 1974, p. 16–17.

[750] Grotius, *De jure belli ac pacis* (Ed. De Kanter-Van Hettinga Tromp – Feenstra – Persenaire), lib. 2, cap. 11, par. 14, p. 335: 'Ut autem promissio ius transferat, acceptatio hic non minus quam in dominii translatione requiritur (…).'

is under no obligation to perform unless the promisee has accepted his promise. Interestingly enough, Grotius rejects Molina's interpretation of the binding force of the *pollicitatio civitati* in Roman law. It may be recalled that, in Molina's view, an unaccepted promise must be binding as a matter of natural law since civil obligation presupposes natural obligation. According to Grotius, Molina is mistaken in his view that D. 50,12 imposed a civil obligation on the *pollicitator civitati*. Grotius refutes Molina's argument by saying that Roman law simply forbade the promisor to revoke his promise.[751] This is precisely the argument that Lessius had employed to counter the view of Molina.[752] There is little doubt, then, that Grotius draws directly on Lessius here.

The fact that Grotius does not explicitly cite Lessius regarding his opinion of the non-binding nature of the *pollicitatio civitati* probably adds weight to the suspicion that Grotius was inspired by Lessius' *De iustitia et iure* also in other places where he does not cite him, rather than the view that Grotius ignored Lessius' teachings on promises altogether. For example, Grotius is rightly famous for having conceived of the perfect promise (*perfecta promissio*) in terms of the transfer of rights (*ius proprium alteri conferre*) and, in regard to promises to do something, in terms of the alienation of a part of the promisor's liberty (*alienatio particulae cuiusdam nostrae libertatis*).[753] The charming simplicity of this enunciation is nothing short of stunning. However, Grotius' 'juridical' conception of promising did not come out of the blue. It is sufficient to recall Lessius' standpoint that the promisor deliberately binds himself to the promisee in order to give or to do something, thereby conferring a right upon the promisee to

---

[751] Grotius, *De jure belli ac pacis* (Ed. De Kanter-Van Hettinga Tromp – Feenstra – Persenaire), lib. 2, cap. 11, par. 14, p. 336: 'Nec obstat quod de pollicitationibus factis civitati iure civile est proditum: quae ratio quosdam induxit, ut iure naturae solum promittentis actum sufficere iudicarent: nam lex Romana non hoc dicit, ante acceptationem pollicitationis plenam esse vim, sed revocari vetat, ut acceptari semper possit: qui effectus non est naturalis, sed mere legitimus.' The opinion according to which 'Molina' should not be connected with 'quosdam' despite the fact that Grotius himself linked it to Molina, seems to complicate matters unnecessarily; see additional note 336a on page 980 of the revised Grotius-edition by De Kanter-Van Hettinga Tromp – Feenstra – Persenaire.

[752] Lessius, *De iustitia et iure*, lib. 2, cap. 18, dub. 6, num. 40, p. 220.

[753] Grotius, *De jure belli ac pacis* (Ed. De Kanter-Van Hettinga Tromp – Feenstra – Persenaire), lib. 2, cap. 11, par. 4, p. 329: 'Tertius gradus est ubi ad determinationem talem accedit signum volendi ius proprium alteri conferre: quae perfecta promissio est, similem habens effectum qualem alienatio dominii. Est enim aut via ad alienationem rei, aut alienatio particulae cuiusdam nostrae libertatis. Illuc pertinent promissa dandi, huc promissa faciendi.'

enforce the promise.[754] Grotius, then, was not an innovator, let alone the pioneer, in analyzing promises in terms of juridical debt.[755] He played a vital role, however, in handing down Lessius 'horizontal' analysis of the binding nature of accepted promises to luminaries such as Robert Joseph Pothier, who made explicit reference to Grotius when espousing the view that unilateral promises without acceptance cannot create contractual obligation.[756]

As indicated before, the scholastic legacy in *De iure belli ac pacis* by no means subtracts from Grotius' creative genius. For one thing, the literary casting of Grotius' exposition on promises creates an atmosphere that is distant from the scholastic universe. Grotius' universe is agreeable to the reader on account of its brevity, its elegance, and its manifold references to both classical and scriptural texts. To the best of our knowledge, there is also no scholastic precedent to Grotius presenting his views on the binding nature of bare agreements in the form of a refutation of the French humanist François Connan.[757] Also, Grotius' conclusions are not all of a piece with scholastic doctrine. A case in point is the doctrine of changed circumstances. Grotius, like the scholastics, conceives of it in terms of a tacit condition (*tacita conditio*) implied in the promise.[758] Yet Grotius seems to have advocated a stricter application of the tacit condition than the majority of the scholastics, or, for that matter, Cicero and Seneca.[759] It is perhaps no coincidence, then, that the doctrine of changed

---

[754] Lessius, *De iustitia et iure*, lib. 2, cap. 18, dub. 8, num. 52, p. 223–224: 'Quia promittere non tantum est affirmare se daturum vel facturum, sed ulterius est se obligare alteri, et consequenter ius illi tribuere ad exigendum. Unde dici solet, *promissionem parere debitum.*' Cf. supra, n. 710.

[755] Lessius, *De iustitia et iure*, lib. 2, cap. 18, dub. 8, num. 55, p. 224 (*omnis obligatio contractuum est obligatio iustitiae*). Cf. supra, n. 711.

[756] Pothier, *Traité des obligations, selon les regles, tant du for de la conscience, que du for extérieur*, part. 1, sec. 1, chap. 1, art. 1 par. 2 (En quoi le contrat differe-t-il de la pollicitation), p. 7: 'La pollicitation est la promesse qui n'est pas encore acceptée par celui à qui elle est faite. [...] La pollicitation aux termes de pur droit naturel ne produit aucune obligation proprement dite, et celui qui a fait cette promesse peut s'en dédire, tant que cette promesse n'a pas été acceptée par celui à qui elle a été faite; car il ne peut y avoir d'obligation, sans un droit qu'acquiert la personne envers qui elle est contractée contre la personne obligée (...).'

[757] For Connan's strict adherance to Labeo's, synallagmatic conception of contract, see Birocchi, *Causa e categoria generale del contratto*, p. 95–136.

[758] Grotius, *De jure belli ac pacis* (Ed. De Kanter-Van Hettinga Tromp – Feenstra – Persenaire), lib. 2, cap. 16, par. 25, p. 421–422: 'Solet et hoc disputari, an promissa in se habeant tacitam conditionem | si res maneant quo sunt loco: quod negandum est, nisi apertissime pateat, statum rerum praesentem in unica illa quam diximus ratione inclusum esse.'

[759] Grotius, *De jure belli ac pacis* (Ed. De Kanter-Van Hettinga Tromp – Feenstra – Persenaire), lib. 2, cap. 16, par. 27, p. 423–424. One should keep in mind, though, that scho-

circumstances seems to have disappeared in the work of natural lawyers such as Pothier. However, there is also evidence to the contrary, namely that to a certain extent, notably in the case of informal contracts, Pothier did accept a kind of theory of changed circumstances.[760]

3.5   CONCLUSION

There is probably no better way of illustrating the turn towards a voluntaristic, consensualist and open law of contact in the early modern period than by recalling Oñate's remarkable praise of 'freedom of contract'. Freedom has wisely been restored to the contracting parties, since they can make any deal that they want and be certain that the court of their choice will universally enforce that contract. Despite the persistence of a plurality of legal traditions, Oñate joyfully observed that in the Spanish empire, canon law, Roman law, statute law and natural law universally agreed on this principle. We have seen Molina expressing the desire that all countries imitate the Spanish model. He wished so for the sake of the salvation of souls. He also believed that the bindingness of all agreements would eventually foster peace in society, even though the rationale for the closed system of contracts in Roman times was thought to be the avoidance of overburdened courts and, hence, the concern for the tranquillity of the republic.

As has been described in the first part of this chapter, the canon law was seminal in attracting the other legal traditions toward the principle that all agreements, however naked, are binding. It might be worthwhile remembering, however, that the canon law itself was basically giving in to

---

lastic views on this topic widely differed, with Juan de Lugo being even more reluctant to grant relief by virtue of changed circumstances than Grotius. It may be worthwhile noting that Lugo's *De iustitia et iure* (1642) was published after the first edition of Grotius' *De iure belli ac pacis* (1625), so maybe Lugo could have become more wary of the tacit condition precisely on account of his familiarity with Grotius' views. However, the final answer to this question remains within the realm of speculation.

760 Pothier, *Traité des obligations, selon les regles, tant du for de la conscience, que du for extérieur*, part. 1, sec. 1, chap. 1, art. 1, par. 1: 'Par exemple, lorsqu'un pere promet à son fils, qui étudie en droit, de lui donner de quoi faire dans les vacances un voyage de récréation, en cas qu'il emploie bien son tems: il est évident que le pere, en faisant cette promesse, n'entend pas contracter evers son fils un engagement proprement dit. Ces promesses produisent bien une obligation imparfaite de les accomplir, *pourvu qu'il ne soit survenu aucune cause*, laquelle, si elle eût été prévue, eût empêché de faire la promesse: mais elles ne forment pas d'engagement, ni par conséquent de contrat.' (Italics are mine). It might be noted that in this context 'cause', just as the Latin word 'causa' means 'circumstance'.

the moral weight of natural law and equity. It remained a matter of dispute, therefore, whether contracts had to be enforced through an ordinary remedy or, rather, as Pope Innocent IV argued, through the extraordinary remedy of evangelical denunciation. Moreover, the freedom inherent in the canon law principle that all agreements are binding was based on moral considerations regarding the salvation of souls. It is therefore not to be confounded with nineteenth century, purely secular accounts of 'freedom of contract', which were chiefly motivated by economic arguments. As Gordley sharply noticed, even though the vocabulary of the canonists and the scholastics may have lived on through the natural lawyers of the seventeenth century, the underlying philosophies changed.[761]

Although deeply rooted in the religious universe of sin and salvation, it has been shown in the second part of this chapter that the moral theologians, particularly the Jesuits, came close to one of the clearest formulations of 'freedom of contract'. It would be no lie to claim that the doctrine of offer and acceptance appears in its fully-developed form in the writings of theologians such as Lessius, Lugo and Oñate. In addition, they based the principle of 'freedom of contract' on a liberal, albeit religious view of man as the owner of his will, thus laying the anthropological foundations of freedom to contract. Contract becomes the instrument of a self-conscious *dominus* who can decide to do whatever he wants with his private property. Through the juridical device of contract, owners can exchange goods *ad libitum*, as if they were private legislators. Importantly, the promisee can enforce a contract because an accepted offer conveys a right to the promisee and imposes an obligation on the promisor. In other words, the moral theologians, specifically the Jesuits, insisted that contractual obligation is of a distinctively juridical nature.

Having laid down 'freedom of contract' as a principle, and having formulated a general category of contract as promise and acceptance, the question to be answered in the following chapters, is whether the moral theologians adhered to 'contractual freedom' unqualifiedly. The next chapter will explore the limitations to 'freedom of contract' that are inherent in the voluntaristic definition of contract. If the entire force of obligation derives from the will, then it would seem that the vices of the will must 'naturally' impede freedom to contract. Individuals' intentions may also be hampered by limitations imposed by the civil authorities, mainly through formality requirements. Hence, the fifth chapter will be devoted

---

[761] Gordley, *The philosophical origins of modern contract doctrine*, p. 112.

to the formal limitations on 'freedom of contract'. 'Freedom of contract' can also be impinged upon by moral objections to the substance of the contract. Accordingly, the sixth chapter will analyze the vivid debate on the validity of contracts for sex. Different from those types of moral considerations are concerns about substantive fairness. The subject of the penultimate chapter is whether 'freedom of contract' can be restricted if there is no equilibrium between the values in an exchange.

CHAPTER FOUR

NATURAL LIMITATIONS ON 'FREEDOM OF CONTRACT'

4.1 INTRODUCTION

The early modern theologians firmly established the concept of contract as a mutually accepted promise that takes the place of law for the contracting parties involved. As a matter of natural law, the essence of a contract consists of mutual consent. Hence, the first, 'natural' obstacle to 'freedom of contract' is the vitiation of consent. The theologians devoted ample space, then, to discussions about the impact of duress (*metus*) and mistake (*error/dolus*) on the validity of contracts.[762] Lack of contractual capacity was also a topic of intensive debates, certainly in regard to minors. In fact, the superabundance of textual material on these subjects largely exceeds the limits that a book chapter on the natural limitations on 'contractual freedom' is bound to observe. Moreover, the complexity of the scholastic treatment of the vices of the will drove Hugo Grotius and Juan de Lugo into despair.

For the sake of clarity a twofold restriction imposed itself upon the following investigation. From a material perspective, duress and mistake are the only vices of the will that have been retained.[763] In respect to the writings of the scholastics themselves, most authority has been given to the Jesuit scholastics at the threshold of the seventeenth century.[764] From a formal perspective, much attention is paid to the question of what kind of nullity the scholastics attached to a contract influenced by either duress or mistake: does coerced or erroneous consent make a contract

---

[762] We chose to translate *metus* alternatively by fear, duress, and compulsion, since all of these terms seem to be present in *metus*. Rendering the concepts of *error* and *dolus* into English is more tricky, because *dolus* and *error* seem to be used as synonyms in the scholastic tradition. Moreover, the concept of *dolus* does not necessarily presuppose evil intentions; cf. Feenstra, *De oorsprong van Hugo de Groot's leer over de dwaling*, p. 87–88.

[763] It seems more appropriate to include the scholastics' doctrine of legal capacity and minors in a monograph on their law of persons.

[764] As pointed out before, they seem to have been the moral theologians who provided us with the most systematic treatments of contract law in general and the vices of the will in particular. Apart from this, the general selection principle as outlined in the chapter on methodology applies.

automatically void (*irritus*) or voidable at the option of the wronged party (*irritandus*)? In the case of mistake, this question goes with an analysis of how the distinction between *contractus bonae fidei* and *stricti iuris* persisted until it was dissolved definitively by Lessius. In the case of duress, it implies a focus on the way Tomás Sánchez treated duress in the context of his law of marriage.

While an attempt has been made to exemplify the casuistry surrounding the issue of duress, no such effort has been made in the examination of mistake. This means that a study of the detailed casuistry on, for instance, the influence of defects in the goods on the validity of sale contracts, has been excluded from this text.[765] Mistake-related issues such as the doctrine of changed circumstances and *laesio enormis* have been ignored, since they are treated in other chapters. In an ideal world it would be interesting to compare the doctrines on duress and mistake in contracts with similar problems in the laws of marriage, oaths, and vows. Such an investigation demands a separate study, however. Moreover, it is to the credit of the early modern scholastics that they neatly distinguished in their treatises between these traditional problematic fields, which were dealt with extensively in the manuals for confessors, and vices of consent in contracts.

4.2   DURESS (*METUS*)

4.2.1   *Foundations*

4.2.1.1   *Romano-canon law*

The theologians of the early modern period are noted for their abundant and ecclectic use of Roman and canon law. The following paragraphs do not mean to be exhaustive when describing the law of duress (*metus*) in Romano-canon law.[766] What we intend to do here is to flag a couple of juridical texts that turned out to be of great importance to the scholastics as they developed their views on duress. The casuistry and rules from Digest title 4,2 (*Quod metus causa gestum erit*) provided the scholastics

---

[765] For this we refer to Decock – Hallebeek, *Pre-contractual duties to inform in early modern scholasticism.*

[766] The late medieval conception of duress has already formed the subject of thorough analysis in Kuttner, *Kanonistische Schuldlehre*, p. 299–314.

with fundamental working materials. Certainly, when it came to defining duress and determining the extent to which relief can be granted for
duress, Digest title 4,2 turned out to be crucial. The canon law provided
the scholastics with important texts to assess the effect of duress on
contractual validity, in particular the canons included in title 1,40 of the
Decretales (*De his quae vi metusve causa fiunt*) and the cases on marital
consent in title 4,1 (*De sponsalibus et matrimoniis*).

Emperor Hadrian had laid down as a general rule that he would not
enforce what was based on duress (*quod metus causa gestum erit, ratum
non habebo*). Mentioning this rule, law *Ait praetor* (D. 4,2,1) specified that
duress is the perturbation of the mind because of an imminent or future
threat (*instans vel futurum periculum*).[767] This threat must concern a major
evil (*major malitas*).[768] Law *Metum autem* (D. 4,2,6) further restricted the
availability of a remedy against duress by pointing out that only duress
that could throw off balance even the most constant man (*homo constantissimus*) could be considered relevant.[769] Every single Latin word in these
definitions would become subject to intense and divergent interpretations
by the scholastics. The same holds true for the casuistry that was meant
to determine which kind of evil could be deemed to intimidate a man of
a steadfast character:[770] fear of death, imprisonment, rape, etc.

---

[767] D. 4,2,1 in *Corporis Iustinianaei Digestum vetus* (ed. Gothofredi), tom. 1, col. 477: 'Ait
praetor: *Quod metus causa gestum erit, ratum non habebo*. Olim ita edicebatur: *quod vi
metusve causa*: vis enim fiebat mentio propter necessitatem impositam contrariam voluntati: metus instantis vel futuri periculi causa mentis trepidatio. Sed postea detracta est vis
mentio ideo, quia quodcumque vi atroci fit, id metu quoque fieri videtur.'

[768] D. 4,2,5 in *Corporis Iustinianaei Digestum vetus* (ed. Gothofredi), tom. 1, col. 478:
'Metum accipiendum Labeo dicit non quemlibet timorem, sed maioris malitatis.'

[769] D. 4,2,6 in *Corporis Iustinianaei Digestum vetus* (ed. Gothofredi), tom. 1, col. 478:
'Metum autem non vani hominis, sed qui merito et in homine constantissimo cadat, ad
hoc edictum pertinere dicemus.'

Some scholars have suggested that the criterion of the 'most constant man' (*homo constantissimus*) is a reflection of the Roman attitude towards the central virtue of constancy
(*constantia*); cf. Zimmermann, *The law of obligations*, p. 653.

Although philosophers like Seneca had elaborated on this virtue before the *Corpus iuris
civilis* was edited, we doubt, however, that the Roman legal text originally intended to
evoke this moral philosophical background. If so, it would have been sufficient to mention the 'constant man' (*homo constans*), without making use of the superlative. Moreover,
as will become clear as we deal with Domingo de Soto, the conjunction of the virtue of
constancy with the Roman legal text takes place explicitly with the early modern scholastics. At the same time (and therefore), they argued that not the 'most constant man'
(*homo constantissimus*), but the 'constant man' (*homo constans*) constituted the standard
of reference: virtue is virtue.

[770] See D. 4,2,3,1; D. 4,2,7,1; D. 4,2,8,2. It should be noted that infamy did not fall into
this category, cf. D. 4,2,7.

The objective and delictual approach to duress in Roman law also left its marks on the scholastic discussion. As is commonly known, the Roman remedy against duress (*actio quod metus causa*) had the characteristics of a real action (*actio in rem scripta*).[771] Hence, the defendant could be either the other party to the contract or any other person who had acquired the object in question. What mattered was the restoration of the wrong done to the intimidated party.[772] Roman law did not consider duress to be a vice of the will. It merely stated that holding parties to *contractus bonae fidei* that had been entered into by duress would go against good morals.[773] Also, the praetor could grant relief to someone who had been coerced into taking possession of a heritage, but duress did not compromise consent as such. In the words of the jurist Paul:[774] 'I agreed despite the fact that I had been coerced' (*coactus volui*). This phrase turned out to be very influential in the scholastic tradition. The gloss explicated that a coerced will remained a will.[775] Part of the success of this rule no doubt derived from the fact that it fitted very well into the Aristotelian-Thomistic tradition on duress.[776]

Canon law dealt with duress in the context of contractual consent, and, particularly, in relation to the validity of coerced consent in marriage contracts. One of the major, albeit indirect contributions of the canon law to the law of contract was its insistence on the absolute liberty with which spouses must enter into a marriage contract. The rule from canon *Gemma* (X 4,1,29) stating that marriages should be free was recognized as a fundamental principle of Church law. The gloss to canon *Gemma* clearly stated that this liberty was to be understood in terms of the absence of coercion

---

[771] Cf. D. 4,2,9,8. Compare D. 4,2,9,1 in *Corporis Iustinianaei Digestum vetus* (ed. Gothofredi), tom. 1, cols. 481–482: 'Animadvertendum autem, quod praetor hoc edicto generaliter et in rem loquitur nec adicit a quo gestum.'

[772] For further details on the Roman law of duress, see Deroussin, *Histoire du droit des obligations*, p. 513–517.

[773] D. 50,17,116 in *Corporis Iustinianaei Digestum novum* (ed. Gothofredi), tom. 3, col. 1901: 'Nihil consensui tam contrarium est, qui ac bonae fidei iudicia sustinet, quam vis atque metus, quem comprobare contra bonos mores est.'

[774] D. 4,2,21,5 in *Corporis Iustinianaei Digestum vetus* (ed. Gothofredi), tom. 1, col. 500: 'Si metu coactus adii hereditatem, puto me heredem effici, quia quamvis si liberum esset noluissem, tamen coactus volui; sed per praetorem restituendus sum, ut abstinendi mihi potestas tribuatur.'

[775] Glossa *Volui* ad D. 4,2,21,5 in *Corporis Iustinianaei Digestum vetus* (ed. Gothofredi), tom. 1, col. 500: 'Et sic nota quod coacta voluntas, voluntas est.'

[776] One might rightly wonder whether the Roman law had not been influenced by Aristotelian thought on duress and (in)voluntary consent in the first place. Cf. A.S. Hartkamp, *Der Zwang im römischen Privatrecht*, Amsterdam 1971, p. 84 and p. 124.

(*ab omni coactione*).[777] Moreover, marriage contracts were thought to require an even higher degree of liberty than other contracts. There were two reasons for that. The first is a theological one. Marriage is a sacrament representing the faithful covenant between Christ and his bride.[778] The second reason is of a more general nature. Freedom of marriage is considered to be the only guarantee that marriage lasts for a life time, which in turn is the best guarantee for the good upbringing of the children (*ad procreationem prolis*).[779]

Other important passages from the Decretales included canon *Abbas* in X 1,40,2 (*quae metu et vi fiunt, de iure debent in irritum revocari*) and canon *Quum dilectus filius* (X 1,40,6). Canon *Quum dilectus filius* constituted a canonical formulation of the Roman criterion of the constant man. Theologians adduced canon *Abbas* to argue that duress resulted in voidability at the option of the intimidated party rather than that the contract was avoided automatically. In 1602, canon *Abbas* would form one of the most authoritative arguments for Tomás Sánchez to defend a general regime of voidability in all contracts affected by duress except marriage.

4.2.1.2   *The Aristotelian-Thomistic tradition*

While the fundamental contribution of Roman and canon law to the development of modern contract law has been widely acknowledged, the philosophical origins of modern contract doctrine have rather been ignored until fairly recently.[780] An elementary understanding of Aristotle's conception of free human agency, certainly in its Thomistic interpretation, nonetheless turns out to be indispensable to anyone trying to

---

[777] Cf. Glossa *Libera debeant* ad X 4,1,29 in: *Corpus juris canonici* (ed. Gregoriana), part. 2, col. 1442, l. 73–74.

[778] E.g. Pedro de Aragón, *In secundam secundae commentaria de iustitia et iure*, Salmanticae 1590, quaest. 89, art. 7, p. 1079: 'Divus Bonaventura atque Durandus dicunt, quod, quia matrimonium Christianorum significat unionem Christi et Ecclesiae, quae est perpetua, perpetuum etiam et indissolubile debet vinculum habere ad quod non solum consensus, verum et liber consensus requiritur, cum nullum violentum possit esse perpetuum.'

[779] This is explained very clearly in Soto, *De iustitia et iure* (ed. fac. V. Diego Carro – M. González Ordóñez, vol. 4), lib. 8, quaest. 1, art. 7, p. 733: 'Quandoquidem et coniugium etiam sub lege quoque naturae liberum requirebat consensum. Dicendum ergo, quod matrimonium ob id a natura ad procreationem prolis constitutum est, ex sua ipsius natura perpetuitatem habet annexam. Alias non esset satis liberis educandis consultum. Perpetuitas autem ex natura rei liberum exigit animi consensum. Nam quae violenta sunt, secundum Aristotelem, nequeunt esse perpetua.'

[780] James Gordley's book on the *Philosophical origins of modern contract doctrine* is a notable exception.

explain the concepts of mistake and duress in the modern law of contract. Also, the Aristotelian account of duress might help to explain the Roman approach to duress in the first place: Aristotle did not consider coerced actions to be entirely involuntary.

At the outset of the third book of the *Nicomachean Ethics*, Aristotle points out that man is responsible for his actions only to the extent that he acts freely and in the absence of ignorance or compulsion.[781] Accordingly, a person can be blamed or praised only for actions that he performs voluntarily. Aristotle indicates that this is an insight for legislators to remember well as they distribute honour and punishment. The question is, however, whether ignorance and compulsion have the same effect upon the voluntariness of an action. Ignorance prevents you from choosing the right course of action since your rational insight into the circumstances of the action is hampered. Put differently, you are mistaken. Compulsion, on the other hand, does not seem to result in involuntary choices automatically.

Take the example of a captain who throws his goods overboard in a storm in order to save the crew. At the moment of action, he definitely wishes to jettison cargo, but he would definitely not have wished to do so in the abstract. Aristotle concludes that there is apparently a category of actions that are mixed, in the sense that they are constituted both by voluntary and involuntary elements.[782] In the end, Aristotle thinks that such mixed acts are more voluntary than involuntary. His explanation runs as follows. True compulsion occurs when the cause of your action is external to you, as when you are carried away by a hurricane. In the case of the captain, however, the cause of his action comes from within himself. True, if circumstances had not been as they were, the captain would have chosen a different course of action. Yet in the circumstances as they occurred to him, he would not have wished to choose any other course of action than to jettison cargo.[783]

Thomas Aquinas carries Aristotle's exposition further. The *Prima Secundae* of his *Summa Theologiae* is entirely dedicated to the philosophy of human action, including fascinating accounts of man's last end, human

---

[781] Aristotle, *Ethica Nicomachea*, 3, 1, 1109b30–34. We used the following edition: *Aristotelis Ethica Nicomachea*, recognovit brevique adnotatione critica instruxit I. Bywater, [Scriptorum classicorum bibliotheca Oxoniensis], Oxonii 1970[15] [= 1894] (hereafter: Ed. Bywater), p. 40.

[782] See Aristotle, *Ethica Nicomachea* (Ed. Bywater), 3, 1, 1110a4–19, p. 40–41.

[783] Aristotle, *Ethica Nicomachea* (Ed. Bywater), 3, 1, 1110b5–9, p. 42.

passions and habits, vice and sin, law and grace. Of particular importance for our present purpose, is question 6 of the *Prima Secundae*, which treats the voluntary and the involuntary in human agency. Aquinas constructs his definition of voluntary action in terms of knowledge of the final end of that action—mistake resulting in involuntariness because of that lack of knowledge. Equally important, however, is the emphasis he puts, in line with Aristotle, on the origins of the action in the person himself for it to be voluntary. This is the point where the discussion on violence and duress enters.

If an action of the will proceeds from an exterior principle, then it falls short of voluntariness. A clear case is violence.[784] But, again, the difficulty concerns the mixed nature of duress. Actions done through fear are partly voluntary and partly involuntary. Thomas recalls the case of the captain who jettisons cargo in order to save his life and that of his crew.[785] Since the principle of action comes from within the captain himself, his action cannot be considered involuntary. The action does not proceed from an external cause. Still there are external circumstances which triggered the internal motivation of the captain. Therefore Thomas says that the captain acted voluntarily simply (*simpliciter*), that is, here and now, and involuntarily in a comparative sense (*secundum quid*), that is, outside the actual circumstances of the case and in comparison with a normal situation.

---

[784] Thomas Aquinas, *Summa Theologiae*, IaIIae, quaest. 6, art. 5 (*Utrum violentia causet involuntarium*), concl., in: *Opera omnia iussu impensaque Leonis XIII edita*, tom. 6: *Prima Secundae Summae Theologiae a quaestione 1 ad quaestionem 70*, Romae 1891 (hereafter: Ed. Leonina, tom. 6), p. 60.

[785] Aquinas, *Summa Theologiae* (Ed. Leonina, tom. 6), IaIIae, quaest. 6, art. 6 (*Utrum metus causet involuntarium simpliciter*), concl., p. 61: 'Unumquodque enim simpliciter esse dicitur secundum quod est in actu: secundum autem quod est in sola apprehensione, non est simpliciter, sed secundum quid. Hoc autem quod per metum agitur, secundum hoc est in actu, secundum quod fit: cum enim actus in singularibus sint, singulare autem, inquantum huiusmodi, est hic et nunc; secundum hoc id quod fit est in actu, secundum quod est hic et nunc et sub aliis conditionibus individualibus. Sic autem hoc quod fit per metum, est voluntarium, inquantum scilicet est hic et nunc, prout scilicet in hoc casu est impedimentum maioris mali quod timebatur: sicut proiectio mercium in mare fit voluntarium tempore tempestatis, propter timorem periculi. Unde manifestum est quod simpliciter voluntarium est. Unde et competit ei ratio voluntarii: quia principium eius est intra. Sed quod accipiatur id quod per metum fit, ut extra hunc casum existens, prout repugnat voluntati, hoc non est nisi secundum considerationem tantum. Et ideo est involuntarium secundum quid, idest prout consideratur extra hunc casum existens.'

This original definition of involuntariness in a comparative sense (*involuntarium secundum quid*) is quite limpid, which cannot necessarily be said of its reception in the later canon law tradition; cf. P. Fedele, *Appunti sui vizii del consenso matrimoniale, Metus ab extrinseco iniuste incussus consulto illatus*, [Biblioteca de 'Il diritto ecclesiastico'], Roma 1934, p. 1–2.

The impact of this Aristotelian-Thomistic account of human action on the subsequent philosophical and juridical tradition has been massive. As has been pointed out by James Gordley, even though the anthropological and moral philosophical account of human agency changed with the advent of empiricist and rationalist philosophies in the modern period, the juridical concepts formed on the basis of Aristotelian-Thomistic philosophy lived on.[786] There should be no surprise about this.

The very scholastic coryphaei who developed modern contract doctrine in their commentaries on the *Secunda Secundae* of Thomas (better known as the treatises *De iustitia et iure* or *De contractibus*) simultaneously wrote extensive commentaries on Thomas' *Prima Secundae*. As is sufficiently well-known, the *Prima Secundae* contained Thomas' ideas on mistake and duress. Limitations of space and time prevent us from a thorough examination of the relationship between the philosophy of the will and the development of contract law in the early modern scholastic period. Yet a brief look at Leonard Lessius' re-working of the Aristotelian-Thomistic teachings on duress should suffice to demonstrate how profoundly aware of this tradition the early modern scholastics were when they dealt with contract law.

In his posthumously published commentary on the *Prima Secundae*, Lessius adopts the conclusion of Aristotle and Thomas: things done under duress are a mix of voluntary and involuntary elements, so that they are voluntary simply (*simpliciter*), but involuntary in a comparative sense (*secundum quid*). Referring to the case of the jettisoned cargo, Lessius concludes that actions under compulsion are to be deemed absolutely voluntary under the circumstances at hand (*circumstantiis*), but unpleasing to the will if considered in the abstract (*nude*).[787] The difference between violence and duress consists in the fact that violence (*violentia*)

---

786 Gordley, *The philosophical origins of modern contract doctrine*, p. 121.

787 Lessius, *In I.II D. Thomae de beatitudine et actibus humanis*, quaest. 6, art. 6, num. 37, in: *De beatitudine, de actibus humanis, de incarnatione Verbi, de sacramentis et censuris praelectiones theologicae posthumae, Accesserunt variorum casuum conscientiae resolutiones*, Lovanii 1645, p. 45: 'Sensus est, utrum id quod metu facimus, alias non facturi, censeatur absolute involuntarium. Conclusio, id quod metu fit, esse mixtum ex voluntario et involuntario, sic tamen ut sit voluntarium simpliciter, involuntarium secundum quid. Ratio est, quia id quod metu fit, acceptum cum circumstantiis quibus fit, est absolute volitum. Cuius signum est, quod ex vi illius voluntatis homo se applicet ad externam operationem, ut patet, cum quis metu naufragii in tempestate proijcit merces. Haec proiecto tali tempore et loco est absolute volita, tamen secundum quid est involuntaria, quia considerata nude extra tale periculum, plane displicet voluntati.'

brutally imposes its effect upon the will, whereas duress inclines the will into wishing, out of its own, what it actually dislikes.[788]

Lessius gives a brilliant psychological account of the process of 'seduction' to which the will is exposed as it is confronted with a fearful event. The psychological process of compulsed assent consists of four stages, illustrated by the example of the jettisoned cargo.[789] Lessius argues that none of them is characterized by involuntariness, while the last stage is entirely voluntary. Firstly, there is the fear of the greater evil (*timor maioris mali*): shipwreck. This fear is not wholly involuntary, since fearing an imminent evil is the opposite of desiring a good. Both proceed from the inclination of the will. Secondly, there is the will to pursue a certain course of action (*volitio alicuius operationis*): throwing off cargo. This is definitely not an involuntary action, since it is willed as such. The third stage consists in a negative experience towards that same course of action considered on its own, because it is unpleasant and damaging (*displicentia illius operationis secundum se consideratae*). Displeasure, however, does not displease the will, so it is not involuntary. Finally, the operation is externalized and effectively takes place (*ipsa externa operatio*). This is a voluntary course of action, since the operation pleases the will under the present circumstances.

Last, in Lessius, we find an explicit testimony to the fact that the scholastics were very well aware of the connection between the more speculative philosophical account of the will and the regulation of practical matters through contract law. From his theoretical account of compulsion and the will, Lessius infers expressly that contracts affected by coerced consent are not void *ab initio*.[790] They do not suffer from lack of consent, since from an absolute point of view, the intimidated party assents voluntarily to the contract. The remedy against duress, then, must be based on the injury from which the intimidated party suffered.

---

[788] Lessius, *In I.II D. Thomae de beatitudine et actibus humanis*, p. 45: 'Violentia non inclinet voluntatem, sed illa omnino repugnante, suum effectum ponat. Metus vero inclinet voluntatem, ut ipsamet aliquid velit et faciat quod per se consideratum illi displicet, idque ad vitandum maius malum.'

[789] Lessius, *In I.II D. Thomae de beatitudine et actibus humanis*, quaest. 6, art. 6, num. 37, p. 45–46.

[790] Lessius, *In I.II D. Thomae de beatitudine et actibus humanis*, quaest. 6, art. 6, num. 38, p. 46: 'Secundo sequitur, contractum metu initum non esse irritum defectu voluntarii, ut multi docent, quia est absolute voluntarius: absoluta autem voluntas sufficiet ad efficiendum validum contractum, modo debita materia interveniat.' For a more extended quote, see below.

4.2.1.3 *Soto: the virtues of constancy and courage*

Soto developed a quite original approach to the question of which kind of
duress meets the constant man test of coercion. In his commentary on the
Sentences Soto considerably enlarges the number of events (*mala*) the fear
of which could result in legitimate fear (*iustus metus*). Also, he formulates
an interesting, virtue-based rule of thumb to know which fear can impress
a constant man. Through the following general rule, Soto fits the Romano-
canon tradition on duress into a moral philosophical framework:[791]

> Fear satisfies the constant man test, if it is compatible with the virtue of
> constancy and courage (*constantia et fortitudo*), and if everybody would feel
> constrained by it; therefore, this kind of fear is an excuse for fault (*a tota
> excusat culpa*).

By redefining the constant man criterion of duress, Soto actually makes it
possible for fear to excuse away fault and sin. For it also pertains to the
virtue of courage to have fear when fear is needed (*una pars fortitudinis
est, timere ubi oportet*).[792]

When law meets virtue, many questions arise. For example, whether
legitimate fear of an evil can justify fault (*culpa*), certainly when this fault
amounts to sin (*peccatum*). Contrary to the common scholastic opinion, Soto thought that duress stemming from the fear of an evil could
sometimes justify sin, indeed, particularly when sin constituted but the
infringement of human law, and not the commitment of an intrinsically
evil act.[793] It would be absurd, Soto says, to think that observing feast
days or Lent is more important than being murdered. If you can only

---

[791] Domingo de Soto, *In quartum sententiarum librum commentarii*, Lovanii 1573, dist. 29,
quaest. 1, art. 2, p. 711: 'Metum ergo cadere in constantem virum est, virtuti constantiae
et fortitudinis non repugnare, metu illo quempiam vinci et cogi. Atque hanc ob rem talis
metus a tota excusat culpa.'

[792] Soto, *De iustitia et iure* (ed. fac. V. Diego Carro – M. González Ordóñez, vol. 4),
lib. 7, quaest. 2, art. 1, p. 633: 'Metus enim ille est cadens in constantem virum, quem
viri constantia secum patitur, scilicet quem stat virum constantem sine suae fortitudinis
vituperatione habere, ita ut non repugnet esse virum constantem et sic metuere. Nam una
pars fortitudinis est, timere ubi oportet. Sed est apprime animadvertendum, quod nullus metus quantumvis in virum constantissimum incidere solitus, a culpa transgressionis
excusat divinae legis et naturalis.'

[793] Soto, *In quartum sententiarum librum commentarii*, dist. 29, quaest. 1, art. 2, p. 712:
'Sed alia posterioris generis, quia non sunt intrinsece mala, possunt quidem bona fieri
quando sunt media cavendi gravioris mali. Ecclesia namque observationem festorum aut
ieiuniorum praecipiens non tam stricto rigore voluit nos obligare, ut pro eorum observatione mortem deberemus obire. Quare qui metu mortis ieiunium vel festum frangit, non
desinit esse constans atque adeo excusatur a culpa.'

escape death through sinning against the duty to abstain from working or drinking, then you cannot be deemed to have become inconstant. Hence, duress excuses your (venial) sin. Soto would elicit heavy criticism for this audacious opinion in Dr. Navarrus' *Manual for confessors*.[794] And we will see Covarruvias invoking the rigorist Augustinian tradition in order to rebuke the standpoint that duress can justify sin.

The key question, however, concerns the effect of duress on the validity of a contract. In his *Commentary on the fourth book of the Sentences*, Soto refutes the late medieval teachings of Duns Scotus and argues that as a matter of natural law marriage contracts affected by duress are voidable (*irritandus*) and not void *ipso facto* (*irritus*). Following the canon *Abbas* (X 1,40,2), Soto holds that, as a matter of natural law, contracts always remain valid even when they are affected by duress.[795] They are voidable, however, at the option of the intimidated party. He concludes from this that the rule that marriage contracts are automatically void when affected by duress must have been introduced by positive, ecclesiastical law. Sánchez and Lessius would make the same point.

4.2.1.4   *Covarruvias at the confluence of scholasticism and humanism*

Diego de Covarruvias y Leyva is undoubtedly the single most distinguished Spanish canonist of the sixteenth century. It is impossible to avoid him when dealing with a concept of general contract law. It is no different this time, as he is commenting on the fourth book of the *Decretales*, dealing with marriage (*connubium*). His commentary on duress would provide the basic elements for the teachings of Sánchez and Lessius, although Covarruvias does not contain a general theory of duress related to a general doctrine of contract. His exposition is a good illustration, however, of the large extent to which humanist jurisprudence became intermingled with the canon law tradition.

---

[794] Azpilcueta, *Enchiridion sive manuale confessariorum et poenitentium*, cap. 22, num. 51, p. 494.

[795] Soto, *In quartum sententiarum librum commentarii*, dist. 29, quaest. 1, art. 3, p. 714: 'Ad secundum simili modo respondetur, quod neque alii contractus, locationis aut venditionis, etc. per metum celebrati, sunt ipso iure nulli, sed debent in irritum revocari, ut cap. Abbas de his quae vi metusve causa fiunt: quia restitutionem expostulant. Et hoc facit pro nobis, quia secundum merum ius naturae etiam matrimonium deberet tenere. At quia rescindi nequit, statutum per ecclesiam est, ut non sit validum.'
Interestingly, in the marginal notes to canon *Abbas* the *correctores Romani* referred several times to Domingo de Soto for its correct interpretation; cf. notae ad glossam *Coactus* ad X 1,40,2 in: *Corpus juris canonici* (ed. Gregoriana), part. 2, cols. 479–480.

He begins with a long meditation on the definition of duress. Covarruvias is careful to stress that the object of fear must be imminent. The 'futurity' of the fearful event mentioned in the definition of duress in D. 4,2,1 (*metus instantis vel futuri periculi causa mentis trepidatio*) must be interpreted as the very near future. For the most fearful event of life, namely death, lies in the future, and still it does not throw anyone off balance. He quotes Aristotle, amongst others, to support this interpretation,[796] and he eventually defines duress as a 'perturbance of the mind, the mind being perturbed by imagining a future and imminent calamity'.[797]

Book four of the *Decretales* is dedicated to marriage, and in commenting upon it, Covarruvias underlines the principle of liberty required by the Church in marital consent. Canons *Veniens* (X 4,1,13) and *Cum locum* (X 4,1,14) are indicative in this respect. Marriage contracts must be free of the slightest form of coercion. The reason being that freedom of marriage is the best safeguard against irresponsible education of the children. The distinctly consensual nature of marriage was promoted by the law of the Church, but Covarruvias is anxious to quote a Roman rule of law (D. 50,17,30) in order to prove that there was also Roman support for the consensual definition of marriage.[798] It did not prevent him, though, from suggesting that the Roman law considered duress as resulting in a delictual action, since damage had to be proven in order for the praetor to grant relief.

If freedom is of paramount importance to the validity of marriage contracts, then it is equally important to know whether all kinds of duress are capable of invalidating a contract. In light of law *Metum autem* (D. 4,2,6) and canon *Quum dilectus filius* (X 1,40,6), this question was traditionally answered in the negative. Law *Metum autem* and canon *Quum dilectus filius* were considered to provide the jurists and theologians with

[796] Aristotle, *Ars rhetorica*, 2, 5, 1382a22–27, in: *Aristotelis Ars rhetorica*, recognovit brevique adnotatione critica instruxit W.D. Ross, [Scriptorum classicorum bibliotheca Oxoniensis], Oxonii 1959, p. 82: '(...) οὐ γὰρ πάντα τὰ κακὰ φοβοῦνται, οἷον εἰ ἔσται ἄδικος ἢ βραδύς, ἀλλ'ὅσα λύπας μεγάλας ἢ φθορὰς δύναται, καὶ ταῦτα ἐὰν μὴ πόρρω ἀλλὰ σύνεγγυς φαίνηται ὥστε μέλλειν. τὰ γὰρ πόρρω σφόδρα οὐ φοβοῦνται· ἴσασι γὰρ πάντες ὅτι ἀποθανοῦνται, ἀλλ'ὅτι οὐκ ἐγγύς, οὐδὲν φροντίζουσιν.'

[797] Covarruvias, *In librum quartum Decretalium epitome*, part. 2, cap. 3, par. 4, num. 1, in: Opera omnia, Augustae Taurinorum 1594, tom. 2, p. 131: 'Est enim metus trepidatio mentis, quia ex imaginatione futuri et propter imminens malum perturbatur mens.'

[798] D. 50,17,30 in *Corporis Iustinianaei Digestum novum* (ed. Gothofredi), tom. 3, col. 1878: 'Nuptias non concubitus, sed consensus facit'. Gloss *Nuptias* to D. 50,17,30 explains that, according to this definition, marriage can exist even if partners do not have sexual intercourse. Conversely, intercourse does not automatically bring about marriage.

a standard to distinguish juridically relevant from juridically irrelevant forms of duress: the criterion of the constant man (*vir constans*). Relying on Thomas Aquinas' commentary on the *Sentences*, Covarruvias defines the constant man as 'the prudent man who knows how to choose a minor evil in order to escape the risk of a greater evil'.[799]

Covarruvias acknowledges in line with the gloss on C. 2,4,13 that in concrete circumstances it is up to judicial discretion (*arbitrium iudicis*) to decide whether fear for a particular evil satisfies the constant man criterion or not.[800] Since sin is always the greater evil, however, it is beyond doubt that no one is allowed to sin in order to escape an evil. In saying so, Covarruvias presumably distances himself from Soto's contrasting opinion. Quoting Augustine and canon *Ita ne* (C.32, q.5, c.3), Covarruvias holds that it is better to suffer all evil than to assent to a sinful act. By the same token, it is not allowed to commit a crime in order to escape an evil. Therefore, Covarruvias rebukes the mythic figure Alcmeon in the lost play of the same name by Euripides for having killed his mother for fear of disappointing his father.[801]

A major question addressed by Covarruvias concerned the impact of duress on women. Drawing on the gloss *Metus* to canon *Cum locum*, our canonist clearly thought that the constant man test had to be specified in the case of women.[802] A judge must allow for a woman's natural weakness of mind and body in comparison to a man's fortitude.[803] After all, prudence and fortitude are not virtues which strive for an objective golden mean. Contrary to justice, the golden mean of fortitude and prudence is

---

[799] Covarruvias, *In librum quartum Decretalium epitome*, part. 2, cap. 3, par. 4, num. 1, p. 131: 'Constantem virum interpretor prudentem, qui sciat eligere minus malum ob maioris mali periculum evitandum.'

[800] Glossa *Cruciatum* ad C. 2,4,13 in *Corporis Iustinianaei Codex* (ed. Gothofredi), tom. 5, col. 322.

[801] Covarruvias, *In librum quartum Decretalium epitome*, part. 2, cap. 3, par. 4, num. 7, p. 132. Covarruvias was well acquainted with Aristotle, of course, who had expressed the same critique in the *Nicomachean Ethics*, 3, 1, 1110a25–30. His philological criticism of a pseudo-commentary on the third book of Aristotle's *Nicomachean Ethics*—ascribed to Eustratius or Aspasius—is another testimony to his familiarity with Aristotelian thought; cf. *In librum quartum Decretalium epitome*, part. 2, cap. 3, par. 4, num. 5, p. 131–132.

[802] Glossa *Metus* ad X 4,1,14 in *Corpus juris canonici* (ed. Gregoriana), part. 2, col. 1429: 'Minor tamen metus magis excusat foeminam quam virum.'

[803] Covarruvias, *In librum quartum Decretalium epitome*, part. 2, cap. 3, par. 4, num. 8, p. 132: 'Hinc etiam iudex arbitrio proprio decernere debet, non ita anxie atque stricte hanc eligendi prudentiam exigendam esse in foeminis, quibus a natura inest minor animi vigor corporisque fortitudo, sed considerandum esse, quid foemina constans eligeret pensata naturali foeminarum prudentia.'

determined by the qualities of the subject who is expected to practice these virtues. Hence the 'natural' prudence of a woman (*naturalis foeminarum prudentia*) is different from the 'natural' prudence of a man.

The issue of women and duress saw Covarruvias ostentatiously distancing himself from Ippolito Marsigli (1450–ca. 1529), a former student of Felinus Sandaeus, legal practitioner, judge and professor of law at the university of Bologna who is mostly remembered for his *Practica causarum criminalium*.[804] One might wonder, however, if this dispute was more than a pretext, again, for Covarruvias to display his humanist erudition. Marsigli had argued that torture must always be applied to men first, because women endure torture far longer than men.[805] Yet Covarruvias draws upon the classics to refute this erratic opinion.[806] Did not Tacitus mention that Nero started torturing women because their bodies are less supportive of pain? Had not Plinius, Tertullian, and Pausanias praised a woman for not having told a secret in spite of long torture, precisely because women cannot be expected to resist torture in the first place? Covarruvias concludes that men are braver than women in tolerating pain and torture, and he quotes the French humanist André Tiraqueau (1488–1558) to give authoritative support to this view. In fact, Tiraqueau argued that in criminal investigation, women had to be submitted to torture before the men, because women were more likely to capitulate faster than the men, thus allowing the judge to discover the truth more rapidly.[807]

---

[804] For more biographical details, see L. Pallotti, s.v. *Ippolito Marsi(g)li*, in: Dizionario biografico degli Italiani, 70 (2008), p. 764–767.

[805] Ippolito Marsigli, *Tractatus de quaestionibus in quo materiae maleficiorum pertractantur*, s.l. 1542, ad l. 1, num. 73, f. 8r: 'Item quantum ad illud quod dicunt praedicti doctores quod incipiendum est potius a femina quam a masculo, quia ipsa est debilior viro et citius iudex habebit veritatem ab ea quam a masculo. Ego in hoc dubito, quia dicit glossa notabiliter in l. nihil interest, ff. de adult., quod mulier patitur maiora vulnera quam masculus, ergo maius tormentum patietur et erit constantior in tortura (...).'; Marsigli, *Repetitio rubricae C. de probationibus*, Lugduni 1531, num. 417, f. 51v: 'Sed ego incidenter dico tibi unum, quod si mulier et vir simul pereant, praesumitur ut supra quod mulier prius decesserit, tamen si moriantur ambo ex vulneribus vir praesumitur prius decessisse quia mulier patitur maiora vulnera quam vir, ita notabiliter dicit glossa in l. nihil interest, ff. de adult.'

[806] For extended references, see Covarruvias, *In librum quartum Decretalium epitome*, part. 2, cap. 3, par. 4, num. 11, p. 132.

[807] André Tiraqueau, *De legibus connubialibus et iure maritali*, Parisiis 1546, l. 9, num. 99, f. 79r: '(...) cum ii primum sint quaestioni subijciendi, a quibus veritas facilius eruitur; (...) ideo prius sunt foeminae quam mares torquendae, ut quae celerius fatebuntur, cum habeant cor momentaneum et instabile (...).' Tiraqueau was known for his misogyny, cf. J.-M. Augustin, s.v. *André Tiraqueau*, in: P. Arabeyre – J.-L. Halpérin – J. Krynen (eds.), Dictionnaire historique des juristes français, XIIᵉ–XXᵉ siècle, Paris 2007, p. 742–743.

A similarly humanist spirit—at least from the point of view of his passion for showing off his classical erudition—runs through Covarruvias' plea for recognizing the fear of losing material goods as duress which meets the constant man test. He quotes Hesiod's verse to the effect that 'money is the soul of miserable man' (*pecunia est anima miseris mortalibus*).[808] This was a popular proverb in the early modern period, just as the saying that money is the sinews of affairs (*pecunia nervus rerum*), which can be traced back at least to Plutarch.[809] From Erasmus' *Adages*,[810] which drew on Hesiod and Plutarch, Covarruvias picks the idea that money is 'life and soul' (*anima et vita*).[811] Moreover, by combining Plutarch and the gospel of Luke, he pretends that in Greek only one word is used to denote both the concept of life and wealth. Unfortunately, he does not mention that magic Greek word.[812] Yet, importantly, from this argument Covarruvias infers that even the loss of only one precious good (*amissio magnae rei*) can constitute a legitimate cause for just fear, let alone the loss of a major part of one's belongings (*amissio maioris partis bonorum*), or the loss of one's entire fortune (*amissio bonorum omnium*).

When it comes to minor fear (*metus levis*), Covarruvias defends the opinion that will later be adopted by Lessius and Grotius. Even if minor fear cannot be considered a sufficient ground for the civil law to grant relief, everything that has been acquired by minor duress must be restored before the court of conscience. In his famous *relectio* on *Regula 'peccatum'*, Covarruvias points out the usual rationale behind the civil law

---

[808] Hesiod, *Works and days*, v. 686, in: *Hesiod, Theogony, Works and days, Testimonia*, edited and translated by G.W. Most, [Loeb Classical Library, 57], Cambridge Mass. – London 2006, vol. 1, p. 142: 'χρήματα γὰρ ψυχὴ πέλεται δειλοῖσι βροτοῖσιν'.

[809] Plutarch, *Kleomenes*, 27,1, in: *Plutarch, Lives*, with an English translation by Bernadotte Perrin, [Loeb Classical Library, 102], Cambridge Mass. – London 1968, vol. 10, p. 110: 'τὰ χρήματα νεῦρα τῶν πραγμάτων'. For further discussion, see M. Stolleis, *Pecunia nervus rerum, Zur Staatsfinanzierung der frühen Neuzeit*, Frankfurt am Main 1983, p. 63–64.

[810] Desiderius Erasmus, *Adagiorum opus*, Basileae 1526, chiliad. 2, cent. 3, adag. 89, p. 428.

[811] If Covarruvias thus stresses the importance of money for the individual, the early modern period also saw the frequent use of the same and similar expressions to insist on the vital character of money for the survival of the State; cf. Stolleis, *Pecunia nervus rerum, Zur Staatsfinanzierung der frühen Neuzeit*, p. 63–68.

[812] Covarruvias, *In librum quartum Decretalium epitome*, part. 2, cap. 3, par. 4, num. 18, p. 133: 'Pecunia extat etiam apud Plutarchum in libello an adolescenti liceat audire poemata. Carmen illud *pergunt alii mihi rodere vitam*, quo in loco Plutarchus opes intelligit. Sic apud Graecos una et eadem dictio vitam significat et facultates, quibus vivitur, quod constat ex evangelio Lucae c. 15 ubi id Erasmus adnotavit.'

regulation.[813] The law of the land does not intend to go against the law of conscience.[814] It merely abstains from reinforcing the law of conscience by means of state power for the sake of the civil good. The civil law presumes that minor fear does not affect 'freedom of contract', even if the truth can be different. For if the civil law was to grant relief on the basis of minor fear, the courts would suffer from over-extension and business would be continually interrupted by law suits.

Of great interest in view of Sánchez's transformation of Covarruvias' ideas are his opinions on reverential fear (*metus reverentialis*). Reverential fear stems from the respect that an inferior person must have toward a superior.[815] Covarruvias claims that reverential fear can become relevant fear only when it is accompanied by lesion beyond moiety (*laesio enormis*).[816] Moreover, he states that this rule holds true both in the case of marriage and other contracts.[817] For example, if in reverence to her

---

[813] This extremely rich *relectio* is investigated in O. Condorelli, *Norma giuridica e norma morale, giustizia e salus animarum secondo Diego de Covarrubias, Riflessioni a margine della Relectio super regula 'Peccatum'*, Rivista internazionale di diritto comune, 19 (2008), p. 163–201.

[814] Diego de Covarruvias y Leyva, *In regulam peccatum, De regulis iuris lib. 6 Relectio*, part. 2, par. 3, num. 7, in: Opera omnia, Augustae Taurinorum 1594, tom. 2, p. 485: 'Non oberunt huic sententiae leges civiles negantes rescissiones contractus metus causa quoties metus levis est nec cadit in constantem virum, quia licet leges civiles non dent in hoc casu ob metum levem repetitionem, nec rescissionem contractus, non tamen approbant eam receptionem, nec eam iustam esse censent, praesumit etenim lex contractum metu levi gestum consensum habuisse liberum et sufficientem ad hoc ut validus is iudicetur. Atque haec praesumptio iuris est et de iure, nam etsi constet de metu, qui tamen levis sit, non permittit lex huius contractus rescissionem ex ea quidem causa, ne passim commercia humana impediantur et ne tot lites ad contractuum rescissiones in republica constituantur.'

[815] For an introduction to reverential fear, see J. du Plessis – R. Zimmermann, *The relevance of reverence, Undue influence civilian style*, Maastricht Journal of European and Comparative Law, 10 (2003), p. 345–379; and Jansen, '*Tief ist der Brunnen der Vergangenheit*', p. 218–220.

[816] We use this translation because it is used in the Louisiana Civil Code, art. 2589 for denoting the same case that in the civilian tradition has become known as 'laesio enormis'. It is ultimately based on an extensive interpretation by the scholastic jurists and theologians of the Roman constitution C. 4,44,2. It holds that the sale of an immovable can be rescinded when the price is less than one half of the just price. In the common law, this concept might also be seen as coming close to 'unconscionability'.

[817] Covarruvias, *In librum quartum Decretalium epitome*, part. 2, cap. 3, par. 6, num. 4, p. 136: 'Cum in matrimonio maior sit exigenda libertas quam in caeteris contractibus, notandum est, caeteros contractus non esse rescindendos ex solo metu reverentiali, nisi praecedentibus minis illatis ab eo qui solet quod minatur exequi. (...) Hi vero omnes quos dixi fateri hanc opinionem esse communem, eandem intelligunt, nisi enormis laesio in contractu contingat cum metu obsequii et reverentiae. Hoc enim solum etiam minus [sic] non probatis sufficiet ad rescindendum contractum. (...) Quae omnia nec temere adduxi-

father a girl agrees to marry a man who is of a far lower status, she can claim rescission. Similarly, a vendor can reclaim rescission if he sold his estate for less than half of its fair market price. Covarruvias, then, does not yet fully distinguish between marriage contracts and other contracts. That contribution to the development of modern doctrines of duress would later be made by Sánchez and Lessius.

Sánchez and Lessius later developed the idea that marriage contracts are not automatically avoided by duress as a matter of natural law, but as a matter of ecclesiastical law. Covarruvias, however, held that marriage contracts falling short of free consent were void from the outset by natural law.[818] Precisely because they wanted to develop a general contract doctrine, while at the same time distinguishing marriage from other contracts, Sánchez and Lessius could no longer say so. As a general principle, Sánchez and Lessius held that duress can only make contracts voidable, not void *ipso facto*. Therefore, they were bound to explain at the same time that the absolute nullity affecting marriage contracts must have been imposed through positive, ecclesiastical law. Covarruvias had not yet reached that level of systematic reflection.

4.2.1.5   *Molina: duress makes contracts void* ab initio

When it comes to duress as a vice of the will, Molina's ideas are scattered. He does not dedicate an autonomous chapter to duress. This is rather remarkable, since Molina is generally known for his vital contribution to the development of a systematic law of contract. The Jesuit from Cuenca deals with duress in the margin of his discussion of two particular contracts, a liberal promise and a loan for consumption. He insists that nullity ensues automatically from coerced consent. In doing so, he defends a view that will eventually be refuted quite radically by Sánchez and Lessius. Looking at the subsequent Jesuit tradition, Molina's brief remarks on duress seem to be the proverbial calm before the storm.

---

mus, sed ut matrimonii contractus nullus omnino sit, eo casu, quo caeteri contractus ex hoc metu sint rescindendi (…).'

[818] Covarruvias, *In librum quartum Decretalium epitome*, part. 2, cap. 3, par. 5, num. 6, p. 134: 'Constat matrimonium metu contractum nullum esse ipso iure ex propria actus natura, non tantum ex constitutione ecclesiae, quod probatur, consensus liber est praecise necessarius ad hunc contractum cap. cum locum de sponsalibus [X 4,1,14]. Hic autem consensus liber non est, ubi metus cadens in constantem virum concurrit. Igitur ex natura sua matrimonium metu contractum est nullum.'

Molina takes it for granted that any form of involuntariness is an impediment to the conveyance of property rights, certainly if liberality is the ultimate cause of the contract.[819] A promise must be deliberate if it is to be considered valid. People who lack full rational capacities can therefore not conclude valid contracts. He believes that there is no reason to elaborate on this, since it speaks for itself.[820] By the same token, promises should not be tainted by deceit, violence or duress. Still, he makes an exception to this rule for contracts that are entered into by legitimate duress (*iuste*), for example because of fear of a just punishment.[821] Another qualification concerns contracts that are not the direct result of duress, for instance when you promise to enter into a contract with somebody so that he helps you out of the difficulty you are in, or when you make a vow to escape assassination. Duress is not the cause (*causa*) but the occasion (*occasio*) to such a contract.[822] Lessius would further develop these ideas.

In respect to the question of reverential fear, Molina is inspired by Sylvester Prierias and Dr. Navarrus. He holds that reverential fear amounts to duress accompanied by threats (*reverentialis metus aequiparatur metui per minas incusso*).[823] Hence, it has the potential of voiding a contract. By

---

[819] Molina, *De iustitia et iure*, tom. 2 (*De contractibus*), tract. 2, disp. 267, col. 67–68, num. 2: 'Tale autem voluntarium mixte satis non est, ut quis dominium vel ius rei suae in alterum transferat, maxime ex mera liberalitate, ut de se est notissimum.'

[820] Molina, *De iustitia et iure*, tom. 2 (*De contractibus*), tract. 2, disp. 267, col. 67, num. 1: 'Ut promissio aut stipulatio valida sit (idemque est de donatione completa), necesse in primis est, ut sit actus humanus plene deliberatus. Qua ratione promissiones et stipulationes eorum, qui rationis usum non habent, invalidae omnino sunt (...) atque ex se est notissimum.'

[821] Molina, *De iustitia et iure*, tom. 2 (*De contractibus*), tract. 2, disp. 267, col. 68, num. 3: 'Quando item iuste metus incuteretur, valida esset promissio, quae ex tali metu oriretur, etiamsi fieret ei, a quo metus provenit. Ut si quis aliquid alicui promitteret, ut iustam poenam ipsi aut alteri condonaret, potestatem haberet ad illam, pro eo pretio aut praemio relaxandam.'

[822] Molina, *De iustitia et iure*, tom. 2 (*De contractibus*), tract. 2, disp. 267, col. 68, num. 3: 'Si autem voluntarium mixte, quo aliquid uni promitteretur, solum sumeret occasionem ex nequitia alterius, minime eum effectum intendentis tunc sufficeret, ut valida esset promissio. Verbi gratia, si quis dum iniuste mors sibi imminet ab aliquo, aliquid Deo voveat, ut ab eo periculo ipsum eripiat, valida est promissio, quoniam licet metu voveat, voluntarium tamen, quod in voto cernitur, solum habuit occasionem ex morte iniusta, qua sibi imminebat.'

[823] Molina, *De iustitia et iure*, tom. 2 (*De contractibus*), tract. 2, disp. 267, col. 68, num. 4: '(...) etiam reverentialem metum, qualis est, quem filius aut filia interdum habet patri, uxor marito, famulus aut vasallus domino, clericus episcopo, et libertus patrono, si involuntariam mixte efficiat promissionem aut stipulationem, reddere illam nullam (...), quoniam reverentialis metus aequiparatur ea in parte metui per minas incusso.'

the same token, he considers minor duress (*metus levis*)—duress which would not throw a constant man off balance—as having a voiding effect on contracts as far as the court of conscience is concerned. He nevertheless admits that minor fear cannot be relevant before the external courts, since no presumption can lie that a contract affected by minor fear was entered into through mixed involuntary consent.[824] Indeed, as Sylvester and Dr. Navarrus had pointed out, nobody can be presumed to be wasting his money for nothing, unless he is affected by just fear. However, this presumption does not lie in the court of conscience, where the truth must prevail.[825]

In treating of usury, Molina expressly attacks the traditional interpretation of canon *Abbas* in X 1,40,2 (*quae metu et vi fiunt, de iure debent irritum revocari*). Usually, canon *Abbas* was thought to imply that duress results in voidability, since, allegedly, it stated that the judge had to intervene to avoid the contract. Molina denies that this is the right interpretation of canon *Abbas*, since he does not think that it says that, if the authority of the judge had not intervened, the contract would have remained valid.[826] According to Molina, contracts affected by duress are void *ipso iure* (*irritus*) and not simply voidable. Although Molina does not mention him, he might have drawn his inspiration from Fortunius Garcia as he defended the nullity *ab initio* resulting from duress.[827] He thinks that the judge is not there to avoid the contract, but merely to express the finding that the contract is already void, and to admonish the illegitimate possessor to make restitution. Molina believes that coerced consent cannot

---

[824] Molina, *De iustitia et iure*, tom. 2 (*De contractibus*), tract. 2, disp. 267, col. 68, num. 5: '(…) in foro conscientiae, etiamsi metus non sit cadens in constantem virum, si tamen promissione revera involuntariam mixte efficiat, reddere illam nullam. (…) In foro autem exteriori, id est, quando metus esset levis, qui in virum constantem, habita qualitate personae, non cadit, non subvenietur ei, qui ex eiusmodi metu promitteret, quod non praesumeretur tam levem metum effecisse promissionem involuntariam mixte.'

[825] Sylvester Prierias, *Summa Sylvestrina*, part. 2, s.v. *restitutio 2*, dict. 7, f. 263r. Compare Azpilcueta, *Enchiridion sive manuale confessariorum et poenitentium*, cap. 17, num. 15, p. 280.

[826] Molina, *De iustitia et iure*, tom. 2 (*De contractibus*), tract. 2, disp. 267, col. 308, num. 14: 'Ad cap. vero *Abbas* dicendum est, verba illius sic habere, *quae metu et vi fiunt de iure debent irritum* (expone, id est, tanquam in se irrita), *revocari*, non quidem invalidum reddendo contractum, quasi seclusa iudicis authoritate esset validus, sed irrita illa pronunciando, praecipiendoque possidenti, ut statim illa restituat, ut continuo in eodem textu subiungitur, quo fit, ut ex illo textu non colligatur, dominium in eo eventu fuisse translatum.'

[827] Fortunius Garcia, *De ultimo fine iuris civilis et canonici*, num. 396, p. 264sqq.

possibly convey property rights.[828] He claims support, in this respect, from Domingo de Soto's alleged view of the automatic nullity of coerced contracts as defended in his *On justice and right*.[829]

4.2.2   *Tomás Sánchez's doctrine of duress*

4.2.2.1   *Duress and the law of marriage*

The enduring influence of classical canon law on the present-day law of marriage in both civil and common law countries is a well-established fact. Less remembered, however, is the fundamental role which the ecclesiastical law of marriage played as a source of inspiration for the establishment of a general law of contract with the scholastics of the early modern period. Indeed, marriage was conceived of as a contract for the exchange of rights over the bodies (*ius in corpus*) of the spouses.[830] Yet this contractual view of marriage in the medieval tradition should not be confounded with the modern conception of marriage as depending solely on the continuing free consent of both parties in the marital relationship.[831] If marital debt (*debitum conjugale*) and the rights over the body of the spouse were a matter of concern to the canonists, then this ensued to a large extent from the unquestioned assumption that marriage entailed an unwavering commitment to the procreation and upbringing of children.

At any rate, the canonists and the scholastics could reason from marriage to other contracts because marriage was essentially thought of in

---

[828] Molina, *De iustitia et iure*, tom. 2 (*De contractibus*), tract. 2, disp. 267, col. 309, num. 14: 'Ex natura ergo rei atque in conscientiae foro, quin et in exteriori de iure praetorio, non censetur translatum dominium, quando aliquid per vim aut metum sufficientem, donatum, traditumque est, sed solum iuris civilis fictione, quondam censebatur translatum.'

[829] This claim is a little bit exaggerated, although it is true that in solving 'that old question on whether usurious giving transfers property' (*vetus illa quaestio utrum per usurariam dationem trasferatur dominium*), Soto concludes that it does not; cf. *De iustitia et iure* (ed. fac. V. Diego Carro – M. González Ordóñez, vol. 3), lib. 6, quaest. 1, art. 4, p. 526–528.

[830] For the origins of the language of rights to describe marriage from the twelfth century up until and including the first Code of Canon law (1917), see, amongst others, M. Madero, *La nature du droit au corps dans le mariage selon la casuistique des XIIe et XIIIe siècles*, Annales, Histoire, Sciences Sociales, 65 (2010), p. 1323–1348; M. Madero, *Sobre el ius in corpus, En torno a una obra de Filippo Vassalli y al debate Francesco Carnelutti-Pio Fedele*, in: E. Conte – M. Madero (eds.), *Entre hecho y derecho, Hacer, poseer, usar en perspectiva histórica*, Buenos Aires 2010, p. 119–134; and Alfieri, *Nella camera degli sposi, Tomás Sánchez, il matrimonio, la sessualità*, p. 143–147.

[831] Ch. Reid, Jr., *Power over the body, equality in the family, Rights and domestic relations in medieval canon law*, Grand Rapids – Cambridge 2004, p. 4–5.

these juristic and contractarian—in the sense of consensualist—terms besides being considered a sacrament.[832] This occurred very clearly in a treatise on marriage law that has probably remained unsurpassed up to this day in its detailed and systematic exposition: the *Disputationes de sancto matrimonii sacramento* by Tomás Sánchez, the great Jesuit theologian from Cordoba.[833] Sánchez's merit consists not only in having stimulated the cross-fertilization between matrimonial law and general contract doctrine, but also in his neatly distinguishing marriage from other contracts when necessary—a disjunction which turns out to be vital precisely in regard to the doctrines of duress.

One of the closest parallels between the law of marriage and other contracts is the huge importance of freedom—in the sense of the absence of coercion—when entering into a marriage. The rules that no one should be compelled to marry (C.31, q.2, c.1) and that marriages should be free (X 4,1,29) were recognized as fundamental principles of Church law. According to the classical canon law of marriage, the exchange of present consent between the spouses or the future consent followed by sexual intercourse was sufficient for the conclusion of a valid marriage.[834] The absence of paternal assent did not invalidate the marriage contract. This case for marital freedom and the irrelevance of parental consent was not made successfully until the advent of Gratian. Before that, it would seem that the Christian tradition remained relatively faithful to the proposition, which it borrowed from Roman law, that fatherly consent was necessary in the making of marriage.[835] It is no secret that the renewed canonical doctrine remained under pressure from practice. Apart from the well-known tendencies in France to introduce paternal assent as a requirement for the valid conclusion of a marriage contract, official Church doctrine also met with continuous resistence from Spain where secular legislation and family custom often required parental assent.[836]

It is important to consider the reasons behind the endorsement of freedom of choice in the classical marriage law of the Church. The reason was

---

[832] The tension between the contractual and the sacramental character of marriage is highlighted in A. Esmein, *Le mariage en droit canonique*, tom. 1, Paris 1929² [= 1891], p. 83–89, and tom. 2, Paris 1935² [= 1891], p. 443–445.

[833] On Sánchez, cf. supra, p. 59–61.

[834] Ch. Donahue, Jr., *Law, marriage and society in the later Middle Ages, Arguments about marriage in five courts*, Cambridge 2007, p. 16–18.

[835] Ch. Reid, Jr., *Power over the body, equality in the family*, p. 30–50.

[836] F.R. Aznar Gil, *El consentimiento paterno o familiar para el matrimonio*, Rivista internazionale di diritto comune, 6 (1995), p. 127–151.

basically that freedom of marriage was the only guarantee that marriage would last for a life time, which in turn was the best guarantee for the good upbringing of the children (*ad procreationem prolis*).[837] The idea of 'freedom of contract' as applied to marital relationships, then, ultimately stems from the concern to assure the good upbringing of future generations. It has hardly anything to do with the modern viewpoint that marriage is a fluid relationship based on voluntary association for the sake of the benefit of the individual parties. As a matter of fact, marriage contracts were thought to require an even higher degree of liberty than other contracts, precisely because once they were concluded, they were indissoluble. Since coercion formed a massive obstacle to freedom of matrimonial consent, Sánchez dedicated the entire fourth book of his *Disputationes de sancto matrimonii sacramento* to the problem (*De consensu coacto*).

Interestingly, in this book on coerced consent Sánchez first systematically expounds the impact of coercion on 'contractual freedom' in general (disp. 1–11). He then proceeds to apply this general theory of coerced consent to marriage contracts in particular (disp. 12–27), while at the same time highlighting the points at which the consequences of compulsion for marriage and other contracts, respectively, diverge. In light of the attention paid to the emergence of a general law of contract in early modern scholasticism, in what comes next we will focus on Sánchez's discussion of *metus* in contracts in general. His elaborate discussion of the impact of coercion on marriage contracts in particular falls outside of our scope.

4.2.2.2   *The constant man test of coercion*

4.2.2.2.1   *Promoting virtue, protecting the weak*
A major concern of the canonists and theologians was of course to limit the scope of coercion (*metus*) as a ground for annulment of a contract. If fear of the slightest kind were considered a relevant ground for frustration of contract, contract would lose its function as an instrument guaranteeing stable relationships altogether. Moreover, as we have seen very clearly in Soto's discussion, accepting simple fear as legitimate fear would have run counter to the Church's more general project of promoting the virtuous life, requiring an attitude of constancy (*constantia*) and courage (*fortitudo*) in the face of danger and adversity. On the other hand, the

---

[837] Soto, *De iustitia et iure* (ed. fac. V. Diego Carro – M. González Ordóñez, vol. 4), lib. 8, quaest. 1, art. 7, p. 733, quoted supra, n. 779.

medieval canonists were not undiscriminately willing to accept, particularly in regard to marriage contracts, the rule of Roman law—reminiscent of Aristotle—that coerced consent is still consent (D. 4,2,21,5).

Drawing on law *Metum autem* (D. 4,2,6)[838] and on canon *Quum dilectus filius* (X 1,40,6) they did find a standard, however, to sort out the juridically relevant forms of coercion: the criterion of the constant man (*vir constans*). Yet the 'constant man' test of coercion only transposed the problem on another level. It is one thing to know that if fear is so serious as to throw even a constant man off balance, it can be considered as a legitimate ground for annulment. But what kind of fear, then, throws a constant man off balance? Accordingly, which fear belongs to the constant man and is justified (*justus*) and probable (*probabilis*)? The perplexity of this question is indicated by the sheer volume of text that is dedicated to its solution (disp. 1–5).

Borrowing from an impressive number of civilians, canonists and theologians, Sánchez gives a decisive impetus to the discussion on the influence of duress on the voluntary consent of the constant man.[839] He lists five conditions for coercion not to fail the 'constant man test'. First of all, the evil feared must be grave in an absolute sense (*malum magnum*). Soto had already insisted on this. He had deemed an ambushed merchant's fear of losing his horse not sufficient grounds for demanding the ransom he had eventually payed to the robbers. Even though from a subjective point of view the merchant might well have considered the loss of his horse as a greater evil (*malum maior*) than the loss of his money, the loss of a horse can never be deemed a grave evil in itself from an objective point of view.[840]

Sánchez calls this opinion of Soto excellent, since freedom of consent (*libertas consensus*) is not hampered by an evil which is feared by a particular person, but minimal from an intrinsic point of view. In order to pass

---

[838] In fact, D. 4,2,6 (Metum autem non vani hominis, sed qui merito et in homine constantissimo cadat, ad hoc edictum pertinere dicemus) speaks of a 'vir constantissimus', thus using the superlative degree of the adjective instead of the positive. Following Philippus Decius (1454–1535), Sánchez nevertheless insists that the right interpretation and sense of 'constantissimus' must be 'constans'; cf. *Disputationes de sancto matrimonii sacramento*, tom. 1, lib. 4, disp. 1, num. 9, p. 325.

[839] Sánchez's doctrine of the constant man test of coercion and its reception in the canon law tradition is subject to a brief treatment in P. Fedele, *Sull'espressione 'metus cadens in virum constantem'*, *Sulla violenza come vizio del consenso matrimoniale, Note e discussioni*, [Biblioteca de 'Il diritto ecclesiastico'], Roma 1935, p. 1–8.

[840] Soto, *In quartum sententiarum librum commentarii*, dist. 29, quaest. 1, art. 2, s.v. *secundo per accidens*, p. 711.

the constancy test, fear must concern grave evil taken on its own (*debere esse timorem gravis mali in se considerati*).[841] Sánchez thus rejects the view of Sylvester Prierias, which had been based on the idea that constancy is the art of choosing the lesser of two evils, thus leaving room for a purely comparative notion of evil.[842] This idea of Sylvester was often based on a literal interpretation of law *Metum* (D. 4,2,5).[843] Sánchez, however, reiterates time and again that there are objective criteria for determining when a contract is null on account of coercion.[844]

The second condition necessary to meet the 'constant man test' is less problematic. The estimation of the evil that is feared must be strong (*aestimatio fortis*). It must be based on right reason and probability, not on vain grounds and levity. In addition to that, the fear must concern an imminent danger (*instans periculum*). This had already been pointed out by Soto and Covarruvias in line with law *Ait praetor* (D. 4,2,1).[845] A danger or damage that lies too far ahead cannot form the object of legitimate fear, according to Sánchez. For future challenges can still be prepared for in many ways (*multis viis occurri potest periculis futuris, longe distantibus*).[846] Still, if entering into the contract in question is the only way left to stave off the future evil, then that fear should be considered to be grave.

There are three further conditions that must be satisfied for fear to be considered as capable of voiding an agreement. All three have to do with the actual danger that must stem from threats and the object of fear. First of all, the extortioner must be capable of putting his threats into practice (*potens minas executioni mandare*).[847] Explicitly relying on Soto, Aragón and Henríquez, our canonist therefore requires the judge to carefully

---

[841] Sánchez, *Disputationes de sancto matrimonii sacramento*, tom. 1, lib. 4, disp. 1, num. 12, p. 325.

[842] Sylvester Prierias, *Summa Sylvestrina*, part. 2, s.v. *metus*, quaest. 1, f. 161r–161v: '(...) generaliter omne maius malum | respectu minoris, quia vir constans seu virtuosus semper consentit in minus malum, ut vitet maius.'

[843] D. 4,2,5 (Metum accipiendum Labeo dicit non quemlibet timorem, sed maioris malitatis) uses the comparative degree 'maior' instead of the positive degree of the adjective 'magnus'.

[844] Sánchez, *Disputationes de sancto matrimonii sacramento*, tom. 1, lib. 4, disp. 2, num. 3, p. 328.

[845] Soto, *In quartum sententiarum librum commentarii*, dist. 29, quaest. 1, art. 2, s.v. *alterum vero*, p. 711; Covarruvias, *In librum quartum Decretalium epitome*, part. 2, cap. 3, par. 4, num. 1, p. 131.

[846] Sánchez, *Disputationes de sancto matrimonii sacramento*, tom. 1, lib. 4, disp. 1, num. 16, p. 326.

[847] Sánchez, *Disputationes de sancto matrimonii sacramento*, tom. 1, lib. 4, disp. 1, num. 19, p. 326–327.

examine the rank and power of the extortioner. Secondly, it does not suffice to show that the extortioner is potentially capable of putting his power into practice. There must be evidence of the extortioner really and regularly having carried through on his threats (*minas exequi solitus sit*).[848] In stating this condition, Sánchez particularly relies on the law *Metum non* (C. 2,19,9) and the common opinion of the jurists in the *ius commune* tradition. Thirdly, the intimidated party must not have had an easy chance of evading the danger (*ne possit timens facile occurrere malis*) by other means save by entering into the contract.[849]

Taking up the old discussion on the respective constancy and strength of men and women, Sánchez does not fail to mention that the 'constant man test' of coercion needs to account for gender. Although there is ample evidence for this in the learned legal and theological tradition, as with Covarruvias, André Tiraqueau once more turns out to be the most reliable authority that can be cited for this slightly problematic claim, more specifically a passage in which Tiraqueau describes women's idle tastes for clothes and jewelry, ascribing that to their softness (*mollities*) and weakness (*imbecillitas*).[850] Sánchez asserts on this basis that 'no matter how capable a woman is of practicing the virtue of constancy, the natural constituency of her sex's body does not allow her to resist coercion as bravely as a man.' 'Women are soft and weak,' Sánchez concludes,[851] 'by their very nature'. Accordingly, women need protection. The criterion of the 'constant man' needs to be applied to women in a particularly mild way.

What is more, the criterion of the 'constant man' must never be applied in an absolute way (*absolute*). The peculiar qualities (*qualitas/conditio*) of the intimidated party involved always matter. The concept of the 'constant man' needs to be specified (*respective*) so as to allow for a different treatment of weaker parties such as children, women and old men. Conversely, in the special case of the military, the 'constant man test' requires an even higher level of constancy and resoluteness. For troops

---

[848] Sánchez, *Disputationes de sancto matrimonii sacramento*, tom. 1, lib. 4, disp. 1, num. 19, p. 326–327.

[849] Sánchez, *Disputationes de sancto matrimonii sacramento*, tom. 1, lib. 4, disp. 1, num. 23, p. 327.

[850] Tiraqueau, *De legibus connubialibus et iure maritali*, l. 3, num. 17, f. 28v.

[851] Sánchez, *Disputationes de sancto matrimonii sacramento*, tom. 1, lib. 4, disp. 3, num. 2, p. 328: 'Et ratio est, quia licet femina habeat virtutem constantiae, propter constitutionem tamen corporis illi sexui naturalem, minus potest resistere metui quam vir. Ergo minor metus sufficiet, ut opprimat cogatque feminam constantem succumbere, quam virum eadem constantia praeditum. Item, quia feminae suapte natura sunt valde imbecilles, ut late Tiraquellus, l. 3, connub., num. 71 [sic] et seq.'

can lawfully be expected to have particularly courageous and dauntless spirits (*affectus*).[852]

4.2.2.2.2 *The constant man, his relatives, and his friends*

As a rule of thumb, compulsion can be a legitimate ground for avoiding a contract, if it is sufficient to sway the will of a constant man or woman (*metus cadens in virum constantem*). Legal practice turns out to be too complex, however, for the 'constant man test' always to be able to provide a clear answer to the question whether or not the intimidated party can claim that the contract was null on account of *metus*. Therefore the doctors unanimously recognized on the basis of law *Metus autem* (D. 4,6,3) that the question should be left to judicial discretion in actual cases (*huius rei disquisitio iudicis est*). To be more precise, in the external court the judge was expected to do so, in the court of conscience a prudent man or confessor could do so.[853]

Still the jurists and theologians tried to formulate an objective doctrine of which types of evil could be considered as satisfying the 'constant man test' of compulsion. What is more, they even tried to figure out if coercion on the part of other persons than the contracting party herself could be considered as fear relevant to the validity of a contract. Sánchez's exposition is both representative and innovative in this respect. Now we will see how he extended the concept of *vir constans* so as to make it include not only the contracting party himself, but also his relatives and friends. In the next paragraph, his list of imminent evils sufficient to throw a constant man off balance reveals the engagement in worldly affairs and the amazing economic insight typical of many of the Jesuits at the turn of the seventeenth century.

In paragraph *Haec* (D. 4,2,8,3) a principle is contained that states that it does not matter for the legal pertinence of an evil feared whether that evil is going to occur to the parents or to their children. Parental affection induces the parents to be more anxious about their children than about themselves anyway (*pro affectu parentes magis in liberis terreantur*). This statement would form the textual basis of the idea that evil events swaying

---

[852] Sánchez, *Disputationes de sancto matrimonii sacramento*, tom. 1, lib. 4, disp. 3, num. 4, p. 329.

[853] Sánchez, *Disputationes de sancto matrimonii sacramento*, tom. 1, lib. 4, disp. 5, num. 1, p. 331–332: 'Primo concors doctorum sententia est, id [sc. quae sint mala gravia et sufficientia metus cadentis in virum constantem] iudicis arbitrio definiendum esse. (...) Et sicut in foro externo relinquitur hoc iudicis arbitrio, ita in foro interno prudentis arbitrio.'

the will of a constant man need not concern the contracting party herself (*in propria persona*). The incumbent evil can also concern people who are close to her. Just how close that tie needed to be was a matter of dispute over the ages of course. But there is no doubting Sánchez's extremely extensive interpretation of this Roman rule.

Sánchez sets out his exposition by repeating the common opinion that the fear of a constant man can also occur to his children or spouse. For as Genesis says, husband and wife are one flesh (*vir et uxor una caro*), and there is a Roman constitution (C. 6,26,11,1) expressly stating that father and son are one person (*pater et filius eadem persona*). Though Sánchez points out that there is further authoritative support for this extension in Thomas, Sylvester, and Angelus, he recognizes that these authors remain vague about extending the fear of a constant man to evil occurring to blood relatives in general (*consanguinei*). Henríquez had expressly included all relatives of the first grade among the persons on account of whom a contracting party might have suffered fear that meets the 'constant man test'.[854]

Yet Sánchez goes further:[855] 'Through love, nature reforges all blood relatives into one flesh composed of the same blood.' A flood of citations are adduced to strengthen the view that evil occurring to blood relatives in general is relevant. Some deal with the annulment of elections because of pressure exerted on blood relatives of the elector, as canon *Sciant cuncti* (VI 1,6,12). Other passages, such as the gloss *Suorum* on canon *Quicumque* (VI 5,11,11) show that blood relatives are legally connected amongst each other since excommunication not only hits the excommunicated person himself but also his blood relatives.[856] Sánchez also adduced the verse, taken from Scripture (Ephesians 5:29) and cited in Gratian's *Decretum* (C.13, q.2, c.19), stating that nobody ever hated his flesh. Antonio Padilla y Meneses' (d. 1598) commentary on law *Interpositas* (C. 2,4,13) is quoted regarding the annulment of a renunciation on account of the fact that

---

[854] Enrique Henríquez, *Summa theologiae moralis tomus primus*, Venetiis 1600, lib. 11 (*de matrimonii sacramento*), cap. 9, num. 5, p. 666: 'Deinde metus gravis dicitur non tantum quando imminet periculum damni in propria persona, sed in persona coniuncta 1. gradu, ut si resultat contra parentes, liberos, et uxorem.'

[855] Sánchez, *Disputationes de sancto matrimonii sacramento*, tom. 1, lib. 4, disp. 4, num. 8, p. 330: 'Quinto dico, idem esse respectu aliorum consanguineorum. Probatur, quia natura ipsa amore conciliat consanguineos tanquam unam carnem, ex eodemque sanguine derivatos.'

[856] For further discussion, see Maihold, *Strafe für fremde Schuld? Die Systematisierung des Strafbegriffs in der Spanischen Spätscholastik und Naturrechtslehre*, p. 314–336.

pressure was exerted on one of the blood relatives of the renouncing beneficee.[857] Sánchez wrongly claims that Padilla's opinion is directly based on a decision of the Rota, the supreme ecclesiastical tribunal.

Sánchez is clearly at pains, then, to find direct canonical support for his claim that evil events scaring *consanguinei* are tantamount to imminent dangers experienced by the contracting party himself. Yet there is even less authoritative support for his claim that paragraph *Haec* (D. 4,2,8,3) must also be extended to in-laws (*affines*) and friends (*amici*). Sánchez holds that through marriage blood relatives of the spouse become like blood relatives of the own family, and hence part of the same flesh (*una caro*). So if you enter into a contract for fear of a grave evil that will otherwise occur to your grandmother-in-law, there is a ground for rescission of the contract. Curiously, Sánchez feels obliged to specify that relatives of a mistress do not become blood relatives of a fornicator, since fornication does not bring about real love.[858]

Last, close friends suffering from pressure can also satisfy the 'constant man test' of coercion, according to Sánchez. 'A friend is an alter ego', our Jesuit argues, quoting Aristotle's *Nicomachean Ethics* (9) and Augustine's *Confessions* (4,6); 'A friend is the other half of his friend's soul', he goes on citing a famous verse of Horace's *Odes* (1,3,8); 'With a friend you share one soul living in two bodies', he finishes his enthusiastic plea by quoting from Aristotle's *Rhetoric* (2,4). Coercion applied to a close friend (*in arctissima amicitia*) sways the will of a constant man or woman. What is more, a friend must reasonably be expected to suffer from his fear that a serious evil will occur to his friend unless he enters into a contract.[859]

---

[857] Antonio Padilla y Meneses, *In titulum de transactionibus Codicis commentarius*, Salmanticae 1566, p. 76, num. 10: 'Non solum autem rescindetur renuntiatio beneficii si metus sit illatus ipsi renuntianti, sed et si consanguineo eius inferatur.'
For scant biographical notices on Padilla, see N. Antonio, *Bibliotheca Hispana nova, sive Hispanorum scriptorum qui ab anno MD ad MDCLXXXIV floruere notitia*, Matriti 1783, p. 148–149.
[858] Sánchez, *Disputationes de sancto matrimonii sacramento*, tom. 1, lib. 4, disp. 4, num. 11, p. 331: 'Sexto dico, similiter esse metum cadentem in virum constantem, quando is incutitur affinibus. Quia sunt velut proprii consanguinei, cum sint consanguinei alterius ex coniugibus et hi sint una caro. (…). Intelligo tamen hoc, quando affinitas provenit ex matrimonio, secus quando ex fornicatione. Quia ex hac nullus amor conciliatur, nec cognoscunt se huiusmodi affines.'
[859] Sánchez, *Disputationes de sancto matrimonii sacramento*, tom. 1, lib. 4, disp. 4, num. 9, p. 331: 'Facit pro hanc sententia clare Alexander de Nevo, c. cum locum, num. 12 de spons, ubi ait esse metum cadentem in constantem virum, sufficientem ad irritandum matrimonium

4.2.2.2.3   *The constant man, his property, and his profits*

As noted above, there was a consensus among the jurists and theologians that the assessment of coercion in actual cases must depend on the judge's discretion. At the same time, learned men as Sánchez did not stop from making lists containing the types of evil that could form a source of unlawful coercion. Such a list ordinarily includes the following evil events (*mala*): death, mutilation, torture, enslavement, captivity, exile, imprisonment,[860] loss of status, loss of honor, rape. Whether infamy and excommunication could count as grave evil was disputed.[861] Sánchez held that legal infamy counted as *metus viri constantis* in any event. The avoidance of factual infamy through entering into a contract could only be deemed a coerced act if there was hardly any alternative way of preventing your reputation from being sullied. The threat of being excommunicated, for its part, was deemed an evil if the excommunication lacked a legitimate ground. Sánchez did not think that fear for a lawfully imposed excommunication could satisfy the constancy test.

The source of a compelling debate concerned the loss of property (*amissio bonorum*) as an evil resulting in relevant duress. Drawing on Hesiod, Plutarch and the Gospel, Covarruvias had pointed out that in Greek 'life' and 'goods' were one and the same concept.[862] In this manner, a traditional obstacle against the relevance of fear for the loss of material riches could be circumvented: canon *Quum dilectus filius* (X 1,40,6). This canon stated that duress could only be deemed relevant if it concerned torture or the loss of one's life (*mors*). Therefore, it had often been cited along with canon *Omnes causationes* (C.32, q.7, c.7) against fear for the loss of material goods as a legitimate ground for rescission of a contract. But in line with Hesiod's interpretation of money and material goods as constituting the living soul of man (*pecunia est anima miseris mortalibus*), this canonical tradition could be by-passed.

---

si inferatur aliis, de quorum personis rationaliter debet timeri ne offendantur. Quod quidem maxime procedere in arctissima amicitia coniunctis, dubitabit nemo.'

[860]   Soto, Aragón, and Henríquez took the view that a short term of imprisonment was not sufficient to meet the 'constant man test' of coercion. See Soto, *In quartum sententiarum librum commentarii*, dist. 29, quaest. 1, art. 2, s.v. *eiusmodi*, p. 711; Aragón, *In secundam secundae commentaria de iustitia et iure*, quaest. 88, art. 3, p. 988; Henríquez, *Summa theologiae moralis*, lib. 11 (*de matrimonii sacramento*), cap. 9, num. 4, p. 666.

[861]   For a detailed account of the debate, see Sánchez, *Disputationes de sancto matrimonii sacramento*, tom. 1, lib. 4, disp. 5, num. 15–18, p. 333–334.

[862]   Cf. supra, n. 812.

As Sánchez puts it, 'fear of losing your property is tantamount to fear of losing your life' (*metus amissionis bonorum aequiparatur metui mortis*).[863] He leaves no doubts about it that the prospect of losing all of your property unless you assent to a contract amounts to duress. Moreover, in his view, losing a substantial part of your property (*amissio maioris partis bonorum*) is sufficient to meet the 'constant man test' of coercion. Again, he thinks that losing a major part of your property amounts to dying, quoting canon *Frequens* (VI 2,5,1) and law *Propter litem* (D. 27,1,21pr.) to grant textual support to the view that the major part of something equals the whole. Covarruvias and Tiraqueau are cited amongst many other authors to prove that this is not a revolutionary idea.[864]

What is interesting about Sánchez is the balanced view he takes. Some had stipulated, for instance, that the goods must always be of great value (*bona magna*) according to objective standards in order for the loss of those goods to be relevant.[865] Sánchez rejects this 'objective' interpretation if it is understood too radically, because the loss of an object which, absolutely speaking, is of small value, can badly affect a poor man.[866] What is to be considered a good of great value (*bonum magnum*) somehow depends on the person in question, too. On the other hand, Sánchez does not accept the other extreme, namely that the criterion of *bona magna* should be of an entirely subjective nature. According to a radically subjective interpretation, a rich man's fear of losing a considerable amount of property would be considered unjust, if he could still sustain himself regardless. Seeking support from Sylvester, Sánchez does not share that subjective interpretation.[867] Even if, relatively speaking, they suffer only a small loss

---

[863] Sánchez, *Disputationes de sancto matrimonii sacramento*, tom. 1, lib. 4, disp. 5, num. 21, p. 334.

[864] For Covarruvias, see higher. Tiraqueau, *De nobilitate et de iure primogeniorum*, Basileae 1561, cap. 31, num. 369, p. 415.

[865] See Azpilcueta, *Enchiridion sive manuale confessariorum et poenitentium*, cap. 22, num. 51, p. 495.

[866] Sánchez, *Disputationes de sancto matrimonii sacramento*, tom. 1, lib. 4, disp. 5, num. 21, p. 334: 'Hanc conclusionem temperant aliqui quando bona quorum amissio timetur, magna sunt. (...) Verum hoc ita absolute dictum displicet mihi. Quia ita gravem iacturam patitur inops ablatis sibi modicis facultatibus vel maiori earum parte ac ditissimus. Imo, multo maiorem ille patitur, quia alia dimidia bonorum parte sibi relicta vitam traducere minime potest. Hic autem potest.'

[867] Sylvester Prierias, *Summa Sylvestrina*, part. 2, s.v. *metus*, quaest. 3, f. 161v: 'Tertio quaeritur utrum metus perdendi bona temporalia vel maiorem partem eorum sit iustus, et dicit Panormitanus (...) quod sic, si non potest quis sustentari sine illis bonis quae perdere timet (...). Abbas extendit hoc non solum quando quis sine illis rebus vivere non potest sed etiam quando gravem patiuntur iacturam, et hoc rationabiliter, quia potest quis esse

of their fortune, the prospect of losing a major part of an estate constitutes just fear.[868] Generally speaking, the criterion for just fear must be objective rather than subjective.

A further testimony to the remarkable willingness of Sánchez to grant relief in case of fear of losing material belongings is his insisting that even the threat of losing a singular precious object (*metus amissionis rei magnae et notabilis*) can sway the will of a constant man. He falsely claims support for this view from Soto, Henríquez and Aragón. There is only one canonist who could rightly be seen as having defended this position before: Covarruvias. Yet Sánchez clearly went further: he even holds that the threat of losing a legal instrument or a notarial deed (*amissio instrumentorum*) certifying the legitimate existence of part of your property meets the 'constant man test' of coercion.[869] He follows Baldus in this. Baldus said that the threat of losing a notarial deed about the entirety of your property, or at least a major part of it, could be tantamount to a threat of being killed.[870]

Even Sánchez, however, tries to limit the scope of threats and fear of evil events leading to the annulment of contracts. A case in point is the loss of profits envisaged if assent to the contract would not be given (*omissio magni lucri*). Put in economic terminology, this raises the question whether the opportunity cost of not giving in to the threats and abstaining from the contract can be a relevant ground for annulment of the contract post factum. For example, you will be appointed heir of an immensely rich testator, if only you yield to my urgent requests to marry Peter. Or

---

ita dives, quod omissa maiori parte bonorum non multum pateretur, ut dicatur iactura gravis respectu incommodi sequentis. Ita enim iactura aliquando potest esse gravior vinculis et verberibus, quae tamen excusantur.'

[868] Sánchez, *Disputationes de sancto matrimonii sacramento*, tom. 1, lib. 4, disp. 5, num. 24, p. 334–335: 'Secundo limitatur eadem conclusio, quando talis est maior pars ea bonorum, ut metum passus absque illa vitam sustentare minime possit. (...) Additque Sylvester vel saltem requiri, ut attentis facultatibus metum passi, gravem patiatur iacturam, sublata maiori bonorum parte. Quia potest (inquit) tam dives esse, ut eam iacturam non faciat, ea ablatione maioris bonorum partis. Caeterum nec haec limitatio placet, sed universaliter credo esse verum, timorem amittendi maiorem bonorum partem esse iustum. Quia est gravis iactura atque ita virum constantem merito movere potest.'

[869] Sánchez, *Disputationes de sancto matrimonii sacramento*, tom. 1, lib. 4, disp. 5, num. 25–26, p. 335.

[870] Baldus de Ubaldis, *In primam Digesti veteris partem commentaria*, Lugduni 1585, ad D. 4,2,8,1, f. 232v: 'Moderni dicunt quod si instrumentum continet quantitatem omnium bonorum vel maioris partis, quod idem est quod quando infertur timor mortis vel poenae capitalis (...).'

you may get promotion, if only you give in to the bosses whims and offer him his favorite services.

In Sánchez's view, it is not impossible to find arguments for the view that fear of letting slip away the opportunity to make profits can set aside a contract. Take his interpretation of paragraph *Si foenerator* (D. 4,2,23,2). It recounts the story of an athlete who is brutally (*inciviliter*) impeded by a money-lender to participate in a competition unless he promises to pay usury. Sánchez takes it to mean that restitution is to be made of money obtained through exercising duress on somebody who feels coerced to assent to the delivery of the money for fear of otherwise losing his profits (*metu perdendi lucri*). He also adduces a viewpoint formulated by Pedro de Navarra, to the effect that if not yielding to urgent pleas (*preces assiduae*) and dissenting (*dissentire*) could lead to an important disadvantage (*magnum incommodum*), the fear of incurring the disadvantage could be deemed a legitimate ground for rescinding the contract.

Pedro de Navarra envisaged the following case, indeed: a pretty woman is unremittingly begged by the local lord or the prince—from whom she expects a favor or a service—to have sexual intercourse with him.[871] Since this woman cannot refuse to have intercourse with this powerful man unless she is prepared to run the risk of missing out on those future benefits (*dissentire sine incommodo non posset*), Navarra concludes that the agreement for sex is entered into by coercion. To be sure, Navarra firmly rejects the idea that importunate begging (*preces importunae*) is always a ground for annulment. In this case, however, which is exceptional because of the opportunity cost involved, Pedro de Navarra believes that the agreement must be set aside.

Sánchez concludes, however, that it is far more likely that fear of missing out on large profits is not sufficient to satisfy the 'constant man test' of coercion. For, actually, this kind of fear (*timor perdendi lucri*) does not constitute fear but rather hope (*passio spei*) and concupiscence (*concupiscentia*).[872] Therefore there is nothing involuntary about the assent of the persons involved in the abovementioned cases, except for

---

[871] Pedro de Navarra, *De ablatorum restitutione in foro conscientiae*, Lugduni 1593, tom. 1, lib. 2, cap. 3, part. 4, dub. 2, par. *Ego vero*, num. 445, p. 203: 'In eo casu hanc sententiam veram putarem, quando dictae assiduae preces essent hominis, a quo illa dissentire sine incommodo non posset, ut si esset eius dominus a quo beneficia sperat, vel princeps a quo favorem et huiusmodi. Is enim metus quidam reverentialis dicitur, causatque involuntarium, ob idque dici solet, preces principum iussa sunt et vim inferunt.'

[872] Sánchez, *Disputationes de sancto matrimonii sacramento*, tom. 1, lib. 4, disp. 5, num. 28, p. 335.

the athlete. The athlete could not merely hope to successfully participate in a competition. He was legally entitled to benefit from his participation. Hence he suffered injustice (*per iniuriam arcetur a lucro ad quod habebat ius*). Accordingly, the loan had to be rescinded.

The argument employed in regard to the athlete in paragraph *Si foenerator* does not apply, however, if a person feels obliged to acquit another person's debt or to give him a present in the hope that that person will some day do him a favor in return. For then, Tomás Sánchez admonishes in the wake of Juan de Medina, those donations are motivated not by fear but by the cupidity to reap a future benefit (*non metui sed cupiditati lucri acquirendi imputanda*).[873] Thomas Aquinas' authority as a psychoanalyst turns out to remain untouched in this regard. As we have noted above, in his *Prima Secundae* (quaest. 6, art. 7) he famously argued that concupiscence does not cause involuntariness, but on the contrary makes something to be even more voluntary. For concupiscence inclines the will to desire the object of concupiscence. As we move on to the next paragraph, this will remain an important idea.

4.2.2.3 *Pressure and flattery*

Sánchez's list of evil events that meet the constancy test is quite lengthy. There is no need to conclude from this, however, that Sánchez endorsed the view that intimidated parties must be granted relief in as many events as possible. A good example of his reluctance in this regard, is the case of pressure (*preces*) and flattery (*blanditiae*). Our Jesuit was basically unwilling to grant relief to people who complained because they had entered into a contract as a way of yielding to someone's importunate pressure or flattery.

As concerns the irrelevance of flattery, Sánchez could simply paraphrase Thomas' *Prima Secundae* (quaest. 6, art. 7): flattery and love do not diminish voluntariness; they rather take away involuntariness. Even if a superior cajoles you into making an agreement with him, the contract remains valid afterwards in spite of the flattery. Only when the superior,

---

[873] Medina, *De poenitentia, restitutione et contractibus*, tom. 2, cod. *De restitutione*, quaest. 3, caus. 2, par. *Si fiat remissio* 3, p. 26: 'Si fiat remissio aut donatio ex metu non acquirendi bonum aut lucrum quod remissione facta obtinere sperat, sive sit metus ad id incussus, sive non, non vitiatur remissio nec donatio, quia talis donatio non metui in casu, sed cupiditati lucri sperati videtur imputanda. Donatio autem ex cupiditate facta non ita vitiatur sicut ea, quae ex metu fit. Haec dixerim, ut occasionem curiosis darem rem particularius investigandi et inter metum et metum in variis casibus distinguendi.'

say a prince, adds real threats to his endearments, can the intimidated party claim relief.[874] By the same token, a fornicator cannot claim restitution from a prostitute, despite the fact that he has been seduced by her blandishments into paying more than her ordinary salary. According to Sánchez, the temptation exercised by a prostitute cannot even result in minor fear. A prudent man does not let himself be dazzled by the fraud typical of women (*muliercula fraus*), which consists in pretending that she is crazy for love for you (*perdite deamare*).[875]

Sánchez could not simply grant relief to people who suffered from simple pressure (*preces*) either. After all, society is structured around hierarchical relationships, to the effect that pressing commands are part and parcel of a smoothly run society. Power in itself and the exercise of pressure that goes with it cannot give rise to relief (*sola potentia non sufficit*).[876] Otherwise, leadership would be frustrated all the time. It would simply not be possible for superiors to give commands any more (*alias principibus nihil petere liceret*). Sánchez quotes a maxim stating that 'it is a leader's job to exercise pressure, namely to exercise this rather vehement kind of commanding' (*est orare ducum, species violenta iubendi*). He borrows this maxim from André Tiraqueau's treatment of duress. Sánchez thinks it is right, except in the case of a tyrant. Also, while Tiraqueau employs the maxim to argue that importunate pressure by a prince constitutes a ground for legitimate fear, Sánchez quotes the maxim to the opposite effect.[877]

The real crux, indeed, concerns pressure that turns out to be manifestly importunate (*preces importunae*). Should not we make a distinction between pressure that is exercised lawfully, and pressure that smacks of brutality and abuse of power? A frightening flood of textual evidence from the Bible and the law of Rome was adduced and manipulated, indeed, to argue that importunate pressure was tantamount to oppression and harassment (*oppressio et vexatio*), both being considered as inducing

---

[874] Sánchez, *Disputationes de sancto matrimonii sacramento*, tom. 1, lib. 4, disp. 7, num. 3, p. 342.

[875] Sánchez, *Disputationes de sancto matrimonii sacramento*, tom. 1, lib. 4, disp. 11, num. 1–3, p. 354–355. This was, of course, a controversial issue. It is occasionally dealt with in the chapter after the next; cf. infra.

[876] Sánchez, *Disputationes de sancto matrimonii sacramento*, tom. 1, lib. 4, disp. 7, num. 1, p. 342.

[877] André Tiraqueau, *De poenis legum ac consuetudinum statutorumque temperandis aut etiam remittendis et id quibus quotque ex causis*, in: Opera omnia, Francoforti ad Moenum 1597, tom. 7, causa 35, num. 2 (*principum preces importunae iustam metuendi causam inducunt*), p. 63.

grave fear.[878] Sánchez nevertheless requires that the importunate pressure be accompanied by reverential fear (*una cum metu reverentiali*) for them to constitute grave fear that meets the constancy test. Only if importunate pressure is induced by a person to whom the intimidated party owes reverence, can it be considered relevant.[879] Reverential fear rightly makes the intimidated party feel weak and timid, while the importunate pressure puts him in a vexed position. Taken together, these factors can impress even a constant man.[880]

In adopting this view, Sánchez follows the practical decisions of Matteo d'Afflitto (1448–1528), amongst other *consilia*. Matteo d'Afflitto had equated the combination of reverential fear for a husband and his importunate pressure with grave fear.[881] Apparently, the sacred court of Naples had set aside a legacy of a house made by a spouse to her husband on those grounds.[882] Moreover, Covarruvias had stated precisely in regard to marriage contracts that importunate pressure along with reverential fear had the same invalidating effect as threats added to reverential fear.[883]

---

[878] A detailed analysis of these references would lead us astray here, but it is worthwhile having a closer look at *Disputationes de sancto matrimonii sacramento*, tom. 1, lib. 4, disp. 7, num. 4, p. 342–343 in order to get a glimpse of Sánchez's use of the humanist-philological method to interpret the Bible and construct his argument.

[879] Sánchez, *Disputationes de sancto matrimonii sacramento*, tom. 1, lib. 4, disp. 7, num. 5, p. 343: 'Secunda sententia limitatius loquitur, asserens preces importunas una cum metu reverentiali, ut si sint personae cui debetur reverentia, incutere metum cadentem in constantem virum.'

[880] Sánchez, *Disputationes de sancto matrimonii sacramento*, tom. 1, lib. 4, disp. 7, num. 7, p. 344: 'Sit conclusio. Inter has sententias secundam reputo probabiliorem. Cum enim ex una parte importunitas, cuiuscumque sit, valde urgeat, ne dicam, vexet et opprimat (…), et ex altera parte reverentia personae petentis debita, pusillanimem ac timidum nec audentem contradicere, rogatum reddat merito; ac iure optimo utraque metuendi causa coniuncta prudentem ac constantem coget ipsiusque consensum extorquebit.'

[881] Matteo d'Afflitto, *Decisionum sacri regii Neapolitani consilii*, Francofurti 1600, ad decis. 69, num. 7, p. 103: '(…) comprobat, ut supra, importunas preces mariti et aliorum coniunctorum metui aequiparari (…)'. On Matteo d'Afflitto, see G. Vallone, *Iurisdictio domini, Introduzione a Matteo d'Afflitto ed alla cultura giuridica meridionale tra Quattro- et cinquecento*, [Collana di studi storici e giuridici, 1], Lecce 1985.

[882] Matteo d'Afflitto, *Decisionum sacri regii Neapolitani consilii*, decis. 69, num. 4, p. 102: 'Fuit visum omnibus doctoribus de sacro consilio, quod attenta fide notarii et iudicis et testium, qui subscripserunt testamentum, quod dictum testamentum sit validum, praeterquam ad legatum domus, ex quo dictum legatum fuit factum per uxorem ob nimiam reverentiam mariti stantis supra eius caput, concurrentibus eius importunis precibus et blanditiis in damnum et praeiudicium Franciscelli patris. Unde sicut actus rescinditur stante metu reverentiali, vel metu verberum vel stantibus minis (…), ita etiam rescinditur legatum metu reverentiali marito factum concurrentibus importunis precibus mariti in damnum alterius.'

[883] Covarruvias, *In librum quartum Decretalium epitome*, part. 2, cap. 3, par. 6, num. 8, p. 136.

Sánchez personally deems it necessary that importunate pressure be extremely urgent, penetrating and without pause.[884] That, however, still leaves the question open of what constitutes reverential fear.

4.2.2.4 *Reverential fear*

The question about the effects of reverential fear (*metus reverentialis*) on the validity of a marriage contract was particularly thorny. On the one hand, consent, certainly to a marriage contract, had to be as free as possible. On the other hand, a due sense of hierarchy and deference to superiors and members of the family, often ending in compulsion, was the structural basis of the early modern society. The dilemma was solved early on by stating that reverential fear on its own was not sufficient to grant relief. An additional condition had to be met: reverential fear must be accompanied by threats (*minae*). Before we go on and examine how Sánchez positioned himself in the debate about the effects of reverential fear on the validity of a contract, it will be useful to know what he understood by that kind of fear in the first place.

With respect to which persons can an intimidated party experience reverential fear? As is expressly recognized by Sánchez, the solution of this problem actually needs to be left to the discretion of a judge or a confessor. The judge is then expected to take into account the special circumstances that make up the case in order to decide on the presence or not of reverential fear. Sánchez, however, wishes to address the question by abstracting from all these particulars (*seclusis particularibus circumstantiis*).[885] In the fashion of the moral theologians, he wants to settle the question in theory by looking at it from the perspective of the 'nature of the affair' (*ex natura ipsa rei*).

In principle, reverential fear is the fear which induces you into a contract out of reverence for anyone who is by right superior to you.[886] For example, a cleric is subjected to a bishop, a civilian to a civil servant, a

---

[884] Sánchez, *Disputationes de sancto matrimonii sacramento*, tom. 1, lib. 4, disp. 7, num. 8, p. 344: 'Monuerim tamen, non quascumque preces assiduas importunas dici, sed quae sunt instantissimae et saepius repetitae et inculcatae.'

[885] Sánchez, *Disputationes de sancto matrimonii sacramento*, tom. 1, lib. 4, disp. 6, num. 24, p. 340.

[886] Sánchez, *Disputationes de sancto matrimonii sacramento*, tom. 1, lib. 4, disp. 6, num. 25, p. 340: 'Metus reverentialis datur in eo, qui iure aliquo subiectionis alteri subest. Ut in clerico respectu episcopi, in seculari respectu magistratus cui subditur, in uxore respectu viri, in filio respectu patris. Conclusio est omnium. Et ratio est manifesta, quia cum hi superiores sint, et alii ipsi subjecti, suapte natura quandam reverentiam et obsequium eis

woman to her husband, and a son to his father. The reason for this is simple: by nature an inferior must pay reverence to his superior and serve him. As a logical consequence, an inferior experiences shame and fear in the presence of his superior so that he is less inclined to contradict him.

Sánchez then extends the reverence a child owes to his parents to the in-laws, since spouses become one flesh through marriage. Since a child owes deference to his grandfather as if his grandfather were his father, Sánchez also thinks that one can suffer from reverential fear in front of ancestors in general. Furthermore, a guardian is to be held in reverence, because he takes the place of a parent. A little more difficult to argue for Sánchez but convincing, anyway, is that a child can also experience reverential fear for his or her mother. Constitution *Quisquis cum militibus* (C. 9,8,5) had stated that women are weak and anxious creatures who, accordingly, cannot easily be the object of fear. Drawing on the consiliary literature, our Jesuit argues that natural law requires a child to pay equal deference to both father and mother.[887] Within a family living in the same house, younger children owe reverence to the elder children, whether boys or girls. Among the authors quoted by Sánchez to support the last claim figures the great Spanish jurist Alfonso de Azevedo (d. 1598), who is famous for his commentary on the *Nueva Recopilación* (1567).[888]

The chances of setting aside a contract are directly proportional, of course, as the number increases of people included in the list of persons to whom reverence is owed. Perhaps it was to avoid the unwelcome consequence of this extensive interpretation, that Sánchez made the appeal to reverential fear as a ground for annulment less evident in another way. For as we will see now, he not only stipulated that reverential fear must be accompanied by threats. The person issuing the threats must also be known to be serious and to have executed his threats in the past. In this manner, the problem of reverential fear seen as a separate category of fear eventually disappeared. For whether fear was reverential or not, Sánchez

---

debent, quae reverentia timorem ac pudorem incutit ut minus audeant ipsorum voluntati contradicere.'

[887] Sánchez, *Disputationes de sancto matrimonii sacramento*, tom. 1, lib. 4, disp. 6, num. 30, p. 340.

[888] Alfonso de Azevedo, *Commentarii iuris civilis in Hispaniae regias consitutiones*, tom. 2 (*quartum librum Novae Recopilationis complectens*), Matritii 1595, ad lib. 4, tit. 21, l. 1, num. 193, p. 720: '(...) inter fratres sicut inter patrem et filium dictus metus reverentialis laesione interveniente attenditur.'

For biographical notes on Azevedo, see Nicolas Antonio, *Bibliotheca Hispana nova, sive Hispanorum scriptorum qui ab anno MD ad MDCLXXXIV floruere notitia*, Matriti 1783, p. 12.

always stipulated that the intimidating party be pronouncing real threats and that he be accustomed to execute his threats in practice. This was an opinion shared by most of the doctors, but certainly not by everybody.

There was a strand of thought holding that simple reverential fear without something more satisfied the 'constant man test' of coercion.[889] To this effect, the rule *Velle* (D. 50,17,4) was quoted, stating that somebody who obeys the order of his father or lord cannot be considered as expressing his will (*velle non creditur, qui obsequitur imperio patris vel domini*). Another important textual argument was based on paragraph *Quae onerandae* (D. 44,5,1,5). It stipulated that relief must be granted (an *exceptio onerandae libertatis causa*) to a freedman who out of reverence (*nimia patrono reverentia*) had assented to a penalty clause if he would ever offend his former master.

The common opinion, however, clearly tried to limit the avoiding character of reverential fear.[890] It was deemed relevant only in cases in which it was compounded by threats or physical compulsion (*minae aut verbera*). Canonical support for this opinion was borrowed from canon *Ex litteris* (X 4,2,11) amongst many other texts. It avoids an engagement contract (*sponsalia*) by taking into account not merely the fear of a daughter for her father, but also the threats he issued. A host of passages from the Digest were quoted to argue that the law of Rome did not recognize simple reverential fear. Among them law *Si patre cogente* (D. 23,2,22). It provided clear evidence that reverential fear without something more was not sufficient to nullify a marriage contract. For a man who, against his own choice, had assented to a marriage for simple fear of offending his father, was not granted relief.[891]

Sánchez endorses this view that had been accepted by the majority of the jurists and theologians. It does not prevent him, however, from adding some personal accents to the common opinion. For example, he points out that in some cases threats may actually be absent and reverential fear still constitute a ground for annulment. This can happen when the intimidator is known to be tremendously cruel by character (*nimis crudelis*). In

---

[889] Sánchez, *Disputationes de sancto matrimonii sacramento*, tom. 1, lib. 4, disp. 6, num. 4–6, p. 336.

[890] Sánchez names dozens of canonists (e.g. Felinus), theologians (e.g. Henríquez), and civilians (e.g. Alciati) in *Disputationes de sancto matrimonii sacramento*, tom. 1, lib. 4, disp. 6, num. 7, p. 337.

[891] D. 23,2,22 in *Corporis Iustinianaei Digestum vetus* (ed. Gothofredi), tom. 1, col. 2111: 'Si patre cogente ducit uxorem, quam non duceret, si sui arbitrii esset, contraxit tamen matrimonium, quod inter invitos non contrahitur: maluisse hoc videtur.'

that event, the threats can be considered as virtually present, while actually absent (*minae actu desint, sunt tamen virtute*).[892] The sole terrifying face of a mighty person, even if he does not express actual threats, reasonably has an effect upon a man of constant character.

Another example of an occasion in which actual threats may be absent and reverential fear nonetheless meets the 'constant man test' is the following. A girl assents to a marriage contract because she fears that otherwise her father will feel horribly offended for the rest of his life (*diuturna indignatio*). If there is absolutely no prospect for the girl of reconciling her with her father (*spes futurae reconciliationis*) unless she assents to the marriage contract he urges her to enter into, she has suffered from real coercion. For is there any constant man, Sánchez asks rhetorically,[893] who would not consider a grave evil the prospect of having to face for the rest of one's life the angry face of a father or another close person. Certainly because offended persons never stop to complain and to speak evil of the persons whom they feel offended by.

Of great interest is Sánchez's reaction to Covarruvias' claim that reverential fear can also become relevant when it is accompanied by lesion beyond moiety (*laesio enormis*).[894] What we have seen Covarruvias stating, indeed, is that reverential fear can still be a ground for rescission, even in the absence of proven threats, provided that the contract is affected by lesion beyond moiety. Moreover, he meant this rule to apply both to marriage contracts and other contracts. For example, if in reverence to her father a girl agrees to marry a man who is of a far lower status, she can claim rescission. Similarly, a vendor can reclaim rescission if he sold his estate for less than half of its fair market price. Yet Sánchez vehemently denies that such an equal treatment of marriage contracts and other contracts is justified.

Sánchez agrees that in other contracts relief can be granted by virtue of sole reverential fear in conjunction with lesion beyond moiety, absent of threats. This is so, because grave lesion always seems to indicate the

---

[892] Sánchez, *Disputationes de sancto matrimonii sacramento*, tom. 1, lib. 4, disp. 6, num. 12, p. 338.

[893] Sánchez, *Disputationes de sancto matrimonii sacramento*, tom. 1, lib. 4, disp. 6, num. 14, p. 338: 'Quis enim vir constans aut prudens non reputabit grave malum, semper coram oculis habere infensum patrem aut virum aut alium a quo pendet et cum quo semper versaturus est, maxime cum vix invenias qui linguam moderari valeat, ne male sentiat, peiusque loquatur de eo, cui infestus est.'

[894] For the use of this translation, borrowed from the Louisiana Civil Code, art. 2589, see supra, n. 816.

presence of deceit (*magna laesio dolum solet arguere*). Grave lesion is not tantamount to deceit, but it raises a presumption of deceit. This actually was an opinion stated by Covarruvias.[895] Sánchez, then, interprets lesion beyond moiety to constitute a mere species of deceit. In this way, he lays the foundation of the distinction between marriage and other contracts. For if it is commonly accepted in the civilian tradition that deceit causing a contract truly vitiates contracts of good faith, it is equally acknowledged that this is not the case with marriage contracts.

Deceit can only avoid marriage if it concerns the identity of the person or his status of being either a slave or a free citizen. Lesion beyond moiety is a species of deceit that is not officially counted among the specific types of deceit that avoid a marriage contract. Consequently, there is a fundamental disparity between marriage and other contracts as regards the effect of reverential fear compounded by *laesio enormis*.[896]

4.2.2.5 *Void* vs *voidable contracts*

Marriage is also neatly distinguished from other contracts when it comes to the effect of duress on the validity of an agreement. In this respect, the dividing line between marriage and other contracts concurs with the division between nullity *ab initio* and voidability. While holding that duress results in a void marriage contract, Sánchez makes a case for considering the avoiding effect of duress on other contracts as merely relative. Put differently, duress causes a marriage contract to be automatically void (*irriti*). Other contracts are voidable (*irritandi*).

---

[895] See Covarruvias, *Relectio in cap. quamvis pactum*, part. 3, par. 4, num. 7, p. 290: 'Laesio maiori vel minori contingens ultra dimidiam iustae aestimationis, simul cum metu reverentiae et obsequii paterni aut maritalis, operatur contractus rescissionem, ut ea fiat ratione metus, licet iuramentum conventioni accesserit. Haec probatur, quia dolus praesumitur in ea conventione adhibitus et oppressio quaedam; alioqui enim non est vero simile, quod tantae laesioni filia vel uxor consensisset.'
[896] Sánchez, *Disputationes de sancto matrimonii sacramento*, tom. 1, lib. 4, disp. 6, num. 15, p. 338–339: 'Et ratio disparitatis inter matrimonium et caeteros contractus, ea est: quod caeteri contractus annullantur ex dolo dante illis causam, quando sunt contractus bonae fidei (...), matrimonium autem minime, sed ex solo errore personae aut conditionis servilis (...). Ratio autem quare magna laesio cum metu reverentiali rescindit caeteros contractus est (...) quia magna laesio dolum solet arguere (...) et dolus hic reipa interveniens ita officit actui ac si ex proposito accederet (...). Non ergo mirum est, si caeteri contractus rescindantur ex metu reverentiali cum enormi laesione, ratione doli illi adiuncti, non autem matrimonium cui dolus ille non nocet, cum non sit circa personam aut conditionem servilem.'

This means that in a normal contract it is up to the party affected by coercion to decide whether he wishes the contract to be rescinded or not. A marriage affected by grave fear, however, is automatically null. Sánchez thus makes an indispensable contribution to the development of one of the most fundamental distinctions in the conceptual fabric of legal thought. In what follows, we will first focus on Sánchez's treatment of contracts other than marriage.

The conceptual difference between void and voidable contracts is of no small practical significance, certainly not when property related issues and contractual consent interfere. In fact, it is precisely on account of the material effects related to a contract that is void *ipso facto*, that some scholars thought of duress as giving rise to automatic nullity in contracts. We have already seen that Molina belonged to this group. As Sánchez demonstrates, there effectively was textual argument that showed property (*dominium*) was not transmitted by means of a contract affected by duress.[897]

Paragraph *Volenti* (D. 4,2,9,4), for instance, states that the intimidated party is granted a real action (*actio in rem*) as well as a personal action (*actio in personam*). From this they concluded that a contract affected by duress must be void *ab initio*. For, from a legal point of view, the existence of a real action indicated that dominion over the thing conveyed had apparently remained in the hands of the intimidated party. Therefore, the intimidated party could avail himself of a *reivindicatio* or secret compensation (*rem propria auctoritate recuperare*).

Other arguments indicating that coerced contracts are automatically void were based on the idea that duress automatically frustrates voluntary consent, since nothing is more contrary to consent than violence and fear (D. 50,17,116). Canon *Cum locum*, which states that consent cannot be found where duress or coercion intervene, was quoted to the same effect.[898] On the basis of paragraph *In hac actione* (D. 4,2,14,3) duress was said to be composed of ignorance, therefore frustrating consent. A lot of these ideas were at variance, of course, with sound Aristotelian-Thomistic philosophy of the will.

---

[897] Sánchez, *Disputationes de sancto matrimonii sacramento*, tom. 1, lib. 4, disp. 8, num. 3, p. 345.

[898] Interestingly, the *correctores Romani* referred to Covarruvias and Soto for further discussion on this canon; cf. nota *Locum* ad X 4,1,14 in *Corpus juris canonici* (ed. Gregoriana), part. 2, col. 1429.

Sánchez himself, however, takes the view that coerced consent does not make contracts void, but voidable, except in the case of marriage. It is undoubtedly due to his familiarity with Aristotle and Thomas that he insisted on the veracity and validity of consent given to a contract affected by coercion (*in consensu metu extorto est verus consensus veraque voluntas*).[899] What is more, he quotes counter-evidence from the law of Rome to support his view, e.g. paragraph *Si metu coactus* included in law *Si mulier* (D. 4,2,21,5). The fact that a future verb is used in the opening verse of D. 4,2,1 is adduced to argue that coerced consent does not avoid a contract automatically but in the future (*Quod metus causa gestum erit ratum non habebo*).[900] Another famous reference includes constitution *Venditiones* (C. 2,19,12).[901] Yet the more convincing quotation comes from canon *Abbas* (X 1,40,2),[902] which clearly indicates that contracts affected by coercion are valid until they are avoided.

Even if it is true that Sánchez could rely on short statements from other learned men, such as Alciati and Henríquez,[903] that duress did not result but in voidability, the juridification and the comprehensiveness of his exposition is baffling. It should suffice here to note that Sánchez expressly inferred from his conclusion that property (*dominium*) is actually and juridically transferred to the other party to the contract—at least in contracts other than marriage.[904] In the wake of the Roman tradition—which considered the *actio quod metus causa* as an *actio in rem scripta*—he also points out that duress can be the effect of either intimidating behavior on

---

[899] Sánchez, *Disputationes de sancto matrimonii sacramento*, tom. 1, lib. 4, disp. 8, num. 4, p. 345.

[900] A similar argument on the contrary was C. 4,44,1, where a verb 'praesentis temporis' is interpreted to mean that nullity is absolute (*mala fide emptio irrita*).

[901] C. 2,19,12: 'Venditiones donationes transactiones, quae per potentiam extortae sunt, praecipimus infirmari.'

[902] X 1,40,2: 'Quae metu et vi fiunt de iure debent in irritum revocari.'

[903] Andrea Alciati, *Responsa*, Lugduni 1561, lib. 1, resp. 5, num. 2, f. 10v: 'Gaspardus contraxit illud matrimonium per metum, quo casu ipso iure est nullum, nam licet regulariter metus interveniens non annullet actum ipso iure, tamen istud non procedit in matrimonio, cuius substantia consistit in mero consensu.'

Henríquez, *Summa theologiae moralis*, lib. 11 (*De matrimonii sacramento*), cap. 9, num. 4, p. 666: '(…) reliquos contractus etiam iuratos metus gravis non irritat iure naturae aut humano, eo quod per iudicem et alia iuris remedia possunt facile rescindi, et in integrum restitui damnum illatum.'

[904] Sánchez, *Disputationes de sancto matrimonii sacramento*, tom. 1, lib. 4, disp. 8, num. 5, p. 346.

the part of the other party to the contract or coercion exercised by a third party outside of the contract itself.[905]

What remains to be examined here is the different manner in which Sánchez deals with the problem of duress in marriage contracts. And his opinion that marriage contracts entered into through coerced consent are not voidable, but void *ipso facto*. For Sánchez, if the coerced party confirms the original marriage while the other party who did not suffer from coercion has not yet revoked his consent, the marriage is confirmed without the need for a new consent by the other party. The crux of the matter lies elsewhere:[906]

> Is a marriage [tainted by coercion] so invalid as to bring about no obligation any more of ratifying it for the contracting party who did not suffer from coercion? Or is it allowed for the uncoerced party to step out of the contract before the coerced party even has the time to confirm his original consent?

As a matter of fact, Sánchez distinguishes two cases. First, it may be that the uncoerced party is free from any fault (*immunis culpae*) since he did not know about the unlawful pressure that led the other party to enter into the contract. In that case, Sánchez does not see why the uncoerced party would have no right to step out of the contract as soon as the coercion and the actual invalidity of the contract came to light. Since he did not commit fraud or deceit, and only promised his commitment provided that the other party committed himself, he should not be forced to stick to the contract.[907] Secondly, the uncoerced party may be the cause of the duress from which the other party suffers. This is the case which sparks off the most intensive debate.

Although we will see Sánchez concluding that a marriage affected by coercion of which the other party is the direct or indirect author is automatically void (*irritus*), he first develops an argument for the contrary

---

[905] Sánchez, *Disputationes de sancto matrimonii sacramento*, tom. 1, lib. 4, disp. 8, num. 6, p. 346: 'Non refert autem, ut contractus metu celebratus rescindatur, sive is in cuius favorem contractus celebratus est, metum gravem intulerit, sive alius.'

[906] Sánchez, *Disputationes de sancto matrimonii sacramento*, tom. 1, lib. 4, disp. 15, num. 3, p. 365: 'Tota autem difficultas est, an matrimonium illud ita invalidum sit, ut nullam prorsus pariat obligationem denuo ratificandi illud, respectu eius qui non est passus metum? Vel an possit hic resilire antequam metum passus ratificet pristinum consensum?'

[907] Sánchez, *Disputationes de sancto matrimonii sacramento*, tom. 1, lib. 4, disp. 8, num. 6, p. 346: 'Et in hoc casu non invenio cur his cogendus sit stare matrimonio et non ab illo resilire possit, eius nullitate cognita, nec priori illo consensu ratificato per coactum. Quia immunis est culpae, nec se obligavit, nisi altero se illi obligante.'

opinion. First of all, he argues that by exercising duress, you cause harm to
the coerced party (*irrogat iniuriam alteri*). This damage (*in-iuria*) can be
undone by giving the right (*ius*) to the coerced party of deciding whether
he wants to repair and confirm the affected contract or not. In this
context, the Jesuit theologian Enrique Henríquez had talked about the
coerced party's right to compell the defrauder (*ius compellendi cogentem*)
so that he is forced to remain bound to the contract if the coerced party
wishes.[908]

The rationale behind this view can be found in the famous canon *Quum
universorum* (X 3,19,8), which draws on D. 16,1,2,3, and states that the law
must protect the defrauded and not the defrauders (*iura deceptis et non
deceptoribus subveniant*). This canon played an important role in the
theologians' treatment of the effects of mistake and deceit. Still, a theologian such as Molina did not found his conclusion on this canon but on
more general principles, namely the common good and 'natural equity'
(*aequitas naturalis*).[909] As will be explained below, Molina argued that a
contract affected by deceit which gave rise to the contract (*dolus causam
dans*) is *ipso facto* void (*irritus*), yet enforceable in favor of the deceived
party on account of this natural equity. In this way, the deceiver can be
compelled by the mistaken party to perform his contractual duties, not
by virtue of the contract itself, but by virtue of the external importance
of equity. Because the injury done to the mistaken party directly created
a right for the mistaken party to demand performance, Molina thought
that he did not have to wait for a sentence by the judge compelling the
deceiver to execute the contract.

Yet this is precisely the point where Sánchez disagrees. Despite the
urgent demonstration in favor of the opinion holding that a coerced marriage is voidable, Sánchez concludes that the opposite opinion is more
probable.[910] His reasoning is quite simple. It might be equitable, indeed,
to have a defrauder stick to the marriage contract on account of his

908 Henríquez, *Summa theologiae moralis*, lib. 11 (*De matrimonii sacramento*), cap. 10,
num. 6, p. 669.
909 Molina, *De iustitia et iure*, tom. 2 (*De contractibus*), tract. 2, disp. 352, col. 413, num. 4:
'Jus humanum videri intendisse tribuere vim consensui dolosi ad eum obligandum ante
latam sententiam, judicisve compulsionem, non solum in poenam doli, sed etiam ex naturali aequitate et quoniam ita bono communi erat expediens.'
910 Sánchez, *Disputationes de sancto matrimonii sacramento*, tom. 1, lib. 4, disp. 15, num. 5,
p. 366: 'Secunda sententia (quam probabiliorem existimo) docet non teneri cogentem
in foro conscientiae perficere illud matrimonium, donec per iudicem condemnetur, sed
libere altero invito posse resilire, nisi aliud damnum secutum sit. Probatur, quia aut tenetur ratione delicti coactionis, in poenam illius, et hoc exigeret iudicis condemnationem,

delictual behavior. If that is the case, however, the obligation to observe the contract is issued in order to punish (*in poenam*) the defrauder for the coercion he exerted, that is for the delict he committed. Since a punishment cannot be imposed but through condemnation by a judge, however, it will depend on the judge and not on the intimidated party whether the contract be brought to live again or not (*exigeret iudicis condemnationem*). In fact, Sánchez applies to marriage contracts affected by duress the same criticism we will see Lessius passing on Molina in the context of mistake.

To sum up, Sánchez considers ordinary contracts affected by duress to be voidable, while marriage contracts deviate from this rule because of the intervention of ecclesiastical law. A marriage contract can be confirmed again, but only by a judge as a measure of punishment. In any event, marriage contracts differ from other contracts when it comes to the effects of duress on its validity:[911]

> The logic is different. Other contracts that have been extorted through duress are legally valid. Only the coerced party is granted a right to rescind the contract. A marriage extorted through duress, however, is totally void.

4.2.3   *The Jesuit moral theologians and the casuistry of duress*

4.2.3.1   *Duress and general contract doctrine*

The impact of Sánchez on future thought about the vices of the will was massive, certainly among his Jesuit successors. This does not mean, however, that some of the most important of his colleagues did not add anything new to the now fully-grown debate about coerced consent and duress anymore. This holds true for famous Jesuits such as Lessius and Lugo, but also for lesser known figures such as the Portuguese Jesuit Fernão Rebelo (1547–1608). Rebelo received his doctorate in theology form the University of Évora, where he became a professor.[912] From his hand we have a

---

ante quam nullus tenetur subire poenam; aut ratione iniuriae illatae per coactionem, et hoc non.'

[911] Sánchez, *Disputationes de sancto matrimonii sacramento*, tom. 1, lib. 4, disp. 15, num. 6, p. 366: 'Dispar est ratio, nam caeteri contractus metu extorti sunt validi ipso iure, et solum metum passo datur ius ad rescindendum. At matrimonium metu extortum est prorsus nullum.'

[912] On Rebelo, see J. Vaz de Carvalho, *Fernão Rebelo*, in: C. O'Neill – J. Domínguez (eds.), Diccionario histórico de la Compañía de Jesús, Biográfico-temático, Roma – Madrid 2001, vol. 4, p. 3303.

compelling work *On the obligations of justice, religion and charity* (*Opus de obligationibus justitiae, religionis et charitatis*) of which, sadly, only the first volume on justice was effectively published in 1608. Rebelo, Lessius and Lugo did not always agree with their celebrated colleague. Nor did they agree among themselves. For another thing, they isolated the debate about vices of the will in contracts from the analysis of particular contracts. It is also worthwhile noting that Lessius further developed the general theory of duress as a vice of the will in his commentary on Thomas' *Prima Secundae*.[913]

In light of the development of a general contract doctrine, it is significant to note that in their treatises *On Justice and Right* Lessius and Lugo inserted their discussion of duress into a special chapter on contract law in general (*De contractibus in genere*). This general chapter precedes the successive chapters on particular contracts—which do not even include marriage anymore. Rebelo, for his part, still deals with marriage contract in his work *On Obligations*. Yet prior to the treatment of particular contracts such as marriage and sale, he gives an exposition of contract law in general (*De contractibus in genere*), including many questions on the vices of the will.

It remained a major concern, certainly for Lessius and Lugo, to find a balance between protecting parties against undue influence, on the one hand, and avoiding excesses in granting relief for duress, on the other. They did not necessarily agree, therefore, on the answer to an important question that had already been raised by Sánchez: does illegitimate duress which is not directly aimed at enticing somebody into a contract (*non incutitur directe ad contractum*) still constitute a ground to set aside the contract in question? Another issue that provoked some controversy concerned the effect of legitimate coercion, certainly when it came to legitimate litigation threats (*ius accusandi*).

Last, a major concern of Sánchez's successors was to determine whether coerced contracts were automatically void or merely voidable at the option of the wronged party. Although Rebelo thought that duress made gratuitous contracts automatically void, Lessius and Lugo eventually established a general regime of voidability regardless of the type of contract and regardless of the kind of vice of the will, that is mistake or duress. Moreover, they compared the remedies for mistake and duress and pondered over the question why the *actio de dolo* was only available

---

[913] Lessius, *In I.II D. Thomae de beatitudine et actibus humanis*, quaest. 6, art. 5–6, p. 45.

against the perpetrator of the deceit, while the *actio quod metus causa* could be brought even against a third party.

4.2.3.2   *Contract as a means of escaping a threat*

Leonardus Lessius is brief and to the point about contracts that have been concluded in order to escape a threatening event. As long as coercion is not exercised with the final objective of making somebody enter into the contract, the contract cannot be subject to annulment.[914] If you make an agreement for another purpose (*ad alium finem*) than the contract itself, e.g. in order to escape an evil event (*ad malum evadendum*), this agreement remains valid. For example, if you are taken hostage by a robber and you promise to pay a certain sum to a third party so that he comes to the rescue of you, this agreement between you and the third party is not affected by coercion. Presumably borrowing from Molina, Lessius holds that this promise cannot be regarded as extorted, since duress was not properly speaking the direct cause (*causa*) behind the contract. It only gave occasion (*occasio*) for the contract to be concluded.

Fernão Rebelo is as careful as Lessius in ruling out the possibility that indirect fear has an avoiding effect upon contracts.[915] He gives the example of a man who enters into a partnership (*societas*) in order to find shelter from an enemy. That contract can certainly not be avoided, since the duress exerted by the enemy is obviously not directed at making that man entering into a partnership with somebody else. In fact, Rebelo also introduced a distinction between two types of duress by analogy with the difference between *dolus causam dans* and *dolus incidens*. In this way he could limit the invalidating effects of duress in an alternative way. If duress had been the necessary motivating factor for the coerced party to

---

[914] Lessius, *De iustitia et iure*, lib. 2, cap. 17, dub. 6, num. 40, p. 203: 'Dixi, *si incussus fuit ad contractum eliciendum*, quia si ob alium finem incussus fuit, et ad illud malum evadendum contractus initus, non potest rescindi. Ut si captus a latrone, promittas tertio qui iniuriae non est particeps, 100 ut te liberet. Tunc enim metus non est proprie causa contractus, sed solum occasio, nec potest dici metu extortus, sed cum iam metus ob aliam causam est iniectus, adhibetur contractus tamquam medium ad illum pellendum. Itaque qui contractum tecum init non infert metum sed aliunde illatum aufert. Unde non meretur ut contractus ei rescindatur.'

[915] Rebelo, *Opus de obligationibus justitiae, religionis et charitatis*, Lugduni 1608, part. 2, lib. 1, quaest. 5, num. 9, p. 208: 'Addidi *ita ut ad extorquendum contractum iniuste inferatur*, quia, si ab hoste iniusto timens pro securitate contractum societatis cum alio inires, non ea de causa contractus foret invalidus.'

enter into the contract (*causa sine qua non*), it was to be deemed relevant.[916] Otherwise, it was not.

Less straightforward is the exposition by Joannes de Lugo about the direct relationship that is required between the evil event and the contract for rescission to be granted. In fact, hiding away behind the authority of 'other scholars', Lugo holds that no direct relationship is required at all for the contract to be avoided.[917] As long as the threats are illegitimate, they do annihilate a contract even if they are not issued with the immediate goal of causing the contract. Lugo admits that his view is not in line with Sánchez's.[918] Lugo is not fair, however, in claiming support from Lessius for this statement. Lessius—as we have just seen—does not at all think, as Lugo does, that 'occasional' yet illegitimate threats are tantamount to threats that have been issued with the direct purpose of causing the contract.

Lugo founds his view on the Roman law *Nec timorem* (D. 4,2,7). In paragraph *Proinde si* of that law it can be read, indeed, that relief on account of duress can be granted to a burglar or an adulterer who entered into an obligation (*se obligavit*) in order to escape the death penalty imposed on his offence if he is caught in the act. Lugo takes the example of a man who deflorates a young lady and is caught (defenceless) in the act by her parents or blood relatives. For fear of vengeance, however illegitimate,[919] and in order to escape death (*ut mortem evadat*), he spontaneously commits himself on the spot to marrying the girl in the presence of her parents.[920]

---

[916] Rebelo, *Opus de obligationibus justitiae, religionis et charitatis*, part. 2, lib. 1, quaest. 5, num. 9, p. 208: 'Dixi si modo metus sit causa sine qua non quia si alioqui, eras eodem modo contracturus, profecto libere simpliciter, et non ex metu contraxisse dicendus eris, ac proinde non est quod minus obligeris, quam si libere omnino faceres.'

[917] Lugo, *De iustitia et iure*, tom. 2, disp. 22, sect. 7, dub. 9, num. 175, p. 43: 'Alii denique aliter distinguunt, et quando metus principalis iuste infertur, concedunt valere matrimonium et alios contractus eo metu factos. Quando vero metus principalis iniuste incutitur eodem modo sentiunt ac si metus ad extorquendum contractum incuteretur.'

[918] Sánchez believes that it is of no importance whether the 'occasional' threats are legitimate or illegitimate. What matters is the direct or indirect relationship between the contract and the threats. Cf. *Disputationes de sancto matrimonii sacramento*, tom. 1, lib. 4, disp. 12, num. 11, p. 356: 'Impertinens est an metus ille conceptus fuerit ex causa iusta necne. Solus enim metus iniuste illatus ad extorquendum matrimonium illud dirimit, ut dixi num. 3.'

[919] Lugo, *De iustitia et iure*, tom. 2, disp. 22, sect. 7, dub. 6, num. 156, p. 39: 'Licet posset impune occidere, non tamen sine peccato mortali iniustitiae, quare metus ille omnino iniuste incutitur et obligat ad restitutionem.'

[920] Lugo, *De iustitia et iure*, tom. 2, disp. 22, sect. 7, dub. 9, num. 174/177, p. 43/44: 'Exemplum est, si aliquis in stupro deprehensus occidendus sit a parentibus vel consanguineis puellae, et ipse nemine petente, sed sponte sua matrimonium offerat, ut mortem evadat.'

According to Lugo, this marriage contract can be avoided on the grounds of coercion, even if the fear illegitimately (*injuste*) exerted by the parents is aimed at taking revenge rather than making the rapist marry their daughter.

Contrary to Sánchez, Rebelo and Lessius, Lugo does grant relief, then, even if the duress was not directed at causing the contract. He does so assuming that the duress was illegitimate. In this respect, the question that will be examined in the next section is different from the cases we have just seen. For it will concern coercion that is legitimately (*juste*) exerted on the contracting party in order to entice him into the contract. On the face of it, neither Lessius nor Lugo is willing to grant relief in that case. A contract entered into through legitimate coercion remains valid. But let us have a closer look at this discussion.

4.2.3.3   *The use and abuse of litigation rights*

Take the following case: a man who deflorates a young lady is caught in the act by her father. The father threatens the man with prosecution unless he enters into a marriage contract with the young lady. It is obvious to both Lessius and Lugo that a father can lawfully (*juste*) issue threats of taking the man to court, even if threatening to kill him would have been illegitimate.[921] Moreover, they agree that a marriage contract, just as any other contract, is not avoided by that kind of rightly exerted duress.

If litigation threats are legitimately issued, precisely because somebody has a right to sue the other party, then contracts entered into for fear of those threats remain valid. As Lessius puts it:[922] 'Those contracts cannot be set aside but on account of injustice. Injustice is absent, however, whenever duress can be exerted lawfully.' The problem with lawfully expressed litigation threats therefore mostly concerns the abuse thereof. For Lugo as well as Lessius the crux concerns people who pretend that they will exercise their legitimate right to litigation, thereby compelling

---

Quo casu parentes non intulerunt metum mortis ad extorquendum matrimonium, sed in vindictam criminis admissi et dedecoris illati, ipse tamen offert matrimonium, ut mortis periculum fugiat.' / 'Unde consequenter probatur eiusmodi metum sufficere ad irritandum matrimonium, professionem et votum, quia metus ille iniustus, qui obligat ad rescindendos alios contractus, sufficit ad haec irritanda (...).'

[921] Lessius, *De iustitia et iure*, lib. 2, cap. 17, dub. 6, num. 41, p. 203 and Lugo, *De iustitia et iure*, tom. 2, disp. 22, sect. 7, dub. 6, num. 155 and num. 158, p. 39–40.

[922] Lessius, *De iustitia et iure*, lib. 2, cap. 17, dub. 6, num. 41, p. 203: 'Ratio est, quia hi contractus non possunt irritari, nisi ratione iniuriae, quae abest, quando metus iuste incuti poterat.'

somebody to enter into a contract, but are actually not intent to do so (*ei qui minabatur accusationem non erat animus accusandi*).[923] Put differently, what are the effects of fictitious threats (*ficte minatus est*)?

Lessius and Lugo faced a dilemma as they tried to come to terms with fictitious litigation threats, because their older colleagues had defended divergent positions. In dealing with gaming contracts, Molina had considered invalid the following obligation entered into by the threatened party: I oblige myself to render the money I have won through a prohibited game in order that you stop threatening me to take me to court. A title (*causa/titulus*) can lie for this transaction, Molina admits, but only provided that the party issuing litigation threats really intends to sue the winner.[924] It is allowed to threaten with a legitimate claim. However, if the loser has no real intention of suing the winner, then he has no legitimate title to recover the money. For, in that event, the extortioner feigns to be intent on claiming back his money in court (*animum repetendi finxit fallacia ac simulatione*), while he merely intends to deter the other player. This is manifestly false.

Lessius shows understanding for Molina's standpoint and explains it as follows. Deceit has been the principal cause behind the transaction (*dolus causam dans*): the extortioner had promised to change minds provided that the other party gives or does something, but actually there had never been a mind to change (*ut deponas animum quem non habes*). At the same time, Lessius chooses not to endorse Molina's view. For he finds Sánchez's contrary standpoint much more probable. Sánchez held that if you have obtained a deal through legitimate litigation threats, this deal is valid, even if you did never have the intention of really taking the other person to court (*quamvis absque animo accusandi*).[925] What counts is that

---

923 Lessius, *De iustitia et iure*, lib. 2, cap. 17, dub. 6, num. 42, p. 203.

924 Molina, *De iustitia et iure*, tom. 2 (*De contractibus*), tract. 2, disp. 514, col. 1176, num. 4: 'Dubium item est, num quando conceditur repetitio pecuniae ludo prohibito acquisitae, fas sit ei, qui ludo illo eam amisit, comminari repetitionem, ac pacisci cum lucrante, ut partem sibi restituat, ne totam in iudicio repetat. Respondendum est affirmanter. Quoniam sicut fas est repetere, ita fas est comminari iustam repetitionem et accipere totum aut partem, ut repetitionem non intentet aut ut ab intentata desistat. Qui tamen, vel ob verecundiam ac infamiam, vel quacumque alia de causa repetiturus non erat, animumque repetendi finxit, ut alius deterritus, partem lucri restitueret, credo retineri id in conscientia non posset. Quoniam, qui ita restituit, iuste illud tanquam suum retinebat, et qui animum repetendi finxit, fallacia ac simulatione iniuste id ita ab illo extraxit, neque causa suberat, ob quam unus id dedit, et ob quam alius poterat iuste illud accipere.'

925 Sánchez, *Disputationes de sancto matrimonii sacramento*, tom. 1, lib. 4, disp. 9, num. 9, p. 349: 'Hinc infertur primo potentem aliquem iuste accusare, eoque timore illato, aliquid extorquentem, ne accuset, minime teneri restituere. Quia iuste poterat accusare,

you are entitled to take somebody to court (*ius accusandi*). Renouncing this right comes at a price for the intimidated party.

Lugo, however, takes sides with Molina. He refuses to share Sánchez's and Lessius' rigorous rights-based talk. Even if you have a right to sue somebody, you are not allowed therefore to coerce somebody into an agreement in exchange for fictitiously renouncing that right. That would definitely be too high a price to pay. It is precisely the will to exercise a right which increases its price.[926] If, in truth, you do not experience that intention, the price of your litigation right is worth much lower a price. Moreover, once deceit causes a contract (*dolus causam dans*) it is not relevant whether the threats constituting the deceit are issued legitimately or illegitimately.[927] Every deceit without which a contract would not have been concluded is to be deemed as unjust.

While Lugo argues that Sánchez's opinion is likely to leave the door wide open to contractual fraud, Lessius defends it obstinately. He admits that from an objective point view, one could maintain that a person who is compelled to do something on the basis of somebody else's right is acting in no less involuntary a way than somebody who is coerced unjustly.[928] He points out, however, that from a subjective point of view just coercion does not result in consent that is to be deemed involuntary. For the fear stemming from just coercion is considered to draw its origins not from a force external to the intimidated party, but from a force that comes from within the person himself (*ab ipsomet*). Hence the assent subsequent to

---

privaturque actione accusandi quam habebat. (...) Et credo id esse verum, quamvis absque animo accusandi minaretur accusationem. Adhuc enim non tenetur eo metu extortum restituere. Quia adhuc privatur iure accusandi, quod pretio aestimabile est.'

[926] Lugo, *De iustitia et iure*, tom. 2, disp. 22, sect. 7, dub. 7, num. 168, p. 42: 'Adde, ius sine voluntate accusandi non tantum valere, quantum pro eo petitur, sed voluntas accusandi auget valorem talis iuris.'

[927] Lugo, *De iustitia et iure*, tom. 2, disp. 22, sect. 7, dub. 7, num. 168, p. 42: 'Gratis dicitur, quod ille dolus sit iustus. Omnis enim dolus qui dat causam contractui eo ipso est iniustus, cum ordinetur ad extorquendum consensum per fraudem et mendacia, et inferat re ipsa damnum contrahenti, cui revera inutilis est ille contractus, cum ius accusandi sine voluntate parum illi noceret.'

[928] Lessius, *De iustitia et iure*, lib. 2, cap. 17, dub. 6, num. 42, p. 203: 'Si physice res consideretur, non minus involuntarie consentit qui iuste cogitur quam qui iniuste. Uterque enim consentit repugnante voluntate, tum per simplicem affectum nolitionis, tum per dolorem animi. Moraliter tamen loquendo, is qui iuste cogitur non censetur involuntarie consentire, quia voluntarie causam metus et coactionis dedit. Unde timor ille mali non censetur extrinsecus inferre, sed ab illomet nasci, ac proinde consensus inde secutus non censetur involutarius, cum sit omnino voluntarius in sua causa. Qui vero iniuste cogitur, censetur involuntarie consentire, quia causa metus non est illi voluntaria, nec ab ipso ortum habuit, sed solum a causa extrinseca.'

this inner coercion is not deemed to be involuntary, since it is entirely voluntary as to its cause (*voluntarius in sua causa*).

Importantly, Lessius insists that 'freedom of contract' is tantamount to absence of external coercion in entering into a contract:[929] 'The doctors talk about free consent, if it has not been extorted through an external cause, namely by unjust duress, or induced through deceit. If you are coerced by a just cause, 'freedom of contract' (*libertas contractuum*) is not affected.' It turns out that for theologians as Lessius, there is simply no contradiction between acting freely and following just causes. After all, man is expected to follow right reason (*recta ratio*), and considered to attain the highest degree of freedom in observing its dictates. A man acts more freely than ever when he internalizes just causes.

What is more, Lessius indicates that fear is about psychology and appearance rather than objective truth and reality. It does not matter whether an evil event is really out there. What counts is the perception of the evil event in the mind of the intimidated party (*malum non causat metum nisi quatenus apprehensum*). This is an analytical insight of Lessius of which even Lugo approves.[930] Applied to our case, however, it means that it is of no relevance whether the litigation threats are based on an actual will to take the intimidated party to court or not. As long as the intimidating party is perceived to have the intention of actually executing his right, the same degree of (legitimate) duress affects the intimidated party.

It needs to be noted, however, that Lessius was also clear about the limits of using litigation rights as a means of pressure. The value of the obligation or the thing the intimidating party receives in exchange for renouncing his litigation right must be proportionate to the value of the litigation right.[931] In other words, one must not abuse his litigation rights.

---

[929] Lessius, *De iustitia et iure*, lib. 2, cap. 17, dub. 6, num. 43, p. 203: 'Liberum vocant, non coactum a causa extrinseca, seu per metum iniustum, et dolo non inductum. Si enim cogaris ex causa iusta, id non officit libertati contractuum.'

[930] Lugo, *De iustitia et iure*, tom. 2, disp. 22, sect. 7, dub. 7, num. 166, p. 41: 'metus non causatur proxime ex malo, sed ex apprehensione illius quae eadem est et aeque moveor, sive animus exsequendi adsit, sive non adsit, ut notavit Lessius (...)'.

[931] Lessius, *De iustitia et iure*, lib. 2, cap. 17, dub. 6, num. 45, p. 204: 'Adverte tamen, si nimis gravis sit obligatio vel res quam metum inferens exigit, et non habeat proportionem cum iure quo ipse cedit, malum intentatum remittens, vel cum opera quam praestat, malum aliunde impendens avertens, posse consensum revocari, quo ad illum excessum, ut contractus ad aequalitatem reducatur, ut si, ne accusem te furti vel alterius criminis, exigam maiorem partem bonorum (...). In his enim aliqua proportio et aequalitas servanda est, prout prudentia determinabit; quae si excedatur, committitur iniustitia, ac proinde tenetur alter ad restitutionem; quam si non fecerit, potest laesus uti occulta compensatione, alia via recuperandi non suppetente.'

A certain proportionality and equality must always be observed in exercising a right (*proportio et aequalitas servanda*). If not, the intimidated party can take the law in his own hands and seek secret compensation (*occulta compensatio*) for the excess value that has been extorted from him. For instance, the litigation right is abandoned in favor of the transfer of almost all of your possessions.

To sum up, then, Lugo is as careful as Molina in avoiding contracts that are based on fictitious litigation threats. Lessius, on the other hand, further develops Sánchez's idea that it is allowed to extort an obligation in exchange for renouncing a litigation right (*ius accusandi*), even if you never seriously considered exercising that right. Lessius does not approve, however, of abuse of litigation rights.

4.2.3.4   *Minor fear*

In view of the lasting influence of the scholastics on Hugo Grotius, it is worthwhile drawing the attention to an important fixation by Lessius of what had hitherto been a point of constant dispute amongst the scholastics: does minor fear (*metus levis*) give rise to annulment or not? Sole reverential fear without threats and importunate pressure without real danger of violence, for instance, were still considered as amounting to minor fear. Yet even Sánchez had remained quite confused about whether minor fear could give rise to annulment of a contract or not—although he seems to have eventually recognized that restitution must be made.[932] Rebelo, for his part, stated that minor fear that had given cause to the contract rendered a contract automatically invalid in the court of conscience. In the external court, he thought minor fear made the contract voidable.[933]

With Lessius, however, we see an unprecedently clear, firm, and well-developed recognition that minor fear has a real effect upon the validity of coerced contracts other than marriage in the court of conscience. For

---

[932] Sánchez, *Disputationes de sancto matrimonii sacramento*, tom. 1, lib. 4, disp. 9–11, p. 348–355.

[933] Rebelo, *Opus de obligationibus justitiae, religionis et charitatis*, part. 2, lib. 1, quaest. 5, num. 17, p. 211: 'Ex dictis habes contractus tam lucrosos quam onerosos extortos tam per metum gravem quam levem, si causa sine qua non sit, in foro conscientiae esse ipso iure irritos. In foro vero iudiciali similiter declarandos esse fuisse etiam irritos, si per gravem metum facti sint; si per levem, rescindi posse si constet metum fuisse eorum causam sine qua non fierent.'

this he quoted Sylvester, Dr. Navarrus, and Covarruvias.[934] Building on these authors, Lessius holds that contracts affected by minor fear are to be considered voidable at the option of the coerced party.[935] He points out that it is not unlikely for minor fear to throw a man off balance as much as grave fear (*non minus perturbat hominem*). Secondly, the goods extorted from the coerced party have been obtained through injury (*iniuria*). Hence, they must be restituted to the injured party. Last, the man who suffers from minor fear is nevertheless unjustly deprived of his freedom (*privatur per iniuriam sua libertate*). Therefore he must get the chance of freely rejecting or confirming the agreement.

Lessius recognizes that minor fear is deemed irrelevant in the external court, to the effect that there are no civil laws which enforce the claims of a party who suffered from *metus levis*. He even thinks that this policy before the external courts is a particularly sound and prudent one. Just as Covarruvias, he points out that, otherwise, the courts would be over-extended (*ne lites in immensum excrescant*).[936] The court of conscience, however, cannot take into account these policy related considerations. The internal forum solely attends the truth, which says that minor fear constitutes a form of injury (*iniuria*). Contrary to Sánchez, therefore, Lessius is not reluctant to grant relief to somebody who assents to a contract for simple reverential fear (*solus metus reverentialis*) or under importunate pressure (*preces importunae*).[937]

4.2.3.5   *Void* vs *voidable contracts*

As we have noted above, one of the most significant contributions of Sánchez to the development of modern contract law concerned his elaborately drawn out distinction between nullity *ab initio* and voidability. He thereby clearly decided to sanction duress with nullity at the option of the

---

934 Sylvester Prierias, *Summa Sylvestrina*, part. 2, s.v. *restitutio* 2, dict. 7, f. 263r: 'Sed in conscientia, ubi dicta praesumptio non habet locum contra veritatem, ubicunque constiterit de qualicunque metu, necessaria est restitutio.' Compare Azpilcueta, *Enchiridion sive manuale confessariorum et poenitentium*, cap. 17, num. 15, p. 280; and Covarruvias, *In regulam peccatum*, part. 2, par. 3, num. 7, p. 485.

935 Lessius, *De iustitia et iure*, lib. 2, cap. 17, dub. 6, num. 46, p. 204: 'Etsi ea quae per metum levem acta sunt, sint aliquo modo valida, nec in foro externo admittatur exceptio huius metus, nec detur actio ad rescindendum contractum, tamen in foro conscientiae possunt in irritum revocari et quae tradita sunt repeti, et qui ea obtinet, tenetur restituere, si metus ille per iniuriam ad illa extorquenda sit incussus.'

936 Lessius, *De iustitia et iure*, lib. 2, cap. 17, dub. 6, num. 49, p. 205.

937 Lessius, *De iustitia et iure*, lib. 2, cap. 17, dub. 6, num. 48, p. 204–205.

wronged party. It is not unlikely, however, that it is to the credit of Lessius to have guaranteed that the recognition of a general regime of voidability to duress eventually became the mainstream opinion. For there definitely was no unanimous agreement on that immediately after Sánchez had tried to settle the discussion.

Within the Jesuit order itself, opinions were divided. We have already seen that only a few years before Sánchez was going to publish his *De matrimonio*, Molina claimed that duress resulted in nullity *ab initio*. After the publication of Sánchez's *magnum opus*, too, this idea remained vivid. Fernão Rebelo claimed that contracts affected by coercion were indiscriminately void from the very outset (*ipso iure irritus*).[938] If duress had been the necessary motivating factor for the coerced party to assent to the contract (*causa sine qua non*), the contract was automatically void. Rebelo argued that this was the case in both the external and the internal forum, provided that the coercion was considerable.

Others treaded a third path to solve the problem. It was ascribed to the Augustinian friar Pedro de Aragón. He allegedly maintained that onerous contracts were voidable, whereas gratuitous contracts tainted by duress were null *ipso facto*.[939] Gratuitous contracts such as liberal promises and donations were thought to require an even higher degree of freedom. Hence duress was thought to have an even more pernicious effect on gratuitous contracts than on onerous contracts. In spite of his otherwise great indebtedness to Sánchez, the Augustinian friar and theologian Basilio Ponce de León (1570–1629) followed Pedro de Aragón's alleged line of thought.[940] This is rather exceptional, since Ponce de León usually followed Sánchez fairly closely. Also, he shared with Sánchez the project of giving a systematic treatment of matrimonial law which was not only useful for theologians, but also for the canonists and the civilians, as is obvious from the addition to the title of this treatise on marriage law (*opus aeque canonici et civilis iuris ac sacrae theologiae professoribus utile ac necessarium*).[941]

---

[938] Rebelo, *Opus de obligationibus justitiae, religionis et charitatis*, part. 2, lib. 1, quaest. 5, num. 17, p. 211 (cited above).

[939] This is not that clear, though, at least not from Aragón, *In secundam secundae commentaria de iustitia et iure*, quaest. 89, art. 7, p. 1007.

[940] Basilio Ponce de León, *De sacramento matrimonii tractatus*, Opus aeque canonici et civilis iuris ac sacrae theologiae professoribus utile ac necessarium, Bruxellis 1632, lib. 4, cap. 6, num. 4, p. 193.

[941] On Ponce de León, see J.F. von Schulte, *Die Geschichte der Quellen und Literatur des canonischen Rechts von Gratian bis auf die Gegenwart*, Buch 3.1: *Vom Concil von Trient bis*

Lessius' plea constituted an almost indispensable support, then, in enhancing the chances of survival for Sánchez's doctrine about the annulment of contracts as a result of duress. This actually seems to have been Lessius' explicit concern, as the whole *dubitatio* on duress is entirely structured around the question whether duress makes contracts void or voidable. He concludes, of course, that coerced contracts are not void but voidable (*irritandi*). But in order to be able to do so, he needs to procede methodically by arguing, first, that duress does not result in automatic nullity as a matter of natural law, and, secondly, that duress does not result in automatic nullity as a matter of positive law. Quoting paragraph *Si metu coactu* from law *Si mulier* (D. 4,2,21,5), constitution *Venditiones* (C. 2,19,12) and canon *Abbas* (X 1,40,2), the latter proved to be an easy job.[942] Lessius' argumentation with respect to natural law turns out to be much more interesting.

Lessius rehearses a standard idea of the early modern scholastics in order to demonstrate that relative nullity is the natural solution to coerced consent: a contract cannot be absolutely void as a matter of natural law but for want of consent (*defectus consensus*) or its containing injustice (*iniuria*).[943] Lessius acknowledges that a party consenting under compulsion suffers from a certain kind of unwillingness (*nolleitas*), but in line with Thomistic psychology he refuses to accord any significance to the element of involuntariness.[944] True, a party would not have consented *if* the evil event had been absent. But the evil was present. The condition that the evil had not been there has not been met (*conditio non extet*).

---

zum Jahre 1870, Das katholische Recht und die katholischen Schriftsteller, Graz 1956 [= Stuttgart 1880], p. 740.

[942] Lugo, on the other hand, painstakingly spent much time considering every single Roman or canon law that could be adduced against or in favor of voidability, only to conclude that Sánchez and Lessius are right (*non invenio firmum fundamentum contra primam sententiam Lessii et Sanchii*). Cf. Lugo, *De iustitia et iure*, tom. 2, disp. 22, sect. 7, dub. 2, num. 118–132, p. 30–33.

[943] Lessius, *De iustitia et iure*, lib. 2, cap. 17, dub. 6, num. 36, p. 201: 'Si est omnino irritus iure naturae, id provenit vel defectu consensus, vel quia intervenit iniuria.'

[944] Lessius, *De iustitia et iure*, lib. 2, cap. 17, dub. 6, num. 36, p. 201: 'Non defectu consensus, quia qui metu coactus consentit, absolute consentit voluntarie: omnibus enim consideratis, vult. Nec obstat, quod illi volitioni iungatur nolitio, quia est solum nolleitas, ut ita dicam, qua nollet, si timor mali abesset; quae proinde est omnino inefficax, cum conditio non extet.'

On *nolleitas* and *velleitas* as well as Thomistic psychology in general, see A. Robiglio, *L'impossibile volere, Tommaso d'Aquino, i tomisti e la volontà*, Milano 2002, esp. p. 40.

In Lessius' view, the contract cannot be declared automatically void on account of injustice either.[945] Injustice cannot be sufficient grounds to set aside a contract automatically (*non sufficiens ut ipsum reddat omnino irritum*). Injustice can be sufficient grounds, however, as a matter of natural law, to revoke consent (*sufficiens causa ad revocandum consensum*). That is the way Lessius had explained that contracts affected by mistake or deceit are not void, but voidable.[946] This is the very point Lessius wants to make: even though coerced contracts are not legally void (*irriti*), they are voidable at the option of the coerced party (*irritandi*). This is also the explicit point he makes in his theoretical discussion of the voluntary and the involuntary in human agency.[947]

Since marriage is a contract, Lessius concludes in his small treatise *De matrimonio* that marriage would also need to be subject to the regime of voidability as a matter of natural law. As a general rule of contract law, coerced consent does not result in the invalidity of the contract automatically, since coerced consent is consent anyway. There is a possibility of rescission at the option of the intimidated party, because in this way the injury which he suffered can be undone. Marriage is an exception to this rule, however, because the positive, ecclesiastical law took away the possibility of rescission at the option of the coerced party, since marriage is indissoluble. Therefore, marriage contracts affected by duress have come to be considered as being absolutely null.[948]

---

[945] Lessius, *De iustitia et iure*, lib. 2, cap. 17, dub. 6, num. 36, p. 202: 'Non etiam ratione iniuriae: tum quia iniuria non est immediata causa contractus, sed consensus contrahentis, tum quia etsi iniuria possit esse sufficiens causa ad revocandum consensum et contractum irritandum, non tamen est sufficiens ut ipsum reddat omnino irritum, ut patet in contractu, cui dolus causam dedit, qui, etsi iniuria interveniat, non tamen est iure naturae irritus, sed irritandus (...).'

[946] See the second part of this chapter.

[947] Lessius, *In I.II D. Thomae de beatitudine et actibus humanis*, quaest. 6, art. 6, num. 38, p. 45: 'Itaque secluso iure positivo, verius existimo, matrimonium metu gravi contractum, esse validum, modo interveniat ultro citroque idonea materia, in qua contractus versetur, nempe personarum habilitas. Idem dico de emptione, venditione, permutatione, locatione, et similibus contractibus. Possunt tamen huiusmodi contractus sic initi, excepto matrimonio, facile irritari, voluntate eius, qui iniuriam passus est, nam potest petere restitutionem in integrum, et agere de damno illato. Excipio matrimonium, quia semel contractum, natura sua est insolubile, unde iure positivo ab initio debuit irritum decerni.'

[948] Lessius, *De matrimonii sacramento*, cap. 4, dub. 8, p. 359, in: *De beatitudine, de actibus humanis, de incarnatione Verbi, de sacramentis et censuris praelectiones theologicae posthumae. Acceserunt variorum casuum conscientiae resolutiones*, Lovanii 1645: 'Cum enim matrimonium natura sua sit insolubile, fit ut semel contractum, sive iure, sive iniuria, non possit dissolvi, sicut possunt alii contractus. Unde merito Ecclesia, ut huic tanto incommodo occurreret, statuit talem contractum ab initio esse irritum, et personas ad sic

To sum up, except for the case of marriage contracts, Lessius equally adopts the regime of relative nullity in the case of mistake and deceit, on the one hand, and the case of duress and coercion, on the other. What is more, he expressly employs the analogy with the doctrine of mistake in order to prove that contracts affected by duress are also voidable at the option of the injured party. This, Lugo points out in an exposition that is heavily indebted to Lessius', is the very advantage Lessius and he have in comparison to Sánchez.[949] Contrary to Lessius and Lugo, Sánchez had not recognized a general regime of voidability for contracts affected by *dolus causam dans*. Therefore he could not, as Lessius and Lugo would, construct an argument based on an analogy with the doctrine of mistake.

4.2.4   *A brief synthesis of the scholastic tradition on duress (Grotius)*

The early modern scholastics' wavering expositions—abounding in juridical technicalities and tough casuistry generated by the direct application of generally established principles to practical cases—make for intellectually stimulating, yet pretty arduous reading. Even if a Jesuit as Lessius gets near to the easy-to-read humanist style of Grotius, it is still a quite delightful experience to switch from the scholastic treatises to Grotius' plain and succinct reflections on duress in his *Law of war and peace*.[950] The great poet, jurist and theologian from Delft comforts his reader by acknowledging that previous attempts to come to grips with coerced contracts have been confusingly complicated (*implicata tractatio*).

This does not mean, however, that there is no use in trying to understand the challenging demonstrations of the scholastic coryphaei. For one thing, Grotius expressly recognizes his debt to the scholastics as he presents his own outline of the doctrine of duress. For another thing, there is much intellectual enjoyment in admiring the elegance with which Grotius

---

contrahendum inhabiles. In caeteris contractibus haec irritatio non erat necessaria, cum voluntate contrahentium solvi possint.'

[949] Lugo, *De iustitia et iure*, tom. 2, disp. 22, sect. 7, dub. 2, num. 119, p. 30: 'Quarto arguitur, quia dolus dans causam contractui reddit illum irritum de iure positivo. Cum ergo dolus et metus aequiparentur, cap. cum contingat, de iureiurando, idem dicendum est de contractibus ex metu factis. Ad hoc conatur Sánchez reddere rationem discriminis inter dolum et metum. Nos tamen facilius negamus antecedens, quia ut diximus sectione praecedenti, contractus etiam ex dolo facti validi sunt, sed rescindendi (...).'

[950] Grotius, *De jure belli ac pacis* (Ed. De Kanter-Van Hettinga Tromp – Feenstra – Persenaire), lib. 2, cap. 11, par. 7, p. 332–333.

offers a synthesis of the doctrines we have seen painstakingly mounted by the early modern canonists and theologians.

A major point where Grotius follows the Aristotelian-Thomistic tradition is in denying that duress results in lack of consent.[951] Contrary to mistake, duress is not actually considered to be a vice of the will in the first place (*consensus hic adfuit absolutus*). He insists, just as Lessius, that there is a problem with duress from the point of view of justice and not from the point of view of consent. He uses the Roman expression 'damage caused by injury' (*damnum iniuria datum*). So tort law, and not contract law, is seen to constitute the basis of the relief that should be granted to the coerced party. Hence, the contract is not automatically void. Robert Joseph Pothier, the famous French natural lawyer, followed Grotius on this point. Consequently, he adopted the scholastic view of duress: the injury which the extortioner inflicts on me through duress liberates me from my contractual obligation, not because a coerced contract is void from the beginning, but by way of compensation for the injustice done.[952]

Moreover, Grotius deems minor fear (*metus levis*) to be tantamount to grave fear.[953] He thereby quotes Sylvester, Dr. Navarrus and Covarruvias—that is, exactly the authors quoted by Lessius in making exactly the same point when he confirms the relevance of minor fear in the court of conscience. As long as the fear is exerted unlawfully (*metus iniustus*), the contract is avoidable at the option of the coerced party.

---

[951] Grotius, *De jure belli ac pacis* (Ed. De Kanter-Van Hettinga Tromp – Feenstra – Persenaire), lib. 2, cap. 11, par. 7, num. 2, p. 332–333: 'Ego omnino illorum accedo sententiae qui existimant, seposita lege civili quae obligationem potest tollere aut minuere, eum qui metu promisit aliquid, obligari: quia consensus hic adfuit, nec conditionalis, ut modo in errante dicebamus, sed absolutus.'

[952] Pothier, *Traité des obligations, selon les regles, tant du for de la conscience, que du for extérieur*, part. 1, sec. 1, art. 3, par. 2 (du défaut de liberté), p. 27: '(...) on ne peut pas dire comme dans le cas de l'erreur, qu'il n'y ait point eu absolument de contrat; il y en a un, mais il est vicieux (...) l'injustice que vous avez commise envers moi, en exerçant cette violence, vous oblige de votre côté à m'indemniser de ce que j'en ai souffert; et cette indemnité consiste à m'acquitter de l'obligation que vous m'avez obligé de contracter; d'où il suit que mon obligation, quand on en supposeroit une, ne peut être valable selon le droit naturel; c'est la raison que donne Grotius.'

[953] Grotius, *De jure belli ac pacis* (Ed. De Kanter-Van Hettinga Tromp – Feenstra – Persenaire), lib. 2, cap. 11, par. 7, num. 2, p. 333: 'Sed illud simul verissimum censeo, si is cui promittitur metum intulerit non iustum, sed iniustum, quamvis levem, atque inde secuta sit promissio, eum teneri ad liberandum promissorem, si promissor velit; non quod inefficax fuerit promissio, sed ob damnum iniuria datum.'

Grotius even seems to have taken seriously what Lessius carefully suggested against the common opinion of the scholastics: the annulment of a contract on account of duress exerted by a third party is based on civil law rather than natural law. Inspired by Lessius, Grotius held that, as a matter of natural law, I am bound to perform a contract, even if I have entered into it because I was coerced by a third party.[954] Hence, the rule that a contract could be avoided because of duress exerted by a third party merely pertained to civil law. Grotius drew criticism for this standpoint in the work of Pothier. The French natural lawyer preferred the contrary opinion as defended by Pufendorf and Barbeyrac: natural law does not oblige me to observe a contract that I have entered into because a third party unduly influenced me.[955] In this manner, Pothier indirectly expressed his preference for the traditional opinion of the scholastics instead of following Lessius' and Grotius' novel idea.

4.3   MISTAKE (*DOLUS/ERROR*)

4.3.1   *Foundations*

4.3.1.1   *Romano-canon law*

The Roman distinction between *actiones bonae fidei* and *stricti iuris* as a basis for dealing with the effects of mistake (*error/dolus*) is sufficiently well-known—at least from its interpretation in the Middle Ages onwards.[956] Paragraph *Actionum autem* (Inst. 4,6,28) in conjunction with paragraph *Societas* (D. 17,2,3,3) could be taken to mean that *bonae fidei* contracts

---

[954] Grotius, *De jure belli ac pacis* (Ed. De Kanter-Van Hettinga Tromp – Feenstra – Persenaire), lib. 2, cap. 11, par. 7, num. 3, p. 333: 'Quod vero quidam actus rescinduntur ob metum ab alio incussum, quam quicum metum est, ex lege est civili, quae saepe etiam actus libere factos ob iudicii firmitatem, aut irritos facit, aut revocabiles.'
Compare with Lessius, *De iustitia et iure*, lib. 2, cap. 17, dub. 6, num. 39, p. 202–203: 'Plerique doctores videntur sentire, ex iure naturae (…) Crediderim tamen, etc…'.
[955] Pothier, *Traité des obligations, selon les regles, tant du for de la conscience, que du for extérieur*, p. 28–29: 'Puffendorf et Barbeyrac pensent au contraire, que dans les termes mêmes du pur droit naturel, lorsque j'ai été contraint par violence à contracter, le contrat ne m'oblige point, quoique celui avec qui j'ai contracté n'ait eu aucune part à la violence.'
[956] See, for instance, Zimmermann, *The law of obligations*, p. 671, and M.J. Schermaier, *Bona fides in Roman contract law*, in: R. Zimmermann – S. Whittaker (eds.), Good faith in European contract law, [The Common Core of European Private Law, Cambridge Studies in International and Comparative Law, 14], Cambridge 2000, p. 63–92.

were void *ipso iure* when entered into because of deceit.[957] On the basis of paragraph *Non solum* (D. 4,3,7,3) in conjunction with law *Dolo vel metu* (C. 8,38,5), amongst other texts, it could be argued that contracts *stricti iuris* were not void automatically, but that the deceived party could be granted relief by means of an *exceptio doli* and an *actio de dolo*.[958]

Even if a combination of other texts and interpretations could have led to other views—as will be attested by Lessius' and Lugo's alternative exegesis—this distinction was sanctified in the thirteenth century by the ordinary gloss *Si in hoc ipso* to law *Et eleganter* (D. 4,3,7pr.). The canon law tradition added further weight to this interpretation through gloss *Bonae fidei* to canon *Quum venerabilis* (X 2,25,6). The latter gloss referred to the abovementioned paragraph *Actionum autem* in Justinian's Institutes to explain which contracts were *bonae fidei* and which were not. In *bonae fidei* contracts, moratory interests were due (*usurae ex tempore morae*) and the judge could add obligations the parties had not thought of. The gloss maintained the distinction between these two types of contracts in regard to the effects of mistake. However, it emphasized that any contract, regardless of whether it is *stricti iuris* or *bonae fidei*, must observe good faith (*bona fides*).[959] If Roman law had given some contracts the more explicit adjective 'of good faith', this merely meant that the office of the judge was even more extended in the interpretation of contracts of good faith than in the interpretation of contracts of strict law.

The distinction between *bonae fidei* and *stricti iuris* contracts was compounded by yet another distinction that arose in the medieval

---

[957] Inst. 4,6,28 in *Corporis Iustinianaei Institutiones* (ed. Gothofredi), tom. 4, col. 492: 'Actionum autem quaedam bonae fidei sunt, quaedam stricti iuris, bonae fidei sunt hae: ex empto, vendito, locato, conducto, negotiorum gestorum, mandati, depositi, pro socio, tutelae, commodati, pigneraticia, familiae erciscundae, communi dividundo, praescriptis verbis quae de aestimato proponitur et ea quae ex permutatione competit, et hereditatis petitio.'

D. 17,2,3,3 in *Corporis Iustinianaei Digestum vetus* (ed. Gothofredi), tom. 1, col. 1685: 'Societas si dolo malo aut fraudandi causa coita sit, ipso iure nullius momenti est, quia fides bona contraria est fraudi et dolo.' Compare D. 4,4,16,1.

[958] C. 8,38,5 in *Corporis Iustinianaei Codex* (ed. Gothofredi), tom. 4, col. 1953: 'Dolo vel metu adhibito actio quidem nascitur, ut subdita stipulatio sit, per doli tamen vel metus exceptionem submoveri petitio debet.'

[959] Gloss *Bonae fidei* to X 2,25,6 in *Corpus juris canonici* (ed. Gregoriana), part. 2, col. 841: 'Non dicuntur bonae fidei, quia in eis tantum servari debeat bona fides, quia in contractibus stricti iuris servari debet bona fides, et in quocunque contractu bona fides intervenire debet. (...) In actionibus bonae fidei multum exuberat officium iudicis et pinguius quam in actionibus stricti iuris, et istis rationibus dicuntur bonae fidei et aliae dicuntur stricti iuris.'

interpretations of the Roman law, particularly of law *Et eleganter*[960]—perhaps under influence of the Aristotelian account of ignorance. Depending on whether the deceit had been fundamental to the conclusion of the contract or merely incidental, *dolus causam dans contractui* was distinguished from *dolus incidens contractui*. In the case of *dolus causam dans*, the deceived party would not have concluded the contract, if he had not been mistaken. Therefore, a *bonae fidei* contract affected by *dolus causam dans* was deemed void. In the case of *dolus incidens*, the party would still have wished to conclude the contract, albeit under more favorable conditions. As a consequence, the contract was not deemed void, although damages could be claimed.

During the Middle Ages, the Roman distinction between *bonae fidei* and *stricti iuris* contracts was generally accepted. In the scholastic tradition, the name of the Orléans professor Pierre de Belleperche became increasingly associated, however, with an alternative opinion, holding that both types of contract are voidable if they are affected by mistake.

Belleperche seems to have defended that contracts affected by fundamental mistake are not void but voidable, indeed. The thrust of Belleperche's argument, however, remains directed towards the idea that all contracts must be performed in good faith, even though there is a category of actions called *stricti iuris* in addition to the category of sixteen actions called *bonae fidei*. The latter are called *bonae fidei* because they are characterized by *bona fides* to a superior degree (*propter exuberantiam bonaefidei*).[961] Yet that does not mean, *a contrario*, that *bona fides* is not required in actions *stricti iuris*.[962] So far, Belleperche's reasoning is just a confirmation of gloss *Bonae fidei* to canon *Quum venerabilis* (X 2,25,6).

What seems novel in Belleperche is that he infers from this that it is not correct to say that contracts *stricti iuris* must be avoided by an *actio*

---

[960] See Glossa *Si in hoc ipso* ad D. 4,3,7pr. in *Corporis Iustinianaei Digestum vetus* (ed. Gothofredi), tom. 1, cols. 508–509.

[961] Pierre de Belleperche, *In libros Institutionum commentarii*, Lugduni 1536, ad Inst. 4,6,28, num. 1, p. 712–713: 'Opponitur, dicitur hic quaedam sunt bonaefidei. Contra divisio habet fieri ex opposito supponit quod actiones stricti iuris non requirunt bonam fidem. Contra C. de actio. et oblig. l. bonamfidem. Dico concedo quod in omnibus contractibus requiritur bonafides, et hoc dicitur hic propter exuberantiam bonaefidei, sic. l. alleg. ff. de verborum obliga. l. qui autem.§.qui id quod.'

[962] Belleperche, *In libros Institutionum commentarii*, ad Inst. 4,6,28, num. 2, p. 713: 'Quare dicuntur bonaefidei istae actiones? Dico non per abnegationem bonaefidei in actionibus stricti iuris: nam in omnibus requiritur bonafides, ut l. alleg. bonamfidem. Sed propter excellentiam quae exuberat vel aliter in l. alleg. in illis maior exuberantia requiritur bonaefidei. Dicit glossa, in multis.'

de dolo, while contracts *bonae fidei* are immediately void because of mistake. Belleperche then tries to propose a regime of voidability for both types of contract.[963] Using distinctively Aristotelian terminology, he distinguishes contracts whose substance (*forma*) is vitiated from contracts whose substance is not vitiated.[964] Mistake is an example of an external cause (*causa extrinseca*), which does not affect the substance of the contract itself. Hence, the contractual obligation ensuing from the contract does not cease to exist.

Belleperche's argument constitutes a compelling deviation from the common opinion—and it would be perceived as such in the subsequent scholastic tradition. To our knowledge, Belleperche did not develop, however, an argument about the equal deficiency of voluntary consent in both *stricti iuris* and *bonae fidei*—as Summenhart later pretended Belleperche did. What is distinctive in Belleperche's treatment of deceit is that he foresees a regime of voidability for both contracts *stricti iuris* and *bonae fidei*. Belleperche's plea in favor of the abolition of the distinction of both types of contract was later confirmed by Cino da Pistoia (c. 1270–1336/7).[965] Just as Belleperche, Cino held that both types of contracts were affected in the same way by deceit. Also, he refused to acknowledge that the superior

---

[963] Belleperche, *In libros Institutionum commentarii*, ad Inst. 4,6,28, num. 3, p. 715: 'Scire debetis quandoque dolus dat causam contractui ubi non eras alias venditurus alias incidit in contracu ubi alias eras venditurus te indui: ut mihi pro minori pretio venderes, ubi dolus dat causam contractui tenet regulariter per rationem legis quae dicit quotiens forma contractus non continet vitium, licet extrinsecatio sit vitiosa mihi, nihilominus obligatio procedit ipso iure. Sed ubi forma in se vitiosa est, non contrahitur obligatio secundum causam, ut promittis interficere hominem primo casu promittis mihi decem ne interficiam, hic contrahitur obligatio licet causa extrinseca inspecta descendat ex dolo. (…) Et nun ubi indui te per dolum ut vendas mihi forma non est vitiosa, ideo, etc.'

[964] The Aristotelian-Thomistic influence on Pierre de Belleperche and the jurists of the school of Orléans in general should not necessarily come as a surprise. Most of the clergy who taught at the law school of Orléans had previously followed 'Thomist type theological studies' in Paris, according to A. Errera, *The role of logic in the legal science of the glossators and commentators, Distinction, dialectical syllogism, and apodictic syllogism, An investigation into the epistemological roots of legal science in the late middle ages*, in: A. Padovani – P. Stein (eds.), The jurists' philosophy of law from Rome to the seventeenth century, [A treatise of legal philosophy and general jurisprudence, 7], Dordrecht – New York 2007, p. 2007, p. 136–141.

[965] Cino da Pistoia, *Lectura super Codice*, Venetiis 1493, ad C. 4,44,2, f. 187v: 'Modo videamus ubi dolo contrahitur, utrum contractus sit nullus. Glossae distinguunt. Aut enim contractus stricti iuris, aut bonaefidei. Si stricti iuris, indistincte tenetur contractus et non est ipso iure nullus. (…) Si est contractus bonae fidei, aut dat causam contractui, et tunc ipso iure non tenetur (…), aut incidit, et tunc tenetur. (…) Istud non reputat Pe[trus Bellapertica] verum esse, sed dicit quod indistincte tenet contractus nec habet legem contra se (…).' [continuation in next footnote]

degree of good faith required in contracts *bonae fidei* meant that those contracts needed to be declared void *ab initio* when affected by deceit.[966] It only meant that they had an action named after their own name instead of the usual *actio de dolo*. He argued that a *bonae fidei* contract must not be automatically void, since a contract affected by duress also involved *dolus* but remained valid at the option of the intimidated party anyway.[967] Cino da Pistoia did not see why the substance of the contract would be vitiated by dolus, therefore concluding with Belleperche that both types of contracts were not automatically void but merely voidable when affected by deceit.[968]

However, the common opinion remained hostile to these new ideas introduced by Belleperche and Cino. The authority of Bartolus de Saxoferrato might have played a crucial role in this regard. In his commentary on law *Et eleganter* (D. 4,3,7pr.), Bartolus rejects the heterodox ideas propounded by Belleperche and Cino, and simply confirms the Roman-based distinction between the two types of contract. The gloss contains the truth in this debate, according to Bartolus.[969] The obligation of a *bonae fidei* contract affected by *dolus causam dans* is impeded from coming into existence.[970]

Bartolus is not convinced about Cino's idea that a contract *bonae fidei* must still be considered somehow valid:[971] 'I say that a *bonae fidei* contract does not contain its substance anymore, since its consent is conditional

---

[966] Cino, *Lectura super Codice*, ad C. 4,44,2, f. 187v: 'Et quod sit verum, probatur, quia sic est in contractibus stricti iuris, et idem in contractibus bonae fidei. Sed contra hoc instatur: quia in bonaefidei contractibus exuberat bona fides, ergo etc. Sed huic respondetur, quod exuberantior bonafides in contractibus bonaefidei operatur ut purgetur dolus per actionem ex eo contractu, sed in stricti iuris purgater per actionem de dolo. (...) Non autem operatur exuberans bonafides ut contractus sit nullus ipso iure.' [continuation in following footnote]

[967] Cino, *Lectura super Codice*, ad C. 4,44,2, f. 187v: 'Et hoc probatur etiam, quia in metu est dolus, et tamen ubi per metum fit contractus bonaefidei non est contractus nullus. (...)'

[968] Cino, *Lectura super Codice*, ad C. 4,44,2, f. 187v: 'Praeterea probat, quia quoties contractus habet suam formam propriam sua essentialia tenet ipso iure nec extrinseca causa eum annulet (...), et propter hoc maxime concludit Petrus quod omnis contractus sive stricti iuris sive bonaefidei indistincte sive dolus dederit causam sive inciderit valet.'

[969] Bartolus, *In primam Digesti veteris partem*, ad D. 4,3,7pr., num. 4, f. 130v: 'Mihi videtur quod glossa nostra dicta puram veritatem.'

[970] Bartolus, *In primam Digesti veteris partem*, ad D. 4,3,7,3, num. 3, f. 130v-131r: 'Sed dolus qui dat causam contractui bonae fidei impedit obligationem oriri ex illo contractu (...), secus si dat causam contractui stricti iuris.'

[971] Bartolus, *In primam Digesti veteris partem*, ad D. 4,3,7pr., num. 6, f. 130v: '(...) dico quod in contractibus bonae fidei non habet sua essentialia, quia ille consensus est conditionalis et conditio [si verum est illud propter quod inducitur ad contrahendum] deficit.

and the condition [if that on account of which he was induced into the contract is true] has not been met. A *stricti iuris* contract, on the other hand, still contains its substance, since that condition is not looked after in such contracts.' Bartolus also rejects the analogy with duress:[972] 'If you consent on account of duress, you are not mistaken about the cause to the consent. You know the cause and your consent is pure, even though it has been given on account of duress. Moreover, the contract is valid. If you consent on account of deceit, however, you are mistaken about the cause of the contract.' In Bartolus' view, this cause has to do with the condition that the facts that make you enter into the contract are true.

Importantly, Bartolus rejects the idea that consent is vitiated by deceit. This is an argument that resonated in the early modern scholastic discussion:[973] 'This argument displeases me. If the contract would be void on account of lack of consent, then, by the same token, we would have to say that a contract *stricti iuris* is void, because it lacks consent.' Contrary to Bartolus, Summenhart would later call this a convincing argument, although he still adopted the traditional conclusion that there is a distinction. Yet Bartolus goes on: 'It is not true that deceit impedes consent to the contract. There is no mistake about the contract, but rather about the *causa* by virtue of which you are impeded from or induced to enter into the contract.'

Different still, is Baldus' treatment of the issue. 'As a matter of canonical equity (*aequitas canonica*),' Baldus claimed, 'I think that all contracts in this world are of good faith.' He did not intend this *bona fides* character of all contracts to be extended to the remedies. What it meant, according to Baldus, is that all contracts are of good faith in regard to their spirit and substantial intent. From this he concluded that any contract affected by fundamental mistake was void *ipso iure*.[974] This standpoint was at odds

---

Sed in contractibus stricti iuris habent sua essentialia, quia talis conditio de stricto iure non attenditur.'

[972] Bartolus, *In primam Digesti veteris partem*, ad D. 4,3,7pr., num. 6, f. 130v: 'Ille qui consentit propter metum non errat in causa consensus, imo scit eam, et pure consentit, propter metum tamen, imo valet contractus. (...) Ille vero qui consentit propter dolum, errat in causa.'

[973] Bartolus, *In primam Digesti veteris partem*, ad D. 4,3,7pr., num. 6, f. 130v: 'Ista ratio non placet mihi, quia si contractus esset nullus propter defectum consensus eadem ratione diceremus nullum contractum stricti iuris, quia consensus deficit. (...) Praeterea non est verum, quod dolus impediat consensum circa contractum, nec erratur in contractu, sed erratur in causa propter quam quis impeditur seu inducitur ad contrahendum.'

[974] Baldus, *Super decretalibus*, ad X 2,11,1, num. 12, f. 144v: 'Ego puto quod de aequitate canonica omnes contractus mundi sint bonae fidei, non dico quantum ad titulum actionis,

both with that of Belleperche and that of Bartolus. Baldus nevertheless thought that fundamental mistake should universally result in automatic nullity, since 'God, who regulates and governs everything, looks after the heart of man', and, secondly, because he could not recall that any such substantial distinction between contracts *bonae fidei* and contracts *stricti iuris* was mentioned in the texts of canon law.[975]

Baldus' references to the canon law suggest that it is not unlikely, indeed, that the process of re-thinking the civilian tradition could not seriously begin until after the spirit of canon law had been brought to bear upon the Roman texts. This process was fulfilled in the works of the moral theologians, who took two canons very seriously. First, canon *Quum universorum* (X 3,19,8), which stated that the law must protect the deceived and not the deceivers (*deceptis et non decipientibus iura subveniant*). If *bonae fidei* contracts were considered void *ipso iure*, deceivers could not be obliged to observe their contractual obligations at the wish of the deceived party by virtue of contract any more, since the contract was considered to be non-existent. At a certain point, the makeshift measures to prevent this from happening would no longer satisfy. The second canon that was going to play a decisive role, was canon *Quum contingat* (X 2,24,28). It expressly recommended that the law of duress and the law of mistake be treated on equal terms. Once Sánchez's regime of voidability in coerced contracts had been established, then, the traditional view that mistake resulted in absolute nullity became subject to questioning.

4.3.1.2   *Aristotelian-Thomistic tradition*

The third book of Aristotle's *Nicomachean Ethics* is famous not only for the influence it has had on the complex and ever-lasting debates on fear and duress. It has also been the starting point of centuries of extremely vast reflection upon the effect of ignorance and mistake on voluntary assent to a contract. As noted before, Aristotle singled out two obstacles to voluntary action: compulsion and ignorance.[976] Nonetheless, compulsion and ignorance do not result in involuntariness indiscriminately. Only

---

sed quo ad mentem et substantiam intentionis, et, ideo, si dolus dat eis causam alias non contracturis, quod contractus sit nullus ipso iure…' [for continuation, see next footnote].

975 Baldus, *Super decretalibus*, ad X 2,11,1, num. 12, f. 144v: '…quia Deus qui regulat et regit omnia respicit cor hominis et in iure canonico non memini hoc notasse in textu aliquot differentiam substantialem inter contractum bonae fidei et stricti iuris.'

976 Aristotle, *Ethica Nicomachea* (Ed. Bywater), 3, 1, 1109b35–36, p. 40: 'δοκεῖ δὴ ἀκούσια εἶναι τὰ βίᾳ ἢ δι'ἄγνοιαν γινόμενα'.

when the moving principle lies entirely outside the human person—the intimidated party contributing nothing—does compulsion result in pure involuntariness. Similarly, for ignorance to result in involuntariness, it is bound to a condition, namely that the mistaken action is followed by a feeling of pain and repentance. Otherwise the ignorant party was simply a not voluntary agent, but not an involuntary agent.

Thomas Aquinas would bring this elementary analysis of ignorance and involuntariness into a more systematic account of human agency. He repeated Aristotle's idea that a movement can only be voluntary when it comes from within the agent. Yet even though movement by an intrinsic principle is a necessary condition for voluntariness, it is nevertheless not sufficient. Imbued with Aristotle's teleological view of movement as expressed in his *Physics*, Thomas makes explicit that the inclination from within must also be directed towards an end.[977] In order for that condition to be met, however, knowledge of this end is required. As a consequence, ignorance—being the opposite of knowledge—vitiates voluntary movement.

So ignorance causes involuntariness, since your rational insight into the end of an action is impaired. Put differently, you are mistaken. Thomas then elaborated on Aristotle's disjunction of a not voluntary agent and an involuntary agent. To this effect, he distinguished a threefold relationship between ignorance and the act of will. Ignorance can precede, accompany or follow an act of will. Accordingly, the ignorance is called antecedent (*antecedens*), concomitant (*concomitans*) or consequent (*consequens*).[978] Concomitant ignorance explains why somebody can be ignorant and still not be a voluntary agent rather than an involuntary agent. If you wish to kill your enemy, for instance, but you do so in ignorance while thinking to kill a stag, your ignorance is concomitant. This kind of mistake might be thought of as coming close to the juridical concept of *dolus incidens*, although no explicit connection is advanced by Thomas.

While concomitant ignorance leads to non-voluntariness, consequent ignorance does lead to involuntariness, but only in a very restricted

---

[977] Aquinas, *Summa Theologiae* (Ed. Leonina, tom. 6), IaIIae, quaest. 6, art. 1 (*Utrum in humanis actibus inveniatur voluntarium*), concl., p. 56: 'Illa perfecte moventur a principio intrinseco, in quibus est aliquod intrinsecum principium non solum ut moveantur, sed ut moveantur in finem. Ad hoc autem quod fiat aliquid propter finem, requiritur cognitio finis aliqualis.'

[978] Aquinas, *Summa Theologiae* (Ed. Leonina, tom. 6), IaIIae, quaest. 6, art. 8 (*Utrum ignorantia causet involuntarium*), concl., p. 62–63. In the early modern scholastic commentaries on this passage, *ignorantia concomitans* is often indicated as *ignorantia comitans*.

sense, since this ignorance is actually consequent to an act of the will, for instance, if you do not want to know something, so that you have an excuse for commiting a sin. This is the first type of consequent ignorance and it is called affected (*affectata*).[979] It leaves the act voluntary, because you are expected to know something. By the same token, not acting or not willing something when it is prescribed to act or to will is a voluntary act.[980] The second type of consequential ignorance stems from negligence. Therefore it is also considered to be voluntary. In both cases of consequent ignorance, Thomas still thinks there is a certain element of involuntariness, because the movement to the (non-)act would not have taken place in the event of knowledge.

Ignorance is preceding the act of will when it is involuntary but still the cause of an act the mistaken agent would not have performed otherwise. A typical example is the accident whereby a hunter kills someone walking down the road. But the concept of antecedent ignorance might also be considered as coming close to the concept of *dolus causam dans*, although Thomas does not mention this.

To summarize, three different degrees of involuntariness correspond to the three different types of ignorance. This will be decisive, of course, in determining the degree to which an ignorant party is responsible for an infringement of the law on account of his ignorance. This question falls outside the scope of our argument.[981] It is worthwhile mentioning, however, that the early modern scholastics wrote vast commentaries on the Aristotelian-Thomistic teachings about duress, ignorance and mistake. Certainly the issue of *ignorantia consequens* seems to have been an issue of particular concern, undoubtedly in light of the questions of responsibility that are attached to it. For example, Lessius distinguishes between *ignorantia affectata*, which is directly voluntary, *crassa*, which is indirectly voluntary through negligence, or *vincibilis*, which is indirectly

---

979 For the canonical roots of this concept, see Kuttner, *Kanonistische Schuldlehre*, p. 141–144.

980 Aquinas, *Summa Theologiae* (Ed. Leonina, tom. 6), IaIIae, quaest. 6, art. 3 (*Utrum voluntarium possit esse absque omni actu*), concl., p. 58: 'Quia igitur voluntas, volendo et agendo, potest impedire hoc quod est non velle et non agere, et aliquando debet; hoc quod est non velle et non agere, imputatur ei, quasi ab ipsa existens. Et sic voluntarium potest esse absque actu.'

981 It is nonetheless worthwhile to examine Thomas Aquinas' influential doctrine on this subject in *Summa Theologiae*, IaIIae, quaest. 76 (*De causis peccati in speciali*), in: *Opera omnia iussu impensaque Leonis XIII edita*, tom. 7: *Prima secundae Summae Theologiae a quaestione LXXI ad quaestionem CXIV*, Romae 1892 [hereafter: Ed. Leonina, tom. 7], p. 52–60.

voluntary through major negligence, while stressing that it is not logically impossible for the voluntary and the involuntary to go together.[982] Some of this might have influenced his idea, also produced by Covarruvias, that mistake does not lead to involuntariness unreservedly.

4.3.2   *Nullity* ipso facto *and the* bonae fidei / stricti iuris *distinction*

4.3.2.1   *Is mistake a vice of the will?*

The influence of the Tübingen professor Conradus Summenhart on the Spanish jurists and moral theologians, certainly in shaping their liberal economic ideas, has been massive. His intensive preccupation with contracts was driven by the desire to guide as many businessmen to God by avoiding the temptations inherent in commercial life. To this effect, he showed them how to observe the virtue of justice in exchange for the most diverse circumstances. The casuistry contained in his *Opus septipertitum de contractibus* is incredibly vast, but very well structured. It is broken up into a series of seven treatises dealing with property law, money-lending, sale-purchase, rents, lease, partnership, and bills of exchange.

There is not really a general law of contract preceding Summenhart's treatise. Yet in his lengthy introduction to fraud in buying and selling he develops important ideas on deceit and mistake that would be summarized by Juan de Medina in his *Treatise on penance, restitution and contracts*. Through Medina, Summenhart's writings would live on in the early modern scholastic tradition, first in commentaries on buying-selling, later in separate chapters on the vices of the will. The fact that Summenhart and Medina were widely consulted for their discussions on mistake, particularly for buying and selling, did not mean, however, that their conclusions were accepted as commonly as they were read by the early modern scholastics. Their strong emphasis on the need for absolutely free and voluntary consent to contracts would expose them to increasing criticism.

Because they were discussing mistake in the context of fraud, justice and restitution in buying and selling, they dealt with the doctrine of lesion beyond—and below—moiety (*laesio enormis*) at the same time. Lesion was considered to be a kind of objective fraud (*defraudatio sine*

---

[982] Lessius, *In I.II D. Thomae de beatitudine et actibus humanis*, quaest. 6, art. 8, dub. 1, p. 49–51.

On the canonical origins of the distinction between vincible and invicible ignorance, see Kuttner, *Kanonistische Schuldlehre*, p. 138–141.

dolo incidens in re ipsa). For objective fraud to lie it sufficed that a price other than the just price (*pretium justum*) had been charged in a contract, regardless of whether the vendor or buyer were aware of that.[983] The theologians borrowed the concept of objective deceit (*dolus re ipsa*) from the *ius commune*. It fitted well into the theologians' concern with commutative justice, which required that there be an objective equilibrium between what is given and received in exchange.[984] Consequently, the idea of objective deceit (*dolus re ipsa*) became quite common in scholastic contract law, in spite of the Portuguese jurist Arias Piñel's (1515–1563) late deconstruction of it. As a result, the scholastics were able to conceive of deceit without there being any trace of evil intention on the part of the 'deceiver'.

With Summenhart and Medina the idea gained ground that objective deceit could not automatically result in nullity.[985] Generally speaking, such a deception in the price merely constituted deceit incidental to the contract (*dolus incidens contractui*) rather than fundamental deceit.[986] This idea can also be found in the manuals for confessors of Angelus and Sylvester.[987] They had been careful to explain that it was up to the buyer to decide whether he wanted the contract to be rescinded or to pay the remainder of the price, even though the vendor suffered the injury. This is basically the original rule according to the medieval interpretation of

---

[983] See the excellent description of 'objective deceit' by Juan de Medina, *De poenitentia, restitutione, et contractibus*, tom. 2, Cod. *De rebus restituendis*, quaest. 33, par. *Sed est dubium*, p. 207: 'Potest praeterea defraudatio fieri sine dolo et dicitur defraudatio incidens in re ipsa, ut si nullus dolus aut mendacium ex parte venditoris apponatur, attamen plus iusto recipit ab emptore. Et potest hoc esse dupliciter; quia vel est defraudatio ultra dimidium iusti pretii vel citra.'

[984] The doctrine of *laesio enormis* and the scholastics' idea of contractual fairness in general, will be touched upon more extensively in the chapter on equilibrium in exchange; cf. infra.

[985] Medina, *De poenitentia, restitutione, et contractibus*, tom. 2, Cod. *De rebus restituendis*, quaest. 33, par. *Secunda propositio*, p. 210: 'Si dolus est incidens in contractu, sive sit defraudatio infra dimidium iusti pretii sive ultra, contractus in utroque foro est validus, ita quod non est eo ipso nullus (…)'.

[986] If the deception about the price had been fundamental in the formation of the contract, then it could still give rise to absolute nullity, according to Medina; cf. infra.

[987] Sylvester Mazzolini da Prierio, *Summa Sylvestrina*, part. 1, s.v. *culpa*, quaest. 7, f. 157r: 'Si vero dolus non dedit causam contractui sed incidit in contractum, tenet quidem contractus, sed in contractibus bonaefidei agitur ex eo contractu ut suppleatur pretium, ff. de act. empt. et vend., l. Iulianus, par. Si venditor. Erit tamen in emptoris arbitrio, vel supplere pretium vel restituere rem si deceptio sit ultra dimidium iusti pretii (…), immo in foro conscientiae etiam si deceptio sit minus dimidio. In contractibus vero stricti iuris agetur de dolo (…).' This is almost a word for word copy of Angelo Carletti de Chivasso, *Summa angelica de casibus conscientiae*, Venetiis 1487, s.v. *dolus*, par. 9, f. 78v.

C. 4,44,2.[988] Summenhart and Medina took this a step further by making an explicit distinction between the remedy (*actio*), on the one hand, and the choice (*optio*) either to rescind the contract or to demand the absolute value of the difference between the actual price and the just price, on the other. They explained in general terms that only the remedy against the objective deceiver belonged to the deceived party (*actio defraudato*). The actual option to choose between rescission or rebalancing pertained to the objective deceiver (*optio defraudanti*).[989] In this manner, both contracting parties were in an equal position (*conditio aequalis*) in regard to the unintended and mutually embarrassing situation of objective deceit.

After Summenhart and Medina, lesion would be increasingly considered as irrelevant to the validity of a contract, even if it were beyond moiety. In fact, they recognized that *laesio* was not a form of deceit in the proper sense of the word. It did not really void contractual consent. To be sure, the restoration of equilibrium in exchange (*aequalitas contrahentium*) mattered. Yet commutative justice needed to be restored without further damage to the contract. If the deceit was only incidental, as was most often the case with lesion below moiety, the validity of the contract did not need to be doubted. The main question, then, concerned the effect of fundamental deceit (*dolus causam dans*) on the validity of contracts *bonae fidei*.[990] Summenhart and Medina made the answer to the question dependent on whether the case was judged before the court of conscience or before the external court.

They deemed the contract absolutely null in conscience.[991] Importantly, they did so on account of a very strict interpretation of the natural definition of contract as consisting of mutual consent and mutual obligation.

---

[988] Glossa *Elegerit* ad C. 4,44,2 in *Corporis Iustinianaei Codex* (ed. Gothofredi), tom. 5, col. 920: 'Est ergo in potestate emptoris, et idem dico econtra emptore decepto esse in potestate venditoris (…).'

[989] Medina, *De poenitentia, restitutione, et contractibus*, tom. 2, Cod. *De rebus restituendis*, quaest. 33, par. *Tertia propositio*, p. 210: 'Si defraudatio eveniat in re, sine dolo contrahentium, et sit defraudatio ultra dimidium iusti pretii, in utroque foro datur actio defraudato contra defraudantem, ut patet: unum de duobus, scilicet, vel quod rescindatur contractus vel quod ad aequalitatem reducatur, et datur optio defraudanti, ut eligat ex his, quod velit.'

[990] Medina does not treat contracts *stricti iuris* altogether in quaest. 33.

[991] Medina, *De poenitentia, restitutione, et contractibus*, tom. 2, Cod. *De rebus restituendis*, quaest. 33, par. *Quibus praemissis*, p. 208: 'Loquendo de contractibus bonae fidei, quando sit contractus cum dolo dante causam contractui, sive apponatur per venditorem sive per mediatorem, ipsis contrahentibus nescientibus, sive sit defraudatio ultra sive citra dimidium iusti pretii, sive in pauco sive in multo, contractus est nullus in conscientia, et unusquisque ex contrahentibus deberet esse contentus rem suam habendo, rescisso

The validity of a contract requires consent, which is absolutely voluntary.⁹⁹²
Indeed, Duns Scotus famously argued that the obligations imposed upon
a person by himself do not exceed the limits of his intention (*in obligationibus privatis nullus obligatur non intendens se obligare*).⁹⁹³ Referring to
Aristotle, Summenhart claimed that voluntary consent is radically vitiated
by fundamental mistake (*talis error causat involuntarium*).⁹⁹⁴ The will
of the mistaken party to bring about an obligation is non-existent. This
implies that the contract is null by definition, since a contract depends
on mutual obligation.

In the external court, a *bonae fidei* contract affected by *dolus causam
dans* was also deemed to be absolutely void. Summenhart and Medina
claimed that the deceived party could nonetheless take the other party to
court and demand that he be condemned to perform his obligations. The
performance of the contract would then be required at the option of the
deceived party after the court decision (*post sententiam*). In other words,
the legal ground that entitled one to enforce the contractual obligations
was not the contract itself (since the contract had been invalidated automatically), but the judge's sentence.⁹⁹⁵

---

contractu.' This radical claim is later mitigated on account of equity (*aequitas*) by Medina
as regards objective deceit and deceit induced by a third party.

⁹⁹² Medina, *De poenitentia, restitutione, et contractibus*, tom. 2, Cod. *De rebus restituendis*, quaest. 33, par. *Quibus praemissis*, p. 208: '(...) ad validitatem contractus in quo
mutuo se obligant contrahentes, necessarius est consensus ipsorum in ipso contractu
consentientium. Sed in casu, is, qui deceptus est ob dolum, dantem causam contractui,
non consensit in illo, cum deceptus et ex errore contraxerit, alias nullatenus contracturus.
Igitur nulla inde in eo fuit orta obligatio, maxime cum obligationes privatae non excedant
metas voluntatis ipsius qui se obligat (...). Ac proinde seclusa iuris dispositione, contractus emptionis dolosae, nullam parit in conscientia obligationem, nec in decepto, nec in
decipiente, cum de ratione contractus sit reciproca obligatio. Est enim contractus ultrocitroque obligatio (...).'
Compare Summenhart, *De contractibus*, Summarium, q. 57, dist. 3, dict. 1, [s.p.]: 'Nemo
incurrit obligationem privatam nisi intendat et velit se obligare, et ita consentiat in obligationem, ut vult Scotus in iii. Distinc. xxxix tractando de iuramento doloso.'

⁹⁹³ Duns Scotus, *Quaestiones in tertium librum Sententiarum*, dist. 39, quaest. 1, num. 10,
in: Ioannis Duns Scoti opera omnia, Hildesheim 1968 [= anastatic reprint of the Lyon 1639
edition], tom. 7, part. 2, p. 1003.

⁹⁹⁴ Summenhart, *De contractibus*, Summarium, q. 57, dist. 3, dict. 1, [s.p.]: 'Talis error
causat involuntarium, iii. Eth., sine autem volitione et consensu non contrahitur privata
obligatio.'

⁹⁹⁵ Medina, *De poenitentia, restitutione, et contractibus*, tom. 2, Cod. *De rebus restituendis*, quaest. 33, par. *Secunda pars*, p. 208: 'Respondetur, quamvis non maneat dolosus
virtute contractus obligatus, cum nullus sit, manet tamen obligatus pro voto decepti, virtute iuris communis ipsum obligantis, stare contractui, si velit deceptus, idque in favorem
seducti et in odium doli.'

Once this judgment has been pronounced in the external court, the contract must also be observed in the court of conscience.[996] Summenhart and Medina motivated this rather pragmatic solution by pointing out that it would have been absurd (*irrationabile*) to leave the deceiver in a better position than the deceived party (*melior esset conditio dolosi*).[997] Moreover, as canon *Quum universorum* (X 3,19,8)[998] indicated, the law must protect the deceived and not the deceivers (*deceptis et non decipientibus iura subveniant*).

It was in order to solve this absurdity in a more radical way that Leonard Lessius would argue later on that, from a conceptual point of view, it was indispensable to adopt a general principle of avoidability of contracts affected by fundamental error. In this manner, the contract would not be automatically null, but voidable at the wish of the deceived party. Until the advent of this logical operation, however, in the footsteps of Summenhart and Medina the early modern scholastics would continue to make variations on the common opinion that *bonae fidei* contracts are *ipso iure* void on account of fundamental mistake.

Before we go on to investigate these variations, one further remark is needed, though. It became common for authors in the tradition subsequent to Summenhart to identify Pierre de Belleperche with a line of thought which was at variance with the common opinion. He argued that *bonae fidei* contracts are merely voidable, just as *stricti iuris* contracts. In the words of Summenhart himself:[999]

> We now know how to refute the arguments of Pierre de Belleperche. He said that if *dolus causam dans contractui bonae fidei* really made that contract void, more precisely because that *dolus* impeded voluntary consent, then that same *dolus* should equally make a contract *stricti iuris* void, because

---

[996] Summenhart, *De contractibus*, Summarium, q. 57, dist. 3, dict. 1, [s.p.]: 'Etiam stante praedicto casu teneretur stare contractui in favorem decepti, etiam in conscientia, quando res iam esset devoluta ad forum contentiosum, et sententia contra eum lata esset de stando in favorem decepti, quia in conscientia sua tenetur parere iudicis decreto.'

[997] Medina, *De poenitentia, restitutione, et contractibus*, tom. 2, Cod. *De rebus restituendis*, quaest. 33, par. *Secunda pars*, p. 208.

[998] This rule was frequently used in the Romano-canon law tradition; see, for example, Hostiensis, *Summa aurea*, lib. 3, tit. *De fideiussoribus*, f. 261v, num. 3.

[999] Summenhart, *De contractibus*, Summarium, q. 57, dist. 3, dict. 1 post decimumquartum: 'Et per hoc patet solutio ad argumentum Petri de Bellapertica dicentis. Si dolus dans causam contractui bonae fidei faceret quod contractus ille ob id esset nullus ipso facto: eo quod ille dolus impediret consensum: tunc etiam dolus dans causam contractui stricti iuris faceret illum contractum esse nullum. Quia etiam ibi dolus impediret consensum. Consequens est falsum. Igitur, etc.'

also in that case *dolus* would impede voluntary consent. This inference would be false, however. Ergo, etc.

Summenhart goes on to say that this would have been a convincing argument, indeed, if only the reason why contracts *bonae fidei* are null were the same in both the external court and the internal court.[1000] This is not the case, however, in Summenhart's view. For the reason why *contractus bonae fidei* are automatically void in the court of conscience is that they fall short of voluntary consent. However, in the external court *contractus bonae fidei* are considered void for another reason, namely because of the authority of the civil law stating that this must be the rule in the external court. In the case of *contractus stricti iuris*, the same authority of the civil law would not have it that way.

Serious doubts could be raised about the authenticity of Summenhart's reference to Belleperche. For one thing, Summenhart does not give any details about the place where he found this alleged argumentation of Pierre de Belleperche. Subsequent authors, such as Covarruvias, pretended that this argumentation could be found in Belleperche's commentary on par. *Actionum autem* (Inst. 4,6,28). Moreover, Covarruvias argued that Johannes Faber and Jean Feu had adopted the same, non-conformist position. There are serious doubts, however, whether Covarruvias' references to these authors are more than false decoration. According to the legal historian Robert Feenstra, Covarruvias almost certainly did not read Pierre de Belleperche and Johannes Faber himself, even though Jean Feu might rightly be said to have advocated the said non-conformist opinion.[1001] For another thing, in his commentary on Inst. 4,6,28, Pierre de Belleperche does not exactly develop the argument which Summenhart ascribes to him.[1002]

In fact, the argument which Summenhart and, subsequently, Covarruvias attribute to Belleperche can be found as a fictitious counter-argument in Bartolus' commentary on law *Et eleganter* (D. 4,3,7)—as we have learned above. Bartolus eventually confirmed the traditional, Roman distinction

---

[1000] Summenhart, *De contractibus*, Summarium, q. 57, dist. 3, dict. 1 post decimumquartum (continuation of citation in preceding footnote): 'Sed dicendum quod bene probaret si nullitas conveniens contractui bonae fidei in foro contentioso: conveniret sibi precise ex illa causa ex qua sibi convenit in foro conscientiae, scilicet ex natura rei. Sed propter hoc inest sibi etiam ex dispositione iuris positivi volentis praedictum contractum bonae fidei esse nullum. Et hoc non voluit de contractu stricti iuris ut supponitur: ideo in illo foro non est ille contractus nullus / sed bene alius.'

[1001] Feenstra, *De oorsprong van Hugo de Groot's leer over de dwaling*, p. 94 (n. 31).

[1002] Cf. supra, p. 276–277.

between *bonae fidei* and *stricti iuris* contracts. Yet it might be useful to recall some of the basics of the scholastic argumentation technique. To escape the accusation of revolutionary novelty, the scholastic theologians and jurists often put forward new ideas by putting them in the mouth of a vague group of scholars (*aliqui*) or in a source that was difficult to verify. They then discussed this counter-opinion at great length, only to refute it rather unconvincingly at the end of their argumentation, or to qualify it as merely probable or not improbable. Finally, a conclusion was reached which was in accordance with safe, traditional doctrine. This logical technique is expressly revealed to us by Lessius.[1003] Incidentally, it has already been pointed out that this scholastic way of arguing was employed with great regularity by Summenhart.[1004]

Bartolus may still have been very antipathetic to this fictitious argument, Summenhart and Covarruvias seem to have considered it as a possible gateway to leaving behind the old distinction between *bonae fidei* and *stricti iuris* contracts. Incidentally, it turns out that Summenhart eventually approves of the reasoning that is ascribed to Belleperche:[1005]

> The civil law has prescribed it that way, even though in the court of conscience both a contract *stricti iuris* and *bonae fidei* are void on account of the lack of consent, as Belleperche's argument convincingly shows.

It would only take one more step, then, namely the rejection of the assumption that voluntary consent entirely vitiates consent,[1006] to be able to argue that both *stricti iuris* and *bonae fidei* contracts needed to be governed by the same law, and that this law should not declare contracts affected by mistake void *ab initio* but voidable.

[1003] Lessius, *De iustitia et iure*, lib. 2, cap. 22, dub. 10, num. 56, p. 303: 'Nec obstat quod Gabriel in respons. ad 3. argumentum contra 4. conclus. addat, *Verum hoc dico recitative et probabiliter, sciens quosdam doctores notabiles haec scripsisse, offero tamen examini peritorum.* Sic enim loqui solemus ad declinandam invidiam, quando aliquid novi et receptae opinioni adversum ex nostra sententia proferimus.'

[1004] O.I. Langholm, *The legacy of scholasticism in economic thought, Antecedents of choice and power*, Cambridge 1998, p. 112.

[1005] Summenhart, *De contractibus*, Summarium, q. 57, dist. 3, dict. 1 post decimumquartum (continuation of citation in preceding footnote): 'Licet in foro conscientiae uterque sit nullus propter defectum consensus ut convincit argumentum praedicti Petri.'

[1006] Which was actually taken by Covarruvias in *Relectio in regulam possessor malae fidei, de regulis iuris*, lib. 6, part. 2, par. 6, num. 6, in: Opera Omnia, Augustae Taurinorum 1594, tom. 2, p. 394. 'Sed quamvis dolus det causam contractui bonae fidei vel stricti iuris, non ex hoc sequitur consensum substantialem contractus defecisse, etenim vere contrahens consensit.' Cf. infra.

4.3.2.2   *A humanist scholastic canon lawyer on good faith* vs *strict law*

Covarruvias fused the manifold juridical and philosophical traditions of
Europe into an extremely rich and potent powder keg of legal thought. His
account of the meaning and the history of the concept of good faith which
precedes his analysis of mistake is an example of humanist erudition at its
best. It provides the immediate context against which the question of the
validity of contracts affected by mistake is dealt with. Covarruvias does
not fundamentally change the traditional analysis of this problem, but the
form of his discussion will undoubtedly have inspired future thinkers such
as Rebelo, and many of the casual remarks he makes will no doubt have
helped Lessius to steer the debate in a new direction.

The first half of Covarruvias' discussion is entirely dedicated to an elucidation of the concept of good faith (*bona fides*). It is structured around
the apparent tension between the universal requirement of good faith
in human affairs, on the one hand, and the seemingly paradoxical fact
that a category of contracts *stricti iuris* exists alongside contracts *bonae
fidei*, on the other.[1007] Covarruvias dissolves the tension by discerning
two meanings behind the single expression 'good faith'. He also uncov-
ers the Roman legal history behind the distinction between *contractus
bonae fidei* and *contractus stricti iuris*. Covarruvias was heavily indebted to
Tiraqueau's impressive treatment of strict law and how it was at odds with
the principles of good faith and equity.[1008] More generally, our canonist's
exposition on equity borrowed from the same humanist authorities that
can be found in Benvenuto Stracca's treatment of the subject, namely Oldendorp, Budé and Tiraqueau.[1009]

In its first meaning, good faith (*bona fides*) is synonymous with a sincere will (*syncera voluntas*). Its antonyms are falsehood (*figmentum*),

---

[1007] Covarruvias, *Relectio in regulam possessor*, part. 2, par. 6, num. 1, p. 391: 'In omnibus
negotiis ratio bonae fidei habenda est, cum ei adversetur mala fides et dolus, qui in republica minime est tolerandus, imo a quocunque negotio summis viribus exterminandus. Hinc
sane quaeritur, quamobrem iure civili actiones quaedam et contractus eo distinguantur,
quod quidam sint bonae fidei, reliqui vero stricti iuris.'
[1008] Tiraqueau, *De utroque retractu, municipali et conventionali, commentarii duo*, in:
Opera omnia, Francoforti ad Moenum 1597, tom. 3, lib. 1, par. 35, glossa 1 (*Stricti iuris*),
p. 330–335.
[1009] Cf. Donahue, *Equity in the courts of merchants*, p. 2. A good introduction to Oldendorp's as well as Budé's conception of equity is included in G. Kisch, *Erasmus und die
Jurisprudenz seiner Zeit*, Studien zum humanistischen Rechtsdenken, [Basler Studien zur
Rechtswissenschaft, 56], Basel 1960, p. 177–259. Contrary to what its title might suggest,
this book is basically a study of the concept of equity in the Aristotelian tradition and in
Renaissance jurisprudence, in particular.

bad faith and deceit (*mala fides et dolus*).[1010] According to Covarruvias, good faith understood in this way is the universal principle underlying all human commerce at least since Antiquity.[1011] The conception of good faith as sincerity remained a constant in the natural law tradition.[1012] Good faith (*fides*) consists in doing what you say. Hence, it is the cornerstone of justice.[1013] Business and exchange must be pervaded by good faith (*in omnibus negotiis ratio bonae fidei habenda*). The ultimate yardstick of good faith is private conscience (*conscientia*).[1014] The identification between good faith and good conscience was a commonplace in the canon law tradition.[1015] The good faith of an action is evaluated by the private judgment of the human person (*iudicium privatum*), who probes the morality of his own actions. This is the meaning of 'good faith' as it applies to 'possession in good faith' or 'concluding a contract in good faith'.[1016]

Even if good faith in the sense of sincerity is required universally, another meaning of good faith exists which is applied more restrictedly.

[1010] Covarruvias, *Relectio in regulam possessor*, part. 2, par. 6, num. 1, p. 391–392.

[1011] Covarruvias cites a plethora of texts from the Corpus Justinianeum, besides a couple of references to verses by actors in the ancient comic plays by Plautus (c. 254–184 BC), *Aulularia*, 4, 6, 1–3, in: *Plaute, Amphitryon – Asinaria – Aulularia*, Texte établi et traduit par Alfred Ernout, [Collection des Universités de France], Paris 1967⁶, p. 187: '[Euclio senex:] Fidei censebam maxumam multo fidem esse: ea sublevit os mihi paenissume. Ni subvenisset corvus, periissem miser.'; and Terentius (c. 195–159 BC), *Heautontimoroumenos*, 4, 5, 759–761, in: *Térence, Heautontimoroumenos—Phormion*, Texte établi et traduit par J. Marouzeau, [Collection des Universités de France], Paris 1964 (hereafter: Ed. Marouzeau), p. 70–71: '[Chremes:] Videre egisse iam nescioquid cum sene. [Syrus:] De illo quod dudum...? Dictum ac factum reddidi. [Chremes:] Bonan fide?' The far-fetched nature of these references demonstrates Covarruvias' desire to show off his humanist erudition at any expense.

[1012] Pothier, *Traité des obligations, selon les regles, tant du for de la conscience, que du for extérieur*, part. 1, sec. 1, art. 3, par. 3 (du dol), p. 29: 'Dans le for intérieur on doit regarder comme contraire à cette bonne foi, tout ce qui s'écarte tant soit peu de la sincérité la plus exacte et la plus scrupuleuse (...).'

[1013] Cicero, *De officiis* (Ed. Testard, vol. 1), 1, 7, 23, p. 115: 'Fundamentum autem est iustitiae fides, id est dictorum conventorumque constantia et veritas.'

[1014] Covarruvias, *Relectio in regulam possessor*, part. 2, par. 6, num. 1, p. 391: 'In summa denique bonam fidem ipse interpretor iudicium illud privatum, quo quisque de rebus propriis diiudicat secum, particulariter quidem de omnibus propriis actibus moralibus. Nam et fides iudicium quoddam est quo credimus aliquid, item et illud, quo proprios nostros actus morales iudicamus. Quamobrem in hac parte fides pro conscientiae adsumitur.'

[1015] J. Gordley, *Good faith in contract law in the medieval ius commune*, in: R. Zimmermann – S. Whittaker (eds.), Good faith in European contract law, [The Common Core of European Private Law, Cambridge Studies in International and Comparative Law, 14], Cambridge 2000, p. 94.

[1016] Covarruvias, *Relectio in regulam possessor*, part. 2, par. 6, num. 1, p. 391: 'Quo fit, ut is dicatur bona fide possidere, bona fide contrahere, qui credit se id iuste facere, et ut dicitur, nullum habens in corde figmentum nec dolum.'

In this sense, good faith is allegedly synonymous with equity. Amongst others, equity says something about the way in which contracts should be interpreted.[1017] Equity in this sense is genuine justice freed from the rigourously cold shackles of strict law (*ius strictum*).[1018] In Covarruvias' view, equity comes down to the mitigation (*mitigatio*) and the moderation (*temperamentum*) of strict law. This is a view expressed also by the Lutheran jurist Johann Oldendorp (ca. 1487–1567), who is expressly referred to by Covarruvias.[1019] Strict law is subtle (*ius subtile*).[1020] It is harsh and bitter (*praedurum et asperum*). It continually runs the risk of overreaching (*summum ius, summa iniuria*).[1021] It does not yield an inch to the interpreter.

[1017] This discussion is part of the larger discussion about the rigorous or equitable interpretation of laws (it might be recalled that contracts were conceived of as privately imposed laws in the first place); cf. E. Cortese, *La norma giuridica, Spunti storici nel diritto comune classico*, [Ius nostrum, 6], Milano 1964, vol. 2, p. 295–362.

[1018] Covarruvias, *Relectio in regulam possessor*, part. 2, par. 6, num. 2, p. 392: 'Verum apud iuris civilis responsa interdum verbum hoc "bona fides" non tam synceram illam voluntatem et animum dolo contrarium quam aequitatem quandam et iustitiam ipsam a rigore quodam summo segregatam et puram significat.'

[1019] Johann Oldendorp, *Formula investigandae actionis per quam unusquisque ius suum in iudicio persequatur, cum deliberatione aequi et boni*, Coloniae 1538, [s.p.]: 'Aequitas autem, quam alias aequum et bonum, alias aequum et iustum, alias aequumbonum sine copula dicimus, alias denique epiikian vocant, est mitigatio legis scriptae in aliqua circumstantia, utpote rerum, personarum ac temporum. Ius est (inquit Donatus), quod omnia recta et inflexibilia exigit. Aequitas est quae ex iure multum remittit.'

[1020] Covarruvias, *Relectio in regulam possessor*, part. 2, par. 6, num. 3, p. 392: 'Hinc denique aequitas rigori et stricto iuri opposita est mitigatio et interpretatio legis scriptae ex aliqua circunstantia personarum, rerum aut temporum. (…) Ex quibus deducitur ius strictum id dici quod praedurum sit et asperum, a quo non liceat nec latum unguem discedere, cuique nihil addi, nec detrahi possit, nisi quod scriptura loquitur. (…) Hocque ius aequitati opponitur, idemque appellatur ius subtile.'

[1021] Covarruvias recounts how this saying has come down to his time from classical Antiquity, citing Terentius, Cicero, Columella and Valerius Maximus. A similar account of the history of the expression 'summum ius summa iniuria' can be found in Budé and Erasmus; cf. Kisch, *Erasmus und die Jurisprudenz seiner Zeit*, p. 190.

Terentius, *Heautontimoroumenos* (Ed. Marouzeau), 4, 5, 796, p. 73: '[Syrus:] Ius summum saepe summa est malitia'. Cicero, *De officiis* (Ed. Testard, vol. 1), 1, 10, 33, p. 120: 'Summum ius summa iniuria'. Columella (d. ca. 70 AD), *De re rustica*, 1, 7, 2, in: *Columella, On Agriculture*, with a recension of the text and an English translation by Harrison Boyd Ash, Cambridge Mass. – London 1960³ [= 1941], p. 78–80: 'Sed nec dominus in unaquaque re, cui colonum obligaverit, tenax esse iuris sui debet, sicut in diebus pecuniarium vel lignis et ceteris parvis accessionibus exigendis, quarum cura maiorem molestiam quam impensam rusticis adfert; nec sane est vindicandum nobis quicquid licet, nam summum ius antiqui summam putabant crucem.'

Covarruvias' reference to Valerius Maximus (1st century AD), *Dicta et facta memorabilia*, 8, 2 (*De privatis iudiciis insignibus*) concerns a section on famous trials, but this text does not contain an explicit reference to the maxim 'summum ius summa iniuria'; cf. *Valerius*

Covarruvias cites a plethora of texts to support his interpretation of equity, although they might actually not always fit as well with his own interpretation as he thought. Reference is made to the Aristotelian concept of equity (ἐπιείκεια).[1022] Aristotle's treatment of equity had drawn a lot of attention at the beginning of Guillaume Budé's commentaries on the Digest, to which Covarruvias expressly refers.[1023] Covarruvias also recalls the famous verse from the *Rhetorica ad Herennium*, the oldest surviving Latin textbook on rhetorics (ca. 90 BC), that justice is equity giving everyone his due according to his 'dignity'.[1024] Furthermore; he refers to the first century rhetorician Quintilianus' admonishment that in dubious cases, where both sides seem to be right, the judge must not try to find out which right is the oldest, but which decision is the most equitable in this particular situation.[1025] All of these texts seem to suggest, indeed, that law should be handled with a certain flexibility.

According to Covarruvias, the distinction between *contractus bonae fidei* and *contractus stricti iuris* has been grafted upon the distinction between equitable and rigourous interpretation of contracts.[1026] Certainly, both contracts must be observed in good faith in the first sense of the word—as gloss *Bonae fidei sunt* to paragraph *Actionum* (Inst. 4,6,28) made explicit.[1027] Yet the obligations ensuing from *stricti iuris* contracts cannot be subject to

---

Maximus, Memorable doings and sayings, edited and translated by D.R. Schackleton Bailey, [Loeb Classical Library, 493], Cambridge Mass. – London 2000, vol. 2, p. 204–210.

[1022] Aristotle, *Ethica Nicomachea* (Ed. Bywater), 5, 10, 1137a31–1138a3, p. 110–111.

[1023] Guillaume Budé, *Annotationes ad viginti quattuor libros Pandectarum*, Parisiis 1508, f. 1r–v.

[1024] *Rhetorica ad Herennium*, 3,3, in: *Rhétorique à Herennius*, Texte établi et traduit par Guy Achard, [Collection des Universités de France], Paris 1989, p. 89: 'Iustitia est aequitas ius uni cuique rei tribuens pro dignitate cuiusque.'

[1025] Quintilianus, *De institutione oratoria*, 7, 7, 8, in: *Quintilien, Institution oratoire, Tome 4, Livres 6–7*, Texte établi et traduit par Jean Cousin, [Collection des Universités de France], Paris 1977, p. 173: 'Plurimum tamen est in hoc, utrum fieri sit melius atque aequius; de quo nihil praecipi, nisi proposita materia, potest.'

[1026] Covarruvias, *Relectio in regulam possessor*, part. 2, par. 6, num. 4, p. 392: 'Igitur ex his apparet ratio, quare contractus quidam bonae fidei dicantur, reliqui vero stricti iuris. Nam bonae fidei contractus ideo quidam censentur, quod in his alter alteri arbitrio et officio aequissimo iudicis teneatur de eo, quod ex bono et aequo praestari oportet, etiam si in conventione id dictum non sit. Habet etenim iudex potestatem in his actionibus iudicandi quod sibi bonum aequumque visum fuerit, quanquam nihil a contrahentibus dictum sit.'

[1027] Glossa *Bonae fidei sunt* ad Inst. 4,6,28 in *Corporis Iustinianaei Institutiones* (ed. Gothofredi), tom. 4 (*Volumen parvum*), col. 492: 'Sed quare magis hae dicuntur bonae fidei quam aliae? Nunquid ideo, quia possit esse mala fides in aliis? Respondetur non, quia in omni contractu debet bona fides intervenire.'

interpretation by the judge.[1028] Apart from the explicitly mentioned obligations between the contracting parties, judicial discretion can impose no additional obligations on the parties to a contract of strict law by virtue of morality and equity (*ex aequo et bono*).

Covarruvias does not content himself with this analytical clarification. True to the spirit of humanism, he goes on to investigate the historical roots of this distinction in the law of Rome. The historical origins of the *bonae fidei* / *stricti iuris* distinction reach back to the *formula* procedure. Covarruvias explains how the Roman praetor first granted a short audience to the litigating parties but then delegated the actual task of judging to civilians. As he left the litigating parties, the praetor sent a formular (*formula*) with them, however, including instructions for the judge as to how he needed to assess the lawsuit. If the praetor added the expression '*ex bona fide*' to the formula, it was allowed for the judge to freely assess the case according to his equitable discretion, without being bound by the formula of the praetor and the stipulations in the contract too strictly.[1029]

Evidence for Covarruvias' historical interpretation is taken from a variety of texts in Cicero, Seneca, and Boethius. Our learned canonist cannot prevent his academic pride from pointing out that formerly, professors of civil and canon law ignored these origins of the *bonae fidei* / *stricti iuris* distinction. He adds to his self-esteem by refuting, on the basis of his wide reading of the classics, an entirely wrong attempt at historical explanation of the distinction by Ullrich Zasius (1461–1535).[1030] Referring to Dionysius Halicarnassus, the humanist jurist Zasius had claimed that some contracts

---

[1028] Glossa *Bonae fidei sunt* ad Inst. 4,6,28 in *Corporis Iustinianaei Institutiones* (ed. Gothofredi), tom. 4 (*Volumen parvum*), col. 492: 'Cum ergo dolus ubique puniatur vel mala fides, ad quid bonae fidei istae dicuntur? Respondetur, aliae stricti iuris dicuntur, quia non venit in eis nisi quod stricte exigit natura actionis. Unde non veniunt usurae ex mora in contractibus stricti iuris (...), sed in contractibus bonae fidei sic (...).'

[1029] Covarruvias, *Relectio in regulam possessor*, part. 2, par. 6, num. 3, p. 392: 'Praetor vero statuta die vocatis ad se litigaturis eisque summatim auditis formulam quandam ex proposita causa concipiebat, quam ad pedaneum iudicem deferent litigatores. Quamque formulam in quibusdam iudiciis stricte in ea fere verba, quibus contrahentes uti fuissent aut in alia ex natura rei ita includebat, ut iudici fas non esset ab eius praescripto discedere, etiam si forte id aequum esse censeret. (...) In quibusdam vero contractibus, his videlicet qui a iurisconsultis bonae fidei dicuntur, praetor cum iudices dabat addere solebat illa verba: ex bona fide; ex qua praetoria formula liberam iudicandi facultatem iudex habebat iuxta id quod sibi aequum visum fuisset, nec tenebatur ad strictam praetoris delegationem, nec ad contractus praeduram verborum conceptionem.'

[1030] Covarruvias, *Relectio in regulam possessor*, part. 2, par. 6, num. 3, p. 393: 'Etenim hanc rationem veteres iuris utriusque professores (...) non omnino ignorarunt, tametsi originis cognitionem minime nacti fuerint. (...) Zasii rationem reiiciendam esse censeo, potissime quia ex variis auctorum locis apparet, apud Romanos contractus istos testibus

were called *bonae fidei* by the Romans, because once upon a time they had been celebrated and concluded in the temple of the Godess Fides.

Once the right meaning of good faith with respect to *contractus bonae fidei* has been definitively settled, Covarruvias turns to the question of mistake. To begin with, he firmly denies that the law of the Church has abandoned the discriminatory treatment of *bonae fidei* and *stricti iuris* contracts. As mentioned above, this had been claimed by Baldus de Ubaldis.[1031] Since the distinction is adopted by the civil law and never explicitly rejected by the canon law, the silence of the canon law must be interpreted as an approval of the civil law regime, according to Covarruvias.[1032] Perhaps Baldus' opinion might be justified in case of pious causes, but pious causes can at most constitute an exception to the rule.

Covarruvias recalls and confirms the *ius commune* rules, which consider that *bonae fidei* contracts affected by *dolus causam dans* are automatically void (*nullus ipso iure*), whereas *stricti iuris* contracts are voidable (*rescindendus*) under the same circumstances. Citing André Tiraqueau and François le Douaren,[1033] he embarks upon a historical investigation, explaining that 'ipso iure' means that the contract is void from the outset because of the fixed rules of civil law (*ius civile*) as opposed to the law created by the moderating intervention of the praetores (*ius praetorium*). From this he infers that it is impossible to believe, as Pierre de Belleperche *cum suis* had done, that contracts *bonae fidei* are voidable.[1034]

---

et arbitris celebrari solere, et eo praesertim, quod non meminerim apud Dionysium Halicarnasseum me legisse quod Zasius ex eodem auctore retulit. (...)'

[1031] Cf. supra, p. 279–280.

[1032] Covarruvias, *Relectio in regulam possessor*, part. 2, par. 6, num. 5, p. 393: 'Quarto subsequitur ex praecedentibus, falsam esse opinionem Baldi qui in cap. 1 de plus petit. in fine scribit iure canonico contractus omnes bonae fidei censeri etiam eos qui iure civili stricti iuris nominantur, atque idcirco iure pontificio sublatam esse distinctionem contractuum stricti iuris a contractibus bonae fidei. (...) Etenim haec conclusio falsa est, nec iure pontificio alicubi haec actionum distinctio reprobata fuit. Unde cum ea iure civili admissa sit, existimandum est in dubio tacite a iure ipso pontificio admitti.'

[1033] André Tiraqueau, *Commentarii in l. Si unquam, C. De revocandis donationibus*, Lugduni 1546, s.v. *revertatur*, num. 119–120, p. 660–661; François le Douaren, *De in litem iurando iudiciisque bonaefidei etiam arbitrariis commentarius*, Lugduni 1542, num. 15–19, p. 25–28.

[1034] Covarruvias, *Relectio in regulam possessor*, part. 2, par. 6, num. 6, p. 394: 'Atque haec ideo praenotata fuere, ut hinc constet apud veteres iurisconsultos verba isthaec, ipso iure, idem significare quod illa, iure civili, ad differentiam iuris praetorii, eiusque aequitatis ac moderationis. (...) Sexto ab huius quaestionis definitione infertur plurima cessare quae per Petrum, Cynum et alios adducuntur adversus communem sententiam (...). Nam ius civile irritum esse censet contractum bonae fidei ab ipso quidem initio (...) Eaque actio de dolo ipsi contractui videtur inesse sicuti et exceptio doli quemadmodum superius probatum, quicquid aliter hac de re doctores nostri scripserint.'

Importantly, in the footsteps of Summenhart, our canonist goes on to rebuke the argumentation of Belleperche.[1035] Yet in the process of doing so, he might actually have sown the seeds for the phoenix from Orléans to rise from his ashes in the work of Leonard Lessius. Belleperche had allegedly argued *ex absurdo* that if the civil law really deemed contracts *bonae fidei* void, that must have been because the contract fell short of consent and hence was vitiated in its very essence (*substantia*). As a matter of natural law, this would hold equally true in the case of contracts *stricti iuris*, however. Therefore, Belleperche was thought to have argued, along these lines contracts *stricti iuris* should have been considered void *ipso iure*, too. Since this is not the case, the common opinion is absurd.

Covarruvias then mentions Summenhart's criticism of Belleperche. Summenhart's is an argument from power. He simply states that civil law prevails, because it has the authority to overrule natural law.[1036] The natural law might consider that substantial consent is equally lacking in both contracts *stricti iuris* and *bonae fidei*. Even so, the civil law is free to rule that both types of contract are subject to differential treatment, according to Summenhart. Now Covarruvias doubts whether it was allowed for Summenhart to accept Belleperche's assumption about the lack of substantial consent in *bonae fidei* contracts in the first place.[1037] For if you accept that mistake undermines substantial consent in *bonae fidei* contracts, it is true that the same must be said about *stricti iuris* contracts.

Our canonist wants to prevent that argument from gaining force, however, and denies, therefore, that *dolus causam dans* affects substantial consent (*sed quamvis dolus det causam contractui bonae fidei vel stricti iuris, non ex hoc sequitur consensum substantialem contractus defecisse,*

[1035] It needs to be recalled that the reference to the alleged argumentation by Pierre de Belleperche is dubious; cf. supra, p. 288.

[1036] Covarruvias, *Relectio in regulam possessor*, part. 2, par. 6, num. 6, p. 394: 'Unde secundum eum [Conradum] etiam si ex natura rei ob deficientem consensum hi contractus bonae fidei et stricti iuris pares sint, tamen quo ad iuris civilis remedia et dispositionem liberam impares censentur et censendi sunt. Cum liberum legi fuerit hoc uni concedere et alteri negare variis ex causis.'

[1037] Covarruvias, *Relectio in regulam possessor*, part. 2, par. 6, num. 6, p. 394: 'Non tamen omnino est admittenda ratio suprascripta, qua diximus dolum dantem causam contractui consensum impedire, quatenus consensus substantia contractus est. (...) Nam si haec fuisset principalis ratio, ex qua ius civile voluit et statuit nullum esse contractum bonae fidei, profecto eadem ratione idem foret in contractibus stricti iuris dicendum, cum et in eis substantia, id est consensus deficeret., quod fatetur Bar. in d.l.et eleganter, col. 3. Sed quamvis dolus det causam contractui bonae fidei vel stricti iuris, non ex hoc sequitur consensum substantialem contractus defecisse, etenim vere contrahens consensit.'

etenim vere contrahens consensit).[1038] This is exactly the kind of reason, however, which could be exploited by a clever theologian as Leonard Lessius in order to advocate a general regime of nullity at the option of the wronged party:[1039] not even a *bonae fidei* contract can be deemed to be entirely void merely on the grounds of mistake.

What is more, Covarruvias ends with an extremely important concession. 'In the court of conscience (*forum animae*)', he concludes with reference to Summenhart,[1040] 'the *bonae fidei* / *stricti iuris* distinction in the event of *dolus causam dans* is irrelevant.' The reason is that the court of conscience merely pays attention to the law of nature (*natura rei*). As a result, Covarruvias' thought offered opportunities for both advocates and adversaries of the *bonae fidei* / *stricti iuris* distinction to vindicate the famous canonist as a partisan of their opinions.

4.3.2.3 *Molina: mistake makes contracts void* ab initio

Contrary to what might be expected, Luis de Molina's treatment of mistake does not mark the beginning of an entirely novel approach to the effects of mistake on contractual validity. As had been the case with Soto, Molina's main discussion of mistake is still part of the specific law of sale.[1041] His conclusions reach a high level of generality, however, so that at the end of his argument, he feels obliged to tell his reader how the general rules which he developed should eventually be applied to the concrete business of buying and selling (*hactenus dicta ad praxim aptantur*).[1042] Moreover, his reflections are of considerable depth and they have been very influential as they formed the implicit background against which Lessius reshaped the whole debate some years later. Neither is his thought a servile imitation of the conclusions reached by Summenhart, Medina, or Covarruvias.

[1038] See the previous note.

[1039] See the remarks made on Summenhart's exposition above.

[1040] Covarruvias, *Relectio in regulam possessor*, part. 2, par. 6, num. 6, p. 394: 'In animae iudicio minime considerandum esse hanc differentiam contractus bonae fidei et stricti iuris, quoties dolus dederit causam contractui (…) siquidem in eo foro non tractatur de subtilitatibus his et distinctionibus iuris civilis a praetorio, sed tantum agitur de natura rei, secundum quam non differt contractus stricti iuris quantum ad hoc a contractu bonae fidei (…).'

[1041] Molina, *De iustitia et iure*, tom. 2 (*De contractibus*), tract. 2, disp. 352 (*validane sit emptio et venditio in qua dolus intervenit*).

[1042] Molina, *De iustitia et iure*, tom. 2 (*De contractibus*), tract. 2, disp. 352, col. 417, num. 16.

To start with, Molina adopts three distinctions that we have already seen in Summenhart and Medina. First, he distinguishes factual deceit (*re ipsa*) from intentional deceit (*a proposito*).[1043] Second, Molina adopts the usual distinction between deceit that turns out to be the final motivating cause of the contract (*dolus causam dans*) and deceit that has been merely incidental to the agreement (*dolus incidens*). Third, he distinguishes between deceit exerted by the other party to the contract (*per ipsummet venditorem*) and deceit stemming from a third party (*per tertium*).[1044] Molina does not include, as Lessius would, a distinction between substantial and accidental deceit. Instead, he adamantly sticks to the difference between contracts *bonae fidei* and *stricti iuris*. It forms the organisational lynchpin of his exposition.

Molina sets out to confirm the distinction made between contracts *stricti iuris* and contracts *bonae fidei* as a matter of civil law.[1045] In the external courts, the former are merely voidable if affected by mistake, while the latter are automatically void. As a matter of conscience, though, he thinks that *bonae fidei* contracts as well as *stricti iuris* contracts are void *ipso facto*, since voluntary consent is equally vitiated through deceit in both cases.[1046] He rejects the opinion of 'the few' who hold that *bonae fidei* contracts are voidable at the option of the deceived party by virtue of an *exceptio doli*.[1047] Molina expressly opposes this adoption of the rules

---

[1043] It needs to be recalled that factual deceit derives from considerations of justice in exchange. This Aristotelian idea was part and parcel of the scholastic tradition, although nowadays it is difficult to think of 'deceit' without evil intentions on the part of one of the contracting parties in the first place. The debate on *laesio enormis* is connected to this concept of factual deceit, which takes place regardless of the intention of the contracting parties.

[1044] As regards deceit exercised by a third party, it needs to be recalled that in the scholastic tradition, it seems to have had a much wider meaning than just persons external to the contract. Under the heading *dolus a tertio* we also see them dealing with material influences external to the contract itself, including changed circumstances.

[1045] Molina, *De iustitia et iure*, tom. 2 (*De contractibus*), tract. 2, disp. 259, col. 27, num. 6.

[1046] Molina, *De iustitia et iure*, tom. 2 (*De contractibus*), tract. 2, disp. 259, col. 28, num. 7: 'Illud cum Conrado et Covarruvia, locis citatis, et cum aliis admonuerim, in conscientiae foro, quando dolus causam dedit contractui, etiam si is sit stricti iuris, esse nullum. Ratio est, quoniam consensus in contractum per dolum, quando secluso dolo eliciendus non fuisset, insufficiens ex ipsa rei natura est, ut ex eo obligatio ratione talis contractus resultet, eo quod non sit tam voluntarius quam ad id est necesse.' Compare Molina, *De iustitia et iure*, tom. 2 (*De contractibus*), tract. 2, disp. 352, col. 416, num. 14.

[1047] Molina, *De iustitia et iure*, tom. 2 (*De contractibus*), tract. 2, disp. 259, cols. 27–28, num. 6: 'Quare reiicienda est paucorum sententia, quos Panormitanus, Covarruvias et Conradus referunt, asserentium, etiam quando dolus dat causam contractui bonae fidei, non esse ipso iure nullum, sed rescindendum esse doli exceptione, non secus ac contractus stricti iuris doli exceptione rescinditur.'

applied to *stricti iuris* contracts in the case of *bonae fidei* contracts, while his younger colleague from Leuven, Lessius, would do precisely that. In the event of onerous *bonae fidei* contracts—except marriage[1048]—Molina always sanctions *dolus causam dans* with nullity *ab initio*. Moreover, he draws an explicit parallel with his solution of duress: mistake and deceit lead to involuntariness and autonomic nullity, just as consent which has been extorted by duress.[1049]

Molina then adds an important modification to this conclusion: although a *bonae fidei* contract affected by mistake is automatically void in both courts, if the deceived party wishes the contract to remain valid, the defrauder must observe the contract. Molina would draw heavy criticism of Lessius for the paradox behind his conclusion that the contract is automatically void at the option of the deceived party (*in decepti favorem ipso iure nullus*).[1050] In taking this view, Molina actually sacrificed juridical logic on the altar of punishment (*in poenam doli*), natural equity (*naturalis aequitas*) and the common good (*bonum commune*).[1051] Just as Summenhart and Medina before him, he realized that the juridical sanctioning of deceit with nullity *ab initio* would favor the deceiver, since he could take advantage of the other party and then simply take to his heels.

[1048] Molina, *De iustitia et iure*, tom. 2 (*De contractibus*), tract. 2, disp. 352, cols. 413–414, num. 5: 'Illud est observandum, quamvis conclusio proposita locum habeat in bonae fidei contractibus onerosis, in matrimonio tamen locum non habere, ut disp. 259 citata dictum est. Si enim quis per dolum, qui causam det contractui, cum aliqua contrahat, affirmans se habere divitias aut esse nobilem vel habere alias qualitates, quas non habeat, sane, interim dum dolus errorem non causet in personam aut in conditionem libertatis, validum est matrimonium propter naturam, indissolubilitatem, ac privilegia eius contractus.'

[1049] Molina, *De iustitia et iure*, tom. 2, (*De contractibus*), tract. 2, disp. 352, col. 412, num. 2: 'Cum ergo error involuntarium in re proposita causet, assensusque extortus sit per dolum ac injustitiam eius, cui consentiens intendebat se per eum obligare, consequens est, ut non magis efficax sit ad obligandum, stando in foro conscientiae ac jure naturali, quam consensus extortus per vim et metum, de quo disp. 326 ad 2 ostendimus non obligare.'

[1050] Molina, *De iustitia et iure*, tom. 2 (*De contractibus*), tract. 2, disp. 352, col. 412, num. 2: 'His ita constitutis, prima conclusio est. Quando dolus causam dat emptioni aut venditioni aut cuicunque alteri contractui bonae fidei, altero contrahente in dolo communicante, contractus neque in conscientiae neque in exteriori foro valet, sed in decepti favorem est ipso iure nullus (…), quod si deceptus velit nihilominus stare contractui, decipiens dissolvere illum non potest, sed cogitur illi stare.'

[1051] Molina, *De iustitia et iure*, tom. 2 (*De contractibus*), tract. 2, disp. 352, col. 413, num. 4: 'Ac sane, quando alter contrahentium sua culpa est per accidens causa, quod ex parte alterius nulla obligatio oriatur, nullum omnino est absurdum, quod ex contractu, ex quo alioqui utrinque obligatio oriretur, nascatur ex altera tantum parte. His accedit, ius humanum videri intendisse tribuere vim consensui dolosi ad eum obligandum ante latam sententiam, iudicisve compulsionem, non solum in poenam doli, sed etiam ex naturali aequitate, et quoniam ita bono communi erat expediens.'

Yet contrary to Summenhart and Medina, Molina did not think that the
deceived party needed to wait for a sentence in court in order to be able
to enforce the contract on the part of the deceiver. He thought it much
more probable that natural equity obligated the deceiver to remain loyal
to the contract even before he was compelled by a judge to fulfill his contractual obligations (*etiam ante ullam iudicis sententiam*).[1052]

There is another point on which Molina departs from the standpoints
of Summenhart and Medina: the influence of *dolus causam dans* exerted
by third parties on the validity of a contract as a matter of natural law. To
be sure, there was no doubt about the validity of contract, no matter how
mistaken one of the parties had been by a third party, as a matter of positive law.[1053] Yet the non-mistaken party to this type of contract could not
be granted a right to enforce the contract before the court of conscience,
according to Summenhart and Medina, since the other party had not
assented voluntarily. By natural definition, a contract consists in mutual
and voluntary consent. They concluded from this that if one of the parties
had not consented voluntarily, the contract had not come into existence
altogether. The non-mistaken party would commit a sin if he nonetheless
wished the mistaken party to honour his contractual obligations.

Molina acknowledged that deceit by a third party remained without
effect on the validity of a contract as a matter of positive law. He did not
think, however, that the court of conscience must be ruled by a different law. As a matter of natural law, too, a contract remains valid even
though one of the parties to the contract has been mistaken by a third
party. What is more, Molina points out,[1054] 'that is precisely the reason
why I did not merely build my argument around involuntariness (*involuntarium*) in my first conclusion, as Summenhart and Medina did, but rather

---

[1052] Molina, *De iustitia et iure*, tom. 2 (*De contractibus*), tract. 2, disp. 352, col. 413,
num. 4: 'Ego probabilius multo arbitror, absolute, quando quis per dolum causam dantem
contractui cum aliquo celebravit contractum, manere obligatum in conscientiae foro ad
standum illi, etiam ante ullam iudicis sententiam aut compulsionem, modo deceptus velit,
idque nihil impediente quod ex parte decepti nec in conscientiae nec in exteriori foro
consurgat obligatio.'
[1053] E.g. Glossa *In hoc ipso*, 3 ad D. 4,3,7 in *Corporis Iustinianaei Digestum vetus* (ed.
Gothofredi), tom. 1, col. 508.
[1054] Molina, *De iustitia et iure*, tom. 2, tract. 2, disp. 352, col. 414, num. 8: 'Arbitror, contractum illum, stando in solo iure naturali, esse validum, falsumque esse fundamentum,
cui Conradus et Medina nituntur, nempe, involuntarium illud sufficiens esse, ut contractus
ille natura rei, standoque in solo iure naturali, sit nullus. Atque hac de causa nos in probatione primae conclusionis innixi non fuimus soli involuntario, ut Conradus et Medina
nituntur, sed potissimum iniuriae ac dolo, quo contrahens ipse, comparatione cuius resul-
tare obligatio debet, consensum extrahit.'

around the injury and deceit (*iniuria ac dolus*) by means of which the deceiving contracting party extorted the other party's contractual obligation towards him.' Indeed, in demonstrating why *bonae fidei* contracts are automatically void, Molina pointed out that the mistaken party had given his consent because the deceiver had elicited this consent through deceit and injustice. The assent was not merely involuntary but extorted through deceit and injustice (*assensus extortus per dolum ac injustitiam*).[1055]

On account of the injury he suffered, the mistaken party is granted an action against the third party who deceived him, according to Molina.[1056] The contract itself, however, remains valid. Involuntary consent stemming from mistake about the motive to the contract (*error penes motivum*) does not affect the validity of onerous contracts as a matter of natural law— although it does invalidate gratuitous contracts.[1057] Similarly, involuntary consent stemming from ignorance of certain decisive circumstances (*ignorantia circunstantiarum*) is irrelevant to the validity of a contract. Molina explains why no contract can be deemed to be made under that condition as a matter of natural law (*ex ipsa natura rei*):[1058] when asked, no contracting party would ever wish that condition (*lex*) to rule the contract, and it would not be expedient to the common good either.

Thus far we have seen Molina's view of the effects of *dolus causam dans*—exerted either by a party to the contract or by a third party—on *bonae fidei* contracts. He thinks they are absolutely void in both the external and internal forum, but on account of equity he still grants the mistaken party a claim to performance if she should wish so.

[1055] Molina, *De iustitia et iure*, tom. 2, tract. 2, disp. 352, col. 412, num. 2, cited above.

[1056] Molina, *De iustitia et iure*, tom. 2, tract. 2, disp. 352, col. 414, num. 7: 'Quando dolus causam quidem dat contractui, sed adhibetur a quodam tertio, non communicante altero contrahente in dolo, validus est contractus, datur tamen decepto actio adversus tertium qui dolum adhibuit.'

[1057] Molina, *De iustitia et iure*, tom. 2, tract. 2, disp. 352, cols. 414–415, num. 8: 'Quo loco observa, quamvis involuntarium, quod oritur ex errore, non quocunque, sed causae, cui donans nititur ad donandum, invalidam reddat donationem, ut disp. 209 late explanatum est. In contractibus tamen onerosis, involuntarium quod ex errore oritur penes motivum unde quis inducitur ad contrahendum cum aliquo, ut ad emendum, permutandum, conducendum, etc. non vitiat contractum ex rei ipsius natura, et multo minus eum vitiat involutarium, quod oritur ex ignorantia aliarum, quas si sciret, non celebraret talem contractum.'

[1058] Molina, *De iustitia et iure*, tom. 2 (*De contractibus*), tract. 2, disp. 352, col. 415, num. 8: 'Ratio autem est, quoniam nullus contrahentium admitteret eam legem, si illam proponeret alter contrahentium, neque ea lex communi expedit bono, quare contractus ex ipsa natura non censentur sub ea lege celebrati.'

When it comes to contracts *stricti iuris* affected by *dolus causam dans*, Molina takes a quite confusing view.[1059] On the one hand, he says that a contract *stricti iuris* affected by mistake is absolutely null (*ipso iure nullus*), citing Summenhart and Covarruvias, but he immediately adds to this that the defrauder is bound to rescind the contract if the mistaken party wishes him to do so—which suggests that the nullity is only relative. Moreover, Molina claims that the law of conscience governing contracts *stricti iuris* affected by mistake should be similar to the law of the land. But the law of the land considers contracts *stricti iuris* to be valid, even if they are affected by mistake, and voidable at the option of the mistaken party. Lugo and Grotius undoubtedly had this passage in mind, amongst other texts, when they deplored the confusion created by the scholastics on the subject of mistake.

Less confusing and quite conventional is Molina's view that *dolus incidens* does not affect the validity of either a contract *bonae fidei* or a contract *stricti iuris* at all. The contract itself remains untouched, because of the rule that what is useful is not vitiated by the useless (*utile per inutile non vitiatur*).[1060] The cases envisaged here are mostly to do with contracts in which commutative justice has been violated through the conveyance of a good in exchange for an unjust price. Contracts *bonae fidei* affected by incidental deceit do give rise to restitution of the excess in the price (*quod ratione doli plus dedit*), even in case of lesion below moiety, before the internal as well as the external forum.[1061] Contracts *stricti iuris* can only give rise to restitution in the court of conscience.[1062]

[1059] Molina, *De iustitia et iure*, tom. 2, (*De contractibus*), tract. 2, disp. 352, col. 416, num. 14: 'Quinta conclusio. Quando dolus causam dedit contractui stricti iuris, validus est contractus in foro exteriori. Conceditur tamen decepto exceptio, quod dolus causam dederit contractui, ut, ope talis exceptionis, non cogatur implere, siquid contractus restat adhuc implendum. Item, si, post contractum impletum, deceptus in aliquo sit damno, conceditur ei actio de dolo adversus decipientem, ut damnum resarciat (…). Hanc etiam conclusionem ex parte stabilivimus disp. 259 citata. Ubi cum Conrado, Covarruvia et aliis diximus, in foro conscientiae contractum esse ipso iure nullum, tenerique dolosum ad rescissionem illius, si deceptus ita velit, eo quod consensus, per dolum et iniuriam extractus, sufficiens non sit ad obligandum deceptum, expedireque ut idem in exteriori foro sanciretur.'
[1060] For the origins of this rule in VI 5,13,37, see D. Liebs, *Lateinische Rechtsregeln und Rechtssprichwörter*, München 2007, p. 239, num. 34–35. It has rightly been argued that this rule draws its origins from the Roman law of testate succession (*favor testamenti*), notably D. 45,1,1,5, and that it was initially restricted to it; cf. Zimmermann, *The law of obligations*, p. 708–709 and 720.
[1061] Molina, *De iustitia et iure*, tom. 2 (*De contractibus*), tract. 2, disp. 352, col. 416, num. 14.
[1062] Molina, *De iustitia et iure*, tom. 2 (*De contractibus*), tract. 2, disp. 352, cols. 416–417, num. 15.

4.3.2.4 Sánchez: delictual and criminal liability

Compared to his elaborate discussion on the impact of duress on the validity of a contract, Sánchez's treatment of deceit and mistake is rather disappointing, at least from the point of view of the development of a general law of contract. He does treat mistake quite extensively as a diriment impediment to marriage,[1063] but he fails to give an elaborate account of the impact of mistake on contractual consent in general. Relevant in this context, however, are a couple of statements made by Sánchez in the framework of his chapter on engagement contracts (*sponsalia*). The question whether such contracts are void ipso facto or only voidable at the option of the mistaken party matters to him, since it determines the applicability or otherwise of the *impedimentum publicae honestatis*. In short, this diriment impediment renders void a marriage between an engaged party and a blood relative of the other engaged party, since the preceding engagement creates a certain bond of conjunction (*vinculum coniunctionis*), which, even though it is less strong than affinity (*affinitas*), dissolves a subsequent marriage of that type.[1064] This impediment cannot come about for either of the parties if the engagement contract is automatically avoided by virtue of mistake.[1065]

While Sánchez considers contracts affected by duress to be voidable at the option of the coerced party, he seems inclined to think that contracts *bonae fidei* affected by *dolus causam dans* are avoided automatically. His argumentation is based on the idea that mistake renders contractual consent involuntary (*error involuntarium causat*), and, hence, radically nullifies contractual obligation.[1066] Sánchez is reluctant, though, to give

---

[1063] Sánchez, *Disputationes de sancto matrimonii sacramento*, tom. 2, lib. 7, disp. 18–24, p. 68–93. Of particular interest is his discussion on the relevance or not of mistake about the quality (*error qualitatis*) of the spouse, which was traditionally thought to be redundant; for a discussion, see P. Fedele, *Error qualitatis redundans in errorem personae*, [Biblioteca de 'Il diritto ecclesiastico'], Roma 1934, p. 5–6.

[1064] Sánchez, *Disputationes de sancto matrimonii sacramento*, tom. 2, lib. 7, disp. 68, num. 1, p. 228.

[1065] Sánchez, *Disputationes de sancto matrimonii sacramento*, tom. 1, lib. 1, disp. 64, num. 1, p. 110: 'Huius rei cognitio necessaria valde est, propter publicae honestatis impedimentum, si enim sponsalia valida sint, quamvis postea irritentur, orietur utique, quod secus est, si ipso iure irrita sint.'

[1066] Sánchez, *Disputationes de sancto matrimonii sacramento*, tom. 1, lib. 1, disp. 64, num. 3, p. 110: 'Et ratio est, quoniam sic deceptus sponsus, consensurus minime erat, sed errore ductus consensit, in quo alter per dolum et iniustitiam participavit, cum ergo error involuntarium causet, assensusque sit per dolum et iniustitiam extortus eius, cui alter consentiens se intendebat obligare, invalidus et inefficax erit.'

a straightforward answer to the question whether the deceiver can still be bound by the engagement contract. He deems it more probable that both parties are delivered from the obligation that was created by giving their word of engagement, although he leaves open the possibility of delictual liability.[1067] His solution is reminiscent of Molina's. He argues that the deceiver can be bound to the engagement contract on account of the wrongful harm that he did to the other party (*ratione damni secuti*), provided that the deceived party wishes the engagement to remain valid. Sánchez expressly refers to the analogous solution in the case of fictitious promises, where the deceiver can also remain bound by virtue of delictual liability.[1068] Also, Sánchez envisages that the deceiver can be held to perform the engagement contract by virtue of criminal liability (*in poenam fraudis*), at least from the moment he has been condemned by the judge.[1069] This solution recalls Summenhart's and Medina's.

In light of his indebtedness to Molina, on the one hand, and to Summenhart and Medina, on the other hand, it is no surprise to find that Sánchez considers the question what effect the deceit by a third party has on the validity of an engagement contract to be very difficult (*maior difficultas*). As mentioned before, Summenhart and Medina acknowledged that deceit by a third party could not compromise the validity of a contract as a matter of positive law, but insisted that the law of conscience must be different. Molina, on the other hand, argued that, even in conscience, a contract affected by deceit exercised by a third party remained valid. Molina admitted that the mistaken party could be granted an action for damages against the deceiver, but confirmed the validity of the contract. At first, Sánchez follows Summenhart and Medina, submitting that deceit, whether stemming from the other party to the contract or from a third party, frustrates voluntary consent, which is the natural prerequisite of contractual obligation.[1070] Eventually, however, Sánchez concludes with Molina that those contracts of good faith, particularly engagement, are not

---

[1067] Sánchez, *Disputationes de sancto matrimonii sacramento*, tom. 1, lib. 1, disp. 64, num. 3, p. 110: 'Et breviter nunc probabilius credo, utrumque liberum esse a fide sponsalium, nisi aliud damnum secutum sit. Ratione enim damni secuti posset decipiens teneri altero volente, sicut de ficte promittente late dixi supra disp. 10.'

[1068] Discussed supra, p. 193–194.

[1069] Sánchez, *Disputationes de sancto matrimonii sacramento*, tom. 1, lib. 1, disp. 64, num. 3, p. 110: 'Posset etiam decipiens in poenam fraudis cogi stare sponsalibus, volente altero. Cum tamen haec poena sit, iudicis sententiam desiderat.'

[1070] Sánchez, *Disputationes de sancto matrimonii sacramento*, tom. 1, lib. 1, disp. 64, num. 4, p. 110: 'Secundo, quia deficit consensus, cum ex errore praestitus sit, et nihil magis contrarium consensui quam error.'

frustrated by deceit from a third party. Citing Bartolus and Covarruvias, he points out that this form of deceit does not concern the substance of the contract, but the cause that leads to the conclusion of the contract.[1071]

4.3.2.5   *A swansong to nullity* ab initio

The huge persistence in the early modern scholastic tradition of the Roman idea that *dolus causam dans* resulted in absolute nullity for *bonae fidei* contracts emerges one last time very clearly from the work *On obligations* by the Portuguese Jesuit Fernão Rebelo. Published in 1608, at the time when Lessius' *On justice and right* had been on the market for about three years, it shows signs of the same turn towards a general law of contract while safeguarding the common opinion that *dolus causam dans contractui bonae fidei* results in absolute nullity.

From an organisational point of view, Rebelo's questions about the effects of mistake on contractual validity are part of a chapter on general contract law (*De contractibus in genere*) preceding a systematic discussion of specific contracts.[1072] Yet despite this modern format, it clings to the traditional view of mistake advocated by the common opinion represented by Molina and Sánchez amongst others. In light of the new approach to this question which had just about been advocated by Lessius (see below), Rebelo's deeply conventional account appears like the swansong of a firmly resisting yet bygone tradition.

Rebelo expressly makes the answer about the effects of mistake on contractual validity dependent on the solution of the larger question whether it makes sense to distinguish contracts *bonae fidei* from contracts *stricti iuris*. In an exposition that paradoxically seems both to imitate and deviate from Covarruvias' ideas, Rebelo arrives at the conclusion that both according to the Roman canon law (*utrumque ius*) and the law of conscience (*forum conscientiae*) the discriminatory treatment of contracts *bonae fidei* and *stricti iuris* is fundamental.[1073]

[1071] Sánchez, *Disputationes de sancto matrimonii sacramento*, tom. 1, lib. 1, disp. 64, num. 5, p. 110: '(...) Non deficit substantialis consensus, ut probat optime Bartolus (...), Covarruvias (...), non enim error contingit circa substantialia contractus, sed circa causam ad contrahendum inducentem (....)'.

[1072] Rebelo, *Opus de obligationibus justitiae, religionis et charitatis*, part. 2, lib. 1, quaest. 2 (*Utrum in contractibus bonae fidei obligatio sit extendenda, in contractibus vero stricti iuris restringenda*) and quaest. 6 (*De dolo sive fraude infirmante contractus*).

[1073] Rebelo, *De obligationibus justitiae, religionis et charitatis*, part. 2, lib. 1, quaest. 2, sect. 1, num. 4, litt. a, p. 198: 'Unde ad quaestionem conclusio sit. Non solum in utroque iure, sed etiam in foro conscientiae admittendum est istud discrimen, ut quidam contractus, vel

Importantly, this means that the interpretation of the extent of the obligations (*ratio obligandi*) deriving from these respective contracts differs: obligations ensuing from contracts *bonae fidei* call for an extensive interpretation (*amplior*), while obligations deriving from contracts *stricti iuris* require a restrictive interpretation (*restrictior*). Rebelo compares the variety in the nature of contracts to the variety in the nature of precious natural materials:[1074] it is possible to extend wax, but it is impossible to extend adamant. He drew this metaphor from the Spanish canonist Francesco Sarmiento de Mendoza (d. 1595), who argued against Baldus that, even as a matter of canon law, not all contracts should be interpreted along the lines of good faith.[1075]

Quoting gloss *Bonae fidei sunt* to paragraph *Actionum* (Inst. 4,6,28) Rebelo indicates just as Sarmiento, that, of course, this distinction does not imply that contracts *stricti iuris* are not governed by good faith, in the sense that deceit and fraud must be absent. Covarruvias, too, had insisted that the word '*bona fides*' can have two senses, depending on whether it is being opposed to fraud or being opposed to strict interpretation. Rebelo recalls that the distinction between contracts *bonae fidei* and *stricti iuris* has only to do with the latter contradistinction, namely with the interpretation of contracts.[1076] The canon law does require all contracts to be concluded in good faith, viz. without deceit, as a matter

---

quasi contractus, quoad obligandi rationem ampliorem, alii restrictiorem interpretationem suapte natura recipere debeant, prout doctores communiter ac iura affirmant.'

[1074] Rebelo, *De obligationibus justitiae, religionis et charitatis*, part. 2, lib. 1, quaest. 2, sect. 1, num. 4, litt. b, p. 198: 'Sicut alia est natura adamantis, saphiri vel alterius lapidis, quam nulla ratione possis extendere; alia vero auri, caerae, panni vel corii, quae extensionem suapte natura possunt recipere, ita proportione quadam de multiplici contractuum natura sive materia philosophandum est.'

[1075] Francesco Sarmiento de Mendoza, *De selectis interpretationibus*, Francoforti ad Moenum 1580, lib. 3, cap. 3, num. 1 (*De iure canonico etiam sunt contractus stricti iuris*), p. 187: 'Si enim materiam ligneam vel lapideam, qualis est materia contractuum stricti iuris, velimus extendere, vel diducere, sicut materiam plumbeam, seu auream, qualis est materia contractuum bonae fidei, non esset ex bono et aequo procedere, sed materiam corrumpere.'

For biographical details of Sarmiento, see Antonio, *Bibliotheca Hispana nova*, p. 476–477.

[1076] Rebelo, *De obligationibus justitiae, religionis et charitatis*, part. 2, lib. 1, quaest. 2, sect. 1, num. 3, litt. d, p. 198: 'Sed cum bona fides dupliciter dicatur, ut notat glossa citata, uno modo, quod contraria sit dolo aut fraudi, quo pacto omnes contractus bonae fidei esse debent, hoc, sine dolo et fraude celebrari ac impleri; altero per antonomasiam, hoc est, propter exuberantem fidem, quae in certis contractibus esse debet (quod scilicet ad multa ex bono et aequo, prout iudex sive vir prudens arbitrabitur, de quibus non fuit actum inter partes, suapte natura extendi debeat) a fide, hoc secundo modo sumpta, contractus dicuntur bonae fidei, ut opponuntur aliis stricti iuris, quia etiam ex eo tales dicuntur,

of course, although it had not blurred the distinction between *bonae fidei* and *stricti iuris* contracts.

Contrary to Covarruvias, Rebelo indicates that the interpretation in contracts *bonae fidei* has nothing to do with the Aristotelian concept of equity (*epieikeia*). Granted, the distinction is closely linked to the interpretation of the extent of contractual obligation rather than to the tolerance of deceit in them. Yet equity (*epieikeia*) implies that the intent of the legislator (*intentio legislatoris*) is taken into consideration rather than the literal wording of the law, because they are thought to be in conflict with each other. The interpretation of a *bonae fidei* contract, on the other hand, is based on the nature of the contract (*natura contractus*),[1077] because the nature of the contract is thought to be tantamount to the declaration or intent of the contracting parties.[1078] By definition, there cannot be a conflict between the nature of the contract and the intent of the parties.

From this theoretical distinction Rebelo infers the common opinion that the effect of *dolus causam dans* on contracts *stricti iuris* is different from the effect of mistake on contracts *bonae fidei*: the former are voidable (*rescindi possunt*), whereas the latter are void (*ipso iure irritus*).[1079] He nevertheless indicates that his own opinion is different. As a matter of fact, in another place of his work, he adopts a general regime of nullity *ab initio* for both *bonae fidei* and *stricti iuris* contracts affected by *dolus*

---

quod natura sua habent, ut in eis non debeat fieri extensio, nisi ad ea, de quibus expressio facta fuit.'

[1077] On this elusive notion, which was frequently distinguished from the 'essence' or 'substance' of the contract, see Birocchi, *Tra elaborazioni nuove e dottrine tradizionali, Il contratto trino e la natura contractus*, passim.

[1078] Rebelo, *De obligationibus justitiae, religionis et charitatis*, part. 2, lib. 1, quaest. 2, sect. 1, num. 3, litt. e-a, p. 198: 'Unde etiam colliges hanc bonam fidem secundo modo acceptam longe diversam esse ab Epicaeia, qua iudex solet iudicare secundum intentionem legislatoris praetermissis interdum verbis legis. Nam in extendenda vel decurtanda sive restringenda obligatione contractus attendi debet semper natura ipsius contractus et in quibusdam amplior, in aliis restrictior interpretatio facienda erit naturae cuiusque contractus congruens; quod ipsum nec verbis nec intentioni contrahentium saltem implicite repugnans est, sed potius consentaneum.'

[1079] Rebelo, *De obligationibus justitiae, religionis et charitatis*, part. 2, lib. 1, quaest. 2, sect. 1, num. 6, litt. b, p. 199: 'Contractus bonae fidei in quo intervenit dolus dans causam contractui est ipso iure irritus, non tamen ii qui sunt stricti riuis, quamvis per exceptionem doli rescindi possint.'

causam dans.[1080] If they are affected merely by *dolus incidens*, say lesion, they remain valid.[1081]

Another inference from this general distinction concerns the irrelevance of changed circumstances on *bonae fidei* contracts.[1082] If you become aware of a circumstance that would have prevented you from entering into a contract if you had known about it at the moment of concluding the contract, you can revoke a *stricti iuris* contract. A *bonae fidei* contract, however, cannot be rescinded if suddenly circumstances change for the worse or a past circumstance is brought to light.

Last, Rebelo argues that the law of duress and the law of mistake are fundamentally different.[1083] Duress makes contracts voidable, while mistake brings about nullity *ab initio*.[1084] Duress does not remove voluntary consent altogether, while mistake and the subsequent ignorance are incompatible with voluntary consent. Only Lessius would succeed in bringing the law of mistake and duress together.

4.3.3   *Voidability and the end of the* bonae fidei / stricti iuris *distinction*

As he returned from an exciting investigation into the long forgotten roots of Grotius' views on mistake, the eminent legal historian Robert Feenstra wondered whether the manifest dependency of Grotius on Lessius meant

---

1080 Rebelo, *De obligationibus justitiae, religionis et charitatis*, part. 2, lib. 1, quaest. 6, sect. 2, num. 9, litt. a, p. 213: 'Si vero dolus causam contractui det, omnis contractus, sive lucrosus ille sit, cuiusmodi est liberalis promissio ac donatio facta homini et intuitu hominis, et alii, in quibus solum ex parte decepti obligatio existit, sive onerosus, in quo utrimque obligatio cernitur, sive sit bonae fidei, sive stricti iuris, in foro quidem conscientiae invalidus est, uno excepto matrimonio (…).'

1081 Rebelo, *De obligationibus justitiae, religionis et charitatis*, part. 2, lib. 1, quaest. 6, sect. 2, num. 8, litt. c–e, p. 213.

1082 Rebelo, *De obligationibus justitiae, religionis et charitatis*, part. 2, lib. 1, quaest. 2, sect. 1, num. 8, litt. d, p. 199: 'Contractus stricti iuris generaliter non extenduntur ad ea quae praecogitata minime sunt. Unde si postquam aliquid v.g. liberaliter pollicitus es, superveniat magna difficultas vel inopinatus eventus, quae si praecogitasses, non promisisses, fas est non stare promissis, ut etiam docet D. Thom. 2.2.quaest.110.art.3.ad.5 communiter receptus. Secus de bonae fidei contractibus dicendum, unde (…) nefas erit ab allis resilire propter inexcogitatum eventum, de quo si praecogitasses, non contraxisses.'

1083 Rebelo, *De obligationibus justitiae, religionis et charitatis*, part. 2, lib. 1, quaest. 6, sect. 2, num. 11, litt. c, p. 214: 'Obiicies rursus, metus dans causam contractui etiam bonae fidei, non reddit illum ipso iure nullum, sed tantum venit rescindendus, si metus probetur (…). Pari ergo ratione nec dolus dans causam contractui bonae fidei illum ipso iure rescindet. Neganda tamen est consequentia.'

1084 In *De obligationibus justitiae, religionis et charitatis*, part. 2, lib. 1, quaest. 5, num. 17, p. 211, Rebelo had claimed that duress results in absolute nullity. Cf. supra, n. 938.

that the cradle of the modern doctrine of mistake must be transferred from present-day Holland to Belgium.[1085] Ever since, scholars have confirmed the seminal contribution of Lessius to the development of our concept of mistake.[1086] Apart from laying bare the obvious influence of Lessius on Grotius, it falls outside the scope of this study, however, to try to weave an almost impossible direct web of lineage between the past and the present. It is a daunting task to try to come to grips with the bright yet somewhat cloud covered minds of the scholastics themselves. Yet there are several good reasons, indeed, for a jurist to investigate Leonard Lessius' analysis of the vices of the will, and of mistake in particular.

4.3.3.1 The format of Lessius' revolution

The first reason why Lessius is worthy of scrutiny has to do with the form and context of his account. He poses the question about the effects of mistake on contractual validity in general terms (*utrum contractus, cui error vel dolus causam dederit, sit validus*), and he does so within the framework of an autonomous chapter on the law of contract in general (*de contractibus in genere*), which preceeds a systematic discussion of the panoply of specific contracts. Hence, the doctrine of mistake ceases to be a commentary on a particular paragraph from the body of Roman or canon law, a special topic of the law of sales, or a gloss to the law of marriage, vows and oaths. Furthermore, Lessius' account of mistake displays three of the central characteristics of his works: brevity, lucidity, and logical consistency. While we have seen his predecessors running into absurd conclusions in order to reconcile the legal tradition with the needs of society, Lessius ingeniously alters the juridical framework itself.

Preceding the actual discussion is a list of three distinctions on which his solution depends.[1087] It is not entirely the same as the list mentioned at the outset of Molina's discussion. First, Lessius distinguishes substantial mistake or deceit (*circa substantiam rei*) from accidental mistake (*circa accidentia et extrinseca*). Second, he mentions the usual distinction between *dolus causam dans* and *dolus incidens*. Third, he points out three different sources of the mistake: the other party to the contract (*a parte*

[1085] Feenstra, *De oorsprong van Hugo de Groot's leer over de dwaling*, p. 100.

[1086] E.g. M.J. Schermaier, *Mistake, misrepresentation and precontractual duties to inform, The civil law tradition*, in: R. Sefton-Green (ed.), Mistake, fraud and duties to inform in European contract law, The Common Core of European Private Law Series, Cambridge 2005, p. 56.

[1087] Lessius, *De iustitia et iure*, lib. 2, cap. 17, dub. 5, num. 27, p. 198.

quae tecum contrahit), an independent third party (*a tertio*), or your own
judgment (*ex propria tua opinione*). In contrast with Molina, the distinction between contracts *bonae fidei* and *stricti iuris* does not play a significant role as an organisational principle in Lessius' exposition any more.
Quite the reverse, it is the convergence of these traditionally distinguished
types of contract that is at the heart of Lessius' argumentation.

Starting with the first distinction, Lessius is capable very quickly of sorting out where the real crux of the debate lies. As soon as mistake concerns a substantial element of a contract, as when a buyer receives glass
instead of a gem, the answer is easy: the contract falls short of substantial
consent (*consensus substantialis*), and, accordingly, is void *ab initio* as a
matter of natural law.[1088] If mistake does not concern a substantial element, the solution bifurcates according to the question whether mistake
is fundamental or incidental to the contract. If mistake is incidental to
the contract (*dolus incidens*) the solution needs no further clarification
either: the contract remains valid. Even in case of lesion beyond moiety
(*laesio enormis*), the only requirement is that equality in exchange be
restored.[1089] Contrary to Molina, Lessius does not differentiate between
contracts *stricti iuris* or *bonae fidei* at all. The more problematic case, however, concerns non-substantial mistake that has been decisive in entering
into the contract (*dolus causam dans*).

In order to come to grips with the rather complicated issue of non-
substantial yet fundamental mistake, Lessius brings in the third distinction, depending on whether the mistake was caused by the other party to
the contract or by another person, including the mistaken party herself.
Both questions are thoroughly dealt with by Lessius. They are the source
of a stimulating and innovative debate toward which we will successively
turn our attention. In the first debate we will see how Lessius brings about
a turnaround in the scholastic tradition by advocating a general regime
of voidability in the case of *dolus causam dans*, thereby removing the

---

[1088] Lessius, *De iustitia et iure*, lib. 2, cap. 17, dub. 5, num. 27, p. 198: 'Quando contingit
in altero contrahentium esse errorem circa substantiam rei, contractus iure naturae est
irritus. (...) Ratio est, quia deest substantialis consensus, nam non consentit in illam rem,
sed in aliam, quam putat subesse istis accidentalibus.'

[1089] Lessius, *De iustitia et iure*, lib. 2, cap. 17, dub. 5, num. 28, p. 198: 'Si non sit error
circa substantiam, contractus est validus, modo dolus non det causam contractui. (...)
Probatur, quia iste vere consentit, v.g. in emptionem istius rei, sciens et volens, absque
metu et fraude. Qui consensus sufficiens est ad contractus validitatem. (...) Hinc sequitur,
contractum esse validum, etiamsi quis deceptus sit in pretio ultra dimidium, quia dolus
non dedit causam contractui, sed solum est causa maioris vel minoris pretii.'

traditional distinction between contracts *bonae fidei* and *stricti iuris*. In the second debate, he first follows Molina, but then curiously argues in favor of a generalized tacit condition allowing a party to rescind a contract—also paying damages if the other party would suffer injury from that—in the event that he realizes that he has been deceived by a third party or by his own wrong understanding of external circumstances.

4.3.3.2   *General application of voidability*

The second reason why it is worthwhile examining Lessius' thought on duress has to do with the content of his argumentation itself. With one stroke of the pen, Lessius overturns what had become established as the common opinion in the sixteenth century.[1090] Lessius comes straight to the point:[1091]

> When deceit is fundamental to the contract and the other party to the contract is its instigator or at least an associate to the deceit, [a] the contract is still not entirely void (*non omnino irritus*) as a matter of natural law, [b] although it is voidable at the option of the deceived party (*pro arbitrio eius qui deceptus est irritari potest*), provided the contract is dissoluble.

This is a statement of which the novelty is probably inversely proportional to its brevity. Lessius proceeds by producing arguments in favor of both of its components before he goes on to refute the traditional distinction made between contracts *stricti iuris* and *bonae fidei* when it comes to the effects of mistake.

As regards the fact that the contract is not entirely void [a], Lessius argues that it follows from the commonly shared assumption that a contract *stricti iuris* remains valid as a matter of civil law even if it is affected by deceit or duress. He indicates that it would have been impossible for the law of the land to take that view if the contract had been absolutely void as a matter of natural law.[1092] For what is void as a matter of natural

---

[1090] Gómez, *Commentarii variaeque resolutiones*, tom. 2, cap. 2, num. 21, p. 224–225.

[1091] Lessius, *De iustitia et iure*, lib. 2, cap. 17, dub. 5, num. 29, p. 199: 'Si dolus det causam contractui, et proveniat ab altera parte, vel saltem illa sit particeps doli, contractus adhuc iure naturae non est omnino irritus, tamen pro arbitrio eius qui deceptus est, (si solubilis sit) irritari potest.'

[1092] Lessius, *De iustitia et iure*, lib. 2, cap. 17, dub. 5, num. 29, p. 199: 'Communis sententia doctorum est, contractum stricti iuris, etiamsi dolus vel metus ei causam dederit, validum esse, doli tamen mali vel metus exceptione actionem elidi, et colligitur ex l. dolo 5, C. de inutilibus stipulationibus, et apertius Institut. de exceptionibus, initio. Hoc autem falsum esset, si iure naturae esset omnino irritus. Quia quod iure naturae est irritum, iure civili non potest esse validum et tribuere actionem.'

law cannot be validated by civil law. The validity of a contract *stricti iuris* affected by deceit or duress as matter of civil law presupposes, then, that a contract is not absolutely void as a matter of natural law either.

From the canon law of marriage, Lessius draws additional support for the claim that contracts affected by deceit or duress are not entirely void. For a marriage contract remains valid even if it has been entered into by deceit or duress. In addition, there is a canon rule of marriage stating that if the mistaken party wishes the contract to be upheld, the deceiver cannot revoke his assent, lest he benefits from his evil act. This is yet another sign for Lessius that the contract cannot have been completely invalidated by the deceit. Last, by hypothesis, the deceit does not concern the substance of the contract. It only concerns the motivation (*causa*) behind the contract, which constitutes a merely extrinsic and accessory element of the contract.

Lessius is careful enough, however, to conclude that a contract affected by *dolus causam dans* is still open to avoidance by the mistaken party herself [b]. He founds the mistaken party's right to avoid the contract both on the contract itself and the extra-contractual liability for fault of the deceiver. The contract can be avoided because of lack of full consent to the contract on the part of the mistaken party (*ratione defectus consensus*) as well as on the injury she incurred (*ratione iniuriae*).[1093] Lessius points out that the difference between duress and mistake lies precisely in the twofold source for restitution in the case of mistake. Contrary to mistake, duress can only be offset on account of the injury done to the intimidated party, since coerced consent is not affected by involuntariness altogether.

By virtue of both of these grounds, the mistaken party is granted a right to withdraw from the contract (*dolus tribuit ius recedendi a contractu*). There is no need for a judge to grant this right to the deceived party. The harm done to the contractual right of the mistaken party is offset by immediately granting him a right to invalidate the contract. The right to revoke his assent is a natural consequence of the injury done to him. This argument actually mirrors the ideas produced by Henríquez and Sánchez in respect to the effect of duress on contractual validity.

[1093] Lessius, *De iustitia et iure*, lib. 2, cap. 17, dub. 5, num. 29, p. 199: 'Itaque duplici iure potest talis contractus rescindi, ratione iniuriae et ratione defectus consensus, qua parte ignoravit. Cum autem metu extortus est, solum ratione iniuriae rescindi potest.'

Lessius' conclusion does not coincide with that of Molina, however. Lessius can logically pretend that the contract remains valid if the mistaken party renounces the right to rescind the contract that is naturally granted to him on account of the extra-contractual fault by the other party to the contract. Molina could not do so without running into absurd conclusions, since he adopted the principle that mistake automatically results in nullity.

There is another important idea put forward by Lessius in order to argue that contracts affected by *dolus causam dans* are voidable at the option of the mistaken party: every contract includes the implicit or tacit condition (*tacita conditio*) that you will fulfill it, unless you discover—even after the conclusion of the contract—that you have been seriously mistaken.[1094] Nobody has the intention of binding himself so strongly that he cannot withdraw from his obligation when he feels he has been gravely mistaken. This is a tacit condition deriving from the law of nations and confirmed by daily practice and custom, according to Lessius.[1095] He nonetheless indicates that a party who avails himself of this tacit condition to withdraw from the contract is bound to make compensation if the other party suffers serious damage from the rescission of the contract.

So far, Lessius has argued in favor of a general principle of voidability *as a matter of natural law* in contracts affected by fundamental mistake. He also argues, however, that the same must hold true *as a matter of civil law*.[1096]

For one thing, Lessius argues that the civil law should adopt the general regime of relative nullity because that would allow the civil law to follow the natural law as closely as possible (*magis consentaneum iuri naturae*)—which is highly recommendable, of course. For another thing, Lessius cites the argument that a system of nullity at the option of the wronged party is much more conducive to the common good (*magis expediens bono*

[1094] Lessius, *De iustitia et iure*, lib. 2, cap. 17, dub. 5, num. 29, p. 199: 'Omnis contractus solubilis iure gentium videtur habere hanc tacitam conditionem, quod contrahens stabit contractu, nisi deprehenderit se graviter deceptum, id est, tali errore qui sit causa contractus. Nemo enim ita intendit inhaerere contractui, ut non possit retrocedere, etiamsi ex gravi errore contraxisset; quia defuit plenus consensus.'

[1095] Lessius, *De iustitia et iure*, lib. 2, cap. 17, dub. 5, num. 33, p. 200–201: 'Quia alter non potest conqueri de iniuria, cum tacita mens contrahentium sit, non obligare se ad implendum contractum, si se deceptos deprehendant, idque confirmat consuetudo passim recepta. Eadem conditio tacite ex usu omnium gentium intelligitur in promissione standi contractu eiusque non revocandi. Si tamen inde alteri damnum obveniret, deberet alter compensare.'

[1096] Lessius, *De iustitia et iure*, lib. 2, cap. 17, dub. 5, num. 31, p. 199–200.

publico). As the saying goes 'whoso diggeth a pit shall fall therein'. In his discussion of gambling and gaming contracts, Lessius insists on it that the law should make sure that defrauders are caught by their own evil acts.[1097]

In arguing that civil law is compatible with the idea of general void-ability, Lessius defies the entire scholastic legal and moral philosophical tradition, of course. Granted, Pierre de Belleperche and other jurists of the Orléans school had taken a similarly unorthodox position, but Lessius acknowledges that their arguments do not hold water. He proposes to endorse their conclusion, but to substitute his own argumentation for theirs.

Lessius starts from a close reading of law *Si dolo* on the alleged nullity *ab initio* of contracts *bonae fidei* affected by mistake (C. 4,44,5) and argues that it actually contains more or less the same formulation as law *Dolo* (C. 8,38,5), which is undisputedly interpreted as prescribing relative nullity in contracts *stricti iuris*. Hence, the text of law *Si dolo* does not suggest that contracts *bonae fidei* are absolutely void, but that they can be rescinded (*posse rescindi*).

An extremely interesting argument from the medieval legal tradition concerns the proposed equal treatment of duress and mistake (*metus et dolus in iure censentur paria*). It is prescribed by canon *Quum contingat* (X 2,24,28). Lessius holds that coerced contracts are always voidable and not void as a matter of both civil and natural law, he infers from this simple syllogism that voidability must also be the solution to contracts affected by mistake in the civil court.

There is still much more to be said about Lessius' use and interpretation of the law of Rome in order to support his view about the general regime of nullity at the option of the deceived party. For exampe, Lessius gives an explanatory account of the Roman law of mistake, which heavily resembles the historical digression developed by Covarruvias. It should suffice here, however, to quote Lessius' conclusion to this argument, which expresses his novel position in his own words:[1098]

[1097] Lessius, *De iustitia et iure*, lib. 2, cap. 26, dub. 2, num. 11, p. 344–345.

[1098] Lessius, *De iustitia et iure*, lib. 2, cap. 17, dub. 5, num. 31, p. 199: 'Ob has rationes sentio esse verius, nullum esse discrimen hac ex parte in foro conscientiae inter contractus bonae fidei et stricti iuris, cum dolus causam dedit, sed utrosque aliquo modo esse validos, et parere aliquam debilem obligationem iure naturae in foro conscientiae, quae tamen dolo detecto possit elidi per eum qui deceptus est. Neque hanc obligationem iure civili impedire.'

For all those reasons I think that the truth is that there is no difference in the court of conscience [when it comes to the effects of mistake on the validity of a contract] between contracts of good faith and of strict law that have been caused by fundamental mistake. Both types of contract are somehow valid and produce an unstable obligation as a matter of natural law before the court of conscience. This obligation can be removed by the mistaken party when he detects the deceit. This obligation cannot be removed as a matter of civil law.

Obviously, Lessius devised a juridical framework that enabled him—and the subsequent juridical tradition—to allow for the interests of the deceived party without needing to commit logical inconsistencies. Molina had not reached that stage of systematical perfection. Accordingly, he drew sharp criticism from Lessius.

It is absurd to believe that the deceiver can still be made to fulfill his contractual obligations before a judge has condemned him to do so (*ante sententiam*), according to Lessius, if a *bonae fidei* contract has first been declared void *ipso iure*.[1099] In that event, the deceiver cannot be held liable on account of the contract (*ratione contractus*) anymore. Consequently, he can only be held to perform as a measure of punishment (*ratione poenae*). Yet nobody can be forced to execute a punishment until condemnation has been pronounced in court (*post sententiam*). Sánchez had passed a similar criticism on Molina's paradoxical defence of automatic nullity of coerced contracts at the option of the intimidated party before the judge's sentence.

4.3.3.3   *General application of the tacit condition*

Even if Lessius criticized his older colleague Molina for his inconsistency, he presumably drew inspiration from him in refuting the idea that mistake induced by a third party resulted in contractual invalidity. As pointed out before, Summenhart and Medina had thought so, because they held that a contract affected by *dolus causam dans a tertio* fell short of voluntariness. No doubt thinking of Molina, yet citing only the gloss, Bartolus, and Covarruvias, Lessius argues that voluntary consent cannot be affected by that kind of deceit, since it does not concern mistake about a substantial element of the contract, but merely an accidental circumstance

---

[1099] Lessius, *De iustitia et iure*, lib. 2, cap. 17, dub. 5, num. 32, p. 200: 'Sed habet difficultatem: si enim non tenetur implere ratione contractus, ergo solum ratione poenae: at nemo tenetur ad poenam nisi post sententiam.'

external to the contract, namely its motive (*ut circa causas quae alliciunt vel avocant a contractu*).[1100] The contract remains absolutely valid.

Only in the event of gratuitous contracts can motivation be considered a sufficient ground to compromise the validity of the contract. As Lessius puts it, you need to take into account the habitual tacit intention (*intentio tacita et habitualis*) behind an act of liberality, because the mere tacit intention takes the form and authority of a law (*lex*) in case of gratuitous contracts—except in the case of vows. This consideration is even recommended in order to avoid needless disputes. With onerous contracts, however, the mistaken party cannot benefit from rescission of the contract. For he should either blame himself for having been negligent, or claim an action against the third party who deceived him.[1101]

Suddenly, Lessius seems to have changed his mind, however, and departed from the viewpoints of Molina in the same way. As we have pointed out before, the scholastics considered a change in circumstances *sensu lato* as almost similar to deceit exerted by a third party, discussing it in the margin of deceit exerted by a third party, accordingly. Molina had expressed his reluctance towards the granting of relief in onerous contracts on the basis of ignorance of certain decisive circumstances at the moment of contract formation, because of the insecurity that would ensue from its recognition.[1102] Lugo would express the same concern half a century later. Lessius departs from that line of thought, though.[1103]

The modification that Lessius makes concerns the case of invincible mistake (*error invincibilis*) from which one of the parties in an onerous contract suffers. Insofar as none of the parties has yet performed (*res adhuc integra*), Lessius thinks that it is nearer to the truth to say that

---

[1100] Lessius, *De iustitia et iure*, lib. 2, cap. 17, dub. 5, num. 33, p. 200.

[1101] Lessius, *De iustitia et iure*, lib. 2, cap. 17, dub. 5, num. 33, p. 200: 'Si vero sit onerosus, maior est difficultas, quia hic contractus pendet etiam ex consensu alterius, qui talem conditionem nollet admittere. Deinde, quia vel tua opinione deceptus es, et sic tibi ipse imputare debes, quod rem melius non examinaveris; vel dolo tertii, et sic in illum actionem habes, ut expresse habetur d. l. Et eleganter 7, ff. de dolo, et l. Si proxeneta 2, ff. de proxeneticis.'

[1102] Molina, *De iustitia et iure*, tom. 2 (*De contractibus*), tract. 2, disp. 352, col. 415, num. 8: 'Ratio autem est, quoniam nullus contrahentium admitteret eam legem, si illam proponeret alter contrahentium, neque ea lex communi expedit bono, quare contractus ex ipsa natura non censentur sub ea lege celebrati.'

[1103] This is a turnaround in Lessius' argumentation which escaped Diesselhorst, *Die Lehre des Hugo Grotius vom Versprechen*, p. 93sq. He is rightly criticized for this by Feenstra, *De oorsprong van Hugo de Groot's leer over de dwaling*, p. 97.

the deceived party can withdraw from the contract as soon as the true circumstances have become clear to him.

He draws an explicit parallel with the acquittal to perform in the event of changed circumstances (*status rerum notabiliter mutatus*).[1104] A past event that comes to light only now is tantamount to a new event that occurs after conclusion of the contract. Moreover, customary law and the law of nations alike recognize the existence of the tacit condition (*tacita conditio*) mentioned before, according to Lessius. The only qualification concerns the need for the party who wants to rescind a contract on account of the tacit condition to compensate the other party for the damage he incurs (*si tamen inde alteri damnum obveniret, deberet alter compensare*).[1105] This is a central idea that will be picked up by Grotius.

When performance has already been made by either one or both of the parties (*res non integra*), Lessius further refines his increasingly casuistical account. If the other party to the contract was aware of the circumstance, say a defect in the merchandise, and he did not reveal that hidden defect to the buyer, the contract is voidable at the option of the mistaken party—at least as a matter of positive law. Lessius believes that a vendor is not under a duty of disclosure as a matter of natural law, unless the buyer explicitly asks for his information about hidden defects.[1106]

To conclude with, Lessius thought it necessary to allow for changed circumstances in both onerous and gratuitous contracts. If we put this in the terminology of Rebelo, Lessius can be said to have wished that the regime adopted in case of contracts *stricti iuris*, namely the recognition of changed circumstances, also be applied to contracts *bonae fidei*.

Lessius does not make use of this terminology himself. Still it sheds light on a striking resemblance between his generalized application of the

---

[1104] Lessius, *De iustitia et iure*, lib. 2, cap. 17, dub. 5, num. 33, p. 200: 'Quia si tale quid post contractum eveniret, non teneretur illum implere, eo quod status rerum sit notabiliter mutatus; ergo etiam non tenebitur, si id quod ab initio latebat, postea se aperiat. Nam paria sunt, supervenire de novo et proferri in lucem seu incipere cognosci.'
  In fact, Lessius' positions seem to be wavering here. In another context, he had explicitly rejected this argument, and he associated it with Medina; cf. *De iustitia et iure*, lib. 2, cap. 21, dub. 5.
[1105] Lessius, *De iustitia et iure*, lib. 2, cap. 17, dub. 5, num. 33, p. 200–201.
[1106] Lessius, *De iustitia et iure*, lib. 2, cap. 17, dub. 5, num. 33, p. 201: 'Si autem is qui tecum contrahit, conscius est vitii, contractus est irritus in tuum favorem, ita ut pro arbitrio tuo, detecto vitio possis illum irritare vel confirmare. (...) Ratio est, quia tunc censetur particeps doli. Nam tenebatur quasi ex officio, saltem iure positivo, aperire tibi omnia occulta rei vitia. (...) Puto tamen, seposito illo iure positivo, illum ex iustitia ad hoc non teneri, nisi rogatum, ut infra cap. 21 dubitatione 11 dicetur.'

regime of nullity at the option of the wronged party (usually associated
with contracts *stricti iuris*) to contracts affected by *dolus causam dans ab
altero*, and his generalized application of the tacit condition (usually associated with contracts *stricti iuris*) to contracts affected by *dolus causam
dans a tertio vel seipso*.

4.3.3.4   *Voidability without tacit condition*

Even if he has been recognized as one of the most outstanding exponents
of the movement himself, Juan de Lugo's assessment of the scholastic
doctrine on mistake was hardly different from Hugo Grotius' conclusion
two decades before him: mere confusion.[1107] Lugo's own analysis of mistake is characterized by the usual breadth and depth of his thought. He
seems inclined to adopt Lessius' conclusion about the universal relative
nullity of contracts affected by mistake, but he is favorable to Molina's
standpoints, too, certainly when it comes to mistake induced by changed
circumstances. Medina's and Sánchez's standpoints on mistake, on the
other hand, are entirely rejected.

Lessius' innovative argumentation is judged extremely convincing by
Lugo (*fortissima argumenta*).[1108] He thinks it is very wise to consider contracts *bonae fidei* voidable (*non nulla sed rescindenda*) on account of law
Si dolo (C. 4,44,5). Moreover, it is entirely true that treating duress and
mistake on equal terms (*dolus et metus aequiparantur*) is recommended
by canon *Quum contingat* (X 2,24,28). Last, a general regime of nullity at
the option of the wronged party is not only in line with the *ius utrumque*.
It is also in perfect conformity with natural law (*magis consentit iuri naturae*) and it is highly conducive to the common good and the prevention
of deceit (*magis expedit ad bonum publicum et ad coercendos eiusmodi
deceptores*).[1109]

Moreover, Lugo goes on to lend additional support to Lessius' thesis.
He argues that a contract affected by mistake cannot be considered null
on account of lack of voluntary consent (*ex involuntario*). Against Medina (and Rebelo for that matter), he argues that voluntary consent is not

---

[1107] Lugo, *De iustitia et iure*, tom. 2, disp. 22, sect. 6, num. 67, p. 18: 'Circa hoc variae
sunt doctorum sententiae propter diversa principia, quae supponunt, et non mediocrem
confusionem pariunt.' As to Grotius, see below.

[1108] Lugo, *De iustitia et iure*, tom. 2, disp. 22, sect. 6, num. 72, p. 19.

[1109] On the late medieval origins of the notion of *bonum publicum*, see K. Pennington, *The prince and the law, 1200–1600, Sovereignty and rights in the Western legal tradition*,
Berkeley 1993, p. 232–235.

wholly vitiated by mistake (*voluntarium simpliciter*). If mistake does not concern a substantial element of the contract, there is no lack of substantial consent either, even though mistaken consent can be considered as being affected by mixed involuntariness (*involuntarium mixtum*).[1110] The fact that contracts are not avoided by ignorance for which the party himself or a third party is responsible,[1111] demonstrates that consent induced by mistake or deceit does not vitiate a contract.[1112]

Lugo also confirms the idea defended by Lessius that the contract cannot be entirely void, albeit voidable still, on account of injury (*ex iniuria*).[1113] Molina and Lessius had already pointed out that the mistaken party benefits from a right to rescind the contract by virtue of the injury done to him. Lugo wants to prevent himself, however, from running into the absurdity Molina had fallen into—but which he attributes to Sánchez without mentioning Molina. He is therefore careful to stress that, formally speaking, the right to rescind the contract is granted by virtue of the contract itself—which is still valid—and not by virtue of the injury (*non nascitur formaliter ex iniuria sed ex ipso contractu*). Consequently, if the mistaken party renounces his right to avoid the contract, he does not need to renew his consent or to beg for the consent of the deceiver. The deceived party can claim performance by the deceiver without the need for a judicial sentence (*ante sententiam*).

So far we have seen how Lugo adopted Lessius' idea of nullity at the option of the wronged party as the appropriate sanction for contracts

---

[1110] Remember the Aristotelian-Thomistic analysis of duress; cf. supra, p. 219–224.

[1111] A fact which Medina had denied; cf. supra, p. 285–286.

[1112] Lugo, *De iustitia et iure*, tom. 2, disp. 22, sect. 6, num. 73, p. 20: 'Secundo probari potest hoc ipsum, quia quod deceptio proveniat ab altero contrahente vel proveniat a te ipso, qui te decepisti, parum refert, cum in utroque casu aeque auferat scientiam requisitam ad voluntarium. Cum ergo validus sit contractus, quando te decepisti, imo quando alius tertius te decepit sine participatione contrahentis, dummodo deceptio non sit circa substantiam, eodem modo validus erit, quando a contrahente deciperis, quod attinet ad consensum requisitum ex parte tua.'

[1113] Lugo, *De iustitia et iure*, tom. 2, disp. 22, sect. 6, num. 78–79, p. 21: 'Similiter ergo contractus dolo factus, quia voluntarius fuit, potuit in decepto obligationem producere, licet ipse deceptus ob iniuriam sibi illatam ius habeat adversus decipientem ad infirmandam obligationem illam, si voluerit. Unde merito dixit Molina, ante iudicis sententiam posse deceptum obligare decipientem ad persistendum in contractu, quia ad hoc sufficit nolle uti iure, quod habet ad rescindendum illum, nam eo ipso obligatio contractus perseverat se ipsa, sine alio adminiculo. (...) Ex quod ad argumenta Sancii supra proposita facile responderi potest. Ad primam dicimus, obligationem decipientis ad implendum contractum non nasci formaliter ex iniuria, sed ex ipso contractu, qui quandiu a decepto non dissolvitur potestate et iure quod habet ad dissolvendum, validus manet et obligat utrumque contrahentem ad sui observationem.'

caused by deceit induced by the other party to the contract. As regards *dolus causam dans* induced by the mistaken party himself or a third party—including external circumstances—Lugo seems to have endorsed the principle that such contracts do not cease to be valid. Abstracting from the complex casuistry surrounding this topic, one might say that this principle had been defended more firmly by Molina than by Lessius. Both were of the view that gratuitous contracts could be avoided on account of initial or subsequent mistake about the circumstances that had led to the contract (*error circa causam sive motivum principale donandi*).[1114] Lessius, however, ultimately indicated that this might well be true also of onerous contracts on account of a kind of tacit condition implicit in every contract as a matter of customary law and the law of nations.

Lugo is wary about making general statements as to the effects of changed circumstances or the supervening knowledge of different circumstances at the moment of the formation of contract. He cites Sánchez's wavering statements as a proof of the intricate complexity of the matter of changed circumstances:[1115] 'Look how difficult it is to unravel the view of the scholastics in this matter. A preeminent doctor as Sánchez, who treated this topic in such a careful and exemplary way, still got caught in the obscurity and inconsistency of his own thought.' It is extremely difficult to state as a general rule that a contracting party is not bound to observe a contract if circumstances change (*status rerum mutatus*).[1116] If circumstances change considerably (*notabiliter*), however, this restraint is subject to interpretation.

Concerning *dolus causam dans contractui* for which the other party cannot be liable in any way, Lugo concludes that it cannot have an avoiding effect upon onerous contracts. He thus adopts the general conclusion of Molina, and implicitly rejects the final observations made by Lessius.

[1114] Cf. supra and Lugo, *De iustitia et iure*, tom. 2, disp. 22, sect. 6, num. 69, p. 19, and num. 89, p. 24.

[1115] Lugo, *De iustitia et iure*, tom. 2, disp. 22, sect. 6, num. 87, p. 23: 'Vides quam difficile investigari possit doctorum sensus in hoc puncto, cum sic doctor, qui cum maiori distinctione hoc tractavit, adeo varie et obscure loquatur.'

[1116] Lugo, *De iustitia et iure*, tom. 2, disp. 22, sect. 6, num. 87, p. 23: 'Advertendum est, regulam illam generalem, quod obligatio cesset, quando id advenit, quod si ab initio fuisset, consensu impediret, difficillimam esse, et de ea late tractat Sánchez (...). Fortissima argumenta contra eam affert, praesertim, quod sequeretur, nullum in rebus humanis contractum firmum manere, quia saepe adveniunt postea aliqua, quae si fuissent praevisa, contractus non fuisset factus, et in universum dicit, promissionem et votum (non tamen loquitur de professione et votis continentibus statum religiosum) non obligare, adveniente notabili rerum mutatione, secus si non esset notabilis (...).'

For the sake of legal security (*propter securitatem contractus*), the smooth practice of contract-based exchange (*usus contrahendi*) and the flourishing of business in general (*commercium humanum*), Lugo rejects the so-called '*clausula rebus sic stantibus*' in contracts entailing mutual obligations.[1117] All onerous contracts must be as secure, stable, and firm as marriage contracts.[1118] Consent to an onerous contract must be unconditional and absolute (*oportet quod consensus sit absolutus*). Parties need to be prudent and thoughtful before they enter into a contract.

Even if, in the footsteps of Lessius, Lugo abandoned the distinction between *bonae fidei* and *stricti iuris* contracts, then, his loyalty to Molina impeded him from adopting the idea that contracts invariably include a tacit condition. Treating gratuitous and onerous contracts on the same terms when it comes to mistake, as will become obvious in the following paragraphs, it seems as though Grotius had remained more faithful to the sole doctrine of Lessius.

4.3.4   *The impossible synthesis of the scholastic tradition on mistake (Grotius)*

Grotius deplores the perplexing state in which he finds the scholastics' treatment of mistake (*perplexa satis tractatio*). As noted above, he expressed a similar critique in regard to their treatment of duress.

Grotius' indebtedness to Lessius' doctrine of mistake is sufficiently well known.[1119] In a couple of seminal contributions, Robert Feenstra

---

[1117] It should be noted that the term '*clausula rebus sic stantibus*' does not figure in any of the scholastic texts themselves.

[1118] Lugo, *De iustitia et iure*, tom. 2, disp. 22, sect. 6, num. 92, p. 24: 'Nam sicut in matrimonio et professione dicebamus propter firmitatem et perpetuitatem status, consensum exigi omnino absolutum, ita in aliis contractibus onerosis exigitur propter securitatem contractus consensus absolutus, quoties non erratur circa substantiam aut dolus ab altero contrahente non apponitur dans causam contractui. Alioquin de omni eiusmodi contractu et de eius valore ac securitate posset dubitari, quod non esset conveniens commercio humano et contrahendi usui, sed expositum innumeris periculis et litibus. Passim enim diceret postea contrahens se deceptum fuisse a semetipso et ductum falsa causa contraxisse. Oportet ergo, quod consensus sit absolutus, et quod contrahentes prius videant bene quid sibi expediat, antequam consentiant, ne postea facile contractus in dubium revocentur.'

[1119] Diesselhorst, *Die Lehre des Hugo Grotius vom Versprechen*, p. 82sq; Feenstra, *De oorsprong van Hugo de Groot's leer over de dwaling*, p. 137–159; Feenstra, *L'influence de la Scolastique espagnole sur Grotius en droit privé, Quelques expériences dans des questions de fond et de forme, concernant notamment les doctrines de l'erreur et de l'enrichissement sans cause*, p. 377–402; N. Jansen, *Seriositätskontrollen existentiell belastender Versprechen*,

demonstrated that Grotius' brief notice on mistake was indebted to Lessius' ideas on mistake down to the smallest details—deeper still than Diesselhorst had dared to imagine and indicate. Schermaier pointed out that the doctrine of Lessius actually came closer to present-day conceptions of substantial mistake than Grotius' calque of it.[1120] Strangely enough, however, on account of the inside perspective on scholastic legal thought taken in this study, it would seem that in other points of his teachings Grotius was even more influenced by Lessius than in his doctrine on mistake.[1121] Granted, Grotius begins his outline by listing almost the same distinctions that Lessius briefly comments upon at the outset of his *dubitatio* on deceit and mistake.[1122] It is also highly probable that the references to Antonine of Florence, Summenhart, Medina, and Navarrus have been directly copied from Lessius.[1123]

Yet the thrust of Grotius' plea seems to correspond to only half of Lessius' argument. Within the context of the alleged absolute nullity (*irritus*) of *bonae fidei* contracts affected by *dolus causam dans* for which the other party to the contract was liable, Lessius had attempted to show that, first of all, it did not make sense to distinguish *bonae fidei* from *stricti iuris* contracts, because, secondly, all contracts affected by *dolus causam dans ab altero* were to be deemed relatively null at the option of the mistaken party (*irritandus*). Grotius' plea, however, is not driven by any of these attempts. True, the absence of any reference to a difference between *stricti iuris* and *bonae fidei* contracts suggests that Grotius had successfully assimilated Lessius' rejection of this distinction. Incidentally, the

---

Rechtsvergleichung, Rechtsgeschichte, und Rechtsdogmatik, in: H. Kötz – R. Zimmermann (eds.), Störungen der Willensbindung bei Vertragsabschluss, Tübingen 2007, p. 136–137.

[1120] Schermaier, *Die Bestimmung des wesentlichen Irrtums von den Glossatoren bis zum BGB*, p. 143.

[1121] See the notes on Grotius in the chapters of this thesis dealing with duress, immoral promises, and equilibrium in exchange.

[1122] Compare Lessius, *De iustitia et iure*, lib. 2, cap. 17, dub. 5, num. 27, p. 198 with Grotius, *De jure belli ac pacis* (Ed. De Kanter-Van Hettinga Tromp – Feenstra – Persenaire), lib. 2, cap. 11, par. 6, num. 1, p. 331: 'De pacto errantis perplexa satis tractatio est. Nam distingui solet inter errorem circa substantiam rei, et qui non sit circa substantiam; an dolus causam dederit contractui, an non; fueritne alter quicum actum est doli particeps; sitne actus stricti iuris, an bonae fidei.'

[1123] See the in-depth analysis by Feenstra, *De oorsprong van Hugo de Groot's leer over de dwaling*, p. 89–95. At first, Feenstra was mistaken about the identity of 'Conum.' [Conradus Summenhart] in Grotius' text, deeming it to be a reference to a certain 'Lancellottus Conradus'. In *L'influence de la Scolastique espagnole sur Grotius en droit privé, Quelques expériences dans des questions de fond et de forme, concernant notamment les doctrines de l'erreur et de l'enrichissement sans cause*, this error was rectified.

same goes for Pothier's treatment of mistake, where the Roman distinction has disappeared.[1124] Yet Grotius does not seem to be concerned about making clear once and for all whether a contract affected by mistake is void or voidable.[1125]

The second part of Lessius' discussion, on the other hand, constitutes the very kernel of Grotius' doctrine of mistake. Lessius famously argued in favor of a tacit condition (*tacita conditio*) intrinsic to all contracts, regardless of whether they were gratuitous or onerous. This condition implied that parties to a contract could withdraw from a contract if they felt they had been seriously mistaken. They needed to compensate the other party for the inconvenience and damage, if necessary. This is exactly the principle that Grotius raises to the main point of his doctrine of mistake:[1126] 'If based on the presumption of a fact which is actually inexistent, a promise is of no validity by nature, since the promisor did not assent to the promise but under a certain condition (*conditio*) which in reality did not exist.'

Grotius' conclusion is based on a comparison with the extent of the obligation stemming from a law (*lex*) based on factual assumptions that turn out to be false:[1127] 'If a law is based on the presumption of a fact, but that fact is actually non-existent, then the law is not binding, since the law falls short of its basis if the fact is not truly there.' It is often thought that the analogy between a contract and a law is an innovation introduced by Grotius in this very context. It is beyond doubt, however, that it dates

---

[1124] Pothier, *Traité des obligations, selon les regles, tant du for de la conscience, que du for extérieur*, part. 1, sec. 1, art. 3, par. 1 (de l'erreur), p. 21–26.

[1125] If considered separately, the only hint in this direction would seem to imply that Grotius is rather in favor of voidness ipso facto of promises affected by mistake; cf. Grotius, *De jure belli ac pacis* (Ed. De Kanter-Van Hettinga Tromp – Feenstra – Persenaire), lib. 2, cap. 11, par. 6, num. 2, p. 332: 'Similiter ergo dicemus, si promissio fundata sit in praesumptione quadam facti quod non ita se habet, naturaliter nullam eius esse vim, quia omnino promissor non consensit in promissum, nisi sub quadam conditione, quae reipsa non exstitit.' Such an interpretation is not accepted, however, by Feenstra, who argues on account of *De jure belli ac pacis* 3, 23, 4 that Grotius considered promises affected by mistake to be voidable rather than void; cf. Feenstra, *De oorsprong van Hugo de Groot's leer over de dwaling*, p. 98 (n. 52) and p. 100 (n. 64).

[1126] See the quotation in the preceding note.

[1127] Grotius, *De jure belli ac pacis* (Ed. De Kanter-Van Hettinga Tromp – Feenstra – Persenaire), lib. 2, cap. 11, par. 6, num. 2, p. 332: '(…) si lex fundetur in praesumptione aliqua facti, quod factum revera ita se non habeat, tunc ea lex non obliget, quia veritate facti deficiente deficit totum legis fundamentum.'

back at least to the *ius commune* and had become a commonplace in early modern scholasticism.[1128]

In the third and last point of his brief account, Grotius notes that a promisor is liable to pay damages to the promisee if he wants to rescind the contract on account of mistake because he has not been careful (*negligens*) in examining the circumstances surrounding the contract or in expressing his consent.[1129] This qualification is reminiscent of Lessius' concession that damages must be payed to the promisee if he is damaged by the rescission of an onerous contract on account of the tacit condition.[1130] There seems to be no parallel in Lessius for Grotius' opinion that a mistaken party has a claim to compensation by virtue of the injury done to him, even though the deceit has not been fundamental to the contract—a mere alternative description for the scholastic concept of *dolus incidens*. But in line with the scholastics, Grotius ends his exposition by indicating that he does consider a promise in which mistake is incidental invalid only pertaining to the part of the promise affected by the mistake.[1131] Grotius was undoubtedly thinking here of the rule that the useful should not be

---

[1128] For the scholastic use of the analogy between *lex* and *contractus*, see our *Jesuit freedom of contract*, p. 441.

[1129] Grotius, *De jure belli ac pacis* (Ed. De Kanter-Van Hettinga Tromp – Feenstra – Persenaire), lib. 2, cap. 11, par. 6, num. 3, p. 332: 'Quod si promissor negligens fuit in re exploranda, aut in sensu suo exprimendo, et damnum inde alter passus sit, tenebitur id resarcire promissor, non ex vi promissionis, sed ex damno per culpam dato, de quo capite infra agemus.'

[1130] There is no need to doubt, as Diesselhorst did, Grotius' dependence on Lessius in this respect; cf. Diesselhorst, *Die Lehre des Hugo Grotius vom Versprechen*, p. 97. Feenstra is right in pointing out that Grotius' remark is slightly more generalizing than Lessius' remark, which concerned onerous contracts in which none of the parties had hitherto performed; cf. *De oorsprong van Hugo de Groot's leer over de dwaling*, p. 98–99 (n. 55–58). It is hard to see, however, why Grotius' explicit addition that this compensation is based on *damnum per culpam datum* would constitute a major (albeit the single one) discrepancy between Grotius and Lessius; cf. *L'influence de la Scolastique espagnole sur Grotius en droit privé, Quelques expériences dans des questions de fond et de forme, concernant notamment les doctrines de l'erreur et de l'enrichissement sans cause*, p. 386. It is exactly to the merit of scholastics, such as Molina and Lessius, to have argued that rescission in contracts tainted by mistake can be equally granted on account of extra-contractual injury and lack of contractual consent.

[1131] Grotius, *De jure belli ac pacis* (Ed. De Kanter-Van Hettinga Tromp – Feenstra – Persenaire), lib. 2, cap. 11, par. 6, num. 3, p. 332: 'Si vero adfuerit quidem error, sed in quo fundata fuerit promissio, ratus erit actus, utpote non deficiente vero consensu: sed hoc quoque casu si is cui promittitur dolo errori causam dederit, quicquid ex eo errore damni promissor fecit, resarcire tenebitur, ex alio illo obligationis capite. Si pro parte fundata erit errore promissio, valebit pro reliqua parte.'

vitiated by the useless (*utile per inutile non vitiatur*), which was expressly used by Molina.

To sum up, there is no doubt about Grotius having been highly familiar with the scholastics in general and Lessius in particular. In addition, the scholastic discussion on mistake influenced Pothier through the work of Grotius. The striking resemblance between major parts of Grotius' *De iure belli ac pacis* and Lessius' *De iustitia et iure* should not make us blind, however, to the differences in scope of their respective doctrines.

4.4 CONCLUSION

Quite unsurprisingly, the scholastics recognized that contractual obligations can be hindered by duress (*metus*) and mistake (*error/dolus*). The reason why they did so, however, might be less obvious and monolithic than expected. It looks as though the weight of the Romano-canon legal tradition and the Aristotelian-Thomistic philosophical tradition prevented them from conceiving of mistake and duress exclusively in terms of lack of voluntary consent. The effect of duress and mistake, respectively, on the validity of a contract is not explained in unanimous terms either. Although it is common for present-day lawyers to think that contracts affected by duress or mistake are voidable at the option of the intimidated or mistaken party, respectively, only at the beginning of the seventeenth century did the scholastics, and Lessius in particular, reach such a generalized conclusion. Presumably, it was the result of an attempt to translate an authentic desire to promote equity into a coherent legal doctrine.

Although fear seems to compromise 'contractual freedom', the Roman law and Aristotle indicated that coerced consent can be voluntary consent anyway. Only when the constant man test is satisfied, can relief be granted. The requirements for meeting this test seem to have been lowered over time. Drawing on Soto and Covarruvias, Sánchez widely extended the evil events that can be deemed to have an effect upon a constant man, for example the loss of a minor part of his property. The extent to which threats to persons other than, albeit related to, the contracting party himself could satisfy the constant man test, was also considerably enlarged, so as to include blood relatives in general and friends. Albeit reluctantly, reverential fear and importunate pressure were sometimes recognized as constituting grave fear. Minor fear was thought to invalidate a contract before the court of conscience. Lessius' endorsement of this view left its marks on Grotius.

The question of duress and contractual validity urged the scholastics to constantly find a balance between the duty to protect contracting parties against undue influence, on the one hand, and the need to provide incentives for people to practise the virtues of constancy and fortitude (as explicited by Soto), on the other. The scope of the invalidating power of duress was therefore also limited, for example by the emphasis on the direct connection that must exist between the evil feared and the conclusion of a contract. The Jesuits were fairly unanimous about that, except for Lugo. A further qualification to the ready granting of relief on account of duress concerned compulsion exercised legitimately. The use and abuse of fictitious litigation threats turned out to be a thorny topic in this respect, which highlighted the importance Sánchez and Lessius attributed to individual rights.

The delictual approach to duress prevailed with the early modern scholastics. As Henríquez and Sánchez put it, the injury done to the intimidated party by compelling him to conclude the contract needed to be reversed by granting him the right to decide whether he wished to avoid the contract or to compel the intimidator in his turn to observe the contract. Sánchez, Lessius and Lugo therefore concluded that duress was sanctioned with nullity at the option of the intimidated party (*irritandus*). Consequently, the intimidated party did not need a renewed assent by the intimidator anymore if he wanted the contract to remain valid despite the injury done to him. Grotius would adopt this idea from Lessius and thus guarantee its survival. This was not an obvious choice at the time. Molina and Rebelo, for instance, had claimed that a contract affected by duress was automatically void (*ipso iure irritus*) on account of lack of consent.

The debate on mistake moved along the same lines of thought. The *ius commune* originally supported the idea that *bonae fidei* contracts affected by fundamental mistake were sanctionned with absolute nullity, while contracts *stricti iuris* remained valid at the option of the mistaken party. Imbued with Aristotelian and Scotist philosophy, Summenhart and Medina concluded that *bonae fidei* contracts affected by fundamental mistake must be void *ab initio* for lack of their essence, namely voluntary consent. In the footsteps of Summenhart, Covarruvias inferred from this that it was not implausible to state that both *bonae fidei* contracts and *stricti iuris* contracts must be absolutely void, since both were equally vitiated in their substance. Yet for their own part they eventually remained loyal to the Roman distinction. Importantly, though, Covarruvias added that he was inclined to think that mistake did vitiate voluntary consent in the end.

Molina therefore thought it safer to argue that the mistaken party is granted a right to decide over the existence of the contract because of the injury that has been done to him, and not merely on account of the possible lack of voluntary consent. Molina believed that the mistaken party could exercise such a right even before a sentence had been pronounced that condemned the deceiver to perform his contractual duties. In this manner, equity needed to prevent that nullity of the contract was to the advantage of the deceiver. A similar concern to protect the deceived party had led Summenhart and Medina to claim that the deceived party could revalidate the contract. Although they equally considered the contract to be void ipso iure (*irritus*), they found it equitable to state that the contract could be revalidated at the option of the deceived party, on the condition that the deceived party had been condemned in court. Sánchez's account indicated the absurdity of Molina's position: if a contract is deemed void in an absolute sense, the deceiver cannot be bound by it anymore, unless by way of punishment pronounced in a court, since contractual obligations have been annihilated *ipso iure* for both parties.

Inspired by the dissenting opinion from the Orléans jurists, Lessius set out to design a more efficacious and logical solution to this problem. He argued that both *bonae fidei* and *stricti iuris* contracts affected by fundamental deceit were voidable at the option of the deceived party (*irritandus*). From this perspective, the deceiver's assent to the contract remained valid, so that he could be urged to fulfill his obligations if the mistaken party wished. The mistaken party was naturally granted a right to confirm or to rescind the contract as a compensation for the injury that had been done to him. The contract was not avoided automatically, because voluntary consent could not be deemed to be entirely vitiated by mistake. Consequently, the distinction between *bonae fidei* / *stricti iuris* contracts had been dissolved.

Within the limits of this investigation, we may conclude that Lessius was the first among the scholastics to have conceived of a general application of nullity at the option of the wronged party as a sanction to both duress and mistake. With one stroke, Lessius devised a juridically consistent way of implementing the concern expressed by canon law to treat mistake and duress on equal terms, and not allowing the law to favor deceivers.

CHAPTER FIVE

FORMAL LIMITATIONS ON 'FREEDOM OF CONTRACT'

5.1 INTRODUCTION

The preceding chapters have highlighted the consolidation of the consensualist principle in early modern scholastic contract doctrine. They also described the concomitant development of a theory of the vices of the will, including mistake and duress. Yet even if offer and acceptance are not vitiated from within, one might wonder if there are external factors which can frustrate individual parties' basic 'freedom of contract'. The law of nature does not stipulate, of course, that naked agreements be embodied in a certain form in order to become enforceable—as was the case in ancient Rome. But does not the natural law at the same time recognize the binding power of statutory law (*ius positivum*) in the court of conscience? And cannot statutory law impose form requirements and conditions (*formulae et conditiones*) on agreements between private individuals for the sake of the common good? Can the essence of a contract always be reduced to mutual consent, or does it sometimes include substantial formalities? Can your action to enforce a contract in the court of conscience, or your right of retention be refused on account of lack of formality? In other words, are there any 'formal' limitations imposed on the free and consensual nature of contractual obligation?

In effect, some of the early modern scholastics recognized that a natural obligation ensuing from a naked agreement could be frustrated by form requirements imposed by statutory law on pain of nullity (*leges irritatoriae*). This, however, was an extremely controversial issue that challenged the greatest minds for ages. Apart from its pressing practical relevance, the question of the binding nature of formalities in conscience made jurists and theologians alike extremely nervous because it touches upon a range of sub-questions that are connected to much larger legal theoretical debates that persist until the present day:[1132] What kind of formalities exist? What is the relationship between the law of the land and the

---

[1132] P. Oestmann, *Die Zwillingsschwester der Freiheit, Die Form im Recht als Problem der Rechtsgeschichte*, in: P. Oestmann (ed.), Zwischen Formstrenge und Billigkeit, [Quellen

law of conscience? What is a contract in terms of a means of exchanging property rights (*dominium*)? What is the extent to which a positive law is binding? What legitimacy is there for political authorities to intervene in contract law? What is the interpretative value of equity (*aequitas*)? The interference with these broader theoretical issues became all the more important, of course, as the early modern scholastics tried and solved specific day-to-day disputes from a systematic perspective.

An important preliminary remark is that one of the main battlefields for discussing the problem of formalism versus consensualism originally was the law of testate succession, particularly the question of the validity of insolemn testaments (*testamentum insolemne*).[1133] Startling though it may sound to the modern reader—for whom compartmentalization is a basic feature of rigorous juristic analysis—the civilians, canonists and theologians of the past reasoned from testaments to contracts. This flexible way of arguing from contracts to last wills and conversely was recognized as a commonplace by the Renaissance jurist Nicolaas Everaerts in his classical work on legal reasoning.[1134] As a matter of fact, the various solutions to the question whether insolemn testaments could still bring about a natural obligation or not, were extended to the issue of formalism versus consensualism in contract law. Only with the Jesuits at the turn of the seventeenth century were these problems dissociated explicitly, even if the debate on the validity of insolemn testament continued to rage on regardless.[1135] At any rate, it should not be a matter of a surprise if the reader discovers that the following paragraphs are relevant to the historical development of a general law of contract as much as to the history of the law of succession.

---

und Forschungen zur höchsten Gerichtsbarkeit im Alten Reich, 56], Köln – Weimar – Wien 2009, p. 1–54.

[1133] This was already the case in Roman law, cf. Zimmermann, *The law of obligations*, p. 87, and it continued in the early modern period, cf. N. Jansen, *Testamentary formalities in early modern Europe*, in: K.G.C. Reid – M.J. De Waal – R. Zimmermann, Comparative succession law, Vol. 1: Testamentary formalities, Oxford 2011, p. 27–50.

[1134] Everaerts, *Topicorum seu de locis legalibus liber*, Lovanii 1516, loc. 17 (*a contractibus ad ultimas voluntates et econtra*), f. 31r.

[1135] This should not come as a surprise; see Waelkens, *Civium causa*, p. 237, observing that the impact of the law of testament in the *ancien régime* was substantial. It guaranteed the transmission of means of subsistence and power at a time when social security was almost lacking and political power was intricately entangled with the fate of kings and dynasties.

5.2   THE POST-GLOSSATORS AND INSOLEMN TESTAMENTS

The seeds of the later scholastic controversy on the binding nature of last wills not complying with form requirements were already present in the conflicting commentaries on law *Cum quis* (C. 1,18,10) of none other than the famous jurist Bartolus de Saxoferrato (1313–1357) and his pupil Baldus de Ubaldis (1327–1400). In the course of their argumentation, we get an early glimpse of the interconnectedness between the debate on voluntarism versus formalism in general, and the validity of defective last wills in particular. The starting point of their debate is the gloss to law *Fideicommissum* (D. 12,6,62). This text was regarded as laying down the rule that a legacy bequested through a last will that did not comply with solemnity requirements is still due to the legatee as a matter of natural debt.[1136] In this respect, they drew a parallel with a bare agreement creating a natural obligation in spite of its lack of form. Pierre de Belleperche had maintained that this was false. He argued that a natural obligation can only arise through mutual consent, while such consent could not be established through an insolemn testament. A lack of form amounted to a lack of essence, so an insolemn testament did not exist in the first place.

5.2.1   *Natural equity*

In Bartolus de Saxoferrato we encounter a first attempt to vindicate the gloss against the objections raised by the likes of Pierre de Belleperche. To start with, he maintains that a natural obligation arises as soon as an obligation lies according to the law of nations (*ius gentium*), which is precisely the case with testaments that do not conform to statutory requirements. All that is needed as a matter of the law of nations are two witnesses who can prove the existence of the testament.[1137] Bartolus points out that a last will which is made up in an informal manner is valid for the military,

---

[1136] We could not find an explicit reference to natural debt in the gloss to D. 12,6,62 in *Corporis Iustinianaei Digestum vetus* (ed. Gothofredi), tom. 1, cols. 1363–1364, although the combined reading of glosses *Non dubium* and *Debetur* leads to the conclusion that a testament which does not observe the solemnity requirements still creates debt. A reference to the natural debt ensuing from an informal last will is made in the gloss *Cum quis* to C. 1,18,10, see *Corporis Iustinianaei Codex* (ed. Gothofredi), tom. 5, col. 232.

[1137] Bartolus de Saxoferrato, *In primam Codicis partem commentaria*, Lugduni 1555, ad C. 1,18,10, num. 9, f. 39r: 'Is naturaliter tenetur, qui de iure gentium tenetur. (...) Sed ego reperio quod remota a testamento omni solemnitate civili remanet debitum de iure gentium, si potest probari relictum per duos testes, ergo naturaliter debetur.'

so the formality requirements cannot be substantial.[1138] On the other hand, consent is sometimes a sufficient, but not always a necessary condition for an obligation to arise. An obligation can arise wherever natural equity (*aequitas naturalis*) comes into play, even in the absence of mutual consent.[1139] Obvious examples include quasi-contractual and delictual obligations, the origins of which are nothing else but natural equity. But the same holds true for testaments, in which natural law judges it only equitable (*aequum*) that the will of a testator be respected by his successor in spite of its lack of solemn expression.[1140]

As regards the objection about the 'lethal' absence of solemnities in an informal last will, Bartolus makes a seminal distinction between form requirements that apply to the validity of the contract, and form requirements that merely apply to the proof of the contract. Presumably, Bartolus was inspired by Jacobo Bottrigari (1274–1347) in making this argument.[1141] Challenged by the argument that formalites are of the essence of a testament, he had argued that those form requirements merely pertained to proof. In true Aristotelian fashion, formalities were considered to be accidental, but not substantial. As in the case of contracts, Bottrigari reasoned, the formalities in testaments were not substantial. They were merely probatory. By the same token, Bartolus admits that some kind of form is lacking in an insolemn testament, yet the formality in question pertains to

---

[1138] See, for example, D. 29,1,1: 'Faciant igitur testamenta quo modo volent, faciant quo modo poterint sufficiatque ad bonorum suorum divisionem faciendam nuda voluntas testatoris.' Similar rules are laid down in D. 29,1,24 and in D. 29,1,40.

[1139] Bartolus, *In primam Codicis partem commentaria*, ad C. 1,18,10, num. 10, f. 39r: 'Praeterea obligatio naturalis oritur quandoque etiam absque consensu, vel ubicumque remanet aequitas naturalis, hoc est de iure gentium.' Incidentally, Cortese notes that in Bartolus' view it pertained to the judge's *arbitrium* to ignore solemnity requirements, because the judge could never go against *aequitas naturalis*, which was the ultimate criterion for his judgment; Cf. Cortese, *La norma giuridica*, vol. 1, p. 163, n. 34.

[1140] Bartolus, *In primam Codicis partem commentaria*, ad C. 1,18,10, num. 10, f. 39r: 'Sed de iure naturali est aequum quod succedens impleat voluntatem defuncti, quantumcumque non sit solemnis. Ergo de iure naturali ad hoc tenetur.'

[1141] Jacobo Bottrigari, *Lectura super codice*, [Opera iuridica rariora, 13], Bononiae 1973 [= anastatic reproduction of the 1516 Paris edition], ad C. 1,18,10, f. 35r: 'Praeterea, ubi deficit forma rei deficit eius esse adeo ut nullum vinculum contrahatur (…) ac in testamento minus solemni deficit eius forma quia solennitas ergo nullum vinculum adest. (…) Non obstat quin dicunt quod ubi deficit forma etc., quia verum quando deficit forma immediata et substantialis, quae hic non deficit nam de substantia legati est quod sit res quae legetur et certa persona cui et a quo solemnitas. Vero non est forma voluntatis defuncti sed scripturae in qua continetur voluntas, et est accidentalis forma, quod patet sic. Quid si contrahimus et instrumentum est minus solemne nunquid viciabitur contractus certe non, quia scriptura non est de substantia contractus, sed fit ad probationem, sed et scriptura testamenti.'

the proof of the will (*forma probationis*), and not to its substance (*forma substantialis*).[1142] The only element essential to the substantial form of a testament, and hence its ability to bring about a natural obligation, is the will of the testator. It is hard to imagine a less formalistic view of testamentary as well as contractual obligation as a matter of natural law. Reactions were bound to follow.

5.2.2   *Substantial formalities*

It was Baldus, of all commentators, who set up a self-conscious, direct attack against the gloss and Bartolus.[1143] Yet true to the scholastic method, Baldus did not go on the offensive before demonstrating sufficient knowledge of the arguments of his opponents. Regretting that the gloss to law *Fideicommissum* had not buttressed its view through solid arguments, Baldus points out that the gloss to law *Cum quis* effectively produced a sound argument in favor of Accursius' thesis that a natural obligation ensues from an insolemn testament. Interestingly, that argument drew on a far-fetched analogy between contracts and testaments. Testaments that did not comply with formality requirements were compared to contracts which were reduced to their status of bare agreements. Hence, they needed to be considered as capable of creating a natural obligation.

Yet Baldus rejects this analogy between contracts and testaments. To the option that lies in contracts of either making an agreement in a solemn or in an insolemn way, no similar choice of type (*species*) corresponds in the field of testaments: there is only one type of last will, according to Baldus, namely the testament that complies with formality requirements.[1144] It is clear, then, that Baldus thinks of solemnities in testaments as belonging to their substance.[1145] To be sure, he is aware that

---

[1142] Bartolus, *In primam Codicis partem commentaria*, ad C. 1,18,10, num. 11, f. 39r: 'Debetis scire quod in ultimis voluntatibus quaedam est forma substantialis, et ista est voluntas defuncti, et ista adest in quaestione proposita, et de illa loquitur ratio facta in contrarium, quando cessat; sed hic non cessat. Quaedam est forma probationis, ut quod sint ibi septem testes et similia. Ista forma licet cesset, non cessat obligatio naturalis, sed cessat probatio.'

[1143] Baldus, *Commentaria in primum, secundum, et tertium Codicis librum*, Lugduni 1585, ad C. 1,18,10, num. 4, f. 80v: 'Sed ego impugno glossam.'

[1144] Baldus, *Commentaria in primum, secundum, et tertium Codicis librum*, num. 5, f. 80v: 'Non obstat argumentum de pacto nudo, quia ibi sunt duae species contrahendi: solenniter et insolenniter; sed in ultima voluntate non est nisi una species, scilicet solennis.'

[1145] He develops the same view in his commentary to C. 4,35,10; cited in Donahue, *Equity in the courts of merchants*, p. 9.

Bartolus claimed that the testator's will constitutes the substantial form or essence—for which Baldus alternatively employs the expression *causa impulsiva sive immediata*—of a testament. Yet he expressly disagrees with that traditional view. From a simple syllogism with as a major premise the Aristotelian-Boethian equivalence of definition and essence, and as a minor the Roman law definition of a testament as constituted by solemnities, Baldus concludes that the formal requirements concerning last wills are part and parcel of their substance.[1146] In analyzing formalities, Baldus discerns three types of form requirements, indeed: those that merely apply to proof (*forma probatoria*), those that solely constitute substance (*forma substantialis*), and finally those that apply to proof as well as validity (*forma substantialis et probatoria*). An eminent example of formalities, which are both probatory and substantial, are the form requirements in testaments.[1147]

Baldus' solution reflects a distinct preference for formalism over Bartolus' equity-based solution.[1148] He seems to be more concerned about the defence of the heir-at-law against conflicting claims by a self-proclaimed testatee than the protection of a veritable testatee against bad faith on the part of the heir-at-law. A lack of form raises suspicions of fraud (*propter suspectam falsitatem*), according to Baldus.[1149] What is more, Baldus thinks that if somebody with the capacity to observe form requirements does not do so in practice, he must not be considered to have wished to make a legacy to the testatee altogether (*non videtur velle*).[1150]

[1146] Baldus, *Commentaria in primum, secundum, et tertium Codicis librum*, num. 5, f. 8ov: 'Quinto sic probatur: in testamento non solenni deficit forma substantialis, ut probabo: ergo non oritur obligatio. Probo maiorem: illa est forma substantialis per quam datur diffinitio. Unde dicit Aristoteles et Boetius quod diffinitio claudit essentiam, descriptio demonstrationes. Sed in diffinitione testamenti ponitur solemnitas, ut ff. de testamentis, l. 1. Ergo solennitas est de substantia.'

[1147] Baldus, *Commentaria in primum, secundum, et tertium Codicis librum*, num. 6, f. 8ov: 'Triplex est forma: quaedam quae requiritur ad esse et ad probationem esse, ut in testamento, et ista est forma substantialis et probatoria; quaedam requiritur ad esse tantum, ut in stipulatione, et ista est forma substantialis, non probatoria (...); quaedam quae requiritur ad solam probationem, non ad essentiam, et ista est forma probatoria, cuius defectus non impedit naturalem vel civilem obligationem, sed elidit probationem minus solemnem (...).'

[1148] This might seem contradictory, given Baldus' reputation as the most philosophical of the jurists (see below). However, Baldus also claimed that written law is preferable either to unspoken norms or to spoken testimony, because its fixation warrants stability; cf. I. Maclean, *Interpretation and meaning in the Renaissance, The case of law*, [Ideas in context, 21], Cambridge 1992, p. 173.

[1149] Baldus, *Commentaria in primum, secundum, et tertium Codicis librum*, num. 7, f. 8ov.

[1150] Baldus, *Commentaria in primum, secundum, et tertium Codicis librum*, num. 5, f. 8ov.

Interestingly, Baldus also formulates an argument against Bartolus that reveals the tensions between the rival normative jurisdictions in the Middle Ages. If we were to allow a last will that is not in compliance with statutory form requirements to bring about a natural obligation, then an intolerable conflict between the law of conscience and the law of the land would arise. For given that a defective testament still creates natural debt, anyone observing statutory law would commit a sin by retaining a legacy that was informally attributed to a testatee (*observatio iuris civilis esset peccatum*).[1151] The compatibility between *ius poli* or *forum conscientiae*, on the one hand, and the *ius fori* or *forum externum*, on the other, was a source of worry, indeed, for jurists such as Baldus. This is further testified by the large discussion, also included in his commentary on C. 1,18,10, in regard to the particular issue of the binding nature of positive law in conscience—whereby Baldus makes sure to stress that he is relying for his views on a discussion amongst the Dominican theologians themselves at their convent in Bologna.[1152] As we will have chance to notice further on in this chapter, the question about the relationship between the law of the land and the law of conscience continued to demand major reflection in the *ius commune* and the subsequent scholastic tradition.

From his formalist solution of the testament problem—even as a matter of natural law—Baldus can safely infer that a heir-at-law does not run the risk of being summoned to appear before an ecclesiastical court *ratione peccati*.[1153] The heir-at-law is neither under a civil nor a natural obligation to transfer a legacy bequeathed through a defective testament. Put differently, in the event of a last will, which does not meet form requirements, a testatee has no retention right (*ius retentionis*) if he has already received the legacy—which is just another proof that the heir-at-law is not liable for any natural debt.[1154]

[1151] Baldus, *Commentaria in primum, secundum, et tertium Codicis librum*, num. 7, f. 80v. It is exactly this argument which returns as the basis for Francisco de Vitoria's vehement refusal to accord any validity to last wills not complying with statutory form requirements (see below).

[1152] Baldus, *Commentaria in primum, secundum, et tertium Codicis librum*, num. 19, f. 81v–82r. As regards the *condictio indebiti*, in particular, Baldus judges that statutory law must conform as much as possible to the law of conscience.

[1153] Baldus, *Commentaria in primum, secundum, et tertium Codicis librum*, num. 9, f. 81r: 'Haeres non potest denunciari coram episcopo ratione peccati, quod bene posset fieri si esset obligatio naturalis.'

[1154] Baldus, *Commentaria in primum, secundum, et tertium Codicis librum*, num. 9, f. 81r.

Yet, as has been stressed by eminent scholars,[1155] Baldus' system was
not as lacking in considerations of equity as might have appeared so far.
In the remainder of his discussion he frequently appeals to the concept in
question. Suppose we have a heir-at-law who effectively conveys a legacy
to the testatee because he mistakenly thinks that he is under a legal duty
to do so, despite the formal defectiveness of the testament. In such a case
of *indebitum solutum*, it was accepted by the common opinion and by Baldus alike that the testatee had a right of retention. For according to standard doctrine, a natural obligation turns into a civil obligation once it has
been peformed, and ignorance of the law is no excuse. Baldus, however,
could not take that view without contradicting himself, since he did not
believe that a natural obligation existed for the heir-at-law to convey the
heritage in the first place. Consequently, he had to find a way out to justify
his solution that the testatee could nevertheless keep the legacy.[1156] He
finds it in the concept of equity (*propter aequitatem*), which, as a result,
ends up being regarded as a moral principle distinct from the natural law
itself.[1157] Equity, then, returns as a crucial concept in Baldus' discussion
of defective testaments, but in a way that differs from its introduction
in Bartolus.

Baldus continues to surprise us as he discusses the binding nature of
naked pacts as a matter of canon law—still in his commentary on law *Cum
quis*. To be sure, he recognizes the fundamentally consensualist approach
of the law of the Church in comparison with the formalism of the civil law.
But in addition to the ordinary requirement of cause (*causa*) for a naked
agreement to produce a natural and canon law obligation (*naturalis et
canonica obligatio*), to the effect that a naked pact can be enforced in
the ecclesiastical courts, Baldus mentions yet another condition: equity

---

[1155] At least since Calasso's mentioning Baldus de Ubaldis as the most philosophical
among the jurists, he has been associated more than any other postglossator with the
transfer of philosophical and canonical ideas into the civilian tradition; cf. F. Calasso,
Medio evo del diritto, Le fonti, Milano 1954, p. 578. This reputation was consecrated through
N. Horn, *Philosophie in der Jurisprudenz der Kommentatoren, Baldus philosophus*, Ius commune, 1 (1967), p. 104–149, and N. Horn, *Aequitas in den Lehren des Baldus*, Köln-Graz 1968.
See also Kriechbaum, *Philosophie und Jurisprudenz bei Baldus de Ubaldis*, p. 299–343.

[1156] Baldus, *Commentaria in primum, secundum, et tertium Codicis librum*, num. 14, f. 81v:
'Secundo quaeritur an solutum ex testamento non solemni repetatur, et distinguo similiter: aut est error iuris, et non repetitur; aut error facti supinus, et idem; aut probabilis et
tunc repetitur (…) et hoc est propter aequitatem, quae in primis duobus casibus impedit
repetitionem, non quod ibi proprie sit naturalis obligatio iure approbata, ut dixi supra.'

[1157] Significantly, unlike Bartolus, Baldus cannot employ the terminology *naturalis
aequitas* in this context anymore.

between the respective performances (*aequitas praestationis*).[1158] In this context, equity seems to have again a slightly different meaning, probably close to equality and justice in economic exchange. This is not a minor provision, in fact, since it applies to the whole category of innominate contracts. As long as neither of the parties to such an innominate agreement has performed his own obligation (*ante impletionem*), no *aequitas praestationis* lies in Baldus' view. They cannot be enforced on a purely consensual basis, accordingly. In other words, *causa* in its canonical sense is a necessary, but not a sufficient condition for all agreements to be enforceable in the ecclesiastical court.[1159] Under the guise of *aequitas praestationis*, Baldus continues to embrace the Roman conception of *causa* in the event of innominate contracts. There is no general principle of 'freedom of contract' in Baldus.

To conclude with, Baldus' rich and dense commentary on C.1,18,10 is an excellent testimony to the intrinsic connections between the debate on defective testaments, on the one hand, and the debate on consensualism versus formalism in contracts, on the other. It also sheds light on the continuing conflict between the rival jurisdictions of the *forum externum* and the *forum internum*, and the corresponding need to reconcile the law of the land with the law of conscience.

5.3   THE DECRETALISTS AND THE CONSENSUALIST TURN

5.3.1   *Contracts, elections, and last wills*

After the postglossators, the philosophically tainted reflections on equity, causality, and the larger problem of the relationship between statutory law and conscience would reappear time and again in the context of the discussion on defective last wills. As a matter of fact, the solution to the testament problem became ever more flexible and multifaceted.

[1158] Baldus, *Commentaria in primum, secundum, et tertium Codicis librum*, num. 22, f. 82r: 'Sed de iure canonico dummodo subsit causa, non requiritur forma verborum. Et ideo ex pacto nudo quod habebat in se aequitatem praestationis, oritur de iure canonico naturalis et canonica obligatio, et per consequens actio (…). Si autem non haberet in se aequitatem praestationis, ut in contractibus innominatis ante impletionem (…) tunc etiam de iure canonico non oritur actio, quia non est ibi naturalis obligatio.'

[1159] On the difference between the meaning of *causa* in the Roman law and in the canon law traditions, respectively, see chapter 3.

Undoubtedly one of the most important contributions to the debate was made by the outstanding canonist Abbas Panormitanus (1386–1455). It occurred in no other way than by free association of doctrines that—in the eyes of the modern reader—constitute entirely different branches of law. Indeed, Panormitanus took the appalling decision of interpreting a discussion on the distinctively administrative law issue of the election of bishops so extensively, that it came to bear on nothing less than the question of formalism versus consensualism in both contracts and last wills—a provocative generalization which proved very successful among most later authors, but at the same time drew criticism of others, such as Francisco de Vitoria.[1160] Panormitanus applied, almost unreservedly, conclusions that actually belonged to just one domain of the law to another—a method of argument which might come across as problematic to the modern jurist. For example, we find Panormitanus making the following, general claim in his commentary on canon *Requisivit* (X 1,41,1):[1161]

> In the court of conscience it is licit to retain all things acquired through a contract or a testament which is not in compliance with statutory solemnity requirements.

Panormitanus explains the reasons why he arrives at this conclusion in his commentary on canon *Quia plerique* (X 3,49,8). There, Panormitanus defends a natural principle of non-formalism simultaneously in contract law ('a natural obligation arises from a contract which is *ipso iure* void on account of a lack of solemnities'), in the law of testament ('in the absence of fraud, a testament exempt of solemnities nevertheless brings about a natural obligation'), and in electoral procedures ('if you have been elected in an electoral procedure that did not comply with solemnity requirements, you still do not have to abandon your position as a matter of conscience').[1162] But before we go deeper into his doctrine, it is necessary to examine its foundations.

[1160] Vitoria, *Commentarii in IIamIIae* (ed. Beltrán de Heredia, tom. 3), quaest. 62, art. 1, p. 91: 'Hinc sumpsit occasionem Panormitanus et alii ponendi de hoc regulam generalem. Sed certe Innocentius, ut constat, particulariter de electione est loquutus. Tamen ipsi putant parem esse rationem de electione et de aliis.'

[1161] Panormitanus, *Commentaria super Decretalibus*, tom. 2 (*Super secunda parte libri primi Decretalium*), ad X 1,41,1, f. 155v, num. 19: 'In foro conscientiae licite retinentur res acquisitae per contractum vel testamentum in quo non sunt adhibitae solemnitates iuris civilis.'

[1162] Panormitanus, *Commentaria super Decretalibus*, tom. 6 (*Ad tertium librum Decretalium*), *summa* ad X 3,49,8, num. 31, f. 231r.: 'Naturalis obligatio oritur ex contractu ipso iure nullo ratione solemnitatis non servatae; Electus licet non solemniter non tenetur in foro

5.3.2   *Formalities against fraud and deceit*

As noted above, it is the redundancy of formalities in elections that constitutes the ultimate cornerstone of Panormitanus's consensualism in the field of contracts and testaments.[1163] Now for this claim, Panormitanus actually relies on the commentaries to the *liber Extra* written by Pope Innocent IV (1243–1254). According to Panormitanus, the consensualist approach to ecclesiastical elections can be ascribed to him.

It remains to be seen, however, if Panormitanus is really ingenuous in founding that idea on the authority of one of the most eminent Decretalists. Granted, in his commentary on canon *Quod sicut* (X 1,6,28)—to which Panormitanus makes reference[1164]—Innocent IV defends the validity of elections that do not meet formality requirements. Although he does not deny that it is hard to think of an election that comes into being without formalities, Innocent IV still confirms the validity of an election that merely came about through consent of the parties involved.[1165] In a loose sense (*large*), an *electio canonica* holds as a matter of natural law

conscientiae renuntiare, quia electio habuit fundamentum naturale, licet solemnitates iuris positivi defecerint.'

Panormitanus is a little bit more nuanced when it comes to defective testaments, although he concludes that when it is clear that there is no fraud involved, the insolemnly expressed will of the testator should be considered valid; ad X 3,49,8, f. 234v, num. 43: 'Respondeo quod me movet est quod solemnitates iuris civilis fuerunt inductae ad falsitates evitandas et de rigore, si ergo constat in foro animae quod nulla falsitas intervenit, debet cessare dispositio iuris positivi et servari aequitas et obligatio naturalis quae oritur ex dispositione defuncti.'

It might be worthwhile noticing that Panormitanus, who was later to be admired by Luther, was the leader of the conciliar party at the Council of Basel. The council refused to obey the papal order by Eugenius IV to dissolve the council at Basel and to meet at Ferrara in January 1438. They declared him deposed and elected a new Pope, Felix V, who withdrew in 1442; cf. Pennington, *Nicolaus de Tudeschis (Panormitanus)*, p. 15. On the struggle between Eugenius IV and the conciliar party, see M. Decaluwe, *A successful defeat, Eugene IV's struggle with the Council of Basel for ultimate authority in the Church, 1431–1449*, [Bibliothèque de l'Institut Historique Belge de Rome, 59], Rome 2010.

[1163] Although not entirely from the same perspective, but rather from the point of view of his conciliarist sympathies, it is worthwhile mentioning that Panormitanus' doctrine of papal elections—not episcopal elections—is studied in O. Condorelli, *Principio elettivo, consenso, rappresentanza, Itinerari canonistici su elezioni episcopali, provvisioni papali e dottrine sulla potestà sacra, Secoli XIV–XV*, Rivista internazionale di diritto comune, 13 (2002), p. 142–157.

[1164] Panormitanus, *Commentaria super Decretalibus*, tom. 6 (*Ad tertium librum Decretalium*), ad X 3,49,8, f. 233v, num. 31.

[1165] Innocentius IV, *In quinque libros Decretalium commentaria*, quibus addita est Margarita Baldi indicis loco, Lugduni 1562, ad X 1,6,28, num. 8, f. 24r: '(...) vix est electio nisi omnia iura solemnia observentur, et tamen ideo non est nulla nec cassatur electio.'

in spite of an absolute lack of formalities as soon as there is consent of
the electoral body and the person elected (*consensus electi et eligentium*),
provided that no fraud or delict (*dolus vel delictum*) was committed by
either of the parties.[1166]

The only reason for the form requirements to have been introduced in
canonical elections, according to Innocent IV, was the avoidance of fraud
and delict, in the interest of the peace among the Churches concerned.[1167]
But if the risk of fraudulent or delictuous behavior, say intrusion of an
illegitimate elector, or simony in bribing the electoral body, does not exist
anymore, there is no reason for adhering to the formalities. Granted, if
among the interested parties somebody takes offence (*contemptus*) at an
unlawful election, he can demand cassation of the election before the
final consecration on account of Gratian's *Decretum*, Dist.62, c.3 (*nullus
non canonice electus ordinetur*).[1168] But in the meantime the elected person can continue holding his benefice against the will of the person who
takes offence until the election has formally been annulled by the judge.

Moreover, Innocent IV acknowledges that an offended party's right
to implore the office of the judge was introduced by strict statutory law
(*hoc officium judicis de rigore juris introductum*). Yet in a moment of provocative lucidity, he judges that equity (*aequitas*) would rather have it
the opposite way. Equity requires that the party who takes offence at an
election that is valid as a matter of natural law be punished himself, rather
than that the naturally valid election be annulled by a judge.[1169]

However, the consensualism advocated by Innocent IV in canon *Quod
sicut* nevertheless does not apply to all kinds of elections. Rather, it is
confined to the specific question of elections of inferior positions and canons (*electio canonicarum*). That, at least, is the conclusion emerging from

---

[1166] Innocentius IV, *In quinque libros Decretalium commentaria*, ad X 1,6,28, num. 8, f. 24r.

[1167] Innocentius IV, *In quinque libros Decretalium commentaria*, ad X 1,6,28, num. 9, f. 24r:
'Sed ius positivum de forma servanda inventum est propter periculum ecclesiarum quae
erant in litibus, quae iam cessant postquam consecratus est pacifice.'

[1168] This is the wording of Innocent IV. Dist.62, c.3 actually reads a little different; cf.
Corpus juris canonici (ed. Gregoriana), part. 1, cols. 415–416: 'Nullus in episcopum, nisi
canonice electum, consecret.'

[1169] Innocentius IV, *In quinque libros Decretalium commentaria*, ad X 1,6,28, num.
8, f. 24r.: 'Hoc enim officium judicis de rigore juris est introductum, nam de aequitate
esset quod contemnentibus eum imponeretur poena et non cassaretur electio a maiori
parte facta etiam quod non imponatur illi qui nullo modo delinquit (...) sicut condemnatus iniuste ad restitutionem rei suae non peccat tenendo eandem rem si non auferatur
per iudicem vel dari praecipiatur sic nec iste qui iure naturali canonice electus est (...).
Consensus tamen legitimus eligentium et electi intervenit qui solus de iure naturali ad
electionem et alios contractus sufficit.'

a more comprehensive reading of passages on electoral procedures in Innocent IV's commentary on the Decretals. For example, in his treatment of canon *Ex parte* (X 3,8,10)—which is not quoted by Panormitanus—Innocent IV defends a consensualist approach to elections for canons, deeming formalities to be unnecessary. But at the same time, there we learn that he makes an important exception to this rule for elections taking place in a widowed church (*electio ecclesiarum viduatarum*)[1170]—that is in a church left alone like a widow after the death of her spiritual spouse, namely the bishop or abbot. In yet another place, namely his commentary on canon *Quia propter* (X 1,6,42), Innocent IV discusses form requirements in episcopal and other prelatical elections, mentioning, amongst other things, the requirement to have a secret vote in a place where the entire chapter has come together.[1171] Moreover, in his treatment of the same canon *Quia propter*, Innocent IV holds that in the event of an *electio* which does not comply with form requirements, the election is null *ipso jure*.[1172]

It is therefore tragic that in his treatment of canon *Quia requisivit* (X 1,41,1) Panormitanus founds his statement about the existence of a right of retention in contracts and in testaments that do not comply with solemnity requirements on the authority of Innocent IV's interpretation of canon *Quia propter*—although he claims that Antonio de Butrio is a better authority to rely on. In effect, Butrio recognized that the law of conscience and positive law were at odds with each other in regard to the validity of an insolemn testament, and he argued that conscience should have precedence. Hence, the legatee was safe in conscience if he retained the legacy. Butrio did not accept the argument that the testator knows that he has to comply with solemnity requirements on pain of nullity of the testament. On the contrary, he argued that the testator knows that his testament is valid as a matter of natural law regardless of the observance of form requirements.[1173]

[1170] Innocentius IV, *In quinque libros Decretalium commentaria*, ad X 3,8,10, num. 4, f. 144r: 'Notandum quod in electione canonicarum non est necessaria forma sed sufficit solus consensus; secus in electione ecclesiarum viduatarum'.

[1171] Innocentius IV, *In quinque libros Decretalium commentaria*, ad X 1,6,42, num. 1, f. 28v.

[1172] Innocentius IV, *In quinque libros Decretalium commentaria*, ad X 1,6,42, num. 8, f. 29r: 'electio facta contra formam nulla est ipso iure'.

[1173] Antonio de Butrio, *Super Decretalibus commentarii*, ad X 3,49,8, tom. 5, f. 205r, num. 9: 'Ex his patet quid de legatis in minus solemni testamento, quia imo est certus quod valebat de lege naturae et conscientiae. Breviter lex naturae suadet retentionem, lex positiva oppositum. An hoc teneatur cum bona conscientia credo quod non, arg. de test. Cum esses et c. Relatum. Et discrepant lex positiva et lex conscientiae, quia positiva sequitur

5.3.3   *A general principle of consensualism*

Panormitan's relatively novel, consensualist approach to elections, contracts, and last wills became the authoritative basis for subsequent
scholars who wished to make the same argument. Therefore, Panormitan's standpoint is worthwhile quoting. Slightly generalizing Antonio de
Butrio's opinion on the validity in conscience of defective testaments, he
argues that:[1174]

> Antonio takes the view that in the court of conscience for a contract to be
> valid it suffices that it be valid within the boundaries of the law of nature,
> that is the law of nations, since as a matter of natural law, or the law of
> nations, consent of itself is sufficient. I utterly agree with this view, and I
> adduce the exceptionally wise words of Pope Innocent IV (ad X. 1,6,42 [sic])
> in support of it: if you have been elected, you remain safe in conscience
> to hold on to your position, as long as the election process has been valid
> according to the law of nations, even if form requirements imposed by statu-
> tory law were not met, since these formalities were introduced just in order
> to avoid scandal and fraud proliferating. Now, no scandal or fraud affecting
> the case at issue and consent being present, in the eyes of God you are safe.
> Be sure always to remember that! For it applies to *every single act* in which
> a solemnity prescribed by statutory law is missing, so that you need have no
> qualms of conscience as long as fraud is absent and consent has been given
> by those who eventually have to render explanation for the act in question
> as a matter of natural law. To sum up, then, in the court of conscience the
> equity of natural law is preferred to the rigor of statutory law.

It would be hard to find a more incisive plea for a general principle of
consensualism and the precedence of equity over formalism than this

---

praesumptionem, lex conscientiae veritatem, et sic de facto per plures rationes consului.
Nec obstat ex quo eligit testari unus solemniter, non videatur voluisse valere testamentum,
quia imo est certus quod valebat de lege naturae et conscientiae. Ita non sumus certi de
mente et tutius eligendum in foro conscientiae.'

[1174] Panormitanus, *Commentaria super Decretalibus*, tom. 2 (*Super secunda parte libri
primi Decretalium*), ad X 1,41,1, f. 155v, num. 19: '[Antonius] dicit enim sufficere quoad
forum conscientiae ut contractus teneat secundum limites iuris naturalis seu gentium.
Nam de iure naturali seu gentium sufficit solus consensus, et haec opinio mihi placet, et
adduco singulare dictum Inn. in ca. quia propter [sic], de elect., ubi dicitur quod electus
est tutus in foro animae si electio sua tenuit de iuregentium, licet non fuerit servata forma
tradita a iure positivo, quia illa forma est introducta propter scandala et deceptiones evitandas. Verumtamen ex quo omnia ista cessaverunt et intervenit consensus satis est is
tutus quo ad Deum et tenebis semper menti illud dictum: quia valet in omni actu in quo
est praetermissa solemnitas iuris positivi ut in foro animae non teneatur quis sibi de hoc
facere conscientiae ex quo non intervenit ibi aliqua deceptio et adfuit consensus haben-
tium actum explicare de iure naturali; ex quo infertur quod in foro conscientiae aequitas
iuris naturalis praefertur rigori iuris positivi.'

simple but highly influential statement of Panormitan. In his commentary on canon *Quia plerique* he insists both on its practical relevance (*saepe occurrit in practica*) and its unique value as an almost universal principle (*singularis quia facit ad multa*).[1175]

As regards the question of testaments which do not comply with form requirements (*testamentum minus solemne*), in particular, we find that Panormitanus radically applies the general consensualist principle to this specific problem. Before he goes on to solve the specific question whether or not a heir-at-law is bound in conscience to transmit the legacy mentioned in a defective testament, Panormitanus indicates that the answer to this specific question merely depends on the outcome of the more general and difficult question of whether a natural obligation arises from a testament that does not meet form requirements.[1176] He eventually takes sides with Bartolus against Baldus, to conclude that if the heir-at-law knew about the will of the testator to make a legacy, he is under a natural obligation to execute the testament, even if it lacks the solemnities required by statutory law.

Arguing that statutory form requirements pertain to the *rigor iuris* with the intention [*causa*] of avoiding fraud and falsehood, Panormitanus holds that once this intention is frustrated [*causa cessante*], the statutory law requirements in question cease to be relevant. As a consequence, positive law must make room for equity to take over and make sure that natural obligations be observed.[1177] Incidentally, an unattributed gloss to this passage might well give us an inkling about a historical reality in the late Middle ages that could have motivated Panormitanus and other jurists in no small a degree to stress the need to give up form requirements if they did not meet their objective any more:[1178] in the event of a plague

---

[1175] Panormitanus, *Commentaria super Decretalibus*, tom. 6 (*Super tertio libro Decretalium*), ad X 3,49,8, f. 233v, num. 31.

[1176] Panormitanus, *Commentaria super Decretalibus*, tom. 6 (*Super tertio libro Decretalium*), ad X 3,49,8, f. 234r, num. 43: 'Haec quaestio dependet ab illa difficili quaestione, an ex testamento minus solemni oriatur obligatio naturalis.'

[1177] Panormitanus, *Commentaria super Decretalibus*, tom. 6 (*Super tertio libro Decretalium*), ad X 3,49,8, f. 234v, num. 43: 'Ratio quae me movet est quod solemnitates iuris civilis fuerunt inductae ad falsitates evitandas et de rigore, si ergo constat in foro animae quod nulla falsitas intervenit, debet cessare dispositio iuris positivi, et servari aequitas et obligatio naturalis quae oritur ex dispositione defuncti.'

[1178] Panormitanus, *Commentaria super Decretalibus*, tom. 6 (*Super tertio libro Decretalium*), ad X 3,49,8, f. 234r, Glossa ad num. 43: 'An ea quae sunt relicta in testamento minus solemni tempore pestis et a pestifero debeant solvi per haeredem: credo quod sic, quia tempore pestis remittuntur solemnitates in testamento requisitae.'

(*tempore pestis*), death could strike so suddenly, that hardly any dying person would have the time to comply with formality requirements, such as going to a notary or finding enough witnesses. Yet that would not prevent the discussion about the suspension of statutory law *cessante causa* from inflaming.

5.3.4 *Teleological interpretations of positive law*

The reasoning of Innocent IV and Panormitanus amounts to the idea that formalities do not matter for the validity of a testament, provided that evidence of the absence of fraud is established by another means. For the *raison d'être* of formalities is merely to avoid fraud. This teleological way of interpreting and explaining the law was typical of the jurists of the (Christian) Middle Ages.[1179] If the reason why a law was enacted (*ratio seu causa*) held no longer true, it was no use to remain loyal to it. Otherwise, the letter of the law would kill the spirit of the law. The glossators used an elegant expression to summarize the idea that a law ceases to apply as soon as its underlying cause no longer applies: *cessante causa/ratione, cessat lex*.[1180] They developed this rule on the basis of D. 3,1,1,5 (irreverence as the motivating 'cause' behind the prohibition on women appearing before a judge). The glossators understood 'cause' in the typically Aristotelian, and, hence, teleological sense of the word. The rule that a law ceases to be binding as soon as its underlying cause is not met anymore became a commonplace in the scholastic, legal and moral theological tradition. Nicolaas Everaerts included it as a *topos* in his work on legal argumenta-

---

[1179] B. Frydman, *Le sens des lois, Histoire de l'interprétation et de la raison juridique*, [Penser le droit, 4], Bruxelles – Paris 2005, p. 143–145.

[1180] Glossa *Causam* ad D. 3,1,1,5, in *Corporis Iustinianaei Digestum vetus* (ed. Gothofredi), tom. 1, col. 330: 'Quid ergo si aliqua bona foemina inveniatur, poteritne postulare? Videtur quod sic, quia causa cessante, cessat effectus (...), sed dico contra, quia illud obtinet in causa finali. Hic autem, sc. improbitas Calphurniae, fuit impulsiva, nam alia fuit finalis, sc. ne contra pudicitiam etc. et ne officiis virilibus etc. (...) et alias est causa impulsiva (...).'

On the distinction between *causa impulsiva* (the immediate occasion which had pushed the legislator into action, e.g. Calpurnia's turpitude) and *causa finalis* (the general aim of that particular law, e.g. prohibiting women from interfering with the business of men), see H. Krause, *Cessante causa cessat lex*, Zeitschrift der Savigny-Stiftung für Rechtsgeschichte, Kanonistische Abteilung, 46 (1960), p. 92–93, and E. Cortese, *La norma giuridica*, vol. 1, p. 217–221. On the *causa seu ratio seu mens legis* more in general, see E. Cortese, *La norma giuridica*, vol. 1, p. 257–296.

tion.[1181] Francisco Suárez dedicated an entire chapter to a discussion of this typically teleological way of interpreting legal obligation.[1182]

If a certain law does not meet its end anymore, you better have it abolished. Canon 41 of Gratian's *Decretum* C.1, q.1—one of the major canonical texts to which the maxim *'cessante causa, cessat lex'* goes back[1183]— actually states that exceptional measures taken in an emergency need to be withdrawn as soon as the state of exception ceases to exist (*quae pro necessitate conceduntur, eadem cessante cessabunt*). If you have assumed a certain office due to an emergency, for instance, you need to leave that office as soon as the normal order has been re-established. If you continue to exercize your office despite the return of normal life, you are guilty of usurpation (*alius est ordo legitimus, alia usurpatio*). By the same token, one might say that a law that continues to claim obedience from its subjects despite its not serving the purposes of the social and divine order anymore, is guilty of usurpation. As Joachim Hopper (1523–1576) points out, laws come into existence for a certain end, and can die as soon as they no longer fulfill that role.[1184]

From the above, it is clear that equity (*aequitas*) is attributed the function of assessing the degree to which the letter of the law still corresponds to its original sense. Without the equitable interpretation of laws, the system of peaceful order turns itself into a brutal system of injustice (*summum ius, summa iniuria*).[1185] Hence, if from the point of view of equity a certain law is considered to be far too ineffective in its application, the letter of the law must be abandoned. Perhaps alluding to C. 3,1,8, which states that equity and justice are to be preferred to the rigour of the law, Panormitanus holds in the last sentence of the quote above that in the court of conscience the equity of natural law is preferred to the rigor of

---

[1181] Everaerts, *Topicorum seu de locis legalibus liber*, loc. 85 (*a cessatione rationis*), f. 96v. Following the gloss, Everaerts is careful to stress that the maxim only holds in regard to the *causa finalis*. On Everaerts, cf. supra, p. 42–43.

[1182] Suárez, *Tractatus de legibus et legislatore Deo*, lib. 6, cap. 9, p. 39–46.

[1183] S. Kuttner, *Urban II and the doctrine of interpretation, A turning point?*, Studia Gratiana, 15 (1972), p. 62, n. 21.

[1184] Cf. Joachim Hopper, *De iuris arte libri tres*, Lovanii 1555, lib. 2, p. 155. On Hopper, who was promoted as *doctor utriusque iuris* with this dissertation in 1553, see the biography by D. van den Auweele in G. Van Dievoet e.a. (eds.), *Lovanium docet, Geschiedenis van de Leuvense Rechtsfaculteit (1425–1914)*, Cataloog bij de tentoonstelling in de Centrale Bibliotheek (25.5–2.7.1988), Leuven 1988, p. 69–72, and G. Janssens, *Hopperus, Joachim*, in: The Oxford encyclopedia of the Reformation, Oxford 1996, p. 254–255.

[1185] For the classical origins of this famous maxim, see Cicero, *De officiis*, 1, 10, 33. Apart from C. 3,1,8, no fragment in the *Corpus Justinianeum* itself comes close to formulating it.

statutory law (*in foro conscientiae aequitas iuris naturalis praefertur rigori iuris positivi*). In this way, he establishes a significant conjunction of conscience, equity and natural law, on the one hand, and associates rigour with statutory law and secular jurisdiction, on the other. In other words, as equity is to the letter of the law, so natural law is to positive law, and the court of conscience to the external court.

Since a discussion on the 'causal' foundation and legitimation of any law enacted by the secular authorities was properly included in Panormitan's treatment of the problem of defective testaments,[1186] the principle '*cessante causa cessat lex*' remained a constant in subsequent scholars' attempts to come to grips with the validity of defective last wills, certainly of those who were in favor of the validity of defective testaments. Indeed, it is not entirely surprising to find that Baldus, who was strongly in favor of respecting form requirements, also rejected the maxim that a law should stop to bind people once its underlying cause had been removed. In Baldus' view, if a statutory law has been enacted by the legitimate authorities, its underlying cause or reason should not be put into question (*supposita potestate, non est quaerendum de ratione*).[1187]

5.3.5 *The triumph of equity and conscience*

In the work of the famous theologian Adrian of Utrecht (1459–1523), the later Pope Adrian VI (1522–1523), we witness how the teleological approach was actually turned into the main angle from which the formalist versus consensualist view of formally defective testaments was examined. Departing from the tradition of the Decretalists who treated defective testaments within the context of their line-by-line commentaries on the *Liber Extra*, Adrian of Utrecht deals with the testament problem within the context of a much larger philosophical debate about the relationship between the law of the land and the law of conscience.

More specifically, in the sixth among his *Quaestiones quodlibeticae*, Adrian sorts out the thorny and politically sensitive problem of whether the violation of a secular law is tantamount to committing a mortal sin (he eventually concludes that it is). But to this end, he needs to tackle

---

[1186] Panormitanus, *Commentaria super Decretalibus*, tom. 6 (*Super tertio libro Decretalium*), ad X 3,49,8, f. 234r, num. 39: 'Lex vel statum emanatum ob aliquam justam causam, an dicta causa cessante, debeant observari?'

[1187] Krause, *Cessante causa cessat lex*, p. 89, n. 28.

the more fundamental question whether statutory law is binding in conscience in the first place. It would seem that human law has no power to bind man in conscience, since an inferior power can hardly be thought of as having jurisdiction in the court of a higher power. On the other hand, the Apostle Paul himself had conceded in his letter to the Romans 13:1–2 that all human power derives from God. Since Adrian formulates his assessment of the binding nature of a defective contract or a defective last will as a corollary following from his solution of this broader political problem, we will now have a closer look at it.

Clearly tapping into the Thomistic tradition of political thought, which requires, amongst other things, that the end of a human law be the common good if it is to be binding in conscience,[1188] Adrian holds that 'a just law (*lex iusta*), that is a just precept issued by a superior lay- or clergyman, is binding in the court of conscience, but only within the boundaries of reason, that is within the limits of the final cause envisaged by the law (*ad metas rationis seu causa finalis*)'.[1189] He then goes on to elaborate on each part of the sentence respectively.

Demonstrating the natural existence of a 'hierarchy of obedience' in any society, Adrian thinks the bindingness of a superior's precept to be obvious. Claiming support from Aristotle's *Nicomachean Ethics* (books 5 and 9), he maintains that to any position or office (*officium*) in society corresponds a duty for those who are subjected to that office to obey the person holding that office. Those offices range from parenthood over the command of an army to the government of a state. As a child obeys its father, a soldier obeys the general, and a head of the family obeys the political authorities. Apart from the 'natural' character of obedience to superiors, there is also Scriptural evidence for the bindingness of a superior's commands and precepts. For example, the injunction in the first letter

---

[1188] Aquinas, *Summa Theologiae* (Ed. Leonina, tom. 7), IaIIae, quaest. 96, art. 4 (*Utrum lex humana imponat homini necessitatem in foro conscientiae*), concl., p. 183: 'Respondeo dicendum quod leges positae humanitus vel sunt iustae vel iniustae. Si quidem iustae sint, habent vim obligandi in foro conscientiae a lege aeterna, a qua derivantur; secundum illud Prov. 8: *Per me reges regnant, et legum conditores iusta decernunt.* Dicuntur autem leges iustae et ex fine, quando scilicet ordinantur ad bonum commune; et ex auctore, quando scilicet lex lata non excedit potestatem ferentis; et ex forma, quando scilicet secundum aequalitatem proportionis imponuntur subditis onera in ordine ad bonum commune.'

[1189] Adrian of Utrecht, *Quaestiones quodlibeticae duodecim, quibus accesserunt Joannis Briardi Athensis quaestiones item quodlibeticae*, Parisiis 1527, quaest. 6, art. 1, concl. 2, litt. g, f. 111r: 'Lex iusta, praeceptum iustum superioris laici vel ecclesiastici ligat in foro conscientiae, sed ad metas solum rationis seu causae finalis quae praetenditur.'

of Peter (1 Pet. 2:13) for subjects always to submit themselves to every human creature for the sake of God (*propter Deum*).

The restraints on human power, however, are implied in the very same injuction to obey the rulers, since the divine origins of power also account for its proper limits. If the divine purpose for which power was conveyed to human beings is no longer served by that power any more, it loses its legitimacy. This is why the two parts of Adrian's thesis form a perfect match for each other. If a law is not enacted for the sake of the final destiny of mankind, its *raison d' être* or final cause is not achieved, thus invalidating its own power to bind in conscience. In the words of Adrian of Utrecht, if the final cause ceases to exist, then the effect, too, must cease to exist (*cessante causa finali, cessare debet effectus*)[1190]—an expression which is evidently reminiscent of the rescripts of Pope Innocent III (1198–1216) in X 2,24,26 and X 2,28,60 (*cessante causa, cesset effectus*).[1191]

What is more, in the footsteps of Panormitan,[1192] Adrian argues that the final reason is not merely the soul of the law, but the law itself (*ratio non solum anima legis sed lex ipsa*). This idea of Panormitanus was widespread by the early sixteenth century. It was confirmed, for instance, by Nicolaas Everaerts, the influential contemporary of Adrian at the University of Leuven.[1193] Adrian seeks support for his claim in law *Non dubium* (C. 1,14,5), which states that the will behind the law (*legis voluntas*) and not the wording of law (*verba legis*) is what really matters. Consequently, not only is a law that does not serve its purpose no longer binding in conscience, it is aborted altogether. If its final cause is missing, the law

[1190] Adrian of Utrecht, *Quaestiones quodlibeticae*, quaest. 6, art. 1, concl. 2, litt. g, f. 111r.

[1191] In his *Lateinische Rechtsregeln und Rechtssprichwörter*, p. 45, num. 23, Liebs also cites X 2,28,16 as an origin of the expression 'cessante causa cessat effectus'. In its explicit form, though, we could only find it in the abovementioned decretals. On this maxim, see Cortese, *La norma giuridica*, vol. 1, p. 238–242 and A. Gouron, *Cessante causa cessat effectus, À la naissance de l'adage*, Comptes-rendus des séances de l'Académie des inscriptions et belles-lettres, 143 (1999), p. 299–309.

[1192] Panormitanus, *Commentaria super Decretalibus*, tom. 6 (*Super tertio libro Decretalium*), ad X 3,49,8, f. 234r, num. 39: 'Si causa est expressa in lege et potest probari causam istam non extitisse in casu occurrenti, non debet servari constitutio, nec in foro animae nec iudiciali, quia ratio legis est lex, et non econtra, unde ubi cessat ratio cessat lex, ut in l. non dubium C. de legi, etc.' This passage is discussed in H. Krause, *Cessante causa cessat lex*, p. 97–98.

[1193] Everaerts, *Topicorum seu de locis legalibus liber*, loc. 34 (*a ratione legis stricta seu limitata ad restrictionem ipsius legis*), f. 43v: 'Ratio legis est anima legis, unde sicut anima dominatur corpori, ita ratio legis vel canonis dominatur verbis.'; loc. 64 (*a lege cessante*), f. 81v: 'Hoc tamen volo te scire, quod ille non loquitur sine lege qui allegat rationem, quia lex est omne quod ratione consistit.'

itself ceases to exist. Interestingly, Adrian then cites Gratian, *Decretum*, C.16, q.1, c.40—a canon that actually prompts a bishop to respect as much as possible a last will made to a good cause—in support of the general ideas we have just about seen laid down.

To summarize, a law is binding in conscience provided it serves its final cause. As a vibrant demonstration of the validity of the rule '*cessante causa cessat lex*', Pope Adrian VI adduces the precept to admonish a brother in the Lord who is sinning (*praeceptum corripiendi fratrem*) mentioned in Matthew 18:15–17, and commonly known as 'fraternal correction'. Being a fundamental instrument of upholding order and peace in the deeply Christian society Europe was until far into the modern period, fraternal correction is always worthy of a legal historian's attention.[1194] It is particularly in this case, not only because fraternal correction was a traditional case to put the theory of the teleological interpretation of legal obligation to the test, but also because it was going to determine the subsequent debate on form requirements in last wills decisively.[1195]

Adrian is of the opinion that the cause underlying the precept to admonish a brother who is sinning is to be identified as the promotion of the spiritual health of that other person's soul (*causa est utilitas spiritualis fratris*).[1196] It should be noted that fraternal correction is not merely conceived of as a counsel or a good deed. Rather, it is a commandment, which requires fulfillment under pain of mortal sin. So, in principle, there is no escaping its execution when necessary. Unless, Adrian would point out, executing the commandment cannot be considered as serving its end any longer, of course. Borrowing from a very influential sermon of Augustine on penance stating that 'if I knew that it were of no use to you, I would not terrify you with my admonishments',[1197] our Adrian asserts that the obligation of fraternal correction cannot obtain in the event that admonishing your neighbour makes no sense. For example, if he is dangerously stubborn, or a recidivist. Then, the cause behind the precept ceases to

---

[1194] On fraternal correction, see chapter 2.4.2.

[1195] A good *status quaestionis* of the debate on the necessity to observe the precept of fraternal correction if it fails to meet its end can be found in Suárez, *Tractatus de legibus et legislatore Deo*, lib. 6, cap. 9, num. 15, p. 44–45.

[1196] Adrian of Utrecht, *Quaestiones quodlibeticae*, quaest. 6, art. 1, concl. 2, litt. h, f. 111v.

[1197] Augustinus, serm. 393 Maur. (= PL 39, c. 1715): 'Nam si scirem non tibi prodesse, non te admonerem, non te terrerem.' This text was integrated, albeit in slightly different terms—as the *correctores Romani* already noted—into the *Tractatus de poenitentia*; Cf. De pen., Dist. 7, c. 4 in *Corpus juris canonici* (ed. Gregoriana), part. 1, cols. 2377–2378.

exist, since its end is never served. Pursuant to the rule 'cessante causa cessat lex', the precept itself ceases to exist, too, accordingly.

For Adrian, the case of fraternal correction is a perfect illustration of how important it is to be concerned with what is really equitable (*verum aequum*), and to have an eye for circumstances that escape the general scope of the law. According to the canon law, for instance, a priest is only allowed to confess a usurer after the sinner in question has made at least partial restitution of his ill-gotten gains as a safeguard (*cautio*) of his future repentance—this being an obligation introduced for the sake of the spiritual welfare of the usurer. Yet assume that a usurer is about to die without having made even the smallest act of restitution, and a medical doctor confirms his imminent death. In this case, the usurer's soul is not served by first trying to fulfill the precept, because then he risks dying without being fortified with the absolution and the rites of the Holy Church. Moreover, there is a canon law precept holding that the final absolution may never be refused to somebody (C.26, q.6, c.13). So if the priest were to stick to the letter of the law (*ad corticem literae*), he would be the murderer of the usurer's soul (*necator animae*).[1198]

Once the general principle 'cessante causa cessat lex' has been established and the case of fraternal correction settled, it is easy for Pope Adrian VI to solve the problem of contracts and last wills, which do not conform to statutory form requirements. Unlike Baldus, but in the footsteps of the gloss, Pope Innocent IV, Bartolus, Butrio and Panormitan, Adrian holds that formalities were introduced as a prevention against fraud and deceit.[1199] As a consequence, the obligation to observe solemnity requirements does not obtain any longer, if the absence of fraud is evident from another source. Adrian acknowledges that a contract may well be void in the external court on account of its lack of formalities, but in the court of conscience it still produces a right of retention as long as fraud is actually absent. Similarly, if the heir-at-law knows for sure that

---

[1198] Adrian of Utrecht, *Quaestiones quodlibeticae*, quaest. 6, art. 1, concl. 2, litt. h, f. 112r.

[1199] Adrian of Utrecht, *Quaestiones quodlibeticae*, quaest. 6, art. 1, concl. 2, illatio 2, litt. k, f. 112r–v: 'Non obstante nullitate contractus ob defectum solemnitatum quae de iure adhiberi debent, potest quis sic adeptum licite servare in foro conscientiae, nisi fraus vel deceptio intervenerit. Ratio est, quia solemnitates adinventae sunt ut fraudibus et dolis obviam iri possit. Ubi ergo fraus dolus vel deceptio nulla intervenerit, dispositio iuris super solemnitatibus adhibendis servanda non est in foro conscientiae. (…) Ex eodem capite Panormitanus tenet haeredem teneri in foro conscientiae ad solvendum legata testamenti minus solemnis si sciverit nullam fraudem intervenisse. Quod intelligo modo ei constet decedentem recte testari voluisse.'

the testator intended the legacy to be conveyed to the legatee mentioned in the defective testament, he is under an obligation in the court of conscience to effectively do so.

A second case to which Adrian applies the principle *'cessante causa cessat lex'* concerns the *Senatusconsultum Macedonianum* (D. 14,6 and C. 4,28), which allowed a son in power to defend himself against the claims of a lender to refund the money lent. This privilege had originally been granted to sons in power by the Emperor Vespasian (69–79) to prevent a *filiusfamilias* from killing his father in order to obtain the heritage and pay his debts with it. But this gave rise to blatant inequity in the event that a *filiusfamilias* would certainly not need to kill his father to render the money to the lender. Hence, Adrian rules that if the cause underlying the *SC Macedonianum* is absent, the son in power loses the privilege. Hence, he commits a sin by still availing himself of the *exceptio* granted by the *Senatusconsultum* when the lender asks him for the money.[1200] In fact, Innocent IV and Panormitanus had reached more or less the same conclusion by reasoning that a precept ceased to be effective if it missed its goal.[1201]

The novelty of Adrian consists in that he not merely dealt with the testament issue *ad hoc*, but within the context of a general exposition on the relationship between statutory law and the law of conscience. He gave clear precedence to the dictates of conscience over the formality requirements imposed by statutory law.[1202] It is not unlikely that this subordination of the formality-issue to the particularly delicate and

---

[1200] Adrian of Utrecht, *Quaestiones quodlibeticae*, quaest. 6, art. 1, concl. 2, illatio 1, litt. j, f. 112r. For dealing with this problem within the context of the issue of formalities in contracts and last wills, Adrian is clearly influenced by Pope Innocent IV and Panormitanus, who did so too.

[1201] Innocent IV, *In quinque libros Decretalium commentaria*, ad X 3,49,8, num. 5, f. 175r: 'constitutio tamen restringenda est ad eum casum ubi fuit iusta constitutio, ut v.g. iusta constitutio quae dat exceptionem Macedoniani propter iustam causam: sed si certum esset quod illa causa non subesset ut si in necessitate mutuasset peccaret qui exceptione se defenderet'.
Panormitanus' elaborations on these ideas from Innocent turn out to have had a profound influence on Adrian; see Panormitanus, *Commentaria super Decretalibus*, tom. 6 (*Super tertio libro Decretalium*), ad X 3,49,8, num. 37 (*constitutio imperatoris contra ius naturale emanata sine causa in nullo foro est servanda*), f. 234r; ad X 3,49,8, f. 234r, num. 39 (*lex vel statum emanatum ob aliquam justam causam, an dicta causa cessante, debeant observari*).

[1202] This is not surprising given Adrian's indefatigable attachment to the idea of moral integrity (*veritas vitae*), guaranteed by the conformity of one's actions to the dictates of *conscientia* or *recta ratio* in the *forum animae*; cf. Hein, 'Gewissen' bei Adrian von Utrecht (Hadrian VI.), Erasmus von Rotterdam und Thomas More, p. 228–232.

conspicuous issue of that tense relationship finally urged a politically sensitive theologian like Francisco de Vitoria to search for the foundations that would allow for a rebuttal of what had become the common, consensualist approach to contracts and testaments. After all, did not *summa aequitas* run the risk of resulting in *summa iniquitas*? Preventing equity from ending in chaos and strengthening the interventionist power of the secular authorities became Vitoria's project.

5.4   THEOLOGIANS FOR FORMALISM I: THE ABSOLUTISTIC VERSION

After the almost unanimous recognition of the juridical validity of contracts that do not meet form requirements in the late medieval canonical tradition, one could think that the question had been settled definitively. Yet the debate would soon lose much of its casual nature as it was integrated into the treatises of the early modern scholastics dealing with justice, law, and contracts from a more systematic perspective. Thus, the question of inheritance through an informal testament became part of a larger debate about property, freedom and the law. The issue of last wills that lack the solemnities prescribed by the law came to bear more than ever before upon such questions as the relationship between natural law and positive human law, and the constraints imposed on a citizen's particular *dominium* by laws issued for the sake of the larger political community.

As we turn to Francisco de Vitoria, it is exciting to see how he feels obliged to draw conclusions that go radically against the common opinion on a specific topic like insolemn testaments, for the mere reason that he must remain consistent with his own, broader legal and political philosophy. Vitoria expressly sets his treatment of the form requirements of contracts and other rights-transferring transactions in relation to a general theory about the natural division of things, man's hold over things (*dominium*), and the natural liberty of man to dispose of those goods through contract freely, though within the limits of positive law. This is clear from the very embeddedness of the debate in his commentary on *quaestio* 62 of the *Secunda Secundae*, which deals with restitution and the *dominium*-issue that inevitably goes with it.

As Domingo de Soto, one of Vitoria's most famous pupils, would point out later in his *De iustitia et iure*, it is necessary to begin any systematic treatment of contracts, commutative justice, and restitution with an elucidation of *dominium*, because this concept is the basis and foundation of

all things done through exchange. All vices opposed to the virtue of justice in transactions amount to violations of *dominia*—restitution being the technique by means of which all these violations are redeemed.[1203]

5.4.1   *Property, contracts, and restitution*

If only because his teachings appear to be floating,[1204] it would be unwise to pretend to give a full account of Vitoria's doctrine of *dominium* in just a few paragraphs. Yet the centrality of the notion of *dominium* to the entire legal undertaking of the early modern scholastics is sufficiently well-known.[1205] It formed the basis of their theories of contract and of restitution.[1206] As a matter of fact, a fundamental discussion of *dominium, ius*, and *divisio rerum* immediately precedes Vitoria's discussion of the case of testaments not satisfying form requirements. Accordingly, it is indispensable reading for a correct understanding of the discussion on formal restraints of 'freedom of contract'.

What matters to Vitoria is to sort out which meaning of *ius* and *dominium*, respectively, is appropriate for the issue of restitution. Vitoria first elucidates his idea of 'right' in the objective and subjective sense. In addition to the rather objective, Thomistic conception of law as that which is licit (*jus nihil aliud est nisi illud quod licet vel quod lege licet*), he borrows from Summenhart the meaning of right in a more subjective sense as a power or faculty pertaining to somebody according to the laws (*jus est potestas vel facultas conveniens alicui secundum leges*).[1207] Subsequently, he discusses three different meanings of *dominium*, ranging from a certain

---

[1203] Soto, *De iustitia et iure* (ed. fac. V. Diego Carro – M. González Ordóñez, vol. 2), lib. 4, prooem., p. 278: 'Enimvero dominium huiusmodi, eorumque divisio, basis fundamentumque est omnium contractuum conventorumque et pactorum, quae per commutativam iustitiam celebrantur. Ac perinde cuncta quae huic virtuti adversantur vitia, violationes quaedam sunt et corruptelae dominiorum, rerumque possessionum, quae subinde iniuriarum genera contractaque debita restitutionis beneficio repensari debent. Quinque ergo convenit de rerum dominio disputare quaestiones.'

[1204] Brett, *Liberty, right, and nature*, p. 124–137 points out the differences between quaest. 57 and quaest. 62 of Vitoria's *Commentarii in IIamIIae*, as well as the diverging approach in his *Relectio de potestate civili*.

[1205] Grossi, *La proprietà nel sistema privatistico della Seconda Scolastica*.

[1206] Condorelli, *Norma giuridica e norma morale, giustizia e salus animarum secondo Diego de Covarrubias*, p. 171–172.

[1207] Vitoria, *Commentarii in IIamIIae* (ed. Beltrán de Heredia, tom. 3), quaest. 62, art. 1, num. 5, p. 64.

eminence or superiority (*eminentia et superioritas*),[1208] over the notion of
property (*proprietas*), to a very large concept including any faculty to use
a good in accordance with rights (*facultas quaedam ad utendum re aliqua
secundum jura*).

Importantly, the third meaning of *dominium* (power or faculty)
coincides with the second meaning of *ius*. Moreover, Vitoria takes this
weaker meaning of *dominium* where it is equivalent to *ius* in a subjective
sense as the starting point of his treatment of restitution and justice in
exchange:[1209]

> In matters related to restitution I use the word *dominium* indiscriminately,
> regardless of whether I am considering the case of a *dominus*, an *usuarius*,
> an *usufructuarius*, or a *possessionarius*, since each of them can suffer injury
> which gives rise to a duty of restitution.

Practically speaking, this use of *dominium* in the wider sense of any kind
of subjective right allows Vitoria to bring all cases under the scope of restitution where somebody has a certain power over a thing, be it property,
use, usufruct, or possession. Consequently, he brings all kinds of transactions that involve man's hold over a thing under the scope of the seventh
commandment not to steal and the virtue of commutative justice (and
hence under the control of the theologians). This is why it may seem to
the modern reader that the entire law of property and contract actually
came to be understood with the early modern scholastics as part of the
law of unjust enrichment. Vitoria's move was not novel. Summenhart had
also equated *ius* in the sense of any real right with *dominium*.[1210] He had

---

[1208] This broader notion of *dominium* in the sense of 'superiority' or even 'lordship'
explains why it is also to do with political authority and not merely with private property; cf. Meccarelli, *Ein Rechtsformat für die Moderne, Lex und Iurisdictio in der spanischen Spätscholastik*, p. 285–311, and D. Quaglioni, 'Dominium', 'iurisdictio', 'imperium', Gli
elementi non-moderni della modernità giuridia, in: G. Dilcher – D. Quaglioni (eds.), Gli inizi
del diritto pubblico, 3: Verso la costruzione del diritto pubblico tra medioevo e modernità,
[Annali dell'Istituto Storico Italo-Germanico in Trento, Contributi, 25], Bologna-Berlin
2011, p. 663–677.

[1209] Vitoria, *Commentarii in IIamIIae* (ed. Beltrán de Heredia, tom. 3), quaest. 62, art. 1,
num. 8, p. 67: 'Et in materia de restitutione indifferenter utemur dominio, scilicet sive sit
dominus, sive usuarius, sive usufructuarius, sive possessionarius, quia in eo etiam cadit
injuria quae est obnoxia restitutioni.'

[1210] Cf. J. Varkemaa, *Summenhart's theory of rights, A culmination of the late medieval
discourse on individual rights*, in: V. Mäkinen – P. Korkman, Transformations in medieval
and early modern rights discourse, [The new synthese historical library, 59], Dordrecht
2006, p. 142–143. In fact, the use of the notion of *dominium* to cover all kinds of real rights
draws on a much older tradition, of which Saint Bonaventure is a famous representative, see

done so precisely to be able to argue that snatching away a *res* against the will of the person who had a *ius* over that *res* was tantamount to theft and, accordingly, gave rise to a duty of restitution to restore justice in exchange—which was the main preoccupation of the theologians in dealing with contracts.

Thomas Aquinas had not gone so far. Rather, Thomas had limited himself like the civilians to equating *dominium* with 'property' (*proprietas*) in treating of restitution.[1211] Vitoria acknowledges, indeed, that 'property' is the meaning of *dominium* originally figuring in Roman law.[1212] He even recognizes that this meaning was adopted by Roman law precisely in order to distinguish 'property' (*dominium*) from other types of real rights such as use, usufruct, and possession. But he is equally explicit in rejecting that distinction, because what he wants is precisely that less absolute rights on goods such as use, usufruct, and possession are also protected by the redeeming measure of restitution. What is more, there is a 'divine element' in Vitoria's concept of *dominium*, which reaches back to the mendicant poverty controversy. It is entirely alien to the Roman law tradition. *Dominium* as a synonym of right in the subjective sense, for Vitoria, as well as for the thirteenth century Franciscans, is imbued with a sense of freedom, since it only pertains to rational, human beings as created in the image of God.[1213]

If *dominium* is the atom of exchange, so to speak, then it matters to know how man can acquire or alienate it. Still more basic a question is how man became entitled to use the goods of the earth in the first place. In this respect, Vitoria develops a theory that explains the division of all created things from the original *dominium* in the state of nature to the present. In the state of nature, *dominium* belonged to the entire community of mankind as a matter of natural law, since the world was created for the sake of man, and it would be impossible for man to survive if he were not able to appropriate and use the rest of created nature to his

---

V. Mäkinen, *Property rights in the late medieval discussion in Franciscan poverty*, [Recherches de Théologie et Philosophie médiévales—Bibliotheca, 3], Leuven 2001, p. 93.

[1211] Brett, *Liberty, right, and nature*, p. 128 (in fine).

[1212] In *Commentarii in IIamIIae*, quaest. 62, art. 1, num. 7, p. 66 he mentions D. 41,2,10–12.

[1213] In this respect, Vitoria disagrees with Summenhart, who had maintained in *De contractibus*, tract. 1, quaest. 3 et 6, that irrational creatures had also been endowed with rights by God. On Summenhart's theory of right and *dominium*, see Varkemaa, *Conrad Summenhart's theory of individual rights*, p. 63–248.

own advantage.[1214] At the same time, *dominium* belonged to every single person in the state of nature, because everyone could claim himself to be the *dominus* of all things created. After all, everybody could appropriate whatever good that pleased him in order to use or to abuse it *ad libitum* as long as he did not harm others or himself.[1215]

An intricate question, however, concerned the transition from a communitarian relationship between man and other things created to the more recent state of individualized *dominium*. Duns Scotus had argued that the original natural law prescribing common *dominium* had been revoked after Adam's fall, thus making way for individual ownership.[1216] But following Thomas' and Summenhart's opinion that the natural law is immutable,[1217] Vitoria could not possibly adopt Scotus' view. Therefore, Vitoria simply holds that the division of things is implied in the original common *dominium* itself: if men are the real *domini* of all things, then we should assume that they are also capable of dividing all created things amongst themselves through mutual consent.[1218] For the original state of common *dominium* was not prescribed by the natural law, but merely

---

[1214] Vitoria, *Commentarii in IIamIIae* (ed. Beltrán de Heredia, tom. 3), quaest. 62, art. 1, num. 13, p. 72–73: 'Item, de jure naturali est quod homo conservet se in esse. Sed hoc non potest sine aliis creaturis, quia omnes aliae creaturae sunt ad conservationem hominum (…), quia Deus et natura nihil faciunt frustra.'

[1215] Vitoria, *Commentarii in IIamIIae* (ed. Beltrán de Heredia, tom. 3), quaest. 62, art. 1, num. 16, p. 74: 'Non solum universitas et communitas humana habet dominium super omnia, sed etiam quilibet homo in statu naturae integrae, id est, stando in solo jure naturali, erat dominus omnium rerum creatarum et poterat uti et abuti omnibus illis.'

[1216] Duns Scotus, *Quaestiones in quartum librum Sententiarum*, dist. 15, quaest. 2, conc. 2, in: Ioannis Duns Scoti opera omnia, Hildesheim 1968 [= anastatic reprint of the Lyon 1639 edition], tom. 9, p. 152: 'Secunda conclusio est, quod illud praeceptum legis naturae, de habendo omnia communia, revocatum est post lapsum, et rationabiliter propter eadem duo. (…)'.

[1217] Aquinas' acceptance of the mutability or otherwise of natural law is more nuanced than suggested by Vitoria; *Summa Theologiae* (Ed. Leonina, tom. 7), IaIIae, quaestio 96, art. 5, concl., p. 172: 'Alio modo intelligitur mutatio legis naturalis per modum subtractionis, ut scilicet aliquid desinat esse de lege naturali, quod prius fuit secundum legem naturalem. Et sic quantum ad prima principia legis naturae, lex naturae est omnino immutabilis. Quantum autem ad secunda praecepta, quae diximus esse quasi quasdam proprias conclusiones propinquas primis principiis, sic lex naturalis non immutatur quin ut in pluribus rectum sit semper quod lex naturalis habet.'

[1218] Vitoria, *Commentarii in IIamIIae* (ed. Beltrán de Heredia, tom. 3), quaest. 62, art. 1, num. 20, p. 77: 'Ergo non opus fuit abrogatione legis naturalis ad dividendas res, ut dicit Scotus, contra quem arguimus. (…) Immo, quia omnia erant communia, ideo de jure naturali potuerunt facere hanc divisionem et appropriationem sibi, quia Deus fecit hominem verum dominum rerum: ergo potuerunt inter se convenire homines taliter quod dicerent: tu cape hoc, et tu hoc, et ego habebo hoc. (…) Et ita si homines erant domini omnium rerum, potuerunt facere quod velint, et dividere, et appropriare.'

conceded. So, by default, natural law had introduced common ownership, but it still allowed for an individualized division of things, which would come into being through an agreement amongst men (*consensu*), that is through human law.

After explaining how the first division of things took place in a consensualist way in Biblical times, Vitoria makes two observations about the present. First, there are still many things that have not been subject to any division amongst men. Referring to D. 41,1,3, on the acquisition of the *dominium* of a *res nullius* through *occupatio*, he concludes that these things belong to the one who first occupies them. Evidence of the direct practical value of these theoretical reflections is Vitoria's subsequent consideration that the Americas cannot be occupied legitimately by the Europeans, since the indigenous people are legitimate *domini* of those lands.[1219] Secondly, he wonders how it came about that people who were originally *domini* of certain goods, now appear to have lost that *dominium*, whereas other people have become the new *domini* of the same goods.

The question of how *dominium* can 'mutate' from one person to another brings us back to the heart of the initial question of justice in exchange, contracts, and restitution. For once the initial division of things has come to an end, there are only two ways—according to Vitoria—in which things can change *dominium*: through the will of the former dominus (*voluntate prioris domini*), or through the authority of the prince (*auctoritate principis*).[1220] These two ways constitute the most important legal titles (*tituli* or *causae*) that can bring about a legitimate change of *dominium*, to which later on, Vitoria adds a third title—not yet elaborated upon by Thomas Aquinas—namely prescription (*praescriptio*).[1221]

[1219] Through insisting on the Christians' right to preach their religion to other people, however, he saves a place for theological argument to underpin the conquest of the Americas; cf. Vitoria, *Commentarii in IIamIIae* (ed. Beltrán de Heredia, tom. 3), quaest. 62, art. 1, num. 28, p. 82. The immediate political significance of the doctrines on *dominium*, the state of nature, and *occupatio* is now laid down in a variety of articles collected in M. Kaufmann – R. Schnepf (eds.), *Politische Metaphysik*, [Treffpunkt Philosophie, 8], Frankfurt am Main e.a. 2007.

[1220] Vitoria, *Commentarii in IIamIIae* (ed. Beltrán de Heredia, tom. 3), quaest. 62, art. 1, num. 27, p. 81: 'Quomodo ergo isti qui modo sunt, facti sunt domini? (...) Facta prima divisione et appropriatione, duobus praecise modis et duobus tantum titulis potuit quis adquirere dominium rerum. Nam etiam duobus potest transferri dominium ad nos ab uno in alium. Et hoc est quod exspectat ad restitutionem. Primo ergo modo potuit transferri dominium ad nos voluntate prioris domini. Alio modo auctoritate principis.'

[1221] Vitoria, *Commentarii in IIamIIae* (ed. Beltrán de Heredia, tom. 3), quaest. 62, art. 1, num. 46–48, p. 102–105.

5.4.2   *Individual property and the State*

With Vitoria, then, the discussion about the formal limitations on 'freedom of contract' becomes embedded in a more general reflection on the juridical titles for conveyance of *dominium*. This *dominium* being understood as right in a large sense and as freedom to enter or not to enter into an act of exchange, the question arises, of course, if there are any limits to a *dominus'* control over his goods. First, Vitoria answers this question in regard to a transfer of *dominium* by virtue of the will of its *dominus* (*ex voluntate domini*). Later on we will see how he discusses the same question from the point of view of the public authorities (*ex auctoritate principis*).

From the point of view of natural law, there cannot be any limitation on an individual's will to transfer his *dominium* over a good to another person, since true *dominium* implies full control over a good. By definition, it is the capacity (*facultas*) to dispose of a thing as one pleases. But Vitoria immediately modifies his account of *dominium* as unbounded power by putting it in the larger framework of the law. I am the new *dominus* of a thing provided that its former holder was its true *dominus* and did not contravene the law in the process of transferring it.[1222] This qualification is not as compromising for a *dominus'* freedom as it might appear. Vitoria indicates that a prodigal promise as well as a transfer of money to a prostitute remain valid, even though these acts may constitute a sin against the law.[1223] For God left the disposal of things entirely to the discretion of mankind. Otherwise, acts of generosity, magnanimity and charity would have been ruled out from the beginning. Still, there are considerable limitations imposed on freedom of exchange based on personal will, as we will see below.

As for now, a more practical and intrinsic limitation to the transfer of *dominium* is worthwhile mentioning. What is questioned is the sufficiency of the will of the *dominus* for making a valid transfer of his ownership, or, rather, the need for expression and acceptance of the *datio*. Vitoria stresses the need for an external expression of the interior intent to con-

---

[1222] Vitoria, *Commentarii in IIamIIae* (ed. Beltrán de Heredia, tom. 3), quaest. 62, art. 1, num. 29, p. 82–83: 'Et generaliter unus titulus ad formandum conscientias est iste, quod si quis verus dominus dat mihi aliquid quod non est lege prohibitum, ego sum vere dominus et non teneor ad restitutionem.'

[1223] On the morality of prodigal promises, see infra, p. 483–485.

vey *dominium*, for the practical reason that otherwise the transferee cannot accept the transfer, acceptance being a necessary requirement of a valid act of conveyance.[1224] His argumentation thus differs from Jacques Almain's. Almain had insisted on the need for an exterior act to transfer *dominium*, but through building on an analogy with a contract for marriage. If exterior consent is needed for the transfer of *dominium* over your body to your spouse, Almain reasoned, then it is required a fortiori for the transfer of other goods.

Vitoria's argument recalls the need for externalization and acceptance stressed by early modern scholastics such as Lessius for the establishment of a valid promise.[1225] The line that Vitoria draws between *datio*, *promissio*, and contract remains unclear, though.[1226] What he is clear about, however, is the adequacy of a mere implicit and voluntary *traditio* as a matter of natural law, although he admits that in the external court, *traditio actualis* is required for a valid conveyance of *dominium*.[1227] We see the natural law origins, here, of the idea, later adopted in the French Civil Code, that property can be transferred on a mere consensual basis, while actual conveyance (*traditio*) is required according to the *ius commune* tradition (C. 2,3,20).[1228] The similarity between the views of Vitoria and Grotius is obvious.[1229]

[1224] Jacques Almain, *De poenitentia sive in quartum lectura*, in: Almaini opuscula, Parisiis 1518, dist. 15, quaest. 2.

[1225] See chapter 3.3.2.

[1226] In an older edition, he makes an explicit distinction between *datio* and *promissio*, claiming that acceptance is not needed in the latter; cf. *Commentarii in IIamIIae* (ed. Beltrán de Heredia, tom. 3), quaest. 62, art. 1, not. 31, p. 84, while that distinction seems to disappear in the edition used in the main text by B. de Heredía, where 'datio' almost disappears altogether, and where Vitoria consistently employs the expression 'transferre dominium', not specifying whether he considers that action to be a *datio*, or a *promissio*.

[1227] Vitoria, *Commentarii in IIamIIae* (ed. Beltrán de Heredia, tom. 3), quaest. 62, art. 1, num. 30, p. 84: 'Sed quidquid sit, nihilominus in jure naturali non requireretur traditio actualis, sed sufficeret acceptatio per voluntatem formalem vel interpretativam.'

[1228] Among the abundant literature on this subject, see I. Birocchi, *Vendita e trasferimento della proprietà nel diritto comune*, in: L. Vacca (ed.), Vendita e trasferimento della proprietà nella prospettiva storico-comparatistica, Atti del Congresso Internazionale Pisa-Viareggio-Lucca, 17–21 aprile 1990, Tom. 1, [Pubblicazioni della Facoltà di Giurisprudenza della Università di Pisa, 115], Milano 1991, p. 139–167; E.J.H. Schrage, *Traditionibus et usucapionibus, non nudis pactis dominia rerum transferuntur, Die Wahl zwischen dem Konsens- und dem Traditionsprinzip in der Geschichte*, in: M. Ascheri e.a. (eds.), Ins Wasser geworfen und Ozeane durchquert, Festschrift für Knut Wolfgang Nörr, Köln-Weimar-Wien 2003, p. 913–958.

[1229] Birocchi, *Vendita e trasferimento della proprietà nel diritto commune*, p. 156–157.

Equally unmistakable is the role that Vitoria attributes to the transferee in the process of exchanging *dominium*. As a result, 'freedom of contract' can be affected if the law has put limitations on the capacity of the transferee to accept *dominium* over a thing. Clearly symptomatic of the central importance of the debate on testaments for the whole of contract doctrine, Vitoria precisely refers to the case of a testament made to the friars of the order of Saint Francis to illustrate this point.[1230] Since the Franciscans had refused to have any legal hold over worldly goods in their attempt to follow Christ's ideal of poverty in a most radical manner—thereby merely claiming factual power over goods (*usus facti*),[1231] they could not be considered to be the lawful beneficiaries of a testament, since they suffered from legal incapacity (*cum illi sint incapaces*). The legal conveyance of *dominium* to the Franciscans would have amounted to a *contradictio in terminis*.[1232] As a result, the heirs-at-law were entitled by law to an inheritance made to the Franciscans, regardless of the testator's will.[1233]

Not until Vitoria moves on to discuss the second legitimate title for the transfer of *dominium*, namely the will of the prince or the public authorities (*ex auctoritate principis*), does the issue of legacies and testaments, as well as the extrinsic or legal limits imposed on 'contractual freedom' gain full prominence.

In this context, a hierarchical relationship between the individual citizen and the state is established, since positive law can modify or limit the

---

[1230] This problem has recently been subject to careful investigation in A. Bartocci, *Ereditare in povertà, Le successioni a favore dei frati minori e la scienza giuridica nell'età avignonese (1309–1376)*, [Pubblicazioni del Dipartimento di Scienze Giuridiche, 32], Napoli 2009.

[1231] On the poverty controversy and *usus facti*, see Brett, *Liberty, right, and nature*, p. 11–20 (including references to further secondary literature), M. Kriechbaum, *Actio, ius und dominium in den Rechtslehren des 13. und 14. Jahrhunderts*, [Abhandlungen zur rechtswissenschaftlichen Grundlagenforschung, 77], Ebelsbach 1996, p. 24–89, and V. Mäkinen, *Property rights in the late medieval discussion in Franciscan poverty*, esp. p. 95–102 and p. 162–190.

[1232] To circumvent this contradiction, there were some medieval jurists, such as the late fourteenth century Bonifacio Ammannati who proposed to create a legal fiction whereby the Churches of the Franciscans were made heirs of the testate succession instead of the monks themselves, so that it would become legally possible for the Franciscans to become the beneficiaries of a last will; cf. A. Bartocci, *Il cardinal Bonifacio Ammannati legista avignonese ed un suo opuscolo 'contra Bartolum' sulla capacità successoria dei Frati Minori*, Rivista internazionale di diritto comune, 17 (2006), p. 260–262.

[1233] Vitoria, *Commentarii in IIamIIae* (ed. Beltrán de Heredia, tom. 3), quaest. 62, art. 1, num. 32, p. 85: 'Quando quis in testamento facit legatum inutile quod non potest sortiri effectum, quando scilicet non tenet datio illa ex iure, legatum illud (...) pertinet ad heredem vel heredes, quantumcumque sit ad pias causas, sicut v.g. facit quis heredes fratres minores (...).'

freedom of disposal of an individual *dominus*. The fact that positive law can change the rules of natural private property should not come as a surprise. As we have just about seen, Vitoria had argued that the institution of private *dominium* was introduced through consent amongst mankind, that is through human positive law itself. Natural law allowed for that change by definition, since *dominium* entailed the liberty for the communitarian *domini* to dispose of their things at will. So if human positive law—enacted by the King, but representing the consent of the people and therefore the consent of every individual *dominus*[1234]—had been able to introduce the division of things, why should that same law not be able to modify or undo the division of things for some sort of justified reason (*ex justa causa*)?

Positive laws do have the power in the court of conscience both to entitle people to certain rights, and to disentitle them from certain rights. Vitoria cites Thomas and Duns Scotus in defence of this view.[1235] Typically, he also gives enormous and very explicit weight to Aristotle's notorious statement in his *Politics* that man is essentially a 'political animal' (ὁ ἄνθρωπος φύσει πολιτικὸν ζῷον).[1236] Accordingly, the State has precedence over the individual, and can dispose of a citizen's person and goods, at least for a legitimate cause.[1237] To sum up, then, there is no doubt for Vitoria that positive human law can restrict the natural freedom of a *dominus* to dispose of his things by means of a contract.[1238]

[1234] Vitoria, *Commentarii in IIamIIae* (ed. Beltrán de Heredia, tom. 3), quaest. 62, art. 1, num. 33, p. 86: 'Est enim jam consensus prioris domini, et leges etiam pendent a consensu reipublicae, licet res eas instituat.'

[1235] Vitoria, *Commentarii in IIamIIae* (ed. Beltrán de Heredia, tom. 3), quaest. 62, art. 1, num. 33, p. 87: 'Haec conclusio est Scoti in 4, d. 15 dicentis quod leges dant et adimunt jus in foro conscientiae. Idem dicit sanctus Thomas 1.2, q. 96, a. 4. Et confirmat hoc Scotus, quia prima rerum divisio facta fuit auctoritate humana. Sed princeps habet hanc auctoritatem ex humana auctoritate. Ergo potest facere hanc divisionem et applicare potestatem unius ad alium, et hoc ex justa causa.'

[1236] Aristotle, *Politica*, 1, 2, 1253a2–3, in: *Aristotelis Politica*, recognovit brevique adnotatione critica instruxit W.D. Ross, [Scriptorum classicorum bibliotheca Oxoniensis], Oxonii 1973⁵ [= 1957], p. 3.

[1237] Vitoria, *Commentarii in IIamIIae* (ed. Beltrán de Heredia, tom. 3), quaest. 62, art. 1, num. 33, p. 86: 'Respondeo, et est fundamentum notandum et quod oportet praemittere ad totam istam materiam, quod homo quantum ad personam, et per consequens quantum ad rem et bona sua, magis est reipublicae quam sui ipsius. Patet ex jure naturali et ex Aristotele, 2 Politicorum.'

[1238] Vitoria, *Commentarii in IIamIIae* (ed. Beltrán de Heredia, tom. 3), quaest. 62, art. 1, num. 34, p. 87: 'In omni contractu, quidquid sit de voluntate dominorum, si tamen talis contractus sit irritus ipso jure, nullum dominium transfertur, nec adquiritur jus in foro conscientiae.'

Given that the existence of positive laws limiting to 'freedom of contract' is beyond doubt, Vitoria then proceeds to point out three well-known cases where such limits are imposed on the (natural) validity of the contract by (positive) law: 1) contracts involving a pupil who acts without the authority of his guardian, no matter how willingly and knowingly he agreed with the terms of the contract; 2) the transfer of ecclesiastical goods without the observation of the necessary solemnities; 3) testaments not satisfying form requirements. To judge these cases, Vitoria starts from a distinction—which he unrightfully ascribes to Abbas Panormitanus—between the case of the pupil (representing the more general problem of contracts in which one of the parties has no legal capacity), and both the case of the ecclesiastical goods and the one about testaments (where formalities imposed by contract law are not satisfied). The former case is easily settled. With the so-called common opinion of the jurists and theologians, Vitoria holds that a contract which is invalid in the external court on the grounds of legal incapacity is equally void of any legal consequence in the court of conscience.[1239]

5.4.3 *The moral enforcement of State regulation*

The problem of a contract that does not satisfy legally imposed form requirements (*contractus factus praeter formam juris*) is clearly not as easy a question to settle as the case of contracting parties suffering from lack of legal capacity. Before entirely rejecting Panormitan's thesis about the natural validity of contracts that fail to satisfy form requirements, Vitoria acknowledges that this is a very delicate issue.[1240] It touches upon questions of a far more general nature, such as the relationship between theology and law, or, more precisely, the tension between state legislation and the regulation of human behavior through moral theology.

Claiming to have thoroughly discussed the matter with his colleagues of the law faculty at Salamanca—who allegedly turned out to be divided on the subject—Vitoria lays down as a general rule that whenever a contract is not deemed valid as a means of transferring and acquiring rights

---

[1239] Vitoria, *Commentarii in IIamIIae* (ed. Beltrán de Heredia, tom. 3), quaest. 62, art. 1, num. 36, p. 89.

[1240] Vitoria, *Commentarii in IIamIIae* (ed. Beltrán de Heredia, tom. 3), quaest. 62, art. 1, num. 37, p. 89–91.

in the civil court, it is also invalid in the court of conscience.[1241] What Vitoria aims at in this context is a far-reaching convergence of two jurisdictions hitherto constantly at loggerheads with each other, namely the law pertaining to the external court and the law ruling the internal court, respectively. He expressly does so for the sake of the tranquillity of the souls (*ob securitatem conscientiarum*), thereby self-confidently rejecting the common opinion of the jurists and theologians in respect to the particular issue of testaments.

From a genuine concern to harmonize the parallel jurisdictions, Vitoria unambiguously draws the conclusion that testaments ruled invalid in the civil court for lack of solemnities are to be deemed equally void in the court of conscience. Ostensibly relying on *quaestio* 96 of the *Prima Secundae*—but omitting Thomas' requirement of a justified cause in order for a positive law to be binding in conscience—Vitoria stresses time and again that positive law has the power to avoid contracts which do not conform to the legally imposed requirements, so that they are deprived of any legal effects in both the civil and the internal court. Testaments lacking the required solemnities are a point in case.

By converging the law of conscience and the law of the land in the particular case of testaments, Vitoria does not mean to say, however, that the experts of these respective laws are granted a right of intervention in one another's affairs. Vitoria emphasizes the need for discretion when it comes to the practical administration of the respective courts. 'Every man to his trade', is the clear message which he sends to the jurists. Moreover, this is exactly the reason why the common opinion on the *contractus praeter formam* is of no argumentative force.[1242] For that common opinion was established by jurists, Vitoria says. Since Panormitanus was a jurist, and a canon laywer in particular, it was actually not within his province to make a valid statement about what ought to be the right judgment in the court of conscience in the first place. Panormitan's as well as other jurists'

[1241] Vitoria, *Commentarii in IIamIIae* (ed. Beltrán de Heredia, tom. 3), quaest. 62, art. 1, num. 38, p. 92: 'Unde ob securitatem conscientiarum pono hanc regulam: quod ex quocumque contractu non datur et adquiritur jus in foro contentioso, nec etiam datur nec adquiritur in foro conscientiae.'

[1242] Vitoria, *Commentarii in IIamIIae* (ed. Beltrán de Heredia, tom. 3), quaest. 62, art. 1, num. 38, p. 92: 'Ut respondeamus istis juristis, dico quod quantumcumque major pars jurisconsultorum et canonistarum amplectatur opinionem Panormitani, nihil tamen refert, quia ipsi parum auctoritatis habent in hujusmodi re. Mittunt siquidem falcem in messem alienam, utpote temporalis tantum est et contentiosa eorum cura, nihilque ad eos expectat judicare de foro conscientiae, sed de contentioso, bene tamen ad theologos.'

competence is confined to the external court, where disputes are settled according to positive law. The court of conscience, on the other hand, is governed fundamentally by the rule of natural and divine law, for which only the theologians are competent.

Granted, a certain exchange between the jurists and the theologians exists and turns out to be inevitable, according to Vitoria. Certainly in view of the relevance of positive law for knowing the rights and obligations that exist in the court of conscience. Yet the relation of a jurist to the court conscience is limited to that of an expert adviser—the executory task of administering justice in the court of conscience is left entirely to the theologians themselves. If, because of its sophisticated nature, theologians are not sure about the meaning of a positive law, they are right to consult a positive lawyer in order to know what the solution of a dispute is according to the written laws of the land. Jurists, then, can help determine the right interpretation of a positive law. But they cannot themselves apply that interpretation to the resolution of a case brought up before the court of conscience.

The competence of administering justice in the internal forum pertains only to the theologians. Hence Vitoria can safely put aside the age-old common opinion on testaments. For it rested on the false authority of jurists acting outside their powers. Moreover, Vitoria argues, since learned men such as Adrian of Utrecht and Sylvester Prierias—who enjoyed theological authority—relied on the jurists' arguments far too heavily, their support for the common opinion is of no real force either.[1243] Vitoria tries to make us understand, then, that there is no authority, neither juridical, nor theological, which stands in the way of his unorthodox position that, even in conscience, 'contractual freedom' is affected by a lack of legally prescribed solemnities.

Moreover, he points out a contradiction in the common opinion.[1244] For one thing, the common opinion has it that contracts in which form requirements are not satisfied do still bring about rights and obligations, because they hold as a matter of natural law—which merely requires true *dominium* for an exchange to be valid. But, on the other hand, they do not recognize the validity of a contract entered into by a minor who has

---

[1243] This is explained more clearly in the alternative version of Vitoria's commentaries; cf. *Commentarii in IIamIIae* (ed. Beltrán de Heredia, tom. 3), quaest. 62, art. 1, not. 38, p. 93: 'Neque auctoritas Hadriani et Silvestri debet movere, quia rationibus canonistarum innititur solum, et non theologicis rationibus.'

[1244] See Vitoria, *Commentarii in IIamIIae*, quaest. 62, art. 1, num. 39, p. 93.

reached full reasoning capacities but acts without his guardian. Still, as a matter of natural law, having the full capacity of reason should be considered sufficient ground to enter into a valid contract. So why do they recognize the invalidating power of positive law in the court of conscience in the case of minors but not in the case of testaments? Furthermore, Vitoria questions the causal relationship between natural law and the court of conscience.[1245] He disconnects nullity in the court of conscience from nullity according to the natural law. For example, elections are in line with the natural law only if a candidate is elected by majority. Still an election can be valid in both the court of conscience and the external court if a candidate was not supported by the majority, say if he got 200 votes behind his name, whereas his two challengers each got 150 votes.

5.4.4   *Against teleological interpretation*

Apart from pointing out contradictions in the counter-opinion, Vitoria also produces very remarkable arguments in favor of his own opinion. In Inst. 2,17,7–8 he finds support for the claim that leaving a testament that does not meet form requirements amounts to dying without any testament at all, therefore leaving the whole heritage to the heirs-at-law.[1246] This attempt to back up his position by reference to the law of Rome would unleash a quest in later authors for texts in the *Corpus Iustinianeum* that could be quoted in defence of the opposite view. Vitoria further holds that the *ratio legis* behind the statutory formality requirements has nothing to do with avoiding falsehood and fraud. An interpretation that clearly goes against mainstream teleological interpretation from Pope Innocent IV over Panormitanus to Pope Adrian VI. In Vitoria's view, the final aim of the form requirements is related to punishing the negligence of testators (*in poenam negligentiae testatoris*). Domingo de Soto would be one of the few authors also to adopt that view.[1247]

[1245] Vitoria, *Commentarii in IIamIIae* (ed. Beltrán de Heredia, tom. 3), quaest. 62, art. 1, num. 41, p. 97: 'Praeterea, ipsi propterea dicunt quod tenet contractus irritus defectu solemnitatis in foro conscientiae, quia est validus in jure naturali stando. Sed contra, aliquis contractus est validus in foro contentioso et in foro conscientiae et tamen est contra jus naturale.'

[1246] Vitoria, *Commentarii in IIamIIae* (ed. Beltrán de Heredia, tom. 3), quaest. 62, art. 1, num. 41, p. 94–95.

[1247] In this manner, Vitoria equates the *ratio legis* behind the Roman law of testament with the *ratio legis* behind the law of prescription. This can be derived, at least indirectly, from Vitoria, *Commentarii in IIamIIae* (ed. Beltrán de Heredia, tom. 3), quaest. 62, art. 1,

Even more crucial—and of the greatest interest from the point of view of the development of the present-day concept of the law as binding universally regardless of particular circumstances and persons—is the fact that Vitoria disagrees with the traditional scholastic method of interpretation. The theologians as well as the jurists tend to call into question the applicability of a law in a particular case by arguing that the *ratio legis* is frustrated under those particular circumstances. Yet Vitoria states that, even if it were true that the main intention behind the statutory form requirements were to prevent deceit, it is of the essence of a law to bind universally, not only in cases where there effectively is a danger of deceit. A legal precept is absolute and universal in its range (*praeceptum absolutum est praeceptum legis*).[1248]

A law intends to bind everybody (*intendit obligare omnes*), for the simple reason that the law itself is unable to distinguish between situations that are likely to be dangerous and other circumstances that are safe from fraud and deceit. For example, if there is a prohibition on the possession of firearms, this prohibitive law applies to every person, even if one citizen in particular is not to be considered a dangerous person. The law itself cannot make the difference between ordinary and extraordinary people (*lex non potest distinguere*). But, one might object, if the law itself is unable to make a distinction, is not there a place for the learned jurists and theologians to come in, and save the sense and meaning of the law by making a distinction? This is precisely what Panormitanus or Adrian of Utrecht had done. Vitoria, however, seems to have been too much in the grip of an absolutist political tendancy to envisage that objection in the first place.

5.4.5 *The politics of conscience*

Should Vitoria's unexpectedly unorthodox position come as a surprise to us? Given its embeddedness in a wider political theology, it must not. Perhaps it simply pertains to the paradoxes and perplexities that ensue

---

num. 47, p. 104: 'Quia mirum est quod potuerit facere lex quod succedat ab intestato propter defectum solemnitatis juris, et faciat illum dominum in poenam negligentiae testatoris, quia scilicet non consuluit doctos ut conderet testamentum, et quod non possit facere dominum habentem jus praescriptionis bonae fidei in poenam negligentiae veri domini, quia scilicet non repetivit.'

[1248] Vitoria, *Commentarii in IIamIIae* (ed. Beltrán de Heredia, tom. 3), quaest. 62, art. 1, num. 45, p. 101.

from the two-track policy of conflict regulation inherent in the early modern confessional state. Too wide a gap between the court of conscience—presided by the most reverend doctors of theology—and the external jurisdictions—organized by the jurists—creates tensions that eventually get out of control. As we have seen, this had already been the explicit concern of Baldus de Ubaldis.

In this manner, the debate about formal limitations on 'freedom of contract' offers an inkling of the tensions that are part and parcel of any normative universe that—contrary to the ideal of present day state monopoly on conflict regulation—moves forward along a double track. In the biblical language from Matthew 16:26, familiar with the Christian audience he is addressing, Vitoria ponders 'what profit it is to a man if he gains the whole world and loses his own soul *because of that law (ex tali lege)*'? As Baldus—who is strangely absent from Vitoria's plea—had pointed out, the observance of the civil law would have implied committing a sin (*observatio iuris civilis esset peccatum*).[1249]

Taking the common opinion on formally defective contracts as a starting point, it is impossible not to conclude that everybody acting according to positive law is endagering his soul. For in following the positive law, one contravenes natural law. So if the common opinion were true, the invalidation of a contract through positive law would be wholly unjust, futile and dangerous for the soul.[1250] For example, if a heir-at-law were to retain the belongings of his father who died without leaving a solemn testament, he would be sinning in the court of conscience, although positive law did grant him a right to the heritage. Worse still, a parish demanding back ecclesiastical goods that were alienated by means of an insolemn contract would be exercising a right based on positive law, yet at the same time committing a mortal sin.

Another *casus perplexus*—frequently mentioned in the early modern scholastic tradition—would concern a guardian of a pupil claiming the heritage of his brother, because the latter left a testament not satisfying

---

[1249] Baldus, *Commentaria in primum, secundum, et tertium Codicis librum*, num. 7, f. 80v (see higher).

[1250] Vitoria, *Commentarii in IIamIIae* (ed. Beltrán de Heredia, tom. 3), quaest. 62, art. 1, num. 41, p. 95–96: 'Esset valde inutilis et periculosa irritatio in foro contentioso defectu solemnitatis, si non valeret in foro conscientiae. Absurdum enim est dicere quod detur in foro contentioso jus cum quo condemnentur homines, cum leges potius provideant saluti animae quam corporis.'

the solemnities required by the law.[1251] If the guardian is sollicited by the pupil to go to court in order to get the heritage, he faces a dilemma. In effectively taking the legatee to court, he acts in accordance with positive law, but sins in conscience. In refusing to go to court, he risks his own fortune since the pupil could take him to court according to positive law for not having looked after his fortune with care. So the guardian is torn between the care for his spiritual and material well-being. Similarly, a lawyer would be sinning in conscience when defending a heir *ab intestato* who is entitled to the inheritance in the external court, even though he is not in the court of conscience because a testament, however defective from a formal point of view, exists.

Interestingly, from all these paradoxes and perplexities Vitoria infers that the jurisdiction of conscience must align with positive law. In theory, he could equally well have argued—as Panormitanus or Adrian of Utrecht would have done—that the positive law has to be put in line with the natural law. But he does not. As a consequence, what Vitoria is doing, at least in this case, is reinforcing secular power by means of conscience, rather than urging secular power to yield to spiritual authority. What at first sight appears to be a minor technical debate on testaments, then, appears to be of tremendous juridical and political significance.

Vitoria explicitly recognized the 'explosive' nature of his argument.[1252] That might explain why at the end of his long-drawn-out and committed attack against the common opinion, he suddenly stops. For the same reason that had driven him first to rebuke the common opinion, he now reverses his conclusions. For the sake of the tranquillity of the souls (*pro securitate conscientiarum*), in particular, he thinks it better to hold in conformity with customary practice (*usus et consuetudo*) that a testate successor has a right of retention as long as the heir-at-law does not take him to court.

Vitoria compares the legal position of the heir-at-law in the case of a defective testament to that of the privileged position of a *filiusfamilias* pursuant to the *SC Macedonianum*, or that of the heirs-at-law thanks to

---

[1251] Vitoria, *Commentarii in IIamIIae* (ed. Beltrán de Heredia, tom. 3), quaest. 62, art. 1, num. 42, p. 98.

[1252] Vitoria, *Commentarii in IIamIIae* (ed. Beltrán de Heredia, tom. 3), quaest. 62, art. 1, num. 44, p. 99: 'Sed tamen, licet ego sim valde tutus cum mea opinione, tamen pro securitate conscientiarum, et ne videamur funditus contrariam explodere opinionem, possumus in hac nostra materia de contractibus dicere sicut dicebamus de senatusconsulto Macedoniano et de lege Falcidia.'

the *lex Falcidia*.[1253] The law that invalidates a testament because it does not meet form requirements, is actually issued in favor of the heirs-at-law, to the effect that they can benefit from the privilege (the invalidation of the testament) that ensues from it.[1254] For that privilege to become effective, however, the heirs-at-law need to take the illegitimate testate successor to court and have their rights enforced by the judge. Consequently, if a heir-at-law is not willing to avail himself of that privilege, or if he is negligent, or ignorant about this law, the testate successor has a right of retention.[1255] In that case, the famous rule applies that the condition of the possessor is the stronger (*melior est conditio possidentis in dubiis*).[1256]

To summarize, if you possess a good on account of a testament or a contract that does not comply with formality requirements, your confessor is allowed to absolve you as long as the legitimate owner has not taken you to court. Yet Vitoria does not conclude in that way without repeating that he takes that view merely to align himself with traditional authority. His own opinion and the truth remain different.[1257]

5.5   THEOLOGIANS FOR FORMALISM II: THE DIPLOMATIC VERSION

5.5.1   *Property, exchange, and the common good*

The shockwaves of Vitoria's provocation can be felt in the subsequent attempt by Domingo de Soto to mediate discreetly between his master's unconventional views and the common opinion of the decretalists. Before

---

[1253] The *Lex Falcidia* (Inst. 2,22; D. 35,1; C. 6,50) imposed limits on the amount of legacies, to the effect that at least a quarter of the inheritance automatically belonged to the heirs-at-law; cf. M. Kaser, *Das Römische Privatrecht*, Erster Abschnitt: Das altrömische, das vorklassische, und klassische Recht, [Handbuch der Altertumswissenschaft, 10.3.3.1], München 1971², p. 756, § 188. On the *SC Macedonianum*, cf. supra, p. 351.

[1254] Vitoria, *Commentarii in IIamIIae* (ed. Beltrán de Heredia, tom. 3), quaest. 62, art. 1, num. 44, p. 100: '(...) lex illa de succedentibus ab intestato, quando ipso jure testamentum est invalidum, est favorabilis illis qui ab intestato decedunt ne patrimonia dilapidentur. Ideo ipse qui succedit potest uti favore illo si vult et tunc obtinebit secure.'

[1255] Vitoria, *Commentarii in IIamIIae* (ed. Beltrán de Heredia, tom. 3), quaest. 62, art. 1, num. 44, p. 100: 'Si tamen non vult illo [favore] uti vel ex ignorantia vel ex negligentia vel ex aliqua causa, alius institutus heres potest cum bona conscientia retinere hereditatem.'

[1256] Vitoria, *Commentarii in IIamIIae* (ed. Beltrán de Heredia, tom. 3), quaest. 62, art. 1, num. 45, p. 101.

[1257] Vitoria, *Commentarii in IIamIIae* (ed. Beltrán de Heredia, tom. 3), quaest. 62, art. 1, num. 44, p. 100: 'Hoc dico magis ut conveniamus cum jurisperitis quam quod in veritate ita sit; nam ad rigorem debebat fieri ut dictum est.'

we go on and examine his diplomatic effort, a preliminary word is needed about the larger context in which Soto tackles the specific problem of formalities in contracts and testaments.

First, it is worth repeating that Soto stresses the need to begin any systematic treatment of contracts by an elucidation of *dominium*, because this concept is the basis and foundation of all things performed through exchange.[1258] Hence it should not come as a surprise that Soto formulates the question of the limits to 'freedom of contract' in terms of the limitations imposed on the free exchange of *dominium*. Incidentally, Soto takes *dominium* in a less wide sense than Vitoria.[1259] While Vitoria and many authors in the scholastic tradition had equated *dominium* with right in the subjective sense, Soto thinks of *ius* in the subjective sense as a much larger category than *dominium*.[1260] For example, in Soto's vocabulary, use or usufruct are not a species of *dominium*, since for someone to be considered a real *dominus*, he must have a faculty over the substance of the good—which, by definition, clearly exceeds the faculty of a usufructuary.[1261] In Soto's definition, *dominium* does not include all forms of right and power, but merely that eminent power over a thing, which allows us to use it according to our own wishes (*pro libito*) for our own utility, and to like it in our own interest.[1262]

A second contextual element worth mentioning concerns the title of the article that opens the question in which the issue of formalities is addressed. It reads as follows: are there any boundaries as a matter of

---

[1258] Soto, *De iustitia et iure*, lib. 4, prooem., cited supra, n. 1203.

[1259] An extensive elucidation of Soto's novel concept of *dominium* is included in Brett, *Liberty, right, and nature*, p. 137–164.

[1260] Soto, *De iustitia et iure* (ed. fac. V. Diego Carro – M. González Ordóñez, vol. 2), lib. 4, quaest. 1, art. 1, p. 279: 'Fit ergo ut ius non convertatur cum dominio, sed sit illi superius et latius patens. Habet enim uxor ius quoddam in maritum, iuxta illud Pauli, 1 ad Corinth., 7, vir sui corporis potestatem non habet, sed mulier. Et filius in parentes, qui curam suorum habere tenentur, ac servi in dominos, a quibus pasci sustentarique debent. Et eadem ratione subditus ius habet in praelatum a quo est instituendus et gubernandus. Et tamen nullus istorum quantumvis nomen extendas, dominus est, appellarive potest sui superioris.'; and *l.c.*, par. *sed ait*: 'Dominium autem non quodcunque ius et potestatem significat, sed certe illam quae est in rem, qua uti pro libito nostro possumus in nostram propriam utilitatem, quamque ob nosipsos diligimus.'

[1261] Soto, *De iustitia et iure* (ed. fac. V. Diego Carro – M. González Ordóñez, vol. 2), lib. 4, quaest. 1, art. 1, p. 281: 'Ex hac constituta definitione dominii colligitur differentia inter ipsum et usum atque usumfructum. Dominium enim est facultas in substantiam rei, ususfructus vero non nisi in eius qualitate et accidentia.'

[1262] Soto, *De iustitia et iure* (ed. fac. V. Diego Carro – M. González Ordóñez, vol. 2), lib. 4, quaest. 1, art. 1, p. 279: 'Dominium autem non quodcunque ius et potestatem significat, sed certe illam quae est in rem qua uti pro libito nostro possumus in nostram propriam utilitatem, quamque ob nosipsos diligimus.'

natural law to the will of an individual to freely dispose of his *dominium*?[1263]
The arguments put forward by those rejecting the idea of unlimited 'contractual liberty' concern precisely both the formal and the substantive
limitations on 'freedom of contract'. As to the substantive limitations—
which will be discussed extensively in the next chapter—the possibility
of immoral contracts like prostitution under a general regime of absolute
'freedom of contract' urges its opponents to make a case for restrictions
on the free exchange of *dominium*.[1264] By the same token, they argue
against unlimited 'freedom of contract' as a matter of natural law considering that:[1265]

> If natural law allowed anybody to be the arbiter of his own will in disposing
> of what belongs to him unlimitedly, it would follow that his will can never
> be refrained by statutory law, since human law can never take precedence
> over natural law (as has been demonstrated in books 1 and 3). But this is a
> false conclusion, as is obvious from widespread custom and practice in well-
> ordered states. For example, minors younger than 25 cannot alienate their
> goods (…) nor can ecclesiastical goods be alienated at will of a prelate or a
> chapter unless by virtue of certain causes (*certis de causis*) and in certain
> well-defined ways (*certis praescriptis modis*).

It is obvious from this passage that the external limitations imposed by
public authorities are mainly felt through requirements on the mode or

---

[1263] Soto, *De iustitia et iure* (ed. fac. V. Diego Carro – M. González Ordóñez, vol. 2),
lib. 4, quaest. 5, art. 1 (*Utrum sua quisque voluntate, naturali iure valeat rei suae dominium
in alterum transferre*), p. 307.

[1264] Soto, *De iustitia et iure* (ed. fac. V. Diego Carro – M. González Ordóñez, vol. 2),
lib. 4, quaest. 5, art. 1, p. 308: 'Si unusquilibet posset suo arbitrio rem suam alienare,
sequeretur eundem perinde posse pretii mercedisque dominium pro re turpi in alterum
traducere. Consequens tamen est falsum, nam qui corrumpendo iudici aut assassino ut
hominem occidat, aut per usuram, aut per symonias quicquam confert, etiam si ultro
id faciat, dominium non transfert, ut iura sancte decernunt. Ergo ius naturae non est ut
quisque potest libere sua donare. Neque vero desunt qui idem de meretrice sentiant quae
merito sui corporis nullius potest mercedis dominium recipere.'

[1265] Soto, *De iustitia et iure* (ed. fac. V. Diego Carro – M. González Ordóñez, vol. 2),
lib. 4, quaest. 5, art. 1, p. 308: 'Si id unicuilibet ius naturale indulgeret, ut suae esset arbiter
voluntatis in rerum suarum dominiis transferendis, sequeretur eiusmodi voluntatem neutiquam civili lege posse cohiberi, nam humanae leges, ut lib. 1 et 3 monstratum est, nullum obtinent contra ius naturae vigorem. Consequens autem creberrimus usus cuiusque
bene institutae reipublicae ostendit esse falsum. Prohibentur namque minores aetate
vigintiquinque annorum sua alienare bona, ut patet ff. eodem titulo, l. 1 [D. 4,4,1]. Item
legibus quorundam regnorum particularibus sic sunt maioratuum iura instituta, ut eorum
possessores nequeant vinculata bona dispendere. Item neque ecclesiae bona alienare pro
libito potest aut praelatus aut capitulum, nisi certis de causis, certisque praescriptis modis,
ut patet ex decreto Leonis, 12, q.2, can. sine exceptione, et toto titulo de reb. eccles. non
alien. [X 3,13].'

form of conclusion of a contract and the capacity to enter into a contract. Soto confirms that there are natural limits to the basic principle of absolute self-determination, since man has the inner, natural predisposition to live the life of a citizen as part of a commonwealth (*homo naturaliter animal civile*).[1266] Yet it is 'naturally' impossible for human beings to peacefully live together in a commonwealth, unless there are public authorities maintaining order and peace.[1267] Public authorities are needed, to act as the guardian of the commonwealth and the administrator of justice. For example, it pertains to the public task of custody to prevent 'citizens whose freedom (*libertas*) is not yet led by the full judgment of reason' from squandering their patrimony, and to the public task of administering justice to punish crimes. By virtue of these public duties, Soto says, the public authorities can take both the property and the life of their citizens. He does not doubt that the public authorities can tax the citizens to collect the money that is necessary for the fulfillment of those tasks, since the parts are subordinate to the whole (*partes sunt propter totum*).

Since the power of the State derives from natural principles, Soto does not see a contradiction between the formal limitations on freedom of exchange, and the natural freedom to dispose of his goods as he likes, from which the *dominus* benefits. Indeed, Soto concludes that every human being has a natural right to dispose of a good of which he is the rightful *dominus* in whatever way he wants, since the natural and the divine foundation of the *dominium* over goods is human reason and freedom (*fundamentum dominii rerum naturale ac divinum esse humanam rationem ac libertatem*).[1268] He supports the existence of this

---

[1266] Soto, *De iustitia et iure* (ed. fac. V. Diego Carro – M. González Ordóñez, vol. 2), lib. 4, quaest. 5, art. 1, p. 309. Interestingly, Domingo de Bañez, who follows Soto's argument very closely, replaces *animal civile* by *animal sociale et politicum*; cf. Bañez, *De iure et iustitia*, ad quaest. 62, p. 151.

[1267] Soto, *De iustitia et iure* (ed. fac. V. Diego Carro – M. González Ordóñez, vol. 2), lib. 4, quaest. 5, art. 1, p. 309: 'Est enim homo naturaliter animal civile. Coalescere autem in unum mortalium vita non potest, nisi a publica authoritate in pace contineantur, quae quidem authoritas tum custos est reipublicae, tum et iustitiae iudex. Ad legitimam vero custodiam primum necessarium est, ut civibus prospiciat, ne antequam eorum libertas pleno iudicio rationis ducatur, sua bona dilapident. Quam ob rem prohibentur pupilli de bonis suis disponere, sic ut eorum alienatio irrita sit et nulla. Secundo et necessarium est sumptus eidem reipublicae necessarios a civibus colligere. Nam iure naturae partes sunt propter totum. Ac demum tamquam iudex custosque iusti ad eum spectat maleficia ulcisci; quare, sicuti vita, ita et bonis potest quemlibet civium expoliare.'

[1268] Soto, *De iustitia et iure* (ed. fac. V. Diego Carro – M. González Ordóñez, vol. 2), lib. 4, quaest. 5, art. 1, p. 308–309: 'Unusquisque mortalium ius habet naturale donandi et quomodocumque alienandi res quarum vere ac legitime dominus est. Conclusio haec ex

natural right to free exchange in two ways. First, by appealing to God's creation of man in His image, that is a rational and free being.[1269] As a result, man's will has the *dominium* over its own actions, and, by this means, also the *dominium* over the goods of the world. 'If a *dominus* is constituted through his will', Soto reasons, 'then it is through the same will that he can abdicate any *dominium* he has.' Indeed, a little further on in his argumentation, Soto cites Inst. 2,1,40, and D. 41,1,9,3 to argue that even Roman law confirms that nothing is more natural and equitable than to respect the naked will of the owner (*quid tam congruum fidei humanae quam ea servare quae inter homines placuerunt*). The second argument which Soto adduces is that everything has been created for the sake of man, so that man can use the things which he possesses as he wishes.[1270] The only limit to a man's *dominium* is his own life. Taking one's own life is strictly forbidden.

Soto sought to demonstrate that the natural law principle that the liberty of man can lawfully be constrained by the State was confirmed by the *ratio scripta* of Justinian's *Corpus iuris civilis*. As a matter of fact, Ulpian claims in D. 4,4,1pr. that it is by virtue of natural equity that minors must be deprived of the capacity to enter freely into a contract.[1271] Considering man as oriented by nature towards the common good of the *respublica* of which he is merely a tiny part, a younger Dominican colleague of Soto, Domingo de Bañez (1528–1604), would even contend that the statutory constraints on an individual man's will were to be deemed more natural

---

superioribus elicitur. Diximus namque fundamentum dominii rerum naturale ac divinum esse humanam rationem ac libertatem.'

[1269] Soto, *De iustitia et iure* (ed. fac. V. Diego Carro – M. González Ordóñez, vol. 2), lib. 4, quaest. 5, art. 1, p. 309: 'Enimvero quia Deus hominem ad sui imaginem condidit, hoc est rationalem ac liberum, per quam rationem et voluntatem dominium habet suarum actionum. Inde factus est rerum dominus, secundum illud Genes. 1, Faciamus hominem ad imaginem et similitudinem nostram, ut praesit piscibus maris, etc. Qua utique de causa soli homini demonstravimus inter sublunares creaturas competere ut sit rei alicuius dominus. Si ergo per voluntatem constituitur dominus, per eandem potest dominium ab se quodcunque abdicare.'

[1270] Soto, *De iustitia et iure* (ed. fac. V. Diego Carro – M. González Ordóñez, vol. 2), lib. 4, quaest. 5, art. 1, p. 309: 'Res universae propter hominem conditae sunt, atque adeo illis quas ipse possidet ad libitum potest uti. Quin vero, ut in definitione dominii supra posita videre est, nihil aliud est dominium rei quam facultas et ius eadem uti, quocunque usu lege permisso, puta donandi, vendendi, consumendi, et quomodocunque alienandi. Res est clarissima. Quin vero non modo res quisque suas, verum et seipsum potest vendere, ut supra assertum est. Nam etsi nemo sit usque adeo sui dominus, ut vita se valeat iure privare, est tamen eius custos, ut quo vitam servet, seipsum vendere queat.'

[1271] D. 4,4,1pr.: 'Hoc edictum praetor naturalem aequitatem secutus proposuit, quo tutelam minorum suscepit.'

than autonomy and absolute freedom of exchange, since those limitations were conducive to the common good (*bonum commune*).[1272]

Soto acknowledges that legal prescriptions issued by the public authorities can legitimately limit individual autonomy in order to protect the weak, to punish delictual behavior, and to promote the common good. Not surprisingly, the first book of Soto's *De iustitia et iure* is largely devoted to the demonstration of the binding nature of positive law in the court of conscience. Moreover, Soto recognizes that by analogy with testaments, law *Hac consultissima* (C. 6,23,21) prescribes solemnities in contracts on pain of absolute nullity.[1273] Against this background, there is not much room left for him to argue that despite its being invalid on account of statutory law, a contract is still capable of transferring *dominium* as a matter of natural law. Still, he would need to find that room in his discussion on defective testaments—precisely within the context of the question of whether a contract which is null as a matter of statutory law still has the force of transferring dominion—if only to bring the argument of his master Vitoria closer to that of the common opinion.

5.5.2   *Technical nuances and academic courtesy*

A subtle way of narrowing the gap between his teacher and the common opinion is for Soto to play down the gravity of the issue. He pretends at the outset of his discussion that the issue of the binding nature of contracts that do not meet solemnity requirements is uncontroversial (*non magnopere inter doctores agitata*).[1274]

Needless to say, this is in stark contrast to the marked liveliness of the debate in the preceding jurists and theologians, as well as its direct relevance for the solution of frequent disputes in everyday practice—first stressed by Panormitanus and still underscored by Luis de Molina at the turn of the seventeenth century. Soto's denial is also strange in view of the

---

1272 Bañez, *De iure et iustitia*, ad quaest. 62, p. 154: 'cum ad bonum commune expedit, ut proprius appetitus et propria voluntas hominis cohibeatur, haec ipsa cohibitio et impeditio magis est homini naturalis quam translatio dominii per propriam voluntatem'.

1273 Soto, *De iustitia et iure* (ed. fac. V. Diego Carro – M. González Ordóñez, vol. 2), lib. 4, quaest. 5, art. 3 (*Utrum per contractum qui nullus est iure civili transferatur dominium*), p. 317: 'Leges civiles, ut libro 1 dictum est, obligant in foro conscientiae, per quas tamen absolute stabiliuntur contractuum solemnitates, sub illo verborum rigore, ut alias contractus pro infecto habeatur, ut de testamento patet, l. hac consultissima, C. de testam.'

1274 Soto, *De iustitia et iure* (ed. fac. V. Diego Carro – M. González Ordóñez, vol. 2), lib. 4, quaest. 5, art. 3, p. 318.

fact that he deemed it necessary to maintain falsely that in his commentary on canon *Quia plerique* (X 3,49,8) Pope Innocent IV had advocated an opinion opposite to that of Panormitanus?[1275] Typically, however, there is no trace in Soto's exposition of an explicit reference to Vitoria's position, let alone to his name. While designating the view of Panormitanus and Adrian of Utrecht as the *communis opinio*, he contents himself to pointing out that for a long time he has heard the opposite view at the university of Salamanca (*in his nostris scholis*).[1276] He even indicates his preference for this alternative viewpoint, deeming it more probable.

Eventually, Soto tries to find a third way to reconcile the genuine standpoint of his teacher with the *communis opinio* by elaborating on the intermediate view briefly suggested by Vitoria at the end of his discussion. 'I do not dare to defend that alternative view in so absolute a manner when I have to judge concrete cases', Soto indicates,[1277] 'I rather take an intermediary position (*media sententia*) of my own that is moderate from both extreme perspectives.' To elucidate his intermediary standpoint, Soto proceeds to point out the two ways in which the public authorities can preclude a transfer of *dominium* from taking place. On the one hand, statutory law can hinder an exchange absolutely. For example, in the case of *minores*. On the other hand, positive law can hinder the transfer of dominion in the same way as it invalidates contracts (*modo contractus*), namely to prevent fraud and falsehood. Instances include solemnity requirements in last wills, and formalities in contracts for conveying *dominium* over ecclesiastical goods.

Soto's intermediary position consists in holding that in contrast to a contract made by a party suffering from incapacity, contracts which are not in compliance with those essential formalities prescribed by the law are not *ipso facto* void in the court of conscience. Rather, the beneficiary of the

---

[1275] Even if the opinion of our canonist is more nuanced than was suggested by Panormitanus (cf. supra), in his commentary on canon *Quia plerique* [X 3,49,8] he does not go as far as to declare void in conscience all contracts that do not comply with solemnity requirements. Rather, Pope Innocent IV claims that all laws enacted by a prince without a cause are of no validity neither in the external nor the internal court.

[1276] Soto, *De iustitia et iure* (ed. fac. V. Diego Carro – M. González Ordóñez, vol. 2), lib. 4, quaest. 5, art. 3, p. 318: 'Audivi ergo iam pridem in his nostris scholis contrariam sententiam, ceu multo probabiliorem defensari, nempe contractum nullum iure civili esse etiam in conscientia nullum.'

[1277] Soto, *De iustitia et iure* (ed. fac. V. Diego Carro – M. González Ordóñez, vol. 2), lib. 4, quaest. 5, art. 3, p. 318: 'Haud tamen ego tam absolute opinionem hanc asserere audio, ubi casus huiusmodi mihi occurrunt, sed mediam sententiam utrinque temperatam pro captu meo amplector.'

privilege granted by the law has to execute his privilege for that contract to become effectively void as a matter of conscience.[1278] For example, if my father makes a legacy through an insolemn testament, as a son and a heir-at-law I am not obliged to execute that legacy. Yet, if the legatee has already taken possession of the legacy, I have to take him to court in order to enforce my privilege based on the nullity of the testament.

Soto is left with two tasks, then. He needs to demonstrate why he thinks the heir-at-law is the ultimate beneficary of a defective testament—which presupposes that a contract or a testament lacking formalities is void. Yet at the same time, an explanation is needed as to why the testatee has a right of retention until he is taken to court and condemned to make restitution—which presupposes that a defective contract or testament is not void *ipso facto*, but voidable. With feigned modesty, Soto reveals his hesitation as he, 'a second-rank theologian', prepares to defend a view that he allegedly could not find expounded by any other authority. In fact, we will see Soto heavily drawing both upon the Spanish Socrates' truly genuine yet provocative opinion (to radically affirm that an informal testament is void), and on Vitoria's final reconciliatory effort (to claim that an informal testament is not immediately affected by its informality).

5.5.3   *The absoluteness of positive law*

Combining the theoretical premise that positive law binds in conscience with the factual evidence of statutory prescribed formalities, Soto has no chance but to state that contracts and testaments have to comply with those form requirements on pain of nullity. Although he does not claim to be exhaustive in citing Roman sources—a task he leaves to the secular judges—Soto recalls that in the civilian tradition the law *Hac consultissima* (C. 6,23,21) along with Inst. 2,10,14 stipulate that seven witnesses be present for a *nuncupatio* to be valid. In Soto's view, this rule has been confirmed by the indigenous Spanish law itself, notably by the *Leyes de Toro*.[1279] Judging from the alienation of ecclesiastical goods, the canon law

---

1278 Soto, *De iustitia et iure* (ed. fac. V. Diego Carro – M. González Ordóñez, vol. 2), lib. 4, quaest. 5, art. 3, p. 318: 'Contractus cui deest essentialis solemnitas iuris, licet in conscientia non sit ipso facto simpliciter nullus, veluti ille qui fieret a pupillo illegitimae aetatis, eatenus tamen est nullus, ut bona conscientia possit quisque legis beneficio in tali casu uti.'

1279 Soto, *De iustitia et iure* (ed. fac. V. Diego Carro – M. González Ordóñez, vol. 2), lib. 4, quaest. 5, art. 3, ad not. marg. *Solemnitas testamentorum describitur*, p. 318; cf.

also turns out to be very strict about formalities and special procedures (C.10, q.2, c.2; C.12, q.2, c.23).

Soto was nonetheless bound to take issue with an objection that stemmed from canon *Cum esses* (X 3,26,10). Here, Pope Alexander III (1159–1181) states that a testament is valid provided that a parishioner makes it before the priest and in the presence of a mere two or three witnesses. It is worth paying attention to Soto's interpretation of this decretale, since canon *Cum esses* would continue to play a role in later discussions among the early modern scholastics (e.g. with Covarruvias and Lessius). Asked by the bishop of Ostia to confirm the practice in that place—almost similar to Roman law—of requiring the written testimony of seven witnesses for a testament to be valid, Pope Alexander III radically disapproved of that practice. Moreover, it was claimed by Soto that the standard gloss suggested that in condemning that practice, Pope Alexander III had abrogated the civil law, replacing it by the natural law. In fact, though, the gloss rejected precisely that suggestion.[1280]

Soto carefully restricts the scope of canon *Cum esses*, to the effect that the requirement of a mere two or three witnesses must be interpreted either as pertaining to the specific case of testaments *ad causam piam* (incidentally, the subject of the following canon, namely X 3,26,11), or as pertaining merely to the diocese of Ostia, which fell under the jurisdiction of the Pope, since it was part of the Church-State.[1281] Otherwise, Pope Alexander III could not possibly be deemed to have had the authority to abolish the civil law, since he had no power to change or contest the civil law but on account of its being at variance with divine law. Domingo de Soto clearly sees no invincible discrepancy between the civil law and

---

Las leyes de Toro glosadas por Diego del Castillo, Burgos 1527, l. 3, f. 17v–18v. In fact this constitution is more flexible than Soto claimed, at least in regard to verbal wills; cf. infra.

[1280] Gloss *Improbamus* ad X 3,26,10 in *Corpus juris canonici* (ed. Gregoriana), part. 2, col. 1174: 'Quidam tamen dicunt, quod per hoc caput quod generaliter loquitur, derogatur omnibus legibus, quae dicunt minus solemnem voluntatem non valere, *quod non credo*, quia non est verisimile quod dominus Papa voluerit unico verbo legibus derogare.' [italics are ours]

[1281] Soto, *De iustitia et iure* (ed. fac. V. Diego Carro – M. González Ordóñez, vol. 2), lib. 4, quaest. 5, art. 3, p. 321–322: 'Igitur illic Pontifex summus non est credendus leges eiusmodi abrogasse, quia non habet autoritatem in leges principum, nisi quatenus sunt contra ius divinum (...), neque abrogationis verbo illic utitur, neque talis abrogatio recepta unquam a principibus fuit. Igitur licet aliis praeterea duobus modis glossa illic textum interpretetur, satis sit nobis altero duorum modorum respondere, scilicet, aut quod id restringendum est ad pia legata (...), quae quidem legata minorem exigunt solemnitatem. Vel forte melius quod cum episcopatus Hostiensis esset in territorio ecclesiae, potuit Papa praecipere ut non servarentur leges civiles.'

divine precepts. In the early seventeenth century, the Jesuit Leonardus Lessius—a fierce adherent of Suárez's political doctrine of the indirect power of the Pope in secular affairs—would maintain that a Pope effectively had this power.[1282]

Soto argues that if natural law requires merely two witnesses, that requirement must definitely be considered to be but a reflection of what the natural law would ordain if men were good and sincere (*ius naturae synceritatis humanae expressivum*).[1283] Of course, if men were sincere and truly lived as Christians, two witnesses would suffice. In the present circumstances, however, where fraud and distrust have poisoned society, that natural law regulation cannot be considered as being prohibitive of measures that are geared towards increasing confidence (*fides*) in economic exchange.

In addition to his large defence of the capacity of human positive law to make statutory form requirements obligatory in conscience, Soto emphasizes the absolute character of a normative precept or law. Presumably relying on Vitoria—but, again, refraining from citing him, Soto holds that a law is universally binding. 'The laws in question do not allow of an exception,' according to Soto,[1284] 'they state universally that a contract is void whenever the solemnities prescribed are lacking.' Consequently, it does not matter whether in a concrete case fraud is entirely absent or not. Similarly, under a general prohibition on the possession of fire-arms, it is forbidden, even for a prudent and wise man to wear a gun, even if he in particular will never pose a threat to the peace and order of the city.

[1282] Lessius, *De iustitia et iure*, lib. 2, cap. 19, dub. 2, num. 6, p. 237: 'Potuit autem Summus Pontifex hac in re legibus civilibus derogare, quia potestatis Ecclesiasticae (cuius plenitudo est in Pontifice) est, ordinare hominum actiones ad finem supernaturalem, qui est salus animae. Et consequenter potest submovere et tollere omnia, quae studium et cursum bonorum operum ad solutem animae pertinentium impediunt. Atqui istae leges in causis piis impedirent studium bonorum operum. Ergo.'

[1283] Soto, *De iustitia et iure* (ed. fac. V. Diego Carro – M. González Ordóñez, vol. 2), lib. 4, quaest. 5, art. 3, p. 321: 'At vero, cum debita reverentia ad textum respondeamus, licet ius naturae sit ut duo vel tres testes sufficiant, nam ubi homines naturali synceritate viverent ille sufficeret numerus, tamen nullatenus negari potest, quin ubi humanae fraudulentiae rempublicam inserperent, nequa tuta esset fides, sanctissimum sit numerum testium lege augere. Nam ius naturae non est prohibitivum, scilicet ne plures exigantur testes, sed synceritatis humanae expressivum, nempe quod vel tres sufficiant, qui ideo numerus, licet plurimum in causis tam civilibus quam ecclesiasticis sufficiat, tamen merito in aliquibus requiruntur plures, ut libr. nos 5. tractabimus.'

[1284] Soto, *De iustitia et iure* (ed. fac. V. Diego Carro – M. González Ordóñez, vol. 2), lib. 4, quaest. 5, art. 3, p. 319: 'Leges eiusmodi nullam prorsus exceptionem faciunt, sed absolute aiunt, ubicunque defuerit talis solemnitas nullum esse contractum.'

Time and again, Soto tries to send the comforting message that there is no need to have qualms of conscience or doubts about the absolute nullity of a contract that is not complying with positive law, the absence of fraud notwithstanding. So even if you know that it was the testator's will to leave a certain amount of the heritage to a third party, but the form requirements were not observed, you as the unique heir-at-law can claim the entire heritage in good conscience. Once the premise about the capacity of the state to control the free will of its citizens is accepted, the need to observe certain procedures and formalities in exchange on pain of nullity must necessarily follow from it.[1285] Explicitly recognizing that the *ratio legis* behind the statutory from requirements is to prevent fraud,[1286] at the same time Soto insists upon the continuing force and validity of those precepts even if in a particular case fraud is certainly absent.[1287] Put differently, a law is either entirely unbinding, or it binds universally. There is no way in between.

Soto also takes issue with Adrian of Utrecht. The analogy with fraternal correction does not hold water, according to Soto, because its final end concerns the good of a particular individual rather than the common good. Whereas the promotion of the individual good can cease to be adequate in certain circumstances, the common good is never cared for well enough.[1288] Apart from this rather novel refutation of Adrian, Soto uses the familiar battery of arguments already deployed by Vitoria to further combat the common opinion. For example, he cites Inst. 2,17,7–8, which holds that leaving a defective testament amounts to dying without any

---

[1285] Soto, *De iustitia et iure* (ed. fac. V. Diego Carro – M. González Ordóñez, vol. 2), lib. 4, quaest. 5, art. 3, p. 319: 'Hanc enim de causa art. 1 dictum est, posse rempublicam naturalem voluntatem civium cohibere in suis dispensandis rebus, atque adeo modum illis praescribere.'

[1286] Typical of Vitoria's constant presence in this argumentation is that Soto also thinks the *ratio legis* is the punishment of negligence on the part of the testator (*in poenam negligentiae testatoris*); cf. Soto, *De iustitia et iure* (ed. fac. V. Diego Carro – M. González Ordóñez, vol. 2), lib. 4, quaest. 5, art. 3, p. 320.

[1287] Soto, *De iustitia et iure* (ed. fac. V. Diego Carro – M. González Ordóñez, vol. 2), lib. 4, quaest. 5, art. 3, p. 319: 'Igitur licet ratio istarum legum fuit ut fraudibus dolisque obviaretur, nihilo minus etsi in aliquo casu finis ille deficiat, lex suum retinet vigorem. Exempla sunt frequentissima ac patentissima, quae demirandum est Panormitanum et suos non inspexisse.'

[1288] Soto, *De iustitia et iure* (ed. fac. V. Diego Carro – M. González Ordóñez, vol. 2), lib. 4, quaest. 5, art. 3, p. 322: 'Quod autem Adrianus subdit de correptione fraterna, nulla similitudine pugnat. Praeceptum namque correptionis fraternae non habet pro fine commune bonum, sed particularem emendationem fratris. Et ideo quando ille cessat, supervacanea esset correptio. Finis autem legum, annullantium illegitimos contractus, est bonum commune, quod numquam cessat.'

testament at all. Yet more importantly, Soto is equally at pains to show the absurdities and the intolerable discrepancy between the internal forum and the external forum that would ensue from the common opinion.

5.5.4   *The equation of legal and spiritual security*

Again, the political dimension of this ostensibly technical debate turns out to be considerable. In the words of Soto, by imposing strict form requirements, the legislator intended to avoid that citizens pin their faith on self-help and appeal to conscience to take the law in their own hands (*noluit legislator cives esse horum iudices*).[1289] Legal 'security', then, as well as 'security' of conscience are of primary concern to Soto.

Just as Baldus and Vitoria, he fears that the casuistic and flexible approach, which is typical of Bartolus, Panormitanus and Adrian of Utrecht, will end in chaos both in the minds of individual citizens and on the level of society as a whole. 'Even if in a particular case there is no single trace of deceit, the vigour of the law should not be affected', Soto argues,[1290] 'because, otherwise, the legal system will needlessly inflate the anxiety of people feeling overburdened with scruples.' For if the judgment on the fraudulent character of a testament is left to the opinion of individuals, no certain criteria will be available to guarantee stability. Allowing people increasingly to take the law in their own hands by appealing to the natural law of conscience in order to promote justice and equity is self-defeating.[1291]

Moreover, as noted above, the debate about formal limitations on 'freedom of contract' also gives us an idea about the tensions that are part and parcel of a double track system of conflict regulation (involving both the court of conscience and the external court). If the laws of the land on

---

[1289] Soto, *De iustitia et iure* (ed. fac. V. Diego Carro – M. González Ordóñez, vol. 2), lib. 4, quaest. 5, art. 3, p. 319: 'Noluit ergo legislator cives esse horum iudices, sed quod syncere auscultarent legi quandiu non esset contrarius naturae.'

[1290] Soto, *De iustitia et iure* (ed. fac. V. Diego Carro – M. González Ordóñez, vol. 2), lib. 4, quaest. 5, art. 3, p. 319: 'Licet in aliquo casu nullus interfuerit dolus, nihilominus vis legis non extinguitur. Et ratio huius est patentissima: quia alioqui leges scrupulos pusillorum conscientiis inijcerent.'

[1291] On the highly political significance of the debate on legal 'self-help' (*occulta compensatio*) in private law matters, see Decock, *Secret compensation*, p. 263–280. It is no coincidence to find that Adrian of Utrecht deals with the question of *occulta compensatio* in the context of the debate on the bindingness of positive law in conscience, and the specific question of the validity of contracts failing to meet form requirements; cf. Adrian of Utrecht, *Quaestiones quodlibeticae*, quaest. 6, art. 1, concl. 2, illatio 4, litt. m, f. 113r.

defective testaments were not binding in conscience, according to Soto, then those laws would be detrimental to the salvation of the soul (*leges illae conscientiarum essent illaqueatrices*)—something the Church could never tolerate.[1292] A precept that cannot be observed without committing a sin, must be abolished. Now from the *fact* that the positive laws imposing formalities have not hitherto been abolished or criticized by the Church, Soto concludes that these laws must not be in conflict with the norms of conscience. Like Vitoria, Soto infers from this *fact* the normative conclusion that the law of conscience should conform itself to statutory law.

Theoretically speaking, they could have drawn the opposite conclusion. They could have demanded the facts to adapt themselves to the law of conscience. Yet, apparently, in the first half of the sixteenth century the balance of power had shifted so much in favor of the secular authorities in the Iberian empire, that—at least as regards the issue of formalities in testaments—it was the Church who was expected to reinforce the law of the land in the internal forum, rather than the secular authorities who felt obliged to enforce the law of conscience by means of the secular courts.[1293] Practically speaking, then, if a testament does not meet form requirements imposed by the State, it does not hold in conscience, even if the confessor and the confessant know for sure that the testator wanted his heritage to be left to a person specified in the defective testament.

5.5.5   Contracts and last wills vs marriage and election

The State-friendly solution of Domingo de Soto would have been too much for a theologian to bear, however, had not a touch of equity been added to it in the form of a qualification of the moment of nullity of a

---

[1292] Soto, *De iustitia et iure* (ed. fac. V. Diego Carro – M. González Ordóñez, vol. 2), lib. 4, quaest. 5, art. 3, p. 320: 'Imo vero si non obligarent in conscientia, tunc leges illae conscientiarum essent illaqueatrices, nec deberent ab ecclesia tolerari, secundum verbum illud in cap. Quoniam, de praescriptionibus, quod absque peccato mortali non potest observari, derogandum est.'

[1293] From the late Middle Ages onwards, the relationship between Church and State had been particularly intense on the Iberian peninsula, of course. In this respect, it is worthwhile mentioning that Alfonso XI, King of Castile and León, promulgated *Ley Paresciendo* (cf. supra, p. 161). This law advocated a consensualist approach to contracts and testaments. The only condition for their bindingness was that the *animus obligandi* and the existence of the contract could be proven in court; cf. Bañez, *De iure et iustitia*, ad quaest. 62, p. 153.

defective testament. To prevent testate successors from the awful experience of being deprived of their freshly gained possessions overnight, Soto adopts the following compromise.

Absent blatant fraud, the heir-at-law does not become the owner of the heritage from the very moment the testament is defective, since a lack of formalities in contracts and testaments does not *ipso facto* prevent *dominium* from nevertheless being transferred. Rather, he has to take the testate successor to court and make the judge invalidate the testament. In Soto's view, the aim of statutory law is to have that kind of contracts avoided in court, but not to have the transfer of ownership invalidated as it takes place (*in iudicio habeantur nulli, non ipso statim facto*).[1294] Citing Lessius, Hugo Grotius would expressly endorse this opinion.[1295] Moreover, a heir-at-law has only himself to blame if eventually he does not take the illegitimate testate successor to court out of ignorance or negligence. The legatee is under no obligation, either, to reveal the unlawfulness of the testament. Any other interpretation would be far too rigorous.

Soto's compromise appears to be indebted to Vitoria. Yet his deliberate choice for this intermediary position—which he says he applied very frequently in his practice as a moral consultant—stands in marked contrast to the openly expressed reluctance with which his master had endorsed it. Subsequent theologians also put this intermediary view on Soto's credit, rather than citing Vitoria. For example, Tomás Sánchez associated the intermediate position with Soto. He summarized it as saying that a defective testament is not entirely void as a matter of conscience, but only inasmuch as the one who first takes possession of the legacy can retain it until he is urged to make restitution by virtue of a court decision.[1296] More-

---

1294 Soto, *De iustitia et iure* (ed. fac. V. Diego Carro – M. González Ordóñez, vol. 2), lib. 4, quaest. 5, art. 3, p. 320–321: 'Nunc igitur explicatione opus est, cur dixerimus, non prorsus per tales contractus impediri dominii translationem. (...) Crediderim ergo quod qui possidet rem aliquam per contractum minus solemnem sibi acquisitam, dummodo fraus omnis, vis, et dolus abfuerit, non tenetur restituere nisi vocatus in iudicium et condemnatus. (...) Et ratio mea est, quod iura humana nihil aliud volunt quam quod in iudicio tales contractus habeantur nulli, non autem quod ipso statim facto translatio sit nulla.'

1295 Grotius, *De jure belli ac pacis* (Ed. De Kanter-Van Hettinga Tromp – Feenstra – Persenaire), lib. 3, cap. 7, par. 6, num. 2, p. 709: 'Tale enim aliquatenus et ius est testamenta nulla dicendi ob deliquium solemnitatis alicuius quam iura civilia praescribant. Probabilior enim sententia est etiam quod tali testamento relictum est retineri salva pietate posse, saltem quamdiu ei non contradicitur.' In the margin, Grotius explicitly refers to Lessius for this standpoint (see note 8 in the edition by De Kanter-Van Hettinga Tromp – Feenstra – Persenaire).

1296 Tomás Sánchez, *Opuscula sive consilia moralia*, Lugduni 1634, tom. 2, lib. 4, cap. 1, dub. 14, num. 5, p. 11: 'Tertia sententia est media, dicitque non esse omnino nullum in

over, he added further weight to Soto's alleged view by arguing that it was based on the principle that, in doubt, the position of the possessor is the stronger in conscience (*in dubio melior est conditio possidentis*).[1297] Consequently, if there was equal doubt about the rights of the legatee and the heir-at-law, the position of the one who first took possession of the inheritance was the stronger, and he need not make restitution.

Another interesting variation on Soto's opinion can be found in Domingo de Bañez. Bañez's statement is worth quoting if only because it is also an excellent example of the casualness with which the early modern theologians move from the law of contract to testaments (it will be criticized by Lessius, accordingly):[1298]

> In that case [of laws nullifying certain contracts that do not comply with solemnity requirements which are essential for their juridical validity] the true dominus is the party in whose favor the contract has been concluded, at least before the sentence of the judge. After the sentence of the judge, he is no longer the dominus and he is bound to make restitution. For example, a dominus of a heritage that belongs to him on account of a testament which lacks the essential solemnities prescribed by the law.

Bañez illustrates his opinion on form requirements in contract law by making reference to the law of testament. Equally significant—and of no small importance to the development of the issue at stake with the Jesuits—is Bañez's excluding two transactions, which he explicitly denotes as 'contracts', from the scope of the general solution he and Soto proposed in matters related to formalities and contracts (*duos contractus excipimus*).[1299]

---

foro conscientiae, sed quoad hoc quod primum occupans haereditatem vel legata in testamento minus solemni potest ea possidere donec condemnetur.'

[1297] Sánchez, *Opuscula sive consilia moralia*, tom. 2, lib. 4, cap. 1, dub. 14, num. 6, p. 11: 'Sit conclusio: licet omnes tres sententiae probabiles sint, at tertia est probabilior. Et ratio est, quia in dubio melior est conditio possidentis, et sic possidens non tenetur restituere. Ergo quando testamentum est minus solemne, cum valde dubium sit uter habet melius ius in foro conscientiae, scilicet haeres ab intestato et institutus in minus solemni testamento, et pro utroque sint opiniones valde probabiles, qui prius occupaverit bona, iuvabitur possessio, meliusque ius habebit in foro conscientiae.'

[1298] Bañez, *De iure et iustitia*, ad quaest. 62, p. 154: 'Tunc enim [quando leges decernunt in contractibus, quos annullat propter defectum solemnitatis essentialis in iure] is, in cuius favorem contractus est celebratus, ante iudicis sententiam est verus dominus; postea vero desinit esse dominus, et tenetur restituere. Exemplum est in eo, qui est dominus per testamentum, cui deficit solemnitas essentialis iuris.'

[1299] Bañez, *De iure et iustitia*, ad quaest. 62, p. 164: 'Duos contractus excipimus, in quibus si solemnitas essentialis iuris desit, nullum transfertur dominium, neque firmum, neque infirmum, neque revocabile, neque irrevocabile.'

The 'contracts' in which Bañez thinks the intermediary position does not apply are marriage (*matrimonium*) and election (*electio*). In view of their singular relevance for society, one must assume that no *dominium* can be transferred through either a marriage 'contract' or an election 'contract' not meeting form requirements, not even before a judge has pronounced a sentence of nullity. Incidentally, this is a beautiful example of the inadequacy of translating the multifaceted concept of '*dominium*'— which, generally speaking, for the scholastics denotes a kind of master-ship over both things and persons—by 'property'. At the same time, it indicates how dependent the concept and definition of 'contract' is on the concept of *dominium*—contract being the instrument of exchanging *dominium*.

If we look at the reasons why Bañez thought marriage and election to be contracts worthy of a special treatment, we need to recall the common knowledge that in the canonical tradition a marriage contract, like a vow, is either irrevocably valid or invalid on account of its sacred indissolubil-ity. In addition, Bañez holds that spiritual jurisdiction is too important a function for its *dominium* to be allowed to pass into other hands by virtue of a defective 'contract'.[1300] It is even forbidden for a prelate 'elect' to accept a benefice that has been attributed to him by a defective elec-tion. The pious clemency, which had inspired Bañez to opt for the third way in order to solve problems related to normal contracts and last wills,[1301] could not be allowed to apply in those special cases.

5.6   EARLY MODERN CANON LAW AND THE IMPERATIVES OF THE STATE

Clemency and a sense of diplomacy had led Soto and Bañez to adopt a 'third way' in between Adrian-like equity and the fervent yet secretive Vitorian rigorism. The canonist Diego de Covarruvias y Leyva (1512–1577), however, would rather come up with a novel compromise of his own than adopt the intermediary position of the Dominicans unthoughtfully. His

---

[1300] Bañez, *De iure et iustitia*, ad quaest. 62, p. 164: 'Alter contractus est electio, quae si iure sit irrita, verosimilius est quod nullum transferat in electum dominium, neque electus potest illam acceptare. Ratio huius exceptionis est. Quoniam per electionem confertur electo iurisdictio spiritualis, quae est res maxime gravis. At rem usque adeo magni momenti, non est tutum concedere quod transferatur per contractum irritum ab ecclesia.'

[1301] Bañez, *De iure et iustitia*, ad quaest. 62, p. 165: 'Ad ultimum respondetur nostram sententiam esse piam et clementem, et idcirco tribuimus dominium licet debile iis qui possident quousque spolientur a iudice.'

debate is quite trying and technical. It is a reaction against the canonical tradition sparked off by Panormitan. On the other hand, he expressly
accepts Panormitan's analogy of reasoning between the problem of the
validity of testaments that do not meet solemnity requirements, elections
that do not occur according to the procedural rules, and contracts that
do not comply with formality requirements (*in contractu, testamento et
electione par ratio extat*).[1302] In other words—and this might surprise
modern readers—he allows one to reason from the conclusions reached
in regard to defective testaments to contracts that are vitiated by lack
of formalities.

To analyze the specific topic of insolemn testaments, Covarruvias
broaches the same general questions about the relationship between
natural law and statutory law that were posed by his predecessors. Con-
comitantly, we also see the debate on contracts for third-party beneficiaries, and more specifically the definition of the *obligatio naturalis*, occupy
a major place in the course of his argumentation on testaments. Although
we will not go deeply into his extensive discussion of the binding nature of
naked pacts within the context of the testament and third party problems,
it is worth recalling that we found this conjunction of themes already in
Baldus. It would gain still further prominence after Covarruvias with the
Jesuits at the turn of the seventeenth century.

Our 'Spanish Bartolus', as he was called, treats insolemn testaments in
two influential *relectiones* of two equally important canons: canon *Quamvis
pactum* (VI 1,18,2) and canon *Cum esses* (X 3, 26, 10).[1303] The former deals
with the problem of insolemn testaments in an indirect, yet fundamental
way, since it develops the theoretical principles that will eventually be
applied to defective contracts and last wills. The latter addresses the issue
of formality requirements directly. We will investigate them successively.

5.6.1   *Contracts for third-party beneficiaries*

In his commentary on canon *Quamvis pactum*, Covarruvias deals extensively with the question whether contracts for a third-party beneficiary

---

[1302] Covarruvias, *In regulam peccatum*, part. 2, par. 3, num. 9, p. 486.
[1303] Diego de Covarruvias y Leyva, *Relectio in cap. quamvis pactum*, part. 2, par. 5,
p. 270–276, and Covarruvias, *In titulum de testamentis interpretatio, cap. 10 (Cum esses)*, in:
Opera omnia, Augustae Taurinorum 1594, tom. 2, p. 43–45, respectively.

are valid or not.[1304] The issue of insolemn testaments and naked pacts are dealt with in the context of this problem. In order to come to terms with the issue of agreements involving a third party, Covarruvias is obliged to elucidate the concept of 'natural obligation' (*obligatio naturalis*). Crucial, too, is an exposition of his view on the relationship between statutory law and natural law.

Those theoretical digressions are necessary for Covarruvias because they enable him to critically assess a statement made by Bartolus de Saxoferrato in his commentary on law *Si quis pro eo* (D. 46,1,56) concerning the validity of contracts for third-party beneficiaries.[1305] For reasons of clarity, this statement of Bartolus can be presented as the outcome of the following syllogism. Take as a major premise that a contract that is neither enforced nor enfeebled by civil law (*contractus cui nec lex assistit nec resistit*) can be confirmed by an oath. Take as a minor premise that a contract for a third-party beneficiary is neither enforced nor enfeebled by civil law. From this we can infer, with Bartolus, that a contract for a third-party beneficiary is valid as soon as it is confirmed by an oath.

The point of controversy for Covarruvias is not the validity of contracts for a third-party beneficiary as a matter of canon law. That discussion he leaves out, even if he maintains that the common opinion, represented by Panormitanus and Felinus, states that contracts in favor of third parties have no more effect as a matter of canon law than by statutory law.[1306] What he does elaborate on, however, is the premise, implicit in Bartolus'

[1304] Although Covarruvias' doctrine would have deserved a more elaborate examination of its own, in a fundamental contribution on the subject Harry Dondorp points out the direct influence of our Spanish canonist's *relectio* on Grotius' *De iure belli ac pacis*, 2, 11, 18, 1. See J. Hallebeek – H. Dondorp (eds.), *Contracts for a third-party beneficiary, A historical and comparative account*, [Legal History Library, Studies in the History of Private Law, 1], Leiden-Boston 2008, p. 56–57.

[1305] Bartolus de Saxoferrato, *In secundam Digesti novi partem commentaria*, Lugduni 1555, ad D. 46,1,56, num. 12, f. 88v.

[1306] Covarruvias, *In cap. quamvis pactum*, part. 2, par. 4, num. 3, p. 270: 'Multa possent in favorem huius opinionis adduci, quae missa facimus, quia omnino expedita non sint, nec admodum urgeant pro eius probatione. Illud tamen omittendum non est, quod huic disputationi causam dedit, nempe ratio Bar. in d. l. si quis pro eo, dum scribit huic stipulationi ius civile nec adsistere, nec resistere, imo ipsam vires iuris naturalis habere.'

In *l.c.*, p. 271, Covarruvias claims that 'Hanc opinionem, quod iure pontificio stipulatio alteri per alterum facta non habeat maiorem effectum quam habet iure civili veriorem esse consentiunt Panormit. et Felin. (. . .) quorum opinio, nisi et in hoc fallor, magis communis est. Quidem tamen, ut ex Felino constat, existimant, iure canonico esse adversus promittentem locum remedio evangelicae denunciationis (. . .).' The latter solution was brought forward by Antonio de Butrio, as is pointed out by Hallebeek in *Contracts for a third-party beneficiary*, p. 27.

conclusion, that Roman civil law neither wanted to enforce nor to enfeeble contracts for third-party beneficiaries. Also, he discusses the concomitant claim that there is a natural obligation ensuing from such a contract (*imo vires iuris naturalis habere*), which can then be enforced before an external court by means of an oath.

According to Covarruvias, it would seem that Roman law did not merely refuse to enforce contracts in favor of third parties, but actually resisted them.[1307] Covarruvias based this conclusion on his interpretation of the gloss to the first rule of law contained in Pope Boniface VIII's Liber Sextus, which states that if the verb *posse* is preceded by a negation, the prohibition expressed through it becomes absolute in scope.[1308] Hence, the canonist held that D. 45,1,38,17 (*alteri stipulari nemo potest*) signified that no obligation whatsoever followed from a contract in favor of a third party. Covarruvias cites contemporary humanists, such as Andrea Alciati (1492–1550), to lend authoritative support to that view.[1309]

5.6.2   *Moral* vs *legal natural debt*

Covarruvias proposes to solve the alleged contradiction between Bartolus and the pristine Roman law by expounding his view of natural obligation and the relationship between natural law and the law of the land. In Covarruvias' view, natural obligation is twofold.[1310] On the one hand, there are natural obligations ensuing from moral debt and honesty (*ex honestate ac debito morali*). On the other hand, we have natural obligations that spring from the constraints imposed by the normative system called natural law (*ex legis ac iuris naturalis vinculo*).[1311]

As has been laid down in the opening chapters of this book, this is a typical scholastic dichotomy we also find expressed later on in authors

---

[1307] Apart from the famous paragraph 'alteri stipulari nemo potest' (D. 45,1,38,17), Covarruvias concedes that the following passages can be used to argue that Roman law expressly excludes the existence of a natural obligation in contracts for third-party beneficiaries: D. 45,1,126,2; D. 45,3,1,1; D. 45,3,1,3; Inst. 3,19,4.

[1308] See glossa *Non potest* ad VI, Reg. iur., 1, *Corpus juris canonici* (ed. Gregoriana), part. 3, col. 780, l. 12–13: 'Haec dictio, potest, negative posita, ut hic, necessitatem importat; cum autem affirmative ponitur, necessitatem non inducit.'

[1309] Alciati, *Pardoxa*, lib. 3, cap. 4, p. 41.

[1310] See Covarruvias, *In cap. quamvis pactum*, part. 2, par. 4, num. 5, p. 271.

[1311] Covarruvias' twofold conception of natural obligation is investigated in Th. Duve, *Obliga en conciencia la naturalis obligatio? Un comentario histórico-jurídico sobre la naturalis obligatio*, in: J. Cruz Cruz, La gravitación moral de la ley según Francisco Suárez, [Colección de pensamiento medieval y renacentista, 109], Pamplona 2009, p. 84–88.

like Juan de Valero and Leonardus Lessius.[1312] Covarruvias holds that it is implicit in Thomas Aquinas' discussion of thankfulness and gratitude in his *Secunda Secundae*, question 106, articles 4–6. There we find Thomas drawing a neat distinction between legal debt (*debitum legale*), which corresponds to the equality principle demanded by the virtue of justice, and moral debt (*debitum morale*), which corresponds to the virtue of gratitude. While the former debt requires equal repayment in due time, the latter is characterized by excess and its repayment until an undetermined point in time.

For Covarruvias, the distinction between a legal and a moral species of natural debt is not merely of theoretical value. As our canonist points out, the differences in juridical consequences that are attached to moral natural debt (*ex honestate*) and legal natural debt (*ex iure naturae*), respectively, are of significant practical relevance.[1313] In this respect, he immediately hints at the issue of the validity of defective testaments—without elaborating on that question, however, in this context.

Moral natural debt (*ex honestate*) underlying a payment is sufficient for the recovery of an *indebitum solutum* to be obstructed in the event that the payment actually took place, even if that payment occurred through ignorance of the law. Assume I transferred the entire inheritance of my father to the legatee mentioned in his last will, ignoring that the *lex Falcidia* allowed me to retain a quarter of the inheritance. I cannot claim back that part of the legacy, since as a matter of honesty, I am under

---

[1312] Consequently, it is important to note that, contrary to ideas of 'natural law' that circulate today, natural law in the scholastic tradition has a distinctively legal character. Natural law is law. It creates legally enforceable debt, its place of enforcement being the court of conscience. It is not what we think of as 'morality' or 'conscience' today. What we now think of as 'morality', in scholastic terminology, corresponds to the natural debt deriving from sources other than the law of nature or the law of the land.

[1313] Covarruvias, *In cap. quamvis pactum*, part. 2, par. 4, num. 5, p. 271: 'Nos item admonuimus hanc distinctionem utilem admodum esse in cap. cum in officiis, de testamentis, num. 10, et in cap. cum esses, eod. tit., num. 9. Qua ratione effectum est, ut apud ius ipsum civile prior naturalis obligatio effectus aliquot habeat quippe quae repetitionem soluti ex errore iuris impediat, secundum Fortun. In l.1, par. ius naturale, ff. de iust. et iure, illat. 10, et sufficiens sit ad novationem, l. 1, ff. de novationib. atque alios, quos modo exponere non vacat. Posterior autem maiorem vim habet, nam exceptionem et retentionem inducit, qui effectus maximi censentur a iuris utriusque interpretibus, atque item in animae iudicio necessitatem solvendi et restituendi omnino imponit sub peccati poena quos equidem effectus prior illa obligatio non habet, quemadmodum ex his, quae in specie statim inferam manifeste constabit, etenim ad multa hanc primam assertionem praemittimus.'

a moral natural debt to respect the testator's will as much as possible.[1314] Or suppose I had been granted debt relief, but then still paid the debt, I cannot by means of a *condictio indebiti* try to recover the money I paid, even if that money was no longer due from a legal point of view. Similarly, I cannot claim back the present I gave you as a sign of gratitude in return for a service you rendered me gratuitously. Beneficence creates a moral natural debt on the part of the beneficee, so that he is bound *ex honestate* to return a favor, i.e. to make a counter-gift (*antidora*).[1315] In fact, that service in return should be of higher value than the value of the favor that has been done to you.[1316] A natural debt of the moral kind is also sufficient ground for the validity of a novation, that is the substitution of a new for an old debt.

The juridical effects of a legal natural debt (*ex iure naturae*), however, are much bigger. A natural debt of the legal kind gives rise both to a remedy (*exceptio*) and a right of retention (*ius retentionis*) in the external, civil and ecclesiastical court. Moreover, in the internal court of conscience a legal natural debt entails an absolute obligation of payment or restitution on pain of mortal sin.

[1314] Covarruvias, *In cap. quamvis pactum*, part. 2, par. 4, num. 8, p. 272: 'Eadem ratione, constat intellectus ad legem primam, l. error, C. ad legem Falcid., cum his, quae notantur in l. 1, ff. de condict. indebi. quib. satis manifestum sit, haeredem solventem integra legata errore iuris non retenta Falcidia, minime posse quartam repetere, id enim procedit propter illam naturalem obligationem, quae ab honestate morali procedit, quo plenior fides era [sic] testatoris voluntatem servetur, d. l. 1, C. ad legem Falcid. Nec enim haeres tenetur naturali obligatione, quae ex debito legali oritur, integra legata solvere non retenta Falcidia. (...)'

[1315] Covarruvias, *In cap. quamvis pactum*, part. 2, par. 4, num. 8, p. 272: 'Etenim in par. praecedenti diximus, liberatum a solutione pecuniae, quam solvere alioqui tenebatur, causa poenae et ad punitionem creditoris, minime teneri in animae iudicio naturaliter ex debito legali ad illius pecuniae solutionem et tamen si solvat non poterit condictione indebiti repetere, tex. in d. l. si poenae causa. Hic enim effectus procedit ab obligatione quadam naturali quae pertinet ad moralem honestatem. Sic et in eo, qui alteri remunerationis causa tenetur moraliter obligatione naturali ad antidoram.'

[1316] Aquinas, *Summa Theologiae* (Ed. Leonina, tom. 9), IIaIIae, quaest. 106, art. 6, concl., p. 403: 'Respondeo dicendum quod, sicut dictum est, recompensatio gratiae respicit beneficium secundum voluntatem beneficiantis. In quo quidem praecipue hoc commendabile videtur quod gratis beneficium contulit ad quod non tenebatur. Et ideo qui beneficium accepit ad hoc obligatur, ex debito honestatis, ut similiter gratis aliquid impendat. Non autem videtur gratis aliquid impendere nisi excedat quantitatem accepti beneficii, quia quandiu recompensat minus vel aequale, non videtur facere gratis, sed reddere quod accepit. Et ideo gratiae recompensatio semper tendit ut, pro suo posse, aliquid maius retribuat.'

5.6.3   *Resisting, assisting or tolerating natural obligation*

Equally important doctrinal viewpoints of Covarruvias concern the interplay between natural law and statutory law. Our canonist leaves no doubt that statutory law can and must limit 'freedom of contract'. More precisely, he thinks that positive law can prevent a natural obligation (of the legal kind) from coming into existence. He is careful to stress that a legal natural obligation is impeded from arising by statutory law in the first place, rather than being allowed to be born and then suffer a sudden death.[1317] It is the will of the testator that is being made impotent, rather than a natural obligation suffering abortion.[1318] Stated in that way, at least the surgery operated by statutory law takes place in a less sanguinary way. Nevertheless, the force of statutory law remains percutaneous.

The power of statutory law is mainly qualified by the typically Thomistic rule that its interventions must be deemed necessary for the public interest or common good (*iuxta utilitatem ipsius humani convictus*). Only if that condition is met can a law be considered just, and, hence, binding in conscience. Certainly, statutory law cannot abolish the first principles of natural law, e.g. that we ought to live in accordance with reason or that we must observe the Decalogue. But the conclusions that follow from the first principles of natural law, 'freedom of contract', for instance, or a certain type of political institution, can be submitted to control for the sake of the social and political community.[1319]

Another qualification implies that 'contractual freedom' may need to be restricted, but not universally. Only where it is most adequate according to place and time should statutory law prevent natural obligations from

---

1317 Covarruvias, *In cap. quamvis pactum*, part. 2, par. 4, num. 6, p. 272: 'Ipse fateor obligationem naturalem lege humana proprie non tolli sed impediri ne oriatur, cum ea producatur a consensu paciscentium legitime, idest lege humana minime reprobato.'

1318 Covarruvias, *In cap. cum esses*, num. 7, p. 45: 'Omnis actus consistit in voluntate et potentia. (...) Per leges autem civiles non potest quis sine solemnitate iuris testari, cum ab eo potentia auferatur.'

1319 Covarruvias, *In cap. quamvis pactum*, part. 2, par. 4, num. 6, p. 271: 'Nam licet ius humanum tollere non possit iura naturalia quod ad prima principia, scilicet ratione vivendum est, nec quo ad ea, quae ex primis principiis necessario sequuntur, qualia sunt Decalogi praecepta, conclusiones tamen, quae ex primis principiis iuris naturalis oriuntur, frequentius non tamen in universum iuris humani dispositioni qua ex pare id utile Reipublicae et communitati sit submittuntur. Hoc ipsum et ratio naturalis dictat, ut leges humanae et hominum instituta mutentur iuxta utilitatem ipsius humani convictus, quod tradit Thomas (...).'

being brought about through mutual consent.[1320] Therefore, Covarruvias indicates that at the same moment the same contract can be invalid in Spain yet valid in Germany. Or, the same contract in the same territory might have been valid before and invalid now.

For Covarruvias, the stakes of the debate are clear. The alternative to state regulation of 'contractual liberty' is chaos. Unless certain contracts are stopped, society will cease to flourish and eventually collapse.[1321] Yet, again, he is careful to refine this general statement. For present purposes, the most crucial refinement Covarruvias makes impinges on the distinction between moral natural obligations and legal natural obligations.

If statutory law resists the validity of a contract (*si lex contractui resistat*), it primarily resists the natural obligation of the legal kind, according to Covarruvias. Human law stops the creation of a legal natural obligation. Sometimes, however, that does not prevent the moral natural obligation, which is based on honesty, still coming into being.[1322] Alternatively, if statutory law neither resists nor assists a contract (*si lex contractui non resistat nec adsistat*), then it lacks enforcement in a civil court, but it is not aborted altogether. Rather, if statutory law remains 'neutral', the power of a contract entirely rests on natural law. Then, it does not only have the potential of bringing about a moral natural obligation, but it is also accompanied by a natural obligation of the legal kind.[1323]

[1320] Covarruvias, *In cap. quamvis pactum*, part. 2, par. 4, num. 6, p. 271: 'Posse contingere contractum aliquem lege humana reprobari ita, ut ei lex resistat, nec ex eo producatur naturalis obligatio, et tamen ex eodem efficacem naturalem et civilem obligationem oriri in his provinciis, ubi eadem humana lex statuta non fuerit.'

[1321] Covarruvias, *In cap. quamvis pactum*, part. 2, par. 4, num. 6, p. 271: 'Praeterea, aut lex humana potest contractum aliquem prohibere et ei resistere aut non. Si potest eadem quidem impedit naturalem obligationem ex vinculo consensus oriri, quia consensum illum irritum facit in foro exteriori et interiori, ut superius dictum est. Si non potest tollitur profecto ubique gentium illa vera hominum consortio et necessaria Reipublicae institutio, quae iuxta tempus et locum debet aliquot conventiones prohibere et improbare.'

[1322] Covarruvias, *In cap. quamvis pactum*, part. 2, par. 4, num. 6, p. 272: 'Nam si lex ipsa contractui resistat et eum reprobet, non producitur ex eo naturalis obligatio quae vinculo iuris naturalis et legis fulcitur, tametsi quandoque adsit quaedam naturalis obligatio ab honestate morali procedens.'

[1323] Covarruvias, *In cap. quamvis pactum*, part. 2, par. 4, num. 6, p. 272: 'At si lex ipsa humana conventioni et contractui non resistat nec adsistat, quippe quae nec ipsum contractum reprobet, nec expressim approbet, ei actionem tribuens et obligationem, imo quandoque expressim eas denegaverit, tunc contractus hic manet destitutus auxilio iuris civilis sub fomento tantum legis naturalis, atque ideo ex eo oritur naturalis obligatio, non tantum ea, quae ad moralem honestatem pertinet, sed et illa, quae a debito legis producitur.'

We are now standing at the point where Covarruvias' analysis of natural debt and his pronounced belief in the interventionist force of statutory
law intersect. This enables us to fully grasp the subtle differences in effects
he attaches to naked pacts (*pacta nuda*), on the one hand, and contracts
in favor of a third party (*stipulatio alteri*) and defective testaments (*testamentum insolemne*), on the other.

This is not the place to dwell on Covarruvias' detailed exposition on the
binding force of naked pacts. It is sufficient to mention that a naked pact
is a perfect example of an informal juridical act that brings about a natural
obligation of the legal kind, without being either supported or resisted by
the civil law. Hence, a naked pact merely produces a right of retention and
an *exceptio* in the external court, but it is fully enforceable in the court
of conscience. Covarruvias wonders whether the civil law must not try to
support the natural obligation ensuing from a naked pact for the sake of
conformity with canon law. This would mean that naked pacts are also
actionable in the external court.[1324] Presumably, Covarruvias' reflections
are reminiscent here of Fortunius Garcia.

Now if we turn our attention to contracts for a third-party beneficiary,
they are taken (by the common opinion) to be subject to the same 'neutral treatment' by the civil law as naked pacts. Consequently, the same
effects described in regard to naked pacts also apply here. The question is
raised, however, whether civil law should not resist the validity of a contract in favor of a third pary rather than adopt a neutral position. Covarruvias tends to answer this question in the affirmative. Hence, contracts
for a third-party beneficiary should not even be deemed actionable in the
court of conscience. Put differently, they do not produce a natural obligation of the legal kind.[1325]

[1324] Covarruvias, *In cap. quamvis pactum*, part. 2, par. 4, num. 13, par. *Quidam*, p. 274.

[1325] Covarruvias, *In cap. quamvis pactum*, part. 2, par. 4, num. 10, p. 273: 'Duodecimo ex
suprascriptis consentaneum est oriri naturalem istam obligationem, quae ad honestatem
pertineat ex promissione et stipulatione alteri per alterum facta. Qua ratione haec stipulatio illos effectus habebit quos habet naturalis obligatio ad moralem honestatem pertinens,
nec in hac conclusione iure poterit controverti, etiam si sequamur opiniones communi
omnium iudicio contrarias, quarum paulo ante meminimus.'
A few paragraphs earlier (at the end of num. 9), Covarruvias had misleadingly held that:
'Undecimo hac in eadem controversia opinamur, ius civile nec adsistere, nec resistere huic
stipulationi, quae alteri per alterum fit, quod ut iam tradidimus, communi fere omnium
iudicio definitum est.'

5.6.4   *The triumph of Spanish statutory law*

In Covarruvias' worst case scenario of the regime of contracts in favor of a third party, it actually coincides with the regime applying to defective testaments. Neither are subject to the 'neutral treatment' by statutory law that we witness in naked pacts. Rather, they suffer from the resistance of statutory law. Nevertheless, this does not prevent a natural obligation of the moral kind from coming into being. This becomes obvious as we turn our attention to Covarruvias' commentary on canon *Cum esses* (X 3,26,10), where he addresses the question of formality requirements for last wills directly.[1326] Here we see Covarruvias making a fierce case for the need to observe formalities imposed by statutory law, only to concede that insolemn testaments still have the power of producing a natural obligation of the moral kind—just like contracts for a third-party beneficiary.

With Covarruvias, we witness the increasing pressure on the theologians and canonists working in Spain during the *Siglo de Oro* to make the law of conscience conform to the law issued by increasingly absolutist princes. The conclusions of the Dominican trio Vitoria-Soto-Bañez as well as the secular bishop and canonist Covarruvias clearly reflect external circumstances different from Panormitan's Sicily and Adrian's Leuven. It is probably not a surprise to find that the reception in a sixteenth century Spanish environment of canon *Cum esses* ended in a stalemate. This canon expressed the twelfth century absolutist tendencies of Pope Alexander III. However, four centuries later, King Philip II dominated Spain in an equally sovereign way. As will be explained in the next paragraph, the indigenous Spanish law had been drawing heavily on the civilian tradition by that time.

Following law *Hac consultissima*, the *Siete Partidas* (1265) stipulated that seven witnesses be present for a written will (*testamentum in scriptis*) to be valid.[1327] Subsequent legislation, particularly the *Ordenanças Reales de Castilla* (1484), *Leyes de Toro* (1505) and the *Nueva Recopilación* (1567),

---

[1326] Covarruvias' discussion of defective testaments in his commentary on canon *Cum esses* is briefly touched upon in Condorelli, *Norma giuridica e norma morale, giustizia e salus animarum secondo Diego de Covarrubias*, p. 186–189.

[1327] *Las Siete Partidas*, tom. 4, part. 6, tit. 1 (*De los testamentos*), p. 3: 'La otra manera es a que dicen en latin testamentum in scriptis, que quiere tanto decir como manda que se face por escripto et non de otra guisa; et tal testamento como este debe seer fecho ante siete testigos que sean llamados et rogados daquel que lo face (...).'

had confirmed that regime.[1328] Indigenous Spanish law had been less consequential, however, when applying the formality requirements stipulated
by law *Hac consultissima* to the verbal wills (*testamentum nuncupativum*).
There was a certain evolution toward flexibility in the interpretation of the
form requirements in verbal wills. As Gregorio López (1497–1560) noted
in what became the standard gloss to the *Siete Partidas*, Alfonso XI had
reduced the requirement of seven witnesses to the mere presence of three
witnesses before a notary, or five witnesses if it were impossible to find a
notary.[1329] This regulation in the *Ordenamiento de Alcalá* was confirmed
by the *Leyes de Toro*.[1330] Three witnesses sufficed without a notary if it was
impossible to find more people capable of being witnesses to the verbal
will. In the early modern Spanish empire, defending this flexibility was
not a matter of pure academic preference. As Juan de Solórzano y Pereira
noted in his *De indiarum iure*, illiteracy was rife among the Indians, and
there were only a handful of notaries and witnesses.[1331]

Indicative of the turn toward flexibility in verbal wills was Covarruvias' emphasizing that in a verbal testament, the testator was not under
an obligation to put his signature under it. Apparently, there was a serious controversy about this issue because a testator or a contracting party
in general was said to be obliged to follow the same protocol the notary
himself had to follow. Signing the verbal will or codicil was part of that.
However, Covarruvias argued that there was absolutely no need of a testator's signature. Three witnesses and a notary would do under normal
circumstances. Five witnesses were required in the absence of a notary.

[1328] *Ordenanças Reales de Castilla [= Ordenamiento de Montalvo]*, Toleti 1549, lib. 5,
tit. 2, l. 1, f. 65r; *Las leyes de Toro glosadas por Diego del Castillo*, l. 3, f. 17v–18v; *Recopilación
de las leyes destos reynos por mandado del Rey Philippe Segundo*, Alcalá de Henares 1569,
lib. 5, tit. 4, l. 2, f. 283v.

[1329] Gregorio López, glossa *Ante siete testigos*, ad *Siete partidas* 6,1,1, in: Las Siete Partidas, p. 3: 'Hodie per legem Ordinamenti Regis Alphonsi, quae servari jubetur in l. 3 Tauri,
sufficiunt quinque testes, quando testamentum nuncupativum fit sine tabellione, et si cum
tabellione, sufficiunt tres.'

[1330] *El Ordenamiento de Alcalá*, ed. I.J. de Assó y del Río – M. de Manuel y Rodríguez,
Madrid 1847, tit. 19, l. 1, p. 28: 'Si alguno ordenare su testament, o otra su postrimera voluntat en qualquier manera con escrivano public, deben y ser presentes a lo ver otorgar tres
testigos a lo menos vecinos del logar, do se fiçiere; et si lo fiçiere sin escrivano public, sean
y cinco a lo menos vecinos, segunt dicho es, si fuere logar do los pudiese aver; et si fuere
tal logar do non puedan ser avisados cinco testigos, que lo menos sean y tres testigos, e
sea valedero lo que ordenare en su potrimera voluntat.' Confirmed in *Las leyes de Toro*,
l. 3, f. 17v–18v.

[1331] Bellomo, *Perché lo storico del diritto europeo deve occuparsi dei giuristi indiani?*,
p. 26–28.

In very extreme circumstances of scarcity of both notaries and witnesses, then only three witnesses. Covarruvias derived this system from the philologically most correct version of the *Ordenanças Reales de Castilla*— which allegedly had been the subject of many interpolations.[1332]

Actually, from this account, one might be tempted to infer that Spanish regulation of verbal testaments at the time of Covarruvias resembled that consecrated in canon *Cum esses*. As we have seen with Domingo de Soto's criticism of it, X 3,26,10 demanded the presence of two or three witnesses before a parish priest. Yet that was clearly not the way Covarruvias thought of it. He is furious about the suggestion that Pope Alexander III's rejection of the practice of requiring extra formalities in the region of Ostia amounts to a condemnation of the civil law as if it were going radically against divine law.[1333] Andrea Alciati is one of the culprits envisaged by Covarruvias. Alciati had suggested that the discussion on civil solemnity requirements in testaments had become futile, since the canon law of testaments, merely demanding that two witnesses be present, had become practiced everywhere.[1334]

Worse still is his anger at those who infer from Pope Alexander III's condemnation that the law of the land should conform itself to the law of conscience and adopt a less formalistic approach towards testaments.

[1332] In a burst of philological frenzy, Covarruvias contends that an exceptional jurist informed him about the corrupted state of more recent editions of the *Ordenanças Reales de Castilla*. Thereupon he had decided to go to the library and consult the most ancient edition of the text. Allegedly, the examination of this ancient version confirmed his interpretation.

Cf. Covarruvias, *In cap. Cum esses*, num. 2, p. 44: 'Admonitus tamen a viro quodam iuris utriusque peritissimo, dictam legem primam, tit. 2, lib. 5 ordin. Vitio scriptorum corruptam fuisse, ea qua potui diligentia codicem vetustissimum legi qui in huius maximi Salvatoris collegii bibliotheca servatur. Atque ex eo sensus Regiae constitutionis hic est, ut testamentum nuncupativum fieri debeat coram notario et tribus testibus. Si vero coram notario non fiat, adesse debere quinque testes, si in eo loco horum sit copia. Alioqui sufficere tres testes ipsi testamento praesentes esse. (...) Quod lectoris iudicio discerni poterit, ex eo praesertim, quod anno MDLXVII Regia Philippi Secundi, regis Catholici ac Domini nostri authoritate et decreto editae fuerint Regiae ordinationes in quarum lib. 5, tit. 4, l. 1 litera constitutionis antiquae in pristinum statum est restituta, sic sane, ut ipse existimem (...).'

[1333] Covarruvias, *In cap. Cum esses*, num. 2, p. 44: 'Secundo, hic textus intelligitur adeo pie, ut eius decisio ubique locum sibi vendicet, etiam in foro seculari, et profanis legatis, explosis iuris civilis solemnitatibus, quasi legi divinae adversis, cum ex ea cuiuscunque rei veritas duobus testibus committatur.'

[1334] E.g. Andrea Alciati, *Ad rescripta principum commentarii*, Lugduni 1535, ad C. 1,2,1, col. 26, l. 1–47.

'For who could stand', Covarruvias declaims,[1335] 'that almost the whole
civil law of last wills, endorsed by scores of mighty emperors and learned
jurists, be abolished on the accusation of being inequitable?' 'What to say,
then,' he goes on,[1336] 'about all those laws, made with so great and exemplary care, but requiring more than two witnesses? Would you dare and
say that each of them runs counter to the law of God?' What is more, he
implicitly criticizes Soto by taking issue with the idea that Pope Alexander III's precept should be interpreted as pertaining to legacies in favor
of charities. That is ridiculous, in Covarruvias' view, given that legacies to
good causes are precisely subject to an assessment in the decretal following on canon *Cum esses*.[1337]

Covarruvias gives a burning defence of Spanish statutory laws requiring formalities in last wills, insisting on their enforceability in the court of
conscience. He insists that formalities are, literally speaking, an essential
component of testaments. Certainly, solemnities are not the substance of
a will. This he concedes in the footsteps of Alciati.[1338] In Covarruvias' view,
the substance of a testament consists in the institution of an heir (*heredis
institutio*)—a view later adopted by Lessius too.[1339] Still, the formalities
required for that institution to be valid, are somehow substantial, too.

Just as Baldus, approximately two centuries before him, and contrary
to Bartolus, Covarruvias holds that testamentary formalities pertain to
the substantial form of a testament (*forma substantialis*). They are not
just necessary as a matter of proof (*forma probatoria*).[1340] Hence solemnities matter, even in the court of conscience.[1341] All other indications or

[1335] Covarruvias, *In cap. Cum esses*, num. 2, p. 44: 'Quis enim ferat, totum fere civile ius
de ordinandis testamentis, a tot caesaribus ac viris sapientissimis comprobatum, iniquitatis causa everti?'
[1336] Covarruvias, *In cap. Cum esses*, num. 2, p. 44: 'Alioqui quid obsecro diceres, tot
legibus, praevia deliberatione statutis, quae plures quam duos testes requirunt? Auderesne
asserere eas omnes divinae legi adversari?'
[1337] Covarruvias, *In cap. Cum esses*, num. 2, p. 44: 'Quae quidem interpretatio manifeste
refellitur ex capite sequenti, quod testamentis in pias causas condendis aliam peculiarem
solemnitatem speciatim aptat.'
[1338] The reference to Alciati is problematical. Perhaps Covarruvias refers to Alciati,
Paradoxa, lib. 1, cap. 15, p. 15: 'Quare aliter ego respondendum censeo. In stipulatione enim
quam maxime operantur verba, in legatis voluntas et praestatio.'
[1339] Lessius, *De iustitia et iure*, lib. 2, cap. 19, dub. 1, num. 1, p. 236.
[1340] Covarruvias, *In cap. Cum esses*, num. 8, p. 45: 'Tamen assumendo substantialem formam
alicuius actus pro ea sine qua actus ipse non valet, nec effectum habere potest, testium solemnitas et numerus in testamentis erit forma substantialis, non tantum probatoria.'
[1341] Covarruvias, *In cap. Cum esses*, num. 8, p. 45: 'Si vero haec solemnitas substantialis
est, nihil refert voluntatem testatoris ex alio exteriori testimonio probari. Ergo nec in foro
animae erit ista minus solemnis voluntas recipienda.'

rumours about the existence of a testament are of little account. The law has imposed substantial form requirements for the sake of the common good (*ad totius reipublicae utilitatem*), since a lack of formalities raises suspicions of fraud. Against the background of their necessity for the public interest, those statutory laws have the status of just laws. Accordingly, they are binding in conscience.[1342]

In the footsteps of Vitoria and Soto, Covarruvias is very concerned about the political and confessional perplexities that ensue from the contrary point of view. An unbearable insecurity of law and endless qualms of conscience would follow from not accepting the binding force of positive law in conscience (*sequeretur leges incertas esse quoad animarum tutelam*).[1343]

For example, the judgments rendered by a judge in a secular court by virtue of statutory law are invested with divine authority, according to Covarruvias. Consequently, they have absolute binding power in the court of conscience. But assume that a judge knows for sure that a testator absolutely intended to leave his goods to a certain legatee, and that there is also certainty about the absence of fraud or falsehood. Still, he judged in favor of the testate successors on account of statutory law. Would not there be an irreconcilable conflict between the judge's conscience and the judgment he rendered unless the law of the land were also binding in conscience?

Another point at which Covarruvias' criticism of Panormitan's and Adrian's flexible account of the law coincides with that of the Dominican theologians from Salamanca concerns the '*causa cessante cessat lex*'-rule. Granted, our canonist acknowledges that a law can lose its binding power if it universally fails to serve its goal. But he is not willing to doubt the validity of a law if in a particular case its application does not serve its ultimate goal.[1344]

[1342] Covarruvias, *In cap. Cum esses*, num. 6, p. 45: 'Lex enim civilis, quae testium solemnitatem induxit testamentis iusta est, quod constat ex reprobatione secundi intellectus. Et probatur, quia hic testandi actus gravis est et mille obnoxius fraudibus. Potuit ergo lex quo tutius et fidelius ageretur, hanc solemnitatem statuere ad totius reipublicae utilitatem. Quod si hoc publicum est commodum iusta erit praedicta lex. Absurdum praeterea existimarem has leges iniquas censeri. Lex vero iusta in animae iudicio est admittenda.'

[1343] Covarruvias, *In cap. Cum esses*, num. 7, p. 45.

[1344] Covarruvias, *In cap. Cum esses*, num. 9, p. 45: 'Non obstat prima ratio, non enim sat est cessare rationem legis in particulari actu, ut cesset ipsa lex, quae data non est ad aliquem particularem finem. Imo, eius ratio continua est, non momentanea. Quamobrem huius legis decisio non cessat, licet eius ratio particulari casu cesset, sed est necessarium cessare rationem legis in communi et universaliter.'

5.6.5   *Defective testaments: naturally binding, but not in conscience*

To summarize, Covarruvias' perspective bears striking similarities to that
of Baldus, Vitoria and Soto. There seems to be no such thing as a 'natural obligation' following from a defective testament. Yet this would be a
premature conclusion. Taking into account the subtle distinction he had
made between natural obligations of the moral kind (*ex honestate*), and
natural obligation of the legal kind (*ex legis ac iuris naturalis vinculo*),
it would be wrong to reduce Covarruvias' standpoint entirely to that of
his predecessors. The originality of his solution rests on the introduction
of his subtle concept of natural obligation. It allows him to eventually
moderate his fervent plea against defective testaments, and to create at
least some space for that much needed, inescapable Christian appeal for
equity. He concludes by admitting that,[1345]

> a certain kind of natural obligation is produced by a testament which does
> not meet formality requirements. It takes its origins from honesty and moral
> debt. But it has nothing to do with the natural obligation that stems from
> the bond of law.

A defective testament might still be thought of as having a certain kind of
binding power, then. Nevertheless, contrary to Vitoria or Soto, for Covarruvias this does not mean that a right of retention is created by a defective testament. If a testatee is already in possession of the inheritance
he is immediately bound to make restitution. In this sense, Covarruvias'
standpoint coincides with the conclusion of his contemporary Antonio
Gómez, professor of Roman law at Salamanca, who held that the testatee of an insolemn testament is not safe in conscience unless he makes
restitution.[1346] And it no doubt encouraged Martín de Ledesma (c. 1509–
1574), who taught theology in Coimbra, to go against the opinion of his
Dominican confrères from Salamanca and hold that restitution of the
inheritance cannot wait until the testatee is finally condemned by a
judge.[1347] According to Covarruvias' line of thought, a defective testament

---

[1345] Covarruvias, *In cap. Cum esses*, num. 9, p. 45: 'Fateor tamen oriri ex testamento
minus solemni quandam obligationem naturalem, quae insurgit ex honestate, et debito
morali, non tamen eam naturalem obligationem, quae ex legis vinculo oritur.'

[1346] Antonio Gómez, *Opus praeclarum et utilissimum super legibus Tauri*, Salmanticae
1598, ad l. 3, num. 123, f. 26r: 'haeres institutus coram duobus testibus non est tutus in
conscientia, sed tenetur restituere'. Neither author cites the other, though, so there is no
direct evidence of mutual influence.

[1347] Martín de Ledesma, *Secunda quartae*, Conimbricae 1560, quaest. 18, art. 1, dub. 12,
concl. 2, f. 227v: 'Sed dico quod statim nullo iudicio spectato tenentur restituere omnia illa

cannot bring about any natural claims of a legal kind, not even in the court of conscience.

5.7   THEOLOGIANS AND FORMALISM III: THE CRITICAL APPROACH

5.7.1   *The disjunction of the debates on testaments and contracts*

Since they were very active in the field of consulting people of all walks of life, and certainly in preparing them to die with a clear conscience, it is by no accident that we find the Jesuits Luis de Molina and Leonardus Lessius dedicating ample space to questions involving testaments. 'This is a very serious and delicate issue,' Molina begins his treatment of statutory formality requirements in last wills,[1348] 'and extremely useful in daily practice.' Even clerics are so much affected by the spirit of the world, Lessius muses, that there is a vast market of consulting them on how to best part with their earthly belongings in a God-pleasing way.[1349] Abuse of power was rife, too. A royal ordinance of 6 April 1588 admonished the Spanish administrators in the Indies to prevent priests from having sick Indians appointing them or their parishes as heirs.[1350]

With Molina, and even more so with Lessius, we find a typical concern to protect as much as possible the will of the testator. Still, Molina is much more cautious than Adrian of Utrecht in allowing considerations of equity to frustrate ordinary formality requirements. Lessius engages in a vivid polemic with Covarruvias to radically defend the voluntaristic account of the law of testament. But he is not as straightforward in applying the consensualist principle unqualifiedly to other juristic acts, like contracts.

As a matter of fact, the major contribution of Molina and Lessius to the debate on formalities appears to be their preparing the disconnection

---

bona vero haeredi, sive iam habuerit illorum possessionem sive non.'

[1348] Molina, *De iustitia et iure*, tom. 1 (*De iustitia ac iure*), tract. 2, disp. 81 (*Utrum per testamentum aut contractum lege humana nullum, comparari possit dominium*), col. 331, num. 16: 'Ut in hac gravi, difficili, quotidiana et perutili quaestione dicam quod sentio, sciendum est.'

[1349] Lessius, *De iustitia et iure*, lib. 2, cap. 19, dub. 4, num. 44, p. 241: 'Et sane mirum est in quibusdam ecclesiasticis tantam esse salutis suae incuriam et futurorum securitatem, ut etiamsi mox ad Christi tribunal rapiendi sint, ea tamen negligant, quibus facile salutem consequi possent, et insuper rem adeo periculosam, ut amicos suos locupletent, audeant attentare. Verum haec est huius saeculi fascinatio, et principis huius mundi, corda mortalium excaecantis, potestas.'

[1350] Bellomo, *Perché lo storico del diritto europeo deve occuparsi dei giuristi indiani?*, p. 29.

of the law of testament and the law of contract. As we will see, Molina makes a sharp distinction between testaments and contracts as he proceeds to solve the question about the necessity of formality requirements. Eventually, he answers the question differently in regard to testaments or contracts respectively. Lessius draws an explicit and compelling parallel between insolemn testaments and naked pacts. He judges both to be entirely valid as a matter of natural law. Nevertheless, he also explains how the basic principle of 'freedom of contract' can be qualified legitimately by form requirements imposed by statutory law. He is wary, like his teacher Francisco Suárez, to extend the superfluity of formalities in testaments to contracts and elections.

This is not to say that the issue of testaments and contracts are already completely dissociated from each other in the works of Molina and Lessius. Lessius deals with testaments as the first instance of a particular contract after his chapter on contracts in general. Molina treats testaments and contracts under the same heading, namely a disputation on the possibility of exchanging *dominium* through either a testament or a contract that is invalid according to statutory law. This perspective is reminiscent of Vitoria, Soto, and Bañez, even if Molina attains a degree of order, comprehensiveness and systematization that clearly distinguishes him from the sometimes fickle stream of thoughts flowing from the pen of the said Dominicans.

The casuistic, dialectic, and practically-oriented nature of Molina's and Lessius' treatises is what still distinguishes their writings from that of a younger Jesuit like Pedro de Oñate. In the latter's vast treatise *On contracts*, we find a theoretical elucidation of the State's power to limit 'freedom of contract'. What we cannot find in his doctrine, however, is a link between the debate on form requirements in contracts, on the one hand, and on testaments, on the other. With Oñate we enter modern times, where contract law does not immediately call forth associations with last wills, let alone elections.

5.7.2   *Moderate formalism in contracts and the resurgence of equity*

If Molina recognizes the importance of the observance of formalities in contracts that is in part because he takes seriously two points that were raised by the Dominicans in the debate on testaments. First, the absurdity that follows from the discrepancy between the law of the land and the

law of conscience.[1351] Assume that a statutory law imposing form requirements in a certain contract does not apply in conscience, so that a natural
obligation is still created by that defective contract. Then a contracting
party commits a mortal sin by taking the other party to court to revoke
the contract on account of the lack of formalities.[1352] Moreover, statutory
law would be sinful in the first place.

Second, the public authorities can impede natural obligations from
coming into existence for a legitimate reason (*causa*), for instance, for the
sake of the common good.[1353] Each individual is a part of the whole, who
has to subordinate its private good to the common good. Consequently,
civil law can impose formality requirements in last wills and contracts
on pain of nullity to prevent fraud.[1354] Moreover, such laws are general
in scope. Adrian of Utrecht's analogy with the precept of fraternal correction does not hold water (*non est par ratio*), according to Molina. He
argues that while the precept of fraternal correction is 'affirmative', and
therefore applicable only when it is useful, the law which stipulates that
formalities are required in contracts on pain of nullity is 'negative' and
absolute in scope.[1355]

[1351] Molina, *De iustitia et iure*, tom. 1 (*De iustitia ac iure*), tract. 2, disp. 81, col. 330,
num. 13: 'Septimo, si contractus, iure canonico aut civili propter defectum solemnitatis
nullus, esset validus in foro conscientiae, sane nullius momenti esset lex, quae illum nullum efficeret, imo vero esset iniqua, quippe cum vi illius talis contractus esset seipso et
in conscientiae foro invalidus, et in exteriori foro absque lethali culpa peti non posset, ut
iuxta eam canonicam aut civilem legem nullus pronunciaretur; quare cum haec absurdis-
sima sint, dicendum proculdubio est eiusmodi contractus nullos re ipsa esse, non minus
in conscientiae quam in exteriori foro.'

[1352] Molina, *De iustitia et iure*, tom. 1 (*De iustitia ac iure*), tract. 2, disp. 81, col. 336,
num. 25: 'Tum etiam quoniam, cum unicuique contrahentium constet se vere celebrasse
eum contractum minus solemnem, sane si ex eo oriretur obligatio naturalis, nullus eorum
posset tuta conscientia ex eo capite illud revocare, quod fuerit minus solemne, nisi forte
petendo, ut in poenam alterius revocaretur.'

[1353] Molina, *De iustitia et iure*, tom. 1 (*De iustitia ac iure*), tract. 2, disp. 81, col. 338,
num. 26.

[1354] Molina, *De iustitia et iure*, tom. 1 (*De iustitia ac iure*), tract. 2, disp. 81, col. 328,
num. 7: 'Respublica seu princeps ad tollendas fraudes et impedienda damna, quae facile
possunt suboriri, habet potestatem condendi leges, quae universim irrita reddant et efficacia ad transferendum dominium in foro conscientiae ac testamenta et contractus quibus
defuerint solemnitates quas iudicaverit expedire.'

[1355] Molina, *De iustitia et iure*, tom. 1 (*De iustitia ac iure*), tract. 2, disp. 81, col. 338,
num. 26: 'Ad confirmationem Adriani neganda est consequentia. Lex namque naturalis
et divina non universim et absolute praecipit correctionem fraternam, sed cum limitatione, praecise quatenus inservit ad fratris emendam. Lex vero humana, quae irrita reddit
testamenta minus solemnia, iuxta opinionem Covarruviae, Ledesmae et Antonii Gomezii

Molina adds to this familiar battery of arguments the novel idea that by
analogy with a marriage contract that does not meet solemnity requirements, defective contracts cannot produce a natural obligation either.[1356]
Indeed, post-Tridentine marriage law was different from before in that it
no longer recognized the validity of a clandestine marriage (*matrimonium
clandestinum*), which was based on mutual consent alone without any
publicity.[1357]

Equity (*aequitas*) is too pervasive an Aristotelian-Christian virtue, however, to remain absent from Molina's seemingly formalistic conclusions.
Even if in principle our Jesuit endorses the moral validity of statutory form
requirements in contracts, he proceeds by making some qualifications to
this general picture. Granted, formalities are needed to protect promisors
against false claims made by self-avowed promisees. But at the same time,
Molina must have been thinking that they should not constitute an excuse
for promisors in bad faith to escape their obligations. Consequently, in the
footsteps of the jurist Luis de Molina y Morales,[1358] he recognizes that
omitting a 'minor' solemnity (*omissio modicae solemnitatis*) does not result

licet originem habeat a fine, a quo legislator fuit motus, irritat tamen ea testamenta, non
praecise, quando est necessarium ad finem, sed absolute et omnino, ut dictum est. Quare
non est par ratio. Adde legem correctionis fraternae esse affirmativam, quae non obligat
ad semper sed aliquando, quando videlicet iuxta finis exigentiam fuerit expediens, leges
vero, de quibus loquimur, esse negativas universim prohibentes, ne talibus contractibus et
(iuxta opinionem Covarruviae) ne talibus testamentis dominium transferatur.'

[1356] Molina, *De iustitia et iure*, tom. 1 (*De iustitia ac iure*), tract. 2, disp. 81, col. 336,
num. 25: 'Tum denique quoniam de matrimonio clandestine celebrato sine solemnitatibus in Concilio Tridentino statutis nullus negare potest non oriri obligationem naturalem,
esseque nullum omnino in foro conscientiae. Eademque est ratio de aliis contractibus
statutis simili modo ipso iure irritis.' (col. 495).

[1357] E.g. Sánchez, *De sancto matrimonii sacramento*, tom. 1, lib. 2 (*De consensu clandestino*), disp. 3, num. 2–3, p. 204: 'Caeterum fides Catholica est, matrimonia clandestine
ante Tridentinum fuisse valida. Id enim definit Alexander III, c. 2 de clandest. despons. et
Tridentinum, sess. 24, c. 1 de matrim. init. anathemate damnans oppositum asserentes.
Et ratio est, quam tradit d. Thomas, 4, d. 28, q. 1, a. 3, quia quoties concurrunt essentialia,
contractus validus est, licet desiderentur solemnitates extrinsecae et accidentales, in matrimonio autem clandestino concurrit tota matrimonii essentia, deficient sola extrinseca
publicitatis solemnitate. Iustissimis autem causis Tridentinum ea irritavit, et iura antiqua
ea prohibuerunt.'

[1358] Cf. Luís de Molina y Morales, *De primogeniorum Hispanorum origine ac natura*
(nova editio cum additionibus Josephi Maldonado Pardo et Fernandi Alfonsi del Aguila
et Roxas), Lugduni 1727, lib. 2, cap. 6, num. 33, p. 292. See the scant notes on this jurist
in N. Antonio, *Bibliotheca Hispana nova, sive Hispanorum scriptorum qui ab anno MD
ad MDCLXXXIV floruere notitia*, Matriti, 1788, p. 52–53, and in M. Rodríguez Gil, *La 'incorporación' de reinos, Notas y textos doctrinales del derecho común*, Cáceres 2002, p. 71–76.

in invalidity—leaving the assessment of the 'minor' or 'major' character of a solemnity to experienced people (*arbitrium prudentis*).[1359]

Moreover, Molina warns that 'it can sometimes be necessary to give up the letter of the law, and to judge according to the norms of equity instead (*aliquando iuris rigor praetermittendus*)'.[1360] For such an equitable judgment to occur, it is necessary to try to imagine what the lawmaker would have decided in the present circumstances. In addition, Molina denies that 'equity and charity require that statutory law, which was issued for the sake of the common good, should be observed,' if doing so would go against equity and charity.

5.7.3   *Restoring the primacy of the will in testaments*

Disconnecting the law of contract and the law of testament, Molina makes a case against formalism in matters related to testaments and last wills despite his bias in favor of form requirements in contract law. Central to his argument is the right interpretation of the sense the lawmakers (*mens legumlatorum*) had intended to give to the passages in the *Corpus Iustinianeum* concerning last wills.[1361]

More than in any other theologian we have seen, the Roman legal texts themselves turn out to play a central role in Molina's debate on formalities. No less than three interpretations of the Roman law of testament are in circulation, according to Molina, to which he adds a fourth of his own.

[1359] Molina, *De iustitia et iure*, tom. 1 (*De iustitia ac iure*), tract. 2, disp. 81, col. 337, num. 25: 'Molina, 2 lib. de primog. cap. 6, n. 33 ex Bart. et aliis quos refert, affirmat omissionem modicae solemnitatis actum non vitiare. Idem dicimus inferius disp. 218 cum multis, quos Greg. Lopez, et Alvar. Valasq. referrunt ac sequuntur, etiam si solemnitas illa sit de forma servari praescripta, ut actus sit validus. Quae autem modica iudicanda sit, arbitrio prudentis est relinquendum.'

[1360] Molina, *De iustitia et iure*, tom. 1 (*De iustitia ac iure*), tract. 2, disp. 81, col. 337, num. 25: 'Illud postremo admonuerim, aliquando iuris rigorem esse praetermittendum, quod ad eiusmodi attinet solemnitates, iudicandumque potius id esse, quod aequitas postulat, quodque verisimiliter ii ipsi legum conditores, si praesentes essent, iudicassent spectatis circunstantiis omnibus concurrentibus. Neque enim prospicere potuerunt omnibus singularibus eventibus, dum id statuerunt, quod ut plurimum communi bono expedire iudicarunt. Neque aequitas et caritas postulat, ut quod pro caritate et communi bono statutum est, executioni mandetur, quando in particulari cum caritate et aequitate pugnare iudicatur.'

[1361] Molina, *De iustitia et iure*, tom. 1 (*De iustitia ac iure*), tract. 2, disp. 81, col. 331, num. 16: 'Sciendum est ex mente legumlatorum circa iura quae quoad invaliditatem testamentorum et contractuum minus solemnium lata sunt pendere, tum legitimam eorundorum iurium interpretationem, tum proinde quaestionis solutionem.'

In this respect, he blames the lack of uniformity in the advise confessors have been giving to the legislators. They should have expressed in clearer terms the goals their laws were expected to serve.[1362]

Some claim that the aim of the laws was not to break the force of the natural obligation of an insolemn testament at all. Statutory law merely introduced a *praesumptio iuris et de iure* to fight fraud and falsehood. As soon as the truth is revealed, for example by a confession of the heir-at-law, natural law should prevail. Others, like Soto, hold that the natural obligation does not cease to exist until the judge has enforced statutory law in court. Molina submits that this is an unwise view, which is unworthy of a powerful legislator.[1363] The view taken by Covarruvias—which is in line with forensic practice—implies that it is a mere manifestation of the power and authority of the legislators (*pro potestate*) that they can impose form requirements on pain of absolute nullity in order to protect the interests of the heirs-at-law. They can do so regardless of the truth. So even if a heir-at-law makes a confession about the true will of the testator, that confession is of no avail to the testatee. Initially, Molina shows sympathy for this opinion, but after closer inspection he rejects it as being at variance with Roman law.[1364]

For the construction of his own view, Molina presumably relies on Bartolus' and Baldus' distinction between substantive formalities (*ad validitatem*) and probatory formalities (*ad probationem*). Still, he does not cite the commentators, and his argument revolves around contemporary Spanish law as much as the law of Rome. In Molina's view, the solemnity requirements were merely imposed for the sake of evidence. Insolemn testaments are not valid as a means of proof (*non admittere eas tanquam legitimas ad probandum*).[1365] Molina argues that this is the true meaning

---

[1362] Molina, *De iustitia et iure*, tom. 1 (*De iustitia ac iure*), tract. 2, disp. 81, col. 336, num. 24: 'Expediret profecto, quandoquidem res haec tota ex legumlatorum mente pendet, ut Christiani legislatores, unusquisque in suo regno, disertis verbis explicarent, num intenderent irritas omnino reddere ultimas voluntates minus solemnes, impedireque ne ex eis obligatio naturalis oriretur (…), an vero eam non impedire (…). Ita enim fieret ut et confessarii essemus unanimes et multo melius conscientiis hominum consuleretur.'
[1363] Molina, *De iustitia et iure*, tom. 1 (*De iustitia ac iure*), tract. 2, disp. 81, col. 336, num. 24: 'Hoc cum Alexandro arbitratae sunt Victoria et Sotus, nec tamen video id iuri alicui inniti, aut legitimatae rationi, quae persuadeat eam fuisse legumlatorum mentem. Quin potius, quicunque id attente expenderit (arbitror) iudicabit illud improbabile, indignumque quod sapiens legislator intenderit.'
[1364] Molina, *De iustitia et iure*, tom. 1 (*De iustitia ac iure*), tract. 2, disp. 81, col. 330, num. 12; col. 339, num. 4.
[1365] Molina, *De iustitia et iure*, tom. 1 (*De iustitia ac iure*), tract. 2, disp. 81, col. 332, num. 16: 'Tertium itaque esse potuit legumlatorum intentum, non quidem irritas reddere

of the Roman texts; it is also the interpretation given to the *Ordenamiento de Montalvo*. This Spanish constitution was considered to say that the law would not admit insolemn testaments as a legitimate means of proof. By the same token, Molina argues that the provisions in the *Leyes de Toro* and their restatement in the *Nueva Recopilación* implied that solemnities were merely of use in regard to the proof of the existence and trustworthiness of the testament in the external court. He does not interpret this text to mean—as we have seen Covarruvias doing—that solemnities are essential to the validity of the testament. Molina submits law *Quaestionem* (C. 6,42,32pr), law *Etsi inutiliter* (C. 6,42,2), and law *Non dubium* (C. 6,23,16) to a detailed exegesis to corroborate his view.[1366]

To conclude, Molina is entirely convinced that contrary to contracts, insolemn testaments are capable of producing an *obligatio naturalis*. This natural obligation is not suppressed by statutory law, as Covarruvias had held. As a consequence, the testatee or legatee has a right of retention and an exception against the heir-at-law as soon as he is in possession of the legacy, since the position of the possessor is the stronger (*melior est conditio possidentis*).[1367] The testatee even has a right to conceal the defective nature of the testament by which he received the inheritance. In addition, in the absence of scandal he can take the law in his own hands (*facere occultam recompensationem*) and steal the inheritance from the heir-at-law—even if the heir-at-law had been granted a right to the inheritance by the judge in the external court.[1368] Conversely, if a heir-at-law secretively knows that the testator's will was to leave his possessions to the testatee, he cannot retain possession of the inheritance, let alone take the testatee to court on pain of mortal sin.

---

minus solemnes testatorum ultimas voluntates, impedireve ne ex eis ea naturalis obligatio emanaret, quae ex natura rei nata est oriri, neque item ex praesumptione falsitatis eas nullas pronunciare iusque concedere haeredibus ab intestate, sed duntaxat non admittere eas tanquam legitimas ad probandum eam fuisse voluntatem testatoris.'

[1366] Molina, *De iustitia et iure*, tom. 1 (*De iustitia ac iure*), tract. 2, disp. 81, cols. 333–334, num. 17–21.

[1367] Molina, *De iustitia et iure*, tom. 1 (*De iustitia ac iure*), tract. 2, disp. 81, col. 334, num. 20.

[1368] Molina, *De iustitia et iure*, tom. 1 (*De iustitia ac iure*), tract. 2, disp. 81, col. 334, num. 22: 'Quod si haec fuit legislatorum mens, sane dicendum est, haeredem in minus solemni testamento institutum, non solum posse occupare ac retinere haereditatem sibi relictam, celareque defectum testamenti, sed etiam posse, cessante scandalo, facere occultam compensationem, si haereditas in exteriori foro haeredi ab intestato adiudicetur. Idem dicendum est de legatario, aut fideicommissario, cui in testamento aut codicillo minus solemni relictum esset legatum, aut fideicommissum.'

Molina opines that if there is doubt about the will of the testator, the heir-at-law who is in possession of the inheritance is bound to make restitution to the testatee in proportion to the doubt (*pro dubii quantitate*).[1369] Molina explicitly denies the validity of the *melior conditio possidentis*-rule in this case. His view will later draw the criticism of Lessius. According to Lessius, the *melior conditio possidentis*-rule applies precisely to cases of doubt, so that the testatee must take the heir-at-law to court before he can claim the inheritance:[1370] 'It is more probable that, in this case, the heir-at-law can retain the possession of the entire inheritance. He has a right which is certain (*ius certum*), and he should not be excluded from it on account of somebody else's right that is hitherto uncertain (*ius incertum*).'

5.7.4   *Formalities, the political contract, and* leges irritatoriae

The change in the larger juridical context where the formalities-issue is dealt with by Lessius is significant of the increasing development of an automous doctrine of contract at the outset of the seventeenth century. Whereas Soto and Molina had still approached the issue of defective testaments and contracts from the angle of the formal limitations on the free exchange of *dominium*, Lessius presents formalities as a qualification of his general principle of consensualism in contracts. Testaments are dealt with as the first instance of a particular contract right after the exposition of his general theory of contract in the two preceding chapters.[1371] In those chapters on general contract doctrine, Lessius has radicalized the consensualist approach to contracts which was handed down to him by the canonical and moral theological tradition. For a contract to be binding, a mutually accepted promise is sufficient in the court of conscience.

[1369] Molina, *De iustitia et iure*, tom. 1 (*De iustitia ac iure*), tract. 2, disp. 81, col. 335, num. 22.

[1370] Lessius, *De iustitia et iure*, lib. 2, cap. 19, dub. 3, num. 21, p. 238: 'Probabilius tamen videtur, heredem ab intestato hoc casu posse totum retinere. Ratio est, quia habet ius certum, a quo non debet excludi per ius alterius dubium. Haec enim est ratio cur melior sit conditio possidentis, quia possidens qui certus est se habere ius possidendi, non tenetur rem nec totam nec partem eius deserere ob ius dubium alterius.'

Only from the second, revised edition onwards (Antverpiae 1609; p. 238) is this modification of the original view of Molina included in Lessius' *De iustitia et iure*. In the first edition (Lovanii 1605; p. 217), Lessius simply adheres to the opinion of Molina, without pointing out his personal, and more probable opinion.

[1371] Lessius, *De iustitia et iure*, lib. 2, cap. 17 (*De contractibus in genere*); lib. 2, cap. 18 (*De promissione et donatione*); lib. 2, cap. 19 (*De testamento et legatis*).

At the same time, though, he adds a marked modification to this consensualist principle by explicitly recognizing the power of the public authorities to limit 'freedom of contract':[1372]

> However naked the agreement, as long as it is freely and spontaneously entered into by parties who have the capacity to make a contract, it entails a natural obligation in the court of conscience. As a consequence, you cannot rescind the contract unless the other party agrees, or unless relative or absolute nullity of the contract is imposed by statutory law (*iure positivo*).

The public authorities can limit the natural 'freedom of contract' precisely by imposing certain clauses and conditions (*certae formulae et conditiones*) on pain of nullity.[1373] Lessius argues that the secular as well as ecclesiastical authorities can do so by analogy with the power of the contracting parties themselves to freely modify a contract by making additional pacts or by inserting certain conditions. Statutory law has the power to nullify the natural obligation produced by a mutually accepted promise in order to protect a certain category of people, to defend the common good, or to promote salvation of the soul. Sometimes, the sanction can be lifted by the protected party itself, for instance by means of an oath.[1374] These conditions imposed by the public authorities concern in essence the formalities of contract.

[1372] Lessius, *De iustitia et iure*, lib. 2, cap. 17, dub. 4, num. 19, p. 197: 'Omnis contractus, etiam nudus, sponte libereque factus, si contrahentes sint habiles, parit obligationem naturalem seu in foro conscientiae, ita ut parte invita non possis rescindere, nisi iure positivo sit irritus vel detur irritandi potestas.'

[1373] Lessius, *De iustitia et iure*, lib. 2, cap. 17, dub. 4, num. 20, p. 197: 'Ratio est, quia sicut duo homines privati seposito omni iure positivo possunt inter se statuere certas formulas et conditiones, sine quibus contractus eorum in posterum non censeantur validi, nec obligationem naturalem possint inducere, ita respublica, quae naturaliter est superior singulorum seu cui naturaliter competit potestas in singulos potest constituere huiusmodi conditiones, et consequenter principes saeculares, in quos suam potestatem respublica transtulit, multoque magis principes Ecclesiae, in iis quae ipsorum gubernationi subsunt, id possunt quatenus necesse est vel expedit ad bonum spirituale subditorum; hanc enim potestatem habent a Christo qui naturaliter supremus est omnium dominus.'
We cannot afford to discuss the conditions the parties themselves are allowed to add to their agreement—there was a most interesting and heated debate about this issue in early modern scholasticism, which is apparent from the mere observation that Lessius' text of *De iustitia et iure*, lib. 2, cap. 18, dub. 15 (*utrum promissio vel donatio conditionalis sit valida, et quam vim habeant conditiones appositae*) considerably differs from one edition to another.

[1374] As Lessius notes, this is a very tricky question, however, if only because it is difficult to determine whether a condition has been imposed for the sake of a particular group of persons ('droit impératif') or for the political community as a whole ('droit impératif d'ordre public'), see Lessius, *De iustitia et iure*, lib. 2, cap. 17, dub. 7, num. 55–59, p. 207–210.

As Francisco Suárez, Lessius' teacher at the *Collegio Romano*, remarks, statutory laws decreeing the nullity of a contract (*leges irritatoriae*) are binding in the court of conscience:[1375]

> If you enter into a contract which is void according to human law, then you are *ipso facto* held in conscience not to retain the good acquired by that contract anymore, or to give up your right to performance, or to abstain from any other effect the contract had entailed if it were not null.

It needs to be stressed that the interference of statutory law with contractual affairs is not as brusque as it might appear on the surface. Political power comes about through free consent by the citizens. At least, it is not at variance with Suárez's and Lessius' theory of political power as deriving from free consent by the members of society.[1376] In Suárezian and Lessian political thought, human authority itself is derived from a free, contractual transfer in the state of nature of the sovereignty and liberty originally resting with the entire community.[1377]

Incidentally, the very contractual relationship between the prince and his people is determined by certain 'conditions' that were stipulated in the political compact. Otherwise, the people would not have parted with their original, supreme jurisdictional power in the state of nature in the first place. Political power, and royal dignity in particular, must have been constituted through a contract. In that contract the people transferred their power upon the prince on condition and under the obligation (*sub onere et obligatione*) that he bears the responsibility for the republic and that he administers justice. Subsequently, along with the power the prince must have accepted this condition (*conditio*). Interestingly, Lessius—who was heavily influenced by Suárez for the development of his political

---

[1375] Suárez, *Tractatus de legibus et legislatore Deo*, lib. 3, cap. 22, num. 9, p. 264: 'Nam qui fecit contractum jure humano irritum, ipso facto, conscientia tenetur, vel rem apud se non retinere, vel alium non obligare, vel denique non uti illo contractu ad alios effectus quos haberet si irritus non fuisset.'

[1376] For a more detailed exposition of Suárez's political theory, see Decock, *Counterreformation diplomacy behind Francisco Suárez's constitutionalist theory*, p. 68–92, including references to further literature.

[1377] This is a basic tenet of Suárez's constitutionalist account of political power as it was directed against Lutheranism and the absolutist tendencies of James I Stuart. See, for instance, *Defensio fidei catholicae*, lib. 3, cap. 1, num. 5, p. 207. In interpreting the famous 'lex regia' (D. 1,4,1 and Inst. 1,2), Suárez insists on the contractual origins of political power, cf. *Defensio fidei catholicae*, lib. 3, cap. 1, num. 12, p. 210: '(...) intelligi debet [lex regia] constituta per modum pacti, quo populus in principem transtulit potestatem sub onere et obligatione gerendi curam reipublicae et justitiam administrandi, et princeps tam potestatem quam conditionem acceptavit (...)'.

ideas—describes the relationship between the Prince and his subjects in terms of an employment contract.[1378] A Prince is to the community as a guardian (*custos*) is to an individual person.

There is no logical contradiction, then, between Lessius' plea for 'freedom of contract' and his acceptance of the interventionist power of the public authorities. For even the latter can eventually be said to be founded on voluntary consent by the parties concerned. Hence, there is no problem about accepting the power of statutory law to avoid a natural obligation. In the mid-seventeenth century, we find Pedro de Oñate reiterating Lessius' statements in an even more systematic way. He leaves no doubt that the possibility exists for the Prince to create or frustrate a natural obligation by introducing form requirements for the sake of the common good (*ad bonum commune*). An analogy is established with the power of private persons to freely add clauses of rescission (*conditiones irritantes*) in view of their private good (*ad bonum cuiusque particularis*).[1379]

Expounding on the *forma contractus*—in the Aristotelian sense of its true nature and essence, Oñate remarks that the substance of a contract is the bond of law (*vinculum iuris*) imposed by the contracting parties upon themselves by offer and acceptance. However, they can turn whatever condition, qualification, or accidental element into a part of the substance of the contract, precisely on account of the typically human freedom in establishing and moulding a contract.[1380] In a blessed moment of academic wonder, Oñate finds that a contract is a product of culture and human inventivity (*res moralis et quasi artificialis*) rather than of nature. Accordingly, its substance can be altered by the contracting parties, for instance by imposing form requirements.[1381]

It is worth recalling, too, that for the scholastics the interaction between naked contractual consensus and statutory law is not merely one of frustration and destruction. Statutory law can impose form requirements on

---

[1378] Suárez, *Tractatus de legibus et legislatore Deo*, lib. 3, cap. 9, num. 4. Compare Lessius, *De iustitia et iure*, lib. 2, cap. 1, dub. 3, num. 13, p. 11: 'Tota respublica se habet ad principem sicut particularis persona ad custodem, quem stipendio ad se tuendum et custodiendum conduxit; et ob hanc causam maxime procuratio boni communis pertinet ad illum architektonikoos.'

[1379] Oñate, *De contractibus*, tom. 1, tract. 1, disp. 1, sect. 6, num. 83, p. 19.

[1380] Oñate, *De contractibus*, tom. 1, tract. 2, disp. 6, sect. 6, num. 111 [summarium], p. 215: 'Contrahentes suo consensu possunt quaecumque accidentalia sumere pro forma contractus; ideo possunt, quia tota substantia contractuum est consensus contrahentium, nec immutant naturam contractuum sed servant, quia sumunt illa pro objecto consensus.'

[1381] Oñate, *De contractibus*, tom. 1, tract. 2, disp. 6, sect. 6, num. 103, p. 215; and num. 111, p. 217.

pain of the annihilation of the natural obligation that would have followed from an accepted promise. But at least two other relationships exist, as became clear in Covarruvias. Pedro de Oñate points out in a brilliant synthesis that 'the civil law either actively supports (*assistit*), or actively resists (*resistit*), or simply ignores (*neque assistit neque resistit*) certain contracts'.[1382] Whereas the civil law can intentionally resist a natural obligation by imposing form requirements on pain of nullity (*leges irritatoriae*), it can also endorse a natural obligation by reinforcing it with an action in the external court (*actio civilis*). A third way of relating to one another is simply characterized by an attitude of non-intervention.

This scheme will turn out to be highly relevant as we fix our attention on the issue of defective testaments again. For Lessius—as it had been for Covarruvias—the key to solving this issue is the correct determination of which of the three types of relationship exists between statutory law and insolemn testaments.

5.7.5 *Lessius against Covarruvias*

Lessius proceeds by consistently distinguishing between the validity of insolemn testaments for pious use (*ad piam causam*) and for non-pious purposes (*ad causam non piam*), respectively.[1383] According to Lessius, both in the civil and in the ecclesiastical court solemnity requirements have already been reduced to a minimum by Pope Alexander III (1159–1181) in canon *Relatum* (X 3,26,12)—an intervention in secular affairs which Lessius defends on account of the indirect secular power of the Church.[1384]

[1382] Oñate, *De contractibus*, tom. 1, tract. 1, disp. 1, sect. 6, num. 87, p. 21.

[1383] On the historical development and the legal nature of the testaments *ad pias causas*, see H. Siems, *Von den 'piae causae' zu den Xenodochien*, in: R.H. Helmholz – R. Zimmermann (eds.), Itinera fiduciae, Trust and Treuhand in historical perspective, [Comparative Studies in Continental and Anglo-American Legal History, 19], Berlin 1998, p. 57–83; E. Conte, *I beni delle 'piae causae' tra beneficenza e vincolo fiduciario*, in: O. Condorelli – F. Roumy – M. Schmoeckel (eds.), Der Einfluß der Kanonistik auf die europäische Rechtskultur, Band 2: Öffentliches Recht, [Norm und Strukter, 37, 2], Köln – Weimar – Wien 2011, p. 295–310. On the similarities between gifts and testaments *ad pias causas* on the Continent and the trust for charitable uses in England, see Helmholz – Zimmermann, *Views of trust and Treuhand, An introduction*, p. 43–44.

[1384] Lessius, *De iustitia et iure*, lib. 2, cap. 19, dub. 2, num. 6, p. 237: 'Potuit autem summus pontifex hac in re legibus civilibus derogare, quia potestatis ecclesiasticae (cuius plenitudo est in pontifice) est, ordinare hominum actiones ad finem supernaturalem, qui est salus animae. Et consequenter potest submovere et tollere omnia, quae studium et cursum bonorum operum ad salutem animae pertinentium impediunt. Atqui istae leges in causis piis impedirent studium bonorum operum. Ergo.'

As a matter of fact, the Church tried to promote testamentary bequests for pious works as best it could, since those bequests were regarded as the best safeguard for the salvation of the soul.[1385] Bequesting money and property to pious works, such as the repair of churches, poor relief, and the upkeep of hospitals, honoured God and the Church.[1386] Canonical intervention in the law of testament was not entirely disinterested, then, as the Church sought to secure enforcement of charitable bequests that mainly supported its own functioning.[1387]

Lessius takes the promotion of charitable giving through testaments a step further. He considers the canonical requirement of two witnesses in testaments for pious uses as necessary for proof only (*ut probari possit*). In his opinion, the requirements of natural law are largely sufficient for an insolemn testament *ad piam causam* to be valid in all the courts. Hence the only prerequisites for making a valid legacy *ad piam causam* are legal ability and liberty of disposition on the part of the testator, and legal capacity on the part of the testatee.[1388]

The crux of the matter, however, concerns testaments *ad causam non piam*, in which (part of) the inheritance is destined to a testatee who is neither a Church, a university, a hospital, or another charity. As we have seen, Diego de Covarruvias y Leyva had taken the view that a testament could only create a natural obligation of the moral kind (*ex honestate*). Yet Lessius mounts a vivid attack against that opinion.

Lessius reproaches Covarruvias because he opposed the common opinion of the *doctores utriusque iuris*. They maintain that a 'natural obligation' ensues from an insolemn testament, thereby understanding 'natural obligation' in a strict, juridical sense.[1389] Also, Lessius turns himself into

---

[1385] S. Herman, *The canonical conception of the trust*, in: R.H. Helmholz – R. Zimmermann (eds.), Itinera fiduciae, Trust and Treuhand in historical perspective, [Comparative Studies in Continental and Anglo-American Legal History, 19], Berlin 1998, p. 102–103.

[1386] G. Jones, *History of the law of charity, 1532–1827*, [Cambridge Studies in English Legal History], Cambridge 1969, p. 3–9.

[1387] Helmholz, *The canon law and ecclesiastical jurisdiction from 597 to the 1640s*, p. 417.

[1388] Lessius, *De iustitia et iure*, lib. 2, cap. 19, dub. 2, num. 7, p. 237: 'Respondeo non esse necessarios (testes). Sufficit enim in his testamentis id, quod iure naturali est sufficiens, nempe ut sit potestas in disponente, capacitas in eo in cuius favorem disponitur et libertas in dispositione. Quod probatur, quia nulla solemnitas iuris civilis in his testamentis est necessaria, ut patet ex cap. Relatum, 1, de testam. Neque etiam necessarii sunt duo testes iure canonico, quia ius canonicum non requirit eos ut dispositio sit valida in foro conscientiae, sed ut possit probari in foro externo, quantum satis est ut iudex pro ea sententiam ferat, ut colligitur ex d. cap. Relatum.'

[1389] Lessius, *De iustitia et iure*, lib. 2, cap. 19, dub. 3, num. 7, p. 237: 'Obligatio naturalis apud iurisperitos vocatur ea quae praeciso omni iure positivo oritur ex natura actus et a iure positivo superveniente non irritatur.'

a fine interpreter of Roman law. The imperial constitutions *Non dubium* (C. 6,23,16), *Etsi inutiliter* (C. 6,42,2), and *Quaestionem* (C. 6,42,32*pr*) are submitted to a detailed exegesis in which Lessius tries to unveil their deeper sense and scope (*mens legislatorum*).[1390] He is heavily indebted to Molina's way of proceeding, in this respect. Still, he applies his own accents.

The most important conclusion Lessius draws from his exegesis is that the Roman regime of insolemn testaments is tantamount to the Roman regime of naked pacts:[1391]

> From these texts it is clear that it was not the intention of the legislators (*mens legislatorum*) to nullify insolemn contracts in the court of conscience. Rather, the aim was merely not to assist them in the civil court, to the effect that you could not get an action to enforce them. By the same token, the Roman legal texts do not grant an action on the basis of a naked promise, unless that naked promise is 'dressed' in a form like the stipulation.

In our Jesuit's view, then, both naked pacts and insolemn testaments produce natural obligations which are neither supported nor frustrated by Roman statutory law (*lex civilis neque assistit neque resistit*).[1392] This is a conclusion diametrically opposed to Covarruvias' contention that insolemn testaments (as well as contracts for a third-party beneficiary) are actually resisted by statutory law. Lessius thinks that the beneficiary of an insolemn last-will can safely retain the legacy as long as he has not been deprived of it for a legitimate reason by the judge.

Interestingly, Lessius also reflects on the legitimate and just grounds (*iustae causae*) that had driven the civil law to take a 'neutral' approach to defective testaments.[1393] First, form requirements are introduced to

---

[1390] Lessius, *De iustitia et iure*, lib. 2, cap. 19, dub. 3, num. 15–20, p. 238.

[1391] Lessius, *De iustitia et iure*, lib. 2, cap. 19, dub. 3, num. 18, p. 238: 'Ex quibus clare patet, non fuisse mentem legislatorum reddere irrita talia testamenta in foro conscientiae, sed tantum in foro externo non assistere, seu non dare actionem. Sicut non dant actionem ex nuda promissione, nisi formula stipulationis vel simili modo sit vestita.'

[1392] Lessius, *De iustitia et iure*, lib. 2, cap. 19, dub. 3, num. 26, p. 237: 'Unde aliter respondetur, illas leges loqui de nullitate in foro externo, quia in foro externo non datur actio ex tali testamento. Lex enim civilis ei non assistit, non tamen ei resistit, ut recte docet Franciscus Sarmiento de reditibus, p. 1, cap. 1, num. 3. Habetur itaque pro infecto, irrito, et nullo in foro externo, quia non conceditur actio ex tali testamento, perinde ac si nullum omnino extaret. Cum hoc tamen consistit, quod ex eo nascatur obligatio naturalis in herede ab intestato ad res illas tradendas, et ius in iis, quibus sic aliquid est relictum, ad exigendum. Sicut patet in pactis nudis, ex quibus etsi nulla oriatur obligatio civilis, oritur tamen obligatio naturalis, ut dictum est cap. 17, dub. 4.'

[1393] Lessius, *De iustitia et iure*, lib. 2, cap. 19, dub. 3, num. 27, p. 239.

prevent the judiciary system getting overloaded because of endless disputes (*ad vitandas plurimas lites*). It will not be a surprise that this is exactly the reason that—in line with the *ius commune* tradition—Lessius had given to account for the unenforceability of naked pacts in Roman law.[1394] Second, form requirements are intended to frustrate cunning attempts to commit fraud (*ad excludendas varias hominum artes et machinationes*). A third reason that explains the Roman law of testament is its bias in favor of the heirs-at-law who have genuinely no idea about the real will of the defunct. Otherwise, on top of their suffering the loss of a beloved relative, they would see themselves painfully deprived of the inheritance (*ne gemino dolore afficerentur*).

To summarize, in matters related to testaments Lessius fully embraces the Roman rule that a last will must be interpreted in the testator's interest. The testator's intention must be observed and intestacy avoided. Hence, an unclear or defective testament should be interpreted benevolently (*benignior interpretatio*).[1395] Lessius cites the words of the Roman lawyer and writer Pliny the Younger (61–113) in his letter to Annianus:[1396] 'I have imposed upon myself the following law: I will always consider and advocate the last will of the defunct as if it were expressed perfectly.' Form requirements in testaments should not be taken into account in the court of conscience. The question remains, though, if this conclusion in regard to testaments can be extended to other juristic acts unqualifiedly, as many jurists and theologians claimed.

Crucially, in Lessius we witness a disjunction of the solution to the problem of defective testaments, on the one hand, and the assessment of the validity of contracts not meeting form requirements, on the other. In fact, Lessius confirms the division introduced by his older colleague Molina:[1397]

[1394] Lessius, *De iustitia et iure*, lib. 2, cap. 17, dub. 4, num. 21, p. 197–198: 'Ratio autem, cur pactum nudum obligationem in foro externo non pariat, est, quia etsi ius civile non resistat talibus contractibus, eos irritando, tamen noluit etiam illis assistere concedendo actionem, ne lites multiplicarentur.'

[1395] On the Roman roots of the principle of benevolent interpretation in the law of testament, see M. Avenarius, *Benignior interpretatio, Origin and transformation of a rule of construction in the law of succession*, Roman Legal Tradition, 6 (2010), p. 1–21.

[1396] Plinius Minor, *Ep.* 2, 16 (ad Annianum), as quoted by Lessius in *De iustitia et iure*, lib. 2, cap. 19, dub. 3, num. 20, p. 238: 'Ego propriam legem mihi dixi, ut defunctorum voluntates, etiamsi deficerent, quasi perfectas tuerer.' Following Covarruvias and Molina, Lessius also quotes Plinius' letter to Calvisius (*Ep.* 5,7) to further strengthen his case.

[1397] Lessius, *De iustitia et iure*, lib. 2, cap. 19, dub. 3, num. 32, p. 240: 'Adverte tertio, ea quae dicta sunt de solemnitate testamentorum a quibusdam extendi ad contractus,

Some pretend that what we have said concerning solemnities in testaments is to be extended to contracts, donations, the distribution of benefices and offices, elections, presentation, and other acts which must meet various solemnity requirements on account of civil or canon law, but the contrary opinion is nearer to the truth and more in line with the law.

As a result, Lessius proceeds,[1398] 'contracts and other acts which fail to meet solemnities imposed by statutory law on pain of absolute nullity do not produce a natural obligation (*contractus quibus deest solemnitas non inducere obligationem naturalem*), unless the law indicates that those solemnities are merely required as a matter of proof in the external court—as is the case with testaments.' Molina and Lessius would be followed in dissociating the law of testaments and the law of contract by no one less than Francisco Suárez. In his *Tractatus de legibus et legislatore Deo* (published in 1612), he firmly rejects the generalizing tendency (*generalitas*) that consists in extending to contracts an unqualified consensualist principle in last wills. Suárez thinks that the opposite rule needs to be enforced:[1399]

> In my opinion, we should rather establish the opposite rule as a general tenet: Those juristic acts are void that lack statutory prescribed solemnities required for the substantial validity of that act, the fact notwithstanding that the act in question really comes about through genuine consent and without breaking the natural law.

Against this background, it is not surprising to find that Lessius takes offence at Bañez's flexible reasoning—quoted above[1400]—in which last wills and contracts are dealt with indiscriminately. Bañez used the

---

donationes, beneficiorum et officiorum collationes, electiones, praesentationes, et similes actus, quia ex dispositione iuris civilis vel canonici requirunt varias solemnitates.'

[1398] Lessius, *De iustitia et iure*, lib. 2, cap. 19, dub. 3, num. 35, p. 240: 'Nihilominus contrarium est iuri conformius, et verius, nimirum huiusmodi actus et contractus, quibus deest solemnitas, sine qua lex illos absolute irritos decernit, non inducere obligationem naturalem, nisi forte alibi explicetur in iure, illam solemnitatem solum requiri ad probationem in iudicio, sicut in testamentis.'

[1399] Suárez, *Tractatus de legibus et legislatore Deo*, lib. 5, cap. 24, num. 4 (*regula generalis vera*), p. 522: 'Quapropter censeo potius contrariam regulam esse generaliter constituendam, scilicet, actus factos contra leges instituentes substantialem solemnitatem tanquam simpliciter necessariam ad eorum valorem, esse nullos ex defectu talis solemnitatis, etiamsi in re fiant ex vero consensu et sine ullo defectu contra legem naturalem.'

[1400] Bañez, *De iure et iustitia*, ad quaest. 62, p. 154: 'Tunc enim [quando leges decernunt in contractibus, quos annullant propter defectum solemnitatis essentialis in iure] is, in cuius favorem contractus est celebratus, ante iudicis sententiam est verus dominus; postea vero desinit esse dominus, et tenetur restituere. Exemplum est in eo, qui est dominus per testamentum, cui deficit solemnitas essentialis iuris.'

example of a testatee in a defective testament to illustrate his point that
a contracting party had a retention right over the goods that had been
conveyed to him through a contract not meeting form requirements—
at least until the moment he was condemned by a judge in an external
court to make restitution. Since this opinion of Bañez presupposes that a
natural obligation exists in spite of the defectiveness of the contract, Lessius cannot agree with it. Again, Lessius and Bañez, who were constantly
at loggerheads with each other in the major theological debate of the day
on divine grace and human free will, take conflicting views.[1401]

According to Lessius, a natural obligation cannot arise out of a contract
that fails to meet substantial form requirements altogether. Still, Lessius
admits that he recognizes that Bañez's opinion is consistent with common practice. It is often too hard (*durum est*) to expect a contracting party
to make restitution spontaneously—without being coerced by a judge's
sentence—of a good he thought he had become the rightful owner of,
since it had been conveyed upon him by mutual consent.[1402]

Quite exceptionally, Lessius refuses to give precedence to custom and
practice over his politically coloured contract theory. That theory is clear
enough: the civil and ecclesiastical authorities (*potestas civilis et ecclesiastica*) have the power to impose contractual form requirements on pain
of nullity in the court of conscience.[1403] By the contracting parties themselves as well as by the public authorities, those formalities can be turned

---

[1401] It is telling, in this respect, that Lessius understands Bañez as the culprit. He could
equally well have criticized Vitoria or Soto, who had first developed the theory here
adhered to by Bañez. On the conflicting points of view of Bañez and Lessius in the debate
on grace and human nature, coupled with an experimental attempt to trace the consequences of those differences in their anthropology in their respective accounts of business ethics, see W. Decock, *Grazia divina e giustizia commutativa, Un confronto tra Bañez
e Lessius*, in: K. Härter – C. Nubola (eds.), Grazia e giustizia, Figure della clemenza fra tardo
medioevo ed età contemporanea, [Annali dell'Istituto storico italo-germancio in Trento,
Quaderni, 81], Bologna 2011, p. 361–388.

[1402] Lessius, *De iustitia et iure*, lib. 2, cap. 19, dub. 3, num. 34, p. 240: 'Videtur haec sententia [sc. per huiusmodi contractus transferri quidem dominium, sed infirmum et revoca-
bile] satis probabilis, maxime spectato usu, qui passim est receptus. Non enim consuetum
est, ut quis ea, quae per tales contractus habet, restituat, nisi cogatur per sententiam.
Durum enim est, ut qui rem habet ex consensu eius qui poterat illam tradere, cogatur
sponte ea cedere, quod non eo loco vel tempore, vel coram illis testibus, quos lex praescribit, tradita fuerit.'

[1403] Lessius, *De iustitia et iure*, lib. 2, cap. 19, dub. 3, num. 35, p. 240: 'Non est dubitandum quin potestas civilis et ecclesiastica possint talem irritationem et nullitatem actibus
inducere ut nullum omnino vim habeant. (...) Quando lex irritum reddit contractum ob
defectum solemnitatis, facit hanc pertinere ad formam essentialem contractus, et adimit
contrahentibus potestatem aliter se invicum obligandi.'

into part of the substance and essence of the contract (*forma essentialis contractus*). Roman law is quoted to confirm the view that positive law can radically resist a natural obligation born out of a contract which fails to meet such formality requirements.[1404]

In any event, if a contract lacks statutory imposed formalities, a party can rescind that contract without the consent of the other party. He can demand to undo the exchange that had occured. Lessius warns, though, that such behavior based on the letter of the law sometimes risks to go against charity (*contra charitatem*).[1405] For example, charity is violated if the other party entered into the contract in good faith (*bona fide*) and suffers considerable damage because he is bound to dissolve the contract on account of the lack of form. Even if Lessius does not use the following expression explicitly, such behavior amounts to 'abuse of law'.

5.8   CONCLUSION

In this chapter we have examined whether the early modern scholastics did not think that the natural law principle of 'freedom of contract' was to be limited from the outside by a basic tenet of their political thought: the admission that ecclesiastical as well as secular authorities have the right to make laws for the common good that are binding in conscience. Part of these statutory laws concern formalities that are required in a great variety of juridical acts on pain of nullity (*leges irritatoriae*).

For a long time the debate on formalities in contracts was dominated by the question of the validity of insolemn testaments. Borrowing from Pope Innocent IV, and perhaps encouraged by reading Bartolus, Panormitanus preached an almost general principle of consensualism in elections, testaments, and contracts as a matter of natural law. It is not unlikely that

---

[1404] He infers from law *In causae cognitione* (D. 4,4,16) that there are a lot of contracts that are so radically voided by an annihilating positive law, that a *beneficium restitutionis* is not necessary anymore for the rescission to take place. He sees law *Qui contra* (D. 46,1,11) as evidence for the fact that contracts which do not meet statutory solemnity require-ments are not admitting of a guarantor anymore.

[1405] This might explain why on another occasion, Lessius maintains that it is 'probable' to think that a contract which is based on mutual consent but fails to meet form require-ments is still valid: cf. *De iustitia et iure*, lib. 2, cap. 17, dub. 7, num. 56, p. 208: 'Probabile est, quando contrahentes sunt habiles et adest utrimque plenus consensus, contractum inducere obligationem naturalem, etiamsi solemnitas iuris non servetur.' At the same time he refers to chapter 19 on testaments for a more elaborate discussion of what he designates as an extremely complex issue (*ea res valde est perplexa apud iurisconsultos*).

this radical consensualist approach was inspired by the typically Christian view that the 'letter kills but the spirit gives life' (2 Cor. 3:6). Pope Adrian VI adopted Panormitan's view, judging that equity did not allow a statutory law imposing formalities to be binding in conscience as soon as it did not serve its purpose anymore.

However, the consensualist view found its counter-reaction in the work of Francisco de Vitoria. Probably inspired by Baldus, Vitoria ruled that formalities imposed by statutory law became part of the very nature and essence of a last will. He inferred from this that a defective testament could not be deemed valid in the court of conscience. Vitoria rebuked excessive regard for the intention and the spirit behind the testament that did not satisfy formality requirements. In addition to the obvious political reasons that lay behind Vitoria's standpoint, he probably realized that 'the letter kills, but the spirit kills as well'.[1406]

Two efforts to reach a compromise between radical formalism and overt consensualism were made. Drawing upon a suggestion made by Vitoria himself, Soto ruled that a testament or a contract lacking formalities imposed by statutory law did not lose its validity in conscience immediately. Its nullity needed to be pronounced by a judge in the external court for the natural obligation to be avoided. Covarruvias stuck to a strict formalist principle, but at the same time left open a small space for equity by claiming that even though a defective testament could not produce a natural obligation of the legal kind, it could still bring about a natural obligation in the moral sense.

Confusion between the regime of last wills and the law of contract continued to surround the debate until the end of the sixteenth century. Eventually, however, the Jesuits introduced a clear distinction between the effects of formality requirements in the law of testate succession, on the one hand, and in the law of contract, on the other. Both Molina and Lessius took a voluntaristic approach to defective testaments, demonstrating that the natural obligation ensuing from the testator's will could not be frustrated by a lack of solemnities. In their treatment of the law of succession, the *favor voluntatis* is neatly translated into *favor testamenti*. Yet

---

[1406] C. Ginzburg, *The letter kills, On some implications of 2 Corinthians 3:6*, History and Theory, 49 (2010), p. 89 (for the German version of this article, see C. Ginzburg, *Der Buchstabe tötet, Einige Schlussfolgerungen aus 2. Korinther 3,6*, in: M. Luminati – W.W. Müller – E. Rudolph – N. Linder (eds.), Spielräume und Grenzen der Interpretation, Philosophie, Theologie und Rechtswissenschaft im Gespräch, [TeNor—Text und Normativität, 1], Basel 2010).

in contractual affairs, they made sure to stress the necessity of complying with statutory form requirements for the natural obligation ensuing from mutual consent to be preserved.

The arguments in favor and against the validity in conscience of contracts and testaments not meeting form requirements impinged on a host of fundamental questions. We have seen how the debate urged jurists and theologians to distinguish carefully substantial formalities from probatory formalities. They had to make a difficult choice between protecting the testator's will or defending the heir-at-law. The protection of the testator's will risked to promote falsehood. Defending the heir-at-law meant running the risk of doing injustice to the truth. Form requirements can prevent consent from being given lightly. At the same time, they may favor a party in bad faith and give him the opportunity to withdraw from a contract on the pretext that the contract lacks formalities.

The formalities-issue also required the scholastics to reflect upon the general bindingness of a statutory law. Does a law hold universally or not? Some accepted the interventionist power of equity unreservedly, because they were convinced that *summum ius* amounts to *summa iniuria*. Others were afraid of an interpretative method which each time subjected the applicability of a law to the question whether its final cause was served in the specific case under scrutiny. After all, too much *aequitas* risked ending in chaos and injustice as well.

Last, the debate brought to light the tense relationship between the two parallel jurisdictions existing in the Iberian empire: the *forum internum* and the *forum externum*. And the concomitant concern not to let that tension get out of control. Some theologians, particularly the Dominicans in the first half of the sixteenth century, seem to have been thinking that they did not have the power anymore to have the secular forces apply the regulations deriving from the natural law. They opted for an affirmation of the statutory law in conscience.

It is difficult to draw general conclusions from a debate that remains compellingly sophisticated. The Jesuits, for example, seem to have demanded statutory law to yield to considerations of equity and natural law in testamentary affairs, whereas their acceptance of statutory form requirements in contracts is quite State-affirming. At least, they seem to have understood that it is unwise to put last wills and contracts in the same box. It is the Jesuits' classifying spirit which will be of no small help as we move from the form requirements in contracts to an examination of the limitations imposed on 'freedom of contract' by the morality of their object.

CHAPTER SIX

SUBSTANTIVE LIMITATIONS ON 'FREEDOM OF CONTRACT'

6.1 INTRODUCTION

After our investigation into aspects of 'freedom of contract' related to the intervention of the State, this chapter will examine the limits imposed on 'contractual freedom' in the court of conscience from the perspective of morality.

The external limitations imposed on the contracting parties through moral or legal restraints were formulated mainly in regard to the morality and lawfulness of the material object of the contract, with the driving factors that ultimately motivated the parties to enter into a contract being considered irrelevant for the validity of contract. But except for Oñate's theoretical reflections on this issue, which will be outlined at the outset of this chapter, the scholastic discussion had organised itself around the hands-on solution of day-to-day cases. Contracts for sex (*contractus cum meretrice*), in particular, proved as pervasive an object of theological consultancy throughout the centuries as its excesses had been an omnipresent nightmare to its societies. Most frequently, the object of a contract for sex was considered to be naturally immoral by itself. Two questions were to become predominant, even if in the beginning they were merely implicit in the debate on restitution rather than formulated in expressly juridical and procedural terms. Firstly, whether the client of the prostitute could claim back his money in court. Secondly, whether the prostitute had a right to claim her due upon completion of her own contractual obligation.

Generally speaking, prostitution agreements as well as other contracts tainted by turpitude or illegality raised the question of the connection between moral or legal 'worthlessness', on the one hand, and juridical 'invalidity', on the other. Are morally objectionable contracts deprived of any legal consequences, to the effect that 'freedom of contract' must be said to be limited by substantive and moral constraints? Or do immoral contracts still produce legal effects? Can parties freely decide to bring about an obligation based on an immoral contract without being frustrated

by the law? As a matter of fact, it was obvious to the scholastics that an
immoral contract was invalid, in the sense that it could not produce any
obligations before any of the parties had carried out his performance
(*ante*). Whether this was still the case after (*post*) one of the parties had
performed, however, turned out to be a much trickier question. It seems
like the scholastics ended up dissociating moral turpitude and legal invalidity at least to a certain extent.

6.2   SEX, THEOLOGIANS AND CONTRACT LAW

6.2.1   *Immoral object* vs *immoral motive*

Consider the following cases: a prostitute and her client making an agreement to have intercourse at a price; two people entering into a contract to
kill somebody; a landlord letting his appartment to a woman who is likely
to use the appartment to receive clients; an arms dealer selling a sword to
a person who will use it to assassinate the king.

It speaks to the analytical skills of the Jesuit scholastics and Pedro de
Oñate in particular to have neatly distinguished between the first two
transactions and the latter on the basis of their intrinsic or extrinsic
immorality, respectively. More precisely, a contract for sex and a contract
for murder are affected by immorality in their very object (*causa materialis*). In the other cases, immoral sexual intercourse and assassination
merely constitute the external motives (*causa finalis*) by virtue of which
at least one of the parties enters into the contract. They do not constitute
the object of the contract. As a consequence, the former contracts are
intrinsically void, whereas the latter contracts may well be disapproved of,
nevertheless their contractual framework and force remains standing.

In fact, a sharp distinction is drawn by Oñate between the final aim of
a contract in general (*finis operis*) and the motives a particular party may
have in concluding a contract (*finis operantis*). Someone may buy a sword
for a variety of reasons, including murder, but also self-protection, self-
display, or mere pleasure. The final aim of a contract itself, however, will
always be the immediate creation of mutual obligation, and, indirectly,
the transferal of a property right, over the sword, for instance.[1407] Even

---

[1407] Oñate, *De contractibus*, tom. 1, tract. 1, disp. 4, sect. 1, num. 7–8, p. 104: 'Prima
conclusio, finis intrinsecus immediatus in omni contractu est constituere seu producere
per contractum obligationem, seu obligare se et alium quocum contrahit. (…) Secunda

though later on he seems to have occasionally ignored his own conclusion, Oñate makes a clear initial statement that, unless the immoral act constitutes its very object (*res turpis*), a contract cannot be invalidated, however unacceptable the final motivation of the parties (*causa finalis operantis*) entering into the contract be:[1408]

> If a contract is really concluded with a view to imposing an obligation upon oneself, and of transferring a property right, it can never ever be vitiated and ruined as to its substance, no matter how depraved and immoral the final motive (*quamlibet pravo et turpi fine*) that underlies it. So even if a marriage contract is concluded for the secret and extrinsic purpose of lust, debauchery or uxoricide; even if the purchase of a sword is concluded for the purpose of regicide or parricide, these motives do not affect the very nature and essence of contract itself, but remain only extrinsically and accidentally connected to it. This holds no longer true, of course, if the parties make a mutual agreement to impose a contractual obligation upon themselves to kill the king or their father. In that event the aim becomes an intrinsic part, that is the object of the obligation itself, and therefore vitiates it. A contract must never have an immoral object (*de re turpi*) as its subject-matter.

In principle, immorality and invalidity of contract do not coincide, then, unless the immorality concerns the object of contract.

Reality proved too complex, however, to leave Oñate with a definitive conception of the relation between juridical validity and moral probity of contract. For on the one hand, he had to recognize—in the wake of the scholastic tradition—that even a contract for prostitution would bring about legal effects upon completion, despite the fundamental juridical invalidity ensuing from its immoral material cause. By the early seventeenth century it had become common opinion, indeed, that a prostitute had a legal and moral claim to her salary, as well as an exception to an action for recovery brought against her by a client. On the other hand, he

---

conclusio, finis mediatus contractuum omnium idemque etiam intrinsecus et necessarius esse debet dominii translatio.'

[1408] Oñate, *De contractibus*, tom. 1, tract. 1, disp. 4, sect. 1, num. 12, p. 105: 'Tertio maxime observandum infertur. Contractum si vere fiat cum intentione se obligandi et transferendi dominium non vitiare et corrumpi in esse contractus, id est non invalidum, et irritum reddi, ex quocumque, quamlibet pravo et turpi fine ad quem ordinetur, v.gr. matrimonium etiam si ordinetur omnino ad libidinem, etiam praeposteram, vel ad uxoricidium secreta et extrinseca intentione; vel emptio ensis ad occidendum regem vel patrem, quia hi fines contractum ipsum in sua natura et essentia non contingunt, sed sunt fines extrinseci accidentaliter coniuncti ei. Secus esset si ipsi contrahentes vellent pacisci et contractu se obligare ad occidendum regem vel patrem. Tunc enim finis ille intrinsice in obligationem ipsam cadit, et est obiectum illius, unde eam vitiat, quia contractus de re turpi esse non potest.'

thought that a contract considered valid as to its material cause while at the same time being immoral on the grounds of its final cause could still be rendered juridically invalid.

Occasionally, we find Oñate maintaining that it is not unlikely for a contract to lose its legal validity because of the evilness of its extrinsic final cause, no matter the intrinsic righteousness of its material cause, citing the very example of the sale of a sword for the purpose of murder to illustrate his case.[1409] Hence, even the upshot of Oñate's systematic reflections on validity and immorality remain confusing every now and then, although he unmistakably makes an attempt to dissociate the spheres of law and morality.

6.2.2   *Roman canon law and the nullity of immoral contracts*

An immoral object of contract, for instance, prostitution, or assassination, immediately nullifies what was still being analyzed as a contract of lease.[1410] To Oñate the invalidity was obvious from the very concept of contract as a personally imposed law (*lex*), which necessarily implied its status as human postive law subordinated to divine positive law within an implicit hierarchy of norms. From Old Testament stories like Eleazar's martyrdom subsequent to his refusal to eat non-kosher meat, and Peter's admonition in Acts to obey God rather than man, a rule of conflict was inferred which affirmed the precedence of divine precepts over human-made contracts.[1411]

[1409] Oñate, *De contractibus*, tom. 1, tract. 2, disp. 5, sect. 3, num. 277, p. 170: 'Dicendum ergo est contractum illicitum, et qui sit peccatum mortale, posse esse nullum, et multoties id contingere, non solum quando illicitus est, quia licet intrinseca omnia habeat iusta et legalia, tamen extrinsece ad finem malum ordinatur. V.gr. si meretrix ad se ornandum ad peccatum emat vestes et iocalia; si alius emat vestes vel equum propter vanam gloriam, vel ensem ad occidendum; sed etiam quando contractus in se ipso prohibetur.'

[1410] Oñate, *De contractibus*, tom. 3, part. 2, tract. 35, disp. 127, sect. 4, num. 66, p. 615: 'Secundus contingere potest [sc. ut locatio prohibita sit] propter malum usum, id est illicitum, et lege naturali vetitum, ut quando meretrix locat operam suam meretriciam, id est se prostituit ad peccandum, vel quando assassinus locat operam suam ad occidendum alium.'

[1411] Oñate, *De contractibus*, tom. 1, tract. 2, disp. 5, sect. 3, num. 267, p. 168: 'Nam si contractus, qui est lex humana, quam sibi sua voluntate imponunt contrahentes, concurrat cum lege Dei, tunc usurpandum est illud Apostolorum, Act. 5, 29: obedire oportet Deo magis quam hominibus et illud Eleazari, 2 Machab. 6, 20: Determinavit non admittere illicita propter vitae amorem, et propter modicum corruptibilis vitae.' Compare *l.c.*, num. 268, p. 169: 'Contractus vero est lex, quam sibimet contrahentes de rebus temporalibus imponunt. Sed stante lege Dei et superioris, cessat lex privatorum, et tunc usurpandum est illud (obedire oportet Deo potius quam hominibus), ergo.'

In no way could eternal salvation be put at risk for the sake of a contract between humans on earth, Oñate concluded from a couple of canon law texts.[1412]

A flood of passages extracted from Roman law were quoted by Oñate to further support the thesis that the immorality of the object of contract inevitably brings about juridical invalidity in its wake. Cunningly misreading paragraph *Si ob maleficium* (D. 2,14,7,3), Oñate molded it to mean that any promise to do moral evil was sanctioned with juridical nullity.[1413] He even held that this rule was confirmed by the famous statements of Ulpian in D. 12,5,4,1 (*in pari causa turpitudinis cessat repetitio*) and in D. 12,5,6 (*condictio ex iniusta causa*)—ignoring that the same texts had been cited by other scholastics precisely to prove that promises invalid on account of their intrinsic immorality could still have legal effects.[1414] Neither will it come as a surprise that our Jesuit made reference to Inst. 3,19,24: 'A promise made for immoral purposes (*turpi ex causa*), e.g. a promise to commit a murder or sacrilege, is not valid.' He produced D. 28,7,15 as an argument to put clauses contrary to good morals (*contra bonos mores*) on a par with impossible clauses: both rendered a transaction invalid. And he could never have dreamt of a better passage to underpin his statements than the famous law *Generaliter* by Ulpian in D. 45,1,26, completed by Pomponius in D. 45,1,27pr., to the effect that: 'As a general rule, we know that immoral stipulations are of no weight. Take the example of a promise to commit a murder or sacrilege.'

Despite the flood of support quoted from the Roman law itself, Oñate deemed it necessary to make reference also to Bartolus' commentary on law *Generaliter* as well as on law *Si plagii* to prove that immoral stipulations were legally void from the outset.[1415] A reference to the ordinary

---

[1412] He refers not wholly without reason to canon *Quum contingat* (X 2,24,28) and to canon *Quamvis pactum* (VI 1,18,2).
[1413] Oñate, *De contractibus*, tom. 1, tract. 2, disp. 5, sect. 3, num. 267, p. 168: 'Probatur iure civili conclusio, ex l. iurisgentium, ff. de pactis, par. maleficium, ubi textus: si ut maleficium fiat promissum sit, nulla est obligatio ex hac conventione.' In fact, the original passage reads: 'Si ob maleficium ne fiat promissum sit, nulla est obligatio ex hac conventione', see *Corpus iuris civilis* (ed. P. Krüger- Th. Mommsen, Dublin-Zürich 1968¹⁶), p. 57, col. 1. Compare the gloss *Nulla* to D. 2,14,7,3 in *Corporis Iustinianaei Digestum vetus* (ed. Gothofredi), tom. 1, col. 262: 'Contra videbatur, quasi causa subesset, sed tamen quia est pro non causa, nulla obligatio nascitur (…).'
[1414] Cf. infra.
[1415] Bartolus, *In secundam Digesti novi partem commentaria*, ad D. 45,1,26, num. 1, f. 15r: 'Generaliter novimus, sitpulatio turpis est ipso iure nulla.'; ad D. 45,1,123, num. 1, f. 56r: 'Promissio facta de praeterito vel de futuro ob turpem causam est ipso iure nulla.'

gloss was made to point out that the immorality pertained to the object of the stipulation.[1416] Finally, a few exhortations not to keep your word in immoral promises that were included in Gratian's *Decretum* and became a rule of law with Boniface VIII (VI, reg. iur. 39) were taken as further evidence of the legal nullity of contracts with an immoral object.[1417] Natural reason (*ratio naturalis*) provided an even more convincing demonstration than legal and theological authority. For the assumption that an immoral object entailed an obligation not to do anything would be logically contradictory to the implication following from a juridically valid contract, namely that an obligation to do something did exist. In addition, man would be totally perplexed if he were to obey a contract which at the same time urged him to disobey God's commandment not to sin.[1418]

On the face of it, the solution to cases involving an immoral material cause should have been easy. An occasional employment contract (*locatio conductio*) involving the performance of sex or murder for an appropriate fee should simply be deemed absolutely void on account of its morally reprehensible object. Similarly, bribing a judge to make him render an unjust sentence could not be enforced any more than an agreement between a pimp and a prostitute.

But there is a catch in this simple way of analyzing things. Did not authoritative sources themselves hold that a judge could retain the bribe he had received? And did not the common opinion think that a prostitute could receive and keep the money paid in exchange for her services? Did not the early modern scholastics generally acknowledge this legal consequence which had come about in spite of the supposed legal nullity of the agreement? Did not Roman law itself expressly recognize that a bribed judge and a prostitute could retain what they had received in exchange for their turpitude?[1419] But how could the scholastics or the Romans have said so without recognizing that at least some kind of legal obligation could be produced by a contract which did not comply with substantive moral standards?

[1416] Glossa *Turpes* to D. 45,1,26 in *Corporis Iustinianaei Digestum novum* (ed. Gothofredi), tom. 3, col. 934: 'Turpes, id est turpitudinem continentes, sive super turpibus rebus interpositas, sed turpiter factae valent, sed obiicitur exceptio.'

[1417] C.22, q.4, c.10: 'Magnae sapientiae est revocare hominem quod male locutus est.' C.22, q.4, c.5: 'In malis promissis rescinde fidem. In turpi voto muta decretum. Quod incaute vovisti non facias. Impia est promissio, quae scelere adimpletur.' Oñate's text, *De contractibus*, tom. 1, tract. 2, disp. 5, sect. 3, num. 268, p. 169, reads 'vero' instead of 'voto'.

[1418] Oñate, *De contractibus*, tom. 1, tract. 2, disp. 5, sect. 3, num. 268, p. 169.

[1419] See D. 12,5,3, and D. 12,5,4*pr.* and 3 respectively.

As a matter of fact, a prostitute was not merely deemed by Oñate to have a remedy to block off an action of recovery by the plaintiff, it had become common scholastic opinion at least by the mid seventeenth century that, once she had rendered her services, a prostitute could bring a suit both in the external and internal court against a fornicator who had defaulted on his promise to pay her.

What, then, makes it possible for a prostitute to receive and to claim money by virtue of what seems, on the face of it, to be a legally void contract? Is free, mutual consent capable of producing legal effects despite the immorality of its object? Finding an answer to this question—not in the least out of an evangelical concern to protect weaker parties such as prostitutes—would constitute the continuous challenge of the scholastic tradition in the face of immoral contracts.

6.3   PROSTITUTION AND THE LAW OF RESTITUTION

6.3.1   *Illicit acquisition* vs *acquisition by virtue of an illicit cause*

The starting point of the medieval theologians in dealing with prostitution was different from a present day lawyer's approach. For Thomas Aquinas, the basic question was not whether a client has a right to recover the money he has transferred to a prostitute, or whether a prostitute can bring an action in either the external or internal court against a client who refuses to pay. Only from the sixteenth century onwards, with theologians such as Domingo de Soto and canonists such as Diego de Covarruvias y Leyva, would that legal approach become fully integrated into the moral theological one, which for its part lies at the crossroads of the virtues of charity and justice.

The medieval theologians envisaged a prostitute plagued by an uneasy conscience about the licitness of her gains, but reassured by the Gospel's message in Luke 16, 9 that she could be purged from sin by investing her ill-gotten gains into charitable causes. They wanted to respond to her qualms of conscience, and notably to the question whether she could really give away her earnings through charitable almsgiving, or if the virtue of justice would rather demand her to make restitution to her client. Augustine had said that almsgiving should be based on clean profits. Usurers, for instance, must return usurious profits to their real owners.[1420] So

---

[1420] See Augustinus, *De Verbis Domini*, sermo 35, 2 (= serm. 113 Maur., 2 = PL 38, c. 649): 'Nolite velle eleemosynas facere de fenore et usuris.'

the question was raised whether, by the same token, a prostitute should not make restitution of her profits to her client rather than spend them on charities, since the client remained the true owner of the money.

In order to decide the question whether a prostitute was either bound to make restitution or to give alms in order to save her soul, Thomas made a distinction between three kinds of acquiring riches in an unlawful way (*illicite acquisitum*). Firstly, the acquisition itself can be illicit (*acquisitio illicita*). Secondly, the acquisition can be founded on an illicit cause (*ex causa turpi*). Thirdly, there is the special case of simony (*simonia*). If the receiving itself is illicit (*acquisitio illicita*), as in the case of theft or a usurious loan, the ownership has actually never been transferred from the robbed person to the receiver. Consequently, the virtue of justice demands that restitution of the goods be made to the original owner. Stolen goods or usurious profits, for instance, could by no means be spent for charitable ends.

In cases like prostitution, however, the taking itself is perfectly lawful, filthy though the source or cause of this acquisition may have been:[1421]

> This is what we call filthy profits (*turpe lucrum*): to the extent that this woman exercises the profession of a prostitute, she behaves filthily and contravenes God's law. But the taking of the money in exchange for her services does not constitute a violation of the law out of itself. Consequently, she can retain what she has earned, and use her profits for almsgiving.

A prostitute acquires legitimate ownership over her profits, even though they are the outcome of an immoral cause (*ex causa turpi*),[1422] that is a

---

[1421] Aquinas, *Summa Theologiae* (Ed. Leonina, tom. 8), IIaIIae, quaest. 32, art. 7, concl., p. 256–257: 'Tertio modo est aliquid illicite acquisitum, non quidem quia ipsa acquisitio sit illicita, sed quia id ex quo acquiritur est illicitum: sicut patet de eo quod mulier acquirit per meretricium. Et hoc proprie vocatur turpe lucrum. Quod enim mulier meretricium exerceat, turpiter agit et contra legem Dei, sed in eo quod accipit, non iniuste agit nec contra legem. Unde quod sic illicite acquisitum est retineri potest, et de eo eleemosyna fieri.'
[1422] Aquinas, *Summa Theologiae* (Ed. Leonina, tom. 9), IIaIIae, quaest. 87, art. 2, ad 2, p. 230: 'Quaedam vero dicuntur male acquisita quia acquiruntur ex turpi causa, sicut de meretricio, de histrionatu, et aliis huiusmodi, quae non tenentur restituere.' Compare Aquinas, *Sententia libri Ethicorum*, lib. 4, lect. 5, in: *Opera Omnia iussu impensaque Leonis XIII*, tom. 47, Romae 1969, p. 216: 'Quorum quidam lucrantur de vilibus et servilibus operationibus; quidem vero lucrantur de turpibus et illicitis, puta de meretricio vel de aliquo simili, sicut leones; quidam vero lucrantur per improbam exactionem, sicut usurarii et qui saltem aliquid parvum volunt lucrari in aliquot multo quod dant vel mutuant. Omnes enim praedicti accipiunt unde non oportet (…) vel quantum non oportet (…). Quibus omnibus commune est quod turpiter lucrantur (…).'

vicious act (*de vitiosis actibus lucratur*).[1423] In particular, these legitimate earnings are the result of an infringement of God's sixth commandment.[1424] But that need not mean that the acquisition itself is void. In this respect, Thomas draws a distinction between filthy profits (*turpe lucrum*) and illicit profits (*lucrum iniquum*). The reason behind the distinction being that in the case of *lucrum iniquum* not only the act on account of which the profits are made, but also the acquisition of the profits themselves itself is expressly forbidden.[1425] *Turpe lucrum*, on the other hand, only indicates that the cause to the acquisition is forbidden.

Consequently, a prostitute is free to choose either to retain her profits, or to give them away as an act of charity. What she cannot do, however, is offer her earnings as an oblation to God in the eucharist as long as she is in a state of sin. For that would give rise to scandal and betray a blatant irreverence for the sacred.[1426]

Thomas' analysis might have been borrowed in part from the canon law doctrine of restitution as expressed in Gratian's *Decretum* C.14, q.5. There scholars have observed a similar distinction between unlawful acquisition *tout court*, on the one hand, and acquisition tainted by an unlawful cause,

---

[1423] Aquinas, *Summa Theologiae* (Ed. Leonina, tom. 9), IIaIIae, quaest. 118, art. 8, ad 4, p. 463: 'Quandoque autem aliquis dicitur illiberalis vel avarus quia excedit in accipiendo. Et hoc dupliciter. Uno modo, quia turpiter lucratur: vel vilia et servilia opera exercendo per *illiberales operationes*; vel quia de aliquibus vitiosis actibus lucratur, sicut de *meretricio*, vel de aliquot huiusmodi; vel quia lucratur de eo quod gratis oportet concedere, sicut *usurarii*; vel quia lucratur *parva cum magno labore*. Alio modo, quia iniuste lucratur: vel vivis vim inferendo, sicut *latrones*; vel *mortuos spoliando*; vel ab amicis auferendo, sicut *aleatores*.'

[1424] Aquinas, *Summa Theologiae* (Ed. Leonina, tom. 7), IaIIae, quaest. 100, art. 11, concl., p. 221–222: 'Sed quia ea quae sunt manifesta, sunt principia cognoscendi eorum quae non sunt manifesta; alia praecepta moralia superaddita decalogo reducuntur ad praecepta decalogi, per modum cuiusdam additionis ad ipsa. (...) Praecepto autem sexto, quod est de prohibitione adulterii, superadditur praeceptum de prohibitione meretricii, secundum illud Deut. 23, *Non erit meretrix de filiabus Israel, neque fornicator de filiis Israel*; et iterum prohibitio vitii contra naturam, secundum illud Levit. 18, *Cum masculo non commisceberis: cum omni pecore non coibis*.'

[1425] Aquinas, *Scriptum super Sententiis magistri Petri Lombardi*, ed. M.F. Moos, Parisiis 1947 [hereafter: Ed. Moos], tom. 4, lib. 4, dist. 15, quast. 2, art. 4, quaestiuncula 3, num. 311–312, p. 693: 'Ad tertiam quaestionem dicendum quod *quando lucrum ipsum est lege prohibitum*, ut rapina, usura et simonia, non solum dicitur turpe lucrum sed iniquum. Et de hoc dictum est qualiter eleemosyna fieri possit vel non possit. Sed *quando actus quo quis lucratus est, lege est prohibitus*, non autem ipsum lucrum, tunc vocatur turpe lucrum sicut est in meretricio vel in similibus. Et tunc de tali eleemosyna fieri potest, quia non tenetur ad restitutionem.'

[1426] Aquinas, *Summa Theologiae* (Ed. Leonina, tom. 8), IIaIIae, quaest. 32, art. 7, arg. 2, p. 256: 'Sed turpe lucrum est quod de meretricio acquiritur: unde et de huiusmodi sacrificium vel oblatio Deo offerri non debet, secundum illud Deut. 23: *Non offeres mercedem prostibuli in domo Dei tui*.'

on the other. The former necessitates restitution to the original owner
of the profits made, whereas the latter still confers legitimate ownership
over the goods acquired in that manner. Accordingly, *turpe lucrum* could
still form the object of almsgiving.[1427] In any event, like Thomas after him,
Gratian insisted in his comments on Augustine that not every ill-gotten
gain must be transformed into a good deed in the same way.[1428] What had
been received through robbery or a usurious loan needed to be restored
to its original owner rather than used for practicing charity.[1429] If the ultimate source of the acquisition had been immoral, however, distributing
the ill-gotten gains among the poor was an option, as when a mathemati-
cian or astrologer had received money for his forecasts and divinations.[1430]

We have already pointed out, however, that Thomas Aquinas also distinguished a third form of acquisition tainted by illicitness: simony (*simonia*). In Thomas' view, this mortal sin must always give rise to almsgiving.
Since both the receiver and the giver had committed a sin in paying or
performing a simoniacal act (*datio et acceptio est contra legem*), no one
of them could pretend to be the legitimate owner of the service fee any
longer. Consequently, the price for the simoniacal service inevitably had
to be destined to charity.[1431] Thus, Thomas did not follow law *Si ob turpem
causam* (D. 12,5,8), stipulating that the position of the possessor is the
stronger in case of equal turpitude on the part of both giver and receiver.
Along that line of reasoning, the supplier of a simoniacal service would
have been allowed to retain the money received. Neither did Thomas
adopt canon *Veniens ad nos* (X 5,3,19), which requires the restitution of
simoniacal gains to the giver.

[1427] Hallebeek, *The concept of unjust enrichment in late scholasticism*, p. 23–24.

[1428] C.14, q.5, c.14. See Augustinus, *De Verbis Domini*, Sermo 35, 2 (= serm. 113 Maur., 2 =
PL 38, c. 649).

[1429] See C.14, q.5, c.1, and C.14, q.5, c.15, §4.

[1430] C.14, q.5, c.14.

[1431] Aquinas, *Summa Theologiae* (Ed. Leonina, tom.8), IIaIIae, quaest. 32, art. 7, concl.,
p. 256: '(…) in simonia, in qua dans et accipiens contra iustitiam legis divinae agit. Unde
non debet fieri restitutio ei qui dedit, sed debet in eleemosynas erogari.'
Compare Aquinas, *Summa Theologiae* (Ed. Leonina, tom. 9), quaest. 62, art. 5, ad 2,
p. 51: 'Ad secundum dicendum quod aliquis dupliciter aliquid illicite dat. Uno modo, quia
ipsa datio est illicita et contra legem: sicut patet in eo qui simoniace aliquid dedit. Talis
meretur amittere quod dedit: unde non debet ei restitutio fieri de his. Et quia etiam ille qui
accepit contra legem accepit, non debet sibi retinere, sed debet in pios usus convertere.
Alio modo aliquis illicite dat quia propter rem illicitam dat, licet ipsa datio non sit illicita:
sicut cum quis dat meretrici propter fornicationem. Unde et mulier potest sibi retinere
quod ei datum est: et si superflue aliquid per fraudem vel dolum extorsisset, tenetur eidem
restituere.'

Despite a certain inconsistency in his overall ideas about restitution,[1432] Thomas leaves no room for doubt about his answer to a prostitute who is in doubt about how to best regain her soul. Irrespective of the unlawfulness of the act of prostituting herself, a prostitute has a choice either to retain or to give away her filthy profits once the act is over. A contract for prostitution does not seem to be wholly deprived of legal effects, then. Nevertheless, in modern terms these effects might be ascribed to an intervention of the law of unjust enrichment rather than to the law of contract. Anyway, the law of restitution and justice in exchange forms the background against which Thomas discusses all contract theory.

6.3.2   *Leasing a right of use over your body*

With the Franciscans, the analysis of prostitution reaches the juridical precision later to be found in its fully-fledged form in the writings of the Jesuits. As if the juridical way of looking at the world had become his second nature, Pierre Jean d'Olivi conceives of prostitution in terms of a contract as a matter of course. Even in so lofty a theological writing as his exegesis of the book of *Genesis*, we find him analyzing the relationship between a fornicator and a whore as a contract in which a prostitute sells, or rather leases the use of her body—over which she has full ownership— at a price.[1433]

No matter how vicious and unlawful the object of a contract for sex may be, a valid lease-hire contract can be established on that basis, given that the formal requirements to make up a valid contract are met: a woman has the ownership over her body, and she can lawfully lease a right of use over part of it at a price. With Olivi, a contract is clearly seen as a vehicle for transferring property rights, that is a technical legal instrument

---

[1432] In his commentary on Peter Lombard's *Sentences* he holds, for instance, that in case of equal turpitude the case of a usurious loan has to be treated on a par with the case of simony: no right of retention to the lender, let alone a right to recovery for the payer of the usurious interest lies. By contrast, a victim of a robbery can claim back the stolen goods since he has never lost his ownership over them. Cf. *Scriptum super sententiis*, lib. 4, dist. 15, quaest. 2, art. 4, quaestiuncula 2, concl.

[1433] Pierre Jean d'Olivi, *Lectura super Genesim*, cap. 38 in: Sancti Thomae Aquinatis opera omnia, Parma 1868, tom. 23: 'Ulterius sciendum, quod licet contractus meretricius sit respectu suae materiae vitiosus, nihilominus ipsa fidelitas, quae includitur in observantia pacti, non est vitiosa, sed bona. Licet etiam mulier corpus vendat sive locet ad usum nefarium, locat tamen rem suam; et ideo vere facit pretium locationis corporis sui: atque ita absque ejus consensu non licet illud alteri dare, imo est sibi solvendum.'

detached from moral considerations. Olivi concludes from this that a client is bound by contract to pay the price for the services he enjoyed. He cannot merely breach his promise and distribute among the poor the money that is contractually due to the prostitute.

Olivi takes his deliciously juridical analysis of prostitution even to higher levels in his treatise *On contracts*, where the starting point is again whether the prostitute has to make restitution to her client of the filthy lucre she has made through him. Hiding away behind the safe excuse of undetermined authority—but actually producing a staggering argument pretty much developed by himself—Olivi maintains that a contract for sex is entirely valid. There is simply nothing in a contract for sex capable of hampering the rights-transferring vehicle called contract. Hence, a prostitute can retain the money she has made, immoral though the services she renders may be:[1434]

> Their reason thereof is that in contracts viciousness and nullity on the formal level (*in sua forma*) are to be neatly distinguished from the viciousness and nullity, not of the intrinsic form of the contract, but of its object or motivating and effective cause (*in sua materia vel causa motiva seu effectiva*). So no matter how vicious the object of prostitution, no matter how vicious the voluntary intention to have sex with a prostitute, or to demand remuneration for this performance, the contractual form of this transaction has still something truly juridical to it. For both parties exchange what truly belongs to them: the prostitute gives over to the client her body which is her personal property (*suum*) according to civil and natural law, and in exchange for that body given to him, the client pays a fee out of his own pocket (*suum*).

6.3.3   *The Saint, the sinner, and the Digest*

As a witness to the brilliance of Olivi's analysis, we find a simple word for word copy of it in a sermon by the fourteenth-century Saint Bernardine of Siena, another Franciscan. He even continues and says, just as Olivi

---

[1434] Pierre Jean d'Olivi, *De contractibus*, part. 3, art. 3, reg. 4, p. 310–311 (ed. Piron 1999): 'Horum autem ratio est quod aliud est contractum esse in sua forma viciosum et nullum, et aliud in sua materia vel causa motiva seu effectiva, non tamen in sua intrinseca forma. Quamvis autem in contractu mercedis pro meretricio sit materia meretricii viciosa et voluntas ad meretricium et ad contractum suae mercedis movens, forma tamen contractus habet in se aliquid veri iuris. Quia sicut meretrix concedit lenoni corpus personaliter et naturaliter ac civiliter suum, sic iste pro corpore meretricis sibi concesso dat aliquid vere suum.'

before him, that if it is possible to donate your property for free, then it should also be possible to demand a price for it, certainly if the receiver derives pleasure and utility from what you give him.[1435] As long as divine or human law does not affect the legitimacy of your jurisdictionary power (*jurisdictio vel potestas*) to dispose of your property as you like, the Franciscan said, your freedom to exercise and transfer you rights through contract should not be nullified because of extrinsic viciousness.

Versed in both the theological and legal tradition, Bernardine would strengthen his argument by making reference to Thomas' distinction between unlawful acquisition and acquisition on the basis of an unlawful cause, on the one hand, and to paragraph *Sed quod meretrici* (D. 12,5,4,3), on the other. Of no small importance to the scholastics' debate, paragraph *Sed quod meretrici* stipulated that a prostitute's client had no right of recovery, because the turpitude concerned only the giver, and not the acquirer. While traditionally analyzing a contract for prostitution as a case of equal turpitude (*turpitudo utriusque*), Roman law came to recognize, indeed, that actually only the giver was tainted by turpitude (*turpitudo dantis*). For the prostitute could only be blamed for being a prostitute, but being one, she could lawfully receive the money.[1436]

Interestingly, Bernardine even proposes a comprehensive interpretation of the entire D. 12,5,4. For this exegesis he distinguishes equal turpitude from turpitude on the sole part of the acquirer or the giver, respectively. Broadly speaking, robbery and usury are presented as instances of turpitude of the acquirer (*turpitudo solius accipientis*), which necessitates restitution to the giver.[1437] Surprisingly, he omits prostitution among his examples of turpitude of the sole giver (*turpitudo solius dantis*). In that category he places robbers and usurers who spend their ill-gotten gains on almsgiving but refuse to refrain from their evil intention to make profits on the basis of immoral activities altogether. Bernardine clearly wants

---

[1435] Bernardine of Siena, *Quadragesimale de Christiana religione*, feria 4, sermo 37, art. 2, cap. 2, in: Opera omnia, Venetiis 1745, tom. 1, p. 167: ' Si autem mihi licitum est dare rem meam gratis, multo magis licitum est mihi dare aliquid pro alio mihi concesso, quamvis mihi illud impie concedatur, et maxime ex quo aliqua temporalitas, sive vere, sive secundum ejus judicium et beneplacitum inde proveniat danti. Si vero jure divino, aut humano non aufertur alicui jurisdictio, vel potestas dandi aliquid meretrici pro locatione sui corporis, aut historioni pro suo histrionatu, et sic de aliis; non oportet ex aliis superannexis vitiositatibus sui juris quamdam aequalitatem et licentiam annullari.' Apart from the omission of some remarks regarding the contract of gaming, this is a mere copy of Pierre Jean d'Olivi, *De contractibus*, part. 3, art. 3, reg. 4, p. 311–312 (ed. Piron 1999).

[1436] Zimmermann, *The law of obligations*, p. 847–848, n. 91.

[1437] Bernardine, *Quadragesimale de Christiana religione*, feria 6, sermo 39, art. 2, cap. 1.

to close the door here to Christians suffering from the diabolic wickedness to pervertedly use a therapy as a strategic means of upholding the
sickness.[1438] A similar concern had been expressed in C.14, q.5, c.14.
Hence Bernardine's conclusion that only if the object of almsgiving really
belonged to lenders and thieves, could it lawfully be retained by the poor,
on condition that the poor had accepted the goods with a clean intention,
of course. If the givers had not had the power to dispose of these goods
(*potestas dandi*), or the poor had acted in bad faith, the profits had to be
restituted to their original owner, that is the robbed person or the borrower of the money.

Even more complex was the case of equal turpitude (*turpitudo utriusque*), in which the basic question was whether the morally questionable act provoked collateral damage or not. A judge or assessor selling
a sentence to the litigating party to whose benefit he would have had to
pass judgment anyway (*iustum iudicium*) was bound to make restitution
to that party on account of his extortionate practice.[1439] If this party had
had an intention of corrupting the judge regardless of the justice of its
claim, he had lost its dominion over the bribes and hence restitution had
to be made through almsgiving. Equal turpitude causing harm to third
parties gave rise to a fit of casuistry. To give just one example, Bernardine
held that a contract for assassination unequivocally entailed an obligation for the hired assassin to make restitution of his service fee to the
heir of the killed person. No considerations of unjustified enrichment are
brought in here—that would be the project of the Dominicans and Jesuits
in early modern times.

6.3.4   Sex for sale

At the outset of the sixteenth century, Tommaso de Vio Cajetan tried to
come to grips with agreements tainted by immorality through a juridical
analysis similar to the one of Olivi. Yet Thomas' heritage would turn out
to be elusive. And Cajetan would never reach the elegance of his Fran-

---

[1438] Bernardine, *Quadragesimale de Christiana religione*, feria 6, sermo 39, art. 2, cap. 2,
p. 179: 'Forte aliquis cogitat, et dicit: Multi sunt christiani divites, avari, cupidi; non habeo
peccatum, si illis abstulero, et pauperibus dedero: unde enim illi nil boni agunt mercedem
habere potero: sed hujusmodi cogitatio ex diaboli calliditate suggeritur. Nam, si totum
tribuat quod abstulerat, addit potius peccatum, quam minuat.'
[1439] Bernardine, *Quadragesimale de Christiana religione*, feria 6, sermo 39, art. 2,
cap. 3.

ciscan predecessor. In his attempt to explain the reasons behind Thomas Aquinas' differential treatment of simony and prostitution, however, he expressed two ideas that would slip through the filter and mind of subsequent authorities.

Firstly, Cajetan argues that giving money in exchange for sexual use of a prostitute's body is evil before the act has taken place (*antequam fiat*), but not once it has happened (*post factum*).[1440] In the former case, the payment takes place out of lust, whereas justice in exchange is the motivation behind the latter case. Paying for a simoniacal act, on the other hand, always implies evil, regardless of whether the service has already been rendered or not. Secondly, from a more technical point of view, Cajetan holds that the object of a contract for prostitution is saleable (*materia vendibilis*), whereas the object of a simoniacal contract is simply impossible. A little awkwardly, he considers prostitution to constitute a sale-purchase contract, in which the object of sale is the sexual use of the prostitute's body (*usus venereus*). Both conclusions of Cajetan would prove to be of massive influence on Soto and the Jesuit theologians.

6.3.5   *The* domina's *(quasi-)contractual claim to a wage*

Even though Cajetan could hope to have explained Thomas' distinction between prostitution and simony, the debate on the alleged distinction between prostitution and usurious contracts left much space for discussion. The critics, as testified in Francisco de Vitoria's commentary on Thomas, claimed that both were instances of extortionary practices:[1441]

[1440] Tommaso de Vio Cajetanus, *Commentaria ad Secundam Secundae divi Thomae*, in: *Sancti Thomae Aquinatis opera omnia iussu impensaque Leonis XIII edita*, tom. 8: *Secunda secundae Summae Theologiae a quaestione I ad quaestionem LVI*, Romae 1895, ad quaest. 32, art. 7, p. 258: 'Signum autem huius differentiae est quod dare mulieri pro venereo usu antequam fiat malum est, pro quanto imperatur a luxuria; post factum autem non est malum, sed actus iustitiae a nullo vitio imperatus: dare autem pro sacris, et huiusmodi, tam ante quam post factum, semper est malum.'

[1441] Francisco de Vitoria, *Commentarii in IIamIIae*, quaest. 32, art. 7, num. 2, in: Francisco de Vitoria, *Comentarios a la Secunda secundae de Santo Tomás*, edición preparada por V. Beltrán de Heredia, tom. 2: *De caritate et prudentia* (qq. 23–56), [Biblioteca de Teólogos Españoles, 3], Salamanca 1932, p. 192 (hereafter: ed. Beltrán de Heredia, tom. 2): 'Sed tamen contra hoc arguitur: quia ille qui paciscitur cum meretrice, ita se habet quod non libere dat, ad minus non magis libere quam ille qui dat ultra sortem. Ubique enim est pactum, ita quod sicut iste non mutuaret nisi acciperet aliquid ultra sortem, ita meretrix non daret corpus nisi acciperet pecuniam. Ergo ita libere dat unus sicut alius. Quare ergo usurarius tenetur ad restitutionem et non meretrix?'

If you make an agreement with a prostitute, you are not acting freely, or at least you are not acting more freely than someone who pays usurious interest payments. For in both cases the performance promised in exchange is rendered on a condition: I lend you money if you pay a surplus on top of the principal; I give you my body if you pay me a fee. So actually there is no difference in the degree of liberty as they pay. Why, then, is a usurer bound to make restitution, whereas a prostitute is not?

Vitoria would answer this question by making a subtle distinction between dominion including all uses over the good owned, and dominion excluding some uses—an argument he wrongly ascribes to Cajetan. Rather, it is much to the credit of Vitoria to have increased the juridical nature of the debate. Someone who is the *dominus* of a loan, for instance, has not the ability to sell that loan. Hence, he cannot lawfully demand a price or interest on top of the principal. In addition, the borrower has the ownership over his money, but not to the extent that he could use it with a view of paying interest on the basis of it. As a result, a usurer is bound to make restitution, not because the borrower entered into the contract involuntarily, but because the lender's ownership over the money does not include the possibility to sell its use (*non est dominus ad vendendum*). A prostitute, on the other hand, owns her body to the extent that she really can sell it (*domina ad vendendum corpus suum*). That is why she does not need to make restitution.

The argument was settled, then, through Vitoria's subtle application of the vocabulary of property law. But that, in turn, would create another problem, in regard to the special treatment of simony, in particular. For how could one claim that the consumer of a simoniacal service had no right to recover his money, since he could hardly be said to have lost his dominion over it through sin. The money could not be destined to almsgiving, then, but needed to be restored to its owner:[1442] 'What is the basis for claiming that, because he sinned in giving the money, he therefore lost dominion? This a non-conclusive argument. We should rather say that the money was his, and that he could not give it away, nor another receive it. Therefore the money remains his all the same.'

At this point, Vitoria pretends that other doctors attribute the standpoint just formulated to positive law. Curiously, he finds himself in need

---

[1442] Vitoria, *Commentarii in IIamIIae* (ed. Beltrán de Heredia, tom. 2), quaest. 32, art. 7, num. 3, p. 193: 'Unde valet: iste peccat dando pecuniam: ergo amittit dominium? Non valet consequentia. Arguitur sic: ista pecunia erat istius; et non potuit dare nec alius accipere: ergo manet ista pecunia sicut a principio.'

to point out that, despite the fact that these doctors never quote a specific passage to defend their views, he would base it on canon *Veniens ad nos* (X 5,3,19). Actually, he thinks this canonical regime to be an expression of the natural law. Natural law dictates that the benefice remains the property of the seller, and the money remains the property of the buyer of the simoniacal service. The obligatory regime of almsgiving that was made to correspond with simony by Thomas, was not the natural regime, according to Vitoria.

To be sure, Vitoria tries to narrow the disparity of opinion between himself and his thirteenth century master by admitting that a subsequent positive law had attached a penal sanction to simony, to the extent that after condemnation in court, the seller of the benefice would be urged to distribute his filthy lucre among the poor. Before that condemnation, however, he would be obliged to make restitution of the money to the buyer.[1443] Only through a penal sanction could the buyer be deprived of the ownership over his money. Thomas had merely envisaged the situation after the seller had been condemned in court, according to Vitoria, who preferred himself to adopt, expressly, the doctrine of the *Liber Extra*.

Vitoria even puts the case of contractual assassination on a par with the case of simony: even if both parties have sinned, the assassin needs to render the fee paid for his services to the principal, for the principal was and still is the owner of the money.[1444] Nevertheless, Vitoria's re-formulation of the case of prostitution in terms of a problem of just wage, to which we will turn now, was later also to become adopted to solve the problem of the contract for assassination: Jesuits like Lessius would simply state that a hired murderer, like a prostitute, had a right to retain a just remuneration for his services.

Vitoria made a major contribution to the debate on prostitution by affirming that a prostitute is entitled to a just remuneration or salary

---

[1443] Vitoria, *Commentarii in IIamIIae* (ed. Beltrán de Heredia, tom. 2), quaest. 32, art. 7, num. 4, p. 193–194: 'Ista est poena, quod detur alteri, non ementi. Ergo ante sententiam judicis non tenetur iste erogare in pauperes, immo debet restituere ei a quo accepit. [...] Et sic dico quod illud statum juris est poenale; non obligat ante prolationem sententiae. Et sic est intelligendus sanctus Thomas, quod pecunia illa non est restituenda ei a quo accepit.'

[1444] Francisco de Vitoria, *Commentarii in Secundam Secundae divi Thomae*, quaest. 62, art. 5, num. 7, p. 162–163: 'Sed pro nunc dico quod, stando solum in jure divino et naturali, secluso jure positivo, illa pecunia cadit sub restitutione, et non debet converti in pios usus, sed est restituenda vero domino, sicut de usuris restitutio facienda est illi a quo pecunia est accepta. Licet enim uterque peccaverit, tamen sic est facienda restitutio. Sicut de illo qui accepit pecunias ut occideret aliquem, tenetur restituere pecunias illi a quo accepit.'

(*stipendium*) for her performance. At the same time he applied Cajetan's ideas by making a fundamental distinction between a salary paid before (*ante*) or after (*post*) sexual intercourse had taken place. Regardless of the existence of a contract, Vitoria stresses that a client is always bound to pay an appropriate price or salary to the prostitute. For a claim to compensation not only lies by virtue of contract, but also on the grounds of what Soto would later interpret as unjust enrichment:[1445]

> A client is bound to pay a salary to the prostitute, not on the basis of contractual agreement alone, but also by virtue of the mere taking place of the deed, which entails a quasi-contract despite the absence of a real contract.

No doubt drawing on Cajetan, he further distinguishes between the giving of the salary as a means of persuading her to have sex (*ad movendum*), on the one hand, which he considers evil (*mala*) because of the evil purpose behind it, and the licit paying of the salary once the prostitute has acted (*peracta re*) on the other. The latter does not constitute a sin given that the final cause to this act of giving is not evil (*finis non est malus*).[1446] It should be noticed, however, that the question Vitoria raises here is of a moral, and not of a juridical nature. Consideration of the final cause concerns the morality, but not the juridical validity of the payment of the salary.

The question as to the just wage of a prostitute would gain increasing interest with Soto as the debate about contracts for sex turned ever more juridical. From now on, the debate would not only concern the dilemma of whether the ill-gotten gains from a somehow immoral contract could be retained, or were rather subject to restitution or almsgiving. Rather, the very initial starting point of the discussion would be questioned. The basic assumption would no longer be that a prostitute retaining a fee was grappling with qualms of conscience regarding the lawfulness of her retention.

[1445] Francisco de Vitoria, *Commentarii in Secundam Secundae divi Thomae*, quaest. 62, art. 5, num. 9, p. 164: 'Tertio dico, quod non solum ex vi pacti, sed ratione actus, etiamsi non facerent pactum, quia virtualiter videntur facere, tenetur vir dare stipendium aliquod.'

[1446] Francisco de Vitoria, *Commentarii in Secundam Secundae divi Thomae*, quaest. 62, art. 5, num. 8, p. 163: 'Respondetur quod dare stipendium scorto non est malum nisi ex fine, quia datio de se est bona, nec illa ideo quod sit meretrix perdit jus ad hoc quod non possit sibi aliquid dari. Unde si datio fiat ad movendum illam ad fornicationem, est mala, et qui dat peccat mortaliter. [...] Secundo dico, quod peracta re, id est post fornicationem, si dat aliquid tamquam mercedem, bene potest ei licite dare, et non est peccatum, quia jam illic finis non est malus.'

Two novel perspectives would substitute for the ancient, restitution-oriented approach. First, the attacks would now be launched from the outside, with the client wondering if he has a legitimate title to bring the prostitute to court and recover the fee he had paid in exchange for her services. And secondly, doubts would now shift towards the question whether the prostitute could obtain a wage altogether if her or his client refused to pay the promised remuneration. A significant part of the solutions Soto would formulate as to those problems were actually inspired by his overt attack against Juan de Medina. That is why we must first turn to the latter's dissonant voice now, before we examine the continuation of the debate in the most influential of Dominican scholastics.

6.4   MORALISTS, REALISTS, THEOLOGIANS AND CANONISTS

6.4.1   *The rigorist approach*

6.4.1.1   *Sex outside wedlock is mortal sin*

Seemingly irritated by the casualness with which his colleagues and predecessors had dealt with contracts for immoral behavior, Juan de Medina was eager to tap into the rigorism of the biblical and patristic tradition in order to advocate and radicalize the rejection of immoral (sexual) behavior. He would even dedicate a whole chapter to the demonstration of the forbidden nature by divine as well as natural law standards of intercourse between two non-married persons (*meretricium seu simplex fornicatio*), and, all the more so, of extra-marital sex involving at least one married person (*moechia seu adulterium*).

Medina advocated a most extensive interpretation, indeed, of the sixth commandment not to commit adultery, so as to make it encompass all sexual intercourse outside wedlock. This exegesis recommended itself, according to him, by analogy with the extensive interpretation the moral theologians were used to apply to the seventh commandment not to steal, to the effect that it included every type of unjust enrichment.[1447]

[1447] Medina, *De poenitentia, restitutione, et contractibus*, tom. 2, Cod. *De rebus restituendis*, quaest. 19, par. *Nec obstant*, p. 127–128: 'Et quamvis nomen moechiae stricte non nisi pro adulterio accipiatur, ex dictis tamen constat etiam ad omnem illicitum concubitum extendi, ut expresse ait Augustinus et habetur 32, q. 4, cap. Meretrices. Et sicut nomine furti omnis illicita rei alienae usurpatio intelligitur, quando in Decalogo furtum prohibetur, ita omnis illicitus concubitus prohiberi intelligitur, quando moechia prohibetur.'

He claimed patristic support for this thesis in Ambrose's and Augustine's commentary on *Exodus* 20, as well as in the ecclesiastical prohibition on extra-marital sex contained in C.32, q.4, c.4. It is commonly known, of course, that the classical canon law took a tough stand on any sort of intercourse outside wedlock (*fornicatio*),[1448] with Gratian considering fornication an equally grave offense as perjury, or even some types of homicide in C.3, q.11, d.p.c.3, and in C.22, q.1, c.17. But Medina also welcomed Emperor Justinian's exhortations to chastity to demonstrate that Roman law, too, prohibited fornication.[1449]

With evidence from the Old Testament, the Gospel, as well as from Paul's letters abounding, Medina had a relatively easy job to argue that simple fornication was not merely prohibited by positive, ecclesiastical and civil law but also by divine law.[1450] As to the possible objection of a couple of stories which could be cited as counter-evidence, Medina was not impressed. He relativized the annoyingly heroic deeds performed by the whore Rachab, who had disobeyed the King of Jericho in order to give shelter to the envoys of Joshua. Neither did he feel bothered by the quite unorthodox story of Tamar, who went unpunished even though she solicited as a prostitute only to get pregnant from Judah, her unsuspecting father-in-law.[1451] The story of Tamar had nevertheless formed the kernel of Adrian of Utrecht's defence of a prostitute's right to retain the money received. Later, it would even be picked up again as a core argument by

---

[1448] As is evident from the terminological digression on the differences in meaning between *fornicatio, stuprum, adulterium, incestus* and *raptus* in C.36, q.1, d.p.c.2, *fornicatio* was used as a generic term to denote any type of sexual intercourse save for that between married persons. In a more specific sense it coincided with *meretricium*, defined in Dist.34, c.16 quite generically as the furnishing of sexual pleasure—a large concept which in the absence of specification seems to have covered any form of promiscuity, whether paid or not. Similarly, Ulpian's understanding in D. 23,2,43,3 of prostitution had not implied mercenariness as of essence.

[1449] E.g. Nov. 14 in *Corporis Iustinianaei Volumen parvum* (ed. Gothofredi), tom. 4, col. 118: 'Sancimus igitur omnes quidem secundum quod possunt castitatem agere. (...) Nulli fiduciam esse pascere meretricem et in domo habere mulieres aut publice prostituere ad luxuriam et pro alio quodam negotio talia mercari (...).'

[1450] Deut. 23:17; Tob. 4:13; Mt. 15:11; 1 Thess. 4:3; Eph. 5; 1 Cor 6:9.

[1451] The story of Tamar is told in Gen. 38, 1–30. References to Rachab are included in Joshua 2 and 6, and Hebr. 11:31. Medina finds an excuse for Tamar's sexually immoral behavior in that she only demanded her due, that is to have children from her husbands, Er and Onan, who had spilled their seed, though, and hence unlawfully denied her the child she barely wanted. Tamar had been driven by a legitimate zeal for justice (*zelo justitiae*), then. As for Rachab, Medina is desperate to show that actually in this context the epithet 'whore' (*meretrix*) has the sole meaning of 'hostess' (*hospita seu caupona*) without implying any promiscuous behavior. Cf. Medina, *De poenitentia, restitutione, et contractibus*, tom. 2, Cod. *De rebus restituendis*, quaest. 19, par. *Iam ad rationes*, p. 128.

Hugo Grotius.[1452] But Medina cleverly tried to hide that such authoritative a scholar as Pope Adrian VI had based his opinion on the story of Judah and Tamar.[1453]

Our radical theologian had a harder job, however, in convincing his audience that simple fornication was also prohibited as a matter of natural law. He argues that natural law was incapable of binding under an eternal penalty of sin, because natural law was ignorant about sanctions in heaven until God's economy of salvation was to be revealed. A vague reference to the third book of Aristotle's *Nicomachean Ethics*, completed by an equally questionable interpretation of Paul's letter to the Romans, is expected to show that in the state of nature mankind could already grasp the notion of mortal sin. Yet regardless of the credibility of these claims about the natural law foundations of the sinfulness of simple fornication, the upshot of Medina's as well Durand de Saint-Pourçain's argument is that sex outside of a legally confirmed stable relationship constitutes mortal sin.[1454] The radical conclusions Medina would draw from this insight in connection with the validity of an agreement to pay for prostitution were not long in coming.

6.4.1.2 *Medina I: radical Augustinianism*

Heavily imbued with Augustinian ideas, Medina opened up a new source to the debate on prostitution that would defy and shake up the Thomistic heritage. It would even create some confusion with Medina himself, since he seems to have been torn between his enthusiastic reading of Augustine's theoretical reflections, on the one hand, and the practical need to safeguard a decent living for a person who was to be considered as a weak and needy creature, on the other.

[1452] Adrian of Utrecht, *Quaestiones in quartum sententiarum praesertim circa sacramenta*, Parisiis 1516, tit. *De restitutione*, par. *Ad quaestionem*, f. 51r. For Grotius, see below.

[1453] Medina, *De poenitentia, restitutione, et contractibus*, tom. 2, Cod. *De rebus restituendis*, quaest. 20, par. *Et per haec*, p. 133: 'Nec placet eorum [sic] sententia qui dicunt meretricem posse licite mercedem pro stibuli recipere per viam mercedis, etiam via donationis seclusa, quod probant exemplo Iudae et Thamar (...)'.

[1454] Medina, *De poenitentia, restitutione, et contractibus*, tom. 2, Cod. *De rebus restituendis*, quaest. 19, par. *Occasione*, p. 125: 'Quod enim sit peccatum, omnes fatentur. Et probat Durandus, quia vel talis actus ordinatur ad delectationem, et sic malus est, cum in malum finem ordinetur; aut ordinatur in prolem, et sic etiam malus est, quia ut plurimum cedit in malum prolis, eo quod cum parentes lege coniugali iuncti non sint, non eam adhibent curam in liberorum educatione quam adhiberent si copulati essent.'

It was a famous passage in Augustine's letter to Macedonius, in particular, which brought Medina to radically question Thomas' position that a prostitute did not need to make restitution. As a Christian, had not a prostitute, by analogy with a lawyer who had accepted a bribe, a duty to make restitution to her client?[1455] Augustine argued, indeed, that it would be appropriate for the lawyer to return the money he had received to plead an unjust case, or to resort to unjust practices to defend his client. That would be real justice, according to Augustine. In so thinking, Augustine formulated a Christian alternative to Paul's idea that no action for recovery could lie for someone who had bribed a judge. The Roman jurist Paul's viewpoint became expressed in law *Ubi* (D. 12,5,3). Augustine acknowledged the realistic attitude behind the civil law regime—where one could find a lawyer willing to spontaneously render the bribes he had received?—but from a man reborn in Christ he would demand an effort to go beyond these natural tendencies and render his ill-gotten gains (*merces iniquitatis*).

By analogy with Augustine's example of the bribed lawyer, Medina argued, an honest prostitute should not retain the salary received in exchange for her inequitable services. Infused with Augustine's argument, he then set out both to strengthen his case about the prostitute's duty to make restitution and to extend it into a general prohibition on the retention of profits deriving from a sinful act (*actus peccaminosus*). Never is it lawful to receive money in exchange for a sinful act, let alone to retain the

---

[1455] Augustinus, *Epistola ad Macedonium* (= PL 33, ep. 153, 6, 25, c. 664–665): 'Verumtamen si iustitia sincerius consulatur, iustius dicitur advocato, Redde quod accepisti, quando contra veritatem stetisti, iniquitati adfuisti, iudicem fefellisti, iustam causam oppressisti, de falsitate vicisti (quod vides multos honestissimos et disertissimos viros, non solum impune, verum etiam gloriose videri sibi committere); quam cuiquam in quolibet officio militanti, Redde quod accepisti, quando iubente iudice cuicumque causae necessarium hominem tenuisti, ne resisteret vinxisti, ne fugeret inclusisti, postremo aut permanente lite exhibuisti, aut finita dimisisti. Sed illud cur advocato non dicatur in promptu est, quia scilicet ita non vult homo repetere quod patrono, ut male vinceret, dedit; sicut non vult reddere quod ab adversario, cum male vicisset, accepit. Quis tandem advocatus, aut ex advocato ita vir optimus facile reperitur, qui suscepto suo dicat: Recipe quod mihi, cum tibi male adessem, dedisti; et redde adversario tuo quod, me agente, inique abstulisti? Et tamen quem prioris non rectae vitae rectissime poenitet, etiam hoc facere debet, ut si ille qui inique litigavit, non vult admonitus corrigere iniquitatem, eius tamen iniquitatis nolit iste habere mercedem: nisi forte restituendum est alienum, quod per furtum clanculo aufertur, et restituendum non est quod in ipso foro ubi peccata puniuntur, decepto iudice, et circumventis legibus obtinetur! Quid dicam de usuris, quas etiam ipsae leges et iudices reddi iubent? An crudelior est qui subtrahit aliquid vel eripit diviti, quam qui trucidat pauperem fenore? Haec atque huiusmodi male utique possidentur, et vellem restituerentur; sed non est quo iudice repetantur.'

ill-gotten gains, unless another just or honest title can legitimize it. This is the point of view with which Medina had 'once' sympathized because he was blinded by his enthusiasm for Augustine.[1456] This first version of Medina's viewpoint (hereafter: Medina I) derived further support from the Gospel story of Judas parting with the money he had received to sell out Jesus.[1457] However, Medina later changed his ideas on the subject (hereafter: Medina II).

Medina I not only relied on theological considerations and radical Augustinianism, but on legal argument, too. He claimed, first, that a sinful good or act is to be deemed unsaleable, given that its market value, just like its moral value, amounts to zero. In the case of a contract for prostitution, for instance, the balance of justice could not possibly be guaranteed, since the value of the remuneration given could never be compensated by the simply non-existing value of the carnal use of a woman's body.[1458] Furthermore, an extensive reading of canon *Veniens ad nos* (X 5,3,19), which introduces an obligation to make restitution of riches obtained through simony, was held necessary.[1459] An equally extensive interpretation was to be applied to canon *Quia plerique* (X 3,49,8), to canon *Quum sit* (X 5,6,16) and to canon *Ad liberandam* (X 5,6,17), which held that whoever sold weapons to the Turkish enemy was obliged to spend his ill-gotten gains on charitable causes supporting the Christian resistance movement in the Holy Land.

But not only canon law could be quoted in favor of a general duty to make restitution of ill-gotten gains. There was Roman law too, according to a naive, or rather a shrewd reading by Medina I. In granting a *condictio ob turpem causam* to the victim of extortionary practices, e.g. to a person forced to pay for a service another person was bound to render him anyway, paragraph *Quod si turpis causa* (D. 12,5,1,2) and paragraph

---

[1456] Medina, *De poenitentia, restitutione, et contractibus*, tom. 2, Cod. *De rebus restituendis*, quaest. 20, par. *Aliquando*, p. 132: 'Aliquando mihi visum fuit generaliter cum illis tenere, qui dicunt quod pro nullo opere peccaminoso, sive commissionis, sive omissionis, quando tale opus in se peccatum est et non solum ob circumstantiam depravantem, licitum est pretium recipere, nec ob illam causam lucrum huiusmodi retinere, nisi alius titulus iustus vel honestus concurrat.'

[1457] Mt. 27: 3–10. Medina falsely claims that Augustine produced this biblical argument to support the views he expounded in his letter to Macedonius.

[1458] Medina, *De poenitentia, restitutione, et contractibus*, tom. 2, Cod. *De rebus restituendis*, quaest. 20, par. *Tertio*, p. 130: 'pretium datum alicuius valoris est, corporis autem traditio, cum peccatum sit in casu, nullius valoris est'.

[1459] Medina seems to endorse Vitoria's criticism of Thomas (cf. supra) that restitution is to be made directly to the giver, and should not take the form of almsgiving.

Item (D. 12,5,2,1) supported the case for a general duty to make restitution of ill-gotten gains. Was not everybody held by precept not to do evil?
Hence, Medina concludes, demanding a price in order to commit a sin is
to be considered an extortionary practice, which gives rise to a claim for
recovery.[1460]

Yet the attack is often the best form of defence, certainly if good
defending starts requiring painstakingly sophisticated contrivances. That
might have been a reason why Medina combined the construction of his
own daring opinion with the mounting of a well-covered but direct attack
upon traditional authority. Cleverly availing himself of the internal conflict that had arisen within the Thomistic tradition itself,[1461] Medina made
no secret of his wondering why the *communis opinio* would recommend
restitution in case of equal turpitude, say simony, while the giver could
hardly be said to have lost the ownership over his money on account of
his shameful act.[1462]

In regard to the traditional, seemingly unproblematic refusal to recognize a right of retention in case of turpitude of the sole receiver, Medina
would boldly challenge the complacency of his adversaries by demonstrating that an unjust receiving did not automatically bar the possibility
of lawful retention at all. Did not secret compensation (*occulta compensatio*), at least when public legal remedies were still available, constitute
an unlawful way of receiving, and yet produce a lawful right of retention?
Did not marrying a woman whom, under oath, you had sworn never to

---

[1460] This syllogism does not hold, of course. The logical conclusion would have been
that charging a price in order *not* to commit a sin is to be considered an extortionary practice which gives rise to a claim for recovery—a conclusion which would obviously have
been of no use for Medina's purposes. Cf. Medina, *De poenitentia, restitutione, et contractibus*, tom. 2, Cod. *De rebus restituendis*, quaest. 20, par. *Quarto*, p. 133: 'Quarto idem videtur,
quia pro opere ad quod quis de praecepto tenetur, non est licitum aliquid recipere. Igitur
nec pro opero peccaminoso, ad cuius oppositum ex praecepto tenetur. Antecedens patet
ff. de condictione ob turpam [sic!] causam. Si dedi tibi ne sacrilegium facias, ne furtum
committas, ne hominem occidas, condici potest. Item si tibi dedero, ut mihi reddas rem
depositam apud te l. 5 titulo allegato, teneris acceptum restituere.' This argument was later
to be refuted by Martín de Azpilcueta in his *Enchiridion sive manuale confessariorum et
poenitentium*, cap. 17, num. 31, p. 288.

[1461] See Vitoria, supra, p. 434.

[1462] Medina, *De poenitentia, restitutione, et contractibus*, tom. 2, Cod. *De rebus restituendis*, quaest. 20, par. *Sunt tamen*, p. 131: 'Sunt tamen in hac praefata responsione aliqua, quae
difficultate non carent. Primum, quia dicunt, quod quando turpitudo se tenet ex parte
dantis, non est illi acceptum restituendum, quia obstat ei sua turpitudo. Nam quamvis
qui turpiter dedit, dignus sit qui rem datam amittat, non tamen ob id quod turpiter dedit,
perdit ius ad rem datam in conscientiam.'

marry, constitute an unlawful way of receiving, and yet produce a lawful right of retention?

The Thomists' conclusion that a duty to make restitution automatically follows from turpitude on the part of the receiver, as in the case of usury or theft, did not universally hold true, then. In this connection, Medina makes reference to the canonical adage (X 3,31,16) that 'there is much that is forbidden, but once it has been performed, it holds' (*multa fieri prohibentur, quae tamen facta tenent*).[1463] This adage would later play an important role in Lessius' thoughts on immoral promises.

6.4.1.3   *Medina II: waiting for the liberal fornicator*

Interestingly, Medina also mentions a third principle that allegedly formed part of the common opinion. In fact, though, it is formulated in a way that sounds more like an anticipation of a ground principle of the ultimate analysis of prostitution and contracts tainted by immorality which he proceeds to make. The doctors are said to be of the view that if the turpitude concerns the circumstances of the acquisition (*ex parte modi aut circumstantiae*) rather than the receiving itself, no restitution is to be made.[1464] Prostitution is thought to fall under this category—a proposition Medina firmly rejects on account of Augustine's admonition to make restitution of ill-gotten gains (*merces iniquitatis*). But together with the idea that there

---

[1463] This maxim is based on X 3,31,16, which litteraly reads as follows in *Corpus juris canonici* (ed. Gregoriana), part. 2, col. 1248, l. 21–23: '(. . .) quia multa fieri prohibentur, quae si facta fuerint, obtinent roboris firmitatem.' The *correctores Romani* observe that the word '*roboris*' is omitted in the oldest and best manuscripts.

This canon draws on a letter written in 1198 by Innocent III to the archbishop of Pisa in which he settles the frequently recurring question whether irregularity ensuing from a novice making his profession during his probationary period invalidates the profession or not. Apparently, the monasteries had been struggling to cope with the rush of people looking after a particularly quick integration into the monastic community in order to be able to benefit from preferential treatment as a monk while sick, but eager to escape the contraints of the monastic life and turn back to the pleasures of the outside world (marriage in particular) as soon as they had recovered. As a means of obtaining dismissal, they then tried to invoke the irregularity that had affected their profession. But Innocent III was intent on eradicating this kind of opportunism, and ruled once and for all that regardless of the forbidden character of a premature profession, it would remain valid once it had taken place.

[1464] Medina, *De poenitentia, restitutione, et contractibus*, tom. 2, Cod. *De rebus restituendis*, quaest. 20, par. *Si vero*, p. 131: 'Si vero turpitudo se tenet ex parte modi aut circumstantiae, ita ut lucri acceptio in se prohibita non sit, tunc sic turpiter acquisitum non est restituendum, ut exemplificant de meretricio lucro, in quo licet modus seu medium per quod acquiritur sit illicitum, non tamen ipsa lucri acceptio: sicut habetur ff. de condictione ob turpem causam, l. 4, par. 1.'

could still be another legitimate title or cause available for remuneration (that is a cause parallel to the intrinsic unlawfulness to receive a fee on the basis of the sinful service itself) the foundations of Medina's revised viewpoint (hereafter: Medina II), have now been laid.

The ultimate and new view of Medina starts from the assumption that there are two kinds of sinful acts (*opus peccaminosum*). That depends on whether the act is intrinsically evil or forbidden, on the one hand, or merely illicit because of circumstances of time and place, on the other. Acquiring and retaining money obtained in exchange for a sinful act is only licit if the act is neither forbidden nor sinful in itself. Otherwise, restitution is to be made.[1465] Yet this most logical and Augustinian-like conclusion would definitely have run counter to another one of Medina's sensitivities, if it had not been slightly modified.

Medina's evangelical concern for the poor and weak urges him, indeed, to acknowledge that even in case of an intrinsically evil transaction, like in the case of prostitution, its performer can still count on some sort of compensation. This reward should not be based on the transaction, however, but on a title (*causa*) entirely extrinsic to the transaction. Practically speaking, donation as an act of the virtue of liberality constitutes this extrinsic title.[1466]

[1465] Medina, *De poenitentia, restitutione, et contractibus*, tom. 2, Cod. *De rebus restituendis*, quaest. 20, par. *Est itaque*, p. 133: 'Est itaque in hac quaestione de opere peccaminoso distinguendum. Nam quoddam est tale ratione sui, quia scilicet vel per se malum est, vel in se prohibitum. Aliud vero est illicitum, non ratione sui, sed ratione circumstantiae, scilicet loci, temporis, scandali, voti, aut iuramenti etc. Pro primo non est licitum pretium recipere nec retinere, bene tamen pro secundo, ut patet ex dictis, maxime si opus tale sit, quod seclusa illa circumstantia est pretio comparabile.'

[1466] Medina, *De poenitentia, restitutione, et contractibus*, tom. 2, Cod. *De rebus restituendis*, par. *Ad aliud secundum*, p. 136: 'Ad aliud secundum, in quo universalius quaerebatur, an sit necessario restituendum, quod per actum peccaminosum est acquisitum, puta, per illicitam negotiationem, patet ex dictis responsio. Nam si negotiatio seu contractus in se illicitus est, nisi interveniat donatio, lucrum sic acquisitum retineri non potest. Si vero sit contractus seu negotiatio in se licita et iusta, ubi scilicet aequalitas inter datum et acceptum servetur, sit tamen ex circumstantia illicita, ratione, scilicet, temporis, loci, personae aut scandali, etc. Tunc non est sic acquisitum necessario restituendum.'
Perhaps Medina was inspired to solve the problem of remunerating prostitutes by making reference to donation as a just cause while reading Adrian of Utrecht's statement that donations have the exceptional quality of not being invalidated where other promises and contracts do. Cf. *Quaestiones in quartum sententiarum*, tit. *De restitutione*, par. *Ad rationes*, f. 51r: 'Sed quidquid de isto sit, nego maiorem argumenti, quia de iure multae stipulationes et promissiones sunt irritae ubi donationes sunt validae. Stipulatur enim meretrix turpiter pro futuro concubitu, et omnis turpis stipulatio est inutilis iuxta l. generaliter, ff. de verb. oblig., et tamen donatio valet etc. Stipulatio qua leno mercedem lenocinii stipulatur non valet, et tamen donata [sic], quia de praesente utriusque turpitudo versatur, tenet.'

As to the question whether, universally speaking, restitution is always necessary if profits have been made through a peccable act, say through an illicit
transaction, this is our solution. If a transaction or contract is intrinsically
illicit, the profits based on it cannot be retained, unless these profits constitute a donation (*nisi interveniat donatio*). If a transaction or contract is licit
and just as it is, on the other hand—which means that equality between
what is given and what is received is observed—and the contract is merely
surrounded by circumstantial illicitness of place, time, person, or scandal,
then the profits are not necessarily to be restored.

At this point, Medina recognizes that an extensive interpretation of canon
Quia plerique (X 3,49,8) does not make sense, given that it is a specific
regulation applying to Jews.[1467] If it were a general rule, then in the same
passage no explicit extension would have been needed to make Turks and
atheists fall within its scope of application. The decretals canon *Quum sit*
(X 5,6,16) and canon *Ad liberandam* (X 5,6,17) are merely to be considered
containing a penal sanction. Hence they do not produce a duty to make
restitution in the court of conscience unless by judicial decision.[1468]

What is more, Medina II opposes the view that the canon law treatment of simony or Augustine's discussion of bribed lawyers can be put
on a par with prostitution. At least twice Medina emphasizes that the
case of prostitution is different (*non est simile*).[1469] Granted, a prostitute
cannot derive any profits from her peccable act, but anything received on
account of donation can be legitimately retained.

Prostitution, then, turns out to be a perfect example of the first sort of
peccable acts (those that are intrinsically evil).[1470] Unlike a sale-purchase
contract between businessmen concluded on a feast-day, in which contractual equilibrium can be established despite the circumstantial illicitness of time, a prostitution agreement is of no worth. As a consequence,
any ill-gotten gain on account of the contract itself is to be restored. By

---

[1467] Medina, *De poenitentia, restitutione, et contractibus*, tom. 2, Cod. *De rebus restituendis*, quaest. 20, par. *Secundo*, p. 136.

[1468] Medina, *De poenitentia, restitutione, et contractibus*, tom. 2, Cod. *De rebus restituendis*, quaest. 20, par. *Ad aliud*, p. 136.

[1469] Medina, *De poenitentia, restitutione, et contractibus*, tom. 2, Cod. *De rebus restituendis*, quaest. 20, par. *Per haec* and par. *Ad tertiam*, p. 135.

[1470] Yet there is no denying that Medina's line of reasoning remains irritatingly wavering. In refuting the analogy with simony, for instance, he explicitly says that the case of
prostitution is different, because it is only illicit as to its *modus*, while the receiving of the
service itself is not illicit; cf. Medina, *De poenitentia, restitutione, et contractibus*, tom. 2,
Cod. *De rebus restituendis*, quaest. 20, par. *Ad tertiam*, p. 135.

definition, you simply cannot receive a salary in exchange for a worthless sexual service:[1471]

> Neither a public nor a secret whore can receive or retain the price rendered for her services as a price corresponding to the value of this unspeakable act. She can, however, if another title (*causa*) is available, namely an entirely free and intentional donation by the giver, notwithstanding the fact that the immoral act is like the *causa sine qua non* of that donation. I disagree with those maintaining that a whore can lawfully receive the price of her services as a salary, regardless of a donation.

Medina simply refuses to think of prostitution in terms of a legally valid contract that is subject to the rules of justice in exchange. Incidentally, he applies the same reasoning to contracts for murder. Every remuneration for such immoral services, then, must take place on another, purely extra-contractual, or moral level. In Medina's eyes, with prostitution or assassination there is no such thing as a contractual performance that needs to be offset by a counterperformance. Contrary to what happens in mainstream scholastic thought on prostitution, then, for Medina *causa* in the more modern sense of final motivating cause, or intention, comes to play a vital role in judging the prostitute's right to retain her ill-gotten profits:[1472]

> The specific intention (*animus*) with which you receive or retain ill-gotten gains is of the greatest importance.

If a client gives money to a whore as a means of paying her for her services, and the prostitute receives the money with the intention of receiving the just salary for her performance, then she cannot retain the money. Only if a client gives money out of liberality, that is without regard to the performance he enjoyed, and the prostitute receives the money knowing that it is not a compensation for her sexual services, does no obligation to

1471 Medina, *De poenitentia, restitutione, et contractibus*, tom. 2, Cod. *De rebus restituendis*, quaest. 20, par. *Et per haec*, p. 133.
1472 Medina, *De poenitentia, restitutione, et contractibus*, tom. 2, Cod. *De rebus restituendis*, quaest. 20, par. *Respondetur*, p. 134: 'Ita in proposito, cum is qui ad meretricem ingreditur sciat opus ipsum fornicarium illicitum esse et animae saltem nihil prodesse, sed mortaliter obesse, et sciens et volens dat aliquid quod valorem operis nefarii cognoscit excedere, videtur condonare quod dat, et ita poterit a meretrice non turpiter, sed licite recipi et retineri, modo illud non tanquam pretium suo operi fornicario debitum accipiat. Nam si sic illud, quia ob ipsum opus sibi debitum accipiat, peccat accipiendo, et si vult illud sic acquisitum licite retinere, opus est animum mutet, quo scilicet velit illud tenere eo modo, quo potest, sive velut pretium corporis, sive velut donatum. Ac proinde non parum refert, quo animo haec turpia lucra accipiantur aut retineantur.'

make restitution arise. If a prostitute receives money as a salary corresponding to the—worthless—value of the use of her body, she has only one chance of lawfully retaining it, namely by changing her mind and considering the money as a present.

It would only take the genius of Domingo de Soto, however, to radically put this subjectivist turn to a halt.

6.4.2   *The pragmatic approach*

6.4.2.1   *Soto on the moral limits to 'freedom of contract'*

Medina had not fundamentally changed the restitution-oriented scope of the debate, nor reached a conclusion that would lead to major practical changes in the patrimonial situation of prostitutes. Still, the alternative theoretical framework he had mounted to challenge the Thomistic tradition would remain a steady, thought-provoking bone of contention. The re-action to Medina would definitely be as strong as his action, which need not come as a surprise, given that those who felt provoked to take up the gauntlet were intellectual giants like Soto and Covarruvias, to whom nothing was left but to show their true colours.

Starting with Soto, an important shift in the scope of the debate took place. To be sure, restitution inevitably remained a central issue for him as well as for other early modern theologians. Yet in his treatise *On justice and right* the problem of prostitution becomes embedded in a context made up of a far more juridical vocabulary. Contract, for example, is fundamentally analyzed again (remember the Franciscans) as a vehicle of transferring property rights (*dominium*).[1473] Occasionally, even a much more procedural approach pops up as claims and remedies before the external court ensuing from a contract for sex are highlighted.

Significantly, we find Soto discussing immoral transactions for the first time as he engages in an explicit debate about the extent of an individual's right to self-determination. The heading of the article in which transactions involving an immoral object are mentioned reads as follows: as a matter of natural law, are there any limits to individual autonomy and the universal right to freely dispose of your *dominium*?[1474] The argument put

---

[1473] For details, see the previous chapter (Formal limitations on 'freedom of contract').
[1474] Soto, *De iustitia et iure* (ed. fac. V. Diego Carro – M. González Ordóñez, vol. 2), lib. 4, quaest. 5, art. 1 (*utrum sua quisque voluntate naturali iure valeat rei suae dominium in alterum transferre*), p. 307.

forward by those rejecting the idea of unlimited 'contractual liberty' is precisely based on a consideration of immoral contracts like prostitution:[1475]

> If anybody were allowed to alienate his *dominium* as he likes, that would
> mean that in exchange for an immoral object he could confer upon another
> the property right over his money by paying a price or a salary. But this
> is a false conclusion. Take the case of someone bribing a judge, hiring an
> assassin, or paying to commit usury or simony. Even if he pays out of his
> own will, the property right over his money will not be conferred upon the
> other party. This is what the laws have decreed, and hence it is not a natural
> law principle that anyone can freely donate his goods. Moreover, some even
> believe that these laws also apply to prostitution, since with good reason a
> whore is denied the acquisition of the property right over any kind of remu-
> neration for the use of her body.

For the first time, then, we see the issue of the moral limits to 'contractual freedom' being formulated as such—with Soto having a dig at
Medina right from the start (some even believe...). Moreover, the moral
constraints to the free power of disposal are formulated in regard to the
object (*res turpis*) of contract as a property-transferring transaction. Put
in Aristotelian terminology, it is the morality of the material cause (*causa
materialis*) which is considered relevant to the juridical validity of a contract, not motivation or final cause.

As to the initial question about the extent of individual freedom, by
bringing Roman law into the debate, Soto tries to ward off the scepticism
that was raised through pointing out the allegedly immoral consequences
that would follow from a recognition of an unlimited right to self-determination. He quotes Inst. 2,1,40, and paragraph *Hae quoque res* (D. 41,1,9,3) to
claim that nothing is more natural and equitable than to respect the will
of the owner.[1476] Soto must have been inspired by the canon law tradition in formulating this argument.[1477] He proceeds to found man's right

---

[1475] Soto, *De iustitia et iure* (ed. fac. V. Diego Carro – M. González Ordóñez, vol. 2),
lib. 4, quaest. 5, art. 1, par. *Tertio*, p. 308, cited above, n. 1265. No doubt Soto was inspired
by Adrian in formulating this hypothetical critique on the approval of prostitution as a
licence for other immoral contracts. Cf. Adrian of Utrecht, *Quaestiones in quartum sententiarum*, tit. *De restitutione*, par. *Quaeritur alia quaestio*, f. 51r: 'Praeterea si donatio facta
meretrici valeret et transferret rei dominium, etiam valeret stipulatio qua ipsi aliquid promittitur. Sed hoc non par. minor [sic] patet, quia omnes stipulationes turpes nullius sunt
momenti aut roboris.'
[1476] D. 41,1,9,3 (Gaius): 'Hae quoque res, quae traditione nostrae fiunt, iure gentium
nobis adquiruntur: nihil enim tam conveniens est naturali aequitati quam voluntatem
domini volentis rem suam in alium transferre ratam haberi.' Justinian simply copied this
passage from Gaius into his own textbook on law (Inst. 2,1,40).
[1477] Notably by Panormitanus and Adrian of Utrecht. See below.

to self-determination on Gen. 1:26, which reveals the creation of man in the image of God. Yet in an Aristolian vein he concludes that there are nonetheless limits to the basic principle of absolute self-determination due to man's social and political nature (*homo naturaliter animal civile*).[1478] The law, issued by the public authorities, can legitimately limit individual autonomy in order to protect the weak, to punish delictual behavior, and to promote the common good. As Cicero underscored, the interest of the individual is identical to the interest of the community.[1479] Moreover, Roman law itself suggests that natural equity implies both absolute and restricted 'freedom of contract', Soto says. On account of natural equity, Ulpian claims in D. 4,4,1pr. that minors must be protected by imposing form requirements. Yet in D. 2,14,1pr. Ulpian makes a case for general enforceability of agreements on the same basis of natural equity.[1480]

As is obvious from the previous chapter on the formal aspects of 'freedom of contract' in early modern scholasticism, the external influence on individuals' transactions exercised by public authority is mainly felt through legally imposed requirements on the conclusion of contract and the abilities to enter into a contract. Moral considerations do matter, too, and find their expression in the prohibition of certain types of contract, like with certain games. There is no doubt, according to Soto, that fornication is immoral as a matter of natural law. Fornication is not merely evil by virtue of a prohibition imposed by positive law.[1481] Soto maintains that the opposite view is heretical.

6.4.2.2   *The market price for sex*

Typical of the persistence of the doctrine of restitution in early modern scholastic contract doctrine, is that we need to turn to Soto's chapters on the ways of making restitution in order to find a discussion of prostitution and a host of other immoral transactions. There we find Soto re-affirming,

---

[1478] Soto, *De iustitia et iure* (ed. fac. V. Diego Carro – M. González Ordóñez, vol. 2), lib. 4, quaest. 5, art. 1, p. 309; quoted above, n. 1266. For parallels in other scholastic authors, see the previous chapter.

[1479] Cicero, *De officiis* (Ed. Testard, vol. 2), 3, 6, 26–27, p. 83: 'Ergo unum debet esse omnibus propositum ut eadem sit utilitas unius cuiusque et universorum; quam si ad se quisque rapiet, dissolvetur omnis humana consortio.'

[1480] D. 2,14,1pr. (Ulpian): 'Huius edicti aequitas naturalis est. Quid enim tam congruum fidei humanae, quam ea quae inter eos placuerunt servare?'; D. 4,4,1pr. (Ulpian): 'Hoc edictum praetor naturalem aequitatem secutus proposuit, quo tutelam minorum suscepit.'

[1481] Soto, *De iustitia et iure* (ed. fac. V. Diego Carro – M. González Ordóñez, vol. 3), lib. 5, quaest. 3, art. 3, p. 420.

at the expense of Medina, the basic distinction Thomas had made between an illicit giving (*datio ipsa est contra legem*), on the one hand, and a giving which is not illicit out of itself but merely as to its cause (*datio ipsa non sit illicita sed causa propter quam datur*), on the other.[1482] He classifies prostitution under the latter category (*ex causa turpi*).

Soto proceeds to deal with the fundamental idea underlying Medina's rejection to grant a prostitute any remuneration by virtue of justice, namely that a morally worthless act can have no value in exchange either. Rather, Soto argues, value in exchange is merely determined by utility and not by morality. Even the use of a prostitute's body is estimated at a certain price in the market. For someone procuring a girl or a boy for satisfying his own sexual desires definitely does derive a pleasure worth a price from that. The seeds of the disconnection between the ontological and the economic order had been sown by Augustine.[1483] Economic value is determined by scarcity, so that a bread can fetch a higher price than a mouse, even though an animal occupies a higher rank than food in the natural order of things. Soto applies this theory of economic value to the controversial issue of prostitution with remarkable consistency:[1484]

> Sinful acts can be bought at a price or a salary—as far as they are useful to human beings—by virtue of the mutual consent between the one hiring out his services and the party deriving pleasure from hiring them. It does not

---

[1482] Soto, *De iustitia et iure* (ed. fac. V. Diego Carro – M. González Ordóñez, vol. 2), lib. 4, quaest. 7, art. 1, p. 359: 'Secus de meretricia mercede, quia dare non est peccatum, licet fornicatio sit peccatum. (...) Ad secundum argumentum respondet divus Thomas sub distinctione. Bifariam enim contingit aliquem quippiam illicite dare. Uno modo quia datio ipsa est contra legem, et tunc, quia dans meretur dominium perdere, quod alter nihilo magis acquirit, restitutio fieri debet, non ei, sed pauperibus. Si vero datio ipsa non sit illicita, sed causa propter quam datur, ut scorti merces, non est restitutioni debita.' It needs to be remarked that, actually, Thomas articulates this distinction in regard to the acquisition, not in regard to the giving.

[1483] Augustinus, *De civitate Dei*, 11, 16, in: *Aureli Augustini opera, Pars XIV, 2*, [Corpus Christianorum Series Latina, 48], Turnholti 1955, p. 336: 'Sed ista praeponuntur naturae ordine; est autem alius atque alius pro suo cuiusque usu aestimationis modus, quo fit, ut quaedam sensu carentia quibusdam sentientibus praeponamus (...). Quis enim non domui suae panem habere quam mures, nummos quam pulices malit? Sed quid mirum, cum in ipsorum etiam hominum aestimatione, quorum certe natura tantae est dignitatis, plerumque carius comparetur equus quam servus, gemma quam famula.'

[1484] Soto, *De iustitia et iure* (ed. fac. V. Diego Carro – M. González Ordóñez, vol. 2), lib. 4, quaest. 7, art. 1, p. 359: 'At vero de peccatis, licet ratione culpae non solum vilia sint nulloque pretio digna, imo abhorrenda et execranda, nihilominus ratione consensus illius qui suas locat operas, rationeque voluptatis illius qui conducit, quatenus ad humanos usus accomodantur, possunt mercede et pretio redimi. Quapropter mulier quae sui corporis copiam facit, mercedem recipere potest pro voluptate quam vir captat, sicut posset ut prolem illi gigneret.'

matter that on account of their peccable nature these services are actually not only vile and unworthy of a price, but also abhorrent and execrable.

Interestingly, Soto even lifts a corner of the veil that covers the logic behind the market for sex. Since pleasure is the measure of all market value, a male prostitute earns more than a female, in Soto's view. For the lust a man can offer to his client is definitely higher than the joy a female prostitute can (sic). In addition, a prostitute can charge a higher price if the client not only derives pleasure from the sinful act, but also wants help in having a child—with Soto pointing out again that a male prostitute's help in obtaining this is worthy of a higher salary. There is a slight gender bias in his market analysis, then, even if he recognizes that women benefit from an even stronger claim to compensation for their services than male prostitutes. For the offer of women wanting to prostitute themselves is certainly much lower than male demand, given that women generally feel far too ashamed to readily indulge in sex outside of wedlock.[1485]

Soto finds additional support for his anti-Medina thesis in the legally recognized status of prostitutes in the civil community. In this manner, positive human law not only seeks to protect prostitutes, but also to enforce their right to a salary in the external court. A client, then, is not merely free to choose and liberally make a donation to a prostitute. On the contrary, a prostitute can take a client to court and have him pay the salary she rightly deserves, as is indicated by the sole name *meretricium* as it is etymologically derived from *mereri*, according to Soto. Consequently, once the client has paid the salary, he has no right to recover it anymore, as is evident from Ulpian in paragraph *Sed quod meretrici* (D. 12,5,4,3).

Soto does not want to deny that a prostitute can benefit from a donation. He defends a prostitute's universal right to receive a donation on account of law *Affectionis* in D. 39,5,5 (*affectionis gratia neque honestae neque inhonestae donationes sunt prohibitae*). The only exception is a case involving a soldier as described in C. 5,163.[1486] Medina had explained the

---

[1485] Soto, *De iustitia et iure* (ed. fac. V. Diego Carro – M. González Ordóñez, vol. 2), lib. 4, quaest. 7, art. 1, p. 359: 'At vero quia foeminis maior inest pudor, ob idque rariores sunt quae illi turpitudini vacent quam viri, pretium ipsae iustius recipiunt.' The natural sense of shame (*verecundia*) of women was a *topos* among the moral theologians ever since Thomas Aquinas, see Alfieri, *Nella camera degli sposi*, p. 212–216.

[1486] Adrian of Utrecht had not even allowed for this exception. He believed that a prostitute could retain a donation made by a soldier as long as she had not been condemned by a judge, because in this case she always benefitted from the '*ignorantia iuris excusat*-rule' (sic); cf. *Quaestiones in quartum sententiarum*, tit. *De restitutione*, par. *si petas*, f. 51r–v: 'Si petas an meretrix iuste servare possit dona qua suscepit a milite (…) respondeo quod

differential treatment for soldiers by noting that if a soldier were allowed
to donate his possessions to a whore, he might end up without the means
to buy weapons and thereby put the whole community at risk.[1487] Soto
did not mention Medina's rationale, however. Neither did he accept Medina's view that a prostitute can only retain the money by virtue of donation. The subjective intention with which a prostitute acquires money is
of no importance to Soto. What matters is justice in exchange between
two objects having a market value, in theory as well as practice.[1488]

6.4.2.3   Theological psychoanalysis

The practice and assessment of prostitution had gradually evolved during
the late Middle Ages, to become a profitable business tolerated by civil
as well as ecclesiastical authorites. As James Brundage has pointed out,
decretists such as Rufinus and Huguccio had already recognized that a
prostitute did no wrong by accepting money for her services, even though
she practiced a most detestable trade.[1489] In the thirteenth century, famous
decretalists such as Cardinal Hostiensis would consider the money a prostitute received as a lawful compensation for her labour, even if they held
it to be entirely wrong to pay in advance in order to persuade her.[1490]
    Relying on the authority of Pope Innocent IV to analyze the relation-
ship between a prostitute and her client as one of equal turpitude, Abbas

---

sic, si alias rite facta sit donatio iuxta metas iuris naturae, quam licite servat quoad usque
per iudices ad restituendum cogatur. Et ubi alias non liceret si iuris peritiam haberent,
ignorantia iuris eos excusat (...). Medina would explicitly reject this statement; cf. Medina,
De poenitentia, restitutione, et contractibus, tom. 2, Cod. *De rebus restituendis*, quaest. 20,
par. *Ad sextam*, p. 135: 'Salva pace Adriani, recipi a meretrice non potest nec retineri, si
sciat iuris dispositionem.'

[1487] Medina, *De poenitentia, restitutione, et contractibus*, tom. 2, Cod. *De rebus restituendis*, quaest. 20, par. *Ad sextam*, p. 136: 'Hoc autem institutum est in favorem militum
armatae militiae, qui pro republica pugnant. Quibus si donare concubinis permitteretur,
accideret eos non habere, quae illis ad pugnandum sunt necessaria, quod in notabilem
reipublicae perniciem cederet.'

[1488] Soto, *De iustitia et iure* (ed. fac. V. Diego Carro – M. González Ordóñez, vol. 2), lib.
4, quaest. 7, art. 1, p. 360: 'Arguitur inquam, quia non tam eius mens existimari debet quam
ipsa traditio. Et re vera consuetissimo usu nemo illis donat, sed pretium solvit, atque ipsae
id plane intelligent, quare semper tenentur ad restitutionem.'

[1489] James Brundage, *Law, sex and Christian society in medieval Europe*, Chicago –
London 1987, p. 309.

[1490] Hostiensis, *In tertium Decretalium librum commentaria*, Torino 1965 [= anastatic
reprint of the Venice 1581 edition], ad X 3,30,23, f. 100v, num. 7: 'Sed contra quia licet meretrix turpiter agat quia meretrix, non tamen turpiter accipit ex quo meretrix, ff. de condi.
ob turpem causam, l. 4, par. quoties, ver. sed. quod meretrici [= D. 12,5,4,3].' For discussion,
see Brundage, *Law, sex, and Christian society*, p. 463–465.

Panormitanus applied the *'melior conditio est possidentis'* rule to the case. Consequently, neither in the court of conscience nor in the external court was a prostitute bound to make restitution of the profits she had made through her trade. The fifteenth century canonist from Palermo believed that nothing was more in line with natural equity than for the law to respect the genuine will of a true owner to convey his belongings, for instance, to a prostitute (*nihil tam naturale quam ut acquisitio fiat secundum voluntatem domini tradentis*).[1491] At the threshold of the sixteenth century, Adrian of Utrecht would rehearse this argument, which was ultimately based on Roman law (D. 41,1,9,3, itself copied into Inst. 2,1,40).[1492] This argument gained prominent place in the subsequent discussions by Soto and by other sixteenth century theologians.

A most striking phenomenon was the transformation of prostitution into a public utility and the increasing involvement of town governments as well as the Church. In sixteenth century Seville, for example, the owners of the brothels did include ecclesiastical corporations. They in turn leased those houses of pleasure to private operators who did not lose their reputation as good christians in keeping them.[1493] Part of this might explain why the remark made by Thomas that a prostitute could not lawfully retain what she had obtained through fraud was now drawing increasing interest.[1494] After all, the profits made by a prostitute not only determined her own fate, but also that of her pimps and employers. So we find Soto explaining that a prostitute is not necessarily liable to make restitution of the money she made by applying fraud and deceit. A client is expected to see through the cunning schemes of prostitutes trying to cajole him into paying her excessively, for instance by pretending to be in love with him.[1495]

[1491] Panormitanus, *Commentaria super Decretalibus*, tom. 6 (*Super tertio libro Decretalium*), ad X 3,49,8, f. 232r, num. 13.

[1492] See higher and Adrian of Utrecht, *Quaestiones in quartum sententiarum*, tit. *De restitutione*, par. *Ad oppositum arguo*, f. 51r: 'Nihil tam naturale est quam ut acquisitio fiat secundum voluntatem domini tradentis.'

[1493] R. Pike, *Aristocrats and traders, Sevillian society in the sixteenth century*, Ithaca 1972, p. 203–206.

[1494] Aquinas, *Summa Theologiae* (Ed. Leonina, tom. 9), IIaIIae, quaest. 62, art. 5, concl., p. 51: '(…) mulier potest sibi retinere quod ei datum est: et si superflue aliquid per fraudem vel dolum extorsisset, tenetur eidem restituere.'

[1495] Soto, *De iustitia et iure* (ed. fac. V. Diego Carro – M. González Ordóñez, vol. 2), lib. 4, quaest. 7, art. 1, p. 360–361: 'Fraus autem est si verbi gratia diceret se esse viro incognitam, aut non nisi semel, idque a magnate; qua fraude plus extorqueret, restituere profecto teneretur. Sed si falso dicat se perdite illum deamare aut facetiis et illectamentis quippiam

Still another issue became relevant once a system of publicly tolerated
brothels had been put in place: is there any reason to treat public and
secret prostitution differently? Antonio Francesco Dottori (1442–1528)
claimed that the distinction between public and 'private' prostitutes had
gained increasing importance in the juridical tradition with Paulo de
Castro's (d. 1441) commentary on D. 12,5,4.[1496] Amongst the theologians,
Medina had argued that public prostitution was evil, but that secret prostitution was worse still. For disputes among public prostitutes and their
clients could be settled before court, whereas simple fornication would
give rise to disputes, not in the least to altercation between rival lovers,
which would not be solved but through vengeance and secret punishment
that could easily upset the order and peace of society. What is more, on
account of their appearance of honesty and virginity, women offering
themselves to have sex outside any legal framework could be expected to
attract even more men, and have them reward their services even more
lavishly.[1497] Secret fornication could impoverish men even more easily,
then, and hence posed a grave threat to the public good.

A wholly different view, but based on no less penetrating a consideration of human psychology, was put forward by Soto. He believes that
these secret prostitutes are merely young girls or married women suffering from a temporary moment of weakness, only one or two times in a
lifetime. Because of their even greater honesty and timidity, these women
entering into an agreement to have sex secretly are even more worthy of
a remuneration, at least before the court of conscience and as a matter
of natural law.[1498] Their legal status is weaker, however. A secret whore

extorserit, fraus illa non obligat ad restitutionem, quoniam probe omnes norunt illas esse
meretricum technas.'

[1496] See Dottori's gloss *De condictione ob turpem causam* [a] in Abbas Panormitanus,
Commentaria in quinque libros Decretalium, Augustae Taurinorum 1577, vol. 2, in cap.
Quia plerique [X 3,49,8], num. 14, f. 232r. We cannot confirm Dottori's claim, at least not
on the basis of Paolo de Castro, *Lectura super Digesto veteri*, Venetiis 1495, ad D. 12,5,4,
f. 207r–208r.'

[1497] Medina, *De poenitentia, restitutione, et contractibus*, tom. 2, Cod. *De rebus restituendis*, quaest. 20, par. *Ad quintam*, p. 135: 'Ratio autem quare diversa sit iuris dispositio de
occultis et de publicis videtur esse, quia si occultae permittantur, multa incommoda in
republica oriri possent, rixae, scilicet, et contentiones inter ribaldos, ut experientia docet.
Similiter tales occultae sub habitu honestatis magis alliciunt homines ad sui amorem,
unde apud eas longe sunt liberaliores, et plus quam convenit illis largiuntur, et inde eos
turpiter in paupertatem incidere accidit, etc. Quae inconvenientia non ita ex publicis
sequuntur, ut patet.'

[1498] Soto, *De iustitia et iure* (ed. fac. V. Diego Carro – M. González Ordóñez, vol. 2),
lib. 4, quaest. 7, art. 1, p. 360: 'Maius autem dubium est an aliae quae non sunt publici-

cannot bring her client to court. Married women and maidens are even susceptible to punishment, although they have a right to retain the money they earned until they are condemned by a judge.[1499] Irrelevant, according to Soto, is the statement in D. 49,14,9 that a woman who tried to poison her husband is condemned to make restitution to the taxman for the profits she made through adulterous sexual relationships, since this rule is rather to be interpreted as a sanction for her attempt to murder her husband.

6.4.3   Thomistic canon law

6.4.3.1   The prostitute's right to remuneration

Sexual offenses accounted for the largest part of business in the local ecclesiastical courts,[1500] so it is hardly surprising to find that the great sixteenth century canonists Martin de Azpilcueta and Diego de Covarruvias y Leyva dedicated thorough and highly influential discussions on it. Engaged in practical affairs as the bishop of Segovia, and trained in the best of sixteenth century canon law scholarship as a student of Martin de Azpilcueta, Covarruvias would strangely enough omit the discussion of his Salamancan master—for reasons that will become obvious later on— yet drive the views of Soto home by adding legal support to it. Covarruvias' discussion could be summarized as follows:[1501]

---

tus expositae, sed maiori cum verecundia copiam sui faciunt, possint pretium recipere. (...) Crediderim has multo iustius posse recipere pretium, quippe quae ob maiorem honestatem pluris sunt aestimandae. (...) Sunt puellae aut maritatae quae semel aut bis collabuntur.'

[1499] Soto, *De iustitia et iure* (ed. fac. V. Diego Carro – M. González Ordóñez, vol. 2), lib. 4, quaest. 7, art. 1, p. 360: 'Sed tamen quantum ad forum iudiciale est differentia inter has mulierum species, quia meretrici datur in iudicio actio petendi pretium, ei autem quae non est publico loco exposita denegabitur, quia illis solis lege decreta sunt pretia. Uxores autem et virgines non solum a iudicio arcentur ne petant, verum in poenam sui criminis privabuntur acquisito pretio. Sed tamen ante condemnationem iure naturae illis debetur.'

[1500] J. Brundage, *Medieval canon law*, London – New York 1995, p. 91, and Ch. Donahue, Jr., *Roman canon law in the medieval English church, Stubbs v. Maitland re-examined after 75 years in the light of some records from the church courts*, Michigan Law Review, 72 (1974), p. 656–661.

[1501] Diego de Covarruvias y Leyva, *In regulam peccatum*, part. 2, par. 2, num. 1, p. 480: 'Unde licet actus venereus ob quem datur pecunia illicitus sit et turpis, ipsa tamen acceptatio pecuniae turpis non est nec iure improbata. Qua ratione sicuti data turpitudine utriusque dantis et accipientis non est locus repetitioni, ita cum ex parte accipientis

Albeit that the venereal act itself, for which the money is given, is illicit and immoral, the acquisition of the money is neither immoral nor forbidden. Therefore, just as in the case of equal turpitude no action for recovery lies, in this not only does an action for recovery not lie [to the client], but rather an action for payment [to the prostitute].

Just as Ulpian in paragraph *Sed quod meretrici* (D. 12,5,4,3), and in line with the Thomistic tradition, Covarruvias did not accept the Roman jurist Paul's view expressed in law *Ubi* (D. 12,5,3), which held that prostitution represented a case of equal turpitude. Rather, a prostitute did not commit an evil act in receiving money in exchange for her services. Consequently, one could certainly not apply to prostitution the rule pertaining to cases of equal turpitude, which said that the position of the possessor is the stronger (*in pari causa turpitudinis potior est possidens*). Hence it was false to pretend that a client who had benefitted from the services of the prostitute was now in the strongest position, and, as a result, could not be forced to pay.

To be sure, Covarruvias accepted the authority of the Digest rules on the *condictio ob turpem causam*, recognizing that D. 12,5,3–4 dispelled any claim for recovery and any action for payment based on a contract involving equal turpitude in the external court. But he added the qualification that this was true only if according to positive law that action (*crimen, scelus, maleficium*) was to be deemed liable to punishment. This subtle interpretation allowed him to defend a prostitute's right of retention and her right to an action for payment, given that Ulpian had allegedly recognized that prostitution was neither prohibited by positive law nor an instance of equal turpitude.[1502] Furthermore, he thought that the civil law regime did not imply that a general right of retention would also lie in the internal court. For in case of simony, for instance, the possessor could not rightfully claim to have become the real owner of the money, given that the service rendered was not vendible. Hence, in such cases, restitution had to be made to the Church, the poor, or the taxman.

---

turpitudo in ipsa acceptione minime datur, non tantum locus non est repetitioni, sed et locus datur exactioni.'

[1502] Diego de Covarruvias y Leyva, *In regulam peccatum*, part. 2, par. 2, num. 6, p. 482: 'Secunda [conclusio]. In pari turpitudinis causa lex humana denegat actionem et repetitionem eius quod propter aliquod scelus committendum datum fuerit. (...). Quarta conclusio. Etiam si propter parem turpitudinis causam quoties datio et receptior [sic] est illicita, minime competat danti repetitio, tamen ubi ipsa receptio est licita, non tantum repetitio negatur, sed et retentio ipsa iustissima est, quod constat ex ratione text. in d. § sed quod meretrici.'

Covarruvias would reject the objection, too, that no action could lie by virtue of any promise made for immoral and evil purposes, as though immorality nullified contract. This objection was based on references to C. 4,7,5 (law *Promercalem*), D. 2,14,7,3 (paragraph *Si ob maleficium*), D. 45,1,26 (law *Generaliter*), and D. 45,1,123 (law *Si plagii*). The story of Judah and Tamar in *Genesis* clearly proved, according to Covarruvias, that an action for payment did lie for a prostitute in the external court.[1503] He despised those arguing that nobody was entitled to ownership over his body, particularly not in order to use it for illicit purposes. On the contrary, a whore was to be considered a rightful owner of her body (*domina sui corporis*), her body a licit object of sale (*materia vendibilis*), and the sale of sex not a contract illicit on account of its object[1504]—a particularly technical argument that reaches back from Soto over Vitoria to Olivi.

6.4.3.2   *Unjust enrichment and secret prostitutes*

Rooted in Vitoria and Soto, yet quite novel in its formulation, and of fundamental importance, was Covarruvias' explicit recognition that the action for payment actually amounted to an action for unjust enrichment. Prostitution was not merely to be considered from the point of view of promises and contracts, according to our canon lawyer. The most important perspective was that taken by the virtue of justice in exchange (*iustitia*

[1503] Diego de Covarruvias y Leyva, *In regulam peccatum*, part. 2, par. 2, num. 1, p. 481: 'Secundo eadem sententia qua asseritur promissionem factam meretrici servandam esse etiam apud iudicem exteriorem et promittentem cogendum fore ad promissi solutionem probatur Genes. c. 38.'

[1504] Diego de Covarruvias y Leyva, *In regulam peccatum*, part. 2, par. 2, num. 1, p. 480: 'Deinde quamvis fornicatio prava sit et iure divino vetita, ipsa tamen meretrix domina est sui corporis, et materia vendibilis est, nec ipsa venditio actus venerei illicita censetur. Et licet actus venereus ex seipso malus sit, eius tamen venditio non est prohibita nec illicita ratione materiae.' Compare *In regulam peccatum*, part. 2, par. 2, num. 2, p. 481: 'Nam licet nemo dominus sit membrorum suorum, est tamen dominus usus proprii corporis, siquidem usum corporis locare potest propter mercedis pretium, sicuti manifeste probatur apud iurisconsultos, qui locationem operarum passim permittunt et probant.' From these quotations it is clear that Covarruvias' distinction between *dominium sui corporis* and *dominium usus sui corporis* was rather vague, and even problematic. Still, as Domingo de Bañez pointed out, the distinction between both concepts mattered; cf. Bañez, *De iure et iustitia*, ad quaest. 62, p. 243: 'Ad argumenta in oppositum respondetur ad primum, quod quamvis foemina non sit domina sui corporis secundum se neque est domina vitae, veruntamen est domina usus sui corporis. Unde sicut potest aliquis locare operas suas vel vendere, v.g. iter facere aut saltare, ita etiam foemina potest vendere illum usum corporis sui.'

commutativa).[1505] It did not matter, then, whether or not an immoral promise was void. To determine the legal effects attached to an immoral contract, it was not sufficient to answer the question whether there were substantial limitations on 'freedom of contract'.

Elaborating on Cajetan's distinction between a prostitute's claim for compensation before (*ante*) and after (*post*) sexual services had been rendered, respectively, Covarruvias argued that once the prostitute had performed, the client was bound to pay as a matter of natural and positive law by virtue of unjustified enrichment. For the services rendered, the labour and utility procured to the client were worth a price. A whore, then, was entitled to a salary (*stipendium*) as a just remuneration for her performances. Covarruvias even maintained that such moral philosophical considerations had been the ultimate rationale behind Ulpian's modification of the analysis of prostitution in paragraph *Sed quod meretrici* (D. 12,5,4,3).

Covarruvias pushes through Soto's analysis of prostitution at the expense of Medina's. He does deal with the question of donation, for example, but merely to prove his point that enforceable contracts can be established between a prostitute and her or his client.[1506] In Covarruvias' as well as in Soto's view, contracts for sex are subject to the law of justice (*lex iustitiae*), and not merely to the virtue of liberality.[1507] Covarruvias extends his critique on Medina to Ullrich Zasius, who in commenting upon D. 45,1,26 had denied that as a matter of justice an action for payment lies for a prostitute or an actor.[1508]

[1505] Diego de Covarruvias y Leyva, *In regulam peccatum*, part. 2, par. 2, num. 1, p. 481: 'Igitur qui meretrici mercedem promisit, iam post ipsum actum venereum cogendus erit eam solvere, etiam si ante coitum pactum fecerit. Cum in hac specie non sit tractandum de promissione aut datione quatenus turpitudinem habet, sed de ea qua ex parte iustitiam respicit commutativam; hic etenim est verus sensus Iurisconsulti in d. § sed et quod meretrici.'

[1506] Cf. *In regulam peccatum*, part. 2, par. 2, num. 2, There Covarruvias also engages in a very interesting discussion with Ullrich Zasius and post-glossators like Cino da Pistoia, Bartolus, Aretinus, Antonio de Butrio, Giasone del Maino, Joannes Lupus, Salicetus, Raphael Cuma, Ancharanus, Ludovicus Romanus on the topic of prostitutes' capacity to inherit and receive donations from clients.

[1507] Covarruvias, *In regulam peccatum*, part. 2, par. 2, num. 4 is entirely dedicated to a refutation of Medina.

[1508] Covarruvias, *In regulam peccatum*, part. 2, par. 2, num. 5, p. 482: 'Hinc etiam infertur, an promissum alicui parasito vel ioculatori ut is inter ludicra et iocos patiatur aliquot alapas et verbera, sit ei necessario solvendum, et promittens solvere cogatur per iudicem? Et quamvis Zasius in d. l. generaliter, num. 31 velit, nullam hic posse dari coactionem iudicis, ego tamen contrarium censeo quoad moderatam actus mercedem.'

Another point on which both Covarruvias and Soto converge in their criticism of Medina is their equal treatment of secret and public prostitutes. According to what Adrian of Utrecht had designated as the *communis opinio*, and what Covarruvias primarily ascribed to Cino da Pistoia, in the external court secret fornication gave no rise to an action to claim a remuneration, nor did it grant a prostitute a right of retention in either the external or the internal tribunal. From law *Lucius Titius* (D. 49,14,9) they would even derive that all profits made through publicly non-recognized sexual activites needed to be restored to the taxman. Drawing on his analysis of agreements for sex from the point of view of contractual equilibrium, Covarruvias rebuked this view entirely. He admitted that in practice a prostitute who had offered her services secretively would, generally speaking, not be granted an action for payment in the external court. But he found that practice unreasonable.[1509]

Assuming that sexual services were worth a just price, he could not see why the question of whether sex had been offered in public or in secret could influence the just remuneration (*justa merces*) corresponding to the value of sexual services. Not to mention that an inheritance case involving poisoning as dealt with in D. 49,14,9 could be brought to bear upon the case of secret prostitution. For poisoning was a punishable act, while prostitution was tolerated by human positive law.[1510] In addition, he could not approve of a right of recovery for the client of a secret prostitute. On the assumption that a public prostitute had a right of retention simply because the object of an agreement for sexual use of her body is saleable (*materia vendibilis*), and not by virtue of a public office, Covarruvias did not understand why a secret whore should be denied a

---

Ullrich Zasius, *In tit. De verborum obligationibus lectura*, Lugduni 1547, ad D. 45,1,26, num. 31, p. 255: 'A mulieribus scenicis pudicitiae ratio non exigitur, quas turpitudo et utilitas vitae legum vinculis dignas non iudicavit. Ista recte etiam conveniunt histrionibus, qui non sunt digni legum vinculis et sic non inhoneste accipiunt.'

[1509] Covarruvias, *In regulam peccatum*, part. 2, par. 2, num. 3, p. 481: 'Quoad primum fateor Cyni sententiam in foro exteriore ob eius et aliorum doctissimorum virorum authoritatem frequentissime admitti, et a plerisque iudicibus eam admittendam fore. At non video qua ratione opinio ista vera sit, cum nihil referat feminam esse publice vel occulte fornicariam ad iustam ipsius venerei usus mercedem.'

[1510] Covarruvias, *In regulam peccatum*, part. 2, par. 2, num. 3, p. 481: 'Satis est distincta iurisconsulti species et eius responsio ab his quae impraesentiarum de meretricio lucro tractantur. Unde mirum est cur Cynus et alii d. l. Lucius ad hanc quaestionem induxerint, cum hic de mercede promissa ob coitum fornicarium tractemus. Qui quidem coitus minime punibilis est lege exteriori et humana.'

right of retention for the money she received in exchange for her equally saleable services.[1511]

This is precisely the point where simony, bribing a judge, and prostitution must be distinguished. Simony and venal justice give rise to an absolute duty to make restitution to a third party, given that they concern unsaleable objects.[1512] But no matter how immoral the final cause of an agreement, whenever its object is saleable and worth a price, a claim of recovery of a salary corresponding to the services rendered is not likely to lie. For example, if a craftsman has been paid for making an unlawful product, he can retain the salary received. By the same token, a soldier who served in an unjust war can retain his salary in the court of conscience, since work and industry need to be counter-balanced by a corresponding price (*iusta merces laboris et industriae*).[1513]

6.4.4   *A moralizing and experienced teacher*

6.4.4.1   *Envy in the canon law faculty*

Diego de Covarruvias y Leyva made a strong case for an action for payment and an exception against recovery in both the internal and external forum. He granted these remedies to public as well as secret prostitutes. By increasingly giving way to philosophical considerations of justice in contractual exchange, Covarruvias borrowed from Soto's teachings. At the same time, he ignored the lessons he had taken with Dr. Navarrus at the canon law faculty of Salamanca. Covarruvias did not even mention his

---

[1511] Covarruvias, *In regulam peccatum*, part. 2, par. 2, num. 3, p. 481: 'Nam si materia hac in specie vendibilis est, parum refert vendatur publice vel secrete, nec item differt venditio fiat ab ea quae vendendi officium publice habet vel ab alia, cum ex propria natura rei materia sit vendibilis, nec eius venditio ratione publici officii permittatur, sed ratione materiae.'

[1512] As to the case of venal justice, see Covarruvias, *In regulam peccatum*, part. 2, par. 3, num. 1, p. 484: 'Opera iustitiae venalia non sunt, nec iustitia est materia vendibilis. Idcirco datio et acceptio sunt contrariae rationi verae venditioni, quae fieri non potest de rebus istis, quibus nulla convenit aestimatio.' He then cites a host of classical authors, like Cicero, Valerius Maximus, Plutarch, Diodorus Siculus, and Aulus Gellius who are said to stress the same point.

[1513] Covarruvias, *In regulam peccatum*, part. 2, par. 2, num. 7, p. 483: 'Quia usus corporis et labor humanus conducitur ad delictum, et ob id conventio iure improba est et illicita ratione turpitudinis utrinque commissa, fortassis accipiens poterit datum retinere in animae iudicio in compensationem arbitrio boni viri ac iustam mercedem laboris impensi et industriae praestitae ad maleficium.'

master's teachings on the subject of prostitution. As we will see in the next paragraphs, Dr. Navarrus was not very pleased with that.

'I find that the most reverent bishop of Segovia does not mention my name,' Dr. Navarrus indicates—tongue in cheek—at the outset of his discussion of prostitution,[1514] 'Still, he has enriched what I taught him as a young boy in an introductory course with a curious sense of erudition.' Visibly irritated, Dr. Navarrus goes on to concede that 'it must have been the modesty so typical of him that had led him to quote me when agreeing with me, and to remove me when I had actually taken another view.' But he could not prevent himself from pointing out the manifest lack of reasonable argument underlying his pupil's endorsement of the traditional Thomistic argument in favor of a prostitute's right of retention.

He expressed his fundamental dissatisfaction with Covarruvias' and the Thomists' founding the prostitute's right of retention on Ulpian's distinction in paragraph *Sed quod meretrici* (D. 12,5,4,3) between the sinfulness of a prostitute's activities, and the lawfulness of her receiving a remuneration for her services. 'I repeat that this argument leaves me completely unsatisfied.'[1515] He would eventually acknowledge, however, that a prostitute had a right of retention to the money paid to her, but not by virtue of this Romano-Thomistic argument endorsed by his former pupil. Academic excellence is to do with elegant and logic reasoning. It does not primarily concern finding solutions, certainly when the demonstration of intellectual superiority is at stake, as when a master is confronted with his pupil.

But there was certainly more to Navarrus' dissonant opinion than mere pleasure in refuting an enviably clever student who had fallen out of his master's favor. There was an element of contradiction inherent in the distinction usually made between the outright evilness of the act of prostitution, on the one hand, and the simple lawfulness of the receiving of a fee in exchange for it, on the other. By slightly changing the interpretation of the rationale behind the Roman laws on prostitution, Dr. Navarrus revealed this contradiction. According to him, law *Ut puta* (D. 12,5,2) states that the

---

[1514] Azpilcueta, *Enchiridion sive manuale confessariorum et poenitentium*, cap. 17, num. 28, p. 285.

[1515] Azpilcueta, *Enchiridion sive manuale confessariorum et poenitentium*, cap. 17, num. 34, p. 291: 'Sed ratio nulla redditarum a praedictis satisfacit. Non quidem prima iurisconsulti in l. 4, par. Sed et quod meretrici, ff. de condictione ob turpem causam, quam etiam ad litteram sequitur Thomas in 2. 2., q. 32, art. 7 et omnes alii post eum, videlicet, quod meretrix licet turpiter faciat eo quod sit meretrix, non tamen turpiter accipit, cum sit meretrix. Non, inquam, satisfacit illa ratio.'

receiving of a price in a contract for murder (*ut hominem occidat*) is evil, precisely because of the turpitude of the act of murder. By the same token, law *Ubi* (D. 12,5,3) labels as evil the judge's receiving of a bribe (*ut inique iudicet*), precisely because of the turpitude of venality in justice. And law *Idem* (D. 12,5,4) considers a young girl's receiving of money in exchange for her defloration (*stuprum*) evil, precisely because defloration outside marriage is evil. Why, then, Dr. Navarrus concludes, would the taking of money in exchange for rendering evil sexual services (*meretricium*) not need to be considered evil?[1516]

To be sure, Ulpian could still be regarded as having linked up a non-contradictory set of conclusions. For positive human law does not necessarily forbid prostitution. Hence Ulpian's statement could be interpreted and defended as being derived from two different approaches: a natural law perspective had brought Ulpian to label prostitution as evil, whereas his approval of the receiving of money by virtue of prostitution drew its inspiration from taking into account human positive law. Yet a theologian could not be saved by that benign exegesis. Since natural law and not human law is the ultimate standard to be applied in the court of conscience, Ulpian's statement in paragraph *Sed quod meretrici* should not be considered as valid within the territory of the human soul (*non satisfacit quoad territorium et forum conscientiae*).[1517] Perhaps influenced by Medina's vast considerations on the absolute turpitude of prostitution as a matter of natural law, Dr. Navarrus insists on the inconsistency in traditional scholastic argument, given that prostitution is thoroughly objectionable according to natural law. The receiving of money in exchange for prostitution should be condemned accordingly, at least if the alleged logic behind the syllogism of the Digest is to be respected.[1518]

Moreover, even if we allow the theologians to apply Ulpian's ambivalent statement in the court of conscience, they are not for that matter absolved from another inconsistency. For adultery, or sexual relationships between lay people and clergy is forbidden even according to positive law, so the scholastics—and Dr. Navarrus is undoubtedly thinking of his pupil Cova-

---

[1516] It will not come as a surprise that Martín de Azpilcueta's interpretation of D. 12,5,2–4 is quite biased.

[1517] Azpilcueta, *Enchiridion sive manuale confessariorum et poenitentium*, cap. 17, num. 34, p. 291: 'Et ita ratio illa non satisfacit quoad territorium et forum conscientiae, licet satisfaciat quoad territorium et forum exterius in quo impune licet meretricari.'

[1518] Azpilcueta, *Enchiridion sive manuale confessariorum et poenitentium*, cap. 17, num. 34, p. 291: 'Cum igitur dicat esse turpe meretricari, cogetur dicere esse turpe propter meretricium accipere.'

rruvias in particular—could not have held against Cino da Pistoia that there is no ground to distinguish between public and secret prostitutes.[1519] Yet they did so, and rightly so, according to Dr. Navarrus, but on the basis of contradictory argument.

Eager to bicker with Covarruvias, Dr. Navarrus wrongly has him say that a right of retention is granted to a prostitute but not to a soldier fighting an unjust war, allegedly because human law tolerates the former while condemning the latter.[1520] It is precisely to Covarruvias' credit, however, that he acknowledged a soldier's right to retention even if hired to fight in an unjust war.[1521] Covarruvias based that view on considerations of unjustified enrichment and the saleability of goods and services (*materia vendibilis*) regardless of their moral value. He did not pay attention to the permissiveness or otherwise of that right of retention by human positive law[1522]—the latter being the major concern with Dr. Navarrus, as we have seen in his exegesis of D. 12,5,4,3.

In fact, Dr. Navarrus could simply not afford to present Covarruvias' argument in an honest way. That would have risked undermining his case for putting forward an alternative argument in order to back a prostitute's right of retention. For he had just about tried to show that his contemporaries' reference to the saleability of evil services was only acknowledged by them in the special case of prostitution, and not in the case of, for instance, a contract for murder. In his view, this proved that the argument of saleability or otherwise was not a solid basis for a satisfactory solution

---

[1519] Azpilcueta, *Enchiridion sive manuale confessariorum et poenitentium*, cap. 17, num. 34, p. 291: 'Ideo non satisfacit praefata ratio, quia concludit necessario unum falsum, scilicet, esse veram opinionem Cini et Angeli in l.2, C. de condict. ob turp. caus. (...)'

[1520] Azpilcueta, *Enchiridion sive manuale confessariorum et poenitentium*, cap. 17, num. 35, p. 292: 'Ratio vero quam praedictus Segobiensis sequutus aliquot alios sentit, videlicet, quod lex permittit et facit iustam operam meretricis, non tamen alias praedictorum operas, non potest defendi.'

[1521] Covarruvias, *In regulam peccatum*, part. 2, par. 2, num. 7, p. 483: 'Item si verum esset quod doctores communiter adnotarunt, sequeretur inde artificem aut fabrum conductum ad fabricandum id quod iure vetitum extat et in maleficium perniciosum fabricatur, teneri ad restitutionem eius quod ob fabricam in mercedem laboris acceperit. Sic et miles conductus ad bellum iniustum, quodque ipse iniquissimum esse certo scit, teneretur restituere mercedem iure conductionis sibi ob militiam praestitam, et tamen nec artificem nec militem ad restitutionem in propositis speciebus ipse non damnarem, nec compellerem in animae iudicio, nec opinor cogi posse.'

[1522] Covarruvias, *In regulam peccatum*, part. 2, par. 2, num. 7, p. 483: 'Quod si materia vendibilis sit, quia usus corporis et labor humanus conducitur ad delictum et ob id conventio iure improba est et illicita ratione turpitudinis utrinque commissa, fortassis accipiens poterit datum retinere in animae iudicio in compensationem arbitrio boni viri ac iustam mercedem laboris impensi et industriae praestitae ad maleficium.'

of contracts involving immorality. In practice people hired for illicit activities other than prostitution were paid.[1523]

Ironically, in refuting Cajetan, Soto, and the scholars of his age, Dr. Navarrus would go as far as to strengthen the unconventional claim of Covarruvias that the argument of unjust enrichment had to be extended to all kind of contracts involving immoral or unlawful acts. He would not have been able to give an honest account of the argument of his pupil without losing his own face entirely.

Altogether indicative of Dr. Navarrus' irritation is his dissatisfaction with Adrian of Utrecht. Adrian argued that a prostitute need not make restitution because the original owner of the money had willingly transferred the ownership of the money to her.[1524] This reasoning was later adopted by Soto and Lessius amongst others. Dr. Navarrus was right to wonder why Adrian of Utrecht had not extended this idea to other instances of delictual contracts as well. Yet at least some of Adrian's and other late scholastics' ideas would become part of Dr. Navarrus' own 'efficacious foundation of the common and age-old recognition of a prostitute's right to retention on a special new argument'.[1525]

6.4.4.2 *Moral worthlessness and lack of economic and juridical force*

That 'new' solution of Dr. Navarrus was based on an attempt—which to a certain extent we have already noticed with Medina—to subordinate

---

[1523] Azpilcueta, *Enchiridion sive manuale confessariorum et poenitentium*, cap. 17, num. 35, p. 292: 'Ratio item Cajetani in 2.2., q. 32, a. 7 videlicet quod usus meretricis est materia vendibilis, et non rei sacrae, quam Sotus et recentiores magni facere videntur, licet aliqua ex parte satisfaciat, quod ponendum differentiam inter acceptum ratione criminis symoniae et acceptum ratione meretricii, quod quam astruendam eam ille reddidit, non tamen satisfacit quoad alia. Nam aeque, imo magis vendibilis est opera eius qui se locat ad militandum in bello iniusto, ad duellum committendum, et ad fuste caedendum vel occidendum alium ac opera meretricis ad explendum libidinem cum ea rem habere volentis. Nam palam et passim conducuntur vel emuntur operae lectorum quos vulgus Hispanum Borreros et Italum Boia appellant. Et l. 1, par. Removet, ff. de postul. [D. 3,1,1,6] edicit de locantibus operas ad pugnandum cum bestiis et idem facit l. in arenam, C. de inoffic. Testam. [C. 3,28,11]. At ipsemet Caiet. et praedicti qui eum sequuntur negant idem esse in aliis delictis in quibus ex utraque parte versatur turpitudo, ergo illa non satisfacit.'

[1524] Adrian of Utrecht, *Quaestiones in quartum sententiarum*, tit. *De restitutione*, par. *Ad rationes*, f. 51r: 'Actus turpis non se habet ut radix respectu huiusmodi lucri seu mercedis, quia radix effective producit ramum. Non sic actus turpis hoc lucrum sed voluntas donantis effective transfert dominium.'

[1525] Azpilcueta, *Enchiridion sive manuale confessariorum et poenitentium*, cap. 17, num. 36, p. 293: 'Quae est conclusio communis et antiqua speciali et nova ratione efficaciter fundata.'

the case of prostitution to a general regulation for transactions involving turpitude:[1526]

> First of all, in the court of conscience, where natural and divine law are enforced, there is no difference between what is received on account of a prostitute's services, on the one hand, and on account of other evil acts tainted by equal turpitude, on the other. In all of these events the giving and receiving takes place in view of an evil deed blameworthy and punishable in that court. In both cases, also, the giving is voluntary on both sides, and the turpitude equally tolerated by both parties, at least in regard to this forum.

This equal treatment of prostitution, and, for instance, a contract for murder, enabled Dr. Navarrus to apply a general rule which he had developed in connection with these other acts of evil to the case of prostitution. According to that rule:[1527]

> Generally speaking, no precept exists saying that what is acquired unjustly but with the consent of the giver's will, so that the turpitude is on both sides, should be restored.

Dr. Navarrus inferred from the absence of a precept to make restitution to a specific person that restitution was only a matter of counsel (*ex consilio*), as when restitution to the poor was recommended.[1528] And in his view,

---

[1526] Azpilcueta, *Enchiridion sive manuale confessariorum et poenitentium*, cap. 17, num. 36, p. 292: 'Quare omnibus omnium dictis ruminatis, asserenda arbitror tria. Primum, quod nulla est differentia quoad forum conscientiae, in quo lex naturalis et divina necessario servanda est, inter acceptum ob operam meretriciam ab una parte et ob operas ad alia maleficia in quibus utrinque turpitudo versatur, ab altera. Quia in omnibus datur et accipitur contemplatione maleficii damnati et punibilis in illo foro et in omnibus aeque voluntarie datur, et in omnibus aeque admittitur turpitudo ab utraque parte, quoad illud forum.'

[1527] Azpilcueta, *Enchiridion sive manuale confessariorum et poenitentium*, cap. 17, num. 30, p. 287: 'Acceptum iniuste de voluntate dantis, ita quod turpitudo versetur ex utraque parte, non est restituendum, saltem regulariter, ulli de praecepto.'

[1528] Azpilcueta, *Enchiridion sive manuale confessariorum et poenitentium*, cap. 17, num. 30, p. 287: 'Est regula Ververcelli (...) quod restitutio quae non est facienda alicui certae personae, sed pauperibus, non debetur ex praecepto, sed solum ex consilio (...).' Compare the somewhat elusive passage in Sylvester Prierias, *Summa Sylvestrina*, part. 2, s.v. *restitutio* 2, par. 3, f. 262: 'Dicitur quod licet meretrix turpiter faciat quod sit meretrix, non tamen turpiter accipit quod ei datur etsi ex meretricio. Et ratio hoc probat quia talis datio acceptio iure naturali tenet quia non tam aequum est quantum quod res secundum domini voluntatem transferatur (...), et consequenter si alias lex positiva hoc non prohibeat, omnino tenet. Et ita tenet Panormitanus post Innocentium (...) et Joannem Andream (...). Et idem Cynus dicens quod de tali potest meretrix disponere et episcopus non se potest impedire (...). Aliae autem mulieres quae non sunt meretrices, id est quae causa libidinis et non quaestus male operantur, secundum Cynum, et sequitur Panormitanus, si quid accipiunt, turpiter accipiunt, et fiscus potest illud auferre, et in conscientia tenentur restituere, et secundum aliquos possunt restituere danti, licet non teneantur, sed

neither on account of divine law, nor by virtue of secular or ecclesiastical law did such a precept exist in regard to cases of equal turpitude.[1529] Other passages proved this *ex silentio*, according to Dr. Navarrus, since they explicitly denied an action for recovery to the giver, and an action for performance to the promisee, but did not contain an explicit precept to make restitution to a particular person of money acquired for the sake of delict.[1530] Combining this general rule for immoral acts with the case of prostitution, by a simple syllogism Dr. Navarrus was able to arrive at the following conclusion:[1531]

> The one true and solid reason why no restitution ought to take place of the gains received through prostitution is that as a matter of precept absolutely no obligation exists (*nulli est de praecepto*) to make restitution to anyone of goods acquired with the consent of the giver's will (*voluntarie*)—so that both parties indulge in equal turpitude—as we have concluded above.

The argument of Dr. Navarrus comes across as easy, indeed. It seems to imply that human will is so free that it is even allowed to bring about a trans-

---

possint dare pauperibus tunc secundum Ververcellum, ubi restitutio non est facienda certae personae est de consilio solum.'

No reference is made to a so-called 'rule of Ververcellus' in Angelus' manual for confessors, although Angelus says that in the event of an agreement tainted by equal turpitude that is not affected by fraud or deceit, no restitution of the filthy profits is to be made. It is not even necessary for the salvation of the soul (*non est de necessitate salutis*) to give the profits away to the poor, since that is merely a matter of counsel (*bonum consilium*); cf. Angelus Carlettus, *Summa angelica de casibus conscientiae*, s.v. *restitutio* (turpe), f. 295r.

[1529] He cites law *Illam* (C. 6,20,19) and canon *Legatur* (C.24, q.2, c.2).

[1530] Azpilcueta, *Enchiridion sive manuale confessariorum et poenitentium*, cap. 17, num. 30, p. 287: 'Statuunt quidem id quod propter delictum datur, repeti non posse, neque quod ob delictum promittitur, peti. Sed non praecipiunt acceptum ob delictum esse alicui reddendum.' From Roman law he quotes paragraph *Si ob maleficium* (D. 2,14,7,3), law *Ubi* (D. 12,5,3) and law *Idem* (D. 12,5,4). The famous canon *In pari delicto* (VI, reg. iur. 65) cited for the canon law.

[1531] Azpilcueta, *Enchiridion sive manuale confessariorum et poenitentium*, cap. 17, num. 36, p. 292–293: 'Ratio solida et vera, quare acceptum ob operam meretriciam non est restituendum, est quod acceptum voluntarie ab alio, ita ut ab utraque parte admittatur turpitudo, nulli est de praecepto restituendum, iuxta conclusa supra, in 2. dicto [cap. 17, num. 30].'

Actually, this amounts to circular reasoning. For one of Dr. Navarrus' arguments to establish the general rule of non-restitution in contracts involving equal turpitude had been a reference to the solution of the case of prostitution; cf. *Enchiridion sive manuale confessariorum et poenitentium*, cap. 17, num. 30, p. 287: 'Quinto, quod ut mox dicemus, meretrix non tenetur de praecepto restituere id quod pro mercede prostibuli accipit, et neque aliae mulieres solutae, conjugatae vel sacrae, et tamen, saltem quoad forum conscientiae, in omnibus eius turpitudo versatur ex utraque parte, ut statim efficaciter probabimus, ergo.'

fer of capital through a morally turpid contract, which remains untouched as long as there is no external precept that intervenes to reverse that shift in property. Dr. Navarrus' insistence on the moral depravity of prostitution does not prevent him from acknowledging man's freedom to bring about a transfer of property by means of such an immoral contract.

Dr. Navarrus repeats time and again that paragraph *Quod si meretrici* cannot be used as a valid argument to underpin this acknowledgment. In the court of conscience, the act of receiving a salary by virtue of prostitution should be considered as ugly as the rendering of sexual services. Ulpian's statement can only be used to defend the acquisition of profits made by prostitution in the external court. What really matters as to the solution in the internal court, according to Dr. Navarrus, is that there is no precept obliging a whore to make restitution of her ill-gotten gains.[1532]

Therefore, our canonist can also claim that there is no reason to treat non-public prostitutes differently from public whores, regardless of human positive law tolerating the latter while punishing the former. Both are equally sinful acts as a matter of natural and divine law.[1533] But again that does not mean that in the court of conscience either a public or a secret prostitute is obliged by precept to make restitution of her ill-gotten gains. Dr. Navarrus argues that a public whore might even be said to sin more deeply. For public prostitution clearly is a sin as a matter of divine positive law, which can be seen from Clem. 5,3,3. From canon *Quam grave* (X 5,31,9) Dr. Navarrus inferred that the ostentatious showing off of her body and clothes involved in alluring clients makes her sin not

---

[1532] Azpilcueta, *Enchiridion sive manuale confessariorum et poenitentium*, cap. 17, num. 36, p. 293: 'Ille par. [D. 12, 5, 4, 3] solum habet locum quoad forum et territorium in quibus opera meretricis est permissa, et non quoad forum et territorium in quo illa est damnata et punitur, quale est forum conscientiae. Et consequenter meretrix quoad forum conscientiae, in quo eius status damnatur, non minus peccat accipiendo mercedem pro illa opera foeda quam praestat quam qui accipiunt mercedem pro operis locatis ad occidendum, ad (ut ita dicam) duellandum, et iniuste bellandum, ac alia huiusmodi, nec consequenter in illo foro tenetur minus ad restituendum quam illi. Sed qui illi per conclusa in praefato dicto secundo [cap. 17, num. 30] non tenentur de praecepto sed de consilio tantum ad restituendum, ita nec ipsa tenebitur de praecepto, sed tantum de consilio restituere.'

[1533] Azpilcueta, *Enchiridion sive manuale confessariorum et poenitentium*, cap. 17, num. 40, p. 295: 'Quarto infertur, necessario idem dicendum esse quoad forum conscientiae de aliis foeminis et maribus cuiuscunque ordinis, qui ob fornicariam operam aliquid accipiunt, quod dictum est de meretricibus, et e contrario. Quia sicut illarum fornicatio est vetita et peccatum mortiferum ut plurimum in utroque foro, sic harum fornicatio est vetita et peccatum mortale in altero, scilicet conscientiae, secundum fidem catholicam, iuxta praedictam Clem. Ad nostrum, de haeret. [Clem. 5,3,3]'.

only against the sixth and the ninth commandment of the Decalogue (You shall not commit adultery / You shall not covet your neighbour's wife), but also against the eighth (You shall not bear false witness against your neighbour).[1534]

Roughly speaking, then, Dr. Navarrus' discussion amounts to a rejection of Soto and Covarruvias, and to a re-appraisal of Medina. With the latter he shares a common refusal, indeed, to fully consider that there is such a thing as a market price for sex. At the outset of the seventeenth century, this would be forcefully denied by Juan de Valero, who was well aware of going against the Dominican and Jesuit position—which by that time had become the common opinion—in following Dr. Navarrus.[1535] In the eyes of Medina, Dr. Navarrus, and Valero, the acquisition of a just wage in exchange for sexual services is wholly inconceivable. Moral turpitude and economic value simply cannot be distinguished.

Never can a sinful act be worthy of a lawful compensation, according to Dr. Navarrus, with the sole exception of prostitution in the external court. The ill-gotten gains cannot be considered as being acquired without sin as the prostitute's rightful due (*debitum*).[1536] By making reference to a host of texts of the *ius commune*, Dr. Navarrus argues that Romano-canon law

---

[1534] Canon *Quam grave* is not directly related to public prostitutes, but can indeed be adduced in this context, since it states that a cleric who takes pride in his sin in public, proclaiming right before the start of a wedding that he had intercourse with the bride, must be suspended (*suspendi debet clericus qui de suo crimine publice gloriatur*); cf. *Corpus juris canonici* (ed. Gregoriana), part. 2, cols. 1785–1786.

[1535] Valero, *Differentiae*, s.v. *restitutio*, diff. 15, f. 306v: 'Unde falsum est praedictas actiones esse coram Deo vendibiles, cum sint a Deo punibiles et reprobae. (...) Quare tam in his quae fiunt contra iustitiam quam in meretricio et aliis non licet in foro conscientiae quicquam tamquam debitum recipere, quamvis in foro exteriori aliquando liceat, quicquid teneat communis in contrarium. (...) Et sic nullo modo dici nec excogitari potest ex his conventionibus, etiam ipsis opere completis, oririi [sic] aliquam obligationem naturalem quae obligat ad aliquid coram Deo.'

Compare Valero, *Differentiae*, s.v. *promissio*, diff. 7–9, in which, contrary to the common opinion, he refuses to grant a secret as well as a public prostitute a claim for payment in the court of conscience. He merely grants a right of retention to a public prostitute; see, for instance, diff. 8, f. 278v: 'Consequens est, promissorem mercedis pro illo usu turpi non teneri conscientia illam solvere, nec ad id posse per confessarium cogi. Tum (ut diximus) ne lucrum ipsa capiat ex eo, quod apud Deum venit punienda. Tum quia ex praedicta promissione tamquam nulla et a Deo reproba nulla potuit oriri obligatio naturalis per quam teneretur promissor mercedem solvere et promissum adimplere, per dictam l. Mercalem.'

[1536] Azpilcueta, *Enchiridion sive manuale confessariorum et poenitentium*, cap. 17, num. 38, p. 293: 'Secundo infertur, opinionem doctissimi Ioannis a Medina in Codice de restitutione, q. 20, quam praedicti doctores Didacus et Sotus penitus carpunt, esse veram, qua parte ait peccare meretrices accipiendo mercedem tanquam debitum operae suae fornicariae.'

clearly confirms Medina's statement that nothing can be promised, given, or received in exchange for an intrinsically evil act.[1537]

Dr. Navarrus disagrees with Medina, however, in that he thinks that a prostitute always has a right to retain what she received, even in the form of a salary, for want of a precept obliging her to make restitution.[1538] More interestingly, he argues that in case of equal turpitude neither a *condictio indebiti* nor a *condictio sine causa* nor a *reivindicatio* lies for somebody who has given money for the sake of an evil deed (*ob maleficium*). To support his view, he gives a most interesting re-interpretation of paragraph *Si ob maleficium* (D. 2,14,7,3), and law *Generaliter* (D. 45,1,26). According to these Roman laws a title or cause (*titulus*) is automatically void if it is the basis for giving something for the sake of an evil deed.[1539] Dr. Navarrus, however, re-interprets these laws.

According to our canonist, paragraph *Si ob maleficium* and law *Generaliter* mean to say that even if an agreement (*pactum vel conventio*) forms the basis for giving something for the sake of an evil deed, it does not become void altogether. Rather, the agreement automatically degenerates into another type of agreement. Hence, a legitimate title or cause for the transfer of the money is still present, albeit in a different shape (*forma*). As a way of punishing the immorality of the giver, the law converts such an agreement into a kind of virtual donation (*donatio quaedam virtualis*) or a watered-down version of the original agreement (*pro derelicto*). As a result, the agreement is not void, and a prostitute, for instance, can retain the goods she obtained by virtue of that agreement.

[1537] He cites the following legal texts: paragraph *Si ob maleficium* (D. 2,14,7,3), title *De condictione ob turpem causam* (D. 12,5), the famous law *Generaliter* (D. 45,1,26), law *Pessimum genus* (D. 47,16,1), title *De condictione ob turpem causam* (C. 4,7); canon *Ad succidendos* (VI 5,3,1), canon *Pro humani* (VI 5,4,1).

[1538] Azpilcueta, *Enchiridion sive manuale confessariorum et poenitentium*, cap. 17, num. 40, p. 294: 'Tertio infertur, opinionem praedicti Medinae non esse veram, qua parte ait, acceptum a meretrice in operae suae foedae mercedem, esse in foro conscientiae restituendum.'

[1539] Azpilcueta, *Enchiridion sive manuale confessariorum et poenitentium*, cap. 17, num. 32, p. 288: 'Non obstat aliud quod plurimum urgere videtur, nempe quod titulus quod aliquid ob maleficium datur, est ipso iure nullus. (...) Quia licet pactum vel conventio qua quid ob maleficium datur, non valeat in illa forma quae partes solae praetendunt facere, valet tamen ut donatio quaedam virtualis, vel ut quidam actus habendi pro derelicto, quod lex in poenam male dantis interpretatur taliter male dantem habere id pro derelicto vel pro donato ad hoc ut ei non debeat necessario reddi, ut alta mente dixit Anton. relatus ibi a Panormitano in cap. quia plerique de immunit. Eccles. Et probatur per l. 2 et 3, 4 ff. de condict. ob turp. caus. ex quibus colligitur non esse paria quod huiusmodi accipiens nullo penitus titulo praecedente accipiat et quod accipiat praedicto quali quali et turpi titulo praecedente.'

Dr. Navarrus is also eager to infer from his conclusions that Bartolus de Saxoferrato was only partly right in interpreting law *Idem* to constitute the basis for the enforceability of a promise for sexual services. 'In the secular court, his view holds good', according to Dr. Navarrus,[1540] 'but not in the court of conscience.' The standard gloss on paragraph *Sed quod meretrici*, which denied an action for payment to a prostitute, had been equally negligent in not differentiating between the *forum internum*—where no action for payment could lie indeed—and the *forum externum*.[1541]

It was no passing concern to Dr. Navarrus, then, to make a clear separation between the court of conscience, where theologians and canonists like him were competent to judge, and the external court. It is worth mentioning, in this respect, that Dr. Navarrus was one of the main advocates of the principle of the non-bindingness of secular laws in what he significantly uses to call the 'territory' (*territorium*) or court (*tribunal*) of conscience.[1542]

6.4.4.3   *College freshmen and the plea against tolerating prostitution*

The fact that we have seen Dr. Navarrus and other scholastics fighting over the issue of prostitution has not solely to do with their well-developed taste for high-quality academic debate. On the contrary, it has to do with their innate concern for finding the most adequate solutions to the most urging problems. It should not come as a surprise, then, that we find Dr. Navarrus sharing with his reader his own experience as a consultant to both prostitutes and their clients.

The case is the following:[1543] a prominent figure had talked a young woman into having sexual intercourse with him by making her large promises of high remuneration. As can be expected, however, he does not act on his promises. What can your woman-client do in order to obtain the money given that actually no action lies for her in the court of conscience? Dr. Navarrus recounts how he advised the woman to write a

---

[1540] Azpilcueta, *Enchiridion sive manuale confessariorum et poenitentium*, cap. 17, num. 41, p. 295.

[1541] Glossa *Sed nova ratione* to D. 12,5,4,3 in *Corporis Iustinianaei Digestum vetus* (ed. Gothofredi), tom. 1, cols. 1323–1324: 'Sed an poterit petere, si sibi est promissum? Respondetur non, quia turpis causa fuit promissionis (...) et quia quaedam honeste accipiuntur, non tamen honeste petuntur.'

[1542] V. Lavenia, *L'infamia e il perdono, Tributi, pene e confessione nella teologia morale della prima età moderna*, Bologna 2004, p. 219–264.

[1543] Azpilcueta, *Enchiridion sive manuale confessariorum et poenitentium*, cap. 17, num. 41, p. 295–296.

letter to the man in which she would beg him to fulfill his promises out of pity, while acknowledging at the same time that she had not the slightest claim to performance as a matter of justice given the nullity of the promise. He invited her to write him about her urgent call for his aid by fulfilling the promises he had made her as a matter of morality and not as a matter of legal debt. In this manner, Dr. Navarrus thought, she would readily obtain more from her client than by having recourse to the external court.[1544] Theologians strived for the promotion of 'mediation' under their supervision at the expense of 'litigation', which became increasingly a monopoly held by the secular state.

A remarkable sense of realism and familiarity with the practice of prostitution allowed Dr. Navarrus to question the toleration exercized by the secular state in regard to prostitution. In his treatment of sinful lease-hire contracts, he explains that there is no point in the commonwealth's permissiveness of prostitution for the sake of public order (*magis expediret non permittere*).[1545] Granted, Augustine and Thomas had recognized that sometimes a lesser evil is to be permitted by the State lest greater evils arise, but Dr. Navarrus explained that this argument actually turned out to be self-defeating.[1546]

Here are but some of the reasons he gives for his scepticism. Many young people begin to sin by engaging in illicit sexual intercourse earlier than if no permission of prostitution existed. Moreover, through indulgence, lust is stimulated rather than inhibited.[1547] Hence chastity is to be considered a much more efficient means of fostering public order and peace. In practice, tolerating prostitution also falls short of another aim:

[1544] Azpilcueta, *Enchiridion sive manuale confessariorum et poenitentium*, cap. 17, num. 41, p. 296: 'Et arbitror, quod ut praedictus homicida per viam iustam plura obtinuit quam obtinuisset per iniustam, ita hae quoque personae impudicae plura consequentur per hanc viam Deo placitam quam per contrariam.'

[1545] Azpilcueta, *Enchiridion sive manuale confessariorum et poenitentium*, cap. 17, num. 195, p. 357.

[1546] Aquinas, *Summa Theologiae* (Ed. Leonina, tom. 8), IIaIIae, quaest. 10, art. 11, concl, p. 93: '(...) humanum regimen derivatur a divino regimine, et ipsum debet imitari. Deus autem, quamvis sit omnipotens et summe bonus, permittit tamen aliqua mala fieri in universo, quae prohibere posset, ne, eis sublatis, maiora bona tollerentur, vel etiam peiora mala sequerentur. Sic igitur et in regimine humano illi qui praesunt recte aliqua mala tolerant, ne aliqua bona impediantur, vel etiam ne aliqua mala peiora incurrantur: sicut Augustinus dicit, in 2. *De ordine, Aufer meretrices de rebus humanis, turbaveris omnia libidinibus.*' Cf. Augustinus, *De ordine*, 2, 4, 12, in: *Aureli Augustini opera, Pars II, 2*, [Corpus Christianorum Series Latina, 29], Turnholti 1970, p. 114. For Azpilcueta's arguments, see *Enchiridion sive manuale confessariorum et poenitentium*, cap. 17, num. 195, p. 357.

[1547] A statement our canonist felt the need to affirm by decretal X 1,34,1.

the preservation and protection of honest women's integrity. Referring to the experience of wise men (*prudentes*), Dr. Navarrus submitted that, actually, men capable of seducing honest women do not visit prostitutes in the first place. In addition, honest women suffer from sexual harassment more often as the 'losers', so to speak, become more addicted to easy sex because they have unhindered access to brothels. Last, our professor of canon law knew from his own experience (*ipsemet novi*) that numerous freshmen are like chaste angels when arriving at the university from places where no single brothel exists, but then rapidly turn into whorehoppers as soon as they are offered the opportunity of paid sex in the university cities—thereby squandering their money, time and talents.

6.5 THE JESUITS AND A GENERAL DOCTRINE OF IMMORAL PROMISES

Perhaps Dr. Navarrus' diatribe against the public toleration of prostitution was just a particularly smart instance of what is perceived to be a general tendency within the post-Tridentine Church to take a harsh stand on prostitution.[1548] Yet this disparaging attitude towards prostitution was definitely not shared by all members of the Counter-Reformation Catholic Church. The Jesuits, in particular, would attempt to increase the protection of a prostitute's claim to a just remuneration by taking a more lenient stand on prostitution. In the next paragraphs, we will focus our attention mostly on Lessius. Parallel doctrinal viewpoints as well as significant deviations in his older colleagues Molina and Suárez will be pointed out occasionally.

By taking seriously Soto's and Covarruvias' considerations on unjustified enrichment and the market price for sex, the Jesuits would defend a general right to payment for anyone who has offered his services in an immoral agreement. Significantly, Lessius would try to ignore Dr. Navarrus' new foundation of a prostitute's (factual) right of retention.[1549] Hardly mentioning Dr. Navarrus, he would simply turn back to the Romano-

---

[1548] Brundage, *Law, sex, and Christian society*, p. 569: 'The new moral climate was particularly hard on the practice of prostitution. Reformers, both Catholic and Protestant, denounced the wickedness of both harlot and client, while fulminating against the involvement of municipalities in operating public brothels.'

[1549] In sharp contrast to Lessius, Molina had no fear of naming his authoritative enemy. Rather, he attacked Dr. Navarrus' positions directly; *De iustitia et iure*, tom. 1 (*De iustitia ac iure*), tract. 2, disp. 94, col. 383, num. 9: 'Navarrus ideo aberrasse videtur, quod non attenderit latissimum discrimen quod est inter pretium pro peccato antequam peccatum committatur et postquam est iam commissum.'

Thomistic distinction between the turpitude of the act of prostitution, for one thing, and the lawfulness of acquiring money by virtue of that act, for another. This is not to say that Lessius' discussion of prostitution is a mere rehearsal of older scholastic thought.

It is to the credit of Jesuits such as Lessius and Molina to have separated the question of whether ill-gotten gains are to be restored or not (*utrum acceptum ob turpem causam sit necessario restituendum et cui*), from the question of the enforceability of promises that involve an immoral object (*utrum promissio ob turpem causam seu propter opus malum—v.g. ob fornicationem, homicidium—obliget*).[1550] For the first time, then, prostitution is becoming a mere instance of a more general doctrine of restitution in connection with ill-gotten gains, on the one hand, and also of a more general doctrine of contracts involving immorality, on the other.

At the same time, Jesuits such as Lessius and Oñate refined Dr. Navarrus' statements on the unlawfulness of lease-hire contracts involving prostitution, only to make an equally important distinction between immoral activities constituting the object of a contract (*causa materialis*), and immoral acts representing a motivating force to another contract (*causa finalis*).[1551]

6.5.1   *The market price for immoral services*

Having reformulated in general terms the question of whether ill-gotten gains (*acceptum ob turpem causam*) ought to be restored as of necessity, Lessius solves it in equally general terms. As a matter of natural law, he does not see why money from a fulfilled, albeit immoral transaction, needs to be returned. For the promisor has willingly and freely given (*libenter et libere dedit*) money in exchange for a service which the promisee is not bound to offer for free.[1552] Moreover, because of its usefulness,

---

[1550] See the headings of the *dubitationes* in Lessius, *De iustitia et iure*, lib. 2, cap. 14, dub. 8, and lib. 2, cap. 18, dub. 3 respectively. Compare Molina, *De iustitia et iure*, tom. 1 (*De iustitia ac iure*), tract. 2, disp. 94 (*quae accipiuntur ob turpem causam, obnoxia ne sint restitutioni et quousque in foro exteriori denegetur eorum repetitio*), and tom. 2, tract. 2, disp. 271 (*de promissione rei impossibilis, illicitae, aut idcirco contra bonos mores, quod occasionem praeberet ruinae et quid si haec ultima iuramento confirmetur*).

[1551] Compare Lessius, *De iustitia et iure*, lib. 2, cap. 18, dub. 3 with lib. 2, cap. 24, dub. 8; for Oñate, see above.

[1552] Lessius, *De iustitia et iure*, lib. 2, cap. 14, dub. 8, num. 52, p. 176. We have already seen this argument put forward by Adrian of Utrecht and Soto above. They both based it on *par. Hae quoque res* (D. 41,1,9,3).

or nuisance, an immoral act has a price regardless of its immorality (*opus pretio aestimabile*). This holds equally true for money given in exchange for prostitution as for bribes given in exchange for an unjust sentence, Lessius argues against common doctrine. From a natural law perspective, an unjust judgement is as saleable as a murder.[1553] To sum up, there is a general, natural right to retention of all ill-gotten gains.[1554] In fact, Luís de Molina had already defended this view some years before, but Lessius does not mention his colleague to support his unconventional view.[1555]

Lessius also finds it advisable for positive law to adopt that general, natural-law based principle that one can claim a right of retention for all ill-gotten gains. He acknowledges that the contrary opinion is common, but he cannot help but indicate the difficulties this view entails in regard to the question to whom restitution should be made:[1556] to the poor, as was commonly pretended (but that was problematic, given that Antoninus and Dr. Navarrus had pointed out that this was merely a matter of counsel and not of obligation), or to the giver, as Soto and Covarruvias had argued (but that was absurd, given that the laws wanted to punish the giver)? So Lessius suggests as a general rule that positive law be interpreted in conformity with natural law as much as possible.[1557]

[1553] Lessius, *De iustitia et iure*, lib. 2, cap. 14, dub. 8, num. 54, p. 176: 'Notandum tamen est, Covarruviam et Caietanum excipere id, quod acceptum est a iudice, ut iniustam sententiam ferat, hoc enim putant iure naturae esse restituendum, quia iniusta sententia et perversio iudicii non est res vendibilis. Sed haec ratio non est firma. Nulla enim est causa, cur magis debeat iure naturae restitui, quod acceptum fuerit pro iniqua sententia, quam quod pro iniqua occisione. Quod tamen etiam illorum iudicio non est necessario restituendum.'

[1554] Lessius, *De iustitia et iure*, lib. 2, cap. 14, dub. 8, num. 52, p. 175: 'Si solum ius naturae spectetur, acceptum ob turpem causam seu propter opus quod est peccatum, opere impleto non necessario est restituendum.'

[1555] Molina, *De iustitia et iure*, tom. 1 (*De iustitia ac iure*), tract. 2, disp. 94, col. 381, num. 6: 'Covarruvias praeterea loco citato n. 7 asseverat, pro ferenda iniusta sententia accipi non posse pretium, etiam postquam ex pacto est iniuste lata, eo quod res illa non sit pretio aestimabilis. Mihi vero longe probabilius est contrarium, nempe exercitium illius actus esse pretio aestimabile.'

[1556] Lessius, *De iustitia et iure*, lib. 2, cap. 14, dub. 8, num. 60–61, p. 174–175: 'Etsi haec verior sit, contraria tamen, quae censet, id quod acceptum fuerit ob crimen legibus punibile, (nisi censeatur donatum) esse restituendum, non est improbabilis. Patet quia est fere communis omnium iurisperitorum. (...) Sed tunc difficultas est, cui restitutio sit facienda.'

[1557] Lessius, *De iustitia et iure*, lib. 2, cap. 14, dub. 8, num. 57, p. 176: 'Ita enim leges positivae sunt interpretandae, si fieri potest, ut dispositioni iuris naturalis consonent.'

To strengthen his case, he quotes the familiar battery of texts from the *ius commune*.[1558] In the wake of Adrian of Utrecht, he pleads for a narrow interpretation of C. 5,16,3, where a soldier's concubine was summoned to make restitution of the gifts she had received.[1559] Of bigger interest, however, is his interpretation of law *Generaliter* (D. 45,1,26), law *Pacta quae contra* (C. 2,3,6), and law *Si plagii* (D. 45,1,123).[1560] Generalizing Molina's restrictive interpretation of law *Si plagii*,[1561] Lessius denies that these laws mean that such agreements cannot constitute a lawful title or cause for transfer of ownership. To put it in Roman law terminology—as Dr. Navarrus had done—a *condictio sine causa*, a *condictio indebiti*, or a *reivindicatio* could not lie, for instance, for the client of a prostitute. Concerned about preserving the obligation to respect the transfer of property on account of an immoral agreement as a matter of natural law, Lessius significantly narrowed the scope of law *Generaliter*, law *Pacta quae contra*, and law *Si plagii*:[1562]

> The laws quoted above and other laws prescribing the rescission of immoral and iniquitous agreements do not for that reason rescind an acquisition of which the cause is such an immoral agreement, nor do they render the promisee incompetent to acquire ownership over the good. What these laws do seem to provide is that before the service has been performed (*ante opus patratum*) these kinds of agreements are invalid in the sense that no civil obligation arises from them which makes the promise enforceable in court.

[1558] Law *Ubi* (D. 12,5,3), which held that in equal turpitude no action for recovery was granted, illustrating this principle with the case of a bribed judge; law *Si ob turpem causam* (D. 12,5,8) (*solutum ob turpem causam non posse repeti*), also provided welcome support for his view, of course; the Codex was thought to underpin the same cf. C. 4,7,2, and C. 4,7,5.

[1559] See Adrian of Utrecht, *Quaestiones in quartum sententiarum*, tit. *De restitutione*, par. *Ad rationes*, f. 51r: 'Speciale est in milite et minore quod non valet.'

[1560] D. 45,1,26: 'generaliter novimus turpes stipulationes nullius esse momenti'; D. 45,1,123: 'si plagii faciendi factive causa concepta sit stipulatio ab initio non valet'; C. 2,3,6: 'pacta quae contra leges constitutionesque vel contra bonos mores fiunt nullam vim habere indubitati iuris est'; cf. Lessius, *De iustitia et iure*, lib. 2, cap. 18, dub. 3, num. 20–21.

[1561] Molina, *De iustitia et iure*, tom. 1 (*De iustitia ac iure*), tract. 2, disp. 94, col. 384, num. 10.

[1562] Lessius, *De iustitia et iure*, lib. 2, cap. 14, dub. 8, num. 57, p. 176: 'Leges istae supra citatae et similes, quae pacta turpia et iniqua rescindunt, non ideo reddunt irritam acquisitionem rei ex tali causa, nec faciunt accipientem inhabilem ad comparandum eius rei dominium, sed tantum videntur decernere, ut ante opus patratum habeantur illa pacta invalida et ne ex illis oriatur obligatio civilis, id est, ob quam possit in iudicio peti promissum.'

The distinction—going back to Cajetan—between enforceability before (*ante*) and after (*post*) performance of the evil service (*maleficium*) would become the pivotal point of the Jesuits' discussion of prostitution and other evil deeds. Molina puts it very clearly:[1563] 'An agreement and the acquisition of a price on account of an evil object are illicit and sinful before (*ante*) such an evil object is performed. After (*post*) performance, however, it is no longer illicit to demand and to accept a price that was formerly agreed on.' In *De iustitia et iure* 2, 18, 3 Lessius, too, would apply this reasoning to promises involving turpitude of object. He fiercely defends the performing party's right to remuneration once he or she has effectively rendered his services (*patrato opere malo*).

In the footsteps of Cajetan, Soto, Covarruvias and Molina, Lessius consistently applies the doctrine of just pricing to the case of evil performances, making a clear distinction between the moral value and the market value of a human act:[1564]

> It does not matter that turpitude is involved in these services, for all these services can be estimated apart from the turpitude of the act (*seorsim*).

Among the services rendered by a prostitute, he counts her labour, by entrusting herself in her client's arms, as well as the lust and pleasure the client derived from that.[1565] None of these performances should be considered gratuitous, Lessius argues against Medina, since we are clearly dealing here with employment contracts, or other forms of onerous agreements that are subject to the law of justice in exchange. Moreover, a hired assassin, a prostitute, or a supplier of simoniacal services, for instance, often run personal risks and danger in performing their services. Like in any market, all of these circumstances are thought to have a price regardless (*abstractim*) of the evilness of the act.[1566]

Lessius takes the price mechanism on the market for evil services, and sex in particular, to correspond to the establishment of a price in the market for luxury goods. Hence, a prostitute has a certain power to determine

---

[1563] Molina, *De iustitia et iure*, tom. 1 (*De iustitia ac iure*), tract. 2, disp. 94, cols. 381–382, num. 8: 'Pactio et acceptio pretii ob rem turpem illicita est et peccatum antequam talis res turpis fiat. Post rem autem patratam illicitum non est petere et accipere pretium antea promissum aut institutum.'

[1564] Lessius, *De iustitia et iure*, lib. 2, cap. 18, dub. 3, num. 19, p. 218: 'Nec refert quod malitia illis sit connexa, quia possunt haec seorsim a malitia operis considerari.'

[1565] Lessius, *De iustitia et iure*, lib. 2, cap. 18, dub. 3, num. 19, p. 218.

[1566] Lessius, *De iustitia et iure*, lib. 2, cap. 18, dub. 3, num. 19, p. 218: 'Ergo similiter in malis poterit periculum abstractim pretio aestimari absque malitia.'

the price according to her own arbitrary will.[1567] In this context, no matter his objections elsewhere, Lessius seems to adopt unqualifiedly the theoretical distinction between the market for necessary goods as opposed to the market for luxury goods as already propounded by Vitoria, Soto and Pedro de Navarra.[1568] So it is difficult to condemn a prostitute who seems to have charged a higher price than what seems to be the common market price for sex. Albeit implicitly, Lessius seems to distance himself here from his colleague Molina who had stressed that the price charged by a prostitute, being either a woman or a man, needed to be moderate.[1569] Moreover, Lessius thinks his opinion to hold particularly true if sex is provided by an otherwise honest woman or a virgin, for that makes the detriment to her even greater.[1570] Like Soto, then, and contrary to Medina, Lessius finds that secret prostitutes may charge a higher price than public ones. Molina also agreed that secret prostitutes have a right to receive a compensation, but he pleaded, again, for moderation in charging a price.[1571]

To conclude, Lessius demonstrates that promises involving turpitude of object can still entail legal consequences, but not before at least one of the parties has performed. After performance, a public prostitute not only has a right of retention in both the external and the internal fora, but also a claim to payment. A secret prostitute benefits from a right of retention and an action for payment in the internal forum. In the external court, she has a right of retention until public condemnation by a judge forces

---

[1567] Lessius, *De iustitia et iure*, lib. 2, cap. 14, dub. 8, num. 53, p. 176: 'Res enim quae certum pretium non habent, nec ad vitam sunt necessariae, sed voluptatis causa quaeruntur, arbitrio venditoris possunt aestimari, ut probabiliter docet Petrus Navarra et alii.'

[1568] In *De iustitia et iure*, lib. 2, cap. 21, dub. 3, num. 16, p. 276, Lessius is much more reluctant to grant a seller arbitrary decision in the market for non-necessary goods, urging him to stick to the market price (conceived of as the common estimation by prudent men) irrespective of the essential or luxurious nature of the goods: 'Non ideo res tanti valet, quia venditori placet eam tanti vendere, sed quia prudentum iudicio omnibus consideratis tanti aestimatur. Ergo non potest eam vendere quanti lubet.' Compare Decock, *Lessius and the breakdown of the scholastic paradigm*, p. 69–70.

[1569] Molina, *De iustitia et iure*, tom. 1 (*De iustitia ac iure*), tract. 2, disp. 94, col. 381, num. 7: 'Dictum est, moderatum et aequale pretium, quoniam sicut in aliis contractibus excessus pretii causa est iniustitiae accipiensque restituere excessum tenetur, sic etiam in re proposita quando de formali aut virtuali voluntate id donandi non constat ex parte dantis.'

[1570] Lessius, *De iustitia et iure*, lib. 2, cap. 14, dub. 8, num. 53, p. 176.

[1571] Molina, *De iustitia et iure*, tom. 1 (*De iustitia ac iure*), tract. 2, disp. 94, col. 385, num. 13: 'Cum enim copia qua illa sui facit multo maioris valoris sit quam ea quam facit publica meretrix, nullaque sit lex positiva quae incapacem illam reddat pretii quod ea de causa accipiat, sane retinere poterit pretium moderatum quod ita acceperit.'

her to make restitution. No action for payment lies to a secret prostitute in the external forum.

6.5.2 *Immoral and impossible conditions*

To explain their attributing legal consequences to immoral agreements in spite of the Jesuits' recognizing the basic invalidity *ante opus* of immoral agreements, one could resort to modern legal terminology. If a Jesuit like Lessius attaches legal consequences to an immoral agreement, he could be said to do so not by virtue of the law of contract, but on account of the law of unjust enrichment. Yet those modern categories were not that clear-cut in his mind, nor in that of the other late scholastics. Lessius, like Oñate almost half a century later, would still try to base the obligation of payment on promise and free consent.

Lessius insists on the free and consensual character of the promise to pay (*libenter et libere dedit*), as we have already noted earlier.[1572] Also, he analyzes a contract for an evil deed in terms of two independent promises. The obligations ensuing from those promises are in a certain sense related to each other like the obligations in a real contract, although Lessius does not say it explicitly. Our Jesuit simply thinks the obligation to pay for an immoral service as deriving from a mere conditional promise (*promissio respectiva seu conditionata*), indeed: the promise of the *conductor* to pay is binding only on condition that the *locator* has rendered his service before.[1573] As with a real contract, then, the performance of the promisor is 'suspended' until the promisee has performed. Conversely, the promise to render the evil service is considered to be made on the condition that payment be obtained.[1574]

[1572] Lessius, *De iustitia et iure*, lib. 2, cap. 14, dub. 8, num. 52, p. 176.

[1573] Lessius, *De iustitia et iure*, lib. 2, cap. 18, dub. 3, num. 17, p. 218: 'Promissor operis non tenetur, quare nec promissor pecuniae, opere nondum praestito, tenetur, cum eius promissio respectiva fuerit, utpote solo intuitu illius operis facta. Imo tenetur illam revocare, tamquam iniquam et ad malum directe allicientem.'

[1574] Lessius, *De iustitia et iure*, lib. 2, cap. 18, dub. 3, num. 19, p. 218. However, the acquisition of the money is only licit if it takes place after the evil deed has been performed. If not, the acquisition of the money implies the evildoer's consent to perform sin, which is contradictory: 'Mercedem opere praestito accipi et exigi posse, quia debetur iure naturali et eam accipiendo non obstringit se ad aliquid quod sit peccatum, nec approbat facinus commissum. (...) Secus si accipiat mercedem ante opus, quia non potest accipere nisi obligando se et promittendo tacite operis executionem. Qui enim accipit pactam mercedem ante opus confirmat se in contractu et spondet opus ut ex parte sua contractum impleat.

Roughly speaking, the promise to pay for an immoral act is always un-enforceable *ante opus* on account of its immoral conditionality before performance. This follows from the rule that nobody can be bound to sin (*nemo potest obligari ad peccatum*), which was inferred from the principle of non-contradiction.[1575] This maxim could be seen as a simple variation on the saying that nobody can be bound to do the impossible (*nemo potest obligari ad impossibile*).

Conditions to a contract were considered by Lessius to be impossible in two ways: either because of physical impossibility (*reipsa*), or because of legal impossibility (*iure*).[1576] This distinction was not uncommon in early modern scholasticism. Molina, too, distinguished between factual impossibility and juridical impossibility.[1577] The former conditions were impossible by nature, say to steal the moon, or in relation to the promisor, say a poor man who promises something on the condition that he will first spend a million guilders. The latter conditions were impossible on account of a violation of positive law, moral turpitude, or uselessness.

The interchangeability of the notions of 'impossibility' and 'turpitude' reached back at least to Roman law.[1578] Pope Boniface VIII canonized the identity between impossibility and immorality (VI, reg. iur. 6). For con-temporaries of the early modern scholastics like those commenting the Roman law in a more traditional way, it was still common to use 'impos-sibility' and 'turpitude' indiscriminately. Even a natural lawyer as Samuel von Pufendorf would still write that conditions to a contract are either

Cumque antea solum esset promissio conditionata seu respectiva, *si solves mercedem*, iam sic absoluta, quia impletur conditio sub qua promiserat opus.'

[1575] See Lessius, *De iustitia et iure*, lib. 2, cap. 18, dub. 1, num. 8, p. 217: 'Nulla potest con-trahi obligatio ad id quod sine peccato praestari non potest, ut patet ex c. ult. de pactis, id enim contradictionem implicat. Sic enim fieret ut idem esset peccatum et virtus, bonum et malum, et ut homo peccaret non minus omittendo peccatum quam faciendo.'; and *De iustitia et iure*, lib. 2, cap. 18, dub. 3, num. 17, p. 218: 'Nemo potest obligari ad peccatum. Hoc enim contradictionem implicat.' Compare Molina, *De iustitia et iure*, tom. 2 (*De contracti-bus*), tract. 2, disp. 271, col. 79, num. 3.

[1576] Lessius, *De iustitia et iure*, lib. 2, cap. 18, dub. 15, num. 121, p. 232: 'Notandum est, conditionem dici dupliciter *impossibilem*, reipsa et iure. *Reipsa impossibilis* est, quae fieri nequit, sive id ex natura rei proveniat, ut si lunam detraxeris, sive ex impotentia illius cui imponitur, ut si pauper millionem aureorum dederis. *Iure impossibilis* dicitur, quae stante iure eoque inviolato fieri nequit, ut est omnis conditio turpis peccatum continens. Item quae nihil boni in se continet et alicui bono est impedimento, qualis olim apud ethnicos erat conditio non nubendi.'

[1577] Molina, *De iustitia et iure*, tom. 2 (*De contractibus*), tract. 2, disp. 271, col. 79, num. 3: 'Sicut impossibilitas facti de qua proxime loquuti sumus, nullam reddit promissionem, sic etiam impossibilitas iuris, sive illa sit divini sive humani iuris.'

[1578] See, for instance, Inst. 3,19,24 and D. 28,7,15.

impossible in a physical or in a moral sense.[1579] Johann Gottlieb Heineccius (1681–1741) would eventually reject this equivocal use of 'impossibility'. He considers the traditional equation between physical and moral impossibility of contractual conditions to be a common, yet blatant misinterpretation of Roman law.[1580]

The key to understanding Lessius' recognition that agreements for prostitution or any other evil deed do still create legal obligations, is his view of the legal consequences that come with impossible conditions to a promise. The case of physically impossible conditions can easily be settled: they are a clear indication of lack of seriousness, and are therefore to be considered as annihilating the legal validity of the contract.[1581] The case of legally or morally impossible conditions is more subtle, however:[1582]

> If a condition is impossible from a moral point of view, it will not invalidate a contract unless it is a condition about the future. An immoral condition in the present or the past cannot invalidate a contract. The reason is that a future condition obliges or allures the other party into sin directly—which is contradictory. (...) But promises do bind if the condition has been fulfilled, because then they do not oblige one to sin any longer.

Lessius would even try to reduce the invalidating potential of immoral, future conditions. In giving a very extensive interpretation to the famous rule that the useful is not vitiated by the useless (*utile per inutile non vitiatur*),[1583] he managed to protect the legal validity of both marriage contracts

---

[1579] Samuel von Pufendorf, *De jure naturae et gentium*, lib. 3, cap. 8, par. 5: 'Conditiones porro impossibiles sunt vel physice tales, vel moraliter: seu quaedam per rerum naturam fieri non possunt, quaedam per leges fieri non debent.'

[1580] Johann Gottlieb Heineccius, *Institutiones jurisprudentiae divinae*, Francofurti – Lipsiae 1688, lib. 2, cap. 6 (*De officio paciscentium*), par. 108, p. 120–121: 'Turpes vero conditiones (...) neque adeo sunt species impossibilium, ut communiter interpretes legum civilium ob non recte intellectam legam Pandectarum volunt.'

[1581] Lessius, *De iustitia et iure*, lib. 2, cap. 18, dub. 15, num. 121, p. 232: 'Igitur si conditio sit priore modo impossibilis, irritum reddit contractum, sive sit de futuro, sive de praesenti vel praeterito, quia talis conditio est signum non adesse consensum serium in contractum, sed dissensum potius.'

[1582] Lessius, *De iustitia et iure*, lib. 2, cap. 18, dub. 15, num. 121, p. 233: 'Si secundo modo dicatur impossibilis, nimirum quia turpis, non irritat contractum, nisi sit conditio de futuro, non autem si de praesenti vel praeterito. Ratio est, quia quando est de futuro, obstringeret vel alliceret alterum directe ad peccatum. Atqui nemo potest obligari ad servandam promissionem, qua alius obstringatur vel alliciatur ad peccatum. Hoc enim contradictionem implicat.' (...) Impleta tamen conditione obligant, quia non amplius ad peccatum obstringunt.' Compare Lessius, *De iustitia et iure*, lib. 2, cap. 18, dub. 3, num. 17, p. 218: 'Nemo potest obligari ad peccatum. Hoc enim contradictionem implicat.'

[1583] Cf. supra, n. 1060.

and testaments despite their containing immoral future conditions.[1584] Lessius was very concerned about protecting the will of the parties. Nevertheless, there is no doubting his bias against purely immoral contracts.

In line with the canon law tradition, Lessius urgently advised people who had agreed to enter into an immoral or illegal contract to revoke their promises as long as no performance of the evil deed on either side had taken place.[1585] There was a canonical maxim (VI, reg. iur. 39), indeed, which expressly stated that it was of no use to be faithful to evil promises (*in malis promissis fidem expedit non observari*). In his mid-fifteenth century commentary on the rules of law of Pope Boniface VIII, Antonine of Florence considered this maxim as a unique exception to the canon law principle of enforceability of naked pacts.[1586] He even cited additional support for it from Gratian's *Decretum*.[1587] Interestingly, Antonine also pointed out that this exception to the rule holds true in case of promises tarnished by an evil object (*mala promissa*), but certainly not in case of promises that are merely affected by formal vices (*male promissa*).[1588] For deceit and duress do not necessarily make it sinful for the wronged party to perform what is still considered a licit object of contract. Hence, the duty to be true to one's word prevails in principle, according to Antonine, no matter how vicious the formation of contract had been.

[1584] If the substantial differences between the discussion of conditions to testaments and marriage contracts in the various editions of *De iustitia et iure*, lib. 2, cap. 18, dub. 15, num. 122–123 both during and after the lifetime of its author are reliable, this was an extremely controversial issue. It falls outside the scope of this book, however, to dwell on this debate.

[1585] Lessius, *De iustitia et iure*, lib. 2, cap. 18, dub. 3, num. 17, p. 218: 'Promissio omnisque pactio ante patrationem operis pravi cuius causa ipsa est facta est invalida, et ultrocitroque nullius roboris. Ratio est, quia nemo potest obligari ad peccatum. Hoc enim contradictionem implicat. Unde promissor operis non tenetur, quare nec promissor pecuniae, opere nondum praestito, tenetur, cum eius promissio respectiva fuerit, utpote solo intuitu illius operis facta. Imo tenetur illam revocare, tamquam iniquam, et ad malum directe allicientem.'

[1586] Antonino di Firenze, *Summa theologica*, Veronae 1740, part. 1, tit. 20, cap. 1, par. 39, col. 871: 'Nota, quod est triplex genus promissionis. Quaedam est, quae sit simplici verbo hominum; quaedam, quae firmatur juramento, et haec fortior; quaedam quae fit voto, et haec fortissima. Quaelibet harum si est de re licita, obligat, nisi superveniat impossiblitas. Etiam simplex promissio obligat in foro conscientiae. (…) Sed in qualibet harum, ubi malum promittatur, servanda est regula ista, ut scilicet non servetur.'

[1587] C.22, q.4, c.3 (Quod David); C.22, q.4, c.8 (Unusquisque); C.22, q.4, c.15 (Non pejerabis); C.22, q.4, c.23 (par. Illicitum).

[1588] Antonino di Firenze, *Summa theologica*, part. 1, tit. 20, cap. 1, par. 39, col. 871: 'Et nota, quod dicit *in malis promissis*. Nam licet mala promissa servari non debeant; tamen interdum male promissa, puta per dolum vel metum, servantur, quando scilicet servari possunt sine interitu salutis aeternae, si juramentum intercessit.'

6.5.3   *Immoral promises invalid as a matter of natural law*

It might be quite unproblematic to hold that future, immoral conditions to a contract as a rule vitiate the juridical validity of that contract. Less clear, however, is the question concerning what actually constitutes those good morals (*boni mores*) that a condition to a contract or a contract itself should not violate. What are the moral limits to 'contractual freedom'? By moral standards, which contracts should be deemed void? In addition, is there a difference between the moral standards imposed by natural law and by positive law? Those are some of the pressing issues Lessius addresses in general terms in the fourth *dubitatio* of his chapter on promises (*quaenam promissiones sunt irritae iure positivo*).

As a matter of natural law, this problem receives a fairly easy answer, although one might have wished Lessius to expound what he represents as a mere hypothesis in a bit more detail:[1589] 'I suppose that according to natural law all promises are void, the performance of which is illicit, since nobody can be obliged to sin.' Examples are lacking in *dubitatio* four, but Lessius certainly would have thought, amongst other things, of a prostitute's promise to give herself away to her client. Such a promise entails the performance of sin and is void on account of that. Hence her client has no action to enforce that promise in court.

Furthermore, it is important to note that there is no means of validating a promise held invalid on account of its violating the natural morals (*boni mores naturales*). A promise that goes against the morality of natural law is absolutely void, and does not admit of validation *ex post* through an oath. With natural good morals (*boni mores naturales*) positively understood to be the morals of the virtuous man, and negatively defined as the opposite of sin.[1590]

[1589] Lessius, *De iustitia et iure*, lib. 2, cap. 18, dub. 4, num. 22, p. 218: 'Iure naturae irritas esse omnes promissiones quarum impletio est illicita, quia nemo potest obligari ad peccatum.'

[1590] Lessius, *De iustitia et iure*, lib. 2, cap. 17, dub. 7, num. 50, p. 205: '*Non est obligatorium iuramentum contra bonos mores praestitum*. Quod intellege de *bonis moribus naturalibus*, unde homo dicitur bonus et quorum contrarium est peccatum, non de *civilibus*, quos tantum expedit esse in republica, ut bene sit ordinata politice.'

Fortunius Garcia, who is not cited by Lessius, defines good morals as follows: 'Et ut sciamus qui sint boni mores, scire debes, bonos mores esse qui congruunt rationi naturali, mali vero, qui a ratione dissentiunt. (...) Ergo boni mores naturales sunt iuris naturalis.' Cf. *De ultimo fine iuris civilis et canonici*, num. 360, p. 240.

As a matter of natural law, the substantive limitations on 'freedom of contract' have to do with a violation of 'possibility' and 'virtue' in the broadest of senses. In his definition of a simple promise, which is not necessarily binding as a matter of justice, Lessius makes this clear right from the outset. What is more, he expressly locates the absence of virtue in the very object (*res*) of promise. Put differently, he connects immorality to the material cause of a promise:[1591]

> A simple promise amounts to a deliberate and spontaneous obligation as a matter of fidelity towards another person in regard to whatever object as long as it is good and possible (*de re quapiam bona et possibili*).

Yet to what extent do these requirements limit the juridical effects of contracts the object of which is not 'good', nor 'possible'? For instance, what about a prodigal promise (*prodiga promissio*)? Should it be considered to bring about no legal effect at all since prodigality is an evil act? Prodigality was commonly held to constitute a sin, even though venial.[1592] Soto, in particular, believed that a promise to pay a prostitute involving prodigality was not legally binding.[1593] Nevertheless, Vitoria had held—as we have seen in the previous chapter—that as a matter of natural law any prodigal promise was entirely valid. For the only title needed for the valid transfer of ownership was that the transferer was the owner of the goods or money transferred.[1594] Molina and Lessius seem to have been inspired by this original position of Vitoria—although they do not quote him. They were followed, in turn, by none other than Grotius.

Lessius acknowledges that prodigality can be considered to be a sin. He nonetheless refuses to infer from this recognition that no juridical effects

---

[1591] Lessius, *De iustitia et iure*, lib. 2, cap. 18, dub. 1, num. 2, p. 216: '*Promissio simplex* est deliberata et spontanea fidei obligatio, facta alteri de re quapiam bona et possibili.'

[1592] See, for instance, Bañez, *De iure et iustitia*, ad quaest. 62, p. 242: 'Prodigalitas saltim est peccatum veniale cum quis propria bona prodigit.'

[1593] Soto, *De iustitia et iure* (ed. fac. V. Diego Carro – M. González Ordóñez, vol. 2), lib. 4, quaest. 7, art. 1, p. 361: 'Si quis illis [meretricibus] superfluum aliquid polliceretur, teneatur promissum solvere? Respondetur teneri in conscientia, quia ius hoc naturale docet, nisi excessus ad prodigalitatem pertingeret. Nam tunc male promissum esset, in quo rescindenda esset fides, etiam si cum iuramento esset promissum, nam iuramentum de re illicita non obligat.'

[1594] Vitoria, *Commentarii in Secundam Secundae divi Thomae*, quaest. 62, art. 1, num. 29, p. 83: 'Et generaliter unus titulus ad formandum conscientias est iste, quod si quis verus dominus dat mihi aliquid quod non est lege prohibitum, ego sum vere dominus et non teneor ad restitutionem. Unde sequitur quod quantumcumque quis sit prodigus, si daret mihi centum milia ducatorum, ego sum dominus, licet alius prodigaliter fecit, quia ille erat dominus et potuit pro arbitrio suo dare cui vellet. Etiamsi daret meretrici, illa esset vera domina et non teneretur ad restitutionem.'

can ensue from a prodigal promise once it has been made. Even a prodigal promisor had been entirely free in making his promise, and, accordingly, in conferring a right upon the promisee to enforce his promise (*ius tribuit*).[1595] Once he had freely chosen to make the prodigal promise, he was bound as a matter of justice to fulfill it. Otherwise he would prejudice the promisee's rights. If a promisor had made a prodigal promise through imprudence, he had only himself to blame, according to Molina.[1596]

Lessius stresses that many actions are imprudent and sinful but still create obligations once they have been performed.[1597] This is not without significance for the law of engagement and marriage. For Molina and Lessius explicitly hold that a lady of noble birth is bound to keep her promise to make a prodigal donation to a poor young man of humble origin.[1598] Even if her father had entirely disagreed to this prodigal promise, she was bound to fulfill that promise in accordance with customary practice in the Catholic Church. For a parent had no right to interfere with a freely made, albeit prodigal promise of engagement by his child. In the wake of

---

[1595] Lessius, *De iustitia et iure*, lib. 2, cap. 18, dub. 1, num. 10, p. 217: 'Ratio est, quia etsi prodiga largitio, quae est executio promissionis, peccatum sit, dum adhuc liber es et nondum obstrictus, tamen postquam te obligasti promissione vel iuramento non est peccatum sed actus iustitiae vel fidei vel religionis, prout te intendisti obligare, neque amplius habet immediate rationem donationis, sed solutionis debiti. Sicut enim prodiga donatio, incipiens a traditione, dominium transfert, ita prodiga promissio ius tribuit, quo iure in altero iam posito, teneris promissum solvere (…).'

[1596] Molina, *De iustitia et iure*, tom. 2 (*De contractibus*), tract. 2, disp. 271, col. 79, num. 5 'Cum in exequutione nulla sit prodigalitas, sed sit adimpletio debiti iam contracti, ut ex iustitia aut ex aequitate morali, post promissionem factam promissor tenetur; certe integram promissionem in conscientiae et exteriori foro tenetur adimplere, nihil impediente, quod promissio prodiga atque cum veniali peccato fuerit, sibique imputare debet promissor imprudentiam ac culpam suam, tantam quantitatem promittendo, neque id praeiudicare potest iuri, quod donatarius ex tali promissione acquiritur.'

[1597] Lessius, *De iustitia et iure*, lib. 2, cap. 18, dub. 1, num. 9, p. 217: 'Non video cur promissio prodiga non obliget, maxime iureiurando accedente, etiamsi ipsa imprudenter et cum peccato facta fuerit. Multa enim imprudenter et cum peccato fiunt, quae tamen facta tenent, nec facile rescindi possunt.'

[1598] Molina, *De iustitia et iure*, tom. 2 (*De contractibus*), tract. 2, disp. 271, col. 79, num. 5: 'Ac certe, si exemplum, quod improbamus, verum esset, sequeretur, puellam nobilem divitem quae male fecit sponsalia contra voluntatem patris cum ignobili ac paupere contrahendo, eo quod exequutio esse non possit sine scandalo aliorum et dedecore ipsius puellae, non teneri implere, quod ita promisit utpote cum peccato, imo et cum prodigalitate promissum. Id autem nullus affirmare potest cum contra praxim sit Ecclesiae. Licet enim puella illa prodiga fuerit, maleque fecerit id promittendo, alius tamen ea promissione ius sibi comparavit iustitiae, ut in ipsius bonum id impleretur, neque puella, supposita promissione, male facit, eam adimplendo, quin potius facit bonum, imo vero facit id, quod ex iustitia tenetur, et quod si omitteret, lethaliter peccaret.' Compare Lessius, *De iustitia et iure*, lib. 2, cap. 18, dub. 1, num. 9, in fine.

his Jesuit colleagues, the great canonist Tomas Sánchez held that it would have been outright sinful for a parent to impede his son or daughter from acting upon his (prodigal) promise.[1599]

6.5.4   *Immoral promises invalid as a matter of positive law*

From the perspective of positive law, Lessius makes a threefold classification of promises that are void on account of their being immoral in one way or another. No doubt he borrowed from Molina in establishing those three categories of promises.[1600] Yet the dichotomy between positive law and natural law, on the one hand, and a parallel distinction between nullity and voidability, on the other, is much more salient in his discussion.

The first category of promises that are void as a matter of positive law are all those 'made on account of a cause that is punished by the laws, even if performance is not illicit'.[1601] Lessius cannot help but insist that it is nearer to the truth for positive law simply to conform to natural law, as he had demonstrated in his interpretation of law *Generaliter*, law *Pacta*, and law *Si plagii*.[1602] At the same time, this exhortation to let positive and natural law coincide highlights the genuine differences between the two systems of law. In view of Lessius' distinction between *boni mores naturales* and *boni mores civiles*—to be explained below—this is not wholly insignificant.

[1599] Sánchez, *Disputationes de sancto matrimonii sacramento*, tom. 1, lib. 1, disp. 14, num. 4, p. 40: 'Hinc infertur, quod docet Gutierrez, ead., q. 20, n. 23, posse patrem impedire sponsalia filii contra ejus voluntatem inita, sane intelligendum esse, nempe quando scandalum dictum probabiliter timetur, alias enim cum filius teneatur fidem servare, ut dixi, num. 2, non poterit pater tuta conscientia impedire ne filius suam obligationem exequatur.' Remark that, unlike Molina, Sánchez thinks that scandal could still be a legitimate ground for a parent to intervene.

[1600] Molina, *De iustitia et iure*, tom. 2 (*De contractibus*), tract. 2, disp. 271, col. 79, num. 6: 'Non solum est nulla promissio quam si exequutioni mandet promittens, transgredietur ius aliquod, atque adeo peccabit venialiter aut lethaliter, sed etiam nulla sunt ea promissio aut pactum quae idcirco sunt contra bonos mores, quod vel manifestam tribuunt peccati occasionem, vel praeiudicium afferunt facileve afferre possunt moribus quos esse expedit in bene instituta republica.'

[1601] Lessius, *De iustitia et iure*, lib. 2, cap. 18, dub. 4, num. 23, p. 218: 'Iure autem positivo probabile est esse irritas, primo, omnes eas promissiones, quae factae sunt ob turpem causam quae legibus punitur, etiamsi earum impletio illicita non sit, quamvis contrarium verius videatur, ut iam dictum est.'

[1602] See above and Lessius, *De iustitia et iure*, lib. 2, cap. 14, dub. 8, num. 57, p. 176: 'Ita enim leges positivae sunt interpretandae, si fieri potest, ut dispositioni iuris naturalis consonent.'

Secondly, all promises that 'can give occasion for sin' are not void *ipso facto* but voidable.[1603] Examples, taken from an extensive interpretation of D. 2,14,27,4, include clauses removing liability for fraud, duress, torts, or theft. A contract that is nullified on that account can be confirmed, however, by the party in whose favor the statutory law ('droit impératif') was established.

Thirdly, promises that go against statutory law and the basic moral principles that underlie and promote the life in society ('droit impératif d'ordre public') are absolutely void. In this respect, Lessius mentions promises in which you renounce the right to freely dispose of your goods.[1604] He founds his claims on an interpretation of law *Stipulatio hoc modo* (D. 45,1,61), and law *Pacta quae contra* (C. 2,3,6).[1605]

6.5.5   *The politics of good morals* (boni mores)

As pointed out before, Lessius draws a sharp distinction between the good morals of society (*boni mores civiles*) and the good morals of nature (*boni mores naturales*). Moreover, he believes that promises violating merely civil morality (*boni mores civiles*), but not virtue (*boni mores naturales*), still do admit of validation by an oath.[1606] Lessius makes a case for a restrictive interpretation of VI, reg. iur. 58, which states that oaths contravening good morals (*boni mores*) are not binding. In Lessius' view, the unenforceability of oaths proposed by Pope Boniface VIII merely concerns oaths that go against good morals in the natural sense of the word (*boni mores naturales*).

[1603] Lessius, *De iustitia et iure*, lib. 2, cap. 18, dub. 4, num. 23, p. 218: 'Irritae sunt omnes promissiones quae praebent occasionem peccandi. (...) Si tamen post iniuriam commissam, libere eam condones, valet condonatio.'

[1604] Lessius, *De iustitia et iure*, lib. 2, cap. 18, dub. 4, num. 24, p. 218: 'Irritae sunt quae adimunt libertatem disponendi de rebus suis, ut si promittas alicui quod illum institues heredem, quod non revocabis testamentum, quod dabis tantum, v.g. 100, si non instituas heredem.'

[1605] Lessius, *De iustitia et iure*, lib. 2, cap. 18, dub. 4, num. 24, p. 219: '*Contra leges* ea dicuntur fieri, in quibus promittitur aliquid quod leges prohibent, ut homicidium, furtum. *Contra bonos mores* fiunt, per quae datur occasio inique agendi, ut in exemplis num. 23, vel impediuntur illi mores quos expedit esse in republica bene instituta.'

[1606] Lessius, *De iustitia et iure*, lib. 2, cap. 18, dub. 4, num. 25, p. 219: 'Adverte tamen, etsi promissiones et pacta quae dicuntur esse contra bonos mores sint per se irrita, tamen si accesserit iuramentum, esse servanda.' In fact, the tricky and perplexing issue of oaths and their power to validate invalid contracts is the subject of a very large and intricate discussion in *De iustitia et iure* lib. 2, cap. 17, dub. 7, num. 50–59, p. 205–210 (*Utrum contractus per se invalidi confirmentur iuramento*) which surpasses the scope of the present discussion.

For example, in what paradoxically seems to imply an extenuation of usury as a matter of natural law, Lessius as well as Molina believe that a promise for usurious interest payments is an example of a promise that goes against civil morality ('droit impératif d'ordre public') but still admits of confirmation through an oath.[1607] Lessius is quick to add that such confirmatory oath is nevertheless dispensable by the bishop.[1608] In this context, both the term *boni mores naturales* and *boni mores civiles*, which Lessius uses, do not figure explicitly in Molina. The theology professor of Evora merely says that there is a difference between good morals in a strict sense, being venial sins against human or divine law, and good morals in a wider sense, amounting to the moral foundations of society.[1609] On other occasions, though, Molina does make an explicit distinction between both civil and natural good morals.[1610] Still, Lessius' discussion of the moral limits to 'contractual freedom' as a matter of positive law gained in precision and robustness in comparison with that of his older colleague.

The pronounced distinction made by Lessius between natural and civil morality is not without political and theological significance. If the role it plays in his discussion of donations is anything to go by, then this distinction seems geared, amongst other things, towards facilitating the incorporation of the genuine Christian doctrine of supererogation and charity into civilian regulations of justice and contract law.[1611]

For example, the Roman prohibitions on donations between husband and wife, and between father and child, respectively, is merely thought by Lessius to constitute a matter of civil morality (*contra bonos mores*

[1607] Molina, *De iustitia et iure*, tom. 2 (*De contractibus*), tract. 2, disp. 271, col. 81, num. 11: 'Promissio illa facta usurario aut grassatori obligat, si iuramento confirmetur, ut disp. 149 ostensum est.'

[1608] Lessius, *De iustitia et iure*, lib. 2, cap. 18, dub. 4, num. 26–27, p. 219: 'Promissio usurarum est contra bonos mores, quia occasionem praebet exigendi usuras. Tamen impleri debet si iuramentum accedat, cap. debitores, de iureiurando. Potest tamen huiusmodi pactis peti dispensatio iuramenti ab episcopo, si in illis aliqua iniuria intercessit et tunc promissionem non servari, ut supra cap. 17, dub. 7 dictum est.'

[1609] Molina, *De iustitia et iure*, tom. 2 (*De contractibus*), tract. 2, disp. 271, cols. 81–82, num. 14: 'Duobus modis dici aliquid contra bonos mores. Uno, presse et proprie, quia videlicet est peccatum, veniale saltem, contra divinum vel humanum ius. Altero late, quia licet in se non sit peccatum, inde tamen bonis moribus quos in bene instituta republica servari decet, potest facile praeiudicium afferri, ut disp. 151 explicatum est.'

[1610] Particularly in connection with oaths not to revoke a testament; cf. Molina, *De iustitia et iure*, tom. 1 (*De iustitia ac iure*), tract. 2, disp. 151, col. 593, num. 10.

[1611] For a more detailed account, see Decock, *Donations, bonnes mœurs et droit naturel*, p. 182–197.

civiles).[1612] For the sake of the stability of the state, husband and wife are to be protected against excessive love for each other lest they do crazy things with their patrimony.[1613] Yet in some cases Christian charity can nonetheless be a licit cause for husband and wife, or father and son, to make excessive donations to each other. Therefore Lessius expressly holds that a natural law obligation to respect the donation still exists. By means of an oath the donation can be confirmed, then, so as to be valid also in the external court.[1614]

By the same token, in the *ius commune* tradition based on law *Stipulatio hoc modo* (D. 45,1,61) a donation of the entirety of your possessions is considered to be invalid as a matter of civil morality (*contra bonos mores civiles*). Yet Lessius argues convincingly that this holds not true as a matter of natural law morality (*boni mores naturales*). The prohibition in question is merely derived from considerations of the political good.[1615] Hence, a donation of the entirety of your possessions could still be validated in the external court by means of an oath. In this manner, Lessius insists that donations of the entirety of your possessions towards the Church or another work of charity needs to be fully recognized by the civil authorities.

The opinion that donations for pious purposes which had not been registered, that is which lacked the *insinuatio*,[1616] could still be considered valid was not uncommon in the civilian tradition. It was also defended, for instance, by Giulio Claro (1525–1575), whom Lessius cites. Claro was a stu-

---

[1612] Lessius cites laws *Cum hic status* (D. 24,1,32), *Si uxor nummis* (D. 24,1,67), *Pater* (C. 3,29,2), and *Cum de bonis* (C. 8,53,11).

[1613] Lessius, *De iustitia et iure*, lib. 2, cap. 18, dub. 12, num. 86, p. 228: 'Donationes coniugum inter se iure communi sunt invalidae, ita ut ad arbitrium donantis sint revocabiles, exceptis quibusdam casibus. (...) Hoc autem ideo iure statutum est, ne coniuges mutuo amore se bonis suis spoliarent.'

[1614] Lessius, *De iustitia et iure*, lib. 2, cap. 17, dub. 7, num. 56, p. 208: 'Exempla, ubi contractus inducit obligationem naturalem sunt (...) donatio inter patrem et filium nondum emancipatum, inter maritum et uxorem.' According to Lessius' personally developed rules about the confirmatory force of oaths, an oath can always confirm an act if that act creates a natural obligation, even if that act is absolutely or relatively void as a matter of civil law: 'Quando actus talis est, ut ipse vel promissio illius ratificandi vel non revocandi inducat obligationem naturalem, confirmatur iuramento, etiamsi alias iure civili sit irritus vel in irritum revocabilis, modo vis vel fraus non intercesserit.'

[1615] Lessius, *De iustitia et iure*, lib. 2, cap. 18, dub. 13, num. 93, p. 229: 'Donatio qua quis donat alicui omnia sua bona tam futura quam praesentia, iure communi est invalida. (...) Ratio est, quia per hanc donationem homo aufert sibi potestatem testandi, quod leges improbant tamquam contra bonos mores quos in republica bene instituta esse decet.'

[1616] In the *ius commune*, there was a requirement of registration (*insinuatio*) for donations exceeding the limit of 500 solidi; cf. Zimmermann, *The law of obligations*, p. 499.

dent of Alciati at Pavia and became a successful lawyer and magistrate in Milan.[1617] In his *Sentences*, which are mostly remembered for their innovative parts on criminal law, he also dealt with the law of gifts, arguing, for instance, that donations to the Church exceeding 500 solidi that lacked the insinuation were still valid.[1618] What singles out Lessius' argument, though, is that he pushes this anti-formalistic reasoning much farther. In his view, the civil law is never to be allowed to prevent a citizen from doing a work of charity through the imposition of form requirements:[1619]

> The civil law should not hinder the performance of duties of piety nor evangelical counsels (*officia pietatis et consilia evangelica*). (…) Secular princes should not make laws that are to the detriment of works of charity and the salvation of souls. They merely have the authority to govern the commonwealth for the sake of temporal order and peace. Their policies should not hinder the pursuit of piety and the means that enables man to attain his supernatural end. Rather, civil policy should serve and promote this spiritual pursuit.

In an indirect, yet no less clear way, the distinction between civil and natural morality reveals Lessius' political convictions about the superiority of the spiritual authorities over secular power in matters that touch the salvation of the soul. Civil law should not limit 'freedom of contract' on account of so-called 'good morals' if 'freedom of contract' without those 'good morals' furthers the interests of the Church and spiritual welfare.

From this it is necessary to draw another conclusion. Remarkably open though Lessius' concept of 'freedom of contract' may be, the political theology behind it does not allow us at all to equate his viewpoints with the modern concept of 'freedom of contract' unqualifiedly. After all, there was a pronounced Counter-Reformation element to Lessius' doctrine of contract.

[1617] Birocchi, *Alla ricerca dell'ordine*, p. 257–261.

[1618] Giulio Claro, *Receptarum sententiarum opera omnia*, Francofurti 1596, lib. 4, par. *Donatio*, quaest. 17, num. 1, p. 117: '(…) hodie tenendum est, quod valet donatio, facta Ecclesiae ultra quingentos solidos sine insinuatione.'

[1619] The passages in translation are based on *De iustitia et iure*, lib. 2, cap. 18, dub. 13, num. 95, p. 229, and lib. 2, cap. 18, dub. 13, num. 102, p. 230 respectively: 'Ius civile non potest impedire officia pietatis et consilia evangelica, atqui talis donatio [omnium bonorum tam futurorum quam praesentium] est officium pietatis et consilium Christi, ergo (…). Principes saeculares non possunt aliquid statuere in praeiudicium bonorum operum et salutis animarum. Solum enim ita possunt gubernare rempublicam ad tranquillitatem temporalem, ut ea gubernatio non impediat studium pietatis et media ad finem supernaturalem, sed potius subserviat et iuvet. Atqui si talis insinuatio esset necessaria in causis piis, saepe bona opera impedirentur, idque cum magno boni spiritualis damno.'

6.5.6   *Morality and the final motivating cause*

This religious aspect of the early modern scholastics' contract doctrine does not mean, however, that they all took rigorous and intransigent views on contracts involving immorality. The Jesuits, in particular, were well known for their leniency. It will not come as a surprise, then, that we find Lessius radically refuting Dr. Navarrus' condemnation of landlords who rent out their houses to prostitutes—although, again, Lessius is careful to cover his dissent with the famous canonist as much as possible.

Firstly, Lessius broadens the scope of the question about lease-hire contracts entered into by some of the contracting parties in view of an immoral final cause. He does not only envisage brothelkeepers, but any landlord or seller who by transferring his property to a person who intends to use this property for immoral purposes, willingly or unwillingly enters into a contract that somehow involves immorality. Secondly, Lessius makes a sharp distinction between contracts in which a person becomes an accessory to the evil doer's purposes in letting or selling his property to him, and contracts in which this person cannot possibly prevent the other party to the contract from pursuing his evil interests.

On top of this, Lessius does not question the juridical validity of such a contract. He merely inquires into the moral quality of such a transaction as a matter of natural law. Prefiguring the more explicit distinction his colleague Pedro de Oñate would make between the *causa materialis* and the *causa finalis* to a contract, Lessius would limit himself to a moral assessment of a lease-hire contract or a sale-purchase agreement by inquiring into what Oñate would later call the *causa finalis operantis*. By this criterion it is possible to evaluate the moral probity of a contracting party, while leaving unquestioned the legal validity of the contract.

As to the concrete solution of the moral probity of contracts involving immoral final causes on the part of the tenant or buyer, Lessius holds that if a shopkeeper sells or rents something with the explicit intention of becoming an accessory to the client's evil purposes, he commits a sin. That would be similar to knowingly selling a weapon to someone whom you know is in a serious dispute over something with somebody.[1620]

[1620]   Lessius, *De iustitia et iure*, lib. 2, cap. 24, dub. 8, num. 39, p. 329: 'Id esse illicitum si vel fiat elocatio in illum finem, vel elocator possit et teneatur peccatum alterius impedire, ut si loces domum furi vel latroni quem putas inde habiturum opportunitatem nocendi civibus; si loces aut vendes arma ei qui contracto litigio parat invadere.'

Equally sinful for a landlord is to rent to a usurer or a prostitute a flat if he is clearly able to prevent the usurer or prostitute from developing his or her sinful activities by not renting the appartment to that person. This is true, for instance, if they would not possibly have been able to find an alternative location in the neighborhood to house their illicit activites.[1621] In that case the landlord has the liberty and the possibility to oppose a sinful deed. By not preventing the prostitute or usurer from developing his activities through granting him a tenancy agreement, he actually becomes a complice.

On the other hand, landlords or shopkeepers most of the time are not aware of the ultimate purposes that drive the other party to enter into an agreement with them. If people do not know about the other party's motives and cannot be expected to know, or to be able to prevent the evil deed, then Lessius thinks that they act without sin, at least in the absence of scandal.[1622] Lessius tries to cite Dr. Navarrus to support that view— which is manifestly false. He is right, however, in quoting John Mair as an authoritative adherent to his position. The Scotsman John Mair had called for a realistic policy in dealing with prostitution. He said that it was 'metaphysical' to think that prostitution could be kept at bay by prohibiting landlords from renting out real estate to prostitutes.[1623]

The ultimate reason why Lessius takes this view is because of his approval of customary practice and elements of general moral theory. If a usurer or a prostitute is likely to get an appartment from another landlord in town, you cannot really make a difference to the common good by refusing to accept them as a contracting party: eventually they will find someone else who is prepared to rent them a house anyway.[1624] Moreover, it is customary practice that prostitutes and usurers are tolerated in

---

[1621] Lessius, *De iustitia et iure*, lib. 2, cap. 24, dub. 8, num. 39, p. 329: 'Imo in hisce duobus casibus, locans censetur praebere auxilium, ac proinde tenetur ad restitutionem damni secuti: si loces domum tuam meretricibus vel usurariis, qui alibi domum commodam non invenirent, idque eo loco, ubi nullo modo expediebat tales permitti.'

[1622] Lessius, *De iustitia et iure*, lib. 2, cap. 24, dub. 8, num. 40, p. 329: 'Si locatio fiat ob finem indifferentem (v.g. ad commodandum dumtaxat de habitatione) et locator non possit aut non teneatur impedire illa peccata quae ibi committentur, non peccat talibus elocando, seposito scandalo.'

[1623] Cf. John Mair, *In quartum sententiarum quaestiones*, Parisiis 1516, dist. 15, quaest. 35, par. *Dubitatur*, f. 107v–108r.

[1624] Lessius, *De iustitia et iure*, lib. 2, cap. 24, dub. 8, num. 40, p. 329: 'Unde sequitur non esse peccatum (si alias absit scandalum) elocare domum meretrici, si vel multae aliae domus aeque commodae non sint ei defuturae, vel si expedit urbi ad maiora mala vitanda, illa permitti: quia tunc vel non possum vel non teneor illarum peccatum impedire.'

almost all parts of the commonwealth. In Lessius' view, even the prohibition contained in canon *Usurarum* (VI 5,5,1) on making a tenancy agreement with a usurer has long been superseded, with secular princes and bishops alike tolerating this practice.[1625]

6.5.7   *Sex as a luxury good and the* stylus aulae

By the mid-seventeenth century, Juan de Lugo would present Lessius' assessment of prostitution agreements as the common opinion.[1626] His own, long-drawn-out discussion of the subject became more descriptive and less polemical. Typically, however, Lugo elaborated on some of the more liberal views Lessius had tried and prudently put forward. The idea of sex as a luxury good, the price of which is set according to the arbitrary will of its seller, was particularly promoted by Lugo:[1627] 'With this kind of good, every individual can determine the price according to his own will, since they are worth so much as the seller estimates his lack of it.'

The maxim extracted from paragraph *Si heres* (D. 36,1,1,16), namely, that a good is worth as much as it can be sold for (*res tantum valet quantum vendi potest*)—one of the basic principles of a liberal market economy—is clearly applied here to the case of prostitution. Lugo does not quote the maxim, though. In a certain sense, a prostitute sells her reputation and honesty, certainly if she is not a public prostitute, and she can demand a price for the detriment she incurs in doing so. Moreover, given that the just price of sex is determined by the will of the prostitute, the benchmark for judging the fairness of the price she demands in a specific case should be the price she commonly demands for parting with her honesty, according to Lugo.[1628]

[1625] Lessius, *De iustitia et iure*, lib. 2, cap. 24, dub. 8, num. 41, p. 330: 'Iure tamen canonico vetitum est ne quis usurariis alienigenis domum elocet (…), hoc tamen non videtur multis locis servari, nam passim principibus et rebuspublicis admittuntur, episcopis minime contradicentibus.'

[1626] Lugo, *De iustitia et iure*, tom. 1, disp. 18, sect. 3, num. 45, p. 499.

[1627] Lugo, *De iustitia et iure*, tom. 1, disp. 18, sect. 3, num. 47, p. 500: 'In eiusmodi enim rebus possunt singuli pretium sibi statuere: tanti enim valent, quanti venditor aestimat illius carentiam. Accipit quippe pretium pro honestate, qua se in gratiam emptoris privat.'

[1628] Lugo, *De iustitia et iure*, tom. 1, disp. 18, sect. 3, num. 47, p. 500: 'Quando vero meretrix non tanti aestimat suam honestatem, cum passim eam aliis minori pretio vendat, excedit iustum valorem et pretium commune rei quam vendit, et ideo restituere tenetur.'

Against the background of his acknowledgment of the arbitrariness of price-making in the market for sex, Lugo's rebuttal of Gabriel Vázquez's partial re-appraisal of Medina might seem to be ironic. Not wholly satisfied with the argument about the saleability of sexual services, the Jesuit Gabriel Vázquez had argued that perhaps it was better to consider a prostitute's profits as having been derived from a free donation.[1629] This was difficult to maintain, according to Lugo, since on that basis, and in the absence of a just price, it would be impossible to judge whether a particular profit was to be considered excessive or not.[1630]

In any event, the argument between Juan de Lugo and Gabriel Vázquez shows that it was not impossible for an individual Jesuit to take views slightly heterodox with respect to the general thrust of opinion within his order. Vázquez's discussion does not contain any reference to Molina, or Lessius, either. Neither were their treatments of the same cases monolithic or repetitive. Depending on their real life experiences as consultants to diverse people, the Jesuits considerably changed the accents in their discussions of the same problems.

For example, we find Lugo dealing with a problem that was not developed at all in Lessius: what about the licitness of retaining money or goods that were given to a prostitute before (*ante*) she performed? On a theoretical level, Lugo distinguishes between acquisitions before sex by virtue of the prostitution agreement itself, and goods or money received before sex as a man's way of seducing a woman into having sex with him.[1631] The former way of acquiring profits could not be considered licit, of course, since it would go against either chastity (if the woman would give in) or justice (if the woman would refuse to make a counter-performance). In the latter case, however, a woman could retain what had been offered to her. Therefore, Lugo tells us, in his consultancy practice he had advised a

[1629] Gabriel Vázquez, *Tractatus de restitutione in foro conscientiae*, cap. 7 (*de turpi lucro*), dub. 1, num. 8, in: *Opuscula moralia*, Compluti 1617, p. 209: 'Mihi videtur, quod alia sit praecipua causa quam quod res illa sit vendibilis. Fateor enim, quod ea est causa sufficiens, qua pretium arbitrio boni viri pro illo actu recipiatur. Praecipua autem ratio est, quam reddidit Navarrus. Quia ille, qui meretrici ob turpem causam aliquid tribuit mere libere tribuit (…). Unde titulo donationis videtur tribuere quidquid dederit meretrici.'

[1630] Lugo, *De iustitia et iure*, tom. 1, disp. 18, sect. 3, num. 47, p. 500: 'Obiicit Vasquez n. 10 quia si donationis titulus separetur, vix posset taxari pretium meretricibus ultra quod tenerentur ad restitutionem. Respondeo, imo tenentur aliquando ad restituendum excessum, quia non intervenit donatio, sed emptio.'

[1631] Lugo, *De iustitia et iure*, tom. 1, disp. 18, sect. 3, num. 49.

noblewoman not to render the necklace of gold a nobleman had given in an attempt to seduce her.[1632]

In royal households, in particular, women servants who let themselves be courted could retain the presents received, even though they knew that these presents were meant as a means of enticing them into sexual intercourse or a marriage they would never consent to. That was just the way things went in a royal household (*stylus aulae*).[1633] What is more, it would be highly objectionable to refuse these presents, since a refusal would almost amount to accusing the most reverend donator of having evil purposes.[1634] No doubt Lugo was mindful here of Antonino Diana (1586–1633), himself born of a noble family in Palermo, who had defended a woman's right to retain the presents, because it would have been a shameful defeat for those lovers to get back what had been meant as a means of seducing a woman.[1635]

6.6   Grotius enjoying scholastic wisdom

The quasi-jurisprudential dimension of the writings of the moral theologians—who were, it needs to be stressed, consultors and judges in the court of conscience—most frequently developed into very lengthy and intellectually demanding discussions that featured both general theoretical principles, and practical solutions to day-to-day cases. In a certain sense it is a relief, then, to move on to a natural lawyer like Hugo Grotius, and find him sketching a simple and easy-to-read theoretical

---

[1632] Lugo, *De iustitia et iure*, tom. 1, disp. 18, sect. 3, num. 49, p. 501: 'Unde ego foeminae nobili, cui nobilis vir torquem aureum magni valoris sinistra intentione donaverat dixi retineri posse (…) quia nec explicite nec implicite sub pacto dederat, sed solum ad eius animum alliciendum.'

[1633] Lugo, *De iustitia et iure*, tom. 1, disp. 18, sect. 3, num. 51, p. 501: 'Quo pacto excusari possunt famulae honorariae regis vel reginae, quae iuxta morem aulicum obsequia et munera ab adolescentibus nobilibus accipiunt. Illa enim munera iuxta stylum aulae nihil turpe significant (…).'

[1634] Lugo, *De iustitia et iure*, tom. 1, disp. 18, sect. 3, num. 51, p. 501: 'Imo neque honeste possent aliquando respui. Esset enim manifestare, et reprobare turpem animum donantis, quem munera ipsa non significabant. Videbantur enim titulo affinitatis vel honestae amicitiae mitti.'

[1635] Antonino Diana, *Resolutiones morales*, Caesaraugustae 1632, tom. 1, part. 2, tract. 2 (miscell.), resol. 40, p. 128–129: 'Dicendum est, contra Lopez, foeminas accipientes munera suis amatoribus, spe consequendi ab ipsis, quod prave concupiscunt, si non consentiant non esse obnoxias restitutioni, quia nullus est amator qui non verecundaretur et erubesceret si praefata munera sibi remitterentur.'

outline of the issue of moral turpitude and juridical (in)validity within the space of only twenty lines.

Typically, Grotius' account appears to be an elegant crystallization of the conclusions that Lessius had reached in the course of a still polarized debate. In general terms, he raises the question whether a cause that is naturally vicious also vitiates the promise that is made on behalf of it, for instance in the case of an assassination agreement.[1636] The promise to pay seems entirely void because of the worthlessness of the murder which constitutes its cause. But not everything that is vicious becomes deprived of juridical effects for that reason, according to Grotius. Our Dutchman notably refers to the case of a prodigal donation—the legal validity of which had been defended precisely by Lessius against the common opinion—to support his view.[1637]

Clearly tapping into the scholastic tradition—he explicitly cites Cajetan – Grotius holds that after performance (*peracto crimine*), a vicious promise can still entail juridical effects.[1638] Alluding to Lessius' idea of a conditional promise (*promissio conditionata seu respectiva*), Grotius analyzes a promise based on a vicious cause as a promise the juridical efficacy of which is suspended (*in pendenti*) until the vicious act is performed.[1639] Moreover, he refers to the story of Judah and Tamar—which had formed the kernel of the argument of his fellow country-man Adrian of Utrecht a century before—to give a concrete example of the juridical validity of a promise involving turpitude.

Interestingly, Grotius would draw criticism by Robert-Joseph Pothier for taking this typically scholastic standpoint. Pothier recalls how Grotius acknowledged the bindingness of an immoral promise as a matter

---

[1636] Grotius, *De jure belli ac pacis* (Ed. De Kanter-Van Hettinga Tromp – Feenstra – Persenaire), lib. 2, cap. 11, par. 9, p. 334: 'Quaeri hic solet, an promissio facta ob causam naturaliter vitiosam ipsa natura valeat, ut si quid promittatur homicidii perpetrandi causa.'

[1637] Grotius, *De jure belli ac pacis* (Ed. De Kanter-Van Hettinga Tromp – Feenstra – Persenaire), lib. 2, cap. 11, par. 9, p. 334: 'Hic ipsam promissionem vitiosam esse satis apparet: in hoc enim adhibetur ut alter impellatur ad malum facinus. Sed non quicquid vitiose sit effectu juris caret, quod in prodiga donatione apparet. Hoc interest, quod donatione facta jam cessat vitiositas: nam sine vitio res relinquitur apud donatarium.'

[1638] Grotius, *De jure belli ac pacis* (Ed. De Kanter-Van Hettinga Tromp – Feenstra – Persenaire), lib. 2, cap. 11, par. 9, p. 334: 'At in promissis ob causam vitiosam manet vitium quamdiu non perpetratum est crimen.'

[1639] Grotius, *De jure belli ac pacis* (Ed. De Kanter-Van Hettinga Tromp – Feenstra – Persenaire), lib. 2, cap. 11, par. 9, p. 403: 'Unde sequitur usque ad id tempus promissionis talis efficaciam esse in pendenti (…); crimine vero perpetrato, jam obligationis vim exseri, quae ab initio non intrinsecus defuit, sed ab accedente vitio fuit impedita.'

of natural law and in the court of conscience after performance of the immoral action.[1640] He points out that Grotius claimed support for this view from the story of Judah and Tamar, and from the argument that once the crime had been committed, the promise no longer allured someone into performing a vicious act and was therefore revived. Pothier rejected Grotius' standpoint, however, arguing that it was immoral. 'Can one imagine,' he asked rhetorically,[1641] 'that natural law should favor criminals to the point of assuring the salary of what they have done?' Seeking support from Pufendorf, he argued that an immoral promise was no less at odds with good morals and natural law after performance of the crime than before.

6.7 CONCLUDING OBSERVATIONS ON SEX AND THE EARLY MODERN THEOLOGIANS

6.7.1 *Classification and analysis of the opinions*

It would be no exaggeration to say that the scholastics' ability to establish a logically coherent doctrine of contract on the manifold traditions of the Bible, patristic authors, canon law, Aristotelian philosophy, and Roman law was put to the ultimate test in their dealing with prostitution and other contracts involving immorality. All of these traditions provided merely partial, ambiguous, and elusive answers to the question of the legal obligations ensuing from morally objectionable agreements. They were interpreted in various and contradictory ways, accordingly.

Two different types of considerations account for the divide between the two main strands of thought within the scholastic tradition—although none of these considerations is developed by the scholastics explicitly. One

---

[1640] Pothier, *Traité des obligations, selon les regles, tant du for de la conscience, que du for extérieur*, part. 1, sec. 1, art. 3, par. 6, p. 44–45: 'Grotius | prétend que ces promesses ne sont pas à la vérité obligatoires, tant que le crime n'a pas été commis, et que jusqu'à ce tems celui qui a fait la promesse peut s'en dédire en donnant un contr'ordre à celui à qui il l'a faite; mais qu'aussi-tôt que le crime a été commis, la promesse devient obligatoire par le droit naturel et dans le for de la conscience: sa raison est que cette promesse est vicieuse en ce qu'elle est un appas au crime; or, ce vice cesse lorsque le crime est commis et consommé: le vice de cette promesse n'existant plus, rien n'empêche qu'elle ne produise son effet, qui est d'obliger à l'accomplissment celui qui l'a faite. Il rapporte l'exemple du patriarche Juda, qui s'acquitta de la promesse qu'il avoit faite à Thamar pour jouir d'elle.'
[1641] Pothier, *Traité des obligations, selon les regles, tant du for de la conscience, que du for extérieur*, p. 46: 'Peut-on penser que la loi naturelle doive favoriser les scélérats jusqu'à leur assurer le salaire de leurs forfaits? Ces raisons me déterminent pour l'avis de Puffendorf.'

school seems to have emphasized the moral objectionability of activities like prostitution and murder, regardless of the circumstances that often surround these agreements. Therefore, they simply refuse to support these agreements through any kind of juridical enforceability. They believe that such activities are not conducive to a virtuous and valuable life, and hence think them to be entirely unworthy of legal effects. Presumably, they think it is beneath the dignity of the law and of the judges in the court of conscience to enforce such agreements.

Another school of thought and 'conscientious' jurisprudence, however, shows greater awareness of the financial interests of those entering into prostitution or murder agreements. They seem to be more attentive to the fact that these kinds of agreements are often accepted by people who are in financial difficulty and have few available options. Most prostitutes had considerably less power than did most of their clients. In a certain sense, it is beneath the dignity of the poor and the weak not to attribute at least some juridically enforceable consequences to these activities. Blaise Pascal's mockery of the Jesuit's defence of a prostitute's or an assassin's right to retain what he or she received in exchange for an immoral service is too cheap, then.[1642] Also, Pascal should have added Soto, Covarruvias, and Grotius to the list of authors who formed the butt of his easy derision.

Both considerations derive from a genuine concern for morality. Yet at the same time they illustrate how big an impact small changes in the analysis of a case can have on its final resolution, even if particularly learned people share a common concern for moral values that are derived from the same (Christian) tradition.

The first 'school', which tasted defeat in the scholastic race, but might have come closer to modern conceptions than their contemporary rivals, chose to identify moral worthlessness with juridical invalidity. No truly juridical obligations or rights could ensue from an evil act such as prostitution, except maybe in a very weak sense as a matter of honesty or liberality. Roughly speaking, that was the point of view of Juan de Medina and Martin de Azpilcueta. Moral turpitude of object and contractual invalidity coincided for them. They had difficulties in granting prostitutes, certainly secret ones, a right of retention as a matter of justice before both

---

[1642] Blaise Pascal, *Les provinciales ou les lettres écrites par Louis de Montalte à un provincial des ses amis, et aux RR. PP. Jésuites: Sur le sujet de la morale, & de la politique de ces pères*, Amsterdam 1657, lettre 8 (Paris, 28 mai, 1656), p. 128.

the internal and the external tribunal, let alone in according them an action for payment. On this account, the moral limitations on 'freedom of contract' were all-pervasive. The juridical order had to reflect the moral order. If moral value was zero, then juridical effects also had to amount to zero.

To a certain extent, this holds true of the second 'school', which represented the majority. Neither Thomas, nor Olivi, Antonine, Bernardine, Cajetan, Vitoria, Soto, Covarruvias, Molina, Lessius, Diana, Lugo or Oñate would have granted a prostitute or any other person performing a morally evil service an action for payment by virtue of a mere consensual agreement. They did not believe that contracts involving immoral activities were enforceable of their own. But they did not believe either that those agreements were utterly lacking in juridical effects. Upon performance, a prostitute has a right as a matter of law and justice both to retain and to claim her profits, certainly in the court of conscience. If she or he was a secret prostitute, payment was even more obligatory. Broadly speaking, these authors did distinguish between value in a moral sense and validity in a juridical sense. Although they acknowledged that prostitution or murder are morally evil, they did not therefore think these activities were of no value on a juridical level.

The attempt at restricting limitations on 'freedom of contract' is particularly clear when we compare how Lessius and Dr. Navarrus, respectively, conceived of the connection that is needed between a contract and an objectionable activity for there to be no juridical obligations on account of turpitude.[1643] Lessius limits the potential of turpitude to avoid a contract to turpitude which concerns the material object to the contract, e.g. a prostitution agreement. Even then, legal obligations still arise after partial performance. Neither is Lessius willing to recognize the law-invalidating potential of turpitude surrounding the final motivation with which one of the parties enters into the contract, e.g. an agreement to rent an appartment to somebody who intends to use it as a brothel. By contrast, Dr. Navarrus inflates the law-invalidating potential of turpitude of object so that no legal obligations can arise out of an agreement tainted by an immoral object anymore. In addition, Dr. Navarrus considers turpitude of the final reasons for which one of the parties enters into the contract to constitute an invalidating factor to the contract.

[1643] For details and references, see above.

Put in scholastic terminology, Lessius brings the invalidating force of immorality only to bear upon the *causa materialis*, while Dr. Navarrus does not flinch from ruining juridical validity by bringing immorality to bear upon both the *causa materialis* and the *causa finalis* in a broad way. To summarize, Lessius would only allow moral considerations to invalidate a contract if that contract requires an immoral activity, whereas Dr. Navarrus would allow turpitude to bring about legal nullity as soon as a contract facilitates an immoral activity.

6.7.2   *Suárez and the protection of 'freedom of contract'*

Lessius' attitude is typical of a general tendency within the early seventeenth century Jesuit order to make a clear distinction between contractual validity, on the one hand, and all kinds of forces limiting the juridical effects of individually established contracts, on the other, whether those limitations derive from natural morality, or from positive human law. On a theoretical level, the debate centered around the correct interpretation of the famous law *Non dubium* (C. 1,14,5), in which, as a general rule, emperors Theodosius and Valentinianus declared void all agreements going against the sense of the law (*contra legis voluntatem*).[1644]

None less than Francisco Suárez made a meritorious attempt to circumscribe the invalidating power of law *Non dubium*. For one thing, he neatly distinguishes laws that radically invalidate agreements (*leges irritantes*), from laws that merely prohibit certain contracts without automatically invalidating them (*leges prohibentes*).[1645] The former take away

---

[1644] Cortese, *La norma giuridica*, vol. 1, p. 27–33. The text of C. 1,14,5 *pr.* et 1 runs as follows: 'Non dubium est in legem committere eum, qui verba legis amplexus contra legis nititur voluntatem: nec poenas insertas legibus evitabit, qui se contra iuris sententiam scaeva praerogativa verborum fraudulenter excusat. Nullum enim pactum, nullam conventionem, nullum contractum inter eos videri volumus subsecutum, qui contrahunt lege contrahere prohibente. Quod ad omnes etiam legum interpretationes tam veteres quam novellas trahi generaliter imperamus, ut legislatori, quod fieri non vult, tantum prohibuisse sufficiat, cetera quasi expressa ex legis liceat voluntate colligere: hoc est ut ea quae lege fieri prohibentur, si fuerint facta, non solum inutilia, sed pro infectis etiam habeantur, licet legislator fieri prohibuerit tantum nec specialiter dixerit inutile esse debere quod factum est. sed et si quid fuerit subsecutum ex eo vel ob id, quod interdicente lege factum est, illud quoque cassum atque inutile esse praecipimus.'

[1645] Suárez, *Tractatus de legibus et legislatore Deo*, lib. 5, cap. 25, num. 22, p. 530: 'Prohibere solum est praecipere et obligare ut actus non fiat; irritare autem non est praecipere, sed facere, scilicet inefficacem reddere voluntatem vel consensum ejus aut inhabilitare personam.'

the juridical effects of a certain act of will, whereas the latter merely pre-
scribe that a certain activity should not take place. Most laws that have
the power to invalidate a contract concern statutory laws imposing form
requirements.[1646] Prohibitive laws are never to be considered invalidating,
unless they expressly mention this fact.[1647] Suárez unremittantly pleads
for a restrictive interpretation of *leges irritantes*. He considers those kinds
of laws to be utterly annoying and against the basic principle of man's
freedom of action.[1648] Suárez thinks that, in a certain sense, an invalidating law (*lex irritans*) robs man of a natural right (*quoddam naturale ius*).

It is no surprise to find, then, that Suárez refers to the very rules of law
laid down by Boniface VIII that form the basis of moral probabilism (a liberal ethical theory centered around human freedom) in order to underpin
his plea for a restrictive interpretation of invalidating laws: VI, reg. iur. 30
(*in obscuris minimum est sequendum*), and VI, reg. iur. 75 (*contra eum qui
legem dicere potuit apertius, est interpretatio facienda*).[1649] What is more,
he expressly points out the basic freedom of man to make contracts, even
involving evil activities, until a superior clearly puts a halt to this freedom
by issuing an invalidating law.[1650] Suárez basically considers a law with
invalidating power as a kind of punishment. As a consequence, it could
only be deemed to be effective, even in the court of conscience, after a
kind of criminal procedure had taken place.[1651]

Referring to Bartolus de Saxoferrato, Suárez argues that nullity *ipso
facto* as propounded in law *Non dubium* is only a kind of legal fiction (*iuris*

[1646] See the previous chapter.

[1647] Suárez would even require canon law regulations to explicitly mention their irritating character. Otherwise they were not supposed to invalidate the juridical effects of
certain acts that did not comply with canon law. See *Tractatus de legibus et legislatore Deo*,
lib. 5, cap. 29, num. 5.

[1648] Suárez, *Tractatus de legibus et legislatore Deo*, lib. 5, cap. 26, num. 24, p. 531: 'In
materia odiosa verba sunt restringenda quoad fieri possit intra eorum proprietates, potius
quam extendenda; sed irritatio actus est valde odiosa et valde repugnans naturae, quia
quodammodo aufert quoddam naturale jus.'

[1649] Suárez, *Tractatus de legibus et legislatore Deo*, lib. 5, cap. 26, num. 24, p. 531.

[1650] Suárez, *Tractatus de legibus et legislatore Deo*, lib. 5, cap. 26, num. 25, p. 531: 'Quia
voluntas humana ex jure naturae habet hanc potestatem contrahendi, donandi, et alia
similia faciendi, quamdiu per superiorem ejus facultas non est ablata vel impedita, etiam
quoad ipsam potestatem et valorem actus. Et ideo non obstat quod actus malus sit. Nam
per actum malum possunt similes effectus valide fieri, ut per se constat.'

[1651] Suárez, *Tractatus de legibus et legislatore Deo*, lib. 5, cap. 28, num. 7, p. 538: 'Quamvis
ex vi illius legis actus sit irritus ipso iure, nihilominus talis irritatio non obligat in conscientiae, nec fit cum effectu, donec per judicem declaretur. Quod probo primo ex principio
supra posito de lege poenali, quod poena etiam ipso facto imposita non incurritur ante
sententiam.'

fictio), leaving the actual value of the juridical act untouched as a matter of natural law. Moreover, the law can only appeal to a legal fiction precisely because in fact there still is a natural obligation.[1652] The only event in which no legal fiction is needed to explain law *Non dubium*, is the case of an agreement that goes against natural morality (*contra bonos mores naturales*). For contracts involving turpitude of object are automatically void, even as a matter of natural law: evil objects are simply incapable of being the source of obligation, according to Suárez.[1653]

6.7.3   *Invalidity versus immorality and illegality*

A practical illustration of the tension between morality in a civil, positive law sense and juridical validity concerns gambling agreements. Those agreements can hardly be said to constitute a sin by nature. In the Aristotelian-Thomistic tradition, play and fun are even considered to be conducive to a happy and virtuous life if enjoyed in the just degree, because man cannot be serious and focus on his work all the time.[1654] Still, certain types

---

[1652] Recently, the late Yan Thomas, like Suárez, emphasized that the main characteristic of legal fictions is that the law wittingly assumes a reality to be true which in fact it knows to be wholly false. Cf. *Les artifices de la vérité en droit commun médiéval*, L'homme, Revue française d'anthropologie, 175–176 (2005), p. 113–130.

For Suárez, see *Tractatus de legibus et legislatore Deo*, lib. 5, cap. 28, num. 10, p. 539: 'Ergo habere aliquid pro infecto nihil aliud est quam incurrisse ipso facto nullitatem, saltem fictione juris. Nam, ut advertit Bart. in dicta l. *Non dubium*, haec verba *pro infectis haberi, censeri*, et similia, secundum juris fictionem significant, et ideo non repugnant naturali valori actus, imo illum supponunt (…) Recte ergo exponitur illa lex de irritatione ipso facto, etiamsi actus non sit omnino nullus in se, et quoad naturalem obligationem, et consequenter optimo conciliantur, quod sit irritus ipso facto fictione juris, et nihilominus non inducatur obligatio in conscientia ad dissolutionem ejus usque ad judicis sententiam.'

[1653] Suárez, *Tractatus de legibus et legislatore Deo*, lib. 5, cap. 28, num. 12, p. 540: 'Talis enim pactio etiam ex natura rei irrita est, non in poenam, sed quia materia ipsa est incapax talis obligationis.'

[1654] Aquinas, *Summa Theologiae*, IIaIIae, quaest. 168, art. 2 (*Utrum in ludis possit esse aliqua virtus*), concl., in: *Opera omnia iussu impensaque Leonis XIII edita*, tom. 10: *Secunda secundae Summae Theologiae a quaestione CXXIII ad quaestionem CLXXXIX*, Romae 1899, p. 351: 'Respondeo dicendum quod, sicut homo indiget corporali quiete ad corporis refocillationem, quod non potest continue laborare, propter hoc quod habet finitam virtutem, quae determinatis laboribus proportionatur; ita etiam est ex parte animae, cuius etiam est virtus finita ad determinatas operationes proportionata, et ideo, quando ultra modum suum in aliquas operationes se extendit, laborat, et ex hoc fatigatur. (…) Sicut autem fatigatio corporalis solvitur per corporis quietem, ita etiam oportet quod fatigatio animalis solvatur per animae quietem. Quies autem animae est delectatio. (…) animus hominis frangeretur, si nunquam a sua intentione relaxaretur. (…) Huiusmodi autem dicta vel facta, in quibus non quaeritur nisi delectatio animalis, vocantur ludicra vel iocosa.'

of gaming or gambling contracts are prohibited by human positive law.[1655] The question which arises, then, is whether the winner of a prohibited game is bound to make restitution.

In this context, Lessius insists on the difference between invalidity, that is absence of juridical obligation (*irritum*) and unlawfulness (*illicitum*).[1656] Not without remembering the classical canon law, Lessius holds that there is much that is unlawful, or forbidden, which nonetheless entails juridical obligations once it has been carried out. Hence, both Suárez and Lessius hold that the winner of a prohibited game has no duty as a matter of natural law to make restitution of his profits, because neither natural law nor positive law can impede the dominion over these profits from being transferred, even if the transfer is based on a prohibited contract.[1657] A law dictating that restitution should be made, must be considered as a penal law. But penal laws can only apply after a due criminal procedure, because otherwise the conscience of the people would be unduly overburdened, according to Lessius, thereby expressing the concern of his master Suárez in a still more concrete way.[1658] This is not to say that the loser is under an obligation to pay.

[1655] Pressure of space dictates that we do not tackle the problem of gambling agreements in early modern scholasticism, which is definitely worthy of a monograph on its own. Lessius lists an overview of gaming contracts prohibited as a matter of civil or canon law in *De iustitia et iure*, lib. 2, cap. 26, dub. 1, num. 4–6.
An excellent account of the theological involvement with gambling contracts in the later Middle Ages is G. Ceccarelli, *Il gioco e il peccato, Economia e rischio nel tardo medioevo*, [Collana di storia dell'economia e del credito promossa dalla fondazione del monte di Bologna e Ravenna, 12], Bologna 2003.

[1656] Lessius, *De iustitia et iure*, lib. 2, cap. 26, dub. 3, num. 17, p. 345: 'Aliud enim est, contractum esse illicitum, aliud esse irritum seu carere vi obligandi. Multa enim illicite fiunt quae tamen facta tenent.' For the latter maxim, see X 3,31,16 quoted above.

[1657] Suárez, *Tractatus de legibus et legislatore Deo*, lib. 5, cap. 25, num. 12, p. 527: 'Licet enim detur actio ei qui perdit ad petendum illa coram judice, nihilominus ante latam sententiam alter restituere non tenetur. Signum ergo est acquisivisse dominium, ac proinde actum fuisse validum, licet postea revocari possit (…) Quae in hoc potissimum fundatur, quod jura prohibentia ludum simpliciter prohibent, et clausulam irritantem non addunt (…).'
Lessius, *De iustitia et iure*, lib. 2, cap. 26, dub. 3, num. 17, p. 345: 'Omnino verius esse, acquisita ludo vetito retineri posse, nec esse obnoxia restitutioni ante sententiam iudicis iubentis restituere. (…) Probatur, quia contractus ludi iure naturae habet vim transferendi dominii; ex eo autem quod talis ludus est prohibitus neque iure naturae neque iure positivo impeditur dominii translatio; ergo acquisita tali ludo non sunt obnoxia restitutioni.'

[1658] Lessius, *De iustitia et iure*, lib. 2, cap. 26, dub. 3, num. 19, p. 345: 'Ratio est, quia haec lex, qua parte iubet solutum reddi, est poenalis, ac proinde non obligat ad id praestandum, quod in poenam statutum est, ante sententiam. (…) Adde, non esse consentaneum moribus hominum, ut victor obligetur ante sententiam, quia rari futuri sunt qui sponte restituent, et ita conscientiae hominum implicarentur absque fructu.'

Before payment is made, the gambling contract is invalid in a relative sense; it is voidable in favor of the loser.[1659] But once the loser has parted with his right not to act on the agreement, granted to him as a kind of a protective measure by the prohibiting law, the contract is entirely valid and productive of juridical effects.

6.7.4   Contract law and unjust enrichment

To return to agreements tainted by natural immorality, it needs to be said that juridical effects to immoral agreements were introduced through what we now understand to be the law of restitution and unjust enrichment, although the scholastics did not necessarily conceive of unjust enrichment as a source of obligations distinct from contract. To be sure, for centuries the *sedes materiae* of the discussion of prostitution had been nothing less than restitution. Moreover, Soto and Covarruvias explicitly refer to unjust enrichment as the basis for their acknowledgement on a normative level of the factual market price for sex.

Typically, with the emergence of an autonomous doctrine of contract distinct from the law of restitution in a moral theologian such as Lessius we also see an attempt to grasp the problem of immoral agreements by means of principles of contract and promise. An agreement for immoral activity is analyzed by Lessius as consisting of two conditional promises (*promissio conditionata seu respectiva*). The promise to pay is not juridically enforceable until the condition for its fulfillment, namely the performance of the immoral activity, has taken place. Grotius varied on this analysis, and it also provided a clue to Pedro de Oñate for solving the dilemma he was faced with.[1660]

To recall Oñate's position as expounded at the outset of this chapter, he had actually set up a sweeping case against the juridical validity

---

[1659] Lessius, *De iustitia et iure*, lib. 2, cap. 26, dub. 4, num. 25, p. 346: 'Quamvis enim lex contractum ludi non reddat proprie irritum (victor enim potest exigere a victo solutionem rei, quam lucratus est, et cum ei tradita fuerit, acquirit eius dominium, nec tenetur eam restituere victo ante sententiam: quod est signum, contractum non fuisse irritum) tamen concedit victo potestatem liberandi se et excutiendi obligationem per contractum inductam, si velit.'

[1660] Oñate, *De contractibus*, tom. 1, tract. 2, disp. 5, sect. 3, num. 276, p. 170: 'Unde ibi duo sunt contractus, quia duo sunt pacta: unus absolutus peccandi, et hic contractus est absolute nullus et invalidus, quia est de re illicita. Alter de solvendis operis mulierculae, et hic est conditionalis, et est licitus et validus in utroque foro, quia mulier implevit conditionem et locavit operas suas (…).'

of contracts involving an immoral object. His argument had been built around the idea of contract as a self-imposed law subject to higher laws within a hierarchy of precepts, the Roman law tradition of law *Generaliter*, and the rational principle of non-contradiction, amongst other evidence. Yet ultimately, Oñate's strong and well-founded argument was crushed by other Roman law principles like Ulpian's paragraph *Sed quod meretrici* from D. 12,5,4,3, and, last, the weight of the scholastic tradition.[1661] He conveys his perplexity as follows:[1662]

> Since a prostitute (and, by analogy, a performer of any other kind of evil activity), does effectively obtain the price for her service; since not only an exception, but also an action lies for her in both the internal and the external court; since the other party to the contract is bound to pay in both courts once the service has been rendered, or otherwise make restitution (according to the common opinion of the doctors, who say that these obligations arise as a matter of justice in exchange, namely by virtue of an employment contract); given all this, how could one claim that the contract is invalid (*quomodo cum hoc stat contractum esse nullum*)?

For Oñate, unjust enrichment is not merely a principle different from contract. He insists on the correlation between the existence of legal obligations and contractual validity. Why must the contract still be valid, according to Oñate? Because the evil service is rendered to the detriment of the one who receives the price, and to the advantage of the one who pays the price.[1663] This is exactly the kind of reasoning a contemporary lawyer would give to invoke the principle of unjust enrichment. Put differently, Oñate cannot conceive of unjust enrichment without maintaining that the contract remains valid, whereas contemporary jurisdictions

---

[1661] Oñate, *De contractibus*, tom. 1, tract. 2, disp. 5, sect. 3, num. 274, p. 169–170: 'Sed certe res haec de meretrice et aliis turpiter contrahentibus (de quibus eadem est ratio) perdifficilis est, et quae multorum torsit ingenia, et in varios modos explicandi fecit abire. (…) Illud in primis urgentissime premit, quod ex sententia omnium fere theologorum (uno excepto Ioanne de Medina q. 20 de restit.) meretrix pretium sui corporis non tenetur restituere. (…) Quin immo meretrices post patratum delictum habent actionem in foro exteriori ut eis solvatur merx conventa, vel (si non convenerit de ea) consueta.'

[1662] Oñate, *De contractibus*, tom. 1, tract. 2, disp. 5, sect. 3, num. 274, p. 170: 'Cum ergo meretrix (et alii dicti) pretium suae meretricationis acquirat, et illud non solum recipere, sed et exigere possit, et contrahens de concubitu post factum teneatur pretium solvere in utroque foro, et restituere, nisi solvat (ut omnes praedicti doctores consentiunt, dicentes, obligationes esse ex iustitia commutativa, ratione contractus locati et conducti), quomodo cum hoc stat contractum esse nullum?'

[1663] Oñate, *De contractibus*, tom. 1, tract. 2, disp. 5, sect. 3, num. 276, p. 170: 'Cum ergo hae operae in detrimentum pretium accipientis, et utilitatem dantis locentur, contractus est validus, et obligationem parit conductori solvendi pretium, et locanti illud exigendi.'

would grant an action by virtue of unjust enrichment precisely because no rights or obligations as a matter of contract or torts lie any more.

For Oñate, and for the scholastics in general, considerations of equilibrium in exchange are simply inherent in contract by definition. If that meant, as is often suggested, that considerations of substantive fairness put serious limitations on 'freedom of contract' in the scholastic tradition, then that is a contention which will be subject to examination in the next chapter.

CHAPTER SEVEN

FAIRNESS IN EXCHANGE

7.1 Introduction

The preceding chapters have conveyed the perplexing feeling that the moral theologians took 'freedom of contract' seriously. External limitations on 'contractual liberty' were carefully circumscribed. However, the modern reader is likely to object that the scholastics' paramount concern with justice in exchange—the subject of the present chapter—is indicative of the fundamental incompatibility between modern and scholastic contract law.[1664] In light of nineteenth century, voluntarist accounts of contract law, this critique is undoubtedly correct. As we have occasionally seen in the discussion on prostitution contracts, the early modern scholastics were concerned with unjust enrichment and fairness in exchange to an extent that seems neither desirable nor feasible to the modern jurist.[1665] As Justice Story put it in 1835,[1666] 'whether bargains are wise and discreet, or profitable or unprofitable, or otherwise, are considerations, not for courts of justice, but for the party himself to deliberate upon'.

However, recent decades have seen a return of the preoccupation with fairness in exchange, notably in consumer contracts.[1667] The concern with justice as an over-arching principle of exchange has also popped up again under the guise of the doctrines of unjust enrichment and restitution.[1668] Hence, the scholastics' battle against exaggeratingly one-sided contracts,

---

[1664] Luhmann, *Das Recht der Gesellschaft*, p. 226–233.

[1665] For a discussion (and refutation) of the arguments that are used by modern jurists to argue against the idea of justice in exchange, see J. Gordley, *Equality in exchange*, California Law Review, 69 (1981), p. 1590–1603.

[1666] Joseph Story, *Commentaries on Equity Jurisprudence* (13th ed.), ed. by M.M. Bigelow, Boston 1886, vol. 1, chapter 6, par. 244, p. 255.

[1667] See, for example, J. Stuyck – E. Terryn – T. Van Dyck, *Confidence through fairness? The new directive on unfair business-to-consumer practices in the internal market*, Common Market Law Review, 43 (2006), p. 107–152, and S. Stijns – E. Swaenepoel, *De evolutie van de basisbeginselen in het contractenrecht, geïllustreerd aan de hand van het contractueel evenwicht*, in: I. Samoy (ed.), Evolutie van de basisbeginselen van het contractenrecht, Antwerpen – Oxford 2010, p. 1–58.

[1668] E.g. V. Sagaert, *Unjust enrichment and change of position*, Maastricht Journal of European and Comparative Law, 11 (2004), p. 159–186.

exploitation of weak parties and unconscionability may actually strike
jurists at the outset of the twenty-first century as not wholly unfamiliar, even if the scholastic conceptual framework behind this battle has
become obsolete. The basic scholastic vocabulary to express the protection against exploitation in contracts, namely justice in exchange (*iustitia commutativa*), just or equal pricing (*iustum seu aequale pretium*) and
lesion beyond moiety (*laesio enormis*), calls forth the wrong associations.
'Justice' is nowadays mostly used with reference to 'social justice' and the
distribution of riches—which it was only to a minor extent for the scholastics. Also, awkward interpretations of the original meaning of the 'just
price' have bestowed a metaphysical taste upon this concept which, originally, it did not have.

The scope of this chapter, then, is to elucidate the conceptual framework of the scholastics' attention paid to what is called 'fairness in
exchange'.[1669] As a matter of fact, the scholastics recognized that natural
law demands two essential things in contracts: mutual consent and justice.[1670] Our first task will be to clarify the natural law precept of commutative justice, the just price as the standard of commutative justice in
contractual exchange, and the remedy by virtue of *laesio enormis* as the
means of guaranteeing fairness in exchange. Against the background of
these fundamental concepts we will be able to understand the conflictual
nature of some of the theological and canonical literature of the first half
of the sixteenth century. The emphasis on fairness in exchange provoked
a clash, indeed, between Roman law and Aristotelian-Thomistic virtue
ethics. It also sharpened tensions between the concurrent jurisdictions of
the *forum internum* and the *forum externum*.

The co-existence of conflicting texts on justice in exchange and the
tension between parallel normative orders stimulated profound reflection on the true meaning of C. 4,44,2. A major part of this chapter is
therefore dedicated to the analysis of two major expositions on the doctrine of *laesio enormis* around the mid-sixteenth century. One is from the

---

[1669] For stylistic reasons alternative designations are used in this chapter to render *iustitia commutativa* into English, including 'commutative justice', 'equilibrium in exchange',
'equality in exchange' and 'substantive fairness'.

[1670] E.g. Lessius, *De iustitia et iure*, lib. 17, cap. 6, num. 36, p. 201: 'Si [contractus] est
omnino irritus iure naturae, id provenit vel defectu consensus vel quia intervenit iniuria.'
Compare K. Luig, *Vertragsfreiheit und Äquivalenzprinzip im gemeinen Recht und im BGB,
Bemerkungen zur Vorgeschichte des § 138 II BGB*, in: Aspekte europäischer Rechtsgeschichte,
Festgabe für Helmut Coing zum 70. Geburtstag, [Ius Commune, Sonderhefte, Texte und
Monographien, 17], Frankfurt am Main 1982, p. 171–206.

canonist Diego de Covarruvias y Leyva, the other from the civilian Arias Piñel. Although Piñel is less classical than Covarruvias in his interpretation, both jurists are each in their own way profoundly indebted to the scholastic tradition, as they take the principle of justice in exchange very seriously. Although this chapter almost exclusively concentrates on the theory behind justice in exchange and the remedy based on C. 4,44,2, an important caveat is added towards the end of the exposition. It needs to be remarked that despite their emphasizing fairness in exchange, many moral theologians have proven themselves to be more liberal than the nineteenth century jurists would even have thought possible when dealing with practical cases.

7.2   THE POINT OF GRAVITY: JUST PRICING

7.2.1   Justitia commutativa

7.2.1.1   *Enriching contracts*

The moral foundations of scholastic contract law largely rest on the Aristotelian-Thomistic virtue of commutative justice. Significantly, Oñate defines contractual obligation in lucrative as well as onerous contracts in terms of justice in exchange.[1671] Until the age of the codifications, justice in exchange forms the common institutional translation of a genuine concern with contractual equilibrium now often associated with social responsibility, consumer protection or unconscionability.[1672] It stipulates that contracts should not suffer from gross disparity or one-sidedness. Contracts should not enrich one party while harming another. In Thomas' vocabulary this means that equality should be preserved between what

---

[1671] Oñate, *De contractibus*, tom. 1, tract. 1, disp. 1, sect. 3, num. 26, p. 7: 'Contractus est pactum obligans ex iustitia commutativa. Quia haec definitio tollit defectus aliarum, datur per verum genus et differentiam, competit contractibus onerosis et lucrativis, et non datur per effectus, sed per essentialia contratus. Et coincidit haec definitio cum definitione Lessii (…)'.

[1672] For the general renaissance of Aristotelian moral philosophy in sixteenth century jurisprudence, cf. Birocchi, *Alla ricerca dell'ordine*, p. 159–164. It may also be recalled that the idea of commutative justice continues to govern the law of contract in many parts of the globe today, not only as a historical relict in minor scraps of the modern codifications, but most of all in Islamic law, which shares the Aristotelian vocabulary with scholastic contract law; see H. Hassan, *Contracts in Islamic law, The principles of commutative justice and liberality*, Journal of Islamic studies, 13 (2002), p. 257–297.

is given and what is received in exchange (*aequalitas inter datum et acceptum*).[1673]

The reason why so much importance was attached to equality in exchange brings us back to the heart of Aristotelian-Thomistic political philosophy. 'Those contracts,' Soto admonishes, 'have been introduced for the common good and for mutual benefit (*in commune bonum aequaleque commodum*)'.[1674] From which Bañez infers that 'what has been introduced for the sake of common utility must not be to the detriment of one party rather than another'.[1675] Referring to Aristotle's *Politics*, the canonist Dr. Navarrus insists that contracts must be concluded for the benefit of both parties to the exchange (*pro communi utilitate ambarum partium*).[1676] To guarantee that exchanges happen for the benefit of both parties to the transaction, equality in exchange must be observed, according to Molina:[1677] 'What has been introduced for the sake of common utility must not be to the detriment of one party rather than another. Natural law demands this, prescribing that you do not unto others what you would not reasonably

---

[1673] This is sufficiently well-known. For an excellent, recent discussion of Aristotle's and Thomas' conception of commutative justice and its lasting influence on the legal tradition, particularly in Scotland, see D. Reid, *Thomas Aquinas and Viscount Stair, The influence of scholastic moral theology on Stair's account of restitution and recompense*, The Journal of Legal History, 29 (2008), p. 189–214.

[1674] Soto, *De iustitia et iure* (ed. fac. V. Diego Carro – M. González Ordóñez, vol. 3), lib. 6, quaest. 3, art. 1, p. 555: 'Si emptio et venditio secundum suam nude naturam contempleris, neutiquam licet rem aut iusto maioris vendere, aut minoris emere. Conclusio est patentissima. Est enim hoc genus contractuum in commune bonum aequaleque commodum introductum. Quod autem sic institutum est, neutram partium gravare debet, sed ad iustitiae aequalitatem est conficiendum.'

[1675] Bañez, *De iure et iustitia*, ad quaest. 77, p. 532: 'Quod autem pro communi utilitate inductum est, non debet esse magis in gravamen unius quam alterius.'

[1676] Azpilcueta, *Relectio in cap. Novit de iudiciis*, not. 6, coroll. 13, num. 44–45, f. 80r: 'Ut Arist. 1 Politicorum tradit, emptio, et venditio et eadem ratione omnis alia commutatio introducta est pro communi utilitate ambarum partium, quarum altera re alterius indiget. Quod autem pro communi duorum utilitate inductum est, non debet esse gravius alteri, quam alteri, ut esset si pretium excederet valorem mercis aut e contrario.' Azpilcueta is undoubtedly referring to Aristotle's exposition on the natural form of wealth-getting and acquisition of property through exchange. Aristotle inferred the naturalness of barter from the fact that some people have too much and others too little of a certain good. See the famous passage in his *Politica* (Ed. Ross), 1, 9, 1257a14–17, p. 15: 'ἔστι γὰρ ἡ μεταβλητικὴ πάντων, ἀρξαμένη τὸ μὲν πρῶτον ἐκ τοῦ κατὰ φύσιν, τῷ τὰ μὲν πλείω τὰ δὲ ἐλάττω τῶν ἱκανῶν ἔχειν τοὺς ἀνθρώπους'.

[1677] Molina, *De iustitia et iure*, tom. 2 (*De contractibus*), tract. 2, disp. 350, col. 405, num. 6: 'Quod autem pro communi utilitate est introductum, esse non debet in gravamen unius potius quam alterius, iure naturali id efflagitante, quod praescribit, ut, quod tibi rationabiliter non vis fieri, alteri non facias; esset autem in gravamen unius potius quam alterius nisi aequalitas servaretur.'

have them do unto you. However, what you do would be to the detriment of one party rather than another unless equality (*aequalitas*) were observed.'

The socio-political dimension of contract law need not conjure up visions of social collectivism. Oñate insists that contracts serve the purpose of benefitting the parties involved (*privata utilitas*), not necessarily society in general.[1678] He thus reacts against the Jesuit Paolo Comitoli (1545–1626), a specialist in Biblical studies, but also the author of a work on contract law (*Doctrina contractuum universa*).[1679] Comitoli had defined contract as 'a legitimate consensus instituted for the sake of society and mankind' (*legitima consensio ad civitatum humanique generis bonum instituta*).[1680] In Oñate's view, the common good of the entire society matters, of course, but it is the object of legal justice (*iustitia legalis*)—alternatively called 'distributive justice'—rather than of commutative justice. Moreover, following Aristotle and Thomas, the scholastics considered the division of things, private property and commercial exchange as part of the same continuum. 'Exchange and the use of contracts have been introduced as matter of *ius gentium*,' Oñate points out,[1681] 'that is the body of law where contracts have taken their origins from, right after the division of things.' Mankind universally started to conclude contracts once the collectivist distribution of things in the state of nature had been replaced by the division of things and the institution of private property.

However, if contract law is a universal product of different peoples' laws (*ius gentium*), how can we justify the requirement to observe equality in exchange, which is a principle of natural law? Oñate tries to explain this as follows:[1682]

[1678] Oñate, *De contractibus*, tom. 1, tract. 1, disp. 1, sect. 3, num. 14, p. 5: 'In fine aberravit Comitolus; finis enim contrahentium, et ipsius contractus, non est publicum bonum (quod respicit iustitia legalis) sed privata utilitas, quam respicit iusititia commutativa.'

[1679] On Comitoli, see J.P. Donnelly, *Paolo Comitoli*, in: C. O'Neill – J. Domínguez (eds.), Diccionario Histórico de la Compañía de Jesús, Biográfico-Temático, Roma-Madrid 2001, vol. 1, p. 874–875.

[1680] Paolo Comitoli, *Doctrina de contractu universe ad scientiae methodum revocato*, Lugduni 1615, part. 1, cap. 4, num. 10, p. 11: 'Contractus est minimum duarum voluntatum, provocantis et provocatae, quae dominio rationis ac rei praeditae sint, legitima consensio ad rem aliquam agendam, vel non agendam, externo aliquo signo declarata, atque ad civitatum humanique generis bonum instituta.'

[1681] Oñate, *De contractibus*, tom. 1, tract. 1, disp. 1pr., num. 9, p. 2: 'Unde permutatio haec et contractuum usus iure gentium invecta est et iam inde originem contractus trahunt, supposita rerum divisione.'

[1682] Oñate, *De contractibus*, tom. 1, tract. 1, disp. 1pr., num. 10, p. 2: 'Quia supposita rerum divisione subintravit protinus naturale ius, in his commutationibus naturalem aequitatem

Given the division of things, natural law suddenly sneaked in again, ordering that natural equity be observed in these exchanges. It prescribed, not
only that you should not do unto others what you would not have them do
unto you, but also that equality be observed between the objects of these
exchanges, as is required by commutative justice. Natural law further prescribed that equality must be restored through restitution if it has been
violated; also, that agreements, once concluded, must be performed with
great fidelity, and that infringers must be restrained through appropriate
penalties.

Although the sudden return of natural law might come across as a fan-
tastic *deus ex machina*, Oñate brilliantly formulates what was standard
scholastic contract doctrine for about half a millennium: equality as a
governing principle of contractual exchange is imposed by the light of
natural reason.

Determining the legal origins of the equality principle was not a
mere scholastic exercise. Certainly as the Protestant reformation gained
momentum, many people, particularly businessmen, appear to have tried
to escape the rulings on commutative justice imposed by the Catholic doctors. They used the argument that the principle of equality in exchange
could not be found in the Bible. However, the confessors invoked the natural roots of the virtue of justice in exchange as a counter-argument. The
emphasis on the natural law basis of contractual equilibrium is particularly evident from Tomás de Mercado's practice-oriented treatise on commerce and contracts.[1683] Natural reason teaches every human being that
he should not receive more than he gave. Natural law has been inscribed
into our hearts. That is precisely why God did not even need to reveal this
principle anymore through the Gospel. Strictly speaking, the Gospel only

---

servandam esse, praecipiens: non solum ut, quod tibi non vis, alteri ne feceris, sed etiam,
ut in his servetur aequalitas rei ad rem, quam iustitia commutativa praescribit, et ut si vio-
lata fuerit per restitutionem resarciatur, et pacta conventa servari magna fide praecipiens,
et violatores congruis esse poenis cohibendos.'

[1683] Tomás de Mercado, *Suma de tratos y contratos*, Sevilla 1587, lib. 1 (*De la ley natural*),
cap. 3 (*De la distinction de la justicia y contratos*), f. 12v–13r: 'De arte que la justicia en todos
los contratos es la igualdad que en ellos se ha de hacer, a lo cual (como extensamente pro-
bamos) nos obliga no sólo la ley divina, sino también la misma natural. Y es suficientísima
causa para reprobar algún negocio, por de gran interés que sea, no ser conforme al recto
dictamen de la razón, porque (según ya hemos claramente mostrado) nos la puso Dios
por ley dentro de nosotros. Y no es maravilla que haya en nuestra alma alguna regla del
Cielo, pues dice el mismo Señor que dentro de nosotros está el Reino de los Cielos. De lo
cual se colige cuánto yerran los hombres que para tener cualquier contrato en particular
por lícito, o al menos por ilícito, quieren que se les traiga texto formal y redondo sagrado
do lo condemna Dios.'

reveals supernatural truths that are outside the reach of reason, such as the need of baptism for the salvation of the soul.

It is no surprise to find, therefore, that the scholastics identify the virtue of commutative justice with the do-no-harm principle of Roman law. Paragraph *Iuris praecepta* of the renowned title *De iustitia et iure* (D. 1,1,10,1) famously stipulated that law consists of three basic precepts: living honestly (*honeste vivere*), not harming anyone (*neminem laedere*) and giving everyone his due (*suum cuique tribuere*).[1684] Tomás de Mercado praises the Christian tradition for expressing the essence of law in even more concise terms: in relation to himself man must be just (*en sí justo*), in relation to others he must not be unjust (*a nadie injusto*).[1685] The former consists of practicing the virtues of prudence, temperance and fortitude; the latter consists of observing the fourth cardinal virtue, namely justice.

The equality principle was a rather minimalistic precept of conduct. Justice in exchange is not conceived of as some kind of high-minded moral principle.[1686] It merely aims at preventing the contracting parties from harming each other. The do-no-harm principle is the minimal yet necessary basis for making life in political society (*policía*) agreeable.[1687] This understanding of 'justice' explains the often liberal flavor to the scholastic treatises 'On justice and right'. What the theologians meant to describe in this type of literature was how contracts had to be concluded in order not to be detrimental to one of the contracting parties. Having laid down that equality between the things exchanged is tantamount to the do-no-harm principle, Mercado emphasizes that the only thing left for him to explain

---

[1684] For a discussion of these principles among the (post-)glossators, certainly of the fact that these three precepts must form the object of a constant and perpetual subjective will (*constans et perpetua voluntas*), see Cortese, *La norma giuridica*, vol. 2, p. 1–37.

[1685] Mercado, *Suma de tratos y contratos*, lib. 1 (*De la ley natural*), cap. 2 (*De los principios de la razon natural*), f. 9v: 'La substancia de todo lo dicho resuelve con artificioso ingenio y suma brevedad Ulpiano en el Digesto diciendo: Tres son los preceptos o partes del derecho: el primero, vivir honestamente; el segundo, no agraviar a nadie; el tercero, dar lo suyo a su dueño. Y nosotros lo podemos en menos palabras resolver, conviene a saber: los preceptos del derecho son ser el hombre en sí justo y a nadie injusto. Para lo primero sirven la prudencia, templanza y fortaleza; para lo segundo, la justicia con sus virtudes anexas y consiguientes, de que ahora no es tiempo de tratar.'

[1686] Cf. Luhmann, *Das Recht der Gesellschaft*, cited supra, n. 294.

[1687] Mercado, *Suma de tratos y contratos*, lib. 1, cap. 2, f. 9v: 'Mas de la justicia y misericordia tiene suma necesidad sólo por la compañía, sin la cual le sería tristísima la misma vida. Y morar en compañía nadie puede con alegría agraviando a los compañeros, porque del agravio no resulta al actor sino tristeza o temor. De aquí es que, como el hombre ama entrañablemente estar en congregación política, así la justicia, que ordena y conserva esta policía, es y ha de ser una constante y firme voluntad de dar a cada uno lo que le pertenece. De esta manera a nadie agraviará y con todos podrá quietamente vivir.'

is 'how this supreme rule applies in concrete cases, since the only thing it teaches is how to do commerce without harming each other'.[1688]

7.2.1.2   *Restitution*

The moral theologians did not limit themselves to relating the Aristotelian-Thomistic virtue of commutative justice to Ulpian's do-no-harm principle. They also brought justice in exchange in connection with the seventh commandment, not to steal, contained in the Old Testament (Ex. 20:15). In this manner, they created a mixture of religious, philosophical and juridical strands of thought that proved to be of tremendous significance for the history of private law.[1689]

The theologians defined restitution as the recovery of equality in exchange. Defined in this manner, restitution is so encompassing that it covers a lot of legal relationships that would never be described in terms of unjust enrichment in the civilian tradition.[1690] It almost made the Roman categories of actions and remedies superfluous. Restitution was seen as a special act of commutative justice that allowed everyone 'his due', broadly understood as every debt owed to him on account of commutative justice. These debts sprang from the law of justice regarding material as well as spiritual goods, the body as well as reputation.[1691] The theologians were extremely worried about giving everyone his due and avoiding any form of theft. For example, they would argue against Inst. 2,1,35 that the possessor in good faith was not entitled to the fruits consumed, and, therefore, liable

---

[1688] Mercado, *Suma de tratos y contratos*, lib. 1, cap. 2, f. 10v: 'Y aun, hablando claro, no resta más en toda la obra de singularizar esta regla tan suprema, pues en toda ella sólo se enseña a tratar unos con otros sin agraviarse.'

[1689] The theologians' doctrine of restitution has received ample attention in the past; e.g. K. Weinzierl, *Die Restitutionslehre der Hochscholastik bis zum hl. Thomas von Aquin*, München 1939; G. Nufer, *Über die Restitutionslehre der spanischen Spätscholastiker und ihre Ausstrahlung auf die Folgezeit*, München 1969 [= doct. diss.]; G. Dolezalek, *The moral theologians' doctrine of restitution and its juridification in the sixteenth and seventeenth centuries*, in: T.W. Bennett e.a. (ed.), Acta juridica, Essays in honour of Wouter de Vos, Cape Town – Wetton – Johannesburg 1992, p. 104–114; R. Feenstra, *Grotius' doctrine of unjust enrichment as a source of obligation, Its origin and its influence in Roman-Dutch law*, in: E.J.H. Schrage (ed.), Unjust enrichment, The comparative legal history of the law of restitution, [Comparative Studies in Continental and Anglo-American Legal History, 15], Berlin 1995, p. 197–236; Hallebeek, *The concept of unjust enrichment in late scholasticism*, passim.

[1690] As is excellently described in Hallebeek, *The concept of unjust enrichment in late scholasticism*, p. 20–22.

[1691] Azpilcueta, *Enchiridion sive manuale confessariorum et poenitentium*, cap. 17, num. 6, p. 276: 'Restitutio apertius et brevius quam hactenus diffiniri potest esse actus iustitiae specialis commutativae, quo redditur alteri quod suum est, vel quod ei debetur lege verae iustitiae, formaliter vel virtualiter, de bonis animi, corporis, honoris vel pecuniae.'

to make restitution after consumption. Interestingly, the civilians eventually adapted their interpretation of Inst. 2,1,35 to this theological way of seeing things, thus accepting an enrichment liability after consumption by the possessor in good faith.[1692]

Through the doctrines of restitution and unjust enrichment, the theologians could grant remedies in cases that could not be subsumed under the law of property, contract or delict. Inspired by the theologians' prohibition on unjust enrichment, the medieval jurists tried to fill those kinds of gaps by stretching existing remedies or creating new ones.[1693] For example, the early glossator Martinus Gosia stretched the action for management of another's affairs (*actio negotiorum gestorum utilis*) to give relief to the builder on another's property, both in good and bad faith, against the enriched landowner. However, in the medieval tradition, as today, the civilians were also at pains to circumscribe the territory of the doctrine of restitution. For the jurists, unjust enrichment and restitution are merely subsidiary remedies. They are only available in the event that no remedies lie by virtue of property, contract or delict. As a matter of fact, the Roman principle that nobody should be enriched at another's expense as expressed in D. 50,17,206 (*iure naturae aequum est, neminem cum alterius detrimento et iniuria fieri locupletiorem*) was not taken to be a general principle of law granting a universal remedy.[1694]

What is important to explain here is why the theologians were so preoccupied with restitution. The answer to this question is fairly easy but drastic in its consequences. It can be found in one of the Bishop of Hippo's influential letters to Macedonius, the vicar of Africa, who was sent to enforce imperial decrees against the Donatists, a Christian sect.[1695] In this letter, Augustine affirms his colleague's disapproval of offenders wishing to remain in possession of the goods that were the object of

---

[1692] J. Hallebeek, *The reception of Inst. 2.1.35 in late scholasticism*, Rivista internazionale di diritto comune, 7 (1996), p. 133. The author goes on to notice, that, on the other hand, the civilians never abandoned the rule from Inst. 2,1,35 that the possessor in good faith acquires ownership of the fruits that are still extant, and they were gradually followed in this by some of the theologians (p. 134).

[1693] For an elaborate account, see Hallebeek, *The concept of unjust enrichment in late scholasticism*, esp. p. 40–41.

[1694] Hallebeek, *The concept of unjust enrichment in late scholasticism*, p. 1.

[1695] G.L. Caldwell, *Augustine's critique of human justice*, Journal of Church and State, 7 (1960), p. 17–20, reprinted in R.O. Brooks – J.B. Murphy (eds.), *Augustine and modern law*, Farnham – Burlington 2011, p. 107–110.

their offence.[1696] According to Augustine, spiritual salvation by means of penitence (*medicina poenitendi*) is beyond reach of such wretched folks. True penitence and the remission of sins are merely possible when the offender makes restitution to the true owner of what he took away from him (*non remittetur peccatum, nisi restituatur ablatum*). This holds true only if restitution is really possible (*cum restitui potest*). Augustine further admonishes creditors to be merciful (*misericordes*) and the episcopal judges to be human (*ne amittat humanitatem*). He also recognizes priestly intercession in favor of criminals and offenders. Yet in order to temper the apparent tendency of the clergy to show too much mercy for the offender and too little concern for the victim, he also declared that a priest who interceded for a man to save him from the duty to make restitution was an accomplice of the 'thief' rather than a saint.

Augustine's qualification of restitution as a prerequisite for the remission of sin became very influential in the entire Christian world. It made its way into the canonical tradition through Gratian's *Decretum* (C.14, q.6, c.1).[1697] Eventually it was listed as one of the general principles

---

[1696] Augustinus, *Epistola ad Macedonium* (= PL 33, ep. 153, 6, 20, c. 662): 'Quod autem in epistola tua sequitur, ubi dicis: *Verum nunc, ut mores nostri sunt, et sceleris poenam cupiunt sibi homines relaxari, et id propter quod scelus admissum est possidere*; pessimum hominum genus commemoras, cui poenitendi medicina omnino non prodest. Si enim res aliena, propter quam peccatum est, cum reddi possit, non redditur, non agitur poenitentia, sed fingitur: si autem veraciter agitur, non remittetur peccatum, nisi restituatur ablatum; sed, ut dixi, cum restitui potest. Plerumque enim qui aufert, amittit; sive alios patiendo malos, sive ipse male vivendo, nec aliud habet unde restituat. Huic certe non possumus dicere, Redde quod abstulisti, nisi cum eum habere credimus et negare. Ubi quidem si aliquos sustinet a repetente cruciatus, dum existimatur habere quod reddat, nulla est iniquitas; quia etsi non est unde luat ablatam pecuniam, merito tamen dum eam per molestias corporales redhibere compellitur, peccati quo male ablata est, poenas luit. Sed inhumanum non est etiam pro talibus intercedere, tamquam pro reis criminum; non ad hoc ut minime restituantur aliena, sed ne frustra homo in hominem saeviat, ille praesertim qui iam remisit culpam, sed quaerit paecuniam, et si fraudari metuit, non expetit vindicari. Denique in talibus causis, si persuadere potuerimus eos pro quibus intervenimus, non habere quod poscitur, continuo nobis eorum molestiae relaxantur. Aliquando autem misericordes et in ipso dubio nolunt homini pro incerta pecunia certa inferre supplicia. Ad hanc misericordiam vos etiam nos provocare et exhortari decet: melius enim, etiamsi habet, amittis, quam si non habet, aut excrucias, aut occidis. Sed pro istis magis apud eos qui repetunt, quam apud eos qui iudicant, intercedere convenit; ne ipse videatur auferre, qui cum habeat potestatem, non cogit reddere: quamvis in cogendo ita debeat adhibere integritatem, ut ne amittat humanitatem.'

[1697] See O. Descamps, *L'influence du droit canonique médiéval sur la formation d'un droit de la responsabilité*, in: O. Condorelli – F. Roumy – M. Schmoeckel (eds.), Der Einfluss der Kanonistik auf die Europäische Rechtskultur, [Norm und Struktur], Köln-Weimar-Wien 2009, p. 160–165.

of law in Pope Boniface VIII's *Liber Sextus* (VI 5,13,4).[1698] The adage that the remission of sin is not possible unless the stolen good is restored formed the backbone of the late medieval theological doctrine of restitution. One of the most elegant expressions of this doctrine can be found in *quaestio* 62 of Thomas' *Summa Theologiae*. It explicitly defines restitution as an act of commutative justice (*actus iustitiae commutativae*), which is necessary for the salvation of the soul (*de necessitate salutis*).[1699] Through restitution, equality as the basic principle of justice in exchange is restored. It balances the equilibrium in between things (*adaequatio rerum*), which cannot occur unless the person who has less than his due receives what is lacking to him.[1700] For this to happen, restitution of the thing must be made to this person by the one who received it without cause.

The confessional context of the duty to make restitution sheds much needed light on why the theologians did go to such great lengths to understand contract law and business in the first place. The material world mattered to the theologians, because spiritual salvation depends on restitution of what belongs to another. This also explains why the theological concept of property or 'lordship' (*dominium*) is much wider than the civilian one. If it is typical of Roman law to distinguish between possession and ownership, the theological approach tends to encapsulate all forms of 'having a good' under the term *dominium* in its weakest sense.[1701] According to this meaning, *dominium* is very broad in scope and tantamount to

---

[1698] Condorelli, *Norma giuridica e norma morale, giustizia e salus animarum secondo Diego de Covarrubias*, p. 165. This article contains references to further literature on the subject of restitution in early modern scholasticism.

[1699] Aquinas, *Summa Theologiae* (Ed. Leonina, tom. 9), IIaIIae, quaest. 62, art. 2, concl., p. 43: 'Respondeo dicendum quod restitutio, sicut dictum est, est actus iustitiae commutativae, quae in quadam aequalitate consistit. Et ideo restituere importat redditionem illius rei quae iniuste ablata est, sic enim per iteratam eius exhibitionem aequalitas reparatur. Si vero iuste ablatum sit, inaequalitas erit ut ei restituatur, quia iustitia in aequalitate consistit. Cum igitur servare iustitiam sit de necessitate salutis, consequens est quod restituere id quod iniuste ablatum est alicui, sit de necessitate salutis.'

[1700] Aquinas, *Summa Theologiae* (Ed. Leonina, tom. 9), IIaIIae, quaest. 62, art. 2, concl., p. 51: 'Respondeo dicendum quod per restitutionem fit reductio ad aequalitatem commutativae iustitiae, quae consistit in rerum adaequatione, sicut dictum est. Huiusmodi autem rerum adaequatio fieri non posset nisi ei qui minus habet quam quod suum est, suppleretur quod deest. Et ad hanc suppletionem faciendam necesse est ut ei fiat restitutio a quo acceptum est.'

[1701] Hallebeek, *The concept of unjust enrichment in late scholasticism*, p. 47.

any kind of subjective right.[1702] It includes every faculty to 'have a good'. As Vitoria famously put it:[1703]

> In matters related to restitution I use the word *dominium* indiscriminately, regardless of whether I am considering the case of a *dominus*, an *usuarius*, an *usufructuarius*, or a *possessionarius*, since each of them can suffer injury which gives rise to a duty of restitution.

Taking *dominium* in its broadest sense as the starting point of his treatment of contracts and commerce allows Vitoria to make the most careful diagnosis of where the do-no-harm principle has been violated. In all cases where somebody has a certain power over a thing, be it property, use, usufruct, or possession, this power can be violated and, accordingly, restitution is required as the necessary remedy in view of the salvation of the soul.

The theologians widened the concept of 'property' so that all kinds of legal relationships could be brought within the territory of the virtue of commutative justice, and, hence, under the 'government' of the theologians. The spiritual realm demanded that everything belonged to its real *dominus* (*es necesario pongamos en todo razón y orden, dando cada cosa a su dueño*).[1704] However, as witnessed by Erasmus of Rotterdam, who chided people's hypocritical tricks to circumvent the principles of justice in exchange, the theologians were struggling to inculcate the masses with the necessity of making restitution.[1705]

Apparently, the need to escape spiritual condemnation for not having made restitution often led people to try to escape by means of 'forum-shopping'. Tomás de Mercado recounts the story of a Salamancan nobleman who confessed himself to Francisco de Vitoria. Learning that this nobleman was guilty of calumny, Vitoria condemned him to stopping the false lawsuit as a way of making restitution. Yet upon hearing this, the

---

[1702] Cf. supra, p. 353–357.
[1703] Vitoria, *Commentarii in IIamIIae*, quaest. 62, art. 1, num. 8, p. 67 (ed. B. de Heredía): 'Et in materia de restitutione indifferenter utemur dominio, scilicet sive sit dominus, sive usuarius, sive usufructuarius, sive possessionarius, quia in eo etiam cadit injuria quae est obnoxia restitutioni.'
[1704] Mercado, *Suma de tratos y contratos*, lib. 6 (*De restitución*), cap. 1 (*Quan necessaria para nuestra salvación es la restitución*), f. 281r.
[1705] Erasmus, *Exomologesis sive modus confitendi*, Antverpiae 1524, [s.p.]: 'Nunc autem quotumcumque reperias, qui non ad omnem occasionem fraude venatur lucellum? Itaque cum mutuo laniatu vivamus omnes, tamen nobis Christiani videmur. Et haec quoniam in consuetudinem abiere ne confitemur quidem, aut si confitemur, satis esse ducimus sacerdoti denarrasse quod gerimus. Iam qui magis sunt obnoxii restitutionibus quam praepotentes? Et tamen ad hos non videtur pertinere restitutio. Confugitur ad compositiones.'

nobleman furiously left Vitoria and went to another confessor. Unfortunately for him, though, the next confessor, Alfonso de Castro, confirmed the judgment rendered by Vitoria. Castro repeated that the nobleman's sin could not be remitted in the *forum internum* as long as restitution had not been made.[1706]

7.2.2   Justum pretium[1707]

7.2.2.1   *Demystifying the just price*

Few concepts in the history of private law provide us with as good an illustration of how difficult it is to move the dead hand of the historiographical past that takes hold of collective memory than the concept of the 'just price'. Even as scholarship evolves,[1708] there seems to be something preventing the common opinion to dissociate itself from Christian Thomasius' famous description of *laesio enormis* and the corresponding doctrine of just pricing as products of mere cerebral phantasy.[1709] It is

---

[1706] Mercado, *Suma de tratos y contratos*, lib. 6 (*De restitución*), cap. 1 (*Quan necessaria para nuestra salvación es la restitución*), f. 281r–281v: 'Acuérdome de un parecer y respuesta notable que se dio los años pasados en Salamanca a un hidalgo que vino de corte a pedir consejo al padre maestro Vitoria, lumbre que fue en sus tiempos de nuestra España, sobre que, movido de pasión, acusó con falsedad a su adversario de un infame delito, por do le habían preso y le querían ajusticiar. Respondióle «Mi parecer es que os dejéis ir al infierno». Atónito el reo de tan absoluta respuesta, preguntóle «¿No habrá algún medio para salvarme?». Respondió «El más cierto a mi juicio es condenaros». Despedido y medio desesperado, fuese al maestro Castro, varón en letras muy eminente, relatándole juntamente el caso y la resolución primera. Díjole «Él os ha respondido con gran prudencia, viendo en vos y vuestro traje que lo que sois obligado a hacer, que es desdeciros ante el juez, no lo habéis hecho, y, no haciéndolo, no hay salvaros».'

[1707] Given its place as a prelude to the discussions on *laesio enormis*, this is but a brief and generalistic account of scholastic just pricing. For further discussion, see W. Decock, *Leonardus Lessius on buying and selling (1605), Translation and introduction*, Journal of Markets and Morality, 10 (2007), p. 433–516, and Decock, *Breaking the limits*, p. 206–374.

[1708] There is abundant literature on the history of the concept of just pricing. For a good, recent overview, see A. Del Vigo Gutiérrez, *Economía y ética en el siglo XVI, Estudio comparativo entre los Padres de la Reforma y la Teología española*, [Biblioteca de Autores Cristianos, 659], Madrid 2006, p. 511–719.

[1709] Christian Thomasius, *Dissertatio iuridica inauguralis de aequitate cerebrina et l. 2, C. de resc. vend. et eius usu practico*, Halae Magdeburgicae 1706, cap. 2, par. 13. For a nuanced contribution on the development in Thomasius' thinking about just pricing, see K. Luig, *Der gerechte Preis in der Rechtstheorie und Rechtspraxis von Christian Thomasius (1655–1728)*, in: Diritto e potere nella storia europea, Atti in onore di Bruno Paradisi, Bd. 2, Firenze 1982, p. 775–803. Thomasius' criticism of equity in general is also apparent in his rejection of laxist interpretations of C. 3,14, which, in his view, unduly extended the category of the *miserabiles personae*; cf. Th. Duve, *Sonderrecht in der Frühen Neuzeit, Studien*

perhaps no coincidence that Thomasius was the first German jurist to systematically defend the teaching of German private law and to consider the Roman legal tradition as something alien to it.[1710] Moreover, in nineteenth and early twentieth century legal and theological historiography, the idea gained ground that the just price was a metaphysically determined, objective value inherent in all goods.[1711]

The attempt to establish a 'historically correct' understanding of just pricing met with renewed interest in the second half of the twentieth century, certainly among historians of economic thought.[1712] However, it would be naive to assess the compelling results of these endeavors without reference to the great twentieth century ideological stalemate between sympathizers of Marx and free market advocates.[1713] Unsurprisingly, some argued that the medieval doctrine of the just price represented a 'labour or cost of production theory of value', while others identified the just price with the 'competitive market price'.[1714] As far as a 'historically cor-

---

zum ius singulare *und den* privilegia miserabilium personarum, senum und indorum *in Alter und Neuer Welt*, [Studien zur europäischen Rechtsgeschichte, 231], Frankfurt am Main 2008, p. 121–124.

[1710] Schäfer, *Juristische Germanistik*, p. 85–86.

[1711] R. Kaulla, *Die geschichtliche Entwicklung der modernen Werttheorien*, Tübingen 1906, p. 53 and M. Zalba, *Theologiae moralis compendium*, [Biblioteca de Autores Cristianos, 175.2], Matriti 1958, vol. 1, p. 1137, num. 2113. For a critical assessment, see O.I. Langholm, *Price and value in the Aristotelian tradition, A study in scholastic economic sources*, Oslo 1979, p. 28–29.

[1712] For a critical evaluation, see O. Hamouda and B.B. Price, *The Justice of the just price*, The European Journal of the History of Economic Thought, 4 (1997), p. 191–216.

[1713] J.W. Baldwin, *The medieval theories of the just price, Romanists, canonists and theologians in the twelfth and thirteenth centuries*, Transactions of the American Philosophical Society, 49 (1959), p. 6–7.

[1714] The 'labour theory of value' was advocated, amongst others, by S. Hagenauer, *Das 'justum pretium' bei Thomas von Aquin, Ein Beitrag zur Geschichte der objektiven Werttheorie*, Stuttgart 1931, p. 12–30, and R.H. Tawney, *Religion and the rise of capitalism*, London 1964 [= 1926]. The 'utility theory of value' was defended, amongst many others, by M. Grice-Hutchinson, *The School of Salamanca, Readings in Spanish monetary theory, 1544–1605*, Oxford 1952, p. 48–49; R. De Roover, *Scholastic economics, Survival and lasting influence from the sixteenth century to Adam Smith*, in: J. Kirshner (ed.), Business, banking and economic thought in late medieval and early modern Europe, Selected studies, Chicago 1974, p. 306–335 [= reprint of R. De Roover, *Scholastic economics, Survival and lasting influence from the sixteenth century to Adam Smith*, Quarterly Journal of Economics, 69 (1955), p. 161–190; A.A. Chafuen, *Christians for freedom, Late-scholastic economics*, San Francisco 1986, passim; R. Beutels, *Leonardus Lessius (1554–1623), Portret van een Zuidnederlandse laat-scholastieke econoom, Een bio-bibliografisch essay*, Wommelgem 1987, p. 68–69; M.N. Rothbard, *Economic thought before Adam Smith, An Austrian perspective on the history of economic thought*, Cheltenham-Northampton, 1999 [= 1995], vol. 1, passim.

rect' insight into the scholastics' concept of the just price is possible in the first place, one would be inclined to favor the latter opinion.[1715]

One of the clearest illustrations of the fact that the scholastics' conception of the just price was neither metaphysical nor Marxist can be found in Covarruvias.[1716] In his commentary on C. 4,44,2, the bishop of Segovia explicitly holds that the just price is never (*nequaquam*) to be based either on the nature of the thing or on the labour of the seller.[1717] Undoubtedly alluding to Augustine's distinction between the ontological order and the economic order, Covarruvias takes the example of a gem, which is generally worth more than a horse on account of utility, even though animate creatures occupy a higher rank in the order of nature than inanimate things. The measure of value in the economic realm is utility.[1718] According to Covarruvias, the common estimation by the people (*communis aestimatio hominum*) is the yardstick of justice in exchange, even if it were insane (*tametsi insana sit*). By the same token, no matter how much costs a merchant from Flanders incurs on his way across the Pyrenees to the Iberian peninsula, in Spain he can only charge the common estimation of his goods in the local market.

[1715] As do Gordley, *The philosophical origins of modern contract doctrine*, p. 94–102, and Zimmermann, *The law of obligations*, p. 264–267. Ironically, the 'labour theory of value' seems to rest at least partially on an ambiguous 13th-century translation of the Greek word 'χρεία' ('need') figuring in Aristotle's *Ethica Nicomachea* (Ed. Bywater), 5, 5, 1133a27, p. 99 with the Latin word 'opus' (which can mean 'need', certainly in the expression 'mihi opus est', but also 'work'); see Langholm, *Price and value*, p. 75–79.

[1716] Covarruvias' brief account of just pricing luckily found its way into Zimmermann, *The law of obligations*, p. 265–266, n. 190–192. It is strange, therefore, to find that scholars continue to characterize Pothier's discussion as a rupture with the canon law tradition; see Deroussin, *Histoire du droit des obligations*, p. 412: 'Le prix d'une chose n'est donc pas un "point indivisible" (Pothier, oblig, n. 33): l'on ne peut mieux rejeter l'idée défendue par les canonistes d'un juste prix et d'une valeur objective et intrinsèque de chaque chose.' In fact, Pothier's ideas on equality in exchange and just pricing could hardly be a better example of the persisting influence of early modern scholastic contract law on the subsequent legal tradition (on the classical scholastic idea of the market price as not being indivisible, cf. infra).

[1717] Covarruvias, *Variarum resolutionum libri quattuor*, lib. 2, cap. 3, num. 4, in: Opera omnia, Augustae Taurinorum 1594, tom. 1, p. 244: 'Primum, in contractibus emptionum et venditionum similibusque permutationibus, nequaquam attendi, ne constitui iustum pretium ex natura rei, sed ex hominum aestimatione, tametsi insana sit aestimatio. (...) Secundo, hinc apparet in pretii iusti aestimatione non esse considerandum quanti res ipsa empta fuerit nec quot labores pro eius acquisitione venditor fuerit perpessus, sed tantum habendam esse rationem communis hominum aestimationis.'

[1718] Augustinus, *De civitate Dei*, 11, 16 (*De gradibus et differentiis creaturarum, quas aliter pendit usus utilitatis, aliter ordo rationis*), cited supra, n. 1483.

7.2.2.2 *Utility and necessity*

A balanced account of the scholastics' market-friendly approach to just pricing must try to discover what was at stake for the medieval and early modern jurists and theologians in identifying the just price with the competitive market price. In this respect, scholars have rightly pointed out that the just price amounted to the price that guaranteed equilibrium in exchange and, hence, protected individual parties from being exploited through one-sided contracts.[1719] It suffices to recall that *pretium iustum* and *pretium aequale* are used interchangeably, precisely because the just price guarantees the equality (*aequalitas*) between what is received and what is given. A market price attains this equality because it is established through common estimation (*communis aestimatio*). It is not dependent on individual wishes and wants. Paradoxically, in a market a price determined subjectively by all becomes objective to each.[1720] Consequently, the risk of exploitation by one contracting party in a peculiar situation of distress is seriously limited.

The just price is neither a metaphysical value nor a product of arbitrary feelings. As the scholastics famously put it by referring to D. 35,2,63, prices are not determined by affection or individual utility, but by common estimation (*pretia rerum non ex affectu, nec utilitate singulorum, sed communiter funguntur*).[1721] Following Augustine, the scholastics would not accept unreservedly that man follows his animal appetite and insatiable thirst always to want to sell for more and to buy for less.[1722] Christian moral theology in general, and scholastic doctrine of just pricing in particular, demand a Stoic control of passions, desires and arbitrary whims. At least

---

[1719] This is the upshot of O.I. Langholm, *The legacy of scholasticism in economic thought, Antecedents of choice and power*, Cambridge 1998.

[1720] J.T. Noonan, Jr., *The scholastic analysis of usury*, Cambridge Mass. 1957, p. 87; Langholm, *The legacy of scholasticism in economic thought*, p. 83.

[1721] The question is, then, how to interpret 'communiter'; see *inter alios*, Gómez Camacho, *Luís de Molina, La teoría del justo precio*, p. 54–57; Langholm, *The legacy of scholasticism in economic thought*, p. 101–102; D. Wood, *Medieval economic thought*, Cambridge 2002, p. 135–136.

[1722] Augustinus, *De Trinitate*, 13, 3, 6, in: *Aureli Augustini opera, Pars XVI, 2*, [Corpus Christianorum Series Latina, 50A], Turnholti 1968, p. 388: 'Et mimus quidem ille vel se ipsum intuendo vel alios quoque experiendo *vili* velle *emere et caro vendere* omnibus id credidit esse commune. Sed quoniam revera vitium est, potest quisque adipisci eiusmodi iustitiam vel alicuius alterius vitii quod huic contrarium est incurrere pestilentiam qua huic resistat et vincat. Nam scio ipse hominem cum venalis codex ei fuisset oblatus pretique eius ignarum et ideo quiddam exiguum poscentem cerneret venditorem, iustum pretium quod multo amplius erat nec opinanti dedisse.'

in this respect, there is an unbridgeable gap between the Christian concept of 'liberty', or that of Plato, Aristotle or the Stoics, for that matter, and that of an instinct-driven consumer society.

The idea that the just price is not just the outcome of a whimsical decision highlights the embeddedness of scholastic contract law in a specific conception of man. Man's will is thought to be auto-nomous, it can create its own laws, but within the hierarchy of laws it remains subject to a plethora of external laws. Those laws include positive human laws, divine law, and, last, natural law, which is regarded by the scholastics as the very source of the precept of justice in exchange. Tomás de Mercado has granted us an invaluable insight into this anthropological foundation of the doctrine of just pricing:[1723]

> Hence, even though we naturally have a free will, we should mind our thinking, not because our liberty and will have abandoned us, but because it is necessary to freely mind our free will and bind it with many ropes, ever since sin has been released. Those ropes are the laws. They teach us not only what we have to do, but also what we have to desire. We are bound to observe them all and implement them in our contracts, so that we do business not according to our desires and appetites, but according to what the laws show and order us to do. The law is the rule of our life through which we render our works measured and balanced.

The disciplined behavior required from the contracting parties expresses itself *par excellence* in what Langholm has famously called the 'double rule of just pricing'.[1724] Parties, particularly vendors, could take into account their own affections, for example, a certain jewel was a family heirloom, but not that of the other party. The utility of the other party (*necessitas seu utilitas alterius contrahentis*) could not influence the price. Essentially,

---

[1723] Mercado, *Suma de tratos y contratos*, lib. 1 (*De la ley natural*), cap. 3 (*De la distinction de la justicia y contratos*), f. 14v: 'De arte que, dado seamos de libre albedrío natural, estamos más cautivos de lo que pensamos, no porque se nos quite nuestra libertad y voluntad, sino porque, según después del pecado es suelta, es menester voluntariamente cautivarla y atarla a muchas maromas, que son estas leyes que nos enseñan no solamente lo que hemos de hacer, sino aun lo que hemos de querer. Y estamos obligados a guardarlas todas y ponerlas en ejecución en nuestros contratos, negociando, no según deseamos y apetecemos, sino según ellas nos mostraren y mandaren. La ley es regla de nuestra vida por do midamos y nivelemos nuestras obras.'

Mercado's doctrine of just pricing is discussed in O. Popescu, *Studies in the history of Latin American economic thought*, London – New York 1997, p. 16–31.

[1724] O.I. Langholm, *The Aristotelian analysis of usury*, Bergen 1984, p. 46–48; O.I. Langholm, *Economics in the medieval schools, Wealth, exchange, value, money and usury according to the Paris theological tradition. 1200–1350*, [Studien und Texte zur Geistesgeschichte des Mittelalters, 29], Leiden 1992, p. 232–234.

this rule goes back to Thomas' admonishment that you cannot sell what is not yours.[1725] However, you can demand the price of the utility the object renders to you, or, of the emotional or material damage you suffer from parting with it for the sake of the other party. An excellent summary of this principle is contained in Thisius' PhD thesis:[1726]

> To prevent you from harming the other party, willing though he is, it is not sufficient that he is absolutely voluntary and involuntary only in a relative sense. Now assume I part with something for the sake of the other party through an onerous contract. It is not licit for me to estimate the utility the other party will procure from this by reason of circumstances that have specifically to do with him; for in regard to goods I give or award to another party through sale-purchase or another onerous contract, it is not licit for me to estimate the value of those goods in regard to their value to the person who concludes the contract with me, but only in regard to their common value or, surely, in regard to their special value for me insofar as I deprive myself of those goods for his sake.

The prohibition on taking into account the utility of the good for a particular buyer allowed the scholastics to offer a guarantee against the exploitation of an individual's need and passions. As Vitoria famously said, while common utility or necessity constitutes the very basis of the price mechanism (*necessitas communis auget pretium rei*), private utility is not allowed to have an influence on the price (*necessitas unius hominis non auget pretium rei*).[1727]

[1725] Aquinas, *Summa Theologiae* (Ed. Leonina, tom. 9), IIaIIae, quaest. 77, art. 1, concl., p. 148: 'Nullus autem debet vendere alteri quod non est suum, licet possit ei vendere damnum quod patitur.'

[1726] Leonardus Ignatius Thisius Mosae-Trajectinus, *Theses theologicae quibus exhibentur quaedam observationes circa aliquot propositiones de furto, compensatione occulta et restitutione inter lxv a Innocentio condemnatas* [praeses: Gummarus Huygens Lyranus; defensio in collegio Adriani VI die 7 decembris 1684], Lovanii 1684, concl. 2, par. 6 [s.p.]: 'Ut injuriam non inferas alteri volenti, non sufficit quod sit voluntarius simpliciter et involuntarius secundum quid. Nec licet in iis quibus nos privamus in gratiam alterius per contractum onerosum pretio aestimare utilitatem quam alter inde accipiet ob circumstantias quae singulariter se tenent parte illius. Siquidem non licet nobis in iis quae per contractum emptionis et venditionis aut alium onerosum alicui damus vel addicimus aestimare valorem quem ista habent respectu illius cum quo contrahimus, sed solummodo valorem communem, vel certe specialem quem habet respectu nostrum, quatenus nosmetipsos in alterius gratiam illis rebus privamus.'

[1727] Compare Vitoria, *Commentarii in IIamIIae*, quaest. 77, art. 1, nrum. 13, p. 129 (ed. B. de Heredía): 'Quia si esset necessitas communis et utilitas, sicut si milites quaerant equos, tunc bene liceret mihi carius vendere equum meum propter hanc necessitatem et utilitatem communem, quia necessitas communis auget pretium rei. Non tamen propter necessitatem et utilitatem privatam licet carius vendere rem, ut intelligit sanctus Thomas, quia necessitas unius hominis non auget pretium rei.'

This explains why the scholastic jurists and theologians were no market fundamentalists either. If market prices were thought to fail to provide a guarantee against exploitation of the necessity or utility of an individual or a group of individuals, such as the poor, the market price needed to be abandoned. This could be the case in particular situations where markets were not competitive, as in the case of monopolies, but also in regard to the sale of particular goods, such as bread or financial products. In such instances, the public authorities were demanded to intervene. It pertained to the prince's office to protect the weak, and, hence, to issue a law that fixed the price.[1728] This was the legitimate price (*pretium legitimum*), as opposed to the market price (*pretium vulgare seu naturale*).

The fact that the scholastics saw the market mechanism as a guarantee against the abuse of particular utility and necessity, not as an end in itself, is also obvious from their emphasis on the human character of market transactions. As John Mair advised, if you want to know what the just price is, then go to the market and see what prudent bussinesmen consider a good price.[1729] Time and again the scholastics insist that the just price is the common estimation by prudent, good and intelligent men. At least in principle, the anthropology underlying the scholastic paradigm in economics is not that of the 'homo economicus' who is but a mechanical part in the wheels of the economy.[1730] Market participants are not just passive price takers, but also morally responsible price makers.[1731] We should

---

[1728] Some theologians, such as Gregorio de Valentia, expressed the idea that in an ideal world all prices must be fixed by the public authorities as a guarantee against exploitation of particular utility and the needy; Gregorio de Valentia, *De discernenda humanorum contractuum iustitia et iniustitia disputatio theologica in celebri et catholica academia Ingolstadiensi anno MDLXXVII die 22 Maij habita*, Ingolstadii 1577, cap. 1, num. 8, p. 2: 'Et consultissimum quidem esset, ut omnium rerum aequalitas lege decerneretur, minor ut locus esset iniquitati. Sed quia id fieri non potest in omnibus, in multis necesse est relinquatur humano arbitrio. Ita tamen, ut non ex singulorum cupiditate, sed communi proborum iudicio, aestimationis humanae quantitas metienda sit.'

[1729] John Mair, *In quartum sententiarum quaestiones*, Parisiis 1516, dist. 15, quaest. 41, par. *Secunda conclusio*, f. 113r: 'Video quomodo prudentes in foro vendunt talem tritici mensuram: tales ulnas panni, et taliter debeo vendere communiter, et ita de aliis rebus quae communiter in usum veniunt. Eodem modo in emendo. Ut si sto prope prudentes ementes pannos: video quanti emunt; scio eos esse prudentes in arte qui non circumvenientur: emo de eodem simili precio.'

[1730] See, especially, F. Gómez Camacho, *Economía y filosofía moral, La formación del pensamiento económico europeo en la Escolástica española*, [Historia del pensamiento económico, 1], Madrid 1998, passim; O. De-Juan and F. Monsalve, *Morally ruled behaviour, The neglected contribution of scholasticism*, The European Journal of the History of Economic Thought, 13 (2006), 99–112.

[1731] However, in the solution of practical cases, moral theologians came amazingly close to the promotion of self-interest and the belief in impersonal market forces. Certainly from

therefore be careful in considering the scholastics' market price (*pretium naturale*) as synonymous with Adam Smith's natural price.[1732] Still, the scholastics are rightly called Smith's direct forefathers on account of their extraordinary analytical insight into the functioning of markets.[1733]

The ordinary market price is called the natural price (*pretium naturale*) in contrast to the price set through a positive legislative act of the prince (*pretium legitimum*). Hence, the content of the concept of 'natural price' is in the first place negative: 'natural' indicates the absence of a positive act of legislation. This is not uncommon in early modern scholasticism. For example, in defining 'natural law', Vitoria opposes it to law that has its basis in a human act of will, namely positive law.[1734] Moreover, Molina expressly confirms this interpretation of 'natural' as 'excluding a human law or constitution' in defining the natural price as derived from the things themselves (*ex ipsismet rebus*), but still dependent on the estimation of human persons and fluctuating on account of a variety of market factors.[1735]

The scholastics had a dynamic view of the market price. Contrary to the legitimate price fixed by the public authorities, the natural or vulgar price could account for fluctuations in the market. The *pretium vulgare seu naturale* of a certain good did not coincide with one specific price (*non in indivisibili*), but rather encompassed a variety of prices within a certain latitude (*latitudo*).[1736] This insight was an essential part of the

the second half of the sixteenth century onwards, a 'depersonalization' or 'objectivization' of the market can be observed. See Langholm, *The legacy of scholasticism in economic thought*, p. 99.

[1732] See F. Gómez Camacho, *El pensamiento económico de la Escolástica española a la Ilustración escocesa*, in: F. Gómez Camacho – R. Robledo (eds.), El pensamiento económico en la escuela de Salamanca, Una visión multidisciplinar, [Acta Salmanticensia, Estudios históricos & geográficos, 107], Salamanca 1998, p. 205–240.

[1733] J.A. Schumpeter, *History of economic analysis*, edited from manuscript by Elizabeth Boody Schumpeter, London 1972 [= 1954], p. 111.

[1734] See Cappellini, *Sulla formazione del moderno concetto di 'dottrina generale del diritto'*, p. 335–336, who quotes Vitoria, *Commentarii in IamIIae Divi Thomae*, Salamanca 1934 (ed. B. de Heredía), tom. 3, quaest. 57, art. 2, p. 7: 'Ius naturale est illud quod est necessarium, puta quod non ex voluntate aliqua dependat.'

[1735] Molina, *De iustitia et iure*, tom. 2 (*De contractibus*), tract. 2, disp. 347, col. 392: 'Quoddam aliud est, quod res ipsa, seclusa quacunque lege humana ac publico decreto, habet. Atque hoc ab Aristotele loco citato et ab aliis pretium naturale nuncupatur, non quod non multum ab hominum aestimatione pendeat (...), non item quod eiusmodi pretium valde inconstans non sit ac varium (...), sed naturale dicitur, quoniam ex ipsismet rebus, seclusa quacunque humana lege ac decreto consurgit, dependenter tamen a multis circumstantiis, quibus variatur, atque ab hominum affectu ac aestimatione (...).'

[1736] *Pro ceteris*, Lessius, *De iustitia et iure*, lib. 2, cap. 21, dub. 2, num. 10–12, p. 275: 'Notandum autem esse discrimen inter haec duo pretia, quod *pretium legitimum* consis-

scholastic tradition in economic thought. One of its most famous advocates was Duns Scotus.[1737] He argued that the latitude of the just price was determined either by a positive law or by custom.[1738] It was perfectly possible, then, for you to buy a good at 95 guilders and subsequently sell it at 105 guilders without committing any injustice. In Lessius' view, the competitive market price of a good depended on a plurality of market factors that varied incessantly: demand and supply of the goods, simultaneous evolutions on the money market, the manner in which the transaction was organized, etc.[1739] Even in fixing the price, the public authorities had to take into account these market factors.

Another element of flexibility concerned the doctrine of extrinsic titles (*causae*). Since the parties could take into account certain personal conditions concerning themselves—not those of the other party to the transaction—they could sometimes invoke a particular cause that allowed a deviation from the common estimation or natural price. They include damages incurred (*damnum emergens*), opportunity costs (*lucrum cessans*),

---

tat in indivisibili, *vulgare* non item, sed habeat quamdam latitudinem, ut docet Scotus d. 15, q. 2 et alii doctores. Ratio est, quia legitimum taxatur ab uno vel a multis in unum convenientibus, vulgare autem a plurimorum iudicio pendet, qui non idem omnino iudicant. Quod enim aliqui aestimant 9, alii aestimant 10, alii 11. Hinc fit ut *pretium vulgare* sit triplex, ut communiter docent doctores. *Infimum* seu pium, *medium, summum* quod et rigorosum dicitur. V.g. pretium medium sit 10, infimum erit 9 plus minus, summum 11. Rursus medium sit 100, infimum 95, summum 105, ut ait Covarruvias supra num. 1. Ipsum quoque medium suam habet latitudinem, similiter infimum et summum.'

[1737] Duns Scotus, *Quaestiones in quartum librum Sententiarum*, dist. 15, quaest. 2, num. 14–15, p. 166: 'Sequitur in illa regula, quod aequalitas valoris est servanda. (...) Ista autem aequalitas secundum rectam rationem non consistit in indivisibili, sicut dicit quidam doctor, motus ex hoc, quia iustitia habet tantum medium rei, sed caeterae virtutes medium rationis. Hoc enim falsum est, ut declaratur lib. 3, dist. 34, quaest. 1. Imo in isto medio, quod iustitia commutativa respicit, est magna latitudo, et intra illam latitudinem non attingendo indivisibilem punctum aequivalentiae rei et rei, quia quoad hoc, quasi impossibile esset commutantem attingere, et in quocunque gradu citra extrema fiat, iuste fit.'

[1738] Duns Scotus, *Quaestiones in quartum librum Sententiarum*, dist. 15, quaest. 2, num. 15, p. 167: 'Quae autem sit latitudo et ad quantum se extendat, quandoque ex lege positiva, quandoque ex consuetudine innotescit (...).'

[1739] *Pro ceteris*, Lessius, *De iustitia et iure*, lib. 2, cap. 21, dub. 2, num. 8, p. 275: 'Accedit quod superiores possunt melius ceteris omnes nosse circumstantias ex quibus aestimatio rerum crescit vel decrescit, quarum quaedam spectantur circa merces ipsas, ut copia, inopia, necessitas et utilitas earum, quaedam circa venditores, ut labores, expensae, pericula, damna in illis comparandis, adducendis et conservandis; item modus vendendi, nempe an ultro offerant an rogati vendant; quaedam circa emptores, sintne multi an pauci, sitne pecuniae copia an inopia.'

affections (*affectus*), gift (*donatio*), etc.[1740] These titles must be negotiated among the parties. They are not presumed altogether. According to the 'double rule of just pricing', the particular utility the other party derives from the transaction (*utilitas alterius contrahentis*) is not an extrinsic title that allows one to receive more than one gives in an exchange.[1741] Utility does play a central role in determining the just price, but, as Vitoria famously said, it is common utility and not individual utility that lies at the basis of the common estimation.

Even more room for negotiation was acknowledged in cases where the price of a specific good had not been determined yet by the prince or the market. This was the case, for example, of exotic birds, precious stones or exceptional paintings. A price established under such circumstances was sometimes called a 'conventional price' (*pretium conventionale*), which could then be distinghuished as a third category of prices alongside the *pretium naturale* and the *pretium legitimum*. There was a discussion among the scholastics whether the Roman maxim that goods are worth the price they are sold for should apply in this case or not.[1742] Some, such as Vitoria, argued that no limitation should be tolerated on the contracting parties' liberty to negotiate the price of such a good. The reason he gave for this returns us to the central point concerning the doctrine of just pricing: preventing the abuse of particular utility or necessity. In Vitoria's view, such a risk was non-existent in the sale of luxury goods (*non est necessitas et coactio*).[1743]

[1740] For an excellent overview, see Gregorio de Valentia, *De discernenda humanorum contractuum iustitia et iniustitia*, cap. 3 (*de causis iustis recipiendi plus quam sit datum*), num. 29–117, p. 6–22. There is a parallel here with the discussion on extrinsic titles in the debate on interest-taking and money-lending. See T. Van Houdt, *Money, time and labour, Leonardus Lessius and the ethics of money-lending and interest-taking*, Ethical Perspectives, 2 (1995), p. 11–27.

[1741] Gregorio de Valentia, *De discernenda humanorum contractuum iustitia et iniustitia*, cap. 4 (*de iniquis causis plus quam datum sit recipiendi*), num. 119, p. 22: 'Prima est utilitas alterius contrahentis, quam illi ex accidenti affert opportunus contractus propter concurrentes circumstantias, minime alioqui pertinentes ad rei quae commutatur aestimationem. Ob eiusmodi enim utilitatem plus petere quam alioqui res cummutata valet iniquum est, quandoquidem ea utilitas non ex rei commutatae valore per se accidit sed aliunde.'

[1742] Cf. T. Van Houdt, *The economics of art in early modern times, Some humanist and scholastic approaches*, in: N. De Marchi – C.D. Goodwin (eds.), Economic engagements with art, [Annual Supplement to Volume 31, History of Political Economy], Durham – London 1999, p. 311–320.

[1743] Vitoria, *Commentarii in IIamIIae*, quaest. 77, art. 1, num. 6, p. 123–124 (ed. B. de Heredía): 'Stando dumtaxat in iure naturali et divino, et non loquendo de iure humano, et loquendo de rebus non necessariis, dico quod licet unicuique hujusmodi res vendere quantum poterit, seclusa fraude et dolo et ignorantia. (…) Probatur, quia volenti non fit

7.2.3   Laesio enormis

7.2.3.1   *C. 4,44,2 and the* ius commune

Against the background of commutative justice and just pricing, lesion beyond half the just price ('beyond moiety') makes perfect sense. It is no surprise to find, then, that as soon as Aristotelian philosophy became integrated into the medieval legal tradition, the doctrine of *laesio enormis* reached its most developed form.[1744] It is highly debatable whether the *Lex secunda*—the *locus classicus* of the doctrine of *laesio enormis* along with the less frequently cited C. 4,44,8—originally meant to be more than a specific measure issued by Diocletian to protect poor peasants forced to sell their real estate. Some scholars have even questioned the authenticity of C. 4,44,2 itself, suggesting that its text might have been the subject of interpolation by Justinian's commission.[1745] The text reads as follows:[1746]

> If you or your father have sold a good worth a very high price at a very low price, it would be human that you restore the price to the buyers and then get back the real estate by virtue of the judge's authority, or, if the buyer prefers so, that you receive the rest of the just price. It seems that we are dealing with a very low price when not even half (*dimidia pars*) of the true price has been paid.

---

iniuria, sed iste qui dat pro illo lapide mille aureos, simpliciter voluntarie dat, et non est | dolus nec ignorantia quia ille bene scit quod non tantum valet, nec est timor nec necessitas et coactio, ergo nulla fit ei iniuria. Ergo iste licite lapidem illum emit et licite alius vendit, et per consequens qui illum vendit non tenetur ad restitutionem.'

[1744] On *laesio enormis* and its development in the late Middle Ages, see Gordley, *Equality in exchange*, p. 1638–1645, and Baldwin, *The medieval theories of the just price*, p. 3–92.

[1745] There is a vast literature on this subject, debated in C. Becker, *Die Lehre von der laesio enormis in der Sicht der heutigen Wucherproblematik, Ausgewogenheit als Vetragsinhalt und § 138 BGB*, [Beiträge zur Neueren Privatrechtsgeschichte, 10], Köln e.a. 1993, p. 10–26; H. Kalb, *Laesio enormis im gelehrten Recht, Kanonistische Studien zur Läsionsanfechtung*, [Kirche und Recht, 19], Wien 1992, p. 11–27; and Zimmermann, *The law of obligations*, p. 259–261, n. 156–169. It is worthwhile noting that Becker and Kalb often disagree with the conclusions reached by René Dekkers in his *La lésion énorme, Introduction à l'histoire des sources du droit*, Paris 1937—a book which formed the basis of Henri De Page's historical reflections on *laesio enormis* in *Le problème de la lésion dans les contrats*, Bruxelles 1946. Even more questionable in light of Kalb's and Becker's scholarship is W.G. Schulze's *Die laesio enormis in der deutschen Privatrechtsgeschichte*, Münster 1973. On the ancient origins of *laesio enormis*, see B. Sirks, *Laesio enormis again*, Revue internationale des droits de l'antiquité, 54 (2007), p. 461–470.

[1746] C. 4,44,2 in *Corporis Iustinianaei Codex* (ed. Gothofredi), tom. 5, col. 920: 'Rem maioris pretii si tu vel pater tuus minoris pretii distraxit, humanum est, ut vel pretium te restituente emptoribus fundum venundatum recipias auctoritate iudicis intercedente, vel, si emptor elegerit, quod deest iusto pretio recipias. Minus autem pretium esse videtur, si nec dimidia pars veri pretii soluta sit.'

Whatever the original meaning of C. 4,44,2, it soon became the *communis opinio* among the civilians and canonists of the late medieval period that a remedy was granted to the *laesus*, that is the vendor, who had sold his estate for less than half the just price.[1747] It was nevertheless up to the *laedens*, that is the buyer, to decide whether he would have the contract rescinded or pay the additional value of the good (*electio est emptoris*).[1748] The remedy of C. 4,44,2 was gradually extended to the buyer who had bought at an excessive price and, hence, was the *laesus* rather than the *laedens*. From sale purchase the *Lex secunda* also became applied more extensively to other contracts of good faith. D. 19,2,22,3 provided the jurists even with an explicit argument from Roman law to extend the doctrine of lesion to lease contracts. Eventually, the doctrine of *laesio enormis* was applied to all contracts of good faith and a large number of contracts of strict law.[1749]

Soon the debate became centered on the right meaning of 'half the just price' (*dimidium/dimidia pars*).[1750] There was almost no controversy about the meaning of 'half' the just price in the case of a vendor. If x is the just price, then a vendor was said to suffer from *laesio enormis* as soon as he received less than $x/2$. However, it was not altogether clear what 'half' the just price should mean in the case of a harmed buyer. According to the ordinary gloss, which became the common opinion, a buyer was deemed to suffer lesion beyond moiety as soon as he paid more than $1{,}5x$.[1751] For example, if the just price is 100, then he suffered harm if he paid more

[1747] For the medieval doctrine of *laesio enormis*, see the excellent synthesis in Feenstra-Ahsmann, *Contract*, p. 26–30. A less succinct but somewhat pedantic account of medieval thinking on *laesio enormis* is contained in G. Fransen, *Le dol dans la conclusion des actes juridiques, Évolution des doctrines et système du Code canonique*, [Universitas Catholica Lovaniensis, Dissertationes ad gradum magistri in Facultate Theologiae vel in Facultate Iuris Canonici consequendum conscriptae, series 2, tom. 37], Gembloux 1946, p. 49–55 and p. 158–170.

[1748] Baldus, *Commentaria in quartum et quintum Codicis libros*, ad C. 4, 44, 2, num. 2, f. 135v.

[1749] Baldus, *Commentaria in quartum et quintum Codicis libros*, num. 17–18, f. 136r: 'Omnium contractuum bonae fidei eadem est aequitas et ratio, ergo idem ius debet esse (...). Dico etiam quod aequitas huius legis extendit se ad contractus stricti iuris, in quibus hinc inde par debet nasci obligatio secundum naturalem aequitatem (...).' See also C. Bekker, *Die Lehre von der laesio enormis*, p. 61–77.

[1750] For a brief overview, see M. Kriechbaum – H. Lange, *Römisches Recht im Mittelalter, Band II: die Kommentatoren*, München 2007, p. 910–911.

[1751] Glossa *Iudicis* to C. 4,44,2 in *Corporis Iustinianaei Codex* (ed. Gothofredi), tom. 5, col. 920: 'Sed quantum est haec dimidia? Dic in emptore decepto, si res valet decem, emit pro xvi, licet alii dicant, emit pro xxi, quod non placet, quia tunc non dimidiam iusti pretii, sed duplum egreditur; in venditore, sicut si res valet decem, vendidit pro quatuor.'

than 150. However, other jurists adamantly claimed that the buyer was harmed only if he had paid more than double the just price or 2x, e.g. more than 200 instead of 100. This approach was advocated in Bologna by Martinus and found fierce defenders in Orléans. It was adopted by Cino da Pistoia and ultimately became the majority view amongst the French humanists. This can be seen, for instance, in François Le Douaren's commentary on D. 45,1,36.[1752]

The interpretation of *dimidium* was not a mere exercise in mathematical prowess. It had a direct impact on the range of the remedy grounded on the *Lex secunda*. By maintaining that a buyer is only harmed if he pays more than double the just price, the doctrine of *laesio enormis* was almost undermined. Unsurprisingly, it is the ordinary gloss to C. 4,44,2 which was later to become the majority opinion among the moral theologians, since it guaranteed a more extended protection of the buyer.

A similar concern to protect the weak might explain why the theologians widely adopted the idea of objective deceit (*dolus re ipsa*) from the post-glossators.[1753] The jurists read the idea of objective deceit into law *Si quis cum aliter* (D. 45,1,36).[1754] This text was held to mean that besides intentional deceit (*dolus ex proposito*), properly described in law

---

[1752] E.g. François Le Douaren, *In lib. 45 Pandectarum, tit. de verborum obligationibus commentarius*, Lugduni 1554, ad D. 45,1,36, f. 21v: 'De emptore circumscripto, nihil scriptum in iure civili comperimus. Nam rescriptum Diocletiani, lex, constitutiove non est. Alioqui generaliter constituendum ab eo fuisset, nec de venditore tantummodo loquendum. Rescripta namque huiusmodi, certarum causarum ac personarum erant, quae Iustinianus in suum codicem congessit, et pro legibus haberi generalibus voluit. Proinde quod de venditore a Diocletiano rescriptum est, ad emptorem ita producere necesse est, ut inter emptorem et venditorem aequalitas et proportio servetur. Idque ut commodius facere possimus, ex ea hypothesi thesis facienda est, et generaliter constituendum, ei, qui ita deceptus est, ut ne dimidium quidem acceperit eius, quod dedit, sive eius, quod accipere debuit, subveniendum esse. Vel ita, quoties id, quod datur, altero tanto amplius est, quam quod accipitur, etc. Quamobrem si ponamus, inversa specie, mercem valere 4., pretium esse 10, dubitandum non est, quin succurratur emptori, quia verum est, eum altero tanto amplius dare quam accipiat, et ne dimidium quidem eius, quod dat, accipere. Quod si ponas, pretium esse septem, aliud dicendum erit, quia hîc non dat emptor altero tanto plus, quam accipiat.'

[1753] On *dolus re ipsa*, see Kalb, *Laesio enormis*, p. 112–116. Becker, *Die Lehre von der laesio enormis*, p. 58–59 points out that from the ninth century onwards a similar distinction between *dolus re ipsa*, on the one hand, signifying *laesio enormis*, and *dolus ex proposito*, on the other, can be found in the Byzantine legal tradition.

[1754] D. 45,1,36: 'Si quis, cum aliter eum convenisset obligari, aliter per machinationem obligatus est, erit quidem subtilitate iuris obstrictus, sed doli exceptione uti potest, quia enim per dolum obligatus est, competit ei exceptio. Idem est etsi nullus dolus intercessit stipulantis, sed ipsa res in se dolum habet, cum enim quis petat ex ea stipulatione, hoc ipso dolo facit, quod petit.' For further discussion of this passage, see below under Piñel's humanist critique of 'objective deceit' (7.5.2).

Et eleganter (D. 4,3,7), there is a form of deceit inherent in the transaction itself. Moreover, they interpreted D. 45,1,36 with reference to C. 4,44,2. Consequently, they thought that *dolus re ipsa* was tantamount to *laesio enormis* as described in the *Lex secunda*.

When it came to distinguishing intentional deceit from *laesio enormis*, despite the fact that both were considered to constitute 'deceit' (*deceptio*), Baldus introduced a compelling pair of new concepts. In his view, the deceit meant in D. 4,3,7 derived from 'deceptive industry' (*deceptio proveniens ex industria deceptiva*), while C. 4,44,2 dealt with deceit stemming from 'commercial industry' (*deceptio proviens ex industria negotiativa*).[1755] In light of this distinction, Baldus could explain why objective deceit was not remedied through the *actio doli* or *exceptio doli*, but rather by means of a remedy of its own, namely the remedy based on the *Lex secunda*.

Whether the notion of 'objective deceit' was successful in the canonical tradition is subject to debate.[1756] In any case, the canonists drew on the civilians' interpretation of C. 4,44,2 in their commentaries on canons *Quum dilecti* (X 3,17,3) and *Quum causa* (X 3,17,6).[1757] They accepted the doctrine of *laesio enormis* and borrowed the idea that it is up to the *laedens* to decide whether the sale could be rescinded or the just price be paid. Before the ecclesiastical courts a remedy was granted against lesion beyond moiety (*ultra dimidium*). Like their colleagues in the secular courts, the canonists accepted the idea expressed in paragraph *Idem Pomponius* (D. 4,4,16,4) that it is naturally permitted for contracting parties to try to outwit each other, provided the lesion did not go beyond moiety.

7.2.3.2   *The Aristotelian-Thomistic tradition*

Mindful of the Aristotelian-Thomistic virtue of commutative justice, the jurists and the theologians held that the slightest deviation from the just price was considered sinful. Consequently, lesion below moiety (*laesio*

[1755] Baldus, *Commentaria in quartum et quintum Codicis libros*, num. 4, f. 135r.

[1756] Kalb maintains not without probability that the notion of *dolus re ipsa* infiltrated into the canonists' commentaries. Yet the ample textual evidence he quotes mostly concerns the debate on nullity (*irritus ipso iure*) versus annullability (*irritandus*) in contracts affected by deceit as well as the question whether lesion is either a form of *dolus incidens* or *dolus causam dans* (see chapter 4). Cf. Kalb, *Laesio enormis*, p. 126–140. Questionable, too, is the claim that the concept of *dolus ex natura*, which apparently figures in Huguccio's commentary on De pen., Dist.5, c.2, is similar to the civilians' notion of *dolus re ipsa*; cf. Kalb, *Laesio enormis*, p. 119–120, n. 41.

[1757] For an extended discussion of these decretals and their reception among the Decretalists, see Kalb, *Laesio enormis*, p. 40–61.

infra dimidium), let alone lesion beyond moiety (*laesio ultra dimidium*), was not accepted in the court of conscience. The canonists themselves often acknowledged that there was a contrast in between the *ius poli* (*forum internum*), and the *ius fori* (*forum externum*), certainly when commenting upon the famous canons *In civitate* (X 5,19,6) and *Naviganti* (X 5,19,19). They admitted that D. 4,4,16,4, which was regarded as tolerating lesion below moiety, applied to the ecclesiastical courts for the sake of the tranquillity of society, although outwitting each other was disallowed as a matter of conscience.

In the light of their care of the soul, the theologians could not possibly agree with the laxity inherent in paragraph *Idem Pomponius*. Thomas Aquinas explains that human law does not punish all that is contrary to virtue, because it applies to all the people, not only to the virtuous.[1758] Its sole aim is to maintain order in society. However, not punishing certain acts is not tantamount to positively approving of them.[1759] It is therefore no contradiction to say that moderate deceit is tolerated by the external courts and yet sinful as a matter of conscience. Contracts have been introduced for the sake of the common good of both parties (*pro communi utilitate utriusque*). There is an absolute prohibition on unjust enrichment

---

[1758] Aquinas, *Summa Theologiae* (Ed. Leonina, tom. 7), IaIIae, quaest. 96, art. 2 (*Utrum ad legem humanam pertineat omnia vitia cohibere*), concl., p. 181: 'Et similiter multa sunt permittenda hominibus non perfectis virtute, quae non essent toleranda in hominibus virtuosis. Lex autem humana ponitur multitudini hominum, in qua maior pars est hominum non perfectorum virtute. Et ideo lege humana non prohibentur omnia vitia, a quibus virtuosi abstinent; sed solum graviora, a quibus possibile est maiorem partem multitudinis abstinere; et praecipue quae sunt in nocumentum aliorum, sine quorum prohibitione societas humana conservari non posset, sicut prohibentur lege humana homicidia et furta et huiusmodi.'

[1759] Aquinas, *Summa Theologiae* (Ed. Leonina, tom. 9), IIaIIae, quaest. 77, art. 1, ad 1, p. 148: 'Ad primum ergo dicendum quod, sicut supra dictum est, lex humana populo datur, in quo sunt multi a virtute deficientes, non autem datur solis virtuosis. Et ideo lex humana non potuit prohibere quidquid est contra virtutem, sed ei sufficit ut prohibeat ea quae destruunt hominum convictum; alia vero habeat quasi licita, non quia ea approbet, sed quia ea non punit. Sic igitur habet quasi licitum, poenam non inducens, si absque fraude venditor rem suam supervendat aut emptor vilius emat, nisi sit nimius excessus, quia tunc etiam lex humana cogit ad restituendum, puta si aliquis sit deceptus ultra dimidiam iusti pretii quantitatem. Sed lex divina nihil impunitum relinquit quod sit virtuti contrarium. Unde secundum divinam legem illicitum reputatur si in emptione et venditione non sit aequalitas iustitiae observata. Et tenetur ille qui plus habet recompensare ei qui damnificatus est, si sit notabile damnum. Quod ideo dico quia iustum pretium rerum quandoque non est punctualiter determinatum, sed magis in quadam aestimatione consistit, ita quod modica additio vel minutio non videtur tollere aequalitatem iustitiae.'

in contractual exchange. Hence, equality must be observed between what is given and received in a sale contract on pain of sin.[1760]

The arguments Thomas developed in rejecting D. 4,4,16,4 became mainstream in the scholastic tradition.[1761] Nevertheless, there was one serious dissident opinion, advocated by Jean Gerson, the Paris theologian widely known for his legacy in political thought, but also the author of a highly influential treatise *De contractibus*. In Gerson's view, *laesio infra dimidiam* does not give rise to a duty to make restitution. Still, he considers lesion below moiety to give rise to a duty to confess. The reason why Gerson does not believe in a duty to make restitution is because he thinks that the maxim that the willing suffer no harm (*volenti et consentienti non fit iniuria*) can be applied to the case of lesion below moiety.[1762] Contrary to the common opinion, he claims that lesion below moiety does not hamper the free and absolutely voluntary consent of the parties.[1763] Put dif-

---

[1760] Aquinas, *Summa Theologiae* (Ed. Leonina, tom. 9), IIaIIae, quaest. 77, art. 1, concl., p. 147: 'Si autem fraus deficit, tunc de emptione et venditione dupliciter loqui possumus. Uno modo, secundum se. Et secundum hoc emptio et venditio videtur esse introducta pro communi utilitate utriusque, dum scilicet unus indiget re alterius et e converso, sicut patet per philosophum, in 1. Politicorum. Quod autem pro communi utilitate est inductum, non debet esse magis in gravamen unius quam alterius. Et ideo debet secundum aequalitatem rei inter eos contractus institui.'

[1761] Cf. supra, p. 509–514.

[1762] Jean Gerson, *De iis ferme rebus quae ad mores conducunt*, Basileae 1518, tom. 2, alphabet. 35 (*Opusculum de contractibus*), part. 2, prop. 11, [s.p.]: 'Quamvis de restitutione varius apud doctores sit sermo, dicentibus aliquibus quod nisi si defraudatio ultra medium iusti pretii defraudans non tenetur ad restitutionem. Et in hoc satis concordant omnes dicentes verum esse in foro exteriori propter irritationem legislatoris, sed de foro conscientiae nulli dubium quin defraudans tenetur confiteri. Utrum autem obligetur restituere non est ita clarum nec concordatum apud omnes praesertim theologos. Non enim videtur necessarium quod ubi concurrunt mutuae voluntates vendentis et ementis ut res suas commutent in alterutrum, quod furtum commitatur vel rapina, iuxta illud: scienti et consentienti non fit iniuria neque dolus, praecipue dum sciens et volens est sui iuris in sua re, quod dicitur propter pupillos et similes; et dum consensus non est lege irritatus, sicut in deceptione ultra medium iusti pretii; si praeterea consensus sit absolutus non solum conditionalis aut secundum quid, sicut Aristoteles loquitur de proijciente merces in mare, et de consensu metu mortis extorto aut per errorem fraudulentem inducto, quoniam ignorantia causat involuntarium vel in toto vel in parte.'

[1763] It is important to distinguish between the validity of the maxim that the willing suffer no harm and the possibility of applying the maxim to the case of lesion. On a formal level, scholastic doctrine would recognize that it is possible to suffer injustice voluntarily. Yet the assent to lesion was never thought to be entirely voluntarily. On the possibility of suffering harm willingly, see Aquinas, *Summa Theologiae* (Ed. Leonina, tom. 9), IIaIIae, quaest. 59, art. 3, ad 3, p. 24: 'Ad tertium dicendum quod passio est effectus actionis exterioris. In hoc autem quod est facere et pati iniustum, id quod materialiter est attenditur secundum id quod exterius agitur, prout in se consideratur, ut dictum est, id autem quod est ibi formale et per se, attenditur secundum voluntatem agentis et patientis, ut ex dictis patet. Dicendum est ergo quod aliquem facere iniustum, et alium pati iniustum,

ferently, he thinks that Aristotle's example of the captain who jettisons cargo—who is not acting absolutely voluntarily—cannot be applied to *laesio infra dimidiam*.

Undoubtedly, Gerson's view was indebted to that of the Franciscan Pier Giovanni Olivi, whose surprisingly liberal standpoints in economic and legal affairs have already been pointed out before.[1764] In any case, his was an opinion that would remain part and parcel of a heterodox strand of scholastic thought, which lived on through the *Summa Rosella*, the influential late fifteenth century manual for confessors written by the Franciscan Giovanni Baptista Trovamala.[1765] However, the oddity of Gerson's position was clearly pointed out by Lessius: if lesion below moiety is subject to confession, it certainly constitutes a sin. If it is a sin, then it is a sin against the virtue of commutative justice.[1766] Yet restoring justice demands restitution. So it goes against all logic to free the *laedens infra dimidiam* of the duty to make restitution. Also, Lessius denies that the maxim that the willing suffer no harm applies to this case, since the *laesus* only consents in a relative sense, just as somebody who has to pay usurious interest rates in order to obtain a loan or a captain who jettisons cargo in order to save his life.

---

materialiter loquendo, semper se concomitantur. Sed si formaliter loquamur, potest aliquis facere iniustum, intendens iniustum facere, tamen alius non patietur iniustum, quia volens patietur. Et e converso potest aliquis pati iniustum, si nolens id quod est iniustum patiatur, et tamen ille qui hoc facit ignorans, non faciet iniustum formaliter, sed materialiter tantum.'

[1764] See chapter 6. Olivi's treatment of *leasio enormis* in his *Tractatus de emptione et venditione* is subject to investigation in Kalb, *Laesio enormis*, p. 145–149.

[1765] Trovamala, *Summa rosella de casibus conscientiae*, Argentinae 1516, f. 74v: (Secus autem si citra dimidiam iusti pretii interveniat deceptio; tunc tam in foro contentioso et ecclesiastico quam in foro animae non tenetur restituere quod habuit. Si vero ultra dimidiam, tunc in omni foro restituere obligatur.'

On Trovamala, see E. Bellone, *Appunti su Battista Trovamala di Sale O.F.M. e la sua 'Summa Casuum'*, Studi Francescani, 74 (1977), p. 375–402; L. Babbini, Tre *'summa casuum' composte da tre francescani piemontesi della provincia di Genova*, Studi Francescani, 78 (1981), p. 159–169; J.A. Brundage, *The rise of professional canonists and the development of the Ius commune*, Zeitschrift der Savigny-Stiftung für Rechtsgeschichte, Kanonistische Abteilung, 81 (1995), p. 26–63; G. Dolezalek, *Lexiques de droit et autres outils pour le 'ius commune'*, in: J. Hamesse (ed.), Les manuscrits des lexiques et glossaires de l'Antiquité tardive à la fin du Moyen Age, [Textes et études du Moyen Age, 4], Louvain-la-Neuve – Turnhout 1996, p. 353–376.

[1766] Lessius, *De iustitia et iure*, lib. 2, cap. 21, dub. 4, num. 22, p. 276–277.

7.3   CONTRACTUAL FAIRNESS IN EARLY MODERN SCHOLASTICISM I

The twin traditions of the *ius commune* and Aristotelian-Thomistic thought would be brought nearer than ever before in the writings of the early modern scholastics. This is particularly evident from Juan de Medina's discussion of lesion. Borrowing from the *ius commune*, he took the idea of *laesio* as a form of objective deceit seriously. Moreover, he expressly connected it with the doctrine of just pricing. We owe to Medina one of the clearest formulations of objective fraud or deceit:[1767]

> Fraud can be committed without deceit and that is called fraud on the level of the thing itself (*defraudatio incidens in re ipsa*), for example when the vendor does not employ deceit or lies, but nevertheless receives more than the just price from the buyer.

As has been pointed out before, Medina does not consider lesion to be a real vice of the will. It cannot vitiate a contract. Normally it is merely a form of incidental deceit (*dolus incidens*). Since an unequal contract is not affected by subjective deceit or evil intentions, it needs to be maintained for both parties' sake. Granted, the fair relationship between the contracting parties (*aequalitas contrahentium*) needs to be restored, yet that does not mean that the contract must be declared null. The *laesus* is granted a remedy (*actio*) against the *laedens*, but the *laedens* has the right to decide (*optio*) whether he prefers the contract to be rescinded or rebalanced. Since neither of the parties is guilty of intentional deceit, their position in 'upgrading' the contract should be equal.[1768]

[1767] Medina, *De poenitentia, restitutione, et contractibus*, tom. 2, Cod. *De rebus restituendis*, quaest. 33, par. *Sed est dubium*, p. 207: 'Potest praeterea defraudatio fieri sine dolo et dicitur defraudatio incidens in re ipsa, ut si nullus dolus aut mendacium ex parte venditoris apponatur, attamen plus iusto recipit ab emptore. Et potest hoc esse dupliciter; quia vel est defraudatio ultra dimidium iusti pretii vel citra.'
Note that Medina uses the term *defraudatio* in order to be able to safeguard the original meaning of *deceptio* as always involving intentional deceit. This is not frequently the case in other scholastic sources.
[1768] Medina, *De poenitentia, restitutione, et contractibus*, tom. 2, Cod. *De rebus restituendis*, quaest. 33, par. *Tertia propositio*, p. 210: 'Si defraudatio eveniat in re, sine dolo contrahentium, et sit defraudatio ultra dimidium iusti pretii, in utroque foro datur actio defraudato contra defraudantem, ut patet: unum de duobus, scilicet, vel quod rescindatur contractus vel quod ad aequalitatem reducatur, et datur optio defraudanti, ut eligat ex his, quod velit. Et in hoc non discrepant doctores, si memini. Nam cum in hoc contractu non interveniat dolus, convenit ut contrahentium aequalitas meliori modo quo potest servetur absque ipsorum contrahentium praeiudicio, quale videtur fieri, si uni contrahentium competeret utrumque, scilicet actio et optio. Nam tunc non esse aequa utriusque conditio.

7.3.1   *A clash between legal and moral principles*

Implicitly drawing on Conrad Summenhart's *Opus septipertitum de contractibus*, Juan de Medina greatly expanded on the tension between the philosophical principle of justice in exchange and the liberal legal maxims taken from Roman law. He opposes the Christian framework of thinking about commerce to famous maxims contained in the Digest and the Code. The result is a compelling overview of the clash of moral and legal principles in scholastic contract law.

7.3.1.1   *Roman maxims* vs *Christian morals*

Let us dwell for a moment on Medina's chapter on sale contracts that violate the rule of just pricing. He first states the principle of justice in exchange. A balanced relationship (*aequalitas*) between the good for sale and the price paid is required on pain of sin. Medina adduces the usual patristic and canonical sources to underscore the principle that contracts must be just: Augustine's *De Trinitate* and paragraph *Hoc ius* from Gratian's *Decretum* (C.10, q.2, c.2).[1769] He also sets the entire discussion on excessive prices in sale contracts (*supervenditio*) against the background of unjust enrichment and the prohibition on theft.

Medina considers unjust contracts as constituting a form of unjust enrichment on account of unjust receiving (*ex iniusta rei alienae acceptione*).[1770] The acceptance itself of the surplus value is unjust, because the *laedens* receives more than his due (*recipit a proximo aliquid alioqui indebitum*). Consequently, restitution should be made as a matter of conscience. Moreover, the *laedens* sins against the principle of charity and the law of nature (*peccat contra charitatem et contra legem naturae*), which hold that you do unto others as you would they should do unto you.[1771]

This basically Christian framework is challenged by four well-known principles based on Roman law. Firstly, it is naturally permitted for

---

Inde, iuxta rectam rationem, iure statutum est, ut in hoc casu alteri competat actio, alteri vero optio.'

[1769]   C.10, q.2, c.2 held that the vendor of ecclesiastical goods must not receive more than the just price, even if the buyer made a higher offer. In *De Trinitate* 13, 3, 6, Augustine condemned as vicious the ordinary practice and wish of people to buy cheap and to sell dear. Cf. supra, n. 1722.

[1770]   Medina, *De poenitentia, restitutione, et contractibus*, tom. 2, Cod. *De rebus restituendis*, quaest. 32, par. *Quod autem*, p. 201 *juncto* par. *Confirmatur*, p. 202.

[1771]   For the identification of *lex naturalis* with the Golden Rule in the *ius commune*, see K. Pennington, *Lex naturalis and ius naturale*, The Jurist, 68 (2008), p. 569–591.

contracting parties to outwit each other (*naturaliter licet invicem se circumvenire*; e.g. D. 4,4,16,4). Secondly, a good is worth as much as it can be sold for (*res tantum valet quantum vendi potest*; e.g. D. 36,1,1,16). Thirdly, everybody is the moderator and arbiter of his own thing (*in re sua unusquisque est moderator et arbiter*; e.g. C. 4,35,21). Fourthly, the willing suffer no harm (*volenti et consentienti non fit iniuria*; e.g. D. 50,17,145).

It has been a constant concern in the scholastic tradition in legal and economic thought to defuse these explosive Roman principles. As a matter of course, the main weapon employed by the scholastics to neutralize these Roman principles was interpretation.

A subtle trick used by Medina to qualify D. 4,4,16,4 is to avoid mentioning the term 'licit' (*licet*) in the abovementioned maxim. He quotes the maxim to the effect that it is naturally granted or permitted (*concessum est et permissum*) for contracting parties to mutually outwit each other.[1772] These are obviously less strong verbs than *licere*. Moreover, he neutralizes 'naturally' (*naturaliter*) by interpreting it to mean 'according to the corrupt nature of man' (*secundum naturam corruptam*). It is 'natural' to cheat among men because they suffer from an innate and depraved cupidity for material things (*ob rerum cupiditatem*).

According to Medina, this actual and natural state of affairs should not be taken as a rule of conduct, since it is clearly at odds with divine law.[1773] In the first letter to the Christians from Thessaloniki, Paul expressly told them to do the opposite: 'do not aggrieve or outwit your brother in doing business, for the Lord will act as an avenger (*vindex*) in all of these matters' (1 Thess. 4:6).

Also, the permission of lesion below moiety before the external, civil and ecclesiastical courts should not be seen as an affirmative authori-

---

[1772] Medina, *De poenitentia, restitutione, et contractibus*, tom. 2, Cod. *De rebus restituendis*, quaest. 32, par. *Nec obstant*, p. 202: 'Nec obstant, quae nonnulli iuristae in oppositum afferunt. Arguunt enim primo, quod excessus, si non sit ultra dimidium iusti pretii, non sit restituendus, quia talis contractus est licitus et iustus, eo quod naturaliter concessum est et permissum contrahentibus se invicem circumvenire atque circumscribere, ut notant iuristae (…).'

[1773] It is difficult to see, then, why Dr. Navarrus implicitly criticizes Medina's interpretation on the ground of a kind of naturalistic fallacy. See Azpilcueta, *In tres de poenitentia distinctiones*, in cap. *Qualitas* (De pen., Dist. 5, cap. 2), num. 44, p. 109: 'Sed contra hos facti, quod parum recte cohaeret secundum hunc sensum illud verbum naturaliter cum illo verbo licet. Nam si haec inclinatio sensualitatis ad illicitum movet, quomodo dicetur naturaliter licere, nisi dicamus secundum inclinationem sensualitatis esse licitum? In quo sensu verum fuerit dicere naturaliter licere fornicari, adulterari, mentiri, quae iurisconsultus minime concessisset.'

zation. Granted, canon *Quum dilecti* (X 3,17,3) confirms the validity of
D. 4,4,16,4 before the ecclesiastical courts. Yet the law of the land does
not approve of contracts affected by lesion below moiety as if they were
honest and just.[1774] For the sake of the common good and peace (*bonum
publicum et communis hominum pax*) the authorities merely connive at
minor deviations from the just price by not punishing these violations of
commutative justice.[1775] Lesion without deceit is not a sufficient ground
to invalidate a contract, but it gives rise to a duty to make restitution as
a matter of conscience.

Medina makes an explicit distinction between the licit or just (*quod
licite et juste fit*) and the lawful (*quod legis authoritate fit*). Referring to
Augustine, he recalls that the dictum according to which all is just that is
lawful does not apply to what is done by virtue of the authority of human
law.[1776] The examples of the discrepancy between transcendental law and
human law are there to be taken: acquisitive prescription in spite of bad
faith, the right of the *pater familias* to kill his children, concubinage, etc.

In light of the usual extension of the permission to outwit one another
in sale contracts (D. 4,4,16,4) to lease contracts (D. 19,2,22,3), Medina deals
with the alleged permission for servants to retain what they extorted from
their bosses. On account of a text by Augustine included by Gratian in
canon *Non sane* (C.14, q.5, c.15), the canonists held that no restitution
ought to be made of extra funds extorted by minor servants.[1777] Yet Medina undermined this line of argument by pointing out that this canon had
been misinterpreted due to a reprehensibly selective quotation by Gratian

---

[1774] Medina, *De poenitentia, restitutione, et contractibus*, tom. 2, Cod. *De rebus restituendis*, quaest. 32, par. *Secundo*, p. 202: 'Respondeo quod nec iura, civile scilicet et canonicum, tales contractus approbant tamquam iustos ac licitos, nec authoritatem praestant,
ut huiusmodi defraudationes fiant.'

[1775] Medina, *De poenitentia, restitutione, et contractibus*, tom. 2, Cod. *De rebus restituendis*, quaest. 32, par. *Secundo*, p. 202 *juncto* par. *Tertio*, p.°203.

[1776] Medina, *De poenitentia, restitutione, et contractibus*, tom. 2, Cod. *De rebus restituendis*, quaest. 32, par. *Secundo*, p. 202: 'Et esto, authoritatem ad id praestarent, non inde fit,
ut licite et iuste fiant, cum multa videamus secundum leges humanas permissa et disposita
quae tamen secundum legem naturalem et divinam sunt damnanda. (...) Unde Augustinus non sine causa id quod dicitur, quod legis authorite fit, iuste fit, non de lege humana
intellexit, sed de divina, ut habetur 23.q.4.cap.qui peccat [C.23, q.4, c.40].'

[1777] See C.14, q.5, c.15 in *Corpus juris canonici* (ed. Gregoriana), part. 1, cols. 1411–1412:
'Non sane, quidquid ab invito sumitur, iniuriose aufertur. Nam plerique nec medico volunt
reddere honorem suum, nec operario mercedem. Nec tamen haec qui ab invito accipiunt,
per iniuriam accipiunt. Quae potius per iniuriam non darentur.'

from Augustine's original letter to Macedonius.[1778] The same critique had been ousted already by Summenhart.[1779]

To Medina's mind, absolute observation of the principle of equality in exchange (*iustitia commutativa*) is equally necessary in lease contracts as it is in sale contracts.[1780] The principle of the just wage is but an extension of the principle of just pricing to the lease of labour. To this effect, Medina quotes John the Baptist's admonition in Lk. 3:14: 'No intimidation! No extortion! Be content with your pay!'

The second (D. 36,1,1,16) and third (C. 4,35,21) maxim posed less difficulties for the scholastics. Medina neutralized them through a simple addition: it is possible to sell a thing for the highest price the buyer is willing to offer as far as that is possible within the limits imposed by the law (*limitandum est ad posse de iure seu licite et rationabiliter*).[1781] In other words, the realm of fact is to be subdued to the realm of law, and the realm of law lives by the norms established by the theologians amongst others. Another escape route from these liberal Roman principles was offered by the market for luxury goods. Undoubtedly inspired by Conrad Summenhart or Francisco de Vitoria,[1782] Medina argues that in their pure form these two maxims are meant to apply to the specific case of the sale of luxury goods, such as ornaments.[1783] They were not meant to be general in scope.

[1778] Medina, *De poenitentia, restitutione, et contractibus*, tom. 2, Cod. *De rebus restituendis*, quaest. 32, par. *Respondetur*, p. 203: 'Itaque defectus Gratiani, infideliter transferendo locum praedictum, causa fuit, ut Innocentius et caeteri post ipsum in hoc loco deciperentur, putantes extorta per praefatos officiales minores non esse restituenda.'

[1779] Summenhart, *De contractibus*, Summarium, q. 57, dist. 3, dict. 2 post decimumquartum, arg. 1: 'Ex quibus patet quod incongrue et prorsus non ad mentem Augustini adducitur praedictum capitulum.'

[1780] Medina, *De poenitentia, restitutione, et contractibus*, tom. 2, Cod. *De rebus restituendis*, quaest. 32, par. *Respondetur*, p. 203: 'Et sicut pro re venali non licet ultra iustum pretium accipere, ita nec pro re locata aut opera alicuius non licet ultra iustum recipere. Et est utrobique eadem ratio, quia utrobique opus est iustitiam commutativam servare.'

[1781] Medina, *De poenitentia, restitutione, et contractibus*, tom. 2, Cod. *De rebus restituendis*, quaest. 32, par. *Confirmatur*, p. 204: 'Ideo dicendum, quod illud dictum, res tantum valet quantum vendi potest, limitandum est ad posse de iure seu licite et rationabiliter, quod fiet, si vendatur iuxta documenta superius posita. Quod autem res possit pro pretio excessivo licite vendi nec ius naturale nec divinum nec humanum authoritatem praestat nec id concedit, etsi id permittat et toleret, ut iam dictum est.'

[1782] Summenhart, *De contractibus*, tract. 3, quaest. 57, concl. 3, par. *In aliis vero mercibus*.

[1783] Medina, *De poenitentia, restitutione, et contractibus*, tom. 2, Cod. *De rebus restituendis*, quaest. 32, par. *Confirmatur*, p. 204: 'Aut dicatur dictum illud vulgare esse limitandum ad res venales quarum pretium nec lege nec communi cursu est determinatum et res tales sunt sine quibus humana vita convenienter transigi potest. (...) Quales sunt res, quae ad ornatum personae vel domus potius quam ad vitae necessitatem pertinent, pro

The maxim stating that the willing and the knowing suffer no harm (D. 50,17,145) was harder to overcome for the scholastics, if only because their conception of contractual obligation was fundamentally based on voluntary consent. According to the objection that there is voluntary consent to the contract on both sides (*mutuae voluntates concurrunt*), the contracting parties are not coerced by necessity (*consentiunt nulla pressi necessitate*) and they do not suffer from ignorance (*nulla ignorantia in eis interveniente*). Hence, no harm is done, and the contract seems to be grounded on solid foundations. Unsurprisingly, Medina's counterargument is rather unconvincing: if this objection were accepted in regard to lesion below moiety, then it would also have to be accepted in the event of lesion beyond moiety—which is not the case.[1784]

The threat posed by D. 50,17,145 shows that in case of conflict, the scholastics' practical concern with the exploitation of the needy and the poor temporarily overrules their theoretical musings about the foundations of contractual obligation. In a profoundly Christian society, the logic of Jesus must take precedence over the logic of Justinian in solving concrete cases. The scholastics may well have advocated the virtue of liberty and 'freedom of contract', Christian liberty also requires that this fundamental principle of action be questioned if necessary. This will also be obvious from Covarruvias' and Piñel's discussion about the (non-)renunciability of the *Lex secunda*.

7.3.1.2 *Just pricing* vs *gift-making*

As we have seen Medina explaining before, a vendor charging more than the just price is thought to receive more than his due (*indebitum*). As a consequence, the acceptance of the surplus value constitutes a form of unjust enrichment, and, in even broader terms, theft.

However, there are three specific grounds (*rationes/causae*) which literally 'ex-c(a)use' a deviation from the just price.[1785] The first two can be

---

quibus etsi aliquid excessivum detur, excessus ob beneplacitum ipsorum ementium videtur condonari.'

[1784] Medina, *De poenitentia, restitutione, et contractibus*, tom. 2, Cod. *De rebus restituendis*, quaest. 32, par. *Respondetur*, p. 204: 'Respondetur, si haec ratio probaret, quod venditor non tenetur restituere excessum citra dimidium, eadem probaret, quod nec tenetur restituere excessum ultra dimidium iusti pretii, cum non minus conveniant sponte in tali contractu quam in alio.'

[1785] Medina, *De poenitentia, restitutione, et contractibus*, tom. 2, Cod. *De rebus restituendis*, quaest. 32, par. *Sed numquid*, p. 204–205: 'Sed numquid id semper sit verum, quod scilicet non liceat rem pro excessivo pretio vendere, et si vendatur, excessus sit semper

dealt with quickly: ignorance (*ratione ignorantiae*) and damages (*ratione interesse*). As long as a vendor is invincibly mistaken about the just price, the contract is safe from fault and vice.[1786] Restitution is due, however, from the moment the vendor realizes what the just price really was.[1787] Similarly, demanding more than the just price does not constitute a sin if the surplus value is a kind of indemnification for the vendor's inconvenience and opportunity costs in selling his goods.[1788] This is a simple application of the so-called 'double rule of just pricing' discussed above. The right to compensation not only suspends, but annuls the duty to make restitution altogether.

The third reason why the excess value may be due to the vendor as a juridical debt on the part of the buyer is by virtue of a concomitant gift (*ratione donationis admixtae*). The surplus value may become a part of the debt the buyer is obliged to pay to the vendor if the buyer himself freely wishes to make a donation (*libera voluntas donandi*).[1789] In that event, no restitution of the excess value should be made anymore.

It is easy to see how the logic of gift could easily undermine the doctrine of just pricing. It sufficed for a vendor to claim that the surplus value was a gift to escape the duty to make restitution in the event of *supervenditio*. The theologians were aware of this loophole and spared no efforts in closing it off. As will be expressed even more clearly in Covarruvias' argumentation, the idea that donation could be presumed in sale pur-

---

restituendus? Respondeo, quod non, sed aliquando licitum est, rem vendere pro maiori pretio, quod totam latitudinem | iusti pretii excedat, idque in tribus casibus in universali, scilicet, ratione ignorantiae, ratione interesse, et ratione donationis admixtae.'

[1786] Medina, *De poenitentia, restitutione, et contractibus*, tom. 2, Cod. *De rebus restituendis*, quaest. 32, par. *Primum*, p. 205: 'Primum fit, quando venditor credit invincibiliter rem, quam vendit, valere id, quod pro ea exigit, scilicet 15, cum re vera non valeat nisi 12 ad summum, excusatur contractus a culpa et vitio.'

[1787] Medina, *De poenitentia, restitutione, et contractibus*, tom. 2, Cod. *De rebus restituendis*, quaest. 32, par. *Tertium*, p. 205: 'Secus in primo casu, quo ex ignorantia res fuit supervendita, quia tunc, durante illa ignorantia, excusatur sicut a culpa, ita a debito restituendi. Superveniente tamen cognitione veritatis, quod scilicet rem plus iusto vendidit, tenetur restituere excessum. Ratio huius clara est, quia ignorantia non tollit, quin emptor fuerit defraudatus, licet a culpa defraudationis excuset.'

[1788] Medina, *De poenitentia, restitutione, et contractibus*, tom. 2, Cod. *De rebus restituendis*, quaest. 32, par. *Secundum*, p. 205: 'Secundum fit, quando venditor ex rei venditione patitur damnum aliquod, aut impeditur ab assequutione alicuius lucri alioqui sibi certi aut probabiliter eventuri. Nam tunc licebit venditori ascendere in pretio, iuxta quantitatem interesse quod ex venditione patitur. Et procedit hoc, quando rem illam vendit ad instantiam emptoris, quia tunc iustum est se servare indemnem.'

[1789] Medina, *De poenitentia, restitutione, et contractibus*, tom. 2, Cod. *De rebus restituendis*, quaest. 32, par. *Quod autem*, p. 201.

chase contracts was fiercely contested. The theologians shifted the onus of proof to the *supervenditor* by maintaining that gifts could never be presumed in business transactions. Hence, a debate took place on how a *supervenditor* could prove that the excess value actually constituted a gift to his advantage.

Copying a check-list drawn up by Summenhart—his usual source of inspiration, Medina concludes that four conditions need to be fulfilled cumulatively.[1790] Firstly, the buyer must be a thoughtful person who knows the value of the good (*persona sagax sciens valorem mercis*). Secondly, the buyer must not give the surplus out of true or presumed simplicity (*non ex mentis levitate vera vel praesumpta*). Consequently, spendthrifts and buyers who suffer from affectional disorder can never be said to make a gift (*excluditur prodigalitas et inordinata affectio*). Thirdly, the buyer must not be compelled to give a surplus out of necessity or coercion (*non ex necessitate vel arctatione*). Lastly, the vendor must be reasonably certain that the three conditions are met in the buyer (*illa tria constent venditori probabili certitudini*).

Unlike Summenhart, Medina qualifies the second and fourth conditions required for proving the donation. Whereas Summerhart insists that receiving a surplus from a prodigal or unstable person is always sinful, Medina objects that reality is more complicated than that. In fact, Medina argues that a distinction should be made between the sinfulness of the giving (*datio*) and the receiving (*receptio*).

The disjunction of *datio* and *receptio* is a distinction that we have seen playing a vital role in the scholastics' discussion of contracts for sex. Unsurprisingly, therefore, Medina illustrates the importance of the distinction by referring to the excusability of a prostitute's receiving the money donated to her, in spite of the fact that the client's giving the money is sinful. By the same token, a rich man giving alms in public for his own glory sins out of affectional disorder (*inordinata affectio*), but the poor man receiving the money can do so with a clear conscience. Medina infers from this that a vendor does not commit a sin in receiving money on top of the just price whenever a prodigal or an unreasonably enthusiastic buyer spontaneously (*sponte*) decides to make him a gift of the excess value.[1791]

[1790] Compare Medina, *De poenitentia, restitutione, et contractibus*, tom. 2, Cod. *De rebus restituendis*, quaest. 32, par. *Circa tertium* with Summenhart, *De contractibus*, tract. 3, quaest. 57, concl. 5 and tract. 3, quaest. 58, concl. 5.

[1791] Medina, *De poenitentia, restitutione, et contractibus*, tom. 2, Cod. *De rebus restituendis*, quaest. 32, par. *Habet tamen*, p. 206: 'Ac proinde si emptor quamvis prodigaliter aut ex

While Medina partly softens the second requirement, he nevertheless concludes that it will almost never happen that the fourth condition be met. According to Medina, it is almost impossible for a vendor to reach probable certainty (*certitudo probabilis*) about the spontaneous, deliberate and entirely voluntary character of the buyer's gift. In most cases, the buyer makes a gift not for the sake of making the gift but for another purpose, for example to win somebody's favor or to boost his own reputation.[1792] These external motivations discredit the vendor's proof of donation.

To sum up, Medina concludes that a vendor will almost never be safe in invoking a donation, even if the other three conditions seem to be fulfilled. A *supervenditor* can almost never attain the degree of moral certainty that is required for the salvation of his soul. This certainty can be reached only where there is an additional ground (*causa*) to presume the logic of gift. As would be repeated time and again by the scholastic theologians, the pre-eminent instances of such a concurrent *causa* are friendship (*amicitia*) and kinship (*cognatio*). Yet outside the inner circle of friends and relatives, the logic of just pricing and *laesio enormis* is presumed almost exclusively.

7.3.2   A clash between secular and spiritual jurisdictions

Medina's discussion of lesion highlights the constant need for the jurists and theologians in the early modern period to try to reconcile the Roman legal tradition with Christian moral principles. Further illustrations of the tension between those conflicting mental worlds in regard to contractual exchange could easily be drawn from other theologians, such as the Dominican friars Domingo de Soto or Domingo Bañez.

---

inordinata affectione quam ad mercem habet, velit pretium excessivum sponte donare, poterit venditor illud recipere nec restituere tenebitur.'

[1792] Medina, *De poenitentia, restitutione, et contractibus*, tom. 2, Cod. *De rebus restituendis*, quaest. 32, par. *Secundo*, p. 207: '(...) venditor cognitis illis conditionibus ex parte emptoris non poterit semper iuste praesumere quod emptor intendat excessum donare, maxime quia ut plurimum emptores pretium excessivum scienter pro merce aliqua non darent, nisi illa simpliciter indigerent, vel saltem secundum quid, puta ad aliquem alium finem, quem ipsi praetendunt, sive praetendant lucrum ex merce illa, sive alicuius amicitiam, cui illam donare intendunt, sive suam propriam complacentiam et voluptatem aut gloriam aliquam seu famam, honorem, aut aliquid huiusmodi, quod non ita sine merce illa assequi sperarent. Quodcunque horum concurrat impedit donationis iustam praesumptionem ac proinde raro erit tutus venditor excessivum pretium accipiens, ob id, quod praesumit emptorem velle donare nisi alia causa id praesumendi concurrat, puta, quia venditor amicus est emptoris aut cognatus cui benefacere solet aut saltem desiderat.'

What is interesting to note is that although they constantly brought to light the discrepancy between the principle of fairness in exchange and the original Roman texts, the canonists and theologians also tried to save the face of Roman law. They would repeat over and over again that D. 4,4,16,4 was not to be interpreted as a licence for cheating, but as the practical toleration of lesion below moiety lest the courts be overextended (*lex permissiva ne lites multiplicarentur*). This was actually considered to be a sound and reasonable policy on the secular level.[1793]

However, a strict observance of just pricing was obligatory as a matter of conscience. This was not just a vague theoretical idea. In the Augustinian tradition, even the slightest degree of lesion gave rise to a natural obligation to make restitution in the court of conscience. How this principle of restitution was to be achieved in practice is abundantly clear from Dr. Navarrus' exposition on *laesio enormis*. It provides us with an excellent illustration of the fierce but often neglected struggle between rival normative powers and their respective jurisdictions in the early modern period.

7.3.2.1 *Enforcing contractual equilibrium*

Even more explicitly than Juan de Medina, Dr. Navarrus puts the *laesio*-prohibition in its original, moral theological context. Dr. Navarrus points directly to the Biblical (Ex. 20) and the canonical roots (C.14, q.5, c.13) of the prohibition to deviate from the just price. Both authoritative texts stipulate that theft is prohibited. Moreover, canon *Poenale* defines theft

---

[1793] Adrian of Utrecht, *Quaestiones quodlibeticae*, quaest. 6, art. 3, litt. f, f. 125r: 'Lex non censetur fovere peccatum quando expedit ad occurrendum pluribus vel gravioribus criminibus. Sic constitutum esse ut in proposito ne passim homines se molestent et infinitis quaestionibus se invicem super contractibus impetant. (…) Patet ergo quomodo lex illa de deceptione citra dimidium iusti pretii neque fovet iniquitatem neque facit eam suam, sed potius occurrit gravioribus et pluribus hominum peccatis, quamquam occasionaliter quidam ex ea fomentum peccandi sumant.'

Soto, *De iustitia et iure* (ed. fac. V. Diego Carro – M. González Ordóñez, vol. 3), lib. 6, quaest. 3, art. 1, p. 552: 'At vero rogas cur ergo tali casu [sc. in laesione infra dimidium] actio non datur? Respondetur inconsultissime (sic) legum latores fecisse. Haud enim illi mortales tanti aestimabant bona haec temporalia ut propter illa tantam sinerent litigationum turbinem quantam nunc videmus, contra documentum Christi admonentis ut ad redimendum tempus petenti a nobis tunicam dimittamus et pallium.'

Bañez, *De iure et iustitia decisiones*, ad quaest. 77, p. 522: 'Ratio autem quare leges permittunt illam iniquitatem et non dant actionem in iudicio damnificato est, quia cum contractus emptionis et venditionis sit frequentissimus in republica, si daretur actio laesis citra dimidium iusti, non sufficerent tribunalia ad dirimendas lites quotidianas quae ex talibus deceptionibus provinerent.'

in a broad sense: as the illicit usurpation of a good that belongs to somebody else.[1794] Damaging, retaining or acquiring a good that is not yours is
prohibited by the seventh commandment not to steal. It is therefore a sin
that cannot be redeemed unless restitution is made:[1795]

> Retaining possession of a good bought at a notably lower price than the
> just price against the free will of the vendor to make a gift is tantamount to
> damaging, retaining or usurping someone else's good against the free will of
> its owner. Consequently, the sin that ensues from this retention cannot be
> redeemed unless restitution is made.

In Dr. Navarrus' exposition, the intricate connection between the seventh
commandment not to steal, the principle of unjust enrichment and the
doctrine of restitution is crystal-clear. The slightest enrichment to the detriment of another constitutes the sin of theft. Hence, unjust enrichment
goes against both natural law and divine law (*locupletari non debet quis
cum aliena iactura*).[1796] Unjust enrichment must be remedied through
restitution, provided restitution is possible. Otherwise, the sin cannot be
redeemed, as canon *Si res aliena* (C.14, q.6, c.1) famously stipulated in the
footsteps of Augustine.[1797] Moreover, the mere fact of possessing something that belongs to another constitutes theft. So even though the possessor does not intend to refrain from restitution, let alone to steal, he sins
as long as he does not actually make restitution.

Referring to Adrian of Utrecht, Dr. Navarrus emphasizes the objective
character of the duty to make restitution.[1798] This follows from the objec-

---

[1794] See C.14, q.5, c.13 in *Corpus juris canonici* (ed. Gregoriana), part. 1, cols. 1409–1410:
'Furti enim nomine bene intelligitur omnis illicita usurpatio rei alienae.'

[1795] Azpilcueta, *Relectio in cap. Novit de iudiciis*, not. 6, coroll. 13, num. 56, f. 81r:
'Postremo, quod omnis damnificatio, retentio et usurpatio rei alienae prohibetur praecepto de non furando, et est peccatum (...). At retentio rei emptae pretio notabiliter
minore iusto contra voluntatem liberam donandi venditoris, est damnificatio, retentio,
vel usurpatio rei alienae contra voluntatem liberam domini. Ergo peccatum inde resultans
non tollitur, nisi per restitutionem.'

[1796] Azpilcueta, *Relectio in cap. Novit de iudiciis*, not. 6, coroll. 13, num. 74, f. 83r.

[1797] See C.14, q.6, c.1 in *Corpus juris canonici* (ed. Gregoriana), part. 1, cols. 1411–1413: 'Si
res aliena, propter quam peccatum est, cum reddi potest, non redditur, non agitur paenitentia, sed fingitur. Si autem veraciter agitur, non remittitur peccatum, nisi restituatur
ablatum, sed, ut dixi, cum restitui potest.'

[1798] Azpilcueta, *Relectio in cap. Novit de iudiciis*, not. 6, coroll. 13, num. 57, f. 81v: 'Quare
doctissimus Adrianus orsurus restitutionis materiam eam appellat cessationem a peccato.
Et postea col. 3 semper et continuo ait obligatum ad restituendum peccare mortaliter
quamdiu detinet alienum invito domino, etiamsi non concipiat propositum non restituendi. Quia satis est ad peccandum, detinere alienum, et non restituere, licet non concipiat propositum non restituendi. Quae omnia etiam alii sentiunt.' Compare *Relectio in cap.
Novit de iudiciis*, not. 6, coroll. 13, num. 79, f. 83v: 'Nihilominus peccare tamen eos contra

tive nature of the virtue of commutative justice. Unless the transaction is taken away from the scope of justice in exchange, e.g. when the parties decide to make a donation (which is then subject to the virtue of liberality), equality should be preserved regardless of the intentions of buyer and vendor. In his commentary on Gratian's *De poenitentia*, Dr. Navarrus gives the example of a vendor who mistakingly believes that he is charging the just price. Even if he does not intend to outwit the buyer, he is under an obligation to make restitution as soon as he finds out that the just price was much lower.[1799] Dr. Navarrus insists that it is not only mortal sin to knowingly deceive and harm the other party to the contract, but also to commit lesion in good faith (*etiam qui bona fide putans se iuste contrahere*).[1800] Consequently, if you thought you concluded a just contract, but afterward discovered that you were mistaken, you have to make restitution on pain of mortal sin. Ignorance and good faith perhaps suspend, but certainly do not abrogate the objective precepts of commutative justice.

The deviation from the just price does not constitute lesion if buyer and vendor can be presumed to have knowingly made a gift (*voluntas libera donandi*). If the price deviates from the just price on another ground (*causa*) than a conscious and deliberate donation, then a duty to make restitution lies. Yet as we have seen with Juan de Medina, and as will be stated even more explicitly by Diego de Covarruvias y Leyva, a presumption of donation barely lies. Dr. Navarrus repeats that the slightest suspicion of exploitation of necessity excludes the presumption of donation. To support this view, Dr. Navarrus relies on a couple of well-known grounds for excluding a presumption of voluntariness, such as ill reputation, captives buying off their liberty, and transactions with a quarrelsome neighbor.[1801] Pietro d'Ancharano (c. 1330–1416), a student of Baldus, had

---

legem Dei non solum scienter ita contrahendo, sed etiam post contractum ita ignoranter factum, non reducendo illum ad aequalitatem iustam.'

[1799] Azpilcueta, *In tres de poenitentia distinctiones*, in cap. *Qualitas*, num. 31, p. 107: 'Infertur et tertio quod etsi forte putarem rem illam octodecim valere et postea comperirem multo minoris pretii esse, ad resarciendum id damnum me teneri.'

[1800] Azpilcueta, *Relectio in cap. Novit de iudiciis*, not. 6, coroll. 13, num. 52, f. 81r: 'Addo his, quod non solum mortaliter peccare is, qui scienter notabiliter laedit aut decipit proximum sic contrahendo contra legem divinam, sed etiam, qui bona fide putans se iuste contrahere, id fecit, si postea cognita veritate id, in quo illum laesit, ei non restituat.'

[1801] Azpilcueta, *Relectio in cap. Novit de iudiciis*, not. 6, coroll. 13, num. 63, f. 82r: 'Concludit [Petrus ab Ancharano] in effectu tunc demum licere praedictam laesionem citra dimidium iusti pretii sine ullo remedio, cum uterque, tam emptor quam venditor, scit illud, et intervenit praesumptio libere donandi excessum, non autem cum fit ob aliquam causam quae tollat praesumptionem liberae voluntatis donandi, puta ob famem suam vel familiae suae, aut ut se vel suos redimat a captivitate, vel ut vicinum rixosum e vicinia

cited these special cases to explain why it could sometimes be manda-
tory for the civil courts (*in foro civili*) to grant relief even for lesion below
moiety if the transaction had been entered into out of extreme necessity
(*suprema necessitas*).[1802] For example, if someone buys dearer because he
wants to escape the harassment by his troublesome neighbor, then the
ground (*causa*) underlying this transaction is not voluntary choice but
necessity. It is unreasonable and compelled. That a voluntary and reasonable *causa* should not be presumed in those cases, not even in the civil
courts, would later be called into question by Arias Piñel.

In particular, the *laesus* can take the *laedens* to an ecclesiastical court
and demand that equality be restored. The remedy available to the *laesus*,
regardless of whether he is a layman or a cleric, is evangelical denunciation (*denuntiatio evangelica*). By virtue of this remedy, a buyer or vendor who does not observe the just price can be forced (*cogi posse*) by
the ecclesiastical judge to satisfy the wronged party.[1803] Why is this so?
Because lesion below moiety is a deadly sin, and all cases involving deadly
sin are declared admissible in the ecclesiastical courts. It lies in the power
of the Church to hear such cases in order to be able to coerce the deceiver
(*ad effectum cogendi decipientem*) through ecclesiastical punishment (*per
censuras ecclesiasticas*) to repent and to make restitution.[1804]

A potential objection might be that the defendant has a means of
defence against the plaintiff who sues him by virtue of evangelical denunciation. Particularly, he can accuse the plaintiff of malice (*malitia*). Such
an exception of malice lies whenever the plaintiff is already granted a

---

tollat, vel ob aliam similem, quia tunc laesus etiam citra dimidium posset petere saltem in
foro canonico, ut illa inaequalitas ad aequitatem reducatur.'

[1802] Pietro d'Ancharano, *Super sexto Decretalium commentaria*, Bononiae 1583, ad VI,
reg. iur. 4, num. 21, p. 531: 'Io. Calderinus sentit, quod ex parte ementis vilius sit peccatum,
et similiter ex parte vendentis carius, quia negari non potest, quin sit iniustitia in tali
excessu. Quod dictum posset tolerari, si maxima subsit necessitas ex parte vendentis vilius,
puta emendo frumentum pro sustentatione familiae tempore magnae famis vel redimendi
se ab hostibus hoc facit, alias non venditurus, vel econverso emit carius a vicino rixoso, vel
inhoneste versante. In istis enim exemplis et similibus iste excessus in pluri
vel in minori fundatur super causa irrationabili et urgenti; ideo subvertendum, nedum in
foro conscientiae, sed in foro civili.'

[1803] Azpilcueta, *Relectio in cap. Novit de iudiciis*, not. 6, coroll. 13, num. 60, f. 81v: 'Pra-
esuppositis ergo his tribus, scilicet, quod huiusmodi deceptor peccat mortaliter, et quod
tenetur ad restituendum, et tamdiu perseverat in peccato, quamdiu detinet alienum, probo
nunc hoc nostrum corollarium, scilicet huiusmodi, de quo agimus emptorem et venditorem etiam si sit laicus cogi posse ab ecclesiastico iudice per viam saltem denunciationis
evangelicae ad satisfaciendum laeso.'

[1804] Azpilcueta, *Relectio in cap. Novit de iudiciis*, not. 6, coroll. 13, num. 60–61, f. 81v.

remedy in the secular court. However, as Dr. Navarrus hastens to reply, the *exceptio malitiae* will normally be dismissed in the event of *laesio*, unless the ecclesiastical court would have had to dismiss the evangelical denunciation in the first place. There is a simple reason for that.[1805] The civil laws do not grant relief for lesion below moiety, so the plaintiff has no remedy in the civil court. Only when the lesion is beyond moiety, can the plaintiff take the *laedens* to a civil court. The relief granted by the ecclesiastical courts by virtue of evangelical denunciation is merely a subsidiary remedy. Put differently, the *exceptio malitiae* is a valid exception only if it comes down to an exception of incompetence of the ecclesiastial courts, but that can only be the case if the lesion is not below moiety.

Since the civil courts do not grant a remedy to the *laesus* unless the lesion is beyond moiety, it is indeed possible for the victim of *laesio infra dimidum* to file an evangelical denunciation against the *laedens* in the ecclesiastical court. Evangelical denunciation fulfills a merely subsidiary role here, so it cannot be opposed by an exception of malice. What is more, the *laesus* not only has the possibility of taking the *laedens* to court (*non solum potest*). As will be explained in the next paragraph, he seems to be obliged in his turn (*videtur teneri*) either to sue the *laedens* or to forgive the remainder of the debt.[1806]

7.3.2.2 *Competing for normative power*

The obligatory character of the evangelical denunciation might strike the modern reader as counterintuitive. However, the omnipresent mental reality of sin urges the theologians and canonists to protect the victim of lesion against violating yet another fundamental divine principle: the Biblical precept of brotherly or fraternal correction (*correctio fraterna*). Briefly,

---

[1805] Azpilcueta, *Relectio in cap. Novit de iudiciis*, not. 6, coroll. 13, num. 61, f. 81v: 'Non, inquam, obstat haec responsio, quia irrefragabiliter replicari potest, quod huiusmodi exceptio malitiae tunc demum habet locum, quando contra talem laesionem proditum est a lege civili remedium per quod illa laesionis iniquitas ad aequitatem reduci potest in foro seculari, ut in 2. difficultate praedixi. At quando tale remedium non est proditum tunc sine ullius eiusmodi exceptionis impedimento coram iudice ecclesiastico potest trahi saltem hac via de qua loquimur denunciationis.'

[1806] Azpilcueta, *Relectio in cap. Novit de iudiciis*, not. 6, coroll. 13, num. 62, f. 81v: 'Secundo et quidem nervosissime licet nove facit, quod eiusdem venditor laesus non solum potest recurrere ad iudicem ecclesiasticum, sed etiam videtur teneri, vel ad remittendum debitum, vel ad repetendum sub poena peccati. Quia omnis Christianus tenetur corripere proximum, quem videt perseverantem in aliquo peccato lethali, et si semel ac iterum monitus non se emendaverit, tenetur eum denunciare ecclesiae, iuxta praeceptum Domini de nos mutuo corripiendo, datum Matthaei 18.'

it means that every Christian is under a duty to talk to his brother in faith about his misbehavior. If the brother in question refuses to listen, then eventually his wrongs should be reported to the Church (Mt. 18:15–17).[1807] In any event, a Christian who sees that his brother is doing wrong must try to have a discussion with him. Since deviating from the just price amounts to the sin of theft, the *laesus* must immediately correct his 'brother' on pain of sinning himself.[1808]

The precept of brotherly correction precedes one of the most important foundational texts for the Church's sacramental and jurisdictionary power: 'I tell you solemnly, whatever you bind on earth shall be considered bound in heaven; whatever you loose on earth shall be considered loosed in heaven' (Mt. 18:18). It is no exaggeration to say that the entire object of study of this monograph would have been a pure mental fiction if Matthew had not written down this verse founding the Church's power of the keys (*potestas clavium*).[1809] By the same token, there seems to be no over-emphasizing the need to contemplate the pair of keys in the Catholic Church's banner, scattered so lavishly on 16th and 17th century Church edifices, to understand why the history of law in the early modern period cannot be written without reference to the Church's spiritual jurisdiction.

It is difficult for the modern reader to imagine how it must have felt to live in a world where spiritual jurisdiction was not just a hidden clerical phantasy or an empty source of anxiety for the flock. Yet no one will doubt that it must have led to a bitter power-struggle between spiritual and secular authorities in early modern times, no matter how close they collobarated at times—or should we rather say, *because* they often collaborated so closely?

[1807] For a more detailed account of the *correctio fraterna*, see chapter 2.4.2.

[1808] Azpilcueta, *Relectio in cap. Novit de iudiciis*, not. 6, coroll. 13, num. 62, f. 81v–82r: 'At omnis venditor huiusmodi, qui vendidit rem emptori credenti vel credere debenti eam multo pluris valere, videtur eum non solum peccasse lethaliter, sive mortaliter, iuxta dicta in 1. praesupposito, sed etiam perseverare in eo non restituendo, iuxta dicta in 2. et 3. praesupposito. Ergo vel debet ei donare quod debet, vel eum monere semel ac iterum, etsi non fuerit auditus, denunciare illius peccatum et perseverantiam ecclesiae, maxime quia is venditor magis quam alii tenetur ad hanc monitionem | et denunciationem. Tum, quia certius novit peccatum eius et perseverantiam quam alii. Tum, quia alii forte putant eum libere ac gratis donasse emptori eam partem qua pretium merx superabat. Tum, quia in ipsum peccat emptor non solum sicut in alios nocendo ei spiritualiter malo exemplo, sed etiam temporaliter damnificando, ut palam est. Et quando sunt multi, qui possunt corripere, ille primo loco ad id tenetur, qui magis est ad id obligatus, iuxta communem sententiam in locis praedictis receptam.'

[1809] For an introduction to the concept of the 'power of the keys', see chapter 2.4.2.

The marks of that clash can easily be traced in Dr. Navarrus' works. For those people who are as impervious as a stone (*saxeus*) to the idea that even laymen can be coerced by the ecclesiastical tribunals to make restitution through the means of evangelical denunciation, he levels the following accusation: 'you are mistaken about the Church's power of the keys' (*est errare in materia clavium*). Worse still, the contrary opinion should inspire terror as it is heretical (*terreat haeresim esse contrarium*).[1810] It is not unlikely that Dr. Navarrus' criticism was levelled primarily at his colleagues in the canon law faculty, who, perhaps, had become sensitive to the Protestant tendency to split the spiritual and the secular spheres of life. In the introduction to his commentary on *De penitentia*, he repeats that the concern with the spiritual sphere and the *forum internum* constitute a great part of canon law. He is sad, therefore, to find that his predecessors have barely turned their attention to these affairs (*adeo frigide tractata*).[1811]

Yet the objections against the enforcement of the dictates of conscience through fraternal correction and evangelical denunciation were equally plain as day. To single out just a few of them as they are listed by Dr. Navarrus himself: 'royal jurisdiction will severely decrease' (*iurisdictio regia maxime diminutum iri*); 'all cases treated by the secular court are transferred or could be transferred to the ecclesiastical court' (*omnes causae fori secularis trahantur trahive possint ad ecclesiasticum*); 'many wealthy people are going to be deprived of their tranquillity and property' (*divites multos deturbatum iri quiete sua et suis*); 'too many lawsuits are detrimental to society (*multas lites nocere reipublicae*)'.[1812]

Dr. Navarrus tries to soothe the nerves of his adversaries. So he simply denies that royal jurisdiction will suffer from the increased competence of the ecclesiastical courts (*negamus*) by referring to his exposition on the nature of lay and ecclesiastical power.[1813] Moreover, he denies that there is a conflict of interests in the first place. Lesion beyond moiety is spiritual business (*negotium spirituale*) for which the secular authorities

---

[1810] Azpilcueta, *Relectio in cap. Novit de iudiciis*, not. 6, coroll. 13, num. 64, f. 82r.

[1811] Azpilcueta, *In tres de poenitentia distinctiones*, [Ad auditores antiquos qui autorem Salmanticae, Tholosae vel Cathurci audiverunt iura pontificia interpretantem]: 'Neque vos latet palam esse spiritualia et ad interius forum pertinentia, quae bona sunt iuris pontificii pars, adeo frigide a nostris antecessoribus tractata esse, ut parum praelegentibus, minusque audientibus placeant.'

[1812] Azpilcueta, *Relectio in cap. Novit de iudiciis*, not. 6, coroll. 13, f. 82v, par. *Confirmato nostro*.

[1813] See the introductory remarks in chapter 2.4.

are simply not competent.[1814] Even if the ecclesiastical courts dismissed these cases, they would be declared inadmissable by the secular courts. Still, he recognizes that sometimes it is possible for both courts to treat the same case, for example homicide. After all, each court examines the case from its own perspective.[1815] The ecclesiastical court is competent to the extent that a particular misbehavior constitutes an offence against God and an impediment to eternal life. The secular courts are competent insofar as the wrong offends another citizen and society.

Dr. Navarrus is not afraid to admit that evangelical denunciation might indeed disturb the peace of rich people. He does not think this is a problem.[1816] There is an evil form of peace (*mala pax*) that needs to be disturbed rather than pursued, because it is the fruit of avarice and complacency. This is the peace Jesus promised to combat with the sword in Mt. 10, 34.[1817] As long as the plight of the poor can be bettered through the increased enforcement of the principle of justice in exchange, Dr. Navarrus does not see why he would not be able to put up with a bunch of angry wealthy people. Similarly, the bishops should not be afraid to be overwhelmed by lawsuits, since these lawsuits are motivated not by avarice, but justice.[1818] Dr. Navarrus is implacable in his condemnation

---

[1814] Azpilcueta, *Relectio in cap. Novit de iudiciis*, not. 6, coroll. 13, num. 69, f. 82v–83r: 'Ad secundum respondeo demirari me solitum illos qui clamant ob hoc minui iurisdictionem regiam. Tum, quia cognoscere de aliqua re, an sit peccatum, et gratiae coelestis impeditivum, et cogere quem ad illius poenitudinem ad nullam potestatem saecularem pertinet (…). Quia hoc negotium spirituale est, terminandum non legibus humanis, non etiam sola naturali, sed supernaturali divinitus in utroque testamento, maxime vero novo revelata. Tum, quia licet ecclesiastica potestas huius rei cognitionem omittat, nihilo magis tamen eam regia capere potest.'

[1815] Azpilcueta, *Relectio in cap. Novit de iudiciis*, not. 6, coroll. 13, num. 71, f. 83r: 'Adde, quod nemo negabit eum qui occidisset aliquem et ob id punitus esset etiam iuste, citra mortem tamen, a iudice seculari, peccati autem non poeniteret, imo diceret placere sibi plurimum id fecisse, posse corripi fraterna correptione, et si non se correxerit, denunciari ecclesiae, et si ab ea monitum non poeniteret, ob contumaciam excommunicari. Quoniam secularis iudex punivit eum ob homicidium, quatenus illud erat crimen civile offendens proximum et rempublicam, ecclesiasticus autem quatenus est offensivum Dei et impeditivum vitae aeternae et quatenus adhuc durat per impoenitentiam illam et contumaciam impedientem vitam spiritualem et aeternam.'

[1816] Azpilcueta, *Relectio in cap. Novit de iudiciis*, not. 6, coroll. 13, num. 76, f. 83v: 'Ad septimum respondeo concedendo aliquot divitibus hoc displiciturum et pacem aliquorum avarorum turbatum iri, dummodo vicissim fateare, quam plurimis pauperibus oppressis (quorum sanguis divitum labris suctus in caelum clamat) placiturum, dum item fateare esse pacem bonam et pacem malam, cum Thoma recepto 2.2.q.29.a.2.ad.3.'

[1817] Mt. 10: 34: 'Do not suppose that I have come to bring peace to the earth: it is not peace I have come to bring, but a sword.'

[1818] Azpilcueta, *Relectio in cap. Novit de iudiciis*, not. 6, coroll. 13, num. 78, f. 83v: 'Cum ergo lites hae quae coram episcopo nostro reverendissimo super hoc articulo moventur

of those merchants who take usurious profit margins of 30% and more through luring simple people into sale contracts. In fact, they should be happy that fraternal correction and evangelical denunciation exist as a last way to save their souls from eternal damnation.[1819]

To sum up, Dr. Navarrus' treatment of lesion gives us a unique insight into the real impact of the *forum internum*. Indeed, through the remedies of fraternal correction, evangelical denunciation, and ecclesiastical sanctions, lay people could be coerced to follow the dictates of conscience (*compellere ad poenitendum*).[1820] Conscience demands that justice in exchange be observed on pain of mortal sin. The seventh commandment not to steal, or, in other words, the prohibition on unjust enrichment, may never be infringed upon. Consequently, Dr. Navarrus insists that it would be a terrible mistake not to grant the remedy of evangelical denunciation to anyone harmed below moiety, if the secular laws do not help him. That would be the blatant denial of the Church's jurisdictional power to prepare mankind for Heaven (*clavibus Ecclesiae derogare videretur*).[1821]

7.4 LESION FOR DUMMIES: THE SYSTEMATIC APPROACH

It is perhaps due to Dr. Navarrus' discussion on the distinctive features of the *forum internum* and the *forum externum* that his pupil's discussion of C. 4,44,2 can be seen to subdivide into a part dealing with *laesio enormis* from the point of view of external jurisdiction and a part tackling lesion

---

non sint vitiosae, non fraudulentae, non filiae avaritiae, sed misericordiae ac pietatis, cum per eas pauperes leventur, eorum oppressores arceantur, animae captivae redimantur, aequalitas sancta in commutationibus introducatur, laudandae sunt et fovendae, imo et qua fieri potest iuvandae.'

[1819] Azpilcueta, *Relectio in cap. Novit de iudiciis*, not. 6, coroll. 13, num. 65–67, f. 82v.

[1820] Azpilcueta, *Relectio in cap. Novit de iudiciis*, not. 6, coroll. 13, num. 79, f. 83v: 'Et ideo etiam si sint laici corripi posse debereque correptione fraterna, et si correpti non se emendarint, denunciari ecclesiasticae protestati, quae, si se blande monentem non audierint, poterit per censuram ecclesiasticam eos compellere principaliter ad poenitendum et per consequutionem ad satisfaciendum parti laesae iuxta regulas denunciationis evangelicae iudicialis vel mixtae.'

[1821] Azpilcueta, *Relectio in cap. Novit de iudiciis*, not. 6, coroll. 13, num. 79, f. 83v: 'Concludamus secundo menti iuris pontificii et sanctitati eius convenire (…) scilicet recta via et sine ambagibus via denunciationis evangelicae competere officium iudicis contra huiusmodi contractores in foro ecclesiastico, quando et quoties nullum remedium praestat eis seculare. Concludamus et tertio tolerari quidem posse illum, qui negarit tale officium competere in tales contractores (quamvis mea sententia inique opinentur) non tamen eum, qui viam denunciationis evangelicae omnino negaret. Quippe qui clavibus Ecclesiae derogare videretur.'

as a matter of conscience. Yet more importantly, the bulk of Covarruvias' commentary is dedicated to three technical questions of great importance. Firstly, whether it is allowed for a party to renounce the remedy which C. 4,44,2 has established in his favor. Secondly, whether the injured party's knowledge of the just price compromises his right to the remedy. Thirdly, whether clauses of donation of the value beyond moiety are valid. Covarruvias' solution of those questions seems to depend on whether he considers them from the point of view of the *forum externum* or of the *forum internum*. In any event, unlike his teacher's exposition, Covarruvias' treatment of *laesio enormis* is mainly technical and less polemical. Still, the influence of theological thinking in his commentary on the *Lex secunda* becomes palpable. Perhaps that is also related to the late influence of Piñel's revolutionary re-interpretation of C. 4,44,2 on Covarruvias' discussion.

7.4.1 The external court

As a matter of positive law, Covarruvias admits that, in principle, lesion beyond moiety gives rise to a remedy grounded on C. 4,44,2. However, he concludes that there are three exceptions to this general rule.[1822] First of all, when the injured party assented to the unequal contract while perfectly knowing the just price. Secondly, when the injured party gave his consent to a specific renunciation clause, to the effect that he abandoned his right to sue the injurer. Thirdly, when the injured party had agreed to donate the excess value. In all of these three cases, the injured party loses the right based on the *Lex secunda* to sue the *laedens*. However, each of these conclusions is equally subject to some form of qualification. Moreover, it seems that the occasional ambiguity of Covarruvias' argument is concerned with his rethinking his own argument on the basis of theological principles. This could be due to his reading Arias Piñel just before the publication of his commentary but after the main structure of his own exposition had already been given shape.

[1822] Covarruvias, *Variarum resolutionum*, lib. 2, cap. 4, num. 6, p. 249: 'Hactenus satis probavimus laesum ultra dimidiam in contractu venditionis posse agere auxilio dictae l. 2, nisi contractui consenserit sciens iustum rei valorem vel actioni sibi competenti et laesioni ultra dimidiam renunciaverit, idem et tertio solet adnotari, ubi laesus alteri donaverit in eodem contractu eam quantitatem quae iusti pretii dimidiam excedit (...).'

7.4.1.1   *The renunciability of C. 4,44,2*

Knowingly entering into a contract which stipulates a price different from the just price was considered to be tantamount to a tacit renunciation clause. The adage borrowed from the *ius commune* stating that he who knows suffers no harm (*scienti non fit iniuria*) was undoubtedly at play here.[1823] Yet Covarruvias does not quote that expression. He simply makes reference to the *communis opinio*, advocated by the Orléans commentators, the Bartolists and, lastly, André Tiraqueau—one of his favorite sources. To be sure, Covarruvias insists that the burden of proof lies on the *laedens*. The presumption that everybody knows the true value of his belongings fails in the case of lesion beyond moiety. So unless the defendant proves that the plaintiff had knowledge of the true price of the good at the moment of the conclusion of the contract, he is liable on the ground of C. 4,44,2.

Moreover, at the end of his life, Covarruvias seems to have changed his mind about the idea of knowledge as a tacit renunciation clause altogether. Eventually, he would not accept any longer the idea that in case of lesion beyond moiety knowledge of the price could frustrate the remedy offered by the *Lex secunda*. At least that is what the additional text to the posthumous *editio Taurinensis* of 1594, directed by a certain Johannes Dominicus Tarinus, suggests.[1824]

Despite his knowledge, a victim of lesion beyond moiety can still vindicate the support of C. 4,44,2. That is a rather new opinion, which departs from the common opinion of the late medieval jurists. It is closer to the views advocated in the penitential literature. As is indicated in the emended edition of his commentary, Covarruvias would have taken this new view under the influence of the Portuguese jurist Arias Piñel, whom we will discuss below. Although the authenticity of this emendation might be questioned, it is excellent proof of the authority Arias Piñel rapidly gained, if not yet with Covarruvias himself, at least among his followers.

Besides the tacit renunciation of the remedy based on the *Lex secunda*, contracting parties can of course stipulate an express renunciation clause. As long as this renunciation clause specifically mentions the abandon-

---

[1823] See D. 50,17,145 and VI 5,13,27.

[1824] Covarruvias, *Variarum resolutionum*, lib. 2, cap. 4, num. 2, p. 248: 'Imo, ut ingenue fatear, et quod mihi magis placet libere explicem, existimo adversus communem iure probari posse, locum esse huius constitutionis actioni, etiam ubi ultra dimidiam laesus sciverit, tempore contractus, verum rei valorem. Quod diligenter probare conatur post huius operis primam editionem Arius Pinel (...).'

ing of the right to use the remedy grounded on C. 4,44,2 in case of lesion beyond moiety, Covarruvias thinks that such a clause is valid. He claims support for this view from André Tiraqueau and the common opinion. What he does not admit of, however, is a general renunciation clause which cannot be interpreted as specifically giving up the remedy provided by the *Lex secunda*.

Even though a particular renunciation (*renunciatio specialis*) is valid in principle, there is a hitch. Covarruvias only thinks a renunciation is valid in the event of so-called moderate lesion beyond moiety (*laesio enormis*). His opinion no longer holds in the case of excessive lesion (*laesio enormissima*).[1825] On the ground of law *Si superstite* (C. 2,20,5), lesion which is more than immense is considered to be taking place on an objective level (*re ipsa*) and is tantamount to bad deceit (*dolus*).

Apparently, for Covarruvias this is not just a subtle theoretical distinction. He cites a recent example from the highest ecclesiastical tribunal in Rome. The majority of the judges in the Rota had ruled that a sale of a thing worth 2300 guilders at 1000 guilders was tainted by *laesio enormissima*. Similarly, he knew from his own experience that the ecclesiastical tribunal at Granada had accepted a claim based on the *Lex secunda* for the sale of a house worth 3500 guilders at 1500 guilders. He thought that this was only equitable (*id maximam aequitatem habet*).

There is a third way in which contracting parties can abandon their right to sue on account of C. 4,44,2: by making a donation of the excess value. Covarruvias insists that this donation clause must explicitly stipulate that the excess value will be donated no matter how far the price exceeds the true value.[1826] Otherwise the clause could be interpreted as being limited to the value within moiety. This is a caveat he borrows from

---

[1825] Covarruvias, *Variarum resolutionum*, lib. 2, cap. 4, num. 5, p. 249: 'Caeterum ubi laesio non tantum contigerit ultra iusti pretii dimidiam, sed praeter ea gravissima, et ut nostrates loquuntur, enormissima sit, adhuc obtinet actio ex dicta l. 2, poteritque deceptus ex ea agere, etiam si expressim renunciaverit eidem constitutioni, eamque renunciationem iuramento praestito stabilierit, donaveritque quantitatem iustum pretium excedentem, eiusve dimidiam partem, praemissa scientiae iusti pretii asseveratione, quandoquidem haec renunciatio, eique adhaerentes clausulae tunc demum vim habent, cum laesio ultra dimidiam mediocris est, non sic ubi is excessus ad gravissimam laesionem pertinet, quo quidem casu laesio, ipsa re contingens dolo comparatur.'

[1826] Covarruvias, *Variarum resolutionum*, lib. 2, cap. 4, num. 6, p. 249: '(...) saltem oportet clausulam istam aperte concipi, ut expressim donetur id quod excedit vel deest ad iusti pretii aestimationem quaecunque ea quantitas sit, alioqui donatio quantitatis deficientis iusto pretio vel id excedentis nihil ad hoc operaretur quia potest intelligi intra dimidiam iusti pretii partem.'

Bartolus and Tiraqueau amongst others.[1827] This form of renunciation is not subject to a lengthy discussion. Yet it does lead to an extended debate about the impact of the three types of renunciation clauses on the nature of the transaction.

7.4.1.2   *Gifts are not presumed*

After expounding the three ways of dispensing with the protection offered by the *Lex secunda*, Covarruvias raises the question whether the various renunciation clauses change the nature of the contract itself. Of particular interest was the question whether onerous contracts containing such a clause became some sort of donation contract. This is a problem that Covarruvias considers to be of direct relevance to practice (*sat utilis et frequens*), since donations exceeding 500 solidi require registration (*insinuatio*).[1828] If the part beyond moiety actually constitutes a true donation because of a renunciation clause, then the rules of donation should apply. However, Covarruvias fiercely rejects this analysis. Apparently, he shares with the theologians a common concern not to confound the law of sale and the law of donation.

The main reason why Covarruvias refuses to interpret renunciations of C. 4,44,2 in terms of a donation is connected with the presumed intention of the contracting parties. In sale there is no reason to believe that the parties intend to make a donation. The intention of the contracting parties is directed towards obtaining a mutually advantageous sale contract. There is nothing they want less than to make a gift.[1829] Even if an element of gift is added to the sale contract in the form of a renunciation, the principal

---

[1827] Bartolus, *In secundam Digesti novi partem commentaria*, ad D. 45,1,36, num. 7, f. 17r: 'Quaero, dicitur in instrumento venditionis, vendidit rem pro tanto, et illud quod plus valet, dedit et donavit. An per hoc cessabunt remedia harum legum? (...) Dico quod si venditor sciebat valorem rei, tunc per talia verba cessant remedia harum legum. Sed si hoc ignorabat, tunc per talia verba non habebat animum donandi, nisi modicum (...), et ideo si quantitas est magna, apparet quod in contractu donationis est laesus et sic habebit remedium huius legis (...).'
Tiraqueau, *De utroque retractu*, lib. 1, par. 1, glossa 18 (*pretium quo res constitit*), num. 11–19, p. 164–165.

[1828] Covarruvias, *Variarum resolutionum*, lib. 2, cap. 4, num. 6, p. 249: 'Superest tandem quaestio non inelegans, imo sat utilis et frequens, an in his tribus casibus quibus laesum ultra dimidiam excludi adnotavimus propter quandam tacitam donationem, sitne donata, ita censenda, ut insinuationem exigat, si quingentos solidos excesserit.'

[1829] Covarruvias, *Variarum resolutionum*, lib. 2, cap. 4, num. 9, p. 250: 'Primum etenim illud est considerandum, quod praecipua contrahentium intentio, totiusque huius intentionis scopus is est, ut emant et vendant, nihilque minus quam gratuitam donationem mente concipiunt. Ideoque, etsi huic contractui mixtum sit aliquid, quod ad donationem

intention to buy or to sell remains the same. The sale contract absorps the adjacent gift.[1830] Its original, onerous nature remains unchanged.

The principle underlying Covarruvias' arguent is clearly that a gift is not presumed (*donatio non praesumitur*). The modern jurist is not wholly unfamiliar with this maxim and it is often traced back to Roman law.[1831] However, it seems probable that this maxim does not appear in this explicit form until later.[1832] It can be found in the writings of French humanists such as André Tiraqueau.[1833] The idea that gifts are not presumed reached a peak in the juristic thought of the moral theologians. We already saw this in Juan de Medina's discussion of *laesio enormis*. Another example is Soto, who frequently repeated that gifts are not presumed unless the evidence is apparent (*nemo praesumitur donare nisi planis documentis constat*).[1834] Following Baldus amongst other jurists, the theologians and canonists thought that presuming gifts in contracts and commercial transactions could be pernicious. Again, we will find Covarruvias giving a rather brief but crystal-clear account of this standard scholastic doctrine.

In a passage absolutely fundamental to understanding scholastic contract law, Covarruvias explains that for a gift to be taken seriously in a

---

pertineat, contractus nomen assumit a principaliori contrahentium actu, et intentione, nempe ab emptione et venditione, non a donatione'.

[1830] Curiously, besides quoting D. 18,1,79, Covarruvias adduces a so-called law *Si quis nec causam*, ff. *Si certum petatur* to strengthen this claim. Yet this particular law does not figure in the Digest. The title *Si certum petatur* is part of the Code but it does not contain a law beginning with *Si quis nec causam*. Interestingly, Jeremy Taylor (1613–1667), who heavily borrowed from the Catholic scholastics in writing his *Ductor dubitantium* (*The Rule of Conscience*), refers to this alleged passage from the Digest as containing the maxim 'In omni dispositione attenditur quod principaliter agitur'. Since the passage referred to does not exist in the first place, this is obviously false. Moreover, the erroneous reference to 'lib. (sic!) *Si quis nec causam*, ff. *Si certum petatur*' adds further weight to the suspicion that Taylor simply copied this reference from another author, perhaps from Covarruvias. See R. Heber (ed.), *The whole works of Jeremy Taylor*, vol. 13 (containing the continuation of *The Rule of Conscience*), London 1828, p. 308.
[1831] See the reference to D. 46,3,50 in Liebs, *Lateinische Rechtsregeln und Rechtssprichwörter*, p. 68, num. 70. However, it is difficult to see how D. 46,3,50 can be interpreted to contain this maxim: 'Si, cum aurum tibi promisissem, ignoranti quasi aurum aes solverim, non liberabor: sed nec repetam hoc quasi indebitum solutum, quod sciens feci. Petentem tamen te aurum exceptione summovebo, si non reddas aes quod accepisti.'
[1832] See A. Wacke, *Europäische Spruchweisheiten über das Schenken und ihr Wert als rechtshistorisches Argument*, in: R. Zimmermann – R. Knütel – J.P. Meincke (eds.), Rechtsgeschichte und Privatrechtsdogmatik, Heidelberg 1999, p. 353–359. The author traces the origins of the maxim back to Johannes Voet (1647–1713).
[1833] Tiraqueau, *De utroque retractu*, lib. 1, par. 36, glossa 2 (*notificatae apud acta*), num. 49, p. 353.
[1834] Soto, *De iustitia et iure* (ed. fac. V. Diego Carro – M. González Ordóñez, vol. 3), lib. 6, quaest. 1, art. 4, p. 527.

sale contract, there must be some kind of cause (*causa*) attached to it.[1835]
There must be a ground (*causa*) that makes a donation look reasonable,
such as friendship (*amicitia*) or an intimate connection between the contracting parties (*necessitudo*). Among strangers there is no reason (*causa*)
to presume donation. A vendor who sells for a much lower price than the
common estimation can do so for a variety of reasons, but unless friendship is involved, most of them are morally suspect. From practical experience Covarruvias concludes that:

> A vendor selling below the market price only does so either because he
> believes that he is selling at the just price, or because he is compelled by
> necessity to sell, or because he is affected by an urgent desire to remove the
> good in question from his own property. This is how it works in practice.
> What kind of reason, then, if any, would tell us to presume that somebody
> who is not thinking about making a gift at all, that somebody who would not
> even be prepared to give a penny to the other party for free, has nevertheless
> the intent of making a gift (*ut animum donandi praesumamus*)?

In other words, Covarruvias states the *donatio non praesumitur*-principle
in an unmistakable way. Moreover, he lists three principal reasons that
explain why the early modern scholastics were so anxious to separate the
law of sale and the law of gifts: (1) The vendor might be mistaken about
the just price of his good; (2) He might be the victim of duress; (3) He
might be driven by the desire to get rid of his goods at any cost—a desire
which the other party should not exploit according to the so-called 'double rule of just pricing'.

[1835] Covarruvias, *Variarum resolutionum*, lib. 2, cap. 4, num. 9, p. 250: 'Secundo, ut ad
institutum peculiare regrediamur, eadem opinio alia ratione constat, vendere etenim rem
viliori pretio non est donatio sed damnosus contractus authore Baldo in rubric. C. de con-
trah. Emptione, num. 11. Is equidem qui rem propriam vendit vilius quam eius sit iusta
aestimatio, cum id agit causa donationis collatae in emptorem qui extraneus est, cum quo
nulla amicitia est, nulla adest necessitudo, ac denique nulla est causa donandi, sed ita
venditor contrahit, vel quia existimat se vendere pretio iusto vel coactus necessitate quadam vendendi, aut voto et desiderio, quod illa res exeat a proprio patrimonio, ut morali
quadam praxi constat. Quae igitur obsecro ratio dictat, ut animum donandi praesumamus
habere eum, qui nullo pacto de donatione cogitat, nec titulo donationis emptori quad-
rantem daret.'

7.4.2   *The internal court*

7.4.2.1   *Reason of sin* vs *reason of state*

The discussion about the presumed donatory character of contracts tainted by lesion brings Covarruvias' discussion to bear on the *forum internum*. The theologians' total rejection of *laesio enormis*, even below moiety, is quoted to the effect that not even the slightest amount of money exceeding the just price can be presumed to constitute a gift. Otherwise the theologians' doctrine that any deviation of the just price is a sin would no longer hold water. In our canonist's view, an assumption resulting in such an absurd conclusion could not possibly be valid.[1836]

In fact, Covarruvias' argument is another testimony to the fundamental interest the theologians must have had in neatly distinguishing the law of sale from the law of donation. Without the support of the *donatio non praesumitur*-principle, the whole doctrine of just pricing would have been constantly put on the defensive. The burden of proof before the court of conscience would have lain with the confessor and not with the confessant.

Interestingly, the bishop from Segovia emphasizes the social significance of contractual exchange. This is the fundamental, natural law basis for the requirement of contractual equilibrium in the court of conscience. The Aristotelian principle of equality in exchange must be observed, since contracts have been instituted by society and human custom precisely to the benefit of both contracting parties (*in utriusque utilitatem*).[1837] Contractual equilibrium is of the highest importance, because contractual exchange should never result in a zero sum game.

Against this background, Covarruvias cannot but endorse the majority standpoint that any deviation from the just price constitutes sin. Lesion, however insignificant, is never permitted in the *forum internum*. Yet that does not mean that the law of the land should be bound by this orthodox view. The external tribunals have to take into consideration the func-

---

[1836] Covarruvias, *Variarum resolutionum*, lib. 2, cap. 4, num. 11, p. 251: 'Quia si donatio circa laesionem intra dimidiam praesumeretur non esset ea laesio ex parte laedentis peccatum, nec is teneretur in animae iudicio restituere eam quantitatem, in qua laesio contingit, quod falum esse apparet, quemadmodum summatim attingam.'

[1837] Covarruvias, *Variarum resolutionum*, lib. 2, cap. 4, num. 11, p. 251: 'Prior opinio verissima est, manifesta et urgenti admodum ratione, quae dictat naturali lege in contractibus commutativis, a republica et hominum moribus in utriusque utilitatem institutis, re ipsa exactam et summam aequalitatem requiri ex iustitia commutativa partis ad partem, secundum Aristotelem (…)'.

tioning of society as a whole (*ratio status*). For that reason, the State can decide not to persecute prostitution or not to enforce naked pacts.[1838] By the same token, a certain form of dissimulation (*dissimulatio quaedam*) for the sake of the stability of the state can be justified in regard to unfair contracts.[1839]

7.4.2.2   Unjust enrichment

As a matter of natural law, even lesion below moiety constitutes a sin against the virtue of justice in exchange. Consequently, contractual equilibrium must be restored before the *forum internum* through an act of restitution. As Covarruvias puts it, disrupting contractual equilibrium is a form of deceit (*deceptio*), which goes against justice in exchange. Yet is the *laedens* bound to make restitution for that matter, even if he truly ignored the just price? Or can the *laesus* claim restitution even if he knew the just price but agreed to a deviating price? Put differently, did the scholastics really believe in some sort of unintentional or objective deceit, regardless of the subjective knowledge of either of the contracting parties?

Covarruvias' answer to these questions turns out to be nuanced. It is articulated in two parts. Firstly, our canonist discusses the impact of the *laedens*' ignorance of the just price on the duty to make restitution. This is a debate which runs into the scholastics' teachings on unjust enrichment. Secondly, the question is raised whether the *laesus*' knowledge of the just price can excuse the lesion in the court of conscience. Here the debate turns on the distinction between the law of sale and the law of gifts.

Let us assume that the *laedens* did not try to deceive the other party on purpose in any way, even though the price to which he assented deviates from the just price. Consequently, he is acting in good faith (*bona fide*), while justice in exchange has been violated. Citing the common opinion, Covarruvias holds that the *laedens* is bound to make restitution regardless.[1840] To be sure, the duty to make restitution cannot be enforced until the *bona fide* party learns that the contractually fixed price did not match

---

[1838] Cf. supra.

[1839] Covarruvias, *Variarum resolutionum*, lib. 2, cap. 4, num. 11, p. 251: 'Leges etenim non omnia quae illicita sunt puniunt nec punire tenentur, nec actionem itidem dare adversus eum, qui iure naturali et iusta ratione quid agere vel restituere debet. Possunt sane legumlatores haec plerunque quibusdam ex causis omittere et dissimulatione quadam tolerare, modo ea curent providere, quae ad hominum coniunctum et reipublicae integrum atque illaesum statum attinent.'

[1840] Covarruvias, *Variarum resolutionum*, lib. 2, cap. 4, num. 11, p. 251: 'Quin et communis opinio adhuc obtinet non solum ubi scienter quis in commutationibus proximum

the just price.[1841] Moreover, the plaintiff's right to recover his property may not have been precluded yet by reason of prescription (*usucapione*).

Covarruvias draws a parallel here with the duty to make restitution which is incumbent on the *bona fide* possessor in general. What is more, he recognizes Thomas Aquinas' doctrine of unjust enrichment—famously expressed in article 62 of the *Secunda Secundae*—as the foundation on which his and the other jurists' opinion relies. According to Aquinas' doctrine of unjust enrichment, even a *bona fide* possessor can be bound to make restitution on the ground of either of the following reasons: unjust receiving (*ratione iniustae acceptionis*), say theft, or the thing received (*ratione rei acceptae*), say a stolen good you bought from a thief. In both cases, the possessor retains something which is actually another person's property (*res aliena*).

The vocabulary Covarruvias uses to denote the two grounds for restitution is not exactly the same as Aquinas', but it helps to clarify the basic Thomistic concepts: unjust detaining against the owner's will (*ratione detentionis iniustae domino invito*) and the thing itself, because it belongs to someone else (*ratione ipsius rei quia aliena est*). In Covarruvias' view, the case of the *laedens bona fide* falls within the scope of unjust detaining against the owner's will. Accordingly, he is bound to compensate for his unjust enrichment.

Interestingly, Covarruvias suggests that the doctrine of unjust enrichment be applied in the *forum externum* as well.[1842] At least when there is purposeful deceit (*dolus ex proposito*) on the part of the *laedens*, Covarruvias thinks that even in the *forum externum* a duty of restitution lies in the event of lesion below moiety (*infra dimidiam*). For that kind of deceit

---

inscium et ignorantem iustum rei valorem laedit, ac decipit, sed etiam si quis bona fide existimans se iusto pretio emere aut vendere, alterum etiam intra dimidiam laeserit.'

[1841] Covarruvias, *Variarum resolutionum*, lib. 2, cap. 4, num. 11, p. 251: 'Quorum opinio communis est, et probatur evidenti ratione, qua constat hunc teneri ad restitutionem postquam cognoverit se proximum laesisse, quia rem alienam detinet invito domino, et causa detentionis iniquae ad restitutionem tenetur, sicut is, qui bona fide rem aliquam acquisivit, et habuit ab eo quem dominum esse existimabat, si, nondum completa usucapione, sciverit rem illam alienam esse, nec domini consensu sibi traditam, tenetur omnino eam domino restituere, vel ratione detentionis iniustae domino invito, vel ratione ipsius rei, quia aliena est, iuxta erudite tradita per Thomam, Caietan, secunda secundae, quaestione 62, articulo 1, 4 et 6.'

[1842] Covarruvias, *Variarum resolutionum*, lib. 2, cap. 4, num. 11, p. 251: 'Verum si quis sciens iustum valorem rei absque mendacio aliave persuasione eam emerit viliori pretio, etiam intra dimidiam ab ignorante, quod sit iustum eius rei pretium fortassis etiam in foro exteriori cogetur iustam rei aestimationem supplere.'

to occur, it is sufficient that the *laedens* knew the just price whereas the other party did not.

In fact, Covarruvias founds this opinion expressly on Augustine. In a passage in *De Trinitate*, Augustine recounts how a buyer who saw that the vendor was selling a book at too low a price still paid the just price to this ignorant vendor.[1843] He regarded this as a virtuous counter-example of the vicious natural tendency men have to try to buy as cheap and to sell as dear as they can. Consequently, Covarruvias considers this story to be a demonstration that wittingly not paying the just price to an ignorant vendor is tantamount to deceit.

This is a conclusion that might seem to be confusing. After all, our canonist has just treated lesion below moiety from the perspective of the *forum internum*. Moreover, he did so assuming precisely that the *laedens* acted in good faith. Yet no matter how unlucky the structure of his argument, Covarruvias' conclusion is nevertheless compelling. It clearly shows how far the jurists were willing to go in order to reconcile the legal tradition with theological principles.

The ignorant victim of lesion—even below moiety—should be allowed to sue the *laedens* and obtain compensation in the *forum externum*. This is certainly true in the ecclesiastical court, where the *laesus* can appeal to the judge's office.[1844] Covarruvias appears to be directly influenced by the doctrine of his teacher Dr. Navarrus here.

7.4.2.3 *Gifts are not presumed*

As has been mentioned before, there is a second question, which concerns the objective or subjective nature of lesion. After discussing the impact of the *laedens'* knowledge on the duty to make restitution, Covarruvias deals with the problem of the *laesus'* knowledge of the just price.[1845] The question is raised whether the *laesus'* knowledge of the just price can excuse the *laedens'* violation of commutative justice. The answer to this question depends on the distinction between sale-purchase and donation.

[1843] Augustinus, *De Trinitate*, 13, 3, 6, cited supra, n. 1722.

[1844] Covarruvias, *Variarum resolutionum*, lib. 2, cap. 4, num. 11, p. 251: 'Sed saltem in foro canonico pluribus placuit, deceptum ignorantem adversus deceptorem ex vera scientia pretii agere posse ad laesionis compensationem apud iudicem ecclesiasticum.'

[1845] Covarruvias, *Variarum resolutionum*, lib. 2, cap. 4, num. 11, p. 251–252: 'Superest casus non omnino facilis, cum quis scilicet scienti iustum valorem eam ei vendiderit carius quam valeat, vel a sciente eam emerit vilius, nam et hunc in conscientiae iudicio peccare et teneri ad restitutionem colligitur ex his rationibus quas in communi sententiae probationem adducit Conradus (...).'

Apparently, Covarruvias has no doubts that in the court of conscience the *laesus*' knowledge of the just price does not excuse the *laedens*. In other words, the maxim that he who knows and consents suffers no harm (*scienti ac volenti non fit iniuria*) does not apply. However, this is not Covarruvias' way of explaining his conclusion. Our canonist points to Summenhart's and Medina's idea that there is no such thing as a presumption of gift (*donationis praesumptio hic non subest*) and that therefore the *laedens* enriches himself unrightfully.

As a result, Covarruvias is at the same time able to claim that the *laedens* is not guilty of violating contractual equilibrium if a presumption of gift can be established after all.[1846] This is the case when the *laesus* could in no way be considered to be the victim of coercion, necessity, or another cause which compelled him to enter into the contract at the given price. In practice this is rarely the case, though, Covarruvias admits.[1847] Moreover, it is very difficult to presume a gift in contractual affairs.[1848]

First of all, gratuitousness is contrary to the very nature of the law of sale-purchase (*ex propria vi et natura non gratuitus*). Again relying on Thomas Aquinas' *Secunda Secundae*, particularly on the famous article 77, our canonist argues that in buying and selling a just price is required, not a gift. Secondly, a gift is not presumed because very frequently compulsion by necessity (*necessitate cogente*) lies at the basis of contracts deviating from the just price. This kind of coercion vitiates the type of unmixed voluntary consent required for donations.

Apart from a reference to a long passage in which Tiraqueau insists on the distinction between gift and sale, a *reductio ad absurdum* further illustrates Covarruvias' point about the essentially distinct nature of the

---

[1846] Covarruvias, *Variarum resolutionum*, lib. 2, cap. 4, num. 11, p. 252: 'Hinc deducitur aliud fore respondendum si possit commode donatio praesumi, nempe si laesus nulla necessitate coactus, nullave alia causa, quae ipsum cogat vendere vel emere, rem illam emerit carius vel vendiderit vilius, certo sciens quis sit eius iustus valor (...).'

[1847] Covarruvias, *Variarum resolutionum*, lib. 2, cap. 4, num. 11, p. 252: 'Quibus omnibus consideratis constat regulariter in his commutativis contractibus non posse donationem praesumi nec eam praemitti, etiam si laesio ultra vel citra dimidiam acciderit.'

[1848] Covarruvias, *Variarum resolutionum*, lib. 2, cap. 4, num. 11, p. 252: 'Quibus et alia ratio adstipulatur, quod contractus emptionis et venditionis ex propria vi et natura non est gratuitus et ideo ad id quod est accidens, nempe ad praesumptam donationem non est advertendum, cum in hoc contractu commutationis de iustitia tractetur, iustumque pretium quaeratur, non donum, sicuti Thomas argumentatur dicta quaestione 77, art. 1. Et praeterea contractus hic frequentissime fit, quadam quasi necessitate cogente, quae inducit in voluntarium mixtum, quod donationem gratuitam impedit.'

law of sale and the law of donation.[1849] If there were no such distinction between sale and donation, the part exceeding the just price could be revoked, just as in a normal gift contract, if the *laedens* were ungrateful or if the *laesus* had a child. Yet this is manifestly false. On top of this, the law of successions would compromise this kind of sale.[1850] One could think of a merchant who sold below the just price and leaves several heirs-at-law who are entitled to their respective *portio legitima*, which is the share in the estate of which they cannot be deprived by will. If the amount below the just price really constituted a gift, and this gift were considered to be an impious gift (*donatio inofficiosa*), then it could be revoked. This amount should then be calculated on the amount of which the testator could dispose. Yet this does not happen in practice and it cannot even be defended in theory, unless this kind of sale is really meant to deprive the children of their legitimate part.

Covarruvias derives from the fundamentally non-gratuitous character of the law of sale that a duty to make restitution of the entire amount of money exceeding the just price is required—even in the external court.[1851] Before the ecclesiastical court and the secular court the *laedens* must not only make restitution of what exceeds half the just price, but of the entire value deviating from the just price. Also, the renuciation of C. 4,44,2 should not be considered a gift in the external court. To summarize, the regulation of *laesio enormis* in the court of conscience seriously left its marks on its treatment in the *forum externum*. Covarruvias' late source of inspiration, Arias Piñel, would only reinforce that cross-fertilization.

[1849] Tiraqueau, *Commentarii in l. Si unquam, C. De revocandis donationibus*, s.v. *donatione*, num. 1–6, p. 269–273.

[1850] Covarruvias, *Variarum resolutionum*, lib. 2, cap. 4, num. 11, p. 252: 'Si hic donationem subesse fateremur, sequeretur, quod venditore habente filios, liberosve, quibus legitima deberetur, hic contractus iure inofficiosae donationis revocaretur ea ex parte, qua iustum pretium deficit vel exceditur, et ea quantitas imputaretur in eam portionem, quae a parentibus exteris legari vel donari iure poterat, quod nec in praxi receptum est, nec iure defendi potest, nisi eo casu, quo facta fuerit venditio in fraudem legitimae portionis filiis debitae.'

[1851] Covarruvias, *Variarum resolutionum*, lib. 2, cap. 4, num. 11, p. 252: 'Unde in foro etiam exteriori cum ad hoc agitur ob laesionem ultra dimidiam, non satisfacit reus restituendo id per quod pretium crescit ultra dimidiam, nec supplendo pretium ad dimidiam usque, quippe qui teneatur integre totum, quod est de justo pretio vel excedit illud, restituere secundum Cynum communiter receptum in d. l.2 quaest. 8.'

7.5 LESION FOR THE ADVANCED: THE CRITICAL APPROACH

In the 1582 edition of the *Corpus iuris canonici*, commissioned by Pope
Gregory XIII, the *correctores Romani* refer to Arias Piñel for further discussion on *laesio enormis*.[1852] Arias Piñel (1515–1563) was a humanist jurist
from Sesimbra near Lisbon. He ranks among those exceptional Renaissance men who continue to appeal to the modern reader both through
depth of knowledge and liveliness of personality. Piñel appears to have
been a successful jurist in his own day.[1853] A popular law professor, first at
Coimbra (1539–1548 / 1556–1559) and later at Salamanca (1559–1563), Piñel
alternated legal scholarship with prestigious lawyering activities, serving,
for example, as an advocate at the Casa de Suplicación in Lisbon.

In light of his own career, it should not come as a surprise that Piñel
cites the famous statement that 'law schools have the laws shoved down
your throat, while the courts make you digest them, since practice is the
science of digestion'. This expression can be traced back at least to Baldus de Ubaldis.[1854] In Piñel's own experience, lawyering without a solid
theoretical basis turns out to be dangerous, but legal scholarship without
practical application proves to be ineffective.[1855] From classical literature
he claims further proof of this insight, citing Pliny the Elder's words that
'the real battle takes place on the *forum*, the school is but a harmless kind
of thing.'

However, if the tremendous erudition displayed by Piñel is anything to
go by, for instance in his very praise of legal practice, then we must conclude from this that the humanist ideal which he ultimately aspired to in
his life can hardly be attained without some degree of academic learning.
Piñel's way of thinking is actually highly reminiscent of that of Diego de

---

[1852] Cf. nota *Vide l.2* ad X 3,17,3 (canon *Quum dilecti*) in *Corpus juris canonici* (ed. Gregoriana), part. 2, col. 1123.

[1853] See J. García Sánchez, *Arias Piñel, Catedrático de Leyes en Coimbra y Salamanca
durante el siglo XVI, La rescisión de la compraventa por "laesio enormis"*, Salamanca 2004,
p. 39–143, along with the review by T. Wallinga in Tijdschrift voor Rechtsgeschiedenis, 74
(2006), p. 185–187.

[1854] Baldus, *In primam Digesti veteris partem commentaria*, ad D. 4,4,38, f. 256v, num. 35:
'Leges in scholis diglutiuntur, in palaciis digeruntur, quia practica est scientia digestiva.'

[1855] Arias Piñel, *Commentarii ad rub. et l. 2, C. de rescindenda venditione, cum annotationibus Emanuelis Soarez a Ribiera. Accessit eiusdem argumenti cap. 3 et 4, lib. 2 resolutionum Didaci Covarruviae*, Antverpiae 1618, ad l. 2, part. 2, cap. 4, num. 2, p. 152: 'Ego autem
post longam legendi professionem, postque diligentissimam foro navatam operam, in ea
sententia sum, ut theorica sine praxi digestam solidamque iuris cognitionem praestare
nequeat, praxisque absque theorica maxime periculosa et manca evadat.'

Covarruvias y Leyva. Covarruvias, too, combined a remarkable passion for humanist learning with a high sensivity for legal practice. His learned and often highly sophisticated commentaries on the *ius commune* were interspersed with quite personal reflections on legal practice, passionate notes on textual criticism and brilliant quotes from ancient literary sources. It is perhaps no coincidence that both Covarruvias and Piñel were students of the humanist-scholastic canonist Martín de Azpilcueta.

7.5.1 *Socio-political foundations*

'The arts, like trees, cannot reach high if they are cut off from their roots'.[1856] In the footsteps of Marcus Tullius Cicero, Piñel is convinced that humanist erudition and a true sense of historical criticism are not just qualities that boost the reputation of a lawyer. They are crucial to the fruitful interpretation of the sacred texts of law in a continuously changing context. Only on the condition that the jurist frees himself from the witches of yesterday can he become an authentic servant of today's society. This explains why Piñel insists on examining the larger historical and philosophical context in which the famous *Lex secunda* originated even before trying to explain the true meaning of C. 4,44,2.

In a two-part commentary *ad rubricam* preceding the actual commentary on the *Lex secunda*, Piñel highlights some of the basic principles that underlie his understanding of C. 4,44,2.[1857] It is impossible in this context to go into the details of Piñel's exposition, but the following points may be worthwhile noting: his emphasizing private property and the prohibition to harm fellow human beings.[1858] Put differently, the commentary *ad rubricam* gives us a good insight into the chief socio-political principles which Piñel endorses.

[1856] Piñel, *Commentarii*, ad rubr., part. 1, cap. 1, p. 1–2*pr*.: 'Artium enim, sicut arborum, altitudo sine radicibus esse non potest, iuxta Ciceronis sententiam.'
The original expression is slightly different, cf. Cicero, *Orator*, 43, 147, in: *Cicéron, L'orateur, Du meilleur genre d'orateurs*, Texte établi et traduit par Albert Yon, [Collection des Universités de France], Paris 1964, p. 53: 'Nam omnium magnarum artium sicut arborum altitudo nos delectat, radices stirpesque non item; sed esse illa sine his non potest.'

[1857] See Piñel, *Commentarii*, p. 1–65 (p. 65 is wrongly indicated as p. 63 in the Antwerp 1618 edition).

[1858] For a more extensive overview of the contents of Piñel's commentary on both the *rubrica* and the *Lex secunda*, see García Sánchez, *Arias Piñel*, p. 201–234.

7.5.1.1 *Individual property and rights*

Piñel starts out with a seemingly theoretical investigation on the origin of the sale-purchase contract. It leads him into vast discussions with the Bartolists and the French humanists on seemingly exotic subjects such as the existence or not of money in the time of the Trojan war. He concludes—in line with traditional teaching—that *emptio venditio* falls under the *ius gentium*. Yet, importantly, Piñel explains why jurists throughout the ages have considered this to be a question worthy of so much debate:[1859] 'they say that this investigation is useful, because the prince can abolish more easily what falls under the *ius civile* than what falls under *ius naturale*, that is *ius gentium*.' Piñel tries to argue, in this respect, that *ius gentium* and *ius naturale* are synonyms.[1860] He cites Oldendorp to bolster this opinion, although this reference is probably a little bit dishonest, since Oldendorp was anxious to stress the differences between *ius gentium* and *ius naturale*.[1861] If any, the theoretical difference between natural law and the law of nations resides in the fact that natural law is shared by animals and human beings alike (D. 1,1,1). So, properly speaking, *ius gentium* and *ius naturale* are only equivalents if *ius naturale* is understood as the *ius naturale* which is proper to the human race.

In any event, Piñel eventually maintains that these distinctions between different types of law are actually superfluous, since all kinds of *ius* must be protected against interference by the prince. Piñel goes to great lengths to combat political absolutism (*absoluta potestas*). In his view, the first kind of harm (*laesio*) that can be done to the citizens is the infringement of their rights by the prince. Moreover, Piñel holds that the prince not only has no right to violate rights which are derived from the *ius gentium*. The prince should in fact never be allowed to violate any transfer of property between citizens, even if their agreement fell under the *ius civile*.[1862]

[1859] Piñel, *Commentarii*, ad rubr., part. 1, cap. 1, num. 31, p. 9: 'Dicunt enim esse utilem eam inspectionem, quia princeps facilius tollere potest, quae sunt iuris civilis, quam ea, quae sunt iuris naturalis vel gentium.'

[1860] Piñel, *Commentarii*, ad rubr., part. 1, cap. 1, num. 18–19, p. 6.

[1861] Johann Oldendorp, *Variae lectiones ad iuris civilis interpretationem*, Lugduni 1546, p. 16: 'Quare cum audis hanc vocem, Ius gentium, non semper exaudiendum est Ius naturale, sed plerumque Ius humanum, ut Livius recte appellat. Neque enim sequitur: Gentes id constituerunt, aut in usum admiserunt: Ergo est ius naturale aut aequum. Imo, saepe iniquissimum est.'

[1862] Piñel, *Commentarii*, ad rubr., part. 1, cap. 2, num. 1, p. 10: 'Demus enim aliquid acquisitum iure civili, prout ex stipulatione vel alia conventione vel obligatione ex iis quas scribentes dicunt esse iuris civilis, per d. l. ex hoc iure. Certe nulla ratio est, cur princeps

Consequently, the traditional distinction between rights deriving from *ius gentium* and rights based on *ius civile* is largely superseded.

Mainstream political thought, which defends absolute power, is to be exterminated, according to Piñel, because it is inhumane (*inhumana*).[1863] In the meantime, princes should be urged to respect private rights as faithfully as possible. They have only limited power. This is the truth that Piñel finds it necessary to investigate and to explain, even if the prince has no superior in his territory. Moreover, he thinks that private individuals have a means of effectively protecting their property against usurpation by the prince—at least if the regime has not turned into a tyranny.

The means of the wronged individual (*pars laesa*) to enforce the protection of his rights are threefold.[1864] First, an individual can make an appeal against the King's order of expropriation (*rescriptum rem suam ei auferens*) with the King himself, who is then obliged to listen to the grievances of the wronged party. Second, if the King refuses him a court hearing, the wronged party can file a complaint with the Pope. Third, the wronged party can claim restoration from the successor to the King, who is then obliged to invalidate the *rescriptum* of his predecessor and correct the wrong that has been done. In any event, Portuguese law stipulates that the judge who officiates the execution of the order of expropriation must again listen to the grievances of the wronged party.[1865]

7.5.1.2 *The do-no-harm principle*

The basis of Piñel's diatribe against political absolutism and interference with private proverty lies in his conception of justice as a kind of

---

auferre possit dominium vel ius quaesitum ex tali conventione iuris civilis, quia in eo laederetur simul lex et ratio naturalis et ius gentium, ut inferius cum Cicerone probabimus.'

[1863] Piñel, *Commentarii*, ad rubr., part. 1, cap. 2, num. 24, p. 18: 'Infertur tandem omnino reijciendam et exterminandam esse inhumanam illam multorum traditionem, cum principi tribuunt plenissimam vel absolutam potestatem, eam ab ordinaria distinguentes, ut ex illa omnia possit, utque facta mentione talis potestatis nulla exceptio obijci valeat.'

[1864] Piñel, *Commentarii*, ad rubr., part. 1, cap. 2, num. 27, p. 21: 'Nec praedicta effectu carebunt, nisi principatus in tyrannidem vertatur. Primo enim pars, quae laeditur ex rescripto rem suam ei auferente, audiri debebit ab eodem principe melius informando. Similiter eodem principe iustitiam negante poterit pars laesa apud summum pontificem conqueri. Sic etiam successor talis principis emendabit eius iniquitatem, et rescindet acta, quae emanarunt ex rescripto vel iussu auferente parti rem suam.'

[1865] Piñel, *Commentarii*, ad rubr., part. 1, cap. 2, num. 28, p. 21: 'Vult igitur lex, ut, quamvis in rescripto committatur executio, audiri debeat pars objiciens vitium aliquod precum seu informationis, ut ita executio impediatur, et iudex cui committebatur executio cognoscet etiam de impedimentis et obiectionibus adversus rescriptum.'

do-no-harm principle. This is a principle dictated by natural reason. It is expressed in the juridical, the religious, and the philosophical traditions from Classical Antiquity:[1866] 'Depriving someone of his property or right (*dominium vel ius suum*) clearly is an offence not only against the civil or man-made written law, but also against natural law or the law of nations, and even against the law of God, since harm (*iniuria*) and injustice (*iniustitia*) are inconsistent with each of these bodies of law.'

Obviously, Ulpian's definition of justice in D. 1,1,1 fits well into Piñel's conception of justice. In Roman law terms, justice is the constant and perpetual will to give everybody his right, to do no harm (*neminem laedere*), and to live honestly.[1867] Following Baldus, Connan and Budé, Piñel repeats that natural reason (*ratio naturalis*) itself dictates that we may do no harm to our neighbors. The text from D. 1,1,3 is a positive legal expression of that natural truth. It says that it is nefarious for man to do harm to another man, since nature made us into 'relatives' of one another.

In principle, Roman law also contains a prohibition on unjust enrichment. Piñel grants that the prohibition contained in D. 12,6,14 (*ne quis cum aliena iactura locupletetur*) can be seen as an expression of natural reason (*ratio naturalis*). However, true to the humanist spirit, he denies that the Roman jurists themselves could have meant this to be an expression of the Judaeo-Christian prohibition on stealing. To be sure, parallels between Roman law and Christian theology in regard to the principle of unjust enrichment do exist. After all, both normative systems have been inspired by natural reason. Yet Piñel rejects the idea that Roman jurisprudence was influenced directly by divine law.[1868]

To Piñel himself, divine law does matter, of course. *Laesio* inflicted by an absolutist prince or by another citizen goes against the 7th Commandment not to steal. In reality, Piñel does not cite the 7th Commandment. He merely refers to *ius divinum* in general. The only Scriptural passages he

---

[1866] Piñel, *Commentarii*, ad rubr., part. 1, cap. 2, num. 26, p. 20: '(...) satis liquere videtur (...) cum alicui dominium vel ius suum aufertur, non tantum ius civile, vel humanum scriptum offendi, sed etiam naturale et gentium, imo et divinum, quibus repugnat iniuria vel iniustitia.'

[1867] D. 1,1,1–3.

[1868] For example, he criticizes the ordinary Gloss on D. 47,2 (*De furtis*) for interpreting natural law as 'divine law' in the Roman text which reads that theft is prohibited as a matter of natural law. According to Piñel, 'that interpretation is miles away from the mind of Paul the jurist; in writing this, Paul did not know about the precepts of divine law and sacred Scripture.'; cf. Piñel, *Commentarii*, ad rubr., part. 1, cap. 1, num. 21, p. 7: 'Patet errasse glossa in d. l. 1 dum exponit *lege naturali*, id est, divina. Id enim prorsus a mente iurisconsulti Pauli ibi, qui praecepta divinae legis et sacrae scripturae non cognovit.'

quotes are the so-called Golden Rule: 'Do to others, what you would have them do to you, that is the entire Law and Prophets' (Mt. 7:12), and the precept to love your neigbor as yourself (Mt. 22:37–39). These prescripts would have been part of Catholic culture in general. Unlike his Protestant counter-parts, Piñel would not have felt the need to get involved in profound Biblical exegesis. In fact, he claims that he borrows the references to these New Testament texts from Augustine's *City of God*.[1869]

Contrary to the meagre attention paid to divine law, Piñel is eager to adduce as many authoritative texts as possible from Greek and Roman philosophers to support his views on justice. Aristotle's argument against tyranny serves as a warning that the more power is concentrated in the hands of the rulers, the more likely it is that political stability will be short-lived, since oligarchy and tyranny are the most unstable forms of government.[1870] Through Ambrose he quotes the typically Stoic maxim that man is born not only with the aim of becoming useful to himself, but also to others (*homo non ut sibi ipsi tantum sed et ut aliis prosit natus*).[1871] To wrong other people is to violate nature (*naturam violat, qui alteri nocet*).[1872]

As is commonly known, patristic social thought, particularly as expressed in Ambrose's *On duties*, is to a very large extent modelled on Cicero's *On duties*. It is hardly surprising, then, to find that Piñel borrows the greatest part of his social views from the famous Roman orator. Accordingly, Piñel regards as one of the most important principles for living in society the universal prohibition on harming another person out of self-interest (*non liceat sui commodi causa nocere alteri*).[1873]

[1869] Piñel undoubtedly refers to Augustinus, *De civitate Dei* (Ed. CCSL 48), 19, 14, p. 681: 'Iam vero quia duo praecipua praecepta, hoc est dilectionem Dei et dilectionem proximi, docet magister Deus, in quibus tria invenit homo quae diligat, Deum, se ipsum et proximum (…).'

[1870] Aristotle, *Politica* (Ed. Ross), 5, 12, 1315b11–12, p. 187: 'καίτοι πασῶν ὀλιγοχρονιώταται τῶν πολιτειῶν εἰσιν ὀλιγαρχία καὶ τυραννίς'.

[1871] This appears to be a free adaptation of Ambrose, *De officiis*, 1, 28, 132, in: *Saint Ambroise, Les devoirs, Livre 1*, Texte établi, traduit et annoté par Maurice Testard, [Collection des Universités de France], Paris 1984, vol. 1, p. 158: 'Quo in loco aiunt placuisse stoicis quae in terris gignantur, omnia ad usus hominum creari; homines autem hominum causa esse generatos ut ipsi inter se aliis alii prodesse possint.'

[1872] An allusion to Ambrose, *De officiis* (Ed. Testard), 3, 4, 24, in: *Saint Ambroise, Les devoirs, Livres 2–3*, Texte établi, traduit et annoté par Maurice Testard, [Collection des Universités de France], Paris 1992, vol. 2, p. 91: 'Hinc ergo colligitur quod homo qui secundum naturae formatus est directionem, ut oboediat sibi, nocere non possit alteri; quod, si qui nocet, naturam violet (…).'

[1873] E.g. Cicero, *De officiis*, 3, 5, 21 (Ed. Testard, vol. 2), p. 81: 'Detrahere igitur alteri aliquid et hominem hominis incommodo suum commodum augere magis est contra

The do-no-harm principle pertains to natural law. It imposes itself upon all human beings, princes and Popes included. It can be regarded as the basis of the *laesio*-interdiction in contractual exchange, in particular.

7.5.2   *A humanist critique*

7.5.2.1   Novum ius

For the majority of the late medieval jurists, the beginning of Piñel's commentary on the *Lex secunda* would have been shocking:[1874]

> Against the gloss and the opinion of all previous writers I strongly believe that the right grounded on C. 4,44,2 was issued for the first time only (*nove*) by Emperors Diocletian and Maximianus. Consequently, this remedy was entirely unknown by the jurists (whose *responsa* we find in the Digest). May the true sense of many laws be revealed through this insight.

Centuries of reading Roman law in light of Christian principles, or, better still, of doing legal scholarship in search of Roman legal texts giving authoritative support to Christian principles are suddenly being thought of as superseded. Highly indebted to the mentality of Renaissance humanism, Piñel looks for nothing but the true meaning (*verus sensus*) of the Roman texts. He wants to understand them in their original context. He wants to highlight the fundamental difference between the pagan world view of the classical jurists and the Christian *ius commune* as it developed in the later Middle Ages.

The classical jurists ignored the remedy now associated with C. 4,44,2. This is what Piñel infers from the absence of even the slightest reference in other imperial consitutions and in the Digest to this remedy or to a concrete determination of the quantity which constitutes *laesio*. If the remedy for lesion had been as crucially important to the pre-Diocletian

---

naturam quam mors, quam paupertas, quam dolor, quam cetera quae possunt aut corpori accidere aut rebus externis.'

[1874] Piñel, *Commentarii*, ad l. 2, part. 1, cap. 1, num. 3, p. 66–67: 'Ego contra glossam et omnes hucusque scribentes verissimum credo, Diocletianum et Maximianum imperatores, nove hoc ius [C. 4,44,2] induxisse, ac proinde iurisconsultis (quorum responsa in libris digestorum habemus) nullatenus hoc remedium cognitum fuisse.' Compare his conclusion in l.c., num. 7, p. 68: 'Nemo igitur iuris vel rationis peritus inauditam nostram sententiam reijciendam putabit, cum tot iuribus, totque fundamentis probetur, ut sic contra glossam et omnes hucusque scribentes maneat, ex constitutione hac Diocletiani novum ius inductum fuisse (…).'

Romans as it was to the late medieval jurists, then we could have expected a more elaborate treatment of it in the *Corpus Justinianeum*.

Moreover, he interprets D. 4,4,16,4 (*in pretio emptionis et venditionis naturaliter licet contrahentibus se circumvenire*) as originally constituting a kind of absolute principle of 'freedom of contract':[1875] 'These words do not admit of imaginery afterthoughts and external restrictions by doctors who seeks to limit them by virtue of C. 4,44,2.' The same holds true for D. 19,2,22,3 (*in locationibus quoque licet invicem se circumscribere*):[1876] 'If we love the truth, we cannot interpret these words as admitting of the violent limitations imposed by the doctors.'

In Piñel's view, the irrelevance of lesion to original Roman law is obvious from various texts in the Digest. First of all, lesion is not listed as a ground for rescission in *De rescindenda venditione* (D. 18,5). Secondly, in obvious cases of lesion the Roman jurists did not provide the *laesus* with a remedy (e.g. D. 42,1,15). Thirdly, in his *On duties*, Cicero recounts the story of a sly and wicked vendor called Pythius who tricked Canius.[1877] He sold him sterile and absolutely worthless lands by persuading him that these lands were in fact the most fruitful lands. Now Cicero apparently did not think Canius could have had any other remedy to defend himself except for the *actio de dolo*, even though this was a clear instance of lesion beyond moiety.

7.5.2.2 *The myth of* dolus re ipsa

Cicero's story of Pythius and Canius leads Piñel to deconstruct yet another mythical notion that was fabricated in the *ius commune*: objective deceit (*dolus re ipsa*). Piñel recognizes that he is afraid (*vereor*) that many will badly bear the new light of truth (*novam veritatis lucem*) he is about to shed on the matter, blinded as they are by an inveterate misinterpretation.[1878] Yet there is no denying a certain feeling of pride and superiority in his voice as he announces his new exegesis. Perhaps this might explain why his pupil, Manuel Soarez a Ribeira, felt the need to soften the impious

---

[1875] Piñel, *Commentarii*, ad l. 2, part. 1, cap. 1, num. 4, p. 67: 'Quae verba non admittunt commenticias subauditiones, extrariasque restrictiones doctorum ea limitantium ex decisione huius l.'

[1876] Piñel, *Commentarii*, ad l. 2, part. 1, cap. 1, num. 4, p. 67: 'Quae verba (si verum amamus) non admittunt violentam doctorum limitationem.'

[1877] Cicero, *De officiis* (Ed. Testard, vol. 2), 3, 14, 58–60, p. 100–102.

[1878] Piñel, *Commentarii*, ad l. 2, part. 1, cap. 1, num. 7, p. 68: 'Vereor tamen ne ex tenebris inveterati erroris plures fortasse novam veritatis lucem aegre sustineant.'

impression his master left. He inserted a gloss on *vereor* in what became the standard edition of Piñel's book. In this gloss, he quoted a couple of verses from Horace's *Letters*, expressing the idea that the elderly do not accept criticism against well-known playwrights, either because they think that the right thing is only what pleases them, or because they do not want to admit that what they learned as young boys was false.[1879] In this manner, Soarez a Ribeira tries to make clear why Piñel had a legitimate reason to be afraid: people tend to be wary of what is new, because innovation is often detrimental to society.

The upshot of Piñel's argument is that the classical jurists were not concerned with *laesio*, whether big or small, as long as it was not accompanied by *dolus*. In the absence of deceit, they would not consider any deviation from some sort of normal price to be relevant. They had no conception of deceit as something intrinsic to the transaction itself. Only in cases of intentional deceit (*interveniente dolo*) could the quantity of the lesion become relevant. The idea of objective deceit could not possibly have made sense to the classical jurists, since the remedy provided in C. 4,44,2 had not come into existence yet.[1880] This is a good example of how important the insight of the novelty of the *Lex secunda* is for a correct understanding of the Digest.

Locus classicus of the debate on objective deceit was law *Si quis cum aliter* (D. 45,1,36). In the medieval *ius commune* it was interpreted as containing a distinction between two types of deceit: deceit by tricks (*dolus ex machinatione*) and objective deceit (*dolus reipsa*).[1881] Lesion beyond moiety was then deemed to be a species of *dolus reipsa*. However, Piñel reads law *Si quis cum aliter* in a completely different way. He does not deny that the text subdivides into two parts that deal with two different

---

[1879] Horace, *Epistulae*, 2, 1, 79–85, in: *Horace, Satires, Epistles, and Ars poetica*, with an English translation by H. Rushton Fairclough, [Loeb Classical Library, 194], Cambridge Mass. – London, p. 402–404: 'Attae fabula si dubitem, clament periisse pudorem cuncti pene patres, ea cum reprehedere coner; quae gravis Aesopus, quae doctus Roscius egit, vel quia nil rectum, nisi quod placuit sibi, dicunt, vel quia turpe putant parere minoribus, et quae imberbes didicere, senes perdenda fateri.'
[1880] Piñel, *Commentarii*, ad l. 2, part. 1, cap. 1, num. 7, p. 68: 'Inde etiam eleganter colligitur, cur tantum interveniente dolo iurisconsulti distinxerunt circa quantitatem (…), quasi cessante dolo non esset differentia inter magnam vel parvam laesionem.'
[1881] D. 45,1,36: 'Si quis, cum aliter eum convenisset obligari, aliter per machinationem obligatus est, erit quidem subtilitati iuris obstrictus, sed doli exceptione uti potest; quia enim per dolum obligatus est, competit ei exceptio. Idem est, et si nullus dolus intercessit stipulantis, sed ipsa res in se dolum habet; cum enim quis petat ex ea stipulatione, hoc ipso dolo facit, quod petit.'

types of deceit. Yet sensitive to the procedural nature of Roman law, he differentiates between deceit at the moment of the conclusion of the contract and deceit which only turns up if the contract becomes the subject of a lawsuit:[1882]

> The true sense of D. 45,1,36 is that both parts of it deal with a plaintiff who committed deceit. The first part concerns deceit right from the inception of the agreement (*a principio conventionis*). The second part concerns deceit at the moment of the lawsuit (*tempore iudicii*). For that reason, the defendant is equally granted an *exceptio doli* against the deceitful plaintiff in both cases.

Departing from a metaphysical reading of the Latin word '*res*', Piñel rightly gives a much more practically significant meaning to it: 'lawsuit'. The sentence which was traditionally seen as the foundation of 'objective deceit' then simply reads as follows: 'the lawsuit itself is affected by deceit' (*ipsa res in se dolum habet*). This new interpretation is illustrated through the following example. Assume that something has been promised or agreed upon in view of a certain reason (*causa*), but that, subsequently, this reason does not come about. There was no deceit at the moment of concluding the contract. Still, the very act of taking the promisor to court would then be deceitful, since the reason that drove the promisor into the contract had not been realized (*causa non secuta*).[1883]

Arias Piñel does not hide the contempt he feels for the *communis opinio*. He deplores that even recent French humanist authors such as Pierre Loriot and Pierre Coustau (Costalius) made the mistake of reading law *Si quis cum aliter* and law *Secunda* together.[1884] Because they did not properly investigate the historical development of C. 4,44,2, they ignored

---

[1882] Piñel, *Commentarii*, ad l. 2, part. 1, cap. 1, num. 8, p. 68: 'Verus ergo sensus d.l. est, quod in utraque parte eius parte, agens dolo erat: in prima vero, fuerat dolus a principio conventionis, in secunda tempore iudicii. Ideoque pariter doli exceptio adversus agentem datur.'

[1883] Piñel, *Commentarii*, ad l. 2, part. 1, cap. 1, num. 8, p. 68–69: 'Exemplum autem secundae partis facile colligitur ex l. 1, ff. de condictione sine causa [D. 12,7,1], melius vero ex l. 2, § circa, ff. de doli exceptione [D. 44,4,2,3], prout quando aliquid promissum vel conventum fuit ob certam causam postea deficientem. Tunc enim in contractu nulla fraus intervenit. Dolose autem ex eo ageretur, causa non secuta.'

[1884] Pierre Coustau, *Adversaria ex Pandectis Iustiniani*, Lugduni 1554, part. 1, ad D. 4,4,16, p. 79: 'Et ex par. Idem Pomponius vulgo omnibus in ore est, et iure civili, et pontificio permissum esse contrahentibus se invicem decipere, quod tamen a bono viro alienum est. Plane si deceptio ex dolo veniat, de dolo actio erit, et contractus rescindetur. Idem si dolus in reipsa est, nempe quia deceptio ultra dimidiam iusti pretii intercessit, tunc enim revocari potest [l. si quis cum aliter]. Quod autem hic ad finem [par. nunc videndum] datur potestas quibusdam iudicibus restitutiones dandi, quibusdam adimitur,

that Emperors Diocletian and Maximianus created a new remedy, which was nonexistent in classical jurisprudential literature. Therefore, they also made a futile effort reading *laesio enormis* into D. 45,1,36.

As critical as a humanist jurist can be, Piñel concludes that traditional authority failed (*hallucinati sunt*).[1885] Originally, Roman law did not care about lesion or some kind of 'objective deceit'. Only if a case of unequal exchange also involved duress or fraud did the classical jurists grant a remedy. Against this background, Piñel feels disappointed by Charles Du Moulin's harsh assessment of C. 4,44,2. How could such a learned man berate Diocletian and Maximianus so severely for not giving relief to a lesioned party unless the lesion was beyond moiety?[1886] In Piñel's view, it is to the credit of the Emperors to have granted relief on the basis of C. 4,44,2 in the first place. Rather than being criticized, they should be praised for their sense of equity.[1887] Incidentally, it might be remarked

---

hodie non est in usu. Iure enim Codicis etiam inferioribus magistratibus hoc competit; est, quod Bartolus hic probat.'

Pierre Loriot, *Tractatus de pactis*, in: De iuris apicibus tractatus octo, et de iuris arte tractatus viginti, Lugduni 1555, axiom. 91, col. 465.

For biographical information on Coustau, see V. Hayaert, *Mens emblematica et humanisme juridique, Le cas du Pegma cum narrationibus philosophicis de Pierre Coustau (1555)*, [Travaux d'Humanisme et Renaissance, 438], Genève 2008, p. 27–48.

For biographical details about Loriot, see J.-L. Thireau, s.v. *Loriot, Pierre*, in: P. Arabeyre – J.-L. Halpérin – J. Krynen (eds.), Dictionnaire historique des juristes français, XIIᵉ–XXᵉ siècle, Paris 2007, p. 518.

[1885] Piñel, *Commentarii*, ad l. 2, part. 1, cap. 1, num. 8, p. 68: 'Ego verius puto doctores cum glossa ad verbos iurisconsulti hallucinatos fuisse, nihilque minus iurisconsultum in l. [D. 45,1,36] ea sensisse quam de remedio huius l. [C. 4,44,2] quod evincitur ex eodem Ulpiano et aliis iurisconsultis in locis supra citatis, dum aperte et indistincte tradunt, laesis in precio nullatenus succurri, nec dolum ex sola laesione censeri.'

[1886] Charles Du Moulin, *Tractatus commerciorum et usurarum redituumque pecunia constitutorum et monetarum*, Lugduni 1558, num. 172, p. 152–153: 'Hic Diocletiano et Maximiano ethnicis visum fuit, satis esse licentiam illam per excessum vel defectum a iusta et vera aequalitate declinandi ad dimidium iusti pretii vel aestimationis, id est ipsius aequalitatis, cohibere, ne ulterius vagari posset. Sed certe haec cohibitio valde disproportionata est, utpote quae proportionem aequalitatis dimidio totius fraudari concedat, et sic inaequalitatem admittit duplae ad subduplam. (…) quod est valde excessivum et a iusta aequalitate et naturali iustitia nimis remotum. (…) Hinc durities dictae legis secundae multum placet et opportuna est viris tyrannicis et pleonecticis, qui sciunt et possunt sibi vigilare et cavere ne unquam decipiantur, ut numquam sibi metuant. (…)'.

[1887] Piñel, *Commentarii*, ad l. 2, part. 1, cap. 1, num. 22, p. 72–73: 'Ex praedictis infertur contra Molinaeum de commerciis, num. 172 qui hanc legem duram et a tyrannis conditam exclamat, arguens, quod maximam iniquitatem permittat non succurrendo laesis, nisi ultra dimidiam iusti precii. Sed miror virum doctum | et ingeniosum inique et incaute in hanc l. invectum, debuit enim potius ex humanitate et aequitate eam laudare, cum antea nullum remedium laesis dabatur, cessante dolo vel metu vel aetatis privilegio, ut supra probavimus, vel debuit saltem cum omnibus agnoscere, ante hanc legem non fuisse aliam quae laesis magis succurreret, ut sic non magis in hanc quam in alias exclamaret.' Pinel

that Du Moulin is often seen as a forerunner of liberal commercial ethics. He nevertheless held on to the principles of equality in exchange and just pricing as tightly as the early modern scholastics.[1888]

7.5.2.3 *Circumscribing* invicem se circumvenire

Apparently, Piñel's enthusiasm for critical legal exegesis never waned. His new interpretation of paragraphs *Idem Pomponius* (D. 4,4,16,4) and *Quemadmodum* (D. 19,2,22,3) challenges the entire tradition of medieval jurisprudence. Traditionally, these passages from the Digest were taken to mean that cheating in sale and lease was allowed as long as the quantity of the harm was moderate. In both the secular and ecclesiastical courts, a remedy was given to the *laesus*, but only if the harm was considerable (*ultra dimidiam*). Yet, again, this conventional interpretation could not satisfy Piñel's insatiable desire for the truth.

If we want to know the true meaning of D. 4,4,16,4 and, by extension, of D. 19,2,22,3, we need to free it from the intellectual world in which the medieval jurists lived, according to Piñel. From the classical jurists' perspective, there is no difference between considerable and unconsiderable *laesio*. Moreover, the general terms in which paragraph *Idem Pomponius* is phrased exclude any distinction between lesion beyond and lesion below moiety.[1889] No matter whether it is big or small, for the Romans any lesion is irrelevant in regard to the validity of a sale contract. In short, traditional opinion has been misguided by not making the effort to read the different texts from the Digest and the Code in their historical context.

The new interpretation of D. 4,4,16,4 suggested by Piñel rests on a reading of the paragraph in its broader textual context. Title 4 of the fourth

---

then goes on to reprehend Du Moulin for having unrightfully criticized the theologians' understanding of *laesio enormis*.

[1888] Du Moulin, *Commentarii in Parisienses consuetudines*, par. 33, gl. 1 in verb. *Droict de relief*, num. 46, p. 438: '(...) quando de laesione et rescissione agitur, iustum pretium ad tantam pecuniam aestimatur, quantum res iuste valet, non quantum repertum fuit aut reperiri posset (...). Et debet esse aequalitas, et eadem commensuratio inter emptorem et venditorem et eadem iuris summetria.'

[1889] Piñel, *Commentarii*, ad l. 2, part. 1, cap. 1, num. 32, p. 74–75: 'Quae verba [sc. in pretio emptionis et venditionis naturaliter licere contrahentibus se circumvenire] accipiunt glossa et omnes ibi, glossa et omnes hic, glossa et omnes in cap. cum dilectus, et noviores infra citandi, ut tantum referantur ad laesionem citra dimidiam. | Ego autem verissimum puto iurisconsultos in illis verbis indistincte de omni laesione sentire, nec aliquid referre ad mentem iurisconsultorum an laesio modica an maxima sit; tum ex generalitate verborum, quae non admittunt communem restrictionem, tum quia eo tempore incognita erat differentia magnae vel modicae laesionis, de qua agit haec lex, ut supra late probavimus.'

book of the Digest concerns minors of age. Law *In causae cognitione*, in particular, deals with the question whether a minor can be granted other remedies than the extraordinary remedy of restitution (*restitutio in integrum*).[1890] According to Piñel, the upshot of the argumentation is that minors cannot appeal to the special remedy of restitution unless the contract they entered into is still valid. Hence, the aim of paragraph *Idem Pomponius* is to determine whether cheating (*circumventio*) invalidates a sale contract or not. If it does, then a minor is granted the ordinary remedies and not restitution.

According to Piñel, what is at stake in D. 4,4,16,4 is the availability of the remedy of *restitutio in integrum* for minors (*principaliter agit de concedenda vel neganda restitutione*).[1891] Since cheating does not invalidate the contract, the conclusion to paragraph *Idem Pomponius* should be that a minor is granted the remedy of restitution in a contract where buyer and seller have tried to outwit each other. So D. 4,4,16,4 is actually about a procedural advantage for minors. The purpose of the argument was not to establish a universal rule of law—rigorous law—that allows buyers and sellers to outwit each other.[1892]

Interestingly, Piñel does not question the incompatibility of D. 4,4,16,4 with the law of the *forum internum*. Conscience requires that equity and good faith be observed down to the last detail.[1893] He does not question either, whether it would be better not to have a general principle allow-

---

[1890] D. 4,4 (*De minoribus vigintiquinque annis*), 16pr.: 'In causae cognitione etiam hoc versabitur, num forte alia actio possit competere citra in integrum restitutionem. Nam si communi auxilio et mero iure munitus sit, non debet ei tribui extraordinarium auxilium, utputa cum pupillo contractum est sine tutoris auctoritate, nec locupletiorem factus est.'

[1891] Piñel, *Commentarii*, ad l. 2, part. 1, cap. 1, num. 33, p. 75: 'Vides igitur, quod dixi contra omnes, quo ad mentem iurisconsulti ibi, dum principaliter agit de concedenda vel neganda restitutione, nullam esse differentiam inter magnam vel modicam laesionem.'

[1892] Piñel, *Commentarii*, ad l. 2, part. 1, cap. 1, num. 34, p. 75: 'Imo si subtilius mens iurisconsulti expendatur, colliges contra glossam et omnes (quod fortasse mirabile videbitur) verba illa, *licere contrahentibus in precio se circumvenire*, principaliter ibi prolata fuisse in favorem et beneficium laesi, nempe minoris, ut scilicet restitutionem habere posset, quia is est scopus iurisconsulti ibi. Non enim pertinebat ad rubricam nec ad ea quae iurisconsultus ibi tractabat, tradere regulam, vel rigorem illum iuris, ut liceat contrahentibus, in precio se circumvenire. Plane igitur mens iurisconsulti eiusque praecipua decisio id petit, ut non obstante qualibet laesione in precio, contractus valeat, et inde sequatur, minorem restituendum fore.'

[1893] Piñel, *Commentarii*, ad l. 2, part. 1, cap. 1, num. 35, p. 75: 'Quae receptior et magis pia traditio satis comprabatur ex iurisconsulto in d. l. iure succursum, 7, § finali, ff. de iure dotali iuncta declaratione superius tradita. Ubi enim exactissime bona fides et aequitas requiritur, prout ibi in causa dotis etiam minor laesio emendari iubetur, quod magis viget in foro conscientiae.'

ing of *laesio* in exchange. Piñel combats the anachronistic reading of D. 4,4,16,4 in the civilian and canon law tradition. True to his humanist ideals, he wants people to see that, originally, paragraph *Idem Pomponius* did not distinguish between cheating beyond or below moiety. It allowed of lesion big and small.[1894] Moreover, by stressing its textual context, he qualifies the opinion that D. 4,4,16,4 should be considered to be a general rule of commerce.

According to Piñel, if paragraph *Idem Pomponius* were a general prescriptive rule, then Pomponius would have contradicted himself.[1895] In D. 23,3,6,2 the Roman jurist demands that any form of *circumventio* in the gift of a dowry be remedied by virtue of equity.[1896] This very text is also concerned about unjust enrichment. So paragraph *Idem Pomponius* should be put into perspective. At the most, it is valid as a principle only in the external court, but even there it must give way to more specific requirements such as D. 23,3,6,3. This is something to keep in mind as we move on to the correct interpretation of the words 'naturally allowed' (*naturaliter licere*).

As it applies to the external court, paragraph *Idem Pomponius* must not be interpreted as a prescriptive rule but rather as a permissive statement. Loyal to the common opinion, for this time at least, Piñel deems 'allowed' (*licere*) to signify merely 'permitted' (*permittitur*) or 'not punished by human law' (*humano iure non punitur*).[1897] Consequently, the external courts do not punish outwitting each other in sale, but they do not want to encourage people to cheat either. However, in the court of conscience, trying to outwit the other party is forbidden. Quoting Baldus, Covarruvias

---

[1894] This might also explain why Piñel was critical of the distinction between *laesio enormis* and *laesio enormissima*; cf. Piñel, *Commentarii*, ad l. 2, part. 3, cap. 1, num. 8, p. 182: 'Nec mihi umquam placuit multorum differentia inter enormem et enormissimam laesionem, quia iure non probatur (…).'

[1895] Piñel, *Commentarii*, ad l. 2, part. 1, cap. 1, num. 36, p. 76: 'Sed ultra scribentes omnes ad d. § idem Pomponius adverto eius verbis nihil obstare legem hanc ut supra explicavi. Minus autem obstare dicta §. Si, l. iure succursum, et sic idem Ulpianus [sic!] secum pugnare videtur: quod enim naturaliter licere uno loco dixit, in alio aequitati et naturae contrarium dixit. Unde ad vitandum repugnantiam iurisconsulti succurrendum est cum praecedenti declaratione theologorum et nostrorum, ut *licere* accipiatur regulariter ad forum exterius, praeterquam ubi exactissima aequitas et bona fides abundare debet, quod iuvabitur ex proximis dicendis num. 39.'

[1896] D. 23,3,6,2 in *Corporis Iustinianaei Digestum vetus* (ed. Gothofredi), tom. 1, cols. 2127–2128: 'Si in dote danda circumventus sit alteruter, etiam maiori annis vigintiquinque succurrendum est, quia bono et aequo non conveniat, aut lucrari aliquem cum damno alterius, aut damnum sentire per alterius lucrum.'

[1897] Piñel, *Commentarii*, ad l. 2, part. 1, cap. 1, num. 35, p. 75.

and Soto, Piñel emphasizes that the regulation in the *forum internum* is different from that in the external court (*diversum in foro conscientiae*).

It is therefore important for Piñel, as it was for the other jurists, to give the right interpretation to 'naturally' (*naturaliter*). To start with, Piñel rejects three famous interpretations of this term. The first was adopted by Fortunius Garcia in the sixteenth century.[1898] It read 'naturally' as meaning 'in good faith, without deceit, not on purpose'. The second line of interpretation read 'naturally' as 'in accordance with the impulses of our sensual nature', or, as Soto alternatively put it, 'according to the common affection of man to crave for profits'. These two interpretations had already been rejected by Dr. Navarrus, one of Piñel's most favorite teachers.[1899] A third opinion, advocated by Du Moulin, amongst others, held that it was 'naturally permitted' for parties to outwit each other, because they were both willing to turn a blind eye to each other's cheating.[1900] Piñel rejects this analysis as unrealistic.

After profound reflection, Piñel thinks the only correct understanding of 'naturally' goes back to the gloss and Thomas Aquinas. Piñel insists that it is dangerous in this context to confound the philosophers' notion of natural law and its juridical meaning. True, Cicero would often have used them as synonyms, but natural law in the sense of natural equity, or the common social bond of love between all men cannot possibly lie behind paragraph *Idem Pomponius*. In this context, the only appropriate meaning of 'naturally' is 'according to the *ius gentium*'.

On account of experience, people from all nations reasoned that lesion should be permitted (*permittenda*) lest commerce be continually disturbed by too strict an observance of contractual equilibrium.[1901] The security of

---

[1898] Fortunius Garcia, *De ultimo fine iuris civilis et canonici*, num. 277, p. 189.

[1899] Azpilcueta, *In tres de poenitentia distinctiones*, in cap. *Qualitas* (De pen., Dist. 5, cap. 2), num. 42–44, p. 107–109.

[1900] Du Moulin, *Tractatus commerciorum*, num. 182, p. 161: 'Nota quod d. l. 2 non est facta, nisi pro veris et naturalibus contractibus commutativis, in quibus tacito quodam naturali sensu partes sibiipsis modicam laesionem mutuo condonare et indulgere videntur.'

[1901] Piñel, *Commentarii*, ad l. 2, part. 1, cap. 1, num. 39, p. 76: 'Ego aliter ea verba explicanda putabam post rem vero satis consideratam, ita credo sensisse gl. In d. § idem Pomponius ad quem nemo advertit. Exponit enim gl. *naturaliter*, id est *iure gentium*. Intelligo autem, ut secundum exactissimam illam priorem aequitatem naturalem non dicatur licere contrahentibus invicem se in precio nec in alia re circumvenire. Nam secundum eam naturae normam omnes homines cognati et mutua dilectionis lege contineri dicuntur (...). Exponitur ergo, *naturaliter*, id est *iure gentium*, quia humana ratione gentiumque et populorum iudicio compertum est, permittendam fuisse eam laesionem in pretio, ne ex nimia aequalitatis observatione commercia turbarentur. Nulla enim conventio securitatem praestaret, nunquam litium finis esset, si ob laesionem in pretio conventa revocarentur.'

transactions and the stability of the legal system prevail. Consequently, what may be wrong on an individual basis may become permitted on the level of society as a whole.[1902] Piñel refers to the debate among humanists such as François Le Douaren and Ullrich Zasius on prescriptive acquisition (*usucapio*). A similar concern for social stability (*tranquillitas reipublicae*) allowed individuals to acquire goods in spite of their bad faith. Interestingly, to support this view, Manuel Soarez a Ribeira adduces Seneca's typically Stoic belief that the Gods care more about the whole than about the individual.[1903] Piñel himself refered to Cicero's statement that the salvation of the people is the supreme law.[1904] In conclusion,[1905]

> The jurists used the expression 'naturally allowed' by reason of a permission by human law, i.e. the law of nations, to the extent that it is more conducive to the stability of the republic to condone lesion in the price. As a result, the contract remains valid regardless of the lesion, so that then, in particular, it became necessary to grant restitution as a remedy to minors. That is what Pomponius' fragment is all about.

7.5.3 Philology meets equity

The humanist flavor of Arias Piñel's legal thought was revealed in his constantly insisting upon the difference between the original sense of the Roman texts and the meaning that was read into them in subsequent ages. The outrage he felt at the abuse of the Digest translated itself into scathing remarks about the historical nonsense of the medieval jurists, which persisted even in contemporary humanist jurisprudence. However, one should not infer from this that Piñel did not share the scholastic jurists'

[1902] Piñel, *Commentarii*, ad l. 2, part. 1, cap. 1, num. 40, p. 77: 'Unde quo ad universos et pro tranquilitate reipublicae potest favorabile censeri, quod singulis separatum (sic) durum videbitur.'

[1903] Seneca, *De divina providentia*, 3, 1, in: *Seneca, Moral Essays*, with an English translation by John W. Basore, [Loeb Classical Library, 214], Cambridge Mass. – London 1963³ [= 1928], vol. 1, p. 14: '(...) pro universis, quorum maior diis cura quam singulorum est (...)'.

[1904] Cicero, *De legibus*, 3, 3, 8, in: *Cicéron, Traité des lois*, Texte établi et traduit par Georges De Plinval, [Collection des Universités de France], Paris 1968² [= 1959], p. 85: 'Salus populi suprema lex esto.'

[1905] Piñel, *Commentarii*, ad l. 2, part. 1, cap. 1, num. 40, p. 77: '*Naturaliter* igitur *licere* dixerunt iurisconsulti ex permissione humani iuris seu gentium, secundum quod ad quietem reipublicae magis consentaneum visum est, eam laesionem in precio remittere, et ideo ea non obstante, semper contractus valet, et consequenter restitutio tunc specialiter minoribus necessaria fuit, ad id enim tendit iurisconsultus in d. § ut supra.'

commitment to adapt legal thinking to the needs of their own, essentially Christian society. His treatment of the renunciability of the remedy grounded on the *Lex secunda* is deeply influenced by the Christian concern to protect the weak and to promote equity (*aequitas*).

7.5.3.1   *The non-renunciability of C. 4,44,2*

In a series of lengthy chapters that follow the historical-critical analysis of Roman texts related to the *laesio*-prohibition, Piñel carefully examines the range of the remedy grounded on C. 4,44,2. Piñel endorses the medieval extension of the *Lex secunda* to all synallagmatic *bonae fidei* contracts and even to contracts of strict law, although he warns that this development is motivated by equity rather than loyalty to the original Roman texts.[1906] He also confirms the common opinion holding that the applicability of C. 4,44,2 should be extended to the buyer. However, he interprets the *dimidium*-rule as it applies to the buyer according to the minority opinion. This minority opinion went back to the jurists from Orléans and was popular among the French humanists. It held that a buyer was granted the remedy provided he paid more than double the just price.[1907] Piñel admitted that the common opinion was more equitable, but he thought that the minority opinion corresponded to the truth.[1908]

Incidentally, Piñel falsely accuses Charles Du Moulin of inconsistency in understanding the *dimidium*-rule as it applies to the buyer, thereby misleadingly citing a passage in Du Moulin's *Consuetudines* that cannot be traced back. In truth, Du Moulin always followed the minority opinion, even though Piñel maintained otherwise.[1909] It would seem that Piñel wished to discredit Du Moulin at any cost. Should we read this as a strategic attempt made by Piñel to avoid the impression among his peers that he was indebted to Du Moulin in following the minority opinion? Du Moulin had not made himself popular among the Catholic theologians, the civilians and the canonists, indeed, in expounding his interpretation of the

---

[1906] Piñel, *Commentarii*, ad l. 2, part. 1, cap. 3, num. 1–7, p. 86–88.

[1907] E.g. Le Douaren, *In lib. 45 Pandectarum, tit. de verborum obligationibus commentarius*, f. 21v (cited supra, n. 1752).

[1908] Piñel, *Commentarii*, ad l. 2, part. 1, cap. 2, num. 7, p. 79: 'In hac doctorum varietate vides opinionem contra glossam et magis communem non paucos habere eam tuentes. Fatetur autem Molinaeus, nec ego negarim communem opinionem aequitate iuvari, contrariam autem veriorem videri.'

[1909] E.g. Du Moulin, *Tractatus commerciorum*, num. 175, p. 154–155; *Commentarii in Parisienses consuetudines*, Francofurti ad Moenum 1597, par. 33, gl. 1 in verb. *Droict de relief*, num. 46, p. 438.

dimidium-rule. As a matter of fact, he accused them of talking rubbish.[1910] Their interpretation was beside the point (*paralogisati sunt*), according to Du Moulin, because it was at odds with practice.[1911]

The medieval jurists not only extended the applicability of C. 4,44,2. They also recognized that contracting parties had the right to renounce the remedy granted to them. Covarruvias left us an interesting discussion of the three main ways of renouncing the remedy of the *Lex Secunda*: through an explicit renunciation clause, a clause of donation of the excess value, or an implicit renunciation, that is by knowingly entering into a contract affected by *laesio enormis*. However, Piñel was highly critical of all of those renunciation clauses. Perhaps he was influenced here by the work of the Antonio Gómez. Gómez had argued that even the combination of a specific renunciation clause and a donation clause could not deprive the *laesus* of his right to seek support from the *Lex secunda*. He reasoned that the same facility (*facilitas*) with which such a party could become the victim of lesion would be at the basis of his renunciation or donation clause.[1912] The singularity of Piñel's discourse, though, is that he would reject the common idea that knowledge on the part of the *laesus* deprives him of the remedy provided by C. 4,44,2. According to our Portuguese jurist, knowledge does not take away that remedy (*scientia laesionis non tollit remedium*).

What motivated Piñel to launch such a straightforward assault on the *communis opinio*? There appear to be three reasons for that. Firstly, Portuguese statute law would nevertheless grant a remedy to a lesioned party who had given up his specific right to sue on account of C. 4,44,2. In fact, Portuguese statute law frustrated two types of renunciation clauses: the tacit renunciation clause based on knowledge (*scientia*) as well as the

---

[1910] Du Moulin, *Commentarii in Parisienses consuetudines*, par. 33, gl. 1 in verb. *Droict de relief*, num. 46, p. 438: 'Nimis ergo paralogisati sunt, et contra communem sensum errarunt omnes fere utriusque iuris et theologi scholastici professores minorem et laesionem et inaequalitatem requirentes ex parte emptoris (…).'

[1911] Du Moulin uses this term (*paralogisati sunt*) also in other contexts to criticize traditional juridical scholarship for its being out of touch with legal practice; cf. J.L. Thireau, *Charles Du Moulin (1500–1566), Étude sur les sources, la méthode, les idées politiques et économiques d'un juriste de la Renaissance*, [Travaux d'Humanisme et Renaissance, 176], Genève 1980, p. 151, n. 251.

[1912] Gómez, *Commentarii variaeque resolutiones*, tom. 2, cap. 2, num. 26, p. 227: 'Item adde, quod talis deceptus poterit agere remedio praedictae legis secundae, etiamsi dixerit, quod donat illud quod plus valeret et insuper renunciavit remedio praedictae legis secundae, quia illa verba non debent referri ad magnum pretium, sed ad modicum (…) Item etiam, quia eadem facilitate qua inducitur ad vendendum, inducitur etiam ad ponendum illam clausulam vel aliam similem (…).'

explicit renunciation clause specifically aimed at giving up the C. 4,44,2 (*renunciatio specialis*).[1913]

The second and the third argument are more important to Piñel: textual truth and Christian morality. 'That whole bunch of scholars have not deterred us,' he declares,[1914] 'because the contrary opinion is more true and more decent to Christians.' Christian morality urges Piñel to take the possibility of abuse of necessity (*necessitas*) seriously. Knowledge of the true price should not be a ground to relinquish the remedy offered by C. 4,44,2, because equity (*aequitas*) lies at the very heart of this constitution.[1915] So this remedy is meant to be of help precisely to someone who knowingly gives up his right. The *Lex secunda*, like laws that protect spendthrifts, applies regardless of a tacit renunciation clause.

However, Piñel's concern for people who are compelled by necessity to contract is not without limits. His discussion of the two cases of exploitation submitted by Ancharano is illustrative in this regard.[1916] One concerns a contracting party who sells or buys in order to save his family from starvation or to buy off his enemies. The other is about avoiding contact with an annoying friend or difficult neighbors. These examples were meant to illustrate Ancharano's point that the restricted use of C. 4,44,2 in the external courts, namely only if there was lesion beyond moiety, was not true in the event of compulsion (*necessitas*). Dr. Navarrus had repeated this view, encouraging a *laesus* to take the *laedens* to an ecclesiastical court if he had assented to an unjust price for another reason (*causa*) than an absolutely free and voluntary donation.[1917]

Piñel's blunt reply to Ancharano is that he has hardly seen the courts taking into consideration the necessity that drove an individual into a

---

[1913] Piñel, *Commentarii*, ad l. 2, part. 1, cap. 2, num. 13, p. 81: 'Apud Lusitanos autem non tantum observabitur, sed indubitabilis erit, ex saluberrima prudentissimaque Ordinatione, lib. 4, tit.30, par. 7 quae aperte decidit, remedium hoc non negari laesis ultra dimidiam, etiamsi probetur eos compertum habuisse verum rei pretium, licet etiam speciatim huic remedio renuncient. In quo ea ordinatio probat quod iudicio meo de iure verius videtur, sed aperte corrigit, quod apud scribentes receptius est.'
[1914] Piñel, *Commentarii*, ad l. 2, part. 1, cap. 2, num. 11, p. 80: 'Sed ea scribentium turba nos non deterruit, quin contrarium verius, et Christianis hominibus decentius putemus.'
[1915] Piñel, *Commentarii*, ad l. 2, part. 1, cap. 2, num. 12, p. 81: 'Suadetur etiam ex aequitate, qua lex haec principaliter nititur, quae militat etiam in eo, qui sciebat verum pretium, potuitque ex necessitate vel alia causa moveri. Iuvatur etiam, quia iura saepe succurrunt hominibus dissipantibus bona sua.'
[1916] Ancharano, *Super sexto Decretalium commentaria*, ad VI, reg. iur., 4, num. 21, p. 531, cited supra, n. 1802.
[1917] Cf. supra, p. 548.

contract.[1918] Piñel finds that necessity is almost always the driving force in the market. Certainly when selling real estate, people are often compelled by necessity to sell. The buyer should not be bothered by that. In conclusion, Ancharano's concern should only matter in the court of conscience, and not in the civil courts. Surprisingly, the Jesuit Leonardus Lessius would argue half a century later that necessity could not even be a valid ground for relief in the court of conscience, since necessity (*necessitas*) is the driving force behind most market transactions. He thus excused the sale of (toxic) credits in the financial market at prices far below their intrinsic value.[1919]

Against this background, it is undoubtedly fair to say that a general concern for equity (*aequitas*) more than a particular fear of exploitation of parties compelled by necessity lay behind Piñel's novel opinion. This is clear also from his addressing the obvious objection to his standpoint, namely that the knowing suffer no harm (*scienti non fit iniuria*).[1920] In fact, Piñel recognizes the truth of this maxim, conceding that the *laesus* probably suffered harm through his own fault. Yet he believes that the iniquity brought about by the *laedens* is graver than the fault of the *laesus* (*iniquitas laedentis praeponderat culpae laesi*). In cases of grave lesion, the law wanted to guarantee equity regardless of the *laesus'* negligence. Therefore, personal conditions of the *laesus* do not matter.[1921] Even if the *laesus* were an expert who knew the correct price, his tacit renunciation would still not affect his ability to invoke C. 4,44,2.

[1918] Piñel, *Commentarii*, ad l. 2, part. 2, cap. 2, num. 36, p. 134 'Ego autem in priori exemplo de emente vel vendente ob necessitatem, scio in iudiciis opinonem Ancharani nullatenus admitti, nec magis succurri laeso ob necessitatem contrahenti, atque ideo etiam in eo servari decisionem huius l. et cap. cum dilecti. (...) Saepissime enim contingit homines (saltem immobilia) non nisi necessitate pressos vendere. Item necessitas vendentis non inducta ex culpa vel facto ementis, non debet emptorem ipsum onerare, quoad forum exterius. Et ideo tantum ad sanitatem conscientiae traditio Ancharani procedet.'

[1919] Lessius, *De iustitia et iure*, lib. 2, cap. 21, num. 8–10.

[1920] Piñel, *Commentarii*, ad l. 2, part. 1, cap. 2, num. 14, p. 81: 'Retenta hac opinione non obstant quae pro communi adducuntur. Et primo illud vulgare, quod scienti non fit iniuria. Respondetur enim quod lex ex aequitate tam graviter laesis succurrere voluit, eo quod iniquitas laedentis, praeponderat culpae laesi, ut ait glossa in d.l. quisquis, infra eod. Albericus hic, Parnormitanus in d. c. cum causa, num. 4. Ideoque scientia laesi tollere non debet hoc remedium, quod probat glossa (ad quam non solet adverti) dum limitat textum ibi, in l. venditor, infra eod.'

[1921] Piñel, *Commentarii*, ad l. 2, part. 1, cap. 2, num. 19, p. 82: 'Inde etiam deducitur, cavendum esse ab aliis, qui male respondebant, remedium huius legis non dari laeso sagaci et experto, ob praesumptionem scientiae. (...) Quod falsum esse, omissis aliis argumentis, satis convincitur ex generalitate huius legis quae non tantum violenter sed inepte et verecunde ad solos ignaros et simplices restringeretur.'

Manuel Soarez a Ribeira, Piñel's commentator, thought that the argument from equity and Christian morality was the most legitimate reason to defy the common opinion on the renunciability *ex scientia*. He was less convinced about Piñel's so-called more true interpretation of the—quite obscure—law *Quisquis* (C. 4,44,15) that served to underpin his maverick opinion.[1922] The upshot of that exegesis was that no presumption lies that everybody knows the value of his property.[1923] By the same token, it is inconsistent to say, as the common opinion does, that a presumption lies that a *laesus infra dimidiam* knows the true value, whereas a *laesus supra dimidiam* does not. According to Piñel, this kind of presumption is absurd, since a contracting party is more likely to be mistaken when the lesion is small.[1924]

To summarize, Piñel radically confronted the traditional view that knowledge of the just price at the moment of concluding the contract frustrated a subsequent appeal to the remedy provided by the *Lex secunda*. Tacit renunciation of that remedy was impossible. In addition, an explicit and specific clause renouncing the remedy grounded in C. 4,44,2 had only limited force. Equity demanded that even a clause in which the *laesus* had knowingly stipulated the donation of the excess value could be undone in court, especially among the Portuguese.[1925] Piñel hailed the practical advantages of his view. In court, the burden of proof now shifted from the

---

[1922] Piñel, *Commentarii*, ad l. 2, part. 1, cap. 2, num. 11, litt. a (annotatione E. Soarez a Ribeira), p. 80: 'Haec nova Pineli sententia mirum in modum placet, etsi illius fundamenta facile dilui ac refelli possint. (...) Sed tamen, ut dixi, quamvis Pineli argumenta faciliter eleventur, eius opinio ob utilitatem publicam recipiendam humaniter videtur ac mihi imprimis placet.'

[1923] Piñel, *Commentarii*, ad l. 2, part. 1, cap. 2, num. 30–33, p. 85.

[1924] Piñel, *Commentarii*, ad l. 2, part. 1, cap. 2, num. 11, p. 80–81: 'Ipsi enim non sibi constant (...). Concedunt enim et agnoscunt omnes, quando laesio est citra dimidiam, praesumi quod laesus sciebat valorem, et ideo ei non succurri. Tunc autem respondent, stante laesione ultra dimidiam, cessare eam praesumptionem et potius errorem praesumi. Ego autem contra eos omnes adverto, praesumptionem scientiae magis | vigere, quando laesio enormis est. Facilius enim errabit quis in modico excessu, ut communi sensu et rerum experimento satis constat.'

[1925] Piñel, *Commentarii*, ad l. 2, part. 1, cap. 2, num. 20, p. 82: 'Ex iisdem infertur ad Bartolum, hic et in d. l. si quis cum aliter, quando in conventione additur clausula, qua invicem sibi donant vel remittunt quod pluris res valet, vel quod plus pro ea datur. Resolvit enim Bartolus non ideo cessare remedium huius legis nisi laesus tunc sciret verum pretium. (...) Qua in re ex coniecturis vel praesumptionibus scientiae, etiam adiecta ea clausula, non est negandum remedium huius legis iuxta supra tradita, maxime apud Lusitanos ex dicta Ordinatione.'

laesus to the *laedens*. The victim of *laesio enormis* would no longer need
to maintain his ignorance, let alone prove it.[1926]

7.5.3.2   *A humanist jurist more Catholic than the theologians?*

A hypercritical scholar, Arias Piñel has thus far also shown himself to be
a jurist sensible to the needs of a truly Christian legal order. In case of
conflict, even his profound, humanist sense of the letter of Roman law
must bend before the spirit of equity. Yet precision, distinction and juristic rigor matter. For instance, he shares the medieval jurists' concern for
the exploitation of the weak, but he refuses to see law *In contractibus*
(C. 2,54,3) in too close a connection with C. 4,44,2. Another one of Diocletian's and Maximianus' constitutions, C. 2,54,3 stipulated that statute law
would protect adults in contracts of good faith through the judge's office
once the case had been heard (*officio iudicis causa cognita*).[1927]

Traditionally, law *In contractibus* was read as an example of the
extended use of the remedy of C. 4,44,2. Yet Piñel regards the remedy
granted by C. 2,54,3 not as an application of C. 4,44,2, but as a separate
remedy, namely restitution. Restitution and the *Lex secunda* are both
there to protect victims of lesion, but on a theoretical level they should
be distinguished. After all, restitution can be granted even in the event of
lesion below moiety. According to Piñel, the reference to the office of the
judge and the hearing of the case clearly indicates that the remedy that
goes with law *In contractibus* is restitution.[1928] C. 2,54,3 provides a general
remedy that stands along C. 4,44,2. A concrete instance of it is provided by
law *Cum de indebito* (D. 22,3,25,1).[1929] Women, peasants, and other people

---

[1926] Piñel, *Commentarii*, ad l. 2, part. 1, cap. 2, num. 16, p. 81–82: 'Infertur similiter necessario, ad praxim et libellum in materia huius legis non esse necessarium articulos vel posi-
tiones formare, quod laesio per ignorantiam contigerit. (...) Ex quo etiam resultat non
solum in processu non oportere probare ignorantiam (...) sed nec eam allegare (...).'

[1927] C. 2,54,3 in *Corporis Iustinianaei Codex* (ed. Gothofredi), tom. 4, col. 479: 'In contractibus, qui bonae fidei sunt, etiam maioribus officio iudicis causa cognita publica iura
subveniunt.'

[1928] Piñel, *Commentarii*, ad l. 2, part. 1, cap. 1, num. 29, p. 74: 'Glossa, Bartolus et alii
ibi variantes circa intellectum illius legis [C. 2,54,3] applicant huius legis [C. 4,44,2] remedium. Sed repugnant verba d.l. ibi, *officio iudicis*, quae exprimere solent restitutionem (...).
Item verba d.l. ibi, *causa cognita*, propria sunt restitutionis (...). Ego adverto eiusdem legis
doctrinam generaliter scriptam particularia exempla habere posse (...).'

[1929] D. 22,3,25,1 in *Corporis Iustinianaei Digestum vetus* (ed. Gothofredi), tom. 1, col. 2079:
'Sin autem is, qui indebitum queritur, vel pupillus, vel minor sit, vel mulier, vel forte vir
quidem perfectae aetatis, sed miles, vel agricultor, et forensium rerum expers, vel alias
simplicitate gaudens, et desidiae deditus, tunc eum, qui accepit pecunias, ostendere bene
eas accepisse, et debitas ei fuisse solutas, et si non ostenderit, eas redhibere.'

who easily fall prey to wicked men because of their ingenuousness (*simplicitas*) benefit from restitution as a remedy.

'The splendor of the Christian faith', according to Piñel,[1930] 'does not admit of deceiving a simple rustic by quibbling.' In a compelling discussion of deceit, our Portuguese jurist runs into some cases that were also the subject of the theologians' preoccupation with law and morality in daily business practice. Most of these concerned precontractual duties to inform. Recent scholarship has revealed that the theologians took an amazingly negative attitude towards such duties.[1931] As a matter of conscience, there was an almost unanimous consensus that a vendor did not have a duty to disclose the intrinsic defects in his merchandise unless he was explicitly asked about them. The theologians had a surprisingly liberal view of the market, considering it as a contest (*certamen*), certainly among professional buyers and sellers.

One example concerned a buyer who told a simple man that he was willing to buy a gem in good conscience, pretending that he was prepared to pay the surplus above the just price as a gift, but nonetheless bought it at far too low a price. The Dominican friar Tommaso de Vio Cajetanus argued that the simple vendor had only himself to blame.[1932] The very suggestion of trustworthiness by the buyer should have made him suspicious. The vendor had not been prudent enough. He should have made inquiries into the true value of his merchandise. If he was mistaken, he

---

[1930] Piñel, *Commentarii*, ad l. 2, part. 3, cap. 2, num. 20, p. 201: 'Nec enim Christianus candor admittit, sub illo verborum aucupio, simplicem rusticum fallere.'

[1931] Cf. Decock – Hallebeek, *Pre-contractual duties to inform in early modern scholasticism*, p. 89–133. For a more thorough analysis of all of the questions dealt with in what follows in the main text, please allow us to refer to this article.

[1932] Tommaso de Vio Cajetanus, *Summula peccatorum*, Venetiis 1571, s.v. *Emptio 2*, p. 104–105: 'Emptio est illicita multipliciter. Primo ex fraude iusti pretii, ut si quis cognoscens pretiosam gemmam, de manu rustici non cognescentis quid habet, emat uno carlino. Nam voluntaria commutatio ex notitia provenit. Simile est enim ac si aurum pro aurichalco ab ignoranter vendente quis emeret. Et tenetur huiusmodi emptor ad restitutionem damni, ultra peccatum. Secus autem esset, si tam emente quam vendente ignorantibus committunt se fortunae, valeat quantum valeat, tunc enim bona fides utriusque et voluntas commutandi cum incuria discussionis transfert dominium licite. Si quis quoque emptor cognoscit pretium gemmae, et monet rusticum, quod ipse vult cum bona conscientia habere absque scrupulo etiamsi valeret mille aureos, et clare explicat quod pro donato habeatur quicquid amplius est, non videtur iniuste emere: ex quo dominus rei monitus cum protestatione non curat discutere rem suam, propterea quia non emit, sed invenit eam. Et emptor non tenetur ei explicite affirmare quantum valet, quum habeat alius unde possit inquirere et scire.'

had only himself to blame.[1933] Piñel, on the other hand, thought that Cajetan's opinion was objectionable, since, in his view, even Roman law would have been more rigorous in judging this buyer.[1934]

To summarize, it turns out that even a civilian jurist such as Piñel was often confused by the conclusions of his colleagues from the faculty of theology. Shocked by their liberal viewpoints on duties to inform, at some points he finds it difficult to restrain his criticism. He finds that even the judges in the external courts would often be more severe with merchants trying to promote their self-interest than confessors in the the court of conscience. To assess Piñel's standpoint, let us go back to the theologians and their discussions on justice in exchange.

7.6   CONTRACTUAL FAIRNESS IN EARLY MODERN SCHOLASTICISM II

The preceding paragraphs have highlighted the omnipresence in the Iberian world of the clash of the so-called liberal Roman principles of commerce and the Aristotelian-Thomistic virtue of justice in exchange. Theologians such as Medina felt the need to defuse Roman maxims by re-interpreting them in light of the theory of just pricing. The work of canonists such as Dr. Navarrus and Covarruvias sheds light on the rivalry between secular and spiritual jurisdictions in the bipolar world of the sixteenth century. Piñel's critical legal scholarship in Roman law did not prevent him from preferring Christian equity to textual purity. Moreover, he was confused by the liberal viewpoints of the moral theologians.

The question arises, then, whether an exclusive focus on the clash between the Roman legal principles and the Christian concern for

---

[1933] Against the background of the conquest of the Americas, this is, of course, a case of particular relevance. A century on, Leonardus Lessius would deal with a similar case, involving a native American selling a gem as if it were a piece of glass to a European buyer; cf. *De iustitia et iure*, lib. 2, cap. 17, dub. 5, num. 27, and lib. 2, cap. 21, dub. 11, num. 84. Generally speaking, the theologians increasingly made a distinction between transaction on a professional market, on the one hand, and commercial dealings involving simple people (to a certain extent the forerunners of our 'consumers'), on the other hand. In the latter type of exchange, professionals were asked to practice the theological virtue of charity. Still, they would not sin against the cardinal virtue of justice if they did not behave in the most charitable way. In other words, they were considered to be able to 'pass' the 'exam' of Last Judgment regardless, albeit without any 'honors'.

[1934] Piñel, *Commentarii*, ad l. 2, part. 3, cap. 2, num. 20, p. 201: 'Ego autem (salvo iudicio sacrae Theologicae facultatis) reijciendam puto eam opinionem Cajetani cum et in foro exteriori talis deceptio reprobetur, secundum Paul. In dicto loco [D. 19,2,22,3], minus ergo probari debet in foro conscientiae.'

commutative justice has not made us blind for the real attitude the early modern scholastics took towards economic liberalism. Textbooks on the history of legal and economic thought usually limit themselves to pointing out the scholastic engagement with the usury doctrine, the theory of just pricing and *laesio enormis*. These classical surveys are then supposed to convey the message that contractual or economic liberalism could not possibly have spread its wings until the advent of the Protestant ethic or the renaissance of genuine Roman sales law. Still, scholarship concentrating on the Catholic moral theologians' solution of practical *cases* rather than theoretical principles has seriously challenged this traditional view. This has already been demonstrated, for instance, in regard to Lessius' usury doctrine.[1935]

7.6.1 Theory: the moral menace of Roman law

To be sure, the aforementioned theory of *laesio enormis* and just pricing continues to play a major role in scholastic legal thought in the second half of the sixteenth and the first half of the seventeenth century. This is abundantly clear from Jesuits such as Luís de Molina, Leonardus Lessius, Juan de Lugo and Pedro de Oñate.

For example, despite his familiarity with Arias Piñel, Molina continues to advocate the concept of objective deceit (*dolus re ipsa*).[1936] At the same time, he follows Antonio Gómez and Arias Piñel in excluding the possibility to renounce the remedy granted by C. 4,44,2.[1937] Lessius, in turn, is merciless in rebuking Gerson's view that the *laedens* is not obliged to

---

[1935] P. Vismara, *Oltre l'usura, La Chiesa moderna e il prestito a interesse*, Soveria Mannelli 2004, p. 156–163; T. Van Houdt, *Implicit intention and the conceptual shift from interesse to interest, An underestimated chapter from the history of scholastic economic thought*, Lias, Sources and documents relating to the early modern history of ideas, 33 (2006), p. 37–58; L. Fontaine, *L'économie morale, Pauvreté, crédit et confiance dans l'Europe préindustrielle*, Paris 2008, p. 190–222.

[1936] Molina, *De iustitia et iure*, tom. 2 (*De contractibus*), tract. 2, disp. 352, col. 411, num. 1: 'Deceptionem posse multis modis provenire. Uno, cum ignorantia decipientis. Ut si quis, existimans se vendere rem iusto pretio, illam vendit plus quam valet. Atque deceptio haec dicitur re ipsa intervenire et non a proposito.'

This is not to say that Piñel had absolutely no influence on the subsequent theological tradition. For example, Domingo Bañez expressly takes over his conclusion that the protection offered by the *Lex secunda* was an entirely new constitution. Cf. *De iure et iustitia*, ad quaest. 77, p. 522: 'Imo vero olim ante legem illam [C. 4,44,2] non dabatur actio in iudicio laesis etiam ultra dimidium pretii.'

[1937] Molina, *De iustitia et iure*, tom. 2 (*De contractibus*), tract. 2, disp. 349, cols. 402–403, num. 16.

make restitution on account of lesion below moiety.[1938] In the footsteps of Dr. Navarrus, Lugo insists on the procedural remedy granted to the victim of lesion below moiety: he can appeal to the judge's office (*officium iudicis*), since ecclesiastical tribunals are always competent for the vindication of mortal sins against justice.[1939]

A systematic refutation of the objections to the *laesio enormis* principle on the basis of Roman legal principles is offered by Oñate.[1940] He follows Molina and Lessius in explaining that D. 4,4,16,4 is to be interpreted as a rule of the law of nations (*ius gentium*). It stipulates that within the limits of the just price (*intra latitudinem iusti pretii*) merchants are allowed to outwit each other. Wholly in the Jesuit spirit, Oñate adds that commercial industry is largely based on this principle (*in hoc maxime industria mercatorum desudat*). It is precisely this kind of cleverness which allows businesmen to make money (*hac praecipue solertia ditantur*). However, beyond the limits of the just price this cleverness turns into sin. Although the tendency to outwit the other party below moiety follows from the natural inclinations of man, it remains a sin, even if it is tolerated by positive human law (*sine poena, non tamen sine culpa*).

In the same way, Oñate neutralizes D. 36,1,1,16 and C. 4,35,21 by adding a typically scholastic restriction. Granted, goods are worth as much as they are sold for, but only within the limits of the just price (*intra latitudinem iusti pretii*). As Oñate frankly admits, if this maxim were to be allowed in its pure Roman form, the entire scholastic enterprise of trying to find out what the just price was, would make no sense (*alias frustra iura et doctores defatigarentur in assignando pretio iusto rebus*). By the same token, everybody may well be the moderator and arbiter of his own things, but that can only be true under the restrictions imposed by civil and natural law (*non ut contra legem naturalem vel civilem*). Since the equality principle is imposed by natural law, contractual fairness must be observed regardless of C. 4,35,21.

Typically, Oñate insists that the logic of gift and the logic of the market are two different things. A gift is not to be presumed in sale contracts (*donatio in venditionibus non praesumitur*). This is his way of refuting

---

[1938] Lessius, *De iustitia et iure*, lib. 2, cap. 21, dub. 4, num. 22.

[1939] Lugo, *De iustitia et iure*, tom. 2, disp. 26, sect. 6, num. 84, p. 322: 'Tertia difficultas esse potest, an laesus citra dimidium iusti pretii possit recurrere ad iudicem ecclesiasticum, ut ratione peccati compellat adversarium ad restitutionem etiam per censuras. Respondetur affirmative, sicut in aliis peccatis mortalibus contra iustitiam id fieri potest (...).'

[1940] Oñate, *De contractibus*, tom. 3, part. 1, tract. 21, disp. 63, sect. 5, num. 141–147, p. 59–60.

the maxim that the willing and the knowing consent voluntarily. This is
rather peculiar. Lessius and Lugo had confronted D. 50,17,145 in another
way. They would deny that a *laedens* could be deemed to have assented
to the contract entirely voluntarily.[1941] In other words, they would assume
that lesion is a vice of the will. Perhaps Oñate sensed the problematical
nature of this perspective: if *laesio enormis* is but a vice of the will, then
why make a separate doctrine out of it? How does one relate it to the idea
of objective deceit?

Oñate left us a systematic outline of the theoretical discussion on *laesio enormis*. Yet, however elegant his synthesis may have been, it makes
one wonder if *laesio enormis* was still more than a well-archived piece of
classical doctrine for students preparing the final exam. For example, in
theory Oñate refuses to extend to other contracts the principle of gaming
contracts according to which the parties are allowed to use good deceit
(*dolus bonus / solertia*). But it is this very idea of contest and playing the
market game that formed the basis of the early modern scholastics' practical solution of daily recurring cases.

7.6.2   *Practice: playing the market game*

The significance of the doctrines of just pricing and *laesio enormis* in dealing with real cases can be questioned, indeed. Better still, our traditional
understanding of the real impact of these doctrines might be in need of
some qualification. For rather than impeding a liberal view of commercial relationships, the consistent application of the doctrine of just pricing
appears to have made astonishingly liberal views on business possible in
the first place. Let us take a quick glance at two famous cases and the way
the Jesuit moral theologians dealt with them: insider trading and asymmetrically distributed information.[1942]

[1941] Lessius, *De iustitia et iure*, lib. 2, cap. 21, dub. 4, num. 22, p. 276–277: '(...) ille non
est absolute volens, sed solum modo explicato, sicut is qui solvit usuras.'

Lugo, *De iustitia et iure*, tom. 2, disp. 26, sect. 6, num. 82, p. 322: 'Respondetur id verum
esse quando voluntarium non est mixtum cum involuntario prout est in casu nostro, in
quo contrahens vel ex ignorantia valoris iusti vel quia aliter vendere aut emere non potest,
cogitur involuntarie in pretium iniustum consentire.'

[1942] For a more detailed account, see W. Decock, *Leonardus Lessius en de koopman
van Rhodos, Een schakelpunt in het denken over economie en ethiek*, De zeventiende
eeuw, 22 (2006), p. 247–261; W. Decock, *At the crossroads of law and morality, Lessius
on precontractual duties to inform about future market conditions*, in: L. Beck Varela –

Among the jurists, insider trading was traditionally considered problematical. Bartolus had condemned a vendor who quickly sold his grain at a high price knowing through his personal contacts with the administration that the authorities would shortly lower the grain price.[1943] According to Bartolus, not sharing this information with the buyer is tantamount to cheating (*circumvenire*). A vendor who knows about a future change in the price should anticipate that in his immediate commercial dealings. This was also the view taken by Juan de Medina.

The majority of the theologians countered that view by making a distinction between intrinsic and extrinsic elements of the good sold. Information about future market conditions pertained to the category of extrinsic information and could therefore not be the subject of a duty to inform. In the civilian tradition, Bartolus and the common opinion of the jurists had been countered quite forcefully by Raffaele Fulgosio (1367–1427), who successively taught civil law at Pavia, Piacenza and Padova.[1944] Fulgosio was a regular counselor to the Republic of Venice. His fame was tainted because of the negative judgment of his work by Giasone del Maino, who accused him of plagiarism. In a surprisingly liberal spirit, Fulgosio defended the clever use of insider information, for instance on the basis of insider knowledge of a future law. He made a radical distinction between the seller's duty to inform about intrinsic qualities of the merchandise he sold, and his right to conceal information about the extrinsic qualities, that is about the future market conditions. Fulgosio underscored that this type of speculative activity pertained to the daily practice of business.[1945]

P. Gutiérrez Vega – A. Spinosa (eds.), Crossing legal cultures, München 2009, p. 243–258, and Decock, *Lessius and the breakdown of the scholastic paradigm*, p. 57–78.

[1943] Bartolus de Saxoferrato, *In secundam Digesti veteris partem*, Venetiis 1570, ad D. 19,1,39, f. 129v: 'Ordinationem qui sciens factam per superiorem quod aliqua res vendatur minori pretio solito, si vendit pro maiori pretio quam fuerit ordinatum, tenetur. (...) Quia videtur facere causa circumveniendi eo ipso, quod scit. (...) Vendidit tibi frumentum pro maiori pretio nec certioraverit te. Certe videtur teneri ad interesse, et ita glos. Sensit in l. contra legem facit, tit. de legibus.'

[1944] For biografical information on Fulgosio, see the extended notes by C. Bukowska Gorgoni in the *Dizionario biografico degli Italiani* (URL: http://www.treccani.it/enciclopedia/raffaele-fulgosio_(Dizionario-Biografico)/).

[1945] Raffaele Fulgosio, *In primam Pandectarum partem commentaria*, Lugduni 1544, ad D. 19,1,39, f. 175r–v: '(...) Et quid dicetis? Nonne cotidie hoc accidit in mercatoribus? Unus mercator recipiat unam litteram recentem, quod galeae, quae veniebant a Flandria fuerunt submersae, vel a barbaris captae, cum super eis esset piper vel aliae merces. Iste mercator ivit et de pipere et aliis mercibus, quae erant super galeis in portu, vel iamdudum reconditis ab aliis mercatoribus emit currenti pretio, cum ipse sciret quod erat futura carior res. At cum notam esset de galeis, quod essent submersae, dicetne quis, quod non valeret talis emptio pro pretio currenti, aut quod rescindi debeat? Non video. Satis est durum hoc

For example, if a merchant was informed that a ship full of pepper on its way from Flanders had sunk or was held hostage by pirates, this merchant would directly buy the pepper supply in his town at the current market price to be able to sell it dear in the future. He wondered why his diligence and industry should not be of benefit to a businessman (*cur non debeat sibi prodesse sua diligentia et solicitudo?*).

In the first half of the seventeenth century, Jesuit theologians such as Lessius and Lugo would defend insider trading on the ground of far-reaching liberal principles. Even if they did not refer to him expressly, they would repeat Raffaele Fulgosio's argument about the need to reward a clever and hard-working merchant and to let him reap the fruits of his good fortune.

Lessius would insist that there is no law forbidding that a businessman uses insider information to his own advantage to sell even more (*plus*) than he originally wanted to. He would rely on the doctrine of just pricing to make this claim. As long as a new law is not officially promulgated, the current price remains the standard of justice in exchange.[1946] Regardless of the vendor's motivations, intentions and personal knowledge, the only criterion to assess the morality of commercial exchange is the just price—and this is the price charged by the insider trader.[1947]

At the heart of Lessius' approval of profit-making based on insider information is the idea of business as a game. This is an idea that reaches back at least to John Mair and to Diego de Covarruvias y Leyva. John

sentire. Et cur non debeat sibi prodesse sua diligentia et solicitudo? Et hoc scio practicatum in civitate Ianuae (...).'

[1946] Lessius, *De iustitia et iure*, lib. 2, cap. 21, dub. 5, num. 46, p. 279: 'Sed contrarium videtur verius, nempe non esse contra iustitiam, etiamsi occasione illius scientiae plus mercium vendas, quod expresse tenet Covarruvias loco citato. Probatur, quia etiamsi sciam decretum a principe vel magistratu conditum circa merces vel monetam, tamen quamdiu illud non est promulgatum, non obligat, nec ullam vim habet, ac proinde antiquum pretium adhuc durat, sictu prior lex vim habet, etiamsi alia quae haec abrogetur, iam sit conscripta, modo tamen non sit promulgata. Ergo possum vendere pretio antiquo.'

[1947] Lessius, *De iustitia et iure*, lib. 2, cap. 21, dub. 5, num. 47, p. 279: 'Sed haec responsio [non posse me ratione notitiae huius decreti vendere plus mercium eo pretio quam alioquin eram venditurus, quia non possum privatim cum aliorum dispendio uti lege quae omnibus debet esse communis] non satisfacit. Primo, quia nulla lex vetat ne utar notitia illius decreti in meum commodum. Secundo, quod vendam aliquid permotus notitia illius decreti vel ob aliam causam nihil facit ad aequalitatem vel inaequalitatem quae servanda est in contractibus. Atqui si vendam modium frumenti pretio currente nihil sciens de illo decreto, erit aequalitas inter rem et pretium, iustaque venditio, nec tenebor ad restitutionem, etiamsi pretium paulo post per decretum minuatur. Ergo etiam erit aequalitas et iusta venditio, etiamsi sciam illud decretum. Tertio, intentio interior non potest facere ut actio exterior alias iusta fiat iniusta et obliget ad restitutionem.'

Mair argued that business is a contest (*certamen*), defining prudence as the ability not to be outwitted in doing commerce.[1948] Covarruvias conceived of cleverness (*dolus bonus sive solertia*)[1949] as an essential part of the natural laws of a gaming contract (*naturalis ludi lex*). On seeing that he has a good hand, a clever player raises stakes.[1950] Lessius transposes this argument to sale contracts, concluding that a merchant can sell even more upon getting his insider information.

Lessius argues that, unlike a civil servant, a citizen is neither expected nor obliged to promote the benefit of others. Lugo would take this argument even a step further. He holds that civil servants and public institutions can themselves take advantage of their insider information. Instead of abuse of power, Lugo considers these speculative activites by the administration itself as pertaining to economic prudence (*prudentia oeconomica*).[1951]

This evolution in moral theological thinking is contrary to Arias Piñel's fierce condemnation of insider trading. In fact, we would expect the reason for his rejection from a theologian rather than from a civilian: 'nobody should be enriched at the expense of another by virtue of a law that is useful for all' (*ne quis ex lege omnibus utili cum alterius iactura inique locupletetur*).[1952]

[1948] See the above quote from John Mair, *In quartum sententiarum quaestiones*, Parisiis 1516, dist. 15, quaest. 41, par. *Secunda conclusio*, f. 113r.

[1949] On the Roman roots of the *dolus bonus* concept (D. 4,3,1,3), see, for instance, A. Wacke, *Circumscribere, gerechter Preis und die Arten der List (Dolus bonus und dolus malus, dolus causam dans und dolus incidens) unter besonderer Berücksichtigung der §§ 138 Abs. II und 123 BGB*, Zeitschrift der Savigny-Stiftung für Rechtsgeschichte, Rom. Abt., 94 (1977), p. 224–230, and Böttcher, *Von der Lüge zur Mentalreservation, Über den Einfluss von Moralphilosophie und—theologie auf das Bürgerliche Recht*, p. 57–59.

[1950] Covarruvias, *In regulam Peccatum*, part. 2, par. 4, p. 486–88.

[1951] Lugo, *De iustitia et iure*, tom. 2, disp. 26, sect. 8, num. 143, p. 303: 'Ratio autem esse potest, quia non apparet cur notitia illa particularis quam habent non possit illis prodesse ad utiliter contrahendum sicut notitia aliarum rerum quam occasione suorum munerum habent, possunt etiam uti ad suum commodum. Si enim consiliarius regis sciat regem velle aliquem subditum ad dignitatem magnam extollere, potest interim offerre ei filiam in uxorem, etc…(…) Ratio est, quia licet lex communis et aequalis esse debeat, eius tamen scientia antequam promulgetur non debet esse omnibus communis sed aliquibus ratione sui muneris potest antea competere. (…) Usus autem scientiae non est usus vel exercitium potestatis sed est actus prudentiae economicae quae ordinatur ad privata commoda. Quare nullus est abusus quod in ea commoda ordinatur.'

[1952] Piñel, *Commentarii*, ad l. 2, part. 3, cap. 2, num. 22, p. 202: 'Sed adhuc non videtur recedendum a recepta opinione, quae specialiter a doctoribus traditur in constitutione publicanda, in qua particularis ratio viget, ne quis ex lege omnibus utili, cum alterius iactura inique locupletetur.'

The argument about the collective utility of laws was actually adopted by Molina to condemn an insider trader who decided to sell even more (*plus*) than he intended to do before he got his inside information. Molina did take a different view than Lessius and Lugo in this respect. Yet Molina would disagree with Bartolus that a merchant with inside information should be worse off than his competitors who had not been informed about the future change of law altogether. His good luck of getting to know something in advance should not be turned into his bad luck. Therefore he was still allowed to sell at the current price, according to Molina.

To sum up, although Luis de Molina would adopt at least part of Piñel's line of argument in regard to insider trading, his younger colleagues Lessius and Lugo would not. This is counter-intuitive for the modern reader. But it also seems to have been perplexing for a sixteenth-century Catholic jurist such as Piñel.

This is also clear from another famous case the moral theologians dealt with in a most liberal way: the Merchant of Rhodes. The theologians' majority solution of this case, which consisted in allowing a merchant to make money on the basis of asymmetrically distributed information, must have fallen short of Piñel's humanist expectations.[1953] Piñel surely approves of the Merchant of Rhodes concealing his information in the external court, deeming his behavior, in Baldus' terms, as pertaining to commercial diligence (*diligentia negociativa non deceptiva*).[1954] Yet he expects the merchant to live up to higher standards as a matter of conscience, notably to the virtue of charity (*charitas*).

However, this is not how the early modern theologians saw it. Apart from Medina's dissident voice, they would generally accept that a sound sense of charity begins with self-love (*ordinata charitas incipit a seipsa*).[1955]

[1953] See Decock, *Leonardus Lessius en de koopman van Rhodos, Een schakelpunt in het denken over economie en ethiek*, p. 247–261. In this article it is also shown how the early modern humanist intellectuals in general, such as Caspar Barlaeus, did return to Cicero's and Ambrose's original condemnation of the merchant who did not share his information about future market developments with the other party to the contract.

[1954] Piñel, *Commentarii*, ad l. 2, part. 3, cap. 2, num. 22, p. 202: 'In his enim et similibus alia inspectio est quoad strictum forum conscientiae et summae bonitatis et charitatis, et tunc non censetur sincere facere qui eo compendio utitur honestum postponendo, quod colligitur ex Cicerone, libro 3 de officiis. Diversa inspectio est, quoad exteriora iudicia et tribunalia: ea enim diligentia negotiativa non deceptiva est (...).'

[1955] See, for example, Summenhart, *De contractibus*, tract. 3, quaest. 62, par. *Secundus modus dicendi*. Still, Summenhart was one of those dissident voices who would not allow the Merchant of Rhodes to capitalize on his dominant information position, because he thought that affected the voluntariness of the transaction on the part of the buyer.

Even the early modern scholastics' concept of charity, then, seems to have been pragmatic rather than idealistic.[1956] In regard to the Merchant of Rhodes, Francisco de Vitoria reasoned that a businessman should not put his own interests at risk by behaving 'like a teacher'. Commercial diligence is a legitimate source of justification in the court of conscience. The ultimate criterion for justice in exchange is the just price. So as long as the vendor who knows that the market price is going to sink in the future charges the current just price, he acts with a clear conscience. There is no need for him to disclose his information about the future market conditions.

The ultimate criterion, then, is the current market price which reflects the information generally available in the market.[1957] The current market price is the just price in regard to which all the merchants carefully plan their transactions. The Jesuits, like Vitoria, point out the absurdities that would ensue from taking into account private information as a price determining factor. The industrious merchants would be worse off, whereas speculation and gaining more information than the other market participants is an essential part of business acumen (*est ars mea quod scio esse sic futurum*).[1958]

The logic of just pricing is clearly different from the logic of gift-making. The logic of just pricing and *laesio enormis* pertains to a moralized worldview on commercial contracts. That does not prevent the moral theologians from solving practical cases in a surprisingly liberal way. The only real limit they would in practice impose on 'contractual freedom' is the exploitation of the needy. As soon as a contract is concluded with a poor or simple man (*simplex vel pauper*) who has no ability whatsoever

---

[1956] As has already been noted by S. Knebel, *Casuistry and the early modern paradigm shift in the notion of charity*, in: J. Kraye – R. Saarinen (ed.), Moral philosophy on the threshold of modernity, [The New Synthese Historical Library, Texts and Studies in the History of Philosophy, 57], Dordrecht 2005, p. 115–139. Certainly in light of Knebel's findings, it would seem that an earlier study on the notion of charity in the late scholastic literature, namely K. Deuringer, *Probleme der Caritas in der Schule von Salamanca*, Freiburg i.Br. 1959 is rather biased.

[1957] Lessius, *De iustitia et iure*, tom. 2, cap. 21, dub. 5, num. 40, p. 279: 'Respondeo, etiamsi venditor sciat futuram pretii remissionem, emptorque nesciat, nihilominus potest res suas absque iniustitia vendere pretio currente. (...) Ratio est, quia res iuste vendi potest iuxta communem aestimationem pro tempore vigentem. Nam iustum pretium est, quod vel principis lege vel communi aestimatione constat. Confirmatur, quia privata scientia venditoris communem sensum et aestimationem non mutat, sicut nec privata scientia emptoris illam mutat.'

[1958] Francisco de Vitoria, *In IIamIIae* (ed. B. de Heredía), quaest. 77, art. 3, ad 4, p. 144, num. 16.

to defend himself, charity (*charitas*) demands that the logic of just pricing be abandoned.[1959]

7.7   GROTIUS AND THE LEGACY OF FAIRNESS IN EXCHANGE

> In the principal act of contracting, equality is demanded, lest more is claimed than is fair. In gratuitous contracts, this is difficult to maintain. (...) Yet in all onerous contracts this principle must be carefully observed. Nobody has a reason to pretend that the surplus value promised by the other party is deemed to have been donated. For this is not usually the intention with which parties enter into those contracts, and it need not be presumed unless it is apparent. What they promise or give must be presumed to be promised or given as if it were a thing equal in value to what they are about to receive themselves, and as if it were owed by reason of this equality.

As is obvious from this quote, there is no need to leave the Aristotelian-Thomistic universe to come to grips with Grotius' contract law.[1960] It is rather difficult to imagine how one could truly understand Grotius' exposition without reference to the conceptual framework developed by the early modern scholastics. His distinguishing the logic of the market from the logic of gift, his emphasizing that donation is not to be presumed, his insisting on equality in exchange, all of these substantial elements of the scholastic discussion on fairness in exchange live on in Grotius' brilliant synthesis.

Samuel von Pufendorf, Grotius' intellectual heir, also appears to be highly indebted to the scholastic views on fairness in exchange.[1961] The

---

[1959] See, for example, Lessius, *De iustitia et iure*, tom. 2, cap. 21, dub. 11, num. 93, p. 286 in regard to the duty to disclose intrinsic defects: 'Etiamsi non sit contra iustitiam non monere emptorem dum suo iudicio fidit, tamen potest esse contra charitatem, ut si videat emptorem ex simplicitate decipi et putet rem ei fore inutilem quamvis aliis inutilis non sit.'

[1960] Grotius, *De jure belli ac pacis* (Ed. De Kanter-Van Hettinga Tromp – Feenstra – Persenaire), lib. 2, cap. 12, par. 11, num. 1, p. 345–346: 'In ipso actu principali haec desideratur aequalitas, ne plus exigatur quam par est. Quod in contractibus bene-|ficis locum vix potest habere. (...) At in permutatoriis omnibus sollicite id observandum est. Nec est quod dicat quispiam id quod pars altera amplius promittit donatum censeri. Neque enim solet hic esse tales contractus ineuntium animus, nec praesumendus est nisi appareat. Quod enim promittunt aut dant credendi sunt promittere aut dare tanquam aequale ei quod accepturi sunt, utque eius aequalitatis ratione debitum.'

[1961] See Kalb's critique of Schulze in *Laesio enormis*, p. 205–206: 'Zusammenfassend ist festzuhalten, dass, entgegen der Ansicht von Schulze [cf. supra, n. 1745], Grotius und Pufendorf im Ergebnis der *aequalitas* und objektiven Wertlehre der aristotelisch-thomistischen Tradition verhaftet sind. Beide akzeptieren auch grundsätzlich die *laesio enormis* als Einrichtung | des positiven Rechts, bzw.—entgegen Schulze—ihre Kritik an diesem Rechts-

same holds true for French natural lawyers such as Robert Joseph Pothier. Pothier asserted that lesion as such, without any intent of deceit on the part of the *laedens*, is sufficient to render the contract vicious.[1962] He went on to explain in truly scholastic fashion that the just price, the guarantor of equality in exchange, did not consist in an indivisible point.[1963] Curiously, the scholastic influence on Pothier is still a matter of dispute in the secondary literature.[1964] It seems to us that the scholastic imprint on Pothier's conception of lesion and just pricing is manifest. The real rupture in thinking about *laesio enormis* may have occurred with Christian Thomasius, who, as was mentioned earlier, considered the doctrine a mere product of learned phantasy.

The center of gravity of Grotius' dealing with contracts and commercial exchange did not shift far away from the moral theologians' legal universe. His doctrine of just pricing and the need to undo unjust enrichment by making restitution mirrors that of the scholastics. His utility-based

---

behelf geht nicht vom Gedanken der Vertragsfreiheit aus, sondern—wie etwa bei den spanischen Spätscholastikern—vom Erfordernis der *aequalitas*.' Compare Wolter's critique on Schulze in *Ius canonicum in iure civili*, [Forschungen zur neueren Privatrechtsgeschichte, 23], Köln-Wien 1975, p. 121, n. 494.

[1962] Pothier, *Traité des obligations, selon les regles, tant du for de la conscience, que du for extérieur*, part. 1, sec. 1, art. 3, par. 4 (de la lésion entre majeurs), p. 35–36: 'L'équité doit régner dans les conventions; d'où il suit que dans les contrats intéressés, dans lesquels l'un des contractans donne ou fait quelque chose, pour recevoir | quelqu'autre chose, comme le prix de ce qu'il donne ou de ce qu'il fait, la lésion que souffre l'un des contractans, quand même l'autre n'auroit recours à aucun artifice pour le tromper, est seule suffisante par elle-même pour rendre ce contrat vicieux. Car l'équité en fait de commerce, consistant dans l'égalité, dès que cette égalité est blessée et que l'un des contractans donne plus qu'il ne reçoit, le contrat est vicieux, parce qu'il péche contre l'équité qui y doit régner.'

[1963] Pothier, *Traité des obligations, selon les regles, tant du for de la conscience, que du for extérieur*, p. 36: 'Le prix des choses ne consiste pas ordinairement dans un point indivisible, il a une certaine étendue, sur laquelle il est permis aux contractans de se débattre.'

[1964] Deroussin, *Histoire du droit des obligations*, p. 412: 'Le prix d'une chose n'est donc pas un "point indivisible" (Pothier, oblig, n. 33): l'on ne peut mieux rejeter l'idée défendue par les canonistes d'un juste prix et d'une valeur objective et intrinsèque de chaque chose.' Drawing on René Dekkers, *La lésion énorme*, p. 147, the opposite view is advocated by C. Becker, *Die Lehre von der laesio enormis*, p. 109: 'Die Anlehnung an das Kirchenrecht kann so weit gehen, dass Robert Joseph Pothier (1699–1772) die *équité* immer dann verletzt sieht, wenn einer der Vertragspartner weniger erhält, als er gibt, jedoch meint, nur im *for intérieur* sei jede beliebige Abweichung erheblich, während im *for extérieur* eine *lésion énorme* erforderlich sei (was klugerweise so eingerichtet sei, weil Sicherheit und Freiheit des Handelns verlangen, dass man Verträge nicht leicht angreifen könne, anderenfalls aus Furcht, der andere könne sich einbilden, übervorteilt zu sein, und überziehe einen mit einem Prozess, niemand es wagte, einen Vertrag zu schliessen). *Dekkers* bezeichnet *Pothier* deswegen geradezu als Kanonisten, dessen Gedanken scheinbar unmittelbar im Mittelalter wurzeln.' See also E. Chevreau – Y. Mausen – C. Bouglé, *Introduction historique au droit des obligations*, Paris 2007, p. 139.

conception of the just price stems from the Aristotelian-Thomistic tradition. The idea that a good is worth as much as it can be sold for commonly
(*communiter*), and that this common estimation has a certain latitude
(*latitudo*), is standard scholastic doctrine. His account of the market factors determining the common estimation as well as the extrinsic titles
that can be invoked to deviate from the market price is a brief synthesis of Lessius, *De iustitia et iure* 2, 21, 2–4.[1965] The claim that Grotius and
Pufendorf deviated from the doctrine of just pricing because they considered affections to be worthy of estimation seems very unlikely in light of
a close-reading of the texts themselves.[1966]

If any, the specific contribution of Grotius consists in introducing the
scholastic doctrines in a new, elegant system of law which nevertheless
bears the marks of the early modern theologians. For example, in his
Inleidinge tot de Hollandse Rechtsgeleerdheid, Grotius distinguishes between
two major sources of obligation: promise (*toezegginge*) and inequality
(*onevenheid*). In his *De iure belli ac pacis*, he subsumes the concept of
'equality in exchange' under a broader concept of equality demanded by
nature.[1967] This concept not only encompasses equality between what is
given and exchanged in a contract (*aequalitas in ipso actu*), but also equal-

---

[1965] Grotius, *De jure belli ac pacis* (Ed. De Kanter-Van Hettinga Tromp – Feenstra –
Persenaire), lib. 2, cap. 12, par. 14, num. 2, p. 348–349: 'In communi autem illo pretio ratio
haberi solet laborum et expensarum quas mercatores | faciunt: soletque subito quoque
mutari ex copia et inopia ementium, pecuniae, mercium. Caeterum possunt et quaedam
esse rei accidentia aestimabilia, ob quae res licite supra aut infra commune pretium ema-
tur vendaturve, puta ob damnum consequens, lucrum cessans, affectum peculiarem, aut
si in gratiam alterius res vendatur ematurve alioqui non emenda aut vendenda; quae ipsa
accidentia ei cum quo agitur indicanda sunt. Eius quoque damni aut lucri cessantis ratio
haberi potest, quod ex pretii solutione dilata aut anticipata nascitur.'
For a translation of the corresponding passages in Lessius, see Decock, *Leonardus Lessius on buying and selling*, p. 466–482.
[1966] The idea of 'pretium affectionis' is connected with Pufendorf in Schermaier, *Mistake, misrepresentation and precontractual duties to inform*, p. 54, n. 74. See also Deroussin,
Histoire du droit des obligations, p. 417. However, further research would be welcome on
this topic. It would seem that Grotius' and Pufendorf's viewpoints on *pretium affectionis*
are not that different from the scholastic views, for example as expressed in Lessius, *De
iustitia et iure*, lib. 2, cap. 21, dub. 3, num. 17, p. 276: 'Adverte tamen, si venditori ei [rei]
valde afficiatur, posse hunc suum affectum aestimare, ut docet Navarrus cap. 23, num. 83,
sed id bona fide fieri debet.' In fact, Pufendorf almost repeats the scholastic 'double rule
of just pricing': 'Sed et illud contingere solet, ut certae quaedam res non communiter,
sed a singulis magni aestimentur, ex peculiari aliquo affectu: id quod vocari solet pretium
affectionis. (...) | Ubi tamen aliqui observant, in emptione et venditione non debere pre-
tium rei intendi ex affectu emptoris, nisi aliae causae pretium intendentes concurrant.' Cf.
Pufendorf, *De iure naturae et gentium*, lib. 5, cap. 1, par. 7, p. 451–452 (ed. Böhling).
[1967] Grotius, *De jure belli ac pacis* (Ed. De Kanter-Van Hettinga Tromp – Feenstra –
Persenaire), lib. 2, cap. 12, par. 8, p. 344: 'In contractibus natura aequalitatem imperat, et ita

ity of information before the parties enter into the contract (*aequalitas in intellectu*) and equality of voluntary consent (*aequalitas in voluntatis usu*).[1968] Still, the manner in which he discusses cases under these headings, e.g. the 'Merchant of Rhodes' in connection with equality of information, are again highly reminiscent of the scholastic debates.[1969]

It would be naive, then, to entirely reduce Grotius' discussion to his scholastic sources of inspiration. As we have had the chance to note on several occasions throughout this book, Grotius' elegant synthesis of the scholastic debates is a relief to the modern reader who just wants to read the upshot of the scholastics' highly technical and mind-bending argumentations. Sometimes he inserts standard scholastic contract law into new contexts, e.g. the law of war and peace. Sometimes he slightly alters the content of scholastic ideas themselves, as is the case with the concept of 'equality'. Also, Grotius' constant referring to Greco-Roman literature—a humanist habit which is even more salient in Pufendorf's discussion of just pricing and lesion—gives his text a seductive flavor which is often lacking in the scholastics' discourse.[1970] It would give him a serious competitive edge over the moral theologians in the struggle to be remembered by future generations of jurists *and* theologians.

7.8   Conclusion

The scholastics loathe gross disparity between what is given and received in contractual exchange. For several reasons, they insist that contracts should not amount to zero-sum games. The principle of equilibrium in exchange—which follows from Aristotle's and Thomas' emphasis on

---

quidem ut ex inaequalitate ius oriatur minus habenti. Haec aequalitas partim consistit in actibus, partim in eo de quo agitur; et in actibus, tum praecedaneis, tum principalibus.'

[1968] Grotius, *De jure belli ac pacis* (Ed. De Kanter-Van Hettinga Tromp – Feenstra – Persenaire), lib. 2, cap. 12, par. 9–13, p. 344–348.

[1969] See Decock, *Lessius and the breakdown of the scholastic paradigm*, p. 67–68.

[1970] This is particularly evident from Grotius' discussion of D. 4,4,16,4; cf. *De jure belli ac pacis* (Ed. De Kanter-Van Hettinga Tromp – Feenstra – Persenaire), lib. 2, cap. 12, par. 26, p. 356–358. Just like the scholastics, he acknowledges that there is a distinction between positive law (*ius gentium voluntarium*) and natural law when it comes to 'naturally allowing parties to outwit each other'. He repeats the scholastics' argument that positive law should prevent the courts from being overstretched, and is therefore allowed to tolerate un-virtuous behavior. Yet, in pointing out that 'naturally' is nothing to do with a possitive approval by natural law, but rather with widespread custom (*recepti moris est*), he cites a plethora of passages from Holy Scripture and from Greek and Roman poets meant to demonstrate that 'naturally' often figures in this sense in Latin texts.

the virtue of commutative justice—stipulates that exchange must not harm any of the contracting parties involved. Moreover, this Aristotelian-Thomistic tradition fits neatly into D. 1,1,10,1, singling out the do-no-harm principle as one of the three major precepts of Roman law. Lastly, the scholastics read these moral philosophical and juridical traditions against the Biblical background of the seventh commandment not to steal. As a result, they treat contract law principally in the light of unjust enrichment and restitution.

Although making generalizations is hazardous, it is fairly safe to claim that the early modern scholastics consider *laesio enormis* as an autonomous ground for the annulment of a contract.[1971] As an external limitation on 'freedom of contract', it cannot be reduced to one of the vices of the will. Hence, we find Arias Piñel stating that the remedy based on C. 4,44,2 is non-renunciable. Renunciation itself is seen as almost positive proof of exploitation of necessity. In principle, the mere discrepancy between the actual price and more than half of the just price is sufficient ground for the contract to be rescinded at the option of the *laedens* if the *laesus* brings a lawsuit against him in a secular or an ecclesiastical court by virtue of the *Lex secunda*. However, the strictest observance of the equality principle is required as a matter of conscience. The slightest deviation from the just price obliges the *laedens* to make restitution of the surplus value on pain of sin.

The age-long career of *laesio enormis* was possible because the scholastics saw in it the best means to protect contracting parties against exploitation of necessity. It required a conceptual framework that was lost in modern times. It is therefore important to recall that the 'just price' was not thought of as a kind of fixed and unchangeable metaphysical value. Generally speaking, the just price was thought of as the ordinary, fluctuating market price. This price was thought to guarantee justice in exchange insofar as it prevented the parties from exploiting each other's individual needs and appetites through personal hard bargaining. To be sure, economic liberalism as we know it since the ninenteenth century denies the existence of such an objective standard, since the value in a contract may also depend upon the purely subjective estimation of the contracting par-

---

[1971] This remains true in the French natural law tradition; see the excellent summary by Deroussin, *Histoire du droit des obligations*, p. 414–415.

ties themselves, not only upon that of the common estimation by other people in the market.[1972]

At least on a theoretical level, the clash between the alleged liberalism of Roman law and Christian morals is apparent. For example, D. 4,4,16,4 and its permission for contracting parties to try to outwit each other was seen in radical opposition to the Golden Rule (*lex naturalis*) that you do not do to others what you would not have done to you. Accordingly, interpretation as a means of neutralizing the moral menace of Roman law was practiced vigorously by the moral theologians. This conflict was confirmed in the struggle between the concurring jurisdictions of the 'soul' and the 'body'. While both the secular and the ecclesiastical courts would only grant a remedy against lesion beyond moiety, canonists and theologians alike were adamant that even lesion below moiety produced an obligation to make restitution in the court of conscience. Anxious for the souls of millions of people, Dr. Navarrus insisted that ecclesiastical judges also grant a remedy for lesion below moiety, since, as Augustine had put it, sin is not forgiven until restitution is made.

It should not necessarily be inferred from this that economic liberalism and scholastic contract law are fundamentally at odds with each other. Firstly, the just price allows of a certain latitude. According to scholastic business ethics, it pertains to commercial acumen precisely to exploit these differences across places and times. Moreover, contractors are allowed to negotiate a deviation from the common estimation in the market on the basis of a series of extrinsic titles. Understandably, these *causae*, particularly donation, cannot be presumed but must be stipulated expressly. The logic of gift is being neatly distinguished from the logic of the market. Otherwise the whole doctrine of just pricing would collapse. Thirdly, the scholastics recognize that the just price of a good can vary depending on the specific type of market. For example, they acknowledge that auctions or markets for luxury goods are steered by a logic of their own.

Lastly, in solving concrete cases, the scholastics tend to advocate confusingly liberal standpoints. Fairness in exchange turns out to be a rather flexible concept. Certainly the Jesuits appear to have gone to unseen lengths in defending industrious businessmen and avid speculators. At the same time, they were careful to delineate the market of professional contractors from exchange between professionals and invincibly weaker parties. There is a striking parallel here with the bipolar nature of

---

[1972] Zimmermann, *The law of obligations*, p. 264.

modern sales law, distinguishing as it does between consumer contracts and standard sales law. As a last remark, it might also strike one as rather counter-intuitive that, while the lasting influence of the scholastic doctrine of fairness in exchange on the Protestant natural lawyers is obvious, that does not prevent them from generally being considered the forerunners of economic liberalism.

CHAPTER EIGHT

THEOLOGIANS AND CONTRACT LAW: COMMON THEMES

Through a close reading of primary sources, the preceding chapters have explored how moral theologians developed substantive doctrines of contract. Taking their elaboration of a general law of contract as a starting point, we proceeded to consider the limitations that they recognized to the natural freedom of the parties to create contractual obligation according to their will. Those limitations derived from vices of the will, statutory form requirements, and the immoral nature of the object of the contract. A remedy was also given to re-balance overly one-sided bargains. Despite the great variety of opinions on almost every subject, and, accordingly, the problematic character of making sweeping generalizations, at this point the lawyerly abilities of the moral theologians should be beyond doubt. This ability is reflected not only in their astounding mastery of technical legal argument, but also in their commitment to finding the right balance between conflicting principles underlying contract law (freedom and justice), between the conflicting values promoted by rivalling institutions of power (Church and State),[1973] and between the opinions of Roman canon authorities and the voices of renewal (medieval and modern). This final chapter proposes to restate some of the major conclusions attained in this study through the lens of those conflicts.

[1973] As a cautionary remark, it needs to be pointed out that a genealogical study of the concept of the 'State' reveals that this term has hardly, if ever, been the subject of a unitary vision. Still, it has been argued, precisely, that the use of the term 'State' to denote a sovereign and absolute power became widespread by the end of the sixteenth century, not in the least under the influence of the early modern scholastics' discussions on *summa potestas*; cf. Q. Skinner, *The sovereign state, A genealogy*, in: H. Kalmo – Q. Skinner (eds.), Sovereignty in fragments, The past, present and future of a contested concept, Cambridge 2010, p. 27–29. See also A.S. Brett, *Scholastic political thought and the modern concept of the State*, in: A. Brett – J. Tully – H. Hamilton-Bleakley (eds.), Rethinking the foundations of modern political thought, Cambridge 2006, p. 130–148; A.S. Brett, *Changes of state, Nature and the limits of the city in early modern natural law*, Princeton 2011, p. 1–10.

8.1   Between freedom and justice

The history of the emergence of the principle that all agreements, however naked, are binding (*pacta quantumcumque nuda sunt servanda*) is
not without its ironies. If 'canon lawyers' such as Huguccio started advocating the enforceability of promises on moral grounds by the end of
the twelfth century, the truly juridical analysis of contractual obligation
was not completed until the beginning of the seventeenth century in the
work of 'moral theologians' such as Lessius.[1974] While Huguccio founded
contractual obligation on the equation of promises and oaths, and on
the sinfulness of violating promises, Lessius explained that the promisor
conveyed a right upon the promisee to enforce the obligation which he
incurred through the promise. In the eyes of the medieval 'canonist', contracts were binding because the promisor otherwise sinned against the
divine prohibition on lying and perjury. In the view of the early modern
'moral theologian', contracts were binding not merely because violating
promises is tantamount to sin, but primarily because the contracting parties establish a horizontal relationship of rights and obligations by virtue
of their mutual consent.

Regardless of the apparent irony—at least in the eyes of a contemporary readership[1975]—that sometimes 'canon lawyers' reasoned in a distinctly moral way and 'moral theologians' in a distinctly juridical way, the
victory of consensualism and the rise of a general category of contract can
be read as the moral transformation of the civilian tradition. The Roman
law was notoriously reluctant to enforce contracts by virtue of consent
alone, except in the case of a limited set of consensual contracts. Elsewhere, *causa* in the sense of *datio* or *factum* beyond consent was required,

---

[1974] Cf. supra p. 123–124 and p. 200–201.

[1975] The irony only holds, of course, if we stick to the conventional classification of
Huguccio as a canonist and Lessius as a moral theologian. In reality, though, those classi-
fications are modern and problematical if applied to the past. For one thing, the origins of
the disciplinary distinction between canon law and theology cannot be traced back earlier
than the eleventh century, but the boundaries between the two disciplines remain very
porous until at least the thirteenth century; cf. J. Gaudemet, *Théologie et droit canonique,
Les leçons de l'histoire*, Revue de droit canonique, 39 (1989), esp. p. 11–12, where he notes
that the Council of Trent and the 'second scholastic' offer particular examples of the
ongoing interconnectedness between canon law and theology. For another, it seems that
the sharp distinction between law, theology and morality is the legacy of the Reformation, particularly of early eighteenth-century Protestant natural lawyers such as Christian
Thomasius.

or, alternatively, a formalistic exchange of promises known as *stipulatio*.[1976]
It was not until the moral approach to contract law prevailed, that this
Roman formalism was radically undermined.[1977] Humanist jurists of the
sixteenth century such as Étienne Forcadel argued desperately for a return
to the Roman system. Yet the weight of generations of canonists eventually prevailed. They advocated consensualism as the best way to conform
the law of the land to divine moral principles. The trickle down from
natural law over canon law to civil law becomes visible in Giasone del
Maino's reflection that even in the civil courts contracts should be liable
to enforcement through evangelical denunciation, which was an extraordinary remedy traditionally intended as the ultimate means to enforce
Christian moral principles in the ecclesiastical courts.[1978]

As a matter of natural law and canon law, the foundation of contractual obligation is mutual consent. To express the simple idea that consent must be real and not mistaken, reference was made to the notion of
causa—different from the Roman concept but without any metaphysical connotation. Consent is sufficient for a natural obligation to arise out
of contract, as was already recognized by the Accursian gloss. The court
of conscience enforced those natural obligations without taking into
account the subtleties and the formalities of civil law. The ecclesiastical
courts readily acknowledged that they had to adopt this principle for the
sake of the salvation of souls, but they required the formal expression of
causa for probatory reasons. In 1568, Matthias van Wezenbeke insisted
that all agreements become enforceable also in the civil courts. In this
manner, he wished to bring civil jurisdiction in line with the dictates of
nature and conscience.[1979] To protect souls from sinning, he argued that
the civil court must adopt the regulations of the canon law in respect to
the bindingness of naked pacts. There was nothing novel about this. The
pressure for civil contract law to conform itself to the law of nature was
initiated already back in 1514 by the Spanish jurist Fortunius Garcia.[1980]

Before we go on to recapitulate the scholastics' amazingly rich view of
the fabric of contractual obligation, it is important to underline the moral
universe in which they operated. As a matter of fact, the Church would

---

[1976] Cf. supra, p. 108 and p. 130–142.

[1977] H. Hübner, *Subjektivismus in der Entwicklung des Privatrechts*, in: K. Luig (ed.),
Heinz Hübner, Rechtsdogmatik und Rechtsgeschichte, Ausgewählte Schriften, Köln e.a.
1997, p. 249.

[1978] Cf. supra, p. 113–114.

[1979] Cf. supra, p. 155–157.

[1980] Cf. supra, p. 158–160.

not have occupied itself with the bindingness of promises and contracts if this issue did not touch upon questions of faith and conscience, notably the salvation of souls (*salus animarum*).[1981] It is wise to keep this difference of perspective in mind. Otherwise, it is easy to conflate the transformation of contract during the early modern period with the victory of the will-theory of contract in the nineteenth century. This modern concept of contract, centered around the 'mystic of the will',[1982] was devoid of any moral content. For example, it despised the typically moral concern for contractual fairness. The moral theologians, or, for that matter, the canonists, would never have subscribed to the famous tenet of the nineteenth century will-theorists of 'who says contractual says just' (*qui dit contractuel dit juste*).[1983] For them, as well as for the subsequent natural lawyers, contractual obligation was not only ruled by the will of the parties, but also by the natural law principle of commutative justice.[1984]

The basis of contractual obligation was clearly thought of as resting on the will, but for the canonists and theologians, contractual exchange, just as other human behavior, was taking place in a moral universe. This world full of moral values where the will creatively lived out its freedom through contractual exchange was not thought of in terms of an obstacle to the individual's autonomy, but rather as its natural precondition.[1985] The will was considered to be its own legislator, but as a privately imposed law, a contract remained subject to higher laws such as the natural law principle that there should be an equilibrium between what is given and received in an exchange. Their notion of *dominium* is astoundingly liberal, but, for example, none of the theologians would have dared to say that man is the owner of his life. Hence, directly taking one's own life was strictly

---

[1981]   Calasso, *Il negozio giuridico*, p. 264.

[1982]   I. Birocchi, *Autonomia privata tra ordini e mercato, Leggendo Rolandino, Domat e Portalis*, in: F. Macario – M.N. Miletti, Tradizione civilistica e complessità del sistema, Valutazioni storiche e prospettive della parte generale del contratto, [Università degli studi di Foggia, Facoltà di Giurisprudenza, Dipartimento di scienze giuridiche privatistiche e pubblicistiche, 28], Milano 2006, p. 128.

[1983]   L. Rolland, *'Qui dit contractuel dit juste' (Fouillée)... en trois petits bonds, à reculons*, McGill Law Journal, 51 (2006), p. 765–780. Interestingly, the author shows how this adage, taken from Alfred Fouillée's (1838–1912) *La science sociale contemporaine* (Paris, 1880) has become the *adage par excellence* to illustrate the centrality of the autonomy of the will as a basic principle of contract law since the nineteenth century, while the socially minded Fouillée did not advocate such a principle altogether.

[1984]   Luig, *Vertragsfreiheit und Äquivalenzprinzip im gemeinen Recht und im BGB*, p. 171–206.

[1985]   Somma, *Autonomia privata*, p. 38; p. 51–52; p. 173–175; Birocchi, *Autonomia privata tra ordini e mercato*, p. 113.

forbidden,[1986] even though theologians such as Lessius would acknowledge that indirect ways of taking one's life could be admitted.[1987]

So, for all the striking parallels, thinking of the triumph of consensualism and the will in the writings of the moral theologians in terms of modern conceptions of the autonomy of the will might fall short of the broader, religious worldview in which they lived. It would be equally misleading, however, to read modern criticisms of 'freedom of contract' into the moral theological sources. Particularly deceptive are some of the historical reconstructions in the French Catholic jurist Emmanuel Gounot's (1885–1960) famous doctoral dissertation where he criticized the emergence of the principle of the autonomy of the will in French private law from the 1880s onward.[1988]

Incidentally, it is worthwhile noting that critical scholarship has confirmed that it was not until the end of the nineteenth century that a spirit of economic individualism and the autonomy of the will were read into the French *Code Civil*.[1989] Deroussin cites the opinion of tribunes Tarrible and Jaubert during the preparation of the *Code*, arguing that the conscience of the contracting parties should form the basis of the obligation and that the legislator should not ignore the rights derived from natural equity.[1990] Tribune Favart asserted that the laws of contract

---

[1986] Soto, *De iustitia et iure* (ed. fac. V. Diego Carro – M. González Ordóñez, vol. 2), lib. 4, quaest. 5, art. 1, p. 309, cited supra, n. 1270. Compare the observations on the impossibility of *dominium corporis et seminis* in Alfieri, *Nella camera degli sposi*, p. 287–289.

[1987] Lessius, *De iustitia et iure*, lib. 2, cap. 9, dub. 6 (*Utrum liceat se ipsum interficere*). The upshot of his argument, which is developed in dialogue with previous contributions on the topic by Vitoria, Dr. Navarrus and Justus Lipsius, is that it is illicit to commit suicide, since as a matter of the natural order (*ordo rerum naturalis*) only God is the master of human life, even if man is the master of life and death over all things that are inferior to him. Lessius allows for indirect suicide, however, by doing or omitting something that will indirectly lead to death. In reference to Lipsius it is worthwhile noting that Lessius and Lipsius were friends. Together they frequently went to visit the thermal baths of Spa, which were famous for their curative qualities; cf. W. Decock, *Leonardus Lessius, Biografie & Hygiasticon*, in: J. De Landtsheer – D. Sacré – C. Coppens (eds.), Justus Lipsius (1547–1606), Een geleerde en zijn Europese netwerk, Leuven 2006, p. 262–268.

[1988] E. Gounot, *Le principe de l'autonomie de la volonté en droit privé, Contribution à l'étude critique de l'individualisme juridique*, Paris 1912.

[1989] See V. Ranouil, *L'autonomie de la volonté, Naissance et évolution d'un concept*, [Travaux et recherches de l'Université de droit, d'économie et de sciences sociales de Paris, Série sciences historiques, 12], Paris 1980, p. 17–18, and Deroussin, *Histoire du droit des obligations*, p. 492–499.

[1990] Deroussin, *Histoire du droit des obligations*, p. 493. For an anthology of texts that illustrate the strong impact of conscience and natural law during the debates on the *Code Civil*, see *Naissance du Code civil, La raison du législateur, Travaux préparatoires du Code*

should be derived from conscience.[1991] The notion that, originally, there was widespread endorsement of a principle of unlimited party autonomy is false. This observation also applies to the development of German doctrines of private law in the nineteenth century. Scholars have pointed out that, generally speaking, the notion of a so-called 'original' principle of unlimited party autonomy in German contract law is a myth.[1992]

To return to Gounot, his analysis seems to have been compromised by his neo-Thomistic assumptions, which were not necessarily identical to the Thomistic principles of earlier times. He proposed that real contracts (*contractus re*), which are not enforceable until one of the parties has performed his obligation, should become the model of contract law in general. Gounot thought that this was the best way to guarantee contractual equilibrium.[1993] Gounot did not give the medieval tradition any credit for having contributed to the rise of 'freedom of contract'. Moreover, he opined that theirs was not a 'theory of the autonomy of the will but a theory of *causa*'. In Gounot's view, the doctrine of *causa* introduced the 'theory of the just objective'. *Causa*, according to Gounot, referred to the moral virtue of commutative justice.[1994]

Indeed, the last century witnessed a sudden feeling, presumably initiated by earlier, moralizing remarks on *cause* in Robert-Joseph Pothier's treatise *On obligations*,[1995] that the morality of contract must have something to do with that mysterious concept of *causa* expressed in art. 1108

---

civil rassemblés par P.A. Fenet, Extraits choisis et présentés sous la direction de François Ewald, Paris 2004, p. 337–364.

[1991] P.A. Fenet, *Recueil complet des travaux préparatoires du Code civil*, Paris 1836, vol. 13, p. 313: 'Le livre où il [le législateur] puise ses lois doit être la conscience; ce livre où tous les hommes trouvent le même langage quand la passion ne les aveugle pas.' Also cited in Foriers, *Espaces de liberté en droit des contrats*, p. 27, n. 5.

[1992] S. Hofer, *Freiheit ohne Grenzen? Privatrechtstheoretische Diskussionen im 19. Jahrhundert*, [Ius privatum, 53], Tübingen 2001, p. 1–4 ('Der Mythos von der grundsätzlich unbeschränkten Privatautonomie') and p. 276–277; S. Hofer, *Vertragsfreiheit am Schneideweg*, [Schriften der Juristischen Studiengesellschaft Regensburg, 29], München 2006; S. Hofer, *Die Diskussion um den Begriff 'Privat-Autonomie' in der ersten Hälfte des 19. Jahrhunderts*, in: P. Collin – G. Bender – S. Ruppert – M. Seckelmann – M. Stolleis (eds.), Selbstregulierung im 19. Jahrhundert—zwischen Autonomie und staatlichen Steuerungsansprüchen, [Studien zur europäischen Rechtsgeschichte, 259; Moderne Regulierungsregime, 1], Frankfurt am Main 2011, p. 63–84.

[1993] Gounot, *Le principe de l'autonomie de la volonté en droit privé*, p. 402–404. For a discussion, see Ranouil, *L'autonomie de la volonté*, p. 144–149.

[1994] Gounot, *Le principe de l'autonomie de la volonté en droit privé*, p. 413–414.

[1995] Gazzaniga, *Domat et Pothier, Le contrat à la fin de l'Ancien Régime*, p. 41.

of the *Code Civil*.[1996] As Italo Birocchi observed, Jean-Étienne-Marie Portalis (1746–1807) introduced the element of *cause* in the *Code Napoléon* (art. 1108) as an element of control and protection against the lapse of contractual liberty.[1997] In this respect, it is not surprising to find that Gounot articulated the particular moral concerns that he felt through the concept of *cause*. However, one should keep in mind that, contrary to the recent, particularly confusing semantic evolution of the concept of *cause*, *causa* in the moral theological literature tells us very little about the morality of contract law. One has a hard time finding a reference to the concept in the writings of the moral theologians, in the first place, and it was definitely not the subject of much debate.[1998] This need not come as a surprise. The moral theologians did not need to bring in an external concept that would enable them to 'control' contractual freedom from an external, moral point of view. In their view, there was no opposition between contract and morality. For them, willing the immoral was as contradictory as willing the impossible. Fairness and other moral principles in matters of

---

[1996] E.g. H. Capitant, *De la cause des obligations (contrats, engagements unilatéraux, legs)*, Paris 1923. Interestingly, Capitant mentioned in his foreword that some of his famous predecessors (e.g. Laurent, Planiol and Dabin) had not arrived at a uniform understanding of *cause* in art. 1108 and 1131–1133 Cod. Civ. He expressed his dissatisfaction at the fact that, generally speaking, they had reduced this notion to something irrelevant, inconsistent and artificial, which could not be neatly distinguished from the object of the contract or the agreement of wills of the parties. Apparently, one of the main reasons that drove Capitant into a search for the true meaning of *cause* in the text of the *Civil code* was his concern that legal doctrine had to be brought in line with the decisions of the courts. The courts had elaborated the concept of *cause* through a great number of decisions, Capitant observed, and importantly, he believed that court decisions are always in line with the original sense of the Civil Code (*la jurisprudence est traditionaliste comme la doctrine; elle n'invente rien*; p. xi). Hence, Capitant reasoned that the courts of the early twentieth century could tell us something about the original meaning of *cause*. He then claimed that this jurisdictional development in the meaning of *cause* was a return to the original meaning of *causa* as it was found in Domat. The meaning of *causa* in Domat is disputed, though, and the quest for the meaning of *cause* in the French Civil Code remains an inexhaustible source of speculation even for the brightest minds; e.g. V. Forray, *Le consensualisme dans la théorie générale du contrat*, [Bibliothèque de droit privé, 480], Paris 2007, p. 373–439. In a spirit that recalls Gounot, Forray claims that *cause* is the instrument allowing the re-equilibration of the economic values in the contract. Forray asserts that the present conception of *cause* means a rupture with the chief source of inspiration of the consensualist theory of contract, namely the natural law tradition (p. 438). We could not agree more.

[1997] Birocchi, *Autonomia privata tra ordini e mercato*, p. 130.

[1998] It may be recalled that *causa* in the moral theological literature refers simply to the absence of mistake and the presence of sufficient consent in a contract; e.g. supra, n. 537 (Sylvester), n. 541 (Lessius), and n. 583 (Gómez). Even the final cause of the contract was considered irrelevant to the juridical validity or invalidity of the contract, cf. n. 1408 (Oñate).

exchange were thought to be part and parcel of any contract. This symbiosis of freedom and morality was destroyed in modern times. Presumably, this evolution urged jurists who felt that morality should be of concern in contracts to bring moral values in from outside the formal Text of the law and then read them into art. 1108 of the *Code*.

In light of the perceived tensions between socialist, moral and liberal approaches to contract law in contemporary scholarship, one might be surprised to find that the Catholic moral theologians of the past argued in favor of a general principle of consensualism without seeing any contradiction between respect for the will of the contracting parties and the observation of commutative justice. These principles were thought to be complementary. The theologians went to great lengths to affirm 'freedom of contract'. At the same time, they gave extensive range to the principle of commutative justice. They unambiguously located the source of contractual obligation in the will and not in an abstract notion of justice. This point merits attention, because recent histories of the rise of 'freedom of contract' have tended to see this evolution in terms of a departure from concerns about justice in exchange. The triumph of contract in the nineteenth century is considered to coincide with the defeat of 'the belief that the justification of contractual obligation is derived from the inherent justice or fairness of an exchange'.[1999] Furthermore, Horwitz claimed that the modern jurists and judges stated 'for the first time' that the source of contractual obligation 'is the convergence of the wills of the contracting parties'.[2000] This suggests that 'freedom of contract', and, for that matter, the rise of modern capitalism, are incompatible with fairness in exchange. Even if this was true in the particular historical experience of the United States and Great Britain, we feel reluctant to apply this broad frame of analysis, regardless of its intrinsic merits, to the particular case of scholastic contract doctrine.

The moral theologians were concerned about fairness in exchange and about the individual's autonomy to freely dispose of his property. Moreover, the moral theologians may have provided the ultimate moral legitimation of the global commercial market economy, which was flourishing right before their eyes. In a stimulating article, Marti Koskenniemi has argued that the real and lasting legacy of the Spanish theologians consists in their capacity to be the 'articulators and ideologists of a global

---

[1999] Horwitz, *The transformation of American law*, p. 160.
[2000] Horwitz, *The transformation of American law*, p. 160.

structure of horizontal relationships between holders of the subjective rights of *dominium*—a structure of human relationships that we have been accustomed to label 'capitalism'.[2001] Indeed, reading the early modern theologians as the architects of an 'empire of private law' does not make for an implausible narrative. It does not contradict the primary sources. Although a thorough-going analysis of the moral theologians' conception of *dominium* falls outside the scope of this study, we have seen them explicitly conceiving of contract as the instrument to exchange property. What is more, 'freedom of contract', in their view, rests on the basic freedom of the *dominus* to do with his property as he likes. Let us recall the brilliant synthesis by Pedro de Oñate, who, incidentally, was very actively involved in the Spanish missions in South-America:[2002]

> Consequently, natural law, canon law and Hispanic law entirely agree, and innumerable difficulties, frauds, litigations and disputes have been removed thanks to such great consensus and clarity in the laws. To the contracting parties, liberty (*libertas*) has very wisely been restored, so that whenever they want to bind themselves through concluding a contract about their goods (*de rebus suis*), this contract will be recognized by whichever of both courts [i.e. the civil or the ecclesiastical court] before which they will have brought their case and it will be upheld as being sacrosanct and inviolable. Therefore, canon law and Hispanic law correct the *ius commune*, since the former grant an action and civil obligation to all bare agreements, while the latter denied them just that.

Property rights are the basis and foundation of contractual exchange (*dominium basis fundamentumque omnium contractuum*), to use Soto's famous words.[2003] Vitoria and Bañez discussed contract law in the context of the exchange of *dominium* by virtue of the will of the *dominus*. Molina explained that the goal of his treatment of contract law was to elucidate the extent to which *dominium* was transferred or not through the will of the contracting parties.[2004] Pushing the proto-liberal tendencies in the sixteenth-century moral theologians to their radical conclusion, Oñate claimed that the will was the sole measure of contractual obligation, citing, amongst other authoritative sources, the Roman maxim that everybody is moderator and arbiter of his own things. More powerful, still, was his appeal to man's being created in God's image, and, consequently,

---

[2001] Koskenniemi, *Empire and international law*, p. 32.
[2002] Oñate, *De contractibus*, tom. 1, tract. 1, disp. 2, sect. 5, num. 166, p. 40. Cited supra, n. 3.
[2003] Cited supra, n. 591 and n. 1203.
[2004] Cited supra, n. 587.

man's *dominium* over the goods of the world and his actions. From this he inferred that God had granted man the freedom to bind himself when and where he wanted. Man could enter into contractual obligation when he wanted and in whatever way he wanted. If not, Oñate literally said, man could not be considered the true and perfect owner of this good.[2005]

Since the will is the foundation of contractual obligation, the intention to bind oneself contractually (*animus obligandi*) is the first requirement for promises to be binding. A mere proposal, plan or indicative statement about future actions was not considered to be a promise. However, moral theologians disagreed over the question whether reliance on an external declaration, which was perceived to be a binding promise, should sometimes prevail over the real will of the promisor.[2006] Tomás Sánchez argued from a voluntaristic standpoint that 'promissary obligation arises out of a private law which the promisor imposes upon himself, but no law is binding unless the legislator intends it to be binding.' Under exceptional circumstances, though, he left room for liability on the grounds of what we would now call 'torts law'.[2007] At the opposite end of the spectrum, we find Gabriel Vázquez, who advocated a radical declaration theory of contractual obligation.[2008] A compromise was reached by Leonardus Lessius, whose argumentation is a harbinger of the contemporary notion of the trust theory of contractual obligation. In Lessius' view, the trust that underlies contractual exchange (*fides contractuum*) will crumble if promisors can withdraw themselves by claiming that they made a fictitious promise.[2009] Also, to protect the reliance of the promisee, Lessius argued that doubtful promises must be interpreted to be valid.

The necessity of the exteriorization and the acceptance of the promise, which the *communis opinio* eventually regarded as the second and third requirement in the formation of contractual obligation, was subject to substantial debate. According to Molina, the inner promise itself was sufficient to create natural obligation. Molina considered the outward expression of the promise and its acceptance by the promisee to be merely instrumental.[2010] Lessius, on the other hand, considered acceptance

---

[2005] Cited supra, n. 608.
[2006] Not surprisingly, this debate rages on in contemporary contract law; cf. J. Smits, *Het vertrouwensbeginsel en de contractuele gebondenheid, Beschouwingen omtrent de dogmatiek van het overeenkomstenrecht*, Arnhem 1995, esp. p. 189–200.
[2007] Cited supra, p. 194.
[2008] Cited supra, n. 693.
[2009] Cited supra, n. 697.
[2010] Cited supra, n. 653.

necessary for the creation of contractual obligation, even in conscience, since he was concerned about giving the promisor the opportunity to revoke his promise (*ius poenitendi*). Therefore, Lessius regarded the acceptance by the promisee as a *conditio sine qua non* that was naturally inherent in both gratuitous and onerous promises.[2011] Moreover, Lessius argued that the exterior signification of a promise was constituitive of the natural obligation. Contractual exchange is a social phenomenon that takes place between men who, unlike God and the angels, cannot perceive the *animus obligandi* of the promisor without communication. According to Lessius, language does not merely convey intention, it contributes to the very creation of that which it signifies.[2012]

Compared with the original idea behind the enforceability of promises, namely that God expects promises to have the same binding force as oaths, Lessius' argument exemplifies the turn towards a more horizontal, social approach to contractual promises. This is something to keep in mind when we address the question concerning what kind of obligation or debt is produced by an accepted promise. Importantly, Thomas Aquinas had distinguished between moral debt and legal debt.[2013] Relationships involving moral debt were thought to be ruled by virtues annexed to justice, such as truth, whereas legal debt was governed by the virtue of justice itself. In the early sixteenth century, Cardinal Cajetan claimed that contractual obligation pertained merely to moral debt. In his view, keeping promises was a matter of honesty, fidelity and truth, but not of justice. Throughout the early modern period, Cajetan would draw heavy criticism for this 'moral' approach to contractual obligation.[2014] As Soto pointed out, promising is not simply a matter of truth, but of commutative justice.[2015] Lessius insisted that all contractual obligations are binding as a matter of justice. Promising entails the transfer of a legal right of enforcement to the promisee (*promittere ius illi tribuere ad exigendum*).[2016]

[2011] Cited supra, n. 681.

[2012] Cited supra, n. 659.

[2013] Explained supra, p. 197–198.

[2014] Curiously enough, though, it is not uncommon to find, even in some of the finest secondary literature on the subject, the claim according to which the moral theologians founded the enforceability of contractual obligation on the 'moral duty of truth and fidelity'. Cf. *inter alia* Wieacker, *Die vertragliche Obligation bei den Klassikern des Vernunftrechts*, p. 16 and p. 21. Those studies may have been misled by an exclusive focus on Cajetan or on the original grounds for enforcing naked pacts in the canon law tradition.

[2015] Cited supra, n. 709.

[2016] Cited supra, n. 710.

It may be concluded that contract was conceived of as the voluntary creation of mutually corresponding legal rights and obligations by the majority of the moral theologians. Still, two potential sources of confusion merit attention. First of all, the question of what determines the character of contractual obligation. The common opinion, represented by Molina, was that the sole will of the promisor was the criterion to decide whether a promise was meant to bind either legally or morally (*pendet ex animo promittentis*).[2017] Lessius, on the other hand, espoused the less common idea that, occasionally, objective circumstances surrounding the promissory declaration needed to be taken into account to protect the promisee's reliance.[2018] The second point worth remembering is the status of gratuitous contracts. Against Soto, but relying on Summenhart, Jesuits such as Molina and Lessius insisted that the obligation brought about by a gratuitous promise bound the promisor legally. Even though they acknowledged that entering a gratuitous contract was a matter of liberality, the obligation resulting from it was regarded as juridically enforceable.[2019]

The differences between the nineteenth century will-theory of contract and the moral theologians' focus on the will as the source of contractual obligation become clear in regard to their analysis of what are known to be the 'vices of the will'. The theologians were divided on whether duress vitiated consent or not. Molina and Rebelo claimed that duress automatically avoided the contract since it vitiated consent. The weight of both Roman law and the Aristotelian-Thomistic tradition, however, impeded the majority of the theologians as well as Grotius from seeing duress exclusively in terms of lack of consent. As Sánchez pointed out, coerced consent does not undermine true consent and true volition (*in consensu metu extorto est verus consensus veraque voluntas*).[2020] Furthermore, classical canon law was cited to argue that contracts affected by duress are voidable at the option of the coerced party rather than void *ipso facto*.[2021] Lessius explained that the party suffering from coerced consent was granted this remedy as a matter of 'tort law' (*iniuria*) and not by virtue of vitiated contractual consent.[2022] Faced with the apparently different regulation in marriage contracts—which were declared void *ab initio* if

---

[2017] Cited supra, n. 719.
[2018] Cited supra, n. 696.
[2019] Cited supra, n. 622.
[2020] Cited supra, n. 899.
[2021] Notably canon *Abbas*, cited on p. 219.
[2022] Cf. supra, p. 270–271.

effected by duress—Sánchez and Lessius said that this discrepancy was merely introduced by positive law.

The debate on how mistake vitiated contractual consent was conditioned to an even higher degree by both the complex Roman canon law on mistake and the subtle doctrine of voluntariness in the Aristotelian-Thomistic tradition. Some argued that mistake did not have the power to vitiate consent automatically, even though Roman law held that *contractus bonae fidei* were avoided *ipso facto* by mistake.[2023] They inferred this conclusion from the existence of a specific remedy to have *contractus stricti iuris* affected by *dolus* declared null by a judge. Others, though, argued that mistake at least if it was fundamental, did vitiate voluntary consent from the outset. They relied upon the philosophical tradition to make this conclusion. However, this conclusion was difficult to reconcile with the moral and canon law principle that the law must protect the deceived party and not the deceiver. The conundrum was solved by Lessius. He blurred the distinction between contracts of good faith and contracts of strict law and introduced a general regime of nullity at the option of the mistaken party (*pro arbitrio eius qui deceptus est irritari potest*).[2024] He arrived at this conclusion by combining elements of both 'torts' (*iniuria*) and contract law. In this way, he even realized the wish expressed in canon law that the regulation of duress and mistake should be identical.

The intricate discussion on mistake allows us to make a short digression into the notion of good faith (*bona fides*). If Christian morality has had any influence on the shaping of modern contract law, then it is generally thought to be through the notion of good faith.[2025] Although there is no reason to call this conventional belief into question, one might be surprised to find how little reference is made to good faith in the moral theological literature on contracts. Perhaps this is just another example of human beings not feeling the need to express the most basic assumptions that underlie their ways of living and thinking, much as fish are unaware

---

[2023] Illustrated supra, p. 314–315.

[2024] Cited supra, n. 1091.

[2025] There is an abundant literature on this subject, which is reviewed in Stolfi, *Bonae fidei interpretatio*, p. 173–189. The notions of *Treu und Glauben* in par. 242 BGB, and *bonne foi* in art. 1134, al. 3 Cod. Civ., which are indebted to the Roman notion of *bona fides*, are discussed by R. Zimmermann and S. Whittaker, *Good faith in European contract law, Surveying the legal landscape*, in: R. Zimmermann – S. Whittaker (eds.), Good faith in European contract law, [The Common Core of European Private Law, Cambridge Studies in International and Comparative Law, 14], Cambridge 2000, p. 18–31 and p. 32–39, respectively.

of the water in which they live.[2026] Yet it has already been pointed out
that in late medieval jurisprudence the concept of 'good faith' is mainly
brought to bear on the acquisition or loss of property through the prescriptive effects of possession in good or bad faith.[2027] In fact, one of the
most interesting expositions on good faith can be found in Covarruvias'
Relectio ad regulam Possessor. To resolve the apparent tension between
the Roman distinction of contracts *bonae fidei* and *stricti iuris*, on the
one hand, and the general Christian duty of good faith, on the other,
Covarruvias explained that 'good faith' had two meanings.[2028] Good faith
in the sense of sincerity is universally required in contracts, while good
faith in the Roman distinction of contracts says something about the
scope or lack of scope for equitable interpretation of contractual obligation by the judge.

The requirement of good faith leads us to the most distinctly 'moral'
element of the theologians' contract law: the virtue of justice in exchange.
It needs to be recalled that the use of modern notions of 'justice' is not
conducive to gaining a better understanding in scholastic contract law of
the early modern period. Still, there is no doubt that the virtue of commutative justice added a moral dimension to contractual exchange which
goes well beyond the focus on the will by nineteenth century will theorists of contract.[2029] To put it another way, the moral theologians would
have accepted that the judge corrected one-sided contracts. The will-
theorists, on the other hand, held parties to their contracts, no matter how
unfair they seemed.[2030] They embraced Joseph Story's famous dictum that
whether bargains are profitable or unprofitable are considerations not for
courts of justice but for the parties themselves to deliberate upon.[2031]

The basic grammar and vocabulary that enabled the theologians to
articulate their moral crusade against 'unconscionable contracts' centered

---

[2026] See the ordinary gloss and Pierre de Belleperche's argument that, obviously, the
Roman category of contracts of strict law should not make us believe that those contracts
did not have to be performed in good faith. The contracts of good faith are so called
because they are characterized by a superabundance of good faith; cf. supra, n. 961.

[2027] Wijffels, *La bonne foi en droit savant médiéval*, p. 26.

[2028] Cf. supra, p. 290–297.

[2029] This remains true of Catholic social doctrine; cf. Pope Leo XIII, *Rerum novarum*,
par. 34: 'Subest tamen semper aliquid ex iustitia naturali, idque libera paciscentium voluntate maius et antiquius.', in: G. Antonazzi (ed.), *L'enciclica Rerum novarum, Testo autentico
e redazioni preparatorie dai documenti originali*, Roma 1957, p. 151, l. 1489–1491.

[2030] Lobban, *Contract*, p. 297.

[2031] Cf. supra, n. 1666.

around the notions of justice in exchange (*iustitia commutativa*), just or equal pricing (*iustum seu aequale pretium*) and lesion beyond moiety (*laesio enormis*). Commutative justice was considered to be an inviolable, natural law principle governing contractual exchange:[2032]

> Given the division of things, natural law suddenly sneaked in again, order-ing that natural equity be observed in these exchanges. It prescribed, not only that you should not do unto others what you would not have them do unto you, but also that equality be observed between the objects of these exchanges, as is required by commutative justice. Natural law further pre-scribed that equality must be restored through restitution if it has been violated; also, that agreements, once concluded, must be performed with great fidelity, and that infringers must be restrained through appropriate penalties.

The reason why contracts must not suffer from gross disparity, is that con-tracts were introduced for the sake of the mutual benefit of the contract-ing parties (*in commune bonum aequaleque commodum*).[2033] Equilibrium or 'equality' between what was given and received in contractual exchange was thought to be a natural law imperative which found its expression in the seventh commandment not to steal and in the do-no-harm principle of the renowned title *De iustitia et iure* of the Roman Digest. Furthermore, the theologians gave an extensive interpretation to the Roman rule that nobody should be enriched at the expense of another person as a matter of natural law (*iure naturae aequum est neminem cum alterius detrimento fieri locupletiorem*).[2034] In this sense, it can readily be argued that the busy, complex, and extremely vast territory of contractual exchange was carefully examined by the theologians through the lens of unjust enrich-ment and restitution. In Thomistic vocabulary, restitution was the act of commutative justice through wich contractual equilibrium was restored, or, alternatively speaking, unjust enrichment undone.

If parties who had enriched themselves at the expense of another failed to make restitution, they jeopardised the salvation of their souls, accord-ing to the absolutely fundamental statement of Augustine that remis-sion of sins is impossible as long as restitution of 'stolen' goods has not been made.[2035] Clearly, commutative justice and restitution were serious

---

[2032] Oñate, *De contractibus*, tom. 1, tract. 1, disp. 1pr., num. 10, p. 2. Cited supra, n. 1682.
[2033] Cf. supra, n. 1674.
[2034] Cf. supra, p. 515.
[2035] Cf. supra, n. 1696.

matters for theologians, as well as for many Christian businessmen in the early modern period, if the busy consultancy practices of the confessors are reliable testimony. One should not infer from this, however, as many interpreters have mistakenly done in the wake of Thomasius, that the moral theologians thought of value and price in 'objective' or 'metaphysical' terms. The 'just' value of a good or product was not based either on the nature of the thing itself or on the labor of the seller. The theologians unanimously agreed that the standard of value in the economic realm is utility. This is expressed through the common estimation of the people, or, the market price. However, because it is not licit to sell what is not yours, one should never take into account the particular utility of the other party to the contract.[2036] This is a fundamental difference between scholastic just pricing and the modern conception of free bargaining.

The moral theologians' remarkable insight into the mechanisms that underlie the formation of a market price need not be recalled here. Soto's, or, for that matter, Lessius' analysis of the market price for sexual services speaks for itself.[2037] The theologians' discussion of contracts for paid intercourse is a fine example of their preoccupation with restitution and unjust enrichment. The question whether a contract with an immoral object can produce contractual remedies remained a thorny issue. But the moral theologians shared a commitment to protect the financial interests of prostitutes. Motivated by the same Christian concern to prevent exploitation in contractual exchange in general, the jurist Arias Piñel declared void all renunciations of the remedy for the relief of lesion. Generally speaking, the moral theologians advocated a remedy for lesion beyond half the price (*laesio enormis*) in the external courts and a remedy for every deviation from the just price, also below moiety, in the court of conscience. Judges in the external court were urged to conform as much as possible to the rules of conscience. Yet that did not prevent the moral theologians from accepting the fact that the secular realm should also be allowed to function according to its own logic. Suárez argued that civil law cannot be expected to forbid anything that goes against moral perfection.[2038]

[2036] Cf. supra, n. 1726.
[2037] Cf. supra, particularly chapters 6.4.2.2, 6.5.1 and 6.5.7.
[2038] Suárez, *Tractatus de legibus et legislatore Deo*, lib. 3, cap. 12, num. 12, p. 219.

8.2   Between Church and State

The Frisian Joachim Hopper, a student of Gabriel Mudaeus (1500–1560),[2039] reflected upon the conflicting regulations in the canon law and the civil law in his dissertation of 1553, which marked one of the apogees of humanist legal scholarship at the University of Leuven. Besides singling out the areas of the law where the disparity between the canon law and the civil law was most apparent, Hopper asked himself why these great bodies of law were divided on so many points. He concluded that they stemmed from a different approach toward the same highest good (*ex diversa summi boni consideratione*).[2040] In domains such as the law of naked pacts, contracts benefitting third-parties, and spurious children, the diversity had to be ascribed to a different conception of 'nature' as the ultimate benchmark and the highest good of the law.[2041] While the civil law adopted the rules stemming from the analysis of nature in its corrupted state (*natura corrupta et depravata*), the canon law was modelled

---

[2039] On the role played by Gabriel Van der Muyden (Mudaeus) from Brecht in spreading legal humanism at the University of Leuven, see Brants, *La faculté de droit de l'Université de Louvain à travers cinq siècles*, *Étude historique*, p. 13–16; p. 113–117; Dekkers, *Het humanisme en de rechtswetenschap in de Nederlanden*, p. 97–143. R. Robaye, *Tradition et humanisme à la Faculté des Lois de Louvain vers 1550, Un initiateur, Gabriel Mudée*, Les Études Classiques, 54 (1986), p. 47–57; J. Papy, *Recht uit Brecht, De Leuvense hoogleraar Gabriel Mudaeus (1500–1560) als Europees humanist en jurist*, Academische lezing naar aanleiding van de 450ste verjaardag van het overlijden van Gabriel Mudaeus, Brecht 2011; J. Papy, *Recht uit Brecht, De Leuvense hoogleraar Gabriel Mudaeus (1500–1560) als Europees humanist en jurist*, Catalogus van de tentoonstelling in het Kempisch Museum Brecht, 31 maart–15 mei 2011, Brecht 2011, p. 13–106.

[2040] Joachim Hopper, *De iuris arte*, lib. 2, p. 158: 'Et sane quod tanta videtur iuris pontificalis et civilis hodie differentia, ex nullo penitus alio proficiscitur, quam ex diversa summi boni consideratione.'

[2041] Characteristically, Hopper remains irritatingly vague about his concept of 'nature' as the divine and highest good, although his account is replete with Stoic and Platonic references. In the canonical tradition, represented, for instance, by Étienne de Tournai (1128–1203), the equation of 'nature' with God (*natura id est Deus*) is a commonplace; cf. Cortese, *La norma giuridica*, vol. 1, p. 45.

Hopper further mentions that the civil goods, namely good health, beauty, power and money, as well as the spiritual goods, namely the virtues of justice, temperance, fortitude and prudence, should ultimately be directed toward the supreme good or God. Hopper also maintains that in the case of the laws of marriage, concubinage, divorce, oaths, usury and testate solemnities, the discrepancy was the result of the use of different, conflicting authoritative texts by the canonists and the civilians, respectively; cf. *De iuris arte*, lib. 2, p. 156–157.

on pure nature (*natura simpliciter*). In Hopper's quite literary, Biblical and Platonic words:[2042]

> One should not ignore that the inspection of the highest and primordial good is twofold. The one is simple, pure, sincere and free from the admixture of any other good. The other is neither pure, nor clear, but troubled as it were by smoke and clouds. It often occurs that what is established in view of the one seems to collide with and dissent from what is made with respect to the other, even though, in fact, they are not at odds altogether, as can be understood from the example of the Mosaic and the Evangelical laws.

The mere title of the chapter in which Hopper treated the apparent mismatch between canon and civil law, namely *On the direction of laws to their ultimate end* (*De directione legum ad ultimum finem*) recalls the wonderful treatise on the ultimate end of canon and civil law by that other sixteenth-century *doctor utriusque iuris*, Fortunius Garcia. Both jurists remind us of the teleological nature of jurisprudence that was typical of the *ius commune* and continued well into the modern age.[2043] It may require an effort of imagination for the modern reader to come to grips with the transcendent concepts of truth, justice, and the final end of all human business—legislation included. But these notions are essential to understand the mission of Fortunius' and Hopper's colleagues in the faculties of theology. If the *summum bonum* did not manifest itself clearly enough to the secular legislators, then it was the task of the moral theologians to hold a mirror up to nature in its simple, pure, and sincere form.

As has been pointed out on several occasions, one should remain careful in making generalizations. The sixteenth century, in particular, witnessed the clash of the 'old' and the 'new', so that it is not unusual to find a plethora of diverging opinions on almost every subject. To cite a famous example that was alluded to before, Dr. Navarrus reprehended

---

[2042] Hopper, *De iuris arte*, lib. 2, p. 157–158: 'Sed iam illud non oportet ignorare, duplicem esse summi primique boni inspectionem. Unam quidem simplicem puram, synceram, et ab omni aliarum rerum admistione seiunctam. Alteram vero, nec puram, nec apertam, sed quibusdam quasi fumis et nubeculis adspersam. Fitque saepenumero, ut quae unius intuitu constituuntur, cum iis, quae alterius respectu fiunt, pugnare ac dissidere videantur, licet reapse tamen nullo modo discrepent, quemadmodum ex Mosaicis et Evangelicis legibus licet intelligere.' The example refers to the fundamental unity of the Old Testament and the New Testament despite their seeming divergences.

[2043] Cortese, *La norma giuridica*, vol. 1, p. 90–96. This also explains the fundamental role of the judge's *arbitrium* in the *ius commune* to safeguard the objective values of justice, truth, and equity—the ultimate standards or ends to which any Christian legal system must aspire; see M. Meccarelli, *Arbitrium, Un aspetto sistematico degli ordinamenti giuridici in età di diritto comune*, Milano 1998, e.g. p. 15.

'the otherwise extremely learned' Fortunius for his lack of precision in discussing the final end of canon law and civil law, respectively.[2044] Making a sharp distinction between the natural and the supernatural dimensions of life and power, Dr. Navarrus insisted that the principal aim of all secular laws was dictated solely by the need for the lay authorities to guarantee a happy, safe and tranquil life on earth. Only in an indirect sense could one say that the canon law and the civil law shared a common conception of the *summum bonum*. For example, because God created nature, or because natural reason was the reference point for the lay legislator.

The assumption that a natural and objective order exists, which is rooted in God's eternal plan for the world (*lex aeterna*), is not insignificant to understand the gradual development from the closed Roman system of contracts to the general principle that all consensual agreements are binding.[2045] In 'simple nature', we find the ultimate criterion to which human activity is bound. As was already recognized by the jurists of the *ius commune*, natural law is the ultimate reference point for all human legislation.[2046] Its light shines on human legislation and drives away the clouds that spoil the view of true nature. To cite Baldus de Ubaldis, this light comes from the sacred art of jurisprudence, and, even more so from theology, to which the sacred laws are subordinated (*leges soli theologiae ancillantes*).[2047] These laws rule and regulate the souls of men (*regulant et regunt hominum animas*). They illuminate life in the inferior spheres so that men are brought closer to the superior life and the participation in God.[2048] Driven by the desire to implement justice in this

---

[2044] Azpilcueta's critical assessment of Fortunius Garcia in his own small treatise on the final end of the laws has been briefly referred to, supra, p. 98–100. See also Azpilcueta, *Relectio in cap. Novit de iudiciis*, not. 3, num. 90–91, f. 70r.

[2045] On the importance of the *lex aeterna*, 'denoting the plan of God directing all things and actions of the world towards an end', for understanding the pre-modern doctrines of natural law, see M. Scattola, *Before and after natural law, Models of natural law in ancient and modern times*, in: T.J. Hochstrasser – P. Schröder (eds.), Early modern natural law theories, Contexts and strategies in the early Enlightenment, [International archives of the history of ideas, 186], Dordrecht 2003, p. 6–7.

[2046] O. Condorelli, *Ius e lex nel sistema del diritto comune (secoli XIV–XV)*, in: A. Fidora – M. Lutz-Bachmann – A. Wagner (eds.), *Lex* and *Ius*, Essays on the foundation of law in medieval and early modern philosophy, [Politische Philosophie und Rechtstheorie des Mittelalters und der Neuzeit, Series 2, Studies, 1], Stuttgart 2010, p. 39.

[2047] This citation is borrowed from A. Padovani, *The metaphysical thought of late medieval jurisprudence*, in: A. Padovani – P. Stein (eds.), The jurists' philosophy of law from Rome to the seventeenth century, [A treatise of legal philosophy and general jurisprudence, 7], Dordrecht – New York 2007, p. 72–73, n. 100–101.

[2048] The moral framework of Baldus' legal thinking as well as his concern with natural law and the salvation of the soul are highlighted in J. Canning, *The political thought of*

transcendental sense into the secular legal order, we find Fortunius Garcia
stating in 1514:[2049]

> It is therefore firmly and singularly established that today we shall have in
> both courts a right of action by virtue of a bare agreement (*in utroque foro
> hodie ex pacto nudo habebimus ius agendi*). For since the civil law showed
> itself negligent in regard to the justice of bare agreements, because it omit-
> ted them, the principle of canon law steps in, which (as I believe) has to be
> observed also in the secular court. Through this rule, justice will be done in
> agreements.

About fifty years later, the principle that naked pacts are enforceable in
the civil courts was confirmed by Matthias van Wezenbeke, another pupil
of Gabriel Mudaeus. Sharing the moral and teleological understanding
of law typical of Fortunius and Hopper, he argued that the civil law of
contract had to model itself on canon law to protect the citizens from
sinning against conscience and natural equity. It may be inferred from
this that the transformative path of the *ius commune* was thought to run
from natural law through canon law to civil law.[2050] To cite Raymond Lull
(c. 1232–1315), 'as a rule, positive law has to be reduced to natural law and
made concordant with it' (*ius positivum ad ius naturale reducatur et cum
ipso concordet*).[2051] The natural law shines at full strength in the court of
conscience, for its radiant light to permeate, first of all, the ecclesiastical courts, and, second, the civil courts. This process of transformation
of the civilian tradition has been slow, bumpy, and limited. Indeed, it
took a couple of centuries for the light of the divine nature to reach the
civil courtrooms in contractual affairs. For example, despite his sharing

---

Baldus de Ubaldis, [Cambridge studies in medieval life and thought, 6], Cambridge 1987,
p. 154–158.

[2049] Cf. supra, n. 420 and n. 575.

[2050] The claim that the civil laws should be corrected by the canon law is well-known;
cf. Glossa *Ambitionis* ad C.1,2,12,1 in *Corporis Iustinianei Codex* (ed. Gothofredi), tom. 5,
col. 35: 'Succumbit ergo lex canoni ubi est ei contraria'. This sounds typically medieval. It
is probably no coincidence that recent scholarship has questioned the authenticity of the
beginning of the Code; cf. L. Waelkens, *L'hérésie des premiers titres du Code de Justinien,
Une hypothèse sur la rédaction tardive de C. 1,1–13*, Tijdschrift voor Rechtsgeschiedenis, 79
(2011), p. 253–296. Another example of the transformative power of natural law is the history of due process; cf. Pennington, *The prince and the law*, p. 119–164.

[2051] Cited from Savigny's edition of Lull's *Ars iuris de regulis iuris* in Cortese, *La norma
giuridica*, vol. 1, p. 91, n. 133. It is worthwhile noting that Professor Richard Helmholz (University of Chicago) is currently working on a promising project that investigates the role
of natural law in practical juridical literature (e.g. *Consilia*) and in court practice on both
the Continent and in the Anglo-American world until the late nineteenth century.

the metaphysical assumptions that contributed to the evolution, Baldus denied that *pacta nuda sunt servanda* applied in the civil courts.[2052]

Baldus is an interesting example for yet another reason. While the dream of the moral theologians was to refashion the civil law in the image of a Christian natural law, Baldus' discussion of formality requirements illustrates that the process could also work the other way round. Against Bartolus, Baldus claimed that solemnities in last wills—which was a proxy for the discussion of form requirements in contracts—were not merely probatory but essential. In other words, positive law could impose form requirements on pain of nullity, even if, in principle, the will is the ultimate criterion in the court of conscience. Hence, the heir-at-law does not sin if he does not respect the disposition of the deceased in a defective last will. This is the only right solution, according to Baldus, since it prevents the creation of unbearable tension between *forum internum* and *forum externum*:[2053] if a natural obligation ensued from a defective testament, then the heir-at-law would be perplexed. By following the civil law, he would endanger his soul.

The perplexity resulting from the discrepancy between spiritual jurisdictions and secular justice could thus be settled in either of two ways. The question of which regulations prevailed does not lend itself to easy answers. In the case of the bindingness of naked agreements, the civil law finally gave in to the law of the Church, but in the case of form requirements, the emphasis on equity and the testator's original intention, which was advocated by many canonists and theologians of the late medieval period, met with resistance from Baldus as well as sixteenth-century moral theologians, such as Francisco de Vitoria and Domingo de Soto. If the harmonization between the parallel jurisdictions was generally desired, the upshot of reconciliatory efforts in concrete cases was much less predictable. The representatives of Church and State were not merely rivals, but also collaborators. Early modern Spain is an excellent point in case.[2054]

[2052] See U. Wolter, *Ius canonicum in iure civili, Studien zur Rechtsquellenlehre in der neueren Privatrechtsgeschichte*, [Forschungen zur neueren Privatrechtsgeschichte, 23], Köln – Wien 1975, p. 49–50. Interestingly, Pietro de Ancharano criticized the civilians for remaining too faithful to the standard gloss on Justinian's law without following the canonists; see Wolter, *Ius canonicum in iure civili*, p. 52, n. 205.

[2053] Cf. supra, n. 1151.

[2054] The interconnectedness of ecclesiastical and secular interests in sixteenth-century Spain is the subject of an in-depth study in A.M. Rouco-Varela, *Staat und Kirche im Spanien des 16. Jahrhunderts*, [Münchener theologische Studien, 23], München 1965, esp. p. 126–149 (*Der Staat im Dienste der Kirche*) and (significantly more voluminous) p. 150–296 (*Ansprüche des Staates an die Kirche*).

It was the kingdom *par excellence* where the clergy asserted themselves as the guardians of the realm and where the secular authorities considered themselves the guardians of the souls.[2055] Consequently, a diplomatic and tactful approach would have worked well on both sides. However, royal control over the Church, particularly through its grip on ecclesiastical jurisdiction, became increasingly pervasive.[2056]

The strong ties between the secular government and the ecclesiastical authorities in sixteenth-century Spain are particularly salient in Vitoria's and Soto's legitimation of the bindingness of statutory formalities in the court of conscience. If 'contractual freedom' is limited in the civil courts through formal constraints, then the court of conscience should enforce that policy. Vitoria rejected the canon law tradition which initially opposed this view. However famous, canonists such as Abbas Panormitanus were not to be considered competent in determining the rules that should govern the court of conscience (*falcem in messem alienam mittunt*). Moreover, theologians such as Pope Adrian VI were not to be taken seriously because they relied too heavily on the canonists. Vitoria and Soto rejected the teleological interpretation of positive law, which was based on the assumption that the law ceases to apply if its underlying reason has been removed. Once it has been laid down, a positive law binds universally. Even in cases where obedience to the law seems to bring about an inequitable result, the force of law remains absolute (*praeceptum absolutum*).

No less important than the recognition of the spiritual duty to observe contractual formalities imposed by human positive law, is what motivated the Dominican theologians to endorse this standpoint. In their opinion, it is necesarry to adopt positive human law as the benchmark of rights and obligations in the spiritual forum to enhance the security of consciences (*ob securitatem conscientiarum*). In other words, the intricate connection between the interests of Church and State is mirrored in the equation of spiritual and legal security. Tranquillity of the soul and the tranquillity of the republic go hand in hand. Peace of mind is the natural corollary of public order and peace. Vitoria and Soto shared the insight, succinctly formulated about a century later in John Selden's (1584–1654) *Table talk*,

---

[2055] H.E. Braun, *Juan de Mariana and early modern Spanish political thought*, Aldershot-Burlington 2007, p. 135–160, and Rouco-Varela, *Staat und Kirche*, p. 46–53.

[2056] A good example is the growing importance of the *recursus ad principem* (*recurso de fuerza*), a royal remedy against usurpation by the ecclesiastical courts; cf. B. Wauters, *Recht als religie, Canonieke onderbouw van de vroegmoderne staatsvorming in de Zuidelijke Nederlanden*, [Symbolae Facultatis Litterarum Lovaniensis, Series B, 35], Leuven 2005, p. 245–266.

that 'generally to pretend conscience against the law is dangerous', or, a little more sarcastically, that a scrupulous man is like an unmanageable horse, 'he starts at every bird that flies out of the hedge'.[2057] Vitoria and Soto were wary of the destabilizing effects of moral scrupulosity. At the same time, they gave in to the pressures that came from the rise of the nation state. They did not poke fun at the court of conscience, however, as Selden did.

Vitoria and Soto were serious about the stability of both the spiritual and the secular order. Moreover, they thought that the cure against perplexed consciences coincided with the prevention of civil chaos. The binding force of contractual form requirements is a case in point, but their discussion of the following case might be even more so. Should the judge decide according to the legitimate outcome of trial procedure if that means that a man whom he truly knows to be innocent will be convicted of a capital crime?[2058] It was part and parcel of the Thomistic tradition that for the sake of his conscience, the judge must follow the evidence and the allegations by the witnesses despite his contrasting private knowledge (*conscientia privata*). Soto forcefully endorsed that legalistic idea. Importantly, he did so not only for the sake of the judge's conscience, but primarily for the sake of the stability of the political order. 'Reason of state' excuses the occasional conviction of innocent people through the strict application of the legitimate rules of procedure:[2059]

> Public trials have been constituted for the sake of the tranquillity and the peaceful state of the republic (*tranquillitas et quietus status reipublicae*), so that there is no way left open for the judge to turn away from the truth wherever he would fancy to do so. Now if he were not bound to judge according to the allegations, the peace of the republic would be disturbed immediately.

[2057] J. Selden, *The table talk* (ed. by S.H. Reynolds), Oxford 1892, ch. 26 (conscience), par. 3, p. 50 and par. 1, p. 49, respectively. It might be noted that Selden's *Table talk* was not published until 1689 by Richard Milward.

[2058] For a more elaborate analysis of this question and its treatment by the early modern scholastics, see Decock, *The judge's conscience and the protection of the criminal defendant*, [forthcoming].

[2059] Soto, *De iustitia et iure* (ed. fac. V. Diego Carro – M. González Ordóñez, vol. 3), lib. 5, quaest. 4, art. 2, p. 438: 'Publica iudicia ob tranquillitatem et quietum statum reipublicae constituta sunt, atque eo pacto ut nulla sit patula iudici via declinandi, ubivis libuerit, a veritate. Si autem non teneretur secundum allegata iudicare, pax ilico reipublicae turbaretur.'

Not only must justice be done, it must also be seen to be done. This, in a nutshell, is the argument behind Soto's legalistic position. The people do not judge what is hidden, such as the judge's private knowledge. Hence, they would cry out against the judicial system if they saw that the judge did not stand by the public proofs. If one has to make a choice between the condemnation of an innocent man and the collapse of public authority, the interest of the State prevails. It is not unusual to find that with the Dominican theologians, certainly in the first half of the sixteenth century, the necessity of upholding public order overrules all other concerns. It is worthwhile, therefore, to point out the slightly different approach which the Jesuit Leonardus Lessius took in this debate about fifty years later. Lessius tried to forge a compromise between the 'legalist opinion' of Soto, and the idea, characteristically defended by Panormitanus amongst others, that the judge should never convict an innocent criminal defendant in spite of the evidence to the contrary. Since the killing of an innocent man is intrinsically evil (*intrinsece malum*), Lessius concluded that in capital cases, the judge's conscience had to prevail over the legitimate outcome of the trial.[2060]

Lessius' viewpoint is certainly indicative of the re-appraisal of the moral order as a system of checks and balances on secular jurisdiction in the specific case of capital trials, but also of a more generally redeemed self-confidence among the moral theologians at the dawn of the seventeenth century. Even though the interconnectedness between secular and spiritual power remained strong throughout the Habsburg empire, it might be argued that the guardians of the *forum internum*, particularly the Jesuits, were less hesitant than the early members of the 'School of Salamanca' to assert their rights. Careful balancing of interests and the subtle arts of diplomacy nevertheless remained fundamental guiding principles. Luis de Molina admitted the binding power of statutory form requirements in contracts, affirming that this was the best guarantee for the security of souls.[2061] The State could also limit 'freedom of contract' for the sake

---

[2060] Lessius, *De iustitia et iure*, lib. 2, cap. 29, dub. 10, num. 78, p. 341: 'Quod autem sit intrinsice malum, probatur. Primo, quia per se malum est adimere alicui vitam sine authoritate; atqui iudex nullam habet authoritatem in vitam innocentis, cum haec soli Deo sit subiecta. Ergo iudicem eam adimere per se malum est. Secundo, si iudex habet hanc authoritatem condemnandi innocentem, id ei concessum est propter bonum reipublicae, atqui ob nullum reipublicae bonum, etsi in proximo periculo versetur, licet directe innocentem occidere, ut ostensum est supra cap. 9, dub. 7. Ergo multo minus licebit ob hoc periculum remotum et cui alia ratione potest obviari.'

[2061] Discussed supra, p. 400–403.

of the *bonum commune*. Yet he vindicated that precious right, attributed to the prudent man's judgment (*arbitrium prudentis*) in the *ius commune* tradition, to let equity prevail over formalism if strict obedience to the letter of the law would end up being absurd.

Equally carefully worded are the observations on the relationship between the individual contracting parties' natural freedom, on the one hand, and statutory constraints, on the other, by that magnificent Jesuit theorician of law, Francisco Suárez. He confirmed positive law's power to avoid contracts.[2062] At the same time, he insisted that the law *Non dubium* (C. 1,14,5), which declared void contracts that infringed upon the civil law, must be interpreted very strictly lest man is robbed of some kind of natural right (*quoddam naturale ius*).[2063] Although it is not desirable in the present context to go into the details of Jesuit political theory, it may be recalled that power, originally resting with the entire community, was thought to have been contractually transferred to the prince under certain conditions. For example, the prince would truly take care of the common good. For Molina, Lessius, and Suárez there is clearly no contradiction, then, between the individual's freedom and the State's interventionist power. The natural law principle that citizens can freely create contractual obligations can be frustrated by the State:[2064]

> However naked the agreement, as long as it is freely and spontaneously entered into by parties who have the capacity to make a contract, it entails a natural obligation in the court of conscience. As a consequence, you cannot rescind the contract, unless the other party agrees, or unless the contract is void or voidable as a matter of statutory law (*iure positivo*).

Through the 'political contract' the public authorities have been granted the power to limit the natural 'freedom of contract' precisely by imposing certain formalities on pain of nullity. It might be recalled that Lessius' (proto-)constitutionalist political views were part and parcel of the early modern scholastic tradition.[2065] In essence, they can be traced

---

[2062] Explained supra, p. 499–501.

[2063] Cited supra, n. 1648.

[2064] Lessius, *De iustitia et iure*, lib. 2, cap. 17, dub. 4, num. 19, p. 197. Cited supra, n. 548 and n. 1372.

[2065] See, *inter alia*, F. Buzzi, *Teologia, politica e diritto tra XVI e XVII secolo*, [Saggi teologici, 28], Genova-Milano 2005, p. 307–367; J.A. Fernández-Santamaría, *Natural law, constitutionalism, reason of state, and war, Counter-Reformation Spanish political thought*, [Renaissance and Baroque studies and texts, 32], New York 2005 [= vol. 1], p. 349–392; B. Hamilton, *Political thought in sixteenth-century Spain, A study of the political ideas of Vitoria, De Soto, Suárez, and Molina*, Oxford 1963, p. 38–41. In a critique of Otto von Gierke's

back to medieval interpretations of the Roman *lex Regia*.[2066] At any rate, since the people had consented to the power of the authorities—at least theoretically, the prince's power to impede natural contractual obligation from coming into existence for the sake of the common good was logically conclusive. Heavily drawing on Aristotle, man's nature as a social animal (*homo animal civile*) was said by Vitoria and Soto to legitimize statutory limitations on the individual's autonomy, even though they fully recognized that the creation of man in the image of God and the centrality of the *dominus*' will in Roman law provided strong arguments in favor of a principle of unlimited contractual exchange.[2067] Domingo de Bañez would even claim that the statutory restraints on free trade were more natural than human freedom.

Yet Lessius, who fought many wars with Bañez, particularly on the topic of divine grace and free will, probably scorned this opinion of his Dominican rival as well.[2068] As mentioned in the introduction, the sometimes ultra-liberal standpoints he defends in concrete business cases are astonishing, although he would certainly not have denied that, in theory, the *bonum commune* prevails over the *bonum particulare*. Admittedly, the doctrines about the constitutionalist origins of power and about the indirect secular power of the Pope can be found equally well in Vitoria, Soto, Bellarmino, Molina as in Lessius.[2069] There are reasons, though, to suspect that the context in which the Jesuits elaborated those old political views provided incentives to adopt a more assertive attitude. For example,

---

attribution of the origins of social contract theory to the sixteenth-century Protestant and Catholic *monarchomachi*, it has been emphasized that the availability of contract terminology is coeval with European political thinking by H. Höpfl – M.P. Thompson, *The history of contract as a motif in political thought*, The American Historical Review, 84 (1979), p. 928; compare A. Black, *The juristic origins of social contract theory*, History of Political Thought, 14 (1993), p. 57–76, and A. Thier, *Klassische Kanonistik und kontraktualistische Tradition*, in: O. Condorelli – F. Roumy – M. Schmoeckel (eds.), Der Einfluß der Kanonistik auf die europäische Rechtskultur, Band 2: Öffentliches Recht, [Norm und Struktur, 37, 2], Köln – Weimar – Wien 2011, p. 61–80.

[2066] On the *lex regia*, mentioned in D. 1,4,1, and the various interpretations it received during the *ius commune*, see E. Cortese, *La norma giuridica*, vol. 2, p. 126–131 and p. 171–191; Q. Skinner, *Foundations*, vol. 2, p. 130–134; R. Tuck, *Natural rights theories, Their origin and development*, Cambridge 1981, p. 39–40; G. van Nifterik, *Vorst tussen volk en wet, Over volkssoevereiniteit en rechtsstatelijkheid in het werk van Fernando Vázquez de Menchaca (1512–1569)*, Rotterdam 1999, p. 109–124.

[2067] Cf. supra, p. 372 and p. 449.

[2068] The confrontation between Bañez and Lessius in the debate on grace and free will is briefly discussed in Decock, *Grazia divina e giustizia commutativa, Un confronto tra Bañez e Lessius*, p. 361–365.

[2069] Hamilton, *Political thought in sixteenth-century Spain*, p. 69–94.

in challenging James I Stuart's theory of the divine right of kings, Suárez affirmed that the belief in the contractual origins of secular power was a fundamental theological axiom.[2070] His doctrine of the indirect secular power of the Church self-confidently proclaimed that the Roman pontiff had the right to intervene in all branches of secular government for the sake of the salvation of souls.[2071]

It has been sharply noticed that 'some of the strongest hierocratic claims made by the church were in fact made in those years when these rights of the church were coming under the strongest attack'.[2072] This is definitely the impression one gets from Lessius' discussion of good morals in contract law. As a matter of natural law, 'contractual freedom' is limited if the performance of the object of the contract constitutes sin. Compared with this simple rule, the substantive limitations on 'freedom of contract' in the civil court are convoluted. First, positive law can avoid contracts because its cause is unlawful. Second, because the promise can give occasion to sin. Third, because the promise violates the laws and the good morals of a well-ordered society. Lessius demands that positive law simply conforms to natural law in articulating the substantive limitations on 'contractual freedom' in regard to the object of the promise. Moreover, using the distinction between 'natural good morals' and 'civil good morals', Lessius argues that contracts violating 'civil good morals' can be ratified, provided that they are not at odds with 'natural good morals'. Here is why:[2073]

[2070] Suárez, *Defensio fidei catholicae*, lib. 3, cap. 2, num. 10, p. 209. On Suárez's constitutionalist theory as essentially an attempt to deconstruct the theory of the divine right of kings, see J.F. Courtine, *Nature et empire de la loi, Études suaréziennes*, Paris 1999. Harro Höpfl notes that Suárez's constitutionalist thought comes much closer to modern versions of social and political contractarianism than any of his predecessors, because with him, contract and consent referred not merely to the conveyance of power from the community as a whole to the prince, but also to the emergence of the political community itself; cf. *Jesuit political thought*, p. 251.

[2071] Suárez, *Defensio fidei catholicae*, lib. 3, cap. 22, num. 10–14, p. 311–313, discussed in Decock, *Counter-Reformation diplomacy behind Francisco Suárez's constitutionalist theory*, p. 85–86. Much could be said about the theory of the indirect worldly power of the Church that would largely exceed the scope of this concluding chapter. Excellent accounts can be found in F.B. Costello, *The political philosophy of Luis de Molina S.J. (1535–1600)*, [Bibliotheca Instituti Historici S.I., 38], Roma 1974, p. 86–94; Höpfl, *Jesuit political thought*, p. 224–262; Wauters, *Recht als religie*, p. 106–110; Fernández-Santamaría, *Natural law, constitutionalism, reason of state, and war*, p. 227–256.

[2072] Helmholz, *The spirit of classical canon law*, p. 141.

[2073] Lessius, *De iustitia et iure*, lib. 2, cap. 18, dub. 13, num. 95, p. 229, and lib. 2, cap. 18, dub. 13, num. 102, p. 230. Cited supra, n. 1619.

The civil law should not hinder the performance of duties of piety nor evangelical counsels (*officia pietatis et consilia evangelica*). (...) Secular princes should not make laws that are to the detriment of works of charity and the salvation of souls. They merely have the authority to govern the commonwealth for the sake of temporal order and peace. Their policies should not hinder the pursuit of piety and the means that enables man to attain his supernatural end. Rather, civil policy should serve and promote this spiritual pursuit.

Christian charity can be a licit cause for a husband and wife, or a father and a son, to make excessive donations to each other, even though such practices go against civil morality. Put differently, the State has a duty, according to Lessius, to allow Christian citizens to practice works of supererogation and mercy. For a leading member of the Church, this was certainly not a wholly disinterested view of the substantive limits on 'contractual freedom'. At one point, Lessius insists that however immoral the alienation of the entirety of a man's belongings may be from the civil point of view, the secular authorities must admit such liberal transactions at least if they are done to the benefit of the Church. The distinction between civil and natural morality reveals that the spiritual forum considered itself superior to the temporal forum. One must be very cautious about generalizing, but this observation suggests that the claim to superiority was more pronounced in some of the Jesuit writers at the dawn of the seventeenth century than in Dominican theologians such as Vitoria and Soto, who, relatively speaking, seem to have been more loyal to secular power.

One probably needs to look in the direction of Dr. Navarrus to find an explanation for the renewed assertiveness of the theologians *vis à vis* secular jurisdiction.[2074] Incidentally, the Salamancan canonist is remembered for his denying the moral bindingness of tax laws and for his scathing remark that Philip II was the greatest prelate in ecclesiastical rents after the Pope.[2075] In this context, we will recall his forceful plea to extend the competence of ecclesiastical tribunals over laymen who violated the

---

[2074] As his *Enchiridion sive manuale confessariorum et poenitentium* became the standard model for Jesuit manuals for confessors, Dr. Navarrus had a profound influence on Jesuit casuistry. The strong ties between the canonist and the Society of Jesus are highlighted in Lavenia, *Martín de Azpilcueta (1492–1586), Un profilo*, p. 103–112.

[2075] V. Lavenia, *Fraus et cautela, Théologie morale et fiscalité au début des temps modernes*, in: S. Boarini (ed.), La casuistique classique, genèse, formes, devenir, Saint-Étienne 2009, p. 50–52, and Braun, *Juan de Mariana*, p. 149, n. 65, respectively. A detailed account of Dr. Navarrus' views of the morality of taxes is contained in Lavenia, *L'infamia e il perdono*, p. 219–264.

just price. He thereby wanted to guarantee the universal enforcement of the natural law principle of contractual fairness. The prospect of disturbing the tranquillity of the State as a result of the strict enforcement of contractual fairness should not scare the authorities, he reassured. While acknowledging the usual rationale behind the reluctance of the secular courts to enforce principles of the *forum internum*—too many lawsuits are detrimental to society, Dr. Navarrus attributed the flooding of the courts to avarice rather than virtue. His colleagues who thought otherwise were accused of being oblivious to the Church's power of the keys (*claves Ecclesiae*).

If self-confidence about the power of the keys became common currency among many Jesuits at the turn of the seventeenth century, their frequently suspect entanglement in worldly affairs as confessors to some of the most powerful men indicates that State-Church relationships in the early modern period remained profoundly ambivalent.[2076] While adumbrating the contractualist origins of political power, Suárez provided the ultimate theoretical framework for the sacralization of secular law by arguing that all laws ultimately derive from God.[2077] Consequently, civil laws, particularly tax laws, are binding in conscience.[2078] Boosted by divine legitimation, it was only a matter of time for secular jurisdiction to outcompete the rival *forum internum* and exclude the moral notion of *summum bonum* from the scope of legislation altogether. In the modern age, *voluntas* and not *veritas* would determine the outcome of legislative activity. One of the things that makes contract law in the moral theological literature so fascinating, is that it offers a unique insight, to

---

[2076] E.g. R. Bireley, *The Jesuits and the Thirty Years War, Kings, courts, and confessors,* Cambridge 2003, p. 1–32.

[2077] See, *inter alia*, the recent observations by Pierre Legendre on Suárez's paramount importance, alongside Hobbes, in the 'theologization' of politics; cf. *L'autre Bible de l'Occident, Le monument romano-canonique, Étude sur l'architecture dogmatique des sociétés,* [Leçons, 9], Paris 2009, p. 74–75 and p. 92.

[2078] Hamilton, *Political thought in sixteenth-century Spain,* p. 56; Lavenia, *Fraus et cautela,* p. 53–54. In regard to the intricate question of the moral bindingness of tax laws, Lavenia's impressive scholarship has revealed that Suárez's position is more State-friendly than Vitoria's. The alleged founder of the 'School of Salamanca' ordered that confessors should abstain from preaching the nullity of tax laws as a matter of conscience, while simultaneously urging them to condone tax evasion in the court of conscience. Vitoria's intermediate position was rejected by the Franciscan theologian Alfonso de Castro (1492–1558), who wished the clergy to collaborate entirely with the taxman and forbid tax evasion on pain of mortal sin; cf. Lavenia, *Fraus et cautela,* p. 48–50. A more extensive analysis of Vitoria's and Castro's moral views of taxation is contained in Lavenia, *L'infamia e il perdono,* p. 163–217.

push Hopper's metaphor a little further, in the stormy process that eventually led to the almost total eclipse of 'simple nature' on official State territory.

8.3   BETWEEN MEDIEVAL AND MODERN

Moral theology is one of the many bridges over which European legal culture passed from the medieval to the modern epoch. This is certainly one of the main upshots of the present investigation into the theologians' contribution to the early modern history of contract law. Yet this is by no means a self-evident conclusion. At the end of the sixteenth century, Bartolomé de Medina could still write that the study of law pertained to the province of both theologians and jurists, albeit with a different end in view.[2079] The theologians investigated laws for the role they played in directing man to the ultimate end of happiness in the Afterlife (*aeterna illa felicitas*), namely the beatific vision of God. The jurists studied laws for the sake of the peace of the republic on earth (*communis pax reipublicae*). At the dawn of the twenty-first century, this bipolar view of life has almost completely collapsed in the West. Consequently, acknowledging the theologians' legacy to contract law requires the strenuous effort of rethinking the plurality of legal cultures in the *ancien régime*.[2080]

The anthropological and jurisdictional background against which the theologians discussed contract law is at variance with 'modern' assumptions about man and law. The ultimate horizon against which they wrote about property and contracts was the preparation for the Afterlife and Last Judgment.[2081] We have seen that this did not prevent the theologians' contract doctrines to survive in more 'modern' and secular contexts, such as in Grotius' *De iure belli ac pacis*. However, the moral theological

---

[2079] Medina, *In primam secundae divi Thomae*, ad quaest. 90, introd., p. 473: 'Theologis et iurisprudentibus communis est disputatio haec de legibus, sed diversa ratione. Nam iurisprudentes de legibus considerant, quatenus ordinant nos in communem pacem reipublicae. At vero theologi tractant de illis, inquantum ordinant nos ad aeternam illam felicitatem, quam in Dei visione sita est.'

[2080] C. Mozzarelli, *Tra ragion di stato e sociabilità, Ipotesi cattoliche di rifondazione del vivere associato*, in: F. Arici – F. Todescan (eds.), Iustus ordo e ordine della natura, Sacra doctrina e saperi politici fra XVI e XVIII, [Biblioteca di Lex naturalis, 5], Milano 2007, p. 63.

[2081] It has been argued that this is a more general characteristic of Spanish legal culture in the Baroque period; cf. A. Botero Bernal, *El culto a la muerte y al fuego como un referente comprensivo de la cultura y del derecho, Análisis de un ejemplo*, Revista Jurídica, Universidad Autónoma de Madrid, 16 (2007), p. 55–70.

literature is primarily indebted to the spirit of 'medieval' canon law. In fact, Pierre Legendre calls the 'second scholastic' the 'second canon law'.[2082] Perhaps the juridification of moral theology was an alternative way of dealing with new challenges posed by the discovery of the Americas to which classical canon law could no longer respond.[2083] Paolo Prodi talks about the 'ossification' that struck post-Tridentine canon law.[2084] Gérard Fransen highlights the positivistic turn in Church law after Trent, which put a brake on the Church's rich jurisprudential tradition.[2085] At any rate, to care for the salvation of souls (*salus animarum*) was the driving force behind the moral theologians' engagement with law. They shared this concern with the canonists of the late medieval period.[2086]

This preoccupation with the soul gives theologians' contract doctrine an outlook which is more 'medieval' than 'modern'. Even when the results of the theologians' sophisticated argumentations sometimes look surprisingly modern, one should bear in mind that the reasons behind their standpoints were significantly alien to modern thinking. For example, 'freedom of contract' may well have been of central value to the theologians, particularly to the Jesuit scholastics, but what motivated them in advocating consensualism and freedom in contracts was the salvation of souls.[2087] The contemporary rationale behind 'freedom of contract' is the smoothness of commerce.[2088] Yet that seems to have been only of secondary relevance to the moral theologians, and even to 'pure' jurists such as Wezenbeke. They were principally concerned with the avoidance of sin.[2089] In fact, even in modern times this 'spiritual' approach to contract law has

---

[2082] P. Legendre, *L'inscription du droit canon dans la théologie, Remarques sur la seconde scolastique*, in: S. Kuttner – K. Pennington (eds.), Proceedings of the fifth international congress of medieval canon law (Salamanca, 21–25 September 1976), [Monumenta iuris canonici, Series C: subsidia, 6], Città del Vaticano 1980, p. 449.

[2083] This challenge is analyzed in A. García y García, *El derecho canónico medieval y los problemas del Neuvo Mundo*, Rivista internazionale di diritto comune, 1 (1990), p. 121–154.

[2084] P. Prodi, *Il paradigmo tridentino, Un'epoca della storia della Chiesa*, Brescia 2010, particularly chapter 5 (Dal *corpus iuris canonici* al diritto pontificio moderno), p. 71–92.

[2085] G. Fransen, *L'application des décrets du Concile de Trente, Les débuts d'un nominalisme canonique*, L'Année canonique, 27 (1983), p. 5–16.

[2086] E.g. Helmholz, *The spirit of classical canon law*, p. 394–399.

[2087] This point receives special attention in Fedele, *Considerazioni sull'efficacia dei patti nudi nel diritto canonico*, p. 57–61.

[2088] The view of contract as the instrument *par excellence* to subsidize economic growth as well as the connection between the rise of a market economy and the development of a will theory of contract is particularly vivid in Horwitz, *The transformation of American law*, esp. p. 160–210.

[2089] Cf. supra, p. 156–157.

not completely disappeared. It suffices to skim through the work of the French jurist Georges Ripert (1880–1958) to become aware of the persistence, however marginalized, of a 'spiritual' dimension in the discussions of contract law. In his famous treatise *The moral rule in civil obligations*, Ripert noticed the following:[2090]

> A jurist should not forget that law must apply itself to a human society founded on Christian morality. On account of its peculiar conception of the ends of man and this world, this morality imposes a series of rules which are not only meant to assure respect for one's neighbor, but also to perfect the soul (*perfectionner l'âme*).

Even if he did not intend to do so, Ripert actually left us an adequate summary of the scholastics' approach to contract law, even if, by his time, the dominant view of contract law did not correspond anymore to the spiritual logic behind the theologians' endorsement of 'freedom of contract'. At least from the nineteenth century onward, it was a liberal economic mindset that dominated modern will theories of contract.

'Freedom of contract' in the canonical and moral theological tradition should not be confused with modern versions of 'freedom of contract' for yet another reason. The scholastic version of 'contractual freedom' relies on a rejection of excessive formality requirements for the validity of contracts, which was typical of Roman law and its obsession with the *stipulation*. However important, the victory over this formalistic approach to the formation of contractual obligation should not be confused with the rise of 'freedom of contract' as the victory of the autonomy of the will in the modern age.[2091] The scholastics endorsed the consensualist principle of canon law because, in their view, the formality requirements of Roman law appeared to be too 'scrupulous' and 'superstitious'.[2092] Right

---

[2090] G. Ripert, *La règle morale dans les obligations civiles*, Paris 1949⁴ [= 1926], p. 27: 'Le juriste ne peut oublier que le droit doit s'appliquer à une société humaine fondée sur la morale chrétienne. Cette morale, par sa conception particulière des fins de l'homme en ce monde, impose une série de règles qui ne tendent pas seulement à assurer le respect du prochain, mais aussi à perfectionner l'âme.' This text is also cited in A.C. van Schaik, *Contractsvrijheid en nietigheid, Beschouwingen vanuit rechtshistorisch en rechtsvergelijkend perspectief over de overeenkomst zonder oorzaak*, Zwolle 1994, p. 100, n. 164.

[2091] Cf. J. Ph. Lévy, preface to Ranouil, *L'autonomie de la volonté*, p. 5–8.

[2092] E.g. Oñate, *De contractibus*, tom. 1, tract. 6, disp. 19, sect. 3, num. 229–231, p. 581: 'Mansit igitur iure Romano (abrogata forma illa nimis scrupulosa et superstitiosa, ut eam olim ipse Iustinianus appellavit) forma nihilominus verborum, quae stipulatio dicitur. (...) Tandem hodie de iure nostro regio Castellae nec concepta verba et superstitiosa illa formula, nec stipulatio ulla requiritur, sed quocumque modo et quibuscumque verbis inter contrahentes de voluntate se obligandi constet, obligatio sequitur, et contractus

conscience and right religion demanded a system other than the 'aberration' of Roman contract law.

Molina exhorted secular jurisdictions to follow the example of Spain and adopt the canon law regulation of contract because that was more advantageous to the peace of souls and, hence, to the peace of the republic than the formalistic, Roman law of contracts. There is a certain amount of irony in this proposition. While the traditional argument in favor of the Roman system of contracts had always been that the tranquillity of the republic would be disturbed if all pacts were to be enforceable in court, Molina, and later Oñate, reversed this argument. In their view, the tranquillity of souls that follows from a regime of 'freedom of contract' is a condition rather than an obstacle to peace in society.[2093] Again, priority is given to moral considerations and the salvation of the soul rather than to the smooth regulation of business and commerce.

The theologians' explanation of liberty of choice in marriage contracts offers a good illustration of the moral motivations behind their wider advocacy of 'freedom of contract'. In line with classical canon law, they thought that the choice to marry should be entirely free and uncoerced.[2094] In equal conformity with standard canon law was the reason they gave for endorsing this consensualist principle. As Soto and Sánchez explained, the perpetual endurance of the marriage of the parents was indispensable for the good upbringing and the education of the children.[2095] The perpetuity of marriage, however, rested on the free and deliberate consent of the spouses. 'Freedom of contract', then, was seen as the best means to attain the goal of giving children the best upbringing. Autonomy was not entirely conceived of as an end in itself. The same *caveat* applies to the apparently minimalistic approach the moral theologians took to moral duties. As soon as one delves into the casuistry of market transactions one is struck by the outspoken liberal standpoints they defended. Yet this moral minimalism was seen as a means and not as an end in itself.

The early modern theologians dreaded the pernicious effects of moral defeatism, which, in their opinion, ensued from urging people to live up to too lofty standards. Rules needed to be set up which even imperfect

---

perficitur, non tantum quoad exceptionem sed etiam quoad obligationem civilem et actionem (...).'

[2093] Cf. supra, p. 164; compare Birocchi, *Saggi sulla formazione storica della categoria generale del contratto*, p. 54.

[2094] E.g. Helmholz, *The spirit of classical canon law*, p. 237–238.

[2095] Cf. supra, p. 219 and 236.

men could endure, so that they may improve with practice and not find themselves easily discouraged.[2096] Moral rigorism not only undermined people's courage to try to live a more virtuous life, but, eventually, it also threatened to destroy the role the clergy played in bringing back the flock to God. The plea for moral realism was an essential feature of the Counter-Reformation spirit. In a disarmingly honest way, Tomás de Mercado explained to his intended readership—ordinary businessmen—that if he were to demand them to live according to the lofty ideals of Saint Paul, he would talk to the deaf. 'Nobody would listen to me,' he conceded,[2097] because 'the people are not as virtuous as Saint Paul wished them to be'. He reassured his readers that he would not attempt to persuade and admonish them to follow the best and the safest path to heaven.[2098] 'I limit myself to teach you what is licit and what is illicit.'

It would be unfair to attribute the legalistic outlook of early modern moral theology to moral laxism on the part of the Jesuits, or, for that matter, the Dominicans.[2099] Much as policy-makers today are trying to find the most efficient ways of raising taxes to feed the State, the moral theo-

---

[2096] This was the traditional argument used by theologians such as Soto and Molina to defend the moral minimalism of state legislation, but now applied to the jurisdiction of conscience; cf. Hamilton, *Political thought in sixteenth-century Spain*, p. 55.

[2097] Mercado, *Suma de tratos y contratos*, lib. 2 (*Del arte del mercader*), cap. 4 (*Del fin e intención que deve tener el mercader en sus tratos*), f. 25r.

[2098] Mercado, *Suma de tratos y contratos*, lib. 2 (*Del arte del mercader*), cap. 3 (*Del grado que tiene el arte del mercader en las cosas morales*), f. 23r. It might be noted that moral theologians until the beginning of the twentieth century continued to define their task in Mercado's terms; cf. Keenan, *A history of Catholic moral theology in the twentieth century*, p. 9–34. The shift toward 'thick' ethics and evangelical morality, welcomed in Protestant circles from their inception in the sixteenth century, was not forcefully initiated in the Catholic Church until the plea for a return to scriptural and patristic sources by Dom Odon Lottin (1880–1965), who studied under Joseph Mercier and Maurice de Wulf at the University of Leuven. His ideas became mainstream through the second Vatican Council. Not surprisingly, after Vatican II the Church simultaneously witnessed one of the strongest anti-nomianist periods in its history, see Donahue, Jr., *A crisis of law?*, p. 22–23.

[2099] One might even add the Protestant casuists to this list, although reformed casuistry is much less technical than its Catholic variant. It is nevertheless worthwhile noting with Margareth Sampson, quoted by James Keenan, that 'casuistry was intended not for the spiritual improvement of the laity but for the pastoral use of the clergy'. Keenan remarks that the Latin, juridic form of the Jesuits' directives made them inaccessible to the laity and, therefore, prevented them from becoming public, permissive norms. Ironically, Pascal's popular attacks in his elegantly written *Lettres provinciales* made them accessible to everyone; cf. Keenan, *William Perkins (1558–1602) and the birth of British casuistry*, p. 108. For a recent deconstruction of Pascal's cheap attacks on the Jesuits, see J.P. Gay, *Le Jésuite improbable, Remarques sur la mise en place du mythe du Jésuite corrupteur de la morale en France à l'époque moderne*, in: P.-A. Fabre – C. Maire (eds.), Les Antijésuites, Discours, figures et lieux de l'antijésuitisme à l'époque moderne, Rennes 2010, p. 305–327.

logians were anxious to find the best way to maximize the fruits of virtuousness to be offered to God. Their minimalistic conception of the task of moral theology fitted into this broader concern. Awareness of these contextual elements is relevant, because it highlights the differences between the rather 'medieval' policy considerations behind the theologians' advocating the principle of 'freedom of contract', on the one hand, and the 'modern' concerns about economic efficiency behind the contemporary plea for 'freedom of contract', on the other hand. The structural parallels between the economy of grace and the economy of public finances as well as the inversion of roles that took place between God and the State are nevertheless fascinating. The liberal character of the theologians' answer to the threat of moral defeatism posed by moral rigorism bears striking similarities to the political answer to the threat of an economic downturn posed by overburdening taxes.

It may be recalled at this point that the contractual view of the relationship between God and man was also related to broader concerns about morality. For example, it was argued by Lessius that, while God must offer the grace to initiate the process of justification, this grace only becomes efficacious on the condition that man's free will decides to accept God's offer.[2100] Justification requires both a divine, graceful offer and free human acceptance of it. There is a parallel here between Lessius' dogmatic views on the conditionality of the promisor's offer in the cooperation between God and man, and his analysis of contract in general as an accepted promise.[2101] This contractual view of the process of salvation was motivated, again, by moral concerns. When explaining his attack on Catholic theologians' embracing mitigated versions of the Protestant doctrines of predestination, Lessius expressed his worry that along those deterministic lines, 'nobody would be able to be converted anymore, unless he already had the right faith; nobody would be able to do a good deed anymore, unless he already was a virtuous man, nobody would be able to gain salvation anymore, unless he was saved already'.[2102]

[2100] For a more detailed analysis, see Decock, *Grazia divina e giustizia commutativa, Un confronto tra Bañez e Lessius*, p. 361–365.

[2101] Lessius, *De gratia efficaci, decretis divinis, libertate arbitrii et praescientia Dei conditionata*, p. 38, p. 102, p. 105–106 and p. 265.

[2102] Lessius, *De gratia efficaci, decretis divinis, libertate arbitrii et praescientia Dei conditionata*, cap. 9, num. 4, p. 82: 'Secundum incommodum quod ex praedicta sententia sequi videtur est: neminem posse converti, nisi qui re ipsa convertitur; neminem posse bene operari, nisi qui bene operatur; neminem posse salvari, nisi qui re ipsa salvatur.'

The moral context of the theologians' defence of the principle of 'freedom of contract' explains the merely instrumental value of the parties' ability to create enforceable contractual obligation whenever they wanted, the way they wanted and to the extent they wanted. Personal autonomy is not an end in itself.[2103] It is a very important means, however, because without genuine freedom of action, leading a moral life is impossible. Created in the image of God, man has to administer both material and spiritual goods as best he can to the glory of himself, his neighbor and God.[2104] This is where the counter-reformation rejection of the doctrine of predestination sneaks in again. Such a pessimistic view of man made the whole moral language of merit and demerit, praise and blame, glory and infamy pointless, according to Lessius.[2105] If man were not free to choose his actions and freely dispose of his material goods through contract, then why would he try to be industrious in the first place? Indeed, Lessius was deeply concerned about dogmatic theological matters such as the relationship between grace and free will, since they had an immediate bearing upon reality. In his view, adopting the doctrine of predestination undermined the zeal and industry of the souls (*videtur tollere zelum animarum*).[2106] Lessius badly deplored the state of desperation and moral paralysis which had ensued from the reformers' doctrine of grace.[2107]

Put differently, Lessius' doctrine of justification illustrates that his as well as many of his colleagues' worldview was expressly centered around the notions of freedom and merit as the best means to give people (souls) the right incentives to take proper care of their material property as well

---

[2103] 'Contractual freedom' was as little an end in itself as private property was thought to be an end itself by the scholastics. Poor people were allowed to steal from the rich in extreme necessity; cf. Gómez Camacho, *Later scholastics, Spanish economic thought in the 16th and 17th centuries*, p. 516–521; Langholm, *The legacy of scholasticism in economic thought*, p. 520–521.

[2104] On the image of God motif, see J. Porter, *Ministers of the law, A natural law theory of legal authority*, Grand Rapids – Cambridge 2010, p. 332–335. It remained a powerful starting point for discussions on property rights and human freedom even in later thinkers such as John Locke; cf. Coleman, *Are there any individual rights or only duties?*, p. 25.

[2105] Lessius, *De gratia efficaci, decretis divinis, libertate arbitrii et praescientia Dei conditionata*, cap. 3, num. 12–13, p. 14–15.

[2106] Lessius, *De praedestinatione et reprobatione angelorum et hominum disputatio*, Antverpiae 1610, sect. 2, rat. 6, num. 15, p. 271.

[2107] Lessius, *De praedestinatione*, ad lectorem, p. 239: 'Causa scribendae huius disputationis fuit, quod longo usu deprehenderim multorum animos praedestinationis consideratione valde perturbari. Scio quosdam inde in gravissimos melancholiae affectus incidisse, alios studium pietatis et perfectionem religionis abiecisse, alios paene per totam vitam in anxietate versari, praedestinationem Dei suspectam semper habentes.'

as their moral lives—the moral life in relationship with people articulating itself through contract. Free choice and human industry are rewarded by God. Man has control over his destiny. Not insignificantly, the Jesuits described the relationship between man and God in terms of a (sacred) employment contract in which man had a duty to work hard to observe God's precepts through his own merits (*per merita*), and God had a corresponding duty to glorify man in exchange for this labor (*pro his operis*).[2108] Conversely—and this has been pointed out by Giorgio Agamben—man had to strive for the glorification of God. Lessius, for instance, asserted that man had to focus on the glory of God as the ultimate goal of his actions.[2109] Indeed, it should not be forgotten that the watchword of the Jesuit order was 'for the greater glory of God' (*ad maiorem Dei gloriam*).

The moral and the religious context of the theologians' contract law reveals at least three things about the intermediary position they took between 'medieval' and 'modern' law. Firstly, they continued the medieval world view that history is essentially a history of salvation, and that law is the instrument which guides man through his earthly journey toward God. The *cura animarum* permeated their entire legal thinking. They agreed with the canonist Giovanni d'Andrea that as God created man in his image, he simultaneously proclaimed natural law, which is derived from man's reasonable nature, as the principal guideline for man on his way to the after-life.[2110] In this respect, it might be remarked, that, conversely, the canon law tradition was probably much closer to theology, natural law and the *forum internum* than has traditionally been suggested.[2111] Abbas Panormitanus provides a particularly good example of the symbiosis of theological and juridical thought in late medieval canon law.[2112] Panormitanus advocated the 'fraternization' of law and

---

[2108] Oñate, *De contractibus*, tom. 2, tract. 8, disp. 24, sect. 5, num. 113, p. 24.

[2109] Lessius, *De perfectionibus moribusque divinis*, Anverpiae 1620, lib. 14, cap. 3, num. 57, p. 539: 'Unde etiam homo non potest sibi excellentius bonum proponere in operando quam gloriam Dei, nec melius actiones suas peragere, quam referendo illas ad gloriam Dei.'
This is undoubtedly the passage referred to in Agamben, *Il regno e la gloria*, p. 240. In light of the reciprocal nature of the glorification that takes place between man and God, the emphasis laid on the fundamentally jealous and egoistic character of God (p. 240–241) could be questioned, though, as is explained by Lessius himself, *De perfectionibus moribusque divinis*, lib. 14, cap. 3, num. 61–63, p. 579.

[2110] Condorelli, *Ius e lex nel sistema del diritto comune (secoli XIV–XV)*, p. 77, n. 135.

[2111] This is brilliantly illustrated by Condorelli, *Ius e lex nel sistema del diritto comune (secoli XIV–XV)*, p. 76–80 (= chapter 7: I canonisti: il diritto nella storia della salvezza—La recezione del pensiero di S. Tommaso).

[2112] Cf. supra, p. 93–94 and p. 337–339.

theology.[2113] It should not come as a surprise, then, that he was one of the most frequently cited canonists in the works of the sixteenth and seventeenth century moral theologians.

Secondly, the moral theologians went significantly further in systematizing contract doctrine than their medieval predecessors.[2114] Significantly, the canonists treated legal problems in the context of commentaries, which strictly followed the order and system of Gratian's *Decretum* or Pope Gregory IX's *Decretales*. The moral theologians, however, re-inserted these doctrines along with material from the civilian tradition into autonomous treatises on rights, laws, and contracts. The moral theological tradition itself underwent an increasing process of autonomization and systematization. While Vitoria remained loyal to the structure of Thomas Aquinas' *Secunda Secundae*—without necessarily being true to the substance of Thomas' thought—Soto designed a more autonomous treatise *De iustitia et iure*. Molina's and Lessius' treatises achieved the creation of systematic doctrines of property law and the law of obligations. As regards the making of a general law of contract, specifically, Lessius' elegantly stuctured treatment of contract law in general (*de contractibus in genere*) probably exceeded the efforts at systematization in the unduly voluminous work of his colleague from Coimbra. Lessius' general law of contract, in turn, was dwarfed two decades after his death by Oñate's *De contractibus*.

Thirdly, while it sets the moral theologians' contract law apart from the teachings of the canonists (and the civilians), the turn towards the construction of autonomous, systematic and comprehensive legal doctrines foreshadows the modern attempts to systematize the law of obligations. This point has already been made by Paolo Cappellini.[2115] The issue of the interconnectedness of 'modern' natural law with sixteenth century moral theology and 'old' natural law traditions continues to be the subject of an incessant stream of excellent scholarship. A recent overview of secondary literature on the topic includes no less than sixty pages replete with

---

[2113] Gaudemet, *Théologie et droit canonique*, p. 12.

[2114] This is not to deny that the canon law tradition, and, more broadly speaking, the late medieval *ius commune*, already made great strides in the shaping of general legal principles and the construction of legal doctrines; see, for instance, P.J. du Plessis, *The creation of legal principle*, Roman Legal Tradition, 4 (2008), p. 46–69 and the contributions collected in J.W. Cairns – P.J. du Plessis (eds.), *The creation of the ius commune, From casus to regula*, [Edinburgh Studies in Law, 7], Edinburgh 2010.

[2115] Cappellini, *Sulla formazione del moderno concetto di 'dottrina generale del diritto'.*

bibliographical references.[2116] In this context, it is appropriate to high-light, once more, the different atmosphere in which apparently similar doctrines were developed. Natural law in the scholastic tradition was connected to the belief that there is an ultimate Legislator, namely God, the creator of all things.[2117] The justification of positive law, in turn, was still thought of in medieval terms and considered to depend on its compliance with transcendent principles such as Truth and Justice.[2118]

If anyone, Hugo Grotius appears to be the ultimate bridge-figure between the moral theologians and the 'modern' natural lawyers. A superficial indication of Grotius' indebtedness to the late medieval *ius commune* and the Spanish scholastics is the great number of references to these sources in the *De iure belli ac pacis*.[2119] On a more substantial level, too, the medieval legacy in Grotius has been evidenced, certainly in the field of international law.[2120] What a close-reading of the relevant passages in Grotius' *De iure belli ac pacis* has revealed is that the theologians' doctrine of

---

[2116] F. Todescan, *Il problema del diritto naturale fra Seconda scolastica e giusnaturalismo laico secentesco, Una introduzione bibliografica*, in: F. Arici – F. Todescan (eds.), Iustus ordo e ordine della natura, Sacra doctrina e saperi politici fra XVI e XVIII, [Biblioteca di Lex naturalis, 5], Milano 2007, p. 1–61.

[2117] J. Schröder, *The concept of (natural) law in the doctrine of law and natural law of the early modern era*, in: L. Daston – M. Stolleis (eds.), Natural law and laws of nature in early modern Europe, Jurisprudence, theology, moral and natural philosophy, Farnham – Burlington 2008, esp. p. 63. Compare Buzzi, *Teologia, politica e diritto tra XVI e XVII secolo*, p. 348.

[2118] M. Stolleis, *The legitimation of law through God, tradition, will, nature and constitution*, in: L. Daston – M. Stolleis (eds.), Natural law and laws of nature in early modern Europe, Jurisprudence, theology, moral and natural philosophy, Farnham – Burlington 2008, esp. p. 49–50.

[2119] R. Feenstra, *Ius commune et droit comparé chez Grotius, Nouvelles remarques sur les sources citées dans ses ouvrages juridiques, à propos d'une réimpression du De iure belli ac pacis*, Rivista internazionale di diritto comune, 3 (1992), p. 7–36 (esp. p. 19–21), which extends the argument already made by the same author, *Quelques remarques sur les sources utilisées par Grotius dans ses travaux de droit naturel*, in: The world of Hugo Grotius (1583–1645), Proceedings of the international colloquium organized by the Grotius Committee of the Royal Netherlands Academy of Arts and Sciences, Rotterdam 6–9 April 1983, Amsterdam – Maarssen 1984, p. 65–81.

[2120] A classic study is P. Haggenmacher, *Grotius et la doctrine de la guerre*, Paris 1983. Grotius' merit in having transposed consensualist contract doctrine on the level of inter-State relationships is highlighted by H. Mohnhaupt, *Vertragskonstruktion und fingierter Vertrag zur Sicherung von Normativität: Gesetz, Privileg, Verfassung*, in: J.-F. Kervégan – H. Mohnhaupt (eds.), Gesellschaftliche Freiheit und vertragliche Bindung in Rechtsgeschichte und Philosophie / Liberté sociale et lien contractuel dans l'histoire du droit et la philosophie, [Ius commune, Sonderhefte, 120], Frankfurt am Main 1999, p. 2–3. Similar points are made in Lesaffer, *The medieval canon law of contract and early modern treaty law*, p. 178–198.

contract left an indelible imprint on Grotius.[2121] There is no reason to doubt the thesis that there is a fundamental continuity—at least on the substantial level—between the contract doctrines of Grotius and the theologians. As Gordley noted, the idea that Grotius rebelled against the scholastic tradition is a myth.[2122] Even in regard to issues of public law, the parallels between Grotius and Suárez appear to be striking.[2123] Grotius' political theory has been called the 'culmination of the interlinkage between Spanish and Dutch political thought'.[2124] It has also been argued that Grotius' conception of natural law is closer to that of the theologians than that of 'modern' natural lawyers.[2125] The medieval and early modern roots of Grotius' concept of natural rights are beyond doubt.[2126] It would almost seem preposterous to recall that the famous 'impious hypothesis', namely that natural law would continue to be valid even if God did not exist, reaches back at least to the Augustinian friar Gregory of Rimini (c. 1300–1358).[2127]

[2121] Cf. supra, p. 81; p. 101–104; p. 208–212; p. 272–274; p. 321–325; p. 359; p. 382; p. 494–496; p. 598–601.

[2122] Gordley, *The philosophical origins of modern contract doctrine*, p. 122.

[2123] Among the recent literature, see Recknagel, *Einheit des Denkens trotz konfessioneller Spaltung, Parallelen zwischen den Rechtslehren von Francisco Suárez und Hugo Grotius*, passim.

[2124] M. Van Gelderen, *From Domingo de Soto to Hugo Grotius, Theories of monarchy and civil power in Spanish and Dutch political thought, 1555–1609*, Pensiero politico, 32 (1999), p. 200.

[2125] M. Scattola, *Das Naturrecht vor dem Naturrecht, Zur Geschichte des 'ius naturae' im 16. Jahrhundert*, [Frühe Neuzeit, 52], Tübingen 1999, p. 217. Conversely, it has been pointed out that the alleged secularization in Grotius' notion of natural law, particularly its increasing alienation from the notion of *lex aeterna*, already occurred in late sixteenth century moral theologians; cf. F. Todescan, *Le radici teologiche del giusnaturalismo laico, I. Il problema della secolarizzazione nel pensiero giuridico di Ugo Grozio*, [Per la storia del pensiero giuridico moderno, 14], Milano 1983, p. 111.

[2126] Tierney, *The idea of natural rights*, p. 316–342 (the footnotes contain useful references to further literature). A contribution that is often omitted in this context but nevertheless valuable is R. Feenstra, *Expropriation et dominium eminens chez Grotius*, in: L. Waelkens et al. (ed.), L'expropriation, [Recueils de la Société Jean Bodin pour l'histoire comparative des institutions, 66], Bruxelles 1999, vol. 1, p. 133–153, esp. p. 144–148 on the Spanish sources of Grotius' concept of *dominium eminens*, particularly by Covarruvias and Suárez.

[2127] See the excellent article by P. Negro, *Intorno alle fonti scolastiche in Hugo Grotius*, Divus Thomas, 27 (2000), p. 236–251; a useful overview of the number of explicit references to moral theologians in several works of Grotius is included on p. 217. Also valuable is A. Dufour, *Les Magni Hispani dans l'œuvre de Grotius*, in: F. Grunert – K. Seelmann (eds.), Die Ordnung der Praxis, Neue Studien zur Spanischen Spätscholastik, [Frühe Neuzeit, 68], Tübingen 2001, p. 351–380.

The rich legacy of moral theology in Grotius should not surprise us. It was recognized—and resented—already by the 'modern' natural lawyers themselves. For example, Johann Gottlieb Heineccius, a Lutheran theologian and jurist, deplored Grotius' endorsement of the 'impious hypothesis', ascribing it to the tyrannical influence of scholasticism.[2128] Interestingly, Robert Joseph Pothier often rejected Grotius' standpoints in favor of following Samuel von Pufendorf precisely on those points where Grotius had been deeply influenced by Lessius, as in the case of immoral agreements and in regard to the validity of contracts affected by duress exercised by a third party.[2129] Incidentally, Pothier's case clearly illustrates that some of the basic principles developed by the moral theologians lived on in the contract doctrines of the 'modern' natural lawyers. As Franz Wieacker noted, the doctrines of these modern writers were more closely connected to the moral theological tradition than to the Roman law tradition, especially on two points: the defence of the principle of commutative justice and the consensualist analysis of contract as *promissio* and *acceptatio*.[2130]

The manner in which Grotius reformulated much of what had previously been expounded by the moral theologians, however, matters as much as the content of these arguments. Grotius was surely synthesizing the work of moral theologians such as Lessius on many occasions, but, unlike Lessius, he also merits the title of 'prince of European literature'.[2131] As we have frequently noted, the refreshing rhetoric that Grotius used to

---

[2128] Cited in Ch. Bergfeld, *Staat und Gesetz, Naturrecht und Vertrag bei Grotius und Heineccius*, in: J.F. Kervégan – H. Mohnhaupt (eds.), Gesellschaftliche Freiheit und vertragliche Bindung in Rechtsgeschichte und Philosophie/Liberté sociale et lien contractuel dans l'histoire du droit et la philosophie, [Ius commune, Sonderhefte, 120], Frankfurt am Main 1999, p. 107, n. 30. For an introduction to Heineccius, who was influenced by Thomasius and the Dutch Elegant School, see Birocchi, *Alla ricerca dell'ordine*, p. 385–387, and R. Feenstra, *Heineccius in den alten Niederlanden, Ein bibliographischer Beitrag*, Tijdschrift voor Rechtsgeschiedenis, 72 (2004), p. 297–326.

[2129] E.g. supra, p. 495–496. On the influence of the scholastic tradition on Pothier, see p. 70–71; p. 80–81; p. 211–212; p. 273–274; p. 323–325; n. 1716; p. 599.

[2130] Wieacker, *Die vertragliche Obligation bei den Klassikern des Vernunftrechts*, p. 21.

[2131] Waelkens, *Civium causa*, p. 117. One is left wondering, though, why Grotius is usually singled out as one of the most important contributors to the development of legal thought, while his fellow-countryman Lessius is not; e.g. R.C. van Caenegem, *Reflexions on the place of the Low Countries in European legal history*, in: N. Horn – K. Luig – A. Söllner (eds.), Europäisches Rechtsdenken in Geschichte und Gegenwart, Festschrift für Helmut Coing zum 70. Geburtstag, München 1982, vol. 1, p. 3–17. See the recent critique by R. Feenstra on another attempt to select 'the most important jurists of the Low Countries' while failing to include Lessius; cf. *Portretten van juristen uit de oude Nederlanden* (Recensie van T. Dankers – P. Delsaerdt, De vele gezichten van het recht, Portretten van juristen uit de oude Nederlanden, s.l. 2009), Tijdschrift voor Rechtsgeschiedenis, 79 (2011), p. 132, n. 15.

turn endlessly detailed scholastic arguments into limpid, succinct humanist phrases is one of the most attractive aspects of his work.[2132] Presumably, it explains why Grotius saved his name for posterity, while most of
the theologians have fallen into oblivion and struggle to find their way
into introductory textbooks in legal history.[2133] Moreover, one should
not underestimate the change in perspective that occurred with Grotius.
While the theologians were still trying to recover from the shattering of
the medieval Christian community,[2134] Grotius was living up to the reality
that several forms of Christianity existed, which in one way or the other
had to be made to live peacefully together. While theologians such as
Mercado were making a last-ditch effort to convince the secular authorities that the political community could not survive without the support of
Catholic confessors and the pastoral care for the souls,[2135] Grotius, just as
Lipsius, was pondering how the foundations could be laid for a state that
could deal with religious pluralism.[2136]

Grotius was a distinguished theologian, in addition to excelling as a
jurist. Pothier was still thinking of the law of obligations in terms of both
the external court and the court of conscience. However, their main ambition was clearly not to guide souls on their earthly way to paradise. This
difference in perspective might be called the true 'secularization' that
took place in Grotius' work in comparison with the religious dimension
underlying the treatises of the Spanish theologians.[2137] This radical differ-

---

[2132] This may help to explain why recent scholarship has been overly reluctant in
acknowledging scholastic influences on Grotius; e.g. B. Straumann, *Hugo Grotius und die
Antike, Römisches Recht und römische Ethik im frühneuzeitlichen Naturrecht*, [Studien zur
Geschichte des Völkerrechts, 14], Baden – Baden 2007.

[2133] Similar observations have been made by historians of philosophy. Trying to explain
why the amazingly rich and abundant Jesuit scholastic philosophy of the seventeenh and
eighteenth centuries has been ignored, it is being found that the philosophers who saved
their name for posterity and are now being studied as the classical thinkers of the period,
such as Descartes, were those who had better literary skills; cf. S. Knebel, *Suarezismus,
Erkenntnistheoretisches aus dem Nachlass des Jesuitengenerals Tirso González de Santalla
(1624–1705), Abhandlung und Edition*, [Bochumer Studien zur Philosophie, 51], Amsterdam
2011, p. 251.

[2134] S. Kuttner, *Reform of the Church and the Council of Trent*, The Jurist, 22 (1962),
p. 33.

[2135] Botero Bernal, *Análisis de la obra 'Suma de tratos y contratos' del Dominico Tomás
de Mercado*, p. 187.

[2136] Of particular relevance in this context is the debate on *ius circa sacra*; cf. A. Fukuoka,
*State, Church and liberty, A comparison between Spinoza's and Hobbes' interpretations of the
Old Testament*, Tokyo 2007, p. 35–78.

[2137] Birocchi, *Alla ricerca dell'ordine*, p. 160. One should not exaggerate, however,
the secularizing tendencies in Grotius, in respect to his views on religion and politics; cf.

ence in scope highlights the distinctive nature of the moral theologians' contract law at the crossroads of the middle ages and the modern period. A less fortunate attempt to distinguish Grotius from the theologians is by making reference to the 'humanist' or 'Renaissance' versus 'scholastic' or 'medieval' nature of their respective thought. It has been noted by eminent scholars that sixteenth-century Spanish thought in general profoundly cross-fertilizes moral theology, humanist literature and laws.[2138] Throughout this monograph the continuous synthesis of 'scholastic jurisprudence', 'Renaissance humanism', and 'medieval philosophy' has been highlighted. The syncretic nature of early modern Spanish culture is apparent, not only in the works of 'pure' moral theologians such as Molina, but also in the work of 'pure canonists' such as Covarruvias, and 'pure jurists' such as Arias Piñel.

To understand why theologians today are not as involved in contract law as their colleagues of the past, it is important to underscore that Catholic 'moral jurisprudence' was no longer fully possible in a modern world. Moral jurisprudence in the sense used by Alfonso de Liguori ran counter, for instance, to the idea that there is no intermediary institution which holds the power of the keys to paradise. This is a major consequence of the Protestant reformations. The existence of moral jurisprudence was at odds, too, with the subjectivization of 'conscience' and the refusal to accept specialist moral experts. This is another major consequence of Luther's and Calvin's reform movements. Moral jurisprudence faltered, eventually, over the collapse of the dualist anthropology which held that man consisted not only of matter but also of soul. In the eyes of the modern reader, the *forum internum*, the tribunal of the truth that belonged to the province of the theologians, has been reduced to a dream. Today,

---

Todescan, *Etiamsi Daremus*, Studio 4: *Secolarizzazione del diritto naturale e jus circa sacra nel pensiero di Ugo Grozio*, esp. p. 74–75.

[2138] E.g. S. Orrego-Sánchez, *The 16th century school of Salamanca as a context of synthesis between the Middle Ages and the Renaissance in theological and philosophical matters*, in: C. Burnett – J. Meirinhos – J. Hamesse (eds.), Continuities and disruptions between the Middle Ages and the Renaissance, [Textes et études du moyen âge, 48], Louvain-la-Neuve 2008, p. 113–138; Braun, *Juan de Mariana*, p. 162, where it is expressly remarked that broad tags such as 'humanism' and 'scholasticism' do not do justice to thinkers such as Mariana (p. 161). The conventional distinction between scholastic and humanist logic has also been called into question by E.J. Ashworth, *Traditional logic*, in: C.B. Schmitt – Q. Skinner – E. Kessler – J. Kraye (eds.), The Cambridge history of Renaissance philosophy, Cambridge 1988, p. 143–172. However, the debate about the humanism/scholasticism distinction remains heated; cf. E. Kessler, *Ethik im Mittelalter und im Frühen Humanismus, Kritische Studie über eine 'Kritische Studie'*, Recherches de Théologie et Philosophie médiévales, 78 (2011), p. 481–505.

the proposition that pastoral care requires expert knowledge of a great number of legal systems, ranging from natural law through canon law and civil law, may even sound preposterous. Conversely, to claim that a modern jurist must respect moral and theological principles would seem to be almost subversive. If anything, economic calculus has replaced canon law as the 'archimedical point' for determining the 'right' legislation and adjudication policies.[2139]

The specialization of disciplines as proposed by Samuel von Pufendorf in the marvellously written introductory note to his work *On Duties* is an ultimate testimony to why 'moral jurisprudence' became unthinkable long before the advent of the Codes. Pufendorf distinghuished three sources of duties, namely reason, civil laws, and divine revelation. He held that it pertained to separate disciplines to analyze the obligations that followed from each of those sources, namely natural law, civil law, and moral theology, respectively.[2140] With Pufendorf, we witness the advent of the Enlightenment.[2141] In Pufendorf's world, moral theologians had no business with natural law or civil law, and law had to distance itself from theology in the first place.[2142] Yet this is not how the Catholic theologians of the early modern period saw it. They shared a widespread view that an expert moral theologian must also peruse the light of reason and the complex body of civil laws.

The theologians of the early modern period spared no effort in assimilating natural law, Roman law, canon law, and positive law into a vast body of moral jurisprudence that reshaped the entire juridical tradition.

[2139] Luhmann, *Das Recht der Gesellschaft*, p. 504.

[2140] Pufendorf, *De officio, Ad lectorem*, cited and translated supra, n. 183.

[2141] F. Todescan, *Le radici teologiche del giusnaturalismo laico, III. Il problema della secolarizzazione nel pensiero giuridico di Samuel Pufendorf*, [Per la storia del pensiero giuridico moderno, 57], Milano 2001, p. 8. At the same time, the author stresses that Pufendorf was more indebted to the scholastic tradition than he would have granted. This is the case, for instance, in regard to his ideas on justice in exchange and restitution, as was noted by Thieme, *Natürliches Privatrecht und Spätscholastik*, p. 1047.

[2142] F. Palladini, *Volontarismo e 'laicità' del diritto naturale, La critica di Samuel Pufendorf a Grozio, De iure belli ac pacis, Prol. II e I, 1, 10*, Roma 1984, p. 32, and Birocchi, *Alla ricerca dell'ordine*, p. 196–197. It might be noted that Pufendorf, who sympathized with the Jansenists, was notoriously hostile to the Jesuits, as is obvious from several of his letters, mostly written in the year 1690; cf. D. Döring (ed.), *Samuel Pufendorf, Briefwechsel*, in: W. Schmidt-Biggemann (ed.), *Samuel Pufendorf, Gesammelte Werke*, Band 1, Berlin 1996, letters 78, 172, 184, 191 and 194. Interestingly, his library contained copies of Covarruvias, Fernando Vázquez de Menchaca, and Juan de Lugo amongst other Spanish and/or scholastic writers; cf. F. Palladini, *La Biblioteca di Samuel Pufendorf, Catalogo dell'asta di Berlin del settembre 1697*, [Wolfenbüttler Schriften zur Geschichte des Buchwesens, 32], Wiesbaden 1999.

The privatization of morality in the modern period has made any return to the ideas of the early modern theologians impossible, but in their own time, the doctrines of the theologians were not a matter of pure intellectual phantasy. The theologians' engagement with law was a matter of necessity in light of the Church's claim that it held the power of the keys to Paradise. Handling those keys required expert knowledge of law to guide man through the labyrinth of life. Before law and moral theology definitively parted ways, the symbiosis of the *ius commune* and the moral tradition reached a peak. As a result, the Catholic theologians bequeathed to the jurists a morally transformed law of contract. As Friedrich Carl von Savigny put it in the context of his monumental system of the modern Roman law:[2143]

> Christianity is not to be regarded merely as a rule of life for us but it has also in fact changed the world so that all our thoughts, however strange and hostile they may appear to it, are nevertheless governed and penetrated by it.

[2143] F.C. von Savigny, *System of the modern Roman Law*, vol. 1, p. 43 (cf. supra, n. 1). On the colonial background against which this translation in English of Savigny's *System des heutigen Römischen Rechts* took place, and the profoundly Christian dimensions to Savigny's doctrines of private law, particularly in regard to family law, see D. Kennedy, *Savigny's family/patrimony distinction and its place in the global genealogy of classical legal thought*, American Journal of Comparative Law, 58 (2010), p. 811–841.

BIBLIOGRAPHY

1. PRIMARY SOURCES

1.1. *Roman, canon and Spanish legislation*

Corpus Iustinianaeum cum commentariis Accursii, scholiis Contii, paratitlis Cujacii, et quo-rundam aliorum doctorum virorum observationibus, Novae accesserunt ad ipsum Accur-sium Dionysii Gothofredi notae, Lugduni 1604 [= 1588] (= ed. Gothofredi).

Corpus iuris civilis, ed. P. Krüger- Th. Mommsen, Dublin – Zürich 1968¹⁶.

Corpus iuris canonici emendatum et notis illustratum, Gregorii XIII iussu editum, Romae 1582 (= ed. Gregoriana).

Corpus iuris canonici, ed. E. Friedberg, Lipsiae 1879–1881.

El ordenamiento de leyes que Alfonso XI hizo en las cortes de Alcalá de Henares (1348), ed. I.J. de Asso y del Río – D.M. de Manuel y Rodriguez, Madrid 1774.

Las leyes de Toro glosadas por Diego del Castillo, Burgos 1527.

Las Siete Partidas de Alfonso El Sabio, cotejadas con varios codices antiguos por la Real Academia de la Historia, y glosadas por Gregorio López, Paris 1851.

Ordenanças Reales de Castilla [= Ordenamiento de Montalvo], Toleti 1549.

Recopilación de las leyes destos reynos por mandado del Rey Philippe Segundo (= Nueva Recopilación), Alcalá de Henares 1569.

Quinque compilationes antiquae nec non collectio canonum Lipsiensis, ed. E. Friedberg, Lipsiae 1882.

1.2. *Classical authors*

Ambrosius, *De officiis*, in: *Saint Ambroise, Les devoirs*, Texte établi, traduit et annoté par Maurice Testard, [Collection des Universités de France], Paris 1984–1992, 2 vols.

Aristoteles, *Ars rhetorica*, recognovit brevique adnotatione critica instruxit W.D. Ross, [Scriptorum classicorum bibliotheca Oxoniensis], Oxonii 1959.

——, *Ethica Nicomachea*, recognovit brevique adnotatione critica instruxit I. Bywater, [Scriptorum classicorum bibliotheca Oxoniensis], Oxonii 1970¹⁵ [= 1894].

——, *Metaphysica*, recognovit brevique adnotatione critica instruxit W. Jaeger, [Scripto-rum classicorum bibliotheca Oxoniensis], Oxonii 1957.

——, *Politica*, recognovit brevique adnotatione critica instruxit W.D. Ross, [Scriptorum classicorum bibliotheca Oxoniensis], Oxonii 1973⁵ [= 1957].

Augustinus, Aurelius, *De civitate Dei*, in: *Aureli Augustini opera, Pars XIV,2*, [Corpus Chris-tianorum Series Latina, 48], Turnholti 1955.

——, *De ordine*, in: *Aureli Augustini opera, Pars II,2*, [Corpus Christianorum Series Latina, 29], Turnholti 1970.

——, *De Trinitate*, lib. 13–15, in: *Aureli Augustini opera, Pars XVI,2*, [Corpus Christianorum Series Latina, 50A], Turnholti 1968.

——, *Epistolae*, in: J.-P. Migne (ed.), Augustini opera omnia post Lovaniensium theologo-rum recensionem, vol. 2, [Patrologia Latina, 33], Parisiis 1845.

——, *Sermones*, in: J.-P. Migne (ed.), Augustini opera omnia post Lovaniensium theologo-rum recensionem, vol. 5, [Patrologia Latina, 38–39], Parisiis 1841.

Cicero, Marcus Tullius, *De legibus*, in: *Cicéron, Traité des lois*, Texte établi et traduit par Georges De Plinval, [Collection des Universités de France], Paris 1968² [= 1959].

——, *De officiis*, in: *Cicéron, Les devoirs*, Texte établi et traduit par Maurice Testard, [Col-lection des Universités de France], Paris 1965–1970, 2 vols.

——, *Orator*, in: *Cicéron, L'orateur, Du meilleur genre d'orateurs*, Texte établi et traduit par Albert Yon, [Collection des Universités de France], Paris 1964.

Columella, Lucius Junius Moderatus, *De re rustica*, 1, 7, 2, in: *Columella, On Agriculture*, with a recension of the text and an English translation by Harrison Boyd Ash, Cambridge Mass. – London 1960³ [= 1941].

Hesiod, *Theogony, Works and days, Testimonia*, edited and translated by G.W. Most, [Loeb Classical Library, 57], Cambridge Mass. – London 2006.

Hispalensis, Isidorus, *Etymologiarum sive originum libri XX*, recognovit brevique adnotatione critica instruxit W.M. Lindsay, [Scriptorum classicorum bibliotheca Oxoniensis], Oxonii 1911.

Homer, *The Odyssey*, Books 1–12, with an English translation by A.T. Murray revised by George E. Dimock, [Loeb Classical Library, 104], Cambridge Mass. – London 1995.

Horatius Flaccus, Quintus, *Epistulae*, in: *Horace, Satires, Epistles, and Ars poetica*, with an English translation by H. Rushton Fairclough, [Loeb Classical Library, 194], Cambridge Mass. – London.

Maximus, Valerius, *Dicta et facta memorabilia*, in: *Valerius Maximus, Memorable doings and sayings*, edited and translated by D.R. Schackleton Bailey, [Loeb Classical Library, 492–3], Cambridge Mass. – London 2000, 2 vols.

Plautus, *Aulularia*, in: *Plaute, Amphitryon—Asinaria—Aulularia*, Texte établi et traduit par Alfred Ernout, [Collection des Universités de France], Paris 1967⁶ [= 1932].

Plutarch, *Kleomenes*, in: *Plutarch, Lives*, with an English translation by Bernadotte Perrin, [Loeb Classical Library, 102], Cambridge Mass. – London 1968, vol. 10.

Quintilianus, *De institutione oratoria*, in: *Quintilien, Institution oratoire, Tome 4, Livres 6–7*, Texte établi et traduit par Jean Cousin, [Collection des Universités de France], Paris 1977.

Rhetorica ad Herennium, in: *Rhétorique à Herennius*, Texte établi et traduit par Guy Achard, [Collection des Universités de France], Paris 1989.

Seneca, Lucius Annaeus, *De beneficiis*, in: *Sénèque, Des bienfaits*, [Collection des Universités de France], Paris 1961.

——, *De divina providentia*, in: *Seneca, Moral Essays*, with an English translation by John W. Basore, [Loeb Classical Library, 214], Cambridge Mass. – London 1963³ [= 1928], vol. 1.

Terentius, Publius Afer, *Heautontimoroumenos*, in: *Térence, Heautontimoroumenos – Phormion*, Texte établi et traduit par J. Marouzeau, [Collection des Universités de France], Paris 1964.

1.3. *Late medieval authors*

Ancharano, Pietro de, *Super sexto Decretalium commentaria*, Bononiae 1583.

Andrea, Giovanni de, *In quinque Decretalium libros novella commentaria*, with an introduction by Stephan Kuttner, Torino 1963 [= anastatic reproduction of the Venice 1581 edition].

Aquinas, Thomas, *Summa Theologiae*, in: *Opera omnia iussu impensaque Leonis XIII edita*, tom. 4–12, Romae 1888–1906.

——, *Scriptum super Sententiis magistri Petri Lombardis*, ed. M.F. Moos, Parisiis 1929–1947.

——, *Sententia libri Ethicorum*, in: *Opera Omnia iussu impensaque Leonis XIII edita*, tom. 47, Romae 1969.

Azo, *Summa Codicis et Institutionum*, Venetiae 1499.

Belleperche, Pierre de, *In libros Institutionum commentarii*, Lugduni 1536.

Bottrigari, Jacobo, *Lectura super Codice*, [Opera iuridica rariora, 13], Bononiae 1973 [= anastatic reproduction of the 1516 Paris edition].

Butrio, Antonio de, *Super Decretalibus commentarii*, Torino 1967 [= anastatic reproduction of the Venice 1578 edition].

Castro, Paolo de, *Lectura super Digesto veteri*, Venetiis 1495.

Duns Scotus, John, *Quaestiones in quattuor libros Sententiarum*, in: Ioannis Duns Scoti opera omnia, Hildesheim 1968 [= anastatic reprint of the Lyon 1639 edition].

Durand, Guillaume, *Speculum iudiciale illustratum et repurgatum a Giovanni Andrea et Baldo degli Ubaldi*, Aalen 1975 [= anastatic reprint of the Basel 1574 edition].

Firenze, Antonino di, *Summa theologica*, Veronae 1740.

Fulgosio, Raffaele, *In primam Pandectarum partem commentaria*, Lugduni 1544.

Gerson, Jean, *De iis ferme rebus quae ad mores conducunt*, Basileae 1518.

Hostiensis, Henricus Cardinalis, *Summa aurea*, Venetiis 1570.

——, *In sex Decretalium libros commentaria*, Torino 1965 [= anastatic reprint of the Venice 1581 edition].

Innocentius IV (Sinibaldo de' Fieschi), *In quinque libros Decretalium commentaria*, quibus addita est Margarita Baldi indicis loco, Lugduni 1562.

Olivi, Pierre Jean de, *De contractibus*, edited by S. Piron in: *Parcours d'un intellectuel franciscain, d'une théologie vers une pensée sociale, L'oeuvre de Pierre Jean d'Olivi (ca. 1248–1298) et son traité De contractibus*, Paris 1999 [unpublished doct. diss. EHESS].

——, *Lectura super Genesim*, in: Sancti Thomae Aquinatis opera omnia, Parma 1868, tom. 23.

Panormitanus, Abbas (Nicolaus de Tudeschis), *Commentaria super Decretalibus*, Augustae Taurinorum 1577.

Pistoia, Cino da, *Lectura super Codice*, Venetiis 1493.

Sandaeus, Felinus, *Commentaria in quinque libros Decretalium*, Basileae 1567.

Saxoferrato, Bartolus de, *In primam Codicis partem commentaria*, Lugduni 1555.

——, *In primam Digesti veteris partem commentaria*, Venetiis 1570.

——, *In secundam Digesti novi partem commentaria*, Lugduni 1555.

——, *In secundam Digesti veteris partem*, Venetiis 1570.

Siena, Bernardine of, *Quadragesimale de Christiana religione*, in: Opera omnia, Venetiis 1745, tom. 1.

Stracca, Benvenuto, *De mercatura*, Venetiis 1553.

Tartagnus Imolensis, Alexander, *Lectura novissima de verborum obligatione*, in: Ad frequentiores Pandectarum titulos, leges et paragraphos, Venetiis 1595.

Trovamala, Giovanni Baptista, *Summa rosella de casibus conscientiae*, Argentinae 1516.

Ubaldis, Baldus de, *Commentaria in quartum et quintum Codicis libros*, Lugduni 1585.

——, *Commentaria in septimum, octavum, nonum, decimum et undecimum Codicis libros*, Lugduni 1585.

——, *In primam Digesti veteris partem commentaria*, Lugduni 1585.

——, *Super Decretalibus*, Lugduni 1564.

1.4. *Early Modern authors*

Adrian of Utrecht, *Quaestiones in quartum sententiarum praesertim circa sacramenta*, Parisiis 1516.

——, *Quaestiones quodlibeticae duodecim, quibus accesserunt Joannis Briardi Athensis quaestiones item quodlibeticae*, Parisiis 1527.

Afflitto, Matteo de, *Decisionum sacri regii Neapolitani consilii*, Francofurti 1600.

Alciati, Andrea, *Paradoxa iuris civilis ad Pratum*, Lugduni 1532.

——, *Ad rescripta principum commentarii*, Lugduni 1535.

——, *Responsa*, Lugduni 1561.

Almain, Jacques, *De poenitentia sive in quartum lectura*, in: Almaini opuscula, Parisiis 1518.

Ames, William, *De conscientia et ejus iure vel casibus libri quinque*, Amstelodami 1631.

Antonio, Nicolas, *Bibliotheca Hispana nova, sive Hispanorum scriptorum qui ab anno 1500 ad 1684 floruere notitia*, Matriti, 1783–1788.

Aragón, Pedro de, *In secundam secundae commentaria de iustitia et iure*, Salmanticae 1590.

Azevedo, Alfonso de, *Commentarii iuris civilis in Hispaniae regias consitutiones*, tom. 2 (*quartum librum Novae Recopilationis complectens*), Matritii 1595.

Azor, Juan, *Institutiones morales*, Lugduni 1612.

Azpilcueta, Martín de (Dr. Navarrus), *In tres de poenitentia distinctiones posteriores commentarii*, Conimbricae 1542.

——, *Enchiridion sive manuale confessariorum et poenitentium*, Antverpiae 1575.

——, *Commentarius de finibus humanarum actuum, in cap. Cum minister*, in: Opera omnia, Venetiis 1601, tom. 1.

——, *Relectio in cap. Novit de iudiciis*, in: Opera Omnia, Venetiis 1601, tom. 3.

Balduin, Friedrich, *Tractatus de casibus conscientiae*, Wittebergae 1628.

Bañez, Domingo de, *De iure et iustitia decisiones*, Salmanticae 1594.

Budé, Guillaume, *Annotationes ad viginti quattuor libros Pandectarum*, Parisiis 1508.

Busenbaum, Hermann, *Medulla theologiae moralis facili ac perspicua methodo resolvens casus conscientiae*, Monasteri Westphaliae 1661.

Cajetanus, Tommaso de Vio, *Summula peccatorum*, Venetiis 1571.

——, *Commentaria ad Secundam Secundae divi Thomae*, in: *Sancti Thomae Aquinatis opera omnia iussu impensaque Leonis XIII edita*, tom. 8: *Secunda secundae Summae Theologiae a quaestione I ad quaestionem LVI*, Romae 1895.

——, *Commentaria ad Secundam Secundae divi Thomae*, in: *Sancti Thomae Aquinatis opera omnia iussu impensaque Leonis XIII edita*, tom. 9: *Secunda secundae Summae Theologiae a quaestione LVII ad quaestionem CXXII*, Romae 1897.

Cano, Melchor, *De locis theologicis*, edición preparada por Juan Belda Plans, [Biblioteca de Autores Cristianos Maior, 85], Madrid 2006.

Carletti de Chivasso, Angelo, *Summa Angelica de casibus conscientiae*, Lugduni 1512.

Claro, Giulio, *Receptarum sententiarum opera omnia*, Francofurti 1596.

Coke, Edward, *Second part of the Institutes of the laws of England*, London 1642.

Comitoli, Paolo, *Doctrina de contractu universe ad scientiae methodum revocato*, Lugduni 1615.

Coustau, Pierre, *Adversaria ex Pandectis Iustiniani*, Lugduni 1554.

Covarruvias y Leyva, Diego de, *Relectio in regulam Peccatum, De regulis iuris, lib. 6*, Salmanticae 1558.

——, *Variarum resolutionum libri quattuor*, in: Opera omnia, Augustae Taurinorum 1594, tom. 1.

——, *In titulum de testamentis interpretatio, cap. 10 (Cum esses)*, in: Opera omnia, Augustae Taurinorum 1594, tom. 2.

——, *In librum quartum Decretalium epitome*, in: Opera omnia, Augustae Taurinorum 1594, tom. 2.

——, *Relectio in cap. Quamvis pactum de pactis, libro 6*, in: Opera omnia, Augustae Taurinorum 1594, tom. 2.

——, *Relectio in regulam Possessor malae fidei, de regulis iuris, lib. 6*, in: Opera Omnia, Augustae Taurinorum 1594, tom. 2.

——, *Relectio in regulam Peccatum, De regulis iuris, lib. 6*, in: Opera omnia, Augustae Taurinorum 1594, tom. 2.

Cujas, Jacques, *Paratitla in libros quinquaginta Digestorum seu Pandectarum Imperatoris Iustiniani*, Coloniae 1570.

Damhouder, Joost de, *Practycke in Civile Saecken*, 's Graven-hage 1626, ed. J. Monballyu – J. Dauwe, Gent 1999.

Diana, Antonino, *Resolutiones morales*, Caesaraugustae 1632.

Doneau, Hugues, *Commentaria iuris civilis*, Hanoviae 1612.

Du Moulin, Charles, *Tractatus commerciorum et usurarum redituumque pecunia constitutorum et monetarum*, Lugduni 1558.

——, *Nova et analytica explicatio Rubricae et legum 1. et 2. de verborum obligationibus ex lectionibus tam Tubingensibus quam Dolanis*, Parisiis 1562.

——, *Commentarii in Parisienses consuetudines*, Francofurti ad Moenum 1597.

Erasmus, Desiderius, *Exomologesis sive modus confitendi*, Antverpiae 1524.

——, *Adagiorum opus*, Basileae 1526.

Everaerts, Nicolaas, *Topicorum seu de locis legalibus liber*, Lovanii 1516.

Figliucci, Vincenzo, *Morales quaestiones de Christianis officiis et casibus conscientiae ad formam cursus qui praelegi solet in Collegio Romano Societatis Iesu*, Lugduni 1622.

——, *Brevis instructio pro confessionibus excipiendis*, Ravenspurgi 1626.

Forcadel, Étienne, *Cupido jurisperitus*, Lugduni 1553.

——, *Necyomantiae sive occultae jurisprudentiae tractatus*, in: Opera Stephani Forcatuli, Parisiis 1595.

Garcia, Fortunius, *Commentarius in l. ut vim, ff. de iustitia et iure*, in: Tractatus in materia defensionis, Coloniae 1580.

——, *De ultimo fine iuris civilis et canonici, de primo principio et subsequentibus praeceptis, de derivatione et differentiis utriusque iuris et quid sit tenendum ipsa iustitia*, Coloniae Agrippinae 1585.

——, *Repetitio super cap. 1 de Pactis*, in: *Commentaria in titulum Digesti de Pactis, difficilem, uberrimum, omniumque contractuum parentem cum repetitione cap. 1 Extra in eodem titulo*, Francoforti 1592.

García, Francisco, *Tratado utilísimo y muy general de todos los contratos*, Valencia 1583, ed. I. Zorroza – H. Rodríguez-Penelas, [Colleción de pensamiento medieval y renacentista, 46], Pamplona 2003.

Gómez, Antonio, *Commentarii variaeque resolutiones iuris civilis, communis et regii, Accesserunt adnotationes Emanuelis Soarez a Ribeira*, Francoforti ad Rhenum 1572.

——, *Opus praeclarum et utilissimum super legibus Tauri*, Salmanticae 1598.

Grotius, Hugo, *De jure belli ac pacis libri tres in quibus ius naturae et gentium item iuris publici praecipua explicantur*, Curavit B.J.A. De Kanter – Van Hettinga Tromp, Editionis anni 1939 exemplar photomechanice iteratum, Annotationes novas addiderunt R. Feenstra et C.E. Persenaire, adiuvante E. Arps-De Wilde, Aalen 1993.

Heineccius, Johann Gottlieb, *Institutiones jurisprudentiae divinae*, Francofurti – Lipsiae 1688.

Henríquez, Enrique, *Summa theologiae moralis tomus primus*, Venetiis 1600.

Hopperus, Joachim, *De iuris arte libri tres*, Lovanii 1555.

Kestner, Heinrich Ernst, *Discursus de jurisprudentia papizante*, Rintelii 1711.

Klock, Kaspar, *Tractatus juridico-politico-polemico-historicus de aerario, sive censu per honesta media absque divexatione populi licite conficiendo, libri duo*, Nürnberg 1651, mit einer Einleitung herausgegeben von Bertram Schefold, Hildesheim – Zürich – New York 2009.

Laymann, Paul, *Theologia moralis*, Monachii 1630.

Ledesma, Martín de, *Secunda quartae*, Conimbricae 1560.

Le Douaren, François, *De in litem iurando iudiciisque bonaefidei etiam arbitrariis commentarius*, Lugduni 1542.

——, *In lib. 45 Pandectarum, tit. de verborum obligationibus commentarius*, Lugduni 1554.

——, *Commentarius in tit. De pactis*, in: Francisci Duareni opera omnia, Lugduni 1554.

——, *De docendi discendique iuris epistola ad Andream Guillartum*, in: Francisci Duareni opera omnia, Lugduni 1554.

Lessius, Leonardus, *De gratia efficaci, decretis divinis, libertate arbitrii et praescientia Dei conditionata disputatio apologetica*, Antverpiae 1610.

——, *De iustitia et iure ceterisque virtutibus cardinalibus*, Lovanii 1605.

——, *De iustitia et iure ceterisque virtutibus cardinalibus*, Antverpiae 1621.

——, *De matrimonii sacramento*, in: De beatitudine, de actibus humanis, de incarnatione Verbi, de sacramentis et censuris praelectiones theologicae posthumae. Accesserunt variorum casuum conscientiae resolutiones, ed. I. Wijns, Lovanii 1645.

——, *De perfectionibus moribusque divinis*, Anverpiae 1620.

——, *De praedestinatione et reprobatione angelorum et hominum disputatio*, Antverpiae 1610.

——, *In I.II D. Thomae de beatitudine et actibus humanis*, in: De beatitudine, de actibus humanis, de incarnatione Verbi, de sacramentis et censuris praelectiones theologicae

posthumae. Accesserunt variorum casuum conscientiae resolutiones, ed. I. Wijns, Lovanii 1645.

——, *In III Partem D. Thomae de Sacramentis et Censuris*, in: De beatitudine, de actibus humanis, de incarnatione Verbi, de sacramentis et censuris praelectiones theologicae posthumae. Accesserunt variorum casuum conscientiae resolutiones, ed. I. Wijns, Lovanii 1645.

Liguori, Alfonso Maria de', *Theologia moralis*, Bassani 1773.

Loriot, Pierre, *Tractatus de pactis*, in: Petri Lorioti de iuris apicibus tractatus octo, et de iuris arte tractatus viginti, Lugduni 1555.

Loysel, Antoine, *Institutes coustumieres ou manuel de plusieurs et diverses reigles, sentences, et proverbes tant anciens que modernes du droict coustumier et plus ordinaire de la France*, Paris 1637.

Luca, Giovanni Battista de, *Theatrum veritatis et iustitiae*, Venetiis 1716.

Lugo, Juan de, *Disputationes scholasticae et morales de virtute et sacramento poenitentiae*, Lugduni 1638.

——, *De iustitia et iure*, Lugduni 1642.

——, *Responsa moralia*, Lugduni 1651.

Maino, Giasone del, *In primam Digesti Veteris partem commentaria*, Venetiis 1579.

Marsigli, Ippolito, *Repetitio rubricae C. de probationibus*, Lugduni 1531.

——, *Tractatus de quaestionibus in quo materiae maleficiorum pertractantur*, s.l. 1542.

Medina, Bartolomé de, *In primam secundae divi Thomae*, Bergomi 1586.

Medina, Juan de, *De poenitentia, restitutione et contractibus*, Farnborough 1967 [= Ingolstadii 1581].

Mercado, Tomás de, *Suma de tratos y contratos*, Sevilla 1587.

Molina, Luís de, *De iustitia et iure*, Moguntiae 1659.

Molina y Morales, Luís de, *De primogeniorum Hispanorum origine ac natura*, nova editio cum additionibus Josephi Maldonado Pardo et Fernandi Alfonsi del Aguila et Roxas, Lugduni 1727.

Navarra, Pedro de, *De ablatorum restitutione in foro conscientiae*, Lugduni 1593.

Noël, François, *Theologiae Francisci Suarez e Societate Jesu summa seu compendium in duas partes divisum, duobusque tractatibus adauctum; primo de justitia et jure, secundo de matrimonio*, Coloniae 1732.

Oldendorp, Johann, *Formula investigandae actionis per quam unusquisque ius suum in iudicio persequatur, cum deliberatione aequi et boni*, Coloniae 1538.

——, *Variae lectiones ad iuris civilis interpretationem*, Lugduni 1546.

Oñate, Pedro de, *De contractibus*, Romae 1646.

Padilla y Meneses, Antonio, *In titulum de transactionibus Codicis commentarius*, Salmanticae 1566.

Pascal, Blaise, *Les Provinciales ou les lettres écrites par Louis De Montalte*, Amsterdam 1657.

Peck, Pieter, *Tractatus de amortizatione bonorum a principe impetranda*, in: Petri Peckii opera omnia, Antverpiae 1679.

Perez, Antonio, *De iustitia et iure et de poenitentia opus posthumum*, Romae 1668.

Piñel, Arias, *Commentarii ad rub. et l. 2, C. de rescindenda venditione, cum annotationibus Emanuelis Soarez a Ribiera. Accessit eiusdem argumenti cap. 3 et 4, lib. 2 resolutionum Didaci Covarruvias*, Antverpiae 1618.

Ponce de León, Basilio, *De sacramento matrimonii tractatus, Opus aeque canonici et civilis iuris ac sacrae theologiae professoribus utile ac necessarium*, Bruxellis 1632.

Pothier, Robert-Joseph, *Traité des obligations, selon les regles, tant du for de la conscience, que du for extérieur*, nouvelle édition, Paris – Orléans 1777.

Prierio, Sylvester (Mazzolini) da, *Summa sylvestrina*, Lugduni 1520.

Pufendorf, Samuel von, *De officio*, ed. G. Hartung, in: W. Schmidt-Biggemann (ed.), Samuel Pufendorf, Gesammelte Werke, Band 2, Berlin 1997.

——, *De jure naturae et gentium, Liber primus—Liber quartus*, ed. F. Böhling, in: W. Schmidt-Biggemann (ed.), Samuel Pufendorf, Gesammelte Werke, Band 4.1, Berlin 1998.

——, *De jure naturae et gentium, Liber quintus—Liber octavus*, ed. F. Böhling, in: W. Schmidt-Biggemann (ed.), Samuel Pufendorf, Gesammelte Werke, Band 4.2, Berlin 1998.

Rebelo, Fernão, *Opus de obligationibus justitiae, religionis et charitatis*, Lugduni 1608.

Regnault, Valère, *Praxis fori poenitentialis ad directionem confessarii in usu sacri sui muneris. Opus tam poenitentibus quam confessariis utile*, Lugduni 1616.

Ruginelli, Giulio Cesare, *Practicarum quaestionum rerumque iudicatarum liber singularis*, Venetiis 1610.

Sá, Manuel de, *Aphorismi confessariorum ex doctorum sententiis collecti*, Antverpiae 1599.

Salas, Juan de, *Disputationes in primam secundae*, Barcinonae 1607.

Sánchez, Tomás, *Disputationes de sancto matrimonii sacramento*, Antverpiae 1620.

——, *Opuscula sive consilia moralia*, Lugduni 1634.

——, *Opus morale in praecepta Decalogi*, Antverpiae 1614.

Sarmiento de Mendoza, Francesco, *De selectis interpretationibus*, Francoforti ad Moenum 1580.

Schwarz, Ignaz, *Institutiones iuris universalis naturae et gentium*, Venetiis 1760.

Selden, John, *The table talk*, ed. S.H. Reynolds, Oxford 1892.

Solórzano y Pereira, Juan de, *De indiarum iure sive de iusta Indiarum Occidentalium inquisitione, acquisitione et retentione*, lib. 1: *De inquisitione Indiarum*, ed. C. Baciero e.a., [Corpus Hispanorum de Pace, Serie 2, 8], Madrid 2001.

Soto, Domingo de, *De iustitia et iure libri decem / De la justicia y del derecho en diez libros*, edición facsimilar de la hecha por D. de Soto en 1556 [Salamanca], con su versión castellana corrrespondiente, Introducción historica y teologico-juridica por Venancio Diego Carro, Versión española de Marcelino González Ordóñez, [Instituto de estudios políticos, Sección de teólogos juristas, 1], Madrid 1967 (vol. 1); 1968 (vol. 4–5).

——, *De iustitia et iure*, Salmanticae 1562.

——, *In quartum sententiarum librum commentarii*, Lovanii 1573.

Stryk, Samuel, *Dissertatio juridica de credentiae revelatione*, quam (...) praeside Samuele Strykio (...) publicae eruditorum disquisitioni exponit Henricus Andreas Breiger, Francofurti ad Viadrum 1675 [= Diss. jur., Frankfurt/Oder, 1675].

——, *Disputatio juridica de conscientia partium in judicio*, quam (...) praeside Samuele Strykio (...) placido eruditorum examini submittit Johannes Christianus John, Francofurti ad Viadrum 1677 [= Diss. jur., Frankfurt/Oder, 1677].

——, *Dissertatio de conscientia advocati*, quam (...) praeside Samuele Strykio (...) placido eruditorum examini sistit Ephraim Nazius, Francofurti ad Viadrum 1677 [= Diss. jur., Frankfurt/Oder, 1677].

Suárez, Francisco, *Commentaria in tertiam partem Divi Thomae, a quaestione 84 usque ad finem*, in: Opera omnia, editio nova a Carolo Berton, Parisiis 1861, tom. 22.

——, *Defensio fidei catholicae adversus Anglicanae sectae errores*, in: Opera omnia, editio nova a Carolo Berton, Parisiis 1859, tom. 24.

——, *Disputationes de censuris in communi et in particulari de excommunicatione, suspensione et interdicto, ac praeterea de irregularitate*, in: Opera omnia, editio nova a Carolo Berton, Parisiis 1861, tom. 23.

——, *Tractatus de anima*, in: Opera omnia, editio nova a D.M. André, Parisiis 1856, tom. 3.

——, *Tractatus de legibus et legislatore Deo*, lib. 1–5, in: Opera omnia, editio nova a Carolo Berton, Parisiis 1856, tom. 5.

——, *Tractatus de legibus et legislatore Deo*, lib. 6–10, in: Opera omnia, editio nova a Carolo Berton, Parisiis 1856, tom. 6.

——, *Tractatus de vitiis et peccatis*, in: Opera omnia, editio nova a D.M. André, Parisiis 1856, tom. 4.

Summenhart, Conradus, *Opus septipertitum de contractibus*, [Augustae Vindelicae 1515].

Thisius Mosae-Trajectinus, Leonardus Ignatius, *Theses theologicae quibus exhibentur quaedam observationes circa aliquot propositiones de furto, compensatione occulta et restitutione inter lxv a Innocentio condemnatas* [praeses: Gummarus Huygens Lyranus; defensio in collegio Adriani VI die 7 decembris 1684], Lovanii 1684.

Thomasius, Christian, *Dissertatio iuridica inauguralis de aequitate cerebrina et l. 2, C. de resc. vend. et eius usu practico*, Halae Magdeburgicae 1706.

Tiraqueau, André, *Commentarii in l. Si unquam, C. De revocandis donationibus*, Lugduni 1546.

———, *De legibus connubialibus et iure maritali*, Parisiis 1546.

———, *De nobilitate et de iure primigeniorum*, Basileae 1561.

———, *De poenis legum ac consuetudinum statutorumque temperandis aut etiam remittendis et id quibus quotque ex causis*, in: Andreae Tiraquelli opera omnia, Francoforti ad Moenum 1597, tom. 7.

———, *De utroque retractu, municipali et conventionali, commentarii duo*, in: Andreae Tiraquelli opera omnia, Francoforti ad Moenum 1597, tom. 3.

Valentia, Gregorio de, *De discernenda humanorum contractuum iustitia et iniustitia disputatio theologica in celebri et catholica academia Ingolstadiensi anno MDLXXVII die 22 Maij habita*, Ingolstadii 1577.

———, *Commentaria theologica in Secundam Secundae D. Thomae*, Ingolstadii 1603.

Valero, Juan de, *Differentiae inter utrumque forum, iudiciale videlicet et conscientiae*, Cartusiae Maioricarum 1616.

Vázquez, Gabriel, *Tractatus de restitutione in foro conscientiae*, in: Opuscula moralia, Compluti 1617.

———, *De matrimonii sacramento*, in: Commentaria ac disputationes in tertiam partem Summae Theologiae divi Thomae, Lugduni 1631.

Vázquez de Menchaca, Fernando, *Controversiae illustres aliaeque usu frequentes*, Francofurti 1668.

Vitoria, Francisco de, *Comentarios a la Secunda secundae de Santo Tomás*, edición preparada por V. Beltrán de Heredia, tom. 2: *De caritate et prudentia* (qq. 23–56), [Biblioteca de Teólogos Españoles, 3], Salamanca 1932.

———, *Comentarios a la Secunda secundae de Santo Tomás*, edición preparada por V. Beltrán de Heredia, tom. 3: *De justitia* (qq. 57–66), [Biblioteca de Teólogos Españoles, 4], Salamanca 1934.

———, *Comentarios a la Secunda secundae de Santo Tomás*, edición preparada por V. Beltrán de Heredia, tom. 4: *De justitia* (qq. 67–88), [Biblioteca de Teólogos Españoles, 5], Salamanca 1934.

———, *Comentarios a la Secunda secundae de Santo Tomás*, edición preparada por V. Beltrán de Heredia, tom. 6, [Biblioteca de Teólogos Españoles, 17], Salamanca 1952.

Vivio, Francisco, *Decisiones regni Neapolitani*, Venetiis 1592.

Vultejus, Hermann, *Jurisprudentia Romana a Justiniano composita*, Marpurgi Cattorum 1628.

Wezenbeke, Matthias van, *Paratitla in Pandectas iuris civilis ab authore recognita et aucta*, Basileae 1568.

Zasius, Ullrich, *In tit. De verborum obligationibus lectura*, Lugduni 1547.

Zypaeus, Franciscus, *Notitia iuris belgici*, Antverpiae 1675.

2. Secondary Literature

Adams, M., *Wat de rechtsvergelijking vermag, Over onderzoeksdesign*, Ars Aequi, 60, (2011), p. 192–201.

Adams, M. – Witteveen, W., *Gedaantewisselingen van het recht*, Nederlands Juristenblad, 9 (2011), p. 540–546.

Agamben, G., *Il regno e la gloria, Per una genealogia teologica dell'economia e del governo*, [Homo Sacer, II. 2], Vicenza 2007.

———, *Opus Dei, Archeologia dell'ufficio*, [Homo Sacer, II. 5], Torino 2012.

Agüero, Alejandro, *Las penas impuestas por el Divino y Supremo Juez, Religión y justicia secular en Córdoba del Tucumán, siglos XVII y XVIII*, Anuario de historia de América Latina, 46 (2009), p. 203–230.

Alonso-Lasheras, D., *Luis de Molina's De iustitia et iure, Justice as virtue in an economic context*, [Studies in the history of Christian traditions, 152], Leiden – Boston 2011.

Ambrosetti, G., *Diritto privato ed economia nella Seconda Scolastica*, in: P. Grossi (ed.), La seconda scolastica nella formazione del diritto privato moderno, [Per la storia del pensiero giuridico moderno, 1], Milano 1973, p. 23–52.

Andujar, E.-Bazán, C., *Aequitas, aequalitas et auctoritas chez les maîtres de l'école espagnole du XVIe siècle*, in: D. Letocha (ed.), Aequitas, aequalitas, auctoritas, Raison théorique et légitimation de l'autorité dans le XVIe siècle européen, Actes du IIe colloque international (1990) du Centre de recherche en philosophie politique et sociale de l'Université d'Ottawa, [De Pétrarque à Descartes, 54], Paris 1992, p. 172–185.

Angelozzi, G., *L'insegnamento dei casi di coscienza nella pratica educativa della Compagnia di Gesù*, in: G.P. Brizzi (ed.), La 'Ratio studiorum', Modelli culturali e pratiche educative dei Gesuiti in Italia tra Cinque e Seicento, [Biblioteca del Cinquecento, 16], Roma 1981, p. 121–162.

Antonazzi, G., (ed.), *L'enciclica Rerum novarum, Testo autentico e redazioni preparatorie dai documenti originali*, Roma 1957.

Anxo Pena González, M., *La Escuela de Salamanca, De la Monarquía hispánica al Orbe católico*, [Biblioteca de Autores Cristianos Maior, 90], Madrid 2009.

Armstrong, L., *Usury and public debt in early Renaissance Florence, Lorenzo Ridolfi on the Monte Comune*, [Studies and Texts, 144], Toronto 2003.

Ascheri, M. – Baumgärtner, I. – Kirshner, J. (eds.), *Legal consulting in the civil law tradition*, Berkeley 1999.

Ascheri, M., *Nicola 'el monaco', consulente, con edizione di due suoi pareri olografi per la Toscana*, in: O. Condorelli (ed.), Niccolò Tedeschi (Abbas Panormitanus) e i suoi Commentaria in Decretales, [I libri di Erice, 25], Roma 2000, p. 37–68.

Ashworth, E.J., *Traditional logic*, in: C.B. Schmitt – Q. Skinner – E. Kessler – J. Kraye (eds.), The Cambridge history of Renaissance philosophy, Cambridge 1988, p. 143–172.

Atiyah, P.S., *The rise and fall of 'freedom of contract'*, Oxford 1979.

Aubert, J.-M., *Le droit romain dans l'œuvre de Saint Thomas*, [Bibliothèque Thomiste, 30], Paris 1955.

Augusto Rodrigues, M., *Note sul 'ius commune' in Portogallo*, Rivista internazionale di diritto comune, 12 (2001), p. 265–287.

Avenarius, M., *Benignior interpretatio, Origin and transformation of a rule of construction in the law of succession*, Roman Legal Tradition, 6 (2010), p. 1–21.

Aznar Gil, F.R., *El consentimiento paterno o familiar para el matrimonio*, Rivista internazionale di diritto comune, 6 (1995), p. 127–151.

Babbini, L., *Tre 'summa casuum' composte da tre francescani piemontesi della provincia di Genova*, Studi Francescani, 78 (1981), p. 159–169.

Baeck, L., *The Mediterranean tradition in economic thought*, London – New York 1994.

——, *Die rechtlichen und scholastischen Wurzeln des ökonomischen Denkens von Leonardus Lessius*, in: B. Schefold (ed.), Leonardus Lessius' De iustitia et iure, Vademecum zu einem Klassiker der Spätscholastischen Wirtschaftsanalyse, [Klassiker der Nationalökonomie], Düsseldorf 1999, p. 39–61.

——, *The legal and scholastic roots of Leonardus Lessius's economic thought*, [Leuven Centre for Economic Studies Discussion Papers], Leuven 1999.

——, *The Mediterranean trajectory of Aristotle's economic canon*, in: M. Psalidopoulos (ed.), The canon in the history of economics, Critical essays, [Routledge Studies in the History of Economics], London – New York 2000, p. 1–23.

Baker, J., *Origins of the 'doctrine' of consideration, 1535–1585*, in: M.S. Arnold (ed.), On the laws and customs of England, Essays in honor of Samuel E. Thorne, Chapel Hill 1981, p. 336–358.

——, *The Oxford history of the laws of England, Vol. 6: 1483–1558*, Oxford 2003.

Baldwin, J.W., *The medieval theories of the just price, Romanists, canonists and theologians in the twelfth and thirteenth centuries*, Transactions of the American Philosophical Society, 49 (1959), p. 3–92.

Barkun, M., *Law without sanctions, Order in primitive societies and the world community*, New Haven – London 1968.

Barrientos García, J., *Un siglo de moral económica (1526–1629), Tom. 1: Francisco de Vitoria y Domingo de Soto*, [Acta Salmanticensia iussu Senatus Universitatis edita, Filosofía y letras, 164], Salamanca 1985.

Barrientos Grandon, J., *El sistema del 'ius commune' en las Indias occidentales*, Rivista internazionale di diritto comune, 10 (1999), p. 53–137.

Bart, J., *Pacte et contrat dans la pratique française (XVIe–XVIIIe siècles)*, in: J. Barton (ed.), Towards a general law of contract, [Comparative Studies in Continental and Anglo-American Legal History, 8], Berlin 1990.

Bartocci, A., *Il cardinal Bonifacio Ammannati legista avignonese ed un suo opuscolo 'contra Bartolum' sulla capacità successoria dei Frati Minori*, Rivista internazionale di diritto comune, 17 (2006), p. 251–297.

——, *Ereditare in povertà, Le successioni a favore dei frati minori e la scienza giuridica nell'età avignonese (1309–1376)*, [Pubblicazioni del Dipartimento di Scienze Giuridiche, 32], Napoli 2009.

Barton, J., *Equity in the medieval common law*, in: R.A. Newman (ed.), Equity in the world's legal systems, A comparative study, Brussels 1973, p. 139–155.

——, (ed.), *Towards a general law of contract*, [Comparative studies in continental and Anglo-American legal history, 8], Berlin 1990.

Bauer, D., *The importance of canon law and the scholastic tradition for the emergence of an international legal order*, in: R. Lesaffer (ed.), Peace treaties and international law in history, Cambridge 2004, p. 198–221.

Baylor, M.G., *Action and Person, Conscience in late scholasticism and the young Luther*, Leiden 1977.

Becker, C., *Die Lehre von der laesio enormis in der Sicht der heutigen Wucherproblematik, Ausgewogenheit als Vetragsinhalt und § 138 BGB*, [Beiträge zur Neueren Privatrechtsgeschichte, 10], Köln et al. 1993.

Begheyn, P., *Gids voor de geschiedenis van de jezuïeten in Nederland, 1540–1850, A guide to the history of the Jesuits in the Netherlands, 1540–1850)*, Amsterdam 2006.

Behrends, O., *Treu und Glauben, Zu den christlichen Grundlagen der Willenstheorie im heutigen Vertragsrecht*, in: L. Lombardi Vallauri – G. Dilcher (eds.), Christentum, Säkularisation und modernes Recht, [Per la storia del pensiero giuridico moderno, 11–12], Baden-Baden/Milano 1981, p. 957–1006.

——, *Die rechtsethischen Grundlagen des Privatrechts*, in: F. Bydlinski – T. Mayer-Maly (eds.), Die ethischen Grundlagen des Privatrechts, Wien – New York 1994.

Belda Plans, J., *La escuela de Salamanca y la renovación de la teología en el siglo XVI*, [Biblioteca de Autores Cristianos Maior, 63], Madrid 2000.

Bellini, P., *L'obbligazione da promessa con oggetto temporale nel sistema canonistico classico, con particolare riferimento ai secoli XII e XIII*, [Università degli Studi di Roma, Monografie dell'Istituto di diritto pubblico della Facoltà di giurisprudenza, Nuova serie, 19], Milano 1964.

——, *'Denunciatio evangelica' e 'denunciatio iudicialis privata', Un capitolo di storia disciplinare della Chiesa*, Milano 1986.

Bellomo, M., *L'Europa del diritto comune*, Roma 1989⁴.

——, *Perché lo storico del diritto europeo deve occuparsi dei giuristi indiani?*, Rivista internazionale di diritto comune, 11 (2000), p. 21–32.

——, *Condividendo, rispondendo, aggiungendo, Riflessioni intorno al 'ius commune'*, Rivista internazionale di diritto comune, 11 (2000), p. 287–296.

Bellone, E., *Appunti su Battista Trovamala di Sale O.F.M. e la sua 'Summa Casuum'*, Studi Francescani, 74 (1977), p. 375–402.

Beltrán de Heredia, V., *Domingo de Soto, O.P., Estudio biográfico documentado*, [Biblioteca de teologos españoles, 20], Salamanca 1960.

Benedict XVI, Pope, *The listening heart, Reflections on the foundations of law*, Address of his Holiness Benedict XIV on the occasion of his visit to the Bundestag (Berlin, 22.09.2011)

[http://www.vatican.va/holy_father/benedict_xvi/speeches/2011/september/documents/ hf_ben-xvi_spe_20110922_reichstag-berlin_en.html (last visited 23.09.2011)].

Bergfeld, Ch., *Die Stellungnahme der spanischen Spätscholastiker zum Versicherungsvertrag,* in: P. Grossi (ed.), La seconda scolastica nella formazione del diritto privato moderno, [Per la storia del pensiero giuridico moderno, 1], Milano 1973, p. 457–474.

——, *Katholische Moraltheologie und Naturrechtslehre,* in: H. Coing (ed.), Handbuch der Quellen und Literatur der neueren europäischen Privatrechtsgeschichte, Band II. Neuere Zeit (1500–1800), Das Zeitalter des gemeinen Rechts, Teilband I.1. Wissenschaft, München 1977, p. 999–1033.

——, *Staat und Gesetz, Naturrecht und Vertrag bei Grotius und Heineccius,* in: J.F. Kervégan – H. Mohnhaupt (eds.), Gesellschaftliche Freiheit und vertragliche Bindung in Rechtsgeschichte und Philosophie / Liberté sociale et lien contractuel dans l'histoire du droit et la philosophie, [Ius commune, Sonderhefte, 120], Frankfurt am Main 1999, p. 95–120.

Berlin, I., *Two concepts of liberty,* in: I. Berlin, Four essays on liberty, Oxford 1969, p. 118–172.

Berman, H.J., *Faith and order, The reconciliation of law and religion,* [Emory studies in law and religion, 3], Grand Rapids – Cambridge 1993.

——, *The religious sources of general contract law, An historical perspective,* Journal of Law and Religion, 4 (1986), p. 103–124 (reprinted in: Faith and order, The reconciliation of law and religion, [Emory studies in law and religion, 3], Grand Rapids – Cambridge 1993, p. 187–208).

——, *Law and revolution II, The impact of the Protestant Reformations on the Western legal tradition,* Cambridge Mass. 2003.

Berman, H.J. – Reid, Ch.J., Jr., *Roman law in Europe and the ius commune, A historical overview with emphasis on the new legal science of the sixteenth century,* Syracuse Journal of International Law and Commerce, 20 (1994), p. 1–32.

Beutels, R., *Leonardus Lessius (1554–1623), Portret van een Zuidnederlandse laat-scholastieke econoom, Een bio-bibliografisch essay,* Wommelgem 1987.

Bezemer, K., *Pierre de Belleperche, Portrait of a legal puritan,* [Studien zur europäischen Rechtsgeschichte, 194], Frankfurt am Main 2005.

Bianchi, L., *Continuity and change in the Aristotelian tradition,* in: J. Hankins (ed.), The Cambridge companion to Renaissance philosophy, Cambridge 2007, p. 49–71.

Bireley, R., *The Counter-Reformation prince, Anti-Machiavellianism or Catholic statecraft in early modern Europe,* Chapel Hill 1990.

——, *The refashioning of Catholicism, 1450–1700, A reassessment of the Counter Reformation,* Washington 1999.

——, *Paul Laymann,* in: C. O'Neill – J. Domínguez (eds.), Diccionario histórico de la Compañía de Jesús, Biográfico-Temático, Roma – Madrid 2001, vol. 3, p. 2297–2298.

——, *The Jesuits and the Thirty Years War, Kings, courts, and confessors,* Cambridge 2003.

Birocchi, I., *Saggi sulla formazione storica della categoria generale del contratto,* Cagliari 1988.

——, *La questione dei patti nella dottrina tedesca dell'Usus modernus,* in: J. Barton (ed.), Towards a general law of contract, [Comparative studies in continental and Anglo-American legal history, 8], Berlin 1990, p. 139–195.

——, *Tra elaborazioni nuove e dottrine tradizionali, Il contratto trino e la natura contractus,* Quaderni fiorentini per la storia del pensiero giuridico moderno, 19 (1990), p. 243–322.

——, *Notazioni sul contratto,* Quaderni fiorentini per la storia del pensiero giuridico moderno, 19 (1990), p. 637–659.

——, *Vendita e trasferimento della proprietà nel diritto comune,* in: L. Vacca (ed.), Vendita e trasferimento della proprietà nella prospettiva storico-comparatistica, Atti del Congresso Internazionale Pisa-Viareggio-Lucca, 17–21 aprile 1990, Tom. I, [Pubblicazioni della Facoltà di Giurisprudenza della Università di Pisa, 115], Milano 1991, p. 139–167.

——, *Causa e categoria generale del contratto, Un problema dogmatico nella cultura privatistica dell'età moderna, I. Il cinquecento,* [Il Diritto nella Storia, 5], Torino 1997.

——, *Causa e definizione del contratto nella dottrina del Cinquecento,* in: L. Vacca (ed.), Causa e contratto nella prospettiva storico-comparatistica, II Congresso Internazionale ARISTEC, Palermo, 7–8 giugno 1995, Torino 1997, p. 189–216.

——, *Alla ricerca dell'ordine, Fonti e cultura giuridica nell'età moderna*, [Il Diritto nella Storia, 9], Torino 2002.

——, *Autonomia privata tra ordini e mercato, Leggendo Rolandino, Domat e Portalis*, in: F. Macario – M.N. Miletti, Tradizione civilistica e complessità del sistema, Valutazioni storiche e prospettive della parte generale del contratto, [Università degli studi di Foggia, Facoltà di Giurisprudenza, Dipartimento di scienze giuridiche privatistiche e pubblicistiche, 28], Milano 2006, p. 95–136.

Bittremieux, J., *Lessius et le droit de guerre, Contribution à l'histoire des doctrines théologiques sur la guerre*, Bruxelles 1920.

Black, A., *The juristic origins of social contract theory*, History of Political Thought, 14 (1993), p. 57–76.

Borobio, D., *The Tridentine model of confession in its historical context*, Concilium, 23 (1967), p. 21–37.

Botero Bernal, A., *El culto a la muerte y al fuego como un referente comprensivo de la cultura y del derecho, Análisis de un ejemplo*, Revista Jurídica, Universidad Autónoma de Madrid, 16 (2007), p. 55–70.

——, A., *Análisis de la obra 'Suma de tratos y contratos' del Dominico Tomás de Mercado*, in: A. Botero Bernal (ed.), Diagnóstico de la eficacia del derecho en Colombia y otros ensayos, Medellín 2003, p. 128–192.

Böttcher, L., *Von der Lüge zur Mentalreservation, Über den Einfluss von Moralphilosophie und -theologie auf das Bürgerliche Recht*, Göttingen 2007.

Boureau, A., *La religion de l'état, La construction de la République étatique dans le discours théologique de l'Occident médiéval (1250–1350)*, Paris 2006.

Braillon, C. – Falzone, E., *Mariage, droit et colonisation(s) en Amérique hispanique et au Congo belge, Quelles concurrences?*, in: S. Eyezo'o – J.-F. Zorn (éds.), Concurrences en mission, Propagandes, conflits, coexistences (XVIe–XXe siècle), Paris 2011, p. 79–105.

Brambilla, E., *Giuristi, teologi e giustizia ecclesiastica dal '500 alla fine del' 700*, in: M.L. Betri – A. Pastore (eds.), Avvocati, medici, ingegneri, Alle origini delle professioni moderne (secoli XVI–XIX), Bologna 1997, p. 169–206.

Brants, V., *Les théories politiques dans les écrits de L. Lessius (1554–1623)*, Revue Néo-Scolastique de Philosophie, 19 (1912), p. 42–85.

——, *L'économie politique et sociale dans les écrits de L. Lessius (1554–1623)*, Revue d'Histoire Ecclésiastique, 13 (1912), p. 73–89.

——, *La faculté de droit de l'Université de Louvain à travers cinq siècles, Étude historique*, Paris-Bruxelles 1917.

Braun, H.E., *Conscience, counsel and theocracy at the Spanish Habsburg court*, in: H.E. Braun – E. Vallance (eds.), Contexts of conscience in early modern Europe, 1500–1700, Basingstoke 2004, p. 56–66.

——, *Juan de Mariana and early modern Spanish political thought*, Aldershot-Burlington 2007.

Brett, A.S., *Liberty, right and nature, Individual rights in later scholastic thought*, [Ideas in Context, 44], Cambridge 1997.

——, *Scholastic political thought and the modern concept of the State*, in: A. Brett – J. Tully – H. Hamilton-Bleakley (eds.), *Rethinking the foundations of modern political thought*, Cambridge 2006, p. 130–148.

——, *Changes of state, Nature and the limits of the city in early modern natural law*, Princeton 2011.

Brieskorn, N., *Luis de Molinas Weiterentwicklung der Kriegsethik und des Kriegsrechts der Scholastik*, in: N. Brieskorn – M. Riedenauer (eds.), Suche nach Frieden, Politische Ethik in der Frühen Neuzeit, I, [Theologie und Frieden, 19], Barsbüttel 2000, p. 167–191.

——, *Skizze des römisch-katholischen Rechtsdenkens im 16. Jahrhundert und seine Spuren im Denken der Societas Jesu und des Petrus Canisius*, in: R. Berndt (ed.), Petrus Canisius SJ (1521–1597), Humanist und Europäer, [Erudiri Sapientia, Studien zum Mittelalter und zu seiner Rezeptionsgeschichte, 1], Berlin 2000, p. 39–75.

——, *Lex Aeterna, Zu Francisco Suárez' 'Tractatus de legibus ac Deo legislatore'*, in: F. Grunert – K. Seelmann (eds.), Die Ordnung der Praxis, Neue Studien zur Spanischen Spätscholastik, [Frühe Neuzeit, 68], Tübingen 2001, p. 49–74.

——, *Diego de Covarrubias y Leyva, Zum Friedens- und Kriegsdenken eines Kanonisten des 16. Jahrhunderts*, in: N. Brieskorn – M. Riedenauer (ed.), Suche nach Frieden, Politische Ethik in der Frühen Neuzeit II, Stuttgart 2002, p. 323–352.

Brooks, R.O. – Murphy, J.B. (eds.), *Augustine and modern law*, Farnham – Burlington 2011.

Brundage, J.A., *Law, sex and Christian society in medieval Europe*, Chicago – London 1990.

——, *Medieval canon law*, London – New York 1995.

——, *The rise of professional canonists and the development of the Ius commune*, Zeitschrift der Savigny-Stiftung für Rechtsgeschichte, Kanonistische Abteilung, 81 (1995), p. 26–63.

——, *Universities and the 'ius commune' in medieval Europe*, Rivista internazionale di diritto comune, 11 (2000), p. 237–253.

Bruschi, C., *Le 'Corpus iuris civilis' dans le premier livre du 'De legibus' de François Suárez*, in: Les représentations du droit romain en Europe aux temps modernes, Collection d'histoire des idées politiques, Aix-Marseille 2007, p. 9–41.

Bukała, M., *Oeconomica mediaevalia of Wroclaw Dominicans, Library and studies of friars and ethical-economic ideas, The example of Silesia*, [Studi del Centro Italiano di Studi sull'Alto Medioevo, 16], Spoleto 2010.

Bunge, K. *Das Verhältnis von universaler Rechtsgemeinschaft und partikularen politischen Gemeinswesen, Zum verständnis des 'totus orbis' bei Francisco de Vitoria*, in: K. Bunge – A. Spindler – A. Wagner (eds.), Die Normativität des Rechts bei Francisco de Vitoria, [Politische Philosophie und Rechtstheorie des Mittelalters und der Neuzeit, Abt. 2: Untersuchungen, 2], Stuttgart 2011, p. 201–227.

Burns, J.H., *Scholasticism, Survival and revival*, in: J.H. Burns – M. Goldie (eds.), The Cambridge history of political thought, 1450–1700, Cambridge e.a. 1991, p. 132–155.

Buzzi, F., *Teologia, politica e diritto tra XVI e XVII secolo*, [Saggi teologici, 28], Genova-Milano 2005.

Cairns, J.W. – du Plessis, P.J. (eds.), *The creation of the ius commune, From casus to regula*, [Edinburgh studies in law, 7], Edinburgh 2010.

Calasso, F., *Diritto volgare, diritti romanzi, diritto comune*, in: Atti del congresso internazionale di diritto Romano e storia del diritto, 2, Milano 1951, p. 357–380.

——, *Introduzione al diritto comune*, Milano 1951.

——, *Medio evo del diritto, Le fonti*, Milano 1954.

——, *Storicità del diritto*, Milano 1966.

——, *Il negozio giuridico, Lezioni di storia del diritto italiano*, Milano 1967².

Caldwell, G.L., *Augustine's critique of human justice*, Journal of Church and State, 7 (1960), p. 7–25, reprinted in R.O. Brooks – J.B. Murphy (eds.), Augustine and modern law, Farnham – Burlington 2011, p. 97–115.

Callewier, H., *Anti-jezuïtisme in de Zuidelijke Nederlanden (1542–1773)*, Trajecta, 16 (2007), p. 30–50.

Canning, J., *The political thought of Baldus de Ubaldis*, [Cambridge studies in medieval life and thought, 6], Cambridge 1987.

Capitant, H., *De la cause des obligations (contrats, engagements unilatéraux, legs)*, Paris 1923.

Cappellini, P., *Sulla formazione del moderno concetto di 'dottrina generale del diritto'* (a proposito di Martin Lipp, *De Bedeutung des Naturrechts für die Ausbildung der allgemeinen Lehren des deutschen Privatrechts*, [Schriften zur Rechtstheorie, 88], Berlin 1980, Quaderni fiorentini per la storia del pensiero giuridico moderno, 10 (1981), p. 323–354.

——, *Systema iuris*, tom. 1: Genesi del sistema e nascita della 'scienza' delle pandette, [Per la storia del pensiero giuridico moderno, 17], Milano 1984.

——, *Systema iuris*, tom. 2: Dal sistema alla teoria generale, [Per la storia del pensiero giuridico moderno, 19], Milano 1985.

——, *Storie di concetti giuridici*, Torino 2010.

Caravale, M., *Alle origini del diritto europeo, Ius commune, droit commun, common law nella dottrina giuridica della prima età moderna*, [Archivio per la storia del diritto medioevale e moderno, 9], Bologna 2005.

Carbasse, J.-M., *Manuel d'introduction historique au droit*, Paris 2007[5].

Carpintero Benitez, F., *'Mos italicus', 'mos gallicus' y el humanismo racionalista, Una contribución a la historia de la metodologia juridica*, Ius commune, 6 (1977), p. 108–171.

——, *Historia del derecho natural, Un ensayo*, [Instituto de Investigaciones Jurídicas, Serie Doctrina Jurídica, 7], México 1999.

——, *Historia breve del derecho natural*, Madrid 2000.

——, *El derecho subjetivo en su historia*, Cádiz 2003.

Cauffman, C., *De verbindende eenzijdige belofte*, Antwerpen 2005.

Cavanna, A., *Storia del diritto moderno in Europa, Le fonti e il pensiero giuridico*, 1, Milano 1979.

Cazal, G., s.v. *Forcadel*, in P. Arabeyre – J.-L. Halpérin – J. Krynen (eds.), Dictionnaire historique des juristes français, XIIᵉ–XXᵉ siècle, Paris 2007, p. 337–338.

Ceccarelli, G., *Il gioco e il peccato, Economia e rischio nel tardo Medioevo*, [Collana di storia dell'economia e del credito promossa dalla fondazione del monte di Bologna e Ravenna, 12], Bologna 2003.

Chafuen, A.A., *Faith and liberty, The economic thought of the late scholastics*, Lanham 2003 [= slightly re-worked version of A.A. Chafuen, *Christians for freedom, Late-scholastic economics*, San Francisco 1986].

Chevreau, E. – Mausen, Y. – Bouglé, C., *Introduction historique au droit des obligations*, Paris 2007.

Chouët, P., *La sacrée Pénitencerie Apostolique, Étude de droit et d'histoire*, Lyon 1908.

Clavero, B., *Religión y derecho. Mentalidades y paradigmas*, Historia, Instituciones y Documentos, 11 (1984), p. 67–92.

——, *Antidora, Antropología católica de la economía moderna*, [Per la storia del pensiero giuridico moderno, 39], Milano 1991.

Coccia, E., *Regula et vita, Il diritto monastico e la regola francescana*, Medioevo e Rinascimento, 20 (2006), p. 97–147.

Coing, H., *English equity and the 'denunciatio evangelica' of the canon law*, Law Quarterly Review, 71 (1955), p. 223–241.

——, (ed.), *Handbuch der Quellen und Literatur der neueren europäischen Privatrechtsgeschichte*, Band II. *Neuere Zeit (1500–1800), Das Zeitalter des gemeinen Rechts*, Teilband I. *Wissenschaft*, München 1977.

——, *Europäisches Privatrecht*. Band I. *Älteres Gemeines Recht (1500 bis 1800)*, München 1985.

——, *Common law and civil law in the development of European civilization – possibilities of comparisons*, in: H. Coing – K.W. Nörr (eds.), Englische und kontinentale Rechtsgeschichte, Ein Forschungsprojekt, [Comparative studies in continental and Anglo-American legal history, 1], Berlin 1985.

Coleman, J., *Are there any individual rights or only duties? On the limits of obedience in the avoidance of sin according to late medieval and early modern scholars*, in: V. Mäkinen – P. Korkman (eds.), Transformations in medieval and early modern rights discourse, [The new synthese historical library, Texts and studies in the history of philosophy, 59], Dordrecht 2006, p. 3–36.

Condorelli, O., *Principio elettivo, consenso, rappresentanza, Itinerari canonistici su elezioni episcopali, provvisioni papali e dottrine sulla potestà sacra nei secoli XII–XIV*, Rivista internazionale di diritto comune, 12 (2001), p. 163–247.

——, *Principio elettivo, consenso, rappresentanza, Itinerari canonistici su elezioni episcopali, provvisioni papali e dottrine sulla potestà sacra, Secoli XIV–XV*, Rivista internazionale di diritto comune, 13 (2002), p. 111–209.

——, *Norma giuridica e norma morale, giustizia e salus animarum secondo Diego de Covarrubias, Riflessioni a margine della Relectio super regula 'Peccatum'*, Rivista internazionale di diritto comune, 19 (2008), p. 163–201.

——, *Il diritto canonico nel tardo Medioevo, Secoli XIV–XV,* Appunti per una discussione, Rivista internazionale di diritto comune, 19 (2008), p. 263–267.

——, *Ius e lex nel sistema del diritto comune (secoli XIV–XV),* in: A. Fidora – M. Lutz-Bachmann – A. Wagner (eds.), *Lex* and *Ius,* Essays on the foundation of law in medieval and early modern philosophy, [Politische Philosophie und Rechtstheorie des Mittelalters und der Neuzeit, Series 2, Studies, 1], Stuttgart 2010, p. 27–88.

Conte, E., *Storia interna e storia esterna, Il diritto medievale da Francesco Calasso alla fine del XX secolo,* Rivista internazionale di diritto comune, 17 (2006), p. 299–322.

——, *Diritto comune, Storia e storiografia di un sistema dinamico,* Bologna 2009.

——, *I beni delle 'piae causae' tra beneficenza e vincolo fiduciario,* in: O. Condorelli – F. Roumy – M. Schmoeckel (eds.), Der Einfluβ der Kanonistik auf die europäische Rechtskultur, Band 2: Öffentliches Recht, [Norm und Strukter, 37, 2], Köln – Weimar – Wien 2011, p. 295–310.

Coppens, E.C., *De 'Ordo Iudiciarius Sapientiam', Een korte inleiding in het vroegste middeleeuwse procesrecht,* in: C.H. van Rhee – F. Stevens – E. Persoons (eds.), Voortschrijdend procesrecht, Een historische verkenning, Leuven 2001, p. 151–169; 218–295.

Cordes, A., *Auf der Suche nach der Rechtswirklichkeit der mittelalterlichen Lex Mercatoria,* Zeitschrift der Savigny-Stiftung für Rechtsgeschichte, Germ. Abt., 118 (2001), p. 168–184.

Cortese, E., *La norma giuridica, Spunti storici nel diritto comune classico,* [Ius nostrum, 6], Milano 1962–64, 2 vols.

——, *Il diritto nella storia medievale, II. Il basso medioevo,* Roma 1995.

Costello, F.B., *The political philosophy of Luis de Molina S.J. (1535–1600),* [Bibliotheca Instituti Historici S.I., 38], Rome 1974.

Courtine, J.-F., *Nature et empire de la loi, Études suaréziennes,* Paris 1999.

Crook, E. – Jennings, M. (ed. and transl.), *Ranulph Higden, Speculum Curatorum, A mirror for curates, Book 1, The commandments,* [Dallas Medieval Texts and Translations, 13], Leuven 2011.

Cruz Cruz, J., *Ius gentium bei Vitoria, Ein eindeutig internationalistischer Ansatz,* in: A. Fidora – M. Lutz-Bachmann – A. Wagner (eds.), *Lex* and *Ius,* Essays on the foundation of law in medieval and early modern philosophy, [Politische Philosophie und Rechtstheorie des Mittelalters und der Neuzeit, Series 2, Studies, 1], Stuttgart 2010, p. 301–332.

Cummings, B., *Conscience and the law in Thomas More,* in: H.E. Braun – E. Vallance (eds.), The Renaissance conscience, [Renaissance Studies Special Issues, 3], Oxford 2011, p. 29–51.

Daniel, W., *The purely penal law theory in the Spanish theologians from Vitoria to Suárez,* Roma 1968.

Daniel, W.L., *The origin, nature, and purpose of canon law in the recent pontifical magisterium,* Studia Canonica, 45 (2011), p. 329–353.

de Boer, W., *The conquest of the soul, Confession, discipline and public order in Counter Reformation Milan,* Leiden 2001.

Decaluwe, M., *A successful defeat, Eugene IV's struggle with the Council of Basel for ultimate authority in the Church, 1431–1449,* [Bibliothèque de l'Institut Historique Belge de Rome, 59], Rome 2010.

Deckers, D., *Gerechtigkeit und Recht, Eine historisch-kritische Untersuchung der Gerechtigkeitslehre des Francisco de Vitoria (1483–1546),* Freiburg – Basel – Wien 1991.

——, s.v. *Vitoria, Francisco de,* in: Theologische Realenzyklopädie, vol. 35, Berlin – New York 2003, p. 169–173.

Decock, W., *Breaking the limits, De 'homo oeconomicus' ontketend in Lessius' denken over markt en prijs? Editie, vertaling en studie van De iustitia et iure, lib.2, cap.21,* Leuven 2005 [unpublished master's thesis KULeuven].

——, *Leonardus Lessius, Biografie & Hygiasticon,* in: J. De Landtsheer – D. Sacré – C. Coppens (eds.), Justus Lipsius (1547–1606), Een geleerde en zijn Europese netwerk, Leuven 2006, p. 262–268.

——, *Leonardus Lessius en de koopman van Rhodos, Een schakelpunt in het denken over economie en ethiek,* De zeventiende eeuw, 22 (2006), p. 247–261.

——, *Leonardus Lessius on buying and selling (1605), Translation and introduction*, Journal of Markets and Morality, 10 (2007), p. 433–516.

——, *L'usure face au marché, Lessius (1554–1623) et l'escompte des lettres obligataires*, in: A. Girollet (ed.), Le droit, les affaires et l'argent, Célébration du bicentenaire du code de commerce, Dijon 2008, p. 221–238.

——, *Lessius and the breakdown of the scholastic paradigm*, Journal of the History of Economic Thought, 31 (2009), p. 57–78.

——, *Freedom, The legacy of early modern scholasticism to contract law*, in: D. Heirbaut – X. Rousseaux – A.A. Wijffels (eds.), Histoire du droit et de la justice, Une nouvelle génération de recherches / Justitie- en rechtsgeschiedenis, Een nieuwe onderzoeksgeneratie, Louvain-la-Neuve 2009, p. 233–245.

——, *At the crossroads of law and morality, Lessius on precontractual duties to inform about future market conditions*, in: L. Beck Varela – P. Gutiérrez Vega – A. Spinosa (eds.), Crossing legal cultures, München 2009, p. 243–258.

——, *Counter-reformation diplomacy behind Francisco Suárez's constitutionalist theory*, Ambiente Jurídico, 11 (2009), p. 68–92.

——, *Leonardus Lessius (1554–1623) y el valor normativo de 'usus et consuetudo mercatorum' para la resolución de algunos casos de conciencia en torno de la compra de papeles de comercio*, in: M. Madero – E. Conte (eds.), Entre hecho y derecho, Tener, poseer, usar en perspectiva histórica, Buenos Aires 2010, p. 75–94.

——, *Jesuit freedom of contract*, Tijdschrift voor Rechtsgeschiedenis, 77 (2009), p. 423–458.

——, *Secret compensation, A friendly and lawful alternative to Lipsius's political thought*, in: E. De Bom – M. Janssens – T. Van Houdt – J. Papy (eds.), (Un)masking the realities of power, Justus Lipsius and the dynamics of political writing in early modern Europe, Leiden – Boston 2011, p. 263–280.

——, *From law to paradise, Confessional Catholicism and legal scholarship*, Rechtsgeschichte, Zeitschrift des Max-Planck-Instituts für europäische Rechtsgeschichte, 18 (2011), p. 12–34.

——, *La transformation de la culture juridique occidentale dans le premier 'tribunal mondial'*, in: B. Coppein – F. Stevens – L. Waelkens (eds.), Modernisme, tradition et acculturation juridique, Actes des Journées internationales de la Société d'histoire du droit tenues à Louvain, 28 mai–1 juin 2008, [Iuris scripta historica, 27], Brussel 2011, p. 125–135.

——, *Law on love's stage, Étienne Forcadel's (c. 1519–1578) Cupido jurisperitus*, in: V. Draganova – S. Kroll – H. Landerer – U. Meyer (eds.), Inszenierung des Rechts, Law on Stage, München 2011, p. 17–36.

——, *Donations, bonnes mœurs et droit naturel, Un débat théologico-politique dans la scolastique des temps modernes*, in: M. Chamocho Cantudo (ed.), Droit et mœurs, Implication et influence des mœurs dans la configuration du droit, Jaén 2011, p. 182–197.

——, *Grazia divina e giustizia commutativa, Un confronto tra Bañez e Lessius*, in: K. Härter – C. Nubola (eds.), Grazia e giustizia, Figure della clemenza fra tardo medioevo ed età contemporanea, [Annali dell'Istituto storico italo-germanico in Trento, Quaderni, 81], Bologna 2011, p. 361–388.

——, *The judge's conscience and the protection of the criminal defendant, Moral safeguards against judicial arbitrariness*, in: M. Dubber – G. Martyn – H. Pihlajamäki (eds.), From 'arbitrium' to the legality principle, [Comparative studies in Anglo-American and continental legal history], Berlin 2012 [forthcoming].

——, *In defense of commercial capitalism (Antwerp, Early 17th century), Lessius, partnerships and the 'contractus trinus'*, in: W. Decock – F. Stevens – B. Van Hofstraeten (eds.), Medieval and modern company law in Europe, [Iuris Scripta Historica], Brussels 2012 [forthcoming].

Decock, W. – Hallebeek, J., *Pre-contractual duties to inform in early modern scholasticism*, Tijdschrift voor Rechtsgeschiedenis, 78 (2010), p. 89–133.

Deflers, I., *Lex und Ordo, Eine rechtshistorische Untersuchung der Rechtsauffassung Melanchtons*, [Schriften zur Rechtsgeschichte, 121], Berlin 2005.

De-Juan, O. – Monsalve, F., *Morally ruled behavior, The neglected contribution of scholasticism*, The European Journal of the History of Economic Thought, 13 (2006), p. 99–112.

Dekkers, R., *Het humanisme en de rechtswetenschap in de Nederlanden*, Antwerpen 1938.

——, *La lésion énorme, Introduction à l'histoire des sources du droit*, Paris 1937.

——, *Bibliotheca Belgica Juridica, Een bio-bibliografisch overzicht der rechtsgeleerdheid in de Nederlanden van de vroegste tijden af tot 1800*, [Verhandelingen van de Koninklijke Vlaamse Academie voor Wetenschappen, Letteren en Schone Kunsten van België, Klasse der Letteren, Jaargang 13, Nr. 14], Brussel 1951.

Del Vigo Gutiérrez, A., *Cambistas, mercaderes y banqueros en el siglo de oro español*, [Biblioteca de Autores Cristianos, 578], Madrid 1997.

——, *Economía y ética en el siglo XVI, Estudio comparativo entre los Padres de la Reforma y la Teología española*, [Biblioteca de Autores Cristianos, 659], Madrid 2006.

De Page, H., *Le problème de la lésion dans les contrats*, Bruxelles 1946.

De Roover, R., *L'Évolution de la lettre de change (14ᵉ–18ᵉ siècles)*, [Affaires et gens d'affaires, 4], Paris 1953.

——, *Scholastic economics, Survival and lasting influence from the sixteenth century to Adam Smith*, in: J. Kirshner (ed.), Business, banking and economic thought in late medieval and early modern Europe, Selected studies, Chicago 1974, p. 306–335 [= reprint of R. De Roover, *Scholastic economics, Survival and lasting influence from the sixteenth century to Adam Smith*, Quarterly Journal of Economics, 69 (1955), p. 161–190].

Deroussin, D., *Histoire du droit des obligations*, Paris 2007.

De ruysscher, D., *Naer het Romeinsch recht alsmede den stiel mercantiel, Handel en recht in de Antwerpse rechtbank (16de–17de eeuw)*, Kortrijk-Heule 2009.

Desan, C., *Beyond commodification, Contract and the credit-based world of modern capitalism*, in: D.W. Hamilton – A.L. Brophy (eds.), Transformations in American legal history, Essays in honor of professor Morton J. Horwitz, Cambridge Mass. 2010, vol. 2, p. 111–142.

Descamps, O., *L'influence du droit canonique médiéval sur la formation d'un droit de la responsabilité*, in: O. Condorelli – F. Roumy – M. Schmoeckel (eds.), Der Einfluss der Kanonistik auf die Europäische Rechtskultur, [Norm und Struktur], Köln – Weimar – Wien 2009, p. 137–167.

Deuringer, K., *Probleme der Caritas in der Schule von Salamanca*, Freiburg i.Br. 1959.

Dickerhof, H., *Land, Reich, Kirche im historischen Lehrbetrieb an der Universität Ingolstadt, Ignaz Schwarz (1690–1763)*, Berlin 1967.

Diego Carro, P.V., *La teología y los teólogos-juristas españoles ante la conquista de América*, Segunda Edición, [Biblioteca de teologos españoles, 18], Madrid 1951.

Diesselhorst, M., *Die Lehre des Hugo Grotius vom Versprechen*, [Forschungen zur neueren Privatrechtsgeschichte, 6], Köln – Graz, 1959.

Diez, A. – Ochoa, X., *Indices canonum, titulorum et capitulorum Corpus Iuris Canonici*, [Institutum iuridicum Claretianum, Universa bibliotheca iuris, Subsidia, Index canonum et legum totius corporis iuris canonici et civilis, 1], Roma 1964.

——, *Indices titulorum et legum Corporis Iuris Civilis*, [Institutum iuridicum Claretianum, Universa bibliotheca iuris, Subsidia, Index canonum et legum totius corporis iuris canonici et civilis, 2], Roma 1965.

Dilcher, G. – Lepsius, S. (eds.), *Max Weber, Zur Geschichte der Handelsgesellschaften im Mittelalter*, [Max Weber Gesammtausgabe, Abt. 1, Band 1], Tübingen 2008.

Dilcher, H., *Der Typenzwang im mittelalterlichen Vertragsrecht*, Zeitschrift der Savigny-Stiftung für Rechtsgeschichte, Rom. Abt., 77 (1960), p. 270–303.

Dolezalek, G., *The moral theologians' doctrine of restitution and its juridification in the sixteenth and seventeenth centuries*, in: T.W. Bennett e.a. (ed.), Acta Juridica, Essays in honour of Wouter de Vos, Cape Town – Wetton – Johannesburg 1992, p. 104–114.

——, *Lexiques de droit et autres outils pour le 'ius commune'*, in: J. Hamesse (ed.), Les manuscrits des lexiques et glossaires de l'Antiquité tardive à la fin du Moyen Age, [Textes et études du Moyen Age, 4], Louvain-la-Neuve – Turnhout 1996, p. 353–376.

Donahue, Ch., Jr., *Roman canon law in the medieval English church, Stubbs v. Maitland re-examined after 75 years in the light of some records from the church courts*, Michigan Law Review 72 (1974), p. 656–661.

——, *Why the history of canon law is not written*, London 1986.

——, *Ius commune, canon law and common law in England*, Tulane Law Review, 66 (1992), p. 1745–1780.

——, *Equity in the courts of merchants*, Tijdschrift voor Rechtsgeschiedenis, 72 (2004), p. 1–35.

——, *A crisis of law? Reflections on the Church and the law over the centuries*, The Jurist, 65 (2005), p. 1–30.

——, *Law, marriage and society in the later Middle Ages, Arguments about marriage in five courts*, Cambridge 2007.

——, *Private law without the State and during its formation*, in: N. Jansen – R. Michaels (eds.), Beyond the State, Rethinking private law, Tübingen 2008, p. 121–144.

Dondorp, H., *Crime and punishment, Negligentia for the canonists and moral theologians*, in: E.J.H. Schrage (ed.), Negligence, The comparative legal history of the law of torts, [Comparative Studies in Continental and Anglo-American Legal History, 22], Berlin 2001, p. 101–128.

——, *The seventeenth and eighteenth centuries*, in: J. Hallebeek – H. Dondorp (eds.), Contracts for a third-party beneficiary, A historical and comparative account, [Legal history library, Studies in the history of private law, 1], Leiden – Boston 2008, p. 47–68.

Donnelly, J.P., *Paolo Comitoli*, in: C. O'Neill – J. Domínguez (eds.), Diccionario Histórico de la Compañía de Jesús, Biográfico-Temático, Roma – Madrid 2001, vol. 1, p. 874–875.

——, *Luis de Molina*, in: C. O'Neill – J. Domínguez (eds.), Diccionario Histórico de la Compañía de Jesús, Biográfico-Temático, Roma – Madrid 2001, vol. 3, p. 2716–2717.

Döring, D. (ed.), *Samuel Pufendorf, Briefwechsel*, in: W. Schmidt-Biggemann (ed.), Samuel Pufendorf, Gesammelte Werke, Band 1, Berlin 1996.

Doyle, J.P., *Francisco Suárez on the law of nations*, in: M.W. Janis – C. Evans (eds.), Religion and international law, London 1999, p. 103–120.

——, *Hispanic scholastic philosophy*, in: J. Hankins (ed.), The Cambridge companion to Renaissance philosophy, Cambridge 2007, p. 250–269.

Dufour, A., *Pufendorf*, in: J.H. Burns – M. Goldie (eds.), The Cambridge History of Political Thought 1450–1700, Cambridge e.a. 1991, p. 561–568.

——, *Les Magni Hispani dans l'œuvre de Grotius*, in: F. Grunert – K. Seelmann (eds.), Die Ordnung der Praxis, Neue Studien zur Spanischen Spätscholastik, [Frühe Neuzeit, 68], Tübingen 2001, p. 351–380.

du Plessis, J. – Zimmermann, R., *The relevance of reverence, Undue influence civilian style*, Maastricht Journal of European and Comparative Law, 10 (2003), p. 345–379.

——, *The Roman concept of 'lex contractus'*, Roman Legal Tradition, 3 (2006), p. 69–94.

——, *The creation of legal principle*, Roman Legal Tradition, 4 (2008), p. 46–69.

Duve, Th., *Sonderrecht in der Frühen Neuzeit, Studien zum ius singulare und den privilegia miserabilium personarum, senum und indorum in Alter und Neuer Welt*, [Studien zur europäischen Rechtsgeschichte, 231], Frankfurt am Main 2008.

——, *Kanonisches Recht und die Ausbildung allgemeiner Vertragslehren in der Spanischen Spätscholastik*, in: O. Condorelli – F. Roumy – M. Schmoeckel (eds.), Der Einfluss der Kanonistik auf die Europäische Rechtskultur, Band 1: Zivil- und Zivilprozessrecht, [Norm und Struktur, 37], Köln – Weimar – Wien 2009, p. 389–408.

——, *Obliga en conciencia la naturalis obligatio? Un comentario histórico-jurídico sobre la naturalis obligatio*, in: J. Cruz Cruz, La gravitación moral de la ley según Francisco Suárez, [Colección de pensamiento medieval y renacentista, 109], Pamplona 2009, p. 83–93.

——, *Katholisches Kirchenrecht und Moraltheologie im 16. Jahrhundert, Eine globale normative Ordnung im Schatten schwacher Staatlichkeit*, in: S. Kadelbach – K. Günther (eds.), Recht ohne Staat? Zur Normativität nichtstaatlicher Rechtsetzung, [Normative Orders, 4], Frankfurt am Main 2011, p. 147–174.

Dziuba, A.F., *Juan Azor S.J., Teólogo moralista del s. XVI–XVII*, Archivo Teológico Granadino, 59 (1996), p. 145–156.

Endemann, W., *Studien in der romanisch-kanonistischen Wirthschafts- und Rechtslehre bis gegen Ende des siebenzehnten Jahrhunderts*, Berlin 1874–1883.

Errera, A., *The role of logic in the legal science of the glossators and commentators, Distinction, dialectical syllogism, and apodictic syllogism, An investigation into the epistemological roots of legal science in the late Middle Ages*, in: A. Padovani – P. Stein (eds.), The jurists' philosophy of law from Rome to the seventeenth century, [A treatise of legal philosophy and general jurisprudence, 7], Dordrecht 2007, p. 79–155.

Escalera, J., s.v. *Perez*, in C. O'Neill – J. Domínguez (eds.), Diccionario histórico de la Compañía de Jesús biográfico-temático, vol. 3, Roma – Madrid 2001, p. 3089–3090.

Esmein, A., *Le mariage en droit canonique*, Paris 1929–1935² [= 1891].

Ewald, F. (ed.), *Naissance du Code civil, La raison du législateur, Travaux préparatoires du Code civil rassemblés par P.A. Fenet*, Paris 2004.

Fabre, P.-A. – Maire, C. (eds.), *Les Antijésuites, Discours, figures et lieux de l'antijésuitisme à l'époque moderne*, Rennes 2010.

Falk, U., *Consilia, Studien zur Praxis der Rechtsgutachten in der frühen Neuzeit*, [Rechtsprechung, 22], Frankfurt am Main 2006.

Falzone, E., *Poena et emenda, Les sanctions pénale et non pénale dans le droit canonique médiéval et la pratique des officialités*, in: M.-A. Bourguignon – B. Dauven – X. Rousseaux (eds.), La sanction juridique du XIIIᵉ au XXᵉ siècle, Actes des journées d'étude (19–20 octobre, Louvain-la-Neuve), Louvain 2012 [forthcoming].

Fantappiè, C., *Chiesa Romana e modernità giuridica*, [Per la storia del pensiero giuridico moderno, 76], Milano 2008.

Fedele, P., *Error qualitatis redundans in errorem personae*, [Biblioteca de 'Il diritto ecclesiastico'], Roma 1934, p. 1–30 [= estratto dalla rivista 'Il diritto ecclesiastico', 45 (1934)].

——, *Appunti sui vizii del consenso matrimoniale, Metus ab extrinseco iniuste incussus consulto illatus*, [Biblioteca de 'Il diritto ecclesiastico'], Roma 1934, p. 1–28 [= estratto dalla rivista 'Il diritto ecclesiastico', 45 (1934)].

——, *Sull'espressione 'metus cadens in virum constantem', Sulla violenza come vizio del consenso matrimoniale, Note e discussioni*, [Biblioteca de 'Il diritto ecclesiastico'], Roma 1935, p. 1–8 [= estratto dalla rivista 'Il diritto ecclesiastico', 46 (1935)].

——, *Considerazioni sull'efficacia dei patti nudi nel diritto canonico*, Tolentino 1937, p. 5–90 [= Estratto degli Annali della R. Università di Macerata, 11].

Feenstra, R., *De oorsprong van Hugo de Groot's leer over de dwaling*, in: L. Jacob (ed.), Met eerbiedigende werking, Opstellen aangeboden aan Prof. Mr. L.J. Hijmans van den Bergh, Deventer 1971, p. 87–101.

——, *De betekenis van De Groot en Huber voor de ontwikkeling van een algemene actie uit ongerechtvaardigde verrijking*, in: Uit het recht, Rechtsgeleerde opstellen aangeboden aan mr. P.J. Verdam, Deventer 1971, p. 137–159.

——, *L'influence de la Scolastique espagnole sur Grotius en droit privé, Quelques expériences dans des questions de fond et de forme, concernant notamment les doctrines de l'erreur et de l'enrichissement sans cause*, in: P. Grossi (ed.), La seconda scolastica nella formazione del diritto privato moderno, [Per la storia del pensiero giuridico moderno, 1], Milano 1973, p. 377–402 [reprinted in *Fata iuris romani*, Leiden 1974, p. 338–363].

——, *Impossibilitas and clausula rebus sic stantibus, Some aspects of frustration of contract in continental legal history up to Grotius*, in: A. Watson (ed.), Daube noster, Essays in legal history for David Daube, Edinburgh-London 1974, p. 77–104, [reprinted in *Fata iuris romani*, Leiden 1974, p. 364–391].

——, *Der Eigentumsbegriff bei Hugo Grotius im Licht einiger mittelalterlicher und spätscholastischer Quellen*, in: O. Behrends (ed.), Festschrift für Franz Wieacker zum 70. Geburtstag, Göttingen 1978, p. 219–226.

——, *Vergelding en vergoeding, Enkele grepen uit de geschiedenis van de onrechtmatige daad*, [Rechtshistorische Cahiers, 6], Deventer 1982.

——, *Quelques remarques sur les sources utilisées par Grotius dans ses travaux de droit naturel*, in: The world of Hugo Grotius (1583–1645), Proceedings of the international colloquium organized by the Grotius Committee of the Royal Netherlands Academy of Arts and Sciences, Rotterdam 6–9 April 1983, Amsterdam – Maarssen 1984, p. 65–81.

——, *Pact and contract in the Low Countries from the 16th to the 18th century*, in: J. Barton (ed.), Towards a general law of contract, [Comparative Studies in Continental and Anglo-American Legal History, 8], Berlin 1990, p. 196–213.

——, *Ius commune et droit comparé chez Grotius, Nouvelles remarques sur les sources citées dans ses ouvrages juridiques, à propos d'une réimpression du De iure belli ac pacis*, Rivista internazionale di diritto comune, 3 (1992), p. 7–36.

——, *Grotius' doctrine of unjust enrichment as a source of obligation, Its origin and its influence in Roman-Dutch law*, in: E.J.H. Schrage (ed.), Unjust enrichment, The comparative legal history of the law of restitution, [Comparative Studies in Continental and Anglo-American Legal History, 15], Berlin 1995, p. 197–236.

——, *Expropriation et dominium eminens chez Grotius*, in: L. Waelkens et al. (ed.), L'expropriation, [Recueils de la Société Jean Bodin pour l'histoire comparative des institutions, 66], Bruxelles 1999, vol. 1, p. 133–153.

——, *Grotius' doctrine of liability for negligence, Its origins and its influence in civil law countries until modern codifications*, in: E.J.H. Schrage (ed.), Negligence, The comparative legal history of the law of torts, [Comparative Studies in Continental and Anglo-American Legal History, 22], Berlin 2001, p. 129–172.

——, *Heineccius in den alten Niederlanden, Ein bibliographischer Beitrag*, Tijdschrift voor Rechtsgeschiedenis, 72 (2004), p. 297–326.

——, *Portretten van juristen uit de oude Nederlanden* (Recensie van T. Dankers – P. Delsaerdt, De vele gezichten van het recht, Portretten van juristen uit de oude Nederlanden, s.l. 2009), Tijdschrift voor Rechtsgeschiedenis, 79 (2011), p. 129–135.

Feenstra, R. – Ahsmann, M., *Contract, aspecten van de begrippen contract en contractsvrijheid in historisch perspectief*, [Rechtshistorische Cahiers, 2], Deventer 1988².

Fenet, P.A., *Recueil complet des travaux préparatoires du Code civil*, Paris 1836.

Fernández, E., s.v. *Oñate*, in: C. O'Neill – J. Domínguez (eds.), Diccionario histórico de la Compañía de Jesús biográfico-temático, vol. 3, Roma – Madrid 2001, p. 2870–2871.

Fernández-Santamaría, J.A., *Natural law, constitutionalism, reason of state, and war, Counter-reformation Spanish political thought*, [Renaissance and Baroque studies and texts, 32–33], New York 2005–2006, 2 vols.

Finestres, J., *El humanismo jurídico en las universidades españolas, Siglos XVI–XVIII*, in: L. Rodríguez – S. Bezares (eds.), Las Universidades Hispánicas de la Monarquía de los Austrias al Centralismo liberal, Salamanca 2000, vol. 1, p. 313–326.

Finnis, J.M., *The truth in legal positivism*, in: R.P. George (ed.), The autonomy of law, Essays on legal positivism, Oxford 1996, p. 195–214 [reprinted in J.M. Finnis, *Philosophy of law, Collected essays*, Oxford 2011, vol. 4, p. 174–188].

Fleischer, H., *Informationsasymmetrie im Vertragsrecht, Eine rechtsvergleichende und interdisziplinäre Abhandlung zu Reichweite und Grenzen vertragsschlussbezogener Aufklärungspflichten*, München 2001.

Flórez Miguel, C., *La Escuela de Salamanca y los orígenes de la economía*, in: F. Gómez Camacho – R. Robledo (eds.), El pensamiento económico en la Escuela de Salamanca, Una visión multidisciplinar, [Acta Salmanticensia, Estudios históricos & geográficos, 107], Salamanca 1998, p. 123–144.

Flume, W., *Studien zur Lehre von der ungerechtfertigten Bereicherung*, herausgegeben von W. Ernst, Tübingen 2003.

Folgado, A., *Los tratados De legibus y De iustitia et iure en los autores españoles del siglo XVI y primera mitad del XVII*, La Ciudad de Dios, 172.3 (1959), p. 284–291.

——, *Evolución historica del concepto del derecho subjetivo, Estudio especial en los teologos-juristas españoles del siglo XVI*, [Pax juris, Escurialensium Utriusque Studiorum Scerpta, 4], Madrid 1960.

Fontaine, L., *L'économie morale, Pauvreté, crédit et confiance dans l'Europe préindustrielle*, Paris 2008.

Foriers, P.A., *Espaces de liberté en droits des contrats*, in: Les espaces de liberté en droit des affaires, Bruxelles 2007, p. 25–60.

Forlivesi, M., *A man, an age, a book*, in: M. Forlivesi (ed.), Rem in seipsa cernere, Saggi sul pensiero filosofico di Bartolomeo Mastri (1602–1673), Atti del Convegno di studi sul pensiero filosofico di Bartolomeo Mastri da Meldola (1602–1673), Meldola-Bertinoro, 20–22 settembre 2002, Padova 2006, p. 23–144.

Forray, V., *Le consensualisme dans la théorie générale du contrat*, [Bibliothèque de droit privé, 480], Paris 2007.

Forster, W., *Das kastilische Privatrecht in der Spanischen Spätscholastik, Luis de Molina S.J. (1535–1600)*, unpublished paper delivered at the symposium *Spanische Spätscholastik-noch Mittelalter oder schon Moderne?* (Hamburg 14–17.09.2008).

Foucault, M., *Les mots et les choses, Une archéologie des sciences humaines*, Paris 1966.

Fransen, G., *Le dol dans la conclusion des actes juridiques, Évolution des doctrines et système du Code canonique*, [Universitas Catholica Lovaniensis, Dissertationes ad gradum magistri in Facultate Theologiae vel in Facultate Iuris Canonici consequendum conscriptae, series 2, tom. 37], Gembloux 1946.

——, *L'application des décrets du Concile de Trente, Les débuts d'un nominalisme canonique*, L'Année canonique, 27 (1983), p. 5–16.

Fries, B., *Forum in der Rechtssprache*, [Münchener Theologische Studien, Kanonistische Abteilung, 17], München 1963.

Frydman, B., *Le sens des lois, Histoire de l'interprétation et de la raison juridique*, [Penser le droit, 4], Bruxelles – Paris 2005.

Fukuoka, A., *State, Church and liberty, A comparison between Spinoza's and Hobbes' interpretations of the Old Testament*, Tokyo 2007.

Fukuyama, F., *The origins of political order*, London 2011.

García Sánchez, J., *Arias Piñel, Catedrático de Leyes en Coimbra y Salamanca durante el siglo XVI, La rescisión de la compraventa por "laesio enormis"*, Salamanca 2004.

García y García, A., *El derecho canónico medieval y los problemas del Nuevo Mundo*, Rivista internazionale di diritto comune, 1 (1990), p. 121–154.

——, *El iusnaturalismo suareciano*, in: R. Pérez Bustamente – F. Súarez Bilbao – Antonio García y García, En el entorno del derecho común, Madrid 1999, p. 189–198 [= reprint from M. Tedeschi (ed.), Il problema del diritto naturale nell'esperienza giuridica della Chiesa, Napoli 1993, p. 154–154].

——, *Derecho romano-canónico medieval en la Península Ibérica*, in: J. Alvarado (ed.), Historia de la literatura jurídica en la España del antiguo régimen, vol.1, Madrid – Barcelona 2000, p. 79–132.

García y García, A. – Alonso Rodríguez, B., *El pensamiento económico y el mundo del derecho hasta el siglo XVI*, in: R. Pérez Bustamente – F. Súarez Bilbao – A. García y García, En el entorno del derecho común, Madrid 1999, p. 200–225 [= reprint from El pensamiento económico en la Escuela de Salamanca, Una visión multidisciplinar, [Acta Salmanticensia, Estudios históricos & geográficos, 107], Salamanca 1998, p. 65–92].

García y García, A. – Alonso Rodríguez, B. – Cantelar Rodríguez, F. (eds.), *Martín Pérez, Libro de las confesiones, Una radiografía de la sociedad medieval española*, [Biblioteca de autores cristianos maior, 69], Madrid 2002.

Gaß, Wilhelm, *Balduin, Friedrich*, in: Allgemeine Deutsche Biographie, 2 (1875), p. 16–17 (URL: http://www.deutsche-biographie.de/pnd116883391.html?anchor=adb).

Gaudemet, J., *Théologie et droit canonique, Les leçons de l'histoire*, Revue de droit canonique, 39 (1989), p. 3–13.

——, *Église et cité, Histoire du droit canonique*, Paris 1994.

——, *L'apport du droit romain à la patristique latine du IVe siècle*, in: Formation du droit canonique et gouvernement de l'Église de l'Antiquité à l'Âge classique, Recueil d'articles, Strasbourg 2008, p. 41–54 [= reprint from *Les transformations de la société chrétienne au*

IVᵉ siècle, Miscellanea historiae ecclesiasticae, [Bibliothèque de la Revue d'Histoire Ecclé-siastique, 67], Louvain-la-Neuve 1983, p. 165–181.

——, *Le droit au service de la pastorale (Décret de Gratien, C. XVI, q. 3)*, in: Formation du droit canonique et gouvernement de l'Église de l'Antiquité à l'Âge classique, Recueil d'articles, Strasbourg 2008, p. 339–349 [= reprint from *Società, istituzioni, spiritualità, Studi in onore di Cinzio Violante*, Spoleto 1994, p. 409–422].

Gay, J.P., *Le Jésuite improbable, Remarques sur la mise en place du mythe du Jésuite corrupteur de la morale en France à l'époque moderne*, in: P.-A. Fabre – C. Maire (eds.), Les Antijésuites, Discours, figures et lieux de l'antijésuitisme à l'époque moderne, Rennes 2010, p. 305–327.

Gazzaniga, J.-L., *Domat et Pothier, Le contrat à la fin de l'Ancien Régime*, Droits, 12 (1990), p. 37–46.

Geens, K., *Hoe het vennootschapsrecht zich met een reverse take over verweert tegen een overnamepoging door het 'beginsel van de juiste prijs'*, in: Synthèses de droit bancaire et financier, Liber amicorum André Bruyneel, Bruxelles 2008, p. 451–468.

Gerkens J.-F., *Comment enseigner le droit privé (romain) en Europe? L'enseignement du droit romain en Europe aujourd'hui (Trento, 12–13 novembre 2010)*, European Review of Private Law, 19 (2011), p. 333–339.

Ghisalberti, A. (ed.), *Dalla prima alla seconda scolastica, Paradigmi e percorsi storiografici*, Bologna 2000.

Gieg, G., *Clausula rebus sic stantibus und Geschäftsgrundlage, Ein Beitrag zur Dogmengeschichte*, Aachen 1994.

Giers, J., *Die Gerechtigkeitslehre des jungen Suárez, Edition und Untersuchung seiner Römischen Vorlesungen De iustitia et iure*, [Freiburger Theologische Studien, 72], Freiburg 1958.

Ginzburg, C., *The letter kills, On some implications of 2 Corinthians 3:6*, History and Theory, 49 (2010), p. 71–89.

Goering, J., *The scholastic turn (1100–1500), Penitential theology and law in the schools*, in: A. Firey (ed.), A new history of penance, [Brill's Companions to the Christian Tradition, 14], Leiden – Boston 2008, p. 219–238.

——, *The internal forum and the literature of penance and confession*, in: W. Hartmann – K. Pennington (eds.), The history of medieval canon law in the classical period, 1140–1234, From Gratian to the decretals of Pope Gregory IX, Washington D.C. 2008, p. 379–428.

Golvers, N., *Building humanistic libraries in Late Imperial China, Circulation of books, prints and letters between Europe and China (XVIIth–XVIIIth cent.) in the framework of the Jesuit Mission*, Roma – Leuven 2011.

Gómez Camacho, F., *Luís de Molina. La teoría del justo precio*, Madrid 1981.

——, *Economía y filosofía moral, La formación del pensamiento económico europeo en la Escolástica española*, [Historia del pensamiento económico, 1], Madrid 1998.

——, *El pensamiento económico de la Escolástica española a la Ilustración escocesa*, in: F. Gómez Camacho – R. Robledo (eds.), El pensamiento económico en la scuela de Salamanca, Una visión multidisciplinar, [Acta Salmanticensia, Estudios históricos & geográficos, 107], Salamanca 1998, p. 205–240.

——, *Later scholastics, Spanish economic thought in the 16th and 17th centuries*, in: S. Todd Lowry – B. Gordon (eds.), Ancient and medieval economic ideas and concepts of social justice, Leiden – New York – Köln 1998, p. 503–562.

Gordley, J., *Equality in exchange*, California Law Review, 69 (1981), p. 1587–1656.

——, *Philosophical origins of modern contract doctrine*, Oxford 1991.

——, *Natural law origins of the common law of contract*, in: J. Barton (ed.), Towards a general law of contract, [Comparative studies in continental and Anglo-American legal history, 8], Berlin 1990, p. 367–465.

——, *Enforcing promises*, California Law Review, 83 (1995), p. 547–614.

——, *Good faith in contract law in the medieval ius commune*, in: R. Zimmermann – S. Whittaker (eds.), Good faith in European contract law, [The Common Core of Euro-

pean Private Law, Cambridge Studies in International and Comparative Law, 14], Cambridge 2000, p. 93–117.

——, *The moral foundations of private law*, The American Journal of Jurisprudence, 47 (2002), p. 1–23.

——, *Reconceptualizing the protection of dignity in early modern Europe, Greek philosophy meets Romanl law*, in: M. Ascheri e.a. (eds.), Ins Wasser geworfen und Ozeane durchquert, Festschrift für Knut Wolfgang Nörr, Köln – Weimar – Wien 2003, p. 281–305.

——, *Foundations of private law, Property, tort, contract, unjust enrichment*, Oxford 2006.

Gounot, E., *Le principe de l'autonomie de la volonté en droit privé, Contribution à l'étude critique de l'individualisme juridique*, Paris 1912.

Gouron, A., *Cessante causa cessat effectus, À la naissance de l'adage*, Comptes-rendus des séances de l'Académie des inscriptions et belles-lettres, 143 (1999), p. 299–309.

——, *Un traité écossais du douzième siècle*, Tijdschrift voor Rechtsgeschiedenis, 78 (2010), p. 1–13.

Grabmann, M., *Geschichte der katholischen Theologie seit dem Ausgang der Väterzeit*, Freiburg im Breisgau 1933.

Graziadei, M., *The development of 'fiducia' in Italian and French law from the 14th century to the end of the Ancien Régime*, in: R.H. Helmholz – R. Zimmermann (eds.), Itinera fiduciae, Trust and Treuhand in historical perspective, [Comparative Studies in Continental and Anglo-American Legal History, 19], Berlin 1998, p. 327–359.

Grice-Hutchinson, M., *The School of Salamanca, Readings in Spanish monetary theory, 1544–1605*, Oxford 1952.

——, *The concept of the School of Salamanca, Its origins and development*, in: L.S. Moss – C.K. Ryan (eds.), Economic thought in Spain, Selected essays of Marjorie Grice-Hutchinson, Cambridge 1993.

Grossi, P., *La proprietà nel sistema privatistico della Seconda Scolastica*, in: P. Grossi (ed.), La seconda scolastica nella formazione del diritto privato moderno, [Per la storia del pensiero giuridico moderno, 1], Milano 1973, p. 117–222.

——, *L'ordine giuridico medievale*, Roma – Bari, 1996².

Grunert, F. – Seelmann, K. (eds.), *Die Ordnung der Praxis, Neue Studien zur Spanischen Spätscholastik*, [Frühe Neuzeit, 68], Tübingen 2001.

——, *Punienda ergo sunt maleficia, Zur Kompetenz des öffentlichen Strafens in der Spanischen Spätscholastik*, in: F. Grunert – K. Seelmann (eds.), Die Ordnung der Praxis, Neue Studien zur Spanischen Spätscholastik, [Frühe Neuzeit, 68], Tübingen 2001, p. 313–332.

Gruys, A., *Cartusiana, vol. 1: Biblioghraphie générale et auteurs cartusiens*, Paris 1976.

Guzmán Brito, A., *La doctrina de Luis de Molina sobra la causa contractual*, in: A. Guzmán Brito (ed.), Actio, negocio, contrato y causa en la tradición del derecho Europeo e Iberoamericano, Navarra 2005, p. 368–440.

——, *Causa del contrato y causa de la obligación en la dogmática de los juristas romanos, medievales y modernos y en la codificación europea y americana*, in: A. Guzmán Brito (ed.), Actio, negocio, contrato y causa en la tradición del derecho Europeo e Iberoamericano, Navarra 2005, p. 197–406 [= reprint of Revista de estudios histórico-jurídicos, 23 (2001), p. 209–367.

——, *La doctrina de la consideration en Blackstone y sus relactiones con la causa en el ius commune*, in: A. Guzmán Brito (ed.), Actio, negocio, contrato y causa en la tradición del derecho Europeo e Iberoamericano, Navarra 2005, p. 441–477 [= reprint from Revista de estudios histórico-jurídicos, 25 (2003), p. 375–406].

Hafner, F. – Loretan, A. – Spenlé, C., *Naturrecht und Menschenrecht, Der Beitrag der Spanischen Spätscholastik zur Entwicklung der Menschenrechte*, in: F. Grunert – K. Seelmann (eds.), Die Ordnung der Praxis, Neue Studien zur Spanischen Spätscholastik, [Frühe Neuzeit, 68], Tübingen 2001, p. 123–153.

Hagenauer, S., *Das 'justum pretium' bei Thomas von Aquin, Ein Beitrag zur Geschichte der objektiven Werttheorie*, Stuttgart 1931.

Haggenmacher, P., *Grotius et la doctrine de la guerre juste*, Paris 1983.

——, *Droits subjectifs et système juridique chez Grotius*, in: L. Foisneau (ed.), Politique, droit et théologie chez Bodin, Grotius et Hobbes, Paris 1997, p. 73–130.

Hallebeek, J., *Sacramenta puberum and laesio enormis, The oath non venire contra by a minor in contracts of sale according to some glossators*, Tijdschrift voor Rechtsgeschiedenis, 58 (1990), p. 55–72.

——, *The concept of unjust enrichment in late scholasticism*, [Rechtshistorische reeks van het Gerard Noodt Instituut, 35], Nijmegen, 1996.

——, *The reception of Inst. 2.1.35 in late scholasticism*, Rivista internazionale di diritto comune, 7 (1996), p. 119–134.

——, *Unjust enrichment as a source of obligation, The genesis of a legal concept in the European ius commune*, Restitution Law Review, 10 (2002), p. 92–99.

——, *Medieval legal scholarship*, in: J. Hallebeek – H. Dondorp (eds.), Contracts for a third-party beneficiary, A historical and comparative account, [Legal history library, Studies in the history of private law, 1], Leiden – Boston 2008, p. 21–46.

Halpérin, J.-L., *Le fondement de l'obligation contractuelle chez les civilistes français du XIX siècle*, in: J.-F. Kervégan – H. Mohnhaupt (eds.), Gesellschaftliche Freiheit und vertragliche Bindung in Rechtsgeschichte und Philosophie / Liberté sociale et lien contractuel dans l'histoire du droit et la philosophie, [Ius commune, Sonderhefte, 120], Frankfurt am Main 1999, p. 323–347.

Hamilton, B., *Political thought in sixteenth-century Spain, A study of the political ideas of Vitoria, De Soto, Suárez, and Molina*, Oxford 1963.

Hamouda, O. – Price, B.B., *The Justice of the just price*, The European Journal of the History of Economic Thought, 4 (1997), p. 191–216.

Hankins, J., *Introduction*, in: J. Hankins (ed.), The Cambridge companion to Renaissance philosophy, Cambridge 2007, p. 1–9.

Harke, J.D., *'Si error aliquis intervenit'—Irrtum im klassischen römischen Vertragsrecht*, [Freiburger Rechtsgeschichtliche Abhandlungen, Neue folge, 45], Berlin 2005.

Hartkamp, A.S., *Der Zwang im römischen Privatrecht*, Amsterdam 1971.

Hartung, G., *Die Naturrechtsdebatte, Geschichte der Obligatio vom 17. bis 20. Jahrhundert*, [Alber praktische Philosophie, 56], Freiburg – München 1998.

——, *Gesetz und Obligation, Die spätscholastische Gesetzestheologie und ihr Einfluß auf die Naturrechtsdebatte der Frühen Neuzeit*, in: F. Grunert – K. Seelmann (eds.), Die Ordnung der Praxis, Neue Studien zur Spanischen Spätscholastik, [Frühe Neuzeit, 68], Tübingen 2001, p. 381–402.

——, *Althusius' Vertragstheorie im Kontext spätmittelalterlicher Jurisprudenz und Scholastik*, in: F.S. Carney – H. Schilling – D. Wyduckel (eds.), Jurisprudenz, Politische Theorie und Politische Theologie, Beiträge des Herborner Symposions zum 400. Jahrestag der Politica des Johannes Althusius 1603–2003, Berlin 2004, p. 287–303.

——, *Zur Genealogie des Versprechens, Ein Versuch über die begriffsgeschichtlichen und anthropologischen Voraussetzungen der modernen Vertragstheorie*, in: M. Schneider (ed.), Die Ordnung des Versprechens, Naturrecht—Institution—Sprechakt, [Literatur und Recht, 1], München 2005.

Hassan, H., *Contracts in Islamic law, The principles of commutative justice and liberality*, Journal of Islamic studies, 13 (2002), p. 257–297.

Hayaert, V., *Mens emblematica et humanisme juridique, Le cas du Pegma cum narrationibus philosophicis de Pierre Coustau (1555)*, [Travaux d'humanisme et Renaissance, 438], Genève 2008.

Heber, R. (ed.), *The whole works of Jeremy Taylor*, London 1828.

Hein, R.B., *'Gewissen' bei Adrian von Utrecht (Hadrian VI.), Erasmus von Rotterdam und Thomas More, Ein Beitrag zur systematischen Analyse des Gewissensbegriffs in der katholischen nordeuropäischen Renaissance*, [Studien zur Moraltheologie, 10], Münster 1999.

Heirbaut, D., *Law*, in: N. Hammerstein, Social sciences, history and law, in: W. Rüegg (ed.), A history of the universities in Europe, Universities since 1945, [A History of the University in Europe, 4], Cambridge 2011, p. 414–422.

Heirbaut, D. – Storme, M.E., *The Belgian legal tradition, From a long quest for legal independence to a longing for dependence?*, European Review of Private Law, 14 (2006), p. 645–683.

——, *The historical evolution of European private law*, in: Ch. Twigg-Flesner (ed.), The Cambridge companion to European Union private law, Cambridge 2010, p. 20–32.

Helmholz, R.H., *Contracts and the canon Law*, in: J. Barton (ed.), Towards a general law of contract, [Comparative Studies in Continental and Anglo-American Legal History, 8], Berlin 1990, p. 49–66.

Helmholz, R.H., *Roman canon law in Reformation England*, Cambridge 1990.

——, *The spirit of classical canon law*, Athens Ga. – London 1996.

——, *The Oxford history of the laws of England, Vol. 1: The canon law and ecclesiastical jurisdiction from 597 to the 1640s*, Oxford 2004.

Helmholz, R.H. – Zimmermann, R. (eds.), *Views of trust and Treuhand, An introduction*, in: R.H. Helmholz – R. Zimmermann (eds.), Itinera fiduciae, Trust and Treuhand in historical perspective, [Comparative Studies in Continental and Anglo-American Legal History, 19], Berlin 1998.

Herman, S., *The canonical conception of the trust*, in: R.H. Helmholz – R. Zimmermann (eds.), Itinera fiduciae, Trust and Treuhand in historical perspective, [Comparative Studies in Continental and Anglo-American Legal History, 19], Berlin 1998, p. 85–109.

Hespanha, A., *Panorama histórico da cultura jurídica europeia*, [Forum da história, 24], Mem Martins 1997.

Heynck, V., *Johannes de Medina über vollkommene und unvollkommene Reue*, Franziskanische Studien, 29 (1942), p. 120–150.

Hoenen, M.J.F.M., *Via antiqua and via moderna in the fifteenth century, Doctrinal, institutional, and Church political factors in the 'Wegestreit'*, in: R.L. Friedman – L.O. Nielsen (eds.), The medieval heritage in early modern metaphysics and modal theory, 1400–1700, [The New Synthese Historical Library, Texts and Studies in the History of Philosophy, 53], p. 9–36.

Hofer, S., *Freiheit ohne Grenzen? Privatrechtstheoretische Diskussionen im 19. Jahrhundert*, [Ius privatum, 53], Tübingen 2001.

——, *Vertragsfreiheit am Schneideweg*, [Schriften der Juristischen Studiengesellschaft Regensburg, 29], München 2006.

——, *Die Diskussion um den Begriff 'Privat-Autonomie' in der ersten Hälfte des 19. Jahrhunderts*, in: P. Collin – G. Bender – S. Ruppert – M. Seckelmann – M. Stolleis (eds.), Selbstregulierung im 19. Jahrhundert – zwischen Autonomie und staatlichen Steuerungsansprüchen, [Studien zur europäischen Rechtsgeschichte, 259; Moderne Regulierungsregime, 1], Frankfurt am Main 2011, p. 63–84.

Höffner, J., *Wirtschaftsethik und Monopole im 15. und 16. Jahrhundert*, Darmstadt 1969.

Holthöfer, E., *Die Literatur zum gemeinen und partikularen Recht in Italien, Frankreich, Spanien und Portugal*, in: H. Coing (ed.), Handbuch der Quellen und Literatur der neueren europäischen Privatrechtsgeschichte, Band II. Neuere Zeit (1500–1800), Das Zeitalter des gemeinen Rechts, Teilband I. Wissenschaft, München 1977, p. 103–500.

Holzhauer, H., *Natur als Argument in der Rechtswissenschaft*, in: G. Köbler – H. Nehlsen (eds.), Wirkungen europäischer Rechtskultur, Festschrift für Karl Kroeschell zum 70. Geburtstag, München 1997, p. 395–417.

Höpfl, H., *Jesuit political thought, The Society of Jesus and the State c. 1540–1630*, [Ideas in context, 70], Cambridge 2004.

——, *Scholasticism in Quentin Skinner's Foundations*, in: A.S. Brett – J. Tully – H. Hamilton-Bleakley (eds.), Rethinking the foundations of modern political thought, Cambridge 2006, p. 113–129.

Höpfl, H. – Thompson, M.P., *The history of contract as a motif in political thought*, The American Historical Review, 84 (1979), p. 919–944.

Horn, N., *Aequitas in den Lehren des Baldus*, [Forschungen zur neueren Privatrechtsgeschichte, 11], Köln – Graz 1968.

Horwitz, M.J., *The transformation of American law, 1780–1860*, Cambridge Mass. – London 1977.

Huber, W., *Rechtfertigung und Recht, Über die christlichen Wurzeln der europäischen Rechts-kultur*, [Würzburger Vorträge zur Rechtsphilosophie, Rechtstheorie und Rechtssoziologie, 27], Baden-Baden 2001.

Hübner, H., *Subjektivismus in der Entwicklung des Privatrechts*, in: K. Luig (ed.), Heinz Hübner, Rechtsdogmatik und Rechtsgeschichte, Ausgewählte Schriften, Köln e.a. 1997, p. 247–270 [= reprint from D. Medicus – H.H. Seiler (eds.), *Festschrift für Max Kaser zum 70. Geburtstag*, München 1976, p. 715–742].

Huesman, W.A., *The doctrine of Leonard Lessius on mortal sin*, Excerpta ex dissertatione ad lauream in Facultate Theologiae Pontificae Universitatis Gregorianae, Romae 1947.

Ibbetson, D., *Consideration and the theory of contract in sixteenth century common law*, in: J. Barton (ed.), Towards a general law of contract, [Comparative studies in continental and Anglo-American legal history, 8], Berlin 1990, p. 67–123.

——, *A Historical introduction to the law of obligations*, Oxford 1999.

Ickx, J., *Ipsa vero officii maioris Penitentiarii institutio non reperitur? La nascità di un Tribunale della coscienza*, in: M. Sodi – J. Ickx (eds.), La penitenzieria apostolica e il sacramento della penitenza, Percorsi storici, giuridici, teologici e prospettive pastorali, Città del Vaticano 2009, p. 19–50.

Jansen, N., *'Tief ist der Brunnen der Vergangenheit', Funktion, Methode und Ausgangspunkt historischer Fragestellungen in der Privatrechtsdogmatik*, Zeitschrift für neuere Rechtsgeschichte, 27 (2005), p. 202–228.

——, *Seriositätskontrollen existentiell belastender Versprechen, Rechtsvergleichung, Rechtsgeschichte, und Rechtsdogmatik*, in: H. Kötz – R. Zimmermann (eds.), Störungen der Willensbindung bei Vertragsabschluss, Tübingen 2007, p. 125–162.

——, *The making of legal authority, Non-legislative codifications in historical and comparative perspective*, Oxford – New York 2010.

——, *Testamentary formalities in early modern Europe*, in: K.G.C. Reid – M.J. De Waal – R. Zimmermann, Comparative succession law, Vol. 1: Testamentary formalities, Oxford 2011, p. 27–50.

Janssens, G., *Hopperus, Joachim*, in: The Oxford encyclopedia of the Reformation, Oxford 1996, p. 254–255.

Jellinek, G., *Die sozialethische Bedeutung von Recht, Unrecht und Strafe*, Berlin 1908.

Jerouschek, G. – Müller, D., *Die Ursprünge der Denunziation im Kanonischen Recht*, in: H. Lück – B. Schildt (eds.), Recht—Idee—Geschichte, Beiträge zur Rechts- und Ideengeschichte für Rolf Lieberwirth anlässlich seines 80. Geburtstages, Köln e.a. 2000, p. 3–24.

Jones, G., *History of the law of charity, 1532–1827*, [Cambridge Studies in English Legal History], Cambridge 1969.

Jugie, M., s.v. *Péché*, in: Dictionnaire de Théologie Catholique, Paris 1933, tom. 12, 1, cols. 140–624.

Kalb, H., *Laesio enormis im gelehrten Recht, Kanonistische Studien zur Läsionsanfechtung*, [Kirche und Recht, 19], Wien 1992.

Kantola, I., *Probability and moral uncertainty in late medieval and early modern times*, [Schriften der Luther-Agricola-Gesellschaft, 32], Helsinki 1994.

Kaser, M., *Das Römische Privatrecht*, Erster Abschnitt: Das altrömische, das vorklassische, und klassische Recht, [Handbuch der Altertumswissenschaft, 10.3.3.1], München 1971².

Kaufmann, M. – Schnepf, R. (eds.), *Politische Metaphysik*, [Treffpunkt Philosophie, 8], Frankfurt am Main e.a. 2007.

Kaulla, R., *Die geschichtliche Entwicklung der modernen Werttheorien*, Tübingen 1906.

Keenan, J.F., *The casuistry of John Mair, Nominalist professor of Paris*, in: J.F. Keenan – Th.A. Shannon (eds.), The context of casuistry, Washington DC 1995, p. 85–102.

——, *William Perkins (1558–1602) and the birth of British casuistry*, in: J.F. Keenan – Th.A. Shannon (eds.), The context of casuistry, Washington DC 1995, p. 105–130.

——, *Was William Perkins' whole Treatise of Cases of Consciences casuistry? Hermeneutics and British practical divinity*, in: H.E. Braun – E. Vallance (eds.), Contexts of conscience in early modern Europe, 1500–1700, Basingstoke 2004, p. 56–66.

——, *A history of Catholic moral theology in the twentieth century, From confessing sins to liberating consciences*, London – New York 2010.

Kempshall, M., *The common good in late medieval political thought*, Oxford 1999.

Kennedy, D., *Primitive legal scholarship*, Harvard International Law Journal, 27 (1986), p. 1–99.

——, *Savigny's family/patrimony distinction and its place in the global genealogy of classical legal thought*, American Journal of Comparative Law, 58 (2010), p. 811–841.

Kessler, E., *Ethik im Mittelalter und im Frühen Humanismus, Kritische Studie über eine 'Kritische Studie'*, Recherches de Théologie et Philosophie médiévales, 78 (2011), p. 481–505.

Kisch, G., *Erasmus und die Jurisprudenz seiner Zeit, Studien zum humanistischen Rechtsdenken*, [Basler Studien zur Rechtswissenschaft, 56], Basel 1960.

Klinck, D.R., *Conscience, equity and the Court of Chancery in early modern England*, Farnham 2010.

Knebel, S., *Wille, Würfel und Wahrscheinlichkeit, Das System der moralischen Notwendigkeit in der Jesuitenscholastik*, [Paradeigmata, 21], Hamburg 2000.

——, *Salamanca und sein Ambiente, Ein Repertorium zur Jesuitenscholastik des 17. Jahrhunderts*, in: F. Grunert – K. Seelmann (eds.), Die Ordnung der Praxis, Neue Studien zur Spanischen Spätscholastik, [Frühe Neuzeit, 68], Tübingen 2001, p. 429–458.

——, *Casuistry and the early modern paradigm shift in the notion of charity*, in: J. Kraye – R. Saarinen (ed.), Moral philosophy on the threshold of modernity, [The New Synthese Historical Library, Texts and Studies in the History of Philosophy, 57], Dordrecht 2005, p. 115–139.

——, *Suarezismus, Erkenntnistheoretisches aus dem Nachlass des Jesuitengenerals Tirso González de Santalla (1624–1705), Abhandlung und Edition*, [Bochumer Studien zur Philosophie, 51], Amsterdam 2011.

Knütel, R., *La causa nella dottrina dei patti*, in: L. Vacca (ed.), Causa e contratto nella prospettiva storico-comparatistica, II Congresso Internazionale ARISTEC, Palermo, 7–8 giugno 1995, Torino 1997, p. 131–144.

Köbler, R., *Die 'Clausula rebus sic stantibus' als allgemeiner Rechtsgrundsatz*, Tübingen 1991.

Köck, H.F., *Der Beitrag der Schule von Salamanca zur Entwicklung der Lehre von den Grundrechten*, [Schriften zur Rechtsgeschichte, 39], Berlin 1987.

Koskenniemi, M., *Empire and international law, The real Spanish contribution*, University of Toronto Law Journal, 61 (2011), p. 1–36.

Koslowski, P. – Schönberger, R., *Was ist Scholastik?*, [Philosophie und Religion, Schriftenreihe des Forschungsinstituts für Philosophie Hannover, 2], Hildesheim 1991.

Krause, H., *Cessante causa cessat lex*, Zeitschrift der Savigny-Stiftung für Rechtsgeschichte, Kanonistische Abteilung, 46 (1960), p. 81–111.

Kriechbaum, M., *Actio, ius und dominium in den Rechtslehren des 13. und 14. Jahrhunderts*, [Abhandlungen zur rechtswissenschaftlichen Grundlagenforschung, 77], Ebelsbach 1996.

——, *Philosophie und Jurisprudenz bei Baldus de Ubaldis, 'Philosophi legum imitati sunt philosophos naturae'*, Ius commune, 27 (2000), p. 299–343.

Kriechbaum, M. – Lange, H. (eds.), *Römisches Recht im Mittelalter, Band II: Die Kommentatoren*, München 2007.

Kuttner, S., *Kanonistische Schuldlehre von Gratian bis auf die Dekretalen Gregors IX, systematisch auf grund der handschriftlichen Quellen dargestellt*, [Studi e testi, 64], Città del Vaticano 1935.

——, *Sur les origines du terme 'droit positif'*, Revue Historique de Droit Français et Étranger, 15 (1936), p. 728–740.

——, *Reform of the Church and the Council of Trent*, The Jurist, 22 (1962), p. 123–142.

——, *Urban II and the doctrine of interpretation, A turning point?*, Studia Gratiana, 15 (1972), p. 55–85.

Landau, P., *Aequitas in the Corpus iuris canonici*, Syracuse Journal of International Law and Commerce, 20 (1994), p. 95–104.

——, *Die Bedeutung des kanonischen Rechts für die Entwicklung einheitlicher Rechtsprinzipien*, in: H. Scholler (ed.), Die Bedeutung des kanonischen Rechts für die Entwicklung einheitlicher Rechtsprinzipien, [Arbeiten zur Rechtsvergleichung, Schriftenreihe der Gesellschaft für Rechtsvergleichung, 177], Baden-Baden 1996, p. 23–48.

——, *Spanische Spätscholastik und kanonistische Lehrbuchliteratur*, in: F. Grunert – K. Seelmann (eds.), Die Ordnung der Praxis, Neue Studien zur Spanischen Spätscholastik, [Frühe Neuzeit, 68], Tübingen 2001, p. 403–426.

——, *Pacta sunt servanda, Zu den kanonistischen Grundlagen der Privatautonomie*, in: M. Ascheri et al. (eds.), Ins wasser geworfen und Ozeane durchquert, Festschrift für Knut Wolfgang Nörr, Köln – Weimar – Wien 2003, p. 457–474.

Langholm, O.I., *Price and value in the Aristotelian tradition, A study in scholastic economic sources*, Oslo 1979.

——, *Economic freedom in scholastic thought*, History of Political Economy, 14 (1982), p. 260–283.

——, *The Aristotelian analysis of usury*, Bergen 1984.

——, *Economics in the medieval schools, Wealth, exchange, value, money and usury according to the Paris theological tradition. 1200–1350*, [Studien und Texte zur Geistesgeschichte des Mittelalters, 29], Leiden 1992.

——, *The legacy of scholasticism in economic thought, Antecedents of choice and power*, Cambridge 1998.

——, *The merchants in the confessional, Trade and price in the pre-Reformation penitential handbooks*, [Studies in Medieval and Reformation Thought, 93], Leiden 2003.

Lardone, F., *Roman law in the works of St Augustine*, Georgetown Law Journal, 21 (1933), p. 435–456, reprinted in: R.O. Brooks – J.B. Murphy (eds.), Augustine and modern law, Farnham – Burlington 2011, p. 229–250.

Larrainzar, C., *Una introducción a Francisco Suárez*, Pamplona 1976.

Lavenia, V., *Martín de Azpilcueta (1492–1586), Un profilo*, Archivio Italiano per la storia della pietà, 16 (2003), p. 15–148.

——, *L'infamia e il perdono, Tributi, pene e confessione nella teologia morale della prima età moderna*, Bologna 2004.

——, *Fraus et cautela, Théologie morale et fiscalité au début des temps modernes*, in: S. Boarini (ed.), La casuistique classique, Genèse, formes, devenir, Saint-Étienne 2009, p. 43–58.

Lefebvre, Ch., *Contribution à l'étude des origines et du développement de la 'denunciatio evangelica' en droit canonique*, in: Ephemerides iuris canonici, 6 (1950), p. 60–93.

——, *L'officium iudicis d'après les canonistes du Moyen Âge*, L'Année canonique, 2 (1953), p. 115–124.

——, *Gratien et les origines de la dénonciation évangélique, De l'accusatio à la denunciatio*, Studia Gratiana, 4 (1956), p. 231–250.

Lefebvre-Teillard, A., *Le droit canonique et la formation des grands principes du droit privé français*, in: H. Scholler (ed.), Die Bedeutung des kanonischen Rechts für die Entwicklung einheitlicher Rechtsprinzipien, [Arbeiten zur Rechtsvergleichung, Schriftenreihe der Gesellschaft für Rechtsvergleichung, 177], Baden-Baden 1996), p. 9–22.

Lefebvre-Teillard, A. – Demoulin, F. – Roumy, F., *De la théologie au droit*, in: R.H. Helmholz et al. (eds.), Grundlagen des Rechts, Festschrift Peter Landau, Paderborn 2000, p. 421–438.

Legendre, P., *L'inscription du droit canon dans la théologie, Remarques sur la seconde scolastique*, in: S. Kuttner – K. Pennington (eds.), Proceedings of the fifth international congress of medieval canon law (Salamanca, 21–25 September 1976), [Monumenta iuris canonici, Series C: subsidia, 6], Città del Vaticano 1980, p. 443–454.

——, *L'autre Bible de l'Occident, Le monument romano-canonique, Étude sur l'architecture dogmatique des sociétés*, [Leçons, 9], Paris 2009.

Leite, A., *Sá, Manuel de*, in: C. O'Neill – J. Domínguez (eds.), Diccionario histórico de la Compañía de Jesús biográfico-temático, Roma – Madrid 2001, vol. 4, p. 34–54.

Leites, E., *Casuistry and character*, in E. Leites (ed.), Conscience and casuistry in early modern Europe, Cambridge 2002 [= 1988]), p. 119–133.

Lepsius, S., *Der Richter und die Zeugen, Eine Untersuchung anhand des Tractatus testimoniorum des Bartolus von Sassoferrato, Mit Edition*, [Studien zur europäischen Rechtsgeschichte, 158], Frankfurt am Main 2003.

——, *Von Zweifeln zur Überzeugung, Der Zeugenbeweis im gelehrten Recht ausgehend von der Abhandlung des Bartolus von Sassoferrato*, [Studien zur europäischen Rechtsgeschichte, 160], Frankfurt am Main 2003.

——, *Juristische Theoriebildung und Philosophische Kategorien, Bemerkungen zur Arbeitsweise des Bartolus von Sassoferrato*, in: M. Kaufhold (ed.), Politische Reflexion in der Welt des späten Mittelalters / Political thought in the ages of scholasticism, Essays in honour of Jürgen Miethke, [Studies in Medieval and Reformation Traditions, 103], Leiden – Boston 2004, p. 287–304.

——, *Rechtsgeschichte und allgemeine Geschichtswissenschaft, Zur Wahrnehmung einer Differenz bei den Historikern Burgdorf und Zwierlein*, Zeitschrift für neuere Rechtsgeschichte, 27 (2005), p. 304–310.

——, *Communis opinio doctorum*, in: A. Cordes – H. Lück – D. Werkmüller (eds.), Handwörterbuch zur deutschen Rechtsgeschichte, Band 1, Lieferung 4, Berlin 2006, cols. 875–877.

——, *Taking the institutional context seriously, A comment on James Gordley*, in: The American Journal of Comparative Law, 56 (2008), p. 655–666 [reprinted in: N. Jansen – R. Michaels (eds.), Beyond the State, Rethinking private law, Tübingen 2008, p. 233–243].

——, *Innominatkontrakt*, in: A. Cordes – H. Lück – D. Werkmüller (eds.), Handwörterbuch zur deutschen Rechtsgeschichte, Band 2, Lieferung 13, Berlin 2011, cols. 1225–1226.

Lesaffer, R., *The medieval canon law of contract and early modern treaty law*, Journal of the history of international law, 2 (2000), p. 178–198.

——, *European legal history, A cultural and political perspective*, Cambridge 2009.

Liebs, D., *Lateinische Rechtsregeln und Rechtssprichwörter*, München 2007.

Lines, D.A., *Aristotle's Ethics in the Italian Renaissance (ca. 1300–1650), The universities and the problem of moral education*, [Education and society in the Middle Ages and Renaissance, 13], Leiden – Boston 2002.

——, *Humanistic and scholastic ethics*, in: J. Hankins, The Cambridge companion to Renaissance philosophy, Cambridge 2007, p. 304–318.

Löber, B., *Das spanische Gesellschaftsrecht im 16. Jahrhundert*, Freiburg im Breisgau 1965.

Luhmann, N., *Das Recht der Gesellschaft*, [Suhrkamp Taschenbuch Wissenschaft, 1183], Frankfurt am Main 1995.

Luig, K., *Der gerechte Preis in der Rechtstheorie und Rechtspraxis von Christian Thomasius (1655–1728)*, in: Diritto e potere nella storia europea, Atti in onore di Bruno Paradisi, Band 2, Firenze 1982, p. 775–803.

——, *Vertragsfreiheit und Äquivalenzprinzip im gemeinen Recht und im BGB, Bemerkungen zur Vorgeschichte des § 138 II BGB*, in: Aspekte europäischer Rechtsgeschichte, Festgabe für Helmut Coing zum 70. Geburtstag, [Ius Commune, Sonderhefte, Texte und Monographien, 17], Frankfurt am Main 1982, p. 171–206.

——, *Das Privatrecht von Christian Thomasius zwischen Absolutismus und Liberalismus*, in: W. Schneiders (ed.), Christian Thomasius, 1655–1728, [Studien zum achtzehnten Jahrhundert, 11], Hamburg 1989, p. 148–172.

——, *Causa und Innominatvertrag in der Vertragslehre zur Zeit des Naturrechts*, in: L. Vacca (ed.), Causa e contratto nella prospettiva storico-comparatistica, II Congresso Internazionale ARISTEC, Palermo, 7–8 giugno 1995, Torino 1997, p. 217–234.

——, *Die Kontinuität allgemeiner Rechtsgrundsätze, Das Beispiel der clausula rebus sic stantibus*, in: R. Zimmermann – R. Knütel – J.P. Meincke (eds.), Rechtsgeschichte und Privatrechtsdogmatik, Heidelberg 1999, p. 171–186.

Maclean, I., *Interpretation and meaning in the Renaissance, The case of law*, [Ideas in context, 21], Cambridge 1992.

Macnair, M., *Equity and conscience*, Oxford Journal of Legal Studies, 27 (2007), p. 659–681.

Madero, M., *Peritaje e impotencia sexual en el De Sancto Matrimonio de Tomás Sánchez*, Eadem utraque Europa (2008), p. 105–136.

——, *La nature du droit au corps dans le mariage selon la casuistique des XIIᵉ et XIIIᵉ siècles*, Annales, Histoire, Sciences Sociales, 65 (2010), p. 1323–1348.

——, *Sobre el ius in corpus, En torno a una obra de Filippo Vassalli y al debate Francesco Carnelutti-Pio Fedele*, in: E. Conte – M. Madero (eds.), Entre hecho y derecho, Hacer, poseer, usar en perspectiva histórica, Buenos Aires 2010, p. 119–134.

Maffei, D., *Gli inizi dell'umanesimo giuridico*, Milano 1972³.

Mahoney, J., *The making of moral theology*, Oxford 1987.

Maihold, H., *Strafe für fremde Schuld ? Die Systematisierung des Strafbegriffs in der Spanischen Spätscholastik und Naturrechtslehre*, [Konflikt, Verbrechen und Sanktion in der Gesellschaft Alteuropas, Symposien und Synthesen, 9], Köln 2005.

Maillard-Luypaert, M., *Les suppliques de la pénitencerie apostolique pour les diocèses de Cambrai, Liège, Thérouanne et Tournai (1410–1411)*, [Analecta Vaticano-Belgica, Série 1, 34], Bruxelles 2003.

Mäkinen, V., *Property rights in the late medieval discussion in Franciscan poverty*, [Recherches de Théologie et Philosophie médiévales—Bibliotheca, 3], Leuven 2001.

——, *Rights and duties in late scholastic discussion on extreme necessity*, in: V. Mäkinen – P. Korkman (eds.), Transformations in medieval and early modern rights discourse, [The New Synthese Historical Library, Texts and Studies in the History of Philosophy, 59], Dordrecht 2006, p. 37–62.

Martínez Tapia, R., *Filosofía política y derecho en el pensamiento español del s. XVI, El canonista Martín de Azpilcueta*, Granada 1997.

Martyn, G., *Het Eeuwig Edict van 12 juli 1611, Zijn genese en zijn rol in de verschriftelijking van het privaatrecht*, [Algemeen Rijksarchief en Rijksarchief in de Provinciën, Studia, 81], Brussel 2000.

——, *Painted Exempla Iustitiae in the Southern Netherlands*, in: R. Schulze (ed.), Symbolische Kommunikation vor Gericht in der Frühen Neuzeit, [Schriften zur Europäischen Rechts- und Verfassungsgeschichte, 51], Berlin 2006, p. 335–356.

Maryks, R.A., *Census of the books written by Jesuits on sacramental confession (1554–1650)*, Annali di Storia moderna e contemporanea, 10 (2004), p. 415–519.

——, *Saint Cicero and the Jesuits, The influence of the liberal arts on the adoption of moral probabilism*, Aldershot – Rome 2008.

Masferrer, A., *Contribución de la teología y ciencia canónica al derecho penal europeo moderno, Materiales y breves notas para su estudio*, in: Europa, sé tú misma, Actas del VI Congreso Católicos y vida pública (Madrid, 19–21 noviembre de 2004), Madrid 2005, vol. 1, p. 185–200.

——, *Spanish legal traditions, A comparative legal history outline*, Madrid 2009.

——, *Spanish legal history, A need for its comparative approach*, in: K.A. Modéer – P. Nilsén (eds.), How to teach European comparative legal history, Lund 2011, p. 107–142.

Massironi, A., *Nell'officina dell'interprete, La qualificazione del contratto nel diritto comune (secoli XIV–XVI)*, Milano 2012.

Mayali, L., *Ius civile et ius commune dans la tradition juridique médiévale*, in: J. Krynen (ed.), Droit romain, jus civile et droit français, [Études d'histoire du droit et des idées politiques, 3], Toulouse 1999, p. 201–217.

Mayer-Maly, T., *Der Konsens als Grundlage des Vertrages*, in: H. Hübner – E. Klingmüller – A. Wacke (eds.), Festschrift Erwin Seidl zum 70. Geburtstag, Köln 1975, p. 118–129.

——, *Die Bedeutung des Konsenses in privatrechtsgeschichtlicher Sicht*, in: G. Jakobs (ed.), Rechtsgeltung und Konsens, [Schriften zur Rechtstheorie, 49], Berlin 1976, p. 91–104.

——, *Die laesio enormis und das kanonische Recht*, in: H. Paarhammer – A. Rinnerthaler (eds.), Scientia Canonum, Festgabe für Franz Pototschnig zum 65. Geburtstag, München 1991, p. 19–26.

——, *Die Rechtslehre des heiligen Thomas von Aquin und die römische Jurisprudenz*, in: J.A. Ankum e.a. (ed.), Mélanges Felix Wubbe offerts par ses collègues et ses amis à l'occasion de son soixante-dixième anniversaire, Fribourg 1993, p. 345–353.

——, *Rechtsgeschichtliche Bibelkunde*, Wien – Köln – Weimar 2003.

Mazzacane, A., *Umanesimo e sistematiche giuridiche in Germania alla fine del Cinquecento, equità e giurisprudenza nelle opere di Herman Vultejus*, Annali di Storia del Diritto, 12–13 (1968–1969), p. 257–319.

Meccarelli, M., *Arbitrium, Un aspetto sistematico degli ordinamenti giuridici in età di diritto comune*, Milano 1998.

——, *Ein Rechtsformat für die Moderne, Lex und Iurisdictio in der spanischen Spätscholastik*, in: C. Strohm – H. de Wall (eds.), Konfessionalität und Jurisprudenz in der frühen Neuzeit, [Historische Forschungen, 89], Berlin 2009, p. 285–311.

Merzbacher, F., *Azpilcueta und Covarruvias, Zur Gewaltendoktrin der spanischen Kanonistik im Goldenen Zeitalter*, in: G. Köbler – H. Drüppel – D. Willoweit (eds.), Friedrich Merzbacher, Recht-Staat-Kirche, Ausgewählte Aufsätze, [Forschungen zur kirchlichen Rechtsgeschichte und zum Kirchenrecht, 18], Wien – Köln – Graz 1989, p. 275–302 [= reprint from F. Merzbacher, *Azpilcueta und Covarruvias, Zur Gewaltendoktrin der spanischen Kanonistik im Goldenen Zeitalter*, Zeitschrift der Savigny-Stiftung für Rechtsgeschichte, Kan. Abt., 46 (1960), p. 317–344].

——, *Kardinal Juan de Lugo als Rechtsdenker*, in: G. Köbler – H. Drüppel – D. Willoweit (eds.), Friedrich Merzbacher, Recht-Staat-Kirche, Ausgewählte Aufsätze, [Forschungen zur kirchlichen Rechtsgeschichte und zum Kirchenrecht, 18], Wien – Köln – Graz 1989, p. 303–317.

——, *Die Regel 'Fidem frangenti fides frangitur' und ihre Anwendung*, in: G. Köbler – H. Drüppel – D. Willoweit (eds.), Friedrich Merzbacher, Recht-Staat-Kirche, Ausgewählte Aufsätze, [Forschungen zur kirchlichen Rechtsgeschichte und zum Kirchenrecht, 18], Wien – Köln – Graz 1989, p. 619–642.

Michaud-Quantin, P., *Sommes de casuistique et manuels de confession au moyen âge (XIIᵉ–XVIᵉ siècles)*, Leuven – Lille – Montréal 1962.

Minnucci, G., *Foro della coscienza e foro esterno nel pensiero giuridico della prima età moderna*, in: G. Dilcher – D. Quaglioni (eds.), Gli inizi del diritto pubblico, 3: Verso la costruzione del diritto pubblico tra medioevo e modernità, [Annali dell'Istituto Storico Italo-Germanico in Trento, Contributi, 25], Bologna – Berlin 2011, p. 55–81.

Mirow, M., *Private law, lawyers and legal institutions in Spanish America, 1500–2000*, Leiden 2003 [= doct. diss.].

——, *Latin American law, A history of private law and institutions in Spanish America*, Austin, TX 2004.

Mizuno, K., *Das 'officium iudicis' und die Parteien im römisch-kanonischen Prozess des Mittelalters, Eine Betrachtung über die 'clausula salutaris'*, Zeitschrift der Savigny-Stiftung für Rechtsgeschichte, Kan. Abt., 97 (2011), p. 76–111.

Mohnhaupt, H., *Vertragskonstruktion und fingierter Vertrag zur Sicherung von Normativität: Gesetz, Privileg, Verfassung*, in: J.-F. Kervégan – H. Mohnhaupt (eds.), Gesellschaftliche Freiheit und vertragliche Bindung in Rechtsgeschichte und Philosophie / Liberté sociale et lien contractuel dans l'histoire du droit et la philosophie, [Ius commune, Sonderhefte, 120], Frankfurt am Main 1999, p. 1–33.

Monballyu, J., *Een kerkelijke rechtbank aan het werk in de contrareformatie, De rechtspraak van de officialiteit van Brugge in 1585–1610*, in: Liber amicorum Monique Van Melkebeke, Brussel 2011, p. 125–161.

Monsalve Serrano, F. – De Juán Asenjo, O., *Juan de Lugo y la libertad en economía, El análisis económico escolástico en transición*, Procesos de mercado, Revista europea de economía política, 2 (2006), p. 217–243.

Moore, E., *Enrique Henríquez*, in: C. O'Neill – J. Domínguez (eds.), Diccionario Histórico de la Compañía de Jesús, Biográfico-Temático, Roma – Madrid 2001, vol. 2, p. 1900–1901.

Mostaza, A., *Forum internum—Forum externum, En torno a la naturaleza jurídica del fuero interno*, Revista Española de Derecho Canonico, 23 (1967), p. 253–331.

Motta, F., *Bellarmino, Una teologia politica della Controriforma*, [Storia, 12], Brescia 2005.

Mozzarelli, C., *Tra ragion di stato e sociabilità, Ipotesi cattoliche di rifondazione del vivere associato*, in: F. Arici – F. Todescan (eds.), Iustus ordo e ordine della natura, Sacra doctrina e saperi politici fra XVI e XVIII, [Biblioteca di Lex naturalis, 5], Milano 2007, p. 63–72.

Müller, D., *Schuld—Geständnis—Buße, Zur theologischen Wurzel von Grundbegriffen des mittelalterlichen Strafprozeßrechts*, in: H. Schlosser – R. Sprandel – D. Willoweit (eds.), Herrschaftliches Strafen seit dem Hochmittelalter, Formen und Entwicklungsstufen, Köln e.a. 2002, p. 403–420.

Müller, W.P., *Huguccio*, [Studies in Medieval and Early Modern Canon Law, 3], Washington D.C. 1994.

Nanz, K.P., *Entstehung des allgemeinen Vertragsbegriffs im 16. bis 18. Jahrhundert*, [Beiträge zur neueren Privatrechtsgeschichte, 9], München 1985.

Negro, P., *Intorno alle fonti scolastiche in Hugo Grotius*, Divus Thomas, 27 (2000), p. 236–251.

Nellen, H., *Hugo de Groot, Een leven in strijd om de vrede (1583–1645)*, Amsterdam 2007.

Nicolini, H. – Sinatti D'Amico, F., *Indices corporis iuris civilis iuxta vetustiores editiones cum criticis collatas, Pars 1: Index titulorum*, [Ius Romanum Medii Aevi, Subsidia 1], Mediolani 1964.

——, *Indices corporis iuris civilis iuxta vetustiores editiones cum criticis collatas, Pars 2: Index legum*, [Ius Romanum Medii Aevi, Subsidia 1], Mediolani 1967.

Noonan, J.T., Jr., *The scholastic analysis of usury*, Cambridge Mass. 1957.

Nörr, K.W., *'Ein Muster damaliger Gelehrsamkeit', Kanonistische Bemerkungen zu zwei Abhandlungen Konrad Summenharts zum Thema der Simonie*, in: S. Lorenz – D. Bauer – O. Auge (eds.), Tübingen in Lehre und Forschung um 1500, Zur Geschichte der Eberhard Karls Universität Tübingen, Festgabe für Ulrich Köpf, [Tübinger Bausteine zur Landesgeschichte, 9], Ostfildern 2008, p. 207–221.

Nuding, M., (ed.), *Matthäus von Krakau, De contractibus*, [Editiones Heidelbergenses, 28], Heidelberg 2000.

——, *Geschäft und Moral, Schriften 'De contractibus' an mitteleuropäischen Universitäten im späten 14. und frühen 15. Jahrhundert*, in: F.P. Knapp – J. Miethke – M. Niesner (eds.), Schriften im Umkreis mitteleuropäischer Universitäten um 1400, Lateinische und volkssprachige Texte aus Prag, Wien und Heidelberg, Unterschiede, Gemeinsamkeiten, Wechselbeziehungen, [Education and Society in the Middle Ages and Renaissance, 20], Leiden – Boston 2004, p. 40–62.

——, *Matthäus von Krakau, Theologe, Politiker, Kirchenreformer in Krakau, Prag und Heidelberg zur Zeit des Großen Abendländischen Schismas*, [Spätmittelalter und Reformation, Neue Reihe, 38], Tübingen 2007.

Nufer, G., *Über die Restitutionslehre der spanischen Spätscholastiker und ihre Ausstrahlung auf die Folgezeit*, München 1969 [= doct. diss.].

Oestmann, P., *Die Zwillingsschwester der Freiheit, Die Form im Recht als Problem der Rechtsgeschichte*, in: P. Oestmann (ed.), Zwischen Formstrenge und Billigkeit, [Quellen und Forschungen zur höchsten Gerichtsbarkeit im Alten Reich, 56], Köln – Weimar – Wien 2009, p. 1–54.

Olivares, E., *Juan de Lugo (1583–1660), Datos biográficos, sus escritos, estudios sobre su doctrina y bibliografía*, Archivo Teológico Granadino, 47 (1984), p. 5–129.

——, *Más datos para una biografía de Tomás Sánchez*, Archivo Teológico Granadino, 60 (1997), p. 25–50.

——, *En el cuarto centenario de la publicación del tratado de Tomás Sánchez, De sancto matrimonii sacramento (1602)*, Archivo Teológico Granadino, 65 (2002), p. 5–38.

O'Malley, J.W., *The first Jesuits*, Cambridge Mass. – London 1994 [= 1993].

Ordóñez, V., s.v. *Salas*, in C. O'Neill – J. Domínguez (eds.), Diccionario histórico de la Compañía de Jesús biográfico-temático, vol. 4, Roma – Madrid 2001, p. 3467.

O'Reilly, F., *Duda y opinion, La conciencia moral en Soto y Medina*, [Cuadernos de pensamiento español, 32], Pamplona 2006.

Orrego-Sánchez, S., *The 16th century school of Salamanca as a context of synthesis between the Middle Ages and the Renaissance in theological and philosophical matters*, in: C. Burnett – J. Meirinhos – J. Hamesse (eds.), Continuities and disruptions between the Middle Ages and the Renaissance, [Textes et études du moyen âge, 48], Louvain-la-Neuve 2008, p. 113–138.

Osler, D.J., *The myth of European legal history*, Rechtshistorisches Journal, 16 (1997), p. 393–410.

——, *The fantasy men*, Rechtsgeschichte, 10 (2007), p. 169–192.

——, *Jurisprudence of the Baroque, A census of seventeenth century Italian legal imprints*, [Studien zur europäischen Rechtsgeschichte, 235–237, Bibliographica Juridica, 4–6], Frankfurt am Main 2009, p. ix–xxiii A-G (vol. 235), H-S (vol. 236), T-Z (vol. 237).

Otte, G., *Das Privatrecht bei Francisco de Vitoria*, [Forschungen zur neueren Privatrechtsgeschichte, 7], Köln – Graz 1964.

——, *Der Probabilismus, Eine Theorie auf der Grenze zwischen Theologie und Jurisprudenz*, in: P. Grossi (ed.), La seconda scolastica nella formazione del diritto privato moderno, [Per la storia del pensiero giuridico moderno, 1], Milano 1973, p. 283–302.

——, *Theologische und juristische Topik im 16. Jahrhundert*, in: J. Schröder (ed.), Entwicklung der Methodenlehre in Rechtswissenschaft und Philosophie vom 16. bis zum 18. Jahrhundert, Beiträge zu einem interdisziplinären Symposion in Tübingen, 18.-20. April 1996, [Contubernium, Tübinger Beiträge zur Universitäts- und Wissenschaftsgeschichte, 46], Stuttgart 1998, p. 17–26.

Padoa-Schioppa, A., *Note sul ruolo del diritto canonico e sulla storiografia giuridica*, in: H. Scholler (ed.), Die Bedeutung des kanonischen Rechts für die Entwicklung einheitlicher Rechtsprinzipien, [Arbeiten zur Rechtsvergleichung, Schriftenreihe der Gesellschaft für Rechtsvergleichung, 177], Baden-Baden 1996, p. 69–80.

——, *Storia del diritto in Europa, Dal medioevo all'età contemporanea*, Bologna 2007.

Padovani, A., *Perché chiedi il mio nome? Dio, natura e diritto nel secolo XII*, [Il diritto nella storia, 6], Torino 1997.

——, *The metaphysical thought of late medieval jurisprudence*, in: A. Padovani – P. Stein (eds.), The jurists' philosophy of law from Rome to the seventeenth century, [A treatise of legal philosophy and general jurisprudence, 7], Dordrecht – New York 2007, p. 31–78.

Pagden, A., *Gentili, Vitoria, and the fabrication of a natural law of nations*, in: B. Kingsbury – B. Straumann (eds.), The Roman foundations of the law of nations, Alberico Gentili and the justice of empire, Oxford – New York 2010, p. 340–362.

Pagden, A. – Lawrance, J. (eds.), *Francisco de Vitoria, Political writings*, Cambridge 2001 [= 1991].

Palladini, F., *Volontarismo e 'laicità' del diritto naturale, La critica di Samuel Pufendorf a Grozio, De iure belli ac pacis*, Prol. 11 e I, 1, 10, Roma 1984.

——, *La Biblioteca di Samuel Pufendorf, Catalogo dell'asta di Berlin del settembre 1697*, [Wolfenbütteler Schriften zur Geschichte des Buchwesens, 32], Wiesbaden 1999.

Pallotti, L., *Ippolito Marsi(g)li*, in: Dizionario biografico degli Italiani, 70 (2008), p. 764–767.

Papy, J., *Recht uit Brecht, De Leuvense hoogleraar Gabriel Mudaeus (1500–1560) als Europees humanist en jurist*, Academische lezing naar aanleiding van de 450ste verjaardag van het overlijden van Gabriel Mudaeus, Brecht 2011.

——, *Recht uit Brecht, De Leuvense hoogleraar Gabriel Mudaeus (1500–1560) als Europees humanist en jurist*, Catalogus van de tentoonstelling in het Kempisch Museum Brecht, 31 maart–15 mei 2011, Brecht 2011.

Parisi, F., *Autonomy and private ordering in contract law*, European Journal of Law and Economics, 1 (1994), p. 213–227.

Peláez, M.J., s.v. *García de Arteaga de Ercilla, Fortún (1494–1543)*, in: M.J. Peláez (ed.), Diccionario crítico de juristas Españoles, Portugueses y Latinoamericanos (Hispánicos,

Brasileños, Quebequenses y restantes francófonos), vol. 1 (A-L), Barcelona – Zaragoza 2005, p. 344.

Pennington, K., *Learned law, droit savant, Gelehrtes Recht, The tyranny of a concept, Rivista internazionale di diritto comune*, 5 (1994), p. 197–209.

——, *Nicolaus de Tudeschis (Panormitanus)*, in: O. Condorelli (ed.), Niccolò Tedeschi (Abbas Panormitanus) e i suoi Commentaria in Decretales, [I libri di Erice, 25], Roma 2000, p. 9–36.

——, *Panormitanus' Additiones to 'Novit ille' (X.2.1.13)*, Rivista internazionale di diritto comune, 13 (2002), p. 39–51.

——, *Lex naturalis and ius naturale*, The Jurist, 68 (2008), p. 569–591.

Pérez Martín, A., *Derecho Común, Derecho Castellano, Derecho Indiano*, Rivista internazionale di diritto comune, 5 (1994), p. 43–90.

Petit, C., *Derecho común y derecho castellano*, Tijdschrift voor Rechtsgeschiedenis, 50 (1982), p. 157–195.

Pezzella, S., s.v. *Angelo Carletti de Chivasso*, in: Dizionario Biografico degli Italiani, 20 (1977), p. 136–138.

Pihlajamäki, H., *Executor divinarum et suarum legum, Criminal law and the Lutheran Reformation*, in: V. Mäkinen (ed.), Lutheran Reformation and the Law, [Studies in Medieval and Reformation Traditions, 112], Leiden – Boston 2006, p. 171–204.

Pike, R., *Aristocrats and traders, Sevillian society in the sixteenth century*, Ithaca 1972.

Pinckaers, S., *Les sources de la morale chrétienne, Sa méthode, son contenu, son histoire*, [Études d'éthique chrétienne, 14], Fribourg 1985.

Pink, T., *Action, will and law in late scholasticism*, in: J. Kraye – R. Saarinen (ed.), Moral philosophy on the threshold of modernity, [The New Synthese Historical Library, Texts and Studies in the History of Philosophy, 57], Dordrecht 2005, p. 31–50.

Piron, S., *Vœu et contrat chez Pierre de Jean Olivi*, Les cahiers du centre de recherches historiques, 16 (1996), p. 43–56.

——, *Marchands et confesseurs, Le Traité des contrats d'Olivi dans son contexte (Narbonne, fin XIIIᵉ–début XIVᵉ siècle)*, in: L'Argent au Moyen Age, XXVIIIᵉ Congrès de la SHMESP (Clermont-Ferrand, 1997), Paris 1998, p. 289–308.

——, *Parcours d'un intellectuel franciscain, D'une théologie vers une pensée sociale, L'oeuvre de Pierre Jean d'Olivi (ca. 1248–1298) et son traité 'De contractibus'*, Paris 1999 [unpublished doct. diss. EHESS].

——, *Le devoir de gratitude, Émergence et vogue de la notion d'antidora au XIIIe siècle*, in: D. Quaglioni – G. Todeschini – M. Varanini (eds.), Credito e usura fra teologia, diritto e amministrazione (sec. XII-XVI), [Collection de l'École française de Rome, 346], Rome 2005, p. 73–101.

Pitkin, B., *Calvin's mosaic harmony, Biblical exegesis and early modern legal history*, The Sixteenth Century Journal, 41 (2010), p. 441–466.

Popescu, O., *Studies in the history of Latin American economic thought*, London – New York 1997.

Porter, J., *Natural and divine law, Reclaiming the tradition for Christian ethics*, Ottawa – Grand Rapids 1999.

——, *Ministers of the law, A natural law theory of legal authority*, Grand Rapids – Cambridge 2010.

Pound, R., *Liberty of contract*, Yale Law Journal, 18 (1909), p. 454–487.

Prodi, P., *Il concilio di Trento di fronte alla politica e al diritto moderno, Introduzione*, in: P. Prodi – W. Reinhard (eds.), Il concilio di Trento e il moderno, Atti della XXXVIII settimana di studio, 11–15 settembre 1995, [Annali dell'Istituto storico italo-germanico, 45], Bologna 1996, p. 7–26.

——, *Il giuramento e il tribunale della coscienza, Dal pluralismo degli ordinamenti giuridici al dualismo tra coscienza e diritto positivo*, in: N. Pirillo (ed.), Il vincolo del giuramento e il tribunale della coscienza, [Annali dell'Istituto storico italo-germanico, 47], Bologna 1997, p. 475–490.

——, *Eine Geschichte der Gerechtigkeit, Vom Recht Gottes zum modernen Rechtsstaat*, München 2003 [= *Una storia della giustizia, Dal pluralismo dei fori al moderno dualismo tra coscienza e diritto*, Bologna 2000].

——, *Conclusioni*, in: D. Quaglioni – G. Todeschini – M. Varanini (eds.), Credito e usura fra teologia, diritto e amministrazione (sec. XII–XVI), [Collection de l'École française de Rome, 346], Roma 2005, p. 291–295.

——, *Settimo non rubare, Furto e mercato nella storia dell'Occidente*, Bologna 2009.

——, *Il paradigmo tridentino, Un'epoca della storia della Chiesa*, Brescia 2010.

Prosperi, A., *La confessione e il foro della coscienza*, in: P. Prodi – W. Reinhard (eds.), Il concilio di Trento e il moderno, Atti della XXXVIII settimana di studio, 11–15 settembre 1995, [Annali dell'Istituto storico italo-germanico, 45], Bologna 1996, p. 225–254.

——, *Tribunali della coscienza, Inquisitori, confessori, missionari*, [Bibliotheca di cultura storica, 214], Torino 1996.

Quaglioni, D., *Standum canonistis? Le usure nella dottrina civilistica medievale*, in: D. Quaglioni – G. Todeschini – M. Varanini (eds.), Credito e usura fra teologia, diritto e amministrazione (sec. XII–XVI), [Collection de l'École française de Rome, 346], Rome 2005, p. 247–264.

——, *'Dominium', 'iurisdictio', 'imperium', Gli elementi non-moderni della modernità giuridia*, in: G. Dilcher – D. Quaglioni (eds.), Gli inizi del diritto pubblico, 3: Verso la costruzione del diritto pubblico tra medioevo e modernità, [Annali dell'Istituto Storico Italo-Germanico in Trento, Contributi, 25], Bologna-Berlin 2011, p. 663–677.

Quinto, R., *Scholastica, Storia di un concetto*, [Subsidia Mediaevalia Patavina, 2], Padova 2001.

Ramírez González, C.I., *La Universidad de Salamanca en el Siglo XVI, Corporación académica y poderes eclesiásticos*, [Acta Salmanticensia, Historia de la Universidad, 68], Salamanca 2002.

Ranouil, V., *L'autonomie de la volonté, Naissance et évolution d'un concept*, [Travaux et recherches de l'Université de droit, d'économie et de sciences sociales de Paris, Série sciences historiques, 12], Paris 1980.

Recknagel, D., *Einheit des Denkens trotz konfessioneller Spaltung, Parallelen zwischen den Rechtslehren von Francisco Suárez und Hugo Grotius*, [Treffpunkt Philosophie, 10], Frankfurt am Main 2010.

Reid, Ch.J., Jr., *Power over the body, Equality in the family*, Grand Rapids – Cambridge 2004.

Reid, D., *Thomas Aquinas and Viscount Stair, The influence of scholastic moral theology on Stair's account of restitution and recompense*, The Journal of Legal History, 29 (2008), p. 189–214.

Renoux-Zagamé, M.-F., *Origines théologiques du concept moderne de propriété*, [Travaux de droit, d'économie, de sciences politiques, de sociologie et d'anthropologie, 153], Genève 1987.

——, *Du droit de Dieu au droit de l'homme*, Paris 2003.

Repgen, T., *Vertragstreue und Erfüllungszwang in der mittelalterlichen Rechtswissenschaft*, [Rechts- und Staatswissenschaftliche Veröffentlichungen der Görres-Gesellschaft, Neue Folge, 73], Paderborn e.a. 1994.

Ripert, G., *La règle morale dans les obligations civiles*, Paris 1949[4] [= 1926].

Rittgers, R.K., *The reformation of the keys, Confession, conscience, and authority in sixteenth-century Germany*, Cambridge Mass. 2004.

Robaye, R., *Tradition et humanisme à la Faculté des Lois de Louvain vers 1550, Un initiateur, Gabriel Mudée*, Les études classiques, 54 (1986), p. 47–57.

Robertson, H.M., *Aspects of the rise of economic individualism, A criticism of Max Weber and his school*, [Cambridge Studies in Economic History, 1], Cambridge, 1933.

Robiglio, A., *L'impossibile volere, Tommaso d'Aquino, i tomisti e la volontà*, Milano 2002.

Rodríguez Gil, M., *La 'incorporación' de reinos, Notas y textos doctrinales del derecho común*, Cáceres 2002.

Rodríguez Penelas, H., *Ética y sistemática del contrato en el siglo de oro, La obra de Francisco García en su contexto jurídico-moral*, [Colleción de pensamiento medieval y renacentista, 82], Pamplona 2007.

Rolland, L., *'Qui dit contractuel dit juste' (Fouillée)... en trois petits bonds, à reculons*, McGill Law Journal, 51 (2006), p. 765–780.

Rose, A., *Studying the past, The nature and development of legal history as an academic discipline*, The Journal of Legal History, 31 (2010), p. 101–128.

Ross, R.J., *Puritan godly discipline in comparative perspective, Legal pluralism and the sources of 'intensity'*, American Historical Review, 113 (2008), p. 975–1002.

Rothbard, M.N., *An Austrian perspective on the history of economic thought*, vol. 1: *Economic thought before Adam Smith*, Aldershot – Brookfield 1995.

Rouco-Varela, A.M., *Staat und Kirche im Spanien des 16. Jahrhunderts*, [Münchener theologische Studien, 23], München 1965.

Roussier, J., *Le fondement de l'obligation contractuelle dans le droit de l'Église*, Paris 1933.

Ruffini Avondo, E., *Il possesso nella teologia morale post-tridentina*, Rivista di storia del diritto italiano, 2 (1929), p. 63–98.

Rummel, E., *The humanist-scholastic debate in the Renaissance and Reformation*, Cambridge Mass. 1995.

Rummel, M., *Die clausula rebus sic stantibus, Eine dogmengeschichtliche Untersuchung unter Berücksichtigung der Zeit von der Rezeption im 14. Jahrhundert bis zum jüngeren Usus Modernus in der ersten Hälfte des 18. Jahrhunderts*, [Fundamenta Juridica, Hannoversche Beiträge zur rechtswissenschaftlichen Grundlagenforschung, 13], Baden-Baden 1991.

Ruppert, S., *Kirchenrecht und Kulturkampf, Historische Legitimation, politische Mitwirkung und wissenschaftliche Begleitung durch die Schule Emil Ludwig Richters*, [Ius Ecclesiasticum, 70], Tübingen 2002.

Rusconi, R., *L'ordine dei peccati, La confessione tra Medioevo ed età moderna*, Bologna 2002.

Sagaert, V., *Unjust enrichment and change of position*, Maastricht Journal of European and Comparative Law, 11 (2004), p. 159–186.

Salas, V.M. (ed.), *J.P. Doyle, Collected studies on Francisco Suárez (1548–1617)*, [Ancient and Medieval philosophy, De Wulf-Mansion Centre, Series 1, 37], Leuven 2010.

Sampson, M., *Laxity and liberty in seventeenth-century English political thought*, in: E. Leites (ed.), Conscience and casuistry in early modern Europe, Cambridge 2002 [= 1988], p. 72–118.

Santarelli, U., *La prohibición de la usura, de canon moral a regla jurídica, Modalidades y éxitos de un transplante*, in: C. Petit (ed.), Del 'Ius mercatorum' al derecho mercantile, III Seminario de Historia del Derecho Privado, Sitges, 28–30 de mayo de 1992, Madrid 1997, p. 237–256.

Santi, F., s.v. *Giasone del Maino*, Dizionario biografico degli Italiani [URL: http://www.treccani.it/enciclopedia/giasone-del-maino_(Dizionario_Biografico)/, last visited 20.09.2011].

Sautel, G. – Boulet-Sautel, M., *Verba ligant homines, taurorum cornia funes*, in: Études d'histoire du droit privé offertes à Pierre Petot, Paris 1959, p. 507–517.

Savelli, R., *Derecho romano y teología reformada, Du Moulin frente al problema del interés del dinero*, in: C. Petit (ed.), Del 'Ius mercatorum' al derecho mercantil, Madrid 1997, p. 257–290.

Scattola, M., *Das Naturrecht vor dem Naturrecht, Zur Geschichte des 'ius naturae' im 16. Jahrhundert*, [Frühe Neuzeit, 52], Tübingen 1999.

——, *Bellum, dominium, ordo, Das Thema des gerechten Krieges in der Theologie des Domingo de Soto*, in: N. Brieskorn – M. Riedenauer (eds.), Suche nach Frieden, Politische Ethik in der Frühen Neuzeit, I, [Theologie und Frieden, 19], Barsbüttel 2000, p. 119–128.

——, *Naturrecht als Rechtstheorie, Die Systematisierung der res scolastica in der Naturrechtslehre des Domingo de Soto*, in: F. Grunert – K. Seelmann (eds.), Die Ordnung der

Praxis, Neue Studien zur Spanischen Spätscholastik, [Frühe Neuzeit, 68], Tübingen 2001, p. 21–48.

——, *Models in history of natural law*, Ius Commune, Zeitschrift für Europäische Rechtsgeschichte, 28 (2001), p. 91–159.

——, *Before and after natural law, Models of natural law in ancient and modern times*, in: T.J. Hochstrasser – P. Schröder (eds.), Early modern natural law theories, Contexts and strategies in the early Enlightenment, [International archives of the history of ideas, 186], Dordrecht 2003, p. 1–30.

——, *Krieg des Wissens – Wissen des Krieges, Konflikt, Erfahrung und System der literarischen Gattungen am Beginn der Frühen Neuzeit*, Padova 2006.

——, *Sklaverei, Krieg und Recht, Die Vorlesung über die Regula 'Peccatum' von Diego de Covarrubias y Leyva*, in: M. Kaufmann – R. Schnepf (eds.), Politische Metaphysik, Die Entstehung moderner Rechtskonzeptionen in der Spanischen Scholastik, [Treffpunkt Philosophie, 8], Frankfurt am Main 2007, p. 303–356.

——, *Eine interkonfessionelle Debatte, Wie die Spanische Spätscholastik die politische Theologie des Mittelalters mit der Hilfe des Aristoteles revidierte*, in: A. Fidora – J. Fried – M. Lutz-Bachmann – L. Schorn-Schütte (eds.), Politischer Aristotelismus und Religion in Mittelalter und Früher Neuzeit, [Wissenskultur und gesellschaftlicher Wandel, 23], Berlin 2007, p. 139–161.

Schäfer, F., *Juristische Germanistik, Eine Geschichte der Wissenschaft vom einheimischen Privatrecht*, [Juristische Abhandlungen, 51], Frankfurt am Main 2008.

Schaub, J.-F., *Suárez, Les lois*, in: O. Cayla – J.-L. Halpérin (eds.), Dictionnaire des grandes œuvres juridiques, Paris 2008, p. 565–570.

Schefold, B. (ed.), *Vademecum zu zwei Klassikern des spanischen Wirtschaftsdenkens, Martin de Azpilcuetas 'Comentario resolutorio de Cambios' und Luis Ortiz' 'Memorial del Contador Luis Ortiz a Felipe II'*, Düsseldorf 1998.

——, *Leonardus Lessius' De iustitia et iure, Vademecum zu einem Klassiker der Spätscholastischen Wirtschaftsanalyse*, Düsseldorf 1999.

——, *Leonardus Lessius, Von der praktischen Tugend der Gerechtigkeit zur Wirtschaftstheorie*, in: B. Schefold, Beiträge zur ökonomischen Dogmengeschichte, ausgewählt und herausgegeben von V. Caspari, Düsseldorf 2004, p. 127–158.

Schermaier, M.J., *Europäische Geistesgeschichte am Beispiel des Irrtumsrechts*, Zeitschrift für europäisches Privatrecht, 6 (1998), p. 60–83.

——, *Die Bestimmung des wesentlichen Irrtums von den Glossatoren bis zum BGB*, [Forschungen zur neueren Privatrechtsgeschichte, 29], Wien – Köln – Weimar 2000.

——, *Bona fides in Roman contract law*, in: R. Zimmermann – S. Whittaker (eds.), Good faith in European contract law, [The Common Core of European Private Law, Cambridge Studies in International and Comparative Law, 14], Cambridge 2000, p. 63–92.

——, *Mistake, misrepresentation and precontractual duties to inform, The civil law tradition*, in: R. Sefton-Green (ed.), Mistake, fraud and duties to inform in European contract law, [The Common Core of European Private Law Series], Cambridge 2005, p. 39–64.

Scherner, K.O., *Die Wissenschaft des Handelsrechts*, in: H. Coing (ed.), Handbuch der Quellen und Literatur der neueren europäischen Privatrechtsgeschichte, Band II. Neuere Zeit (1500–1800), Das Zeitalter des gemeinen Rechts, Teilband I.1. Wissenschaft, München 1977, p. 797–997.

——, *Lex mercatoria – Realität, Geschichtsbild oder Vision?*, Zeitschrift für Rechtsgeschichte der Savigny-Stiftung, Germ. Abt., 118 (2001), p. 148–167.

Scherrer, W., *Die geschichtliche Entwicklung des Prinzips der Vertragsfreiheit*, [Basler Studien zur Rechtswissenschaft, 20], Basel 1948.

Schmidt-Biggemann, W. (ed.), *Samuel Pufendorf, Gesammelte Werke*, Berlin 1996–2004.

Schmitz, H.J., *Die Bussbücher und Bussdisziplin der Kirche*, Mainz 1883.

Schmitz, Ph., *Busembaum*, in: C. O'Neill – J. Domínguez (eds.), Diccionario histórico de la Compañía de Jesús, Biográfico-temático, Roma – Madrid 2001, vol. 1, p. 578.

——, *Probabilismus – das jesuitischste der Moralsysteme*, in: M. Sievernich – G. Switek (eds.), Ignatianisch, Eigenart und Methode der Gesellschaft Jesu, Freiburg – Basel – Wien 1990, p. 354–368.

——, *Kasuistik, Ein wiederentdecktes Kapitel der Jesuitenmoral*, Theologie und Philosophie, 67 (1992), p. 29–59.

Schmoeckel, M., *Das Gesetz Gottes als Ausgangspunkt christlicher Ethik? Zu calvinistischen Traditionen des 16. Jh.s im Hinblick auf ihre rechtshistorische Relevanz*, in: Ius commune, 25 (1998), p. 347–366.

——, *Humanität und Staatsraison, Die Abschaffung der Folter in Europa und die Entwicklung des gemeinen Strafprozeß- und Beweisrechts seit dem hohen Mittelalter*, Köln e.a. 2000.

——, *Rechtsgeschichte im 21. Jahrhundert, Ein Diskussionsbeitrag zur Standortbestimmung*, Forum Historiae Iuris (2000) [URL: http://www.forhistiur.de/zitat/0005schmoeckel.htm; last visited on 25.07.2011].

——, *Der Entwurf eines Strafrechts der Gegenreformation*, in: M. Cavina, Tiberio Deciani (1509–1582), Alle origini del pensiero giuridico moderno, Udine 2004, p. 207–234.

——, *Fragen zur Konfession des Rechts im 16. Jahrhundert am Beispiel des Strafrechts*, in: I. Dingel – W.-F. Schäufele (eds.), Kommunikation und Transfer im Christentum der Frühen Neuzeit, [Veröffentlichungen des Instituts für Europäische Geschichte Mainz, Beihefte, 74], Mainz 2008, p. 157–191.

Schmugge, L., *Verwaltung des Gewissens, Beobachtungen zu den Registern der päpstlichen Pönitentiarie*, Rivista internazionale di diritto comune, 7 (1996), p. 47–76.

Schmutz, J., *Bulletin de scolastique moderne* (1), Revue thomiste, 100 (2000), p. 270–341.

Schnapper, B., *Les rentes au XVIᵉ siècle, Histoire d'un instrument de crédit*, [Affaires et Gens d'Affaires, 12], Paris 1957.

Schnepf, R., *Francisco Suárez über die Veränderbarkeit von Gesetzen durch Interpretation*, in: F. Grunert – K. Seelmann (eds.), Die Ordnung der Praxis, Neue Studien zur Spanischen Spätscholastik, [Frühe Neuzeit, 68], Tübingen 2001, p. 75–108.

Schrage, E.J.H., *Actio en subjectief recht, Over Romeinse en middeleeuwse wortels van een modern begrip*, Openbare les—in verkorte vorm—uitgesproken bij de aanvaarding van het ambt van gewoon lector in het Romeinse recht aan de faculteit der rechtsgeleerdheid van de Vrije Universiteit te Amsterdam op 31 maart 1977, Amsterdam 1977.

——, *Utrumque Ius, Eine Einführung in das Studium der Quellen des mittelalterlichen gelehrten Rechts*, [Schriften zur europäischen Rechts- und Verfassungsgeschichte, 8], Berlin 1992.

——, *Utrumque Ius, Über das römisch-kanonische ius commune als Grundlage europäischer Rechtseinheit*, Revue Internationale des Droits de l'Antiquité, 39 (1992), p. 383–412 [Reprinted in: E.J.H. Schrage, *Non quia Romanum sed quia ius, Das Entstehen eines europäischen Rechtsbewußtseins im Mittelalter*, [Bibliotheca Eruditorum, Internationale Bibliothek der Wissenschaften, 17], Goldbach 1996, p. 273–302].

——, *Traditionibus et usucapionibus, non nudis pactis dominia rerum transferuntur, Die Wahl zwischen dem Konsens- und dem Traditionsprinzip in der Geschichte*, in: M. Ascherie.a. (eds.), Ins Wasser geworfen und Ozeane durchquert, Festschrift für Knut Wolfgang Nörr, Köln – Weimar – Wien 2003, p. 913–958.

Schröder, J., *Entwicklung der Methodenlehre in Rechtswissenschaft und Philosophie vom 16. bis zum 18. Jahrhundert*, [Beiträge zu einem interdisziplinären Symposion in Tübingen, 18.-20. April 1996, Contubernium, Tübinger Beiträge zur Universitäts- und Wissenschaftsgeschichte, 46], Stuttgart 1998.

——, *Rhetorik und juristische Hermeneutik in der frühen Neuzeit*, in: R.H. Helmholz et al., Grundlagen des Rechts, Festschrift Peter Landau, Paderborn 2000, p. 677–696.

——, *Recht als Wissenschaft, Geschichte der juristischen Methode vom Humanismus bis zur historischen Schule (1500–1850)*, München 2001.

——, (ed.), *Theorie der Interpretation vom Humanismus bis zur Romantik – Rechtswissenschaft, Philosophie, Theologie*, [Beiträge zu einem interdisziplinären Symposion in

Tübingen, 29. September bis 1. Oktober 1999, Contubernium, Tübinger Beiträge zur Universitäts- und Wissenschaftsgeschichte, 58], Stuttgart 2001.

——, *The concept of (natural) law in the doctrine of law and natural law of the early modern era*, in: L. Daston – M. Stolleis (eds.), Natural law and laws of nature in early modern Europe, Jurisprudence, theology, moral and natural philosophy, Farnham – Burlington 2008, p. 57–72.

Schüßler, R. *Moral im Zweifel*, Band I: *Die scholastische Theorie des Entscheidens unter moralischer Unsicherheit*, Paderborn 2003.

——, *On the anatomy of probabilism*, in: J. Kraye – R. Saarinen (eds.), Moral philosophy on the threshold of modernity, [The New Synthese Historical Library, Texts and Studies in the History of Philosophy, 57], Dordrecht 2005, p. 91–114.

——, *Moral im Zweifel*, Band II: *Die Herausforderung des Probabilismus*, Paderborn 2006.

——, *Moral self-ownership and 'ius possessionis' in scholastics*, in: V. Mäkinen – P. Korkman (eds.), Transformations in medieval and early modern rights discourse, [The New Synthese Historical Library, 59], Dordrecht 2006, p. 149–172.

——, *Jean Gerson, moral certainty and the renaissance of ancient skepticism*, in: H.E. Braun – E. Vallance (eds.), The Renaissance conscience, [Renaissance Studies Special Issues, 3], Oxford 2011, p. 11–28.

Schulte, Friedrich von, *Kestner, Heinrich Ernst*, in: Allgemeine Deutsche Biographie, 15 (1882), p. 664 [URL: http://www.deutsche-biographie.de/pnd122950054.html?anchor=adb'; last visited on 20.09.2011].

Schulze, W.G., *Die laesio enormis in der deutschen Privatrechtsgeschichte*, Münster 1973.

Schumpeter, J.A., *History of economic analysis*, edited from manuscript by Elizabeth Boody Schumpeter, London 1972 [= 1954].

Seelmann, K., *Die Lehre des Fernando Vazquez de Menchaca vom Dominium*, [Annales Universitatis Saraviensis, Rechts- und Wirtschaftswissenschaftliche Abteilung, 89], Köln e.a. 1979.

——, *Theologie und Jurisprudenz an der Schwelle zur Moderne, Die Geburt des neuzeitlichen Naturrechts in der iberischen Spätscholastik*, [Würzburger Vorträge zur Rechtsphilosophie, Rechtstheorie und Rechtssoziologie, 20], Baden-Baden 1997.

——, *Thomas von Aquin am Schnittpunkt von Recht und Theologie, Die Bedeutung der Thomas-Renaissance für die Moderne*, [Luzerner Hochschulreden, 11], Luzern 2000.

——, (ed.), *Wirtschaftsethik und Recht*, Vorträge der Tagung der Schweizer Sektion der internationalen Vereinigung für Rechts- und Sozialphilosophie (Oktober 2000 in Fribourg), [Archiv für Rechts- und Sozialphilosophie, 81], Stuttgart 2001.

Sefton-Green, R., *General introduction and comparative conclusions*, in: R. Sefton-Green (ed.), Mistake, fraud and duties to inform in European contract law, The Common Core of European Private Law Series, Cambridge 2005, p. 1–38; 369–400.

Selderhuis (ed.), H.J., *Calvin Handbuch*, Tübingen 2008.

Selzner, C., *Les forges des philistins, La problématique d'une casuistique réformée en Angleterre de William Perkins à Jeremy Taylor*, in: S. Boarini (ed.), La casuistique classique, Genèse, formes, devenir, Saint-Étienne 2009, p. 73–86.

Seuffert, L., *Zur Geschichte der obligatorischen Verträge*, Nördlingen 1881.

Siems, H., *Von den piae causae zu den Xenodochien*, in: R.H. Helmholz – R. Zimmermann (eds.), Itinera fiduciae, Trust and Treuhand in historical perspective, [Comparative Studies in Continental and Anglo-American Legal History, 19], Berlin 1998, p. 57–83.

Simon, C., *Comment Lessius traite le droit*, Louvain 1975.

Sirks, B., *Laesio enormis again*, Revue internationale des droits de l'antiquité, 54 (2007), p. 461–470.

Skinner, Q., *The sovereign state, A genealogy*, in: H. Kalmo – Q. Skinner (eds.), Sovereignty in fragments, The past, present and future of a contested concept, Cambridge 2010, p. 26–46.

Smith, S.A., *Contract theory*, Oxford 2004.

Smits, J., *Het vertrouwensbeginsel en de contractuele gebondenheid, Beschouwingen omtrent de dogmatiek van het overeenkomstenrecht*, Arnhem 1995.

——, *Van wil, causa en verrijking, Over een alternatieve route naar de contractuele gebon-denheid*, Stellenbosch Law Review, 8 (1997), p. 280–295.

——, *The making of European private law, Toward a ius commune Europaeum as a mixed legal system*, Antwerp – Oxford – New York 2002.

Soetermeer, F., s.v. *Belleperche*, in: P. Arabeyre – J.-L. Halpérin – J. Krynen (eds.), Diction-naire historique des juristes français, XIIe–XXe siècle, Paris 2007, p. 61–62.

Somma, A., *Autonomia privata e struttura del consenso contrattuale, Aspetti storico-compa-rativi di una vicenda concettuale*, [Problemi di diritto comparato, 4], Milano 2000.

Specht, R., *Die Spanische Spätscholastik im Kontext ihrer Zeit*, in: F. Grunert – K. Seelmann (eds.), Die Ordnung der Praxis, Neue Studien zur Spanischen Spätscholastik, [Frühe Neuzeit, 68], Tübingen 2001, p. 3–18.

Spies, F., *De l'observation des simples conventions en droit canonique*, Paris 1928.

Stäudlin, K.F., *Geschichte der christlichen Moral seit dem Wiederaufleben der Wissenschaf-ten*, [Geschichte der Künste und Wissenschaften, 2], Göttingen 1808.

Stein, P., *Systematisation of private law in the sixteenth and seventeenth centuries*, in: J. Schröder, Entwicklung der Methodenlehre in Rechtswissenschaft und Philosophie vom 16. bis zum 18. Jahrhundert, [Beiträge zu einem interdisziplinären Symposion in Tübingen, 18.–20. April 1996, Contubernium, Tübinger Beiträge zur Universitäts- und Wissenschaftsgeschichte, 46], Stuttgart 1998, p. 117–126.

Stijns, S. – Swaenepoel, E., *De evolutie van de basisbeginselen in het contractenrecht, geïl-lustreerd aan de hand van het contractueel evenwicht*, in: I. Samoy (ed.), Evolutie van de basisbeginselen van het contractenrecht, Antwerpen – Oxford 2010, p. 1–58.

Stolfi, E., *Bonae fidei interpretatio, Ricerche sull'interpretazione di buona fede fra esperienza romana e tradizione romanistica*, [Università di Torino, Memorie del Dipartimento di Scienze Giuridiche, Serie 5, 21], Napoli 2004.

Stolleis, M., *Pecunia nervus rerum, Zur Staatsfinanzierung der frühen Neuzeit*, Frankfurt am Main 1983.

——, *Geschichte des öffentlichen Rechts in Deutschland, Band I: Reichspublizistik und Policeywissenschaft 1600–1800*, München 1988.

——, *The influence of 'ius commune' in Germany in the early modern period on the rise of the modern state*, Rivista internazionale di diritto comune, 11 (2000), p. 275–285.

——, *Das Auge des Gesetzes, Geschichte einer Metapher*, München 2004.

——, *The legitimation of law through God, tradition, will, nature and constitution*, in: L. Das-ton – M. Stolleis (eds.), Natural law and laws of nature in early modern Europe, Jurispru-dence, theology, moral and natural philosophy, Farnham – Burlington 2008, p. 45–56.

Story, J., *Commentaries on Equity jurisprudence*, ed. M.M. Bigelow, Boston 1886[13].

Stöve, E., s.v. *De Vio, Tommaso*, in: Dizionario biografico degli Italiani [URL: http://www.treccani.it/enciclopedia/tommaso-de-vio_(Dizionario-Biografico)/ last visited 12.09.2011].

Straumann, B., *Hugo Grotius und die Antike, Römisches Recht und römische Ethik im früh-neuzeitlichen Naturrecht*, [Studien zur Geschichte des Völkerrechts, 14], Baden-Baden 2007.

Strohm, Ch., *Ethik im frühen Calvinismus, Humanistische Einflüsse, philosophische, juri-stische und theologische Argumentationen sowie mentalitätsgeschichtliche Aspekte am Beispiel des Calvin-Schülers Lambertus Danaeus*, [Arbeiten zur Kirchengeschichte, 65], Berlin – New York 1996.

——, *Calvinismus und Recht, Weltanschaulich-konfessionelle Aspekte im Werk reformierter Juristen in der Frühen Neuzeit*, [Spätmittelalter, Humanismus, Reformation, 42], Tübin-gen 2008.

——, *Weltanschaulich-konfessionelle Aspekte im Werk reformierter Juristen*, Rechtsge-schichte, Zeitschrift des Max-Planck-Instituts für europäische Rechtsgeschichte, 15 (2009), p. 14–32.

Stuyck, J. – Terryn, E. – Van Dyck, T., *Confidence through fairness? The new directive on unfair business-to-consumer practices in the internal market*, Common Market Law Review, 43 (2006), p. 107–152.

Sumner Maine, H., *Ancient law, its connections with the early history of society and its relation to modern ideas*, London 1883⁹.

Tawney, R.H., *Religion and the rise of capitalism*, London 1964 [= 1926].

Tejero, E., *El Doctor Navarro en la historia de la doctrina canónica y moral*, in: Estudios sobre el Doctor Navarro en el IV centenario de la muerte de Martín de Azpilcueta, Pamplona 1988, p. 125–180.

Tellegen-Couperus, O., *Law and religion in the Roman Republic*, [Mnemosyne, Supplements, 336], Boston – Leiden 2011.

Thayer, A.T., *Judge and doctor, Images of the confessor in printed model sermon collections, 1450–1520*, in K.J. Lualdi – A.T. Thayer (eds.), Penitance in the age of reformations, Aldershot 2000, p. 10–29.

Thieme, H., *Qu'est ce que nous, les juristes, devons à la Seconde Scolastique espagnole ?*, in: P. Grossi (ed.), La seconda scolastica nella formazione del diritto privato moderno, [Per la storia del pensiero giuridico moderno, 1], Milano 1973, p. 7–22.

——, *Natürliches Privatrecht und Spätscholastik*, in: H. Thieme (ed.), Ideengeschichte und Rechtsgeschichte, Gesammelte Schriften, Band II, [Forschungen zur neueren Privatrechtsgeschichte, 25], Köln – Wien 1986 [= 1953], p. 871–908.

Thier, A., *Ecclesia vivit lege Romana*, in: A. Cordes – H. Lück – D. Werkmüller (eds.), Handwörterbuch zur deutschen Rechtsgeschichte, Lieferung 5, Berlin 2007, cols. 1176–1177.

——, *Legal history*, in: E. Hondius – H.C. Grigoleit (eds.), Unexpected circumstances in European contract law, [The common core of European private law], Cambridge 2011, p. 15–32.

——, *Klassische Kanonistik und kontraktualistische Tradition*, in: O. Condorelli – F. Roumy – M. Schmoeckel (eds.), Der Einfluβ der Kanonistik auf die europäische Rechtskultur, Band 2: Öffentliches Recht, [Norm und Strukter, 37, 2], Köln – Weimar – Wien 2011, p. 61–80.

Thireau, J.-L., *Charles Du Moulin (1500–1566), Étude sur les sources, la méthode, les idées politiques et économiques d'un juriste de la Renaissance*, [Travaux d'Humanisme et Renaissance, 176], Genève 1980.

——, *Loriot, Pierre*, in: P. Arabeyre – J.-L. Halpérin – J. Krynen (eds.), Dictionnaire historique des juristes français, XIIᵉ–XXᵉ siècle, Paris 2007, p. 518.

Thomas, K., *Cases of conscience in seventeenth-century England*, in: J. Morrill – P. Slack – D. Woolf (eds.), Public duty and private conscience in seventeenth-century England, Essays presented to G.E. Aylmer, Oxford 1993, p. 29–56.

Thomas, Y, review of Carlos Cossio, La causa y la comprension en el derecho, Buenos Aires 1969, in: Dimensions religieuses du droit et notamment sur l'apport de Saint Thomas D'Aquin, [Archives de philosophie du droit, 18], Paris 1973, p. 464–467.

——, *Le langage du droit romain, Problèmes et methodes*, in: Le langage du droit, [Archives de philosophie du droit, 19], Paris 1974, p. 339–346.

——, *Les artifices de la vérité en droit commun médiéval*, L'homme, Revue française d'anthropologie, 175–176 (2005), p. 113–130.

Tierney, B., *The idea of natural rights, Studies on natural rights, natural law, and Church law, 1150–1650*, [Emory Studies in Law and Religion, 5], Grand Rapids – Cambridge 2001.

——, *Dominion of self and natural rights before Locke and after*, in in: V. Mäkinen – P. Korkman (eds.), Transformations in medieval and early modern rights discourse, [The New Synthese Historical Library, 59], Dordrecht 2006, p. 173–203.

Todescan, F., *Lex, natura, beatitudo, Il problema della legge nella scolastica Spagnola del sec. XVI*, [Pubblicazioni della Facoltà di Giurisprudenza dell'Università di Padova, 65], Padova 1973.

——, *Le radici teologiche del giusnaturalismo laico, I. Il problema della secolarizzazione nel pensiero giuridico di Ugo Grozio*, [Per la storia del pensiero giuridico moderno, 14], Milano 1983.

——, *Le radici teologiche del giusnaturalismo laico, II. Il problema della secolarizzazione nel pensiero giuridico di Jean Domat*, [Per la storia del pensiero giuridico moderno, 26], Milano 1987.

——, *Le radici teologiche del giusnaturalismo laico, III. Il problema della secolarizzazione nel pensiero giuridico di Samuel Pufendorf*, [Per la storia del pensiero giuridico moderno, 57], Milano 2001.

——, *Etiamsi daremus, Studi sinfonici sul diritto naturale*, [Biblioteca di Lex naturalis, 1], Padova 2003.

Todeschini, G., *Il prezzo della salvezza, Lessici medievali del pensiero economico*, Roma 1994.

——, *I mercanti e il tempio, La società cristiana e il circolo virtuoso della ricchezza fra Medioevo ed Età Moderna*, Bologna 2002.

Tomas y Valiente, F., *Manual de historia del derecho Español*, Madrid 1980².

Totzeck, Markus M., *A Lutheran jurist and the emergence of modern European states – Dietrich Reinking and his late work 'Biblische Policey' (1653)*, Zeitschrift der Savigny-Stiftung für Rechtsgeschichte, Kan. Abt., 97 (2011), p. 304–356.

Trebilcock, M.J., *The limits of freedom of contract*, Cambridge Mass. 1993.

Trusen, W., *Äquivalenzprinzip und gerechter Preis im Spätmittelalter*, in: F. Mayer (ed.), Staat und Gesellschaft, Festschrift für Günter Küchenhof zum 70. Geburtstag, Göttingen 1967, p. 247–263.

——, *Forum internum und gelehrtes Recht im Spätmittelalter, Summae confessorum und Traktate als Wegbereiter der Rezeption*, Zeitschrift der Savigny-Stiftung für Rechtsgeschichte, Kan. Abt., 57 (1971), p. 83–126.

——, *Zur Bedeutung des geistlichen Forum internum und externum für die spätmittelalterliche Gesellschaft*, Zeitschrift der Savigny-Stiftung für Rechtsgeschichte, Kan. Abt., 76 (1990), p. 254–285.

Tuck, R., *Natural rights theories, Their origin and development*, Cambridge 1981.

Turrini, M., *La coscienza e le leggi, Morale e diritto nei testi per la confessione delle prima età moderna*, [Annali dell'Istituto storico italo-germanico, Monografie, 13], Bologna 1991.

——, *Il giudice della coscienza e la coscienza del giudice*, in: P. Prodi – C. Penuti (eds.), Disciplina dell'anima, disciplina del corpo e disciplina della società tra medioevo ed età moderna, [Annali dell'Istituto storico italo-germanico, 40], Bologna 1994, p. 279–294.

——, *Tra diritto e teologia in età moderna, Spunti di indagine*, in: P. Prodi – W. Reinhard (eds.), Il concilio di Trento e il moderno, Atti della XXXVIII settimana di studio, 11–15 settembre 1995, [Annali dell'Istituto storico italo-germanico, 45], Bologna 1996, p. 255–270.

Tutino, S., *Law and conscience, Catholicism in early modern England, 1570–1625*, Catholic Christendom 1300–1700, Aldershot 2007.

——, *Empire of souls, Robert Bellarmine and the Christian Commonwealth*, Oxford 2010.

——, *Nothing but the truth? Hermeneutics and morality in the doctrines of equivocation and mental reservation in early modern Europe*, Renaissance Quarterly, 64 (2011), p. 115–155.

Vallone, G., *Iurisdictio domini, Introduzione a Matteo d'Afflitto ed alla cultura giuridica meridionale tra quattro- et cinquecento*, [Collana di studi storici e giuridici, 1], Lecce 1985.

van Caenegem, R.C., *Ouvrages de droit romain dans les catalogues des anciens Pays-Bas méridionaux (XIIIᵉ–XVIᵉ siècle)*, Tijdschrift voor Rechtsgeschiedenis, 28 (1960), p. 403–437.

——, *Reflexions on the place of the Low Countries in European legal history*, in: N. Horn – K. Luig – A. Söllner (eds.), Europäisches Rechtsdenken in Geschichte und Gegenwart, Festschrift für Helmut Coing zum 70. Geburtstag, München 1982.

——, *An historical introduction to private law*, Cambridge 1992.

——, *Clio and the humanities, Alma Mater and prodigal sons?*, in: L. Milis et al. (eds.), Law, history, the Low Countries and Europe: R.C. van Caenegem, London – Rio Grande 1994, p. 27–35.

van den Auweele, D., s.v. *Nicolaas Everaerts*, in G. Van Dievoet e.a. (eds.), Lovanium docet, Geschiedenis van de Leuvense Rechtsfaculteit (1425–1914), Cataloog bij de tentoonstelling in de Centrale Bibliotheek (25.5–2.7.1988), Leuven 1988, p. 60–63.

——, *Joachim Hopperus*, in G. Van Dievoet e.a. (eds.), Lovanium docet, Geschiedenis van de Leuvense Rechtsfaculteit (1425–1914), Cataloog bij de tentoonstelling in de Centrale Bibliotheek (25.5–2.7.1988), Leuven 1988, p. 69–72.

Van der Wee, H., *The Low Countries in the early modern world*, Aldershot-Brookfield 1993.

Van de Wiel, C., *Geschiedenis van het kerkelijk recht*, Leuven 1986.

Van Dievoet, G. e.a. (eds.), *Lovanium docet, Geschiedenis van de Leuvense Rechtsfaculteit (1425–1914)*, Cataloog bij de tentoonstelling in de Centrale Bibliotheek (25.5–2.7.1988), Leuven 1988.

Van Gelderen, M., *From Domingo de Soto to Hugo Grotius, Theories of monarchy and civil power in Spanish and Dutch political thought, 1555–1609*, Pensiero politico, 32 (1999), p. 186–206.

Van Hofstraeten, B., *Juridisch humanisme en costumiere acculturatie, Inhouds- en vormbepalende factoren van de Antwerpse Consuetudines compilatae (1608) en het Gelderse Land- en Stadsrecht (1620)*, Maastricht 2008.

Van Houdt, T., *Money, time and labour, Leonardus Lessius and the ethics of money-lending and interest-taking*, Ethical Perspectives, 2 (1995), p. 11–27.

——, *De economische ethiek van de Zuid-Nederlandse jezuïet Leonardus Lessius (1554–1623), Een geval van jezuïtisme?*, De zeventiende eeuw, 14 (1998), p. 27–37.

——, *Leonardus Lessius over lening, intrest en woeker, De iustitia et iure, lib.2, cap.20, Editie, vertaling en commentaar*, [Verhandelingen van de Koninklijke Academie voor Wetenschappen, Letteren en Schone Kunsten van België, Klasse der Letteren, Jaargang 60, Nr. 162], Brussel 1998.

——, *The economics of art in early modern times, Some humanist and scholastic approaches*, in: N. De Marchi – C.D. Goodwin (eds.), Economic engagements with art, [Annual Supplement to Volume 31, History of Political Economy], Durham – London 1999.

——, *Implicit intention and the conceptual shift from interesse to interest, An underestimated chapter from the history of scholastic economic thought*, Lias, Sources and documents relating to the early modern history of ideas, 33 (2006), p. 37–58.

Van Houdt, T. – Decock, W., *Leonardus Lessius, Traditie en vernieuwing*, Antwerpen 2005.

Van Houdt, T. – Golvers, N. – Soetaert, P., *Tussen woeker en weldadigheid, Leonardus Lessius over de Bergen van Barmhartigheid (1621), Vertaling, inleiding en aantekeningen*, Leuven-Amersfoort 1992.

Van Hove, A., *Prolegomena ad Codicem iuris canonici*, [Commentarium Lovaniense in Codicem iuris canonici, 1.1], Mechliniae – Romae 1945.

——, *De oorsprong van de kerkelijke rechtswetenschap en de scholastiek*, [Mededeelingen van de Koninklijke Vlaamsche Academie voor Wetenschappen, Letteren en Schoone Kunsten van België, Klasse der Letteren, Jaargang 6, Nr. 3], Antwerpen – Utrecht 1946.

van Nifterik, G.P., *Vorst tussen volk en wet, Over volkssoevereiniteit en rechtsstatelijkheid in het werk van Fernando Vázquez de Menchaca (1512–1569)*, Rotterdam 1999.

van Schaik, A.C., *Contractsvrijheid en nietigheid, Beschouwingen vanuit rechtshistorisch en rechtsvergelijkend perspectief over de overeenkomst zonder oorzaak*, Zwolle 1994.

Varkemaa, J., *Summenhart's theory of rights, A culmination of the late medieval discourse on individual rights*, in: V. Mäkinen – P. Korkman (eds.), Transformations in medieval and early modern rights discourse, [The New Synthese Historical Library, 59], Dordrecht 2006, p. 119–147.

——, *Conrad Summenhart's theory of individual rights and its medieval background*, Helsinki 2009 [= doct. diss.].

——, *Conrad Summenhart's theory of individual rights*, [Studies in Medieval and Reformation Traditions, 159], Leiden – Boston 2012.

Vaz de Carvalho, J., *Fernão Rebelo*, in: C. O'Neill – J. Domínguez (eds.), Diccionario histórico de la Compañía de Jesús, Biográfico-temático, Roma – Madrid 2001, vol. 4, p. 3303.

Vereecke, L., *De Guillaume D'Ockham à Saint Alphonse de Liguori, Études d'histoire de la théologie morale moderne 1300–1787*, [Bibliotheca Historica Congregationis Sanctissimi Redemptoris, 12], Romae 1986.

——, *Théologie morale et magistère, avant et après le Concile de Trente*, Le Supplément, Revue d'éthique et théologie morale, 177 (1991), p. 7–22.

——, *Le probabilisme*, Le Supplément, Revue d'éthique et théologie morale, 177 (1991), p. 23–31.

Vervaart, O.M.D.F., *Studies over Nicolaas Everaerts (1462–1532) en zijn Topica*, Arnhem 1994 [= doct. diss.].

Villey, M., *La promotion de la loi et du droit subjectif dans la Seconde Scolastique*, in: P. Grossi (ed.), La seconda scolastica nella formazione del diritto privato moderno, [Per la storia del pensiero giuridico moderno, 1], Milano 1973, p. 53–72.

——, *Bible et philosophie gréco-romaine, De saint Thomas au droit moderne*, in: Dimensions religieuses du droit et notamment sur l'apport de Saint Thomas D'Aquin, [Archives de Philosophie du Droit, 18], Paris 1973, p. 27–57.

——, *La formation de la pensée juridique moderne*, Cours d'histoire de la philosophie du droit, nouvelle édition corrigée, Paris 1975.

Vismara, P., *Oltre l'usura, La Chiesa moderna e il prestito a interesse*, Soveria Mannelli 2004.

Volante, R., *Il sistema contrattuale del diritto comune classico, Struttura dei patti e individuazione del tipo, glossatori e ultramontani*, [Per la storia del pensiero giuridico moderno, 60], Milano 2001.

von Kaltenborn-Stachau, C., *Die Vorläufer des Hugo Grotius auf dem Gebiete des ius Naturae et Gentium sowie der Politik im Reformationszeitalter*, Leipzig 1848.

von Schulte, J.F., *Die Geschichte der Quellen und Literatur des canonischen Rechts von Gratian bis auf die Gegenwart*, Graz 1956 [= Stuttgart 1875–1880].

Wacke, A., *Circumscribere, gerechter Preis und die Arten der List (Dolus bonus und dolus malus, dolus causam dans und dolus incidens) unter besonderer Berücksichtigung der §§ 138 Abs. II und 123 BGB*, Zeitschrift der Savigny-Stiftung für Rechtsgeschichte, Rom. Abt., 94 (1977), p. 184–246.

——, *Europäische Spruchweisheiten über das Schenken und ihr Wert als rechtshistorisches Argument*, in: R. Zimmermann – R. Knütel – J.P. Meincke (eds.), Rechtsgeschichte und Privatrechtsdogmatik, Heidelberg 1999, p. 325–369.

Waelkens, L., *Nicolaas Everaerts, Un célèbre méconnu du droit commun (1463/4–1532)*, Rivista internazionale di diritto comune, 15 (2004), p. 173–183.

——, *Was er in de zestiende eeuw een Leuvense invloed op het Europese contractenrecht?*, in: B. Tilleman – A. Verbeke (eds.), Actualia vermogensrecht, Brugge 2005, p. 3–16.

——, *Le rôle de l'appel judiciaire romain dans la formation des Pays Bas au seizième siècle*, in: Podział władzy i parlamentaryzm w preszłosci i współczesnie, Prawo, doktryna, praktyka, Warschau 2007, p. 75–85.

——, *La cause de D. 44,4,2,3*, Tijdschrift voor Rechtsgeschiedenis, 75 (2007), p. 199–212.

——, *Civium causa, Handboek Romeins recht*, Leuven 2008.

——, *Droit germanique, La fin d'un mythe? À propos d'un ouvrage récent*, Revue historique de droit français et étranger, 87 (2009), p. 415–426.

——, *De oorsprong van de causaliteit bij contractuele verbintenissen*, in: B. Dauwe e.a. (eds.), Liber Amicorum Ludovic De Gryse, Brussel 2010, p. 669–679.

——, *Réception ou refoulement? Pour une lecture grecque de l'histoire du droit de la Renaissance*, in: B. Coppein – F. Stevens – L. Waelkens (eds.), Modernisme, tradition et acculturation juridique, Actes des Journées internationales de la Société d'Histoire du Droit, Louvain 29 mai–1 juin 2008, [Iuris Scripta Historica, 27], Brussel 2011, p. 137–149.

Wagner, A., *Francisco de Vitoria and Alberico Gentili on the legal character of the global commonwealth*, Oxford Journal of Legal Studies, 31 (2011), p. 565–582.

Waibel, D., *Aufstieg und 'Fall' des alexandrinischen Getreidehändlers, Ausgewählte Informationsprobleme beim Kauf von Cicero bis Savigny*, in: M. Ascheri e.a. (eds.), Ins Wasser geworfen und Ozeane durchquert. Festschrift für Knut Wolfgang Nörr, Köln – Weimar – Wien 2003, p. 1057–1074.

Waldron, J., *A religious view of the foundations of international law*, [NYU School of Law, Public law and legal theory research paper series, 11–29], New York 2011.

Waldstein, W., *Ins Herz geschrieben, Das Naturrecht als Fundament einer menschlichen Gesellschaft*, Augsburg 2010.

Wallinga, T., *La libertad contractual – de Roma al derecho privado europeo*, in: J. Miranda (ed.), O sistema contractual romano, De Roma ao direito actual, Coimbra 2010, p. 985–1002.

Warembourg, N., *Le 'droit commun coutumier', Un exemple paradoxal d'acculturation juridique*, in: B. Coppein – F. Stevens – L. Waelkens (eds.), Modernisme, tradition et acculturation juridique, Actes des Journées internationales de la Société d'Histoire du Droit, Louvain 29 mai -1 juin 2008, [Iuris Scripta Historica, 27], Brussel 2011, p. 161–171.

Wasserschleben, F.W.H., *Die Bussordnungen der abendländischen Kirche*, Halle 1851.

Wauters, B., *Recht als religie, Canonieke onderbouw van de vroegmoderne staatsvorming in de Zuidelijke Nederlanden*, [Symbolae Facultatis Litterarum Lovaniensis, Series B, 35], Leuven 2005.

Weber, W., *Wirtschaftsethik am Vorabend des Liberalismus, Höhepunkt und Abschluss der scholastischen Wirtschaftsbetrachtung durch Ludwig Molina SJ (1535–1600)*, [Schriften des Instituts für christliche Sozialwissenschaften der westfälischen Wilhelms-Universität Münster, 7], Münster 1959.

——, *Geld und Zins in der spanischen Spätscholastik*, [Schriften des Instituts für christliche Sozialwissenschaften der westfälischen Wilhelms-Universität Münster, 13], Münster 1962.

Weiler, A.G., *Het morele veld van de Moderne Devotie, weerspiegeld in de Gnotosolitos parvus van Arnold Gheyloven van Rotterdam, 1423, Een Summa van moraaltheologie, kerkelijk recht en spiritualiteit voor studenten in Leuven en Deventer*, [Middeleeuwse studies en bronnen, 96], Hilversum 2006.

Weinzierl, K., *Die Restitutionslehre der Hochscholastik bis zum hl. Thomas von Aquin*, Münich 1939.

Westerman, P.C., *Some objections to an aspirational system of law*, in: N.E.H.M. Zeegers et al. (eds.), Social and symbolic effects of legislation on the rule of law, Lewiston 2004, p. 299–315.

——, *The emergence of new types of norms*, in: L.J. Wintgens (ed.), Legislation in context, Essays in legisprudence, Aldershot 2007.

Whitman, J.Q., *The moral menace of Roman law and the making of commerce, Some Dutch evidence*, The Yale Law Journal, 105 (1996), p. 1841–1889.

——, *Zum Thema der Selbsthilfe in der Rechtsgeschichte*, in: W. Fikentscher (ed.), Begegnung und Konflikt, Eine kulturanthropologische Bestandsaufnahme, [Bayerische Akademie der Wissenschaften, Philosophisch-historische Klasse, Neue folge, 120], München 2001, p. 97–105.

——, *The origins of reasonable doubt, Theological roots of the criminal trial*, New Haven – London 2008.

Whittaker, S. – Zimmermann, R., *Good faith in European contract law, Surveying the legal landscape*, in: R. Zimmermann – S. Whittaker (eds.), Good faith in European contract law, [The Common Core of European Private Law, Cambridge Studies in International and Comparative Law, 14], Cambridge 2000, p. 7–62.

Wieacker, F., *Privatrechtsgeschichte der Neuzeit unter besonderer Berücksichtigung der deutschen Entwicklung*, Göttingen 1967.

——, *Contractus und Obligatio im Naturrecht zwischen Spätscholastik und Aufklärung*, in: P. Grossi (ed.), La seconda scolastica nella formazione del diritto privato moderno, [Per la storia del pensiero giuridico moderno, 1], Milano 1973, p. 223–239.

——, *Die vertragliche Obligation bei den Klassikern des Vernunftrechts*, in: G. Stratenwerth et al. (eds.), Festschrift für Hans Welzel zum 70. Geburtstag, Berlin – New York 1974, p. 7–22.

Wijffels, A.A., *La bonne foi en droit savant médiéval, Bona fides – mala fides dans les consilia d'Alexander Tartagnus (Imolensis)*, in: La bonne foi, [Cahiers du centre de recherches en histoire du droit et des institutions, 10], Bruxelles 1998, p. 23–52.

——, *Qu'est ce que le ius commune?*, in: A.A. Wijffels (ed.), Le Code civil entre ius commune et droit privé européen, Bruxelles 2005, p. 643–661.

——, *Justitie en behoorlijk bestuur, Hans Vredeman de Vries' schilderijen in het stadhuis van Danzig (Gdánsk)*, Pro Memorie, 13 (2011), p. 103–118.

Winkel, L.C., *Die Irrtumslehre*, in: R. Feenstra – R. Zimmermann, Das römisch-holländische Recht, Fortschritte des Zivilrechts im 17. und 18. Jahrhundert, [Schriften zum Europäischen Rechts- und Verfassungsgeschichte, 7], Berlin 1992, p. 225–244.

——, *Alcune osservazioni sulla classificazione delle obbligazioni e sui contratti nominati nel diritto romano*, in: M. Talamanca (ed.), Bullettino dell'Instituto di Diritto Romano 'Vittoria Scialoja', IIIa serie, CIII–CIV (2000–2001), Milano 2009, p. 51–66.

Wisse, M. – Sarot, M. – Otten, W. (eds.), *Scholasticism reformed, Essays in honour of Willem J. van Asselt*, [Studies in Theology and Religion, 14], Leiden – Boston 2010.

Witschen, D., *Zur Bestimmung supererogatorischer Handlungen, Der Beitrag des Thomas von Aquin*, Freiburger Zeitschrift für Philosophie und Theologie, 5 (2004), p. 27–40.

Witte, J., Jr., *Law and protestantism, The legal teachings of the Lutheran reformation*, Cambridge 2002.

Wolter, U., *Ius canonicum in iure civili, Studien zur Rechtsquellenlehre in der neueren Privatrechtsgeschichte*, [Forschungen zur neueren Privatrechtsgeschichte, 23], Köln – Wien 1975.

Wood, D., *Medieval economic thought*, Cambridge 2002.

Zalba, M., *Theologiae moralis compendium*, [Biblioteca de autores cristianos, 175.2], Matriti 1958.

Zanfredini, M., *Vincenzo Figliucci*, in: C. O'Neill – J. Domínguez (eds.), Diccionario histórico de la Compañía de Jesús, Biográfico-temático, Roma – Madrid 2001, vol. 2, p. 1416.

Zendri, C., *L'usura nella dottrina dei giuristi umanisti, Martin de Azpilcueta (1492–1586)*, in: D. Quaglioni – G. Todeschini – M. Varanini (eds.), Credito e usura fra teologia, diritto e amministrazione (sec. XII–XVI), [Collection de l'École française de Rome, 346], Rome 2005, p. 265–290.

Zimmermann, R., *The law of obligations, Roman foundations of the civilian tradition*, Cape Town – Wetton – Johannesburg 1990.

——, *'Heard melodies are sweet, but those unheard are sweeter' – Conditio tacita, implied condition und die Fortbildung des Europäischen Vertragsrechts*, Archiv für die civilistische Praxis, 193 (1993), p. 121–173.

——, (ed.), *Globalisierung und Entstaatlichung des Rechts, Teilband II: Nichtstaatliches Privatrecht, Geltung und Genese*, Tübingen 2008.

INDEX OF NAMES

INDEX OF TERMS

absolutism
    interpretation of laws and   292 n. 1017,
        345, 568–569
    political (*see* power)   8, 10, 15 n. 50, 27
        n. 95, 29–30, 33 n. 124, 37 n. 142, 40,
        49, 76, 97–98, 102, 116, 142, 158, 202
        n. 718, 330, 347, 352, 354 n. 1208, 357
        n. 1219, 361, 366, 368, 378, 380, 390,
        397, 407 n. 1374, 408, 416–417, 449,
        487–489, 510, 513, 534, 567–569, 571,
        605 n. 1973, 627, 629–630, 631 n. 2070,
        633, 639, 644, 646
abuse   600
    of law   205, 292, 345, 416
    of litigation rights   266–267
    of necessity   82, 473, 543, 547, 584,
        602, 649
    of power   248, 399, 595, 600
acceptance (*acceptatio*)
    grace and   639
    theory of offer and   107, 163, 177–178,
        187–192, 213, 329, 409, 614–615, 639
acceptatio occulta (*see* compensation,
    secret
accessorium sequitur principale   112
acquisition (*acquisitio*)
    illicit – *vs* – by virtue of an illicit cause
        (*ex causa turpi*)   426–428, 431, 450,
        456, 476, 478 n. 1574
action (*actio*)
    bonae fidei/stricti iuris   216, 274–277,
        278 nn. 966, 968, 970, 279–280, 284
        n. 967, 285 n. 990, 287–290, 293–299,
        302, 305–308, 310–312, 314, 317–318,
        321–322, 530 n. 1749, 617–618
    doli   260, 275–278, 295 n. 1034, 302
        n. 1059, 532, 573, 575 n. 1884
    quod metus causa   216–218, 256, 261
action (*condictio*)   423, 442 n. 1460, 443
    n. 1464, 456, 461 n. 1515, 469, 475, 575
    n. 1883
    causa data causa non secuta   133,
        136 n. 499, 137, 575
    ex canone iuramenti   124 n. 541, 125,
        127–128, 129 n. 476
    indebiti   335 n. 1152, 389, 469, 475
    ob turpem causam   133 n. 486, 423
        n. 115, 441, 443 n. 1464, 452 n. 1490,
        454 n. 1496, 461 n. 1515, 469 n. 1537

actor (*see* plaintiff)
actus peccaminosus (also *opus
    peccaminosum*) (*see* sinful act)
adultery   63, 172, 437, 462, 468
aequalitas (*see* equality)
aequitas (*see* equity)
affectional disorder (*see* donation)
agency (*negotiorum gestio*) (*see also*
    mandate)   3, 68, 173, 275 n. 957, 515
agreement (*pactum*)
    bindingness of naked (*pacta
        quantumcumque nuda servanda*)   42,
        93, 106, 110, 112 n. 411, 118, 122–124,
        126–130, 332 n. 1140, 392, 606–607,
        627
    naked *vs* clothed (*pactum nudum/
        vestitum*)   19 n. 67, 107, 109–111,
        113, 119 n. 434, 121, 125–128, 136
        n. 499, 138, 140 n. 515, 142–143,
        146 n. 525, 147, 329, 336, 413 n. 1394,
        625
Alcalá de Henares   40, 53–54, 57, 59, 67,
    203 n. 720
alienation (*alienatio*)
    of ecclesiastical goods   367, 371,
        375–376
    of freedom   210, 355, 632
    of property in general   17, 102, 448
almsgiving (*eleemosyna*)   425–426, 427
    n. 1425, 428, 431–432, 434–436, 441
    n. 1459, 543
anima legis (*see* soul of the law)
animal civile (*see* political animal)
animal sociale et politicum (*see* political
    animal)
animus donandi (*see* donation)
animus obligandi (*see* intention / will)
annullability (*see* voidability)
anthropology
    difference between Lutheran and
        Jesuit   46–47
    dualistic   9, 26, 647
    underlying liberal view of contract
        law   162, 168, 213, 634, 636
    underlying probabilism   5, 76
antidora (*see* counter-gift)
anti-Jesuitism   16 n. 57, 497, 638 n. 2099
anti-nomianism   25, 638 n. 2098
anti-papalism   47

n. 1762, 535 n. 1764, 536, 539, 545 n. 1793,
556, 561–563, 573–576, 580, 588, 589
n. 1934, 590, 592, 595, 599, 617
bad (*malus*) 436, 439 n. 1454, 457
n. 1504, 500 n. 1650, 556, 595 n. 1949
commercial (*ex industria
negotiativa*) 532, 596
fundamental (*causam dans*) 258, 261,
264–265, 272, 276, 278, 282, 284–287,
295–303, 305, 307–310, 312–313, 315,
318, 320, 322, 327, 532 n. 1756, 595
n. 1949, 617
good (*dolus bonus/solertia*) 591–592,
595
incidental (*incidens*) 261, 276, 281,
284, 285, 298, 302, 308–310, 324,
532 n. 1756, 536
intentional (*ex proposito*) 254 n. 896,
298, 531–532, 536, 562, 574
it is naturally permitted to outwit each
other (*naturaliter licet invicem se
circumvenire*) 532, 538, 578–580,
591, 595, 601 n. 1970, 603
laws must protect the deceived, not
the deceivers (*deceptis et non
decipientibus iura subveniant*) 258,
280, 287
objective (*reipsa*) 284–585, 531–532,
536, 561, 573–576, 590
*deceptis et non decipientibus iura
subveniant* (*see* deceit)
defamation 64, 172
defects in goods sold 216, 317, 588, 598
n. 1959
defendant (*reus*) 64, 71, 78–79, 87,
100–101, 128 n. 471, 138, 140 n. 515, 141,
167, 218, 548, 555, 565 n. 1851, 575, 628
defraudatio 283, 285, 536
deliberation (*deliberatio*) 117, 180
denunciatio canonica (*see* canonical
denunciation)
denunciatio evangelica (*see* evangelical
denunciation)
denunciatio judicialis (*see* judicial
denunciation)
deposit (*depositum*) 64, 172–173, 175, 205,
442 n. 1460
detraction 64, 172
discretion (*arbitrium*) 227, 252 n. 891,
284 n. 987, 293 n. 1026, 311, 317, 332
n. 1139, 371 n. 1264, 403, 477 n. 1567,
483 n. 1594, 488 n. 1613, 525 n. 1728, 617,
622 n. 2043, 629

of the judge 227, 240, 243, 250, 294,
332 n. 1139, 622 n. 2043
of wise and prudent men 240, 403,
460 n. 1513, 463 n. 1522, 493 n. 1629,
629
dispensation 61
dissimulation 561
distracts (*distractus*) 173
distributive justice 64, 347 n. 1188, 511
divine law (see also *ius divinum*) 27, 58,
83, 118, 130, 364, 377, 395, 438, 465–467,
487, 523, 538, 546, 570–571
division of things (*divisio rerum*) 164,
352–353, 356–357, 361, 511–512, 619
divorce 61, 621 n. 2041
dolus (*see* deceit)
Dominicans 39, 45–46, 49–51, 53–54, 65,
75, 103, 149, 165, 175, 335, 373, 384, 393,
397–398, 400, 418, 432, 437, 468, 544,
588, 626, 628, 630, 632, 638
dominion (*dominium*)
Christ's 166
conceptions of 613
dominion of one's actions 169, 373, 614
dominion of the self 167, 171
everybody is the moderator and
arbiter of his own thing (*in re
sua unusquisque est moderator et
arbiter*) 169, 538, 591, 613
modes of transferring 164–165,
358–360, 374–375, 384, 447
relation to other real rights 353–355
restitution and 355
shared dominion in the state of
nature 355–357
donation (*donatio*) 61, 64, 68, 81, 113,
139–140, 150, 169 n. 606, 172–175, 184–186,
190–191, 208, 232 n. 820, 247, 256 n. 901,
269, 301 n. 1057, 308 n. 1080, 407 n. 1373,
410 n. 1383, 414, 439 n. 1453, 444–452,
458, 475, 489, 493, 495, 528, 542–544,
546–547, 557–561, 563–565, 579, 583–591,
597–598, 603
affectional disorder and 543
as a contract 139–140, 175–177
between husband and wife 487–488,
632
impious (*inofficiosa*) 565
intention of (*animus donandi*) 139
is not presumed (*nemo praesumitur
donare*) 139, 557–560, 563–565, 591
of the entirety of one's
possessions 488
virtual 469

poena (*see* punishment)
poenitentia (*see* penance)
policía 513
political animal 361, 372, 449, 630
  limits to contract law and man as a
    361, 372
political thought (*see also* power) 98,
  347, 408, 416, 534, 569, 644
  discussion on statutory form
    requirements and 366–369,
    380–381, 406–410
  in early modern canon law 97–101,
    384, 621–634
pollicitatio (*see* offer)
poor (*pauperes*) 53, 96 n. 358, 244,
  411, 428, 430, 432, 432 n. 1438, 435,
  435 n. 1443, 440 n. 1455, 444, 450 n. 1482,
  465, 466 n. 1528, 474, 479, 484, 497, 525,
  529, 541, 543, 552, 597, 640 n. 2103
portio legitima (*see* inheritance law)
positive law (*see* law, positive)
positivism, legal 22, 80 n. 293, 83 n. 307,
  86, 101, 635
possession (*see also* doubt) 63, 76 n. 279,
  77, 82, 164, 167, 171, 185–186, 192, 196,
  218, 267, 291, 354–355, 366, 376, 378,
  382–383, 398, 405–406, 452, 488, 515,
  517–518, 546, 618
  in good faith 291
potestas (*see* power)
poverty (*paupertas*) 166, 355, 360, 572
power (*potestas*) 1, 7–10, 26, 27 n. 95, 29,
  34–35, 38, 43, 45, 56, 84, 86, 88–89, 93,
  97–98, 101, 122, 133 n. 489, 152 n. 542, 184
  n. 650, 218 n. 774, 353, 399 n. 1349, 407
  nn. 1372–1373, 411 n. 1388, 415, 431–432,
  497, 499–500, 518, 545, 548–551, 552
  n. 1814, 553, 568–569, 571, 575 n. 1884,
  595, 605, 617, 621 n. 2041, 623, 624
  n. 2050, 628–633, 647, 649
  absolute (*potestas absoluta*) 568–569,
    605 n. 1973
  alleged superiority of spiritual 43, 94,
    489
  Church's indirect secular (*potestas
    indirecta*) 98–99, 410, 630–632
  civil (*potestas civilis*) 415, 368, 632
  lawful (*potestas legitima*) 84
  of jurisdiction (*potestas iurisdictionis*)
    89
  of the keys (*potestas clavium*) 88–89,
    550–551, 553, 633, 647, 649
practice 28–30, 32–34, 39, 42, 71–72, 74,
  109, 141, 143, 153, 155–156, 184, 191, 197,

228, 235, 238–240, 252, 313, 321, 334, 368,
  371, 374, 377, 382, 395, 399, 404, 415, 432,
  440, 452, 459, 464, 471, 472 n. 1548, 484,
  491–493, 512, 537 n. 1769, 545, 557, 559,
  564–567, 583, 588, 589 n. 1933, 592–593,
  567, 624 n. 2051, 632, 638
praying 64
praeceptum (*see* precept)
praesumptio levitatis (*see* presumptions)
precept(s) (*praeceptum*) 61, 79, 81–82,
  88, 90, 347, 349–351, 356 n. 1216, 366,
  378–379, 381, 396, 401, 422, 427 n. 1424,
  465–467, 469, 504, 508, 513, 523,
  547, 549–550, 570 n. 1868, 571, 602,
  626, 641
preces importunae (*see* importunate
  begging)
predestination 639–640
prescription (*usucapio*) 63, 77, 165, 171,
  357, 365 n. 1247, 374, 539, 562, 581
presumptions (*praesumptiones*) 73,
  117–118, 151, 230, 268, 323, 342, 404–405,
  544 n. 1792, 547 n. 1801, 564, 585
  n. 1921, 586 nn. 1924–1925
  gifts are not presumed 541–544,
    557–560, 563–566
  irrelevant in conscience 73
  of levity as basis of non-bindingness of
    naked pacts 117
pretium affectionis (*see* price)
price (*pretium*)
  conventional (*conventionale*) 528
  double rule of just pricing 523, 528,
    542, 559, 600 n. 1966
  just or equal (*iustum seu aequale*) 508,
    619
  latitude of (*latitudo*) 526–527, 542
    n. 1785, 591
  legitimate (*legitimum*) 525–528
  market 231, 253, 468, 472, 477, 503,
    520, 521 n. 1716, 522, 525–527, 559,
    594, 597, 600, 602, 620
  natural (*naturale seu vulgare*)
    525–528
  of affections (*affectionis*) 600 n. 1966
  of sex 449, 468, 472, 477, 492, 503,
    620
prince (*princeps*)
  authority of the 165, 357, 358, 360
  role and duties of the 53, 360,
    401 n. 1354, 408–409, 489, 508, 525,
    528, 568–569, 572, 629, 632
privity of contract (*see* third parties)
probabilism (*see also* certainty *and* doubt)

secular power (*see* power, civil)
secularization   99–100, 644 n. 2125, 646
security (*securitas*)
  legal   208, 321, 380, 580–581, 628
  spiritual   380, 626, 628
Selbsthilfe (*see* self-help / compensation, secret)
self-help (*see also* compensation, secret)   27 n. 95, 88, 102–103, 380
Senatusconsultum Macedonianum   351, 368
sense (*sensus*)
  five meanings of 'I will give you a horse tomorrow'   181–182
  of contract *vs* its wording (*see* will)
  of law *vs* its wording (*see* law)
sentence of the judge (*sententia iudicis*)   11 n. 1388, 15 n. 1402, 74 n. 1553, 86 n. 316, 258–259, 286, 299–300, 304, 315, 319, 383, 414 n. 1900, 435 n. 1443, 500 n. 1651, 501 n. 1652, 502 n. 1657, 503 n. 1659, 552
servitudes (*servitudines*)   63, 171, 173
settlement agreement (*transactio*)   173
Sevilla   60
sex
  contractual freedom and   419
  market for   450–451, 468, 472, 476–477, 492–493, 503, 620
  right over the body and   429, 433, 457
  unjust enrichment and   429, 436–437, 450, 457, 503–505, 620
shame (*see also verecundia*)   251
Siete Partidas   33–34, 393–394
simony (*simonia*)   64, 173, 340, 426, 427 n. 1425, 428, 429 n. 1432, 433–435, 441–442, 445, 448, 456, 460
simplicity (*simplicitas*)   543, 587 n. 1929, 588, 598 n. 1959
sin (*peccatum*)   75
  as source of jurisdiction   92 n. 335, 94, 96–97, 100, 335, 591 n. 1939
  mortal *vs* venal   149–150, 157, 194, 199, 200, 202, 225, 346, 349, 367, 389, 401, 428, 439, 487, 547, 553, 591, 633 n. 2078
  nobody can be bound to sin (*nemo potest obligari ad peccatum*)   479, 480 n. 1582, 481 n. 1585, 482 n. 1589
  remission of   516–517, 619
sincerity (*synceritas*)
  good faith as   291, 618
  highest end of law and   622
  human   378

sinful act (*opus peccaminosum*)   440, 444, 450–451, 467–468
smoothness of commerce   635, 637
societas (*see* partnership)
softness (*mollities*)   239
soldiers
  fighting in an unjust war   460, 463
  prostitutes and   451–452, 475
solemnities (*see* formalities)
solertia (*see* deceit, good)
sortes (*see* lottery agreement)
soul (*anima*)
  immortality of the   144
  of the law (*anima legis*)   348
  pre-modern anthropology and (*see* anthropology)
  salvation of the (*salus animarum*)   5–6, 26, 72, 98, 109, 126, 138, 145, 151, 212–213, 381, 407, 411, 466 n. 1528, 489, 513, 517–518, 544, 581 n. 1904, 607–608, 619, 623 n. 2048, 631–632, 635, 637
sovereignty   408, 605 n. 1973
Spanish legal culture
  indebtedness to Roman law   33–35
  influence of Church on   34, 625–626
specific performance   110 n. 401, 194
sponsalia (*see* engagement contract)
sponsio (*see* gambling and gaming contracts)
state
  of exception (*see* necessity)
  of pure nature   58, 100
  reason of (*see* reason)
  religious   64
stipendium (*see* wage)
stipulation (*stipulatio*)   108, 112, 119 n. 434, 124 n. 451, 127 n. 468, 130–131, 136, 138–139, 146, 149, 154, 161, 173, 177, 191, 294, 412, 424, 607, 636
stylus aulae   494
subjective approach (*see* interpretation of contracts)
subtleties, legal (*subtilitates*)   145–146, 155, 160, 607
summum bonum (*see* good)
summum ius summa iniuria (*see* abuse of law)
supererogation (*supererogatio*)   81, 487, 632
superstition   64
suretyship (*fideiussio*)   18 n. 62, 64, 147 n. 530, 148, 172, 287 n. 998

Printed in the United States
by Baker & Taylor Publisher Services